JOHN PRITCHARD

THE PENGUIN GUIDE TO THE LAW

SECOND EDITION

VIKING

VIKING
Penguin Books Ltd, Harmondsworth, Middlesex, England
Viking Penguin Inc., 40 West 23rd Street, New York, New York 10010, U.S.A.
Penguin Books Australia Ltd, Ringwood, Victoria, Australia
Penguin Books Canada Ltd, 2801 John Street, Markham, Ontario, Canada L3R 1B4
Penguin Books (N.Z.) Ltd, 182–190 Wairau Road, Auckland 10, New Zealand

First published 1983
Reprinted with minor revisions 1983
Second edition 1985
Published simultaneously by Penguin Books

Copyright © John Pritchard, 1982, 1985
The acknowledgements on page 898 constitute an extension of this copyright page

Typeset in Linotron Times by
Filmtype Services Limited, Scarborough, North Yorkshire
Printed in Great Britain by
William Clowes Limited, Beccles and London

British Library Cataloguing in Publication Data available

ISBN 0-670-80332-4

To Mary, who helped;
also to Tom, Sam, and Becky – who didn't

Contents

Acknowledgements

This is the 'thank you' page. As such, it is often skipped by the reader, but to the author it is perhaps the most important page of all. Without the help of the people mentioned below, this book would not have taken on its final form.

My acknowledgements fall into four categories:

The experts. The manuscript was carefully checked by Susan Maidment; Howell Lewis; Bill Thomas; Joe O'Hara; Greg Powell; Stephen Gold; Tony Lynes; and staff at the DHSS.

I am grateful to all the above for their help and constructive suggestions. For any errors that remain, I alone am responsible.

The publishers. My thanks to Michael Dover, editor at Penguin, and to the late Professor Harry Street, the consultant editor, for being bold enough to commission me at the age of twenty-seven to write this book and for being patient enough to wait for the manuscript to be delivered.

Readers. Many people who bought the first edition were kind enough to write to me with comments and suggestions. My thanks to them. If you have any comments, write to me c/o Penguin Books. Also, if you have any grouses about the law in general, or ideas for law reform, let me know.

Family and friends. Here the list could be very long. Special mention must go to my colleagues at Powell Magrath & Spencer. Chief thanks must go to my wife, Mary Pritchard. This is not just a marital thank you but an acknowledgement of the work she put in during the planning and writing of the first edition. Her experience as a Citizens' Advice Bureau worker has been a great asset. In particular, her task has been to keep the content of the book down to a realistic level and to prevent me being carried away on points of legal interest that are not strictly relevant to a book of this sort. It takes a CAB worker to bring one down to the reality of everyday law on topics such as dismissal, housing and consumer complaints. To Mary, my especial thanks.

Note To avoid the irksome repetition of 'he or she', 'he' has sometimes been used to indicate either sex.

Introduction

This book cannot tell you all the law. No one knows all the law, not even the most eminent judge – and certainly not me!

The law is as huge as it is indefinable. Suffice to say that it is impossible to compress more than just a smattering of knowledge into a book of this size. All I can do is to try to extract those parts of the law that seem – to me – to be most relevant and useful to the general reader. So if you see this book as a substitute for the considered advice of a solicitor or barrister, think again.

What a guide of this sort can do is to introduce the reader to the complexities of the law, to remove some of the mysteries that shroud it, and to give an overall view of the law. I hope that information will be sufficient to enable the reader to identify the legal element in a problem and to point him in the right direction towards solving that problem.

This book is one man's view of the law. As such, it differs from most recent laymen's guides, which are produced by an amalgam of consultative committees, editors and graphic designers. Since this is a personal view of the law it must inevitably reflect my prejudices and own interests, as well as my professional experience and practice as a solicitor in N W London. Thus, topics such as housing and employment receive greater coverage than, for instance, bankruptcy, tax, and other commercial matters. Overall, my aim has been to concentrate on the topics that directly affect private individuals.

Finally, two cautionary notes. Firstly, the law changes quickly and any part of this book might be out of date when you read it, so do not treat what is written here as being gospel truth. Secondly, remember that 'a little knowledge can be a dangerous thing'; this book presents a condensed view of the law and it may be that the details that have been omitted are crucial in deciding the answer to your particular legal problem. If in doubt, take legal advice.

The law as described here is up to date to September 1985; it applies only to England and Wales, since Scotland and Northern Ireland have their own laws.

John Pritchard, September 1985

PART ONE

THE FAMILY

1 Getting Married

Becoming engaged

The law attaches little significance to engagement; it is only when the couple come to marry that the law lays down detailed requirements as to their status and age. Similarly, the legal effects of an engagement are few, whereas the legal effects of a marriage are many – ranging from the duty to cohabit to the obligation to maintain and provide for the spouse.

Engagement requires no legal formalities; no one's consent needs to be obtained and the couple do not even have to be over the age of sixteen. This is because the engagement has no legal effect and cannot be enforced by the courts.

Prior to 1970, a contract to marry (i.e. an engagement) was like any other contract, and if it was broken the rejected suitor could sue for breach of contract. But the right to sue has now been abolished and so an agreement to marry (i.e. an engagement) is no longer a legally binding contract. Further, the rejected suitor cannot even sue to recover any losses or expenses incurred in planning and preparing for the marriage. For example, the jilted groom may have booked hotel rooms, or the jilted bride may have spent money on a trousseau, dress, cake, and all the other costs of a reception; none of the expenses can be recovered from the other party unless it was specifically agreed beforehand that he or she would pay them. Similarly, if the father of the rejected bride booked a hall for the reception, he cannot sue the ex-fiancé or even demand that he pay half the booking fee.

Returning the gifts on cancellation

If the couple were sent presents before the wedding was cancelled, then generally those presents must be returned to the people who gave them. The law assumes that the gifts were given on the understanding that the couple were to be married, and so if the marriage is called off they are no longer entitled to the presents. If the people who gave the presents do not want them back, the law will usually allow the man to keep the gifts from his friends and relatives and the woman to keep the gifts from her friends and relatives.

The same applies to gifts made by the couple to each other. The law assumes that the gifts were conditional on the marriage taking place, and so should be returned if the marriage is called off. It makes no difference who is to blame for the cancellation of the marriage – the 'guilty' lover is still entitled to have his or her presents returned.

The only exception to this is the engagement ring; the woman can nearly always hold on to this even if it is her fault that the marriage has been cancelled. Only in exceptional cases would a court order her to return the ring; when the ring was a family heirloom, for example, and the man had only given it to her on the clear understanding that if she did not become a member of his family then the ring was to be returned.

All these rules are based on a presumption that the gifts were conditional on the marriage taking place. So, if a present was not conditional on the marriage, it would not be returnable. Thus, Christmas and birthday presents will not normally have to be returned.

Property bought jointly

Sometimes an engaged couple will buy a house together before their wedding day. If the wedding is cancelled what happens to the house?

If they cannot agree on what to do with the house or flat, the court will normally order that it be sold. After paying off the mortgage, and the estate agent's and solicitor's fees, the remaining money will be divided between them. The amount that each will receive will depend upon their percentage share in the house, which will partly depend upon how much each put into the purchase. Often, the money will be split fifty-fifty unless there is clear evidence for dividing it in some other way – for instance, they may have agreed on a one-third/two-thirds ownership when the property was bought.

Warning: complications can arise if the property was not bought in the couple's joint names. See page 90 for the principles that apply.

Similar rules apply to furniture and other possessions bought by the couple. If they cannot agree, either can ask the court to order the sale of the items concerned – although it is obviously best to do everything possible to avoid the expense of going to court.

Marriage formalities

Generally, romantic love is the basis of marriage in this country, but this is a relatively recent development. In the past bride seizure, payment, and parental arrangement were regarded as the normal methods for deciding on marriage partners.

To be legally valid, a marriage must be:
1. Voluntary.
2. Between two single people.
3. Who are over sixteen.
4. Of the opposite sex.
5. And not closely related.

1. 'Voluntary'

Both man and woman must be acting voluntarily. Force, fear, and duress will all invalidate the marriage. But it must be real duress; for instance, social pressure and the desire to please one's parents do not invalidate the marriage.

The marriage will also be invalid if one of the couple does.not realize what he or she is doing (e.g. if drink or old age affects their awareness of what is happening).

Similarly, if there was a mistake as to the identity of the other partner the marriage would be invalid. But other mistakes will not invalidate it. For instance, if the man is mistaken as to the financial standing, social status, or career prospects of his wife, he cannot argue that he would not otherwise have married her and so claim that the marriage is invalid. Duress and social pressure can also invalidate the marriage. This can be a particular problem with arranged marriages:

A nineteen-year-old Hindu girl was forced into an arranged marriage. Had she not agreed, her parents would have thrown her out of the house leaving her homeless and penniless. The Court of Appeal granted a declaration that the marriage was a nullity – 'the crucial question in these cases . . . is whether the threats, pressure, or whatever it is, is such as to destroy the reality of the consent and overbear the will of the individual'. So, in many ways it was the threat of homelessness and social ostracism that were the key factors in this case, and not so much the mere parental and social pressure. Hirani (1983)

This case should not be taken as showing that all arranged marriages can be set aside, but it is clear evidence of a change of attitude by the courts in being prepared to tackle this difficult problem.

2. 'Between two single people'

Neither party can be already married. So they must both be either single, widowed, or divorced. If either is married at the time of the ceremony the marriage will be void and the offence of bigamy will have been committed (but see polygamy, page 19). In fact, bigamy prosecutions are relatively rare these days because the police do not prosecute if the sole purpose was to allow the couple to live respectably as man and wife. Only 20 per cent or so of bigamy cases are prosecuted. Obviously if the bigamist was acting maliciously or fraudulently then he or she would be prosecuted.

Problems arise when a married person separated from the other spouse many years ago and now wishes to remarry. To avoid the risk of a bigamy prosecution, the court should be asked to grant a decree of presumption of death and divorce, or to grant a divorce based on five years' separation (see page 37). Unless such an order is obtained there is always a risk that the second marriage will be bigamous, although there is a special defence for those who have not heard from their spouse for at least seven years and who have no reason to suppose that he or she is still alive. This defence, even if it reduces the risks of a bigamy conviction, may not be enough to save the second marriage. Almost certainly, the second, bigamous, marriage will be null and void, so the couple will be in the same position as if they had never been married.

3. 'Who are over sixteen'

Since 1929, the minimum age for marriage has been sixteen. Before then, it was fourteen for boys and twelve for girls.

If a boy or girl of under sixteen is married, the marriage will be null and void. In addition, the child will be committing a criminal offence.

A person under the age of eighteen needs to obtain parental, or other, consent to the marriage. If the consent is forged, or if the child states that he or she is over eighteen in order to make consent unnecessary, the marriage will remain valid, but the child will be committing a criminal offence. The marriage will only be invalid if the child is under sixteen.

Consents. A sixteen- or seventeen-year-old will need the signed consent of both parents: but see the table below.

Circumstances	Consent needed from
One of the parents has died	the surviving parent and any guardian
The parents are divorced or separated	the parent awarded custody; if both parents have custody then both must consent
One parent has been deserted by the other	the deserted parent
The child is adopted	the adoptive parents
The child is a ward of court	the court
The child is in the care of the local authority	the local authority
Both parents are dead but the child has not been adopted	the guardian

If for some reason one of the parents cannot give consent (e.g. because s/he cannot be traced), then special consent will be needed; the registrar of marriages can provide details.

If the parents refuse their consent the child can apply to the court for its consent. Although the application can be to a magistrates' court, a county court, or the High Court, it is usually most convenient to apply to the local magistrates' court. The child should go to the court as though he or she wanted to issue a summons and explain the position to the warrant officer (see page 886).

4. 'Of the opposite sex'

Gay (i.e. homosexual or lesbian) marriages have no legal validity. Nor do sex-change marriages:

April Ashley was born a man. In 1960 he had undergone a sex-change operation involving removal of the testicles and most of the scrotum, and the formation of an artificial vagina. In September 1963 April Ashley married a man – who was aware of the sex change – and they lived together as man and wife. Three months later the man asked that the marriage be declared null and void because it was a marriage between two men. April Ashley disagreed, saying it was a marriage between a man and a woman. Held: It was not a valid marriage. April Ashley had been born a man and by all medical criteria he was a male, although psychologically he was trans-sexual. The sex change had not altered his biological (legal) sex and so the marriage was void.

In addition, the marriage could be annulled on the grounds of non-consummation since the artificial vagina did not allow of true intercourse. Corbett (1970)

5. 'And not closely related'

Society disapproves of marriages between people from the same family. This is so even when one of the parties is adopted into the family or is now divorced out of the family. So, for example, whilst a man may marry his female cousin, he cannot marry his son's divorced wife or his brother's adopted daughter.

'The Prohibited Degrees': When Marriage within a Family is Prohibited

A man cannot marry his:	*A woman cannot marry her*:
mother	father
daughter	son
grandmother	grandfather
granddaughter	grandson
sister	brother
mother-in-law	father-in-law
stepdaughter	stepson
stepmother	stepfather
daughter-in-law	son-in-law
grandfather's wife	grandmother's husband
wife's grandmother	husband's grandfather
wife's granddaughter	husband's grandson
grandson's wife	granddaughter's husband
aunt	uncle
niece	nephew

Polygamous marriages

No marriage that takes place in this country can be valid if one of the parties is already married. Such a marriage is void and also bigamous (see page 17). But some societies allow a man to have more than one wife and the question then arises of whether our courts will recognize all the marriages made by a polygamous foreigner or whether they will recognize only the first marriage and regard the others as bigamous. The position is complicated, but basically our courts will recognize all the marriages if:

1. The marriages complied with the laws of the country where they took place.

A Sikh marriage took place in India. The husband was abroad but was represented at the marriage ceremony by a photograph of himself. Held: This was a valid marriage in India and so it could be recognized in this country. Birang (1977)

2. The spouses must also have been capable of marrying (i.e. of age, not within the

prohibited degrees, etc.) according to the laws of their respective countries of domicile (see page 21).

However, the law is complex and anyone in doubt should take legal advice.

The formalities of marriage

The Marriage Act 1949 sets out the formalities for a valid marriage. But the Act largely repeats the law that has evolved over the centuries and so the result is a confusing muddle.

There are two basic methods of marrying: in a Church of England ceremony or in a civil ceremony.

Church of England marriages

Before the couple can be married they must comply with the formalities. There are four ways in which they can do this:

Banns. The names of the couple are read out in their parish churches on three Sundays. The marriage must then take place within three months of the last reading of the banns.

Common licence. This is a licence granted by a diocesan bishop and it is valid for three months. It will only be granted if one of the couple has lived for the preceding fifteen days in the parish where the marriage is to take place.

Special licence. This can only be granted by the Archbishop of Canterbury and it allows the marriage to take place anywhere and at any time.

Superintendent registrar's certificate. Both bride and groom must give at least seven days' notice of their intention to marry to the civil registry office for the area in which they live. A certificate allowing the marriage to take place will be issued twenty-one days after notice was given.

Civil marriages

Unless the marriage is to be by Church of England ceremony, it can only take place if a superintendent registrar's certificate has been issued. There are two alternatives. The certificate can be issued 'with a licence' or 'without a licence'.

A certificate without a licence. Allows the marriage to take place twenty-one days after the notice was given to the registrars for the areas where both parties live. There is a seven-day residence requirement.

A certificate with a licence. Allows the marriage to take place one day after the notice was given. Notice need only be given to one registrar, but one of the parties must have been resident in that area for at least fifteen days beforehand.

The marriage ceremony must take place in the registrar's office, or in a church, chapel, synagogue, or meeting-house appropriate to the couple's religion.

The legal effects of marriage

Getting married leads to the creation of new rights and new obligations between the couple. Amongst other things, they have a duty to maintain one another, to live together, and they impliedly agree to have sex with each other.

Marriage: the legal consequences for the woman

A new name?

For a woman the most obvious change brought about by the marriage will usually be a change of name. However, it is only tradition that requires the woman to take her husband's name. There is no legal obligation on her to change her name and she can retain her maiden name if she wishes.

In practice, most women follow the social convention and adopt the husband's name on marriage. The woman is then entitled to keep her husband's name (and any title) even after he dies or after they divorce and re-marry. Alternatively, she can revert to her maiden name if she prefers.

In English law, anybody can call themselves by whatever name they choose, and they can change their names as and when they wish (see page 97).

A new nationality?

No. Nationality is a political status of an individual and this is not affected by marriage. A British national who marries a foreigner retains his/her nationality – but may have dual nationality.

A new domicile?

A wife need not acquire her husband's domicile, although in practice she will often do so. Domicile should not be confused with nationality, citizenship, or residence. *Domicile* is where a person has his/her permanent home or, if he/she is living abroad, where he/she intends to return to permanently. *Residence* is the place where a person happens to be living; a person can be resident in several countries at the same time but can only have one domicile.

How domicile is decided. At birth, a baby will normally acquire its father's domicile, or if the father is dead, its mother's domicile. This is called the 'domicile of origin'.

In practice it is very difficult to change that domicile until the child is sixteen, but thereafter the child can acquire a 'domicile of choice', depending on the place where he or she is now permanently resident or intends to reside permanently.

Although a wife need not acquire her husband's domicile on marriage, it will usually be the case that she will live with him and that she will plan to spend her life with him in his domicile. Thus, in practice, she will usually acquire that new domicile.

A new passport?

The newly married woman can, if she chooses, have a new passport in her married name. In practice, the bride-to-be who is planning a foreign honeymoon can obtain a passport in her married name before the wedding takes place, although she must agree to surrender it should the marriage be cancelled.

An existing passport can be altered to the woman's new name by sending the passport and the marriage certificate to the Passport Office. They will amend the passport to show her new name.

A newly married wife is not obliged to have a passport in her married name, for she can continue to use her existing passport until it expires. The new passport will then have to be in her married name – assuming, of course, that she has adopted her husband's name and has not retained her maiden name.

Another alternative is for the newly married wife to have her name included in a joint passport with her husband.

The Passport Office will accept the title 'Ms'.

A new bank account?

If a newly married woman adopts her husband's name she should ensure that her bank changes her account name.

The couple may also consider opening a joint bank account. Generally, this is a good idea but it should be realized that if the marriage breaks down it is quite likely that the money in the account will be divided equally between the couple. As a general guide it can be said that if the wife is dependent on the husband she ought to insist on a joint account; and if he is dependent on her, then he should insist on a joint account (see page 53).

The financial effects of marriage

Marriage may result in:

New tax arrangements. Not only are there different allowances for married people, but the date of the marriage may affect tax liability (see page 52).

New entitlement to DHSS benefits. The wife will probably be eligible for national insurance widow's benefit and other benefits if her husband dies before her (see page 753).

New inheritance rights. If a married person dies without having made a will, then most of his or her possessions will pass to the surviving spouse. If there is a will, but it leaves little or nothing to the surviving spouse, then the court can intervene to award him or her a fair share of the estate (see page 181).

New credit rights. A wife may be able to make her husband liable to pay some of the household bills she incurs (see page 54).

New property rights. Both husband and wife will be able to claim a share in their joint assets (see page 54).

Maintenance. Both husband and wife are liable to maintain one another (see page 54).

A new home?

When a couple marry they impliedly agree to live together; this is the 'duty to cohabit'. Married couples are obliged to live together and to give each other the benefit of their company and support; the legal phrase for this is 'consortium'.

But the courts will not enforce these obligations by making the parties live together or by preventing one spouse from leaving the other. The law regards either spouse as being free to leave if s/he wishes but, by doing so, that spouse will be in desertion and so may be liable to be divorced and be ordered to pay maintenance to the other. In practice, though, many women are not free to leave the marital home when they might otherwise choose to do so; their financial dependence on their husbands, and the need for a home for themselves and the children, prevent them from leaving.

Given that the couple are expected to live together, which one of them can choose where the home is to be? Obviously, the views of both husband and wife should be taken into account, but all things being equal, it is the need to be near the bread-winner's place of work that will decide the issue. In practice, it is usually the man who has the final say and if his wife refuses to move with him to a new work place, she may well be in desertion. But all the circumstances must be considered, and so in the exceptional case, the health of the wife, or the schooling of the children may be held as sufficient reasons to justify a wife's refusal to move home. Obviously, if both husband and wife are at work, the parties have equal say in the matter and the other circumstances may be decisive.

But, overall, such questions are usually of academic interest only. If the couple cannot agree on where to live, it is likely that this is merely a symptom of a deeper problem in their relationship and that the argument over moving is merely a means of expressing their discontent.

A new bedfellow

Sex is part of the duty to cohabit, for by marrying the couple impliedly agree to have sexual intercourse with each other.

But, as with so many things legal, the concept of 'reasonableness' prevails and so marriage is taken as an implied consent to a reasonable amount of sex. So, excessive demands for sex or a virtual refusal to have sex will be unreasonable and may justify a petition for divorce on the grounds of 'unreasonable behaviour'. It all depends on the circumstances. For example, a refusal of sex by an invalid may be reasonable, but a refusal of sex by a healthy virile person is probably unreasonable. So also will be an insistence on always using contraceptives so that the couple will never have any children.

Note also, that if the marriage is never consummated (i.e. no sex), it may be annulled (see page 51).

Because marriage gives an implied consent to sexual intercourse, it is legally impossible for a man to rape his wife. As long as the duty to cohabit continues he has her implied consent to intercourse. Only when the duty to cohabit is ended can this consent be withdrawn and then the husband who forces his wife to have sex can be prosecuted for rape. The duty to cohabit only ends if:

- because of violence, a magistrates' court has made an exclusion or personal-protection order, or a county court has granted an injunction (see page 83);
- divorce proceedings have been started and either:
  – the wife has been granted an injunction which orders the husband not to molest her, *or*
  – the decree nisi has been granted;

O'Brien forced his wife to have sex with him, only two days after she had obtained a decree nisi against him. Held: He could be convicted of rape. If he had raped her two days earlier, he could not have been convicted. O'Brien (1974)

- husband and wife have signed a separation agreement which contains a non-molestation clause.

Finally, if the woman becomes pregnant the husband cannot stop her having an abortion to destroy the foetus.

A wife asked for an abortion and two doctors certified that continuing the pregnancy could injure her health. She had not consulted her husband, so he sought an injunction forbidding her to have the abortion. Held: No. A husband does not have a legal right to stop his wife having a legal abortion. Paton (1978)

It might be possible, though, for a husband to use his wife's insistence on an abortion as evidence of 'unreasonable behaviour' for a divorce petition.

Contractual obligations between man and wife

Marriage is a contract, but the courts will not enforce the contract between husband and wife. For instance, if the woman was persuaded to marry the man because he said he was wealthy, she cannot sue him for misrepresentation if he lied about his supposed wealth.

The courts will not interfere with a working marriage. So if a husband arranges to meet his wife at twelve o'clock but she does not keep the appointment, he cannot hold her liable for the losses and expenses he has suffered. This is all part of the wear and tear of marriage. The courts will only intervene if the couple clearly intended a legal relationship to follow on from an agreement, such as when they are discussing a business matter.

Different considerations arise if the marriage is breaking down. If it is no longer a working marriage the courts will intervene in extreme situations. So, if the couple decided to separate and drew up a separation agreement, the courts would probably enforce it if one of the parties did not carry out his (or her) part of the bargain (although the court could override the terms of the agreement if it was unfair). See page 48.

Marital confidences and secrets

Most married people tell one another things that they would not tell other people. If necessary, these marital confidences and secrets will be respected by the courts.

So, in a criminal trial, the husband or wife of the accused cannot normally be called to give evidence for the prosecution; neither can he or she be forced to give evidence for the defence. Similarly, in a civil case, whilst the spouse can be called or sub-poenaed to give evidence, the judge will excuse the spouse from answering questions, if to do so would involve a breach of marital confidences.

If one of the spouses plans to publish the marital secrets the courts may grant an injunction to stop the publication.

The Duke of Argyll divorced the Duchess of Argyll because of her adultery. A year later, the Duke wrote an article for the People *in which he disclosed secrets of the Duchess's personal life and conduct, based on what she had told him when they were married. The Duchess applied for an injunction. Held: The injunction would be granted since the articles were a breach of marital confidences.* Argyll (1965)

But, the granting of an injunction is a discretionary remedy, and the court will refuse an injunction to someone who has previously been willing to publicize his private life. For instance:

John Lennon, the ex-Beatle, applied for an injunction to stop his former wife, Cynthia Lennon, from writing newspaper articles about their married life. Held: An injunction would be refused. Both John and Cynthia Lennon had previously made public – in return for payment – intimate details of their relationship. An injunction would not be appropriate. Lennon (1978)

2 Separation and Divorce

In this chapter we are concerned with marriages that are no longer working properly; for some reason the marriage has broken down and either, or both, of the parties now want to separate and perhaps put an end to the marriage.

These days the law does not look closely at the conduct of the parties when a marriage is failing. Blame will only be relevant in exceptional cases, for the courts are generally most concerned to safeguard the welfare of any children and to ensure that a dead marriage is not perpetuated as a sham.

When a marriage is in trouble, most people immediately think of divorce as the obvious legal remedy, but there are, in fact, five legal remedies that can be used.

Legal remedy	See page	Effect
1. Divorce	27	These legally end the marriage (i.e. the husband and wife are both single people again)
2. Annulment (rare)	50	
3. Judicial separation (rare)	49	These do not legally end the marriage – they just end the obligation to cohabit; the parties cannot remarry
4. Separation by informal agreement	48	
5. Separation under a written deed	48	

With all five procedures the courts have wide powers to sort out the couple's financial affairs; just how this is done is explained in Chapter 3.

Which to choose

Each of the six remedies has its uses, its advantages, and its disadvantages. But the basic decision is to choose between ending the marriage (usually by divorce) or simply separating and keeping the marriage legally alive. Which to choose will obviously depend on individual circumstances and individual emotions. If there is any prospect of a reconciliation then separation is the better choice, since divorce effectively terminates the marriage.

When a husband abandons his wife

Whichever long-term remedy the woman decides to pursue, she must ensure she immediately takes steps to protect herself in the short term.

Housing. She should check that her husband is still paying the rent or mortgage. If he is not, she should arrange to do so herself. A landlord or building society cannot refuse to accept payment from her just because the home is in his name. See page 265.

Financial. She should claim supplementary benefit if she has little or no money (see page 744). She should also consider applying for maintenance for herself and the children. If she has a joint bank account with her husband she should make sure he cannot draw out all the money – perhaps she should even draw it out before he does!

Violence. If her husband has been violent and there is danger of further violence, she should see a solicitor. It might be possible to have her husband excluded from the home (see page 83).

DIVORCE

The modern divorce laws

In the last 150 years divorce has changed from being the exclusive right of the very rich to being the right of everybody; changes in the law and the introduction of legal aid have combined to make divorce a growth industry.

Originally, the church courts dealt with all matrimonial matters and those who wanted a divorce had to obtain a special Act of Parliament. The Victorians changed the law to allow a husband to obtain a divorce on the ground of his wife's adultery; later, women were also permitted to obtain a divorce on the ground of adultery. And that was the position until 1937. In that year, A. P. Herbert sponsored an Act which allowed divorce if any one of several 'matrimonial offences' could be proved – such as adultery, desertion, and cruelty. This was a radical reform and it made divorce more easily obtainable.

But its disadvantage was that it emphasized the 'matrimonial offence' and the need to find the other spouse guilty of misconduct. Thus 'conduct' became very important, for only the sinned-against could start divorce proceedings. The sinner could not initiate the divorce. The concept of the matrimonial offence as the basis of our divorce laws was removed in 1969 when Leo Abse piloted the Divorce Reform Act through Parliament, an Act which aroused bitter controversy and claims that it was a Casanova's charter.

Gone is the concept of the matrimonial offence; instead we have the overall question: 'Has the marriage broken down irretrievably?' If so (and this has to be proved by showing one of five facts, such as unreasonable behaviour) then the marriage will be ended, irrespective of who is to blame. The 'sinner' as well as the 'sinned-against' can now petition for divorce.

Has the 1969 Act been a Casanova's charter? It seems not, for although the divorce rate has risen dramatically, marriage remains as popular as ever and the courts are now simply putting an end to 'sham' marriages that under the old law would have limped along.

But the figures for divorces are staggering. There are now some 150,000 divorces each year – a doubling of the divorce rate since 1970. The divorce-to-marriage ratio is now 1:2·4. However, although that is an oft-quoted statistic, it is extremely misleading, because it compares one year's marriages with one year's divorces – but the divorces cover marriages of all married people, not just those married in one year. (Think about it!)

Divorce: the two hurdles

The modern divorce law requires the petitioner (the person asking for the divorce) to clear two hurdles before the divorce can be given:

Hurdle No. 1   Has the marriage lasted a year?

Hurdle No. 2   Has the marriage broken down irretrievably? This is shown by proving one of five sets of circumstances.

In addition, the petitioner must be resident or domiciled in this country (see page 39).

Divorce Hurdle No.1. Has the marriage lasted a year?

No one can apply for a divorce unless they have been married for at least a year. This is an absolute rule – there are no exceptions. If a married person wants a divorce within the one-year period, all s/he can do is to leave the spouse and wait for the year to expire before filing a divorce petition. See page 48 for separation. In practical terms no one can obtain a divorce until about eighteen months after marriage. This is because the one-year rule prevents them starting the divorce proceedings for twelve months, and then it generally takes at least six months for the divorce to go through.

Divorce Hurdle No.2. Has the marriage broken down irretrievably?

The court wants dead marriages to be ended gracefully. But the law insists that the marriage must be dead. The phrase used is 'that the marriage has irretrievably broken down'. If the marriage has not died – for instance if it has just temporarily broken down – then divorce is not allowed.

Before the courts will be persuaded that a marriage has irretrievably broken down, the petitioner must first prove that one of five factors, or sets of circumstances, exists. If the petitioner cannot bring his or her case within one of these five grounds for divorce, then the court cannot say that the marriage has irretrievably broken down – and so no divorce can be granted.

In practice, once the petitioner can show that one of the five factors exists, then the court will more or less presume that the marriage has irretrievably broken down. So, in effect, divorce is now automatically available on any one of these five grounds:

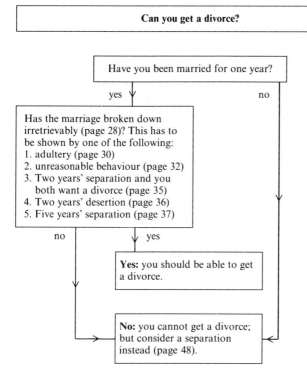

1. The other spouse has committed *adultery* and it is intolerable to live with him/her;
2. The other spouse has *behaved unreasonably*;
3. Husband and wife both want a divorce and have been *separated (living apart) for at least two years*;
4. The other spouse has been in *desertion for at least two years*;
5. Husband and wife have been *separated (living apart) for at least five years*.

Note, in particular, No.2, 'the other spouse has behaved unreasonably' – this is a catch-all phrase that covers marital misconduct that does not come within any of the four other factors.

Generally, the courts are not very demanding in the standard of proof they require. In an undefended case the registrar will often give the petitioner the benefit of the doubt, even when the evidence is rather weak. The courts will not obstruct the dissolution of dead marriages. This is why it is usually unwise to defend a divorce petition; the mere fact that the couple have got to the divorce court will often be a clear indication that the marriage is not working, and both parties are likely to be advised that there is little point in defending the divorce. This does not, of course, prevent them from defending claims for maintenance, a share of the family assets, or applying for custody of the children. So, although the divorce may go through 'on-the-nod', there can still be a long and bitter argument about children and finances – those matters are distinct from the question of whether or not there should be a divorce. The divorce may be undefended, even though everything else is disputed.

Grounds for divorce

1. The other spouse has committed adultery

More than mere adultery is needed. The law requires two things:
- that the other spouse has committed adultery, *and*
- that the petitioner finds it intolerable to live with the other spouse, for whatever reason.

So, strictly speaking, proving adultery is not enough, for the petitioner must also convince the court that s/he finds it intolerable to live with his/her spouse. In practice, though, the courts will readily assume that if there has been adultery, the petitioner finds it intolerable to live with the other spouse.

What is adultery?

Everyone knows what adultery is: it is voluntary sex between two people of different sexes, either or both of them being married. The courts have decided that actual sexual intercourse, involving penetration, but not necessarily orgasm, is necessary for there to be adultery. Sexual familiarity, foreplay, or masturbation, is not enough. Since adultery must be a voluntary act, sex when drunk or when raped cannot count as adultery. Artificial insemination is not adultery – although it might be grounds for divorce based on 'unreasonable behaviour' if it took place without the consent of the other spouse.

Proving adultery

Fortunately, the courts do not require eyewitness evidence of adultery. They will look at the surrounding circumstances; usually, if the petitioner can show inclination and opportunity, then the court will assume that intercourse took place. Circumstantial evidence will usually suffice: for instance, that the couple have been seen holding hands, kissing, or in a parked car together late at night when they are supposed to be somewhere else; love letters or the contracting of venereal disease may also be sufficient evidence. Similarly, if a wife has a child when it was impossible for the husband to have been the father, that will be proof of her adultery.

Blood tests can also be used to show that the husband is not the father of his wife's child. Blood tests cannot prove who is the father, but they can often show that a particular man cannot be the father.

If the petitioner thinks his/her spouse is committing adultery but has no evidence, s/he may have to hire an inquiry agent to obtain evidence. He will watch the spouse and keep a record of when and where s/he met his/her lover. However, inquiry agents are expensive to hire and it would be unwise for a suspicious husband or wife to hire an agent without first taking advice from a solicitor.

Usually there will be no need for the adultery to be proved by an inquiry agent or by other circumstantial evidence. More often than not, the adulterous spouse will sign a 'confession statement', which is a simple admission setting out when and where the adultery took place and with whom. Only rarely will the court allow the name of the other person (the 'co-respondent') to be kept secret, however.

Under the old, pre-1969, divorce law, the courts were very concerned with which spouse was the 'guilty party', and in those days an admission of adultery might have seriously affected the rights of that spouse when the court came to decide custody of the children, the division of the family assets, and the payment of maintenance. Now, 'guilt' is usually ignored (see page 60) and so the adulterous spouse can sign a confession statement knowing that it will probably make no difference to his or her position when the court decides on custody of the children and how the money is to be divided.

Carrying on living with the adulterous spouse

At one time, a petitioner had to show that s/he had stopped living with his/her spouse as soon as s/he had learnt of the adultery. If s/he cohabited with him or her s/he would probably be held to have forgiven him or her and so lost the right to petition for divorce. That rule has now been changed so that the petitioner can live with the adulterer for up to six months without it being held against him or her. This is sometimes called the 'kiss-and-make-up rule' – so called, because it allows the couple a chance to try living together and working out their problems without prejudicing their divorce rights.

The six-month period need not be one single period, but can be the total of several short periods of cohabitation. For instance, a husband may commit adultery in January. If the wife continues living with him until March, but then moves out, and returns again in July, she has until September to decide whether to rely on the January adultery as grounds for a divorce. Once the six months is exceeded, that act of adultery cannot be used as a ground for divorce, except as evidence of the other spouse's 'unreasonable behaviour' if that is made the ground for divorce.

In October 1973 the wife obtained a decree nisi on the ground of her husband's adultery. In January 1974 they started living together again, and the wife told her solicitors not to apply for the decree nisi to be made a decree absolute. In December 1974 the relationship deteriorated and in June 1975 the wife applied for the decree nisi to be made absolute. Held: No. There had been more than six months' cohabitation and so there could be no decree absolute. Biggs (1976)

If a further act of adultery occurs, a new six-month period starts.

Is it intolerable to live with the adulterous spouse?

The law requires the petitioner to prove more than a simple act of adultery; s/he must also show that s/he finds it intolerable to carry on living with his/her spouse. As explained above, the court will usually accept the act of adultery as being enough to make living together intolerable. The mere fact that the couple lived together for up to six months following the adultery cannot be used to suggest that it is not intolerable for the couple to live together.

The position of the co-respondent

Finally, what of the co-respondent – the person with whom the adultery was committed? The petitioning spouse can name the co-respondent in the divorce petition and ask that the legal costs be paid by the adulterous spouse and/or the co-respondent.

Usually, the co-respondent's identity – if known – cannot be kept secret:

> *A husband wished to divorce his wife because of her adultery with three men, but only to name one as a co-respondent since the other two were happily married. The husband, therefore, asked the court for leave not to name the two men. Held: The names should be disclosed. Whilst it was unfortunate that the two men's marriages might be put at risk, the interests of justice demanded that their names be disclosed. C (1977)*

The co-respondent can defend the charge even if the respondent does not. It sometimes happens that the court finds that the respondent did commit adultery but dismisses the case against the co-respondent for lack of evidence.

In practice, it is rare for the co-respondent to have to pay more than nominal costs. Years ago, petitioners used to be able to sue the co-respondent for having sex with the other spouse, but this is no longer possible.

2. The other spouse has behaved unreasonably

'Unreasonable behaviour' is a vague and imprecise phrase; deliberately so, for this is the 'catch-all' ground for divorce. Neither Parliament nor the courts have laid down a precise definition of 'unreasonable behaviour' because to do so might narrow the scope of this ground for divorce.

Instead, we have an overall test – is the behaviour so 'grave and weighty' that the petitioner cannot reasonably be expected to carry on living with the husband or wife? So it all depends on the facts of the individual case; how serious is the misconduct and what is its effect on the petitioner?

If there is clear physical violence to the petitioner or the children that will undoubtedly be 'unreasonable behaviour'. But few cases are that straightforward – usually there is not one single incident but a succession of small, seemingly trivial, events which together combine to make the behaviour unreasonable. So small incidents can together add up to unreasonable behaviour, whether the misbehaviour is aimed at the children or the petitioner.

Unreasonable behaviour is now the most popular ground for divorce. Some 90 per cent of petitioners using this ground are women.

What is unreasonable behaviour?

Examples are given of the sort of conduct that the courts will look at to see if there has been 'unreasonable behaviour' and, if so, whether the marriage has broken down. Remember that it is impossible to give a simple guide to behaviour that will be regarded as grounds for divorce; it always depends on the circumstances. But examples of conduct that have been held to be 'unreasonable behaviour' include:

● physical assault or ill-treatment, whether or not it causes personal injury, and whether it is aimed at the petitioner or at the children;

● verbal assault (i.e. ill-treatment of a non-physical kind) such as persistent nagging, insults, unkindness, or persistently ignoring the other spouse; threats of assault; boasting of sexual experiences with other people – whether true or not;

● sexual activity with another person which, while improper, is not adultery, such as a lesbian or homosexual relationship, bestiality or petting and kissing;

● adultery followed by over six months' cohabitation as husband and wife;

● unreasonable sexual activity, such as excessive sexual demands on the petitioner, or a complete refusal to have sex or to have sex without using contraceptives, or sodomy and other unnatural sexual activities forced on the petitioner;

● refusal to have children;

● obsessive tidiness; persistent nagging; dirty habits;

● frequent drunkenness – although much will depend upon the effect of the drunkenness; drug taking;

● financial irresponsibility, such as failure to provide sufficient housekeeping money; failure to look after the home; irresponsible gambling; refusal to work when a reasonable job is available.

A few cases will illustrate how the courts decide whether or not there is 'unreasonable behaviour'.

Cases where the behaviour was unreasonable

A religious wife refused to allow her husband to smoke or drink, and she only allowed him to watch a strictly limited amount of TV. He was not allowed to entertain himself on Sundays, and in addition she would refuse to go to any social function with him – whatever the day of the week. Held: Unreasonable behaviour. (Allen, 1976)

The husband was retired and decided to renovate the house. He took up floorboards, mixed cement in the living room, and removed the lavatory door for six months. Held: Unreasonable behaviour. (O'Neill, 1975)

The wife suffered from fits and her physical and mental condition deteriorated as a result. She was an in-patient for eighteen months and then went home to see if her husband could cope with looking after her. He did everything for her for three weeks but became tense, nervous, and irritable. The wife also threw things at the husband's mother, who lived with them. Held:

33

Unreasonable behaviour, despite the fact that her behaviour was due to a mental condition. (Thurlow, 1975)

Cases where the behaviour was not unreasonable

Attitudes change. In a 1947 case a judge could say: 'It may no doubt be galling – or in some sense of the word humiliating – for the wife to find that the husband prefers the company of his men-friends, his club, his newspapers, his games, his hobbies, or indeed his own society, to association with her . . . But this may be called the reasonable wear and tear of married life.' Forty years later, these complaints would be sufficient to justify a divorce petition. Nowadays, the courts do not require serious misbehaviour.

The couple had been married for six years and had two children when the husband suddenly lost interest in his wife and was no longer sexually attracted by her. He went out a lot and became absorbed in sports. He refused to visit a marriage guidance counsellor, and eventually he left the home. Held: This was not unreasonable behaviour. (However, he was in desertion and so his wife would have been able to obtain a divorce on that ground after two years; see page 36.) (Stringfellow, 1976)

The husband left his wife because she did not show her affection openly. His nature was such that he required open, loving demonstration and reassurance. Held: The wife had not behaved unreasonably. (Pheasant, 1972)

The wife petitioned for divorce on the grounds of unreasonable behaviour because of her husband's low sex-drive. Held: Although intercourse was infrequent and unsatisfactory, and despite the fact that this made the wife unhappy, this did not of itself amount to unreasonable behaviour. (Dowder, 1978)

Proving the unreasonable behaviour

It is obviously desirable to have evidence from other people to back up an allegation of unreasonable behaviour. For instance, if a wife has been assaulted by her husband and she received hospital treatment, she should obtain a certificate from the hospital confirming the date, time, and nature of the treatment. Similarly, if her GP has been consulted in connection with the marital difficulties, he should write a letter confirming the attendance and his opinion as to the cause. Medical evidence showing that the marriage problems are getting on top of the petitioner can be invaluable.

Friends, neighbours, and relatives may also be able to give evidence as to loss of weight, nervousness, tension, sleeplessness, depression, inability to concentrate at work, lack of interest in hobbies, and also of weepiness.

The petitioner should also try to keep a record or diary of the husband's (or wife's) behaviour (i.e. noting, on the day, any way in which he abused or insulted her).

This evidence may be sufficient to prove the case, for the court will not expect to be presented with independent eyewitness evidence of assaults or other grave misbehaviour. Usually circumstantial evidence, and evidence of the effect of the misbehaviour, will be sufficient.

Carrying on living with the 'unreasonable' spouse

As with adultery, there is a six-month 'kiss-and-make-up' period for a petitioner relying on unreasonable behaviour. This means that s/he can live with the spouse, and have sexual relations, for a total of up to six months after the last act of misbehaviour. Cohabitation during this kiss-and-make-up period will not be held against him/her. However, once they have lived together for six months then the cohabitation during the kiss-and-make-up period can be taken into account by the court. So the misbehaviour can still be used as the basis of an 'unreasonable behaviour' claim – but their continued living together becomes more relevant.

3. The husband and wife both want a divorce and have been separated (living apart) for at least two years

This is the 'divorce by consent' provision that aroused such controversy when the 1969 reforms were introduced. In essence it allows a couple who have been living apart for two years to end the marriage mutually.

But if only one of them wants a divorce and the other will not consent, there can be no divorce until they have been living apart for five years (see page 37).

The main difficulties that arise concern the meaning of 'living apart', for with the housing shortage it is often unrealistic to expect one of the couple to be able to move out and obtain accommodation elsewhere. To meet this situation, the courts have held that a couple can be living in the same house and yet be living apart, if they have 'separate households'. So, although they may share the same kitchen and bathroom, they must not share the same bedroom or living-room, nor should they cook for one another, spend their evenings together, and watch TV together. In other words, they should cease living as a couple and act as though they were two strangers sharing the same house.

If the couple have shared the same accommodation, and yet claim that they have not been living together, they will need to produce independent evidence confirming the state of affairs and how they have ceased to cohabit.

When the two-year period starts

The two-year period of separation starts either from the date when the couple started living apart *or* from the date when they decided that the marriage was over – whichever is the later. Usually, of course, this will mean the date the couple started living apart, but this need not always be so.

Illustration. *A couple may be arguing and decide that a 'trial separation' would help them sort out their problems. They then separate but both have an intention of resuming cohabitation in the future. However, suppose that soon afterwards the wife decides that the marriage is dead and that there is no point in their resuming cohabitation together; in that case, the two-year period does not run from the date when they started living apart, but from the date when it was decided that the marriage was at an end.*

35

The effect of living together during the two-year period

As with adultery and unreasonable behaviour, there is a six-month 'kiss-and-make-up' period for the two-year separation. This allows the couple to resume cohabitation for up to six months without that ending their separation. If they decide to carry on living apart before the six months are up, then the two-year period of separation carries on as before.

Illustration. *Suppose a couple decide to separate and do so for twelve months. They then resume cohabitation for three months, live apart again for six months, and then cohabit again for two months. So far they have lived eighteen months apart and five months together; as long as they do not resume cohabitation for more than a month, they will be able to petition for divorce after a further six months of living apart.*

Changing your mind

Before the divorce is made either the husband or wife can change his/her mind and withdraw consent for the divorce. If the decree nisi has been granted, the husband or wife can still apply to the judge on financial grounds, and the judge will not make the decree absolute unless he is satisfied that:
• the petitioner has made reasonable provision for the other spouse or has promised to do so, *or*
• the other spouse does not need maintenance.

4. The other spouse has been in desertion for at least two years

Desertion is now rarely used as a ground for divorce. However, it was a popular ground before the 1969 reforms and it has evolved into a complex and technical subject. What follows is only an outline, and it is usually wise to take legal advice before petitioning for divorce on the ground of desertion.
There are four elements to desertion:
• living apart
• with the intention of deserting
• against the wishes of the other spouse
• and without justifiable cause.

'Living apart'. This means that there must be two separate households. But it is possible for the couple to live in the same house and yet be living apart (see page 35).

'With the intention of deserting'. Desertion must be a voluntary act. So if a spouse is in prison or in hospital it will usually not be desertion.

'Against the wishes of the other spouse'. If they both agree to live apart it is 'separation', not desertion.

'Without justifiable cause'. Obviously if a wife is driven out of the family home by her husband's unreasonable behaviour, she will not be in desertion. But he will be – even though he remains in the family home. This is called 'constructive desertion' and

arises where a spouse has behaved in such a way that he (or she) should have realized that the other spouse would be forced to leave. Constructive desertion cases are rare these days since such behaviour will usually be sufficient to justify a petition on the ground of 'unreasonable behaviour'.

Ending the desertion

The main ways of ending desertion are:
• *by a separation agreement*: if the couple agree to separate and draw up a separation agreement (see page 48), then the living apart will no longer be against the wishes of one of them, so it will become separation, not desertion;
• *by a judicial separation order*: this ends the marital duty to cohabit and so there can no longer be desertion;
• *if the deserter's offer to come home is rejected by the deserted husband or wife*: if an honest and genuine offer to return is made, the deserted spouse will become the deserter if the offer is rejected.

The effect of living together again

As with the other grounds of divorce, there is a six-month kiss-and-make-up period in desertion cases. This allows a deserted spouse to resume cohabiting with the other spouse and know that their living together will not end the desertion until they have cohabited for a total of six months. In effect it allows the two-year period to be interrupted for trial periods of reconciliation.

5. Husband and wife have been separated (living apart) for at least five years

This allows a blameless spouse to be divorced against his or her will. Subject only to the 'hardship' exception, explained below, there is virtually no way that the petitioner can be prevented from obtaining a divorce.

Living apart

The couple must be living in separate households throughout the five-year period. But it is possible for them to be living in the same house and yet be living in 'separate households' (see page 35).

The effect of living together during the five-year period

As with the other grounds for divorce, the six months' kiss-and-make-up rule applies. So the five-year period can be interrupted by up to six months' resumption of cohabitation, but once they have lived together for more than six months, the five-year period has to start running again.

The Family: Marriage and Divorce

A couple separated in 1970, but the husband visited the wife regularly, spending weekends and sometimes several weekday nights with her. On three occasions he spent a whole week with her, and between January and March 1975 he lived there continuously. In September 1975 he petitioned for divorce but the wife disputed that they had been living apart for five years. Held: The couple had not been legally 'living together' since they had separated in 1970. They had been keeping separate households since then and his visits had not altered the nature of the relationship. Piper (1978)

However, this was a borderline decision.

The 'hardship' exception

There is a special defence available in five-year separation cases. This allows the respondent (i.e. the defending spouse) to oppose the petition on the grounds that granting the divorce would cause him or her 'grave financial or other hardship, and that in all the circumstances it would be wrong (i.e. unjust) to dissolve the marriage'.

At first glance, this seems to be a defence that could be raised in many cases, especially those in which the respondent is a wife with several children who will be forced to accept a drastic reduction in her living standards. However, the courts have applied it very narrowly, for if the defence were of general application it would undermine the policy of the divorce laws – namely that dead marriages should be ended and not allowed to continue against the wishes of one of the parties.

In 1947, the husband, a Pole, had married his wife, a Sicilian, but the marriage had failed by the end of the year. The wife then went to live in Sicily with the new-born child. In 1972 the husband petitioned for divorce on the ground of five years' separation. The wife said divorce would cause her 'grave hardship' because (a) she was Roman Catholic and divorce was anathema to her, and (b) divorce would result in her and her son being socially ostracized in Sicily to such an extent that they would not be able to continue living there. Held: This was not sufficient hardship. Divorce granted. Rukat (1975)

Husband, aged sixty-seven, was divorcing wife aged sixty-three. She pleaded 'other grave hardship' because she was looking after their invalid son and a divorce would cause her great hardship. The trial judge held this was 'grave hardship' and refused the divorce. The husband appealed and, before the appeal was heard, the invalid son died. Held: The divorce would be granted. Lee (1973)

Wife opposed the divorce because she and her husband belonged to a backward Hindu caste, and divorce would result in a serious social stigma and reduce their daughter's marriage prospects. Held: The divorce would be granted. Balraj (1981)

In fact, the 'grave financial or other hardship' defence has only succeeded in a handful of cases. This was one of those exceptional cases:

H and W married in 1943. H was now sixty-one, and W was fifty-five. The three children had left home. H had deserted some nine years ago. He was a policeman and if W survived him she would receive an index-linked pension of nearly £2,000 a year. H had no other financial resources and was too old to insure his life. So the divorce petition was refused because if it was granted W would suffer 'grave financial hardship'. Johnson (1982)

The courts have made it clear that the defence is more likely to protect women than men, and that it is intended to benefit older women, rather than those who are young and healthy and who might remarry.

Financial arrangements

The judge can grant a decree nisi but refuse to make it absolute until he is satisfied that adequate financial provision has been made for the other spouse. This is the same as with the two-year separation by mutual agreement but, in practice, it only applies to a few cases.

Divorce: domicile and residence qualifications

Our courts can only grant a divorce if either husband or wife:
● *has been resident* in England or Wales for one year prior to filing the divorce petition; *or*
● *is domiciled* in England or Wales (i.e. England or Wales must be his or her home country). The domicile can be a domicile of choice or of origin (see page 21).

The defences to a divorce petition

If you are served with a petition for divorce and you do not want to be divorced, are there any defences you can raise to stop the divorce? It will be clear from the above section on the five grounds for divorce that the only possible defences are:
1. That the facts set out in the petition are not true and so the petitioner is not entitled to a divorce (e.g. you have not behaved unreasonably, or committed adultery).
2. Although the facts specified in the petition are true, you do not agree that the marriage has broken down irretrievably. It will be remembered that the five grounds for divorce are no more than the permitted ways of showing irretrievable breakdown and that, in theory, one of the grounds can exist without the marriage having broken down. But, in practice, if the petitioner says s/he regards the marriage as having irretrievably broken down, there is usually little that you can do to disprove it.

   The following was an unusual case:

   > The wife committed adultery and, despite telling her husband that she would end the affair, she continued to see the man involved. She then petitioned for divorce on the grounds of her husband's unreasonable behaviour. She complained that the husband was sulking because they had intercourse so rarely. The husband did not ask for a divorce. Held: The wife's petition was refused. The marital breakdown was not necessarily irretrievable. Welfare (1977)

3. There has been more than the six months' cohabitation allowed under the kiss-and-make-up rule. All the grounds for divorce allow trial reconciliation periods

of up to six months without prejudicing the divorce petition (for instance, you can sleep together for up to six months after adultery; you can cohabit for up to six months during a two-year separation period). If you want to argue that there has been more than six months' cohabitation you will have to produce supporting evidence, such as a diary or the evidence of friends.

4. If you are being divorced against your will under No.5 (husband and wife have been separated at least five years), then you may be able to raise the special defence that the divorce will cause you 'grave financial or other hardship'. But it is virtually unknown for the defence to succeed and for all practical purposes it might just as well not exist, so limited is its application.

5. If you are being divorced under No.3 (husband and wife both want a divorce and have been separated for at least two years) or No.5 (husband and wife have been separated for at least five years) then you can object to the decree nisi being made absolute if the financial arrangements made for you are inadequate (see page 39). But in practice this defence is rarely used because the courts feel that financial matters are best dealt with separately, and kept distinct from the decision whether or not to grant the divorce.

These are the only defences that can be raised to a divorce petition. Generally, therefore, a well-grounded divorce petition cannot be defended. This is reflected in the fact that 99 per cent of petitions are undefended – although this does not mean that the parties are in agreement about the financial arrangements or the future of the children.

These matters – together referred to as 'ancillary relief' – are dealt with in a private hearing in the judge's chambers, and are separate from the question of whether or not there should be a divorce. The point to grasp is that a divorce can be 'undefended' even though the couple are at loggerheads about everything else. The divorce, being undefended, will be simple and straightforward even if there are then long and difficult negotiations (and court hearings) about the children and the finances.

If the divorce is defended – and only 1 per cent are – legal aid may be available. It is not available for undefended divorces although the green-form scheme may provide some of the cost of legal advice and assistance (see page 868).

Getting a divorce

How much will it cost?

The cost will vary according to the complexity of the case. The more work involved, the more a solicitor will charge. The basic factor will be whether or not the divorce is defended by the other spouse. If it is defended then the costs will rise dramatically, but only a few divorces are in fact defended. In addition, the costs will increase if there are complicated financial disputes or if there is disagreement over the arrangements for the children.

The petitioner cannot be sure that the case will be undefended until the day of the court hearing, for either spouse can change his or her mind right up until the last moment. Usually, though, the petitioner will know when the respondent returns the divorce papers to the court, for amongst the questions is one asking whether or not it is intended to defend the case. If s/he says 'yes' the case is defended and is transferred from the county court to the High Court. If it is defended, legal advice will be necessary, and legal aid may be available to help with the cost.

How much? It all depends therefore on the extent of the disagreement between the husband and wife. In most cases, the divorce is undefended and one could think in terms of a solicitor charging between £100 and £200 (plus VAT), to which would have to be added the court fee of approximately £40. Generally, solicitors in the south charge more than those in the north! If there is a dispute, and so the case has to go to a trial, one must accept that the legal costs will be high. A defended divorce will probably cost each spouse over £1,000. A dispute over maintenance would probably cost some £250. Custody applications probably start at about £500, but could go up to £1,500 if several hearings were needed (although the involvement of 'experts', such as psychiatrists and welfare officers, can result in a bill running into several thousand pounds). In short, therefore, the size of the legal bill will depend upon the extent of the disagreement between the parties.

Remember that legal aid may be available, but a husband or wife on legal aid usually ends up paying their own legal fees (since the family assets will often be used towards repaying the legal aid costs). This is a most important point that is overlooked; see page 858 for how the rules work. The moral is that there are sound financial reasons for spouses to try to reach some sort of compromise rather than throw away their money on legal costs.

Will legal aid pay the costs?

The rules as to financial eligibility for legal aid are set out on page 850. Many middle-class wives who, when securely married, were outside the legal-aid limits, may well be eligible when at loggerheads with their husbands and so deprived of their income.

Defended divorces. Defended divorces can be very expensive. However, legal aid is available to help with all or part of the legal costs – assuming that the applicant comes within the current financial limits.

Undefended divorces. Legal aid is not available for undefended divorces, although it may be available to cover the costs of disputes over the children and/or money matters. This general denial of legal aid is, however, subject to two exceptions.

1. Legal advice may be available under the green-form scheme

The green-form scheme is technically different from legal aid (which covers court proceedings) in that it covers 'legal advice and assistance' – that is, everything except court proceedings. (See page 864 for how the green-form scheme works and the financial limits.)

So although a petitioner may not be entitled to full legal aid for an undefended divorce, he or she may be able to obtain legal advice and assistance under the green-form scheme, covering solicitor's fees up to £90. This will usually be enough to allow the solicitor to draft the divorce petition, give general advice on the divorce, and perhaps write a few letters. In short, he can do most of the work in the case, except take the actual steps in the proceedings. These must be done by the petitioner, since the green-form scheme does not cover a solicitor's costs in court proceedings, although it will cover the solicitor's fees in telling the petitioner what to do.

2. Legal aid may be granted in more complicated cases

If the case raises difficulties the petitioner may be able to obtain legal aid, even though the divorce is undefended. If legal aid is granted it will cover the solicitor's fees in conducting the divorce for the petitioner – unlike the green-form scheme, which only covers advice and assistance from the solicitor.

Only exceptionally will legal aid be granted for an undefended divorce (e.g. if one of the parties does not speak English, or is subnormal). But remember that the fact that the divorce is undefended does not mean that there cannot be disputes and arguments over the children and over the finances – and legal aid may well be available for those disputes (even if not for the divorce).

In an undefended case there is an alternative to paying a solicitor to handle the divorce. Both petitioner and respondent can act for themselves – a summary of the steps to be taken in a do-it-yourself divorce is set out on page 44.

Whilst a petitioner or respondent is entitled to act for himself (or herself) in a defended divorce case, this is usually unwise. The complexity of the procedures and the issues involved make it advisable to use a solicitor.

Consulting a solicitor

For how to find a solicitor, see page 820. But remember that solicitors specialize, and the solicitor who handled a friend's conveyance may not be as efficient or knowledgeable when conducting a divorce. So it is wise to ask the solicitor whether he or she does a lot of matrimonial work; if s/he does not, consider going elsewhere.

Many people find it embarrassing to have to tell a complete stranger the full details of their marital affairs, including, perhaps, their sexual relationship. However, a lawyer will treat their information as strictly confidential and will not tell anyone else about it. He will not be shocked or embarrassed by anything he may be told; in all probability, he will 'have heard it all before' and will treat the matter in as unemotional a manner as would a doctor. It is not for him to become emotionally involved in the case. He is paid to provide objective advice and he cannot do that if his judgement is clouded by prejudice in favour of his client.

He will also test the strength of his client's case by asking the sort of questions that the other spouse's solicitor may, in time, ask. Some people are surprised when they are cross-examined by their own solicitor in this way; the reason is that the solicitor wants to find out the weaknesses in the case so that he can then take steps to strengthen them.

A client who is not happy with his or her choice of solicitor should consider changing to another firm. But this should only be a last resort.

In particular it is important not to blame the solicitor for the law. Just because a solicitor tells a client that the case is hopeless it does not follow that the solicitor is incompetent, or that s/he dislikes the client. If the law does not support the case then it will be pointless to go to another solicitor.

Reconciliation

Divorce is only for dead marriages. If there is any possibility of a reconciliation then the divorce should not go through. There are numerous agencies that will give advice and help to a couple in difficulties; for instance, priests, doctors, the Marriage Guidance Council, and, for more specialized problems, the Family Planning Association, the probation service, child-care officers, etc. Some courts also run conciliation schemes, but all conciliation schemes depend upon both partners being involved – they will never be imposed on an unwilling spouse. The local CAB (or the local divorce county court) will be able to advise as to what conciliation schemes are available.

How much publicity for the divorce?

Generally, a divorce will receive no publicity; with over 150,000 divorces each year, the press are only likely to be interested if one of the parties is a public figure.

Undefended divorces are generally arranged by post so there is no court hearing. Defended cases are always heard in open court, however, and the press and public can attend if they wish. But discussion of money matters and arrangements for the children (called 'ancillary matters') is heard in private, in what are called 'chambers', so these matters are always kept secret.

In addition, the press are subject to strict regulations as to what they can report, namely only:

1. The names, addresses and occupations of those involved.
2. Any charges, defences, and counter-charges, that are supported by evidence – but not the evidence given.
3. Any submission on a point of law (and the court's decision).
4. The court's judgement and any observations made by the judge when giving judgement and during his summing up. So the judge can use this indirect route to allow the evidence to be reported.

The divorce certificate

When the court grants a divorce it will first issue a decree nisi. The decree absolute is applied for six weeks later, and is usually a formality. It is the certificate of the decree absolute that is needed as a divorce certificate (e.g. if asked for by the taxman, or by the local authority when applying for rehousing). Copies can be obtained either from the divorce registry or from the county court that granted the divorce.

DIY divorce: the undefended divorce petition

Two factors have made DIY divorce popular in recent years. Firstly, legal aid is no longer available for undefended divorces and, secondly, the procedure involved has been considerably simplified.

It is not difficult to conduct your own undefended divorce case. But be sure that you are not making a false economy in saving on solicitor's fees. If there is a considerable amount of money to be argued over or if there are children involved, it is usually wiser to take legal advice rather than risk making a mess of your case. Similarly, it is unwise to act for yourself if the case is defended. Defended cases are heard in the High Court where the procedure is much more formal and legalistic than in the county court, where undefended divorces are heard. If your spouse is likely to be obstructive in any way you would probably be advised to employ a solicitor.

When you start the divorce proceedings (see page 46) you may not know whether your spouse will defend the petition. It is not uncommon for the spouse to say initially that s/he will defend the petition when this is in fact no more than a bargaining tactic in the dispute over the children and/or money. Usually a compromise is worked out and the case ends up as undefended.

For instance, a wife may petition for divorce on the grounds of her husband's unreasonable behaviour. He denies this and cross-petitions (i.e. asks for a divorce from her) on the grounds of her adultery. She admits that she has committed adultery. Both sides want a divorce but are raising issues against the other in an attempt to secure more of the family assets or to improve their chances of gaining custody of the children. In the end, the husband allows the wife to have her divorce if she accepts only 25 per cent of the value of the matrimonial home, rather than the larger amount she might otherwise have received. If this should happen to you, consult a solicitor before agreeing to anything.

Often the petition will be based on multiple facts; in other words, it will claim that there is more than one ground for divorce. This is especially advisable when the parties have agreed on a divorce by consent after two years' separation (see page 35), for that consent can always be withdrawn at the last moment. Sometimes, a spouse will withdraw consent and refuse to agree to the divorce unless the petitioner agrees to give up more of the family finances than was previously agreed. By basing the petition on several grounds, the opportunities for such arm-twisting tactics are reduced.

It must be appreciated that the tactics in a divorce case are these days really aimed at the negotiations over money matters and over the children. The divorce itself is usually regarded as of relatively minor importance, since it is probably a foregone conclusion that the divorce petition will succeed.

For how the courts deal with money matters and children, see Chapters 3 and 8.

Undefended divorce: Children's arrangements

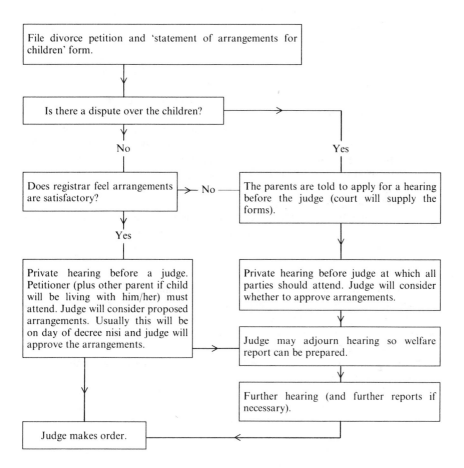

File divorce petition and 'statement of arrangements for children' form.

Is there a dispute over the children?

No

Yes

Does registrar feel arrangements are satisfactory?

No

The parents are told to apply for a hearing before the judge (court will supply the forms).

Yes

Private hearing before a judge. Petitioner (plus other parent if child will be living with him/her) must attend. Judge will consider proposed arrangements. Usually this will be on day of decree nisi and judge will approve the arrangements.

Private hearing before judge at which all parties should attend. Judge will consider whether to approve arrangements.

Judge may adjourn hearing so welfare report can be prepared.

Further hearing (and further reports if necessary).

Judge makes order.

A summary of how to obtain your own undefended divorce

1. Obtain a copy of your marriage certificate.
2. Draft the divorce petition.
    (a) Go to the local divorce county court and obtain:
      • three copies (four if an adultery case) of the standard divorce petition form (ask for form D8);
      • if there are children, three copies of the standard Statement of Arrangements for Children form (ask for form D8A);
      • a copy of the notes for guidance on filling in the forms and the free booklet on DIY divorce.
    (b) Fill in all the copies of the divorce petition form and the Statement of Arrangements for Children form, if applicable (see specimens on pages 900–901). Use the notes for guidance, the free booklet, and the books recommended below for advice on how to fill in the forms.
3. Start the divorce proceedings.
    Take or send to the court:
    • two copies of the completed divorce petition form and two copies of the Statement of Arrangements form (if there are any children). If the case is based on adultery then give the court:
    • three copies of the divorce petition;
    • the copy marriage certificate;
    • the fee of £40 (people of limited means are exempted – ask at the court);
    Note: if you are claiming a share in the family home you may also need to register your claim against the land (see page 78).
4. The court allocates a reference number to the case and sends the respondent (i.e. your husband or wife):
    • a copy of the divorce petition form and Statement of Arrangements form (if there are any children);
    • a Notice of Proceedings form;
    • a form for him/her to acknowledge that s/he has been served with (i.e. received) these documents. This is called the Acknowledgement of Service form.
5. The respondent signs the Acknowledgement of Service form stating that s/he does not intend to defend the petition, and sends it to the court.
6. The court will then send you:
    • a copy of the Acknowledgement of Service form;
    • a standard form for you to request Directions for Trial;
    • a standard form of affidavit for you to complete. This will set out the basis of your petition and the evidence in support.
7. Sign the completed affidavit of your evidence and the copy Acknowledgement of Service form in front of a solicitor or a court official. Send those documents to the court together with the completed form asking for Directions for Trial.
8. The affidavit and evidence goes before a registrar. If he thinks the evidence is

sufficient to entitle you to a divorce, he will issue a certificate, a copy of which is sent to both spouses. He also fixes a date for either:

(a) *if there are no children* – the pronouncement of the decree nisi (there is no need for either spouse to attend court on that day), *or*

(b) *if there are children* – the date of the appointment before the judge. Both husband and wife should attend (although, strictly speaking, only the petitioner need attend), when the judge, in a private hearing, will consider the proposed arrangements for the children. This is called the children's appointment. If the judge is not satisfied, he will adjourn the proceedings until the problems are resolved, and if he does not have sufficient information he may well order a welfare officer's report.

9. Once the decree nisi has been pronounced a copy is sent to both spouses, together with a copy of the judge's order concerning the children.

10. Obtain the standard form applying for the decree nisi to be made absolute, and send it to the court at least six weeks after the decree nisi is pronounced.

11. The registrar makes the decree absolute and a certificate of decree absolute is sent to both spouses.

And that's all there is to it! Ninety-seven per cent of all divorces follow the procedure set out above without the parties appearing in open court. Note that if there are no children, there is no need for the spouses to attend court at all – it is all done through the post. If there are children a court attendance will be necessary. This will be for the children's appointment (see 8(b) above), which will be a private hearing in front of a judge. The petitioner should take a copy of the petition and the Statement of Arrangements for Children and tell the judge if there are any changes in the arrangements. The judge may question the petitioner about any relevant matters, for instance, about the security of tenure of the proposed home. There will be no need for either the husband or the wife to have a solicitor present, although the Law Society has suggested that if there are any particular difficulties (e.g., if the petitioner is especially nervous or inarticulate) it is a good idea for the petitioner's solicitor to write to the judge beforehand, explaining the position.

Further information

There are several DIY divorce books on the market. Recommended is *Getting a Divorce* (Edith Rudinger, Consumers' Association). Also, there is a useful thirty-page booklet called *Undefended Divorce*, obtainable free from any county court. In a completely straightforward case it will be a sufficient guide.

ALTERNATIVES TO DIVORCE

The usual alternative to a divorce is separation. Another, much less common, alternative is to have the marriage annulled (see page 50).

Separation

There are four ways of legally separating:

1. A simple agreement to live apart.
2. A formalized agreement to live apart, set out in a deed.
3. By magistrates' court order. This used to be called a non-cohabitation order, but is now known as an exclusion order.
4. By judicial separation (relatively rare).

1. An informal separation agreement

The couple may simply decide to separate, and not reach any formal agreement about maintenance or the custody of the children. Alternatively, they may swap letters and accept those letters as binding. But the trouble is that the law might not regard the agreement as binding. Firstly, the courts do not like to enforce contracts made between husband and wife (see page 24) and, secondly, they may have scant regard for an agreement that was made without the parties having had the benefit of legal advice. Accordingly, it is usually better to consult solicitors, obtain their advice and then have the terms of the agreement set out in a deed.

> *A couple married in 1954. The wife worked and managed the family finances although the house was bought with equal contributions of capital by both husband and wife, and they both contributed to the mortgage repayments. In 1973, the wife left the husband and went off with another man, taking one of the two children with her. The husband took legal advice and his solicitors drew up a document transferring the house from joint ownership to the husband. The wife did not take legal advice before she signed. In 1975 the wife applied for a share in the family assets. Held: The 1973 transfer should be overruled since it was made at a time of emotional stress. The wife should have a share in the value of the house, on the basis of its 1973 value.* B (1977)

However, if the husband's solicitors had fully explained the effect of the transfer to the wife and urged her to take legal advice, it is likely that the transaction would have been allowed to stand.

Another problem with an informal separation agreement is that the taxman might not accept that the couple are living apart. This could then lead to problems in their claiming separate tax allowances, and also in the husband getting tax-relief on any maintenance payments he makes (see page 71). These problems will not arise if there is a formal separation deed.

2. A formal separation deed

The courts can vary and alter the terms of a formal separation deed, but they are much less likely to do so than if it was just an informal agreement. This is because a formal deed indicates an intention for the parties to be legally bound and it also shows that they took legal advice before signing the agreement.

Apart from the tax advantages of a separation deed, a deed will also reduce the likelihood of future argument as to exactly what was agreed.

The typical separation deed will contain a maintenance agreement, arrangements for the children, and a mutual covenant releasing the other spouse from the marital duty to cohabit. It may also go on to divide up the family assets between the couple.

But the terms of the deed can never be totally binding. The court always has the power to alter and vary the terms if it thinks that would be just – for instance, if the husband's income had increased significantly, or if he had deliberately concealed the true size of his wealth and so 'conned' the wife into under-settling. One point to note is that a provision that the wife will accept a stated level of maintenance payment for the rest of her life will always be void. Also, there used to be a rule that the court could only *reduce* the amount that the husband pays the wife if there was a specific clause in the agreement allowing it to do so. Today, a husband's solicitors will probably still insist on such a clause.

From the wife's point of view it is important that the deed should entitle her to maintenance. It may be that at the moment she does not need maintenance from her husband but she should always protect her position by inserting an obligation on the husband to pay her a nominal sum – even if it is only 5p a year. As long as a specific sum is stated she can always go to the courts and ask for it to be increased. If no sum is stated, she might not be entitled to maintenance and may find it difficult at a later date to persuade the court to order that she be paid any.

It is usually wise to specify the circumstances that will bring the agreement to an end. These could include the death of either spouse, the commencement of divorce proceedings (in which case the court could make an order for maintenance, etc.) or if the wife should cohabit with another man.

If the agreement releases the spouses from their mutual duty to cohabit then neither can later petition for divorce on the grounds of the other's desertion. If there is no duty to cohabit there can be no desertion.

The Inland Revenue can be very fussy about the wording of separation deeds. Accordingly, it is usually advisable to consult a solicitor when drafting the deed for otherwise the full tax advantages may be lost.

3. A magistrates' court order

A magistrates' court can order the couple to live apart. Usually this is only done when there is a real danger of violence to the wife or children. These exclusion, and personal-protection, orders are discussed in Chapter 4 (page 83). For maintenance orders in magistrates' courts see page 63.

4. Judicial separation

Judicial separation is a rarely used alternative to divorce proceedings. There are generally only some 1,600 decrees each year, and of these over 90 per cent are presented by women. Judicial separation does not end the marriage in the same way that a divorce does. Accordingly, the parties are not free to remarry. But it does end the parties' obligation to live together. If one of the spouses dies intestate (i.e. without a will) the survivor will not be able to claim the estate as the surviving spouse.

To obtain a judicial separation, the petitioner has to prove one of the same five grounds as is used to obtain a divorce (see page 29). However, there is no need to show that the marriage has broken down irretrievably. The main procedural difference is that there is no three-year rule and so the petitioner can get a judicial separation when s/he would not be able to obtain a divorce.

Judicial separation is of limited use these days. It is mainly used by petitioners who have religious scruples about divorcing, but it does not prevent the other spouse from obtaining a divorce if s/he can – and don't forget that after five years' separation s/he can get a divorce against the wishes of the other spouse. A decree of judicial separation can usually be converted into one of divorce very easily.

Annulment

Annulment is like divorce in that it ends a marriage. But, whereas divorce is granted because the marriage has now broken down irretrievably, an annulment is granted if the marriage was not valid in the first place or if it is defective in some way. Annulments are relatively rare these days for most eligible couples are able to obtain a divorce instead. There are about a thousand applications each year – compared with some 150,000 divorce petitions. But the one advantage of an annulment claim is that there is no need for the marriage to have lasted a year before the proceedings can be started (cf. the rule in divorce cases, page 28). As with divorce, the court can also make orders concerning maintenance, money, and the children.

The law distinguishes between two types of annulled marriages – those that are *void* and those that are *voidable*. The distinction is of little practical importance and basically amounts to the fact that (in theory) with the former there was never a marriage, whereas with the latter, there was a marriage but it was defective. The children of a voidable marriage will always be legitimate; with a void marriage the children will only be illegitimate if at the time of the conception one of the parents knew that the marriage was probably invalid (which is, of course, extremely rare in practice).

The grounds for annulling a marriage

Void

1. The couple are too closely related.
2. Either was under sixteen at the time of marriage.
3. Certain marriage formalities were not followed.
4. It is bigamous.
5. The couple are of the same sex.
6. Invalid polygamous marriage – because, although the marriage was valid abroad, one of the parties was domiciled here at the time of the marriage.

Voidable

7. No consummation of the marriage because one of the couple was incapable. Consummation is any one act of sexual intercourse involving full penetration and a sustained erection; ejaculation is not necessary. Premarital sex does not count as consummation.*

8. Wilful refusal by the other spouse to consummate the marriage. 'Wilful refusal' means a determined refusal, persisted in over a period of time. It does not cover nervous first-night fears! Only one act of intercourse is necessary for the marriage to have been consummated, but if a spouse then refuses any further sexual advances, s/he is almost certainly guilty of 'unreasonable behaviour' justifying the other spouse in obtaining a divorce (see page 16).*

9. Lack of consent at the time of the marriage (e.g. the spouse was drunk, coerced, etc., see page 16); or 'mental disorder' as defined by the Mental Health Act (see page 698).*†

10. At the time of the marriage the other spouse was suffering from communicable venereal disease.*†

11. At the time of the marriage the woman was pregnant by another man.*†

* The other spouse can defend the petition if s/he can show both (1) that the petitioner knew of the ground and yet led him/her into believing it would not be used against him/her and also that (2) it would be unjust to grant the decree. Generally this covers the situation where the petitioning spouse had accepted the position and treated the marriage as a proper one, but now wants an excuse to end it. Similarly, it would cover the case of a man who advertised for a housekeeper and then proposed marriage to her as a matter of convenience only. If it was clear that there was an implied no-sex agreement then nullity on the ground of wilful refusal to consummate would be refused.

† Proceedings must normally be started within three years of the marriage, otherwise the claim will not be allowed.

3 Money Matters

Married couples are not just legally united; they are also financially united. Both have an obligation to maintain the other and both can claim a share of the joint family assets if the marriage breaks down.

This chapter looks at how the law treats the finances of a married couple. For the law on the finances of an unmarried couple see Chapter 5.

Tax and marriage

On marriage, the wife's income is treated as that of her husband. She loses her personal allowance but in return the husband is given an increased personal allowance (£3,455 instead of £2,205: 1985/6 figures) and an allowance for part of his wife's earned income (up to £2,205: 1985/6 figures). Note that the wife's earned-income allowance is the same amount as the single person's allowance, but it applies only to earnings – it cannot be set against income from investments. Alternatively, the couple may opt to be treated as two separate people for tax purposes, although this is only worth while for those with large incomes. This is called 'separate taxation', or 'wife's earnings election'. Each spouse is entitled to a single person's allowance but they lose the married man's allowance and the wife's earned-income relief. But since each is a separate tax entity the effect is to defer the level of income at which they pay more than the basic rate (30 per cent) tax. Thus each partner can earn up to £16,201 taxable income (1985/6) before reaching a higher tax rate.

The figure when separate taxation becomes worth while changes every year as the tax rates and personal allowances alter. In 1985 the couple would have needed at least £26,000 between them, with the wife's share at least £7,000. In practice, a larger sum would usually be needed, since any mortgage interest paid should be added on to that figure.

Separate assessment is different from separate taxation. Separate assessment merely allows each spouse to be responsible for his/her own tax. The couple's total tax bill remains unaltered and they receive the usual reliefs of the married man's allowance and the wife's earned-income allowance.

Tax in the year of marriage

If the marriage takes place after 6 April, then for the rest of the tax year (i.e. until the next 5 April) each spouse will be treated as a single person and can claim a single person's allowance (£2,205 in 1985/6). However the husband can claim a married man's allowance (£3,455) instead of the single person's allowance for that proportion of the tax year during which he was married (e.g. if he married between 6 April and 5 May he can claim 12/12 of £3,455, and so on). His wife will still retain her single person's allowance.

Gifts between spouses

Usually it is obvious if a gift is intended; for instance, if a woman buys her husband a set of cuff-links they can be presumed to be a present.

But it is not always so straightforward. If an item is to be transferred from one spouse to the other then problems can arise. This is because the law is not satisfied with a simple statement of 'you can have my ... (e.g. car) ..., dear'. The law demands that not only should there be an intention to hand over the item, but there should be either a deed recording the transfer or, at the least, a physical delivery of the item from one spouse to the other. In fact, these rules apply to all gifts, whether they be to a spouse, child, or friend. But with husband and wife there is more of a risk that the rules will not be complied with. Often, though, they are complied with – but more by luck than design.

For instance, if a husband decides to give his wife his car because he is buying another, it is more likely than not that they will tell the registration authority of the change of ownership, and in addition, he will obviously give her the keys to the car, so the legal requirements are met. Similarly, with land, it is usual for the legal formalities to be met, because most people know that transferring land is complicated; the couple will probably instruct a solicitor to do the necessary work and so the legal formalities will be followed.

But these rules can cause hardship. Suppose a man owns valuable antique furniture which he decides to give to his wife. He tells her she can have the furniture but the gift is not recorded in writing and clearly there will be no physical transfer of the furniture; it simply stays where it is. Years later, if the husband should become bankrupt and have his assets seized, the wife would lose the furniture. She would be unable to show that it had been given to her by her husband and so it could be seized by the creditors. If the husband had known of the law he could have avoided this by making a signed deed, giving the furniture to his wife – although, obviously, it would have been invalid had it been done just to defraud his creditors.

Joint bank accounts

It is advisable for a couple to have a joint bank account, especially if one of the couple is dependent on the other.

If there is a joint account the court will assume that it is owned equally, unless the contrary can be proved. For instance, if one spouse made *all* the payments into the account then s/he may be able to claim all the money in it. But the general rule is that if both husband and wife pay money into the account at various times, they will both be entitled to a half share, even if one spouse contributed more than the other.

Usually, though, if there is a dispute it is likely to be just part of a larger dispute over dividing up the family assets because the marriage has broken down. In that case, the court can make whatever order it thinks fair and the money in the joint account is likely to be dealt with as part of an overall financial settlement (for instance, the money in the joint account may go to the husband, whilst the wife receives a larger share in the matrimonial home).

A husband's liabilities for his wife's debts

An old legal rule says that a husband can be responsible for his wife's household debts. In practice, though, this rarely happens.

The basis of the rule is that a man living with a woman impliedly takes on liability for necessary household goods and services – whether or not the couple are married. Thus, in theory, if a woman's housekeeping is insufficient she can simply buy household items (what the law calls 'necessaries') and leave it for her husband (or cohabitee) to pick up the bill. But this assumes that the woman is able to buy household goods on credit, which is not always the case.

The man has a legal defence to a claim against him if he can show that he did, in fact, pay the woman a reasonable amount of housekeeping, bearing in mind her needs; if the woman's inability to pay arises from her own bad management then the man is not liable. Obviously, this puts the trader in a difficult position; how is he to know how much housekeeping the woman receives?

The man can end his obligation to meet the household debts if he notifies the trader accordingly. This usually requires a letter since an advertisement in the local paper is ineffective unless it can be proved that the particular trader saw it.

Maintenance payments and division of the family assets when the marriage has come to an end

There are two fundamental principles:

1. **Every wife has a right to be maintained by her husband and every husband has a right to be maintained by his wife.** This mutual obligation to maintain is one of the legal consequences of marriage and the duty to cohabit together. Even if the couple stop cohabiting, the wife (or husband) may still be able to obtain maintenance for herself and she will certainly be able to obtain maintenance for the children.
2. **When the marriage ends, the courts have a free hand in dividing up the family assets between the couple.** For instance, the house may be in the husband's name, yet the court can order that it be transferred to the wife. One of the most common misapprehensions is that when a marriage ends the husband and wife split everything fifty/fifty. This is not so. More likely the wife will be awarded maintenance and between one third and a half of the family assets (such as the house).

How can you get maintenance?

If your husband/wife will voluntarily agree to pay you maintenance there will be no need to go to court. Usually, though, a court application is necessary. The procedure to be followed will depend upon whether or not you want a divorce:

• *if you do want a divorce*: once divorce proceedings have been begun you can apply to the divorce court (i.e. the county court in an undefended divorce; the High Court in a defended case). The court can order maintenance even before the divorce is granted – this is called a maintenance pending suit (see page 67).

• *if you don't want a divorce*: apply to the magistrates' court for maintenance – this is a simple, quick, and cheap procedure (see page 63).

How can you get a share of the family assets?

Unless your spouse will voluntarily agree to transferring a fair share of the assets a court application will be necessary. The procedure to be followed will depend upon whether or not you want a divorce.

• *if you do want a divorce*: the divorce court can divide up the family assets and property as it thinks fit when the divorce is granted. Often the court will simply be rubber-stamping an agreement worked out beforehand by the couple and their lawyers.

• *if you don't want a divorce*: the county court can divide up the family assets and order that they be sold. But the court will look only at the true ownership of the property; for instance, if the wife is not named on the title deeds she will not receive a share of the matrimonial home unless she contributed money towards its purchase. The court will not apply the one-third rule but will apply the same rules as with an unmarried couple who are in dispute over property (see page 90). Thus, a wife will usually be better off if she petitions for a divorce or for judicial separation, for then the court has a wider discretion and will generally give her a larger share.

How much?

The basic rules used in deciding how much maintenance and what share of the family assets a wife should receive are the same whichever court the application is made in; this can be the High Court, county court, or magistrates' court, depending upon the circumstances and the type of order sought.

A set of guidelines has emerged over the years and all the courts apply them, although each court will vary slightly in the terms of the orders it will make. Remember that every case is unique, with its own particular facts and its own set of circumstances. So what follows can only be a guide – it does not claim to be a guarantee of what will happen in any particular case. See the warning on page 81!

For advice on how to apply to the different courts for the different orders see page 62.

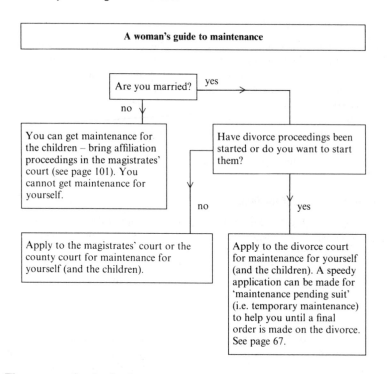

There are no fixed rules, but . . .

The starting-point is to give the wife:

- one third of the *family assets* and
- *maintenance* so that her total income will be one third of their combined gross incomes.

This is the so-called 'one-third' rule – but it isn't really a rule, it is just a starting-point. The court has to start from somewhere and it will probably start by seeing how a one-third division would work out. The figures will then have to be adjusted – either up or down – to reach the fairest result.

It is vital to realize that:

- there is no hard and fast rule which says how much each spouse is to get;
- no two cases are ever identical, so it is always impossible to be 100 per cent sure about what a court would order;
- in practice, there is rarely enough money to go around. What might have been a reasonable income for the maintenance of one household will often be totally inadequate for two households. So, usually, both husband and wife must resign themselves to a drop in their living standards;
- going to court to argue about 'who gets what' is expensive. Even a person on legal aid will probably have to put some of his/her share towards the legal costs (see

page 858), so it is usually better to do everything possible to reach a compromise agreement by negotiation. The only people who benefit when a case goes to court are the lawyers!

So, what follows is no more than a rough guide – each case has its own facts (and its own problems). See the warning on page 81!

What does the court look at?

In practice then the court will aim at giving one third of the family assets and the family income to the wife. In doing so, the courts are supposed to take into account a host of different considerations. By section 25 of the Matrimonial Causes Act 1973 any court that is considering maintenance or a division of the family assets must take into account: the house, capital earning capacity, and responsibilities of the spouses; their standard of living, their age and how long the marriage lasted; and the contributions they have both made to the welfare of the family. In practice, of course, it is usually a matter of seeing whether the one-third rule can be applied and, if not, trying to reach a settlement that comes as near to the one-third rule as seems fair. But, overall, the wife usually receives 25–35 per cent of the joint gross income.

The aim of the court

The court will realize that it cannot hope to put the parties in the same financial position as if there had not been a divorce: there is unlikely to be enough money for that. The court will look at all the circumstances but place particular emphasis on the welfare of the children, and the desirability of the couple becoming financially independent.

1. Maintenance

Wachtel (1973) was the case that first spelt out the one-third rule. But even then it was emphasized that it was no more than a starting-point. As Lord Denning said,

There may be cases where more than one third is right. There are likely to be many others where less than one third is the only practicable solution. But one third as a flexible starting-point is in general more likely to lead to the correct final result than a starting-point of equality or one quarter.

In *Wachtel*, both husband and wife were aged forty-six. The husband was earning £6,000 p.a. and the wife's earning capacity was £750 p.a. The only asset was the house, worth some £20,000. The wife received £1,500 p.a. maintenance:

husband's income (gross)	£6,000
add wife's income (net)	£ 750
	£6,750
divide by 3	£2,250
deduct wife's income	£ 750
maintenance payable	£1,500

The wife also received a lump sum of £6,000 (one third of the family assets would have been £6,666).

Maintenance: the calculation

The lawyers begin by taking the combined gross (not net of tax) earnings of both spouses. National insurance and some other outgoings (but not tax) are deducted. The court then sees how much maintenance the wife would need to give her one third of that total figure. For instance, at its simplest, this might be:

husband's earnings	£14,000
wife's earnings	£ 4,000
total gross earnings	£18,000
one third is	£ 6,000
deduct wife's earnings	£ 4,000
maintenance is therefore	£ 2,000

For a more complicated example, suppose the husband earns £15,000 (plus various other perks), and the wife earns £3,000, with the only child going to a private school. The starting-point would be:

husband's salary	£15,000	
value of company car (say)	£1,250	
phone bills paid by employer	£250	
	£16,500	
wife's earnings	£3,000	
total gross income		£19,500
less		
NI contributions for husband	£1,350	
NI contributions for wife	£315	
pension contributions	£300	
school fees	£1,800	
wife's travel expenses	£150	
total outgoings		£3,915
total net income		£15,585
one third is		£ 5,189
but wife already receives*		£2,535
So, think in terms of maintenance of		£2,654 p.a.

*i.e. £3,000 less NI of £315 and travel of £150.

But this is no more than a starting-point. The next stage is to see how this would affect each of the parties. So the court might then work out the net income of both husband and wife (after tax) if such a one-third order was made; the total household budgets would therefore be calculated (in a fairly rough-and-ready way). The earnings of any new boy-friend or girl-friend would probably be taken into account; tax,

NI, mortgage or rent payments, heating, gas, phone, electricity, HP payments, etc. would all be deducted. At the end of this one could see whether both spouses could afford to live on their respective incomes – and how much, if anything, would be left at the end of the week. If there was a wide disparity (e.g. the wife having £50 left to save at the end of each week, and the husband only having £15) then the court would probably juggle the figures and partly redress the balance (e.g. by reducing the wife's maintenance by £10 per week, so that she would be left with £40 per week, and the husband with £25).

In short, it is a case of juggling the figures to make the best of a bad job. Summarized, it is a two-step procedure:

1. Try to give the wife one third of the combined gross incomes.
2. See how this would work in practice, after allowing for living expenses. Would the outcome be roughly fair? If not, then try adjusting the figures to see if a fairer outcome can be arranged.

Maintenance: when the wife earns more

Sometimes the wife will earn a wage that is more than one third of the combined incomes. In such a case the one-third approach may be varied so that the wife still receives some maintenance – but not much.

Alternatively, the court may decide that the wife should not receive any maintenance – or just give her maintenance for a short period. This is because the modern trend is to end the financial interdependence of the couple (so that there is a 'clean break', enabling them to start again). Thus, if the wife can be financially independent (or could be working), then she may well be denied maintenance.

Maintenance: when there isn't enough money

Often the courts cannot apply the one-third rule because the husband's income cannot stretch to supporting two households. In such a case, all the court can do is to order the husband to pay as much as it thinks he can afford.

But the court will not order the husband to pay so much that he will end up with less than the current social-security subsistence levels. As an illustration, supplementary-benefit rates in 1985 were (approximately): married couple, £46; single householder, £28; single non-householder, £23; dependent child (aged eleven to fifteen), £15; dependent child (under eleven), £10. (To this would be added normally full rent via housing benefit.)

An example

A husband leaves his wife and their two children to live with his mistress, who also has two children. Both homes are council houses, with rents of £20 p.w. each. He earns £100 p.w. gross (£80 net) but his wife does not work. The one-third calculation by *Wachtel* would be:

his gross income	£100
deduct N I and travel	£10
total combined income	£90
divide by 3	£30
(the wife has no income to be taken into account)	
total maintenance due to wife	£30 p.w.

This will leave the husband with a pre-tax income of £60 p.w. But in addition he will have to pay maintenance for his two children at, say, £13 p.w. each. Thus, his pre-tax income is reduced to £34.

However, he also has to maintain his mistress and her two children. Suppose social-security subsistence levels for such a family are approximately £55 p.w. Accordingly, the court will not order him to pay maintenance that will leave him with less than £55 p.w.

But in fact he will usually be allowed more than that. In practice, the court may well end up by allowing him

• the supplementary-benefit scale allowance for himself and his dependants
• his rent
• and a quarter of his total net earnings.

In this case this would be approximately £70, plus £20, plus £22 (a quarter of £90), i.e. a total of £112. Since this is more than he earns, he would not be ordered to pay maintenance (apart from a nominal few pence per week to his children).

The wife will, however, be able to claim supplementary benefit for herself and the two children.

So in poorer families the one-third rule can have no application as regards maintenance payments. Bear in mind that a wage of £10,000 p.a. can seem a lot for one household – but for two households it will certainly be inadequate.

Maintenance: the relevance of the wife's conduct

If the wife has been adulterous, can she still expect to receive one third of the family assets and combined income? The answer is basically 'yes'. The same applies to other types of misconduct, such as cruelty, for the court is only supposed to take it into account if it would be 'inequitable' not to. This is a hopelessly vague phrase but in practical terms it generally means that the courts will not ignore bad behaviour if it would be really unfair to do so. In effect, this means that if the husband is totally innocent and the wife totally 'guilty', then the court might reduce her maintenance (although the children's maintenance could never be reduced because of the parent's conduct). Usually, the courts will be more subtle than this – they won't openly say they are reducing a wife's maintenance because of her conduct, but they will simply round down the figures and give her slightly less than might otherwise have been the case.

Maintenance: The effect of adultery

Thirty years ago, a wife who committed adultery would usually forfeit her right to maintenance. Now, however, adultery is just a factor to be taken into account and normally the court will attach little significance to it. However, if the wife is cohabiting with another man the law will assume that her new man is supporting her, and so her husband will no longer be bound to maintain her. He will, of course, still be liable to maintain the children.

Maintenance: Short marriages

If the marriage is short-lived the wife may not be entitled to anything. For instance:

A wife deserted the husband after a year of marriage. They were both in their twenties and the wife had a steady job as a nurse. A magistrates' court ordered the husband to pay her £8 p.w. He appealed. Held: When the marriage is short and the parties are young and capable of earning a living, only a nominal order should be made. She was entitled to 10p p.w. The judge said, 'In these days of women's lib., there is no reason why a wife whose marriage has not lasted long, and has no child, should have a bread ticket for life.' Graves (1973)

However, if the marriage lasts a few years, the wife will almost certainly be entitled to a third, although, in one case, a four-year marriage was regarded as 'short' (and so the wife got no share of the husband's assets). But there were no children in that case and it is best regarded as very much an exceptional decision. This is more typical:

H and W married when W was twenty-four and H was twenty-one. They parted two years later, there being no children. Both had jobs but he earned more than her (so he was left with about £25 p.w. after expenses, and she had only £5 p.w.). Held: She was only entitled to nominal maintenance (i.e. £1 a year). She should not receive normal maintenance despite the fact that H was much better off than she was. Frisby (1984)

If the husband drives the wife out she is more likely to receive one third (but – as always – remember that one third is only a rough-and-ready guide). Once there is a child of the marriage, the courts tend to pay little attention to the length of the marriage.

Maintenance: The children's maintenance

On any divorce, the court's overriding concern will be with the welfare of the children. So, proper maintenance for the children will take precedence over the financial claims of the parents. The court will want to do what is best for the children. For example, it may allow the wife to continue living in the home because she will be looking after the children – and their need for a home will take precedence over the father's desire to realize his share of the property's value (see *Mesher*, page 75).

If a man has to pay maintenance to his wife and to his children, it will usually be in the wife's interests to have a relatively large sum apportioned to the children and paid direct to them. This way, the mother will receive a tax benefit, unless she pays little or no tax. See 'Tax on maintenance payments', page 71.

How much maintenance the wife receives for the children will depend on the financial circumstances. As a guide, many practising solicitors take the current supplementary-benefit allowance for children (see page 744) as a starting-point. It has been calculated that, on average, the maintenance for each child is 7½ per cent of the father's gross income, but obviously such an arithmetical calculation is no more than a rough guide to the likely figures.

Maintenance: The effect of remarriage on maintenance payments

A wife will lose her right to maintenance payments as soon as she remarries. However, her former husband will still be liable to pay maintenance to his children; that liability will be unaffected by the mother's remarriage.

If the ex-wife decides to cohabit with another man, but not marry him, she may still forfeit her maintenance. The court always has the power to vary the amount of maintenance she should receive, and if it was felt that the woman had set up a 'household' with the man then the court would probably regard it as akin to a marriage and so considerably reduce her maintenance. However, it would be up to the husband to apply to the court to reduce the maintenance. Mere sexual liaisons will not affect the wife's right to maintenance. But once the relationship develops from that of 'boy-friend' to that of 'cohabitee', then the ex-husband might well be able to apply to the court for his ex-wife's maintenance payments to be reduced (or stopped altogether).

Property orders are not affected by a remarriage. So if a wife was given a third of the matrimonial home and then remarried, the husband could not ask the court to reverse its previous decision. So a wife who is negotiating financial arrangements with her husband should ask for a high property settlement, or lump sum, and a low maintenance payment, if she plans to remarry afterwards.

The man's remarriage does not bring his maintenance obligations to an end. However, his new commitments may be a ground for his asking that the amount of the maintenance payments be reduced.

How to apply for maintenance

A wife or husband can apply for a maintenance order whether or not divorce proceedings have been started. If divorce proceedings have begun, the application is made to the divorce court (i.e. the county court or the High Court). If divorce proceedings have not begun, the application is made to the local magistrates' court, or to the divorce county court.

Both the divorce courts and the magistrates' courts have wide powers that allow them to order one spouse to pay maintenance to the other, although in practice it will nearly always be the husband who is ordered to pay maintenance to the wife. In addition, the court can order maintenance to cover the needs of the children.

The principles used in the different courts are the same, although there are differences in the way in which the application to the court is made.

Although the different courts have similar powers to order maintenance payments, they have different powers when it comes to dividing up the family assets and property, such as the home and possessions. Basically, the magistrates' courts cannot make these orders, for it is only the divorce court that has these powers. So, if a wife (or husband) wants the court to divide up the family property, in addition to ordering maintenance, then divorce or judicial separation proceedings must be begun.

Virtually all maintenance applications are made by wives against husbands. However, it is possible for a man to apply for maintenance from his wife, for instance if he is unable to work, or if the wife is wealthy, or if he gave up his job or home by marrying her, or if he is looking after the children.

Applying for maintenance in the magistrates' court

It is quite easy to apply for a maintenance order in the magistrates' court without the help of a solicitor. Only if the sums involved are large, or if there are any particular difficulties, is a solicitor advisable.

To start the proceedings the wife goes to the local magistrates' court; this can be any magistrates' court in the county where either her husband, or she, lives. If she is embarrassed about applying in a court near her home she can go to another court in the same county, although the proceedings could be transferred to her home town if that would be more convenient to everyone else. The wife should try to be at the court by 9.45 a.m.

At the court she should ask for the warrant officer and tell him that she wishes to apply for a maintenance order – and any other order she may be seeking, such as an exclusion order (see page 83). The wife will then have to fill in a form, which is her formal complaint. She then appears before a magistrate, who will probably ask her a few questions before he issues a summons against the husband. The summons is the court's order telling him to appear at the court on a particular day to defend the maintenance claim. The issuing of the summons does not mean that the wife has been, or will be, awarded maintenance; it just signifies the start of the legal proceedings. The court staff will arrange for the summons to be served on the husband.

It will probably be a week or so before the case is heard. In the meantime, the wife can apply to the DHSS for supplementary benefit (see page 744).

Both the wife and her husband will have to attend the court hearing. Maintenance applications are 'domestic proceedings' and must, therefore, be heard in private. There must be either two or three magistrates hearing the application, and if possible, they should include members of both sexes. In the large cities, a full-time stipendiary magistrate can hear the application by himself (see page 767).

Both the wife and her husband will be asked about their family finances, where they are both living, the age of any children, their income, and so on. It is helpful if they have documentary evidence to put before the magistrates so there can be no dispute as to their financial commitments; for instance, wage slips, bank statements, mortgage agreement, rent books, savings books, and hire-purchase agreements.

Having heard the evidence in a fairly informal manner, the magistrates will decide whether the wife should receive maintenance, and if so, how much. They will also decide whether maintenance should be paid in respect of the children.

The court will only order maintenance if it is satisfied that the husband (or, exceptionally, the wife) has either

• failed to provide the wife, or the children, with a reasonable amount of maintenance, *or*

• behaved in such a way that the wife cannot reasonably be expected to live with him, *or*

• deserted the wife.

The amount of maintenance will depend on the facts of the individual case. But the basic principles used in deciding 'how much' will generally be based on Lord Denning's judgement in *Wachtel*, i.e. one third of the combined incomes (see page 56). However, magistrates' courts are generally more cautious than divorce courts and a magistrates' court may well give the wife slightly less than she would have received in the divorce court, although this is not a hard and fast rule. Also, magistrates' courts tend to be more influenced by the good or bad conduct of the parties than are the divorce courts.

It should not be forgotten that the magistrates are unlikely to order the husband to pay a sum of maintenance that will leave him (and his new family, if he has one) on less than social-security subsistence levels. In practice, the magistrates will probably make sure that the husband is left with:

• one quarter of his net (i.e. take-home) pay, *plus*

• his rent, *plus*

• supplementary-benefit rate sums for himself (and for his new family, if any).

So the maintenance for the ex-wife will be limited to whatever figure would ensure that he is not left with less than this amount. If this means that she is left with insufficient maintenance, then she will have to claim supplementary benefit. See page 59 for more detail on this rule, and an example of how it works.

If the wife is on supplementary benefit it is advisable for her to ask the court to 'make the maintenance order over to the DHSS'. (See page 66 for more details.)

Maintenance: Changing the amount of the order

The wife can go back to the court at any time, if she wants the amount increased, either for herself or for the children. Similarly, the husband can go back to the court if he wants it reduced. But the court will only increase or decrease the amount if good grounds for doing so can be shown – for instance if the husband has had a wage rise or become unemployed. If the wife commits adultery the husband can apply for her maintenance (but not the children's) to be reduced, but these days adultery, by itself, is unlikely to lose the wife her maintenance.

The amount of the maintenance can be increased any time after the original order – even if it is decades later:

*A couple married in 1942 and lived together for two years. In 1945, the wife obtained main-
tenance of £2 p.w., which was reduced to £1.50 p.w. in 1948. In 1953 she obtained a divorce
because of her husband's desertion. She had a job until 1970 when she was forced to retire because
of ill health. In 1977, she was living on state benefits and the £1.50 p.w. maintenance. The
husband was earning £110 p.w. She applied for increased maintenance. Held: She should receive
£12 p.w. (which was approximately the value of £2 in 1945). She would have received more if the
marriage had not been so short, and if it had not ended so long ago. McGrady (1977)*

Maintenance: When does the maintenance end?

The wife's right to maintenance will automatically end if she remarries, or if she
resumes cohabitation with her husband for a continuous period of six months. If the
woman starts living with another man, the ex-husband may be able to get the court
to reduce (or even stop) the wife's maintenance – but not the children's.

A child's maintenance order will continue until the first birthday after he reaches
the minimum school-leaving age of sixteen (see page 117). However, the court can
order it to continue until he is eighteen (e.g. if he is still at school) and even beyond
the age of eighteen if the child is undergoing further education, or if there is some
other reason justifying such an order.

The wife's and the children's maintenance will also end if the man dies, although
both wife and children can apply to the court for a share of his estate (see page 183).
The child's maintenance will also end if he is adopted, as the parents' duty to maintain him will then cease.

Maintenance: If the husband stops paying

The husband is supposed to pay the maintenance to the court every week (or month).
The court should then post the maintenance to the wife. If he stops paying, she will
have to go back to the court and ask for the order to be enforced. She should go to
the warrant officer and tell him she wishes to apply for 'an arrears of maintenance
summons'. Some magistrates' clerks are reluctant to issue these summonses unless
the arrears are considerable; however, they have no right to refuse to do so, even if
there is only one week of arrears. So the wife should be prepared to insist on her
rights. The summons will be issued and served on the husband by the court. When
the date of the hearing arrives both husband and wife will have to attend court. The
husband will have to explain why he has not paid the maintenance. If he can show
good cause (e.g. he has become unemployed; he has moved in with another woman
and so has additional financial responsibilities) then the magistrate may reduce the
amount of the maintenance order. Generally, though, the husband is simply told to
pay up.

He will probably be told to pay off the arrears of maintenance by instalments, but
any arrears of more than twelve months will usually be written off. The magistrates
may back up their order by threatening an attachment of earnings order, or even
imprisonment.

Attachment of earnings. If the man has a steady job, an attachment of earnings order can be a good way of enforcing the maintenance order. It is a court order telling the man's employer to deduct the maintenance from the man's wage packet and pass it on to the court. Thus, the maintenance is deducted before the man receives his wages. Obviously, such an order is of no use when the man is unemployed, self-employed, or flitting from job to job. (For more information see page 885.)

Imprisoning the husband. If the magistrates are satisfied that the husband has not paid the maintenance because of 'wilful default or culpable neglect' (i.e. if he could have paid it, but didn't) then he can be sent to prison. But prison is the last resort and will only be ordered against a persistent offender and where an attachment of earnings order would not be appropriate. No more than six weeks' imprisonment will be imposed: see the table on page 806.

Often the magistrates will sentence the husband to prison but say that the sentence will be suspended if he pays the maintenance, plus the arrears, in instalments. Thus, the man is given one more chance; if he does not keep up the payments, he will go to prison. Usually, these 'suspended orders' are successful, but in about 10 per cent of cases the husband still refuses to pay the money and so he ends up in prison.

Going to prison does not wipe out the arrears of maintenance. The husband will still be liable to pay them off when he comes out. But, in practice, the man will often avoid having to pay the arrears, because the court may decide to give him a fresh start by cancelling the debt ('remitting the arrears' is the term used), and, more important, he cannot be sent back to prison for a second time because of the same arrears. Thus the wife's chances of recovering the arrears are usually non-existent.

Maintenance: Signing the maintenance order over to the DHSS

Often, a wife who is separated from her husband will be totally dependent on her maintenance; it will be her only income. If the husband stops paying she will have to apply to the DHSS for supplementary benefit. She may, therefore, be living from week to week; one week the maintenance arrives, but next week it does not and she will have to go down to the DHSS office to queue for supplementary benefit.

The solution is for the maintenance order to be made over to the DHSS. If the husband pays the maintenance, then the DHSS will receive it direct from the court; if he does not, then the DHSS can try to enforce the maintenance order against him. But the wife will be relieved of worrying whether the maintenance will be paid. She will receive supplementary benefit each week and although the amounts may not be large at least they will be regular. She now has a guaranteed regular income which arrives on the same day each week, and she will no longer have to worry about whether he will pay up each week (and nor will she have the problem of having to go back to the court to try to enforce the maintenance order).

So the wife whose maintenance is less than the supplementary-benefit level should always ask the magistrates' court clerk if the order can be signed over to the DHSS. See page 744 for the approximate benefit levels. If her maintenance is less than these supplementary-benefit levels then the magistrates' court clerk should agree without too much difficulty. If it is more than the SB level then an application to the court may well be necessary – and a signing-over order is unlikely to be made unless the husband has previously defaulted on his payments.

In practical terms, the importance of being able to sign over the maintenance to the DHSS cannot be over-emphasized. It is estimated that as many as three quarters of all maintenance orders are signed over in this way.

Maintenance: Applying for maintenance in the county court

If a wife does not want to commence divorce proceedings she has two alternative methods of obtaining a maintenance order against her husband:
- she can apply to the magistrates' court (see above), *or*
- she can apply to the county court on the basis of her husband's failure to maintain her or the children.

The county court can make a maintenance order if there has been a failure to provide 'reasonable maintenance' for the other spouse or for one of the children. Basically, the court will decide an application on the merits of the case, using similar principles to those used in the magistrates' court and in the High Court on a divorce. In practical terms, it is easier and simpler to apply in the magistrates' court. Also, legal aid is more readily obtainable for magistrates' court applications and so most women do, in fact, apply to the magistrates' and not to the county court.

Whilst it is usually possible to get a maintenance order in the magistrates' court within two or three weeks, it can take two or three months in the county courts. The other disadvantage of applying in the county court is that the county court cannot enforce its maintenance order if the husband defaults – to enforce a county-court maintenance order, you generally go back to the magistrates' court (see page 65).

Maintenance: Applying for maintenance in the divorce court

When a wife (or a husband) files a petition for divorce, she can include a request for maintenance for herself and/or the children. The form, filled in when filing the divorce petition, contains a section for requesting maintenance. There is no need to wait for the divorce to be granted before asking for maintenance.

Maintenance can be awarded before the divorce petition is heard. This is called *maintenance pending suit* and will only be a temporary award until a proper, final award is made.

If the couple cannot reach an agreement about maintenance pending suit, the wife should file a notice in the county court, which is then served on her husband. He has fourteen days in which to file an affidavit setting out details of his income, capital, and expenses. The court arranges a private hearing before the registrar, who hears the evidence and then decides on how much maintenance pending suit should be paid. The order remains effective until the decree absolute.

There is no obligation on a wife (or indeed a husband) to apply for maintenance pending suit. If a temporary agreement can be worked out between the couple then no application is needed, but this may affect the tax position (see page 72).

An application for maintenance proper should be made as soon as the divorce proceedings are started. The application must be supported by an affidavit of means setting out the applicant's finances and an estimate of the other spouse's financial status. The husband (or wife) will also have to file an affidavit of means. Legal aid can cover maintenance disputes, even if the divorce itself is undefended.

When the maintenance application is heard by the registrar, in his chambers, he will go through the affidavits and probably question both husband and wife. If necessary, he can call for papers and other documents. Sometimes it is not easy to work out a man's income – if, for instance, he is self-employed in a cash business. In such a case the court might base its order on his apparent standard of living; it would not necessarily accept that the figures on his income-tax return were accurate. The wife's lawyers would, of course, arrange for his accounts to be carefully examined by an independent accountant.

The amount of maintenance awarded will usually be determined on the principles set out in the *Wachtel* case – i.e. the one-third-of-combined-incomes rule (see page 57). Obviously, though, if the wife is receiving an unusually large share of the house or a lump-sum payment, then she will probably have to accept a smaller amount of maintenance.

The wife should always ask for the maintenance order to be registered in the magistrates' court – this will simplify matters if the husband stops paying (see page 65). But, in practice, the High Court and county court both come under a lot of pressure from the magistrates' courts not to allow orders to be registered in the magistrates' court (basically, magistrates' court clerks think they already have too much work). Usually, therefore, the High Court and county court will only agree to registration in the magistrates' court if the husband already has a bad payment record and it seems likely that he will default in the future.

Divorce Court: If the husband stops paying the maintenance

If the husband stops paying, he will have broken the court order. The wife's remedy is to go back to the court and ask it to enforce the order against him – either by giving him a warning, making an attachment of earnings order, or by sending him to prison.

However, it is easier to apply to the magistrates' court than to the divorce court (i.e. High Court or county court). With a magistrates' court order the wife can simply go along to the court and a summons will be issued against her husband straight away; the case will probably be heard in a week or two. In the divorce court it is likely to be several weeks (or even months!) before the application is heard.

This difficulty can be overcome if the divorce court's maintenance order is registered with the magistrates' court – in other words, the divorce court makes the maintenance order but it then gives the magistrates' court the power to enforce it. If the husband stops paying, the wife can go along to the magistrates' court and issue an 'arrears of maintenance summons' in the usual way (see page 65). The procedure then is exactly as though the original maintenance order had been made by the magistrates' court and not the divorce court.

Another advantage of registering the maintenance order with the magistrates' court is that it allows it to be made over to the DHSS in cases where the maintenance is less than the supplementary benefit (see page 66).

Maintenance: Is it worth applying for maintenance?

Many women find that it is not worth applying for maintenance when they part from their husbands. Rather than go to the magistrates' court and ask for maintenance (see page 63) they wait until the divorce is granted. In the meantime the woman claims supplementary benefit.

If she does claim supplementary benefit, the DHSS cannot force her to start maintenance proceedings against her husband. In fact, deserted wives are now given a pamphlet by the DHSS which makes it clear that it is for the woman alone to decide whether to apply for maintenance; the DHSS will not pressurize her into applying to the court. (The SB handbook says 'it is left entirely to her to decide whether she wishes to take civil action. No pressure is put upon her to do so, and it is emphasized that whatever decision she reaches will not affect her entitlement to supplementary benefit.') However, the DHSS can, itself, apply for maintenance for her (if the couple are not yet divorced), and for the children.

There are two main reasons why the woman may decide it is not worth applying for a maintenance order:
• it may be unlikely that her husband would pay the maintenance;
• any maintenance would probably reduce the amount of her supplementary benefit.

If the woman is in full-time employment she will not be eligible for supplementary benefit, however poor she may be (see page 744). However, she might be able to claim family income supplement (FIS; see page 742). If in receipt of FIS she might well decide that it would be better not to claim maintenance from her husband. This is because the maintenance would be treated as income and it might increase her income so as to make her ineligible for FIS. Apart from losing FIS, she would automatically lose other welfare benefits that are given to those on FIS (such as free prescriptions, glasses, dental treatment, school dinners for children and free legal advice under the green-form scheme). If she had maintenance she would be in danger of falling into the 'poverty trap', when a small increase in income results in a larger loss of welfare benefits.

So, the best order will often be for the wife to get the matrimonial home (which will not prevent her claiming benefit), with no order for her maintenance. If the couple do not own their own home, but pay rent, then a lump sum will probably be better than regular maintenance (although problems can arise when it is more than £3,000 since she will then be ineligible for supplementary benefit – see page 744).

When the divorce is granted, the court can make maintenance orders and also property orders (for instance, giving the wife a lump sum or transferring the house to her). The normal rule is to give the wife maintenance of one third of their joint incomes and one third of the matrimonial home (see page 56). But, if resources are limited, the wife might be better advised to forgo maintenance, and negotiate instead for a lump sum and/or transfer of the home (or its tenancy) to her. This may be a more sensible course of action because:

1. The husband may not pay the maintenance.
2. Maintenance will affect her supplementary benefit (or FIS) eligibility. A capital sum of up to £3,000 will not. An even larger amount will be ignored by the DHSS if it is to be used by the wife to buy a home.
3. A lump sum can be used as a deposit for a house purchase. Note also that building societies will usually take the woman's weekly supplementary benefit payment into account as 'regular income' when assessing her mortgage application.
4. If she remarries, her maintenance payments would end, but she would not have to refund any lump sum she received.
5. If the home is transferred to her, the mortgage interest can be met by supplementary benefit (see page 744).

An out-of-court agreement

Often the husband and wife will be able to work out a satisfactory financial arrangement between themselves. It is usually advisable to have the terms of the agreement drawn up into a formal document which can then be placed before the divorce judge. He will then make a 'consent order' which confirms that both husband and wife agree to the terms and that it is now an order of the court.

If the court order does not entitle the wife to be paid any maintenance (for instance, she might be given the matrimonial home and in return agree to forgo maintenance), she cannot later change her mind and reapply to the court for maintenance. The courts say that when there is a clean break between the spouses in this way, the consent order should normally be binding. For instance:

Mr and Mrs Minton were divorced in 1972. In 1973 they reached an agreement about the family assets and it was agreed that Mrs Minton would be given the matrimonial home in return for £10,000 cash and for agreeing to forgo any maintenance. The agreement was made a consent order by the court. However, the bargain proved disastrous from Mrs Minton's point of view, for she soon found herself deep in debt, in poor health, and with the children to bring up. In 1976 she applied to the court for maintenance for herself. Held: She was not entitled to maintenance. By agreeing to the consent order she had forfeited her right to claim maintenance, and it was only fair on her husband that there should be a clean break between them. However, this did not, of course, prevent the court increasing the amount of maintenance for the children, their maintenance settlement being completely separate from that of their mother. Minton (1979)

Maintenance: When the DHSS can claim the maintenance

A man is legally obliged to maintain his wife and children. If he does not maintain them, and they claim supplementary benefit (SB, as it is usually called), then the DHSS can take him to court to recover the SB payments they have paid out. These are called 'liable-relative proceedings' (i.e. because the man is sued for maintenance in respect of relatives for whom he is liable).

Prior to divorce, liable-relative proceedings can be brought by the DHSS for money paid to both the wife and the children. After divorce, the husband is no longer obliged to maintain his ex-wife (unless a maintenance order was made in the divorce proceedings) and so liable-relative proceedings can only be brought in respect of the children – the obligation to maintain them is not ended by the divorce. This is an important point and should be remembered by a husband who is trying to negotiate a clean break with his wife and children. The wife may suggest that he gives her the house and that she have no maintenance: this will leave her free to claim SB (whereas if she had maintenance payments they would simply reduce her SB entitlement – see above). The attraction for the husband will be that he can make a fresh start and not be burdened by future maintenance payments. But, if the wife claims SB for the children, there is a risk that the DHSS will claim from the ex-husband, and if necessary start liable-relative proceedings against him. So a husband should not negotiate a clean break from the children if the wife and children will have to claim SB.

Liable-relative proceedings. If the DHSS do go to court, they will get reimbursement for payments made to the wife (if there has not been a divorce, assuming no maintenance order) or to the children. But they will make sure that the husband is left enough to live on. The court will not order the husband to reimburse the DHSS if the result would be to leave him with less than his own financial needs. To calculate how much that will be, refer back to page 59, since the same test is used as when assessing a husband's ability to pay maintenance to his wife and children.

Tax on maintenance payments

The general rule is that maintenance payments are taxable income and so the husband pays the wife the net amount (i.e. the amount due, minus tax of 30 per cent). He is then taxed on the full (100 per cent) amount. At the same time, the husband is supposed to give his wife a certificate (form R 185) stating how much tax he has deducted. If she does not pay tax, or is entitled to a refund, she can produce the certificate to the Inland Revenue and reclaim the tax deducted. Her husband must supply form R 185 if she asks him for it. He can obtain blank forms from his tax office. The husband can deduct the gross amount of the maintenance from his taxable income when he himself is assessed for tax.

Illustration. *The wife is entitled to maintenance of £100 p.w. Husband deducts tax of £30 and pays her £70. The £30 goes to the Inland Revenue. The wife can reclaim the £30 if she is not liable to tax. The husband can deduct £100 from his income when assessing it for tax.*

But there are three major exceptions to the general rule, as follows.

1. If the maintenance is paid voluntarily

If there is no legal obligation on the husband to pay the maintenance then the wife is not liable to pay tax on the money she receives; conversely, the husband cannot deduct the amount paid when assessing his taxable income. He can, however, still claim the married man's personal allowance. For instance, using the figures in the above illustration, the husband would pay £100 to his wife, who would not have to pay any tax on that sum. However, the husband would not be able to deduct £100 from his income when assessing it for tax.

2. If the maintenance order is 'free of tax'

Sometimes maintenance is declared to be 'free of tax', which means that the maintenance is paid without any tax being deducted. However, the husband is still liable to pay the tax on the grossed-up amount.

Illustration. *A wife is entitled to maintenance of '£70 p.w. free of tax'. The husband pays her £70 and he pays £30 to the Revenue. He can deduct £100 from his income when assessing it for tax.*

Orders 'free of tax' are rarely found these days.

3. If the amount of maintenance is small

If the woman is not liable to pay tax then it is inconvenient and time-wasting for her to be paid the net sum (e.g. £70) and then have to reclaim the tax deducted (e.g. £30). If she is not liable to tax, it is simpler for her husband to pay her the £100 straight away.

So special rules exist for what are called 'small maintenance payments'. These are orders that entitle the wife to £33 p.w. (£143 per month) or less, for her own maintenance, plus the same amount for each of the children. These amounts can be paid gross by the husband, so that she receives the full amount.

These rules make no difference to the total amount of maintenance paid by the husband or the amount eventually received by the wife. All they do is to allow the wife to receive the full amount straight away.

Illustration (a). *In the above example the wife is entitled to maintenance of £100 p.w. This is more than the small maintenance levels and so she has tax deducted and receives £70 p.w.*

Illustration (b). *If the wife was entitled to maintenance of £30 p.w. she would be within the small maintenance rules. Thus she would receive the full £30 without any tax being deducted.*

Illustration (c). *If the wife is entitled to maintenance of £40 p.w. for herself and £8 p.w. for her child (i.e. a total of £48) her own maintenance is outside the small maintenance limit and so she receives the £40 minus tax at 30 per cent (i.e. £12 = £28 net). The child's maintenance payment is within the small maintenance rules and so is paid without deduction, i.e. the full £8. The payment therefore, totals £36, although the wife will probably be able to reclaim the £12 tax at a later date.*

But in this case it might be better to alter the maintenance figures so the wife is entitled to £33 p.w. and the child to £15 (i.e. still a total of £48 so there is no disadvantage to the husband). Both payments are now within the small maintenance rules and so she receives a total of £48 straight away.

Note that the small maintenance rules only apply to maintenance paid under a court order. (If paid voluntarily or under a binding written agreement, tax must be deducted.)

If the maintenance is paid under the terms of a court order or if it is paid under the terms of a properly worded formal separation deed then the taxman will regard it as being paid under a legal obligation and so deductible by the husband. Thus, an informal separation agreement (see page 48) may be less beneficial from a tax point of view than a formal agreement.

Usually, maintenance agreements are made orders of the court ('consent orders') for this reason. The general test for deciding whether a maintenance agreement is a 'legally binding agreement' is: 'Could the wife take court action for arrears if the payments were not made?'

Tax on maintenance payments to children

Tax planning can be especially important with maintenance payments to children, where the child's own personal tax allowance can be utilized. Briefly, the alternatives are for the maintenance to be:
* *paid voluntarily:* husband cannot deduct the maintenance. The wife is not taxed on the maintenance received by the children or by herself.
* *paid under a binding written agreement:* husband can deduct the maintenance when assessing his taxable income and thus he is better off, but the woman will be taxed on the total maintenance received by the children and herself. Thus, she will be worse off.
* *paid under a court order:* husband can deduct maintenance when assessing his taxable income. The woman will be taxed on her share of the maintenance but she will not be taxed on the maintenance paid to the children. Each child will have a personal tax allowance (£2,205 in 1985/6) and only the excess would be taxable. Accordingly, this is usually the best solution.

How the woman can receive overpaid income tax

If the husband mistakenly deducted tax from her maintenance payments, the woman can apply to the Revenue for the tax deducted to be refunded to her. On making the claim, she will be asked to:
* complete a claim form, setting out details of all her income;
* supply a completed form R 185 from her husband;

- forward evidence that the maintenance is paid under a 'legally binding agreement' (e.g. copy of court order or separation deed).

How income tax personal allowances are treated

In the tax year in which the couple separate:
- *the man* has the full married man's allowance for that year;
- *the woman* is given the full single person's allowance from the date of separation and, if working, she can claim the wife's earned income allowance (up to the amount of her earnings if less than the allowance) for the period up to the date of separation.

Different rules apply in the following tax years:
- *the man* receives a single person allowance, unless he wholly maintains his wife with his voluntary payments. If so, he can claim the married man's allowance until the date their divorce is made absolute;
- *the woman* receives a single person's allowance.

The Inland Revenue publish a free pamphlet on *Separation and Divorce*. Ask for IR 30.

2. Dealing with the family home

In addition to maintenance, a wife may be entitled to a share of the family property and assets, such as the house and the car.

Such an order can only be made by the divorce court and so it will be necessary to start divorce (or judicial separation) proceedings. When granting the divorce, the court has a complete discretion as to how it divides up the property. As always, the main concern will be with the welfare of the children – and who is to have the home will often depend on who is to have the children.

The magistrates cannot divide up the family property or transfer it from one spouse to another. Apart from ordering maintenance payments, all they can do is order the payment of a lump sum of up to £500, although this can be done more than once. They can also order that the lump sum be paid by instalments.

The court's order will depend upon whether the home is owned or rented.

1. Owner-occupiers

Often the only substantial asset will be the family home in which the children are living. This presents a grave problem because if the assets are to be divided up the house will have to be sold, and often the parent with custody of the children will be unable to afford to buy another property. When that is the case, the courts insist that the financial entitlements of the two spouses should take second place to the needs of the children; the availability of the home for the children must be ensured.

In practical terms, there are usually three possibilities:

A. Transfer the house to one of the spouses

For instance, if there are children – and they will be living with the woman – the court might give the house totally to the wife. In practice:

• the court will rarely make such an order of its own accord (although it has, exceptionally, been ordered);

• it is quite common, however, for it to be agreed to by the parties as the best arrangement. Usually, in return for her husband's agreement, the wife will agree to abandon any right to maintenance for herself. Thus, there is a clean break – husband gives her the house, and knows that he will not have the burden of maintenance payments hanging over him for years to come;

• similarly, such an arrangement is often agreed if the wife has left the home to go and live with another man. The ex-husband may then buy out her share for a lump-sum payment.

B. Sell the property and divide the money

This may well be the best solution if neither can afford to keep the house or flat. Often it is agreed to sell the house so that the proceeds can be used to enable the wife to buy a cheaper home, with the husband giving her a larger-than-normal share of the proceeds in return for a reduced (or nil) maintenance entitlement.

A practical problem can arise if one (or both) of the parties is on legal-aid. If the home is sold then the Law Society might be able to claim some or all of the money towards repaying the legal costs. This is because the 'proceeds' of a case can be used to reimburse the legal-aid fund (see page 858 for details). On the other hand, if the house is not sold, then the Law Society will wait until the house is eventually sold before claiming repayment (and, indeed, will probably wait until even later if a replacement house is bought). So it might be better to keep the home rather than sell it, in order to avoid an immediate repayment of legal-aid costs. Often the best solution is to keep the home until after the case has been settled, and then sell – that way the legal-aid costs can probably be postponed until that replacement house is sold.

C. Keep the house, for the wife to live in

This is the order that is often made if there are young children – indeed it is often the only feasible solution. The typical order will then be for the wife to live in the house with the children, and for the house to be sold when the youngest child reaches eighteen. For instance:

A couple married in 1956. In 1970 the husband left the matrimonial home and the wife obtained a divorce and custody of their only child, a girl. The wife asked for the house to be transferred to her. Both husband and wife were planning new marriages; the husband had already bought a house with his cohabitee, and the wife's new partner had transferred his house to his ex-wife. Held: The husband should not lose all his share in the home. The property would be held jointly until the daughter was seventeen, when it could be sold. In the meantime, the wife should pay all the outgoings, including the mortgage. Mesher (1973)

That was a 1973 case, and since then the courts have refined the orders a bit. Now, generally, sale will also be ordered if the wife dies, remarries, or if she wishes to move home.

The problem with this sort of order is that the wife can find herself homeless in middle age (when the youngest child reaches eighteen or so), with only a share in the proceeds of sale – and a share that may not be enough to buy anywhere else (and a further difficulty may well be that her age and limited earnings prevent her from taking on a mortgage). To try to avoid this problem, some judges prefer to say that the property should only be sold on the wife's death, marriage, or her wishing to move (i.e. no mention of a sale on the children reaching eighteen). Thus, the wife has long-term security but at the price of depriving the husband of his share of the capital for what may turn out to be a very long time – and many judges take the view that this is too unfair on the husband.

The problem is, of course, that there is no satisfactory solution – there usually is not enough money available to finance the purchase and maintenance of two homes. Because of these difficulties, sometimes the court will order the husband to buy out the wife and so order a 'clean break'. For instance:

The husband moved out after seventeen years' marriage, leaving the wife and the three children in the house (worth £18,500). The trial judge ordered that the property be kept until the youngest child left home and that then it be sold, with the proceeds being divided fifty/fifty. In the meantime, the wife should pay 'rent' to the husband for the use of the house. On appeal, the court decided that this was an impracticable order; the wife would not have the money to pay any rent to the husband. Instead, the husband was ordered to accept the wife's offer to buy out his share in the house for £2,500. This would give him a deposit for a new house, and he would be able to afford mortgage repayments. The wife would be left with the house, which would give her long-term housing security, but no maintenance (she could claim supplementary benefit if necessary). Scipio (1983)

Does it matter whose name the house is in?

It used to matter a lot. Before 1970 the courts adopted a very legalistic approach and were primarily concerned with whose name was on the title deeds. Often a wife was refused a share in the matrimonial home simply because her name was not on the deeds.

After years of agitation by Lord Denning and others, Parliament changed the law. Now the courts are not so concerned with whose name is on the deeds, although it is still a relevant factor.

If the house, or flat, is held in joint names (i.e. both spouses' names appear on the deeds) then it is virtually certain that they own the property jointly. Often the wife will receive half the value of the house plus maintenance, although sometimes the value of the maintenance will be offset against her share and so what she will receive will be nearer one third than one half. For instance, the house in one case was in joint names but the wife was only deemed to be entitled to a one-third share. However, if there were no children, and both husband and wife had contributed to the house bills, then both would probably receive half – especially if the wife was working and would receive only a small maintenance award.

If the house is not in joint names (i.e. it is in the name of only one of the couple) then the position may occasionally be different. The courts will then be more ready to deny the other spouse a one-third share of the home, but this will only happen in exceptional circumstances, such as with a very short marriage, or where the other spouse has behaved very badly or is wealthy and yet did not provide any money for the house.

But in the vast majority of marriages that last more than a few years the wife will be given a half share, whether or not she is on the deeds. Even though her husband may have put up all the money for the house, it is likely that the court will see her contribution in terms of being a home-maker, cook, and mother, and so she will have earned her share in that way. As Lord Denning said in *Wachtel*:

. . . Parliament recognized that the wife who looks after the home and family contributes as much to the family assets as the wife who goes out to work. The one contributes in kind. The other in money or money's worth. If the court comes to the conclusion that the home has been acquired and maintained by the joint efforts of both, then, when the marriage breaks down, it should be regarded as the joint property of both of them, no matter in whose name it stands.

Although the courts will usually give the wife a half share whether or not she is on the title deeds, it is preferable for her to insist that the house be in their joint names. But it must be remembered that no two cases are the same: it is impossible to generalize, and there is no rule that says the wife must have a half share. It could be more; it could be less. See the warning on page 81.

The importance of staying at home with the children

The court will nearly always award the house to the spouse who has remained living there with the children. In practice this means that if the wife can remain in the house with the children, and get her husband out, she is almost certain to be awarded the property by the divorce court. As we have seen (above) this is likely to mean either:
• she occupies the house until the children grow up, whereupon it is sold and the proceeds divided between the spouses, *or*
• she becomes sole owner of the house immediately, forfeiting about one third of her maintenance as payment for her husband's share.

Thus, there is every reason for the wife to refuse to move out. Since her husband's legal advisers may well have informed him that if he moves out he is likely to lose the house, there is every likelihood of a domestic confrontation. Quite simply, neither dares move out. When this situation develops the law favours the wife, since she can get an exclusion order ordering the man out of the house if the strain becomes too great (see the example of *Spindlow* on page 84). Thus, an unscrupulous wife might apply for an exclusion order so as to cement her claim to the family home.

Stopping a sale before the divorce goes through

If the house is not in joint names, but (for instance) in the sole name of the husband there is an added danger; he may sell the house before the court makes an order and then disappear with the proceeds.

However, this can be prevented. The wife can register her interest in the house and so stop it being sold against her wishes. She can do this at any time – not just when she has fallen out with her husband. Her husband will probably not learn of the registration until he attempts to sell the property or to raise a new mortgage on it.

This system of registration is set out in the Matrimonial Homes Act 1983. It allows the non-owning spouse, whether wife or husband, to register a charge on the property. This gives her (or him) a legal right to occupy the home and so no one would buy the property (or lend money on its security) until she removed her registration. In effect, she can make the property unsellable and she can therefore be sure that the property will not be sold behind her back. The only transaction that the registration is ineffective against is if the building society (or other lender) forecloses on the mortgage and repossesses the house because the instalments were not paid. But otherwise it gives her complete protection. Also, if her husband should try to evict her forcibly from the house she can apply to the court for an injunction (see page 83).

This right of occupation can be registered simply, easily, and cheaply. It is best done by a solicitor, and he should be asked to 'register a Class F land charge under the Matrimonial Homes Act'. The solicitor's fee would probably be between £10 and £25 (the green-form, legal-advice scheme might cover the cost – see page 864).

A non-owning spouse who has any doubts as to the loyalty of the other spouse is always well advised to register a Class F land charge.

Ordering the other spouse out of the home

Once the divorce is heard the court can make whatever order it wishes and it may well order one of the spouses to leave the matrimonial home. Usually, the court will only order a spouse out of the home *before* the divorce is granted if he (or she) has been violent to the other spouse or to the children (see page 83).

Summary

With owner-occupied property, the woman has the following rights even if her name is not on the title deeds:
- she can live in the home until a court order is made evicting her;
- she can ask the divorce court to transfer the home to her sole name;
- in the meantime, she can prevent the home being sold, by registering a charge. She can also obtain an injunction if her husband tries to throw her out of the house.

2. Rented property

The divorce court can order that the tenancy be transferred to one of the spouses.

(a) Privately rented property

The position depends upon the terms of the tenancy, and whether there is any restriction on the tenancy being assigned (i.e. transferred).

If there is no written tenancy agreement. It will be assumed that the tenant can assign the tenancy, even if the landlord does not want him to. Thus, the court will feel able to transfer the tenancy to the other spouse even if the landlord and the original tenant object.

If there is a written tenancy agreement. The position here is more complicated. There are three possibilities:

(i) *If the agreement does not contain a clause forbidding the assignment of the tenancy* then the tenant is able to assign and so the court will feel able to transfer the tenancy to the other spouse. In other words, the position is identical to that when there is no written tenancy agreement.

(ii) *If the agreement contains a clause stating that the tenancy can only be assigned with the consent of the landlord* then the law will imply a qualification to this by saying that the landlord cannot 'unreasonably' withhold his consent. Thus, if the spouse to whom the tenancy would be granted is a 'reasonable' prospect as a tenant, then the landlord cannot object to the transfer of the tenancy. On the other hand, if it would not be 'unreasonable' for the landlord to object (e.g. the spouse cannot supply references, has no money, has previously been a bad tenant) then he cannot be forced to agree to the assignment. If the spouse is a 'reasonable' prospect then the court will feel able to transfer the tenancy, even if both landlord and tenant object. If the spouse is not a reasonable prospect then the court will not agree to the transfer. Usually, of course, there is no suggestion that the spouse (probably the wife) would not make a suitable tenant and so the problem rarely arises.

(iii) *If the tenancy agreement contains a clause stating that the tenancy cannot be assigned (and there is no clause saying that the landlord's consent is needed)* then the landlord cannot be forced to accept an assignment. Thus, the court will probably feel unable to transfer the tenancy to the other spouse.

(b) Council property

The council will only transfer the tenancy from one tenant to another if a court order has been made. The court can only make an order on divorce or judicial separation. The position will therefore depend upon whether one or both of the spouses are tenants.

• if the council flat or house is in joint names (i.e. both spouses' names are on the rent book) and the court does not order a transfer of the tenancy, then they can both stay there. This is commonly what happens when there are no children; neither spouse has anywhere else to live and so the divorced couple are forced to continue living together. If this happens, the only hope is for one of the spouses to be able to show that her (or his) mental or physical health is suffering as a result of the arrangement. If this can be shown the divorce court may order the other spouse out or the council may agree to rehouse the ill spouse.

• if the council house or flat is in the name of only one of the spouses and the divorce court does not transfer the tenancy to the other spouse, then the other spouse will have to leave if ordered to do so by the spouse who is the tenant, once the divorce has been made absolute. Until that time, s/he has a right to remain in occupation. After the decree absolute, the spouse who is the tenant can apply to the county court for an eviction order (and if necessary an injunction) against the other spouse.

• if the council house or flat is in the name of only one of the spouses and the divorce court transfers the tenancy to the other spouse, then the original tenant will have to leave. Generally, the court will transfer the tenancy to the spouse who has custody of the children and will require the other spouse to leave.

Similar rules apply when renting from a housing association.

Does it matter whose name is on the rent book?

Generally, the answer to this is 'no' for, as explained above, the court can order that the tenancy be transferred from one spouse to another. However, if the rent book or lease is in the names of both spouses then they can both continue living there unless the court says otherwise. So it is always an advantage for a spouse to have his, or her, name on the rent book or lease – in the same way that it is always better to have both names on the title deeds if the couple are owner-occupiers.

Sometimes a rented home will be in the name of the husband only and, following a matrimonial dispute, he simply walks out and does not return. When this happens, the wife can continue living in the home and she can insist that the landlord accepts rent from her as though she was the tenant. In effect, she takes over in place of her husband, although she will have to pay off any rent arrears that may have built up. This provision, in the Matrimonial Homes Act 1983, also applies to husbands who are deserted by their wives. However, it does not apply to unmarried couples – the deserted common-law wife cannot insist that she be allowed to remain in her ex-lover's rented house or flat.

Ordering the husband out before there is a divorce

This is often ordered when the husband has been violent to his wife or the children. In fact the husband can be ordered out even if he has not been guilty of physical violence (see page 83).

Summary: the finances of a split-up

This chapter has gone through the principles applied by the courts when working out maintenance and the division of the family assets on a matrimonial breakdown. It will be clear that there are numerous factors to be taken into account and accordingly it is impossible to give simplified advice that will apply in every case.

However, a few years ago in his book, *Divorce and Your Money* (Allen & Unwin, 1979), W.M.Harper attempted an analysis of reported decisions to see whether there are any mathematical constants in the decisions of the judges. Surprisingly, he found that there was an overall consistency in the approach of the judges in typical middle-class cases. His findings are summarized in the chart overleaf, although it should be emphasized that this should not be regarded as an infallible guide to the outcome of any individual case. In particular, if the parties are rich or poor, as opposed to being of average income, the chart will not be applicable. Also, the courts have become more flexible in recent years – they are now less likely to adopt rigid ideas of one third or one half. They also put greater emphasis on the position of the children and the desirability of the couple becoming financially independent. **So treat this chart and this example with great caution.**

An example

The husband earns £150 p.w. gross, and the wife £30 p.w. gross. They have three children. The husband has left the matrimonial home, which is worth £50,000, but subject to a £10,000 mortgage.

Maintenance. The wife will receive a third of the joint income, less her own: a third of £180 (£60), less £30. Thus, she receives £30 a week. Each child will receive 7½ per cent of her husband's income (i.e. £11.25 each). But there will be a slight discount for wife's earnings so each is likely to receive £10 a week. For the three this totals £30 per week. Thus the total maintenance is £60. But this is 40 per cent of the husband's income. Final maintenance is likely to be the average of 30 and 40 per cent (i.e. 35 per cent), which is £52.50 a week.

The house. This is likely to go to the wife. But she will then probably lose a third or more of her maintenance. Her final total maintenance is thus likely to be in the region of £30 to £35 a week.

Money matters: conclusion and warning

Please remember what has been repeated again and again. In a book of this sort the author can only give general guidance. Please do not think (for instance) that a wife is automatically entitled to one third income plus half the house. It is not as simple as that. Every case depends on its own circumstances – and the courts will throw away the rule book to do what is best in the particular circumstances.

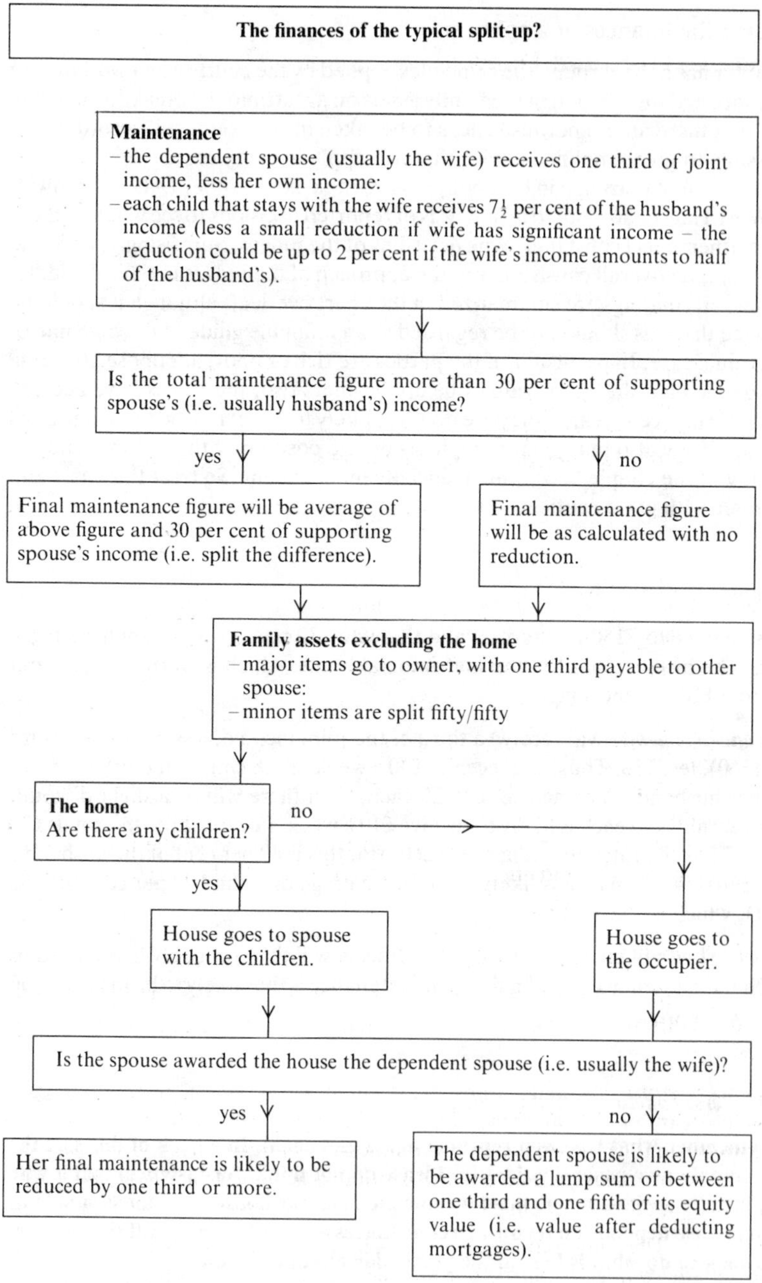

The finances of the typical split-up?

Maintenance
- the dependent spouse (usually the wife) receives one third of joint income, less her own income:
- each child that stays with the wife receives $7\frac{1}{2}$ per cent of the husband's income (less a small reduction if wife has significant income – the reduction could be up to 2 per cent if the wife's income amounts to half of the husband's).

Is the total maintenance figure more than 30 per cent of supporting spouse's (i.e. usually husband's) income?

yes

Final maintenance figure will be average of above figure and 30 per cent of supporting spouse's income (i.e. split the difference).

no

Final maintenance figure will be as calculated with no reduction.

Family assets excluding the home
- major items go to owner, with one third payable to other spouse:
- minor items are split fifty/fifty

The home
Are there any children?

no

yes

House goes to spouse with the children.

House goes to the occupier.

Is the spouse awarded the house the dependent spouse (i.e. usually the wife)?

yes

Her final maintenance is likely to be reduced by one third or more.

no

The dependent spouse is likely to be awarded a lump sum of between one third and one fifth of its equity value (i.e. value after deducting mortgages).

Based on a chart in *Divorce and Your Money* (Allen & Unwin, 1979) by W.M. Harper.
Treat this chart with caution! See warning on page 81!

4 Battered Wives and Domestic Violence

It is only recently that the law has woken up to the plight of battered wives, for until a few years ago the courts were unable to offer any effective remedy. Fortunately, Parliament has since introduced new laws and new remedies to protect the victims of domestic violence (including women who are not married), although there can still be problems in applying the remedies effectively.

There are now several remedies available but before looking at their individual merits, it should be stressed that:

● common-law wives (i.e. a woman living with a man but not married to him) *can* get protection;

● the court procedures in domestic violence cases are often complicated. It is always advisable to take legal advice and the woman should instruct a solicitor to act for her. Legal aid is available; since the husband's income will be ignored, most battered women will be eligible for free legal advice (see page 851).

How the law can protect the wife and children

The court can do two things; firstly, it can order the husband/man to stop assaulting or threatening the wife and/or children. This is called a non-molestation or personal protection order. Secondly, it can order the husband/man out of the matrimonial home, so leaving the wife and children in peace. This is called an exclusion order.

Which court to apply to?

There are three different courts that can help in wife-battering cases. The procedure in each court is different, and each has its own particular advantages and disadvantages.

The magistrates' court. The magistrates' court can make a personal protection order and/or exclusion order but only *if the couple are married.* It cannot help if the couple are unmarried and it cannot make an order unless the husband has been violent to the wife or child (or unless he had been violent to someone else and now threatens to use violence on the wife or child).

The county court. The county court can grant an injunction and/or a non-molestation order *whether the couple are married or unmarried.* The county court can make an order even if there has been no physical violence or threats of violence. For instance, see *Spindlow* (1978) below.

The divorce court. The divorce court can make a non-molestation order and/or an exclusion order, but only if divorce proceedings have been started. Obviously, this can only apply to *married* couples.

Note: unmarried women can only apply to the county court, not the magistrates' court or the divorce court.

The choice of court will depend upon the circumstances of the individual case. For instance, if the couple are unmarried the woman will have no choice but to apply to the county court. If divorce proceedings have been started, then the application will have to be made to the divorce court (i.e. the High Court in a defended divorce case; the county court in an undefended divorce).

If the couple are married and divorce proceedings have not been started, the wife has a choice; she can apply to either the magistrates' court or the county court. They have broadly similar powers and so it will often be a matter of deciding which is the more convenient. Generally, the county court is preferred.

Procedure in the magistrates' court is very informal and the wife could probably act for herself if she wanted to. However, this would rarely be necessary since she would probably be eligible for legal aid and so could have a solicitor to act for her. A disadvantage of magistrates' courts is that the magistrates are usually part-time amateurs, and there is a lack of consistency in the decisions of magistrates' courts that is not so common in the county court, where cases are decided by experienced professional judges. But the wife may find that the decision is taken out of her hands: the legal aid will probably be for the cheaper court – the magistrates' court.

In addition, the county court can make an order even if violence has not been threatened. In the magistrates' court, an act of violence is usually a pre-condition of being able to apply for an order.

'Mr and Mrs' Spindlow were unmarried; they lived in a council house with their two children. Mrs Spindlow applied to the county court (under the Domestic Violence and Matrimonial Proceedings Act 1976) for an injunction ordering Mr Spindlow to leave the matrimonial home. There had not been any real physical violence although there was evidence of one incident when Mr Spindlow had pushed Mrs Spindlow on to the settee. But Mrs Spindlow said that unless Mr Spindlow left she would leave with the children and since there was nowhere else for her to go the children would have to go into care. Held: An injunction would be granted. The welfare of the children was the court's main concern, and since Mrs Spindlow was the only person able to look after them, the court would accept the reality of the situation; she would not live with Mr Spindlow and so he would have to go. The 1976 Act allowed the court to order a spouse or cohabitee out of the home even if there had been no violence (cf. the position in the magistrates' court). Spindlow (1978)

One other advantage of the county court is that the magistrates are more likely to want the man to be given advance notice of the application to the court.

Domestic Violence: Magistrates' Court or County Court?

Giving evidence	The county court is better, since the wife can give written evidence by way of affidavit. In the magistrates' court she must attend in person and give evidence in the witness box.
Legal aid	Legal aid is available in both courts. Usually the wife will be eligible for legal aid, since her husband's income and capital will be ignored when considering her finances. In the magistrates' court, financial eligibility will be decided under the green form rules (see page 866); in the county court it will be under the civil legal-aid rules (see page 850). Because of the difference between the two, the wife should check which is financially more advantageous.
Do-it-yourself	Usually this will not be necessary, because of the availability of legal aid. But if the woman wishes to act for herself, she should choose the magistrates' court, where the procedures are less formal than in the county court.
The court's order	There are two procedural advantages of the county court. First, the county court order may last for two or three months, whereas the magistrates' court will probably say that the order will only last for a month or so. Second, the county court rules on serving the order are better, since they allow the woman's solicitor to serve the order for her. In the magistrates' court the order will be served by the police, and, in practice, they do not regard this as a priority task. Delay often occurs and they may make no great effort to track down the husband.
Children	If there are children, the wife should choose the county court. It is generally the better place for making orders affecting children.
If no violence has occurred	Only the county court can make an order if there has not already been violence. See above.
The court	There are many more magistrates' courts than county courts, so it may be more convenient to choose the magistrates' court.

The county court injunction

If the wife (married or common-law) needs help as a matter of urgency, she should apply to the county court or divorce court for an injunction against the man. An injunction is a court order directing a person not to behave in a particular way; in domestic violence cases, the injunction tells the husband not to molest the woman and children and/or not to re-enter the matrimonial home.

Orders that could be included in an injunction are:
- not to assault the woman (called a 'non-molestation order');

- not to assault the children;
- to leave the home and not return (called an 'exclusion order' or 'an ouster');
- to allow the woman back into the home;
- to keep away from the home (e.g. not to come within a quarter of a mile of the home).

If the man breaks the injunction (for instance by hitting the woman, or trying to re-enter the home) he can be brought before the court and punished – if necessary, by imprisonment. However, it can take time to summons him before the court, and a more effective way of enforcing the injunction is to allow the police to enforce it. The problem is that the police will not normally intervene in what they call 'domestic disputes', and so they will usually refuse to eject the husband even if he has broken an injunction. The only exception is where the court backed up the injunction by attaching 'a power of arrest' to it. If there is a 'power of arrest' then the police will have no choice but to intervene and enforce the injunction if asked to do so.

Thus, it is usual for the wife's lawyer to ask the court to attach a power of arrest to the injunction, so that the husband can be arrested if he breaks it. But, in practice, county courts often refuse to attach a power of arrest, unless the case is particularly serious. Certainly a power of arrest will not be granted unless there is clear evidence that the woman or child has suffered actual bodily harm.

If there is a power of arrest and the man breaks the injunction, the police can keep him in custody for up to twenty-four hours before bringing him before a judge for punishment. If there is no power of arrest, then the police cannot intervene and the woman will have to give the man at least two days' notice if she intends to apply for him to be committed to prison because he has broken the injunction. During that two-day period the woman is often at risk.

Ordering the man out of the home

It is much more difficult to persuade the court to grant an exclusion order, ordering the man out of the home, than it is to obtain a non-molestation or personal protection order, which merely orders him to stop assaulting and threatening the wife and children.

Whether or not an exclusion order will be made will depend on all the circumstances – in particular, how quickly the wife has gone to court, and the extent of the violence. It is important to realize that a domestic-violence injunction is only a temporary remedy; the courts take the view that it is reasonable to evict a man from his home for three months or so but then permanent arrangements must be worked out. For instance:

Ms O'Neill and Mr Williams cohabited in a flat, which they owned in their joint names. In August he assaulted her and so she moved out. She hoped there would be a reconciliation and so it was not until October that she went to see solicitors. They applied for legal aid (to cover the costs of going to court for an exclusion order against Williams) but legal aid was not granted until February. The court then held that it was too late: exclusion orders are designed to give temporary, emergency, relief whilst long-term solutions are sorted out. Now that six months had passed, it would not be right to order Williams to leave the flat in which he had a half-share. So, the injunction was refused and Ms O'Neill would have to apply to the court for an order that the flat be sold and the proceeds split fifty/fifty. O'Neill (1984)

Apart from the question of urgency or delay, the court will also look at:

1. Whose name is the property in (whether it be owned or rented)? If the property is in the sole name of the woman she will find it much easier to obtain an order than if it is in the sole name of the husband. This is particularly so if the couple are not married. If the couple are unmarried and the property is in the sole name of the man, the woman may obtain an exclusion order but it will not be permanent. The court will not deprive the man of his property permanently, so the woman can only expect three to six months' protection. The aim of an injunction is to give the woman a chance to find somewhere else to live. This is so whether the house is owned or rented.
2. How large is the property? Could it be divided up so that the couple could lead separate lives?
3. Is there anywhere else for the husband (or boy-friend) to go? Has he friends or relatives he can stay with?
4. What assaults or threats have been made to the woman or children? When was the most recent? Are further attacks likely? If not, there is virtually no chance of the man being ordered out. Has the man since made a sincere apology and promised to behave himself in the future? If so, what are the chances of his keeping his word?
5. Is it likely to cause mental or physical suffering to the woman and/or the children if the man is allowed to continue living in the same house? In short, is it impossible for her to continue living with him?

Applying 'on notice' or 'ex parte'

Applications to a court are usually made after notifying the defendant (i.e. the man) of the date of the application and the type of order that the court is being asked to make. Such an application is said to be made 'on notice'.

However, it is not always necessary to warn the defendant beforehand. In emergency cases the application to the court can be made without notice; such an application is said to be made '*ex parte*'.

Usually, of course, the battered woman would prefer that the application be made *ex parte*, so that the man does not know about it until after the injunction or order has been granted. Naturally, she will be worried that he will assault her if he is given notice of the proposed application. However, *ex parte* applications are only for real emergencies – i.e. more-serious-than-average cases where there is real immediate danger of serious injury or irreparable damage. Whilst non-molestation and personal protection orders can be obtained without difficulty *ex parte*, it is much more difficult to obtain an exclusion order *ex parte*. This is because the courts are reluctant to exclude a man from his home without giving him a full chance of explaining himself to the court and of being able to call witnesses to support his version of events. This is particularly so when the home is either rented or owned in the sole name of the man. The woman's solicitor will be able to advise her whether the case is sufficiently grave to justify an *ex parte* application.

Obtaining the injunction

If she wishes, the woman can act for herself and apply to the court without the help of a solicitor. However, in practice it is advisable to use a solicitor since s/he will be more familiar with the procedure and can act more speedily. Legal aid will usually be available (see page 849). Relatively few solicitors specialize in this sort of work so it is advisable to ask at a Citizens' Advice Bureau or Women's Aid Centre for the name of an experienced, competent, solicitor. Then:

1. The solicitor will type out an originating application asking the county court to grant an injunction and specifying the type of injunction sought. Two extra copies will be made – one for the court and one for the man.
2. The solicitor will take a detailed statement from the woman, which will then be set out as a formal affidavit to be signed by the woman (see the example on page 902; note that it does not only deal with the last violent incident but also explains why further violence is likely). Sometimes an affidavit will also be taken from a witness.
3. The solicitor will then take the papers to the court and pay a £15 fee; legal aid may pay the fee. In an exceptional emergency, the application can be made *ex parte*, and the hearing will take place immediately. In less exceptional circumstances the application must be on notice, and the man must be given at least four days' advance warning.
4. The application will be heard before the judge. The hearing will be in chambers, a private room, and not in a public courtroom.
5. The judge makes his order. If he grants an injunction (see pages 85, 903), the solicitor will ask him to attach a power of arrest (see page 86). The importance of this is that the police must arrest the man if he breaks the injunction. But courts are reluctant to attach a power of arrest – the Court of Appeal has said it is only for 'exceptional circumstances, where the man or woman persisted in disobeying an injunction'. Even if a power of arrest is granted, it is unlikely to be valid for more than three months.
6. The injunction must be served on the man. Only then does it become effective, unless a power of arrest is attached. The solicitor will usually arrange for service.
7. If the man disobeys the injunction the position depends upon whether the injunction had a power of arrest attached:
   • *if there was a power of arrest* the woman should contact the police, who will already have a copy of the injunction. They should arrest the man (although often they refuse to) and keep him in custody until he appears before the judge, usually within the next twenty-four hours. The woman should attend that

hearing, having sworn an affidavit setting out the details of how the injunction was broken.

● *if there was no power of arrest* the woman will have to go back to the county court. Her solicitor will try to arrange a speedy hearing in front of the judge who granted the injunction. The man must be given at least two days' notice of the hearing and the woman will have to swear an affidavit setting out how the injunction was broken. In practice, there is likely to be a delay of at least a week between the woman contacting her solicitor again and the case being heard by the judge. This is the disadvantage of not having a power of arrest.

Either way, the judge will read the affidavits and listen to what the man has to say. The man may be given another chance or he may be sent to prison for contempt of court. However, if he tells the judge he is sorry and that he will not break the injunction again, he is unlikely to go to prison. Similarly, if he is sent to prison he will probably be released as soon as he apologizes to the court and promises not to break the injunction again.

A set of legal documents from a typical domestic-violence case is shown on pages 902–3.

If the couple are unmarried

If the couple are unmarried, there is a loophole in the legislation that can mean the woman has only a pyrrhic victory. If the furniture in the home belongs to the man the court cannot prevent it being removed on his behalf. So, although the woman will have possession of the house or flat, the court cannot ensure that she also has the use of the furniture. If the woman has limited means – as is often the case – her inability to buy new furniture will make her court order of limited practical value. This is a loophole in the law that should be closed.

If the woman is homeless

The local authority has a duty to house homeless people who have a 'priority need' (see page 722). The government's Code of Guidance (see page 723) says that battered women with children are always a priority need. If there are no children, the woman should be regarded as a priority need if she risks further violence by returning home. Note that the council cannot argue that a battered woman is 'intentionally' homeless in an attempt to avoid their duty to house: the Code of Guidance says 'a battered woman who has fled the marital home should never be regarded as having become homeless intentionally, because it would clearly not be reasonable for her to remain'.

5 The Unmarried Couple

The law has yet to come to terms with the fact that many couples, living together, are not married and that society now generally regards the common-law wife as entitled to fair treatment from the courts as a form of quasi-wife.

The main differences in the legal positions of the married and unmarried couple are set out in the table on page 94 and it will be seen that there are two major areas in which the common-law wife is seriously disadvantaged:

• firstly, she cannot claim maintenance for herself (although she can, of course, claim maintenance for the children);

• secondly, she has fewer rights over the family home:

• unless she is the owner of the home (or joint owner) she can be evicted by the man;

• she can only exceptionally claim a share in the value of the home if it is owned solely by the man. (If the couple were married, she would be entitled to claim a share of its value.)

The family home

When the home is privately owned

If a couple are married, the law assumes that they are both entitled to a share in the value of the family home. The fact that the house or flat may be legally owned in the name of the husband only is usually irrelevant. The court will regard the home as a family asset to be divided up between husband and wife should the marriage end in divorce. Generally, the wife will receive up to half its value, plus the right to maintenance (see page 54).

But if the couple are unmarried the law does not take such a generous view, for it is primarily concerned with who is the strict legal owner of the property. Since there was no marriage, the courts will not presume that the home is family property to be divided up when the relationship ends. So, more often than not, the house or flat will go to the person whose name is on the title deeds. Thus, if the property is in the sole name of the man, it is likely that he alone will be entitled to it. By the same reasoning, if the property is in their joint names then they will probably be regarded as joint owners with both of them entitled to 50 per cent of its value.

So if the couple are unmarried the legal starting-point is to say that the house or flat should go to the person who owns it; the fact that it has been used as a family home is not important.

But this presumption is rebuttable. In other words, the person who is not on the title deeds can claim a share of the property if s/he can show that it is, in fact, jointly owned. Often, though, it will be difficult to prove this.

The sort of evidence that must be produced to show that the house is jointly owned would include:

• correspondence between the couple which supports the contention that the property was to be jointly owned even though it was to be put in the sole name of one of them;

• if the deposit for the property was provided by the person whose name is not on the title deeds;

• if the mortgage repayments were financed by the person whose name is not on the title deeds, even though the mortgage was taken out in the name of the 'owner';

• if the person whose name is not on the title deeds has done *a great deal* of work to the property and so increased its value. But this requires more than, for example, helping to redecorate or carrying out simple maintenance or repairs. The work must have been more than the average husband/wife would have done – in short, a great deal of work. Generally, it is very difficult for an unmarried partner to claim a share of the property in this way. There is no reported case of a mistress being awarded more than 25 per cent of the value in such a claim.

If there is a dispute as to whether the house or flat is jointly owned the person whose name is not on the title deeds should take legal advice. If it seems that s/he is entitled to a share of the property, the solicitor will start proceedings under the Law of Property Act 1925, which allows the court to pronounce on the true ownership of property and give the applicant whatever percentage of the value of the property s/he is entitled to. These proceedings will be expensive (unless legal aid is available) and slow – probably taking about nine months or so. In the meantime the 'owner' should be prevented from selling it. This can be done by the solicitor registering the non-owner's claim as a charge against the property and so making it virtually unsellable until the dispute has been resolved.

If the property is in the man's name

If the house is in the name of the man and the court is unable to find that the woman contributed to the purchase and upkeep of the property then it cannot give her a share of the sale proceeds. The most that she can hope for is that the court will decide that there was an implied contract with the man whereby he would not evict her from the property. Thus, if he tries to do so she can apply for an injunction. In one case, the Court of Appeal used this breach of contract device to give a dispossessed mistress £2,000 compensation, but such cases are very rare. Only if the woman made a substantial sacrifice by going to live with the man (e.g. she gave up a Rent Act tenancy) can she hope for any compensation if the man orders her to leave. Generally, the courts take a tough line. For instance, in a 1983 case, the Court of Appeal dealt with one woman's claim by saying 'she had lived with him for nineteen years as man and wife, and at the end had no rights against him. But the unfairness of that was not a matter in which the courts had control. It was a matter for Parliament' (*Burns*, 1984). Similarly, in another 1983 case, the Court of Appeal refused to give a common-law wife a share of the family home larger than that based upon her original financial contribution – as far as the court was concerned, it was to be a purely financial calculation, and the court would not top-up her share 'on the basis of some broad notion of what would be fair' simply because the house had been bought and used as a family home.

In short, common-law spouses do not build up any property rights. The moral is clear: they should always insist on having their names on the title deeds. Otherwise the courts – regrettably – are not prepared to help.

If the property is in joint names

Usually the proceeds of the sale will be divided fifty/fifty. If one of the parties thinks s/he is entitled to more than 50 per cent then s/he can apply to the court under the 1925 Act (see above).

It sometimes happens that only one of the joint owners wants to sell, whilst the other wants to keep the property. In these cases, the person who wants to sell can usually insist on a sale and, if necessary, obtain a court order against his reluctant co-owner. If the property has been a family home, then the court may occasionally decide that it should remain a family home until the youngest child reaches eighteen. Thus, a sale may be refused until that time – but note that this will only apply if the home was in joint names. If it is in one name only, then almost certainly the court will say that the other partner has no claim on it, and that it would be wrong to prevent the sale (see above).

Finally, note that the fact that both of the parties have their names on the title deeds does not *guarantee* that they will both have a share in the property. If the court decides that one of them only put his name to the purchase to help with the mortgage application (but did not, in fact, make any real financial contribution to the mortgage payments), then it may be the case that he is not entitled to a share in the property. But such cases are rare, and the general rule remains that a joint owner can expect a half-share in the property – for, usually, the court will find that there was some home-making contribution (e.g. bringing up the children) that should be taken into account, even if there was no financial contribution.

When the home is rented

When a marriage ends the courts can often transfer a tenancy from one spouse to another. Thus, it is usually irrelevant whose name is on the rent book or lease, for the court can simply override that and transfer the tenancy as it thinks fit (see page 79).

However, the courts do not have these powers when the relationship between an unmarried couple ends. The courts cannot simply transfer the tenancy as they think best, but must allow it to remain with the lawful tenant.

Thus it is of crucial importance to see whose name is on the rent book or lease. That person will be the tenant and can evict the other party (after giving reasonable notice, of course). Alternatively, s/he can surrender the tenancy to the landlord without being obliged to offer it to the ex-partner first.

Only rarely can the person whose name is not on the rent book or lease claim to be a tenant. He or she would have to produce sufficient evidence to show that it was intended by the couple that they should both be tenants. Generally this is difficult to prove.

Sometimes the man is the tenant and he simply abandons the woman and children in the rented flat. Since the woman is not the tenant she has no right to stay on in the flat and so the landlord can apply to the court for an eviction order against her. (If the couple were married, the landlord would have to accept the wife as the new tenant – see page 80). The abandoned common-law wife cannot remain in the rented home unless the landlord is prepared to agree to her staying there. The woman who is caught in this position is best advised to say nothing and just carry on paying the rent. Once the landlord has accepted her rent it will be difficult for him to deny that she is the lawful tenant, although the landlord can overcome this if he can prove that he thought the man was still living there and that the woman was merely acting as his agent in paying the rent.

If the man is the tenant of the family home and he dies, the woman can claim the tenancy as his 'survivor'. This is because the Rent Acts specifically allow a tenancy to be inherited by a 'member of the family' who was living with the deceased tenant. The courts have held that a mistress, or common-law wife, can be included as a 'member of the family' for this purpose. Similarly, if the woman is the tenant, the man can inherit the tenancy on her death (see page 265).

Injuctions against cohabitees: see page 83.

A List of the Main Differences in the Legal Position of the Married and Unmarried Couple

	Married couple	*Unmarried couple*
Maintenance	Husband and wife have obligation to maintain one another during the marriage and perhaps afterwards as well.	Neither has a duty to maintain his or her partner, either when they are living together or after they have broken up.
Maintenance for the children	Husband has obligation to maintain the children during the marriage and afterwards as well. He is assumed to be the father of all the children born during the marriage.	Man is not automatically bound to maintain his children. The mother must apply for an affiliation order and this will only be granted if she applies within three years of the birth or if she can show that the man maintained the child for any time during those first three years (see page 101).
Rights over the children	Both husband and wife have an equal say in the child's upbringing – unless the court makes a custody order, etc.	The father has no rights, for all the parental rights are in the mother alone. Only in an exceptional case will the court grant him custody.
Income tax	A married couple have bigger personal allowances than an unmarried couple. They are treated as one person for tax purposes, but if that is to their disadvantage they can elect to be treated as separate individuals; this is only beneficial if their joint income is £24,000 plus. They can only claim one £30,000 mortgage tax allowance.	An unmarried couple can only claim their single person's allowances, and must always be separately assessed for tax purposes. They can claim two mortgage allowances (i.e. $2 \times £30,000$).
Capital transfer tax	Transfer of property between spouses is exempt.	Transfer between the couple may be taxable.
State pension	A married woman can earn a state pension in her own right, but if she has not made enough contributions she may well be able to claim a pension by virtue of her husband's contributions.	An unmarried woman can only claim a state pension by virtue of her own contributions; she cannot claim a pension by virtue of the man's contributions.
Other state benefits	1. Lump-sum maternity grant can be claimed on the basis of the woman's NI contributions or those of her husband. Weekly maternity allowance is only payable on the woman's own NI contributions.	Lump-sum maternity grant and weekly maternity allowance can only be claimed on the basis of the woman's NI contributions – not on her lover's contributions.

	Married couple	Unmarried couple
	2. Other benefits: the married woman is eligible for widow's allowance, widowed mother's allowance and widow's pension.	The unmarried woman is not eligible for any of the widow's benefits.
	3. Legal aid: when one spouse applies for legal aid the finances of the other spouse will be taken into account, unless the couple are in dispute (e.g. divorce proceedings).	A cohabitee's finances are not taken into account when assessing financial eligibility.
Insurance	A married couple can take out insurance against each other's death.	An unmarried couple cannot take out insurance against each other's death; instead they have to insure their own lives and then legally assign the benefit of the insurance policy to their cohabitee.
Inheritance on death	1. If s/he makes a will that does not provide sufficiently for the other spouse (or the children) the court will alter the will.	1. If s/he makes a will that does not provide sufficiently for the other cohabitee (or the children) the court can alter the will.
	2. If s/he dies without a will, most of his/her property will go to the other spouse.	2. If s/he dies without making a will all his/her property will go to the family (see list on page 180) and not to the other cohabitee. However, it may be possible to get the court to order that part of the estate goes to the cohabitee or the children.
	3. Survivor will inherit funds in joint bank account.	3. Survivor will inherit funds in joint bank account.
Immigration	Either can usually join the spouse who is settled in UK.	Unmarried partner unlikely to be able to join partner who is settled in UK.
Right to occupy the home	Both spouses have equal rights to occupy the matrimonial home, until the marriage is ended by a decree absolute.	Only the owner of the flat/house has a right to occupy it. The other cohabitee can be evicted after due notice – unless s/he has obtained an injunction excluding the owner from the home because of 'wife battering', etc.

	Married couple	*Unmarried couple*
Rent/mortgage arrears	Other spouse can compel landlord/mortgagee to accept rent/mortgage payments from him or her.	Other partner cannot compel landlord/mortgagee to accept payments from him or her (unless is joint tenant or joint borrower).
Inheriting a tenancy of the family home	Will be inherited by surviving spouse (see page 265).	Will be inherited by the other partner (see page 265).
Right to a share of the family assets	On the breakup of the marriage the wife can claim a share of all the family assets even if they are in the husband's sole name (e.g. the house). Often she will be awarded one half of the assets (see page 56).	The woman can only claim what is legally hers – she cannot automatically claim a share of her cohabitee's assets (e.g. his house or car). Only if she can show that she helped pay for the property (e.g. by mortgage instalments) or perhaps if she increased its value (e.g. helped modernize it) can she claim a share of it. If the property is jointly owned it will usually be divided fifty/fifty.
Wife battering	The wife can get her violent husband excluded from the home by applying to the magistrates' court, the county court, or the divorce court. The question of whose name is on the title deeds or rent book is virtually irrelevant (see page 83).	The woman can get her violent cohabitee excluded from the home by applying to the county court. The question of whose name is on the title deeds or rent book, whilst not a major factor, is more relevant than it would be if they were a married couple (see page 83).
Ending the relationship	A marriage can only be ended by a court order (i.e. divorce, nullity, etc.). There can be no divorce in the first year of marriage.	The cohabitation arrangement can be ended without notice and without any legal formalities at any time either of the couple chooses to terminate it.

6 Change of Name

An adult can use whatever surname he or she chooses to use. It is the name by which s/he is commonly called that is the correct surname. Thus, a person called Brown can simply decide to adopt the name Smith, and the change of name will be valid. The only restriction on this is that the change of name must not have a fraudulent intent (e.g. to use someone else's cheque book).

It also follows from this that a married woman need not take her husband's surname (see page 21), and indeed her husband is free to take her name if he so chooses.

Therefore, from the law's point of view, anyone can simply change their name as and when they choose, as long as they then use that name in everyday life.

However, other people may not be prepared to accept such an informal change of name; in particular, banks, the DHSS, and other people who pay money to the person will want more formal proof of the new name. On marriage, a copy of the marriage certificate will generally be accepted as sufficient evidence, but otherwise the person may need to produce one of the three following documents.

- *A note signed by a respected member of the community (e.g. solicitor, JP, doctor, clergyman).* The note should confirm that the new name is the name by which the person is commonly known; however, an unofficial document of this sort is unlikely to impress a bank or other institution (although the passport office will usually accept it).
- *A statutory declaration.* The statutory declaration is an official way of formalizing the change of name; it is a sworn statement (similar to an affidavit); a solicitor would probably charge £20–£30 for preparing it. A typical statutory declaration is shown overleaf.
- *A deed poll.* This is the most formal method of regularizing the change of name and, in practice, is the method most commonly used. A solicitor prepares a formal deed which is signed by the person (i.e. both the old and new names) in front of a solicitor (it must be a solicitor from a different firm of solicitors). The deed might also need to be enrolled with the Supreme Court if the person is a member of one of the professions, so that the deed poll is kept as a permanent record of the change of name. A solicitor would probably charge £10–£30 for preparing and stamping a deed poll.

Changing a Christian or forename. These rules apply to surnames; surprisingly, it can be more difficult to change a forename, especially if the person has been baptized.

In practice, most people just overlook these problems and carry on as if it was the surname only that was being changed.

Changing the name of children

The name of a legitimate child cannot be changed without the consent of the father, although exceptionally the court will order that the father's consent is not necessary (see page 182). The name of an illegitimate child can be changed by the mother alone, unless the child's birth was registered in the father's name. It is not possible to alter the name on a birth certificate. The normal rule is that a birth certificate cannot be altered more than twelve months after registration. During that time, the child's name can be altered without question. After that time, however, it is possible to make a change – provided the parents can show the registrar some proof that the child was called by this name during the twelve-month period (e.g. baptismal certificate; post-office book; GP's registration card, etc.). But, unless the name was used in the twelve-month period, there is no way that the birth certificate can be altered after that time has elapsed.

How to change your name

Usually, a statutory declaration is the best method. Prepare a document along the lines of the one below, and then go to a solicitor and 'swear' it in front of him (he will charge a £3 fee).

I ... [*old* name, plus address and occupation] do solemnly and sincerely declare that:

1. I absolutely and entirely renounce, relinquish and abandon the use of my said former surname of ... and assume, adopt and determine to take and use from the date hereof the surname of ... in substitution for my former surname of ...

2. I shall at all times hereafter in all records, deeds and other writings and in all actions and proceedings, as in all dealings and transactions and on all occasions whatsoever, use and subscribe the said name of ... as my surname in substitution for my former surname of ... so relinquished as aforesaid to the intent that I may hereafter be called, known or distinguished not by the former surname of ... but by the surname of ... only.

3. I authorize and require all persons at all times to designate, describe and address me by the adopted surname of ...

AND I make this solemn declaration conscientiously believing the same to be true and by virtue of the provisions of the Statutory Declarations Act 1835.

Declared at ...
this ... day of ... 198– ... [signature] ...
before me, ...,
a solicitor
empowered to administer
oaths

7 Parents and Children

Legitimate or illegitimate?

Some 9 per cent of births are illegitimate. At one time, the illegitimate child was given virtually no legal rights against his parents and 'bastardy' carried a grave social and legal disadvantage. Today, the legal disadvantages have been largely removed, even if the social disadvantages do, to some extent, linger on.

The old test for deciding whether a child was illegitimate was to ask whether it was born 'outside wedlock'. But the law has now been reformed so that a child is presumed to be legitimate if the parents were *either* married at the time of conception *or* married at the time of birth:

The parents were married at the time of conception. It does not matter if the parents divorce between the conception and the birth. However, if they were legally separated from each other at the time of conception, the presumption of legitimacy will not apply. This is because legal separation ends the marital duty to cohabit.

The parents were married at the time of birth. It does not matter if the parents were unmarried at the time of conception – even if they were then married to other people. Further, it is presumed by the law that the child of a married woman is the child of the woman and her husband, and so the child is presumed to be legitimate.

All these presumptions can be rebutted if it can be shown that it is 'more probable than not' that the child is illegitimate. For instance, if the father was abroad at the time of conception, then the presumption of legitimacy will be rebutted and the child will be illegitimate. The same will apply if the alleged (putative) father can produce other evidence to show that the child was not his, and this will usually be by way of a blood test.

Blood tests

By comparing the blood of the man with that of the child it is sometimes possible to show that the man could not be the child's father. But blood tests can never prove that the man was the father – their sole use is in showing who could not have been the father. If the man is not the father, a blood test will have a 93 per cent chance of proving this. The point to grasp is that a blood test cannot prove paternity, only who was not the father.

The court cannot order the man to undergo a blood test but the court can of course

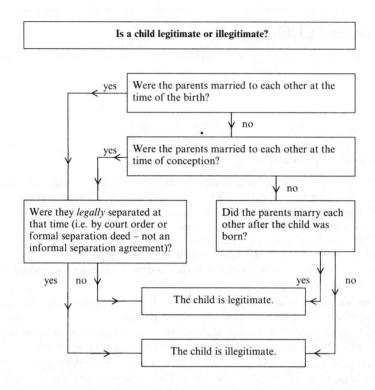

draw its own conclusions if he refuses to agree to the test. As regards the child, it is for the person with care and control of the child to give his/her consent to the blood test (see page 126 for who has care and control). But sometimes the court will intervene to stop the blood test, if it would be against the child's interests. Thus, if a child is thought to be legitimate and the only effect of the blood test would be to make him illegitimate, with no father, the court might refuse to allow the test to take place. On the other hand, if the child is already illegitimate, it is unlikely that he will suffer by having the blood test and so the test will usually be allowed. Certainly, in affiliation cases blood tests are very rarely refused.

Surprisingly, a man cannot apply for a court order declaring him to be the father of an illegitimate child.

Legitimation

Although a child may be born illegitimate, it can subsequently be made legitimate. This happens if:
● the parents marry, *or*

• the child is adopted jointly by the mother and her husband (who is not the father of the child), *or*

• the child is adopted by the mother alone. But this will only be possible if the father is dead, or missing, or if there is some good reason for excluding him from the child's future.

This is called legitimation. It is sometimes wrongly said that a child will be legitimated if the father's name is put on the birth certificate; that is not so.

A legitimated child is in virtually the same position as a legitimate child. The only differences are in complex rules as to inheritance and property rights, such as the legitimated child being unable to inherit its father's title.

If the parents do marry and so legitimate the child, they should re-register the child's birth as though the child had been born legitimate. The father will have to attend the registration to confirm his paternity, unless he was originally registered as the father or was ordered to make affiliation payments to the mother. The application for re-registration is made on form LA1, obtainable from any register office.

Affiliation: maintenance for the illegitimate child

The father of an illegitimate child is legally bound to contribute towards the child's maintenance. If he will not voluntarily agree to make reasonable payments, the mother (or the DHSS) can start affiliation proceedings against him.

Voluntary agreements

The father of an illegitimate child may voluntarily agree to pay maintenance for the child. The woman should always get the man to sign a written agreement which she would be able to produce in court if the man defaulted. The voluntary agreement does not prevent the mother from applying to the magistrates' court if she wishes. The National Council for One-Parent Families can provide a standard form of agreement for the father to sign. This agreement will be enforced by the courts, but the courts do have the power to alter the arrangement if they think fit. So if the father's income is increased, the mother can usually ask for increased affiliation payments.

Generally, the more formal the document, the more likely it is that the court will uphold it. The position is the same as with voluntary separation and maintenance agreements between a husband and wife (see page 48).

Affiliation proceedings

Few unmarried mothers apply to the courts for affiliation orders (i.e. maintenance for the child). This is partly because of the complexity of the law and partly because of the possible embarrassment of a court hearing.

The mother applies for the order in the magistrates' court. She should issue a summons in the usual way and tell the warrant officer, and then the magistrates, that she wants an affiliation order in respect of her child. (See page 886 for how to issue a summons in the magistrates' court.) A date will then be fixed for the hearing of the case. Legal aid may be available under the green-form scheme (see page 864).

The case will be heard in private, as are all 'domestic proceedings'. To obtain an order against the man, the mother will have to prove that (1) she is a single woman, (2) she has applied in time, and (3) the man is the child's father:

She is a single woman. She will be single if she is divorced, widowed, or unmarried. In addition she can be a 'single woman' even if she is married, if she is separated from her husband and has lost the right to be maintained by him. Usually, of course, she will have done so by committing adultery and bearing another man's child. She must have been single either at the time of the birth or at the time she applies to the court.

She has applied in time. She must apply no later than three years after the birth. However, if she can show that the man contributed to the child's upkeep (for instance, by paying for clothes, or making a cash payment) within that three-year period, she can apply any time thereafter.

The man is the child's father. If the man does not admit to being the father, she will have to produce evidence to support her contention. This can be done by calling as a witness someone to whom the man has admitted his paternity or by producing letters that indicate paternity. Similarly, evidence that the man has already contributed to the child's maintenance will usually prove paternity. Evidence showing that the couple probably had sex at the probable time of conception will also be accepted. If the man is not the father he will probably ask for a blood test, and this will usually be ordered.

The possible embarrassment and unpleasantness of proving paternity explains why so few affiliation applications are made.

The court's order

If the court is satisfied that the man is the child's father, it will make an affiliation order against him. The order can cover the expenses of birth, including the layette, an order for weekly maintenance payments, and the payment of a lump sum of up to £500. The order will normally run until the child's sixteenth birthday.

The amount to be paid will depend on the circumstances, such as the means and needs of both parents and the age of the child. Generally, with maintenance and affiliation payments for children, the court attempts to make the payments at least equal the current supplementary-benefit allowance for children. But often the man's low income will make such an order impossible. For instance:

An unemployed bricklayer had an affiliation order of £1 p.w. made against him. He was living on supplementary benefit and appealed the amount of the order. Held: The order should be a nominal 5p p.w. He should not be left with less than his normal supplementary allowance (although obviously the woman could reapply if he got a job and his finances improved). Haldane (1983)

The order can run from the date of the application, unless the application is made

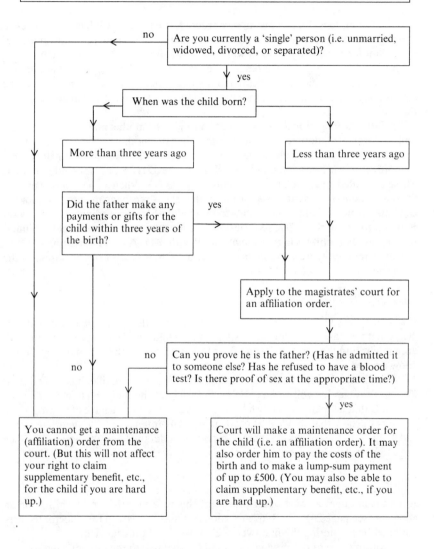

Unmarried mothers
Can you get maintenance for the child?

no — Are you currently a 'single' person (i.e. unmarried, widowed, divorced, or separated)?

yes

When was the child born?

More than three years ago

Less than three years ago

Did the father make any payments or gifts for the child within three years of the birth?

yes

Apply to the magistrates' court for an affiliation order.

no — Can you prove he is the father? (Has he admitted it to someone else? Has he refused to have a blood test? Is there proof of sex at the appropriate time?)

no

yes

You cannot get a maintenance (affiliation) order from the court. (But this will not affect your right to claim supplementary benefit, etc., for the child if you are hard up.)

Court will make a maintenance order for the child (i.e. an affiliation order). It may also order him to pay the costs of the birth and to make a lump-sum payment of up to £500. (You may also be able to claim supplementary benefit, etc., if you are hard up.)

within two months of the birth, in which case it can be backdated to the date of birth. Orders generally end on the child's sixteenth birthday, but can be continued (usually not beyond the twenty-first birthday) until the child ends his or her full-time education.

If the father does not pay the money ordered, the mother will have to go back to the magistrates' court and ask for another summons to be issued, this time for arrears of affiliation payments. The court will then decide how to enforce the order (see 'If the husband stops paying maintenance', page 65 where the position is the same).

The order is not unalterable. Either father or mother can apply to the court for the amount payable to be altered. Once the child reaches sixteen, s/he can also apply for the order to be varied.

The father's obligation does not come to an end if the mother marries another man. Only if the child is adopted by someone other than the mother need he stop paying.

If the mother is on supplementary benefit, the DHSS may apply for the affiliation order, in which case the money will go to the DHSS and not to the mother. These are called 'liable-relative proceedings' (page 71). When a single parent applies for supplementary benefit she is asked whether she is receiving maintenance for the child and, if not, whether she wishes to bring affiliation proceedings. If she refuses to name the father the DHSS will not pressure her or withhold benefit. Similar rules apply if the child is in the care of a local authority. A foster parent or adopting parent cannot apply for an affiliation order, but a person with custodianship of the child can.

Inheritance by illegitimate children

If a man leaves his property to his 'children', this will be assumed to include his illegitimate children and not just his legitimate children. Thus, the legitimate children might find themselves sharing their father's estate with someone they did not know existed.

However, the father is not obliged to leave his property to his illegitimate children. He can draw up his will as he chooses and exclude the illegitimate children if he wishes. If that happens, the only hope the illegitimate children have of sharing in the estate is to show that they were receiving some maintenance from their late father and to apply to the court for a share of his estate under the family provision laws (see page 184 for details).

Abortion

A man cannot get a court order preventing his wife or girl-friend from having an abortion (see page 24). The 1967 Abortion Act makes it lawful for a doctor to carry out an abortion during the first twenty-eight weeks of pregnancy if:
- the continuance of the pregnancy would involve risk to the mother's life, *or*
- the continuance of the pregnancy would involve risk to the physical or mental health of the mother or her other children (social circumstances can thus be taken into account), *or*

- there is a substantial risk that the child would be born with a physical or mental abnormality that would make it seriously handicapped.

The consent of two doctors is needed; a doctor or nurse can refuse to take part in an abortion on the grounds of conscience. The NHS will not always provide a free abortion and often the mother will have to go to a fee-paying clinic. A mother who is having difficulty in arranging an abortion should contact one of the pro-abortion charities, such as the British Pregnancy Advisory Service

Unplanned children. On a related topic, what happens if a man or woman has a vasectomy or sterilization operation but then has a child? Some judges have held that it is wrong for the parents to then be able to sue over the birth of the child – taking the view that it is against public policy for a claim to be based upon a child having been wrongly born. But not all judges share this view:

> *A vasectomy was carried out properly but the doctor forgot to tell the man that it could not be 100 per cent guaranteed that he would not father a child. When a child was born, the man sued for breach of contract. Held: Damages should be awarded. The man and his wife were awarded a total of £8,600 damages (£2,000 for her loss of earnings between the birth and the time the child started school; the rest being the cost of upbringing, based on SB rates). Thake (1985)*

Thus, damages may be claimed if a sterilization or vasectomy operation goes wrong.

Children: whose responsibility?

Someone has to be legally responsible for a child until it grows up and reaches the age of eighteen. Disputes can arise as to who is responsible and who has authority over the child. As a last resort, the court can resolve the argument, but when doing so the court's first concern will be the welfare of the child and not the feelings of the parents.

Legitimate children

Under the old law, the father had sole parental rights and responsibilities. But since the Guardianship Act 1973 both mother and father have equal rights and these rights 'shall be equal and exercisable by either without the other'. Thus, either mother or father can make major decisions concerning the child without the consent of the other, but the other parent can apply to the court for any dispute to be resolved. The court will decide the matter by deciding what is in the best interests of the child.

If one of the parents dies, then the surviving parent will usually assume sole authority and responsibility for the child. However, if the dead parent left a will which appointed someone as the child's guardian, then the survivor will share the parental rights and responsibilities with that person. This means that major decisions affecting the child must be taken in consultation with the guardian, for otherwise the guardian would be able to apply to the court for it to intervene. In practice, this rarely happens and the surviving parent is usually left to bring up the child with the guardian only intervening in the most exceptional circumstances.

The Family: Children

If the child's parents divorce, then the authority and responsibility for the child will pass to the parent who is given custody by the court. If neither parent is given custody, then the position continues as before, with custody being shared by both parents.

Exceptionally, one parent is given custody and the other parent is given 'care and control'. When this happens, the child lives with the parent who has care and control, but the parent with custody has to be consulted about major decisions affecting the child (see also page 126).

Illegitimate children

The mother has sole parental rights and responsibilities. The father generally has no say in how the child is brought up, even if he is paying maintenance towards its upkeep. If the father is worried about the way the child is being brought up he can apply for custody or access, or apply for the child to be made a ward of court (see page 133); alternatively he could ask the Social Services Department to intervene and, in an extreme case, they might take the child into care. The father cannot object if the mother proposes to change the child's name. Note that there is no legal procedure that allows the father to establish his paternity without the mother's consent and cooperation.

Losing parental rights and authority

A parent can lose his/her rights and authority by the child being taken into care or being made a ward of court, or if custody is granted to the other parent (see page 127).

Step-parents

If a child's mother or father remarries, then the parent's new spouse will be the child's step-parent. Yet although the child may regard the step-parent as its 'new' mother or father, the law does not recognize that there is a parental relationship between them.

Unless the step-parent acquires some legal status vis-à-vis the child (and that would be done by adoption or a custody order, see page 126), s/he will have no rights over the child. But if the step-parent accepts the child as a member of the family, then the step-parent will become liable for its maintenance. So, on divorce, the step-parent can be made to pay maintenance to the child.

But the real difficulties arise when the natural parent dies. Usually the step-parent will have no legal rights over the child unless adoption or custody has been arranged. If the natural parent was divorced, it is likely that the only person with parental rights over the child will be the other divorced parent, if still alive. If so, that parent can theoretically take the child away from its home. But even if the other parent is dead or if the child was illegitimate, the step-parent will still not have any legal rights over the child, simply because the law does not recognize the relationship of step-parent and stepchild. The step-parent can, however, apply to be made guardian or to be granted custodianship or to adopt the child, but an application for the child to be made a ward of court (see page 133) is usually the best step to take.

Adoption by a step-parent

About half of all adoptions are made by a parent and step-parent. It is the most complete way of forming a legal relationship between the child and its step-parent.

If the child is legitimate and the other parent is still alive then his/her consent will usually be needed for the adoption. Without that consent the adoption is unlikely to be allowed because the courts will very rarely force the parent to consent. When this happens, the best the step-parent can hope for is a custodianship order (in effect, custody for non-parents) and not adoption. But even if the other parent does consent, the court may well be reluctant to sever the child's links with its natural parent and so the step-parent will often only be granted custody.

If the child is illegitimate then there will be no need to obtain the consent of the other natural parent (i.e. the father). The same will be true if the child was legitimate but the other parent has since died without appointing a guardian. However, even in these cases, the court will not always approve an adoption order; it might make a custodianship order instead.

Custody to a step-parent

Whilst the courts are reluctant to allow a step-parent to adopt a stepchild, they will usually encourage the step-parent to obtain custody of the child. This can be done by applying to the court and asking for the original custody order to be varied so that custody is now shared jointly by the natural parent and his, or her, new spouse, the step-parent.

One of the main problems that arises between step-parents and stepchildren is over the child's surname. Generally, the surname cannot be changed to that of the step-parent unless the other parent agrees or unless s/he has died without appointing a guardian. If the child is illegitimate then the father's consent will generally not be needed.

This is frequently a source of great discontent. See, generally, page 132.

Grandparents

Grandparents do not normally have an automatic legal right to see (i.e. have access to) their grandchildren. If there is matrimonial breakup, and one of the parents is applying to the court for custody, then a grandparent can apply to the court for access. In practice, the court welfare officer will then prepare a report with a recommendation as to whether or not access should be allowed. But (except via wardship) there is usually no other way that a grandparent can apply to a court for an access order.

Guardians

Guardians can be appointed by the parents (under a will or a parental deed) or by the court. A guardian has full parental rights as if s/he were the natural parent.

If a guardian has been appointed by one parent then he will act jointly with the surviving parent. Where either objects to this arrangement, the court can give sole rights to one of them.

A guardian cannot appoint someone else to act as guardian on his/her own death.

Registering a child's birth

A child's birth must be registered, with the District Registrar for Births, Marriages and Deaths, within six weeks of the birth.

The registrar will take details of the date and place of birth; the name, surname, and maiden name of the mother; the name, surname, and occupation of the father (if the child is legitimate); and the child's sex and names. Following social convention, the legitimate child will usually take its father's surname.

Illegitimate children

Naming the father on the registration of the birth has no direct legal consequences, but in practice this is very useful evidence of paternity for a later affiliation claim. However, the birth can only be registered with the father's name:

● at the joint request of both mother and father, *or*

● at the request of the mother if she produces a statutory declaration sworn by the father in which he declares that he is the father;

● when section 95 of the Children Act 1975 is brought into operation, by a third method – at the request of the mother if she produces an affiliation order which names the man as the father.

Note that there is no way in which the father can insist that he be named unless the mother agrees. Also, until the 1975 Act comes into effect, there is no way that the mother can insist that he be named unless he agrees.

A child will usually take its father's surname (unless illegitimate) but this is not mandatory. The mother of an illegitimate child can register the birth in whatever name she chooses, including that of the father and even if he denies paternity. The name can be changed within twelve months of the registration. Thereafter, the child's name can only be changed to the father's name if the mother and father apply jointly or if the mother obtains an affiliation order against the father.

The birth certificate

There are two types of birth certificate. The short certificate does not give full particulars of the parents and thus conceals the fact that the child is illegitimate; one copy is provided free at the time of registration. The long form of birth certificate includes the parental details. The long and short forms are equally valid.

If a child is legitimated by the marriage of its parents, the birth should be re-registered (see page 100). The new birth certificate will be indistinguishable from that of a child who is born legitimate except that the date of re-registration will be marked, together with the words 'on the Authority of the Registrar General'.

Adopted children

When a child is adopted the Registrar General enters the adoption in the Adopted Children's Register, which sets out the date, country, district, and subdistrict of the birth, the new names of the child, its sex, the name, address, and occupation of the adopters, the date when the adoption order was made, and the court that made the order. This is the child's new full birth certificate, and should be used in place of the previous birth certificate.

The full birth certificate shows that the child is adopted. As with an ordinary birth certificate it is possible to obtain a short form of birth certificate which makes no mention of adoption.

The original record of the child's birth is still kept on file, but is marked 'adopted'. This is confidential and cannot be inspected by the public. It can only be disclosed on order of a court or on application by the adopted person. The adopted person must be over eighteen, and if adopted before November 1975 will have to be interviewed by a social worker before the application can be considered. The application is made to the General Register Office, Titchfield, Fareham, Hampshire.

Parental duties

Parenthood involves the assumption of various responsibilities and duties. Generally, though, the child cannot enforce these duties against the parent. For instance, if the parent does not send the child to school, the child cannot sue the parent for its 'lost' education. However, these duties can usually be enforced indirectly, for if the parent fails to look after the child, the local authority may intervene and take the child into care. In addition, parental neglect or ill-treatment of the child may be a criminal offence.

Maintenance

The parent has a legal duty to maintain the child. Generally this duty is enforced against the father by the mother seeking a maintenance order (or affiliation order if the child is illegitimate). See page 62.

Treatment when ill

The parent must behave as a 'reasonable parent' would. If a reasonable parent would send for a doctor or allow an operation, then so should the child's parent. Religious objections are not allowed to override the test of how a reasonable parent would behave. If neither parent will consent to a necessary operation on the child, the hospital will probably inform the Social Services Department of the local authority and the child may then be taken into care. The parental powers and duties would then be vested. in the local authority, which could then consent to the operation. Any concerned person can apply for the child to be made a ward of court (see page 133) if there is concern over the medical condition of the child.

Injuring the child

Obviously the parent has a duty to look after the child and to avoid injuring it. Whilst deliberate injury or irresponsible neglect might well give rise to criminal proceedings and reception into care, there is also the more general question of the parent's liability if s/he should negligently injure the child.

The law allows the child to sue the parent for negligent injury. The most common example of this is when the child is injured when a passenger in a car driven by its father; if the father was driving negligently then he has broken his duty of care of the child, and so he can be sued. In practice, of course, the father will have motor insurance to cover his liability for negligent driving and the child will be able to claim compensation from the insurance company. A child cannot sue in its own name, however, so the action is brought in the name of an adult who is said to act as the child's 'next friend' for the purposes of the action (see page 124).

But a child cannot sue its parents for injuries caused to it before its birth. For instance, if a child is born retarded because its mother smoked cigarettes (or took drugs) during pregnancy, the child cannot sue its mother for negligence.

Corporal punishment

The law allows parents to impose 'reasonable chastisement' on their children. The test, therefore, is whether a reasonable parent would impose that punishment. Thus, a smack is allowed and will not be an illegal assault on the child. On the other hand, a punch in the face will be unreasonable and will be a criminal offence. In addition, of course, conduct of that sort is likely to lead to the child being taken into care by the local authority. Unnatural punishments, such as keeping the child locked up, are also illegal.

A mother asked her boy-friend to 'smack' her six-year-old boy, for disobedience. The boy-friend hit the boy twice with his belt – bruising him. The social worker saw the bruises, and the boy was taken to hospital. The boy-friend was prosecuted for causing actual bodily harm to the boy. Held: He was guilty. Smith (1985)

When a child goes to school the staff of the school also have power to impose 'reasonable chastisement' (see page 116).

Violent parents

Neighbours and relatives who think that a child is receiving excessive punishment should report their fears to the Social Services Department of the local authority or the NSPCC. The NSPCC will handle the matter confidentially, and cannot be made to disclose a complainant's identity:

The NSPCC received a complaint about the mistreatment of a fourteen-month-old girl. An NSPCC inspector visited the parents and the mother called the family doctor, who examined the child and found it to be unmarked. The mother, who was very upset, sued the NSPCC and demanded to know the name of the informant. The NSPCC refused to disclose the informant's identity. Held: The need for confidentiality overrode the other claims, and so the NSPCC were not obliged to disclose the identity of the informant. NSPCC (1977)

If the father is violent towards the child, the mother can petition for a divorce on the ground of her husband's unreasonable behaviour (see page 32). In addition, she will probably be able to obtain an injunction which forbids the father from harming the child and which, in some instances, excludes him from entering the family home (see page 83).

Cruelty to children

There are numerous criminal charges that can be brought against parents who assault or harm their children. The main offence is the 'cruelty to children' provision in the Children and Young Persons Act of 1933 which protects children under sixteen. The accused person must have had 'custody, charge or care' of the child and must have assaulted, ill-treated, neglected, abandoned, or exposed the child – which is sufficiently wide to cover general abuse and threats. But, in addition, the prosecution must show that the neglect was 'wilful', in that the act of cruelty was deliberate even if its effect was not anticipated. The offence is triable in the magistrates' court (maximum £2,000 fine and/or six months' prison) or the crown court (up to two years' prison and unlimited fine).

In practice, relatively few prosecutions are brought. The more sensible remedy is to remove the child from the position of danger. This is done either by the local authority taking the child into care or by the non-violent parent asking for an injunction to exclude the violent parent.

The child's education

The Education Act 1944 imposes a duty on parents to ensure that their children are educated and a duty on local education authorities (LEAs) to provide suitable schools.

If a child is of compulsory school age (between five and sixteen) s/he must 'receive efficient full-time education suitable to his age, ability, and aptitude'. This duty falls on the person with actual custody of the child (usually both parents) and if the local authority thinks that this duty is not being fulfilled, it can give the parent fourteen days to prove that the child is receiving suitable education. If the local authority is not satisfied with the explanation offered, it will serve a *school attendance order* on the parents. If this is ignored, the parents will be summonsed to appear in the magistrates' court.

Thus parents cannot refuse their child an education. However, it does not necessarily follow that the child has to go to school; the parents can discharge their duty to provide suitable efficient full-time education by, for example, employing a tutor or teaching the child themselves. The parent who chooses to do this need not notify the local education authority beforehand, but once the local education authority learns that the child is not attending school it will require the parents to prove that the child is being properly educated.

The 1944 Act does not define what is a 'suitable' education, other than to say it must be full-time, and suited to the child's age, ability, and aptitude. Much is, therefore, left to the discretion of the LEA, but it cannot insist that the child be taught the same range of subjects as is available at the local school or even that its education be as efficient. There is no need for the parents who are teaching their own children to be qualified teachers, although if they are suitably qualified that will be an important factor in deciding the authority's attitude.

If the parents cannot satisfy the LEA that the child's education meets the statutory standard they will first be given formal warning that the LEA intends to serve a school attendance order. The parents may be able to delay matters by appealing against the LEA's choice of school, but the end result may well be the service of a school attendance order, followed by an appearance in the magistrates' court (see 'Truancy and School Attendance', page 114). In addition, the LEA could apply for the child to be taken into care if it is not receiving official full-time education.

Types of schools

The Education Acts refer to a confusing variety of schools. Officially, the categories are:

County schools. Entirely financed by LEAs. Most primary and secondary schools come within this category;

Voluntary schools. These get some financial help from the LEA and are of three types:

- *controlled schools:* run by voluntary organizations, but the LEA will nominate two thirds of the governors, and pay all the running costs (and appoint the teachers);
- *aided schools:* receive 85 per cent of their running costs from the Secretary of State or the LEA. Two thirds of the governors are appointed by the voluntary body (the others by the LEA);
- *special-agreement schools* are relatively rare (about one hundred or so, mostly Catholic, with some Church of England).

Special schools: for those with a 'learning difficulty' (see page 114).

Direct-grant schools receive some grant aid. Most are former grammar schools which opted to go 'independent' rather than be drawn more closely into the county schools system.

There is no duty on LEAs to provide comprehensive education. A 1976 Act did introduce such a duty, but it was repealed in 1979, so now there is just a power for LEAs to impose the comprehensive system.

Choosing the school

The Education Act 1981 gives parents some say in the choice of their children's school. But it is not a right to insist on a particular school, nor is it a right to veto the local authority's choice of school.

The choice of school is made by the person having custody of the child, which will usually, of course, be the parents.

Finding out about the local schools. Most parents will find about their local schools through informal contacts – friends, neighbours, etc. But, in addition, the LEA is obliged to provide certain basic information. The Education (School Information) Regulations of 1981 require that the local authority should let inquirers know:
- the number of children that will be admitted to a school in the coming year;
- the admission arrangements for children who do not live in the authority's area;
- transport arrangements (and whether help is given towards travel costs);
- the functions of the authority and the school governors as regards admissions.

The local authority's decision. The education authority need not accept the parent's choice of school. Under section 6 of the Education Act 1981, the authority can use one of three excuses:
- it would prejudice the provision of efficient education, or the efficient use of resources. This is a very wide let-out clause but it will generally be used when there are no spaces available in the school, or if preference is to be given to children who live more locally to the school;
- when it would be incompatible with the normal admission policy of the school (e.g. a church school that only takes children from a particular parish);
- when the child is refused admission because of 'ability or aptitude' (e.g. if there is an 11-plus exam, which the child has not passed).

The authority's decision can usually be appealed. The authority should provide details of the procedure, but all appeals must be in writing; a time limit for making the appeal will usually be laid down, but this cannot be less than fourteen days. Usually, a simple letter of appeal will be enough but it is important to give a reason for the appeal. The sort of reasons that are more likely to be taken seriously are: that the child does live in the school's catchment area; brothers and sisters go to the school or to another school in that area; that older brothers and sisters had been to the school that was being rejected (i.e. the parents have had one child there and do not want another to go); if the child's home is very close to the school; when there are genuine medical or social reasons (but try to get a doctor's certificate in support). On the other hand, the sort of reasons that are less likely to make the authority change its mind would include: convenience for mother's shopping or child-minding arrangements; parents wish to have the child educated at single sex (or coed) school; better sports facilities at a particular school; the child's friends will be going to the school.

In practice, it is difficult to win an appeal for a child who lives outside the school's catchment area. If a written appeal is made, there will eventually be a private hearing at which the parent can argue his/her case. After the appeal, a dissatisfied parent can complain to the Secretary of State for Education that the authority's admission arrangements are 'unreasonable', but in practice such complaints very rarely succeed.

Special schools

The Education Act 1981 saw a change in the way of dealing with children who have 'special educational needs'. The previous policy had been to send them to special schools but the 1981 Act introduced a policy, wherever possible, of keeping such children in ordinary schools (i.e. they are not to be segregated into special schools). In practice, this has been no more than a statement of intent because lack of money has prevented it being implemented.

The LEA can decide that a child has 'special educational needs', in which case the parent must be told, and be consulted. The LEA can then go on to make a formal assessment. The procedures are extremely complex but involve the LEA in preparing a written statement of the child's special needs, which can be appealed by the parent. The parent can also ask for reassessment. Advice on the procedures (and the tactics of appealing) can be obtained from a CAB, and from one of the specialist educational advice bodies.

Truancy and school attendance

A parent commits an offence if the child does not regularly attend the school where it is registered, unless, of course, the child is receiving suitable full-time education elsewhere (s.39, 1944 Act).

The offence is committed even if the parents were unaware that the child was not attending school. The only defences to the charge are:
- the child did not attend school because of sickness, *or*
- the child could not attend school because of some unavoidable cause affecting the child (i.e. not affecting the parent), *or*
- the child was absent on days set aside for religious observance (either the parents or the child must follow that religion), *or*
- the school is not within walking distance of the child's home, and the local education authority has not provided transport or arranged for transfer to a nearer school. ('Walking distance' for children under eight is two miles, and for those over eight, it is three miles; distances are measured by the shortest practicable route, i.e. disregard heavy traffic – but the child is not expected to use isolated track.)

In practice, prosecution is a last resort. The first step will be for an education welfare officer to call on the parents to discuss why the child is not attending school. If it is simply because the parents are too poor to pay for a school uniform, the local authority may help with the cost. A prosecution for truancy (i.e. failing to secure regular attendance of child at school) is a different offence from failing to register a child at school. If the parents do not register the child at school, then they will probably be served with a school-attendance order. See page 112.

If it seems to be the *parents* who are at fault, the LEA will usually serve a warning notice on them. If there is no improvement, the parents will be prosecuted and arrangements may be made for the child to be taken into care (maximum penalty, £400 fine, and one month's prison).

If it is the *child* who is at fault, the case will go before the juvenile court. The court will consider reports from the education welfare service and will usually adjourn the case for four weeks to give the child a last chance. Most children heed this warning, but if the child continues to play truant, the next step will probably be a referral to a child guidance clinic and then, if necessary, putting the child into care.

School rules

Local education authorities can lay down rules covering such matters as dress, length of hair, and discipline, and these rules can apply not just while the child is at the school, but on his way to and from the school. If the child breaks these rules (e.g. because he is improperly dressed) then the school can refuse to admit him. The child's parents will then be failing in their duty to ensure that the child is being educated.

The School Regulations of 1959 govern the exclusion of children from school. There are, in fact, three different sanctions available and they have different consequences:
- exclusion.
- expulsion.
- suspension.

Exclusion. A child can be excluded on medical grounds (for instance if it is infected with vermin, or otherwise medically unfit to be at school). In practice, pregnant girls are often excluded from school on this ground. Confusingly, some LEAs also use the word exclusion when suspending a child who has not complied with one of the school rules (e.g. as to dress).

Expulsion. This is the ultimate sanction. However, this is reserved for serious breaches of discipline, since if the child is of compulsory school age (see below) he must receive schooling from the LEA. This means that if he is expelled, the LEA must find another school for him.

It is not within the power of a head teacher of a school to expel a pupil. The articles of government of the school will lay down who has the authority to expel; it will be either the LEA or the governors, or a combined decision of the LEA with the governors. It will never be the head who expels.

In practice, expulsions are rare and are usually dressed up as suspensions. This avoids the LEA having to provide a place in another school for the child.

Suspension. This is primarily designed for use against children who break school rules (e.g. against the wearing of jewellery). A suspended child remains on the school register and accordingly there is no need for the LEA to find another school place for the child. Accordingly, it is a temptation for LEAs to suspend pupils rather than expel them. However, by suspending a child for an indeterminate length of time, the practical effect is the same as that of expulsion – the child does not attend school.

The procedure for suspending a child will be set out in the school's articles of government. These may differ from one LEA to another but it is likely that they conform to the Model Articles, which state that the head teacher shall 'have the power of suspending pupils from attendance for any cause which s/he considers adequate, but on suspending a pupil s/he shall forthwith report the case to the governors who shall consult the local education authority'. Sometimes the consent of the governors is also needed before a child can be suspended.

A parent has no legal right to see the school's articles of government, although in practice most head teachers will show them to an interested parent.

When a child is suspended, the parent should write to the head teacher asking for details as to why the suspension took place and for how long it is to last. They should also ask whether they have the right of appeal; copies of the letter should be sent to the governors and to the LEA. It is important that the head teacher is asked to specify the length of the suspension; this will help prevent the suspension becoming indeterminate in length.

Corporal punishment

Teachers have a right to inflict corporal punishment on their pupils.

Schools must record corporal punishment in a punishment book kept by the head teacher, who is responsible for its accuracy and completeness. The punishment book must be kept for at least three years after the date of the punishment.

The law lays down a 'reasonableness' test as to the amount of corporal punishment that can be inflicted. The general limits were laid down in an 1860 case (*R* v. *Hopley*):

> If it be administered for the gratification of passion or of rage, or it be immoderate and excessive in its nature or degree, or if it be protracted beyond a child's power of endurance, or with an instrument unfitted for its purpose, or calculated to produce danger to life or limb, in all such cases, the punishment is excessive, the violence is unlawful, and if evil consequences to life and limb ensue, the person inflicting it is answerable to the law.

In short, it is a matter of what is reasonable. It depends on the circumstances and, often, on the attitudes of individual judges. Boxing the ears has been held to be unreasonable, whereas the inflicting of a blow which broke a boy's jaw in two places was once held to be reasonable – the judge said he had a special duty to protect society from 'an excess of sentimentality or sloppy thinking'. In a 1961 case, sixteen strokes of a cane on the hands of a fourteen-year-old girl were held not to be excessive, despite there being marks on her hands four weeks later.

The 1944 Education Act gives LEAs the power to issue regulations controlling corporal punishment. About three quarters of LEAs have issued regulations.

If parents object to corporal punishment it seems that there is little they can do to prevent it. The Society of Teachers Opposed to Physical Punishment (STOPP) publishes a form for parents to fill in, requesting the LEA not to use corporal punishment. But it is unlikely that this has the legal effect of countermanding a teacher's powers to impose corporal punishment. In practice, though, most schools will respect parents' wishes and not impose corporal punishment in these circumstances. Also relevant is a decision of the European Court of Human Rights in 1982; that case held that corporal punishment must not be used against the wishes of a parent, and also that a child cannot be suspended from school for refusing corporal punishment. Although that decision is not legally binding in the UK, most LEAS follow it. In addition, a new law may be in effect soon. This may allow schools to abolish caning and corporal punishment. Furthermore, parents may be able to opt out – they may be able to give written notice to the school, requiring that their children are not subjected to corporal punishment.

Parents who object to their child being struck by school staff should obtain a copy of the school's rules and also ask to see the relevant entries in the school's punishment book. If they think the punishment was excessive, they can prosecute the offending teacher for assault or sue him/her for damages; this is done by issuing a summons in the magistrates' court for a private prosecution (see page 779) or by suing in the county court (see page 872).

Starting school

Schooling is compulsory from the beginning of the first term after the child's fifth birthday. In practice, many education authorities are prepared to take children before that age.

Leaving school

The minimum leaving age is sixteen, but a child cannot necessarily leave on his or her sixteenth birthday. By the Education Act 1962:

Date child becomes sixteen	When he can leave school
1 September to 31 January	End of spring term
1 February to the end of May	End of May
End of May to 31 August	End of summer term

The Family: Children

Sixteen-to-nineteen-year-olds

The duty of the LEA to educate extends to sixteen-, seventeen-, and eighteen-year-olds. There is a duty to provide suitable facilities for children of that age group who wish to receive full-time education. As regards those aged nineteen and over, there is a duty to provide further education for those who want it (but since it need not be in the local area, this duty is – in practical terms – meaningless). As for fees, LEAS can charge for non-advanced further education (which means below GCE A-level standard); until recently, few LEAS did charge, but some authorities have now introduced charges.

Sex education

Parents cannot insist that their children should not have sex-education lessons. There is no duty on the LEA to provide such lessons, and there is no right for the parent to object to such lessons. In practice, all the parent can do is to attempt to reach an informal agreement with the head that the child be excluded from those classes.

School uniforms

Head teachers can lay down rules that require the wearing of certain items and which forbid the wearing of others (e.g. Doc Marten boots). But the rules must be 'reasonable' and it would not be reasonable for the head to insist that particular types of garment (e.g. a special type of blazer) be worn when cheaper, otherwise similar, items can be bought elsewhere. Similar principles apply when dealing with problems of appearance (e.g. long hair, jewellery, make-up) – it is all a matter of reasonableness. In practice, the head teacher is in a powerful position and failure to comply with the school rules as to uniform and appearance may eventually lead to suspension – it being treated as a discipline problem. The concerned parent should begin by discussing the problem with the head. The next step is to ask the LEA for a copy of its *Information for Parents* booklet to see whether the head teacher is complying with it (1981 regulations require that the LEA must publish details of its schools' uniform and dress rules). Otherwise, the only hope is to complain to the LEA.

The child and religion

Parents have no duty to bring children up with religious beliefs. The courts will not interfere unless the child is being exposed to a religious belief that will harm it – but, of course, such cases are few and far between.

Schools are required by law to start the day with collective worship and they must also provide RI classes. Many schools ignore this legal requirement. A parent has a legal right to withdraw the child from the collective worship or from the RI classes. In county schools, the collective worship must be non-denominational.

School records

All schools keep records on pupils, but those records are confidential and need not be shown to either the pupils or the parents.

School charges

State education should be free. In practice, many schools ask parents to contribute towards the cost of books, craft materials,and also to pay for swimming and music lessons. Such charges are probably illegal (certainly, the courts have held that fees for music lessons carried out on school premises are illegal). However, the school can certainly charge for activities and trips which are outside the normal curriculum, and since 1980 schools have been free to charge what they like for school meals (and indeed for school milk). As regards fares for school buses, the LEA cannot charge anything if the child lives further than 'walking distance' (see page 114 for what this means), but otherwise the authority can charge what it wishes.

Size of classes

There is no fixed maximum number of pupils per class; the Schools Regulations 1959 simply state that classes should not be 'overcrowded'.

Accidents at school

A school is responsible for the safety and well-being of its pupils. If the school or its staff is negligent then the school will be liable in damages. Similarly, the school will be liable if the premises are unsafe:

> *Two boys were playing with a swing door. As a result of horseplay, a child put his hand through a glass panel in the door. The glass was an eighth of an inch thick. Held: The school was liable. Whilst the glass was thick enough for normal domestic use it was not suitable for the rough and tumble of school life.* Lyes (1962)

> *Was it negligent to allow a child – aged seven years and two months – to select sharp-pointed scissors for use in an art class? Held: The teacher had been negligent, and the education authority was liable for £10,000 damages for the serious eye injury caused.* Black (1983)

The child's nationality

A child takes the nationality (i.e. citizenship) of its father or the place where it was born. If these are different, the child can choose either, or alternatively it can have dual nationality, keeping both.

If a legitimate child, born abroad, has a mother with UK nationality but a foreign father, the parents can apply for the child to be registered as a UK citizen. The decision is in the hands of the Secretary of State.

The Family: Children

An illegitimate child born abroad has no right to UK citizenship even if the mother and father are both UK nationals. The only exception is if the illegitimate child is stateless, in which case the Secretary of State may register it as a UK national.

If the child is born on a ship, aircraft, or hovercraft which is registered in the UK, that child will be deemed to have been born in the UK. For example, if a child is born in the course of a British Airways flight to Iran, the child will be a UK national. However, if the flight was on an Iranian plane the child would not be of UK nationality unless its father has UK nationality.

Growing up

Although the law will rarely allow a contract to be enforced against a child, it does allow children to own money, possessions, and property, but not land (which includes houses). Generally, though, children's possessions are held in trust for them by their parents until the child is old enough to manage its own affairs. If the parent betrays the trust by using the money for his/her own uses, the child can sue the parent for the money lost. The parent is, however, allowed to withdraw money to pay for the child's upkeep, board, and education.

Large amounts of money are usually held by independent trustees such as solicitors or bank managers. Generally, they will only release money for the child's maintenance and will not part with other sums unless the permission of the court has been obtained.

As the law stands, a child under sixteen cannot be given advice or treatment on contraception or abortion without parental consent – unless it is an emergency. This is what the Court of Appeal decided in *Gillick* (1984).

Taking a job

For the rules on the employment of children see page 399.

Leaving home

Although the age of majority is eighteen, the courts will only rarely intervene to stop a child in its mid or late teens from leaving home.

Generally, if the child has reached 'the age of discretion' (approximately fourteen for boys and sixteen for girls) the court will not intervene. Whilst the parents could apply for the child to be made a ward of court (see page 133), the court would be unlikely to intervene unless it could be shown that the child was in danger (e.g. keeping bad company).

Another possibility is for the child to be taken into care by the local authority as being in need of 'care and protection' (see page 135).

Generally, the child who has reached the age of discretion, has found a job, and is leading a steady life is unlikely to be troubled by the law. The child will not be able to claim supplementary benefit for him/herself until aged sixteen.

Parents' liability for children

Liability for contracts

In legal theory, a parent is only liable for his children's contracts if the parent told the child to make the contract or if he allowed the child to appear to be his agent (e.g. if the child orders groceries from the local shop the grocer is entitled to believe that the child is acting on its parents' behalf).

But in practice parents are often made liable for their children's contracts because the parent signs an indemnity or a guarantee agreement. This makes the parent personally liable if the child defaults on payment. Usually, no trader will accept a sizeable order from a child unless the child's parent signs a guarantee or indemnity (in which case the parent is liable – see page 572).

The child itself is unlikely to be liable to carry out the contract. Only if the contract is for 'necessary' items, or if it is to his/her definite advantage, will it be enforced against him/her. But this probably does not prevent the child enforcing the contract against the other, adult, party to the contract, although some lawyers dispute this.

Liability for the child's negligence

Negligence is a failure to take 'reasonable care' (see page 653). But obviously a different standard of 'reasonableness' has to be applied to a child than to an adult. A child may therefore be able to do an act that injures another person or which damages property and yet not be legally liable, whereas if that same act had been done by an adult, the adult would be legally liable.

So the 'reasonable behaviour' test has to be modified when dealing with children. A seven-year-old boy who injures someone with a catapult will probably not be liable, for the court would be likely to decide that a typical seven-year-old would not appreciate the harm a catapult might do. But if the child was ten, the court might well think that a ten-year-old should have realized the dangers of a catapult and so he would be liable in negligence. The additional problem that arises when suing a child is that the child is unlikely to have any money with which to pay any damages. Usually, the child's parents will not be liable on behalf of their child and so they cannot be made to pay the damages. The practical result of this is that it is only rarely worth suing a negligent child.

But can the parent be sued for the child's negligence? Generally the answer will be 'no'. The parent is not automatically liable for the child's negligence and the parent will only be liable if he (or she) was himself negligent. For instance, the court might find that the parent was negligent to give a seven-year-old child a catapult, for if the child is too young to appreciate the dangers of a catapult, perhaps he should not be given one. Thus the person injured by the catapult might be able to sue the parent, not for the child's negligence, but for the parent's own negligence in letting the child have the catapult.

121

Growing Up: the Law's Minimum Ages

Age

At birth	A bank or building society account can be opened in the child's name and s/he can own premium bonds.
6 weeks	The child can be handed to prospective adopters.
4½ months	The child can be adopted.
2	The child can join a nursery school.
3	The child must be paid for on public transport.
5	The child must receive full-time education (see page 111) and can drink alcohol in private.
7	The child can draw money from a TSB or PO savings account.
10	The child can be convicted of a crime if it can be shown that s/he knew it was 'wrong' (page 144).
12	The child can buy a pet.
13	The child can open a current bank account, at the discretion of the bank manager.

14 The child:

- can take a part-time job (see page 399)

- can be convicted of a criminal offence as if an adult (although the mode of trial and the sentence will be different); can also be fined up to £200 and sent to a detention centre

- must pay full fare on British Rail

- can own an airgun

- can go into a bar with an adult but cannot buy or consume an alcoholic drink.

A boy can be convicted of rape and unlawful intercourse with a girl under sixteen.

The police can take the child's finger and palm prints if they have obtained a magistrates' court order.

15 The child can:

- own a shotgun and ammunition

- be sent to youth custody.

- be admitted to a film rated 15

16 The child:

- can marry if there is parental consent (see page 18)

- can apply for supplementary benefit in its own right

- can buy fireworks

- can consent to medical treatment and choose his/her own doctor

- can leave school (see page 117) and then work full time

- can buy a ticket in a registered public lottery

- can join a trade union
- can drink beer, cider, porter or perry in a pub, but only with a meal in a part of the pub that serves meals, not at the bar
- can drive a moped or tractor
- can fly solo in a glider
- can buy cigarettes (s/he can smoke at any age)
- has to pay prescription charges
- has to pay the full fare on buses and on the Underground
- A boy can join the armed forces, with parental consent
- A girl can consent to sexual intercourse. (A boy can consent at any age)

16½ The child can receive sickness and unemployment benefit.

17 The child can:

- drive a car or motor cycle
- go into a betting shop (but not bet)
- have an airgun in a public place
- fly a plane solo
- be tried on any charge in an adult court; can also be sent to prison
- A girl can join the armed forces, with parental consent.

18 *The child becomes an adult and can:*

- vote
- sue in his/her own name
- marry without parental consent
- change his/her name
- apply for a passport
- own land (including a house)
- enter into binding contracts
- obtain credit (including HP) and have a cheque or credit card
- be eligible for jury service
- buy drinks in the bar of a pub
- be tattooed
- donate blood and organs
- bet
- make a will
- join the armed forces without parental consent
- be admitted to a film rated 18.

21 *The adult can now:*

- stand in a general or local election
- apply for a liquor licence
- if male, consent to homosexual acts in private
- drive a lorry or bus.

Such cases are rare, but one was reported:

Was a father liable when a house fire was caused by his fourteen-year-old son playing with candles? The son had not been warned of the dangers of candles. It was held that the father was liable for the son's negligence and so the father had to pay damages to a man who was burned in the fire. (In practice, of course, it would have been the father's insurance company – not the father himself – who would have had to pay.) Jauffur (1984)

Thus a parent is not automatically liable for the child's negligence. If a child breaks a neighbour's window, the parent is only liable if he told the child to break the window or if he failed to exercise reasonable and adequate control over the child. In practice, the parent will rarely be liable and so the neighbour cannot legally insist on compensation.

How a child sues

A child cannot sue in his or her own name. But this does not prevent the child from suing in the courts. Instead of the action being in the child's name, it is brought on his or her behalf by a parent, guardian, relative, or other close friend. Usually, of course, it will be one of the parents who lends his or her name and who, technically, brings the action. The person bringing the action is called the 'next friend' of the child.

The next friend brings the court proceedings on the child's behalf, but s/he must employ a solicitor. This is to minimize the risk of the next friend accidentally under-settling the child's claim. The next friend makes himself or herself liable in two ways:

Costs. If the child's claim is unsuccessful and the court orders that the defendant's costs be paid by the child, it is the next friend who will have to pay them. However, if the claim is financed by legal aid, the liability of the losing party will, in practice, be limited (see page 860).

Under-settling the claim. If the next friend under-settles the claim, the child may be able to sue him/her for negligence when s/he reaches the age of eighteen.

However, if the claim is settled only after court proceedings have begun, then the settlement must be approved by the court before it becomes binding. This will be done in an informal hearing in chambers (a private room) at the court. If the settlement is approved, then the next friend can be certain that it is a reasonable settlement and that there can be no risk of his/her having negligently under-settled the claim.

But relatively few cases are settled after court proceedings have been begun. In most cases, the defendant makes an offer before the court proceedings have been commenced. In these cases, the next friend may simply have written to the defendant, setting out the details of the child's claim and then received a compromise offer in settlement. The risk is that, if s/he settles the case now, it might later turn out that s/he under-settled it. So, to avoid this risk, the next friend should take legal advice and ask a solicitor to look at the papers and confirm that the settlement is satisfactory. It is especially important to do this if the claim is for damages following an injury to the child. What may seem to be a trivial injury can sometimes turn out to be more serious. If the solicitor approves the settlement, that will almost certainly safeguard the next friend's position. If the claim is for more than £500, the solicitor's costs will have to be paid by the other side (see page 840).

An added protection is to ask the court to approve the settlement. This can be done even though court proceedings have not been commenced. The solicitor will advise as to whether this is worth doing. Certainly, if the claim is for several hundred pounds or more, and there is any doubt as to the proper value of the claim, court approval should always be obtained. (Legal aid will be available, see page 849.) In addition, if the claim is for more than £500, the legal costs will probably have to be paid by the defendant (see page 840).

Children and the courts

Age	10–13	14–16	17	18–20	21
Civil cases	infant or minor			adult	
Criminal cases (i) Court in which case will be tried	juvenile court			adult court	
Criminal cases (ii) Category for deciding what sentence can be imposed for a criminal offence	child	young person		young offender	adult

Time limits when a child sues

The law lays down time limits within which court proceedings must be started. For instance, if a person is injured by another person's negligence, court proceedings must be started within three years of the date of the accident. (See page 773 for further details, and also the 'limitation periods' that apply to other types of claims.)

But for children the law is different. The limitation period runs from the time the child reaches its eighteenth birthday, and not from the time of the accident.

Illustration. *Jane is fourteen years old. Last week she was injured in a road accident. She wants to sue for negligence; negligence claims have a three-year limitation period, so if she was an adult Jane would have to start court proceedings within three years of the date of the accident. However, since she is an infant, she has until three years after the date when she reaches eighteen – i.e. she has seven years in which to bring her claim.*

Note: the courts do not approve of children taking undue advantage of these extended limitation periods. The defendant (i.e. the person sued) will probably be able to argue that he has been prejudiced by the delay, and this may well have an indirect effect on the result. These extended limitation periods are designed to protect children whose parents or guardians did not sue for them. Normally, the claim should be brought without delay.

8 Disputes over Children

When parents fall out, it is often the children who are caught in the middle as mother and father argue over who is to 'have them'.

The law's main concern is for the welfare of the children and not the hurt feelings and pride of the parents. Generally, though, the courts feel that a child's welfare is best protected by ensuring that it retains links with both parents. Often the court will make an order that allows both parents to play some part in the child's upbringing. In doing so, the law distinguishes between custody of children, care and control, and access.

Custody

This is the right to take the long-term decisions that affect the child. A parent with custody (properly called *legal custody*) has the ultimate legal responsibility for the child, but it does not necessarily follow that the child will live with that parent, since *legal custody* does not always equal *physical custody* of the child. Usually, the parent with custody will also have actual physical custody of the child but not always; the two can be separated, with custody going to one parent and 'care and control' going to the other (although such 'split orders' are very rare these days). The most common order is for one parent to have sole custody, since this is a straightforward arrangement and is the least likely to give rise to misunderstandings and arguments. Sometimes a joint-custody order will be made (custody to both parents jointly, but with only one of them having care and control), but such an order is unlikely to be made unless the parents are in total agreement about the arrangements.

The sort of decision that the parent with custody can make is: choosing the method of education; the choice of religion; administering the child's property; vetoing the issue of a passport to the child; withholding consent to the child's marriage. Normally, the parent with custody must get court consent before taking the child abroad (or consent of the other parent if there is no custody order).

Care and control

This covers the day-to-day care of the child, and the responsibility for looking after it. It is nowadays called *actual custody* of the child, but does not include the right to make the sort of decisions that go with *legal custody*. Usually, of course, one parent will be given both legal and actual custody of the child. But sometimes the court will separate the two by making a joint order which gives legal custody to both parents jointly and actual custody to just one of them. By doing this, both parents are able to retain some influence over the child and neither feels totally excluded.

Access

This allows the parent who does not have care and control to visit the child. The courts will only rarely refuse to allow access for they are always reluctant to sever a child's links with its natural parents. Only if the visits are likely to harm the child will access be refused, for the general rule is that the parent who fails to obtain custody will be granted access.

Usually, the court will order 'reasonable access' (i.e. no fixed times) and will often allow more access as the child grows older. By the time the child is a teenager, it might be allowed to spend weekends with the parent or go away on holiday with him/her, although this will largely depend on the character and wishes of the child and the parents. These arrangements are usually agreed by parents – not ordered by the court.

The court's paramount aim will not be to please the parents but to make access arrangements that benefit the child. Usually, however, it will be held to be in the child's interests to see both its parents. These are two typical cases:

An unmarried couple had a child in January 1976. The father paid £7 p.w. towards the child's maintenance and was granted access by the magistrates. The mother appealed, saying access would put the child in a position of strain between the parents, and she herself wanted to start a new life. Held: Appeal dismissed. It was in the child's interests to see his father. S (1977)

In 1973 a nineteen-year-old woman and thirty-nine-year-old man started living together. A child was born in 1975, but by the end of 1976 the couple had split up. The father lived in a pub, had a drink problem, had threatened to abduct the child, and had attempted suicide. He applied for access. Held: No. The child's welfare was the prime concern and the court agreed with the mother that access might adversely affect the child. M (1977)

Note that the right to apply for custody and/or access is not confined to the parents of legitimate children. For instance, the father of an illegitimate child can apply for custody and/or access.

However, grandparents do not have a general right to apply for access. Generally, they can only apply if custody or divorce proceedings have been begun. For instance, if Mr and Mrs Brown obtain a divorce and Mrs Brown is given custody of the children, and she then marries Mr Smith who refuses to allow Mr Brown's parents access to their grandchildren, Mr Brown's parents will have no right to apply to the court for access to see their grandchildren.

The rights of the parent without custody

Even if a parent does not have custody, the courts will normally allow him (or her) reasonable access (see above). In addition, there will always be the right: to refuse to allow the child to be adopted; to prevent the child's surname being changed (see page 132); to object if the local authority tries to assume parental rights (see page 135); and to ask the court to resolve a dispute on any important matter.

Who has the children on divorce or separation?

On separation

If the parents are married, there is nothing to stop them coming to a voluntary agreement between themselves as to custody, care and control, and access. However, such an agreement will not be binding and it is always possible for one of the parents to apply to the court for it to vary the terms of the agreement.

Whether or not the court will override the agreement will depend upon whether the agreement is in the best interests of the child. This is the court's main concern.

In addition the court will look at the general validity of the agreement. If it is set out in a formal document, prepared by solicitors, it is more likely to be upheld than if it is set out in letters between the parents. The general principles are similar to those applying to voluntary separation agreements (see page 48).

If the separating parents cannot come to a voluntary agreement, application should be made to the local magistrates' court or the divorce court.

If the parents are not married, custody will automatically go to the mother (see page 106). The father can apply for access and/or custody.

On divorce

No divorce decree can be made absolute without the court being satisfied as to the arrangements made for the children of the family. This is so even when the divorce is with the consent of both husband and wife.

The children of the family whose welfare has to be considered include the couple's legitimate, legitimated, and adopted children. It also includes any child that has been 'treated' by both of them as a child of the family. So, the arrangements made for a stepchild will also have to be approved by the court.

Normally, the court will only be concerned with the arrangements for children under sixteen, unless the child is undergoing education, training, or an apprenticeship, in which case the age limit is eighteen. Custody orders cannot be made for a child over eighteen, but financial orders (e.g. maintenance) can.

When the parents agree over the children

Usually the parents are able to work out some satisfactory arrangement that they can both agree to. For instance, they may agree that the children are to live with the mother whilst the father has access every Sunday afternoon and for one week of the summer holidays.

When filing the divorce papers, the petitioner must lodge a document called

Statement of Arrangements for Children of the Family. This sets out the proposed arrangements which then have to go before the judge for his approval. The couple will have to attend before the judge in a private hearing in chambers (see step 8(b) in the DIY divorce guide on page 46). This is so even if the divorce is undefended. If children are involved, the petitioner must attend court, for divorce through the post is only available when there are no children. Usually, the judge will approve the arrangement but if he has any doubts he will refer the case to the court's welfare officer so that a thorough investigation can be made and a welfare report prepared.

The welfare officer will then visit both the parents at home, and discuss the children and their relationship with them. If the mother or father has acquired a new partner, the officer may well want to know how s/he feels about looking after the children. The officer will also talk to other people who have relevant information – such as a social worker who has been involved with the parents and, sometimes, the child's schoolteacher. The child's views will also be noted if he, or she, is old enough, say ten years old.

The welfare report will then go to the judge. The parents are entitled to copies of the report. The judge will then decide whether to approve the parents' proposals, and if not, will announce the order. Only then can the decree nisi be made absolute, and the parents be formally divorced. For a summary, see the chart on page 45.

When the parents cannot agree over the children

If the couple cannot reach agreement, this will *not* make the divorce a 'defended divorce'.

Applications for custody in disputed cases are best made by a solicitor; legal aid should be available.

In a disputed case, a welfare report may be prepared and copies can be supplied to both parents. The solicitors will draw up formal affidavits setting out their clients' respective claims to the children and the reasons why the children should go to a particular parent. All these papers will be put before the judge when he hears the case, in private, in his chambers. He will want both parents to be present so he can question them.

The judge will then make his order. In about 80 per cent of cases the judge follows the advice of the welfare officer; if he does not, he will say why.

The decision as to who has custody of the children will usually be vital in deciding which spouse is to have the matrimonial home (i.e. possible transfer of a tenancy or transfer of owner-occupied home), or in persuading the local authority to rehouse that parent – since the home will normally go to the parent who has custody.

The factors that decide a custody case

There are numerous matters that have to be taken into consideration. But the overriding principle is that 'the court . . . shall regard the welfare of the minor as the first and paramount consideration' (s.1, Guardianship of Minors Act 1971). The court will look for the solution that offers the best prospects of protecting the child's physical, moral, and emotional well-being, and which will cause it the least disruption. For instance:

Husband and wife separated, and the wife took the eight-year-old son with her. Later, the husband obtained a custody order from the magistrates' court, and then divorced his wife on the grounds of her adultery. The divorce court judge confirmed that the husband should have custody of the boy, noting that the father had a steady job and lived with his parents, whom the boy was fond of. The wife appealed to the Court of Appeal. Held: Custody should go to the wife. The wife had remarried and was pregnant. It would be in the best interests of the child to have a full-time mother and the prospect of brothers and sisters. This would be better for him than having a part-time father. P (1973)

Generally, the courts decide that a child's welfare is best protected by being with its mother, rather than with the father. However, this is only a general rule, and whilst a young girl will almost certainly go to the mother, it is not unusual for older boys to be handed to the father. Before giving care and control of the child to one of the parents the court will look at:

The parents' characters. Obviously this is basic. For instance, the court will not make an order that will put the child into contact with a violent parent. Overall, it is a matter of trying to assess which will be a better parent. If either parent is remarrying then the suitability of their new partner as a step-parent must also be considered. An unconventional life-style may reduce a parent's chances of obtaining an order for custody.

The parents' conduct. The conduct of the parents will usually be irrelevant, unless it is such as to expose the child to moral or physical danger. For example, the mere fact that the mother committed adultery, which led to the divorce, should not be held against her; however, if she was a prostitute, that would be relevant. This is a relatively new approach, and there can be no doubt that sometimes the courts do consider a spouse's conduct. As an illustration of the old approach, in a 1962 case the court gave care and control of two girls (four and six) to the father, and Lord Denning commented, 'Whilst the welfare of the children is the first and paramount consideration, the claims of justice cannot be overlooked', and so the 'adulterous' wife lost her children. However, times have changed, and since the divorce reforms of 1969 have come into effect, it is unlikely that the same decision would be made today. The modern approach is illustrated by a 1977 case:

The husband was a clergyman. His wife had an affair with a member of the church youth group and she told her husband that she intended to leave, taking the two young children with her. Husband applied for custody. Held: The welfare of the children was the court's paramount concern. Despite the fact that the husband was a clergyman and of unimpeachable conduct it was in the best interests of the children that they be with their mother – despite her being the 'guilty' party. Custody of both children to the wife. Re K (1977)

The fact that, for instance, the mother has several boy-friends will not normally be held against her. Similarly, the mere fact that the mother has adopted a lesbian partner will not be fatal to her custody application (unless of course the court thinks the child might be corrupted). However, a parent who walks out on the family and leaves the other parent to cope may be at a disadvantage when claiming custody. A woman who does so, on the assumption that 'the children always go to the mother', may well jeopardize her claim.

Social and medical evidence. The court will be interested to hear independent evidence as to the likely effect on the child of living with a particular parent. Until recently, the courts adopted a rather brusque attitude to children's emotions, but now there is a growing awareness of the dangers of upsetting a child by moving it. This is why it is always an advantage for a parent to have care and control of the child whilst the case is pending – the courts are reluctant to disturb a stable home life.

The child's sex and age. Normally the mother will be awarded care and control of a young, or sickly child, especially if a girl. Older boys will often go to the father. The following is a *very* rough-and-ready guide (remember that the ages are only approximate):

- *children under six* are better cared for by the mother, assuming that all other things are equal;
- *children aged six to eleven*: the mother will probably be preferred to the father on grounds of practicality; however, if he could show equally good arrangements for feeding them, looking after (especially in the daytime) and caring for them, he would probably have as good a claim as the mother;
- *children over eleven*: the parents have equal claims. Often boys go to the father and girls to the mother. But this is subject to the proviso that the court will try to avoid splitting brothers and sisters. In addition, the court will probably favour maintaining the status quo and avoid a decision which will involve a change of home, school, etc. (Remember that these age figures are for rough guidance only.)

Splitting the family. This is always regarded as undesirable. So if there is a young girl in the family she will probably have to go to the mother and, consequently, the other children will too, unless they are near the age of majority or unless good access arrangements can be made.

The child's wishes. Judges pay little attention to the wishes of the child, unless s/he is of the age of discretion (see page 120). This is simply because experience shows that a child will often have been indoctrinated or coerced by one parent to say it does not want to live with the other parent.

The standard of living offered. What if one parent can offer the child a substantially higher standard of living and material advantage than the other parent? This will generally be ignored since the court will look for the arrangement that brings the greatest happiness to the child, not the greatest material benefits. However, if one of the parents cannot offer proper accommodation, that will be an important consideration. But a parent (especially a mother) should not be deterred from asking for custody just because s/he does not have permanent accommodation. If custody is granted, that will give the parent a much better chance of obtaining permanent accommodation (for instance, from the council or by transfer of the matrimonial home by the divorce court).

Emigration. If there is a likelihood of one of the parents emigrating, that must be taken into consideration. If the child has been brought up in this country, the court may disapprove of him being taken abroad and so having his education interrupted and an alien culture imposed on him. If the child is very young, then the risks attached are, of course, considerably reduced.

The other difficulty with allowing the child to emigrate is that this makes it unlikely that s/he will ever see the other parent again. This can be heart-breaking for the parent, but the court's concern must be with the welfare of the child, not with the feelings of the parent.

Interim custody. The question of custody is usually decided as part of divorce or judicial separation proceedings but sometimes an interim order (i.e. a temporary, emergency order) is made, for instance if there is a danger that the children may be snatched back by one of the parents. Similarly an interim order might be sought to ensure rehousing by the council, since some local authorities will only treat the wife and children as a separate family unit if the wife has custody of the children. Interim applications for custody are best handled by a solicitor. Legal aid will usually be available (see page 849).

Changing the child's name

The child's surname cannot be changed unless both parents consent. This is so even if the parents have divorced or separated.

This can cause problems. For instance, suppose that Mrs Smith divorces Mr Smith and is awarded care and control of the daughter Miss Smith. Mrs Smith then marries Mr Brown and becomes Mrs Brown. But her daughter cannot change her name to Miss Brown; she remains Miss Smith despite the fact that her mother, her stepfather, and stepbrother and stepsister are called Brown. This can cause the child great embarrassment. The only way this can be avoided is by obtaining the written consent of Mr Smith to her changing her name to Brown, unless, of course, Mr Smith has died.

The courts do have the power to allow a change of name without the other parent's consent, but in practice this power is very rarely exercised. For instance:

The mother of two children, aged three and four, had remarried. She applied for leave to change their name to that of their new stepfather but the natural father would not agree. Held: Changing a child's name is a matter of importance affecting the best interests and the psychological welfare of the child. The natural father was someone with whom it would be beneficial for the children to maintain a close connection. A marriage could be dissolved, but not parenthood. So leave to change the names was refused. L (1978)

However, this and similar decisions were greatly criticized and some judges are now prepared to order a change of name. Obviously the law needs clarification. For more on changing children's names, see pages 97 and 108.

Emergency disputes: making the child a ward of court

Sometimes the court has to act quickly to protect a child. For example, the parents might break up and one of them might try to snatch the child, and perhaps take it abroad. Similarly, the child may need to be prevented from doing something that would be to its own disadvantage – for instance, a young heiress might need to be stopped from marrying a philanderer. In these situations – and child-snatching is the typical occasion – a speedy remedy is needed. One answer is to make the child a ward of court – in other words, transferring the legal custody of the child (although not its physical custody) to the court. Thus, the court's permission is needed before the child can be taken out of the country or before the child can take any major decisions. To take a ward of court out of the country is contempt. Every wardship application has clearly printed on it: 'IMPORTANT NOTICE: it is contempt of court, which may be punished by imprisonment, to take any child named in this summons out of England and Wales, even to Scotland, Northern Ireland, the Republic of Ireland, the Channel Islands or the Isle of Man, without the leave of the court.'

The application for wardship need not be made by a parent, and in fact it is often made by a concerned relative or friend. The application should be made through a solicitor (legal aid is available) who will file an application with the High Court which will immediately make the child a ward of court. As soon as the application is lodged with the court office, the child becomes a ward, even though there has not been a court hearing. The applicant then has twenty-one days in which to apply to the court for the wardship to be extended, for otherwise the wardship automatically ends after twenty-one days. Despite this, the actual hearing of the application does not have to be within the twenty-one-day period; it is sufficient if the solicitor applies for an appointment even if the date (as is likely) is weeks later.

Wardship is an effective remedy in emergency cases, but it will not be used to protect the child from every harm. For instance:

A fourteen-year-old boy lived with his mother and stepfather. His father was dead and the child had been taught to respect his late father. A book was to be published which would describe the father as a depraved individual, obscene and a drunkard. Since the boy was highly strung, it was feared the publication of the book would cause him gross psychological injury. The step-parent asked for the child to be made a ward of court and for the court then to grant an injunction stopping the publication. Held: No. The interests of a free press were paramount and wardship was not necessary. An injunction was refused. Despite the refusal of wardship, Lord Denning did say that wardship is 'to protect the young against injury of whatever kind, from whatever source'.
Re X (1975)

Generally, wardship applications are made with a view to:
- preventing the child being kidnapped and taken abroad;
- preventing an undesirable association;
- protecting the child – for instance:

An eleven-year-old girl was to be sterilized because she suffered from a congenital abnormality. Her mother had consented to the sterilization. A local authority social worker applied for the child to be made a ward of court so the court could then refuse to give the necessary consent for

The Family: Children

the operation to take place. The application was successful and the sterilization prevented. Re D (1976)

A child was born with Down's syndrome, and also with an intestinal blockage – which would prove fatal if not operated on within a few days. The parents thought it would be kinder to let the child die and so they refused to consent to the operation. The local authority then applied to the court and the child was made a ward of court. The local authority then asked for the court's permission for the operation to be carried out. The trial judge refused but on appeal the Court of Appeal overruled his decision. The real question was to decide what was in the interests of the child – not simply to respect the wishes of the parents. The court was not convinced that the life of a person with Down's syndrome was such that the child should be condemned to die. The operation was carried out. Re B (1981)

- allowing non-parents to apply for care and control of children they have been looking after for some time (e.g. relatives). For instance, they might not be able to adopt the child because of parental objections, so wardship would give them care and control. (Note: when the custodianship provisions of the Children Act 1975 come into effect, such people could apply for custodianship instead.)

Wardship is not the only remedy in child-snatching cases. Unless the case is a real emergency, it might be better to apply to the magistrates' court or county court for a custody order or, if divorce proceedings are under way, to apply to the divorce court for custody. This will usually take a few weeks, but once custody is obtained it will be a contempt of court for the other parent to seize the child. Once the court has made a custody or care and control order, the child cannot be taken out of England and Wales unless the court gives permission or unless the order says otherwise.

If there is any danger of the child being taken abroad or to Scotland or Ireland (and so outside the jurisdiction of the courts) a wardship application should be made without delay. As soon as the application is made, the court will supply a 'Home Office letter' which instructs all ports and airports to keep a look-out for the child. Finally, it should not be forgotten that taking a child abroad without the consent of the court (or of the other parent if there is no custody order) is a criminal offence (i.e. of kidnapping, and also under the Child Abduction Act 1984).

Taking the child into care

When a child goes into 'care' the local authority takes over the parents' rights and responsibilities. It has most of the rights and duties of the natural parents and has very wide powers to decide how, and where, the child shall be looked after. Thus, the local authority (in practice, the social services department) can place the child in a home, with foster parents, or even with friends, relations, and, in some cases, the parents themselves; also the authority can deny the parents access to the child.

There are various statutory provisions allowing local authorities to take children into care. Apart from being incredibly complex, they are also very wide and are designed to cover any occasion when a child might be in need of outside help. In addition, there are provisions which allow for parents to put their children into care voluntarily: when the parents are unable to cope, for example, because they have become homeless, or the mother has become ill and cannot look after them. At any time, there are roughly 100,000 children in care. Of these, about 90 per cent are in voluntarily – their parents have voluntarily agreed that the children should be put in care. Thus, in practical terms, voluntary care is much more important than the situations when the council (or the court) force a child to be put into care. Voluntary care is dealt with under section 1 below.

The care laws are designed to deal with three sets of circumstances:

1. *When the parents can't cope or can't be found.* For instance, the mother is ill or the family have been made homeless, and so the parents agree that the child should be taken into care. Alternatively, the parents may have abandoned or ill-treated the child or it may have become lost.
2. *When the child is 'troublesome'.* If it has committed an offence and is in need of care and control. The juvenile court can order that the child be put into care, even if the parents do not agree.
3. *Emergency problems.* For instance, in cases of child battering, when the child is being neglected or has been abandoned. The child can be taken to a place of safety for up to twenty-eight days – a community home, a police station, hostel, or any other suitable place that will accept it.

1. When the parents can't cope

Voluntary care can be arranged under section 2 of the Child Care Act 1980. The conditions that must exist are set out in the chart on pages 136–7. The emphasis is on the inadequacy or default of the *parents* – as opposed to the child – for instance, if they cannot provide proper housing, or if they are ill or inadequate. Also covered are situations in which the child is parentless, for instance, if he has been abandoned, is lost, or if his parents are dead.

Since it is voluntary care, the parents can demand the child back at any time. However, once the child has been in care for six months, the parents must give at least twenty-eight days' notice before reclaiming the child. This gives the local authority time in which to decide whether to make a 'section 3 resolution'.

Voluntary care can be made permanent by the local authority passing a resolution under section 3 of the Child Care Act 1980. The chart sets out the occasions when the authority can pass this 'section 3 resolution', which gives the authority the rights and duties of a natural parent. Before the resolution is passed, the parents should be given written notice that the authority is considering passing a resolution and the parents should also be told why the resolution is being made. A government circular also says that parents should be able to give their side of the story to the authority. If the resolution is passed it will be made by a committee of councillors on the social services committee – the decision is made (in theory, anyway!) not by the council staff but by the elected councillors. Once the local authority has given the parents notice, they have twenty-eight days to object to the passing of the resolution. If they do object, the case goes to the juvenile court and the magistrates decide whether the

135

The Family: Children

WHEN THE PARENTS CAN'T COPE because of temporary difficulties, such as illness or bad housing. Or if the child has been lost or abandoned (although a Place of Safety Order might be a more suitable alternative).

↓

WHEN THE CHILD IS IN DANGER Emergency powers allow the child to be put in a 'place of safety' (e.g. police station, community home, hospital); for instance, if it has violent or neglectful parents.

↓

The local authority must receive a child into *care* if s/he
– has no parents or guardian
– has been abandoned
– is lost
– can't be looked after by the parents
– because of homelessness, sickness, etc.
The local authority will also want to be sure that its intervention is necessary in the interests of the child's welfare (s.2 Child Care Act 1980). This is voluntary care and cannot be done against parents' wishes.

Local authority, police, or NSPCC can apply to a magistrate or to the juvenile court for a *place of safety order*. Usually this will last for 8 days, but it can be for up to 28 days.
(Children and Young Persons Acts 1939 and 1969). The magistrate must be satisfied that:
– the child's development (or that of a brother or sister) is being impaired, *or*
– the child is exposed to moral danger, *or*
– the child is beyond control, *or*
– the child is not receiving a full-time education, *or*
– the child has committed an offence.
But he need not decide that the child is in need of care and control.

Taking the child out of care: the parents can demand the child back at any time, unless it has been in care for 6 months. If so, they must give at least 28 days' notice.

Making the arrangement permanent: the local authority can take over the parental rights by passing a resolution (s.3 Child Care Act 1980), but only if:
– the parents are dead and there is no guardian, *or*
– the parents or guardian have a permanent disability, *or*
– the parents or guardian lead an unsatisfactory way of life or have been irresponsible, *or*
– the child has been abandoned, *or*
– the parents or guardian have mental disability and can't cope, *or*
– the child has been in care for three years or more.

Making the arrangement permanent: for the local authority to take over the parental rights a *care order* must be made. Do the parents object to a care order being made?

no — yes

Parents don't object Child can be taken into care under s.2, Child Care Act 1980.

Parents do object Apply for child to be taken into care under Children and Young Persons Act 1969.

Do the parents object?

yes ↓ — no ↓

Parents can object within 28 days.

Parents don't object.

Juvenile court decides. There is no appeal. Local authority must apply to juvenile court within 14 days of parents' objection.

Getting the child out of care:
1. The local authority must review the position at least once every 6 months. If the authority decides that it is in the interests of the child that the care ends, it can apply to the court.
2. Application can be made to the juvenile court for the care order to be ended as not being in the child's interest.

Local authority assumes parental rights.

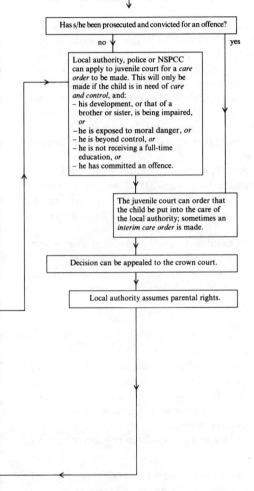

TROUBLESOME CHILDREN
When the child has committed an offence
or is otherwise in need of care and
control – for instance, he plays truant.
(Children and Young Persons Act 1969).

Has s/he been prosecuted and convicted for an offence?

no   yes

Local authority, police or NSPCC
can apply to juvenile court for a *care
order* to be made. This will only be
made if the child is in need of *care
and control*, and:
– his development, or that of a
  brother or sister, is being impaired,
  or
– he is exposed to moral danger, *or*
– he is beyond control, *or*
– he is not receiving a full-time
  education, *or*
– he has committed an offence.

The juvenile court can order that
the child be put into the care of
the local authority; sometimes an
interim care order is made.

Decision can be appealed to the crown court.

Local authority assumes parental rights.

resolution should be confirmed. Otherwise, if the parents do not object, the resolution automatically remains in force.

In addition, when a divorce court is considering the custody of a child it has power to put a child of not more than sixteen years of age into care. This would be done if there were exceptional circumstances making it impractical for the child to be entrusted to the parents or any other person.

Putting a child into care because there are short-term difficulties in the family may seem to be an attractive course of action. But it should not be done without carefully thinking through the possible consequences. In particular, the following points should be borne in mind:

• *supplementary benefit*: the parents will lose that part of the benefit which relates to the child. If the parent is a 'single-parent family' then because s/he will no longer have direct responsibility for the child, s/he will have to register for employment before s/he can claim supplementary benefit (see page 744). If the parent is not on supplementary benefit (or is not a low earner) then s/he will have to pay the council a contribution towards the child's upkeep.

• *housing*: a parent with a child has a 'priority need' for rehousing and will usually be rehoused by the local authority if homeless (see page 723). If the child is in care, the local authority will probably argue that the parent is no longer a priority need, although strictly speaking that may not be a correct application of the law and the parent may be able to challenge it.

• *changing your mind*: during the first six months the child is in voluntary care and the parent can take the child out of care without giving any notice to the council. But in practice this right can be denied to the parent since there are various ways in which the Social Services Department can apply for the care to be made continuous against the wishes of the parent (e.g. a section 3 resolution).

2. When the child is troublesome

The Children and Young Persons Act 1969 contains care provisions for children who are in trouble, or who need care and control. Under the Child Care Act 1980 (see above) the emphasis is on situations in which the *parents* are inadequate, at fault, or cannot be found. Under the 1969 Act, the concern is with situations in which the conduct of the *child*, or his or her character, is in issue.

The 1969 Act allows the juvenile court to make a care order in two sets of circumstances:

(a) If the child has been convicted by the court of an offence that could be punished with imprisonment if committed by an adult. So minor offences cannot, by themselves, lead to a care order.

(b) The police, the local authority, or the NSPCC can apply to the juvenile court for a care order to be made. The conditions to be met are set out in section 1 of the 1969 Act and are summarized in the chart. The overall concern is that the child is in need of 'care and control' – for instance, if s/he won't go to school. Both the child and its parents can be legally represented at the court hearing. Both parents and child can get legal aid. The child can appeal (the parents can do this for the child unless the child is separately represented).

A care order is only one of the orders the juvenile court can make. Other orders include: a supervision order (a juvenile version of probation, see page 149); a hospital or guardianship order (where the child's mental condition warrants his or her detention in hospital or under the guardianship of the local authority's health department); and, in care applications – (b) above – a parental recognizance order (the parent voluntarily agrees to take proper care of the child and control him/her properly, and enters into a recognizance of up to £1,000).

Frequently, an interim care order will be made. This can be made by a single magistrate and it can be for up to twenty-eight days. It is usually made when the juvenile court requires further information and it asks for a welfare report to be prepared. The child goes into care for the interim period. Some juvenile courts seem to use the interim care order as a 'frightener' for troublesome teenagers. If a child has committed an offence the court will sometimes make an interim care order; the child is taken from its parents and so given a warning as to what will happen if it commits any further offences. This is, of course, definitely not the aim of the legislation.

If the juvenile court does make a care order, it can be appealed to the crown court within twenty-one days.

3. Emergency problems

Child-battering, child abuse, sex attacks, and other emergencies require special remedies. The Children and Young Persons Act 1969 (s.28) allows *a place of safety order* to be made by a single JP, although such an order should preferably be made by a juvenile court if one is sitting. The application is usually made by the local authority, the police, or the NSPCC, but any concerned individual (e.g. a relative) can apply. In an emergency, the order could be made by a single magistrate at his home, without a court hearing. The child and parent have no legal right to be present to argue their case, and they will not normally be allowed to do so. The magistrate will need to be satisfied that the child is in need of help (e.g. he is being ill-treated) but in practice the magistrate does not question the evidence too closely at this stage. The order can be for up to twenty-eight days. This gives the local authority sufficient time to decide what to do next.

In addition the police can detain a child for up to eight days without a warrant if they have reason to believe that there are grounds upon which a juvenile court could make a care order (i.e. under 2(b) above). Also, the police can apply for a warrant to search premises in which they believe there is a child in need of urgent protection. A place of safety order is not a care order. The parents cannot challenge or appeal against the making of a place of safety order, nor do they have any rights to see the child.

When the place of safety order expires, the local authority has three options:

(a) Let the child return to its parents.

(b) Persuade the parents to agree to a voluntary care order under the Child Care Act 1980 (see 1, above).

(c) Ask the juvenile court to make a care order under the Children and Young Persons Act 1969 (see 2, above); often the court will make an interim care order while the case is properly investigated.

Reviewing the position

A local authority must review the position of every child in its care at least once every six months. If necessary, the authority must consider whether it should apply to the court for the care order to be discharged. The difficulty, of course, is that neither the child nor the parent has the legal right to attend the review hearing – and, in practice, few authorities are prepared to give the necessary permission. This is surprising, given the importance of the decision to the child and the parents. For instance, it does seem unreasonable not to consult a teenage child about the options being considered (e.g.: How would he feel about being fostered out? Would it be feasible for him to live with an adult friend? Would he mind moving to a different home, if it meant being separated from the friends he had already made in care?) In theory, the local authority must consider the child's wishes – but it need not consult the child.

The legal effect of a care order

The effect of a care order is to give the local authority the legal custody (i.e. the parental rights and powers) of the child. This lasts until the order is discharged or until the child reaches eighteen (unless the child was over sixteen when s/he was put into care, in which case the order lasts until s/he is nineteen).

However, it does not necessarily follow that the local authority will put the child into a children's home or similar institution. The local authority, as legal custodian of the child, can delegate the care and control of the child to someone else, and so hand the child to foster parents, relatives, or family friends. Sometimes a child in care will be handed back to the parents, who are, in effect, given another chance, but this time under the watchful eye of the local authority, which can reclaim the child at any time it wishes.

In practice, problems often arise over visits by the parents. Whilst exceptionally the local authority can keep the location of the child a secret from the parent, the general rule is that the authority must place the child as near as possible to its home area. Although this principle is made law by a 1983 Act, it is often not possible for authorities to comply. The shortage of children's homes means that children are often sent a long way from their local areas. If (as is often the case) this causes financial problems because the parents cannot afford the fares, they should ask their social worker to apply for travel costs from the local authority (under section 26 of the 1980 Child Care Act). Exceptionally, the local authority can refuse to allow the parents access to the child. If this happens, the parents must be served with a formal notice. They can then apply to the magistrates' court, which will then decide whether or not access should be allowed. Legal aid would be available for the application to the magistrates' court.

Contributing towards the costs. The local authority can make the parents contribute towards the costs of keeping the child in care. But if the parent is on SB or FIS, no contribution can be demanded. Also, the father of an illegitimate child can only be asked to pay if he already has an affiliation (i.e. maintenance) order against him. The rules on parental contributions are complicated; the best source of advice is an excellent booklet from the Family Rights Group, *In Care: Money Guide For Families'* (1984, £2.50).

Legal aid. The parents will be able to apply for legal aid to prepare for the care hearing. The child will also have legal aid and, almost certainly, a different solicitor. The parents should be sure to try to find a solicitor who has knowledge and experience of care cases, since the whole area is a legal minefield. A CAB should be able to suggest a suitable solicitor – who will probably be on the child-care panel (i.e. a panel of solicitors with proven experience of care cases).

Appealing a care order. Normally, the parents cannot appeal if a care order is made by the magistrates. The child can appeal – but the child will have separate legal representation, and a court-appointed 'guardian' will (with the help of an independent solicitor) decide what is in the best interests of the child. So, there is no way that the parents can force the matter to appeal – it is out of their hands. Bearing in mind the seriousness of depriving a parent of the child, it does seem incredible that the parent cannot appeal (incidentally, until 1984 there was a right of appeal).

Finally, note also that these sweeping powers have the practical effect of invalidating several legal principles. For example, the law states that a child under ten can never commit a criminal offence, since s/he cannot know the difference between right and wrong. Thus, it might be thought that a nine-year-old could commit offences with impunity. But this is not so, for the care provisions would almost certainly apply and, whilst the child could not face a criminal charge, s/he might well face care proceedings in the juvenile court and so end up in a children's home.

Private fostering

Fostering is usually used when parents are temporarily unable to look after their children, yet do not want the children to be adopted or to go into care. The eventual aim is often for the child to be reunited with its parents.

Fostering is arranged through the local authority (if the child is in care) or privately. If private, the Children Act 1975 requires the foster parents to notify the local authority of the fostering, between two and four weeks beforehand, unless:

The Family: Children

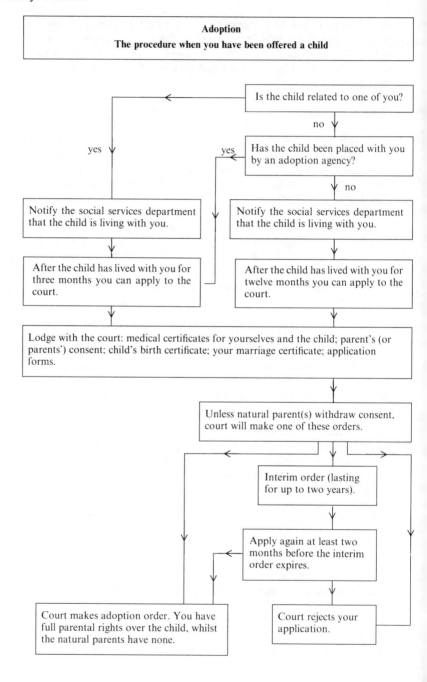

Adoption
The procedure when you have been offered a child

Is the child related to one of you?

no

yes

yes   Has the child been placed with you by an adoption agency?

no

Notify the social services department that the child is living with you.

Notify the social services department that the child is living with you.

After the child has lived with you for three months you can apply to the court.

After the child has lived with you for twelve months you can apply to the court.

Lodge with the court: medical certificates for yourselves and the child; parent's (or parents') consent; child's birth certificate; your marriage certificate; application forms.

Unless natural parent(s) withdraw consent, court will make one of these orders.

Interim order (lasting for up to two years).

Apply again at least two months before the interim order expires.

Court makes adoption order. You have full parental rights over the child, whilst the natural parents have none.

Court rejects your application.

142

- the foster parent is a relation, guardian or custodian of the child, *or*
- the fostering is for not more than six days (twenty-seven days if the foster parent does not take a foster child each year).

Note that it is not only commercial fostering that has to be registered – even if the foster parents do not receive payment, the fostering must still be registered.

The idea of registering the fostering is to allow the local authority to check the suitability of the proposed foster home. The local authority has power to remove the child and can also impose conditions as to the number of children in the house and their ages, sex, accommodation, and so on.

In practice, these regulations are largely ignored, for relatively few private fostering arrangements are registered with the local authorities.

A person who would like to be a foster parent should contact the social services department of the local authority, who will then inspect the home. If approved, the foster parent will be paid a weekly sum for the child's maintenance.

The local authority can always reclaim a child from its foster parents. If it is private fostering, the parents can also demand it back from the foster parents (however much heartache this causes the child and foster parents). But:

- *adoption*: if the child has been fostered for a year, the foster parents can apply for adoption. If the fostering has been for five years or more, natural parents cannot remove the child while the case is waiting to be heard.
- *custodianship*: this allows a non-parent to apply for custody. If the child has been fostered for three years then the foster parent can apply for a custodianship order (the period is one year if the natural parent will agree to the custodianship application). The natural parents cannot remove the child while the case is waiting to be heard. (Note: these custodianship provisions are set out in the Children Act 1975 and are only likely to become law at the end of 1985.)

Adoption

See the chart on page 142 for the procedure on adopting a child. An adoption application can be made by: a married couple (both must be at least twenty-one); parent and step-parent (but often a custody order will be preferred – see page 106); or a single person (must be at least twenty-one and unmarried – or if married, spouse permanently living apart). Unmarried couples cannot jointly adopt a child; however, one of them can apply as a single person to adopt.

In practice, of course, the fundamental problem is finding a child to adopt. Begin by asking the adoption officer in the local social services department to provide a list of adoption agencies.

9 Children and Crime

Criminal charges against children are heard in the juvenile court and not in the adult courts such as the magistrates' court or crown court. The criminal responsibility of a child will depend upon its age.

Under ten

The child cannot be found guilty of any criminal offence and so is immune from prosecution. But this does not mean that the child can commit offences with impunity, for the persistent offender may well be put into the care of the local authority.

Between ten and fourteen

The child can only be found guilty of a criminal offence if it can be proved that he knew what he was doing was 'wrong'. The child need not realize that it is a criminal offence, but if he realizes that it is morally wrong, then he will be assumed to know it was legally 'wrong'. In practice, the court has a wide discretion in deciding whether the child knew it was 'wrong'. The courts generally apply a robust, down-to-earth attitude rather than a legalistic approach. The closer the child is to the age of fourteen, the more easily can it be shown that he knew what he was doing was 'wrong'. Even if he is not criminally liable, the juvenile court can deal with him by making a care order.

Between fourteen and seventeen

The child is subject to the same laws as an adult. Thus he is assumed to know the law, and to know what is an offence. Although subject to the adult's law, he will usually be tried in the juvenile court and, if found guilty, is likely to receive a different sentence than he would if he were an adult. In addition to the usual sentences (see page 148) he can, of course, be put into care.

Over seventeen

The child is an adult in the eyes of the criminal law.

Police investigations

The Children and Young Persons Act 1969 is still the principal statute dealing with children and crime. It is based on the premise that the child who commits an offence probably has social problems, and so the aim should be to help the child and enable him to mend his ways. Prosecution should be the last resort, being used only when the social-work approach will not, by itself, reform the child.

Some magistrates complained that the 1969 Act left them virtually powerless to deal with persistent child criminals who are beyond help. They argued that the good intentions of the 1969 Act had misfired, with the result that juvenile offenders were no longer taught to respect and obey the law. As a result, the sentencing rules were toughened up in 1982.

Often the first the parent knows of the offence is when a policeman calls at the house. If that happens, the parent should discuss the case with the policeman, out of earshot of the child. The policeman may then ask to speak to the child. If he does, the parent should insist on being present.

As a general rule, the police are told that they should only interview children in the presence of a parent or guardian. If a parent or guardian is not available, then the interview should be in the presence of some other person who is of the same sex as the child, and who is not a police officer (e.g. teacher, social worker, or relative). The police are advised to take great efforts to avoid arresting or interviewing a child at school if it can possibly be avoided; even if they have no choice but to interview the child at school, this should only be done with the consent, and in the presence of, the head teacher. In practice, of course, these are only guidelines and there will be little the parent can do if the police break them.

If the offence is serious the parent may feel it is best that the child does not answer any questions until a solicitor has been instructed. This is one of the rights of any accused person, whether a child or an adult (see page 664).

Remember that legal aid will be available for a child involved in criminal proceedings. The child's financial eligibility will be assessed on the basis of its parents' income and capital.

If the child admits the offence

If the child admits that he is guilty, the police may decide simply to caution him rather than prosecute. A caution is, in effect, a dressing-down from a senior police officer. The child is given a severe warning and told that he will not be dealt with so leniently next time. The caution does not go down as a criminal record, although it can be referred to if he should ever come before a juvenile court in the future.

Whilst the idea of cautioning a child as an alternative to prosecuting is clearly sensible, there is one major disadvantage. A caution will only be given to a child who admits his guilt and, since many children regard a caution as 'getting off', there is a danger that the innocent child will wrongly admit his guilt, just to avoid the anxiety and worry of a juvenile court appearance. Thus, the caution can sometimes be an inducement to plead guilty. That caution can, at a later date, be used as evidence of previous bad character if the child is prosecuted.

Prosecution is seen as a last resort, to be used only when the child refuses to admit his guilt, or in more serious cases where prosecution cannot be avoided, or where the child has previously been cautioned, or the police regard prosecution as desirable because of the child's home or his conduct at school.

Many police forces have specialist juvenile bureaux to deal with juvenile offenders. If the child admits the offence, and if the offence is not too serious, the papers will go to the bureau. They will investigate the facts and background, considering such things as the child's home life, character, and past record. The bureau will then decide whether to prosecute the child, whether to give him a caution, or whether to drop the matter. As an approximate guide, it seems that of all the children reported to the bureaux, about half are prosecuted, a third are cautioned, and the remainder have the cases against them dropped. The police have a complete discretion in deciding whether to prosecute, except for serious offences (e.g. rape, arson, aggravated assault, etc.), which must be prosecuted. Also, if the young person has been arrested and cautioned on three previous occasions then prosecution – not a caution – will follow (although practices vary with different police forces).

If the child denies the offence

If the child refuses to admit his guilt, then the police have to decide whether to prosecute or to drop the matter. The child cannot simply be given a caution if he will not admit his guilt.

If the police decide to prosecute, the next step will usually be for them to obtain a summons and serve it on the parents. This will tell the parents and child to attend the juvenile court at a stated time for the trial of the case. Only in particularly serious cases will the police issue a warrant for the arrest of the child and take him to the police station; if this should happen, the parents should immediately instruct a solicitor.

Which court?

Most children accused of crimes appear before the juvenile court. This is a private sitting of what is, in effect, a specially constituted magistrates' court. The bench will be made up of two or three magistrates drawn from a special panel of JPs. The magistrates who go on the panel are supposed to be those who have a knowledge and experience of children. At the time of being appointed to the panel they must be under fifty (preferably under forty) and they must retire at the age of sixty-five.

Procedure in the juvenile court is similar to that in the magistrates' court (see page 786). The main consequence of this is that the case is tried *summarily* – i.e. without a jury. Virtually all children charged with criminal offences do not have the right of a jury trial, which they might have if they were adult. One exception is when a juvenile is accused of homicide or an offence for which an adult could be imprisoned for fourteen years or more; the magistrates can then decide that the juvenile be tried in the crown court.

The other exception is when a juvenile is charged jointly with a non-juvenile. When this happens the juvenile will probably be tried in the adult courts beside his co-defendant.

Illustration. A sixteen-year-old (juvenile) and a seventeen-year-old (adult) are jointly accused of stealing a car. The seventeen-year-old can opt for trial in either the magistrates' court or the crown court. If the seventeen-year-old opts for a magistrates' court trial the sixteen-year-old will be tried with him. But if the sixteen-year-old is found guilty, he will be passed on to the juvenile court for sentencing. However, if the magistrates wish to fine him, bind over his parents, or give him an absolute or conditional discharge, they can impose that sentence themselves. If the seventeen-year-old opts for a crown court trial the sixteen-year-old will almost certainly be tried with him. But if the sixteen-year-old is found guilty, he will almost always be passed back to the juvenile court for sentencing.

In theory, the juvenile should only be tried in the crown court if it is necessary in the interests of justice. But in practice, he is nearly always tried in the crown court. This is because the prosecution do not want to risk one offender being acquitted and the other being convicted on the same evidence but in a different court.

The sixteen-year-old offender

The juvenile court normally hears cases involving children up to the age of seventeen. Frequently, a child will be sixteen at the time when he is charged and yet, because of the delay in cases coming to trial, he will be seventeen by the time the case is heard. The general rule is that he should then be tried in the adult courts – that is, the magistrates' court or the crown court. (See page 785 for how to decide which court an adult is tried in.)

Procedure in the juvenile court

When the parent and child attend court, they will probably find that the court is in the same building as the local magistrates' court and, indeed, the hearing will often take place in the courtroom that is used by the magistrates. There may, however, be a separate entrance to the court building.

The procedure in court will be similar to that in a magistrates' court trial (see page 786), the magistrates acting as judge and jury. The procedure will certainly be less formal than in a normal magistrates' court case but to a young child it can still be a bewildering and frightening experience.

The hearing is in private, so the general public cannot attend. However, there will often be a surprising number of people in the courtroom: the magistrates, their clerk, an usher, the child, the child's parents and lawyers, the police, the LEA representative, and a probation officer. In addition, a representative of the press can be present, although only rarely will one attend, since the name, address, or school of the child, or any other information that might identify him, cannot be published.

The parents are expected to attend and, indeed, can be ordered to, if necessary. If there is some reason why they cannot attend (e.g. illness), then the magistrates will probably accept another family member, such as an older brother or sister, as a substitute. Otherwise, the case may be adjourned, especially if the young person does not have a solicitor appearing for him. In some courts, the juvenile will be referred to the court's duty solicitor, who will then act for him or her.

To make the proceedings less intimidating, the juvenile is normally referred to by his christian name; he is asked whether he 'admits' or 'denies' the offence, rather than whether he pleads guilty or not guilty; and witnesses 'promise' to tell the truth as opposed to swearing. In addition, juveniles are not 'convicted' or 'sentenced' – they are euphemistically 'dealt with'. If the child is found guilty, the parents and child will both be given an opportunity of making a statement to the magistrates. The magistrates will then move on to consider what would be the appropriate sentence. In this, they will be largely influenced by social reports.

Home-surroundings reports

If no report has yet been prepared the court will adjourn so that social workers can make inquiries and draw up a 'home-surroundings report'. In many areas this is done prior to the court appearance in all but the most trivial cases, and if a report has been prepared the magistrates will be able to sentence the child without further delay. If an adjournment is necessary, the juvenile will probably be granted bail (although it is common for parents to be asked to act as sureties – see page 784; conditions may also be imposed, such as the juvenile not going to certain places, or being in by a particular time at night). If bail is not granted, the child will probably be kept in the care of the local social services department, although exceptionally a child will be kept in custody (at a remand centre).

If the child is under thirteen, the report will usually be prepared by the local authority. If the child is over thirteen, it is normally the probation service or a social worker that prepares it. The typical home-surroundings report will set out details of the family structure, the conditions of the home, and the standard of living. The child's character and personality will be discussed, and reference will be made to his school attendance record, and any relevant medical history. The child's attitude to the offence and any mitigating circumstances will also be included. In addition, the home-surroundings report may be supplemented by reports from the local education authority and others.

The reports need not be read out aloud in court. In fact, the parents and the child can be ordered out of the courtroom whilst the reports are being discussed. Whatever happens, the court should tell the parents or the child the substance of any information in the report that will affect the sentence.

The court's sentence

Discharge. Absolute discharges and conditional discharges (see page 804) are common sentences in juvenile courts. They provide a warning to the child and yet avoid the stigma that might attach to a more serious sentence.

Binding over. The court can bind the child over which, in effect, warns him not to commit another offence within a specified period (see page 807). Usually, though, a conditional discharge is imposed instead. In addition, the parents can be bound over to take proper care and control of a young offender (i.e. aged fourteen to sixteen), but this can only be done with the parents' consent, and, in practice, is rare.

Deferred sentence. This allows the court to defer imposing a sentence for up to six months. When the court reconvenes it will consider how the child has behaved in that intervening period. If he has behaved himself, he will usually be given an absolute or conditional discharge or a fine. In practice, many juvenile courts do not bother to defer sentence but simply impose a conditional discharge.

Fine. If the child is under fourteen, the maximum fine is £100; over fourteen it is £400. In addition (or as an alternative) the child can be ordered to pay compensation of up to £2,000 for each offence. If the court feels that the offender cannot afford to pay both a fine and compensation, then preference is given to ordering compensation and not ordering a fine (see page 714 for when a compensation order can be made). The normal court order is for the parent or guardian to pay the fine/compensation, although the court can agree not to do this if it would be 'unreasonable'. The family's finances must be taken into account when fixing the level of the fine or compensation, and the parent or guardian must be given a chance to speak to the court before the sentence is imposed.

Attendance centre order. This requires the child to attend a local centre at stated times. The usual sentence is for a total of twelve hours, being served by between one and three hours on alternate Saturday afternoons. It is thus particularly suitable for football hooligans, but generally it achieves little. An added problem is that few areas have enough attendance centres available and so some other sentence has to be imposed. It can be imposed on offenders aged ten to twenty-one. The maximum number of hours that can be imposed is: aged ten to thirteen, twelve hours; fourteen to sixteen, twenty-four hours; seventeen to twenty, thirty-five hours. If the offender does not attend when he should, then he can be brought back and a different sentence imposed.

Supervision order. This is the juvenile court's equivalent of a probation order. The aim is to give the child long-term help without removing him from home. Apart from allowing general supervision of the child, the order can require him to receive treatment, such as character training, away from home, and also to attend for psychiatric treatment. The order can only be made against a child who is under seventeen. Often conditions will be imposed (e.g. to live with parents; curfew; regular appointments with supervisor; to undergo medical treatment). If the offender does not comply with the supervision order he can be brought back and another sentence imposed (care order; attendance centre order; fine of up to £50).

Care order. The court can put the child into the care of the local authority, which then assumes all parental rights over him (see page 134). The local authority must review the order every six months. It is the local authority that decides what sort of home the child should be sent to but, more often than not, it is a question of finding any home with vacancies that is prepared to take the child. Sometimes, the child will be allowed to remain at home even though s/he is in the care of the local authority; the child will know that if further offences are committed then transfer to a children's home is likely to result.

Detention centre. This is intended as a short sharp shock. The order can be made for any boy between the ages of fourteen and twenty-one and can be for a period of from twenty-one days to four months. An order can only be made if he has been found guilty of an offence that an adult could have gone to prison for. The regime is both strict and rigorous (e.g. square-bashing and PE). There is no attempt at rehabilitation or education.

Community service. This is unpaid voluntary work. The rules are the same as for adult offenders (see page 806) but it cannot be ordered for a child under sixteen. The maximum sentence for a sixteen-year-old is 120 hours.

Youth custody. In reality, this has replaced borstal. It is for offenders aged fifteen or over and can be for up to six months per offence (maximum twelve months). The usual minimum sentence is four months. The aim is to provide an element of training and education (unlike detention centre).

Prison. No juvenile (i.e. under seventeen) can be sentenced to prison, but the crown court can sentence the child to be detained during Her Majesty's pleasure, usually in a young person's prison. This is called detention.

The sentences in practice

Although this may appear a formidable list of sentences, in practice it is not. Fines are largely unenforceable and have little effect on most offenders. In addition, there seems to be no way that the court can order a child into residential accommodation of a humane and rehabilitating nature, since admission to 'community homes with education' (CHE) is at the discretion of the local authority. Not only are there too few of them but the court cannot order them to accept individual children. Thus, all too often the juvenile court is faced with the stark alternatives of virtually letting the offender off or removing him from home into a punitive and severe institution. There is no provision for a half-way house that can accommodate the child and try to help rather than punish.

(See also 'Sentencing Offenders', page 802.)

10 Wills

Probate is the general name given to the law of wills, succession, inheritance, intestacy, and administration. It is one of the traditionally important legal topics and a subject that concerns us all, for while one may possibly go through life unaffected by, for instance, conveyancing or matrimonial legislation, no one has yet succeeded in avoiding the attention of the probate laws.

Whilst death destroys a person's human personality it does not terminate his legal personality. His assets and liabilities will live on after him as his 'estate', being held by his 'personal representatives'. They will hold the estate for him until the debts and liabilities have been satisfied and the remaining assets distributed in accordance with his wishes – subject, of course, to his having made reasonable provision for his spouse and dependants. The personal representatives will find out his wishes, either by looking at his written will or by consulting the rules laid down by Parliament as to the presumed wishes of the average person who dies without leaving a will (i.e. intestate).

The probate laws have three objectives:
- to safeguard the dead person's creditors;
- to ensure that reasonable provision is made for the dead person's dependants;
- to distribute the balance of the estate in accordance with the known – or presumed – intentions of the dead person.

The common law laid down its own rules for securing these objectives, but these laws have been replaced by detailed statutory laws, mainly of nineteenth-century origin, which lay down rules as to how a valid will is to be made, how personal representatives are appointed, the extent of their powers and duties, and, finally, how the assets are to be distributed and to whom.

Why make a will?

If a person dies without leaving a will, he is said to die intestate. His property will pass to his relatives in accordance with the rules laid down by Parliament (see page 180). Generally, this means that the surviving husband or wife receives the first £85,000 (or £40,000 if there are any children), plus a life share in half the balance. Problems, therefore, arise if the deceased does not want his spouse to take such a large share (for instance, they might have separated) or if he wants her to receive a larger amount. Many lawyers these days advise that a surviving spouse should be left all the estate unless it amounts to well over £100,000. This is because inflation can soon reduce the value of that lump sum; even with inflation at only 5 per cent a year, £100,000 today would be worth only £46,500 in fifteen years. So, a man worth £100,000 with a wife and child would be well advised to sign a will leaving everything to his wife, rather than rely on the intestacy laws (in which case his wife would only get £40,000, plus a half-share in the other £60,000).

So a will is advisable when the intestacy laws will not produce a satisfactory distribution of the estate. Since circumstances can change (for instance, a person might not think his estate is worth more than £40,000 or £85,000, but a few years of house price inflation can drastically alter the position), it is always sensible to make a will and avoid possible problems in the future. One way of reducing the impact of inflation on a will is to express gifts in terms of fractions or percentages of the estate so that the relative value of each gift is maintained at the same level.

In more complicated situations the advantages of a will are obvious. Apart from ensuring that the estate is given to the right people in the right proportions, a will can avoid family squabbles and jealousies, reduce the amount of capital transfer tax payable, and also simplify the task of the personal representatives. An additional benefit is that the person who leaves a will can choose who will be his executors; if he dies intestate they will be selected by following an arbitrary set of rules (see page 170).

Making a will is not expensive. Solicitors generally charge between £15 and £50 for drawing up a straightforward will, but despite this, many people put off making a will until it is too late: 'I feel better now, doctor' are famous last words.

Making a will

The intention

Anybody who is over eighteen and of sound mind can make a will. But not every written document that sets out how one's property is to be disposed of on death is a will, for it must be intended to act as a will and to be its maker's 'last will and testament'. Under the common law, a man's 'will' dealt with his land whilst his 'testament' disposed of all his other property, and although this distinction has long since been abolished, many lawyers still like to commence a will with the formal words 'This is the last will and testament of . . .'

Unless the document is intended to be a will it will not be enforced by the courts, or, to put this in more sophisticated language, a will is only valid if it is made with the necessary testamentary intention. Thus if a person is of unsound mind, or doubtful mental capacity, his will may be invalid. Because of this, when an aged and perhaps senile person makes a will it is advisable to have a doctor as one of the witnesses, and the doctor should check that the old or infirm person is capable of making a will and that he understands what is written in the will. If the doctor makes a record of his examination it may be valuable evidence should the will ever be challenged on the grounds of mental incapacity.

Foolishness, eccentricity, or social pressure are not enough to invalidate a will. However, fear, fraud, or coercion are; for instance, a person who signs a will at gunpoint is not making a valid will. Thus, if a solicitor or doctor takes advantage of his position of trust so that he benefits under the will, the gift to him will probably not take effect. Similarly, if a person is nagged and pestered by a begging relative, that too may amount to undue influence.

In any case in which testamentary capacity is in doubt it is important to take legal advice straight away.

The formalities

There are detailed rules on how to sign and witness a will. These are set out in section 9 of the Wills Act 1837 (and, in fact, the rules were much stricter until sensible changes were introduced in 1982). Now, the rules are that:

- the will must be in writing (so a video will would not be valid!), *and*
- it must have been signed; *and*
- there must be signatures from at least two witnesses, who both saw the testator sign and who both then signed in his/her presence.

If the will does not comply with these requirements, it will be invalid. Its author will, therefore, die intestate, and his personal representatives may be forced by the intestacy rules to distribute the estate in a way that he did not intend.

Although the Wills Act requirements seem straightforward, numerous wills have been turned down over the years because of a failure to meet the strict wording of the provisions. Although these rules may seem strict, the rules were even stricter before 1982 and it is likely that in the future many fewer wills will fail than was previously the case. For example, before 1982 the testator had to sign at the foot of the will – if he wrote anything after his signature, then that part of the will was ignored. Now, he can sign wherever he likes as long as it is clear that he wants the whole document to be treated as his will. In practice, of course, the will should still be signed at the end so as to avoid any arguments, but the 1982 changes have meant that if a mistake is made it is now less likely to cause major problems.

Witnesses

There must be at least two witnesses to the will. Any adult, except someone who is blind, can be a witness, but the witness must see the testator sign, and then sign the will himself. The will is not valid if the witness does not see the testator sign or if the testator signs after the witness.

The witness need not see the contents of the will; all he is doing is witnessing the testator's signature, not the contents of the will. He is there as an independent witness that the person signed the will freely and voluntarily. Because he is an independent person, he cannot benefit from the will, nor can the witness's husband or wife benefit. Any gift to the witness (or the witness's spouse) will be invalid and the property that would have gone to them will form part of the residue of the estate.

However, if the witness and the beneficiary marry after the will is made this rule will not apply and the beneficiary can take the gift.

It is vital, therefore, that a beneficiary or the spouse of a beneficiary under a will should not witness it. If he does witness it, and so causes the gift to be forfeited, that will not affect the validity of the rest of the will; it will remain valid subject to his (or his spouse's) gift being struck out.

People often ask close relatives to witness their wills. In such a case the witness should check whether he (or his spouse) will benefit from the will; if so, someone else will have to witness the will. This is most important!

Drafting a will

A will that complies with the rules and which was made with testamentary intention will be upheld by the courts as a valid and binding will. Therefore, the personal representatives will have to follow its instructions exactly – even if it is clear that the testator made a mistake when drafting it. This is because the law requires the written directions of the testator to be followed, and if he leaves clear and unambiguous instructions they must be obeyed. Only if there is some ambiguity or uncertainty in the will itself can the court consider other evidence, such as letters written by the deceased, or memories of conversations with him. Thus, the language of a will must be clear and unambiguous, and the wording carefully chosen.

If ambiguous words are used, there are two possible consequences. Firstly, the gift might not go to the correct people. For instance, suppose a man leaves his property to 'my children' and at the time of his death he has three children, including one stepchild. In such a case the law will construe 'my children' as meaning 'my own children of the whole blood', and so the stepchild will not receive anything. The property will all go to the other two children.

The second possible consequence of unclear wording is that the gift will fail altogether, because the court cannot decide what the testator meant. For instance, suppose a man leaves his house to his wife for her lifetime and then on her death the house is to be sold and the proceeds shared by 'her and my relatives'. What does 'her and my relatives' mean? There are three ways of interpreting it:

- his relations alive at his death and her relations alive at her death, *or*
- his relations and her relations alive at the time of her death, *or*
- his relations and her relations alive at his death.

The court has to decide which of these equally plausible interpretations is the correct one. In such a case, the court might even decide that it has no idea what he intended, and so the proceeds of sale should not be divided among the relations but instead be put into the residue of the estate, which could mean someone else taking the money. Thus, a slight carelessness in the choice of words when drafting the will can alter its whole effect. Even if the court does work out the dead person's intentions (e.g. by looking at his letters), a lot of money and time (and heartache) will have been wasted in taking the case to court. The moral is to avoid difficulties by using clear, unambiguous language when drawing up a will.

Because of pitfalls such as these, words used in a will must be chosen with great care. Whilst the layman can draft his own will if it is simple (for instance leaving all his property to one person), it is unwise to draft one's own will if there are several beneficiaries involved, or if the value of the estate is considerable. In these cases it is worth paying a small amount for a solicitor to draft the will. In fact, many solicitors make a loss on will drafting, but are prepared to do the task cheaply in the hope that they will be asked to take over the rewarding work of administering the estate when the testator dies. Bear in mind also that capital transfer tax can begin to bite on an estate worth around about £70,000; will-drafting by a solicitor may pay for itself many times over if the solicitor can draw up the will so as to reduce the CTT payable. Generally, therefore, it is wise to use a solicitor for drafting a will; this does not, of course, mean that there will be any obligation to let the solicitor administer the estate when the time comes.

A person who is not prepared to go to a solicitor and who insists on writing his own will should use one of the will forms obtainable from stationers. These forms have the Wills Act requirements incorporated into them and give basic instructions for completion. Despite these precautions, people still make mistakes when using these forms. Also, the forms give little help on how to word the gifts correctly.

Words in wills

Wills drawn up by solicitors often seem verbose and full of antiquated legal jargon. Usually there is a reason for this; the solicitor is carefully using words and phrases that are known to have a well-defined legal meaning, usually as a result of court decisions which have laid down what these phrases mean. Generally, though, most people's wills can be written in modern English, uncluttered by the 'hereinafters', 'abovementioneds', 'hereinbeforementioneds', 'provided howevers', etc., that one frequently associates with legal documents. But whatever words he uses – ancient or modern – the draftsman will need to choose his vocabulary with care, and also to ensure that the will envisages and deals with all possible eventualities.

Words that are frequently used

bequeath. The word 'bequeath' is used to refer to a gift of anything other than land (i.e. houses, flats, land). If the gift is of land, the word 'devise' is used. For instance, a testator 'bequeaths' a car, or a gift or £x, but he 'devises' his house.

children. This includes both legitimate and illegitimate children, whether boys or girls. Adopted children are included if the will was made after the date of the formal adoption order; if it was made before the order, it will probably not include that child. Stepchildren do not always come within the definition of 'children' unless all the children are stepchildren and there are no other children alive at the date the will was made, or unless it is clear that the stepchildren were intended to be included.

If a gift is made to a child, but the child dies before the testator, the gift to the child is still valid. This is an exception to the general rule that a beneficiary must be living at the time of the testator's death. The gift will pass into the estate of the dead child rather than pass automatically to the grandchildren.

descendants. This means children, grandchildren, great-grandchildren, great-great-grandchildren, etc., whether male or female. If property is left to 'all my descendants' each individual descendant will have an equal share of the estate, whereas it will often have been the intention of the testator that each of his children (or the child's family if the child has died) should receive an equal share. If this is intended, the words '*per stirpes*' should be used.

family. This word has been held to have several different meanings. Generally, it means the same as 'children', but the careful will-drafter will avoid using the word 'family' because of the confusion over its meaning.

free of tax. Any capital transfer tax payable on a gift usually comes from the gift, or is paid by the beneficiary. For instance, if tax of £50 was payable on a pecuniary legacy (i.e. money gift) of £1,000, the beneficiary would receive £950. But if the gift was 'free of tax' the beneficiary would receive the full £1,000 and the tax would be paid out of the residue of the estate.

infant. This means the same as 'a minor', i.e. a person under eighteen. People under eighteen cannot own land and they cannot give a valid receipt to the personal representatives for money or chattels. It is, therefore, impossible for a gift to go direct to a minor. In the case of land, it will be held by trustees until the child is eighteen, and with other property the usual device is to word the will so that the gift goes to the parents or other trustees, who are asked to apply it for the child's benefit.

issue. This has basically the same meaning as 'descendants', but occasionally it has been held to have a different meaning. Therefore, the word 'issue' is avoided by experienced will-drafters.

nephews and nieces. The general rule is that this phrase only includes the testator's own nephews and nieces, and not those of his/her spouse. For the avoidance of doubt, it is wise to name the children rather than simply describe them as 'my nephews and nieces'.

next of kin. This will be the person who is the closest blood relative of the testator.

pecuniary legacy. This is the term used to describe a gift of cash.

residue. The residue is what is left after paying all the specific legacies and devises (i.e. after all specific gifts have been made).

testamentary expenses. These are the expenses of administering the estate: e.g. expenses of the executors, lawyers' fees, costs of adverts, tracing beneficiaries, etc.

Making a will: thinking ahead

The draftsman of a will has to think ahead and envisage all possible circumstances, such as the death of the main beneficiary, a change in the size of the estate, or even a change in the tax laws. These are some of the points that a solicitor would want his client to consider:

• are some people to be allowed to select mementoes or souvenirs from the testator's personal possessions? If so, it is wise to fix a maximum value per person, and to give the personal representatives overall discretion.

• is there a gift of the *residue*? The residue is the property that is not specifically given away as named items or as money legacies. If there is no gift of the 'remainder of my property', the residue will not pass under the will but be distributed as though the testator had died intestate (see page 180).

• is a gift to be free of capital transfer tax? Unless the will says otherwise, a gift is assumed to bear its own CTT, which is thus paid by the beneficiary. If the gift is 'free of tax' the tax will be paid out of the residue. Would that be fair on the residuary beneficiary?

• if a house is to be given to a beneficiary, are any mortgages to be paid off? If so, it is the residue that will suffer. Would that be fair? At this point it is worth noting that confusion can arise over the effect of a mortgage protection policy. This is an insurance policy that pays out enough money on death to pay off the mortgage. However, it does not always follow that the insurance money must be used to pay off the mortgage; to avoid doubt it is wise to have a clause in the will which makes it clear that the policy moneys are to be used to pay off the mortgage.

• should a particular beneficiary be given a first option to buy a specific item from the estate and, if so, on what terms?

• what if a beneficiary should die before the testator? Normally, a dead person cannot inherit under a will. So, if the beneficiary is already dead when the testator dies, then the gift will fail. In this case, the property that should have gone to the dead person will remain in the testator's estate – and go to those people who are entitled to the residue. However, there is one exception. If the gift was to a child (or grandchild) of the testator, then it passes to that child's (or grandchild's) children. But, if the dead child did not have any children, then the gift will fail – it will pass into residue (and not, for instance, go to the dead child's spouse). It is therefore important when making a will to consider making substitutional gifts, to deal with the eventuality of someone dying. Bear in mind that if a specific gift does lapse, it will be added into the residue. Would that be an unfair benefit to the person entitled to the residue?

• what will happen if the person who is to receive the residue should die before the testator? Unless other arrangements are set out in the will the residue would then pass under the intestacy rules (see page 180).

• are there any adopted, legitimated, or illegitimate children? Although such children are assumed to be included in the phrase 'children' (see above), it is best to avoid any doubt by specifically naming them.

- does the will revoke all previous wills made by the testator?
- is it possible that the testator will not own the property specifically named when he dies? Obviously, if he does not own the property at the time of his death, he will not be able to give it to the beneficiary, and so the testator should consider this possibility by including an alternative gift when drafting the will. Lawyers say that a will 'speaks from death' which means that one must look at the position at the time of death, not at the time the will was written. For example, if a person makes a gift of 'my sports car' but by the time of his death he has traded in the sports car for a saloon model, then the proposed beneficiary will take nothing; the correct way to word the will is to give 'my car' or 'my sports car or any other car I may own at the time of my death'. A gift that fails in this way is said to have been 'adeemed'.
- does the testator have any children? If so, should the will appoint guardians in case the other parent also dies and the children are left without parents?
- is there a gift subject to a condition? Such a clause requires very careful drafting. The solicitor will word it so that the condition is for an event to happen before the gift is made, rather than for the gift to be forfeited on the event happening. Also, the condition should be drafted in such a way that it will be easy for the personal representatives to decide whether or not the condition has been satisfied.
- the will should name the executors (personal representatives who are named in a will are called executors). Should substitutes be named in case the named executors have died or are unable to take on the job? Two is generally regarded as the ideal number of executors. Are the executors to be paid for their services? If so, the will must specifically authorize their payment. Before naming someone as an executor, the testator should check that the person is willing to be an executor; a person named as an executor can decline to act. It is not essential to name executors: it will still be a valid will even if executors are not named.
- does the will specifically state that it is 'signed by the testator in our presence and then by us as witnesses in his presence'? This confirms that the main requirements of the Wills Act have been observed and is called an 'attestation clause'. Its omission will result in the personal representatives being unable to prove the will until they obtain evidence from the witnesses that the Wills Act rules were observed. Accordingly, an attestation clause will save time, expense, and inconvenience after the death.
- should a trust be set up? A trust is an arrangement whereby property is given to someone to hold for someone else's use until the occurrence of some event, such as their death. The concept is very simple but, unfortunately, the more one goes into it the more complicated it becomes. Suffice it to say that if I had £100,000 and a mistress (I have neither), I might leave the money to a solicitor to hold on trust for my mistress until her death; although the solicitor (the 'trustee') would be the legal owner of the money, it would be my mistress (the 'beneficiary') who would receive the benefit of the gift. However, she would not receive the capital sum itself; my solicitor would have to invest the money and the mistress would only be entitled to receive the interest or income from it – she could not touch the capital. On the

mistress's death, the £100,000 would revert back into my estate and be distributed by my personal representatives in accordance with the terms of my will.

A trust is an effective method of giving a person the benefit of property without actually giving them the property itself. The beneficiary of a trust can be anyone – an infant, a Mental Health Act patient, a spouse, etc. – but the main use of the trust has been to enable wealthy families to pass their money down through the generations without the risk of it being squandered by one spendthrift member of the family. The trust is also used in schemes to minimize the amount of income tax and CTT paid by members of a family, and was greatly used in estate duty avoidance schemes. If complex trusts are being contemplated, specialist legal advice will be needed.

Making a will: a summary of the steps to be taken

1. Draw up a list of the estate. This will be all the assets, such as land, property, money, cars, valuables, etc., less debts (i.e. mortgage, bank overdraft, debts, bills). The net figure is the likely estate.
2. Draw up a list of beneficiaries: the people who are to benefit.
3. Work out who is to receive what. Check that all eventualities are covered. Is the bulk of the estate to pass under the gift of the residue or is that just a tidying-up clause?
4. The will should be set out on a clean sheet of paper. Whilst it can be handwritten, it is advisable to type it and so avoid any problems of illegible handwriting.
5. The first clause of the will should set out the correct and full baptismal names of the testator. If s/he does not always use that name, the words 'sometimes known as . . . ' should be stated. To avoid doubt it is best to state specifically that all previous wills are revoked. There is no need to start with the words 'This is the last will and testament of' although many lawyers like to use these words.

   A typical first clause will simply state:

   'I . . . (name, address, occupation) hereby revoke all previous wills and testamentary dispositions made by me and declare this to be my last will.'
6. The next clause should appoint the executors. Note that the executor(s) can be beneficiaries under the will (but witnesses cannot, see page 153). In a typical will the testator leaves all his property to his spouse and in such a case it is usual to appoint the spouse as the sole executrix, with a named alternative in case the spouse cannot act for some reason. If a professional executor, such as a solicitor, is to be appointed then the clause should specifically allow him to charge the estate for his work. In such a case, the testator should inquire what the executor's likely fee will be.
7. The will should next deal with all the gifts of money and property other than land (which includes houses and flats). These are the legacies – 'chattels' is the word used to describe all such property, except for money. A typical clause will state: 'I give to (*name*) absolutely such of my chattels and effects of personal domestic or household use or ornament as are not hereby otherwise specifically disposed of', and then go on to deal with specific gifts: 'I give the following specific legacies absolutely:
   (a) to my daughter (*name*) my gold watch,

(b) to my grandson (*name*) the tools which belonged to my late husband', and finally deal with pecuniary legacies: 'I give the following pecuniary legacies absolutely and free of all taxes:

(a) to (*name*) the sum of £x

(b) to each of my grandchildren living at my death (absolutely and free of all taxes*) the sum of £x.'

8. Next come the devises of real property (i.e. land, houses, and flats). Sometimes these devises are held via trusts, in which case complicated provisions may apply. Legal advice is then essential. Often, though, the property (generally the family house) will go to the testator's spouse along with all the other property. Then a typical clause will read: 'I devise and bequeath all my estate both real and personal whatsoever and wheresoever, subject to the payment of my debts and funeral and testamentary expenses unto my said wife/husband (*name*) if s/he survives me by twenty-eight clear days but if s/he should fail to survive me as aforesaid the succeeding provisions of this Will shall take effect (*then set out the alternative provisions*) . . .'

9. Who is the residue (i.e. the net estate after making all the other gifts) to go to? Usually it is left to the surviving spouse in which case the above clause can be used. Otherwise, a different clause will be needed, such as: 'I give the residue of my estate to my two sons (*names*) equally, but if either of them dies before me leaving children then those children shall on reaching eighteen take equally the share which their father would otherwise have taken.' If the residue is not left to anybody it will be distributed under the intestacy rules (see page 180). When working out entitlement under the intestacy rules, any benefits received under the will are taken into account. For instance, if a surviving spouse has already received £20,000 under the will then she will only be absolutely entitled to £65,000 of the residue (£20,000 if there are any children).

10. Finally, the testator should sign in the presence of his two witnesses. Remember that neither the witnesses nor their spouses can be beneficiaries. Typical wording is:

In witness whereof I have hereunto set my hand this . . . day of . . . 19—.
Signed by the above-named (*name*) in
our presence and then by us in his:..
(*signature*)

....
(*signature*)

(*name, address, occupation*)

....
(*signature*)

(*name, address, occupation*)

*Optional (see page 156).

11. The will should be kept in a safe place; it is advisable to make photocopies. Solicitors and banks will usually hold wills. Alternatively, the will can be lodged for safekeeping with the Principal Registry (at Somerset House) – contact any district probate registry for details of this service (which costs £1). This ensures that the will is available when anyone attempts to become a personal representative and so there can be no risk of the testator dying intestate. The executors and the family should be told where the original will is kept and a note of the place written on a copy of the will kept with the other papers.

12. The really conscientious will-maker will try to make things easy for his/her relatives by making a comprehensive note of all the personal details that might be needed after death, e.g. names and addresses of: doctor, trade union, bank, accountant, solicitor, landlord, employer, building society, bank, anyone who is a beneficiary or who should be told of the death. Also, where the following documents can be found: birth and marriage certificates, driving licence, insurance policies, title deeds, HP agreements, building-society and bank books, rent book, passport, share certificates, NI card, etc.

13. It should be remembered that marriage revokes a will so always make a new will on remarriage (and also on divorce – see below).

Revoking or altering the contents of a will

The usual way of cancelling a will is by making a new one and commencing it with the phrase 'I hereby revoke all former wills and codicils made by me'. If the revocation clause was not included, the new will would only revoke the earlier will in so far as it was inconsistent with it.

As might be expected, the deliberate burning, tearing up or destroying of a will is assumed to destroy it. But merely writing 'revoked' across the face of the will may not be enough.

The revocation of a will may not always be effective if it was done on a false assumption. For example, suppose a testator makes a new will and then tears up his old will. If his new will should be held to be invalid for some reason, he would seem to be left without a valid will. However, in these circumstances, the court might say that the revocation of the old will was conditional on the new will being valid and, since that is not so, the revocation of the first will would be ineffective and it would still be a valid will. The jargon for this conditional revocation is 'dependent relative revocation' – a phrase that endows a straightforward idea with an unnecessary aura of complexity. For instance:

In August 1966, Mr Carey, a widower, made a will leaving his estate to his sister-in-law. He left the will with his solicitors but in 1972 he reclaimed it saying that he had nothing to leave and so he was going to destroy the will. In 1973 his sister died leaving him £40,000. In 1976 Mr Carey died without leaving a will. The sister-in-law asked the court to enforce the 1966 will on the basis that it had been revoked by Mr Carey in the mistaken belief that he had nothing to leave. Held: The 1966 will remained valid. Carey (1977)

Marriage and Divorce

Marriage. Revocation is automatic on the marriage of the testator. The logic behind this rule is that Parliament in 1837 assumed that most testators would want to leave their property to their spouse but a newly married testator might forget to alter his will, which might not mention the spouse as a beneficiary. Thus, the Wills Act provides that unless the testator makes a new will after his marriage, he will die intestate and so the spouse will inherit some, if not all, of the estate under the intestacy rules (see below). The only exception to this rule is when the gift was clearly made in contemplation of the marriage, for then the testator can be assumed to have had his spouse-to-be in mind when he drafted the will; this applies even if the will leaves nothing to the spouse, for Parliament did not think it proper in 1837 to interfere with the right of a man to dispose of his property as he wished. Now, of course, the family-provision legislation allows the courts to award shares of the estate to a spouse and other dependants (see page 183).

If a will is made before a marriage it should always state that 'This will is made in contemplation of my marriage with —'. If the marriage does not take place such a will would remain valid, and so it is usual to add 'and is conditional on the marriage taking place within . . . months'. Unless clear wording is used, the courts will not be able to uphold the will as having been made in contemplation of marriage.

Divorce. Divorce does not invalidate a will but may make it largely ineffective. This is because any gift to the former spouse will no longer take effect, and nor will the appointment of the ex-husband/wife as executor. In effect, the ex-spouse is cut out of the will, but the rest of the will takes effect in the usual way. This rule is subject to there being no 'contrary intention' in the will – so if it is made clear that the spouse is to have the gift even if there is a divorce, then the gift will remain valid. Remember, though, that if the divorce is followed by a remarriage then the new marriage will invalidate the will (see above) and so the ex-spouse will get nothing – unless a new will is executed in which a gift is made to her (or unless she can apply to the court under the family-provision legislation – see page 183).

If a divorced husband/wife is cut out of the will in this way, then his/her share will go to the person who is entitled to the residue (i.e. all parts of the estate that are not specifically given to other people). Sometimes, of course, this is not what was intended. For instance, suppose a husband makes a will leaving his house to his wife, but if she should die before him, it is to go to the children. The residue is to go to his brother. If they are then divorced, and he does not rewrite his will, then on his death the house will not go to the wife. She will have been cut out. However, it will not go to the children – as was probably intended – but will go to the brother (i.e. because he takes the residue). So, if you are getting divorced, your ex-spouse will be cut out of the will – but you should think carefully about what will happen to his/her share. If you do not want it to go to the person who is entitled to the residue, then you should alter your will to deal specifically with the point.

Can you agree not to alter your will?

The general rule is that a will is not a contract and so a disappointed beneficiary cannot sue for breach of contract if he is not left what he was promised by the testator. This is because a person is free to alter his or her will as s/he pleases. For instance, if a poor relative of a rich person agrees to be housekeeper for that person – on the basis that 'you will have the house when I've gone' – then the poor relative cannot claim off the estate if, in fact, the house is left to someone else. However, there is one exception to this. If there was a binding contract between the testator and the disappointed beneficiary, then the estate will be bound to honour that contract – and so the beneficiary could sue the estate for the value of the gift that had been promised. For this to happen there must have been a specific contract – and usually this will have to be in the form of a deed (i.e. a professionally prepared document that is formally witnessed, etc.). If there was such a document, then the disappointed beneficiary (e.g. the poor relative who had been promised the house) could sue the estate.

But unless there is a formal agreement of this sort, it is legally unwise to rely on a promise of being left something in a will – ask for a formal deed to be prepared, for otherwise the promise will be worthless.

Alterations

Any alteration to a will should be treated as a new will, with all the Wills Act formalities being observed, even if the alteration or amendment is only minor. Amendments are usually put into 'codicils' at the end of the will, and apart from ensuring that the codicil is properly signed and attested, it is wise to state that 'in all other respects I confirm my will' so there can be no suggestion that the codicil was meant to revoke the whole will. However, if the layman wishes to alter his will it is better to rewrite the whole will in its amended form rather than add on codicils.

Two sample wills, one invalid and one valid, are shown on pages 164 and 165.

Two sample wills: *John James wants to leave everything to his cohabitee, and nothing to the wife from whom he is separated*

An Invalid Will

I John James of 2 Abingdon Cottages, London NE1 make this my Will, as set out in the Schedule hereto.
Signed by me, John James, on the 2nd of November 1985

....

(signature)

Witnesses: Mabel Smith

                  ....

                  (signature)

                  Fred Evans

                  ....

                  (signature)

The Schedule

I give the whole of my estate to my common-law wife Mabel Smith and nothing to my lawful wife Anne James.

Defects in this invalid will

1. The testator, John James, has not signed at the end of the will. It will not be invalid, but the Probate Registry will probably query the signature (causing delay and probably expense).
2. The beneficiary is Mabel Smith, yet she is one of the witnesses. The gift to her would therefore fail and the estate would pass under the laws of intestacy to Anne James, the testator's surviving spouse (and, if the estate was of sufficient size, to children or other relatives; see page 180).
3. Although there are two witnesses, it is not stated that they saw the testator sign and that they then signed in his presence. Whilst such a clause is not essential, the Probate Registry will not grant probate until it has been confirmed that the proper formalities were observed. If the witnesses cannot be traced, this can cause delay and difficulty.
4. The will does not state that it revokes all previous wills. If there is no revocation clause the will only revokes an earlier will in so far as it is inconsistent with it. In this example, it would probably make no difference but it is always wise to avoid doubt by inserting a revocation clause.
5. A properly drafted will would appoint executors.

Summary. The will fails completely. Thus, John James will die intestate and all or part of his property will pass to his wife, Anne James, which is precisely what he wanted to avoid. The only hope that Mabel Smith, his common-law wife, will have of inheriting any of the estate is to apply to the court under the family-provision legislation (see page 183).

A Valid Will

I, John James, of 2 Abingdon Cottages, London NE1, a fitter, hereby revoke all previous Wills and Testamentary dispositions made by me and declare this to be my last Will.

1. I appoint Mabel Smith of 2 Abingdon Cottages, London NE1 to be the executor of this my Will but if she should be unwilling or unable to act as my executor I appoint my son, John James of 93 Clifton Road, London NE5, to be my executor.

2. I devise and bequeath all my estate both real and personal whatsoever and wheresoever subject to the payment of my debts and funeral and testamentary expenses unto Mabel Smith of 2 Abingdon Cottages, London NE1, but if she should pre-decease me I leave all my said estate to my son John James of 93 Clifton Road, London NE5.

In witness whereof I have hereunto set my hand this 2nd day of November 1985

Signed by the above-named   John James
John James in our presence   ....
and then by us in his: *(signature)*

Fred Evans
(1a Abingdon Cottages, London NE1, postman)

Mavis Evans
(1a Abingdon Cottages, London NE1, housewife)

Note. This will is for illustration purposes only. Do not risk adapting it to other circumstances. Many stationers sell pre-printed wills that can be used to cover most contingencies and one of those forms should be used if a solicitor is not used to draft the will.

11 When Someone Dies

Check-list of steps to be taken on death

Before personal representatives are appointed (see below) there are several administrative tasks that have to be carried out. Ideally, of course, the person who is likely to be the personal representative should take control and carry out these steps:

1. Immediately on death

If death occurred at home

Inform:
- the family doctor
- relatives, and perhaps the priest, vicar, etc.
- the police, if the death was violent, accidental, or in suspicious circumstances.

If the doctor attended the deceased during his terminal illness, the doctor will give the relatives:
- a free medical certificate, showing the cause of death. This will be in a sealed envelope addressed to the registrar of deaths, *and*
- a formal notice stating that he has signed a medical certificate, and which also explains the procedure for registering the death.

Alternatively, the doctor will report the death to the coroner if:
- the deceased was not seen by a doctor during his last illness, or within fourteen days of death, *or*
- if the cause of death is uncertain, *or*
- if the death was sudden, violent, or caused by an accident, *or*
- if the death resulted from an industrial disease.

If death occurred in hospital

The ward sister will inform the nearest relative of the death (the police will do this if the death followed an accident). The relative will have to attend the hospital to collect the deceased's possessions and also identify the body, unless the deceased had been an in-patient.

If the cause of death is clear, the hospital doctor will give the relatives a free

166

medical certificate and a formal notice (as with a death at home, above). In addition, he will usually carry out a post-mortem, if the relatives agree.

Alternatively, he will report the death to the coroner if:

- the cause of death is uncertain, *or*
- the death was sudden, violent, or caused by an accident, *or*
- if the death resulted from an industrial disease, *or*
- if the death occurred during the course of an operation or while the deceased was under anaesthetic.

2. If the coroner is notified of the death

Whether the death was in hospital or not, the coroner will usually arrange for a post-mortem to be held; the relatives' consent is not needed, although they can retain a doctor to be present during the post-mortem.

The coroner may also decide to hold an inquest. He will generally do so if the cause of death:

- was violent, *or*
- was accidental, *or*
- resulted from an industrial disease, *or*
- remains uncertain.

If an inquest is held, the coroner will normally hold a preliminary hearing within a week or so of death. This hearing will be for purposes of identification only and formal evidence of the identity of the body will have to be given. The coroner will then release the body and so allow the funeral or cremation to take place. The inquest proper will usually take place some weeks later and will be an inquiry into the cause of death. The coroner may decide to sit with a jury.

Before the burial can take place, the coroner must first issue a disposal certificate (either an order for burial or a certificate for cremation). This will normally be provided, free of charge, after the post-mortem or after the preliminary inquest hearing.

In addition, the coroner must also issue a cause of death certificate, so that the death can be registered. There are two possibilities:

(a) If the post-mortem shows that death was by natural causes, the coroner will normally provide a pink form addressed to the registrar of deaths in a sealed envelope. Sometimes he will simply send the form direct to the registrar, in which case the relatives will be notified of its issue.

(b) If a full inquest was held, the coroner will send a cause of death certificate direct to the registrar of deaths.

3. Registration of the death

Register the death with the local Registrar of Births, Marriages and Deaths (address in the telephone book).

If the death has been reported to the coroner it cannot be registered until the coroner has provided the necessary pink form or certificate (see above). Thus, there is nothing to be done until the coroner notifies the relatives that the pink form or certificate has been issued.

If the death has not been reported to the coroner, it must be registered within five days. Documents needed are:

- evidence of the cause of death (i.e. medical certificate provided by the doctor and/ or pink form provided by a coroner);
- the deceased's NHS card, if available;
- any war pension order book of the deceased (if applicable and if available).

The registrar will want to know:

- date and place of death;
- deceased's usual address;
- full christian and surnames of the deceased (and maiden name, if a married woman);
- deceased's occupation (and that of her husband if a married woman or a widow);
- deceased's date of birth, and town, county, and country of birth;
- date of birth of deceased's surviving spouse (if applicable);
- whether the deceased was receiving any state benefits.

The registrar will then register the death and provide the applicant with:

(a) A certificate for disposal, unless the coroner has already issued one. This will have to be produced to the funeral director before the burial or cremation can take place.

(b) A certificate of registration of death. This is for social-security purposes and upon production at the local DHSS office will prove entitlement to the death grant (see page 738) and widow's benefit (see page 753). Extra copies can be obtained for a small fee and may be needed for claims on insurance policies, etc.

(c) Pamphlets on welfare benefits that might be available (see page 738) and form PR 48 which gives guidance on obtaining a Grant of Probate.

4. The funeral arrangements

These cannot be finalized until it is known whether the death will be reported to the coroner, for this will affect the date when the body can be released for burial or cremation.

Check the deceased's will to see if it contains instructions as to whether he is to be buried or cremated. Note that there is no legal obligation on the executors or next-of-kin to follow these instructions: it is for them to decide whether to bury or cremate.

It is advisable to use a funeral director who belongs to the National Association of Funeral Directors (NAFD) since they are bound by a code of practice agreed with the Office of Fair Trading. In particular, an NAFD member must provide a full estimate in advance, and this must include the estimate for the cost of a basic, simple, funeral (i.e. exclusive of church fees, flowers, notices in local paper, but inclusive of a coffin, collection or delivery of the body up to ten miles, care of the deceased, and provision of a hearse and one following car to the nearest local cemetery or crematorium, together with conductors and bearers as necessary).

The death grant (page 738) can be used towards the cost of the funeral. Supplementary-benefit payments may be made if the person responsible for paying for the funeral is on, or near, supplementary-benefit level; application should be made before the funeral is arranged. Otherwise the deceased's estate can be used to meet the bill, but most of the assets will only be available when probate has been obtained, and that will take some time. However, some institutions (e.g. building societies, banks) may be prepared to release up to £5,000 worth of assets on production of the death certificate alone (see step 30, page 179).

The funeral cannot take place until a disposal certificate has been handed to the funeral director.

Burial

Check the deceased's personal papers and will to see if he has already paid for a plot in a graveyard or churchyard (the documents are called a grave deed or a deed of grant and a faculty, respectively). If not, a plot will have to be bought. The funeral director will provide details.

The burial will only take place when the following documents have been produced:

● either a certificate for burial (the disposal certificate) from the registrar of deaths, *or*, if there has been an inquest, the coroner's order for burial;

● application for burial – addressed to the cemetery and signed by the executor or next-of-kin. The funeral director will provide this form;

● grave deed or faculty, from the cemetery or diocese, which entitles the deceased to be buried in a particular plot.

Cremation

A cremation involves more formalities than a burial. It is necessary to have *one* of the following:

(a) A certificate for cremation (the disposal certificate) from the registrar of deaths, plus two cremation certificates. One is signed by the family doctor and the other by another doctor; both doctors will probably charge a fee.

(b) If the death was reported to the coroner, then after a post-mortem or inquest he will provide a free certificate for cremation.

The following documents are also needed:

(c) A cremation certificate signed by the medical referee at the crematorium. His fee will usually be included in the crematorium's charge.

(d) Two forms signed by the executor or next-of-kin. One applies for the cremation, whilst the other confirms the arrangements and gives instructions for disposal of the ashes.

Other steps to be taken

1. Return any pension book or welfare benefit book to the DHSS; the book is the property of the DHSS.
2. Go through the provisions of the will.
3. Apply for the death grant and other appropriate welfare benefits (see page 738).
4. Inform the deceased's bank and insurance companies of the death. The bank will stop all the deceased's cheques. Deposit any season ticket with bus or rail authorities so that a refund can be obtained.
5. If the deceased's car is to be used, obtain a new insurance certificate.
6. End all credit-card accounts. Do not pay the bills yet.
7. Work out who will be the personal representative(s) – see below. Having done that, begin administering the estate. (Turn to the check-list on page 176 for a step-by-step guide.)

The personal representatives

The personal representatives are the guardians of the deceased's legal personality. They can sue on his behalf (strictly speaking, on behalf of his estate) if, for instance, he was owed money under a contract and, conversely, they can be sued (i.e. the estate can be sued) by the deceased's creditors.

The personal representatives are not personally liable to pay the deceased's debts, nor can they personally claim any damages recovered; it is the estate that is suing, or being sued, and the personal representatives are the mere nominees through whom the estate acts.

There are two types of personal representatives; those appointed by a will, and those not appointed by a will:

• personal representatives appointed by a will are called *'executors'* (female, executrix);

• personal representatives not appointed by a will are called *'administrators'*.

Both types (collectively called personal representatives) have similar powers and duties. Only one personal representative is needed to administer an estate.

A personal representative's task is similar to that of a trustee. Various statutes lay down detailed rules as to what a trustee or personal representative should, and should not, do. The basic rules are that they should be familiar with the terms of the will and not deviate from them; they must take care of the property and assets as though they were their own; they must keep full accounts and keep the beneficiaries fully informed; they must consult with any other trustees, and not make unilateral decisions, and if in doubt, they should take legal advice. They must not make a profit from their position, although they can recover their out-of-pocket expenses; neither must they put themselves in a position where there is a conflict of interest between themselves and the estate – thus a personal representative cannot buy anything from the estate unless all the beneficiaries are adults and they all consent.

If they fail to live up to the high standards required, the beneficiaries can sue them for negligence or fraud; if the claim is upheld they will be personally liable to compensate the estate, unless they can persuade the court that they acted 'honestly and reasonably, and ought fairly to be excused', in which case the court has a discretion to let them off.

Clearly, then, being a personal representative, or the trustee of a trust, is no sinecure. However, the prospective applicant should not be alarmed for, in practice, most estates are straightforward and are simple to administer, involving the personal representative(s) in little or no personal risk. In addition, of course, many personal representatives choose to seek the help of a solicitor and charge up his fees to the estate.

Who will be the personal representatives?

Different rules apply depending upon whether there is a will or not.

If there is a will

In this case the starting-point will be to see whether the will names any executors. If they are willing to act, they will have to do the job. However, an executor is not obliged to act and if he does not wish to, he should make his position clear. This is best done by sending a written letter of 'renunciation' to the other people concerned, in case it is suggested that he has accepted some of the duties involved and so become obliged to take on all the responsibilities.

If the will does not name any executors, or if the named executors all renounce the job, someone else will have to apply for the grant. The persons entitled, in order of priority, are:

• the trustees and beneficiaries of any trust set up under the will; in practice, it is rare for there to be a trust and so those next entitled are:

• the persons entitled under the will to the residue of the estate (see page 156).

• those entitled to inherit the estate under the intestacy rules (see page 180).

Whoever takes on the task will be an administrator, not an executor, since he was not appointed by will.

Why appoint an executor? It is sensible to appoint an executor – although it is not compulsory to do so. The best advice is to appoint a friend or relative. Alternatively, a bank, or solicitor, can be appointed. But if a solicitor or bank is appointed then your family will be committed to using that solicitor or bank to administer the estate. This can be extremely expensive (see below). It might be much better simply to appoint a friend or relative, because at least that person will have the option of administering the estate themselves, rather than incur professional fees. See page 176 for the steps to be taken. Another disadvantage of naming a particular bank or solicitor is if the person chosen should turn out to be inefficient and slow. If that happens, then there is not much that the beneficiaries (i.e. your family and relatives) can do to hurry matters up. It is very difficult for beneficiaries to bring pressure to bear on a slow solicitor or bank – it would be much better if they themselves were the executors, in which case they could sack the slow bank or solicitor, and transfer the papers to someone who was likely to be more helpful.

If there is no will

If there is no will the estate will be vested in one or more administrators. Parliament has laid down an order of priority between competing applicants based largely on the closeness of the applicant's family links with the deceased. The order of priority is:
- surviving spouse, *next*
- issue (i.e. children, grandchildren, etc., whether adopted, illegitimate, etc.), *next*
- parents, *next*
- brothers and sisters of the whole blood (or their issue), *next*
- the Treasury Solicitor *unless* there is no surviving spouse, in which case the order continues:
    - brothers and sisters of the half blood (or their issue), *next*
    - grandparents, *next*
    - uncles and aunts of the whole blood (or their issue), *next*
    - uncles and aunts of the half blood (or their issue), *next*
    - the Treasury Solicitor.

Between those of equal priority there is no order of priority (e.g. eldest son and youngest daughter have equal priority). Sometimes it may even depend upon who 'gets in first', but it is obviously better if the family can agree as to who will act.

Remember: this is just the order for deciding who is to be the administrator; there is a different order of priority for deciding how the estate is to be divided up (see page 180).

The appointment of the personal representative(s)

Once it has been decided who is entitled to become the personal representative(s), the prospective executor or administrator must apply to the Probate Registry for the court's written confirmation of his appointment.

The court's confirmation is in the form of a certificate called a 'grant', and this is the personal representative's formal proof to the rest of the world that the deceased's estate is vested in him. The grant made to an executor (i.e. if appointed by the will) is called a 'Grant of Probate', while the grant to an administrator (i.e. when there is an intestacy) is a 'Grant of Administration'; in addition, there is also a 'Grant of Administration with the Will Annexed', which covers the hybrid situation of a will but no executors. Although these three grants have different names, their effect is the same – namely, to vest the deceased's assets and liabilities in the personal representative(s) as from the date of death, not just from the date of the grant. Thus, there is no period of time when the deceased's legal personality is neither in the deceased nor in the personal representative(s), and so the myth that death does not destroy the legal personality is preserved.

When there is no need for a grant

It may not be necessary to have a grant, because:
- small sums in National Savings, etc. can be paid out without a grant (see page 179). So also can 'nominations' (see page 180);
- cash, jewellery, etc. can be divided up between the relatives and beneficiaries (if they all agree) without a grant (see page 180);
- jointly held assets will normally pass automatically to the survivor (e.g. jointly owned house, or bank account) and so a grant may not be necessary.

Do-it-yourself probate

Many personal representatives simply instruct a firm of solicitors to supervise the administration of the estate, and the duties of the personal representative are then restricted to signing forms prepared by the solicitors. The solicitor's fees will be paid out of the estate. Alternatively, a bank will usually be prepared to administer the estate, provided all the executors renounce probate and agreement can be reached over payment of the bank's (usually high) fees.

However, the personal representative need not retain a bank or solicitor to help him with his duties. He can instead do the administering of the estate himself and so save the legal fees that the estate would otherwise have paid. The savings can be considerable (see 'Legal fees in probate work', below).

In view of the potential liabilities of being a personal representative (above) DIY probate is not something that should be taken on lightly. However, when the estate is small, or if there are few beneficiaries, it is usually a straightforward, if time-consuming, business of writing letters to banks, creditors, and insurance companies. On the other hand, there are some more complicated situations when it is inadvisable to do the work oneself, and instead the executor or administrator should instruct a solicitor or a bank to administer the estate for him. This would generally be so if:
- the estate is worth a large amount (or, conversely, it is not large enough to pay the debts);
- the dead person has set up a trust;
- some of the beneficiaries cannot be traced;
- the dead person did not leave a will and it is known that there are untraced relatives who might have a claim on the estate;
- the testator was under eighteen when he made his will;
- the will does not contain an attestation clause (see page 158);
- the will contains unsigned alterations;
- the will shows signs of burning, tearing, erasions, or of another document having been attached (e.g. staple holes);

173

- the will refers to another document or deals with property outside the UK;
- one of the beneficiaries under the will witnessed the will (or is married to one of the witnesses);
- the will is ambiguous or unclear;
- the will does not dispose of the residue of the estate;
- there is a possibility of a relative or dependant making a family-provision claim (see page 183).

Legal fees in probate work

The saving of legal fees is likely to be the main reason why a personal representative decides to administer the estate himself.

Solicitors' fees are assessed on the same basis as fees in any other non-contentious (i.e. non-court) legal work, such as conveyancing. The seven factors to be considered when deciding what is a 'fair and reasonable' fee are set out on page 834. But with probate work, the size of the estate is usually taken as the most important single factor. If the solicitor charges on a time basis, the Law Society would generally approve a bill which comprised a charge for the time spent, plus 25–30 per cent typing and services, plus 1 per cent of the value of the gross estate. For instance if the administration of an estate of £120,000 took twenty hours, and time was charged at £25 per hour, the bill might be

20 × £25	£500
plus 30 per cent	150
plus 1 per cent of £120,000	1,200
	£1,850 (not incl. VAT and disbursements)

However, it is usual to value property that was jointly owned at half its normal value and take the principal residence at half its market value when charging. For instance, if the £120,000 estate included an £80,000 house that the deceased owned jointly with his spouse, that house would be valued at £20,000 (half his half share), and so the 1 per cent would only be charged on £60,000 rather than £120,000.

If the solicitor is an executor under the will (especially if he is a sole executor with added responsibilities) it is usual to increase the 1 per cent charge to 1½ per cent.

Grant only

If the solicitor takes out only the Grant of Probate or Letters of Administration, and takes no part in administering the estate, the 1 per cent is generally reduced to ⅙ per cent. For instance, if taking out a grant on an estate worth £120,000 took four hours, and time was charged at £25 per hour, the bill might be

4 × 25	£100
plus 30 per cent	30
plus ⅙ per cent of £120,000	200
	£330 (not incl. VAT and disbursements)

If it included a jointly owned main house worth £80,000, the ⅙ per cent would be £100 and the total bill £220.

It must be stressed that the above figures are only a guide. In difficult cases the solicitor can charge more. Conversely, the charge will often be considerably less. As always, to avoid difficulties, it is advisable to obtain a firm estimate from the solicitor before instructing him to act.

Disputes over fees. Solicitors' fees for probate work come under the general non-contentious costs rules (see page 834). In particular, if the personal representative thinks the solicitor's fee is too high, he could ask the solicitor to obtain a remuneration certificate from the Law Society and he can ask for the fees to be taxed (see page 835). This is one major advantage of using a solicitor, rather than a bank: with banks, there are no controls over the fees charged (and, in any event, they nearly always charge more than solicitors).

Banks

Banks lay down their own scale of fees. Because banks usually charge a lot it is essential to discuss the fee before committing oneself to using the bank. Relatively few people realize just how much banks charge. For instance, in 1985, Barclays charged a basic £500 'responsibility fee' for taking on the estate. There would then be a charge of 2½ per cent on the first £250,000 value of the estate. In addition, there would be 'activity fees' – their charge was £265 for every 'relevant beneficiary', plus £50 for handling every asset worth over £500. Lloyds and Midland both had a basic charge of 3 per cent on estates up to £100,000, with 2 per cent on the next £250,000. In addition, Lloyds charged £40 for handling each asset, £24 for handling each liability (e.g. gas bill), and £16 for selling a share. The Midland charged a fee based on 'units' at £11.50 each, with a minimum per estate of £250. The National Westminster Bank charged a basic 5 per cent on the first £50,000, 3 per cent on the next £50,000, plus 2 per cent on extra amounts. They too had additional fees for the amount of work done – but they were not prepared to publish them!

The end result is an extremely large bill. Generally, solicitors' charges are considerably less. As a rough guide, on an estate of £20,000 a solicitor would be likely to charge £550 (plus VAT) whereas a bank might charge approximately £1,200 (plus VAT). In addition, there would be disbursements (i.e. out-of-pocket expenses, see page 832) incurred by the solicitor or the bank, the main one being probate fees paid to the court when taking out the grant. These are charged on the size of the *net* estate. The net estate is the amount left for distributing to the beneficiaries after paying funeral, probate, and testamentary expenses.

A 1983 survey for *Planned Savings* magazine showed figures for an estate of £25,000, without a house (all figures exclude VAT), of:

Barclays	£1,400	Devon solicitors	£200
NatWest	£1,250	London solicitors	£500–£750
Lloyds	£1,016	Law Society estimate of	
Midland	£1,200	solicitor's charges	£1,500

Finally, if the property contains a house or flat, there will be solicitor's conveyancing fees for transferring the property to the beneficiary, or for acting on the sale of the property (see page 222 for conveyancing fees). If the property is sold, the solicitor's conveyancing fee will be calculated on the usual basis (see page 222). However, if the property is merely transferred to a beneficiary (by what is called an 'assent') the fee will be much less, since little work will be involved.

Administering an estate: a step-by-step guide

Obviously, no two estates are the same but the procedure to be followed will always be similar. This check-list summarizes the main steps to be taken by a personal representative who decides to administer the estate himself, whether he be an executor (i.e. there is a will) or an administrator (i.e. there is no will).

Before obtaining the grant

1. Follow 'Steps to be taken on death', page 166.
2. Examine all the deceased's papers and find out where all his property is. A full list of his assets and liabilities will eventually have to be prepared.
3. Write to the bank for a statement showing balance, interest and any bank charges. What cheques have not yet been paid in? Ask whether the bank holds any securities for the dead person. Ask a bank to open an executor's account; the account need not be with the deceased's own bank.
4. Find out the details of any life-assurance policies held by the deceased. Write to the company notifying them of the death and enclosing a copy of the death certificate. Ask for details of the amount that will be paid; ask for a claim form. The amount due under the policy will not form part of the estate if either (i) it was taken out by the deceased's spouse, on the deceased's life, or (ii) it was taken out under the Married Woman's Property Act (in which case the policy is deemed to be held for the wife and children).
5. Draw up a list of any shares held by the deceased. These will have to be valued as at the date of death; the bank manager will probably be able to find out the valuation. Otherwise, contact the brokers, or look up the shares in the Stock Exchange official list for the date of death.
6. If there is a mortgage, notify the building society and enclose a copy of the death certificate. Ask for details of the amount owed at the date of death.

7. Value any real property, such as a house or flat. The district valuer of the Inland Revenue will agree to fix a valuation after the papers have been lodged with the Probate Registry (see below).

8. Contact any pension fund (or employer) enclosing a copy of the death certificate and asking for full details of any sums due on death (e.g. under an occupational pension scheme). Ask whether the sum is to be treated as part of the estate or not, as this can affect the question of tax.

9. If the deceased held any savings certificates, write to the Savings Certificate Office, Durham, enclosing a copy of the death certificate. Ask for a full list of all certificates held, their date of purchase, and value at the date of death.

10. If the deceased held any premium bonds, write to the Bond and Stock Office, Lytham St Annes, Lancashire, giving the full name and bond numbers. For the moment the bonds can be left in the draw and only cashed shortly before the estate is distributed to the beneficiaries (bonds can remain in the draw for up to twelve months after death).

11. With savings, as in the National Savings Bank or a building society, send the savings book or deposit book to the institution, enclose a copy of the death certificate, and ask for the book to be made up and interest calculated to the date of death. Ask for a withdrawal form.

12. Value all the personal assets of the deceased. A valuer or secondhand-furniture dealer can value the furniture if a personal estimate is felt to be insufficient. Use a garage to value a car, or look up its value in trade publications.

13. Notify the Inland Revenue of death. Is the deceased entitled to a tax refund or does he owe tax?

14. Draw up a list of people who owed money to the deceased.

15. Draw up a list of people who are owed money.

16. Once all this information has been collected, the personal representative will be in a position to complete the forms needed to apply for probate or for letters of administration.

Applying for probate

17. Find out the location of the nearest local probate registry or probate office from the telephone directory. Write for the necessary forms. There are four forms:
    - form 38 (white application form)
    - form 44 (blue form for capital transfer tax calculations)
    - form 37B (yellow form for listing real property such as houses, flats, land)
    - form 40 (yellow form for listing stocks and shares).

    These forms are lengthy but each is straightforward. Do not be frightened by their seeming complexity. Forms 38 and 44 must always be completed; forms 37B and 40 need only be completed if the estate includes real property and shares. Generally, if the estate is not worth more than £40,000, it will not be necessary to fill in any capital transfer tax forms.

18. Send to the Probate Registry (not the probate office):
    - the four forms, duly completed
    - the death certificate
    - the will (keep a copy in case the original is lost in the post)
    - a covering letter. As a personal applicant the personal representative will have to attend for an interview, either at the Probate Registry or the probate office. He should state which he wishes to attend and he should state any dates or times of the day when he cannot attend.
19. The applicant will be given an interview appointment. The object of the interview is to sort out any difficulties or ambiguities and to ensure that the forms have been completed correctly. The applicant will also have to formally swear a Capital Transfer Tax Account Form, and sign a Capital Transfer Tax Warrant. The interview will be informal.
20. Some three or four weeks after the interview the applicant will be sent a set of forms. These forms are the application forms for the Grant of Probate. These should be completed and returned. The full list of items to be returned is:
    - the Capital Transfer Tax Account Form
    - the forms originally filled in (see 17, above)
    - the Capital Transfer Tax Warrant, with a copy of the will annexed to it
    - a cheque for the capital transfer tax in favour of the Inland Revenue. The amount of tax payable is set out on page 12 of the Capital Transfer Tax Account Form. In fact, few people have to fill in CTT forms – let alone pay any tax. The forms need only be filled in if the estate is worth more than £40,000, and tax will only be payable if it is worth over £65,000 (1984 figures). However, it is not necessary at this stage to pay tax arising because of land (i.e. house, flat, etc.) or certain shares in a private company. The personal representative may have to arrange to borrow money from a bank to pay the tax, for even if the amount in the deceased's own account is enough to meet the bill it cannot be touched until after probate is granted. However, if the account was a joint account the survivor can operate it and may be prepared to advance enough money to pay the tax. There is a special scheme to allow National Savings to be used to meet the tax bill; for details, contact the tax office.
    - a cheque for the probate fee. Make the cheque in favour of the District Probate Registrar
    - a covering letter requesting two photocopies of the Grant of Probate.
21. Some three weeks later the executor will be sent the Grant of Probate plus the two photocopies.

Administering the estate

22. Open a bank account in the name of the estate.
23. Collect any debts owed to the deceased, sums payable on insurance policies, sums in banks, building societies, unclaimed pension benefits, premium bonds, etc. Pay the moneys into the estate's bank account, especially if it was overdrawn

to pay out the tax and other sums mentioned in 20 above. A copy of the Grant of Probate will probably have to be produced before the debtor, or institution, will pay out the money due (but see 30, below).

24. Ask the Inland Revenue to pay over any tax refund.

25. Pay the debts owed by the deceased, funeral bills, testamentary expenses and CTT. If there is not sufficient cash available, sell off assets. Unless the will states which assets are to be used, the money should be raised, in order, from:
    - property not dealt with under the will (i.e. property in respect of which the testator died intestate), *next*
    - the residue, *next*
    - property specifically left for the payment of debts (note that this property is *not* the first property used to pay the debts), *next*
    - any fund left to pay pecuniary legacies, *next*
    - property specifically devised or bequeathed (a proportion of the money from each).

26. Advertise for any creditors. Place adverts in the *London Gazette* and, if the deceased held land, in a local paper in the area. Forms can be obtained from Oyez Publishing Limited (see page 894); ask for forms Pro. 36A, 36B and 36C. The estate should not be distributed until two months after the placing of the advertisements, for otherwise the executor may be personally liable to the creditor. Once the two months has expired the executor is not personally liable, although the debt remains legally valid and the creditor can sue the estate and, if necessary, recover the money from the beneficiaries. If the advertisements result in claims these must be investigated before the estate is distributed.

27. Consider whether there is any possibility of a family-provision claim (see page 183), i.e. are there any children, mistresses, ex-wives, or others who might have a claim on the estate? If there is any possibility of there being such a person, do not distribute the estate until six months after obtaining the grant.

28. Sell off assets that are not specifically devised or bequeathed, and which are not wanted by any of the beneficiaries. If they realize more (or less) than their original valuation, additional (or less) CTT may be payable. Apply to the Revenue on form D3.

29. The next step is to distribute the assets. Note:
    - the cost of maintaining any property specifically devised or bequeathed (e.g. insurance, packing, repairs) is borne by the beneficiary; similarly, legal fees on conveying land to a beneficiary are borne by the beneficiary;
    - if property specifically devised or bequeathed produces income (e.g. dividends on shares) the beneficiary is entitled to all the income since the date of death;
    - a pecuniary legacy accrues interest at 6 per cent per annum but generally this only arises as from one year after the death.

Small estates – no need for probate

30. Small amounts of money due to the estate from building societies, the National

Savings Bank, savings certificates, premium savings bonds, government stocks, banks, etc., may be payable without the need to obtain, or produce, a Grant of Probate. If the amount due from each institution is no more than £5,000 that institution may agree to pay out the money without the need for a Grant of Probate. However, the institution can insist on production of a Grant of Probate if it so wishes. Note that there can be up to £5,000 in each institution, so the total amount coming within this 'small estates' exception can be quite large. Also, any cash and personal effects (e.g. jewellery, furniture) can be dealt with without the need for a grant – provided that all the relatives and beneficiaries can agree on how it is to be split up.

Money 'nominated' before death

31. A person with money in a friendly society, trade union, trustee savings bank, or the National Savings Bank can instruct the society or bank to pay the money to a nominee when he dies. The nominee will be entitled to the money on production of the death certificate; he need not wait until a Grant of Probate or Letters of Administration have been obtained. Thus, money 'nominated' in this way can be a useful source of ready cash when someone dies. However, the total amount that can be nominated with each institution is £500. If more than £500 is nominated, probate or administration papers will be required.

   A person who wants to nominate money in this way must write to the bank or society setting out his wishes; some bodies (e.g. NSB, TSB) have a special form for this. The nomination can be cancelled at any time by giving written notice to the institution. It will automatically be cancelled if the nominator marries or if the nominee dies first. It is not cancelled by a will which leaves the money to someone else.

   When the death occurs, the nominee simply writes to the institution setting out the circumstances and enclosing a death certificate. He may be asked to complete a form.

   Premium bonds, giro accounts, building society accounts, and ordinary bank accounts cannot be nominated in this way. Government stocks and National Savings Bank accounts could be nominated until May 1981, but no new nominations have been allowed since then.

Intestacy: when there is no will

If there is no will, the personal representatives will distribute the estate in accordance with the intestacy rules laid down in the Administration of Estates Act 1925 and the Intestates' Estates Act 1952. The order of entitlement laid down in these Acts was drawn up after a detailed examination of the way people tended to leave their property in wills, and so these Acts can be said to give effect to the 'presumed intentions' of the deceased – i.e. what he would have done had he left a will.

The rules are complicated and are best understood by considering, in turn, the position of the spouse, then the issue, and finally, the other relatives.

The surviving spouse

The spouse will always inherit the deceased's 'personal chattels', which include things such as household goods, car, clothes, but exclude any items from a business. In addition, the spouse receives £40,000 net (with interest at 6 per cent from the date of death), assuming that the estate is worth that much. If there are any assets remaining, the spouse's additional share depends on:

● *if there are any children* one half of the remaining assets will be put on trust for the rest of her/his life, giving a right to the interest but not the capital sum, *or*

● *if there are no children, but there are parents, brothers or sisters (or their children)*, the spouse will receive an extra £45,000 with interest (i.e. a total of £85,000) plus one half of any excess remaining, *or*

● *if there are no children, parents, brothers or sisters* the spouse takes everything.

The issue (i.e. children, grandchildren, etc.)

What the issue receive will depend upon whether the deceased parent left a surviving spouse:

● *if there is a surviving spouse* the issue take one half of the residue (i.e. the amount left after the spouse has deducted the chattels and £40,000). The other half of the residue will go to the surviving spouse for life and will then pass to the issue on his/her death.

● *if there is no surviving spouse* the issue inherit the whole estate. The estate is held for them so that they all have equal shares when they reach eighteen or when they marry (if earlier).

The other relatives (i.e. parents, brothers, sisters, or their children)

Entitlement here will depend upon whether there is a surviving spouse and/or any issue (children, grandchildren, etc.):

● *if there are any issue* the other relatives will not receive anything.

● *if there is a surviving spouse, but no issue* the other relatives receive one half of the residue left after the surviving spouse has deducted the chattels and £85,000. The half will go to the parents of the deceased in equal shares, but if there are no parents living, it will go to the deceased's brothers and sisters (or their children) in equal shares.

● *if there is no surviving spouse and no issue* the other relatives inherit all the estate. The order of entitlement is:

● to the parents, but if none
● to brothers and sisters, but if none
● to half-brothers and half-sisters, but if none

- to grandparents, but if none
- to uncles and aunts of the whole blood (i.e. brothers and sisters of one of the deceased's parents), but if none
- to uncles and aunts of the half-blood (i.e. half-brothers and half-sisters of one of the deceased's parents) but if none
- the estate passes to the Crown. In practice, the Crown will often pay all or part to someone who seems morally entitled to a share.

Note: if, under the intestacy rules, a share passes to a child, brother, sister, uncle or aunt, who died before the deceased, then the share passes to that person's descendants (usually their children).

Illustration. *Fred Jones died intestate leaving an estate of £130,000. He was survived by his wife Mabel, but they had no children. Other relatives include two nephews – the sons of Fred's brother Michael, and a niece – the daughter of his brother Frank. The estate will be divided as follows:*
- his wife Mabel *will take the personal chattels plus £85,000, plus one half of the remaining £45,000 (i.e. £22,500). A total of £107,500 plus chattels.*
- the nephews and the niece *will take the share their parents would have taken. As brothers of Fred, each would have been entitled to an equal share of the £22,500 left after Mabel had taken her share. Thus, the niece inherits £11,250 and the two nephews inherit £5,625 each.*

Mistresses, common-law spouses

The intestacy rules only recognize the claims of relatives. Mistresses, lovers, close friends, and others do not have any claim under the intestacy rules. However, they may be able to qualify as 'dependants' and so bring a claim under the family-provision legislation for a share of the estate (see below).

Partial intestacy

If a person dies leaving a will, but the will does not dispose of all his estate, he is said to have died partially intestate. For instance, if the residue is left equally between two people, but one dies before the testator, then his share will pass as on an intestacy. Note that if the gift was to the two people jointly, then the survivor would take the whole gift.

The usual rules on intestacy apply to that part of his estate but the spouse and issue must take their benefits under the will into account when working out their shares under the intestacy rules. For instance, a widow who received £10,000 under the will would not take the first £40,000 of the undisposed-of estate, but only the first £30,000.

12 The Family-Provision Legislation: Fair Shares for Family and Dependants

Only in 1938 did Parliament decide that a testator's moral duty to provide for his family should become a legal obligation.

It had long been a principle of English law that a man could dispose of his property as he wished. Thus, a man was free to leave his family and dependants destitute – a principle that was alien to most Continental legal systems and to the laws of Scotland too. The only relaxation of this strict rule was by virtue of several old common-law doctrines (such as dower, escheat and curtesy) that sometimes allowed the spouse and children to claim part of the estate, but these laws were repealed by a series of statutes from 1833 onwards. The law of the nineteenth century was a *laissez-faire* law, in which the right to dispose freely of one's property was inviolable. The family-provision legislation of 1938 scotched this notion, and it provides yet another example of the free-enterprise spirit of Victorian law being overturned by a twentieth-century Parliament which is more concerned with social justice than jurisprudential consistencies.

The 1938 Inheritance (Family Provision) Act was replaced in 1975 by the Inheritance (Provision for Family and Dependants) Act. This statute extended the protection to dependants such as mistresses, and did away with some of the more restrictive rules affecting the entitlement to provision and the form the provision was to take.

The 1975 Act (usually called the 'family-provision legislation' – despite the fact that it includes dependants who are not members of the family) envisages three categories of claimants – the surviving spouse, the children, and, finally, other dependants whether members of the family or not. The Act is strengthened by provisions which make it difficult for the testator to concoct schemes that may get around the legislation. Application under the Act is made by way of an originating summons to the High Court, unless the estate is worth less than £30,000, in which case the county court can hear the claim.

The application must be made within six months of the grant being issued by the Probate Registry, although the court does have power to allow late applications in exceptional circumstances (for instance, on the late discovery of a will). This six-month time-limit poses a problem to many claimants, such as spouses who have been deserted by the deceased and who may not have heard of his/her death. To prevent the estate being distributed without his/her knowledge, the potential claimant can register a 'caveat' in the Probate Registry, which prevents a grant being made for the following six months without his/her knowledge and approval. An alternative and simpler safeguard is for the potential claimant to make a 'standing search' at the Probate Registry (fee £1) which entitles him/her to a copy of any grant during the next six months, and also to any grant taken out in the last twelve months. The search can, of course, be renewed every six months.

The surviving spouse

The court will act as though it was considering the financial arrangements to be made on a divorce; thus, the factors and principles considered by the divorce court (see page 54) will be applied to the family-provision claim. Most important, the issue before the court is not whether the deceased made reasonable provision for the *maintenance* of the spouse, but whether the deceased left his spouse (whether by will or under the intestacy rules) a 'fair share of the family assets' – which may, of course, be considerably more than is needed for maintenance alone. This test is more generous than that applied to the children and other dependants who are only entitled to reasonable provision for their maintenance.

If the surviving spouse was divorced or judicially separated from the deceased, it is probable that there will have been an earlier court hearing when the family assets were divided between them. In such a case, although the surviving spouse can apply under the family-provision legislation, the earlier division may well reduce the chances of a successful claim. If the former spouse remarries, he or she automatically loses all rights to maintenance or a share of the assets under the family-provision legislation, and any order (e.g. for maintenance) is cancelled.

When deciding the sort of order to be made, the court has similar powers to those of the divorce court in matrimonial cases. For instance, the order can be for periodic payments, a lump sum (or a lump sum payable by instalments), or the transfer and purchase of property. A 'fair share' of the assets is determined on an objective basis, depending on the commitments and wealth of the deceased at the time of his death.

The children

The children do not fare as well as the surviving spouse. The test is whether the deceased parent made 'reasonable provision' for their maintenance. This is all they are entitled to – maintenance only, not a share of the family assets. 'Children' in this context includes any child of the family who was maintained by the deceased prior to his death; the child's age, marital status, or illegitimacy is irrelevant.

Other dependants

The final category of claimants under the 1975 Act is that of other dependants who were partly or wholly maintained by the deceased at the time of his death. This includes common-law wives and mistresses. Many cases of hardship arose from the exclusion of such people from the 1938 Act, for when the deceased died intestate the estate would pass to relatives (e.g. an undivorced, but separated, wife) and not to the common-law spouse. Although the common-law spouse is now included in the legislation, s/he is still discriminated against, for the Act only permits a claim for 'reasonable provision for maintenance', and not for a share of the family assets. In addition, of course, the common-law spouse is wholly excluded from the intestacy rules (above), does not have full protection under the Rent Acts (see page 269), and is not eligible for such DHSS benefits as the widow's pension (see page 753).

Family-provision legislation in practice

In 1971, the testator made a will leaving all his property to his only son. In 1972, he started living with his mistress, who became his common-law wife, and the mistress's daughter was adopted by him on his own insistence. In 1974 the couple had a son. In 1976, the testator died not having revoked his 1971 will, which left his estate to the older son. The common-law wife applied to the court for a share of the estate. Held: She would be awarded £5,000, and the remainder of the estate (valued at between £25,000 and £35,000) would be split between the two boys. The daughter would receive nothing. CA (1978)

On the other hand:

A stepdaughter was awarded £19,000 out of a £45,000 intestate estate. This was despite the fact that she was now aged fifty-five, having made her own way in life since aged twenty-one. Leach (1984)

Husband and wife had been separated for forty-three years – although before their separation, they had been married for nineteen years. He died, leaving £100,000. She applied for a share of the estate – but was only awarded £3,000. Rolands (1984)

A mistress can use the legislation to claim a share of the estate. For instance:

Mr Harrison was separated from his wife in 1939. From 1958 until his death in 1977 he cohabited with and supported a mistress and her son. From 1965 he had maintained another mistress for whom he had bought a flat in Malta. He also paid her an allowance of some £60 per month. When Harrison died he made provision for the mistress with whom he had been living and for her son. No provision was made for the other mistress, who then applied to the court for a share of the estate. Held: She was entitled to financial provision since Harrison had made himself responsible for her maintenance; apart from her share in the flat she should receive £30,000 which represented her maintenance for the years to come. Malone (1979)

Since the cost of taking a disputed case to court can often be a substantial part of the value of the estate, the courts discourage claims over relatively small estates.

PART TWO

HOUSING

13 Home Ownership

This chapter looks at the law for the home-owner. The law on renting a home is dealt with in Chapters 16 to 18.

The purchase of a house or flat is quite unlike the buying of a car, fridge, caravan, or other physical commodity. This is partly because the land on which a house or flat stands is indestructible and will never wear out; in addition, land can be subject to a whole host of rights and liabilities that cannot apply to other things: rights of way, rights of light, restrictive covenants, and so on. Thus, the ownership of land (and the houses and flats on the land) can only be transferred by following a set procedure involving inspection and transfer of formal documents of title, a process that usually takes three months from start to finish. In comparison, the purchase of, say, a fridge or a car is comparatively straightforward, for then it is largely a question of seeing the item, satisfying oneself that it belongs to the seller, paying the purchase price, and then taking possession of the item.

This is why conveyancing has traditionally been such a long-winded and complicated process. The pressure for change is now immense and it is hoped that conveyancing procedures will be streamlined and simplified in the next few years. The first step has been the abolition of the solicitor's monopoly, which effectively meant that only solicitors could act on the sale and purchase of properties. That monopoly has now gone, but without leaving a free-for-all. Licensed conveyancers are now to be allowed to do conveyancing but there are still strict qualifying rules which mean that the numbers of non-solicitor conveyancers will still be relatively few (see page 223). Until more fundamental reforms come about (e.g. more computerization at the Land Registry; the widespread use of electronic mail) conveyancers will continue to have to operate the present inefficient and time-wasting system. The real power to introduce change lies with the finance houses – the banks and the building societies.

The ownership of land, houses, and flats

Traditionally, the law has always been concerned with 'land' rather than the houses, flats, garages, and other buildings on the land. Even today, the law technically still looks at the transfer and ownership of the land, not the flat, semi-detached house, or other building on the land. The building is seen as a mere incidental to the purchase of the land. For instance, the standard legal phrase for describing a house is 'all that land situate and known as (*address*) together with the dwelling house

189

situate thereon' (see the contract on page 210), as though the land was the important thing to the purchaser, not the house.

So the first step towards understanding conveyancing is to appreciate that when a lawyer talks of 'land', he is also referring to the house or flat, or whatever stands on the land; 'land' does not just mean allotments, gardens, and country estates.

Freehold or leasehold?

Householders can have either a freehold or a leasehold interest in their property.

The freeholder owns the land for ever and he has fairly wide powers to do with the land as he wishes. The leaseholder owns the land for a fixed period only, and at the end of that period the land will go back to the freeholder (but see the Leasehold Reform Act, page 231). In the meantime the leaseholder will have to pay ground rent to the freeholder and observe the terms of the lease granted by the freeholder.

Clearly, then, a freehold interest is more desirable than a leasehold interest and it may seem surprising that anyone would accept a leasehold and not insist on having the freehold. The answer lies in the enforcing of obligations and restrictions between neighbouring home-owners. It is very difficult to give one freeholder the power legally to restrict another freeholder's use of his land (see 'Restrictive covenants', page 335). But with leaseholds the position is different; the leases can be worded so as to allow one leaseholder to enforce covenants against another leaseholder. This is absolutely essential with flats because, for instance, the owner of a first-floor flat must be able to make the owner of the ground-floor flat maintain his flat so that the first-floor flat does not lose its structural support. Conversely, the owner of the ground-floor flat will want to be sure that he can force the owner of the top-floor flat to maintain the roof. Mutual repairing obligations are needed between flat-owners and this is something that the law allows only between leaseholders, not freeholders. Thus, flat-owners nearly always have leases. On the other hand, the need to enforce mutual covenants is not generally needed for houses and so most house-owners have freehold, and not leasehold, interests. Generally, it is only if mutual covenants are needed (e.g. in some new town-house developments) that the householder will have a lease, and not the freehold.

It is usually possible to buy the freehold of *houses* (but not flats) held on a long lease (see Chapter 15).

The main differences in the positions of freeholders and leaseholders are set out in the table on pages 192–3.

Shared ownership. This is a hybrid form of home ownership – in effect it is a half-way house between owning the house (whether by having a leasehold or freehold) and renting it. It is only available to secure tenants (i.e. council tenants, housing-association tenants, etc. – but not tenants of private landlords). See page 299.

Time-shares. How does a time-sharing agreement fit into these legal structures? The answer is that it doesn't: lawyers have had great difficulty in finding a satisfactory legal framework for time-shares. A time-sharer will have a limited interest in the land (e.g. for one week a year, for a period of ninety-nine years). Various legal devices have been used but few of them stand up to close examination. In practice, the best schemes will involve the participation of one of the major banks (or some other reputable institution), which will hold the land and property and then act as trustee; each time-sharer will have a contract with the trustee, and the chances are that there will not be any problems. The difficulties, in practice, arise when the property is held by a management company that is in financial difficulties, or which starts over-charging the time-sharers through excessive service charges. This is especially so with speculative developments abroad. The unfortunate reality is that our old-fashioned system of land law has not been able to adapt sufficiently to meet the new problems of time-share agreements.

'Ownership' of land

Beyond distinguishing between freehold and leasehold interests, it is difficult to define the word 'ownership' when it is applied to land. The layman may be satisfied with the short dictionary definition of its meaning 'to hold', but the lawyer requires more precision. If his client is spending thousands of pounds on purchas-ing the 'ownership' of a plot of land, he must know exactly what 'ownership' means.

Clearly, there can be no such thing as the *absolute* ownership' of land today, for the Planning Acts, police rights of entry, public footpaths, etc., have all made a nonsense of the adage that 'an Englishman's home is his castle'.

The concept of ownership is also weakened in less obvious ways. For instance, suppose someone buys a flat on a ninety-nine-year lease, with the help of a building society mortgage, and then lets out part of the flat. Who 'owns' that flat? To the layman the answer is simple enough: the owner is the leaseholder. That is true enough, but consider the position in more detail. The building society has a mortgage deed which entitles it to be repaid in full, and which allows it to enter and sell the property if the instalments are not paid or if the borrower breaks any of the other clauses in the mortgage deed. Further, the property is on a lease, so there is a freeholder who may be able to reclaim the flat at the end of the ninety-nine years. In addition, there may be a Rent Act tenant who has possession and who cannot be evicted without a court order. Thus, although we say that the leaseholder 'owns' the flat, the reality is that the building society, the freeholder, and the Rent Act tenant all have rights over the flat which significantly erode the extent of the leaseholder's 'ownership' of it.

Accordingly, to speak in simple terms of 'owning' a home can be misleading, for 'ownership' is a meaningless description until one knows what rights other people have over that property. Thus, 'ownership' is a relative concept; it can mean one thing to one home-owner and a completely different thing to another home-owner. This is another illustration of the inadequacy of words as a means of accurately describing legal concepts; as Humpty Dumpty said to Alice, 'When *I* use a word it means just what I choose it to mean' (see page 829).

Freehold and Leasehold: the Main Differences

	Freehold	*Leasehold*
Mortgage availability	Mortgages on houses should be easy to obtain (subject to satisfactory survey, etc.). Mortgages on freehold flats are very difficult to obtain since maintenance and repair of common parts, stairs, structure, etc., cannot easily be enforced.	Building societies like there to be at least thirty to forty years of the lease left *after* the date of paying off the mortgage. They will inspect the maintenance and repair provisions of a flat lease to ensure that they can be properly enforced.
Rent	No rent payable, unless property is subject to a rent charge (unlikely outside Manchester and Bristol).	Annual ground rent payable according to terms of lease; usually increases as the lease expires, generally between £50 and £150 p.a. Will rarely be such that it could be two thirds of the property's rateable value, since Rent Act protection might then come into effect. In addition, leaseholder may have to pay a maintenance charge.
Security	The owner cannot be dispossessed (i.e. evicted) except by: (i) compulsory purchase (ii) foreclosure by building society if he fails to pay the instalments or breaks the terms of the mortgage deed (e.g. by letting the property).	The owner cannot be dispossessed except by: (i) compulsory purchase (ii) foreclosure by building society if he fails to pay the instalments or otherwise breaks the terms of the mortgage deed (iii) eviction by freeholder if he fails to observe the terms of the lease (e.g. does not pay the ground rent) (iv) eviction by freeholder on expiry of the lease (unless Leasehold Reform Act 1967 applies; see Chapter 15).
Obligation to repair	None, unless: (i) insisted on by the building society. (The mortgage deed will impose repairing and maintenance obligations on the borrower.)	The lease will probably require the tenant to keep the property in a good state of repair and to maintain it properly (e.g. repaint the interior every three years). There may also be an obligation to

	Freehold	*Leasehold*
	(ii) if the building is of special architectural or historic note, the local authority can make an order requiring repairs or maintenance to be carried out.	pay a proportionate part of the cost of maintaining/repairing common parts of a block of flats. In addition: (i) Building societies may insist on repairs and maintenance as a condition of their mortgage loan (ii) if building is of special architectural or historic note, the local authority can make an order requiring repair or maintenance to be carried out.
Alterations, extensions, change of use	Owner can do as he wishes, subject to: (i) obtaining any necessary planning permission (ii) satisfying any building regulations (iii) observing any restrictive covenants, rights of light and support, etc. affecting the property (iv) the mortgage deed, which will probably require him to obtain the building society's consent.	Position is similar to that of freeholder, but in addition restrictions will probably be set out in the lease (e.g. that property be only used for residential purposes and that freeholder's consent be obtained for any alterations and extensions).

'Rights' over land

The rights that a freeholder or leaseholder has over his land (to live there, to chop down trees, etc.) are limited by:

● *rights vested in the community and its representatives* (e.g. to use the planning laws to control development on the land, to allow the police to enter with a search warrant, to dig trenches for public sewers), *and*

● *rights of other people* (e.g. the Rent Act tenant who lives there, or the next-door neighbour, who can prevent the erection of buildings that obstruct the light to the next-door property).

All any home-owner has is a 'bundle of rights' over the land, house, or flat. The extent of his bundle of rights will depend on the rights enjoyed over the land by other people and by the community. If 'ownership' can be understood in this way, one can soon appreciate what a conveyancer does when he acts for the buyer of a house or flat; he is looking to see what 'rights' the seller has over the land, how many of those 'rights' will be transferred to the buyer, and what 'rights' other people and the

The Householder Owns a 'Bundle of Rights' Affecting his Land

The owner's 'rights'

- to live in the property
- to let the property
- to keep, sell, or destroy, anything on the property
- to build on the land
- to sell the land to whom-ever he likes, when he likes
- to give the land (or part of it) away; to bequeath it in his will
- to fish in any river that flows through the land
- to do what he likes on the property, whenever he likes
- to sue for trespass by other people, or their possessions (including tree roots and branches)
- to sue for nuisance, if his 'quiet enjoyment' is disturbed (for example, by noise and vibration), etc.

The 'rights' that other individuals may have over the property

- as tenant under a lease for more than twenty-one years (the 'rights' will be set out in the lease and in the Leasehold Reform Act 1967)
- as tenant under a lease (the 'rights' will be set out in the Rent Acts, and in the lease, if any)
- as building society that lent money on a mortgage (the 'rights' of possession and sale will be set out in the mortgage deed)
- my neighbour's 'right' to prevent me from obstructing the light that enters his adjoining buildings
- my neighbour's 'right' to prevent me from removing soil that would affect the support and structure of his soil (and, maybe, his buildings)
- a 'right of way' to pass over the land
- a 'right' of possession gained by twelve years squatting on the land
- 'rights' under restrictive covenants to control and prevent development on the land or a change in its use
- 'rights' granted by custom, to graze cattle on my land, dig turf for fuel, etc.

'Rights' vested in the community

- to enforce standards of hygiene and cleanliness
- to control development, erection of buildings, signs, conversions, etc.
- to control a change of use of the property
- to control the quality and nature of building works
- to restrict the type of fuel burnt on the property
- to allow planes to trespass over the land and through its airspace
- to claim gold, silver and oil found on the land
- to claim any treasure trove found on the land, on behalf of the Crown
- to regulate the number of persons living there
- to restrict the amount of water that can be abstracted from any rivers that flow across the land
- to prevent the property being used for certain dangerous purposes (e.g. involving radioactive fuels)
- to sue for nuisance if the landowner disturbs others, or allows dangerous commodities to escape from the land
- powers of entry given to police, gas board officials, etc.
- the right to compulsory purchase of the land
- the right for certain works to be carried out on the land (e.g. digging of pipes and laying of cables), etc.

community have over the land which may adversely affect the buyer's use and enjoyment of it. The table on page 194 gives an idea of the sort of 'rights' that can affect land, and how some of these 'rights' are vested in the owner, some in other individuals, and others in the community at large.

The community's rights over private land

Acts of Parliament lay down various rights that apply over all land, such as the law that all houses are subject to the planning controls laid down by Parliament, or that aircraft are free to fly over private land and through the air space that technically belongs to the owner of the land. These rights are of general application, as are the other examples listed in the table, and they are all illustrations of how the traditional sanctity of private property has been eroded.

Other people's rights over private land

Of more immediate concern to the conveyancer are those rights that other private individuals have over the land. The problem is to find out what rights exist, and whether those rights can be enforced against a purchaser of the land. Clearly, not all these rights will survive against the purchaser; for example, the seller's building society will have powerful rights of entry and sale by virtue of the mortgage deed, but the purchaser's solicitor will insist that the mortgage be repaid (and so the building society's rights destroyed) before the purchase is completed. However, some of the other rights might bind the purchaser (e.g. a right of way over the land). The list in the table opposite gives some of the more important rights that outsiders may have over private land.

How other people acquire rights over private land

Apart from statute, the main ways in which outsiders can acquire rights over private land are either by deed (as with the building society and its mortgage deed) or by continued assertion and use of the right over a period of years.

When the right is created by statute or deed the position is clear enough, since the purchaser simply has to refer to the lease, title document, will, Rent Act, or whatever to see the extent of those rights. The problems arise when there is no written statement of the rights, as happens when they are acquired by long usage – by what is called *prescription*.

Prescription assumes that someone has a legal right to do something when they have been doing it continuously over a period of years in such a way as to indicate that they have a legal right to do it. For example, if a person parks his car on his neighbour's plot of land for year after year, he may acquire the legal right to keep on parking his car there and that right may be taken over by whoever owns his house in later years. But if he had first asked for permission to park the car or if he had occasionally bought his neighbour a small gift as a 'thank you', then he would – by implication – have admitted that he did not have the legal right to park there and so he could not acquire the right to park there by prescription. Similarly, if the neighbour had told him not to park there, his claim would be defeated.

The right must be exercised without permission, force, or secrecy, before it can become a legal right by way of prescription. In addition, the right must have been exercised fairly continuously over the years; if the householder only parks on his neighbour's land once every few years then he cannot claim the right to do so by prescription. The real problem is in deciding how long the right has to be exercised before prescription can apply. At common law, the rule was that the right must have existed since 'time immemorial' which – for sake of convenience – was arbitrarily fixed at the start of Richard I's reign, 1189. This was a hopelessly strict test, and so the courts decided that the right might be assumed to exist if it could be shown to have been in use for as long as could be remembered by those in the area. But these tests were not applied with any uniformity and so Parliament has now passed several statutes laying down various periods of time for the acquisition of rights by prescription. Generally, twenty years' regular use will be enough, assuming that it was without permission, force, or secrecy in the first place.

The rights that outsiders can acquire

The rights that outsiders can have over other people's land are numerous. Those listed in the table are merely illustrations of the more common rights.

Many of these rights date back to feudal days when, for example, the rights to cut turf or to cut wood for making agricultural implements were of some importance. Nowadays, such rights of 'turbary' and 'ploughbote' are few and far between, and the conveyancer will be more concerned with rights of way, rights of light, etc., over the land. Even if the right is unlikely to be used by the outsider, the conveyancer will still want to know the full extent of it. The fact that it would be unfair for the outsider to be allowed to exercise his right is not relevant, for a court would not consider the merits of the case – only whether the right is valid and enforceable. Thus, for example, it might be unfair for the neighbour of a cricket club to exercise his ancient right of cutting turf for his hearth, but the court would still enforce the right even if it meant destroying the cricket pitch; this can be compared with the French and German legal systems, where rights cannot be exercised if they can have no other purpose than to harm someone else.

See Chapter 20 for when these rights can apply.

Tax relief and the owner-occupier

Owner-occupiers receive relief on both income tax and capital gains tax liabilities.

Income tax relief

Tax relief is allowed on interest paid to buy or improve the taxpayer's only or main residence. Typically, this will be interest on mortgage repayments.

Detailed points to note include:
- the property must be in the UK or Eire. It need not be a house or a flat but could, for instance, be a houseboat or caravan.
- only interest on the first £30,000 (1985) of the loan is deductible. Married couples are allowed only £30,000 between them, unless they are separated. Unmarried joint purchasers split the tax relief on the basis of their respective shares in the property.
- the relief does not only apply to loans to buy the property. A loan to improve or develop a property will also be allowed. For instance, installing central heating or double glazing; building a garage, garden shed, extension, swimming pool or patio; converting the house into flats. If the loan is used to carry out repairs it will not generally qualify unless it covers the repair of dilapidations arising before the purchase of the property.
- the property must be the taxpayer's only or main residence. If he has more than one residence it is a question of fact which is the main residence; he cannot arbitrarily choose for himself (cf. capital gains tax).
- it does not matter to whom the interest is paid. Typically, it will be a building society or bank, but loans from other sources (e.g. private loans) are also eligible. But tax relief on interest on bank overdrafts and on credit cards is not allowed, so improvements should be financed by a bank loan, not by overdraft or Access/Barclaycard.
- generally, in order to qualify for relief the taxpayer has up to twelve months to move into the property after buying it, although the Revenue will often agree a longer period. Generally, up to four years' absence will be allowed if the taxpayer's job requires him to move for a period not exceeding four years, and if he is likely to return to the property at the end of that time. Similarly, if the taxpayer moves into his new home before selling the old home, tax relief will be allowed on both the old and the new loan (usually a bridging loan) for at least twelve months. The old loan will also be ignored for the purpose of the £30,000 limit. The Revenue will usually extend the twelve months' period if there is a genuine difficulty (for instance, if a property slump makes it difficult to sell the old house).

Capital gains tax relief

The general rule is that the profit arising on the sale of any capital item (such as a house) is subject to capital gains tax at 30 per cent. However, if the property was the taxpayer's only or main residence during the period of ownership, the whole of the profit will be exempt from tax.

Detailed points to note include:
- if a tax-payer has more than one residence he can choose which is to qualify for the CGT relief. But he must serve a formal notice on the Revenue within two years of the start of the date when he claims it became his main residence.
- if the property was not the only or main residence for the whole period of ownership, then tax will have to be paid proportionately on the profit. But temporary periods of absence are ignored. This covers:

– periods (together not exceeding three years) when the taxpayer was employed outside the UK, *and/or*
– periods (together not exceeding four years) when the taxpayer (or spouse) could not live in the property because of the location of his job or because of a condition imposed by his employer, *and*
– the last two years of ownership is always ignored.
If applicable, all of these periods can be added together and claimed cumulatively.
● an apportionment will also be needed if part of the property is used for business purposes (e.g. offices; or let as a flat) since it will not have been used solely as a main residence. Lettings by resident landlords get the benefit of a special relief: the capital gain attributable to the rented property is taxed only if it exceeds £20,000 (1985), or if it exceeds the capital gain attributable to that part of the property used as the main residence (whichever is the lower). Only the excess is taxable. For instance:

A house was owned for fifteen years; one third of it was let for ten years. The capital gain on its sale is £180,000; the taxable portion of this is 10/45 of £180,000, that is £40,000. So tax is charged on £20,000 (the excess over £20,000), at 30 per cent.

● land belonging to the residence may not be exempt from tax. Generally, only one acre of land can get the benefit of being part of the residence. However, this is not a hard and fast rule. Similar problems can arise when selling off part of a garden. Usually, one can sell off part of a garden before selling the house, but not sell the house and then sell the garden. Professional advice is needed in such cases.
● husband and wife can only have one main residence between them, unless separated. Complications can arise on divorce when the ex-wife is given the right to live in a property partly owned by her ex-husband, with his being entitled to a share in the proceeds when it is eventually sold. Professional advice is needed in such a case.

Mortgages

The costs of mortgages vary from time to time, as interest rates and tax rates change. The figures in the tables below give a rough comparison of the various types of mortgages available. For most young people starting out on the property-buying business, the best advice is to go for the cheapest possible monthly repayment – do not worry

Loan of £10,000 repayable over twenty-five years, monthly payments

	Annuity (repayment) mortgage (10·25%)	With-profits endowment mortgage (10·50%)	Low-cost endowment mortgage (10·50%)
Actual monthly repayment to building society net of tax relief	£72.90	£61.25	£61.25
Insurance premium	—	£37.65	£17.65
Total cost	£72.90	£98.90	£78.90
Possible bonus	—	£20,000.00	£2,500.00

about long-term bonus payments, etc. A pound or two saved now (when you are hard up!) is probably more valuable than a lump sum in twenty-five years' time.

The table on page 198 shows that the average monthly cost of a low-cost endowment mortgage is marginally higher than that for an annuity mortgage.

Monthly repayments on a £10,000 loan with mortgage interest relief

Interest rate (%)		Twenty-year term	Twenty-five year term	Thirty-year term
8.00	(5.60 net)	£70.40	£62.80	£58.00
8.50	(5.95 net)	72.40	64.90	60.30
9.00	(6.30 net)	74.50	67.10	62.50
9.50	(6.65 net)	76.60	69.30	64.90
10.00	(7.00 net)	78.70	71.60	67.20
10.50	(7.35 net)	80.90	73.80	69.60
11.00	(7.70 net)	83.00	76.00	72.00
11.50	(8.05 net)	85.20	78.40	74.40
12.00	(8.40 net)	87.50	80.80	76.90
12.50	(8.75 net)	89.70	83.20	79.40
13.00	(9.10 net)	92.00	85.60	81.90
13.50	(9.45 net)	94.30	88.00	84.40
14.00	(9.80 net)	96.60	90.40	87.00
14.50	(10.15 net)	98.90	92.90	89.60
15.00	(10.50 net)	100.30	95.40	92.20

The Homeloan scheme. First-time buyers often overlook the existence of this scheme. It gives a loan of £600 (interest-free for five years), plus a cash sum of up to £110. The catch is that you must have been saving with a building society, national savings, or girobank, for at least a year. A first-time buyer who thinks he or she comes within those rules should ask the building society, etc. for details of the Homeloan scheme.

Mortgages: getting into arrears

The general rule for the borrower is to warn the lender if he is in financial difficulties. It is important not to allow arrears to build up without having first told the lender. If all else fails, and the arrears become sizeable, the lender will take steps to obtain a possession order from the court. This gives him the power to evict the borrower and sell the house to repay the loan; any money left after paying off the mortgage will go to the borrower.

The usual sequence of events is:

1. Borrower falls into arrears.
2. Lender asks that arrears be paid off.
3. Lender threatens legal proceedings.
4. Lender instructs solicitors. They start court proceedings and a possession summons is served on the borrower. This states the date for the court hearing.

5. At the court hearing the borrower explains his problems to the court. It is advisable to make an offer to pay off the arrears, if only by regular instalments. The court is likely to:

    • dismiss the lender's application if the borrower can immediately pay off the arrears and show he is unlikely to fall into arrears again, *or*

    • grant a suspended possession order if a sensible and realistic offer of instalment payments is made; if the borrower pays the instalments no further action can be taken; if he falls into arrears the lender can ask the bailiff to evict without having to reapply to the court, *or*

    • grant a possession order if there are no prospects of paying off the arrears.

6. The ultimate step is for the bailiff to evict the borrower. The property is then sold, sometimes by auction, which tends to realize a lower price than in a private market sale. All the mortgages are then paid off, legal costs are deducted, and the balance (if any) is paid to the borrower.

Mortgages and supplementary benefit

A person in receipt of supplementary benefit (see page 744) should receive an allowance sufficient to cover the full interest (not capital payments) due under the mortgage. Note that most building societies will agree to forgo capital repayments if the borrower is on supplementary benefit.

14 Conveyancing

The conveyancing transaction

What follows is not a comprehensive guide to the buying and selling of houses; several excellent books have been written on the subject, and the limited aim of this description is to reveal some of the mysteries of the conveyancing machinery, which are so often shrouded in obscure legal phraseology. The following description is intended to strike a balance between the detailed knowledge needed by a DIY conveyancer and the over-simplified impression given by the many newspaper articles on the subject, such as the one which started 'a purchaser's solicitor sends a form to the local council and another form to the vendor's solicitor; then he exchanges contracts'. Regrettably, there is more to it than that!

The step-by-step guide illustrates the sequence of events in the purchase of a freehold house. The procedure when buying a leasehold flat (or even a leasehold house) is the same, except that it will be necessary to examine the lease to see how long it has to run, whether there have been breaches of its terms, how much the rent is, and how the repairing covenants are to be enforced, etc.

But first, there are certain points to be borne in mind:

1. A *conveyance* is simply a written deed. It can also be called a *transfer*.
2. For historical reasons, lawyers describe the seller as the *vendor*.
3. There are two systems of conveyancing in England and Wales, depending on whether the land (i.e. house, flat, etc.) is registered or unregistered.

Registration of land was first introduced in the 1860s and, in time, all land will eventually be registered; at the moment about 85 per cent of homes are registered. It tends to be the rural areas that are still unregistered.

It is easy to find out whether land is registered or not; telephone the nearest District Land Registry and ask whether the land is in an area of 'compulsory registration', and if so, when it became a registered area. If the property has been sold or mortgaged since then, it will be registered.

If land is registered, the purchaser knows that the seller's title has been checked and that it is virtually guaranteed by the government; all he has to do is to inspect the Land Registry certificate for the property and check the entries. If the land is not registered, the checking of title is more laborious for it involves inspecting the 'chain of conveyances' to the present seller, although it is only necessary to go back to the first conveyance that is over fifteen years old. For example, if the land was sold as follows:

1950 Henry to Harry
1952 Harry to Freddy
1975 Freddy to Bertie
1977 Bertie to Basil

then a purchaser from Basil would want to see the conveyances of 1977, 1975 and of 1952 (since that would be the first conveyance outside the fifteen-year period). Title would be checked by examining these three documents and seeing that the property was properly described in each, that stamp duty was paid on each transaction, and so on. This is called 'deducing title' and it obviously involves much more work (and legal knowledge) than the purchase of a registered property. So, the step-by-step guide (below) deals only with registered properties.

The conveyancing transaction is in two halves:

– The first half is the stage between the seller's acceptance of the purchaser's offer and the time when the parties sign binding contracts (called 'exchange of contracts'). During this period the purchaser will be arranging his mortgage and perhaps obtaining a surveyor's report, whilst his conveyancer will be checking that there are no planning restrictions, road proposals, etc., that could affect the property. In short, during this stage, the nature and character of the property is being examined, and either buyer or seller can back out without giving any reason.

– After exchange of contracts, there is the second half of the transaction when the buyer's conveyancer checks the seller's right to sell the property (i.e. he looks at the Land Registry certificate or the chain of conveyances) and prepares the transfer (sale) document. Once these inquiries have been completed the transaction can be completed by the purchaser paying the balance of the price and the seller signing the transfer deed. During this second stage neither side can back out and they are bound to proceed with the purchase and sale.

Buying a house: a step-by-step guide to the conveyancing process

The chart on pages 218–9 shows the sequence of events from the buyer's point of view; the seller's steps follow on from what the buyer does. Refer to the chart when reading this step-by-step summary of the conveyancing procedures:

Step-by-step conveyancing: 1

Buyer chooses property, makes offer 'subject to contract', which is accepted by the seller, and pays a small deposit to the estate agent

'Subject to contract'

Any offer to buy or sell a house should specifically state that it is 'subject to contract';

this is a golden rule that must always be followed, for otherwise a binding contract may be made unintentionally before a party has made all his arrangements (e.g. obtained a mortgage).

A contract to buy or sell land (and thus houses, flats, garages, etc.) is unlike a contract to buy or sell any other commodity in that generally it must be in writing. By section 40, Law of Property Act 1925, a contract to sell or buy land must be in writing, and it must name the property, the price, and the names of the parties, and it must be signed by the party to be bound by it. The contract need not be in any set form, so any letter (e.g. confirming the offer) could form a valid and binding contract. Thus, for instance, the buyer could find himself in the position where he was bound to buy, but the seller – who had not signed such a letter – could not be made to sell. By inserting 'subject to contract' on all correspondence and paperwork, the parties prevent this happening, for they are imposing a condition that allows them to back out of the transaction any time before the mutual signing of contracts. This was confirmed by the Court of Appeal, under Lord Denning, in 1974:

Property dealers agreed on the sale of a building for £190,000. Both parties instructed solicitors, and the purchaser's solicitor wrote a letter to the vendor's solicitor: 'Empire House: we understand you act for the vendor in respect of the proposed sale of the above-mentioned property to our clients Wearwell Ltd at £190,000 leasehold, subject to contract.' However, within a few days the purchasers changed their minds and decided not to proceed with the purchase. The vendors argued that the purchasers were bound to buy the property; the solicitor's letter was binding on them since it was a written, signed confirmation of the deal. Held: The words 'subject to contract' prevented the letter from being a binding commitment to purchase. But if those words had not been used they might have been forced to go ahead with the purchase. Tiverton Estates (1974)

Similarly:

Landlords wrote to a prospective purchaser offering him a flat on a ninety-nine-year lease for £20,000 – 'subject to contract'. Neither side proceeded with the transaction, but nine months later the landlords' representative offered the flat at £17,000 with a ground rent of £50; nothing was said about that offer being 'subject to contract'. The prospective purchaser paid £50 ground rent and then arranged for a builder to carry out improvements and alterations. The landlord then refused to sell him the flat. Held: The court would not order a sale at £17,000. The negotiations were still 'subject to contract'. Cohen (1981)

Only exceptionally will the courts enforce an oral (i.e. spoken) contract for the sale of land, for the general rule is that the contract must be in writing. However, if buyer and seller come to an agreement and one of them unequivocally acts on that agreement (e.g. the buyer pays the purchase price and moves into the property with the seller's consent), the court may uphold the oral contract. But such exceptions are rare.

The important point to remember is that at this subject-to-contract stage of the transaction either buyer or seller can back out. It is only when there is a signed contract that either the buyer or seller is bound. Thus if, for example, a purchaser finds dry rot in the roof of the house, he can refuse to proceed with the transaction if he has not yet signed and handed over the contract; once he has exchanged contracts it is too late for him to back out, and he takes the property subject to any dry rot that it contains. Similarly, the seller can change his mind and refuse to sell the property to the buyer until he has signed and handed over a contract; from then on he is bound, and he cannot back out if, for example, someone else offers him a higher price for the house or flat.

The preliminary deposit

The estate agent will probably ask the buyer for a deposit to show the 'seriousness of his intentions'. As explained above, if the offer is subject to contract, the payment of a deposit to an estate agent at this stage will not legally commit either the buyer or the seller, and so the paying of such a deposit is no more than an indication of the moral commitment between the parties. Accordingly, there is little reason to pay a deposit at this stage, and if one is required it should be no more than a nominal sum, say £50 or £100. Some agents ask for more (sometimes as much as 5 per cent of the purchase price), but if they do they must give the purchaser the interest if it comes to more than £10, and if more than £500 was taken as the deposit (see page 226). Obviously, the purchaser should refuse to pay more than a nominal sum and he may find it necessary to ask the seller to tell the agents to accept a smaller amount than they want; there is, of course, no loss to the seller in his agreeing to this.

If a deposit is paid to an estate agent (or indeed to anyone, including a solicitor) he should confirm in writing that he holds it as 'stakeholder' (i.e. as a neutral agent of the parties), rather than as 'agent for the vendor' (which would be the same as paying it to the seller himself). If the parties should later have a dispute, this makes it less likely that the deposit will be paid to the seller.

If the transaction should fall through before contracts are signed, any preliminary deposit will be returned to the purchaser. This is so even if the buyer backs out without any good reason (e.g. simply because he changes his mind).

Step-by-step conveyancing: 2
Buyer instructs surveyor to inspect the property

A buyer takes a house or flat 'as he finds it'. The seller gives no guarantee as to the condition of the property unless, of course, he specifically makes claims that turn out to be untrue (e.g. if he says it has cavity-wall insulation, when it does not). See 'Misrepresentations', page 513.

A survey is, therefore, essential; the Royal Institution of Chartered Surveyors and the Society of Valuers and Auctioneers can suggest the names of suitable surveyors. The buyer should not use a surveyor from the firm of estate agents involved in the sale, since he will not be independent.

Many purchasers do not bother to obtain a surveyor's report. This is usually because they begrudge spending money in the expectation of being told that there is nothing wrong with the property. In addition, some people are prepared to rely on the building society's survey on the basis that 'if the building society are lending their money, it must be all right, mustn't it?' 'Not at all' is the answer, for the building society's survey is a relatively cursory affair that is only designed to check that the building society will recover its money should they ever have to foreclose and sell; it will not go into the sort of detail required by most buyers (see page 207).

As regards 'wasting £100 or more on a report' the buyer should bear in mind that the report may well pay for itself by revealing hidden defects in the property. It may be a remote chance that the house/flat is defective, but property repairs cost so much that few buyers can afford to take the risk. In addition, a well-written survey report can often be used to negotiate a reduction in the price.

However, a survey will rarely be 100 per cent comprehensive, since a complete survey would require removal of ceilings, lifting of floorboards, etc., all of which are unlikely to be agreed to by the seller.

Illustration. *Mr and Mrs Gill bought a flat. On the advice of their solicitor they had it surveyed, and the survey report was satisfactory, revealing no major defects. Within a month of buying the flat, the roof of the kitchen extension had fallen in, and they were faced with a bill for £600. Their first reaction was to blame the surveyor for not noticing the fault, but closer examination revealed that the fault in the roof-beams could only have been discovered by removing the kitchen ceiling. This was clearly impracticable and so the surveyor had not been at fault.*

With flats, there is the additional problem that a proper survey really requires a full examination of the other flats in the block, since a failure to repair one flat may have disastrous consequences for everyone else in the block. Also, most flat-owners pay a percentage service charge towards the cost of maintaining the whole block of flats, and so they have to pay just as much towards the cost of a structural repair to one part of the building as they do another part of the building (e.g. the owner of a ground-floor flat usually pays a proportion of the costs of repairing the roof, even though his flat is not directly underneath the roof). So to discover the likely level of the service charge, a surveyor would have to survey the whole block of flats! Usually, it is impracticable to inspect the other flats and so the survey can only be of limited value.

A normal structural survey does not include electrical or gas services, drains, or woodworm, etc. although these can be inspected at further cost. The buyer should be sure to ask the surveyor exactly what is included in the survey fee.

Most surveyors charge between £100 and £150 for a full written report. However, if the surveyor is also carrying out a survey for a building society, then he will charge a reduced sum to the purchaser. If the same surveyor is to be used, it is essential that the building society is informed as soon as the mortgage application is submitted; otherwise the surveyor may have made his inspection for the society without realizing that he is also to prepare a private survey report for the purchaser.

When reading a surveyor's report, the buyer should look for any wording that is open to a double interpretation and try to pin the surveyor down to a definite opinion. If the report finds fault with the property, it is usually advisable to show it to the seller and argue that the price should be reduced. In this way, a survey report can often pay for itself.

The NHBC guarantee

The buyer may decide to dispense with a survey because the estate agent tells him that the property has a ten-year National House Building Council (NHBC) guarantee. But a buyer should not take such a 'guarantee' as being all-embracing for it is of limited value except during the two years following its issue, when nearly all defects have to be put right by the builder (but, even then, not all defects are covered – normal wear and tear, and normal shrinkage, are excluded as are fences and lifts. Central-heating boilers and any other electrical moving parts are only covered for one year). For the next eight years (i.e. until ten years after construction), the guarantee only covers major structural defects, and not hidden defects such as faulty wiring, or poorly connected plumbing. For the guarantee to take effect, the defect must be 'severe' and it must be a structural defect that has caused major damage (e.g. collapse or serious distortion of joists or roof structure; dry rot; failure of a damp-proof course). Subsidence and settlement will only be covered if not covered by the householder's own insurance policy. Minor structural defects, and non-structural problems, are excluded (e.g. leaking gutters, twisted doors, cracked fittings). In short, the NHBC guarantee is not much of a guarantee and, in practice, many people mistakenly think it offers more protection than it actually does. At the end of the ten-year period, the guarantee expires and is of no value at all.

A further weakness is that since 1979 the maximum cover given by the guarantee is the original price of the house (i.e. the price paid by the first purchaser) up to a maximum price of about £50,000. The cover then increases at the rate of 15 per cent compound interest each year. The risk is that this increase of cover will not be sufficient to cover the high inflationary rises in building and repair costs.

The NHBC guarantee is therefore of limited value. However, the guarantee does show that a certain level of workmanship was used during the construction of the building and it does provide some protection against major defects. Clearly, though, the mere presence of an NHBC guarantee should not necessarily mean that there is no need to have the property surveyed.

Other guarantees

If the property has been treated for woodworm, dry rot, or wet rot during say the last twenty-one years, there may be a guarantee that goes with the house or flat. The purchaser should check the wording of such a guarantee very carefully to see exactly what is promised. The guarantee should specifically state that it benefits future owners of the property and not just the person who originally had the work done. Also the guarantee will usually be worthless without the original survey report and the original estimate, since the guarantee will often state that 'a claim can only be entertained on production of the survey report and estimate'. More often than not, either or both of these documents has been lost. In addition, there is always the risk that the company which issued the guarantee has since gone out of business, in which case the guarantee will be worthless.

Step-by-step conveyancing: 3
Buyer applies to a building society for a mortgage

Most people need a mortgage to help finance their purchase of a home; the average advance is some 65 per cent of the total purchase price (with first-time buyers, the average figure is nearly 80 per cent).

People who have difficulty in obtaining mortgages often use the services of so-called 'mortgage brokers', who advertise that they can 'procure advances'. Unfortunately, many of these firms charge excessive fees (e.g. 1 per cent of the mortgage sum) and should be avoided. Even if no mortgage can be arranged, some of these firms still try to charge for their services, although the Consumer Credit Act does state that if no mortgage is arranged within six months, the customer cannot be liable for a fee of more than £3 (see page 574). Mortgage brokers should not be confused with 'insurance brokers', who receive their fees from insurance companies in the form of commission.

Solicitors and estate agents often have agencies with building societies, and may be able to help the buyer obtain a mortgage.

The buyer will have to pay a valuation fee to the building society. This covers the fee of a surveyor who will inspect the property for the society, check its condition, and also value it. His fee will have to be paid even if the society refuses to grant a mortgage and even if the purchase falls through.

The fee is on a scale depending upon the price of the property (not the amount of the mortgage). If the price is £12,000 then the fee is likely to be some £30; on a £25,000 purchase it would be approximately £46; on £50,000, it would be £64. Bear in mind that these figures are only approximate; in addition, many building societies give the buyer a choice and allow him to have a much more detailed survey carried out for (approximately) an additional £50 or £60.

Building society surveys are relatively cursory. The surveyor is likely to spend considerably less time examining the property than if he were carrying out a full private survey and the buyer should not rely on the building society's survey as being conclusive proof that the property is in good condition. It is therefore advisable for him to arrange his own private survey, in addition to the building society survey. However, only about 10 to 15 per cent of buyers do this.

The building society surveys the property for the building society, not the purchaser – although the purchaser pays for it. It used to be thought that if the building society surveyor carried out the survey negligently, the purchaser would not be able to sue the surveyor. But, that all changed in 1981, with this case:

The Halifax was going to lend money so that Mr and Mrs Yianni could buy a house. The Halifax asked a local firm of surveyors to survey the house – for the Halifax, not for the Yiannis. The surveyors were negligent and failed to spot major defects: within nine months there were subsidence cracks, and one wall was eventually rebuilt, and others underpinned. The Yiannis sued the surveyors, who argued that the survey had been for the Halifax, not the Yiannis and, anyway, the Halifax mortgage application form had a printed recommendation that anyone applying for a mortgage should get their own independent survey. Held: The surveyors were liable to the Yiannis. The surveyors knew that their valuation would be passed on to the Yiannis, and that they would rely on it. Yianni (1981)

Until recently, building societies never supplied copies of their surveyors' reports to purchasers; this practice is now changing and it is now normal for the society to enclose a copy of the report (usually called a 'valuation report'), when sending the mortgage offer to the purchaser.

Mortgage rates. See page 198 for information on mortgage rates, and also for information on the Homeloan scheme (a government scheme giving grants to first-time buyers).

Step-by-step conveyancing: 4
The buyer's conveyancer receives title documents from the seller's solicitor

These documents are:
- the draft contract
- a copy of the Land Registry certificate for the property
- a copy of the lease (if the property is leasehold).

The draft contract

This is the contract that the seller wants the buyer to sign on exchange of contracts. It sets out the terms of the transaction and what is being sold. The contract will usually be one of two pre-printed standard forms used by the legal profession. One is published by Oyez Publishing Ltd and is called 'The National Conditions of Sale'; the other, published by the Law Society, is known as 'The Law Society's Conditions of Sale'. Both contracts comprise four sides of print, the front and back pages of the 'National Conditions' being illustrated on pages 210–11. The two inside pages (not illustrated) contain the detailed provisions that govern the contract and which apply in the event of a dispute – these run to some 8,000 words! The contract is called a *draft* contract at this stage because the purchaser's solicitor may wish to amend it slightly, although usually there are few changes that need to be made.

Fixtures and fittings

The buyer and seller should come to an agreement as to what is, and what is not, included in the sale price. If no specific arrangements are made, the purchaser will be entitled to claim the 'fixtures and fittings' that are permanently attached to the property. This seemingly straightforward test can often be difficult to apply in practice, and the best way to avoid problems is for the parties to make a list of what is included in the price. The value of the curtains, furniture, etc., can be taken off when working out the sale price for stamp-duty purposes. (See page 225.)

It will be seen from the table on page 209 that several items fall into the 'doubtful' category and it is arguable whether or not they are removable. Generally, the answer will depend upon the extent of the damage that would be caused by their removal. For instance, fitted shelves might be held to be removable if the damage caused by taking them was easily made good – for instance, by filling in the holes and repapering – although it would be the responsibility of the seller to do this work.

A person who buys a property and moves in to find that the seller has taken fixtures and fittings should immediately report the matter to his conveyancer. The conveyancer will complain to the seller's conveyancer and demand that the items be replaced, or alternatively that the purchaser be compensated for the loss of value; obviously, this will include the cost of making good any damage caused in removal of the unauthorized items. If the seller refuses to compensate the buyer, then the buyer should consider starting county-court proceedings. If the items are within the 'not removable' category, then the purchaser would have excellent prospects of success.

Fixtures and fittings

Removable	Not removable	Doubtful
cooker (unless built-in)	wiring	curtain rails
fridge	plumbing	fitted shelves
washing machine	bathroom suite	greenhouse without
dishwasher	central heating	foundation
hanging light fittings	built-in cupboards	wall lights
(but not the bulb	purpose-built cupboards	fitted decorative wall
holders or sockets)	garden shrubs and plants	mirrors
gas fires (unless built in)	greenhouse on foundations	TV aerial
carpets, lino, curtains	towel rail	
garden furniture	wall-mounted bathroom	
fitted wardrobe designed	heater	
to be removable	coal bunker	
	toilet-roll holder	

A copy of the Land Registry certificate

This is the title deed. See specimen on pages 905–6. The buyer's conveyancer will want to check the plan on the certificate to see that it tallies with what the buyer thinks he is buying. In addition, he will look for restrictive covenants (see page 335) which might affect the land.

If the property is unregistered, there will be no Land Registry certificate. Instead, the buyer's conveyancer will usually be sent a plan (probably taken from an old conveyance), and a copy of any restrictive covenants mentioned in the deeds.

Step-by-step conveyancing: 5
Buyer's conveyancer sends two inquiry forms to the local authority

There will be numerous points to be checked with the local authority. For example:

A deposit of 10 per cent is payable when contracts are signed and exchanged

There are thirteen Land Registries, each with its own area of the country

Every registered property has its own individual title number

Note the unnecessarily wordy description: the postal address alone would suffice

This means the seller owns the property himself. He could be selling as a personal representative or as part-owner, for example

This form is copyright. It can only be purchased by solicitors

CONTRACT OF SALE
The National Conditions of Sale, Twentieth Edition

Vendor John David Evans of 200 Morrison Lane, Maida Vale, W.9, in the County of Greater London

Purchaser Michael Peter Jones and Mary Ann Jones (his wife) both of 12 Springsteen Grove, Lower Norwood, in the County of Greater London

Registered Land		
District Land Registry: Harrow	Purchase price	£ 60,500 —
Title Number: NGL1234567	Deposit	£ 6,050 —
Agreed rate of interest:	Balance payable	£ 66,550 —
	Price fixed for chattels or valuation money (if any)	£ 250 —
	Total	£ 66,800 —

Property and interest therein sold

ALL THAT freehold land situate at and known as No. 96 Clifton Road, Maida Vale, W9, in the County of Greater London as the same is registered at H as Land Registry with Title Absolute.

Vendor sells as beneficial owner   Completion date: 18th October 1986

AGREED that the Vendor sells and the Purchaser buys as above, subject to the Special Conditions endorsed hereon and to the National Conditions of Sale Twentieth Edition so far as the latter Conditions are not inconsistent with the Special Conditions.

Signed J.D. Evans

Date 20th September   1986

Completion will usually be arranged for 4 weeks after the date of exchanging contracts

This is the rate of interest that the buyer will have
to pay to the seller if he delays completion
(see page 220).

Re: 200 Morrison Lane, :   Evans to Jones
London W.9.   and Jones

SPECIAL CONDITIONS OF SALE

A. The prescribed rate of interest is   15%

B. Title shall be deduced ~~and shall commence as follows:~~

in accordance with s.110 of the Land Registration Act 1925.

This means that the
buyer will be provided
with a copy of the
Land Registry
certificate and an
authority to inspect the
certificate.

C. The sale is with vacant possession/~~subject to the existing tenancy of which details have been supplied to the Purchaser/subject to the following tenancies:~~

This confirms that
there are no tenants
occupying the
property.

D. The property is sold on the footing that the authorized use thereof for the purposes of the Planning Acts is ~~the use (if any) specified in the particulars of sale~~/use as

a private dwelling house.

E. The sale includes the chattels, fittings and separate items specified in the inventory annexed, which are to be taken by the purchaser for a sum (additional to the purchase price of the property) of £250 — ~~/to be ascertained by a valuation to be made by at the expense of~~

F. The property is sold subject, so far as they are still subsisting and capable of being enforced or of taking effect, to the restrictions and stipulations

set out in Entries Nos. 1, 2 and 3 on the Charges Register

The property is subject
to restrictive covenants
(see page 335). These are
set out in the Land
Registry Certificate
(see illustration on
pages 905–6).

Is there a possibility of road development? Was planning permission granted when the property was built? Are there compulsory-purchase proposals? Are there any tree-preservation orders? Is the property connected to the mains sewer? Is the road a public highway? Have any public-health orders been made? Is it a slum-clearance area, a development area, a conservation area, a clean-air zone, etc.?

Fortunately, all these questions are printed on a standard form of inquiry which the purchaser's solicitor simply sends to the local authority. After some two to four weeks he will receive replies. A fee of approximately £15 will have to be paid.

The pre-printed form of inquiries has been criticized for not being comprehensive enough (e.g. it asks for details of roads planned within 200 yards of the property; what happens if the road will be 201 yards from the property?). In addition, of course, an answer may be correct today but wrong tomorrow as a result of a change in council policy – such changes may, of course, happen even before the contract is made and the buyer committed.

Delay in receiving replies from the local authority is one of the main reasons why it can take over a month before a buyer can sign a contract. It will be a condition of the mortgage offer that there is a clear local-authority search; the purchaser cannot risk exchanging contracts (and so committing himself to the purchase) until a clear search has been received, otherwise he might find himself committed to buying the property but having lost his mortgage because of an adverse local search.

A cash-buyer can reduce the delay by going in person to the council offices and taking the standard inquiry form from department to department. But a 'personal search' of this sort would not be guaranteed as accurate by the council, and so it would be unacceptable to a building society.

Step-by-step conveyancing: 6
Buyer's conveyancer sends preliminary-inquiries form to the seller's conveyancer

There are many questions to be asked of the seller. For example: Is there an NHBC guarantee? Are there any tenants in the property? What fixtures and fittings are included? Who maintains the boundary walls and fences? Is there mains water? Are there any adverse rights known? What is the rateable value? And so on.

Most of these questions are asked by the purchaser's solicitor sending a pre-printed form to the seller's solicitor, which he returns duly answered. In the same way that the local-authority forms have been criticized, these forms have also been accused of being defective. The seller's solicitor will put these questions to his client, but the solicitor will probably not reply fully to the purchaser's questions, for fear of binding the client to an answer that is later found to be inaccurate. Thus, the solicitor's replies are likely to be evasive and unhelpful, and in addition, the form states that the answers are not to be binding! However, despite these apparently major defects in the system of inquiries, the procedure usually works well enough, although this is probably only due to the fact that most people are honest and trustworthy. Clearly, if there are any particular points that concern the buyer he should specifically mention them to his solicitor/conveyancer so that he can attempt to deal with them.

Remember, the buyer takes the property as it is, and it is up to him to check these matters before he signs the contract.

Step-by-step conveyancing: 7
If a mortgage is granted the building society (or bank) may appoint its own conveyancer

Usually, the building society will appoint the buyer's conveyancer to look after its interests in the transaction. Sometimes, however, if the buyer's conveyancer is not on the building society's list of approved conveyancers, the society will ask another firm of conveyancers to act for it. Also, some of the smaller building societies prefer – as a matter of policy – to appoint independent solicitors, rather than rely on the buyer's own conveyancer.

This is an important point for the prospective purchaser, since the building society will expect him to pay its legal fees. Thus, a buyer who has a building-society mortgage will have to pay his own legal fees, plus either:
● an additional fee charged by his conveyancer for acting for the building society, *or*
● a separate fee to another firm of solicitors/conveyancers.

If a separate firm is used by the building society, the buyer's own conveyancer will expect his client to pay him for the extra work arising from the correspondence, etc., with the other firm. It is therefore cheaper for a buyer if his own conveyancer also acts for the bank or building society (see also page 224).

Step-by-step conveyancing: 8
If the buyer's conveyancer has received satisfactory replies

The buyer will be ready to commit himself once his conveyancer has received satisfactory:
● surveyor's report (see step 2)
● mortgage offer (see step 3)
● answers to any queries on the draft contract (see step 4)
● local-authority search (see step 5)
● replies to preliminary inquiries (see step 6)
Generally, this stage will not have been reached for at least a month after the buyer had his offer for the property accepted. Replies to local-authority searches and mortgage applications generally take a month or so to process, and until both have been received he dare not commit himself by exchanging contracts.

Step-by-step conveyancing: 9
The buyer signs the contract and sends it with a 10 per cent deposit to the seller's conveyancer

This is the last opportunity for the buyer and seller to back out. Exchange of contracts will take place when the seller has received the buyer's signed contract (plus his deposit cheque), and when the seller has, in turn, posted his own signed contract to the buyer.

Usually, a 10 per cent deposit is paid (less any preliminary deposit that may have been paid to the estate agents). The buyer will have to raise this money, either from his savings or by borrowing it from his bank (a 'bridging loan'). He cannot use his mortgage money since he will not have that until the purchase is finally completed – probably one month later. To avoid the expense and inconvenience of borrowing the full 10 per cent deposit, he could try asking whether the seller would accept less (e.g. 5 per cent). Remember that the interest on the deposit money (if it is put on deposit between exchange and completion) will probably not go to the seller but to his solicitor/conveyancer – so the seller will probably not mind accepting a smaller deposit, as long as he feels it is enough to cover his losses should the buyer wrongfully back out of the purchase. The other way of avoiding having to borrow the deposit is for the buyer – if he is selling his own property – to ask the person buying from him whether the deposit on the sale can be used on his purchase.

The idea of a deposit is to provide the seller with some security, in case the buyer backs out at the last minute; if that happens, the seller may be able to forfeit the deposit (in practice, this virtually never happens since a buyer will nearly always make some arrangement to avoid losing his deposit). In many ways, the idea of paying a deposit is old-fashioned. A much simpler (and cheaper) way of giving the seller some security against the buyer backing out would be to replace deposits with guarantees. Such a guarantee would be provided by the buyer's bank or building society, which would promise to pay up if the buyer defaulted.

The completion date

'Completion' is when the deal is completed – the buyer pays the rest of the money and is then allowed to move in. Normally, this will be four weeks after the day on which the contracts were exchanged. But, this four-week rule is no more than a convenience – if both buyer and seller want it to be more (or less), then that can be agreed. In practical terms, however, a gap of ten days between exchange and completion is likely to be the shortest that can be agreed by the conveyancers, since it usually takes that long to do the searches and to obtain the money from the building society or bank. Also, if there is a chain of transactions, then it is often difficult to get everyone to agree on a specific date, in which case the usual four-week period is adopted.

Moving in before completion

If the house is empty, the buyer might wonder whether he can move in before completion. Generally, the answer will be 'no' – the seller's conveyancer will be worried about the practical difficulties of evicting the buyer should he default and refuse to pay up on the completion date! However, the seller may agree to allow the buyer access so he can measure up, and even have building works done. Normally this can be agreed – but there is no obligation on the seller to agree, and it will normally be on the strict understanding that the buyer is not to take advantage of the seller's generosity and move in to the property. It follows that if a buyer wants access to an empty property between exchange and completion he should tell his conveyancer to make this a term of the contract, so it can be agreed to before exchange of contracts: he will then be sure that he and his builders can have access.

Step-by-step conveyancing: 10
The buyer's building society (or bank) insures the property

The buyer has signed a contract to buy the property. From now on he is, in theory, the legal owner of the property and the seller holds it for him as a trustee, looking after it for him until the purchase price is paid. This will usually be some four weeks later, and only then can the buyer move in.

If the property is destroyed or damaged between now and completion it will be the buyer's loss. Accordingly, he must insure it straight away, preferably on a 'comprehensive' basis. In fact, this will automatically be done by the building society and so the buyer will not have to do anything about it. But the seller must look after the property until completion takes place. If he does not, he will be liable to the buyer.

Mr Lucie-Smith contracted to buy Mr Gorman's house. Contracts were exchanged with completion to be on 31 January. Gorman moved out on 24 January without notifying Lucie-Smith. Completion was delayed because of a delay on the part of Gorman. Unfortunately the house was flooded early in February when a frozen pipe burst: it turned out that Gorman had not turned the water off when he had left on 24 January. Lucie-Smith claimed damages for the cost of repairing the damage. Held: Gorman was liable. He should have turned off the water supply. Lucie-Smith (1981)

The seller will probably keep his own insurance on during this period rather than risk relying on the buyer's insurance.

Step-by-step conveyancing: 11
The buyer's conveyancer receives a signed copy of the contract from the seller's conveyancer

Contracts have now been exchanged and both parties are bound to proceed with the transaction. Both will have a copy of the contract signed by the other.

Step-by-step conveyancing: 12
The buyer's conveyancer receives permission to inspect the Land Registry register

The seller's conveyancer will now give permission for the buyer's conveyancer to contact the Land Registry and check the seller's legal title to the property (e.g. whether he is really the owner or any claims have been registered against the title).

Step-by-step conveyancing: 13
The buyer's conveyancer sends his queries on title to the seller's solicitor

The seller is now asked to answer any queries as to the title. The buyer's conveyancer will use a pre-printed form that contains most of the usual points arising (e.g. asking when the seller's mortgage will be paid off). These queries are called 'requisitions'. The seller's conveyancer will answer them by filling in the blanks on the form sent to him.

Step-by-step conveyancing: 14
Buyer's conveyancer prepares draft transfer (i.e. the sale deed)

Whereas it was the seller's conveyancer who prepared the draft contract, it is the buyer's conveyancer who prepares the draft transfer (called a 'conveyance' if the land is unregistered). The seller's solicitor may ask for changes to be made, although this rarely happens (usually, only if the seller's conveyancer made a mistake when filling in the standard form – such as misspelling a name). There is a specimen form printed on page 904.

Step-by-step conveyancing: 15
The seller's conveyancer sends a completion statement to the buyer's conveyancer

The completion statement sets out how much money has to be paid on completion. Generally, this will be the balance of the purchase moneys (i.e. the purchase price less any deposit already paid) plus a sum to allow for any rates, water rates (and, if leasehold, any service charge, rent, or insurance) paid in advance – or owed – by the seller. These sums will be apportioned so that the seller pays for the period up to completion and the buyer pays for the period from completion.

Rates and water rates are personal debts. This means that they are debts of the individual occupier of a property and do not attach to the property itself. Thus, if the seller fails to pay his rates or water rates, the buyer is not liable to the council or the Water Board for the arrears. The purchaser is only liable as from the date he buys the property. (With the rates he may only be liable for the period from when he moves into the property; check with the council whether they charge rates on un-occupied property.)

Service charges, rent, and insurance due on a leasehold property are debts that go with the property. Thus, the buyer is liable for any arrears. This means that the buyer will be liable for the seller's unpaid bills – so the buyer's conveyancer will want to check that all bills have been paid up to date. With service charges on flats this can be a problem; often, service charges are invoiced on an annual basis at the end of the year and so neither buyer nor seller will know just how much the eventual bill will be. Either money will have to be kept back (which is highly inconvenient) or buyer and seller will just have to make the best guess that they can.

216

Step-by-step conveyancing: 16
Buyer's conveyancer checks that the buyer is not bankrupt, and that the seller has a proper title

The buyer's conveyancer will need to prove to the building society that his client is not bankrupt before they will agree to part with the mortgage money. Thus, one week or so before completion the solicitor obtains a certificate confirming this from the Land Charges Department (Burrington Way, Plymouth), where a register of bankruptcies is kept. He will also check the seller's legal title to the property by posting a search-form to the Land Registry. This will show whether there have been any recent changes, or if there are any problems.

Step-by-step conveyancing: 17
Completion takes place

Completion is when the transaction is finalized. In return for his money, the buyer receives the title deeds (and the keys!). Until a few years ago this used to be done by the two sets of solicitors meeting in the office of the seller's solicitor and physically handing over bank drafts, deeds, keys, etc. Now, the vast majority of completions take place by post – the buyer's conveyancer simply tells his bank to transfer the money immediately from his bank account to the account of the seller's conveyancer. In return, the seller's conveyancer will phone and promise to put the deeds and other documents in the post. The handing over of the keys will probably be sorted out by the buyer and seller themselves, or by the estate agents. There should be no need for the buyer (or the seller) to have to go to the conveyancer's office since all the signing of paperwork, and paying over of money, should have been sorted out in advance.

Finally, note that completion is usually four weeks from the day when contracts are exchanged. But this four-week period is no more than a traditional convention – see page 214. Completion must take place on a weekday (i.e. when the parties' conveyancers are open for business) – not on a weekend.

Step-by-step conveyancing: 18
The buyer can now move in

Step-by-step conveyancing: 19
The conveyancers finalize the transaction

To complete the paperwork:
● the seller's mortgage will be paid off. The seller's conveyancer will do this with the money received from the buyer, and afterwards send a building-society (or bank) receipt to the buyer's conveyancer.
● the buyer's solicitor will send the purchase deed to the Inland Revenue, and pay any stamp duty (see page 225).

Housing: Owner-Occupiers

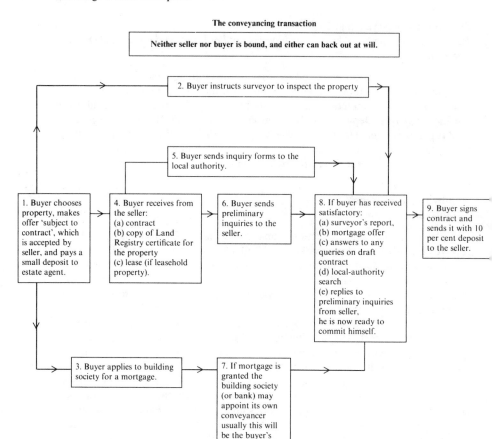

The conveyancing transaction

Neither seller nor buyer is bound, and either can back out at will.

2. Buyer instructs surveyor to inspect the property

5. Buyer sends inquiry forms to the local authority.

1. Buyer chooses property, makes offer 'subject to contract', which is accepted by seller, and pays a small deposit to estate agent.

4. Buyer receives from the seller:
(a) contract
(b) copy of Land Registry certificate for the property
(c) lease (if leasehold property).

6. Buyer sends preliminary inquiries to the seller.

8. If buyer has received satisfactory:
(a) surveyor's report,
(b) mortgage offer
(c) answers to any queries on draft contract
(d) local-authority search
(e) replies to preliminary inquiries from seller,
he is now ready to commit himself.

9. Buyer signs contract and sends it with 10 per cent deposit to the seller.

3. Buyer applies to building society for a mortgage.

7. If mortgage is granted the building society (or bank) may appoint its own conveyancer usually this will be the buyer's own conveyancer.

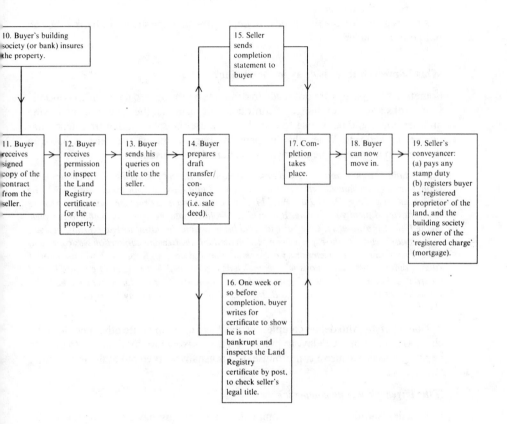

Both buyer and seller are bound and neither can back out without the other's consent.

10. Buyer's building society (or bank) insures the property.

11. Buyer receives signed copy of the contract from the seller.

12. Buyer receives permission to inspect the Land Registry certificate for the property.

13. Buyer sends his queries on title to the seller.

14. Buyer prepares draft transfer/conveyance (i.e. sale deed).

15. Seller sends completion statement to buyer

16. One week or so before completion, buyer writes for certificate to show he is not bankrupt and inspects the Land Registry certificate by post, to check seller's legal title.

17. Completion takes place.

18. Buyer can now move in.

19. Seller's conveyancer: (a) pays any stamp duty (b) registers buyer as 'registered proprietor' of the land, and the building society as owner of the 'registered charge' (mortgage).

- finally, the buyer's conveyancer will send the papers (i.e. the purchase deed, the title certificate, the mortgage deed, receipt for the seller's paid-off mortgage) to the Land Registry. He will also pay the Land Registry fee, and then the seller will be registered as the owner.

After registration the title deeds are kept by the building society or bank – they do not go to the buyer.

What happens if there is delay in completing?

Sometimes the parties are not ready to complete on the agreed date, which is usually four weeks after the exchange of contracts. For example, the seller may be buying another house and be unable to complete because the seller in that transaction has not yet moved out. When this happens the person causing the delay is liable in damages to all the people affected by his default. For instance:

> In a chain of transactions A agreed to sell his house to B, and B agreed to sell his house to C. Contracts were exchanged between A and B, and B and C, with both transactions due to be completed on 12 July. On 11 July, A told B that he would have to delay the completion because A was having difficulty in moving. B immediately told C that they would be unable to complete on the 12th. Unfortunately, C had already sold his house and his furniture was on route in a van to B's house, ready for the expected completion on the 12th. Because completion was cancelled, C was forced to move into temporary accommodation and store his furniture. It was not until 11 August that the two transactions were completed. C then sued B for the extra expense he had incurred; B in turn sued A, arguing that A should indemnify B for the damages due to C. Held: B was liable to C, and A was liable to B. In effect, therefore, A had to pay C's expenses. Raineri (1980)

Thus a person who delays completion may have to compensate other people in the chain as a result of the delay. In practice, it is relatively rare for damages to have to be paid. This is because a compromise deal is usually worked out at the last minute.

If the buyer is delaying completion

If the seller is willing and able to complete, the buyer must pay interest on the money due (i.e. on the purchase price minus the 10 per cent deposit). The rate of interest will be as stated in the contract – see Special Condition A in the specimen contract on page 211.

Also, the seller can serve a 'notice to complete' on the buyer. This means that unless the buyer completes within (usually) about three weeks the seller will be able to forfeit the 10 per cent deposit and sue the buyer for any other losses incurred. The deposit can be forfeited even if the seller re-sells the property for a profit. A striking illustration of how this can work was provided by a case in which a property company agreed to sell a site for £2,350,000; the buyer paid £235,000 deposit but then refused to complete. The seller then took the deposit and sold the property to another buyer for £2,500,000. Thus, as a result of the original purchaser defaulting, the seller had made an extra £385,000 (the deposit plus the increase in the selling price).

If the seller delays completion

The buyer is in a less strong position since he may not be able to demand interest. However, he can serve a 'notice to complete' and if the seller does not complete within twenty-eight days the buyer can:

- cancel the contract and have his deposit returned, *or*
- sue for breach of contract and obtain damages for any losses, *or*
- go to court for an order that the seller be forced to complete.

However, in practice, the buyer is in a weaker position than the seller, since he cannot charge the seller interest if there is delay in completing. Whilst, in theory, he may be able to sue for damages (see above), this only happens rarely (when the losses involved justify the cost and inconvenience of suing).

Why does conveyancing take so long?

Most conveyancing transactions take about three months from start to finish. Why is this? There are three main reasons:

1. The buyer cannot commit himself until he has received a clear local search (i.e. step 5 above; see page 209). Many authorities, especially the London boroughs, take a month or so to reply.
2. The buyer cannot commit himself until he has received a definite mortgage offer. This will rarely take less than three weeks, will often take four weeks, and can exceptionally take two months. During this time the building society will check the applicant's income and survey the property.
3. Each transaction will probably be dependent on one or more other transactions. For instance, if A is buying from B, and B is buying from C, and C is buying from D, then A cannot proceed until B, C, and D are all ready to go ahead. They will all want to exchange contracts simultaneously so that no one will be in the position of being committed to buying without having his sale also finalized, and vice versa. So a chain of conveyances can build up, with everyone being held up by one person in the chain.

The only feasible way of reducing the delay would seem to be for local authorities to provide a return-of-post service for local searches (presumably at an increased fee) and for building societies to speed up their process for offering mortgages. This saving of time would then reduce the likelihood of delay in the chain. Conveyancers could also improve the efficiency of the operation by the seller's conveyancer automatically providing the purchaser's conveyancer with replies to the standard preliminary inquiries, rather than waiting to be asked (i.e. step 6 above; see page 212). Also the usual twenty-eight-day period between exchange of contracts and completion could be reduced to, say, fourteen days; this can be done now, although generally people do in fact want a month in which to finalize removal arrangements, etc. Increased computerization might also help. It goes without saying that the whole process would be quicker and cheaper if all the searches could be done by computer links, and if conveyancers had compatible software systems. These changes are on the way.

The expenses of buying and selling property

As a result of a typical conveyancing transaction, the following bills will have to be paid:

Seller pays

- his conveyancer's fee
- his estate agent's fee.

Buyer pays

- his conveyancer's fee for acting on the purchase
- the legal fees for the building-society work. This will depend upon whether his conveyancer also acted for the building society. He will pay *either*:
  - the building-society conveyancer's fees, plus a small additional fee to his own conveyancer for the extra work involved in writing to the building society's conveyancer, *or*
  - his ownconveyancer's fee for acting for the building society
- fees for local-authority and bankruptcy searches
- stamp duty
- Land Registry fee
- building society's surveyor's fee
- perhaps, surveyor's fee.

Conveyancing fees

Until 1973 solicitors' conveyancing fees were on a scale basis: the more the house was worth, the more the solicitor charged. The drawback of this system was its inflexibility and the absurdity of the notion that the complexity of the transaction was related to the value of the property. Its advantage was that everyone knew where they stood; the client knew in advance how much he would be charged and there was little scope for misunderstanding.

In 1973 conveyancing fees were put on the same basis as other non-contentious (i.e. non-court) work done by solicitors. The solicitor should charge what is 'fair and reasonable', having regard to eight factors (such as the complexity of the transaction, its urgency, whether the land is registered, etc.). See page 834 for a full list of the eight factors and for how solicitors' fees are worked out.

See page 835 for how to complain about a solicitor's bill. In particular, note that there is a procedure allowing the client to have the bill checked by the Law Society; see 'Remuneration Certificates', page 836.

Since the scale fees have been abolished, it is not possible to give a detailed guide as to likely solicitor's fees. However, as a general guide one can say that the solicitor's fee for acting on a purchase or sale (exclusive of VAT, stamp duty, building-society legal work, etc.) is rarely likely to be less than $\frac{1}{2}$ per cent of the price of the property, and it is rarely likely to exceed $1\frac{1}{4}$ per cent of the price. Generally, sales are cheaper than purchases, and usually the fee is likely to be nearer the 1 per cent level until the price rises to over £25,000–£30,000. For instance, a typical price on a £20,000 sale might be £200, and on a £20,000 purchase, £220. For a £40,000 sale the fee might be £300, and for a £40,000 purchase, approximately £350. Some solicitors think in terms of charging $\frac{1}{2}$ a per cent (of the price) plus £50 (for instance, on a £30,000 purchase, this would be £200, plus VAT – plus the fee for acting for the building society). But there is no uniformity in solicitors' charges.

It must be remembered that these are rough guides only. The longer a transaction takes and the more complicated it is, the more the solicitor is likely to charge. Many solicitors' firms keep a time record and charge their clients on the basis of how much time was spent on the transaction. In such cases, the Law Society will generally approve a bill drawn up on the basis of the time spent, with an additional 25–35 per cent to cover typing and other services, plus $\frac{1}{2}$ a per cent of the purchase/sale price. For instance, if a purchase of a £60,000 house took eight hours and time was charged at £25 per hour, the bill might be: £200 (8 × £25) plus £60 (30 per cent) plus £300 ($\frac{1}{2}$ per cent of £60,000) = £560 (plus VAT and disbursements). (Note: surveys by the 1979 Royal Commission on Legal Services showed that a typical sale took a solicitor approximately seven hours, and a purchase approximately eight hours, although the time tended to increase as the value of the property rose.)

In practice, the Law Society-approved fees are often at the upper end of the scale and most solicitors would charge less than £560 for a £60,000 purchase; generally, solicitors have to give quotes in advance and then they usually give a lower figure. Perhaps £350–£450 would be a more typical figure for a £60,000 purchase.

Licensed conveyancers. *Licensed conveyancers are non-solicitors who are licensed to do conveyancing work. Generally, they tend to be former legal executives (see page 820) who have taken extra exams and who have specialized in conveyancing. The first licensed conveyancers were only appointed in 1985 and so the system of licensed conveyancers is still in its early days. Generally the qualification requirements are quite strict, so one should expect a similar standard of service and competence as from a solicitor. As regards fees, it is too soon to tell whether they are cheaper than solicitors. Certainly, many solicitors market their services more aggressively than they did a few years ago, and the result seems to have been that one can find good value. The simple answer is to shop around for quotes. When doing

*The laws allowing licensed conveyancers are likely to be introduced soon after publication of this book. To simplify matters we have assumed that the changes are now in force.

this, be sure to compare like with like, and in particular check whether a quote is exclusive of VAT, search fees, Land Registry fees, stamp duty, and building-society legal fees. For instance, a quote on a £40,000 purchase of £700 inclusive of all those items would be cheaper than a quote of £250 exclusive of them all. Because of the wide variations in the fees charged by different solicitors' firms, you should always get a firm estimate in advance. In 1984, it became possible for solicitors to advertise. The immediate effect was a general reduction in conveyancing fees – a few solicitors began advertising nationally, and the end result was a general lowering of fees. It is thus more difficult than ever to quote typical prices – different firms' charges can vary enormously, and the best advice is to shop around.

Do not forget that the conveyancer will charge even if the transaction falls through. His fee is based on the work done, not on whether the property is bought or sold.

Building society's legal fees

If a purchase is partly financed by a mortgage, the building society (or bank) will instruct a conveyancer to prepare the mortgage deed and generally to protect its interests. They will normally use the buyer's own conveyancer but a different firm might be instructed if, for instance:

● the purchaser does not have a conveyancer because he is doing his own conveyancing or is using an unlicensed conveyancing firm (see page 230).

● the purchaser's conveyancer is not on the building society's panel of conveyancers. Some building societies restrict the number of conveyancers they use.

The fees will depend upon whether or not the buyer's conveyancer also acts for the building society.

When the purchaser's own conveyancer also does the building society's legal work

The fee will be on a scale recommended by the Building Societies' Association. If the fee is more, complain to the building society. Many conveyancers charge less.

Amount of mortgage	Conveyancer's fee* (plus VAT)	Amount of mortgage	Conveyancer's fee* (plus VAT)
£10,000	£52.50	£30,000	£75.00
£15,000	£62.50	£35,000	£76.25
£20,000	£67.50	£40,000	£76.75
£25,000	£72.50	£50,000	£77.25

*In the case of an endowment mortgage the fee will be 25 per cent higher.

When the conveyancer who does the building-society work does not act on the purchase as well

In this case there is no scale fee and the charge must be 'fair and reasonable'. In practice, it is likely to be 50–60 per cent more than the scale fee charged by a conveyancer who also acts on the purchase (e.g. on a £30,000 mortgage the fee is likely to be some £115–£120 plus VAT).

Stamp duty

Stamp duty is paid by the buyer of a property worth more than £30,000. Above that figure, the duty is 1 per cent (e.g. £350 on a £35,000 property: £900 on a £90,000 property, etc.). If the property is not worth more than £30,000 then no stamp duty is paid (e.g. on a £29,000 – or even a £30,000 – purchase, no duty is paid). The stamp duty is paid on the whole of the purchase price – not just the excess over £30,000. For instance, the tax on (1985 figures) a £30,000 purchase is nil; but on a £40,000 purchase it is £400. The tax is levied on the whole £40,000, not just the £10,000 over the £30,000.

If the price of the property is at the bottom level of stamp-duty liability (i.e. £30,000 in 1985), then it might be possible to value the curtains, fittings, and furniture separately, and so reduce the price to below the stamp-duty threshold. For instance, on a £30,500 purchase, if £500 can legitimately be apportioned to the furniture, then the price of the property can be stated as £30,000 and no stamp duty will have to be paid (i.e. a saving of £305).

Land Registry fees

These are paid when a buyer of a property is registered as the owner. The fee is on a sliding scale, rising with the value of the house. There are two different scales, depending upon whether or not the property is being registered for the first time (i.e. is it the first purchase since the area became an area of compulsory registration? See page 201). Typical fees would be: £45 on a £20,000 purchase; £90 on a £40,000 purchase; £140 on a £60,000 purchase; £190 on a £80,000 purchase; and £240 on a £100,000 purchase.

Estate agents' fees

Estate agents' fees vary enormously, but are generally very high. Commission is usually $1\frac{1}{2}$, 2, or $2\frac{1}{2}$ per cent of the selling price, although some agents operate a sliding scale (e.g. $2\frac{1}{2}$ per cent on the first £5,000, and $1\frac{1}{2}$ per cent on the rest). In London $2\frac{1}{2}$ per cent is common. Thus, on a £35,000 house, the agent's fee may be £875 which, with the addition of VAT means a bill to the seller of over £1,000. In comparison, the conveyancing fees, Land Registry fees and stamp duty paid by a purchaser can often fade into insignificance!

Since the legal controls on estate agents are few, it is important that the seller agrees the agent's rate of commission in advance. The seller should insist on written confirmation of the rate, and he should check that he will not be charged for advertisements, etc., placed by the agent. In addition, the seller should check carefully on the following points.

Sole agency. This means that the estate agent is the only agent for the property. It is advisable to put a time limit on his sole agency.

Sole selling rights. Do not confuse a sole agency with sole selling rights, which means that he alone can sell the property so, for instance, if the seller sells privately to a friend, the agent can still claim his commission. The general rule is never agree to sole selling rights.

Multiple agency. In this case the agent is not the only agent with the property on his books. The disadvantage is that the agent may not try as hard as if he had a sole agency; also, there can be arguments between agents as to which is entitled to the commission if the buyer contacted both of them.

It is also important to agree in advance exactly when the agent should be entitled to commission. Some agents have a standard contract that entitles them to commission on 'introducing a buyer ready, willing and able to buy'. It might be argued that this commits the seller to paying the agent even if the seller changes his mind and subsequently withdraws from the transaction or if he sells privately to a friend in preference to someone sent from the agents. Such a clause should never be accepted; the seller should insist that the agent is only to be paid if the buyer introduced by him actually buys the property.

The Estate Agents Act 1979 makes it compulsory for an estate agent to inform his client of the scale of fees and when they will become payable. This information must be provided before the contract is made with the client; if it is not provided, then the court can declare that the contract is not binding on the client, and so no fee, or only part of the fee, is payable. Estate agents must also:

- pay interest to clients on deposits, but only if the deposit is over £500 and the interest is at least £10;
- declare any personal interest they have in a transaction. For instance, if an estate agent is selling a flat that is owned by an associate (e.g. a nominee company with a different name) then the buyer must be told (although, in practice, this will not be until the buyer is on the verge of signing the purchase contract). The idea of requiring estate agents to disclose their interests is, of course, to make buyers realize that the agent cannot be trusted to be an impartial middleman;
- the agent must keep proper books and accounts and these must be audited every year.

Do-it-yourself and cut-price conveyancing

No one is bound to use a solicitor or a licensed conveyancer when buying or selling a house or a flat; either or both of the parties are free to do their own conveyancing if they so wish.

Before deciding whether to do one's own conveyancing, there are two questions that need to be answered:

- what is the saving in legal fees?
- how difficult is conveyancing?

The costs of moving: purchasing a house or flat

	£	See page
Conveyancer's fee for purchase	...	222
Conveyancer's fee for building-society work	...	224
Local-authority and bankruptcy search fees	...	209, 217
Land Registry fee*	...	225
Stamp duty	...	225
Building society's surveyor's fee	...	207
Surveyor's fee	...	204
Removal firm's charge	...	
Total		

*Note. With unregistered property there will be no Land Registry fee (unless the property now has to be registered), but the conveyancer's increased charge for the legal work will offset this saving.

The costs of moving: selling a house or flat

	£	See page
Conveyancer's fee on sale	...	222
Estate agent's fee	...	225
Removal firm's charge	...	
Total		

The first question can be answered by looking at the above section on 'The expenses of buying and selling property'. However, it should be borne in mind that the conveyancer's fee is only one of the expenses arising and that all the other fees (such as the building society's legal charges, stamp duty, estate agent's fees, Land Registry fees) will still have to be paid by the DIY conveyancer. Thus, the saving may not be as great as it seems at first glance.

The feasibility of DIY conveyancing

It is the alleged difficulty of conveyancing that is the real point of contention between those who advocate DIY conveyancing and those who say that it is an unwise and risky venture. The first part of this chapter mentioned some of the complicated adverse rights that can arise in the course of a conveyance, and which go some way towards justifying Dickens's contention that English land law was the son of the devil. Against that, of course, one can argue that most of the legal theory just does not arise in practice when dealing with a typical residential property. For example, a leading textbook devotes a hundred pages to a discussion of the complications that can arise with mortgages, yet all the buyer of a house needs to know is that the seller's mortgage must be paid off by completion and that he should keep up to date on his mortgage repayments! However, conveyancing can be complicated and it should be appreciated that the transaction described above is of the simplest type; frequently, the transaction will raise more difficult problems.

Arguments in favour of DIY conveyancing

- the saving in legal fees can be considerable;
- the vast majority of house conveyances are straightforward and do not raise complicated matters of law;
- there are several good books available on DIY conveyancing, which, if followed carefully, virtually guarantee success;
- much of the terminology used in conveyancing is less complicated than it seems at first glance (e.g. the words engrossment, abstract of title, peruse, requisitions, all sound more intimidating than they really are);
- most of the standard forms used by conveyancers can be purchased by members of the public;
- many firms use unqualified clerks to do most of their conveyancing, so often the person is not in reality paying for the advice and experience of a qualified solicitor or licensed conveyancer;
- the conveyancing procedure as conducted by conveyancers is not particularly efficient or comprehensive (e.g. see criticisms made of the pre-contract searches and inquiries above); a person acting for himself can do a more thorough job.

Arguments against DIY conveyancing

- people do not like the responsibility of handling large sums of money.
- the conveyancing transaction takes place over some two or three months and most people would prefer to pay a professional person to take over the responsibility and worry during this time. An analogy can be made with repairs to a car: the layman can buy a workshop manual telling him how to repair his car and he can then spend his leisure hours working on the car; however, most people prefer to pay a specialist to repair their car for them. So it is with conveyancing; most people who buy and sell property prefer to pay a conveyancer to do the work for them.
- although most conveyances are straightforward, how does the layman know that his will not be the exceptional case that does raise difficult legal problems?
- will the layman be able to recognize a defect in the title or a legal problem if one arises?
- the DIY books cannot foresee every problem that might arise. If lawyers' textbooks are several thousand pages long, how can DIY manuals of a few hundred pages cover all eventualities?

- the DIY conveyancer will still have all the other fees to be paid (and, in particular, increased building-society legal fees, see page 224).
- the conveyancer does not just provide his 'legal' services; in addition he will usually advise on insurance, mortgages, and surveys, and he will be able to arrange a convenient completion date. With his experience, he is better able to do this than a DIY conveyancer.

A *personal opinion*

The opinion of this conveyancing solicitor is:

Buying freehold property (i.e. usually houses). It can be seen from the chart on page 218 that there is much more work to buying than there is to selling. In addition, of course, a mistake will probably have more disastrous consequences for a buyer than for a seller. A distinction should be made between:

(a) *Registered property*. A person of average intelligence can safely do his own purchase, so long as he approaches the task with care;

(b) *Unregistered property*. Most people would find the complication of checking a chain of title deeds totally confusing. This work is best left to a qualified lawyer.

Selling freehold property. A person of average intelligence can safely sell his registered freehold property. If the title is unregistered, then there are more complications, but these can be overcome (although, in fact, relatively few people try to do their own unregistered sales). Do not forget that the major expense on a sale is likely to be on estate agent's fees, and these will usually be much more than those of a conveyancer. So anyone trying to save money might be well advised to concentrate his energies on finding a buyer without using an estate agent.

Buying leasehold property (i.e. usually flats). The extra complications with a leasehold property arise from the need to check the clauses of the lease (e.g. have there been breaches of the terms? Are the repairing covenants properly framed and enforceable?). Although these need not be difficult to understand, they usually are – largely because most leases are drawn up in unnecessarily complicated legal jargon. It is probably best to use a solicitor for a leasehold purchase.

Selling leasehold property (i.e. usually flats). The complications of a leasehold title are of more concern to the buyer than the seller. A fair summary of the position might be to say that you can do your own sale of a lease with a registered title, but not of one with an unregistered title.

Buying a new property (whether a house or a flat). This presents extra complications. For instance, the contract may have to be signed before the property is built, and it is then essential to have properly drafted clauses in the contract as to the quality of the building work, specifications, materials to be used, and the date by which it should be finished. In addition, the purchaser will have to sign the NHBC guarantee agreement (see page 206). Because of these complications, it is generally unwise to act for oneself when buying a new property.

In conclusion, there are several points that must be stressed. Firstly, conveyancing can be very time-consuming and it also takes time and patience to familiarize oneself with the terminology used by the legal profession.

Secondly, those who decide to do their own conveyancing should not rely on just one DIY book; there are several guides available and it is best to have as many as possible, together with access to a comprehensive law book for the occasional technical problem.

Thirdly, bear in mind that all the DIY guides assume that there is a solicitor or licensed conveyancer acting for the other party. It is very unwise to risk doing one's own conveyance if the other person is also acting for himself. If there is a conveyancer on the other side, he is likely to stop the DIY conveyancer from completely messing up his conveyance.

Fourthly, if a defect in title is not noticed when the property is bought it can cause considerable delay when the property is sold, for the purchaser will want the defect corrected.

Finally, no DIY conveyancer should be afraid of going to a conveyancer if difficulties arise. The sums of money involved in property transactions make it foolish to risk thousands of pounds for the sake of a relatively small saving on legal fees.

Cut-price conveyancing firms

In 1984 it was announced that non-solicitors would be allowed to set up as licensed conveyancers. The qualification requirements for licensed conveyancers are very strict and thus it would seem that they will be able to provide a competent and professional service. Time alone will tell whether they are a better buy than solicitors. Already they have had a beneficial effect – the threat of competition has led to many bargain offers on conveyancing and this can only be to the benefit of the consumer. Similarly, the introduction of advertising by solicitors, and their being able to act as estate agents by selling property, is directly attributable to the 'threat' posed by the new licensed conveyancers. In addition, reform and simplification of the conveyancing process is promised, and this should result in further economies when buying and selling property.

But the new licensed conveyancers should not be confused with their predecessors – unlicensed conveyancers. Some (but not all) of these firms offer a competent and competitive service, but it is difficult to see why anyone should bother to use such a firm (and save perhaps a few pounds), now that there is greater competition than there was a few years ago. Generally, the best advice would seem to be to go to a solicitor or a licensed conveyancer (or do it yourself).

15 Leasehold Reform

Converting a long lease into a freehold

The differences between a freehold and leasehold have already been explained (see page 190). The essential difference is that the leaseholder's interest in the property comes to an end when his lease expires and so he may well lose his home.

This harshness of the law has been softened to some extent by the provisions of the Leasehold Reform Act 1967. This allows householders who have long leases to buy the freehold to the house or, alternatively, to obtain a fifty-year extension of their leases. The Act is a complicated piece of law; its provisions are technical and no layman should use them without having taken full legal advice.

The basic requirements of the Act are set out in the chart overleaf. There are three basic points:

1. The Act only applies to houses, not flats. As a policy decision, flats were excluded, but there is now some pressure for the Act to be amended so as to include them. Not surprisingly, disputes have arisen over what is a 'house', but it seems clear that if a property is divided vertically into separate dwellings, then those dwellings will be 'houses' (as with a terrace). However, if the property is divided horizontally, the dwellings will be flats and so outside the 1967 Act.

2. The lease must be a long lease. It must originally have been for more than twenty-one years, even if it now has only a few years left to run. The annual ground rent paid under the lease must be less than two thirds of the rateable value as at 1965; if the ground rent is as much as that, then the house will probably be within the Rent Acts and the leaseholder will probably have little need of Leasehold Reform Act protection. As with the Rent Acts, the Leasehold Reform Act does not apply to luxury dwellings (e.g. if the rateable value in 1965 was over £750, or £1,500 in London).

3. The leaseholder himself, or his family, must have lived in the house for the last three years (or have lived there for a total of three years during the last ten years).

If all these conditions are met, the leaseholder can either buy the freehold (often at a bargain price) or demand that his lease be extended for fifty years. If the leaseholder opts for a fifty-year extension, the ground rent will be set at a modern level (e.g. £50 p.a.), not the level contained in the old lease; in addition, there will be a rent review after twenty-five years. More important, once the original lease has expired the leaseholder cannot later change his mind and decide to buy the freehold

How a tenant may be able to buy the freehold to his house

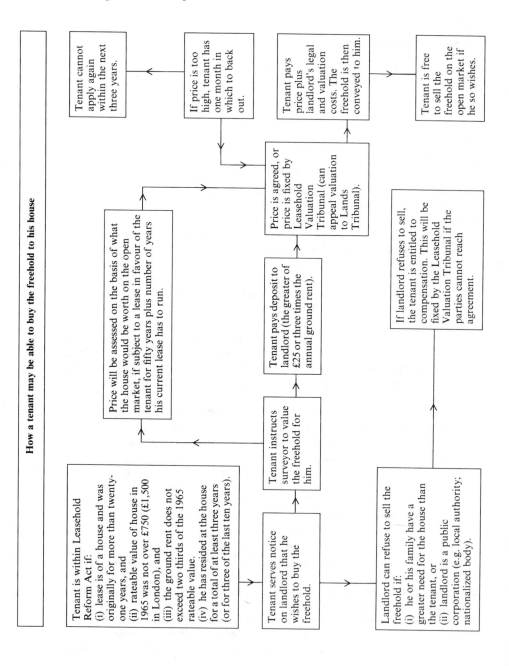

Tenant is within Leasehold Reform Act if:
(i) lease is of a house and was originally for more than twenty-one years, and
(ii) rateable value of house in 1965 was not over £750 (£1,500 in London), and
(iii) the ground rent does not exceed two thirds of the 1965 rateable value.
(iv) he has resided at the house for a total of at least three years (or for three of the last ten years).

Tenant serves notice on landlord that he wishes to buy the freehold.

Landlord can refuse to sell the freehold if:
(i) he or his family have a greater need for the house than the tenant, or
(ii) landlord is a public corporation (e.g. local authority; nationalized body).

Tenant instructs surveyor to value the freehold for him.

Price will be assessed on the basis of what the house would be worth on the open market, if subject to a lease in favour of the tenant for fifty years plus number of years his current lease has to run.

Tenant pays deposit to landlord (the greater of £25 or three times the annual ground rent).

If landlord refuses to sell, the tenant is entitled to compensation. This will be fixed by the Leasehold Valuation Tribunal if the parties cannot reach agreement.

Price is agreed, or price is fixed by Leasehold Valuation Tribunal (can appeal valuation to Lands Tribunal).

If price is too high, tenant has one month in which to back out.

Tenant cannot apply again within the next three years.

Tenant pays price plus landlord's legal and valuation costs. The freehold is then conveyed to him.

Tenant is free to sell the freehold on the open market if he so wishes.

instead; at the end of the fifty-year period the freeholder will be able to recover possession of the house. The fifty-year extension is unlike a Rent Act granting of security from eviction; with the Rent Act the security is personal to the tenant (and his family) but under the Leasehold Reform Act it is not personal. Thus the leaseholder can sell the lease if he wants to.

If the leaseholder qualifies under the Act, there is usually no way the freeholder can deny him his rights, unless the freeholder is a public body and can show that the property will be needed for development within the next ten years. (Even then, though, compensation would have to be paid to the leaseholder.) However, if the freeholder acquired the freehold before February 1966 he may be able to argue that he and his family have a greater need of the house than the leaseholder and his family. In such a case the Lands Tribunal would consider whether greater hardship would be caused to the freeholder by allowing the tenant to exercise his rights under the 1967 Act. Even so, the freeholder would have to pay compensation to the leaseholder. Subject to these limited exceptions, the rule is that the leaseholder can insist on the freehold being sold to him.

The cost

The central issue for the leaseholder will be: 'What price must I pay for the freehold?' Unfortunately, there is no simple answer. Each case has to be looked at individually, and if the parties cannot reach agreement then the Leasehold Valuation Tribunal will assess a fair price. In valuing the freehold, the parties (or the Tribunal) try to decide how much it would be worth with the tenant in occupation but on the assumption that the tenant cannot buy the freehold; this is obviously an artificial calculation and one that the parties will only be able to do with expert advice. Generally, though, it means that the leaseholder gets a good bargain if the lease has only a few years left to run. As an example, if a house is on a lease that has thirty years left to go, and the rent is £5 p.a. but the modern ground rent would be approximately £100 the freehold would probably cost the leaseholder some £175. Generally, the price increases as the lease runs out. On the other hand, leases that have a very long life will go for a nominal amount – for instance, the price to pay for a lease with 950 years unexpired might be £100 or so. (Note: different valuation rules apply to high-value premises.)

Finally, the leaseholder must pay the 'reasonable' costs and expenses of the freeholder. Thus, the leaseholder must budget for paying the price of the freehold, and also the costs of two sets of solicitors (and probably surveyors as well). It may be because of this that surprisingly few leaseholders have taken advantage of their rights under the Act. In fact, it should not be difficult to borrow money for the purchase, since the lender can always take the newly purchased freehold as security for the loan.

The alternative: becoming a Rent Act tenant

The tenant with a long lease may not always be able to take advantage of the Leasehold Reform Act provisions when his lease comes to an end; for instance, if he occupies a flat rather than a house or has not lived in the house for three years.

Some long leaseholders can become Rent Act tenants, and so be safe from eviction. Part 1 of the 1954 Landlord and Tenant Act gives this protection to leaseholders whose original lease was for more than twenty-one years, and whose annual rent is less than two thirds of the March 1965 rateable value of their property. Generally, the Rent Acts do not apply to such tenants (see page 240), but an exception is made for long leasehold tenants on the expiry of their leases. However, the tenancy must otherwise meet all the requirements needed for it to be a *regulated* Rent Act tenancy; see the chart on page 238.

If this provision applies, the leaseholder need not leave on the expiry of his lease. However, on the ending of the lease, the landlord can serve a possession notice on him, and he will be entitled to evict the leaseholder if he can show that one of five situations exists. These grounds for eviction are described in the chart on page 266 as 'alternative accommodation', 'breach of tenancy', 'rent arrears', 'nuisance to neighbours', and 'required for the landlord or his family'. Unless one of these grounds exists, the leaseholder can remain in possession.

The landlord can treat the leaseholder as a *regulated* tenant. He can, therefore, apply to the rent officer for a fair rent to be registered, and this will, of course, be considerably more than the nominal ground rent the leaseholder was previously paying. The grounds for evicting the leaseholder will be those applying to any regulated tenant (see page 260).

16 Renting from a Private Landlord

The Rent Acts are absurdly complicated. As a result this chapter may seem difficult to follow, but do not despair. For most people the rules are relatively straightforward, and a lot of the complexities can be safely ignored. The best way to begin is to skip through to the various summaries and the charts; these set out the basic rules (which probably apply in 99 per cent of cases). Having got an idea of the basics, you can then go back and read the detail.

Whilst nearly everyone has heard of the Rent Acts and knows that they protect tenants from arbitrary eviction and excessive rent levels, few laymen have any idea as to how the Acts operate. This is largely because of their complexity, which has three main causes.

1. The Rent Acts are a twentieth-century innovation which has been super-imposed upon a legal concept of land ownership that dates back to the Middle Ages. Quite simply, the law is a horrendous mixture of new and old, with the old common-law rules being used where necessary to resolve ambiguities in the Acts and to fill in any gaps. In addition, the judiciary have occasionally used the common-law rules to try to avoid the full effects of the Rent Acts when they have felt that the Acts were too radical.
2. Housing, and the extent of tenants' protection, is largely a political issue. Over the decades, different governments have altered the rules, sometimes to increase and sometimes to decrease the protection given to tenants. Each change in the law has been imposed on the then-existing law. Thus, one finds that the laws to be applied will differ depending upon the date a tenancy started. For instance, prior to the Rent Act 1974, greater protection was given to unfurnished tenants than to furnished tenants, but after that Act the vital distinction was between tenants who had landlords resident on the premises and those that did not. But the status quo as at 14 August 1974 (when the Rent Act 1974 was introduced) had to be maintained and so we now have different rules for pre-August-1974 tenants than for post-August-1974 tenants. Similarly, the Rent Acts of 1957 and 1965 introduced new criteria, and so the present legislation is a mixture of some fifty statutes.
3. The Rent Acts have been designed to deal with the landlord who will try to evade the law. The Acts, therefore, assume the lowest common denominator, and

contain detailed anti-avoidance provisions designed to prevent the bad landlord from avoiding his legal obligations.

It is, therefore, impossible to summarize neatly the landlord and tenant laws. The layman who wants to know what the law is must be prepared to wade through a mass of complex detail before he can be sure that he has found the correct answer.

The types of tenancies

An A–Z glossary of the jargon used in the law of landlord and tenant:

assured tenancy. A letting by an 'approved' landlord of property, the building of which started after August 1980. The rent can be at an open-market level – i.e. higher than a *registered rent* under a *full protection tenancy*.

contractual tenancy. A contractual tenancy can be either (a) a *fixed-term tenancy* (e.g. a pre-arranged period of six months that has not yet expired) or (b) a *periodic tenancy* (e.g. by the week, month) that has not been ended by a notice to quit. In both situations, the original contract between landlord and tenant remains in force, not having expired or been ended. So it is called a contractual tenancy.

controlled tenancy. A Rent Act tenancy that started before 1957, with the tenant usually paying an extremely low rent. Abolished in 1981, when they became *regulated tenancies*, allowing the landlord to register a higher rent.

fixed-term tenancy. The tenancy is for a pre-arranged period (e.g. a year). Neither landlord nor tenant can unilaterally end the agreement before that date. When it expires the tenant can remain in possession as a *statutory tenant*.

full protection tenancy. A *protected tenancy* with the tenant being able to register the rent and being protected from eviction except on strictly controlled grounds.

licence. A person who has a licence may not have a tenancy, in which case he will have little protection from eviction (being treated in the same way as a tenant with a resident landlord).

periodic tenancy. The tenancy is of undetermined length, not being for a fixed term. Instead the tenant pays rent periodically (e.g. monthly, weekly) and so it is, for example, a monthly, or weekly, periodic tenancy.

protected tenancy. A tenancy that has full protection, being either a *regulated tenancy* or a *shorthold tenancy*.

regulated tenancy. This is a type of *full protection tenancy* with the tenant being able to register the rent and also being fully protected from eviction.

restricted contracts. Another name for a *restricted protection tenancy*.

restricted protection tenancy. A *restricted tenancy*. The tenant is able to register the rent but the landlord can easily obtain an eviction order.

restricted tenancy. The tenant has restricted protection (mainly tenants with resident landlords).

secure tenancy. A tenancy of a council or housing-association property (also included is a tenancy from a New Town Commission, development corporation, housing corporation or charitable housing trust). The tenant can only be evicted on strictly controlled grounds.

service occupancy. The landlord is the tenant's employer and the tenant lives in the property because he has to in order to carry out his job or because his employment requires him to. The landlord can easily obtain an eviction order when the job ends. (Note: agricultural workers are given special protection.)

shorthold tenancy. A *protected tenancy* where the property is let for a fixed period of from one to five years, although the tenant can end the tenancy earlier if he wishes. The landlord must have given notice to the tenant that he could easily evict the tenant at the end of the fixed term. In Greater London only, the rent must have been registered at the start of the letting.

statutory tenancy. The *contractual tenancy* has been ended because either (a) the pre-arranged fixed term has expired or (b) a *periodic tenancy* (e.g. weekly, monthly) has been ended by the expiry of a landlord's notice to quit. The tenant can continue in occupation. The Rent Act will give him the right to stay there and so he is said to have a statutory tenancy.

When considering any landlord-and-tenant question, the way to approach it is to ask:
1. **Do the Rent Acts apply? (See page 237.)**
2. **If the Rent Acts do apply, is it a case of 'full protection' or 'restricted protection', since different rules apply to each? (See page 241.)**

1. Do the Rent Acts apply?

The basic rule is that most people who rent private residential premises are within the Rent Acts. But for most purposes it suffices to know that the typical residential tenant is within the Rent Acts.

The chart overleaf, 'Is a tenancy within the Rent Acts or not?', contains a check-list of questions for working out whether the Rent Acts apply. Once again, the details are complicated, but bear in mind that virtually all residential tenants are within the Rent Acts. Particular problems to watch out for are:

Running a business from home

The tenant who uses his home for business purposes may find that he has taken himself out of the Rent Acts. This is because the Rent Acts aim to protect people's homes, not their businesses. For instance:

A tenant conducted an import business from his flat, although he used a local Post Office box number as his business address. Held: The business use was a significant part of the occupation and so the tenant was outside the Rent Acts. Cheryl Investments (1978)

The tenant was chairman of the Turkish Cypriot organization in London. He had no other job,

237

Is a tenancy within the Rent Acts or not?

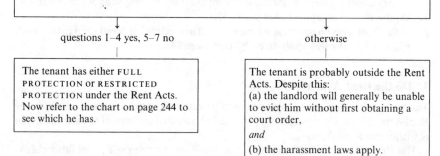

Can *all* these questions be answered 'yes'?

1. *The home:* is it a tenancy of a residential dwelling (e.g. flat, house, bed-sit, as opposed to a hotel room, hostel, office)?

2. *Exclusive possession:* is there exclusive possession of at least part of the property – even if it is only one room?

3. *The rateable value:* was the rateable value of tenant's part of the property, in April 1973, less than £750 (£1,500 if in Greater London)?

4. *The rent:* is the rent at least two thirds of the March 1965 rateable value of the tenant's part of the property?

Can *all* the following questions be answered 'no'?

5. *Holiday lets:* is it a holiday let (see page 239).

6. *Board:* is the tenant provided with substantial board (e.g. full meals each day) (see page 246)?

7. *The tenant's job:* is the tenancy an essential part of the job?

questions 1–4 yes, 5–7 no	otherwise

The tenant has either FULL PROTECTION or RESTRICTED PROTECTION under the Rent Acts. Now refer to the chart on page 244 to see which he has.	The tenant is probably outside the Rent Acts. Despite this: (a) the landlord will generally be unable to evict him without first obtaining a court order, *and* (b) the harassment laws apply.

SUMMARY: The basic rule is that a tenant of a flat or house is within the Rent Acts and so has protection from eviction and from excessive rents.

and there were regular meetings of the ten-man executive in the flat. He received about fifteen letters a day there. Held: He was outside the Rent Acts since he was no longer using the flat for normal residential and domestic activities. Florent (1983)

Compare:

An elderly lady took lodgers into her home. The landlord argued that this was a business and so she was not protected by the Rent Acts. In reply, she pointed out that she made a very small profit and so it could not be a business. Held: The tenant must be engaged in commercial activities to be outside the Rent Acts, and the degree of profit involved here was so small that it could not fairly be called a business. But if she had been making a good profit from her lodgers she would probably have lost her Rent Act protection. Lewis (1978)

A tenant should therefore be careful not to take too much work home. If he converts a room into an office and conducts some of his business from that office (e.g. receives visitors, makes phone calls), he might be held to be outside the Rent Acts. If he is held to be carrying on a business and so not Rent Act protected he will generally have some protection from eviction under the business tenancies legislation (see page 607), unless his lease prohibited any business use, in which case he could probably not even claim business tenancy protection.

Company lets

A company cannot have a 'residence'. So, any letting to a company must be outside the Rents Acts (since the company cannot claim to be using the property as a residence). This will be so even if the company allows its directors or employees to live there. This explains why so many adverts for flats say 'company lets only' – the landlord knows he can let the flat and be sure to recover possession at the end of the lease. Note that whilst the Rent Act rules on security of tenure (i.e. the right to stay on at the end of the lease) do not apply to company lets, the rent-restriction rules (see page 250) do apply. So if a company is charged more than the registered rent it can refuse to pay the excess and it can sue for return of the over-payments (see page 256).

Holiday lets

Genuine holiday lets are always outside the Rent Acts. The holiday-maker can never acquire Rent Act protection. Some disreputable landlords have tried to use this provision to avoid the Rent Acts by calling their lettings 'holiday lets'. Such devices are usually doomed to failure; the Rent Acts are only avoided if it is a *genuine* holiday let. Thus, it must have been intended by both landlord and tenant that it be a holiday let and not a normal residential letting dressed up as a holiday let. If the landlord knew that the property would be the tenant's main residence he may well find it difficult to convince a court that it was a genuine holiday let. For instance:

Four single people rented a flat together in West London. They signed what was called a holiday agreement, lasting three months. At the end of the three months the landlord applied for an eviction order against the tenants but they claimed that it was not a genuine holiday letting and so they were entitled to the protection of the Rent Acts. Held: It was not a genuine holiday let. The court pointed out that West London was not noted as a holiday area, that the tenants all lived and worked in London and had no other home, and it was held that there had never been a joint intention by both landlord and tenants that the accommodation would only be used for holiday purposes. Kemp (1975)

Holiday homes that are let out of season (i.e. not holiday lets) are within the Rent Acts but there are special provisions; if the letting was for no more than eight months and the tenant was warned that possession would be required, the court must make a possession order (see page 267 for details).

Some student lettings

Lettings to students are not necessarily outside the Rent Acts. However, an exception is made for certain specified educational institutions (e.g. universities, polytechnics). Lettings by such bodies are outside the Rent Acts. Thus, a student in a college hall of residence cannot claim that his tenancy has Rent Act protection. It must be stressed that other lettings to students come within the Rent Acts in the normal way.

Low-rent lettings

If the rent is less than two thirds of the rateable value of the property when it was let then the letting will be outside the Rent Acts. This is designed to exclude owners of properties on long leases who pay a small ground rent to the landlord. Service and maintenance charges are generally ignored when assessing the amount of the rent.

Licences

Many landlords used to (and some still do) grant licences rather than tenancies. Their aim was to avoid the full rigours of the Rent Acts, since a licensee (i.e. a person with a licence) was not thought to have full Rent Act protection. But a 1985 case made it clear that this dodge would not work, and so virtually all licensees do, in fact, have tenancies – and Rent Act protection. See page 278.

Some people still have licence agreements (e.g. they may have signed them before the 1985 case was decided; their landlord may still think – wrongly – that the licence dodge will work). Despite the fact that those written agreements call themselves licences, they are not licences – and the 'licensees' have Rent Act protection. The only occasion when a licence may indeed be upheld as a licence (in which case there would be no Rent Act protection) is if the person is really a lodger – a person who receives meals, cleaning, etc.

To summarize:

1. The licence dodge does not work.
2. The courts will treat a licensee as a Rent Act tenant – unless he is no more than a lodger.

2. If the Rent Acts do apply, is it a case of full protection or restricted protection?

There are different categories of Rent Act tenants. Once it is clear that the tenancy is within the Rent Acts, it is necessary to see what category of protection applies. There are two main categories: full protection and restricted protection. As one would expect, tenants with restricted protection have fewer legal rights than those with full protection.

The chart on page 244 gives a check-list for working out whether a Rent Act tenant has full protection or restricted protection. As always, the rules are complicated but it is normally enough to know that:

– **If the tenancy started after 13 August 1974** the tenant will have full protection unless his landlord lives in the same house (i.e. he is a resident landlord) or unless it is a shorthold letting (i.e. fixed term, in which it has always been agreed that the tenant will have to leave at the end of the lease).

– **If the tenancy started before 14 August 1974** the position is more complicated, but the basic rule is that if the property was unfurnished then the tenant will have full protection. If it was furnished, he will have full protection unless the landlord has been resident on the premises since 14 August 1974.

– **if he has a valid licence** (but this is unlikely – see page 278) he will have restricted protection only (and be treated in the same way as a person with a resident landlord).

In short, the general rule is that the tenant will have full Rent Act protection unless he has a resident landlord or unless he has a valid licence (in which case he will only have restricted Rent Act protection). Additional factors that can cause the tenant to lose full protection and have only restricted protection are:
• if the landlord shares some of the tenant's living accommodation;
• if the landlord provides certain types of services.

What is a resident landlord?

The crucial question is usually: Is there a resident landlord?' If so, the tenant is likely to have only restricted protection.

A landlord will be resident if he uses part of the building as a residence – even if it is not his only residence. The important point to grasp is that the landlord need not be resident in the same part of the building as the tenant; he can still be a resident landlord if he occupies a separate flat in the building. Only if the building is a purpose-built block of flats will this not be so. If the building is not purpose-built flats (for instance, it is divided into flats but the conversion was done after the building was constructed as a single dwelling) then the landlord is a resident landlord even if his flat is on a different floor from the tenant's and even if they have separate entrances. This is so even if the property was converted into flats some decades ago – or even in the last century!

A large Victorian house was divided into flats in 1959. In 1979 (i.e. twenty years later) Ms Barnes took a tenancy of one of the flats. The landlord lived in one of the other flats in the building. Did she have a resident landlord or not? She pointed out that the conversion work had been done twenty years ago and that she did not live in the same flat as the landlord. Held: She had a resident landlord. The house had not originally been built as flats and so it was not a purpose-built block of flats – and thus her landlord was resident. Barnes (1982)

So a resident landlord need not share any of the premises with the tenant although often, of course, he will do so.

Difficulties have arisen with landlords who have kept a room in each of their several properties and then claimed to be resident in each. However, the courts have made it clear that such a dodge will not work. The landlord must have a genuine intention to use the room(s) as a home, and not just as a device for denying the tenant full protection. It is possible for the landlord to have more than one home if he can show a genuine intention to live in each home, and if he leaves signs of his continuing occupation in each (for instance, furniture, family). However, the courts are sceptical of claims by landlords that they have more than one home. Few such claims are upheld and the few that are tend to be cases in which the landlord's wife occupies the other premises for him.

A company has no natural life and so it cannot 'reside' somewhere. Thus, if a tenant's landlord is a company, the tenant can be sure that he does not have a resident landlord and accordingly the tenant knows that he has full protection rather than restricted protection.

For a resident landlord to deny full protection to a tenant, the landlord must have been resident not only at the start of the tenancy, but also ever since. Alternatively, if the resident landlord bought the house subject to the tenancy, then the person who sold to him must also have been a resident landlord. The resident landlord status can be transferred from one resident landlord to another, but a landlord cannot buy a house in which there is a tenant with full protection and then move into the house and claim to be a resident landlord; in such a case, the tenant retains his full protection.

If a tenant has joint landlords (e.g. two brothers own a property jointly), but only one is resident, then he will still have a resident landlord (i.e. there is no need for both the landlords to be resident).

When the resident landlord sells

If a resident landlord sells the house, the new owner has twenty-eight days in which either to move in or to serve a notice on the tenant that he intends to use the house as his home and so will be a resident landlord, as was his predecessor. The new owner then has an additional six months in which to move in; if he does not move in within that time, the resident-landlord status will be lost and the tenant will have full protection, not restricted protection. Thus there could be up to seven months' delay without the new owner losing resident-landlord status.

When the resident landlord dies

If a resident landlord dies, his part of the house can remain unoccupied for up to two years before the resident-landlord status is lost. If the executors do not sell to a new landlord who moves in within that twenty-four-month period, the tenant will be entitled to full protection and not restricted protection.

The executors can evict the tenant or they can sell with the tenant in occupation:
- evicting the tenant: if a resident landlord dies, the executors have two years in which to serve a Notice to Quit on the tenant. The possession proceedings (see page 258) will be heard as though the tenant still had a resident landlord – i.e. possession will normally be granted (see page 271).
- selling the house: if the executors sell within two years of the landlord's death, the purchaser will take the house subject to the tenancy, but if he takes up residence at the property he can claim to be a resident landlord (as above).

Losing resident-landlord status

The landlord will lose his resident-landlord status if he moves out of the premises, or if he buys another property and no longer regards the original premises as his home.

When the landlord and tenant share living accommodation

If the tenant shares some of the living accommodation with his landlord, he will automatically have restricted protection, not full protection.

This is a different rule from that on resident landlords, for a landlord can be a resident landlord and yet not share any living accommodation with the tenant. If the landlord does share living accommodation then he will obviously also be a resident landlord.

Living accommodation does not include a bathroom or a lavatory. A kitchen will usually be living accommodation, even if it is only used for cooking and not eating. The question here is whether the accommodation is shared with the *landlord*; the mere fact that a tenant shares accommodation with other *tenants* will not affect the position.

When the landlord provides services

Services are generally of three types: furniture, attendances, and board.

Furniture

Until 1974 the question of whether the landlord provided furniture was basic in deciding whether a tenant had full protection or restricted protection. The rule was that unfurnished tenancies had full protection, and furnished tenancies had restricted

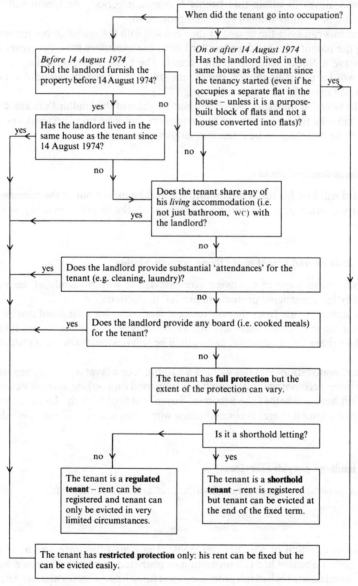

Full protection or restricted protection?

You should only refer to this chart after using the chart on page 238 to check that the tenancy is within the Rent Acts. This chart will show how much protection the tenant has.

When did the tenant go into occupation?

Before 14 August 1974
Did the landlord furnish the property before 14 August 1974?

On or after 14 August 1974
Has the landlord lived in the same house as the tenant since the tenancy started (even if he occupies a separate flat in the house – unless it is a purpose-built block of flats and not a house converted into flats)?

yes

Has the landlord lived in the same house as the tenant since 14 August 1974?

Does the tenant share any of his *living* accommodation (i.e. not just bathroom, wc) with the landlord?

Does the landlord provide substantial 'attendances' for the tenant (e.g. cleaning, laundry)?

Does the landlord provide any board (i.e. cooked meals) for the tenant?

The tenant has **full protection** but the extent of the protection can vary.

Is it a shorthold letting?

The tenant is a **regulated tenant** – rent can be registered and tenant can only be evicted in very limited circumstances.

The tenant is a **shorthold tenant** – rent is registered but tenant can be evicted at the end of the fixed term.

The tenant has **restricted protection** only: his rent can be fixed but he can be evicted easily.

Summary: the basic rule is that a tenant has full protection unless he has a resident landlord.

protection. The importance of that distinction was largely abolished when the Rent Act 1974 introduced the rule that tenants with resident landlords have restricted protection, and most other tenants have full protection.

But what of the tenant who in 1974 had an unfurnished tenancy (full protection) with a resident landlord (at that time, not a relevant factor)? Would the tenant lose full-protection status and change to restricted protection because of the new 'resident landlord' criteria? It was decided that this would be unfair and that the status quo should be maintained. Thus, the tenant with an unfurnished tenancy that started before 14 August 1974 will have full protection even if he has a resident landlord. If the tenancy was furnished the tenant will now have full protection (whereas previously he had restricted protection) unless his landlord has been resident since 14 August 1974. Such are the complexities caused when a new Rent Act is passed!

Occasionally, therefore, it will still be important to know whether a tenancy is furnished or unfurnished, for the pre-August-1974 unfurnished tenant can have full protection even if he has a resident landlord (but not, of course, if he shares living accommodation with the landlord, see above). To decide whether the tenancy is furnished or unfurnished, one must work out whether the rent for the furniture forms a *substantial* part of the total rent. The calculation generally involves three steps:

1. What was the value of the furniture at the start of the tenancy to the tenant? Usually, this will be its second-hand value but if it was worth more/less to that particular tenant then that should be reflected in the figure assessed.
2. What is 20 per cent of that figure?
3. What percentage of the total annual rent is the 20 per cent figure? If it is less than 10 per cent it will probably not be a 'substantial' amount and so the premises will be regarded as unfurnished. Over 20 per cent will probably be substantial, and so the premises will be treated as furnished. Between 10 and 20 per cent it is a matter of argument.

Attendances

These are personal services provided for the tenant by the landlord or his representative. They must be personal to the tenant; thus, cleaning of communal stairs or rooms would not count. But cleaning of the tenant's room or provision of laundry would be attendances.

If the landlord provides *substantial* attendances then the tenant has restricted protection. If the value of the attendances to the *tenant* are not a *substantial* part of the total rent, the tenant has full protection – unless, of course, he has a resident landlord, which is very likely, in which case he will have restricted protection. The difficulty, of course, lies in deciding what is substantial. In practice, the courts try to adapt the test used when deciding whether a substantial amount of furniture is provided (see above).

The reason for the distinction is that Rent Act full protection is not designed for occupiers of hotel rooms and hostels.

Housing: Tenants

Board

A tenant has board if he has at least one cooked meal each day. If the landlord provides *substantial* board (e.g. as in bed-and-breakfast accommodation) the tenant is completely outside the Rent Acts (see chart on page 238). If a small amount of board is provided the tenant will only have restricted protection, for the tenant who has board is never entitled to full protection. On the other hand, if the amount of board is trivial (e.g. a cup of tea) then it can be ignored and the tenant will still have full protection. For instance, some landlords try to exploit this potential loophole by providing a very nominal amount of board (e.g. a packet of cornflakes and a can of dried milk; a tin of baked beans each day). Usually, the courts take a fairly tough line on such tactics and will decide that this is not enough to amount to 'board' (although not all county-court judges are that sympathetic to tenants, so one does occasionally come across such arrangements being upheld). The difficulties arise when more than a trivial amount is supplied and one then has to decide whether it forms a 'substantial' part of the rent or not. Usually, the courts try to adapt the test used in furniture cases – see above.

A further problem is that if the tenant tries to get the rent registered (see page 254), the rent officer may decide that he is not prepared to become involved in the argument as to whether or not there is board provided – in which case he may refuse to register the rent. The tenant is then in a difficult position; at that stage it is best to seek legal advice (with a view to applying to the court for a declaration that the tenant does not receive board and thus has full Rent Act protection).

Shorthold tenancies

Most full-protection tenants have:
● the right to have a fair *rent* registered for the property. This then becomes the maximum rent they can be charged, *and*
● the right not to be *evicted* unless they misbehave (or unless certain narrowly defined situations exist).
These are the rights of a *regulated* full-protection tenant.

However, the Housing Act 1980 complicated the position by introducing a new type of full-protection tenancy, but one that gives less protection to the tenant. This is called a *shorthold* tenancy. This is a fixed-term letting of between one and five years, but the tenant has no protection from eviction at the end of the term. The landlord can always get an eviction order from the court at the end of the fixed term (or afterwards) and need not rely on the normal grounds for possession.

When shorthold tenancies were introduced, the rule was that the rent had to be registered from start to finish of the letting. But, that rule was altered and it is now only lettings in Greater London that need to have a registered rent.

A tenancy will only be *shorthold* if:
1. It started after 27 November 1980.
2. The letting was for a fixed period of one to five years.

3. The landlord gave written notice to the tenant that it was a shorthold tenancy. This must have been done on an approved form, and the notice must have been given to the tenant before the agreement was made – not afterwards.
4. If the property is in Greater London, then the rent must have been registered at the start of the letting.
5. The tenant was not already a *regulated* full-protection tenant of the landlord. The aim of this rule is to prevent a landlord from tricking a *regulated* full-protection tenant into signing a new *shorthold* agreement, so forfeiting his protection from eviction.

The general principle is that if any of the above requirements are not met, then the tenancy will not be a *shorthold* tenancy – it will be a *regulated* tenancy, with the tenant thus having full rent protection and also full protection from eviction. He will therefore not have to leave when the fixed term ends. But the Housing Act 1980 gives the county court a discretion to waive conditions 3 and 4 above, if it thinks it would be 'just and equitable to do so'.

To sum up. In Greater London, the landlord can trade off the disadvantage of having a fair rent registered against the certainty that he can recover possession. Outside Greater London he need not even register the rent. In those cases, the effect is that a fixed-term tenancy of between one and five years can be entered into with the landlord knowing he can get possession at the end of the period.

Controlled tenancies

Prior to 1981 there used to be a special category of full-protection tenant, called controlled tenants. These were tenants holding under a tenancy that had started before 1957. Generally, they paid extremely low rents. In 1981 controlled tenancies were abolished and turned into regulated tenancies (i.e. full protection).

To summarize: a Rent Act tenancy can have either FULL PROTECTION or RE-STRICTED PROTECTION. If it has full protection it will be either a regulated tenancy or a shorthold tenancy.

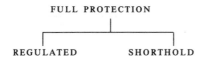

FULL PROTECTION

REGULATED   SHORTHOLD

RESTRICTED PROTECTION
(mainly licensees and tenants
with resident landlords)

**Summary of the Differences between Tenancies with Full Protection
and with Restricted Protection**

Rent

FULL PROTECTION

IF A REGULATED TENANCY, the rent can be registered by the rent officer, and will then be the maximum rent that any tenant can be charged – despite any agreement to the contrary (page 250).

IF A SHORTHOLD TENANCY in Greater London the rent must have been registered by the rent officer when the tenancy began and that will then be the maximum rent that can be charged (see page 246). Outside London the rent need not be registered.

RESTRICTED PROTECTION

The rent can be registered by the rent tribunal and that will then be the maximum rent that any tenant can be charged – despite any agreement to the contrary (see page 256).

Eviction

FULL PROTECTION

IF A REGULATED TENANCY, the court will only order the tenant's eviction in a few clearly defined circumstances. Usually, this means that the tenant with a regulated tenancy has long-term security from eviction (see page 260).

IF A SHORTHOLD TENANCY the tenant has full protection from eviction until the fixed-term agreement (one to five years) expires. Then the landlord can start possession proceedings and the court is bound to make an eviction order (see page 264).

RESTRICTED PROTECTION

The tenant (or licensee) has little security of tenure. When possession proceedings are commenced, the court can postpone the eviction for some months, but it has no power to postpone the eviction for a long period. This is so even if he is a 'good' tenant (see page 271).

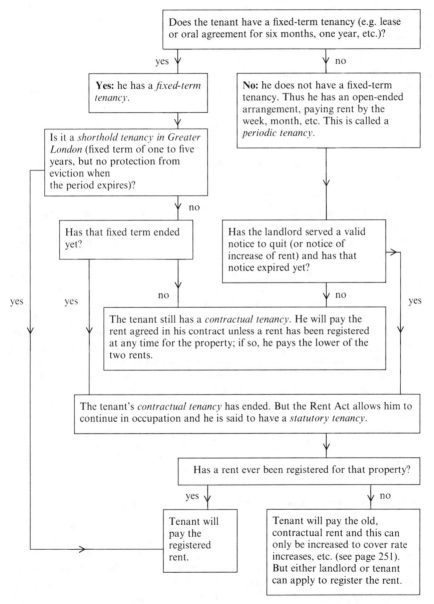

Rent control

This chart shows how to work out the maximum rent. It applies to all Rent Act tenants.

Does the tenant have a fixed-term tenancy (e.g. lease or oral agreement for six months, one year, etc.)?

yes

Yes: he has a *fixed-term tenancy.*

no

No: he does not have a fixed-term tenancy. Thus he has an open-ended arrangement, paying rent by the week, month, etc. This is called a *periodic tenancy.*

Is it a *shorthold tenancy in Greater London* (fixed term of one to five years, but no protection from eviction when the period expires)?

no

Has that fixed term ended yet?

Has the landlord served a valid notice to quit (or notice of increase of rent) and has that notice expired yet?

yes   yes   no   no   yes

The tenant still has a *contractual tenancy.* He will pay the rent agreed in his contract unless a rent has been registered at any time for the property; if so, he pays the lower of the two rents.

The tenant's *contractual tenancy* has ended. But the Rent Act allows him to continue in occupation and he is said to have a *statutory tenancy.*

Has a rent ever been registered for that property?

yes

Tenant will pay the registered rent.

no

Tenant will pay the old, contractual rent and this can only be increased to cover rate increases, etc. (see page 251). But either landlord or tenant can apply to register the rent.

Summary: the basic rule is that a tenant does not have to pay more than the registered rent.

RENT CONTROL

Summary: Any Rent Act tenant can apply to have the rent for his property registered. Once the rent is registered, that will be the maximum amount that the landlord can charge. So a tenant who is paying more (e.g. under a lease) can then instead pay the lower registered amount.

The basic rules are therefore straightforward. Unfortunately, as is usually the case with the Rent Acts, there are different detailed rules for the two different categories of tenants: (1) those with *full protection*; and (2) those with *restricted protection* (usually, because they have a resident landlord).

Rent control: tenants with full protection

Tenants with full protection can be either *regulated* tenants or *shorthold* tenants (see above).

For a tenant with full protection:

A fair rent can be registered by the rent officer and that will then be the maximum rent that can be charged despite any agreement to the contrary. If a fair rent has not been registered, the tenant will pay according to the terms of his present (or past) contract.

That is the basic position. With a *shorthold tenancy in Greater London*, the rent must have been registered when the tenancy began; otherwise it cannot be a shorthold tenancy. That registered rent will then be the maximum rent that can be charged. That rent cannot be increased unless the registered rent is increased, and an application to re-register can only be made at intervals of not less than two years.

With a *regulated* tenancy, the rent need not be registered. However, either landlord or tenant can apply for the rent to be registered at any time, if he so wishes. With a regulated tenancy, the rent to be paid will not only depend upon whether a fair rent has been registered with the rent office, but also whether there is still an existing contract between the landlord and the tenant. Deciding whether there is still a valid contract between the parties is not just important in determining the rent of regulated tenants, for it comes up again and again when applying the Rent Acts; in particular, it can be of vital importance when considering whether a tenant is liable to be evicted.

When is there a contract between the landlord and the tenant?

If a landlord agrees to let premises to a tenant for a fixed term (e.g. for one year) then the landlord and tenant will have entered into a contract for that period of time. Thus, the tenant is said to have a *contractual tenancy*. When the contract expires at the end of the year (or whatever period the contract was for) the *contractual tenancy* ends. But the Rent Acts allow the tenant to stay on in occupation beyond the end of the contractual tenancy. The tenancy is then called a *statutory tenancy* (since it is derived from a statute, the Rent Act). In short, the statutory tenancy starts when the contractual tenancy ends.

The contract between the landlord and tenant can be either for a fixed term (e.g. six months, one year) or for an open-ended, undetermined period with the tenant paying his rent every week or month, etc. The former is called a *fixed-term tenancy*; the latter, a *periodic tenancy*. Both are *contractual tenancies*. The fixed-term contractual tenancy ends when the fixed term expires, whereas the periodic contractual tenancy usually ends when the landlord gives the tenant notice to quit and that expires (see page 261).

The regulated tenant's rent when there is still a contract

When there is still a contractual tenancy the regulated tenant will pay the rent agreed in his contract (i.e. in the lease or verbal agreement). But, as we have already seen, if there is a 'fair rent' registered for the property, that is the maximum rent that can be charged. Thus, the tenant will pay the registered rent if it is lower than the contractual rent, but if the registered rent is higher he will pay the contractual rent. In short, he will pay whichever is the lower of the registered rent and the contractual rent.

The regulated tenant's rent when the contract has ended

When the contractual tenancy has ended, the amount of rent to be paid will depend upon whether a 'fair rent' has been registered for the property.

If no fair rent has been registered the tenant will pay the same amount as under his old contract, although he may be liable to bear increases in the rates and part of the cost of improvements, etc. (see below).

If a fair rent has been registered that will be the maximum rent and if it is higher than the old contractual rent the landlord can increase the tenant's rent up to the registered amount (but a notice of increase will be needed, and the increase will have to be phased; see below).

This is shown diagrammatically in the chart on page 249.

Finding out if there is a registered rent

The rent officer (address in telephone book) keeps a register of all rents that have been registered. He will usually state on the telephone whether there is a registered rent for a particular property. The tenant should check that the registered rent is binding – in particular, is he renting the same number of rooms and are the rooms furnished when perhaps the registration was for unfurnished property?

Increases for rates, improvements, and services: when can they be passed on to the tenant?

To understand this section, you must first read 'When is There a Contract between the Landlord and the Tenant?' on page 250.

251

Rates

When there is still a contract. No increase unless the contract specifically permits it.
When the contract has ended.

    (a) If no fair rent has been registered, the landlord can pass any rate increase on to the tenant (but a notice of increase will be needed, and this can only be back-dated by six weeks; phasing does not apply; see below).

    (b) If a fair rent has been registered, the landlord can pass any rate increase on to the tenant (no notice of increase needed; phasing does not apply).

Services and furniture

When there is still a contract. No increase unless the contract specifically permits it.
When the contract has ended.

    (a) If no fair rent has been registered, the landlord can pass on any increased cost (no notice of increase needed; phasing does not apply; see below).

    (b) If a fair rent has been registered, no increase *unless* the rent register specifically permits it.

Improvements

When there is still a contract. No increase unless the contract specifically permits it.
When the contract has ended.

    (a) If no fair rent has been registered, the landlord cannot pass on any increase to the tenant, unless the expired contract would have allowed him to. The landlord's remedy is to apply for a fair rent to be registered.

    (b) If a fair rent has been registered, the landlord cannot pass on the increase. He should ask for the registered figure to be reassessed in the light of the improvements.

Note: generally the landlord must obtain the tenant's consent before he can improve the property; see page 300.

Repairs

The cost can never be passed on to the tenant if it was the landlord's duty to carry out the repairs (see Chapter 18).

Phasing of rent increases

If a regulated tenant's rent is being increased, the new rent level must normally be phased in over a two-year period. The rule is that the landlord can increase the rent by up to one half of the increase each year.

Illustration. *A tenant's rent is registered at £6 p.w. The rent officer re-registers it at £10.50 p.w. The landlord can increase the rent:*

year one (i.e. immediately) – to £8.25 p.w.
year two (i.e. one year later) – to £10.50 p.w.

Phasing applies only to increases in rent; it does not apply to increases for services which are included in the rent.

Illustration. A tenant's rent is registered at £20 p.w. inclusive of £4 p.w. for services. The rent officer registered the rent at £30 p.w. inclusive of £6 p.w. for services. The increase in services (£2 per week) can be charged immediately, but the rent increase (£8 per week) must be phased:

year one (i.e. immediately) – to £26 p.w. (£20 + £6)
year two (i.e. one year later) – to £30 p.w. (£24 + £6)

Illustration. A tenant's rent is registered at £10 p.w. plus £3 p.w. for services, and he also pays rates of £2 p.w., making a total of £15 p.w. The registered rent is increased to £13 p.w. plus £5 p.w. for services, and his rates are increased to £5 p.w. In year one (i.e. immediately) he will pay one half of the rent increase (i.e. £1.50), all of the service increase, and all of the rate increase (i.e. a total of £21.50).

Before a rent increase can be phased, the tenant must first have been served with a notice of increase.

Notice of increase of rent

A landlord will often need to serve a formal notice of increase on the tenant before he can charge increased rent (and rates). The rules are ridiculously complicated, but a notice will be needed if:
– the landlord wants to increase the rent (either on the end of the contractual tenancy, or because a new registered rent has been fixed);
– the landlord wants to pass on a rates increase to the tenant (but no notice of increase is needed if the rent is registered).

Because the rules are so complicated it is best to get advice on whether or not a notice of increase is needed. If a notice is needed, it must be in the correct form laid down by Parliament (copies can be obtained from major stationers). If it does not use the correct wording, the tenant can probably ignore it (or sue to recover his overpayments).

The tenant had a lease of a flat. The lease said that she was to bear any increases in rates. The lease ended and she paid the increased rates when the landlord asked for them. Later she got into arrears and the landlord started possession proceedings. The tenant countered this by pointing out that the demands for the increased rates should have been in the proper Notice of Increase form. The landlord said the tenant had waived this mistake by paying the rates – it was no more than an oversight. Held: The tenant could recover the overpayments. Proper notices should have been served. Aristocrat Property (1982)

Pre-printed forms can be purchased from the larger stationery shops. (See also 'A Typical Notice to Quit', page 262.)

What if the tenant will agree to a rent increase?

Often a tenant will informally agree to pay a higher rent. However, an informal agreement will generally not be binding. The Rent Act lays down procedures that must be followed:

• *if there is no fair rent registered*: if the tenant will agree to a rent increase, this should be recorded in a 'rent agreement'. This must be signed by both tenant and landlord, and it must remind the tenant of his legal rights. If these formalities are not complied with, the tenant can refuse to pay the increase and continue to pay the original rent. Moreover, he can sue the landlord for up to one year's excess rent.

• *if there is a fair rent registered*: the new rent should be registered as the fair rent. Landlord and tenant can make a joint application to the rent officer for this registration. If this is not done, and the tenant pays the increased rent, he can back out of the agreement and only pay the original registered rent. In addition, he can sue the landlord for up to two years' excess rent.

In practice, relatively few landlords and tenants know of these provisions, and many tenants do not realize that informally agreed rent increases are not binding. It is yet another example of the unnecessary complexities of the Rent Acts. Why on earth can't they be overhauled!

Registering a 'fair rent'

The landlord, tenant, or local authority can apply to the rent officer for a fair rent to be determined and then registered. Once registered, the fair rent cannot be questioned or reviewed for at least two years, unless there has been such a change of circumstances that it can no longer be regarded as a fair rent (e.g. the condition of the property has changed). The registration will outlast the tenancy during which it was registered, and will apply to all subsequent tenants until there is a fresh registration. For instance, a rent registered in 1970 will be the maximum rent that can be charged in 1987 unless a new rent is registered in the meantime or unless the landlord had the registration vacated while the property is empty (see page 255).

The registration procedure is informal. If the landlord and tenant cannot agree a 'fair rent' the rent officer will inspect the premises and then hold an informal hearing at which both sides are free to put forward their arguments.

In deciding a fair rent, the rent officer will obviously consider the age, character, and location of the property. But he will ignore the financial status of the landlord and of the tenant, and in addition he will ignore any improvements that the tenant himself has made to the property (and conversely, any damage done by the tenant will be ignored – he pays rent on its original, undamaged condition). However, most important of all, the rent officer will assume that there is no housing shortage, and so he will ignore the scarcity-value of the accommodation. If – as is usually the case – demand for rented property exceeds the supply, the result will be that the fair rent is artificially low (some say an average of 20 per cent lower). The justification for this is, of course, that Parliament wants landlords to have a fair return from their properties, but it does not want them to be able to exploit the housing shortage by charging scarcity rents.

The rent officer will want to hear evidence of the registered fair rents for comparable properties in the same neighbourhood. Anyone attending a rent officer hearing should previously inspect the rent officer's register of rents – which is open to the public (see page 251) – and try to find registered rents for similar flats and/or houses. The floor area, condition, and location of the properties should be as similar as possible. The date of a comparable registration should also be noted; inflation may have made the comparison valueless. Remember that registered rents are always exclusive of rates, so a tenant whose rent includes rates should always deduct the rates when comparing his present rent level with those in the rent officer's register.

Once the rent officer has decided what is a fair rent, the landlord and tenant both have twenty-eight days in which to appeal to the Rent Assessment Committee if dissatisfied. The committee will examine the registration anew; generally, the committee allow higher rents (10 per cent or so, on average) than rent officers, so tenants are rarely advised to appeal.

There is a specimen rent-registration certificate on page 907.

When does the registered rent take effect?

If the registered rent is *higher* than the rent the tenant had been paying, the landlord cannot backdate the new rent. The higher rent only applies from the next date when the rent is due after the date of the rent officer's decision. In addition, the landlord will have to serve a notice of increase on the tenant, although this can be backdated by up to four weeks. The increase in rent will have to be phased.

Illustration. *A tenant pays rent quarterly on 1 January, 1 April, 1 July, and 1 October. On 1 February an increased fair rent is registered. The landlord cannot claim the increased rent until 1 April. He would have to serve a Notice of Increase but he is allowed to backdate it by up to four weeks so he could get away with not serving it until 28 April.*

Do not forget that a tenant pays whichever is the *lower* of the contractual rent and the registered rent. So, if his contract has not expired yet (see page 250) and if the registered rent is higher than the contractual rent, he can continue paying the lower, contractual, amount.

If the registered rent is *lower* than the rent the tenant had been paying, the tenant pays the lesser amount. He cannot backdate the reduction in his rent to the date of the application to the rent officer.

How long does the registered rent last?

The registered rent is the maximum rent payable for those premises until either a new registered rent is registered or the registration is vacated. A new application to the rent officer cannot be made until at least two years have elapsed since the registration of the registered rent. At the end of the two-year period, the landlord (or tenant) can apply for a new rent to be registered and the tenant (or landlord) will be able to oppose that application. However, if there is no tenant in occupation at that time, the landlord can simply have the registered rent cancelled; the entry on the register is said to be 'vacated'. This allows the landlord to re-let the premises at a contractual rent which exceeds the old registered rent. A new tenant can, of course, immediately apply for a fair rent to be registered, but, in practice, most tenants do not bother to do so.

If the tenant pays more than the registered rent

A tenant cannot be charged more than the registered rent for the property. If he is, then he can recover up to two years' overpayments: either he can sue in the court, or he can simply deduct the amount he is owed from his future rent payments. But it is important to check that the tenant has in fact been overcharged. Bear in mind that a tenant with an unregistered rent will often have his rates paid by the landlord, whereas a tenant with a registered rent will normally have to pay his own rates. So it is usually necessary to work out the rates and add them to the registered rent figure: that will normally be the amount the tenant should pay. If he has been paying more than that then he has almost certainly been overcharged and he should reclaim the overpayments (for up to two years).

Another point to check is that the registered rent was for the same furnished or unfurnished property (i.e. a registered rent for the unfurnished property will not be binding if the property is then let furnished).

Tenants with restricted protection

The basic rule is that a tenant with a resident landlord will only have restricted protection under the Rent Acts.

If a tenant has restricted protection:

A reasonable rent can be registered by the rent tribunal and that will then be the maximum rent that can be charged – despite any agreement to the contrary. If a reasonable rent has not been registered, the tenant will pay according to the terms of his contract.

This summary sets out the basic position. But remember that a tenant or licensee with restricted protection has very little security from eviction and only sometimes does he have short-term security (see page 271). Thus, it will usually be unwise for a tenant to register the rent and so incur his landlord's wrath, since a notice to quit might well result. What follows should be read subject to this major proviso.

Registering a 'reasonable rent'

In the same way that the rent of a full-protection tenant (regulated or shorthold) can be registered, so can the rent of a tenant with restricted protection. The basic principles of registration are similar, with the registration taking effect for at least two years as the maximum rent that can be charged (see above, page 255). See the chart on page 249.

However, the registration of restricted-protection rents is supervised by the rent tribunal; this is completely separate from the rent officer, who supervises the registration of regulated rents. Also, the registered rent of a regulated property is called a 'fair rent' whereas for the restricted-protection property it is called a 'reasonable rent'. Despite this, basically similar procedures, rules, and considerations apply to both systems.

When does the registered rent take effect?

The new rent becomes chargeable as from the date of its registration by the rent tribunal.

If the registered rent is lower *than the rent the tenant has been paying* the tenant cannot claim any of the excess back to the date of his application to the rent tribunal. The new lower rent comes into effect on the date of registration.

If the registered rent is higher *than the rent the tenant has been paying* the landlord cannot backdate the new rent. The higher rent only applies from the next date after registration when it is due. No notice of increase is needed. Phasing does not apply.

Illustration. *A tenant pays £60 per month rent. On 1 January the landlord asks the rent tribunal to register a reasonable rent. On 1 March the rent tribunal registers a rent of £70 per month. The landlord can only charge the new rent as from 1 April.*

Paying more than the registered rent

If the tenant pays more than the registered reasonable rent he can reclaim the excess for up to six years (cf. the two-year period for fair rents; see page 256). But the excess cannot be deducted from future rent and must be sued for (see page 872 for how to sue in the county court). Overcharging a tenant with restricted protection is a criminal offence and should be reported to the tenancy relations or harassment officer. (Overcharging a tenant with full protection is not a criminal offence.)

How long does the registered rent last for?

The registered rent is the maximum rent payable for those premises until either a new registered rent is registered or the registration is vacated. A new application to the rent officer cannot be made until at least two years have elapsed since the registration of the registered rent. At the end of the two-year period, the landlord (or tenant) can apply for a new rent to be registered, and the tenant (or landlord) will be able to oppose that application. However, if there is no tenant in occupation at that time, the landlord can simply have the registered rent cancelled (the entry on the register is said to be 'vacated'). This allows the landlord to re-let the premises at a contractual rent which exceeds the old registered rent. A new tenant can of course immediately apply for a fair rent to be registered, but, in practice, many tenants do not bother to do so. In practice, a tenant will often not risk offending his landlord by applying for the rent to be registered. This is because a tenant with restricted protection has virtually no long-term protection from eviction (see page 271).

Increases for rates, improvements, and services: when can they be passed on to the tenant?

With both types of full-protection tenancies, increases in the cost of these items can often be passed on to the tenant. However, with restricted-protection tenancies, only *rate* increases can be passed on to the tenant. The rule is that the tenant pays the full amount of any rates increase. However, the landlord can ask the rent tribunal to register a new reasonable rent to take account of a change of circumstances (e.g. improvements).

EVICTION

No one can be evicted from his home without a court order

This is so important that it is worth repeating: no one can be evicted from his home without a court order. This is so whether the person has full protection under the Rent Acts, or only restricted protection (e.g. because he has a resident landlord, or a licence – although few licences are legally valid: see page 278).

Thus, the question is not 'When can my landlord evict me?' but 'Will the court make an order that I am to be evicted?' This will depend upon whether the tenant is within the Rent Acts (page 237) and, if so, whether he has full protection or restricted protection (see page 241).

1. If the occupier is not a Rent Act tenant

If the tenant has neither full protection nor restricted protection (e.g. if he is a student in a hostel, or a guest in a hotel) the court must make an eviction order if asked to do so by the landlord or owner.

2. If the occupier is a Rent Act tenant

Before deciding whether to make the order the court will want to know whether the tenant has full protection or restricted protection.

A tenant with full protection. A tenant with full protection will normally be safe from eviction and the court would only make an order if he had misbehaved or if one of several specified circumstances applied. Thus, he usually has long-term security from eviction. However, if he is a *shorthold* tenant with a fixed-term agreement of one to five years, whilst he cannot be evicted during that pre-arranged fixed period, the landlord can easily obtain an eviction order once that period has expired (see page 264).

A tenant with restricted protection. A tenant with restricted protection has no long-term security from eviction. In practice, the most he could hope for is that no court order will be made for three months (see page 271).

The eviction order

If the landlord thinks he might be entitled to an eviction order he should apply to the county court. There will be a delay of a few weeks before his case comes up for hearing. The speed with which his case proceeds will largely depend upon the grounds on which he is seeking possession. The list on pages 266–7 sets out the sixteen different grounds.

If the landlord is using a ground under which the court MUST grant possession (i.e. numbers 11–16 in the list) a speedy procedure allows the case to be heard quickly. The tenant need only be given a week's notice of the hearing and the hearing can be in chambers (i.e. in private).

If the landlord is using a ground under which the court MAY grant possession (i.e. numbers 1–10 in the list) the speedy procedure is not available. Instead, the tenant must be given at least three weeks' notice of the hearing and the hearing must be in open court before a judge; because of the pressure of work on judges, such a case is unlikely to come to court within six weeks of the proceedings being started.

If the court decides to grant an eviction order (called a *possession order*), there are three alternatives available.

1. An outright order

This takes effect immediately. The occupier is not given any time in which to make moving arrangements. The landlord can ask the bailiff to go in straight away and evict the occupier. However, it would be almost unheard of for such an order to be made against a tenant. Generally, it is used against trespassers (see 'Squatting', page 280).

2. A twenty-eight-day order

This takes effect after a short delay. Generally, the occupier is given four weeks (sometimes six) in which to move out. Only when that period has elapsed can the landlord ask the bailiff to go in and evict the occupier. This would be a typical order made against a tenant, assuming of course that the court decided to make a possession order. The court would normally order that the tenant continue to pay his rent during that period.

If the tenant was a full-protection tenant being evicted under one of the grounds when the court had no discretion (see numbers 11–16 in the list on page 267) then the Housing Act 1980 requires the court to allow the tenant only fourteen days in which to move out; only in exceptional cases can that be extended, and in no case beyond six weeks. This stricter rule does not apply if the court was not obliged to evict (i.e. numbers 1–10 in the list on page 266) or if the tenant had a resident landlord.

3. A suspended order

This is a possession order that is either suspended for more than six weeks or is suspended indefinitely, subject to the tenant meeting certain conditions. For instance, if a tenant is in rent arrears the court might make a possession order but suspend it indefinitely, subject to the tenant paying off the arrears at a specified rate and also not falling into any new arrears. If the tenant did not meet these conditions, the landlord could reapply to the court and ask that the suspended order be made an outright order. If a tenant has a suspended order made against him he should apply to the court for it to be discharged once he has fulfilled all the conditions (e.g. paid off rent arrears). Otherwise the landlord will be able to reactivate the order at short notice if he should ever get into arrears again.

Eviction by the bailiff

If the tenant remains in possession after the date fixed by the court for him to leave, the landlord should not eject him, but instead ask the court bailiff to carry out the eviction. There will usually be a delay of ten days or so before the bailiff carries out the eviction. Most tenants, of course, leave on the date ordered by the court and do not wait to be evicted by the bailiff. Tenants who are facing eviction and have nowhere to go should consider whether the council has a duty to rehouse them (see 'Homelessness', page 722).

Eviction: tenants with full protection

It will be recalled that there are two types of full-protection tenancies – regulated and shorthold tenancies (see page 241).

Most full-protection tenants are regulated tenants and can only be evicted if they misbehave. But shorthold tenants are in a different position. A shorthold tenant will have been granted a tenancy for a pre-arranged fixed period of between one and five years; before the tenancy began, he will have been told that he could be evicted at the end of the period (see page 246 for the detailed rules). See below for eviction of shorthold tenants.

Regulated tenants

As with rent control, the position on evicting a regulated tenant depends partly upon whether or not there is an existing contract (e.g. an expired lease) between the landlord and the tenant. Refer to page 250 for guidance on whether or not the contractual tenancy is still in existence.

Eviction when there is still a contract

Since the tenant has a contract that allows him to live in the rented property, he cannot be evicted unless he breaks his part of the contract (e.g. fails to pay the rent; sublets without permission). Then the landlord might be able to go to the court for an eviction order.

In short, the tenant cannot be evicted while the contract is still in existence. But the question arises, how can the landlord bring the contract to an end? With fixed-term agreements (e.g. an agreement for six months, two years, etc.) the answer is that he cannot normally bring the contract to an end until it has run its normal course. Once that period expires the contract will automatically end without any move on the part of the landlord (i.e. the landlord need not serve a notice to quit on the tenant). The tenant can, of course, stay in possession as a *statutory tenant* (see page 250) and need not leave unless a court makes a possession order against him.

If the agreement is not for a fixed term, it will be periodic. For instance, the tenant will simply pay his rent each week or month, and the length of the tenancy will not have been decided in advance. A periodic tenancy can be brought to an end by either landlord or tenant giving the other notice. Usually, this is a notice from the landlord to the tenant, and this is called a 'notice to quit'.

Notice to quit

The rules on serving a notice to quit are largely derived from the old common law. They are extremely complex and it is easy for a landlord to break them inadvertently. To avoid this, it is usual for the landlord to cover himself by giving notice to quit 'on . . . (*date*) . . . or at the end of the period of your tenancy expiring next four weeks after service of this notice on you'. This should ensure that the notice to quit is effective.

If a notice to quit does not comply with the legal requirements it will be ineffective; it will be as though the tenant was never given a notice to quit. If the landlord starts a possession action on the basis of an incorrect notice to quit, the court will dismiss his application. He will then have to start again, issuing a fresh notice to quit.

Pre-printed notices to quit can be purchased from the larger stationery shops.

To complicate the position still further, under a full-protection tenancy a notice of increase of rent (see page 253) can take effect as a notice to quit if it is served sufficiently far in advance to comply with the notice-to-quit rules (outlined above). So if a tenant has been served with either a valid notice to quit or a valid notice of increase, his contractual tenancy will have ended.

If the rented property is in a Housing Action Area, the landlord must send a copy of the notice to quit to the local authority, otherwise he commits a criminal offence.

A Typical Notice To Quit

Sir, I, (*name*), of (*address*), hereby give you notice to quit and deliver up possession of the [house, flat, etc.] and premises, with the appurtenances, situate at (*address*) in the county of ———, which you hold of me as tenant thereof, on the (*date*) day of (*month*) 19—, or at the expiration of the week of your tenancy which shall expire next after the expiration of four weeks from the service upon you of this notice.

The information prescribed by the Notices to Quit (Prescribed Information) Regulations 1980 is contained in the Schedule hereto.

Dated the (*date*) day of (*month*) 19—.

....
(Signed)

SCHEDULE

Prescribed Information

1. If the tenant does not leave the dwelling, the landlord must get an order for possession from the court before the tenant can lawfully be evicted. The landlord cannot apply for such an order before the notice to quit has run out.

2. A tenant who does not know if he has any right to remain in possession after a notice to quit runs out, or is otherwise unsure of his rights, can obtain advice from a solicitor. Help with all or part of the cost of legal advice and assistance may be available under the legal-aid scheme. He should also be able to obtain information from a Citizens' Advice Bureau, a Housing Aid Centre, a rent officer or a rent-tribunal office.

Eviction when the contract has ended

If the lease expires, or if the weekly, monthly, etc. periodic tenancy is ended by a notice to quit (or notice of increase) the contract will come to an end. But the tenant does not have to leave. The Rent Acts allow him to carry on living there until such time as the court orders him to leave – and that will only be in a few, well-defined circumstances.

The 'grounds for possession' are given on pages 266–7.

Only if one of these grounds exists can the court make an eviction order. But even then, it will be seen that the court usually has to be satisfied that to evict the tenant would be reasonable in all the circumstances; thus, the landlord usually has to do more than simply show that one of the grounds for possession exists.

The owner-occupier as landlord

We have seen that if a landlord lets part of his property and continues living in the other part, the tenant will only have restricted protection. But if the landlord does not live in the property, the tenant will have full protection.

It is a common misconception that the owner-occupier who parts with possession of his house will never be able to evict the tenant. This is not so.

The owner-occupier can recover possession from a tenant with full protection if:
● he lived in the property before he let it, *and*
● before the property was let, the tenant was given written notice by the owner-occupier that this might happen (in fact the court does have a discretion to make an eviction order even if the written notice was not given to the tenant; but it is obviously best always to give proper notice), *and*
● the contract must now have come to an end (i.e. the lease must have expired), or a periodic tenancy must have been ended by service of a notice to quit or notice of increase *and*
● vacant possession is needed because:
  – the owner now wants it back to live there himself, or it is needed for a member of his family who used to live there with him, *or*
  – the owner has died and vacant possession is needed to sell the property or a member of his family who was living with him at the time of his death wants to move into the property, *or*
  – the property is not reasonably suited to the owner's place of work and he needs vacant possession to be able to sell and use the money to buy a more suitable property.

If these requirements are met the court has no discretion; it *must* grant the possession order.

In particular, the landlord does not have to be acting reasonably in wanting the property back:

Mr and Mrs Kennealy lived in their flat from 1957 to 1968 when Mr Kennealy was posted abroad. They then let the flat to Mr Dunne on a weekly tenancy. In 1974 they came back from abroad and sought possession of the flat. In the meantime they lived in a house that they also owned. The county court judge refused to make a possession order against Mr Dunne since he did not think Mr and Mrs Kennealy reasonably needed the flat as their residence. On appeal, held: A possession order would be granted. If the owner-occupier 'required' his flat back then an order must be made: there was no rule of law that he had to 'reasonably' require the flat. Kennealy (1977)

Note that this special protection for owner-occupiers is not restricted to house-owners who go abroad; it applies even if the owner-occupier remains in this country.

The vital requirement is that the tenant is given advance notice that the landlord is an owner-occupier and that he might want the property back. The best way to do this is to:

1. Write a letter to the tenant before the tenant signs an agreement or goes into occupation, saying, 'As you know, I am the owner-occupier of the property within the meaning of section 105 of the Rent Act 1977, and I would now repeat what I have already told you, namely that I may require possession of the property as a residence for myself or a member of my family. It is only on this basis that I am prepared to consider letting the property to you.' The tenant should be asked to sign a copy of the letter.
2. The tenancy agreement should repeat this warning. A formal clause might read: 'The tenant

hereby acknowledges that prior to the execution of this Agreement he received notice from the landlord that the landlord is the owner-occupier of the property within the meaning of section 105 Rent Act 1977 or within the meaning of Case 11 of Part II of Schedule 15 to the Rent Act 1977 and that possession of the property may be recovered by the landlord under the said section 105 or the said Case 11 and by virtue of section 98(2) Rent Act 1977 as may be appropriate.' Less formal wording would still work.

If these formalities are observed, the owner-occupier will have no difficulty in obtaining a possession order when the tenancy ends. Often the court will arrange a speedy hearing of the application within two or three weeks, instead of the usual six weeks or so. Even if this written notice is not given, the court still has a discretion to make a possession order if it thinks it would be 'just and equitable to do so'.

Summary: letting your home

1. *If you continue living there* – **you will be a resident landlord. The tenant will only have restricted protection under the Rent Acts; in particular, you will be able to get an eviction order relatively easily.**
2. *If you move somewhere else* – **you will not be a resident landlord (since you are not residing there!) but you can stop the tenant getting full Rent Act protection from eviction. Do this by serving a notice (as on page 263). You will then have no difficulty in getting the property back when you want to live there again.**

Retirement homes; lettings by servicemen

Similar provisions allow a landlord to obtain vacant possession if he wishes to use the property as his retirement home or if he is a member of the Forces who needs his home back. The conditions are as with owner-occupiers (above) and, in particular, the tenant must have been given advance warning that this could happen before he was granted the tenancy.

Shorthold lettings

A shorthold let is a tenancy for a pre-arranged period of between one and five years. The tenant must have been given advance warning that he could be evicted at the end of the term (see page 246 for the detailed rules).

The whole idea of the shorthold letting is to allow the landlord to recover possession at the end of the fixed term; none of the above grounds for possession need apply. Once the period is ended the landlord can simply start possession proceedings in the county court and the court *must* make an eviction order.

The landlord can apply to the county court any time after the fixed period; he cannot apply before the end of the period unless the tenant has committed a serious breach of the tenancy (e.g. large rent arrears). It does not matter if the landlord waits until after the end of the fixed period, for the rule is 'once a shorthold always a shorthold', even if the tenant stays in possession for a long time after the end of the period. This is so even if the tenant signs a new tenancy agreement that is not a shorthold agreement and even if the tenancy is inherited by his family on his death (see below).

However, shorthold tenants must be given at least three months' warning before the possession proceedings are started, but the written notice can only be served during the three months immediately before the end of the fixed period, or its anniversary if it has already expired. Once again, we find that the rules are unnecessarily complicated.

Illustration. *The landlord grants a two-year shorthold tenancy on 1 June 1985, expiring 30 May 1987. The landlord must give notice in March, April or May 1987, or March, April, May of succeeding years. The notice must be of at least three months' duration.*

Once the notice has expired the landlord can start his possession proceedings. The court must make an eviction order; it cannot suspend, postpone, or delay the eviction order (cf. the usual position, page 259) so the tenant must leave.

Eviction of the tenant's family

What happens when a tenant dies, or if he simply leaves the rented property? Do the people living with him have to leave, or can they carry on living there?

Husbands, wives, children, and relatives

When the tenant dies. When a tenant dies, the tenancy passes automatically to the spouse (if s/he was living in the property). S/he takes over as the tenant and is in exactly the same position vis-à-vis the landlord as was the late husband or wife. If the tenant did not leave a spouse, the tenancy can pass to any *member of the family* who was living there during the last six months. For instance:

> *Mr Murch left his own rented house following a row with his wife; Mrs Murch remained in the matrimonial home. Mr Murch went to live with his mother. When the mother died, he claimed the tenancy as her successor, having lived there with her for the previous six months. Held: Yes, he was 'residing' there and so he was entitled to the tenancy.* Morgan (1970)

If several members of the family claim the tenancy, the county court can decide who has the best claim.

Two points should be noted:

1. These inheritance provisions only apply twice. On the third death, the landlord can claim the property back. For instance, suppose a husband is the tenant and he dies; the tenancy then passes to his widow. On her death, it might pass to a son. But on the son's death the landlord can recover possession.
2. These inheritance provisions only apply to tenants with full protection (see

(*Continued on page 269.*)

Grounds for possession of regulated (and shorthold) tenancies

---

The tenant **may** *be evicted on the following grounds*

1. *Rent arrears.* Usually the order will only be made if the tenant has a very bad rent record. If the arrears can be paid off by instalments the court might make an order, but suspend it; the order will then come into effect if the tenant does not pay the instalments. If the rent arrears are paid off before the court hearing, it is almost certain that no eviction order will be made.
2. *Breach of tenancy.* If the tenant has broken the terms of the tenancy agreement. However, no order will be made if the breach is only minor and the tenant agrees to remedy it.
3. *Alternative accommodation.* If the landlord can show that suitable alternative accommodation is available. Size, rent, security of tenure, and convenience to the tenant's work place will all be relevant.
4. *Subletting.* If the tenant has sublet the whole of the premises without the landlord's consent. Alternatively, if he has charged a lawful subtenant (of all or part of the property) more than the registered rent for the subtenant's part of the property.
5. *Damage.* If the tenant (or any person for whom he is responsible, such as a lodger or subtenant) has damaged the property or furniture, or made unauthorized alterations to the premises. Or if the damage was by a lodger or subtenant, if the tenant has not taken steps to remove him.
6. *Employment.* If the tenant was let the property as an employee, but he no longer works for the landlord and the property is now needed for a full-time employee of the landlord.
7. *Nuisance.* If the tenant has been a nuisance to neighbours. Or if the nuisance has been caused by someone for whom the tenant is responsible and whom he has not taken steps to remove (see *Damage,* above).
8. *Illegal use.* If the tenant (or someone for whom he is responsible) has received a criminal conviction for using the premises for illegal or immoral purposes.
9. *Tenant's notice to quit.* If the tenant now refuses to leave the property having previously given notice that he would. But the landlord must be able to show that he is seriously prejudiced by the tenant's change of mind (e.g. he has contracted to sell the property with vacant possession). This only applies if the tenant's notice to quit was valid legally (see page 275 for the rules).
10. *Required for landlord.* If the landlord now needs the property for himself or his family (i.e. parent or child over eighteen). But he must show he will otherwise suffer greater hardship than the tenant. Note: this ground will not apply to a landlord who bought the property subject to the tenancy.

Note: with all the above grounds the landlord must, in addition, convince the judge that it would be reasonable to evict the tenant.

The tenant must be evicted on the following grounds

11. *Owner-occupier.* The landlord lived in the property before letting it off and he now wants it back to live there (see page 262). However, the tenant must usually have been given notice of the possibility before he was granted the tenancy.

12. *Retirement home.* The landlord has now retired and wants to live in the property, or has died and the property is wanted as a residence by a member of his family who lived with him at the time of his death. However, the tenant must usually have been given notice of this possibility before he was granted the tenancy.

13. *Armed forces.* The landlord was a member of the armed forces both when he acquired the property and when he let it. He now needs the property back to live there (or he has died). However, the tenant must usually have been given notice of this possibility before he was granted the tenancy.

14. *Holiday home.* The property must have been used for a holiday within the twelve months prior to the tenancy starting. The tenancy must be for a fixed term not exceeding eight months, and the tenant must usually have been warned of this possibility before he was granted the tenancy. Similar provisions apply to premises normally let to students, which are let during the off-season or during a year in which the demand for student lets is unusually low.

15. *Overcrowding.* The tenant has been found guilty of an overcrowding offence at the premises (see page 286).

16. *Shorthold.* The tenant signed a shorthold-tenancy agreement (i.e. pre-arranged minimum duration of one to five years, signed after 28 November 1980, the tenant being notified in advance that he could be evicted at the end of the period).

Note: with the above six grounds there is no need for the landlord to convince the judge that it would be reasonable to evict the tenant.

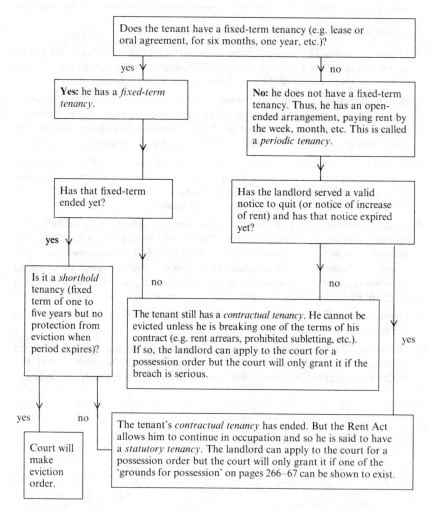

Eviction controls for tenants with full protection

Does the tenant have a fixed-term tenancy (e.g. lease or oral agreement, for six months, one year, etc.)?

yes → **Yes:** he has a *fixed-term tenancy*.

no → **No:** he does not have a fixed-term tenancy. Thus, he has an open-ended arrangement, paying rent by the week, month, etc. This is called a *periodic tenancy*.

Has that fixed-term ended yet?

Has the landlord served a valid notice to quit (or notice of increase of rent) and has that notice expired yet?

yes →

Is it a *shorthold* tenancy (fixed term of one to five years but no protection from eviction when period expires)?

no → The tenant still has a *contractual tenancy*. He cannot be evicted unless he is breaking one of the terms of his contract (e.g. rent arrears, prohibited subletting, etc.). If so, the landlord can apply to the court for a possession order but the court will only grant it if the breach is serious.

no →

yes →

yes → Court will make eviction order.

no → The tenant's *contractual tenancy* has ended. But the Rent Act allows him to continue in occupation and so he is said to have a *statutory tenancy*. The landlord can apply to the court for a possession order but the court will only grant it if one of the 'grounds for possession' on pages 266–67 can be shown to exist.

Summary: the basic rule is that a tenant with *full protection* (generally a tenant without a resident landlord) can only be evicted if he is a 'bad' tenant, or if he has a shorthold agreement that has expired.

page 241). On the death of a tenant with restricted protection (e.g. with a resident landlord, see page 241) the tenancy ends automatically and neither the surviving spouse nor members of the family can demand that they be allowed to inherit the tenancy.

When the tenant deserts his or her family the abandoned husband or wife can stay on in occupation with full Rent Act rights against the landlord (Matrimonial Homes Act 1983). Other members of the family have no such right, so if a single tenant abandons her aged mother, the mother cannot stay on in the rented property.

On divorce. On divorce, the spouse who is not the tenant will automatically lose the right to carry on living there, unless the court makes an order transferring the tenancy to him or her.

Under the Matrimonial Homes Act 1983, the court has full power to transfer a tenancy with full protection (but not restricted protection) from one spouse to another even if the lease or tenancy agreement specifically prohibits its assignment. Under the Matrimonial Causes Act 1973 the court has more limited powers, for it can only transfer a contractual tenancy (see page 250) before the contract has ended, and only if the lease or tenancy agreement does not prohibit assignment; however, the 1973 Act applies to both full-protection and restricted-protection tenancies. See page 79 for the courts' attitude to transferring tenancies on a marriage breakdown.

Mistresses

Mistresses, common-law spouses, etc., have little protection.

When the tenant dies. The unmarried partner may be able to inherit the tenancy as 'a member of the family' (see above). This will depend upon how long their relationship has existed and whether they had sexual relations. If there were children, then the unmarried partner will almost certainly be regarded as a member of the family and so be able to inherit the tenancy. But if there were no children, the position is much more difficult, and unless a long and stable relationship existed – such as to give an impression of permanence – it is unlikely that the partner will qualify as a member of the family.

Ms Fox lived with the tenant of a house for twenty-one years until his death in 1961. She remained in the house, paying rent to the landlords. In 1973 they discovered she had not been married to the tenant and so asked her to leave. She argued that she had inherited the tenancy as a member of the dead tenant's 'family'. Held: The word 'family' was to be given an ordinary, everyday meaning and on this basis she was certainly a member of his family. She had inherited the tenancy. Dyson Holdings (1975)

In 1958 Mr Lucas moved into his girl-friend's flat. Mr Lucas was married but his wife had left him a few years before; they never divorced. In 1977 the girl-friend died and Mr Lucas claimed that he could succeed to the tenancy as a member of her family. The landlord argued that Mr Lucas was not entitled to take over the tenancy, firstly, because he and his girl-friend had kept their separate surnames and secondly because Mr Lucas was still a married man – how could he have two families? Held: Mr Lucas was 'a member of the family'. If the relationship looked like a marriage in the old sense of a lifelong union with nothing temporary or casual about it, then it was a family. Thus, Mr Lucas could take over the tenancy. Watson (1980)

However, the relationship must be of a fairly permanent nature for the common-law spouse to be treated as 'family'. For this reason most relationships between young people will not be sufficiently permanent to transfer the tenancy on the early death of the tenant. For instance:

In 1972 Mr Rafferty moved into his girl-friend's flat and they lived as man and wife. In 1977 the girl-friend died after three years of illness during which Mr Rafferty had cared for her as would any loving husband. When she died, the landlady asked Mr Rafferty to leave but he claimed to be entitled to the tenancy as a member of his late girl-friend's 'family'. Held: No. The couple had not pretended they were married and there was evidence that the girl-friend had wanted to remain single. In these circumstances, Mr Rafferty could not be called a member of her family. Helby (1978)

Generally, therefore, it is important that the couple should have outwardly appeared to be married (e.g. sharing a common surname).

When the tenant deserts the unmarried partner. The unmarried partner cannot take over the tenancy as could a deserted spouse. The only hope is for the abandoned partner to get the landlord to accept him/her as the new tenant (e.g. by accepting several rent payments from him/her). If not, the abandoned partner will have to leave when the contractual tenancy ends (page 250) for s/he will have no Rent Act rights against the landlord.

Friends

A person may have been living with the tenant without having been a tenant and without there having been a heterosexual relationship between them.

When the tenant dies. The friend has no right to inherit the tenancy. He or she cannot claim to be a member of the tenant's family and so claim the tenancy by inheritance.

In 1958 Mr Sharratt moved into a flat rented by an elderly widow and he lived there until her death in 1976. Their relationship was platonic and was recognized by her family as that of 'aunt' and 'nephew'. When she died, Mr Sharratt claimed that he was entitled to inherit the tenancy as a member of her 'family'. Held: No. A platonic relationship between two adults, for however many years, cannot make them members of each other's 'family'. Carega Properties (1979)

The same applies to gay couples:

After a tenant died, her former gay lover applied to the court for the tenancy to be transferred to her. This was on the basis that any ordinary person would have said that the two women were living together as husband and wife. Held: The gay lover was not to be treated as a member of the tenant's 'family'. She could not claim the tenancy. Harrogate Borough Council (1984)

When the tenant leaves the friend. The abandoned friend cannot take over the tenancy. The position is identical to that of an abandoned common-law wife or mistress (above).

Eviction: tenants with restricted protection

Remember that it is tenants with resident landlords, (and the few people with legally valid licences – see page 278), that are most likely to have only restricted protection under the Rent Acts. See page 241 for more details on how to decide whether there is restricted protection or full protection. Tenants with restricted protection have no long-term security from eviction and only occasionally will they have short-term security, of a few months.

The position depends partly upon whether or not there is still an existing contract (e.g. unexpired lease) between the landlord and the tenant. Refer to page 250 for guidance on whether or not a contract is still in existence. Do not forget that, whatever the case, the landlord cannot evict the tenant without first obtaining a court order.

Eviction when there is still a contract

Since the tenant has a contract that allows him to live in the rented property, he cannot be evicted unless he breaks his part of the contract (e.g. fails to pay the rent; sublets without permission). Then the landlord might be able to go to the court for an eviction order. But, even then, if the contract was in writing (e.g. a lease) the court would want the contract to state specifically that the tenant's breach allowed the landlord to forfeit the agreement; if there was no such specific clause in the contract, eviction would be refused.

In short, the tenant cannot be evicted while the contract is still in existence.

Eviction when the contract has ended

If the licence expires, or if the weekly (monthly, etc.) tenancy is ended by a notice to quit, the contract will come to an end (see page 250). But the tenant or licensee does not have to leave. The Protection from Eviction Act 1977 allows him to carry on living there until such time as the court orders him to leave.

Once the contract has ended the landlord can start possession proceedings in the county court. When the court hears the case (generally there is a delay of four to six weeks before the case is heard) the judge *must* make a possession order as soon as it becomes clear that the tenant only has restricted protection. This means that a licensee or a tenant with a resident landlord cannot hope to defend possession proceedings successfully once the contract has ended. The most that the tenant can hope for is that the judge will agree to postpone the date when the possession order comes into effect; he can do that for up to three months. This gives the tenant a period of time to arrange his departure from the premises.

For pre-28 November 1980 tenants, it is also possible to apply to the Rent Tribunal for a Notice to Quit to be extended. A solicitor, or CAB, can provide details.

Harassment and illegal eviction

The various protections given to tenants by the Rent Acts would be useless unless there were sanctions that could be applied against landlords who flouted the Rent Acts.

To ensure that the Rent Acts are obeyed, the law provides two distinct remedies:
• *a criminal remedy*: prosecution for the criminal offences of harassment and illegal eviction, *and*
• *a civil remedy*: allowing the tenant to sue in the civil courts for damages, and for an injunction ordering the landlord to stop or remedy his unlawful behaviour.

The two remedies are completely distinct: they are sought in different courts and their aims are different. The criminal prosecution aims to punish the landlord, whereas the civil action aims to compensate the tenant.

In practice, the civil remedy is far more effective and the tenant who has been illegally evicted or who is being harassed should take legal advice immediately with a view to starting a civil claim against his landlord.

Remember it will be unlawful to evict a tenant, former tenant, or licensee who had a contractual term, without a possession order from the court (see page 258).

The civil claim

Civil claims are brought in either the county court or the High Court (see page 764). Most harassment and illegal eviction claims are brought in the county court, partly because the procedure in the county court is more informal than in the High Court, and also because few claims are for more than £5,000, which is the maximum amount that can be claimed in the county court.

As with any civil claim the action must be based on a claim that the landlord has committed a tort (a civil wrong) such as assault on the tenant, trespass (e.g. entering the flat), breach of contract (e.g. refusing use of wc that the tenant is entitled to use under the tenancy agreement), or nuisance (e.g. banging on the walls at night). In effect, the claim has to be couched in a sufficiently legal manner and this is one reason why a tenant bringing such a claim should always seek legal advice rather than act for himself.

The tenant will ask the court for an injunction and for damages

An injunction. This is a court order directing someone to stop doing an unlawful act. For instance, it could order a landlord not to keep the tenant's electricity supply disconnected, or not to prevent the tenant from re-entering the rented property.

An injunction is an effective remedy. But it will only be granted in a sufficiently serious case and only if the tenant acts quickly. He must show that his case is an emergency and if he delays before going to court, the judge will assume that it is not an emergency. Speed is therefore of the essence – which is another reason why the court case should be handled by a lawyer who is familiar with court procedures, and not by the tenant in person.

If the complaint is serious – and any illegal eviction will be taken seriously by the court – the judge will grant an injunction straight away, without giving the landlord a chance to put his side of the case. The judge will read the tenant's sworn statement set out in an affidavit and grant an injunction immediately. This injunction will last for a week or so, when there will be a proper hearing which the landlord can attend and so argue his side of the case. This injunction is called an *interim injunction* because it is ordered at an interim stage of the case, not at the end of the action. It might also be described as being an *ex parte injunction* if it was made without one of the parties (i.e. the landlord) being present.

In illegal eviction cases there is an additional reason for starting court proceedings quickly. If the landlord re-lets the vacant property the court is unlikely to grant an injunction ordering the ex-tenant back into the property because this would necessitate the eviction of the new tenant. So a tenant who has been illegally evicted should not waste any time before taking legal advice with a view to applying for an injunction.

Damages. The court can also order the landlord to pay money compensation to the tenant who has been harassed or illegally evicted. The damages can provide compensation for expenses incurred by the tenant and also for inconvenience and general disturbance. If the court thinks that the landlord has calculated that the property with vacant possession will be worth more than any damages he may have to pay the tenant, the court can impose exemplary damages so that he forfeits the profit.

There is an increasing tendency for the civil courts to recognize that illegal eviction is a serious matter, and in the words of Lord Justice Lawton it is 'one of the worst torts that can be committed'.

A tenant had his rent registered. A week later the tenant found that cronies of his landlord had bolted the door and thrown out all his property. The tenant obtained an injunction but the landlord appealed and did not obey the injunction. In all the tenant had to sleep on the floor of a friend's house for ten weeks. The tenant claimed £1,000 damages. Held: The landlord's behaviour was 'monstrous' and the tenant should be awarded the full £1,000. Drane (1978)

The tenant lived in a flat in a three-storey house. The house was bought by a developer who wanted to convert it into modernized flats that could then be sold. He harassed the tenant for many months, and in the end he removed all gas pipes, leaving the tenant without gas for his cooker, water heater or gas fires. An injunction was obtained and the gas was eventually reconnected. The judge awarded the tenant £500 damages. De Silva (1984)

The landlord's son removed the front door to the tenant's flat and threw out all his possessions. The tenant lost his flat and was not able to return. The court awarded him £1,000 damages. Taibi (1981)

Although the judges talk in terms of giving adequate compensation to tenants it will be seen that the sums are relatively small – especially when compared to the large amounts that an unscrupulous property-owner might realize through throwing out the tenant and selling off the flat.

The criminal remedy

If a landlord illegally evicts a tenant or if he harasses a tenant, the landlord will almost certainly be committing a criminal offence. On conviction he could face a fine of up to £2,000 plus six months' imprisonment (in the magistrates' court), or an unlimited fine and up to two years' imprisonment (if tried in the crown court).

At first sight this would seem an effective remedy. In practice it is not. This is largely because the criminal courts refuse to regard harassment and illegal eviction as serious offences. Despite the potentially severe penalties for these offences, the average penalty in the magistrates' court is a fine of *less than £20*. A further reason why the criminal sanction is of little weight is that the police will not prosecute for harassment or illegal eviction. They will only intervene if some other offence (such as an assault) is being committed, for as a matter of policy the police try to avoid involvement in landlord-and-tenant disputes, in the same way that they will not normally prosecute in domestic and matrimonial disputes (page 86). The prosecution, therefore, has to be brought either by the tenant himself (but this is a risky step since he might have to pay the landlord's legal costs if the prosecution failed – see page 779, 'Bringing a Private Prosecution'), or by the tenancy relations officer or harassment officer appointed by the local authority. These officers specialize in resolving landlord-and-tenant disputes but some of them prefer to use conciliation rather than prosecution. In addition, the decision on whether to prosecute is usually taken by the local authority's legal department and not by the officer and, in practice, the legal department often decides that there is insufficient evidence to be able to prove harassment to a magistrates' court. The ineffectiveness of the harassment laws can be shown by the simple fact that the first conviction of a company for harassment did not take place until 1984!

Harassment

Section 1(3) of the Protection from Eviction Act 1977 makes harassment of any residential occupier a criminal offence.

Harassment is any act which is done with the intention of causing the occupier to give up possession of all or part of his property, or which is intended to stop him exercising his legal rights (e.g. to use the services in the premises, to apply for the rent to be registered). Obvious examples of harassment include:

- locking the tenant out of the building
- changing the locks
- assaulting the tenant or his family
- turning off the gas, electricity, or water
- taking up the floorboards every weekend on the pretext of repairing the electric wiring
- removing slates from the roof
- deliberately blocking a shared wc
- leaving hi-fi on so as to disturb the tenant

- the landlord kicking the door whenever he passes it
- the landlord saying 'You will have to be out by the weekend, you know' every time he sees the tenant
- interfering with the tenant's hot-water supply
- removing light bulbs from the hall so that the passage becomes unsafe
- insulting, or swearing at, the tenant or his family.

The offence is committed even if the harassment is unsuccessful; for instance, if the tenant does not leave the premises or refuses to be intimidated.

Illegal eviction

Section 1(2) of the Protection from Eviction Act 1977 makes it a criminal offence to deprive a residential occupier of all or part of his premises or to attempt to do so. Since the basic rule is that no residential occupier can be evicted without there being a court order it follows that nearly all unauthorized attempts at eviction will be 'unlawful' and so caught by section 1. Virtually the only exceptions are trespassers (see 'Squatting', page 280) and some former licensees, but even in these cases there are risks of breaking the Criminal Law Act 1977, and so, in practice, no landlord should risk eviction without a court order.

OTHER POINTS

Ending a tenancy: when a tenant wants to leave

Strictly speaking, a tenant who wishes to leave his rented property and end his tenancy should give his landlord advance notice. The only exception is when the agreement was for a fixed period (e.g. one year) and the tenant leaves on the expiry date. Then no notice need be given to the landlord.

In every other case, the landlord should be given advance notice by the tenant sending him a written notice to quit. This does not have to be in any particular form (cf. a notice to quit served by a landlord on a tenant, page 261) but must state the date when the tenant intends to end the tenancy.

The length of the advance notice must be at least four weeks. However, sometimes it should be longer:

- if the tenant had a periodic tenancy (e.g. monthly, quarterly) then the notice must be at least as long as that period, subject to it being not less than twenty-eight days. For instance, a weekly tenancy needs twenty-eight days' notice, a quarterly tenancy needs three months' notice. Confusingly, a yearly periodic tenancy only needs six months' notice to quit.
- if the tenant has a fixed-term tenancy (e.g. pre-arranged period of one year) he cannot leave before the end of that period.
- if a tenant has a shorthold tenancy (i.e. a tenancy of predetermined duration when it is agreed in advance that the landlord can recover possession at the end of the fixed term; see page 246). A shorthold tenant can end the tenancy before the fixed period

has expired although obviously the landlord cannot. However, he must give proper notice to the landlord. If the agreed period was for over two years then he must give at least three months' notice; if it was for two years or less then the minimum period of notice is one month. If the fixed term has already expired and the landlord has allowed the tenant to remain in possession, then the tenant must give at least twenty-eight days' notice if he decides to leave.

In practice, many tenants do not give proper notice to quit to their landlords. If inadequate notice is given the landlord may be able to claim damages, equal to the rent for the period when notice was not given. For instance, if a weekly tenant leaves, he should give four weeks' notice; if he only gives one week's notice, his landlord can claim three weeks' rent as damages, either by suing him in the county court or, more usually, by forfeiting the deposit paid by the tenant.

However, the law also requires the landlord to 'mitigate his loss' – in short, to take every step to ensure that his losses are kept to a minimum. This means that he must re-let the property if he can. Since there is generally a great shortage of rented accommodation, the court will normally hold that a landlord could have re-let the premises within, say, one week. Thus, the landlord will only be entitled to one week's lost rent and will forfeit any excess. The practical effect of this is that if a tenant gives one week's notice to quit he should resist any attempt by the landlord to charge him rent for the extra period when notice should have been given. In practice, of course, the landlord will usually refuse to hand back the tenant's deposit and – in practical terms – there will be little that the tenant can do about it, since he himself will have acted wrongly in not giving adequate notice. Only if the balance of the deposit is a large amount is it likely to be worth his while suing.

Subtenants, joint tenants, sharers, etc.

Subtenants

A landlord can himself be a tenant. For instance, if landlord L lets a house to tenant T1 and T1 then lets part of the house to another tenant T2, T1 will be T2's landlord. What is T2's position as regards T1, and also as regards L? As with any Rent Acts question, the answer is not simple.

If T1 *was allowed to sublet* to T2, then T2 will have normal Rent Act protection against T1, with the extent of his rights depending upon whether he has full protection or restricted protection. In practice, one finds that most subtenants rent part of their landlord's own home and so the subtenant has a resident landlord, which means T2 only has restricted protection. Often T2's tenancy will also be binding on L, and if T1 should give up his own tenancy this will not affect T2; T2 will carry on as the tenant of L and he will have full protection or restricted protection depending upon the circumstances. But if T2 has restricted protection he will only become a tenant of the landlord if:

● T1 had a contractual tenancy, not a statutory tenancy (i.e. T1's original letting had not expired, see page 250), *and*

• the tenancy was ended by T1 giving notice to quit to L, or by T1 surrendering his tenancy to L.

Unless both these requirements are met, a T2 with restricted protection will not be able to carry on as a tenant of the landlord.

That is the theory: a subtenant has full Rent Act rights. Unfortunately, in practice T2 often has no protection. T2 only has Rent Act rights if T1 was allowed to sublet to T2. If T1 *was not allowed to sublet*, then the law does not recognize T2's tenancy: he is an illegal subtenant and, as such, his tenancy only binds T1, not L.

Most written tenancy agreements contain a clause that prohibits subletting; it is a standard clause in most pre-printed rent books and in most leases or agreements drawn up by solicitors.

Such a prohibition can be of two kinds:

1. 'The tenant may not sublet without first obtaining the consent of the landlord'; if T1 does not obtain L's consent, the subletting to T2 will be illegal. But if T1 asks L for his consent, the law says that L cannot 'unreasonably' withhold his consent. Usually he can only withhold consent if T2 is unsuitable (e.g. a prostitute, has a bad rent record).
2. 'The tenant may not sublet': this is an absolute prohibition on subletting and the landlord need not give his consent unless he wishes to. Otherwise, any subletting will be illegal.

If the subletting to T2 is in breach of such a clause, it will be illegal. It can only be legalized by L knowingly waiving the breach of the clause. For instance, if L accepts several rent payments from T1, realizing that the money is from T2 and not T1, and knowing that T2 is in occupation, he will be taken to have agreed to the subletting and so legalized it.

The landlords let a flat to T1 in 1972; the lease was for three years and it specifically prohibited any subletting. In 1975, T1 sublet to T2. T2 paid the rent to T1, who in turn paid to the landlords. T2 lived openly in the flat for three years, to the knowledge of the landlords' porters. The landlords then sought an eviction order on the grounds that T2 was an illegal subtenant. Held: The landlords had waived the illegality of the subletting and T2 was now the lawful tenant. The porters were under a duty to report changes of personnel to the landlords and by continuing to accept rent the landlords had waived the breach. Metropolitan (1979)

If T2's subtenancy is illegal

As against T1. The position is unchanged – it is as though he were a legal subtenant. He therefore has full protection or restricted protection depending upon the circumstances. T1 cannot use the illegality of the subtenancy against T2.

As against L. He has no status. If T1's tenancy ends (for instance L may ask the court to evict T1 because of his illegal subletting to T2) then T2 cannot stay on in the property. He has no Rent Act rights. This is so even if T2 did not realize that he was an illegal subtenant. Often a subtenant does not realize that his landlord is himself a tenant. The only exception is if T1 had a contractual tenancy (not a statutory tenancy) and gave notice to quit to L or if he surrendered the lease. If that happened, even the illegal subtenant, T2, would become the tenant of the landlord L.

Otherwise T2's only hope is for the landlord to accept rent and so waive the breach (as above).

Shorthold tenancies. If a shorthold tenancy is sublet the subtenant (T2) takes it subject to the shorthold rules. In brief, he can be evicted at the end of the fixed period – even if he did not know that his own landlord (T1) only had a shorthold tenancy.

Joint tenants

A tenancy can be shared by several people with each of them being a tenant and having equal rights in the rented property. For instance, if there are three joint tenants, they are all equally entitled to every part of the rented property; they do not each have exclusive rights to a third of the property. If one of the three moves out of the property, the other two will take over his share and so they will now hold the entire property as two joint tenants.

The remaining joint tenants cannot ask someone to move in with them and then give him a share of their joint tenancy. If that was allowed, they would be able to force the landlord to accept a person as his tenant and the law rules that a landlord cannot have a new tenant forced on to him. Thus, if someone moves in to replace the previous joint tenant, the new person will not be a joint tenant unless the landlord agrees to his coming in as a tenant or unless the landlord knowingly accepts rent from him. Generally, this will have to be more than one payment of rent so that it cannot be dismissed by the landlord as a mere oversight on his part. The landlord will be bound even if the rent payments are made to managing agents or if they go through a computer.

If the landlord does not accept the new person as one of the joint tenants then the new occupier will probably be a licensee and so have few Rent Act rights; occasionally, he might be a subtenant of the joint tenants.

Licensees

A licensee is a person who is allowed on to someone else's property on sufferance or with permission but without legal rights. For instance, dinner guests, friends and relatives staying overnight, and repairers fixing items inside a building are all licensees. They are not tenants.

Similarly, a person who stays in a hotel room is a licensee, not a tenant; he cannot use the full weight of the Rent Acts against the hotel.

Many landlords used to grant licences (sometimes called non-exclusive occupation agreements), rather than tenancies. This was to get around the Rent Acts, since it was wrongly believed that these documents would ensure that the tenant was treated as a licensee, rather than as a Rent Act tenant.

A 1985 case has made it clear the licence dodge is doomed to failure:

Mrs Mountford took furnished rooms in Boscombe, for £37 per week, from Mr Street. He was a solicitor and had drawn up a carefully worded licence agreement. The agreement called itself a 'licence' (not a tenancy) and referred to 'licence fee' (not rent). It ended with: 'I understand and accept that a licence in the above form does not and is not intended to give me a tenancy protected under the Rent Acts.' That was followed by Mrs Mountford's signature. Eventually, Mr Street wanted the rooms back; Mrs Mountford argued that she was entitled to continue living there since she had full Rent Act protection. Mr Street said she did not – she was merely a licensee, which would mean that he could easily get an eviction order.

The House of Lords held that Mrs Mountford was a tenant. One looks at the reality of the agreement – not what it calls itself. ('The manufacture of a five-pronged implement for manual digging results in a fork even if the manufacturer, unfamiliar with the English language, insists that he intended to make and has made a spade.') If rooms were let exclusively to one person (or a group of people) then there was a tenancy. Only if Mrs Mountford had been a lodger (i.e. if she had received food, cleaning services, etc.) would the court have been prepared to regard her as a licensee. Since that was not the case, she had full Rent Act protection. Street (1985)

The end result is that only house guests, hotel guests, and lodgers are likely to be licensees. Anyone else with sole use of the room (or rooms) is likely to be a Rent Act tenant.

Flat-sharers

The law does not recognize the arrangement of flat-sharing or room-sharing and so it has to be fitted into one of the existing legal categories of occupation. There are usually several possibilities:

• all the sharers are joint tenants

• only one of them is a tenant, and the others are either his subtenants or licensees.

Unfortunately, there is no easy answer to the question of which applies. Refer to 'Joint tenants', 'Subtenants', 'Licensees' (above) to work out which applies to a particular case (do not be worried if you find it absurdly complicated: most solicitors find it difficult to understand these rules!).

Assigning a tenancy

'Assignment' is the legal word for transferring a tenancy from one person to another.

Only a contractual tenancy (page 250) can be assigned. Once the contract has expired the tenant carries on by virtue of his Rent Act rights and this right to stay in occupation is a personal right which cannot be assigned to someone else.

The tenancy can be assigned unless the contract (e.g. lease, rent book) says otherwise. In practice, most leases and rent books do prohibit assigning, although such clauses can be of two types (the position is the same as with clauses regarding subtenants, see page 276).

If the contract prohibits assignment, then any unauthorized assignment will be illegal and the landlord can recover possession of the premises from the illegal assignee – unless, of course, the landlord waived the breach (as with waiving an illegal subletting; see above). However, a *shorthold* (see page 246) tenancy can never be assigned – any attempted assignment will be ineffective.

For this reason, a person who is buying an existing lease should check that the assignment will not be illegal, for otherwise he may well be paying for something that can be taken from him. Note also that any payment he makes for the assignment may be unlawful and so recoverable (see page 282). The assignment should preferably be by deed and in writing.

Squatting

The word 'squatting' is not known to the law. A person who occupies premises without permission is, in the eyes of the law, a trespasser and, as such, has no rights over the land on which he is trespassing. Until recently, any trespasser could be physically ejected, using 'reasonable force', but now the law prohibits violence except in certain well-defined instances.

The only type of squatter who is not a trespasser is the squatter who is allowed into short-life property by the owner (for instance, a council). Such squatters are licensees (see page 278), not trespassers.

A person who is considering trespassing as a squatter should bear in mind that he will often be committing a criminal offence. Although squatting itself is not illegal, it can lead to the committing of other criminal offences. For instance, if the squatter damages the property in any way when entering (e.g. breaking a window, forcing a padlock) he can be prosecuted for causing criminal damage. In addition, there are three offences created by the Criminal Law Act 1977 which are specially designed to include squatters:

Trespassing with an offensive weapon

If the squatter enters with an offensive weapon he commits an offence for which he can be fined up to £2,000 and imprisoned for up to three months. The offence is easily committed when one remembers that the term 'offensive weapon' does not just include obviously dangerous implements such as knives and coshes, but also items that could be an offensive weapon (e.g. a spanner, heavy torch).

Refusing to leave when requested

Once the squatter is inside the premises he commits an offence if he refuses to leave when asked by someone who was previously living there or who now wants to live there. Such a person will be one of the following:
● a displaced residential occupier: this is a person who was using the premises as his home prior to the squatter entering. Thus, a tenant or owner-occupier who went

away on holiday and returned to find a squatter in occupation would be covered. Another squatter, living there until ousted by the new squatter, would not be included.

• a protected intending occupier: this is someone who was intending to move into the premises as his home and would have done so but for the squatting. Owner-occupiers and those with leases for over twenty-one years are covered. Intending tenants or private landlords are not included, for otherwise the owner of the property might let it to a tenant as a device for getting rid of the squatters. However, tenants and licensees offered the premises by a council or housing association are included.

The important point is that the squatter does not commit an offence if he refuses to leave when asked to by someone who does *not* have his home in the premises. Only if the person comes into one of the two categories above is an offence committed.

If the offence is committed, there is a maximum penalty of a £2,000 fine and six months in prison.

Resisting or obstructing a bailiff

A squatter who resists or intentionally obstructs an officer of the court who is executing (i.e. enforcing) a possession order commits an offence. The maximum penalty is a £2,000 fine and six months in prison.

Evicting the squatter

Until 1977 the squatter could be physically ejected without the need for a court order. The law has now been changed so that it is an offence to threaten or use violence to secure entry to premises if it is known that there is someone on the premises who is opposed to the entry. In effect, therefore, it is illegal to threaten violence to get into a squat. The maximum penalty is a £2,000 fine and six months in prison.

However, the offence cannot be committed by a 'displaced residential occupier' (i.e. someone who had his home there prior to the squat). So a displaced residential occupier, such as an owner-occupier or Rent Act tenant, can use threats of violence (but not acts of violence) to secure entry. However, such a course of action is extremely unwise, for there are numerous other offences that can be committed if violence is used, such as assault, grievous bodily harm, etc.

Because of this, the best course of action is to apply to the civil courts for a possession order against the squatters. Speedy procedures exist which allow the High Court or county court to make an order within five days of the proceedings being started, even if the squatters cannot be identified, in which case they will simply be described as 'persons unknown'.

When the application is heard the possession order must be granted once the person has shown that he is entitled to the property and that the occupiers are mere trespassers. The squatters can be ordered to pay the legal costs, although it is unlikely that the plaintiff will ever recover the money from them. He cannot get damages for nuisance, damage, etc., by using these speedy procedures; to do that he must start a default action (see page 878).

Once a possession order has been made, the next step will be for the bailiff to be sent in to evict the squatters. There will normally be a delay of a week or two before that happens.

Further protection for tenants

Premiums and deposits

The whole idea of rent control could be undermined if a landlord were able to charge a lump sum to a would-be tenant for the right to move into a house or flat. Accordingly, such premiums (or 'key money') are illegal and can be recovered.

Merely asking for a premium is a criminal offence – whether or not the tenant actually pays it. However, only the local authority can prosecute for the offence, and so complaint should always be made to the local tenancy relations officer. Although the tenant cannot himself prosecute, he can sue for the return of the money in a civil action.

Premiums can also arise in less obvious ways. For example, a tenant may move into an unfurnished flat and agree to buy the 'fixtures and fittings' for £1,000. But if the fixtures and fittings are only worth £600, the balance of £400 will be an illegal premium. The tenant can, therefore, move into the flat, and then sue for the return of the £400. The same applies to someone who buys a tenancy from a tenant by paying for it to be assigned to him. Any excess above the true value of the furniture and fittings will be recoverable.

Similarly, if a landlord asks for a payment to cover his legal costs in granting the tenancy, if the amount is unreasonable, the excess will be an illegal premium.

An unreasonably large deposit will also be an illegal premium. The Housing Act 1980 states that if the deposit does not exceed two months' rent and is 'reasonable in relation to the potential liability', then it will not be an illegal premium; accordingly, a deposit of more than two months' rent would normally seem to be illegal.

Accommodation agent's commission

The Accommodation Agencies Act of 1953 limits the occasions when an agent who helps a tenant to find a home can charge the tenant.

The Act strictly limits the occasions when the tenant is liable to pay the agent's fee. Basically, a charge can only be made if the agency does find accommodation for the tenant and, in addition, if the fee only becomes payable after the accommodation has been found and the tenancy arranged. Otherwise, no fee can be charged, even if the agency has done its best to help the tenant.

In practice, many agents ignore the Act and attempt to impose a charge for putting the tenant's name 'on the books' or send a bill for work done even when they failed to find accommodation for the tenant. If a tenant pays such a fee he can sue the agent for its recovery; in addition, the tenant should complain to the local authority.

Rent books

Only weekly tenants and licensees need be provided with a rent book. A weekly tenant is a periodic tenant (see page 236) who pays his rent on a weekly basis, as do most council tenants.

The rent book must be in the prescribed form, which tells the tenant of his legal rights – including his right to stay in the accommodation until a court order is made – and also informs him of such things as the name and address of his landlord and the weekly rent he should be paying. His weekly payments of rent are also recorded in the book. Failure to provide a proper rent book – even if the tenant does not ask for one – is a criminal offence (maximum penalty, £1,000).

The rent book is therefore more of a receipt book, with certain additional information printed on it, than a record of the terms of the contract (i.e. tenancy) made between the landlord and the tenant. Copies of properly worded rent books can be obtained from major stationers.

Gas and electricity charges

Each gas and electricity board lays down the maximum price that can be charged for the resale of gas and electricity, which is technically what happens when a landlord charges a tenant for the supply. Similarly, there is a maximum amount that can be charged for renting out a meter. Gas and electricity showrooms can provide the details.

If the landlord overcharges the tenant by exceeding these maximum prices, the tenant can recover the excess from him.

If money is stolen from a meter there will probably be a dispute as to who is liable to replace it. The gas or electricity board's hire agreement will almost certainly require the 'hirer' of the meter to make good the loss, and generally the landlord will be the 'hirer' unless it was the tenant who signed the hire agreement with the board. But if there is a written lease or tenancy agreement, it may require the tenant to recompense the landlord for any money stolen from a meter. In practice, the board will often inquire as to who took the money. If it was a member of the tenant's household then the tenant will probably be expected to pay. If it is obvious that an outsider stole the money then the board may well be persuaded to waive repayment by the tenant (especially if the tenant has little money).

Landlord's name and address

Obviously, a tenant can only exercise his legal rights against his landlord if he knows who the landlord is. Thus, the Housing Act 1974 allows any tenant to ask the person who collects his rent for the name and address of the landlord. An offence is committed if the details are not provided, in writing, within twenty-one-days. If the landlord is a company, the tenant can then ask for the names and addresses of the directors and secretary; once again, there is a twenty-one-day period for compliance. (Maximum penalty for non-compliance is a £1,000 fine.)

Rent allowances and rate rebates

Tenants may be able to claim a rent allowance and/or rate rebate from the local authority. Both schemes apply to all tenants, whether they rent from a private landlord, the council, or a housing association. In addition, owner-occupiers are eligible for rate rebate. See 'Housing Benefit', page 743

Service charges

Most Rent Act tenants with registered rents pay a fixed rent that includes the cost of any services provided. Only occasionally can an increase in the cost of these services be passed on to the tenant (see page 251).

However, some tenants – and this includes virtually all tenants with long leases (for instance, for ninety-nine years) – have a rent that is subject to an additional charge for the cost of services, and that additional sum can vary each year. To prevent landlords levying unfair and unreasonable service charges, the Housing Act 1980 contains detailed rules as to how and when service charges can be levied, and how tenants should be consulted.

What is a service charge?

A service charge covers the cost of such items as electricity, gas, heating, repairs, porterage, maintenance, redecoration, insurance, and the landlord's administration charges. If the service charge can vary from year to year then the Housing Act provisions apply – whether the tenant is for example a Rent Act shorthold tenant, or 'an owner' with a ninety-nine-year lease.

The duty to consult the tenants

The landlord must obtain estimates and consult the tenants before incurring expenditure over a certain value. That value is the greater of £500 or £25 per flat in the building. This means that if the expenditure does not exceed £500 then the tenants need not be consulted. But if there are more than twenty flats, then the £500 figure is increased (e.g. it would be £2,500 if there were 100 flats in the block).

For works above that value, the landlord must:

• obtain at least two estimates (one from a person with whom he is not connected in any way), *and*

• prepare a notice to the tenants describing the works to be carried out and inviting observations on the works and the estimates. The notice must specify a date (at least one month ahead) as a closing date for observations.

● then he must either send a notice (with a copy of the estimates) to each tenant or display a notice (and copy estimates) in the building in a place where it is 'likely to come to the notice of all those tenants'. In addition, if there is a tenants' association, the notice and copy estimates must be given to the association's secretary.

● the landlord must then wait until the closing date for observations and have due regard to any points raised. He cannot start any works before that date unless the works are urgently needed.

If the landlord does not follow this procedure he cannot charge the excess above the '£500/£25 per flat' figure. For instance, if the unauthorized work cost £1,600, and there are forty flats, the landlord could not recover the excess over £1,000 (i.e. £600 is unrecoverable) unless a court considers that he could not have reasonably been expected to comply with the above requirements.

Is a service charge reasonable?

The Housing Act 1980 also prevents landlords from levying unreasonably high service charges (e.g. charging for work that is not needed).

A tenant need only pay a service charge if

● the costs are reasonably incurred; in effect, this means:
  – was it reasonable to have the work done and to incur the expense?
  – was the amount paid reasonable for the work done?
● the works (or services) were provided or carried out to a reasonable standard;
● the consultation procedure (above) was followed, if applicable.

It is for the landlord to justify the expenditure and to show it was 'reasonable'. If necessary, the county court will make a declaration as to whether or not it was reasonable. Generally, though, it is preferable for the parties to agree to ask an arbitrator to decide the issue; a chartered surveyor will usually agree to act as an arbitrator.

If the service charge is held to be unreasonable the tenant need not pay it; often the court will order that he just pays the reasonable sum and need not pay the excess.

In theory, these provisions provide extensive protection for tenants. In practice, they are little used. Few tenants are prepared to incur the expense and inconvenience of court proceedings. In addition, it really requires the cooperation of all the tenants, with all of them refusing to pay the sums demanded; more often than not, some of the tenants in the block are not prepared to get involved and would rather pay the excessive amount demanded. Another problem is that a long-running service charge dispute may put off prospective buyers when the flat is sold, and so many long-lessees think it is better to pay up if they have any plans to sell in the near future. The net effect of these difficulties is that, in practice, it is only the most blatant examples of overcharging that reach the courts.

Obtaining a detailed breakdown from the landlord

Any tenant can ask the landlord for a written summary of how the service charge is calculated. Within six months of the landlord providing a written summary, the tenant can apply in writing to inspect the accounts, receipts, and other papers, and to be allowed to take copies. The landlord then has one month in which to make the papers available and he must then ensure that they remain available for a further two months.

If there are more than four flats in the building or if the service charge covers more than one building, the landlord's written summary must be certified by an accountant. The accountant's fees will obviously form part of the service charge to be paid by all the tenants.

Sanctions

If the landlord does not comply with these service-charge procedures, he runs the risk of not being able to charge the tenants for all or part of the work. Further, he can be prosecuted in the magistrates' court (maximum penalty £500 fine). If the landlord is a company, its officers (e.g. directors) can be prosecuted and cannot escape behind the identity of the company. In practice, these provisions are a dead letter.

Overcrowding

Finally, a mention of overcrowding. In fact, this legislation may work to the detriment of a tenant, for it may result in his eviction.

A criminal offence may be committed if premises are overcrowded. But the overcrowding rules only apply to separate dwellings where only one family is in residence. If more than one family live in the building it will be a case of 'multiple occupation' (see page 319).

From the tenant's point of view, the important thing about overcrowding is that it allows the landlord to evict him (see under 'Grounds for Possession', page 267(15)). But if the tenant is on the council's housing waiting list, he has a defence to the proceedings and thus cannot be evicted.

What is overcrowding?

Sleeping arrangements. Do two, or more, people over the age of nine, and who are of the opposite sex, sleep in the same room? If so, there is overcrowding, unless they are living together as man and wife (whether married or not).

Number of rooms. Add up the total number of occupants, counting children under ten as half a person, and ignoring those under one year old. Now refer to the table below: if the number of rooms occupied is less than the figure for that number of people, there is overcrowding. Count living-rooms and bedrooms only.

Number of people		2	3	5	7½	10	12	14	16
Number of rooms		1	2	3	4	5	6	7	8

Size of accommodation. Add up the total number of people living there, as above (i.e. children under ten only count as half a person, etc.). Then work out the square footage of each room. Use the table below to work out how many people can occupy each room, then add up the total of the permitted number of occupants. If more people live there than is permitted, the property is overcrowded.

Number of people	0	½	1	1½	2
Size of room (sq. ft)	0–50	50–70	70–90	90–110	100+

This is a very low standard. For instance, the average two-storey terraced house (with three bedrooms and two living-rooms) could be occupied by six adults and eight children under ten without being overcrowded, assuming, of course, that the square-footage requirements were met.

17 Renting from a Council or Housing Association

COUNCIL HOUSING

Whereas the Rent Acts – which control relations between landlords and tenants of privately rented properties – are of awesome complexity, the law for council tenants is relatively straightforward. In short, council tenants have considerable protection from eviction, but little or no protection from rent increases.

Rent

A council tenant will have to pay whatever the local authority thinks is 'reasonable'.

Eviction

A council tenant can only be evicted by a court order. This will only be made in certain well-defined circumstances and if it would be reasonable to evict, or if alternative accommodation is available.

The provision of accommodation

Local authorities have considerable discretion in deciding how many council houses or flats to build and to whom they should be let. In short the 'general management, regulation, and control' of local-authority housing is within the hands of the local council, but this is subject to influence and pressure from central government as to the design and layout of the houses.

Sometimes a simple waiting list is the sole criterion in the selection of tenants, although it is more usual for it to be combined with a *points system* that takes into account such things as:
- room deficiencies, including mixed sleeping
- whether the family has been broken up as a result of their poor housing conditions
- the absence of facilities such as a bath, wc, cooker, etc.
- the fact that the accommodation is shared with other people
- the inadequacy of the facilities provided; for example, if the cooker is on the landing or the wc is in the back yard
- personal health, age, and disability
- length of time the family has been living in the borough

• length of time the family has been on the housing waiting list.

Different boroughs award different numbers of points for these varying factors, for the government has not laid down any fixed guidelines. Councils must provide written summaries of their selection and priority rules if requested.

When it is decided that an applicant should be offered a house or flat, the usual procedure is for him to be visited by a member of the council's housing department. The council official will try to form an impression of the applicant's standards and his general desirability as a tenant. Thus, tenants are often informally graded so that a high-quality home will not be given to an unsatisfactory tenant and a tenant with financial problems will probably be offered a cheaper property than would otherwise be the case.

Rehousing

Generally, therefore, the council has a wide discretion when deciding how to allocate its accommodation. However, there is one restriction on this discretion, for it must, by law, rehouse any person made homeless by compulsory purchase, redevelopment, demolition, etc., on the part of the council; in such a case the council must provide 'suitable alternative accommodation on reasonable terms' if the applicant cannot find such accommodation for himself. Generally, therefore, the council has to rehouse in these cases.

For whether the council has to rehouse in other cases, see 'Homelessness', page 722.

The council tenancy: a secure tenancy

In law, a council tenancy is usually called a 'secure tenancy'. The rules on rent and eviction set out in this chapter only apply to secure tenants which, in practice, includes the vast majority of council tenants.

But the following council tenants are excluded and will not have secure tenancies:
• lettings of non-residential property
• fixed-term lettings for a period of over twenty-one years
• some lettings to students
• lettings to council employees when 'the house comes with the job'.

In addition, short-term temporary accommodation will not be protected since there will not be a secure tenancy. This covers property let:
• as short-life lettings pending development of the land. For instance, many councils allow squatting groups to occupy short-term property that is due for redevelopment or demolition; those squatters would not be secure tenants.
• to homeless people under the Housing Homeless Persons Act 1977. There is a twelve-month period before they become secure tenants, so during that time the council can evict them more easily. At the end of the twelve-month period (or earlier if rehoused elsewhere by the council) the tenant becomes a secure tenant and so has the benefit of the stricter controls on eviction.

• to job seekers. If a person moves into a district or London borough to take up a job, the local authority can give him accommodation without his becoming a secure tenant. But he must have been given written notice of this before the letting began and, in any event, the restriction only lasts twelve months. At the end of that time, he will become a secure tenant.

• when the council itself only has a short let. If the council then lets the property, that tenant will not be a secure tenant.

The terms of the tenancy

When an applicant is offered a council house or flat he will have to accept the terms of the tenancy offered by the council. The terms will vary from council to council since there is no standardized set of terms laid down by central government.

Some councils require the tenants to sign a formal tenancy agreement, while others simply set out the main terms in the rent book. A rent book must be provided if the tenant pays his rent on a weekly basis.

The tenant will probably have to pay his rent each week on Monday, one week in advance. He will also have to pay the water rates and general rates of the property.

Allowing the tenant to make improvements

One of the more absurd clauses that used to be found in council letting agreements was a restriction preventing tenants from carrying out improvements to their homes. The Housing Act 1980 removed this restriction by providing that the tenant must ask the council for permission but the council cannot unreasonably withhold its consent.

This applies to any alteration or improvement, e.g. changing bathroom fittings, erecting an exterior TV aerial, painting the outside. But in every case, the council's permission must be asked before the work can be done.

Subletting part

A lodger lives with the family; for instance, he shares meals and is taken into the home to live more or less as a member of the family. A council tenant need not obtain the council's prior permission before taking in a lodger. But if part of the property is let off to a subtenant, not a lodger, the council's approval must first be obtained.

So the tenant must ask the council for permission and the council will want to know who is to be the subtenant. The council cannot unreasonably withhold its consent, but if there are reasonable grounds for refusing permission (e.g. there would be overcrowding) then the subletting will be prohibited. If the council gives a reason that seems unreasonable, the county court will decide the issue, but the burden would be on the council to show that it is not being unreasonable.

If part of the house or flat is sublet unlawfully (because the council's permission was not obtained or because it was sublet in defiance of the council's reasonable objections) the subtenant will be an 'illegal subtenant' (see page 276) and the council will be able to evict him. However, the subtenant's own landlord – i.e. the council tenant – will not be able to use the illegality of the subletting as a ground for evicting the subtenant; only the council can do that.

In practice, the subtenant will have little security vis-à-vis his landlord, the council tenant. This is because his landlord will be a resident landlord and so the subtenant will only have restricted protection (see page 271 for the eviction of tenants with restricted protection).

Subletting/assigning the whole tenancy

If the tenant parts with possession of the whole of the property he will no longer be a secure tenant, nor will the person who takes over from him. The council would be able to obtain possession very quickly.

The general rule is that a secure tenancy cannot be given away or sold to someone else unless, of course, the council will give its consent. But transfer is allowed:

• when one secure tenant exchanges (swaps) with another;
• when the court orders a transfer of the tenancy to husband or wife in divorce proceedings;
• when the tenant dies and a member of his family 'succeeds to the tenancy' (see page 292).

Rent

Unlike Rent Act tenants, the tenants of council houses and flats do not have the benefit of rent-control legislation. So the council can increase the rent at any time it chooses and by any amount – subject, of course, to the new rent being 'reasonable'.

The tenant must be given four weeks' notice of the proposed rent increase. The increase does not have to be phased, but a notice of increase must be served. Rent and rate rebates are available to council tenants (see 'Housing Benefit', page 743).

Increases for rates, improvements, services, etc.: when can they be passed on to the tenant?

The tenant pays any increase in the rates, but is not liable to pay the council's increased costs in providing services or for carrying out repairs and improvements to the property. However, the council can simply increase the rent to cover these extra costs.

Notices of increase and phasing (see page 252) do not apply to council tenants as regards rates, improvements, services, etc.

Service charges

The normal rules for protecting tenants against unreasonable service charges (see page 284) do not apply to council tenants, unless the tenant has a fixed-term lease of over twenty-one years – which is very unlikely.

Eviction

The Housing Act 1980 severely restricts the occasions when a council can obtain a court order to evict a council tenant. Before that Act was passed, councils could easily obtain eviction orders and the courts had no choice but to grant orders even when it was clear that the council was acting unreasonably.

Evicting the tenant

Like any landlord, the council must obtain a court order before it evicts a tenant. If a tenant is evicted without there being a court order it will be an illegal eviction and, generally, a criminal offence (see page 274).

The procedure to be followed is in two steps:

- first, the council must serve a preliminary notice on the tenant;
- second, at least four weeks later, court proceedings can be begun.

The preliminary notice to the tenant

The first requirement is for the council to serve a written notice on the tenant, stating the ground on which the council will apply to the court for possession.

In many ways, this preliminary notice is similar to the notice to quit that is often served by a private landlord on a Rent Act tenant (see page 262). It must give at least four weeks' warning of the commencement of proceedings. Exceptionally, the warning period will have to be even longer – for instance, if the tenant pays his rent on a quarterly basis, then three months' notice must be given.

The preliminary notice has a life of twelve months. If proceedings are not commenced within that time, the council will have to serve a fresh notice and wait for the minimum period of four weeks to expire before starting the court proceedings.

The court proceedings

It is for the county court to decide whether a possession (i.e. eviction) order should be made. The general rule is that a well-behaved tenant will not be evicted unless his home is needed and even then he will have to be rehoused by the council. The detailed grounds for possession are set out on pages 294–5.

Eviction of the tenant's family, etc.

What happens if the council tenant dies or leaves the rented property: do the people living with him have to leave as well or can they carry on living there?

Members of the tenant's family

When the tenant dies. The secure tenancy can be inherited by members of the tenant's family. Those entitled to inherit are:

292

- the husband/wife of the dead tenant, provided that it was his/her main home at the time of the death. He or she will always have first claim to the tenancy.
- any other member of the family who lived in the property for twelve months before the death and who regarded it as his/her main home.

'Family' means common-law husband or wife, parents, grandparents, children, grandchildren, brothers, sisters, uncles, aunts, nephews and nieces. If there is a dispute as to which member of the family should succeed to the tenancy, the landlord can select the new tenant.

These rules are similar to those that apply on the death of a Rent Act tenant (see page 265). One difference is that succession can only take place once – on the second death the tenancy ends and cannot be passed on (e.g. father dies and mother inherits; on mother's death the son cannot succeed to the tenancy).

In addition, the tenancy cannot be inherited if the dead tenant:
- was a sole tenant who had previously been a joint tenant, *or*
- had the tenancy assigned to him, since he would then already have been the second tenant to hold under that tenancy.

When the tenant deserts his family. The abandoned husband or wife cannot automatically take over the tenancy, but the landlord is obliged to accept rent from him/her (Matrimonial Homes Act 1983); the landlord cannot argue that the tenant has left and that accordingly the remaining spouse must also leave.

Although the council must accept rent from the remaining spouse, they may refuse to transfer the tenancy to that spouse unless the court has made an order to that effect. However, the court will only make an order in a divorce or judicial separation. If there are no divorce or judicial separation proceedings, then the court cannot order a transfer of the tenancy.

Other members of the family have no such right to remain in occupation. For instance, if the tenant is a single woman and she abandons her aged mother, her mother cannot demand to be allowed to stay on in the rented property.

On divorce. The divorce court can order the secure tenancy to be transferred from one spouse to another, or from joint names into the name of one spouse only. If there are children, the tenancy is likely to be transferred to the spouse who has custody of the children. The council is unlikely to transfer the tenancy unless there is a court order.

Common-law husbands/wives

When the tenant dies. The common-law spouse can inherit the tenancy (see the above section).

When the tenant deserts the common-law spouse. The abandoned partner has no legal right to claim the tenancy or to insist that the council accept his/her payments of rent. However, if the unmarried couple originally took out the council tenancy together, then they will almost certainly both have their names on the rent book. Thus the departure of one of them would not affect the other, for s/he would be a joint tenant and would be able to carry on living there. For joint tenants see page 278.

Council tenants: grounds for possession

When it must be 'reasonable' to evict

The court will only make a possession order if it would be 'reasonable' to do so. For instance, not every act of damage will result in a court making an eviction order – the court will want to be sure that it is reasonable for that damage to lead to the tenant's eviction.

1. *Rent arrears.* Usually the order will only be made if the tenant has a very bad rent record. If the arrears can be paid off by instalments the court might make an order, but suspend it. The order will then come into effect if the tenant does not pay the instalments. If the arrears are paid off before the court hearing, it is almost certain that no eviction order will be made.
2. *Breach of tenancy.* The tenant has broken the terms of the tenancy agreement (e.g. unreasonable subletting). However no order will be made if the breach is only minor and the tenant agrees to remedy it.
3. *Nuisance, annoyance, illegality, immorality.* The tenant, or anyone living with him, has been guilty of such conduct.
4. *Damage.* The tenant has damaged the property or the furniture or allowed it to fall into disrepair. If a lodger or subtenant was to blame, the tenant must have failed to take steps to evict him.
5. (a) *False statement.* The tenant made a false statement, knowingly or recklessly, to persuade the council to grant him the tenancy.
   (b) *Selling the tenancy.* When the tenant has bought, sold, or swapped his tenancy.
6. *Temporary accommodation.* When the tenant has been allowed to live in the property while building works were being carried out to his own home.

When the council must provide suitable alternative accommodation

The court will only make a possession order if it is satisfied that the council can offer the tenant suitable alternative accommodation. In short, this means that the tenant must have security of tenure – it will be either another secure tenancy or a private protected tenancy where the court is not forced to evict (see page 266), and in addition the property must be suitable for the tenant and his family – distance from work, size, terms of the tenancy, any furniture provided, will all be relevant.

7. *Overcrowding.* The premises are overcrowded (see page 286 for what this means).
8. *Demolition, reconstruction.* The council reasonably needs possession to demolish or reconstruct the premises within a reasonable period.
9. *Charitable housing trust.* The landlord is not a council but a charitable housing

trust and the tenant's occupation conflicts with the charity's objects (e.g. a person in housing for the blind is no longer blind).

When the council must prove it is reasonable to evict and *must also provide suitable alternative accommodation*

In these cases, a double test has to be satisfied – reasonableness *and* provision of suitable alternative accommodation.

10. *Disabled accommodation.* The property is suitable for disabled persons but the tenant is not a disabled person.
11. *People difficult to house.* If a housing association lets property to people who are difficult to house and the present tenant is either not within such a category or has been offered a secure council tenancy.
12. *Special needs.* If the property is one of a group let to people with special needs, where special services are provided, and the present tenant does not have special needs.
13. *Overhoused.* The accommodation is more extensive than is reasonably needed. But the tenant must have been a 'successor' to the original tenant (see page 293) and he must have been given at least six months' notice of court proceedings before this ground can apply.

The repair and maintenance of council properties

Contrary to popular belief, councils are not exempt from the laws on maintenance and repair of rented property. See next chapter.

The council tenant's right to buy his home

The Housing Act 1980 allows council tenants to buy their homes. No such right is given to tenants of private landlords.

The tenant (or his spouse) must have been in occupation for at least two years. The price to be paid will be the open-market price, less a discount which varies with the length of the tenant's occupation:

• up to two years, 32 per cent discount

• over two years, 32 per cent discount plus 1 per cent for every year over two years (e.g. ten years equals 40 per cent) subject to a maximum discount of 60 per cent and the maximum figure being £25,000.

The price will initially be fixed by the council but the tenant can appeal this valuation to the district valuer within three months. His decision is final.

If the tenant re-sells within five years of his purchase he must repay part of the discount to the council:

Time since purchase	Percentage of discount to be repaid
under one year	100 per cent
after one year	80 per cent
after two years	60 per cent
after three years	40 per cent
after four years	20 per cent
after five years	nil

The tenant can claim a council mortgage to finance his purchase. This can be up to 100 per cent of the price, subject to the tenant's income entitling him to a loan of that amount.

If the tenant cannot afford to buy, he can opt for shared ownership instead (see page 299).

Most housing-association tenants also have a right to buy (see page 299).

HOUSING ASSOCIATIONS

Housing associations are now seen as the second line of state-financed housing. Basically, the idea is that a group of people can register themselves as a housing association with a view to constructing new homes or converting existing buildings into modern housing; if the government approves of the scheme it will finance the building works and capital costs through full grants from the Housing Corporation, and when the work is completed the housing association will rent out the properties at 'fair rents'.

The concept of housing associations is not new and dates from the mid nineteenth century. However, the early housing associations soon found that their economic-cost rents were too expensive for the 'labouring classes' for whom the accommodation was intended. Thus, it was left to private foundations such as the Guinness, Peabody, and Bournville Trusts to subsidize various schemes, and it was not until the 1960s that the state began to take an active interest in financing housing associations. Since then, the housing-association movement has expanded rapidly.

Since there are many similarities between housing associations and local-authority housing programmes, it is not surprising that housing associations are expected to have motives that go beyond the rehousing of the people who formed the association. The government (through the Housing Corporation) will want to be sure that it is lending money to a deserving cause and, in particular, will look for evidence that the association is concerned with improving housing conditions in an area where they are poor. In addition, housing associations are expected to behave like local authorities in allocating housing to those with special needs – such as the infirm and those with social problems that make it difficult for them to find accommodation.

The position of the tenant in a housing association

For rent purposes the housing-association tenant receives the protection of a private (Rent Act) tenant, but for eviction purposes he is treated in the same way as a public (council) tenant.

Rent

A tenant of a housing association will pay a 'fair rent', as registered by the rent officer.

Eviction

A tenant of a housing association has a secure tenancy and can only be evicted by court order in certain well-defined circumstances, and only if either it would be reasonable to evict him or if alternative accommodation can be provided for him.

When a housing association buys tenanted property

What happens if the private landlord of a tenant with Rent Act protection sells the property to a housing association? Does the tenant retain his Rent Act protection or does he lose it and have the lesser protection of a secure tenant? The answer is that he becomes a secure tenant and is in the same position as any other housing-association tenant. Thus, his rent can now be increased more easily than when he was the tenant of a private landlord.

Rent

Housing associations charge 'fair rents' as assessed by the rent officer (see page 254 for how fair rents are assessed and registered).

Housing-association tenants are covered by the rules as to notices of increase and phasing of rent increases (see page 252).

Redevelopment and rent increases

There is an increasing tendency for housing associations to concentrate on refurbishing and modernizing existing dilapidated houses rather than building new houses.

In cases of refurbishment, there is often a tenant living in the unmodernized property, and it is not uncommon for the tenant to refuse to move out. The housing association will be able to obtain an eviction order from the county court, although it will have to rehouse him (he may also be entitled to a home-loss grant). If the tenant is allowed to move back in once the building work has been completed he will then be charged a 'fair rent' for the property, and this is likely to exceed the amount he paid for the old, unmodernized accommodation; although the tenant may argue that this is unfair ('I didn't ask for the work to be done, did I?'), he is bound to pay the increased rent. This is a problem that arises particularly with old people who have lived in a property for many years. Any rent increase will, of course, be phased (see page 252).

Increases for rates, services, improvements, etc.

The position is as with council tenants (see page 291).

Rent allowances and rate rebates

Housing-association tenants are eligible for both of these benefits (see page 743).

Eviction

The tenant of a registered housing association has a 'secure' tenancy and can only be evicted by a court order obtained in certain well-defined circumstances. The position is exactly the same as for council tenants (see page 292).

Eviction of the tenant's family, etc.

What happens if a housing-association tenant dies, leaves the rented property, or divorces his/her spouse? Briefly, the position of the spouse and family will be exactly the same as if they were in council housing (see page 292).

Similarly, the position of a mistress (etc.) is as if the property was rented from the council (see page 293).

Repair and maintenance of housing-association properties

The normal rules as to the repair and maintenance of the rented property apply to housing associations (see Chapter 18).

The 'right to buy': housing-association tenants

Many housing-association tenants have the right to buy their homes from their landlords – as if they were council tenants. See page 296 for how the discount is calculated, and the rules on re-sale. But not all housing-association tenants have the right to buy. The rules are complicated and it will usually be necessary to ask the housing association whether it is subject to the right-to-buy provisions. Note that tenants of housing associations which are *charities* do not have a right to buy their own homes but are given a chance to buy other properties. The basics of the scheme are that the housing association calculates the value of the discount that the tenant would have received if he had been able to use the right to buy. The tenant can then ask the housing association to buy a different property, and then re-sell it to him at a discount (i.e. at the price the association paid, less the value of the discount). However, the government has only made a small amount of money available for this scheme and as a result few tenants of charitable housing associations have been lucky enough to be selected for the scheme.

SHARED OWNERSHIP

Tenants of local councils, housing associations, and certain other bodies can opt for shared ownership. This is when the buyer does not buy the whole house or flat but buys a percentage share in it (usually because he cannot afford 100 per cent ownership). For instance, suppose a house is bought from a new-town corporation on a 75 per cent shared-ownership basis. The buyer will pay 75 per cent of the market price (usually, of course, with a mortgage), plus he will pay 25 per cent of the normal rent for that property. The buyer can change his mind at a later date and buy out the other 25 per cent if he wants to. If he doesn't then when he comes to sell he will have to split the proceeds (i.e. in this case 25 per cent would go to the new-town corporation).

Shared ownership is only available to secure tenants (see page 289 for what this means); a tenant with a private landlord cannot demand shared ownership.

One point that a shared-owner should bear in mind is that he will become fully liable for all repairs on the property – he does not share those costs with the council or landlord. To offset this increased liability, the rent he pays is reduced by 25 per cent (e.g. if the rent is £50, but he then buys a 50 per cent share, then future rent will be £25 less 25 per cent = £18·75).

Tenants' Exchange Scheme. Council and housing-association tenants who want to move to another part of the country should register under the Tenants' Exchange Scheme. Each month a list of secure tenants who want to move is sent to each local council, and tenants are encouraged to contact other people on the list to see if they can agree a swap. If so, the council or housing association, etc. will normally agree.

18 Rented Property: Its Repair and Maintenance

The law on repairing rented accommodation is both complicated and difficult to enforce. Ideally, the law should be set out in one easily understood Act. But in practice this is not the case, for the law may be contained in any one of several unrelated statutes or in the terms of a tenancy agreement between the landlord and the tenant. Often a tenant will find that he has more than one remedy and that these different remedies originate from different Acts; he will then have to decide which to pursue first.

There are eleven major repairing remedies that may be available to the tenant; these are set out in the table on page 303. Few of the remedies have any connection with each other; each remedy has its own rules as to when it is available and the tenant has to work his way through the list finding out which remedies are applicable to his particular problem. But to complicate matters further, the different remedies are enforced in different ways, and whereas some remedies are relatively speedy to put into effect, others are not.

So the starting-point is to check which remedies might be applicable to the problem in hand; the next stage is to see which remedy is the most easily enforced in the shortest possible time. (A helpful hint – usually Repairing Remedy No. 1 (on page 304) – will be the most useful starting-point.)

It may be a good idea to refer first to the full-page diagram on page 302; this illustrates some of the common housing defects and suggests the remedies that might be available.

What if the landlord wants to repair, but the tenant won't let him?

Most of this chapter deals with the position when a landlord is reluctant to repair and so a tenant has to use a legal remedy to ensure that the necessary repairs are carried out. However, it sometimes happens that the position is reversed, and it is the landlord who wants to carry out the building works but the tenant refuses to give his consent. What can the landlord do?

Firstly, a landlord has the right to enter the property (after giving reasonable notice) and carry out necessary *repairs* if:

● there is a specific clause in a lease or tenancy agreement that gives him that right, *or*

● the repairs are his legal responsibility under tenant's Remedy No. 1 or No. 4 (see table, page 303).

300

Otherwise the landlord cannot force repairs on the tenant; if he tries to do so, he may be liable for harassment (see page 274).

Secondly, the landlord might want to *improve, modernize, extend* or *convert* the property, as opposed to merely carrying out repairs. If so, does he have the right to enter the property and carry out the work? Generally, the tenant can refuse him entry unless there is a specific clause in the lease that allows him entry. The only exception is when the landlord wishes to install 'standard amenities' (i.e. bath/shower, washbasin and sink, all with hot and cold water) which are eligible for a local authority Intermediate Grant (see page 322). If the tenant will not give his consent, the landlord can try to obtain an order from the county court. Otherwise, repairs and improvements cannot be forced on a tenant. However, if the tenant has very little security from eviction (e.g. he has a resident landlord) the tenant may have no choice but to agree or be evicted.

Repair or improvement?

Be careful to distinguish repair from improvement.

Repair includes

- remedying a defective damp-proof course
- repointing brickwork
- eliminating dry rot and replacing the affected timbers but not removing the cause (e.g. lack of a damp-proof course)
- renewing crumbling plaster
- maintaining an existing water heater
- replacing worn-out fixtures
- rewiring
- replumbing.

Improvement includes

- putting in a bathroom
- installing extra electrical sockets when rewiring
- installing damp-proof course
- replacing fixtures put in by a tenant.

A tenant's remedies when his landlord will not carry out repairs

There are eleven major repairing remedies. The tenant must work his way through the list and see which remedies apply to his case; he then selects the remedy that seems to be most effective. In practice, Remedy No. 1 (see page 304) will probably be the most helpful.

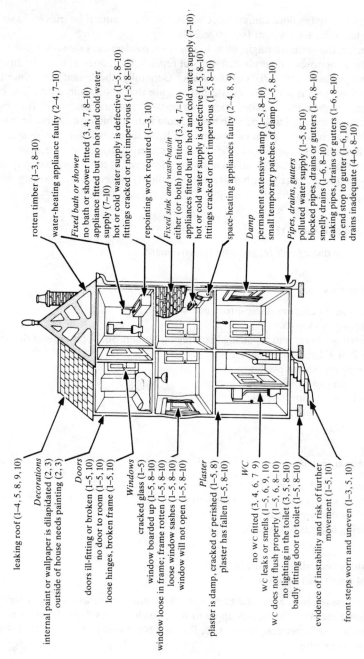

rotten timber (1–3, 8–10)

water-heating appliance faulty (2–4, 7–10)

Fixed bath or shower
no bath or shower fitted (3, 4, 7, 8–10)
appliance fitted but no hot and cold water supply (7–10)
hot or cold water supply is defective (1–5, 8–10)
fittings cracked or not impervious (1–5, 8–10)

repointing work required (1–3, 10)

Fixed sink and wash-basin
either (or both) not fitted (3, 4, 7–10)
appliances fitted but no hot and cold water supply (7–10)
hot or cold water supply is defective (1–5, 8–10)
fittings cracked or not impervious (1–5, 8–10)

space-heating appliances faulty (2–4, 8, 9)

Damp
permanent extensive damp (1–5, 8–10)
small temporary patches of damp (1–5, 8–10)

Pipes, drains, gutters
polluted water supply (1–5, 8–10)
blocked pipes, drains or gutters (1–6, 8–10)
smelly drains (1–6, 8–10)
leaking pipes, drains or gutters (1–6, 8–10)
no end stop to gutter (1–6, 10)
drains inadequate (4–6, 8–10)

leaking roof (1–4, 5, 8, 9, 10)

Decorations
internal paint or wallpaper is dilapidated (2, 3)
outside of house needs painting (2, 3)

Doors
doors ill-fitting or broken (1–5, 10)
no door to room (1–5, 10)
loose hinges, broken frame (1–5, 10)

Windows
cracked glass (1–5)
window boarded up (1–5, 8–10)
window loose in frame; frame rotten (1–5, 8–10)
loose window sashes (1–5, 8–10)
window will not open (1–5, 8–10)

Plaster
plaster is damp, cracked or perished (1–5, 8)
plaster has fallen (1–5, 8–10)

WC
no WC fitted (3, 4, 6, 7, 9)
WC leaks or smells (1–5, 6, 9, 10)
WC does not flush properly (1–5, 6, 8–10)
no lighting in the toilet (3, 5, 8–10)
badly fitting door to toilet (1–5, 8–10)

evidence of instability and risk of further movement (1–5, 10)

front steps worn and uneven (1–3, 5, 10)

The tenant's possible remedies are numbered in the brackets: see page 303 for key

A tenant's possible repairing remedies

Remedy	Who enforces it?	Council tenants included?	See page
1. *Letting of less than seven years*, so landlord responsible for drains, heating, structure, etc.	tenant only	yes	304
2. *Written tenancy agreement* with specific clauses on responsibility for repairs	tenant only	yes	305
3. *No written tenancy agreement*, so several implied terms are assumed to apply	tenant only	yes	306
4. *Lettings at a very low rent*, so landlord must keep premises 'fit for human habitation'	tenant only	yes	306
5. Breach of the *general public health laws*	either tenant or local authority	yes	308
6. Breach of special public-health laws relating to *w cs, drains, and sewers*	either tenant or local authority	yes	311
7. *A basic ('standard') amenity is missing*, so the landlord may be forced to install it	local authority only	no	312
8. The premises are *'unfit for human habitation'* and cannot be repaired at reasonable expense	local authority only	no	315
9. The premises are *'unfit for human habitation'* and can be repaired at reasonable expense	local authority only	no	316
10. The premises are in *'substantial disrepair'* yet not unfit for human habitation	local authority only	no	316
11. More than one family live in the premises and so the *multiple occupation* laws may apply	local authority only	no	319

303

Housing: Tenants

A. Remedies enforceable by the tenant only

Repairing Remedy No. 1

In lettings of less than seven years, the landlord is responsible for maintaining and repairing:
- *structure and exterior of the building*
- *drains, gutters, and external pipes*
- *water, gas, and electricity supplies*
- *sanitary installations such as sinks, baths, and wcs*
- *space-heating (e.g. gas fires) and water-heating appliances.*

Most rented accommodation is covered by this, which is based on section 32 of the Housing Act 1961. Note that the obligation on the landlord is only to repair and maintain; he need not (for instance) install water heaters or gas fires if they were not there when the tenant first rented the property. Summarized, it makes the landlord liable for the repair and maintenance of the structure of the building (e.g. outside walls, roof, foundations, stairs) and of the electrical, gas, and plumbing systems.

The remedy is only available if the original letting was to be for less than seven years (e.g. lease for six years; weekly tenancy) although it still applies if the tenant stays on for more than seven years. It therefore covers all periodic tenancies, and the vast majority of Rent Act lettings. In addition, pre-1961 lettings are excluded unless the rent register specifically states that the landlord has agreed to accept the Act's repairing obligations – as it often does.

The landlord cannot evade responsibility by putting a clause in a lease which states that the Act shall not apply.

The tenant's use of the property. However, the landlord will be able to avoid liability if the disrepair arose through the tenant not behaving properly, such as failing to 'behave in a tenant-like manner'. Thus, if the tenant is going

away for the winter he must turn off the water and empty the boiler. He must clean the chimneys when necessary, and also the windows. He must mend the electric light when it fuses. He must unstop the sink when it is blocked by his waste. In short, he must do the little jobs about the place which a reasonable tenant would do. (Lord Denning, 1954)

Consequential loss. Even if the landlord is clearly liable to repair the property, there may be a dispute as to the cost of loss and damage caused by the defect. For example, if the roof leaks and rain damage is caused to interior decorations, who pays for the cost of redecorating? Even worse, suppose the roof leaks so badly that a bedroom ceiling falls on the tenant, injuring him; can he sue the landlord for his personal injury and loss of wages while off work? As regards the cost of repairing the roof and the ceiling there can be no argument, for the Act clearly makes this the landlord's responsibility. But as regards the consequential loss (i.e. the cost of redecorations, the injury compensation, loss of wages) the landlord will only be liable if he had notice of the defect. Thus, if the tenant had earlier warned the landlord that the ceiling looked unsafe, the landlord would be liable. Or, if the landlord's builder had inspected the property and seen the defect (or if he *ought* to have seen it) the landlord would be liable. But not otherwise. For instance:

> *Mr O'Brien was the tenant of a flat. In 1965 he had complained to his landlord about stamping on the ceiling from the flat above, although he had not suggested that the ceiling was defective in any way. In 1968 the ceiling fell in and Mr O'Brien was injured. He sued the landlord, arguing that there had been a breach of section 32, Housing Act 1961. Held: The landlord was only liable to remedy the defective ceiling when he knew that it was defective; he had not been given notice of any defect and so he was not liable.* O'Brien (1973)

So the advice for any tenant is to carry out regular inspections of his rented property, and give the landlord written notice of any possible defect.

The main drawbacks of this remedy are that it cannot be used:

● to require structural alterations or improvements (and installing a damp-proof course would probably come within this category – although there are cases in which a landlord has had to repair an existing d.p.c.);

● when the tenant has not given the landlord notice of the disrepair;

● to require hot water or space heating if there was none in the property at the start of the letting;

● generally, it does not apply to communal parts (e.g. shared hallway or a wc on the landing).

Despite these drawbacks, the remedy applies to virtually all Rent Act tenants and will often be the main remedy available.

Enforcing the remedy. See page 307.

Repairing Remedy No. 2

When there is a written agreement there may be a specific clause in the lease or tenancy agreement that states who is responsible for carrying out the repairs.

If a tenant has a lease, it is likely that several clauses will deal with responsibility for repairs – generally imposing many obligations on the tenant but few on the landlord. However, an express clause of this sort cannot override a repairing obligation imposed by an Act of Parliament; for example Remedy No. 1 (Housing Act 1961) cannot be evaded by putting in a clause saying the Act shall not apply (see above).

Most leases exempt the tenant from responsibility for damage, etc., caused through 'fair wear and tear'. This exempts him

from liability for repairs that are decorative and for remedying parts that wear and come adrift in the course of reasonable use, but it does not exempt him from anything further. If further damage is likely to flow from that wear and tear, he must do such repairs as are necessary to stop that further damage. If a slate falls off the roof through wear and tear . . . the tenant is not responsible for the slate coming off, but he ought to put in another so as to prevent further damage. (Lord Denning)

He could, of course, charge the cost of replacing the slate to the landlord.

The tenant's use of the property; consequential loss. The position is the same as under Remedy No. 1, see page 304.

Enforcing the remedy. See page 304.

Repairing Remedy No. 3

When there is no written agreement, the law puts several fairly minor repairing obligations on the landlord.

Often there will be no written contract or agreement between the landlord and tenant, and so there is an 'oral' tenancy. In this case, the common law implies several terms into their oral agreement, as being the law's assumption of what they would have agreed had the terms been put into writing.

Furnished lettings. The courts have held that there is an implied covenant that furnished premises are 'fit for human habitation' at the time the letting starts. This should not be confused with the statutory requirement that all dwelling-houses be fit for human habitation (see Remedy No. 8, page 315). Generally, a lower standard is expected than under the statutory provisions and in practice this remedy is of virtually no use.

Weekly tenancies. There may be an implied term that the landlord will be responsible for the repair and maintenance of the outside structure of the building, if it is a weekly tenancy (i.e. the tenant pays his rent week by week – as do most council tenants). However, the law is not clear; one case says there is an implied term making the landlord liable, but another case says he is not responsible. Once again, the remedy is of very little practical use. Repairing Remedy 1 (above) is much more likely to be of use.

Safety of common parts. The landlord must take reasonable care to keep the common parts (e.g. steps, stairs, passages, roof, shared wc) in safe condition.

The tenant's use of the property; consequential loss. The position is the same as under Remedy No. 1, see page 304.

Enforcing the remedy. See page 307.

Repairing Remedy No. 4

In lettings at a very low rent there is an implied term that the landlord will keep the premises 'fit for human habitation'.

Remedy No. 4 is based on section 6 of the Housing Act 1957. It only applies if the rent at the start of the tenancy was less than £52 p.a. (£80 p.a. if in Inner London) unless the tenancy pre-dates the Act, in which case the rent levels are halved. Thus few tenants come within the scope of this remedy. Even if they do, the standard of repair is not high; all that is required is that the premises should be 'fit for human habitation'; see page 315 for what this means. The end result is that this remedy is of little practical use to a tenant.

The tenant's use of the property; consequential loss. The position is the same as under Remedy No. 1, see page 304.

Enforcing the remedy. See below.

Enforcing Remedies 1–4

These remedies can only be enforced by the tenant himself; he cannot ask the local authority to enforce them for him. The tenant will probably want to know whether he can claim damages and also get the repairs done.

Damages

The landlord is liable in damages as from the date he knew of the defect. He can be sued, generally in the county court, but the compensation is unlikely to be substantial unless the tenant suffered specific loss, as opposed to general inconvenience. The courts are not generous; most cases are not worth even £500, and only in the worst case could the tenant expect to receive as much as £1,000 damages.

Getting the repairs done

This will be the tenant's main concern. He can either start court proceedings or get the repairs done himself.

Starting court proceedings. Generally the tenant will bring his claim in the county court. He can ask the court for an *injunction*, which in effect orders the landlord to do the work, as does an *order of specific performance*, which is another type of order that he might ask for. Alternatively, the landlord may agree to give an *undertaking* to the court to do the repairs, without the need for the case and evidence to be heard.

But these three courses of action (the injunction, order for specific performance, and the undertaking) all presuppose that the tenant is able and willing to go to court. Although legal aid (see page 849) may be available, the court case will probably involve expense, inconvenience, and – most important – delay. So the tenant may do better to get the repairs done himself.

Doing the repairs yourself. The tenant can get the work done himself and deduct the cost from his future payments of rent. However, the danger of this is that the landlord will say that the tenant has failed to pay his proper rent and serve a notice to quit, with a view to bringing a county-court claim for an eviction order. To avoid this danger, the tenant should play safe and give the landlord written notice of his intention. The landlord should be given a chance to do the work himself – say twenty-eight days, or seven days if it is really urgent. The tenant should obtain more than one estimate for the work and give the landlord a chance to challenge them. Only then should the work be done and the cost deducted from future rent payments.

Obviously, the tenant should be sure that the landlord is legally liable to do the work before he risks doing the work himself and deducting the cost from his rent. As a less risky alternative, the tenant could still do the work himself but then sue the landlord in the county court (see page 872 for the procedure) for the cost – rather than deducting the cost from his rent payments. That way he cannot be said to have got into rent arrears.

B. Remedies enforceable by either the tenant or the local authority

The next two remedies can be enforced by either the tenant or the local authority. They are speedy and effective remedies, and are derived from the public health legislation, which reflects society's concern that everyone should live in hygienic, healthy surroundings. However, in practice, local authorities are reluctant to get involved in anything that might require them to spend money and so often it is only in the worst cases that they are prepared to intervene.

Repairing Remedy No. 5

Has there been a breach of the public-health laws because the premises are in such a state as to be:
- *likely to cause injury, or*
- *a nuisance to the occupiers and neighbours?*

The unusual feature of this remedy is that it *requires* the local authority to take action against the landlord if the public-health provisions have been broken. The local authority has no discretion.

The remedy applies to two different sets of circumstances: firstly, when the premises are a legal 'nuisance' (see page 347) and, secondly, when they are 'injurious to the public health'. It is the 'injury to health' claim that is likely to be of most use to a tenant.

To the layman, the idea of a breach of the Public Health Acts conjures up images of a house infested with rats and cockroaches, or with foul drains. Although the Acts do cover such blatant examples of uncleanliness, they also encompass much less obvious health hazards that might not, at first sight, seem to be public-health matters. A look at the illustration on page 302 will indicate the wide range of items that can come within the scope of this remedy; for example, dampness, defective sanitary fittings, ill-fitting windows or doors, leaking rainwater gutters, defective roofs, damp plasterwork, etc.

But it must be appreciated that it is not the defect itself that gives rise to a public-health remedy – it is the *consequence* of the defect that raises a matter of public-health concern. As an illustration, consider a window that will not open because the wooden frame has rotted; in itself this will not be a public-health matter, but if that is the only window in the room the result will be that there is no ventilation in the room and that will be a public-health matter, since it is 'injurious to health'

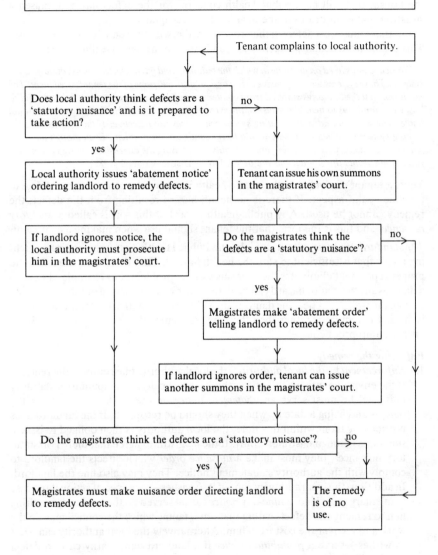

Repairing Remedy No. 5
When defects are 'injurious to health'

Tenant complains to local authority.

Does local authority think defects are a 'statutory nuisance' and is it prepared to take action?

no

yes

Local authority issues 'abatement notice' ordering landlord to remedy defects.

Tenant can issue his own summons in the magistrates' court.

If landlord ignores notice, the local authority must prosecute him in the magistrates' court.

Do the magistrates think the defects are a 'statutory nuisance'?

no

yes

Magistrates make 'abatement order' telling landlord to remedy defects.

If landlord ignores order, tenant can issue another summons in the magistrates' court.

Do the magistrates think the defects are a 'statutory nuisance'?

no

yes

Magistrates must make nuisance order directing landlord to remedy defects.

The remedy is of no use.

to occupy an unventilated room. Similarly, suppose the defect is a holed roof; of itself, that will not be a public-health matter, but as soon as it rains and water enters the house, that will be a public-health concern, for the defect has now caused a situation that is 'injurious to the health' of the occupants.

But there must be a defect in the property. Otherwise the remedy will be of no use. This can be a particular problem with condensation, as this case illustrates:

> *Council tenants lived on an estate in which the buildings had gas or electric background-heating systems. These systems were expensive to run and, in practice, none of the tenants used them. The result was that the buildings suffered from condensation. The tenants complained that the buildings were 'injurious to health' because of the extensive condensation. Held: The council was not liable. There was an adequate heating system which was not defective. If the tenants used the heating system provided then there would be no condensation problem. Even though the court felt that the tenants were not acting unreasonably in not using the expensive heating systems, the fact remained that the council was not liable.* Dover District Council (1982)

Thus, a tenant can only use the public-health remedy if he can tie up the defect to a public-health aspect. If there is no health hazard resulting from the defect, the remedy cannot be used. Any public-health hazard of this sort is called a *'statutory nuisance'* and this is the term that the tenant should use when making a complaint.

The standard of repair. Unfortunately, the Public Health Acts only require a patching repair that is sufficient to stop the health hazard. They do not require a full and proper repair that eliminates the root cause of the problem. For example, if there is a damp wall, the health hazard can be overcome by simply drying out the wall, even though the wall might become damp again within a few months; the temporary repair is all that is required, rather than the long-term cure of, for example, installing a proper damp-proof course.

Enforcing the remedy.
1. *Enforcement by the local authority* – the local authority must enforce the remedy. If the environmental health officer thinks that the defects amount to a 'statutory nuisance' he must serve an *abatement notice* on the landlord, specifying the defects and fixing a date by when they should be remedied. If the landlord does not remedy them within this time, the local authority is then obliged to issue a summons in the magistrates' court. If the magistrates agree that there is a 'statutory nuisance', they must make a *nuisance order* which directs the landlord to comply with the authority's abatement notice. They may also fine the landlord. In addition, the local authority can – if it so wishes – take special action if the case is an emergency. If so, a *nine-day notice* can be served on the landlord, requiring him to remedy the defects within that time, failing which the council may do the work and recover the cost from him. Alternatively the local authority can – if it so wishes – serve a *prohibition notice* if a landlord temporarily cures a defect which is likely to occur again (e.g. he puts a poor-quality patch on a leaking roof). But note that the council has a discretion in deciding whether to issue a nine-day notice or a prohibition notice; in the case of the abatement notice the council has no choice.

But this assumes that the local authority is helpful and prepared to act on the tenant's behalf. If the council fails to serve an abatement notice, the tenant could probably go to the High Court for an order telling the council to carry out its duty; however, this is unnecessarily complicated, for all the tenant has to do is to start proceedings against the landlord himself.

2. *Enforcement by the tenant* – the tenant may find it quicker to take action himself rather than wait for the local authority to do so. The tenant should go to his local magistrates' court and ask to issue a summons under section 99 of the Public Health Act 1936. (See page 886 for the procedure on issuing a summons, but legal aid will not be available for this.) Once the summons has been issued, the court will serve it on the landlord and arrange a date for the hearing of the case. If the magistrates decide there is a statutory nuisance, they must issue an abatement notice (see chart, page 309).

Some magistrates' courts take a fairly robust view of what constitutes a health hazard and is thus a statutory nuisance. However, it must be remembered that several seemingly trivial defects can, when taken together, amount to a statutory nuisance. Although this is undoubtedly the law, some magistrates' courts are reluctant to convict in such cases, and need to be reminded of the law. For instance:

Mr Patel issued a section 99 summons against his landlord. At the hearing the evidence was given by a self-employed public health adviser and by the local council's environmental health officer; both described the property's defects in detail and stated that they were 'prejudicial to health'. Despite this expert evidence, the magistrates did not convict the landlord. They said 'it appeared from the unchallenged evidence that the alleged defects to the premises existed and that the standard of those premises was undesirably low. The majority of the defects were trivial and appear to have been contributed to, if not caused by, the neglect of the occupiers [i.e. the Patels]. They constituted an inconvenience rather than a health hazard.'

Mr Patel appealed to the divisional court. Held: The magistrates were ordered to convict the landlord. Magistrates should not substitute their own opinion for those of informed expert witnesses. Patel (1980)

From the tenant's point of view, the main problem with this repairing remedy is that it can be very difficult to get the local authority to act (especially if the council is itself the landlord!). The other problem is that legal aid is not available to the tenant who wants to take the case to court himself.

Repairing Remedy No. 6

Has there been a breach of the special public-health laws relating to drains, soil pipes, and wcs?

Whereas Remedy No. 5 is concerned with general health hazards, this remedy is specifically designed to deal with unhygienic sanitary facilities.

Briefly, the provisions are:

● *insufficient wcs or drains.* The local authority *must* require the landlord to provide more or to replace the existing ones.

● *repair of wcs, drains, and private sewers.* The local authority *must* require the owner (i.e. landlord) to repair or replace broken wcs, drains, and private sewers.

● *blockage of wcs.* The local authority *may* (NB, the local authority has a discretion) order the owner to unblock it within forty-eight hours, failing which the local authority can do the work and then recover the cost from the landlord.

● *shared wcs.* If the wc is shared by several families, it is an offence to injure, block, or improperly foul it (50p fine). The people using it are responsible for cleaning it and the approach to it.

Enforcing the remedy. A prosecution can be brought in the magistrates' court by either the local authority or the tenant. In practice, the council will probably only intervene in the worst cases.

C. Remedies enforceable by the local authority only

The next five remedies can only be enforced by the local authority. With all of them, the local authority has a complete discretion in deciding whether to take action; there is nothing the tenant can do to make the council help him.

All the tenant can do is to lobby the housing department, his local councillor, and his MP to see whether pressure can be brought to bear. Once again, the council may well be reluctant to help.

All these remedies are derived from the Housing Acts, which reflect society's concern that individual houses should be kept in good repair and not allowed to deteriorate, for otherwise the nation's housing stock would be reduced.

Repairing Remedy No. 7

When certain basic amenities are missing, the landlord can be forced to install them – but the tenant's rent may well be increased as a result (Part VIII, Housing Act 1974).

Strictly speaking, this remedy is not for repair, but for improvement; however, it is closely related to the repairing provisions and is best seen as part of the armoury of remedies available to a tenant who wishes to improve his housing conditions.

If a tenant does not have all of the following *standard amenities* he can ask the local authority to order the landlord to install them. The standard amenities are:

● a fixed bath or shower, with hot and cold water
● a wash-hand basin with hot and cold water
● a sink with hot and cold water
● a wc.

These are all eligible for a local-authority Intermediate Grant (see page 312).

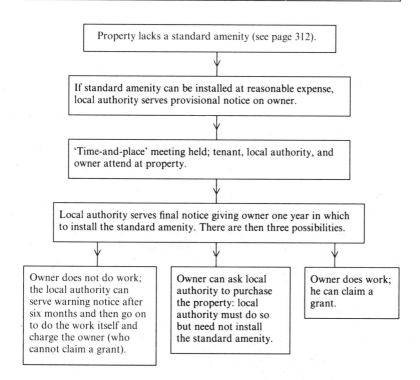

Repairing Remedy No. 7
Compulsory installation of standard amenities

Property lacks a standard amenity (see page 312).

↓

If standard amenity can be installed at reasonable expense, local authority serves provisional notice on owner.

↓

'Time-and-place' meeting held; tenant, local authority, and owner attend at property.

↓

Local authority serves final notice giving owner one year in which to install the standard amenity. There are then three possibilities.

↓

Owner does not do work; the local authority can serve warning notice after six months and then go on to do the work itself and charge the owner (who cannot claim a grant).

Owner can ask local authority to purchase the property: local authority must do so but need not install the standard amenity.

Owner does work; he can claim a grant.

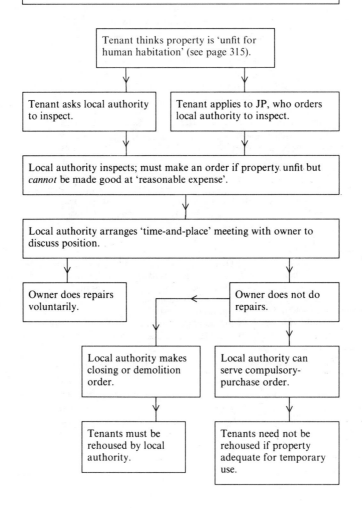

Repairing Remedy No. 8
Unfit and *not* repairable at reasonable expense

Tenant thinks property is 'unfit for human habitation' (see page 315).

Tenant asks local authority to inspect.

Tenant applies to JP, who orders local authority to inspect.

Local authority inspects; must make an order if property unfit but *cannot* be made good at 'reasonable expense'.

Local authority arranges 'time-and-place' meeting with owner to discuss position.

Owner does repairs voluntarily.

Owner does not do repairs.

Local authority makes closing or demolition order.

Local authority can serve compulsory-purchase order.

Tenants must be rehoused by local authority.

Tenants need not be rehoused if property adequate for temporary use.

The remedy is only available to houses and flats that were created – whether by construction or conversion – before October 1961. It does not matter if the tenancy was created after 1961. For details, see the chart on page 313.

Repairing Remedy No. 8

Is the condition of the property so bad that it is 'unfit for human habitation', and it is not repairable at reasonable expense? If so, the local authority may order that it be demolished or that no one be allowed to live there (s. 17, Housing Act 1957).

The first step is for the council to decide whether the property is 'unfit for human habitation'. This is decided by reference to the *nine-point standard*, which considers the state of repair, stability, damp, natural lighting, ventilation, water supply, drainage, wcs, and cooking facilities. Only matters on this list are considered; thus, a house may be infested with bugs and not have any electricity, and yet be legally 'fit for human habitation'. On the other hand, there was one case in which it was held that a broken sash-cord in a bedroom window made the whole house unfit for human habitation (since it was not properly ventilated). Obviously, most cases do not come within these extremes but the general rule is that many old and tatty properties are, strictly speaking, legally unfit for human habitation.

If it is decided that the property is unfit for human habitation, the local authority must then decide whether it is repairable at reasonable expense; if 'yes', then Remedy No. 9 may be used. If 'no', then this remedy can be employed.

The council will discuss the position with the landlord but can make:

• a demolition order: this orders that the building be pulled down. The landlord can appeal to the county court.

• a closing order: this is the equivalent of a demolition order when the unfit premises form part of a larger building (e.g. a flat in a house, or a semi-detached house which partly supports the next-door house). In such a case demolition could not be ordered and so a closing order is made which directs that no one is to live in the unfit premises. The landlord can appeal to the county court. For details of the procedure, see the chart on page 314.

The position of the tenant. Clearly, this is a drastic remedy, for the tenant will lose his home. However, the council is obliged to rehouse the tenant so it may well be an admirable remedy from the tenant's point of view. In addition, the tenant may be able to claim:

• a home-loss payment: if the tenant was resident there for at least five years he can claim a home-loss payment. The claim must be made within six months of moving out of the premises.

• a disturbance payment. This covers reasonable costs incurred in moving (e.g. the hire of a removal van).

Repairing Remedy No. 9

Is the condition of the property so bad that it is 'unfit for human habitation', but it is repairable at reasonable expense? If so, the local authority must order the owner to carry out the necessary repairs (s. 9, Housing Act 1957).

The first step is to determine whether the property is 'unfit for human habitation' – see Remedy No. 8, above, for the standard applied.

Remedy No. 8 applies if an unfit property *cannot* be repaired at reasonable expense. This remedy, No. 9, applies if the unfit property *is* repairable at reasonable expense.

If it is repairable at reasonable expense, the local authority must serve a notice on the owner requiring him to carry out the necessary works within twenty-one days – a 'twenty-one-day notice'. If the owner does not do the works, the authority *may* do it and charge the owner; in practice, of course, most local authorities are reluctant to incur the expenditure and so they do not do the work in default.

It can often be difficult to persuade the local authority to inspect premises. If they do not come when requested, the best remedy is to apply to a JP (i.e. magistrate), and describe the state of the premises; if he thinks that they are unfit for human habitation, he will order the authority to inspect. Once the authority inspects and agrees that the premises are unfit and repairable at reasonable expense, it *must* serve a notice on the owner. The full procedure is set out in the chart on page 317. The council will normally have to give grants to help with the cost of the work (see page 322), which is why councils are usually reluctant to use this repairing remedy.

Repairing Remedy No. 10

Is the property fit for human habitation but yet in 'substantial disrepair'? If so, the local authority may order the owner to carry out necessary repairs (s. 9(1A), Housing Act 1957).

Even if the property is not 'unfit for human habitation' (see Remedies 8 and 9), the local authority still has power to order the owner to carry out necessary works. This can be done if the property is in 'substantial disrepair'. There is no definition of what is substantial disrepair but it generally means that the authority can order such works as are needed to bring the property up to a reasonable standard having regard to its age, character, and locality.

Note that there is no obligation on the local authority to order the owner to carry out these works; compare the position with Remedies 8 and 9 when the authority must take steps. Once again, the council may be reluctant to intervene because it will probably have to give the landlord a grant to help with the cost of the works.

For the procedure, see the chart on page 318.

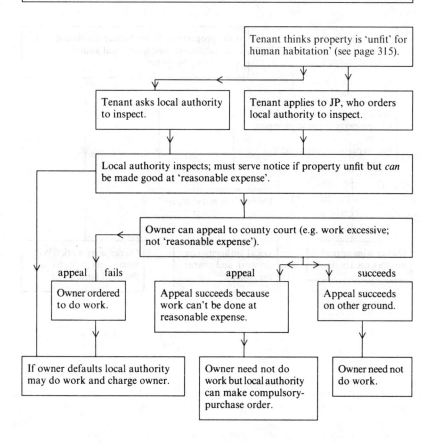

Repairing Remedy No. 9
Unfit and *repairable* at reasonable expense

Tenant thinks property is 'unfit' for human habitation' (see page 315).

Tenant asks local authority to inspect.

Tenant applies to JP, who orders local authority to inspect.

Local authority inspects; must serve notice if property unfit but *can* be made good at 'reasonable expense'.

Owner can appeal to county court (e.g. work excessive; not 'reasonable expense').

appeal | fails

appeal

succeeds

Owner ordered to do work.

Appeal succeeds because work can't be done at reasonable expense.

Appeal succeeds on other ground.

If owner defaults local authority may do work and charge owner.

Owner need not do work but local authority can make compulsory-purchase order.

Owner need not do work.

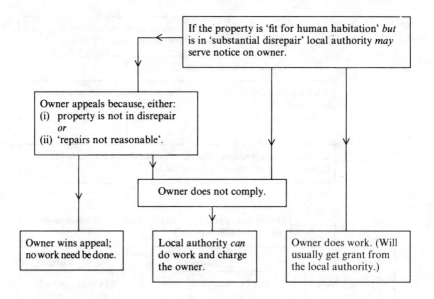

Repairing Remedy No. 10
Properties in 'substantial disrepair'

If the property is 'fit for human habitation' *but* is in 'substantial disrepair' local authority *may* serve notice on owner.

Owner appeals because, either:
(i) property is not in disrepair
   or
(ii) 'repairs not reasonable'.

Owner does not comply.

Owner wins appeal; no work need be done.

Local authority *can* do work and charge the owner.

Owner does work. (Will usually get grant from the local authority.)

Repairing Remedy No. 11

If more than one family lives in the property, then there are special rules as to 'multiple occupation'. These allow the council to order the owner to carry out repairs.

Multiple occupation exists when a house or flat – which is meant to be lived in by only one household – now accommodates more than one family. Thus, an owner-occupier who lets off part of his house will own a house in 'multiple occupation'. Do not confuse multiple occupation with 'overcrowding', which exists when one house or flat has only one family in it but there are too many of them for the size of the property (see page 286).

Multiple occupation is when one property houses several households, even if they are in self-contained flats. The main examples are:

● when a house is occupied by two households;

● when a house is shared by several people, but the relationship between them is so tenuous that they cannot be regarded as one collective household;

● when lodgers are taken in – having a person 'living in' on a small scale need not be multiple occupation but if the householder caters for lodgers on a substantial scale, as a business enterprise, it is likely to be multiple occupation. Thus, many resident landlords are likely to own houses in multiple occupation.

If there is multiple occupation the local authority can order the owner to carry out necessary works connected with lighting, ventilation, water supply, personal washing facilities, drainage and wcs, the facilities for storage, preparation and cooking of food, the disposal of waste water, the installation and use of space-heating appliances (e.g. safe use of paraffin heaters), and fire escape and fire proofing.

The landlord has twenty-one days in which to comply with the order, failing which the local authority can do the work itself and recover the cost from him.

In addition, the council can lay down a 'management code' for the organization and running of the property (e.g. arrangements as to cleansing and maintenance of the water supply, drains, passages, electrical supply, etc.). A more drastic step is for the council to serve a control order which authorizes the council to take over control of the premises, to collect rents, and to carry out repairs. Such orders are rare; a complicated procedure has to be followed, and local authorities are reluctant to make such orders because of the administrative and management work involved.

The local authority can also limit the number of people allowed to live in the premises. (The maximum penalty for the landlord is a £50 fine and £2 a day if the offence continues.)

The position of the tenant. The multiple-occupation rules do not always work to the advantage of the tenants, although usually they will. Some councils have tried to apply the legislation to owner-occupiers who let out part of their house and so come within the scope of the rules. The tenants of such owner-occupiers only have restricted protection under the Rent Acts (see page 241) and can be evicted within a relatively short period. So, to avoid the expense of carrying out repairs, smaller landlords may evict their tenants, thus taking the property outside the definition of 'multiple occupation', since the amount of rent they receive does not make it worth their while to go to the expense of having all the extra building work carried out.

19 Home Improvements, Modernization, and Planning Controls

The householder who wishes to modernize, convert, or improve his property has three hurdles to overcome before he can put his plans into effect.

Firstly, he must raise the money; a local authority grant (see below) may cover part of the cost, but he may also need to raise money by loan or mortgage (page 327). Once it is clear that finance is available, he must next consider whether the local authority's consent should be sought, either for planning permission (page 327) or for Building Regulations approval (page 334). Finally, he must obtain any other necessary consents, for example, from his building society or neighbours (page 335).

Only then can he start work.

Raising the money: 1. Local-authority grants

The householder with plans to modernize or improve his property may be eligible for a local-authority grant. There are two main grants – one claimable as of right from the local authority and the other payable at its discretion. Neither is subject to a means test.

Intermediate Grants. These cover part of the cost of putting in basic living amenities (e.g. bath, hot and cold water, plus associated repairs and replacements). If the applicant is eligible, *the local authority cannot refuse to pay* him the grant (see page 322).

Improvement Grants. These cover part of the cost of improving or modernizing a home beyond installing basic living amenities. *The local authority has complete discretion* in deciding whether to make a grant to the householder (see page 324).

Claiming a grant

The detailed rules on eligibility vary with the different types of grants (see below). However, anyone applying for a grant should bear in mind that it may take several months for his application to be processed by the council. This may delay his building plans, for the grant must be confirmed before any building works are started.

In addition, the council may well require the householder to do work that he would not otherwise have done, so that the whole property is brought up to a satisfactory standard; this extra work may not be eligible for a grant and so the financial gain arising from the grant will be partly offset by the cost of this additional work. For instance, a grant may not be available for repairing an existing damp-proof course, as opposed to installing a new one, yet the council may insist that the property be free of damp if a grant is to be given.

In addition, the carrying-out of grant-aided work will usually result in the council increasing the rateable value of the property. This can often make substantial inroads into the cash benefit of the grant.

The general rule is that the grant covers 50 per cent of the cost of the work, up to certain amounts varying with the type of grant. A householder cannot claim 50 per cent of the estimated cost of having a builder do the work and then economize by doing it himself; in that case he could only claim 50 per cent of the cost of the materials.

In all probability, the boom days of housing grants are now over. Government has cut back the amount of money that is available, and there are suggestions of scrapping the existing grants rules. In many areas, the waiting-list for grants is so long that people are deciding it is not worth applying.

Who can apply?

Owner-occupiers. This covers a person who lives in the property and who owns the freehold or has a lease with at least five years left to run.

The owner-occupier will have to sign a certificate stating that he (or a close relative) will occupy the property for the next five years. If he does not comply with this undertaking (e.g. he uses the property as a second home) the council can reclaim the grant, with interest. If the owner-occupier sells the property within the five-year period then the new owner will have to repay the grant, unless he too is an owner-occupier. One point to watch is that many councils will not consider an application until the applicant has already qualified for the grant (e.g. by buying the home and becoming an owner-occupier). So, prospective buyers cannot apply for a grant before they complete their purchase – they will normally have to wait. In addition, some councils insist that the applicant becomes the registered owner of the property (i.e. registered as the owner at the Land Registry, if the property is in an area where properties have to be registered – see page 201). There can often be a delay of weeks (and even months) between buying a property and being registered as the owner, so it is always advisable to find out beforehand whether the council insists upon the applicant being registered. If so, the applicant should specifically tell his solicitor/ conveyancer that he wants the registration to be done quickly (which can usually be arranged for an extra £15 Land Registry fee). Otherwise there is likely to be a frustrating wait between buying the home and being able to submit the grant application.

Tenants. They must first ask their landlord for permission. This permission cannot be unreasonably withheld by the landlord and, if necessary, the tenant can get an order from the county court if consent is unreasonably withheld. Any improvements or works carried out with the help of a grant will be ignored when the tenant's rent is next registered or reviewed. Thus, the landlord does not benefit in the short term from the tenant having carried out the works. But in the long term he does. This is because the landlord need not compensate the tenant for the cost of the improvements when the tenancy ends and the tenant leaves. For this reason, few tenants apply for grants.

Landlords. If the property is to be let on a residential basis, a landlord can also apply for a grant (but not, for instance, if it is to be used for holiday lets). If necessary, the county court can order a tenant to allow the landlord to carry out grant-aided works, even if the tenant does not want his home improved. The improvements can, of course, be taken into account when registering or reviewing the rent. If the landlord does not let the property for at least five years, then the council can reclaim the grant, plus interest – for instance, if he sells the property within that time.

Breaking the terms of the grant. A grant might be paid to someone as (for instance) an owner-occupier. What happens if there is then a breach of the grant terms – e.g. if he moves elsewhere and just uses this property as a holiday home? The council can then ask for all the grant money back, plus compound interest. In practice, they will often accept a lesser sum if a good reason can be given. Similarly, if the person given the grant wants to, he can buy it out by offering a repayment to the council. Although the council could legally demand the whole amount of the grant (plus compound interest) the usual practice – based on Ministry advice – is to reduce the amount by one-fifth for each of the five years that has passed since the grant was paid (e.g. if the grant is bought out after three years the council will probably accept 40 per cent reimbursement).

Intermediate Grants: non-discretionary grants for basic amenities

What is covered?

Intermediate Grants cover part of the cost of putting in basic living amenities (referred to as *standard amenities*). The amenities included are fairly unsophisticated, and are merely enough to bring the property up to the minimum standard used by councils in their own housing. The amenities are:
- a bath or shower, with a hot-and-cold-water supply
- a wash-basin, with a hot-and-cold-water supply
- a kitchen sink, with a hot-and-cold-water supply
- a wc, normally indoors.

If the property does not have all of these standard amenities, the council *must* give a grant towards the cost of installing them. But the grant will only provide one of each amenity, and so it cannot finance, for instance, the installation of a second wash-basin unless the property is shared, in which case the council will require that there be separate basic amenities for each family or household in the property.

A grant will only cover the bare minimum of work necessary for the installation of the amenity. It will not cover other incidental work; for example, the grant will pay part of the cost of installing a wc, bath, and hand basin, but it will not finance the erection of a bathroom in which to put these amenities (but an improvement grant might be available, see below). However, part of the grant can be used to pay for general repairs and replacements needed to bring the property as a whole up to a fit state of repair. Note that this only applies to 'repairs and replacements', not to 'improvements' – see below for the difference between them.

The council will want to be sure that the property will be fit for human habitation once the work has been carried out. Even if the property does not fulfil those criteria the council can give a grant if it wishes – it has a discretion to do so if it thinks it would be reasonable to do so.

Since a house can be fit for human habitation without having all the standard amenities, it follows that a grant can be obtained for the partial, piecemeal, improvement of a property. For instance, if the householder wants to install an inside toilet he can normally get a grant for that without having to do other work.

How much?

The grant will be a fixed *percentage* of the cost (up to a *maximum cost*) of installing the standard amenity:

The percentage. Generally the grant is 50 per cent of the cost, up to the maximum cost figures, given below. But this can be increased to

- 60 per cent if the property is in a general improvement area;
- 75 per cent if the property is in a Housing Action Area or if it is a 'priority case'. This generally covers properties in especially bad condition, even if not in a Housing Action Area (for instance, unfit for human habitation, lacking standard amenities, or in need of substantial and structural repair). The percentage allowed used to be 90 per cent (between 1982 and 1984). But that was only a temporary increase and the normal levels are as above.
- exceptionally the grant can be increased by up to 15 per cent if the council decides that the applicant could not do the work without undue hardship.

The maximum cost

	Greater London	Elsewhere
Fixed bath or shower (normally in a bathroom)	£450	£340
Wash-hand basin	175	130
Sink	450	340
Hot and cold water at a:		
Fixed bath or shower	570	430
Wash-hand basin	300	230
Sink	380	290
wc (normally inside the dwelling)	680	515
Total	3,005	2,275

For example, a priority house in London: maximum intermediate grant is 75 per cent of £3,005.

If other repairs are being carried out extra money can be claimed on top of the figures set out above. The householder has a choice. He can either:

• bring the whole property up to what the council regards as a reasonable standard of repair – basically, to make it fit for habitation. If he does this, he can claim an extra 'repairs element' of 50 per cent – or more, see above – of up to £4,200 in Greater London, or £3,000 elsewhere, *or*

• do piecemeal repairs without having to meet the council's required standard. If he does this he can claim an extra 'repairs element' of 50 per cent – or more, see above – of up to £420 per standard amenity and a total of £1,680 if in Greater London. Elsewhere, the figures are £300 and £1,200. But these extra sums are available only for *repairs and replacements*, not for *improvements*. It is therefore important to distinguish between them.

Repairs and replacements. Tackling signs of damp and rot; rewiring; replacing old gas pipes; re-slating the roof; replacing defective gutters; repointing brickwork; repairs to doors; repairing broken window-frames; removing unused chimney stacks.

Improvements. Installing a damp-proof course; strengthening single brick walls; making gutters and drains; rebuilding brickwork; making basement rooms up to modern standards; laying paths to front and back doors; insulating walls; replacing an old, winding staircase; replacing a damp or rotten floor; all the work involved in converting a house into flats; redecoration resulting from the improvements (but not other redecoration); knocking out an unused chimney breast. See also page 301.

Payment of the grant

The grant is not paid until the work has been completed. Exceptionally, if the works are major, the council may agree to pay part of the grant in advance instalments, as work progresses. It is essential that work is not started before the council has confirmed that it will make a grant; this is a common cause of misunderstanding and many people lose their entitlement to a grant because they do not wait.

Improvement Grants: a discretionary grant for improvements and conversions

Since most properties have the basic living amenities of wc, bath, etc., an Improvement Grant is more likely to be of use to a householder than the basic Intermediate Grant described above.

What is covered?

An Improvement Grant covers part of the cost of improvements, together with incidental repairs and replacements. However, exactly what is included varies from one council to another, since it is entirely in their discretion when to award a grant. Thus, what follows should be taken as a general guide only. In practice, of course, many councils simply do not have enough money to be able to pay grants.

It should be remembered that Improvement Grants are designed to help bring homes up to a good standard. Thus a grant will not be available to improve satisfactory modern houses or to fully equipped houses that are already in good condition. Similarly, a grant will not be paid to enlarge a house to provide another bedroom; likewise central heating will not be grant-aided unless it forms part of a major scheme of improvement.

The council will want to be sure that the property will be in a satisfactory condition once the works have been completed. This means that a grant will only be given if the property will:

- have a useful life of at least thirty years, *and*
- be in 'reasonable' repair, *and*
- have all the 'standard amenities' (see page 322 for what this means), *and*
- will be fit for human habitation (see page 315 for what this means), *and*
- will have adequate loft insulation (but see page 326 for insulation grants).

Rateable value limits

An Improvement Grant cannot be made if the house or flat has a rateable value of over £400 in Greater London, or £225 elsewhere, unless the property is in a Housing Action Area. If it is in such an area, there are no rateable value limits. Similarly, there are no limits if the house is for a disabled person. Generally, flat conversions are also exempt from the rateable value limits. Note too that Intermediate Grants (above) are not subject to any rateable value limits – so a person with a large or expensive house who might be outside the Improvement Grant limits may still be able to obtain an Intermediate Grant.

How much?

The grant will be a fixed *percentage* of the cost (up to a maximum *cost*).

The percentage. Generally the grant is 50 per cent of the cost, up to the maximum cost figures, given below. But this can be increased to

- 60 per cent if the property is in a general improvement area;
- 75 per cent if in a Housing Action Area or if it is a 'priority case' (see page 323, for what this means). 'Priority' is given a wide meaning and the point to grasp is that it is the condition of the property, not the finances of the applicant, that decides whether it is a priority. An added bonus is that if it does qualify as a priority case, then the increased percentage (i.e. 75 per cent) is of a larger amount (see the figures below);
- exceptionally, by another 15 per cent in cases of undue hardship (see page 232).

The maximum cost

	Greater London	*Elsewhere*
For priority cases or in a Housing Action Area	£13,800	£10,200
In other cases	£9,000	£6,600

For example, a house in a Housing Action Area in Manchester: maximum improvement grant is 75 per cent of £10,200.

Other grants

There are several other local-authority grants that the householder might be able to obtain. All but one of these are discretionary, so the council does not have to award them. Different rules apply to each, so the district council should be consulted for full details.

Home Insulation Grants

Grants are available to help with the cost of roof insulation, for lagging cold-water tanks and pipes in a loft, and lagging hot-water tanks. The grant is 66 per cent of the cost, up to a maximum of £69.

The grant is only paid when there is no insulation at the time of the application; it cannot be given for increasing the insulation to the current standard of 80 mm thickness. Nor can it be given for lagging pipes and tanks only (e.g. if the loft already has insulation). Tenants and owner-occupiers can apply. Application is made to the local authority. The local authority has no discretion: it cannot refuse a grant to an eligible householder unless the authority does not have sufficient money to pay the grant, in which case it may tell the applicant to reapply in the next financial year.

Special Grants

These are for houses in multiple occupation (see page 319), i.e. those in which there is more than one household. The grants are for the installation of standard amenities eligible for an Intermediate Grant, but different rules apply. The grants can also cover the cost of fire-escape equipment.

Repairs Grants

These cover substantial and structural repairs to pre-1919 houses. The grant is discretionary and is designed to cover the case of an old house which is in need of repair but is not being improved. Routine maintenance (e.g. rewiring, replacing old baths) is not eligible. Rateable value limits are as with Improvement Grants (see page 325).

The grant will be a percentage (as for Improvement Grants, see page 325) up to a maximum of £6,600 in Central London and £4,800 elsewhere.

Fireplace Grants

These cover the cost of modifying chimneys or fireplaces to burn smokeless fuel, in order to comply with the Clean Air Acts.

System buildings

Owners of defective 'system-built' properties (e.g. Airey) can apply for special grants to cover the cost of repairs. This is because some of these system-built properties have fundamental defects in their design.

Special grants for listed buildings

Buildings of 'special architectural or historic interest' may be eligible for special grants. If the building is 'listed' by the Secretary of State, the local authority can give a grant even if the building is not within the council's geographical area. However, if the building is not 'listed' the local authority can only give a grant if it considers it to be of architectural or historic interest, and if it is situated in its area.

In addition, the Historic Buildings Council can award grants for buildings of architectural or historic interest.

Raising the money: 2. Borrowing to finance the work

The first place to try for a loan is the building society that originally gave a mortgage for the house purchase; they may well be sympathetic to a proposal that increases the value of the property. However, building societies only lend money for work on properties that are already mortgaged to them, and it would be most unusual for them to finance repairs and improvements to a house that was mortgaged to another society.

Tax relief can be claimed on interest paid on all forms of home-improvement loan except for a bank overdraft (see page 196).

Obtaining consent from the local authority

The householder will have to consider whether he needs planning permission and/or Building Regulations approval.

Planning permission

The wish of the householder to improve, modernize, or convert his home must be balanced against the effect the works will have on the local area and its amenities.

The control of such development is provided by the planning system introduced in 1948 by the Town and Country Planning Act.

Planning permission is needed for any *development*. However, the word 'development' is given an unusually wide definition by the planning laws. Thus, not only does it cover straightforward building work such as the erection of an extension, but it includes any plan which involves a change of the use to which the building is put. For example, converting a house into two flats, or into an office, will be a change of use and so require planning permission; this is so even if no building work is needed to carry out the change of use.

Thus, when the town-planner talks of 'development' he is giving the word a much wider meaning than does the layman. The result of this wide definition is to bring most projects for the improvement, modernization, conversion, and repair of homes within the scope of the planning laws. Fortunately, though, the fine detail of the Acts exempts many of the minor household 'developments' from the need to apply for planning permission.

So it is possible for a householder to carry out a 'development' and yet not have to obtain planning permission. The summaries, below, set out the rules that apply to the more usual household developments.

Applying for planning permission

Forms can be obtained from the district council (or London borough council). It is wise to discuss the plans with the council officers before filling in the forms.

Detailed plans will have to be lodged with the application unless outline planning permission only is being sought. For outline permission, the plans need only indicate the size and form of the development. If approved, the outline permission would have to be followed up by a further application to approve all the details; this is called an 'application for approval of reserved matters'. The outline planning permission procedure is not available for a 'change of use' application.

Applications generally take about two months to process. A fee is usually payable. If permission is refused, or is granted subject to conditions, the council must give an explanation to the applicant; he then has six months in which to appeal to the Secretary of State.

Flouting the planning laws

Do not be tempted to ignore the need for planning permission and assume that once the development has been completed the local authority will be unable, or unwilling, to do anything about it. The developer in such a case is likely to be served with an 'enforcement notice' requiring him to put the property back to its original (undeveloped) condition, regardless of the cost and inconvenience of doing so. If the 'enforcement notice' is not obeyed, the local authority may start criminal proceedings against the developer.

If the unauthorized development involved *building works* then an enforcement notice must be served within four years of the works being carried out. Once the four years has expired it is too late for the council to serve an enforcement notice and so the unauthorized development is allowed to stand. However, if the unauthorized development did not involve building works but was a *change of use* (e.g. converting an office into a flat) then there is a longer time limit for serving an enforcement notice. Unauthorized changes of use can never acquire legality by the passage of time, except that pre-1964 breaches cannot now be challenged (on request, the council will issue an 'established use certificate' confirming that the change of use was made prior to 1964).

Is planning permission needed?

The summaries, below, set out the usual position for household developments, *but* bear in mind that:
- they deal with houses (for flats and maisonettes the answers may be different);
- whether or not planning permission is needed, do not forget to consider the need for Building Regulations approval (see page 334);
- an existing planning permission may cover the property and lay down special conditions that override the normal rules;
- special conditions can apply in Conservation Areas and to listed buildings; also, the position in London may be different by virtue of the London Building Acts;
- the full details are set out in the Town and Country Planning General Development Orders 1977 & 1981.

Changing the use of a property

Planning permission is needed for 'a material change of use'. Thus, it will be needed if, for instance, a shop is to be changed into a residential house or a factory is to be changed into a supermarket. This is so even if no building works are needed to bring about the change.

In particular, the Town and Country Planning Act 1971 states that the conversion of one house into two or more dwellings is a material change of use and so planning permission is needed. All conversions of houses into flats must therefore be approved by the planners.

Not all changes of use are so clearly within the planning laws. The difficulty lies in deciding what is a 'material' change of use. Guidelines were laid down in a ministry circular some thirty years ago:

A proposed change of use constitutes development only if the new use is *substantially* different from the old. A change in *kind* will always be material – e.g. from house to shop, or from shop to factory. A change in the *degree* of an existing use may be 'material' but only if it is very marked. For instance, the fact that lodgers are taken privately in a family dwelling house would not in the Minister's view constitute a material change of use in itself so long as the use of the house remains substantially that of a private residence. On the other hand, the change from a

(*Continued on page 334*)

Is Planning Permission Necessary?

Advertisements No. But separate control-of-advertisements rules might apply (these do not apply to signs for jumble sales, etc.)

Aerials No.

Central-heating tanks Yes. Unless all of the following apply:
- the tank must be for domestic heating purposes, and be in the garden
- it must not exceed 3,500 litres in capacity, or be more than 3 m above ground level
- it should not project beyond the front line of the house where it faces on to a public road or path, nor be positioned where it might obstruct the view of a road user.

Demolition No. Unless the building is listed as being of special architectural or historic interest.

Detached structures Yes. This covers such separate buildings as a shed, greenhouse, aviary, kennel, summer-house, swimming pool, sauna cabin, etc. However, there will be no need for planning permission if all the following apply:
- the structure is for the use of the residents of the main house, and is connected with the residential use of the home (i.e. it cannot benefit other people or have a business use)
- it does not project beyond the front line of the house, where it faces on to a public road or path
- the height does not exceed 3 m (or 4 m if it has a ridged roof)
- less than half of the garden is covered by the new structure or other structures built since the erection of the house or since 1948 (whichever is later)
- it does not obstruct the view of road users and is not in a position to cause them danger.

Driveway or path Yes. Unless the drive or path gives access to an unclassified road. If the drive or path will cross the footway, pavement, or verge of a road, it will also be necessary to obtain consent from the highway authority.

Extensions Yes. But if the extension is for the use of the residents of the house (i.e. it will not be a separate dwelling), there will be no need for planning permission if all the following conditions are met:
- the volume of the house as originally built (or in 1948, if built before then) will not be increased by more than 70 m³, or 15 per cent, up to a maximum of 115 m³, whichever is the greater. Stricter limits apply to terraced houses; then the maximum increases are 50 m³, 10% and 115 m³.
- the extension will not be higher than the original house (but if it will be within 2 m of the perimeter, then it must not exceed 4 m in height);
- it will not project beyond the front line of the house where it fronts on to a public road or path;
- it will not obstruct the view of road users or cause them danger.
Finally, if the extension will go over an existing drain or sewer, special permission will be needed from the district council. (The above rules are shown in the diagram on pages 332–3.)

Fences and walls	Yes.	Unless it is not higher than 1 m if it faces on to a road; otherwise not higher than 2 m. In addition, the fence or wall must not obstruct the view of road users or cause them danger.
Flats	Yes.	There is a material change of use. In particular, permission is needed to convert a house into two or more flats. Permission is needed even if no building works are needed for the conversion.
Greenhouse	Yes.	See 'Detached Structures', opposite.
Hardstanding for a car	No.	Unless a new means of access will be required (see 'Driveway or Path', opposite).
Hedges	No.	cf. 'Fences and Walls', above.
Improvements	No.	Unless the front line of the house is extended in any way. Thus, changing flat sash windows into bay windows might require planning permission, whereas a change from sash window to casement window would not. See also 'Internal Alterations' and 'Maintenance' below.
Internal alterations	No.	Unless there is a change of use (e.g. erecting a new staircase for the purpose of converting a house into a flat and an office) or unless it is a listed building. Otherwise, the householder can do what he likes to the interior of his house, subject of course to the building regulations. See also 'Extensions', 'Improvements', 'Maintenance'.
Keeping a boat or caravan in the garden	No.	Unless the caravan is used as a separate dwelling. However, many local authorities have local by-laws that restrict the keeping of boats and caravans in gardens, so check with the local council.
Loft conversion	No.	Unless the volume of the loft will be increased; see 'Extensions' opposite.
Maintenance	No.	For example, redecorating the inside and outside, repointing brickwork, pebble dashing, sandblasting, fitting shutters to windows, etc. All of these can be done without planning permission, even if the external appearance of the house is altered.
Office	Yes.	Using part, or all, of a house as an office will be a change of use and so will need planning permission. Similarly, a householder who decides to work from home, give lessons at home, or store business goods in a spare room, will technically require planning permission, although councils will often turn a blind eye to minor infringements (see page 329).
Porch	Yes.	Unless all the following conditions are met: • the floor area does not exceed 2 m²; • no part of the porch is more than 3 m above ground level; • no part of the porch is within 2 m of a boundary facing on to a road or footpath.
Shed	Yes.	See 'Detached Structures', opposite.
Sun-lounge	Yes.	See 'Extensions' opposite.
Tree lopping or felling	No.	But check that the council has not made a tree preservation order (see page 356).
Walls	Yes.	But see exceptions in 'Fences and Walls', above.

Extensions: Is Planning Permission Necessary?   (And see page 330)

YES

extension is larger than 15 per cent of the size of the original house, and is larger than 70 m³

NO

extension is within the 15 per cent (70 m³) size limit

1930 house

1971 garage

YES

extension is within the 15 per cent size limit, but the limit has already been taken up by the garage

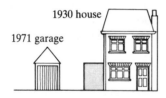

road

YES

extension is above the height of the original house. Front fence (facing road) can only be up to 1 m high

road

NO

extension does not exceed height of original house

YES
extension is in front of original house, facing a road

road

NO
extension does not face a road and is at rear of the original house

road

original house
extension
unclassified road
drive
classified road B123

YES
extension has a new access on to a classified road

extension drive
unclassified road
original house
classified road B123

NO
extension has a new access but it is not on to a classified road

private residence with lodgers to a declared guest house, boarding house, or private hotel would be 'material'. In the case of a change of use involving only part of a building, which would nevertheless continue to be used as a whole . . . the question . . . should be decided in relation to the whole premises and not merely in relation to the part, i.e. the point at issue is whether the character of the whole existing use will be substantially affected . . . He would not, for instance, regard as constituting a material change of use the use by a professional man – say a doctor or a dentist – of one or two rooms in his private dwelling for the purposes of consultation with his patients so long as this remained ancillary to the main residential use . . . The use, however, of a part of a private residence for a shop would clearly be a material change of use since even if the shop were to be confined to part of the building, its establishment would involve a change in the kind of use.

Booklet. Anyone who has a planning-permission query should begin by obtaining a copy of an excellent booklet called *Planning Permission, a Guide for Householders* (free from councils and CABs).

Building Regulations approval

The Building Regulations are made under the Public Health Acts and are primarily concerned with the structural safety of buildings and the safeguarding of public health through proper building standards. The Regulations cover such items as building materials, damp-proofing, fire resistance, ventilation, weather resistance, structural safety, thermal and sound insulation, room heights, fire escape, drainage, sanitation, and so on.

The Regulations were first introduced in 1965 and are now set out in the Building Regulations 1976. They are usually administered by building-control officers of the district councils. Their permission is needed before *any* structural work, or work involving a change of use of premises, is started. Any new building, the erection of an extension, or the conversion of a house into an office, would require consent. Repairing an existing building, or replacing parts of it, would not require consent unless structural work or a change of use was involved.

Even if the building-control officer has approved building plans it will still be necessary to give him twenty-four hours' notice before carrying out such work as covering a drain, or installing a damp-proof course or new foundations; this enables him to inspect the work.

If unauthorized work is carried out the council can require the building to be put back into its original state. In practice, if more than one year has elapsed since the work was done there is little the council can do.

London

Different Building Regulations apply in London. These are laid down under the London Building Acts rather than the Public Health Acts. The Regulations are enforced by district surveyors who are directly responsible for work done within a London borough. The Regulations are similar to those made under the Building Regulations but generally tend to be more detailed.

Obtaining other consents

Even if the householder has raised enough money to finance his improvements or modernization, and he has obtained any necessary permission from the local authority, he may not, even yet, be able to start work.

There may be other people whose consent he has to obtain before starting work. In particular, he may have to ask permission of someone with the benefit of a restrictive covenant over his land; a ground landlord; the building society that gave him a mortgage to buy the property; or a tenant who lives in it. Some, none, or all of these consents may have to be obtained.

Restrictive covenants

Restrictive covenants may limit the freedom of the freeholder to do what he likes with his property. Frequently, such restrictions are imposed by the developer of a building project when he sells off the plots, so as to preserve the character and amenities of the area or of his neighbouring piece of land. In essence, the present owner of land A can stop the present owner of land B from doing what is expressly forbidden by a restrictive covenant in land B's title deeds.

Typical restrictive covenants are shown in the specimen Land Registry certificate on page 905; other restrictive covenants that are frequently met forbid the erection of fences, construction of extensions, use of premises as an office, etc.

The law on restrictive covenants is complicated and in some respects out of date. Detailed rules decide when a restrictive covenant is enforceable. The solicitor who acted on the purchase of the property should be able to advise the owner whether the land is subject to any restrictive covenants, and if so, he may also be able to say who they benefit.

In practice, many of the restrictive covenants in title deeds are unenforceable because they do not comply with the strict rules as to enforceability; such covenants can be safely ignored by the householder, but obviously this is something that should only be done after taking full legal advice.

If there is a valid restrictive covenant that affects the building work proposed by the landowner, he has four possible lines of action:
1. Approach the holder of the restrictive covenant and negotiate (i.e. buy) his consent.
2. Apply to the Lands Tribunal for the restrictive covenant to be cancelled or altered. Basically, the landowner will have to prove that:
   - there has been a change in the character of the area, *or*
   - no one would be injured by the cancellation or amendment, *or*
   - the restrictive covenant impedes the reasonable use of the land.
   In practice the landowner has to make out a very good case, and sometimes he has to pay compensation. It will probably cost him several hundred pounds to make the application and his plans will be held up for months while the case waits to be heard.

3. If the proposed works involve the conversion of a house into two or more dwellings, the landowner can apply to the county court for the restrictive covenant to be cancelled or altered. Once again, cost and delay are factors to be borne in mind.
4. The householder can simply insure, so that if the restrictive covenant should be enforced against him, he will be compensated. Obviously, cover is only available when it is most unlikely that the covenant is enforceable. Premiums vary considerably but a typical rate would be 50p per £100 covered.

Is a restrictive covenant enforceable? Suppose my land has the benefit of restrictive covenants affecting my neighbour's land. Can I enforce the covenants? Only if:

● *my neighbour's title deeds make it clear that the restrictive covenant is to benefit my land* (unless they were both part of an estate developed and sold off by one person, in which case special rules apply), *and*

● *the restrictive covenant can be observed without the need for my neighbour to spend money.* (For example, a clause to 'maintain a fence' cannot be a restrictive covenant since it requires money to be spent, as does a clause 'not to allow a party wall to fall into disrepair'. But compare 'not to use the premises for business purposes' or 'not to build on the garden' – these do not require the spending of money, and so can be valid restrictive covenants.)

Covenants in a long lease

In the same way that a freeholder's rights may be limited by restrictive covenants, a leaseholder's rights may be limited by clauses in his lease. Moreover, the advantage of a lease is that it allows positive covenants (e.g. to spend money on repairing a fence) to be enforced. This is why most flats are sold on a leasehold, not freehold, basis.

Most long leases (i.e. leases for a fixed term over twenty-one years) require the leaseholder to obtain the landlord's consent before he erects an extension or carries out any other building work. Such consent should always be obtained, for otherwise the landlord might be able to terminate the lease for breach of covenant by the tenant; only dispense with consent after taking full legal advice.

As with restrictive covenants, the Lands Tribunal and the county court have powers to cancel and amend such clauses in long leases. The grounds of application are identical to those for restrictive covenants, above.

With most Rent Act tenancies (i.e. lettings for under twenty-one years) the tenant must ask the landlord for permission before he can carry out any improvements. However, under a full-protection tenancy, a shorthold tenancy, or a secure tenancy (see table on page 236 for explanation of these terms), the landlord cannot unreasonably refuse to give permission for any improvement or alteration.

Building-society consent

Most mortgage deeds contain provisions which require the borrower to obtain the lender's consent before he carries out alterations or building works to the mortgaged property.

Usually, the obtaining of such consent is no more than a formality since the building society (or other mortgagee) will be only too pleased to approve works that increase the value of the property. However, the consent should always be obtained, for otherwise – in theory, anyway – the building society might be entitled to reclaim its loan.

Party walls

A neighbour may have a 'right of support' from the land or buildings on the householder's land. If so, the householder must not carry out any works that would interfere with that right. In effect, both property owners are prevented from pulling down the party wall.

In London there are special laws that allow a householder to develop a party wall after giving notice to the neighbour. If the neighbour will not consent to the works, permission to carry them out can be obtained from the court, which can also order the neighbour to contribute towards the costs of the works if he will benefit from them.

Rights of light

Check that the building works will not interfere with a neighbour's right of light (see page 345).

A tenant's consent

If there is a tenant living in the property, it may well be necessary to obtain his consent before any building work can be carried out. There are strict rules about forcing unwanted repairs and improvements on to tenants (see page 345).

20 Neighbours

Every householder has certain rights over his property; and similarly, his neighbours will have rights over their property. At times, these rights and interests will clash, and then the law must resolve the ensuing dispute.

But the law is a clumsy instrument for dealing with such a delicate relationship and the aggrieved householder will probably do better to use tact, persuasion, and diplomacy, rather than move in with a blunt statement of his legal rights. All solicitors know from experience how neighbour disputes can easily erupt into lengthy, expensive, and bitter litigation, with the real cause of the argument being lost in a web of hurt feelings and self-justification. Often, too, neither party is satisfied with the outcome.

If the parties cannot reach a satisfactory compromise, what is the legal position? What are the rights and responsibilities of the householder vis-à-vis his neighbours?

My rights – my neighbour's rights

We have already seen that there is no such thing as the 'absolute ownership' of land or the complete freedom to do as one wishes in one's house or garden (see page 193). This is because the householder's right to 'use and enjoy' his property is subject to the rights enjoyed by the community and by other individuals over that land. A glance back at the table on page 194 will illustrate this; the owner's rights seem at first sight to be all-embracing, but we see that in fact his rights are subject to:
- rights vested in the community (e.g. to enforce public-health standards of hygiene on the property; to control the erection and design of buildings; to allow police and gas board officials to enter the house, etc.);
- rights that other individuals have over the property (e.g. a right of way to walk over the land; the power to stop nuisance-making activities, etc.). These are the sort of rights that neighbours can have over one's land, and are therefore the concern of this chapter.

Thus, my right to use and enjoy my land freely is limited by my neighbour's rights. Conversely, the extent of my rights over his land affects the extent of his ability to use and enjoy his land.

The point to be repeated (again and again!) is that the law should be the last resort in a neighbour dispute. Conciliation, not confrontation or litigation, is likely to yield the best results.

Troublesome Neighbours

Possible legal remedies

Suing for trespass (see page 339) e.g. to tackle overhanging tree branches; intrusion on to one's land, etc.

Suing for legal nuisance (see page 347) e.g. to tackle noise, smells, fumes, etc.

Complaining to the Public Health Department (see page 308) e.g. to tackle smells, dirt, dust

Complaining to the Planning Department (see page 308) e.g. to tackle problems raised by commercial use of a residential house

Issuing a summons under the Control of Pollution Act (see page 350) e.g. to tackle persistent noise

---

Trespass

'Keep Out – Private Property' is a concise statement of the law. If someone owns a plot of land, a house, or a garden, it is up to him to decide who can come on to his property. This is, of course, subject to the community's right to send in the police or to allow gas pipes to be laid, etc. But as regards other private individuals, such as his neighbours, he can generally say 'Keep Out – Private Property; You are Trespassing.'

What if the trespasser defies his wishes and comes on to the property; what can be done? Firstly, the landowner can eject him, after first asking him to leave, using no more force than is necessary. But this is unwise, for the trespasser might allege that unnecessary force was used and so prosecute for assault.

Secondly, the landowner could sue the trespasser for damages, to obtain compensation for any loss caused. Unless the intruder had damaged the house, trampled on the garden, or broken a fence, it would be unlikely that the landowner would have suffered any loss and so claiming damages would be a pointless exercise. He would probably only recover nominal damages of a few pence, and the court might show its disapproval of his suing over such a petty matter by not awarding him his legal costs.

Does this mean that there is no remedy against the trespasser? Against the casual trespasser – such as the country walker who takes a short cut across a field – the answer is 'yes' for, in practice, the landowner can do nothing unless real damage is caused. However, the landowner could ask the court for an *injunction* against a persistent trespasser, ordering him not to trespass in the future; if he ignored that order he would be in contempt of court and so be liable to fining or imprisonment. Thus, if a person regularly uses someone else's back garden as a short cut, or if they frequently park their car on someone else's lawn, the law can be used to stop the trespassing.

Housing: The Householder and the Law

As for signs that proclaim 'Trespassers Will be Prosecuted', these are pure bluff on the part of the landowner. Trespass is a wrong to the landowner and he can sue in the civil courts for damages and/or an injunction. He cannot prosecute, since trespass is not, of itself, a criminal offence. Exceptionally, the person who trespasses in a building by squatting may be committing a criminal offence, but the general rule remains that trespass is a civil, not a criminal, wrong.

Squatters' rights

For the law on squatting in residential premises, see page 280.
If a person trespasses on land for twelve years he may acquire the legal title or ownership of that land. In fact, there is no need for him to live there for that twelve-year period, for all he has to do is to openly assert his authority and ownership during that time, without acknowledging the owner's right to the land (for example, by asking his permission to stay there or by paying him rent). In addition, the owner must not have been in possession himself or have asserted his rights over the land (for instance, by asking the squatter to leave).

The strict requirements of this *adverse possession* by the squatter mean that it would be most unusual for a squatter in a housing squat to acquire a title in this way, for few householders would completely ignore the possession for twelve years. However, it has been known to happen. In contrast, in agricultural areas it is not uncommon for a farmer to acquire title; for instance, when renewing his fence he may erect the new fence a few yards on the wrong side of his neighbour's boundary, and perhaps acquire the title to the land after grazing his animals there for twelve years.

Rights of way

The general rule is that a person who goes on to another's land without permission will be a trespasser. Footpaths and other rights of way allow the use of private land without trespassing.

Private footpaths

A person may have the right to use a footpath across private land. That right can be given by written deed, or it can be acquired by using the footpath for a sufficiently long period.

Some legal rights can be acquired by continued usage over a long period of time – by what the law calls *prescription* (see page 195). So it is with footpaths – a person who openly crosses another's land for twenty years or more can acquire the right to do so for the years to come. However, for prescription to apply, he must have acted as though he had the legal right to use the path and the landowner must have impliedly accepted that right (e.g. by not challenging his use or by not doing anything inconsistent with it). So if he asked for permission or offered payment, or if the owner told him to stop using the path, the prescription rule could not apply.

If a person has a right of way across another's land then he will not be a trespasser as long as he keeps to the footpath. If he deviates from the path, he will become a trespasser.

Public rights of way

In the same way that an individual can acquire a private footpath right, so the public at large can gain a public right of way. Public rights of way can be created after twenty years' use, but only if the route is used:

- by the public at large (i.e. not just by the landowner's staff), *and*
- as of right (i.e. without permission having been asked for or given), *and*
- over a defined route (cf. general access to a hillside).

After twenty years' use by the public, the law presumes that the landowner has dedicated the land as a public highway (Highways Act 1980). To avoid this happening, a landowner should publicly show that he does not want a public right of way to be created. This can be done by displaying a sign stating that the land is not being dedicated as a public highway, or by depositing a formal notice with the local authority. Alternatively, the landowner can protect his position by blocking off the road or path for one day every year (as is done in the Temple area of London), so as to assert his ownership and indicate that the use of the path is by courtesy only.

A right of way, whether public or private, can be restricted to a particular class of user. In cases of uncertainty, one should inspect the local authority's definitive map showing all highways in their area. By the National Parks and Access to the Countryside Act 1948 and the Countryside Act 1968 all highways have to be categorized as either:

- *footpaths:* pedestrians only
- *bridleways:* pedestrians and horses only
- *by-ways open to all traffic:* i.e. cart-ways open to pedestrians, horses, carts, and cars.

The district and county councils keep copies of the definitive map, which shows the location and classification of every public right of way. If a path is marked on a definitive map that will be conclusive evidence that it is open to the public, but just because a path is not on the map it does not follow that it is not open to the public. So public paths can still be created and can therefore exist even when not marked on the definitive map. Obviously, in such a case it is sensible to ask the county council to include the path on the definitive map when it is next revised.

A footpath cannot be lost by disuse; once a footpath exists it remains a footpath, until closed by an order made under a statute. Such an order might be made, for example, to divert a path in order that a building estate can be constructed.

Use of a footpath

A public footpath can be used by anyone, but only for passing along it in the course of a bona fide journey. Whilst the walker can stop for a rest he cannot use the footpath for camping on or for some other use unconnected with travelling along the path. If the path is not used for its proper purpose, the walker becomes a trespasser.

A footpath ran beside a field where horses were trained. A journalist walked backwards and forwards over a fifteen-yard stretch of the path for an hour and a half, making notes on the performance of the various horses. Held: He was a trespasser since he was not just using the path for a bona fide journey. Whilst it would not be unreasonable for a walker to sit down to rest, or even to stop to make a sketch, it was unreasonable to use the footpath as a means of spying on the training of horses. Hickman (1900)

The general rule is that it is a criminal offence to ride a motor bike, or drive a car, on a footpath or bridleway. Although horse riders are not allowed to use footpaths they do not, in fact, commit any criminal offence in doing so; the only remedies are for the council to put up barriers (but leaving sufficient space for walkers), or for the landowner to sue for trespass. Finally, a walker can take a dog with him on a footpath, but obviously it must not be allowed to stray on to the neighbouring land.

Maintenance of footpaths and bridleways

The general rule is that it is the duty of the county council, or London borough council, to maintain public footpaths and bridleways in its area; the only exceptions are footpaths created since 1949 which the council has not agreed to maintain. By section 130 of the Highways Act 1980, county councils have a duty 'to assert and protect the rights of the public to the use and enjoyment' of paths in their area and 'to prevent as far as possible the stopping up or obstruction' of paths.

The council's duty is only to maintain the surface of the path. There is no duty to maintain the subsoil on which it rests. For example, if a towpath collapses into a canal the council need not repair the path since it has now disappeared!

A council is not expected to maintain a path in perfect condition. As long as it is safe and fit to carry its usual amount of traffic that will be sufficient. The rambler cannot expect a little-used path to be fully cleared. Ministry guidelines to councils state:

Where paths are used mainly for pleasure by ramblers, it will no doubt generally be sufficient that they should be free from obstructions or impassable water or mud, and that they should be inconspicuously but sufficiently signposted or marked where necessary. The main consideration is clearly that they should serve their purpose, whether business or pleasure, and not that they should conform to some arbitrary standard of construction.

If the county council, as the highway authority, fails to maintain paths to this standard, it can be taken to court by any private individual and ordered to repair the path or bridleway. For instance:

Over the years a public footpath had become increasingly obstructed by fences and buildings put up by adjoining landowners. Since 1969 the parish council, local residents and local organizations had been urging the county council to use its powers and force the landowners to remove the various obstructions. Eventually the parish council sought a court order requiring the county council to take action. Held: Yes. The Highways Act required the county council 'to take proper proceedings' to remove obstructions. It had not done so. The court would order the county council to take action. Surrey County Council (1980)

In addition, if the authority fails to inspect the paths reasonably often and then carry out any necessary works, it may well be liable in damages to anyone injured because of the lack of repair. However, it is rare for such a liability to arise since the courts do not expect councils to carry out frequent inspections of their footpaths.

Mrs Whiting was injured while walking on a footpath; she stepped into undergrowth beside the path to let another walker pass, and hurt herself on a concealed tree stump. She sued the council, but the council argued that it had not been negligent. The path had been inspected in July, cleared the following February, and the accident happened a month later. Held: The council had acted reasonably and was not liable. Whiting (1970)

Whilst the duty to maintain the surface of a footpath falls on the council, the duty to maintain stiles and gates rests on the owner of the land. His obligation is to keep stiles and gates 'in safe condition, and to the standard of repair required to prevent unreasonable interference with the rights of persons using the footpath or bridleway' (Countryside Act 1968). The council must contribute at least a quarter of the maintenance costs. If the landowner does not maintain the stiles and fences, the council can give him fourteen days' notice and then do the work itself, but at the expense of the landowner and without any contribution from the council. Alternatively, the council or any private individual can apply to the magistrates' court for an order requiring the landowner to do the necessary works.

In theory, county councils are under a duty to put up signposts whenever a public right of way meets a metalled (i.e. tarmac) road. But the Act does not lay down a time period within which this must be done and so, in practical terms, councils cannot legally be forced to put up signposts.

Obstructions on footpaths and bridleways

Anyone who 'wilfully obstructs the free passage along a highway' can be fined up to £400 (s. 137 Highways Act 1980). The prosecution need not be brought by the highway authority but can be brought by a private individual or even an amenity group (see page 779 for how to bring a private prosecution).

It is not necessary that the obstruction should completely block the path; it is sufficient that it blocks part of it or that it makes walking along the path more difficult. For instance, a farmer who dumps refuse on part of the path or who padlocks a gate can be prosecuted. Similarly, if a farmer allows crops to grow on the footpath or bridleway, that too may be an obstruction.

Although the magistrates can fine the offender, they cannot order him to remove the obstruction. If successive fines fail to induce the offender to remove it, the Attorney-General might agree to an injunction being sought against him. If the landowner obstructs the path or bridleway, it will not be trespass for members of the public to go on to his land in order to get past the obstruction.

The ploughing up of a path or bridleway is not, of itself, an obstruction unless, of course, it makes it impossible to use the route. In theory, ploughing might be a legal nuisance and those affected could start an action in the civil courts for damages and an injunction. In practice, the difficulty and expense of bringing such an action would deter most people from trying to take action against the farmer. Thus there is little that can be done when a footpath is ploughed. If crops have grown where the ploughing was carried out, the walker can walk through the crops provided he causes as little damage as possible.

If a walker or rider comes across an obstruction he can remove it himself, but only in so far as it is necessary for him to be able to continue his journey. So if the path is only partly obstructed the walker cannot remove the obstruction if he could continue his walk without removing it. He is only allowed to do what is essential.

Mr Slama had a café by the seafront in Hastings. Access to the café was by three public footpaths which crossed Mr Seaton's land. Mr Seaton erected a fence which blocked all three paths. Slama took down 180 yards of fence and burnt part of it, claiming that he was exercising his right to remove obstructions from a public footpath. Held: No. The judge said: 'If the gate is locked he may be entitled to break the lock. If there is a fence across the entrance to the way he may be justified in removing a sufficient part of the fence to enable him to have free access to the way.' But he could do no more than that. Seaton (1932)

In addition, this form of self-help is only available to someone who is genuinely using the path for a journey. So a rambler who sets out with the sole object of removing obstructions cannot claim to be acting lawfully; apart from being sued for trespass, he might be prosecuted for criminal damage. In practice, of course, it would be difficult for the landowner to prove that the rambler did not genuinely intend using the path for a journey.

The experienced walker will probably come across two other problems – usually resulting from farmers who resent public use of footpaths. Firstly, there is the 'misleading sign' ploy (e.g. a 'Private' sign). This is illegal if the sign is designed to deter the use of a public right of way marked on the definitive map (see page 341). Report the offence to the county council. The second tactic is the 'bull in the field' ploy. Since 1981 all dairy bulls have been banned from fields that are crossed by public paths, and other types of bulls can only be permitted if accompanied by cows or heifers. Prosecution is difficult because no specific criminal offence arises (although the police might decide that the business being carried on is endangering the public, and so prosecute under the Health & Safety At Work laws).

Airspace

The rules of trespass are not confined to the land itself. In legal theory, a landowner owns not only the land, but the air above it and the soil beneath it. Thus, an unreasonable intrusion into another person's airspace will be a trespass, although whether he will be awarded any damages will depend upon his being able to show a resulting loss.

Mr Kelsen had a tobacconist's shop in Islington. His landlords allowed a tobacco company to erect a large 'Players Please' sign which projected eight inches into the airspace above his shop. Mr Kelsen sued for trespass. Held: Yes, it was a trespass and the sign should be removed. Kelsen (1957)

When planes first started flying, their pilots faced trespass claims from the owners of the land flown over. To get around this problem, the Civil Aviation Act 1949 exempts over-flying aircraft from trespass claims, for otherwise home-owners near airports would be able to obtain injunctions against the airline operators and so ground all flights. How-ever, the Act does not protect planes that are flying 'unreasonably low' and in that case there may be a trespass; generally, the minimum height for a light aircraft is about 1,000 ft and 2,000 ft for other aircraft except, of course, when landing and taking off.

The protection given by the 1949 Act covers any flight which is at a reasonable height, even when the object of the flight is not just to pass over the land en route to the plane's destination.

Skyviews were a firm that took aerial photographs of people's houses and then offered to sell photographs to the householder. One person whose home was photographed in this way was Lord Bernstein. He took exception to this invasion of his privacy and sued Skyviews for trespass. In their defence, Skyviews relied upon the protection given by the Civil Aviation Act 1949. Held: A landowner only has rights in his airspace to such a height as is necessary for the use and enjoyment of his land. The flight by Skyviews had been at a reasonable height and was thus protected. There had been no trespass. Bernstein (1977)

Light

Although a landowner owns the airspace above his property, he does not have an automatic right to have light enter his airspace or land. Thus, if his neighbour wants to build a high boundary wall that will put his house into shade there may be nothing he can do about it, beyond opposing the neighbour's application for planning per-mission to erect the wall (see page 331).

Acquiring a 'right to light'

That would be the landowner's only remedy unless the property had acquired a 'right to light', either by written agreement with his neighbour or by *prescription* (i.e. continuous use) over twenty years or more. So, if the house is over twenty years old, the householder will probably have acquired a right to light and will be able to prevent the erection of any structure that would seriously reduce the amount of light. Similarly, if the house is new, but is built on the site of an old property that had acquired a right to light, then the new house will normally inherit that right to light, unless it is radically different in size and character from the old house.

This twenty-year rule only applies to rights to light for buildings, and not for gardens and other open spaces, such as allotments; so if the proposed wall would put a rose garden into shadow the landowner could probably not claim a right to light to prevent its erection.

The extent of the right

If a right to light exists, it is not a right to prevent any obstruction, but just a right to ensure that a minimum level of light is maintained. If the light is reduced, but the selling and letting value of the house is unchanged and the comfort of its occupants not reduced, then there will not have been any infringement of the right to light. Thus, the question is not 'How much light has been taken away?' but 'How much light remains?'

In deciding what is the minimum level required the court will consider such factors as the nature of the locality and the type of room affected; for instance, a bedroom needs less light than a lounge, and this will be so even if, for example, the bedroom is used for an activity that requires good lighting, such as sewing and embroidery.

Conversely, if the normal use of a building requires it to have an unusually high level of light, then the right to light will have been infringed if the level is reduced to a level which is insufficient for its normal use. For instance:

Mr and Mrs Allen had a greenhouse in their back garden. It had been there for over twenty years, so when their neighbours erected a fence beside it, they asked for the fence to be removed on the grounds that it infringed their right to light. In particular, their tomatoes no longer grew properly because the greenhouse was now in shadow. The neighbours refused to move the fence and argued that a right to light only covers a 'normal' amount of light – not the exceptional amount needed by a greenhouse. Held: A right to light extends to the amount of light needed by a building for its normal use. The greenhouse needed a lot of light, and so the right to light had been infringed. The fence had to be taken down. Allen (1979)

(This case also shows that a householder is entitled to sunlight, not just illumination, which could be important if solar heating panels became more widespread.)

If a householder does not have a right to light (for instance, if he owns a new house on a new site) there is nothing he can do to stop his neighbours blocking off the light apart, of course, from using this as a ground for opposing the granting of planning permission. If, despite his efforts, planning permission is granted, he will just have to accept the resulting inconvenience and reduction in the value of his property.

Finally, a word of warning: it is possible to own a twenty-year-old house and yet not have a right to light. This can happen when the title deeds specifically say that a right to light cannot be acquired. For instance, if a householder sells off half his garden for development, he might insert a clause preventing a right to light being acquired by the purchaser and his successors; otherwise, if he wanted to build on the other half of the garden in over twenty years' time, he might be prevented on the ground that the proposed building would infringe the other property's right to light. By suitably wording the original conveyance he can prevent the right to light being acquired. It is not unusual for the conveyance to state that the buyer cannot acquire a right to light over the seller's land, whilst specifically giving the seller a right to light over the buyer's land.

Mr Howells decided to put up an extension. His neighbours the Pughs objected – pointing out it would interfere with their right to light. Despite clear warnings on this, Mr Howells went ahead. The Pughs then went to court, asking for an order that the extension be removed. Held: The extension did interfere with the light to the Pughs' house. Howells had been given ample warning but decided to go ahead heedless. An order was made that the extension should be knocked down. Pugh (1984)

The other method of stopping a right to light from being acquired is under the Rights to Light Act 1959. This little-used Act allows a landowner to register a notice with the local authority stating that an adjoining building is not acquiring a right to light by the passage of time. The registration only lasts for one year but it would only need to be renewed every twenty years so as to stop a fresh period of twenty years running.

Protecting a view

English law does not recognize the right to a view from one's house and, unlike a right to light, it is not possible to acquire the right to an uninterrupted view by twenty years' usage.

Thus, a householder cannot go to court if his neighbour erects a building or plants a tree that will ruin the view from his house, even if it takes thousands of pounds off its value.

Nuisance

Trespass covers *physical* intrusions by a neighbour, but if the interference with a householder's rights is of a less tangible nature, trespass will be of no use; for instance, noise and smells cannot be stopped by bringing an action for trespass since there has been no physical encroachment on to the property. However, for these *intangible* intrusions, the law provides another remedy – bringing an action for 'nuisance'.

When a lawyer talks of a 'nuisance' he is using the word in a well-defined legal sense. Not every antisocial act by my neighbour will be a legal 'nuisance', although I might well regard it as a damned nuisance.

The 'nuisance' claim covers behaviour that causes injury to land or, alternatively, substantially interferes with the enjoyment of land. Vibrations from a nearby factory that cause damage to the foundations of my house; heavy smoke from a coal fire; strong smells from a neighbour's septic tank; noise from machinery in a factory or noise from late-night parties: these are the sort of antisocial acts that can amount to a legal 'nuisance'.

The law expects neighbours to give and take. When people live in close proximity to one another they must be prepared to compromise and to take account of the reasonable wishes of their neighbours. In fact, the word 'reasonable' occurs again and again in the courts' decisions on nuisance cases, for the courts apply an objective test of how the 'reasonable man' would behave and how he would react to the behaviour in question.

Does a 'nuisance' exist?

The first step is to consider whether the plaintiff (i.e. the complainant) is justified in going to court. Clearly, if he or his land has suffered material physical damage, he is entitled to bring a claim (e.g. if his crops have died from factory fumes). If he is complaining of an interference with the use and enjoyment of his land (e.g. unpleasant smells) then the courts will want to be sure that there is a serious or substantial interference, and that he is not being over-fussy or fastidious. Thus, the extent and duration of the interference becomes relevant (e.g. a party every night is unreasonable, but one a week is probably not). What is the nature and character of the harm? Is the plaintiff's use of the land suitable for the neighbourhood and locality (e.g. he may want peace for his animals to graze – in the country this might be reasonable, but in central London it would be unreasonable)? Could he have easily avoided the consequences of his neighbour's behaviour or is he being bloody-minded?

If the plaintiff passes these hurdles on the 'reasonable man' test, the court goes on to consider the behaviour of his troublesome neighbour, the defendant. An important factor will be whether his use of the land is reasonable for the area and locality (e.g. keeping a dozen pigs may be reasonable in the country, but it would be considered unreasonable in central London). Is his aim innocent or is he, in fact, acting with malice by trying to annoy the plaintiff (e.g. is his sole motive for practising drum solos to annoy his neighbour or is he really a music student with nowhere else to practise?)? Has he taken all reasonable steps to minimize the effects of his actions (e.g. does he try to muffle the sound of his drums? Does he practise in daylight hours only?)? Once again, a 'reasonable man' test is applied, and if the defendant has not behaved reasonably the court will award damages to the plaintiff and probably grant an injunction ordering the defendant to stop his nuisance-making activities.

Clearly, then, what will be a nuisance in one part of the country may not be a nuisance in another area; what may be a nuisance to one plaintiff will not be a nuisance to another plaintiff. It all depends on the facts of the case and whether our 'reasonable man' would tolerate the neighbour's behaviour. But nuisance claims are not confined to such obvious complaints as noise and smells. Anything that substantially interferes with a householder's or landowner's enjoyment of his property can be a nuisance. For instance:

Two prostitutes lived in a house in Mayfair. Their neighbours applied to the court for an injunction ordering the girls not to use their house for prostitution, on the ground that the frequent callers and the general misbehaviour was a legal nuisance. Held: Yes, there was a nuisance, and an injunction was granted. Thompson-Schwab (1956)

A company bought a shop in an area that was residential, but which included restaurants, snack-bars, etc. Previously the shop had been a dress shop; the company converted it to a sex shop, with illuminated signs describing its wares. Local residents brought a nuisance claim against the company, claiming damages and an injunction. Held: A sex shop could be a legal 'nuisance'. Anything that was an affront to the reasonable susceptibilities of ordinary people and which interfered with reasonable domestic enjoyment of property could be a nuisance. An interlocutory injunction would be granted. Laws (1981)

A motor company had a lease of premises next to some open land owned by the local council. Gipsies moved on to the land, and despite complaints, the number of gipsies increased over the years. The council got a court order against the gipsies but never evicted them. The garage company sued for damages – complaining that they had suffered a major loss in trade due to the presence of the gipsies. Held: The council were liable in nuisance. They owned the land and should have taken more prompt steps to get rid of the gipsies. Page Motors (1981)

Noise

When considering a nuisance claim for noise, the court will consider all the factors mentioned above. For example, in a 1914 case, a hotel was able to stop building operations on an adjacent plot because they prevented the residents from sleeping and after-dinner speakers from making themselves heard. But the court only ordered the builders to stop their pile-driving between 10 p.m. and 6.30 a.m. – so what may be a nuisance at night need not be a nuisance in the daytime.

The nature of the locality will also be important. For instance:

Mr Leeman bought a house in an area that was partly residential and partly rural. His neighbour had an orchard 100 yards away, in which he kept 750 cockerels. The crowing of the cockerels prevented Mr Leeman from sleeping, so he brought a nuisance claim against his neighbour. Held: The cockerels were a nuisance, although they would probably not have been a nuisance in a non-residential area. Leeman (1936)

Why does the plaintiff need peace and quiet? Is his neighbour's noise really a nuisance or is the plaintiff being fussy? For instance, when the vicar of a Brighton church went to court over the hum from nearby electrical machinery, his claim failed because the court did not regard the noise as a sufficiently serious annoyance, since he was still able to preach and conduct services.

Sometimes it is a new neighbour who has just moved into the area who complains about the defendant's noisy behaviour. The defendant might argue that 'I was making the noise before he came; he didn't have to come and live here.' That argument will not succeed, and the defendant will have to stop his antisocial behaviour if it is a nuisance to his new neighbour – as with Mr Leeman's neighbour who kept the cockerels in his orchard (above). The fact that Mr Leeman was new to the area did not prevent him from having an existing nuisance stopped.

Mrs Kennaway owned land beside a man-made lake, which was used by a skiing club. The club had been using the lake since the early 1960s. In 1969 Mrs Kennaway got planning permission to build a house which she started occupying in 1972. From 1969 onwards the motor-boat activities steadily increased and by 1977 the lake was used each weekend for races and practice. In 1977 Mrs Kennaway started court proceedings. She wanted an injunction but the trial judge would only award her damages (£1,000 for past nuisance, and £15,000 for future nuisance). She appealed. Held: An injunction would be granted allowing only limited use of the lake by the club. Damages should only be awarded in place of an injunction in the most exceptional circumstances. Kennaway (1980)

On the other hand, the defendant may be able successfully to argue the 'long usage' defence against a neighbour who has tolerated it for twenty years or more; for example, if Mr Leeman had waited twenty years before complaining, he might well have lost his case.

Even noisy children can be a legal nuisance. For instance:

*Mr and Mrs Dunton owned a small hotel with a pleasant garden and grazing land beyond it.
The council built a housing estate on the grazing land, with a playground next to the hotel garden.
The playground was open from dawn to dusk and was used by children of all ages. The noise was
so intolerable that Mrs Dunton moved out of the hotel. Mr Dunton brought a nuisance claim
against the council. Held: The playground was a nuisance. The council was ordered to limit its
use to children under twelve, and to restrict the opening hours to between 10 a.m. and 6.30 p.m.
In addition, Mr Dunton was awarded £200 damages.* Dunton (1977)

If an injunction is granted, it may be suspended in order to give the defendant time
in which to reorganize his business:

*Mr and Mrs Allison lived in a council house next door to a hospital boiler room. The noise,
a continuous low-pitched hum, interfered with Mr Allison's sleep and caused him a significant
degree of nervous agitation, as well as bouts of depression. Held: The noise was a nuisance. The
hospital would be given twelve months in which to cure the noise, and in the meantime, the
Allisons would be paid £850 damages.* Allison (1975)

The problem is, of course, that going to court – and asking for an injunction – is
usually an expensive process.

Other remedies for noise

Bringing an action for nuisance is only one of the remedies available against noisy
neighbours. Because of the cost of bringing such a civil action the householder will
probably be reluctant to sue for nuisance and might prefer to try a cheaper remedy.
The Control of Pollution Act 1974 contains various provisions that can be used to
control excessive noise.

The first step is to complain to the Environmental Health Department of the local
authority that the noise is a 'nuisance' under the 1974 Act. Evidence that it interferes
with sleep, or causes disturbance, will probably be needed. If the council agrees that
the noise is a nuisance, it can serve a noise-abatement notice on the owner or
occupier of the building. The notice will forbid the making of the noise, or restrict
it to certain noise-levels, at certain times of the day. If the noise-abatement notice
is not complied with, the council can prosecute in the magistrates' court, and unless
the offender can show that he used the 'best practicable means' to avoid making the
noise (e.g. if he used the latest, quietest machinery in his factory and he had all the
usual noise-reduction devices) he will be guilty (maximum penalty £200 fine for first
offence, £400 for subsequent offences).

If the council refuses to issue a noise-abatement notice, or if it refuses to prosecute for its breach, the householder himself can complain to the magistrates'
court. A summons is issued in the usual way (see 'How to Bring a Private
Prosecution', page 779) and if the magistrates agree that the noise is a nuisance under
the 1974 Act, they will issue a noise-abatement notice. As with a notice issued by the
council, the offender can be fined if he does not observe the terms of the notice. A
householder who applies to the magistrates' court for a noise-abatement order

should produce evidence to support the contention that the noise is a nuisance (for instance, statements of other neighbours, a note from a doctor as to the effect the noise is having on the householder and his family, etc.).

Another way of taking action against noise is to prosecute under local by-laws. Most local authorities have by-laws that can be used to control noise. Usually, a private individual can prosecute for breach of the by-laws, although it is always advisable to try to persuade the council to prosecute. The maximum penalty is usually a £50 fine. The householder should check whether there are relevant by-laws by inquiring in the Environmental Health Department; anti-noise by-laws are usually contained in the 'Good Rule and Government' section of the by-laws. The following are typical anti-noise by-laws:

Radio, stereo, etc. Such noise is prohibited if it is so loud and so continuous that it is an annoyance to occupiers of premises in the neighbourhood. Generally, the complainant must first give fourteen days' written notice to the offender that he regards the noise as a nuisance, and the notice must also be signed by two other householders within hearing distance. Only if the noise continues beyond the fourteen-day period can the offender be prosecuted in the magistrates' court.

Alarm bells. It is often an offence to leave an alarm bell ringing for so long that it becomes an annoyance to local residents. However, the offender will usually have a defence if he can show that the noisy alarm was not his fault (e.g. there was an unknown electrical fault).

Noisy animals. It is usually an offence to keep a noisy animal if it causes a serious nuisance to residents in the neighbourhood. As with the radio and stereo by-law (above) the offender must first be given fourteen days' notice, signed by a total of three householders.

Music near houses. It is usually an offence to play any 'musical or noisy instrument' or sing in a street or public place that is within 100 yards of a house or office. However, the noise must have been sufficient to have interfered with the ordinary activities carried on in the building (e.g. sleeping, if outside a house at night) or to have been otherwise unreasonable.

Two other common sources of noise are also subject to legal restriction.

Car horns. The Road Traffic Act 1974 makes it illegal to sound a horn while the car is stationary or to sound the horn on a moving car in a restricted road (unless there is danger to another moving vehicle) between 11.30 p.m. and 7 a.m. Both offences carry a maximum penalty of a £1,000 fine. Prosecutions are extremely rare.

Chimes and loudspeakers. The Control of Pollution Act 1974 makes it illegal to operate a loudspeaker or chime in a street. The main exception is for food and drink vehicles, which can use loudspeakers and chimes between noon and 7 p.m., but only if the noise does not cause unreasonable annoyance to local residents. Thus, short bursts on an ice-cream chime are allowed but long tunes are not. The maximum penalty, on conviction, is a £2,000 fine and £50 for each day the noise continues after conviction.

Noisy vehicles

Maximum noise levels for vehicles are laid down in the Motor Vehicles (Construction and Use) Regulations. The maximum fine for breach is £1,000. In practice these noise restrictions are of limited value because the police lack the facilities for monitoring noise levels. In addition, it can often be difficult to prove that a particular vehicle was causing excessive noise if it was one of several vehicles on the road at that time.

Complaints about routeing and regulation of traffic should be made to the local traffic authority.

Noise from planes

There is little that can be done about noise from planes. The normal remedies of applying for a noise-abatement order or of bringing a nuisance action do not apply, since various statutes exempt aircraft from these controls.

Complaints about noise from aircraft using an airport should be made to the airport operator. Complaints about military aircraft should be made to the Ministry of Defence, Provost and Security Services UK, Government Building, Bromyard Avenue, London w3, and to the station commanding officer.

Grants for insulating against traffic noise

The Noise Insulation Regulations 1975 provide for grants to help insulate homes affected by traffic noise.

The scheme only covers new roads or roads which have an extra carriageway added to them. This is a major flaw, because it means that existing roads which suddenly have more traffic (for instance, because a new motorway exit is opened) are not included.

A complicated noise test is used to determine whether a particular residential building is eligible. When the road (or extra carriageway) is built the local authority must write to the occupiers of all eligible properties offering them the grant. The amount paid will depend upon what would be a 'reasonable cost' for the works.

Local authorities also have a *discretionary* power to make grants to people living near roads that have had their location, width, or level altered, and who would otherwise be ineligible for a grant.

For full details see *Insulation against Traffic Noise* (No.5 in the 'Land Compensation – Your Rights Explained' series published by the Department of the Environment).

Smells

What if a neighbour has a compost heap in his garden and, because of the exceptionally dry weather, it smells? Probably there is no nuisance, because it is only a temporary annoyance and it is quite reasonable to have a compost heap in one's garden. However, if the neighbour uses the heap as a general dump for all his household refuse, that would probably be unreasonable, and so a nuisance.

What is an objectionable smell in one neighbourhood may be perfectly normal elsewhere. A person who lives in a steel town is expected to tolerate smells that would be regarded as a nuisance in other areas; as one Victorian judge said, 'What would be a nuisance in Belgrave Square would not necessarily be so in Bermondsey.' Thus, the smell from a fish-and-chip shop was held to be a nuisance, even though it would not have been a nuisance in a less fashionable district one mile away.

Assessing damages in 'smell' cases can be difficult. For when no direct physical harm has been caused, the judge has to put a monetary value on the joys of fresh air and the enjoyment of one's home. Not surprisingly, awards vary enormously, but a 1975 case provides a useful guide. In that case, the two plaintiffs went to court over smells from the defendant's pig farm; they were awarded £1,000 each for two years' loss of amenity and enjoyment of their land.

As with noise, the householder who suffers from offensive smells in the neighbourhood may have additional remedies apart from an action for nuisance. Complaint should be made to the environmental health officer of the local authority, for there are several statutory provisions that can be used to control the source of the smells.

Building works

The nuisance action can sometimes be of help to the landowner disturbed by nearby building operations. If noise, dust, and fumes result, he may be able to obtain an injunction to stop the work continuing, although the court will probably confine the ban to the night hours and insist that the builders take all reasonable steps to minimize the inconvenience (as in the hotel case on page 349). However, some disruption and inconvenience may have to be accepted by the landowner, for it is not unreasonable to build on one's land (or carry out DIY works) as long as the inconvenience to others is minimized.

Local authorities have special powers to control noise from building sites, so complaint should be made in the first place to the local authority.

Subsidence

But what of the damaging effect that the building works may have on one's own property? If a neighbour digs a hole on his side of a boundary fence, he may well cause subsidence to the soil on the other side. Can he be ordered to stop digging, in order to prevent the subsidence? The answer is 'yes', for a neighbour cannot excavate his land if it will cause another's soil to fall in.

But this *right of support* only applies to earth and soil – it is not assumed to apply to buildings. This may seem ridiculous, but if the excavations cause his house to collapse the householder may not have any remedy, unless his soil would have fallen

353

in anyway, whether or not there was a building there! In short, the right of support only covers soil and earth, not buildings.

However, it is possible to acquire a right of support for buildings, so that they are protected in the same way as soil and earth. This could be done by a written deed or restrictive covenant (see page 335), but the usual method is to acquire it by twenty years' usage (i.e. *prescription*) in the same way that a right to light is acquired after twenty years (see page 345). If the house has had the benefit of a support for twenty years or more, then the law presumes that it has the right to be supported by next-door's soil. Also, if a house stands on the site of an old house that had itself acquired the right of support, then the new house will probably inherit that right. Once acquired, the right continues for ever. Otherwise there will be no right of support for a house, just for the earth and soil. However, if subsidence is caused to a house by a neighbour's tree roots, the landowner can sue even if there is no right of support (see below).

Trees

Trees can also amount to a nuisance at law.

Overhanging branches

If the branches of a neighbour's trees interfere with a landowner's enjoyment of his property, it may amount to a nuisance.

The usual way of tackling a legal nuisance is to take the matter to court and ask for damages and/or an order that the offending item be removed. This is an un-necessarily complicated and expensive procedure for so small a matter as an over-hanging branch. If the neighbour refuses to prune the tree, the landowner is allowed to resort to *self-help* and cut off the branches himself. However, the branches will not be his property (and nor will the fruit on them) so the law-abiding landowner should return them to his neighbour.

This is one of the few occasions when the law does not frown upon self-help, for generally the courts do not approve of people taking the law into their own hands. It is, though, important that the landowner be able to show that he acted reasonably in chopping off the branches; probably the best safeguard is for him to write a letter to the neighbour setting out his complaint, and stating a date by when the tree should be pruned, failing which he will prune it himself.

If the tree branches do not overhang the landowner's property, but merely block the light, there is probably no remedy for the landowner unless he has a right to light (see page 345).

Tree roots

As with tree branches, so with tree roots; if the roots of a neighbour's tree intrude into another's property, the landowner can either cut off the roots or take the neighbour to court for damages and/or an order that the roots be removed. In view of the cost of digging up tree roots, it is usually advisable for the landowner to obtain a court order beforehand, rather than do the work himself and then recover the cost from his neighbour. Apart from paying for the cost of digging up the roots, the neighbour would also be liable for incidental expenses, such as returfing a lawn.

The tree owner will also be liable for any damage caused to neighbouring buildings. This does not just apply to trees owned by neighbours; it also applies if the trees are on the council's pavement:

Two old oak-trees were growing in the pavement outside a house. They were about 150 years old. The council was told that the trees were causing damage but nothing was done. Held: The council was liable for the damage caused to the foundations. Russell (1984)

But this does not mean that every council is liable for all damage caused by trees on pavements. For example:

Eight metres from a house was a sixty-foot-high horse-chestnut tree. In the 1976 drought, the roots dehydrated the soil and caused subsidence. The householder sued for the cost of the £5,000 underpinning. Held: The council was not liable. The risk of this sort of damage arising had been too vague and remote. It would not be right to make the council liable. Solloway (1981)

The moral from this case is to make sure that the council is given good advance notice if there is any possibility that the roots might cause damage.

It is no defence for the tree owner to argue that the damaged building should have been constructed more soundly.

A block of flats was built near the boundary of a plot of land. On the other side of the boundary were tall trees. Within ten years the foundations of the flats were affected by subsidence, caused by the trees which were reducing the moisture level of the soil. The tree owner was sued, but he argued that the flats were of faulty construction. Held: The tree owner was liable. He could not blame the faulty construction of the building; that would only be relevant if the defects had been so overwhelming as to make the effect of the roots insignificant. Moreover, the fact that the trees had been there before the block of flats was no defence in a nuisance claim. The tree owner was liable for the full cost of repairs. Bunclark (1977)

Falling trees and branches

The owner of any item or piece of property is liable for damage or injury caused if he was negligent. So it is with trees, and the householder will be liable for damage caused by a falling tree or branch, if he was negligent. So if the accident occurred without warning (for instance, because of a gale, lightning, or other unforeseen weather conditions) he would not have been negligent. But if the tree fell down because of old age or disease he would probably have been negligent for not inspecting the tree regularly, and so he would be liable in damages. The prudent tree owner would probably be expected to inspect his trees at least once a year and perhaps twice a year.

Tree-preservation orders

A tree-preservation order (TPO) is an order made by the local planning authority which makes it illegal to prune, fell, uproot, or lop that particular tree. When a TPO is made the owner is given notice by the local authority, and he then has twenty-eight days in which to make representations.

The TPO is binding on all subsequent owners of the land, not just the person who was the owner at the time the order was made. This is so even if the offender does not know of the existence of the TPO:

> *Mr Mortimer cut down an oak tree that was subject to a tree-preservation order. He was prosecuted but argued that he could not be guilty since he had not known about the TPO. Held: This was not a defence. He was guilty.* Maidstone (1980)

For how to find out whether a particular tree is covered by a TPO see Appendix 1. The maximum penalty for felling a protected tree is a fine of £2,000, or up to twice the timber value of the tree, whichever is the greater. For otherwise damaging a protected tree, the maximum penalty is £1,000 fine.

Even if a tree is not subject to a TPO, the owner may be subject to restrictions on lopping, pruning, felling, or uprooting the tree. If it is within a Conservation Area he must give at least six weeks' notice to the local authority, so they can decide whether to make a TPO. Failure to give notice is an offence (same penalties as for breach of a TPO). A person who thinks that a particular tree should be subject to a TPO should apply to the local planning authority for an order to be made. In deciding whether to make a TPO, the authority will refer to a 1966 circular sent out by the ministry. This states:

> Local planning authorities can make a tree-preservation order only if they find it expedient in the interests of amenity. The amenity should be one enjoyed by the public at large, and the local planning authority should be able to show that without the order there would be a risk of amenity being spoiled. The degree of risk should be assessed realistically but it is not suggested that orders should be made only when there is an immediate threat of felling. Areas should be chosen with discrimination and not so as to blanket extensive areas with a view to maintaining a general control over a whole district. Orders should not be made for shrubs or bushes but only for trees with real amenity value . . . Precautionary orders may be desirable to protect trees of special amenity value, for example in urban areas where trees are few and far between.

Liability for escaping water, oil, etc.

If a householder chooses to store water on his land, is he liable if it escapes? For example, suppose he builds a rock garden with fountains and fish ponds; what happens if the supporting walls give way and the escaping water floods his neighbour's cellar? The courts would say that the householder was liable even if he had no reason to suspect that the walls might give way; thus, his having acted 'reasonably', without negligence, would be irrelevant. The court would simply say that if he chose to store water on his land, he did so in the knowledge that it might cause damage if it escaped. He knew the risks and it would be for the householder to compensate his neighbours if an accident occurred. This strict rule was laid down in a case that is famous amongst lawyers – *Rylands* v. *Fletcher*, 1868.

Mill-owners built a reservoir to hold water for their mill. Unfortunately, the water percolated down disused mine workings and flooded a nearby mine. The mill-owners had not been negligent, but it was held that they must compensate the mine-owner for the damage done. A 'person who for his own purposes, brings on his land and collects and keeps there anything likely to do mischief if it escapes, must keep it at his peril'. Rylands (1868)

Since then it has been extended to cover the storage and escape of other potentially dangerous substances, such as electricity, smuts, gas, and even sewage in a septic tank. Similarly, if the householder builds a tank to hold central-heating oil, but the tank fractures and the escaping oil ruins his neighbour's garden, then he is liable to the neighbour – whether or not it was the householder's fault.

It is this element of *strict liability* (irrespective of negligence, nuisance, reasonableness, and the other usual tests of liability) that makes the rule in *Rylands* v. *Fletcher* so unusual. Generally, English law disapproves of strict liability. Normally, negligence by the neighbour must be shown; if it *is* shown then he will be liable. For instance:

A basement was used for storing goods. The next-door building was derelict and the basement owners made lots of complaints about tramps wandering around the next-door building. Eventually, burglars broke through the dividing wall and stole valuable goods. Held: The owners of the derelict building had been negligent in not taking reasonable security precautions. Perl (1983)

Rivers, fishing rights

Although a landowner owns the air above and soil below his property, he does not own the water that runs across his land in rivers.

Navigation. The public can navigate on a tidal river up to the point where the tide ebbs and flows. Beyond that point the public only have a right to navigate if such a right has been acquired by long usage over the years (in the same way that the public can acquire a right of way over land – see page 341).

Fishing. The public can fish in a tidal river up to the point where the tide ebbs and flows. Beyond that point, fishing rights are vested in the landowner. Even if the public have acquired a right to navigate over this non-tidal part of the river, that navigation right will not include the right to fish.

Abstracting water. A landowner used to be able to take water from rivers and streams that flowed through his land. However, the Water Resources Act 1963 now requires the landowner to obtain a licence to abstract from the local water authority, although no licence is needed if no more than 1,000 gallons are abstracted, or if the water is taken for domestic purposes.

Boundary fences and walls

'Good fences make good neighbours,' wrote Robert Frost. But the law does not usually require a landowner to fence his property or even maintain an existing fence or wall.

Despite this, neighbours often have disputes over the responsibility for maintaining their boundary fences. The first point to note is that there is only rarely a legal obligation on a landowner to fence his property. Generally, this will be as a result of a covenant in the title deeds or lease which obliges him to fence. Conversely, the property may be in an open-plan estate in which case it is likely that the title deeds will contain a covenant prohibiting him from fencing.

But in the absence of such a legal obligation, the householder is free to decide for himself whether or not he wants to fence his property, and similarly whether he wants to maintain an existing fence or wall.

Fences. If the deeds make no provision, a general guide for deciding the ownership of a fence is to say that it belongs to the land on the side of the vertical support posts.

Boundaries. When it comes to considering the ownership (and even the location) of a disputed boundary, the court will look, firstly, at the title documents to see if they give any guidance (e.g. 'T' marks). But often the deeds are of little help, being imprecisely worded, or incorporating a map of such a small scale as to be useless. However, if there is a hedge and a ditch, the court will assume that the person who dug the ditch did so at the boundary of his own land, and then planted the hedge on top of the earth from that ditch; so the boundary is then assumed to run along the edge of the ditch furthest away from the hedge. The rather strained logic behind this rule can be overruled by other evidence; for example, if the other landowner has traditionally maintained the hedge, it might be held that it – and not the ditch – formed the boundary. Similarly, if the title deeds define the property by reference to Ordnance Survey maps, the hedge-and-ditch rule might not apply, for the OS always draw boundaries along the middle of hedges rather than along the edges of ditches.

Responsibility for damage caused by animals

What if a pet escapes and causes damage to a neighbour's garden or injures him; can he sue? Generally, the answer will depend upon whether the pet's owner was *negligent*, and so his conduct will be judged according to the standard set by the mythical 'reasonable man'.

Thus, if an animal wanders out on to the public highway and causes an accident, the owner will only be liable if his behaviour fell below that expected from a reasonable man. For example, it may be reasonable to leave an untethered dog in an ungated garden if the property is beside a quiet country road; however, if the same behaviour took place in the centre of a town the owner would almost certainly be liable if, for example, the dog ran out into the road and caused a motor-cyclist to swerve and fall off his machine.

Ms Sudron bought a pedigree puppy. To stop it escaping she had repairs done to her fence and gate. One afternoon, when she was out, her boy-friend failed to notice that a visitor had forgotten to close the gate. The puppy darted out and caused a moped-rider to crash. He sued. Held: Ms Sudron was not liable. She had not been negligent since she had taken all the precautions that one could reasonably expect. The injured moped-rider went without compensation. Smith (1982)

Although the animal owner will normally be liable only if he was negligent, there are three exceptions to this rule.

1. Dangerous animals

If a person chooses to keep an animal belonging to a *dangerous species* he does so at his own risk. So he will be liable if the animal escapes and causes damage, even if he was not negligent and could not be blamed for the accident.

Certain animals are obviously dangerous, such as lions, tigers, elephants, etc., and so if one of these animals escapes from a zoo, the zoo-keepers would be liable whether or not the accident was their fault. The Animals Act 1971 says that an animal is of a 'dangerous species' if it is not usually domesticated in this country and is, when fully grown, likely to cause severe damage unless restrained.

2. Animals that are normally harmless but for some reason are dangerous

The same rule of strict liability without the need to show negligence will apply to damage caused by animals that are not from a 'dangerous species', yet have unusual characteristics known to the owner. This is because an animal may normally be harmless but, in a particular set of circumstances, can be dangerous. For example, a dog is not normally dangerous, yet if a bitch has a litter of puppies it is quite likely that she will bite an approaching stranger; thus, the owner of the bitch should keep her under strict control during this dangerous period. Similarly, a dog with rabies is, in the circumstances, dangerous and so if it bites someone the owner will be liable – assuming of course that he knew it had rabies.

It is this requirement that the owner should know of the special circumstances that makes the animal dangerous which gives rise to the phrase 'every dog is allowed one bite'. Until that first bite, the owner has no reason to suppose that his seemingly normal dog is unusually aggressive and dangerous; however, after that bite he is assumed to know of its dangerous temperament and so he should take precautions to ensure that it does not hurt anybody. But there is no need to show that the animal was known to be vicious – merely that it was bad-tempered may be enough.

A groom was injured whilst leading a horse into a trailer. The horse, which was known to be temperamental and nervous, suddenly became violent and her arm was crushed. Held: The stable owner was liable. There was no need to show that the horse had a vicious tendency to injure people; it was known to be unpredictable and unreliable, and that made it dangerous. Wallace (1982)

3. Straying livestock

We have seen that an animal owner is not usually liable if his pet strays, unless he was negligent. However, for *livestock* the position is different, and the owner may be liable whether or not he was negligent; this applies when the animals stray on to private property, such as a neighbour's front lawn.

This strict liability rule only applies to livestock, as defined in the Animals Act 1971. The definition includes cattle, horses, asses, mules, sheep, pigs, goats, fowls, turkeys, geese, ducks, pigeons, peacocks, and other poultry; it does not include cats and dogs.

Thus, if a householder chooses to keep a goat in his garden, and the goat enters his neighbour's garden through a hole in the hedge, the householder will be liable for any damage caused by the goat – even if he thought that the goat was properly tethered and he did not know about the hole in the hedge. His only defence would be if it was the neighbour's own fault (e.g. in leaving a gate open), or if the livestock strayed on to the neighbour's land from the public highway (if they were lawfully on it in the first place). Remember that if livestock stray on to the road then the owner will only be liable if he was negligent (page 358).

Guard dogs

The Guard Dog Act 1975 lays down special rules for the use of guard dogs on commercial premises. Unfortunately, the Act does not apply to private houses or to agricultural land.

The main requirement of the Act is that the dog should be under the immediate control of its handler or, alternatively, that it be tethered so it cannot roam freely. In addition, a warning notice must be displayed. Breach of these laws is a criminal offence, triable in the magistrates' court (maximum penalty, a fine up to £2,000). However, breach of the Act does not automatically mean that the dog's owner would be liable in damages if a civil claim was brought (e.g. if someone was mauled by an untethered guard dog). This is because the Act is only concerned with the criminal law, and not with the civil law of damages for injury and loss caused to someone else. Despite this, though, the fact that the dog was allowed to roam freely would probably be regarded as 'unreasonable behaviour' on the part of the owner, if he was sued for negligence.

Keeping animals

Most domestic animals need not be licensed, although dogs are a major exception to this rule. It is a common belief that cats are beyond the law, and that a cat owner cannot be responsible for the actions of his pet; this is not true, and a negligent cat owner will be liable in the same way as any other pet owner, although, in practice, proof of such negligence would probably be extremely difficult.

A local-authority licence is needed to keep a dangerous wild animal (e.g. alligator, cobra, cheetah, lion, gibbon, ostrich, etc. – a full list is set out in the Dangerous Wild Animals Act 1976). The maximum penalty for not having a licence is a £2,000 fine, plus disqualification from holding a licence.

Any animal imported into the country must go into quarantine for six months. There are no exceptions to this rule; it applies to all live animals (not just dogs and cats), even if they have been inoculated against rabies and other diseases. The importation should be arranged through an authorized 'carrying agent' who will bring the animal in under licence and leave it at approved kennels. The animal owner is liable for all the costs of importation, kennelling, etc.

Most animals from abroad can only be imported under licence (unless the animal comes from Northern Ireland, Eire, the Channel Islands or the Isle of Man, and has been there for the previous six months). Applications for a licence should be made to the Ministry of Agriculture, Fisheries and Food, Government Buildings, Hook Rise, South Tolworth, Surbiton, Surrey. The application should be made at least four (preferably eight) weeks in advance.

It is a criminal offence to evade quarantine (maximum penalty, an unlimited fine or one year's imprisonment).

Dogs and the criminal law

Various statutes contain provisions aimed at controlling dogs, and also at protecting animals from their owners. In practice, prosecutions are rare: apart from the difficulties of identifying the owner of a particular dog, the police tend to refuse to prosecute in all but the most serious cases. The main laws are:

Dogs roaming in the road. Local authorities can designate particular roads as being roads in which any dog must be on a lead. The maximum penalty for breach is a £50 fine.

Dangerous dogs. The Dogs Act 1871 allows the magistrates to take action against dogs that are both dangerous and not under proper control. The mere fact that a dog is dangerous is not sufficient; the magistrates will also want to be sure that it is not under sufficient control. In practice, the easiest way to prove that a dog is dangerous is to show that it has attacked someone; once again, therefore, there is some truth in the adage that 'every dog is allowed one bite'.

If the case is proved, the magistrates can order the owner to keep the dog under proper control, or they can order its destruction, in which case the owner has fourteen days to appeal to the crown court.

Private prosecutions are permitted for Dogs Act offences (see page 779 for how to bring a private prosecution).

Collarless dogs. Under the Control of Dogs Order 1930 it is compulsory for a dog on a highway or in any 'place of public resort' to wear a collar stating the name and address of the dog's owner. Maximum penalty for breach of the order is a £400 fine.

Fouling the footpath. Most local authorities have by-laws which provide that 'no person being in charge of a dog shall allow the dog to foul the footpath . . . provided that a person shall not be liable if he satisfies the court that the fouling of the footway was not due to culpable neglect or default on his part'. Maximum penalty is usually a £50 fine. Private prosecutions are permitted.

Noisy dogs. By-laws usually contain provisions that can be used to control noisy dogs (see page 351).

Worrying livestock or poultry. Under the Dogs (Protection of Livestock) Act 1953 it is an offence for a dog to 'worry' livestock on agricultural land if it could reasonably be expected to cause injury or suffering to the livestock. Maximum penalty is a fine of £200. If the dog actually injures cattle or poultry, or chases sheep, it can be treated as a 'dangerous dog' (see page 361). Private prosecutions are permitted.

The Dogs Act 1926 makes the owner liable if the dog injures poultry, cattle, or sheep. He can be sued for damages and it is not necessary for the farmer to show that the dog's owner was negligent or that he had reason to think the dog might attack the animals.

A trespassing dog can only be shot if it is worrying or attacking animals or human beings, and if it was reasonable in the circumstances to shoot it.

Cruelty to dogs. Under the Protection of Animals Act 1911, it is an offence to be cruel to any animal, including a dog. The maximum penalty is £50 fine and three months' imprisonment, plus disqualification from keeping a dog for a stated period. Private prosecutions are permitted.

Abandoning a dog. The Abandonment of Animals Act 1960 makes it illegal temporarily or permanently to abandon any animal without reasonable cause, if it is likely to cause unnecessary suffering to the animal. The penalties are the same as for cruelty. Private prosecutions are permitted.

Accidents at home

What happens if someone is injured because of a defect in the home, such as an uneven path or a falling slate; is the householder liable for the state of his property?

The simple answer is 'yes'. The general rule is that the owner of the premises will be liable if he was negligent. This is the rule applied if the person injured is on the road or if he is the next-door neighbour. Thus, if a slate falls off the roof and hits the neighbour's car the question to be asked is: was the householder negligent? If he knew the slate was loose, or if he had not inspected the roof for a long time, then he would be liable. On the other hand, if the falling slate was the result of an unusually fierce storm, he might not be liable, since then he might not have been negligent.

The same rule applies if a tenant has a flat, and he is injured by something falling from the landlord's part of the building:

> *Mrs Cunard was injured when part of the roof and some guttering fell on her. Mr and Mrs Cunard were tenants of part of the building, but the roof and guttering were retained by the landlord. Held: The landlord had been negligent and so he was liable to pay damages to Mrs Cunard.* Cunard (1932)

Visitors, etc.

Complications arise if the accident involves someone who is visiting the house. Whilst the general rule is that the occupier is liable if he was negligent, the rule has to be modified to deal with uninvited guests: burglars, squatters, and other trespassers. It would be unfair to make the occupier liable to these trespassers and so the law provides that he is not liable even if he was negligent. For instance, if a burglar trips over an uneven step, he cannot sue the householder. But even this rule is subject to exceptions:

1. The occupier cannot take advantage of this freedom from liability deliberately to lay traps that might injure a trespasser. For instance, it is wrong to leave a man-trap to catch a burglar, and the householder who did so would be liable in damages. In short, the householder need not take steps to ensure that trespassers are not injured but he must not deliberately take steps that will cause them to be injured.
2. Children cannot be expected to stay off private property. Children are naturally adventurous and curious. The householder must therefore take precautions to prevent children from entering his dangerous property – if he does not, and the children are injured, he cannot argue that they were trespassers. The precautions to be taken will largely depend upon the extent of the risk.

But this is not an absolute duty. The occupier (or the owner of the land) just has to take the precautions that a sensible and humane adult would. It is a matter of protecting children from themselves, but there is a limit to the precautions that can reasonably be taken:

Northampton Council owned a rubbish tip. At one end it adjoined houses, but the railings between the two had been broken down. The council knew that children played on the tip, and staff chased them off whenever dumping was being carried out. It would have been prohibitively expensive to fence the whole site. Several children lit a fire on the site and one of them threw an empty aerosol can into it. It exploded, burning one of the children. Held: The council was not liable. The risks did not warrant the expensive precautions required to make the site child-proof.
Penny (1974)

So, if a person is injured on someone else's property (or if his property is damaged), he will be able to sue the negligent householder, unless he himself was a trespasser. But, in addition, there may be other people who can also be sued:

The landlord. If the property is rented, the landlord will probably be liable for accidents caused by defects in the property. (See Chapter 18 for when a landlord is obliged to repair a tenant's home.) However, the landlord will only be liable if:
• he knew of the defect, *or*
• he should have known of the defect (see page 304).

Building contractors. If the householder employs a contractor to carry out work and a visitor is injured through the contractor's negligence, the contractor will be liable.

Building contractors were employed to remove a sloping ramp leading to the front door of a house. They told the householder to use a side route until the work was completed. The side route passed close to a small sunken area. One night a seventy-one-year-old friend of the householder left by the side route and was injured. Held: The negligent contractors were liable to her. Billings (1957)

Professional advisers. They owe a duty to all people who might reasonably be on the property. For instance:

During demolition works, an architect advised that a wall was safe and that it could be left standing. In fact, it was not safe – as any expert should have known. A labourer was hurt when the wall collapsed. Held: He could sue the negligent architect. Clay (1963)

The local authority. The local authority has a duty to take care when it inspects new buildings for Building Regulations approval. If someone is later injured, or suffers loss, the council might be liable if their inspector should have checked the premises more thoroughly.

In 1962 a local authority approved the plans for a block of flats that was built later that year. By 1970 structural cracks had appeared in the walls due to subsidence and it was discovered that the local authority's building inspector had not properly inspected the foundations to see that they had been prepared in accordance with the approved plans. The owners of the flats sued the council for negligence. Held: The council was liable, for it had a duty to the future owners and occupiers of the flats to take care. Anns (1977)

Insurance

Most house-owners have a building policy that provides cover for damage to the home by fire, explosion, etc. In addition, this policy is likely to provide cover for liability arising from accidents caused by the defective state of the premises. Thus, most house-owners are insured against a claim for damages.

Tenants, however, are often not insured, since they rarely take out a building policy. However, the landlord will be liable if he should have known of the defect and if it was his responsibility (see above) and it is usual for a landlord to have a building policy. More often than not, therefore, an insurance company will have to pay any damages.

PART THREE

EMPLOYMENT

21 The Worker's Contract of Employment

Despite all the recent legislation, the basis of modern employment law is still the idea that each employee has his own contract of employment. The theory is that each employee individually enters into a legally binding contract with his employer; the employee provides his working skills and, in return, the employer pays him wages.

The contract of employment was, and still is, at the heart of the employment relationship or, as it was called until recently, the 'master and servant relationship'.

But the use of the word 'contract' suggests that there was a bargaining session at which employer and employee negotiated the terms of an agreement. This is, of course, not so. The idea of a freely negotiated employment contract is a myth – a legal fiction. Life is not like that. The unemployed worker does not negotiate with the personnel manager to secure the best terms. What is more likely is that he will have been sent to the firm by the Job Centre, be told the rate of pay and what the job involves. He will then have to take it or leave it. If he accepts the job, then the lawyer will say that there is now an employment contract between the employer and the employee, even though there is no written agreement, and even though few of the terms of employment were expressly agreed.

A contract does not have to be in writing to be legally binding, and employment contracts are no different from other contracts in this respect. The law will enforce the terms of the contract, and if the parties did not specifically agree on all the terms, then the law will work out what they intended – the *implied* terms. So terms as to overtime, holiday arrangements, sick pay, discipline, can all be implied if no express agreement was reached.

Every employee has a contract of employment with his employer. It is impossible to be an employee without having an employment contract.

Workers who are self-employed are not 'employees'. They do not benefit from all the numerous employment protection rights given to employees. It is not always easy to decide whether a worker is employed or self-employed. See page 382.

The employment contract

The employment contract is important because it is the peg from which all the employee's rights hang. It is the starting-point in deciding whether he has been unfairly dismissed or been made redundant. It decides whether he can be forced to do overtime, how much holiday he can take, whether he can demand sick pay, the extent to which he can be disciplined by the employer. It is the very basis of the employer/employee relationship, and hardly any employment law dispute can be resolved without considering the terms of the employment contract.

This is, of course, an artificial approach. It virtually ignores the existence of collective bargaining – a grave fault, since some 65 per cent of British employees have their conditions of employment determined by reference to collective agreements. All the law can do is to imply some – but not all – of the terms of the collective agreement into the individual's employment contract and so legal theory is half-heartedly reconciled with industrial reality.

Putting the employment contract into writing

It is better for both employer and employee if the contract of employment is set out in writing. Both of them then know where they stand and there is unlikely to be a dispute over the terms and conditions.

Although the law does not insist that the employment contract be in writing, it encourages the employer to set out some of the terms in writing:

1. The employer *must* provide the employee with a written statement of the main terms of the employment contract within thirteen weeks of the employee starting work. This written statement (usually called the 'written particulars') aims to be a true record of the more important terms of the contract, although it is not the contract itself. But often the written statement will be the only written record of what was agreed and so it will, more often than not, be taken as a summary of the employment contract. Since the employer has to prepare the written statement he might just as well set out the whole of the contract in writing.
2. Industrial tribunals look with disfavour on employers who do not put the terms of the employment contract into writing. If there should ever be a dispute between employer and employee – such as an unfair-dismissal claim – the industrial tribunal might well give the benefit of any doubt as to the terms to the employee.

This is underlined by the Industrial Relations Code of Practice, which sets out the behaviour expected of the 'reasonable' employer. Whilst it is not an offence to ignore the Code of Practice, an employer who fails to follow its recommendations may well find that an industrial tribunal will regard him with disfavour. Paragraph 62 of the Code of Practice states:

Apart from the statutory requirements, management should ensure that each employee is given information about:
  (i) the requirements of his job and to whom he is directly responsible;
  (ii) disciplinary rules and procedures and the types of circumstances which can lead to suspension or dismissal;
  (iii) trade-union arrangements;
  (iv) opportunities for promotion and any training necessary to achieve it;
  (v) social or welfare facilities;
  (vi) fire prevention and safety and health rules;
  (vii) any suggestion schemes.

The obvious way for the employer to prove that he has 'informed' the employee of these items is to set them out in the employee's employment contract.

Drawing up a written employment contract

Ideally, the written employment contract will set out all the terms and conditions of the employer/employee relationship. It should be as comprehensive as possible. So that nothing is overlooked, it is best to:

1. List all the points that must be included in the written statement, which has to be prepared within thirteen weeks of the job starting. See page 374 for all the matters that must be mentioned in these 'written particulars'. If the written contract covers all these points there will be no need to prepare separate written particulars; the written contract will suffice.
2. Next, deal with the seven points listed in the Code of Practice above.
3. Finally, consider whether there are any other matters that should be included. In practice, employers often forget to ask themselves whether they need specific clauses dealing with:

   • *job mobility*: will the employee be expected to move home if the employer wants him to work elsewhere?

   • *job flexibility*: will the employee be expected to change his duties if asked? If the contract sets out a very narrow job description the employee will probably be able to refuse to alter his duties.

   • *overtime*: will the employee be expected to work compulsory overtime when required?

   • *works rules*: works rules and disciplinary codes will probably be *implied* into the contract anyway (see page 373). But to remove any doubt it is best to refer to them specifically in the written contract.

   • *restrictions on future employment*: should there be a clause limiting the employee's future choice of jobs (for instance, if he knows trade secrets or lists of customers)? See page 422.

When there is no written employment contract: working out the terms

When there is no written contract of employment, the law will look at all the surrounding circumstances and work out what it thinks the parties meant to agree. These are *implied* terms, and can be derived from:

1. The duties imposed on all employ*ers* by the law.
2. The duties imposed on all employ*ees* by the law.
3. Obvious terms.
4. Custom and practice.
5. The conduct of employer and employee.
6. Collective agreements.
7. Works rules and disciplinary codes.
8. The 'written particulars' supplied to the employee.

1. The duties imposed on all employers

Every employer is expected to:
- *pay his staff* (see page 383 for the law on 'pay');
- *provide a safe system of work* by taking reasonable care of his staff. This means supplying proper, safe equipment, competent fellow-workers, adequate supervision, and proper instruction. If an employee is injured because his employer failed to provide a safe working environment, the employee can sue the employer for negligence – even if the injury resulted from the negligence of a fellow-employee (for instance, if an employee trips over an uneven floor, is injured by an unfenced machine, or knocked over by another employee, then almost certainly the employer – through his insurance company – will have to pay him compensation). For examples, see page 410.

Similarly, if an employer breaks the law and the employee is sued as a result, then the employee can demand that the employer pays the damages:

> *Mr Gregory was injured when a lorry driven by Thomas Hill knocked him off his motor bike. At the time Hill was driving his employer's lorry in the course of his job. Unknown to him, his employers had not insured the lorry. Mr Gregory sued him for damages because of his negligent driving. Could he sue his employers to recompense him for the damages he had to pay Mr Gregory? Held: Yes. It was an implied term of Hill's employment contract that his employer would obey the law and insure the lorry: 'There was an implied term in the contract of service that the employer would comply with [the law] from which it would follow that the servant would be indemnified . . . for any damage caused by his negligence.'* Gregory (1951)

In addition, the employer must obey the law by giving the employee the benefit of his rights under the employment-protection laws. Thus, eligible staff must be allowed to claim maternity pay and their job back after pregnancy, to be paid a guarantee payment if laid off, or put on short time, to take time off for trade-union duties or activities, and so on. But note that there is no general implied obligation on employers to provide their staff with any work (see page 401) or to supply them with references when they leave (see page 422).

2. The duties imposed on all employees

To work. Employees must turn up for work and work to a reasonable standard. But if they are sacked for absenteeism or poor work they may still be able to bring an unfair-dismissal claim (see page 433).

To obey orders. But an employee need only obey lawful orders. So if he is asked to do something dangerous or unlawful – such as operate an unsafe machine, or 'cook the books' – he can refuse. Also, the orders must be within the terms of the employment contract: a fitter need not obey an order to clean the toilets, because those duties are outside his employment contract.

To take reasonable care. The employee must take reasonable care when carrying out his duties. If he is negligent then he can be sued by his employer for the resulting loss.

But he will not be liable if he acted reasonably – the courts 'apply the standards of men, and not those of angels'.

It may seem incredible that an employer can sue his negligent employee, but this was laid down in a House of Lords decision of 1957:

Martin Lister and his father both worked for the same Romford firm. While reversing the firm's lorry into a yard, Martin negligently drove into his father. His father then sued the firm, saying it was liable for the negligent acts of its employees. But the company's insurers argued that if they were liable to Martin's father – which they clearly were – then they could recover their losses from Martin himself. Held: Yes. Martin owed his employers a duty to take care. Since he hadn't taken care they could sue him for his negligence. Lister (1957)

Surprisingly, that case remains the law today. This was confirmed in a Court of Appeal decision, when a bank successfully sued a former assistant general manager for £36,000. The employee had been negligent in granting overdrafts and the bank was able to sue him for its losses (*Janata Bank*, 1981). In practice, it is extremely rare for an employer to sue his staff in this way: usually the employer will be covered by insurance and insurers do not sue because it is bad for their image! But, legally, the principle remains valid.

Not to betray his employer's trust. An employee must not give away his employer's trade secrets or confidential information. Often there will be an express clause in a written contract of employment restricting the employee's future activities (see page 422).

There is *no* general duty on an employee to cooperate with his employer. As long as he fulfils the terms of his employment contract that is sufficient. The basic rule is that he cannot be expected to do more than comply with his contractual obligations. However, the court will usually decide that an employee is contractually obliged to do whatever is necessary to keep the employer's business running reasonably smoothly (e.g. as in a 1972 case, railway workers who went on a work-to-rule were held to be in breach of their contracts of employment). In addition, if the employer is under a statutory duty to fence machinery or ensure that safety equipment is worn, then the employee must cooperate to help the employer meet these obligations.

3. Obvious terms

Some terms are so obvious that they 'go without saying'. For instance, if an employer advertises for a lorry driver, it is an assumed part of the employment contract that the employee will be able to drive a lorry. If the employee didn't know how to drive, the employer could dismiss him without risk of an unfair-dismissal or redundancy claim.

4. Custom and practice

The custom and practice in an industry as a whole can also be relevant. For instance, if an employer can show that it is normal practice, or customary, for workers of that sort to be 'mobile' then the court will imply such a term into the contract of employment. On this basis a job-mobility clause might well be implied into an actor's employment contract, but not into a solicitor's.

But the courts will only recognize a custom if it is 'reasonable, certain, and notorious'. 'Notorious' means that it must be very well known in the industry.

Traditionally Lancashire weavers had deductions made from their wages for bad workmanship. Nothing was said about this practice in any written employment contract and so one worker took his employer to court arguing that the deductions were unlawful. Held: No. 'A Lancashire weaver knows and has for very many years past known precisely what his position was as regards deductions for bad work in accepting employment in a Lancashire mill.' So it was a valid custom. Sagar (1931)

5. The conduct of employer and employee

The parties' conduct during the employment can be used to work out what they originally agreed. For instance, suppose that an employee is told that he will have to move to a new plant a hundred miles away. Whether the employee can refuse to move (and so claim unfair dismissal or redundancy if he is sacked for refusing to move) will depend upon whether his employment contract contains a job-mobility clause. If there is no express clause, then the law looks at, amongst other things, the past conduct. So, if the employee has previously moved home at the employer's request, that will probably be evidence of an implied job-mobility clause.

6. Collective agreements

Some two thirds of the working population have their terms and conditions of employment set by collective agreements. Yet only 50 per cent of the working population are union members. Do the terms of a collective agreement bind the individual worker?

If the individual's employment contract specifically refers to the 'current collective agreement' then there can be no doubt. He is subject to the terms of the agreement even if negotiated without his knowledge and against his will.

Mr Callison was a first-rate spray painter. He worked for Fords and his employment contract was subject to the terms agreed from time to time between his union and Fords. Fords and the union negotiated a reorganization which made spray painters of his ability unnecessary and so he was regraded as a Class C sprayer. He left, and claimed wrongful dismissal and redundancy. Held: No. The new arrangements had been agreed with the union, and since his employment contract bound him to accept the terms negotiated by the union, the company had not acted wrongly. Callison (1969)

Difficulties arise when the employee's employment contract does not make any mention of a collective agreement. In these circumstances it is more difficult for an employer to argue that the employee is bound by the terms negotiated with the union. But, in practice, employees are usually bound by the terms of collective agreements – especially if they have accepted the terms of the agreements in the past. Often, in the absence of objection, the employee will be assumed to accept the new collective agreement. Generally, this will be so whether or not he is a member of the union.

7. Works rules and disciplinary codes

These days, employers are expected to have comprehensive disciplinary codes and disciplinary procedures. To what extent are these, and other works rules, binding on the individual employee?

If the rules are specifically referred to in the employee's contract of employment then there can be no doubt that he is bound by them. So the wise employer ensures that his staff have written contracts that state 'I have read the works rules and regulations contained in the works rules booklet and accept the conditions of employment set out in that booklet.' Also, if he signs that he accepts the job 'on the usual conditions', that will usually be enough to make him bound by the rules.

But few employers are that legally minded. Usually there is no express reference to the works or disciplinary rules. When this happens, the employee will generally be held to be bound by them if they are reasonable and likely to be regarded as binding by the staff. If the rules are on display in the office or factory then they will generally be regarded as binding.

However, this does not mean that the employer can simply alter the terms of the employment contract by pinning up a new set of works or disciplinary rules. If the orders are changed to such an extent that they alter the contract of employment, then the employee can protest.

8. The written particulars supplied to the employee

If there is no comprehensive written employment contract the employer must provide the employee with a written summary of the contract (see below). Often these 'written particulars' are the only written evidence of the contract and so, more often than not, they are accepted as the best evidence of what was agreed between employer and employee unless the employee can convince the industrial tribunal that his recollection of what was originally said is correct. For instance:

Mr Rump started work as a heavy-goods-vehicle driver in 1973. The company asked him to sign a contract of employment form which said that he would be liable to work anywhere in the United Kingdom. However, one of the company's managers orally promised him that he would only have to work in the south of England owing to his family circumstances. As a result of this promise, Mr Rump signed the form.

In 1976, Mr Rump signed a copy of his written particulars of employment which stated 'you may be required to transfer from one workplace to another on the instruction of the employer'.

All went well until February 1978, when Mr Rump was ordered to work outside the south of England. He refused, resigned, and then claimed unfair dismissal. Held: It had been an original oral term of his employment that he would not have to work outside the south of England. The

1976 written particulars could not alter the contract of employment. Accordingly, he was justified in resigning once the company insisted that he work outside the south of England. He was entitled to unfair-dismissal compensation. Hawker Siddeley (1979)

If an employee does not agree with the details set out in the written summary, it is important that he makes this clear to the employer. If he does nothing he will later find it difficult to argue that the summary is not a true record of what was agreed.

Employment rights

The longer you have worked for your employer, the more rights you are entitled to:

Period of employment	Rights	See page
1 month	If sacked, you must be given at least one week's notice; you are entitled to guarantee payments if laid off, on short time, or if you are suspended on certain medical grounds.	415 389
13 weeks	You should have received written particulars of your contract of employment by now.	374
26 weeks	If sacked, you can demand a written statement of the reason for your sacking.	418
2 years	You are within the unfair-dismissal legislation	425
	If sacked, you must be given at least two weeks' notice.	415
	You are within the redundancy-payments legislation.	464
	You can have reasonable time off to look for a job if you are being made redundant.	478
	You are entitled to maternity pay and also to return to your job after confinement for pregnancy.	404
4–12 years	If sacked, you must be given one week's notice for each year of your employment.	415
over 12 years	If sacked, you must be given at least twelve weeks' notice.	415

Providing 'written particulars' of the employment contract

Employers must provide each member of staff with a written summary of the main terms of his employment contract. This must be provided within thirteen weeks of starting work.

But it is not the actual contract of employment that need be provided. The 'written particulars' are just a summary of the terms of the contract – not the contract itself. However, as already explained, the written particulars will usually be the best record of the terms of the contract and so, for all practical purposes, will be the contract. But in theory they are not.

The written particulars can be handed or posted to the employee within the thirteen-week period. All the particulars need not be contained in one document, so the employee can be given a piece of paper that refers him to another document – such as a works rules booklet or a pension-scheme handbook. If he is not given a copy of the other document, there must be one available for him to inspect at work and he should be told where it is. So a worker could be referred to 'the terms of the current collective agreement made between the firm and the recognized trade unions, a copy of which is available for inspection in the personnel department offices'.

Obviously, it is better if each employee is given his own individual written particulars with all the information contained in the one document. But, as the law stands, this is not necessary.

The sensible employer will:

1. Prepare the written particulars as soon as the employee is recruited, rather than wait until the end of the thirteen-week period. By serving the written particulars straight away he is reducing the scope for future argument.
2. Include all the other terms in the contracts of employment and not confine himself to those points required by law (see page 378). He will thus end up with a comprehensive, written employment contract.
3. Ask the employee to sign that he accepts the written particulars as representing the terms of his contract. By doing this the employee will almost certainly be committing himself to accepting the terms set out in the written particulars – even if they are not a true record of what was originally agreed.

If the written particulars are wrong

If an employee accepts incorrect written particulars he will probably find that he is bound by the error. For instance, suppose that the particulars state that he is entitled to sick pay at two thirds of the normal rate, whereas full sick pay was agreed when he was offered the job; if he does not query the error he will later find it very difficult to prove what was originally agreed. More often than not, his silence in not querying the error will be taken as acceptance of the terms.

An employee should write to his employer pointing out any errors. If the employer refuses to accept that there is an error, the employee can ask an industrial tribunal to decide who is right.

Mr Churcher was sent written particulars which described him as 'planner and associated duties'. He thought he should be 'senior planning engineer'. The firm did not agree and so he took the matter to an industrial tribunal. Held: His proper job title should be 'planning engineer'. Churcher (1976)

Employee's rights

		Written particulars of the employment contract (see page 374)	Notice (see page 415)	Unfair dismissal (see page 425)	Written reasons for dismissal (see page 418)	Redundancy payment (see page 464)
	The right					
Eligible employees	(see remedy below)	1	2	3	4	5
Self-employed; partner; freelance		no	no	no	no	no
Over the normal retirement age for the job, even if under sixty or sixty-five		yes	yes	no	yes	yes
Of retirement pension age, i.e. sixty-five for men, sixty for women		yes	yes	no	yes	no
Aged under eighteen		yes	yes	yes	yes	no
Less than one calendar month's continuous employment		no	no	no	no	no
Less than two years' continuous employment		yes	yes	yes	no	no
Fixed-term contract for over one year which specifically excludes these rights		yes	yes	no	yes	no

What sanction can be imposed (usually by industrial tribunal)?
The remedy

1 *Declare what particulars should be*
2 *Sue for wages in county court*
3 *Award reinstatement, re-engagement, or compensation.*
4 *Can award up to two weeks' pay*
5 *Cash compensation*
6 *Up to six weeks' wages at 90 per cent of net pay*

Ineligible employees. In addition various other groups of employees are ineligible: registered dock workers, Crown servants, public officials, shore fishermen, those who work outside Great Britain, and employees who work for a spouse are excluded from virtually all these employment-protection rights. So too are 'part-timers', but there is a complicated definition of what is a part-

Maternity pay and leave (see page 404)	Itemized pay statement (see page 383)	Equal pay (see page 391)	Guarantee pay on lay-off and short-time (see page 389)	Rights on employer's insolvency (see page 421)	Trade-union activities (see page 479)	Time off for union officials (see page 481)	Time off for public duties (see page 399)	Time off for antenatal care (see page 403)
6	7	8	9	10	11	12	13	14
no	no	no	no	no	no	no	no	no
yes	yes	yes	yes	yes	yes	yes	yes	yes
yes	yes	yes	yes	yes	yes	yes	yes	yes
yes	yes	yes	yes	yes	yes	yes	yes	yes
no	yes	yes	no	yes	yes	yes	yes	yes
no	yes	yes	yes	yes	yes	yes	yes	yes
yes	yes	yes	yes	yes	yes	yes	yes	yes

7 *Award up to thirteen weeks' worth of the 'deductions'*
8 *Wage imbalance for up to two years*
9 *Five days' pay per quarter*
10 *The Secretary of State can pay the arrears due*

11 *Can award compensation*
12 *Can award compensation*
13 *Can award compensation*
14 *Can award compensation of wages due during time off*

timer (i.e. a person who works fewer than sixteen hours per week, unless employed for five years or more, in which case it is a person employed for fewer than eight hours per week). Also excluded are seasonal workers – that is, employees taken on for a fixed period of twelve weeks or less.

The contents of the 'written particulars'

By section 1 of the 1978 Act, an employee's written particulars must state:

1. The *names* of both employer and employee.
2. The *date* when the employment began. Also whether any previous service will count as continuous employment for working out eligibility for employment law rights.
3. *Pay* – the rate of pay, or the method of calculating it. Also whether he is to be paid by the week, month, or year.
4. *Job title*. But it need not be a job description. If it is a detailed description of the job, rather than a mere job title, it may well be taken, at a later date, as restricting the employer's ability to ask the employee to do other work. The employee should object if the particulars contain a job description which is very wide since this may restrict his/her right to refuse a 'suitable alternative job' if s/he is made redundant or if she returns to work after pregnancy.
5. *Holiday entitlement*. What are the holidays? Are they paid? When does the firm's holiday year begin?
6. *Pension*. Is there a pension scheme? If so, what are the details? Usually the employee is referred to a separate pensions booklet.
7. *Sickness and injury*. The firm's rules about sickness. Is the employee entitled to sick pay? If so, for how long? Can the employer deduct DHSS sickness benefit from the sick pay? What procedure is to be followed for deciding whether an employee is so ill that he should be dismissed? What are the rules about production of sick notes? Can the employer insist on a medical examination by the firm's doctor?
8. *Notice*. Both employer and employee must give the other notice if the employment is to be ended by sacking or resignation. The minimum periods of notice must be set out, but they cannot be less than the statutory minimum periods (see page 415).
9. *Hours of work*. What is the length of the normal working week? An employee need not work overtime unless it is a term of his employment contract. So if the employer wants to be able to insist on compulsory overtime, there should be a specific clause saying so.
10. *Discipline at work*. Employers are expected to draw up disciplinary rules and disciplinary procedures. The employee should be told of them. Usually this will be done by referring him to a separate booklet, such as the works rules. He should also be told of the disciplinary appeals procedure.
11. *Complaints*. The employee should be told to whom he can complain if he has a grievance.

If the written particulars are not provided

If the written particulars are not provided, the employee can complain to an industrial tribunal. He can complain at any time during his employment, or within three months of his leaving the job. The industrial tribunal can then declare what the written particulars should say.

But beyond that, there is no real sanction on the employer who does not supply the written particulars. The employee will probably be reluctant to complain to his employer or to make an issue out of it. Certainly complaining to an industrial tribunal is hardly likely to increase his promotion prospects within the firm!

Asking for your written particulars

1. Check that you are entitled to receive 'written particulars'. A few workers (such as part-timers) are excluded: see 'Ineligible Employees', below.
2. Check that your employer has not complied with his legal obligation by handing you a note which refers you to other document(s); see page 375.
3. Once you have been employed for thirteen weeks you can demand the written particulars. If they have not been supplied check that this is not through an oversight or clerical error.
4. A letter is now needed. Write asking your employer for 'the written particulars of my contract of employment, which you are required to provide to me, in accordance with section 1 of the Employment Protection (Consolidation) Act 1978'. Keep a copy of the letter.
5. If you still do not receive the written particulars you will have to decide how far you are prepared to take the matter. You can complain to an industrial tribunal but you might do best to draw up your own set of written particulars and send them to your employer. You will then have gone on record as setting out what you regard as the main terms of the employment contract. This should safeguard your position for the future. But, whatever you decide to do, it might be sensible to wait until you have been employed for fifty-two weeks. Then you will be eligible for compensation for unfair dismissal and will have some protection if your employer decides you are a trouble-maker and sacks you. Alternatively, you might ask a trade union for help, especially if it is recognized by your employer.

Ineligible employees. Not all employees are entitled to written particulars (e.g. part-timers). For full details see the chart on page 376.

Employed or self-employed?

Only 'employees' are eligible for the various employment-protection rights (except the discrimination and equal-pay laws) that have been introduced in recent years, such as unfair dismissal, redundancy, the right to notice, maternity pay, and so on.

A person who is self-employed cannot claim any of these rights, for he does not have a contract of employment. Instead he is an independent contractor, employed on a contract for services.

Usually it is obvious whether a worker is an employee or not. The question can often be answered by simply asking, 'Who pays the national insurance contributions?' and, 'Does he pay tax by PAYE?' However, these factors are not conclusive – a worker can have claimed the tax benefits of being self-employed, and yet still be held to be an employee:

Mr Davis was a lecturer at the New England College, Arundel. He was taken on as an employee in 1971, but later he asked the college to treat him as self-employed 'for fiscal reasons'. Thereafter the college no longer deducted tax or national insurance contributions from his pay. Later, Mr Davis was sacked and the question that arose was whether he was eligible for unfair dismissal. The college argued that he was self-employed and so not eligible. Held: He was an employee. The relationship between Davis and the college was that of employer and employee, and this had not been altered by the tax and NI arrangements. Davis (1977)

So it is not so much the label that the parties put on their relationship (i.e. employee or self-employed) but the reality of the relationship. For instance:

Under the 'lump' system, building labourers are said to be self-employed, whereas in reality they are treated as employees. The device was widely used as a tax-dodge until the tax laws were tightened up. In one case, a lump worker was injured and sued the contractor for negligence. If the worker was an employee, the contractor would have been liable; if the worker was self-employed, the contractor would probably not have been liable. Held: He was an employee. The mere fact that he was called 'self-employed' could not hide the real nature of the employer/ employee relationship. The judge said, 'I regard the lump . . . as no more than a device which each side regarded as being capable of being put to his own advantage . . . but which in reality did not affect the relationship of the parties . . . the reality of the relationship was employer and employee.' Ferguson (1976)

Similarly:

Mr West was a sheet-metal worker. He asked his employers to treat him as self-employed and they did so. He was paid without deductions and he received no holiday or sick-pay entitlement. But otherwise there was no difference between his working conditions and those of his PAYE workmates. The employers told him that they did not need him any more and he claimed unfair dismissal. The employers argued that he was not eligible for unfair-dismissal compensation since he was self-employed, not an employee. Held: West was really an employee – it was impossible to regard him as being in business on his own account – so he was within the unfair-dismissal legislation. Young & Woods (1980)

However, this is probably a more typical case:

An architect worked for a housing association for a period of twenty-one months, averaging twenty-eight hours' work each week. He did not receive sick pay or holiday pay. Was he employed or self-employed? Held: He was self-employed. But this was largely because he did not undertake or promise to turn up at the office at any particular time and nor did he promise to do a particular number of hours each week. Basically, all he had promised was to do architectural work during the hours that he chose to work. WPHT (1981)

Undoubtedly, many people claim to be self-employed and yet they work for only one person, turn up at that person's office, and do the work they are told to do, during the hours laid down for them. Accordingly, it would seem that such people are not genuinely self-employed – and they and their employers should beware (because the DHSS might claim that the more expensive employee's NI stamps should be paid, and the taxman may claim that the self-employed person's tax benefits should not apply).

Home workers can be employees; once again, the issue is decided by looking at the totality of the relationship. Most home workers are self-employed but some may be surprised to learn that they are not (or, more likely, their employers would be horrified to learn that the home workers are employees!). For instance:

A clothing factory made men's trousers. Machinists worked in the factory and they were all employees. However, there were also out-workers who worked at home, sewing pockets into the trousers. They were paid on piece-rate and they decided themselves how much work they wanted to do (usually, it was about four to seven hours a day). There was an argument over holiday pay, and it ended with two of the home workers claiming unfair dismissal. So the question then arose of whether they were employees or self-employed. Held: They were employees. Nethermere (St Neots) (1984)

This decision was greeted with some amazement at the time and so it is probably best seen as an extreme example. The position remains that most home workers are probably self-employed but they may turn out to be employed; a lot will depend upon the extent to which the employer supervises their work and lays down the working hours, etc. Similarly, casual workers can also be employees, although they will normally be regarded as self-employed unless they have to work as and when requested by the employer.

Company directors can often be in a difficult position. It is not always easy to decide whether they are employees or self-employed. Usually, the control test (can he be told how to do his job?) will decide the issue. If the director is in reality his own boss, he will not be an employee. For instance, a director who owns a majority of the shares in a company will be self-employed.

Full-time directors are more likely to be regarded as employees than part-time directors. But even a full-time director will be self-employed if his position is inconsistent with his being an employee.

The three Parsons brothers inherited their father's haulage business and ran it, although most of the shares were owned by their mother. But the brothers argued and Leonard Parsons was voted off the board. He claimed unfair dismissal, but the company argued that he was not an employee and so he was not eligible. Although Leonard did not have a contract with the company he was a director for life. Held: By looking at all the circumstances, it was clear that Leonard was self-employed. His pay was described as director emoluments and he paid tax and NI contributions as a self-employed person; thus he could not claim unfair dismissal. On these facts, the court could not agree that he was an employee. Parsons (1979)

Employed and Self-employed: the Differences

	Employee	*Self-employed*
Tax	PAYE deducted by employer assessed under Schedule E	Pays Schedule D; generally has more deductible expenses and so pays less tax; will usually pay tax in arrears
NI	Paid partly by employer and partly by employee	All paid by the self-employed worker
Occupational pension	Probably entitled to a pension, partly financed by employer	Must pay own pension contributions
Sickness	Entitled to statutory sick pay from employer, or sickness (or supplementary) benefit from DHSS	No entitlement to sick pay or statutory sick pay. Can claim sickness (or supplementary) benefit from DHSS
Unemployment benefit	Eligible	Ineligible
Unfair dismissal	Eligible	Ineligible
Redundancy payments	Eligible	Ineligible
Holidays	Usually receives paid holiday	Not paid
Notice	Entitled to statutory minimum period of notice (see page 374)	Need not be given any notice, unless contract says otherwise
VAT	Not liable	Must be charged if turnover over £19,500 p.a. (1985)

22   At Work

Wages

Itemized pay statements

Employers must provide their staff with itemized pay statements (s. 8, Employment Protection (Consolidation) Act 1978), specifying:

- the gross pay
- the net pay
- any deductions from the gross pay, stating the amounts deducted and why the deductions are made.

The employee should therefore be able to work out how his pay is made up. The itemized pay statement need not repeat the fixed deductions that are made from every pay slip if the employee has been given (within the last year) a 'standing statement of fixed deductions' setting out the amount of the deductions, when they are made, and why they are made. So fixed deductions, such as trade-union membership fees and staff club contributions, need not be set out separately on every pay slip.

The aim of the legislation is that every employee should be able to work out how his net pay is calculated. Unfortunately, the Act does not lay down any standard form of pay slip, and an employer can provide his staff with computerized pay statements that comply with the legislation, but which are nevertheless difficult to understand.

If an employee is not given an itemized pay statement, or if he is given an incomplete statement, he can apply to an industrial tribunal (the usual application form, IT1, is used; see page 449). The application can be made at any time during the employment, or within three months of the ending of the employment. The tribunal can decide what the statement should have said. But that by itself is no real sanction. So an additional sanction is provided by allowing the tribunal, in effect, to 'fine' the employer. He can be ordered to pay the employee an amount up to the total of all the unnotified deductions made during the thirteen weeks before his application to the tribunal. So the employer can be ordered to pay a sum equal to the employee's tax, NI, pension, and other contributions – even though the employer was entitled to deduct them in the first place. For instance:

Mr and Mrs Davies were employed as steward and stewardess at a labour club in Cardiff for three months. They were not given an itemized pay statement despite having asked for one. They complained to an industrial tribunal. Held: The tribunal calculated Mr Davies's unnotified

383

deductions at £181.35 and Mrs Davies's at £62.30. The tribunal awarded Mr Davies £150 and Mrs Davies £50. This was despite the fact that neither Mr nor Mrs Davies had suffered any loss through the club's failure to supply itemized pay statements. Davies (1979)

Ineligible employees. Not all employees can demand an itemized pay statement (e.g. part-timers are not eligible). For a full list, see the chart on pages 376–7.

Being paid in cash

Only shop assistants and those in 'manual labour' can demand their wages in cash – other employees cannot complain if they are paid by cheque. This law derives from the Truck Acts 1831–1940. These Acts were primarily aimed at banning the practice of 'trucking', under which employers paid their staff in kind, or by vouchers which could only be spent at the employer's 'tommy shop' where goods would be marked up in price. The Acts require 'workmen' and shop assistants to be paid in cash and they also lay down strict rules on the deductions that can be made from their pay packets.

The courts have had some difficulty in deciding which employees qualify as 'workmen', and so must be paid in cash. The Truck Acts specifically exclude 'seamen, domestics, and menial servants' so they can be paid by cheque or in kind. 'Workman' means an employee who is engaged in 'manual labour', but the difficulties arise when an employee's job is part manual and part non-manual. The courts have not found a satisfactory test, beyond asking whether the job involves a 'real and substantial' amount of manual labour or whether it was merely 'incidental' to the work done. This has led to some strange distinctions being made; for instance, a warehouse packer's job has been held to be 'manual labour', but those of a greengrocer's assistant, a hairdresser, a research chemist, and a guard of a goods train do not, according to the courts, involve 'manual labour'. The courts have held that 'manual labour' does not mean that the job must involve an element of hard physical labour, and so a TV repairman has been held to be employed in 'manual labour'.

So, as the law stands, the position is unclear. There seems to be little justification for the continued retention of the Truck Acts nowadays, and it might be best to repeal them. One side-effect of the Acts is that they prevent blue-collar staff from being given the perks and bonuses that their white-collar colleagues receive. The giving of luncheon vouchers, shares in the company, and other perks to 'manual workers' is illegal. In fact, the government has announced its intention of abolishing the Truck Acts, so these laws may soon be no more than history.

Being paid by cheque

Employees who are not shop assistants or 'workmen' cannot object if they are paid by cheque or Giro.

A Truck Act 'workman' can only be paid by cheque if he makes a written request to his employer and if the employer agrees to pay him by cheque (Payment of Wages Act 1960). But the arrangement can be cancelled by either employer or employee giving the other four weeks' notice. The 1960 Act was introduced as an attempt to cut down the amount of cash used in paying wages and so reduce the likelihood of a wages snatch. In practice, it is only rarely used.

Deductions from wages

An employer can always deduct items such as tax, national insurance contributions and pension contributions from an employee's wages. But the deductions must be set out in an itemized pay statement (see page 383).

If the employee is a Truck Act 'workman' (see above) then there are special restrictions on the additional deductions that the employer can make. Briefly, the employer can only deduct the true value of rent, food prepared and eaten on the premises, medicine and medical care, fuel, miners' tools, and certain animal foodstuffs. Also the employee must sign that he agrees to the deductions being made.

Deductions from the 'workman's' wages because of his bad workmanship can only be made if the deduction represents the true loss, and is 'fair and reasonable having regard to all the circumstances'. The deductions can only be made if the employee signs a contract allowing deductions for bad workmanship or if there is a notice, clearly displayed, notifying the staff that such deductions can be made.

The Truck Acts are enforced by wages inspectors of the Department of Employment. They will advise a 'workman' who thinks his employer is making illegal deductions. Guilty employers can be fined up to £400 in the magistrates' court. In addition, the employee can recover the illegal deductions by suing the employer in the courts (in addition he might be able to persuade the magistrates to order the employer to compensate him when convicting the employer; see 'Criminal Compensation Order', page 714).

Two employees were sacked by a self-service petrol station. Both had till shortages and the employers had deducted the shortages from their wages. The employers were prosecuted in the magistrates' court. Held: The petrol station staff were 'manual workers' and so they came within the Truck Acts. The deductions from their wages were therefore illegal. The employers were fined £200 on each charge and ordered to pay full compensation to the ex-employees. Wells (1983)

In practice, it is not uncommon for till staff to have 'shortages' deducted from their wages. This case shows that these deductions can be illegal – but bear in mind that the deductions will only be illegal if (1) the employee is a 'manual worker', and (2) the employee has not signed an agreement allowing these deductions to be made.

Finally, it is also illegal for an employer to make any deductions from an employee's wages in respect of safety equipment which is specifically required by statute – e.g. goggles for a lathe operator (s. 9, Health and Safety at Work Act 1974). He can be fined up to £400 in the magistrates' court. This provision does not apply to the employer's general (i.e. non-statutory) duty to take reasonable care for the safety of his staff; accordingly, an employer can (for instance) charge his staff for gloves used for lifting, since he is not under a statutory obligation to supply the gloves.

Being overpaid

If the employer makes a mistake and overpays the employee, then generally the employee will have to give the money back. This is because of the general rule of law that you cannot hold on to money that has been paid to you by mistake. However, it would probably be unreasonable for the employer to deduct the whole amount from the next wage packet (unless the sum was very small) – normally, it should be done by reasonable instalments. Also, the deductions should be properly itemized in the pay statements (see page 383). In one case, an employee owed £111 to his employers and they deducted it from his pay as 'miscellaneous deductions'. It was held that the deduction should have been properly itemized, and so the employee was awarded £25 compensation – even though he had known that he owed the £111.

Exceptionally, the employee may not have to repay the overpaid wages:

A gym teacher was overpaid by £1,007 over a two-year period due to a computer error. By then he had spent most of the money and had retired. Held: The council had led him to believe the money was his and it would be wrong to now expect him to repay it. Avon CC (1983)

So, while each case depends on its own facts, the basic rule would seem to be that the longer the mistake is made, and the more 'innocent' the employee is, then the less likely it is that the court will order the money to be repaid.

Suing for arrears of pay

An employee who is owed wages can sue his employer. The claim is brought in the county court, unless the amount involved exceeds £5,000, in which case it is heard in the High Court.

This is one of the few occasions when an employment dispute is heard by the civil courts and not by an industrial tribunal. There are plans to transfer these claims to industrial tribunals, but as yet the necessary regulations have not been made.

Special provisions apply when an employer becomes insolvent. His staff can claim money due from the Department of Employment (see page 421).

The right to sick pay

Whether or not an employee can demand sick pay from his employer will depend upon the terms of his employment contract. If there is a written contract with a clause giving (or denying him) the right to sick pay, then that will be conclusive.

But few employees have written employment contracts and so the law has to work out what the parties intended the position to be. Usually by far the best evidence of this will be the 'written particulars' of the employment contract, sent to the employee within thirteen weeks of his starting work (see page 374). The written particulars should state whether sick pay is payable. In the absence of other clear evidence, the law will accept the position as set out in the written particulars.

If the written particulars do not mention sick pay (or if the employee is not sent any written particulars) the law will look at the custom and practice in the firm or industry, and see what has happened in the past. There is no definite rule that an employee is automatically entitled to sick pay, unless the contract says otherwise. The court will usually be able to come to a decision based on past practice in the firm, what was said when the employee was first offered a job, and so on. But if there is no evidence either way, then the likely outcome is that the employee will be presumed to be entitled to sick pay.

An employee was off sick for seven of his fourteen months' employment, before he resigned. He claimed that he was entitled to sick pay. Held: There was no automatic entitlement to sick pay. One had to look at the details of the case. Since the 'written particulars' did not cover the point, this meant looking at the past history. Since he had not sent in any sick notes, and no one else had been paid whilst off sick, it was decided that there was no implied term that he should be paid whilst off sick. Mears (1982)

Even if there is an implied right to sick pay, it will normally only be payable for a 'reasonable' length of time – not indefinitely. In cases of serious, lengthy, sickness the employer may be able to say that the employment has automatically been brought to an end (because the illness has 'frustrated' it). See page 417.

Statutory sick pay

Most employees are entitled to statutory sick pay (SSP). This is a cash payment made by the employer, for which the employer later claims a refund from the state. It is payable for up to eight weeks (after which time the employee will normally have to claim sickness benefit from the DHSS). But the rules will change soon. As from April 1986, SSP will be paid for twenty-eight weeks by the employer, and at the end of that time most employees have to start claiming invalidity benefit (see page 741).

Since only employees can claim SSP, it follows that a self-employed person cannot claim it (instead, he should claim sickness benefit from the DHSS). Also a few categories of employees are excluded – see the chart, overleaf.

SSP is only payable when the employee has been ill for four days in a row (note that this includes non-working days, such as Saturdays and Sundays). But he does not actually have to be paid any SSP unless he has been sick for three 'qualifying days' (i.e. days on which he would normally have worked) in any two-week period. Once the employee is eligible it is for the employer to pay the SSP to the employee; this will be at one of three different rates, depending upon the employee's earnings. Considerable discretion is given to employees as to the rules they want to lay down for notification of sickness but the basic requirement is that the employer must be notified no later than one week after the first 'qualifying day' (i.e. within one week of the first work-day being missed). If the illness is for seven days or less, most employers will accept a self-certificate (i.e. a form filled in by the employee stating that he was ill); for longer periods, it is usual to ask for a doctor's certificate.

A simple guide to SSP is contained in DHSS pamphlet N1244; full details will be found in a sixty-page pamphlet, N1227.

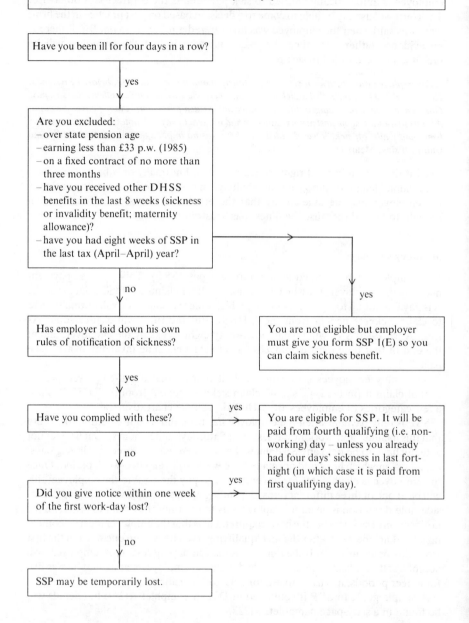

Statutory sick pay

Have you been ill for four days in a row?

↓ yes

Are you excluded:
– over state pension age
– earning less than £33 p.w. (1985)
– on a fixed contract of no more than
   three months
– have you received other DHSS
   benefits in the last 8 weeks (sickness
   or invalidity benefit; maternity
   allowance)?
– have you had eight weeks of SSP in
   the last tax (April–April) year?

→ yes

You are not eligible but employer must give you form SSP 1(E) so you can claim sickness benefit.

↓ no

Has employer laid down his own rules of notification of sickness?

↓ yes

Have you complied with these? → yes →

You are eligible for SSP. It will be paid from fourth qualifying (i.e. non-working) day – unless you already had four days' sickness in last fort-night (in which case it is paid from first qualifying day).

↓ no

Did you give notice within one week of the first work-day lost? → yes →

↓ no

SSP may be temporarily lost.

Medical suspension pay

A healthy employee might be laid off because of dangerous conditions at work. If so, he can claim full (basic only) pay from his employer for a period of up to twenty-six weeks, unless he has unreasonably refused an offer of suitable alternative work from the employer (s. 19, Employment Protection (Consolidation) Act 1978).

This right to medical suspension pay only applies to certain industries such as paint, vitreous enamelling, lead smelting, certain chemicals, india rubber, radio-active substances, asbestos, and pottery dust. For instance, an employee working with radioactive substances may be laid off if the radiation levels become too high.

Ineligible employees. Not all employees can demand medical suspension pay (e.g. part-timers). For a full list, see the chart on pages 376–7.

Wages during lay-off or short time

Industrial action, recession, bad weather, and breakdown can all lead to short-time working, or even lay-offs. Can the staff demand their full wages?

As with any employment question, the first place to look for an answer is the individual employee's contract of employment. If it says that he is entitled to a certain amount (or nothing) during lay-offs or short time, then that will be the position. If the employment contract says nothing about lay-off or short time, the employee must be paid in full. He should receive his normal wage or salary; if paid by piece rate or commission, he should receive his average pay.

Many employees are subject to 'Guaranteed Work Agreements' (GWAs) negotiated by their unions and the employer. Typically, GWAs:

• expect the employee to be prepared to do another job if it is necessary to keep production going;

• only apply to staff who have been employed for a stated minimum period;

• are usually subject to exceptions and restrictions that mean an employee will not receive his full pay;

• are often limited in duration, and only cover temporary interruptions in produc-tion caused by breakdown of machinery. Usually, lay-off caused by industrial action is specifically excluded.

Frequently GWAs are a bad deal from the employee's point of view. This is because the law assumes that an employee is entitled to be paid during lay-off or short time unless the employment contract says otherwise. So, often the employee will be better off if his employment contract or his written particulars say nothing about short-time and lay-off pay than if they incorporate a GWA.

Guarantee payments

Even if the employment contract says the employee is not to be paid, it is probable that he can claim some pay from his employer. By section 12 of the Employment

Protection (Consolidation) Act 1978, an employer must make a 'guarantee payment' to an employee who has been laid off and lost a full day's work. But the payment need not be made if the employee has unreasonably rejected an offer of suitable alternative work from the employer or if the lay-off is caused by an industrial dispute in the firm or an associated firm.

The lay-off, or short-time working, must be due to an 'occurrence' such as a fall in orders, fire, flood, bankruptcy of a customer, etc. But no money has to be paid if it is due to an industrial dispute involving any of the employer's staff (in either that or an associated company – even if at a different location).

In any event, the amount payable is very small. The employee can be paid for no more than five days off in any three-month period. So he cannot receive more than twenty days' guarantee pay in a year.

More important, the maximum amount that the employer is required by law to pay is £10.50 a day (1985 figures).

Illustration. *Frank Jones is a gardener in a private school. He is laid off because a heating breakdown has closed his school. He is paid £2.75 per hour for a basic thirty-seven-hour week. But he usually works an extra four hours each week, at £3 per hour. He can claim a guarantee payment:*

$$\frac{\text{pay}}{\text{hours}} = \frac{\text{£2.75} \times 37 \text{ and £3} \times 4}{41} = \frac{\text{£101.75} + \text{£12}}{41} = \text{£2.78 per hour}$$

The guarantee payment for one day will be 8·2 hours at £2.78 per hour = £22.80. But the maximum amount payable is £10.50, so that is all he receives.

Guarantee payments need only be made for days when the employee's employment contract requires him to work. So if the employee *accepts* a shorter working week, he cannot then claim a guarantee payment for the days he is laid off:

Mrs Clemens worked a four-day week. But business declined and so she agreed to work a two-day week and this amendment was recorded in her contract of employment. She claimed a guarantee payment for the other two days when she was laid off. Held: No. She was ineligible because she had accepted the shorter working week. Clemens (1977)

If the employer does not pay the employee his guarantee payment, the employee can take his claim to an industrial tribunal which can order the employer to pay him. There is no criminal penalty imposed on the employer.

Ineligible employees. Staff with less than a month's service and part-timers cannot claim guarantee payments. For a full list, see the chart on pages 367–7.

The statutory right to a guarantee payment was a well-intentioned innovation. However, the amounts that are paid are so unrealistically low that the scheme may do more harm than good. This is because some employers are taking the '£10.50 per day and five days per quarter' levels as being the maximum that they should pay staff who are laid off. Some employees seem unaware that they can still claim their full wages from the employer (unless there is a GWA) under the old rule of law that an employee is entitled to be paid while laid off unless his employment contract says otherwise. So the danger is that employees will only claim a small proportion of the wages that are actually due to them.

Minimum wages for certain industries

There are some industries in which trade unions are notoriously weak, mainly those employing large numbers of women and part-timers. To protect these workers, Wages Councils have been formed to lay down minimum terms and conditions in each industry. In particular, the Wages Councils can lay down minimum rates of pay and holiday entitlement, and they also have the power to lay down any other terms and conditions of employment.

There are some 3½ million workers in the industries that are subject to Wages Councils. There are some fifty Wages Councils, and they include most jobs in:
- retail shops (including supermarkets, but excluding chemists and butchers)
- the catering trades (excluding canteens and boarding houses)
- hairdressing
- clothing trades
- toy manufacture
- laundries (excluding dry cleaners and launderettes)
- agricultural jobs (which are largely governed by Agricultural Wages Boards).

The orders made by Wages Councils are enforced by the Wages Inspectorate of the Department of Employment. They can provide a full list of the trades covered by Wages Councils and they will prosecute employers who pay less than the minimum rates (maximum £400 fine for each offence). In practice, the inspectors are so few on the ground that they can only prosecute in the worst cases. A much better course of action is likely to be for the employee to sue the employer (in the county court) for the underpaid wages. He (or more probably, she) can sue for up to six years' under-payments. (See page 872 for how to sue in the county court; legal aid may well be available.)

Statutory fair wages

There are several Acts of Parliament that require 'fair wages' to be paid in particular industries or firms. These statutes cover the nationalized industries and some private firms which are government-aided or which operate under licence. There are statutes covering the coal, gas, electricity, civil-aviation, road-transport, atomic-energy, road-haulage, sugar-beet-refining, film-making, and TV industries, and the NHS.

Equal pay for men and women

The Equal Pay Act 1970 requires equal pay for 'like work' regardless of the employee's sex. That seemingly straightforward aim has, however, been partly frustrated by a series of court decisions that have made the legislation extremely complex and difficult to apply.

The woman can compare herself with a man employed in the same firm, if (i) they do 'like work', or (ii) a job-evaluation scheme has compared their jobs, or (iii) her job is of 'equal value' (i.e. the demands made on her – effort, skill, decision, etc. – are of equal value to those made on the man). There are thus three routes to an equal-pay claim. But the laws are complicated and an employer can often get away with paying the woman less:

1. Regrading of jobs may put women in lower categories, and there are some jobs (e.g. office cleaning) that are rarely done by men. This can make even 'equal value' claims difficult.

2. The Act allows inequality of pay where there is a 'difference of *practical* importance in the work done'. In other words, the employer can then argue that it is not 'like' work. So, if the man is doing a more responsible job, a wage differential is justifiable. If the man can be said to be using different equipment, to have extra duties, or to be working on a different stage of the same work process there may well be a 'practical difference' justifying the inequality.

3. There may be a 'material difference' between the man's job and the woman's job. A 'material difference' allows a more general, wider, comparison than under the 'practical difference' rules, above. Generally, 'practical difference' relates to the work done, whereas 'material differences' are concerned with who does it. For example, inequality is allowed if:

   • the wages include a bonus element, and so the man earns a larger bonus because his output is greater;

   • the wages include a 'service' element determined by the length of service with the firm. The man can be paid more if he has worked longer than the woman;

   • a new male recruit may be appointed at the same salary as an existing female employee who has better qualifications and more experience, although he cannot be paid more than her.

The employee's remedy

The employee can apply to an industrial tribunal at any time during the employment or within six months of leaving the job. The tribunal can award damages, including pay due to the employee if she is being paid less than a man. No more than two years' arrears can be awarded.

Before going to an industrial tribunal the employee would be well advised to contact the Equal Opportunities Commission (EOC). The EOC can advise as to the prospects of success and, in exceptional cases, will help bring the claim.

Anyone thinking of bringing an equal-pay claim should take specialist advice from a solicitor or trade-union representative. The decisions of the courts have made the legislation a minefield for the unwary. Certainly, reading the reported cases, one has the impression that the tribunals and the courts have decided to

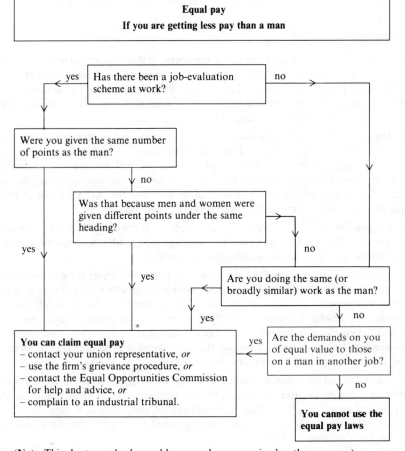

Equal pay
If you are getting less pay than a man

yes — Has there been a job-evaluation scheme at work? — no

Were you given the same number of points as the man?

no

Was that because men and women were given different points under the same heading?

yes

yes

yes

Are you doing the same (or broadly similar) work as the man?

no

yes

You can claim equal pay
– contact your union representative, *or*
– use the firm's grievance procedure, *or*
– contact the Equal Opportunities Commission for help and advice, *or*
– complain to an industrial tribunal.

yes

Are the demands on you of equal value to those on a man in another job?

no

You cannot use the equal pay laws

(**Note.** This chart can also be used by men who are earning less than women.)

apply a very restrictive interpretation to the Act. Often, 'material differences' and 'practical differences' are found where – to the layman – they do not exist.

Discipline

It is an implied term of any contract of employment that the employee will obey his employer's reasonable, lawful commands, and that he will behave himself at work.

What happens if the employee is in breach of this implied duty? If he misbehaves or is disobedient the employer may want to discipline him. But there are legal constraints on the disciplinary action that he can take.

1. *Dismissal*. The employer can dismiss the employee, but the employee will probably be able to bring an unfair-dismissal claim. The claim will succeed unless the employer can show that the employee's behaviour justified the sacking, and that he, the employer, acted reasonably in the way he carried out the sacking. Often, this will mean that the employer has to show that he followed the ACAS Code of Practice on Disciplinary Rules and Procedures (see page 395).

2. *Suspension on full pay*. Generally, an employer is not obliged to supply his staff with work, as long as he pays them their wages (see page 401). So suspension on full pay will be a proper, and legal, disciplinary sanction.

3. *Suspension without pay*. This will usually be unlawful. Whilst the employer need not provide his staff with work, he must provide them with their full wages unless their employment contracts say otherwise. So suspension on less than full pay will usually be unlawful – unless specifically allowed by the contract of employment, or unless the employee's behaviour had been so bad that the employer was entitled to dismiss him (in which case, of course, the employee might be prepared to accept a day's loss of wages as an alternative to dismissal).

4. *Warnings and reprimands*. An employee cannot object if he is reprimanded and given a warning (written or verbal) by his employer. If he does not think the reprimand or warning is justified he should say so, preferably in writing. But there is no legal remedy – he cannot, for instance, complain to an industrial tribunal that he has been unfairly told off.

5. *Fines and deductions*. These will be unlawful unless permitted by the employee's contract of employment. Generally, a specific clause will be needed, but occasionally the courts will recognize the existence of a trade practice or custom allowing the deduction (but it is rare that this happens: see page 386). The Truck Acts impose special restrictions on fines and deductions imposed on 'workmen', so refer to page 385).

6. *Demotion*. This will be a breach of contract on the part of the employer. The employee can thus regard himself as having been sacked, and so he can resign and then claim unfair dismissal.

7. *Transfer to another location*. This also will be a breach of contract unless a job-mobility clause exists (see page 472).

The importance of disciplinary rules and procedures

The Advisory, Conciliation and Arbitration Service (ACAS) has published a Code of Practice on disciplinary rules and disciplinary procedures. The Code sets out the behaviour required of a reasonable employer.

Whilst it is not illegal to fail to observe the Code, an employer who does so will find it more difficult to defend an unfair-dismissal claim.

Accordingly, the Code is one of the fundamental documents in modern employment law. Both employers and employees should know what it says (see below). Anyone involved in a dispute over discipline at work – and in how arguments should be resolved – should always begin by reading through the Code of Practice to see whether the 'other side' have followed it. But the industrial tribunals do not expect 'blind obedience' to the Code – for instance, if the employee has been guilty of a very grave offence, it will probably make little difference if the employer does not follow the procedures recommended by the Code. (For more on this, see page 447.)

The main parts of the Code are set out below, but the most important paragraphs are those on how an employer should deal with a disciplinary matter. The sequence of events is:

1. Tell the employee of the complaint being made against him.
2. Give him a chance to explain himself.
3. Take a decision on what is the appropriate disciplinary action. The disciplinary action will normally be:
   - *formal oral warning, or*
   - *formal written warning* for 'more serious issues'; the warning should set out the offence and the likely consequences if it is repeated, *or*
   - *final written warning* saying that further breaches of discipline will lead to a specified step, such as dismissal or suspension;
   - *dismissal* (or suspension without pay, if allowed by the employment contract).

The main provisions of the Code of Practice

[Paragraphs 1–5 omitted]

6. When drawing up rules the aim should be to specify clearly and concisely those necessary for the efficient and safe performance of work and for the maintenance of satisfactory relations within the work force and between employees and management. Rules should not be so general as to be meaningless.
7. Rules should be readily available and management should make every effort to ensure that employees know and understand them. This may be best achieved by giving every employee a copy of the rules and by explaining them orally. In the case of new employees this should form part of an induction programme.
8. Employees should be made aware of the likely consequences of breaking rules and in particular they should be given a clear indication of the type of conduct which may warrant summary dismissal.

9. Disciplinary procedures should not be viewed primarily as a means of imposing sanctions. They should also be designed to emphasize and encourage improvements in individual conduct.

10. Disciplinary procedures should:
   (a) Be in writing.
   (b) Specify to whom they apply.
   (c) Provide for matters to be dealt with quickly.
   (d) Indicate the disciplinary actions which may be taken.
   (e) Specify the levels of management which have the authority to take the various forms of disciplinary action, ensuring that immediate superiors do not normally have the power to dismiss without reference to senior management.
   (f) Provide for individuals to be informed of the complaints against them and to be given an opportunity to state their case before decisions are reached.
   (g) Give individuals the right to be accompanied by a trade-union representative or by a fellow employee of their choice.
   (h) Ensure that, except for gross misconduct, no employees are dismissed for a first breach of discipline.
   (i) Ensure that disciplinary action is not taken until the case has been carefully investigated.
   (j) Ensure that individuals are given an explanation for any penalty imposed.
   (k) Provide a right of appeal and specify the procedure to be followed.

11. When a disciplinary matter arises, the supervisor or manager should first establish the facts promptly before recollections fade, taking into account the statements of any available witnesses. In serious cases consideration should be given to a brief period of suspension while the case is investigated and this suspension should be with pay. Before a decision is made or penalty imposed the individual should be interviewed and given the opportunity to state his or her case and should be advised of any rights under the procedure, including the right to be accompanied.

12. Often supervisors will give informal oral warnings for the purpose of improving conduct when employees commit minor infringements of the established standards of conduct. However, where the facts of a case appear to call for disciplinary action, other than summary dismissal, the following procedure should normally be observed:
   (a) In the case of minor offences the individual should be given a formal oral warning or if the issue is more serious, there should be a written warning setting out the nature of the offence and the likely consequences of further offences. In either case the individual should be advised that the warning constitutes the first formal stage of the procedure.
   (b) Further misconduct might warrant a final written warning which should contain a statement that any recurrence would lead to suspension or dismissal or some other penalty, as the case may be.
   (c) The final step might be disciplinary transfer, or disciplinary suspension without pay (but only if these are allowed for by an express or implied condition of the contract of employment), or dismissal, according to the nature of the misconduct. Special consideration should be given before imposing disciplinary suspension without pay and it should not normally be for a prolonged period.

13. Except in the event of an oral warning, details of any disciplinary action should be given in writing to the employee and, if desired, to his or her representative. At the same time the employee should be told of any right of appeal, how to make it and to whom.

14. When determining the disciplinary action to be taken the supervisor or manager should bear in mind the need to satisfy the test of reasonableness in all the circumstances. So far as possible, account should be taken of the employee's record and any other relevant factors.
15. Special consideration should be given to the way in which disciplinary procedures are to operate in exceptional cases. For example:
    (a) *Employees to whom the full procedure is not immediately available.* . . .
    (b) *Trade-union officials.* . . .
    (c) *Criminal offences outside employment.* These should not be treated as automatic reasons for dismissal regardless of whether the offence has any relevance to the duties of the individual as an employee. The main considerations should be whether the offence is one that makes the individual unsuitable for his or her type of work or unacceptable to other employees. Employees should not be dismissed solely because a charge against them is pending or because they are absent through having been remanded in custody.

For cases of unfair dismissal and disciplinary offences, see pages 433–46.

Hours

Overtime

An employee must work for the number of hours stated in his contract, but no more. Theoretically, therefore, he can refuse to work overtime unless his employment contract specifically requires him to do so.

The length of the working week, and any overtime requirements, should be included in the written particulars sent to the employee within thirteen weeks of his starting work (see page 374).

But if an employee regularly agrees to work overtime he might then find that he is unable to refuse overtime in the future. He might be held to have impliedly agreed to change his contract so that overtime is now compulsory:

Mr Tovey was a lorry driver. On 18 November he, and other drivers, changed to a new wage structure agreed with the company. The new agreement did not deal with the question of overtime payments. Three days later he was asked to do unpaid overtime, but said he would only do overtime if he was paid. He was sacked and then claimed unfair dismissal. Held: Tovey had accepted the new arrangement and there was evidence that other drivers customarily worked short periods of overtime without extra pay. Accordingly, he was now bound to work overtime and his dismissal was not unfair. Tovey (1975)

Senior staff may find it more difficult to refuse to work overtime. The law will often assume that there is an implied term in a manager's or senior executive's employment contract that he will work overtime when required – even if it is unpaid overtime. Whether this will be so will depend on the nature of the job and the practice in the trade or profession.

An employee who need not work overtime but who is dismissed for refusing to do it can claim unfair dismissal. But the tribunal might find his refusal unreasonable and so reduce the amount of compensation he receives. This is especially likely to be so if other staff have agreed to work overtime, or if the employer wants to reorganize his work arrangements more efficiently. In recent years the tribunals have been more ready to find that employees should cooperate with work-place reorganizations and it is therefore likely that an employee who sticks to the strict wording of his employment contract will be treated unsympathetically by the tribunal.

Maximum hours of work

There is no general restriction on the length of the working week. Instead there are various provisions mainly aimed at protecting women and children. In addition, there are miscellaneous statutes limiting the hours that men can work in mines, in night work at bakeries, as shop workers, in the sheet-glass industry, and in the transport industry.

Women

There are two main sets of restrictions on employing women.

Night-time work. Basically, women cannot be employed on night-time work in industrial undertakings. But there are exceptions.

Factory workers. Complicated provisions supplement the ban on night-time working. But these additional restraints only apply if the woman works in a factory (see page 412). The Health and Safety Executive can grant exemptions from these restrictions.

Women and young people in factories

Maximum hours per week	Forty-eight hours; for boys and girls under sixteen, the maximum is forty-four
Maximum hours per day to be worked (i.e. excluding tea, meal breaks, etc.)	Ten hours, unless factory is on a six-day week, when it is nine hours per day
Maximum hours per day including tea, meal breaks, etc.	Twelve hours, unless factory is on a six-day week, when it is eleven hours per day (Saturday, six hours only)
Maximum uninterrupted spell of work	Four and a half hours, but if ten-minute break is given, then five hours
Sunday hours	Generally Sunday working is prohibited
Earliest time for starting work	7 a.m. (exceptionally 6 a.m.)
Latest time for finishing work	8 p.m. (Saturdays, 1 p.m.); for boys and girls under sixteen, 6 p.m.
After childbirth	Cannot work within four weeks of giving birth

The Health and Safety Executive will give advice on whether the detailed rules are being broken. Various exceptions apply to different industries so its opinion should always be sought.

At Work

Children

There are various laws that restrict the employment of children. Unfortunately, the position is complex:

- *children under thirteen* can never be employed unless the local education authority (LEA) has agreed a lower age. This is usually done to allow children to work with their parents in light agricultural and horticultural work.
- *children between thirteen and school-leaving age* generally cannot work:
  - for more than two hours on school days or Sundays
  - before 7 a.m. or after 7 p.m.
  - until after school hours on school days. But many LEAs alter this and allow one hour's work before school, thus permitting paper rounds, etc.
  - without obtaining a licence if there is a performance at which a charge is to be made; school performances are exempt, as are performances amounting to fewer than three days in a six-month period.

  Note that school-leaving age is not necessarily sixteen – see page 117.
- *children between thirteen and sixteen* cannot:
  - do any work involving heavy lifting or carrying
  - work in manufacturing, demolition, building, transport, or mining.
- *children under seventeen* cannot take part in street trading (e.g. working at stalls, selling flowers or papers)
- *children under eighteen* cannot work in a bar. But a child of thirteen or more can work in licensed premises where drinks are served with meals (e.g. restaurants, canteens).

Taking time off for public duties

An employee can take unpaid time off work to carry out his duties (s.29 Employment Protection (Consolidation) Act 1978) as a:
- magistrate
- local councillor
- member of a tribunal
- regional or area-health-authority worker
- water-authority or river-purification board member

The employee can only take a 'reasonable' amount of time off. Clearly, the size of the firm, his position in the firm, and the amount of time needed for the duties, will all be relevant. Often employees who are members of these various public bodies will also be trade-union officials and so allowed to take paid leave for those duties (see page 481). If that is the case, then time already taken off for union duties can be taken into account when deciding what is a reasonable amount of leave for the public duties.

If the employee is entitled to time off, the employer cannot expect him to work evenings to catch up with his work:

A college lecturer asked for time off when he became a local councillor. The employers rearranged his teaching timetable so that he could attend council meetings but he was still required

399

to do the same amount of teaching. As a result he had to work in the evenings and at weekends. He complained to an industrial tribunal that the college had not given him time off work. Held: He was right. The college had not given him time off. All they had done was to swap his hours around. Ratcliffe (1978)

An employee who is refused time off has three months in which to complain to an industrial tribunal (using the usual Form IT1). The tribunal can order the employer to pay him cash compensation.

Although there is no Act dealing with the point, an employee should always be allowed time off work for jury service (although he need not be paid). See page 801.

Ineligible employees. Not all employees can claim unpaid leave for public duties. (e.g. part-timers). For a full list, see the chart on pages 376–7.

Time off for other purposes

Officers of recognized trade unions can take paid leave so as to carry out their union duties and to undergo training (see page 481). Members of recognized trade unions can take unpaid time off work to take part in union activities (see page 481). Redundant workers can take unpaid leave to look for a new job or to arrange training (see page 478). For jury service, see page 801.

Holidays

An employee is always entitled to take public holidays as holidays unless his employment contract requires him to work then. (The days covered by this are New Year's Day, Good Friday, Easter Monday, spring holiday, late summer holiday, Christmas Day and Boxing Day.)

Generally, the courts will find that there is an implied right for an employee to take a reasonable amount of paid holiday. So, in practice, unless the employment contract or the written particulars specifically say otherwise, the employee can claim a paid holiday. The amount of holiday will depend on the general practice and custom in the industry; in short, how much holiday do other workers of similar standing and length of employment receive? So, if an employee was sacked for taking a holiday of a reasonable length, he would almost certainly win his unfair-dismissal claim.

An employee who returns to work late after his holiday will obviously be in breach of his contract of employment but it seems that the tribunals do not regard a twenty-four-hour lateness as justifying dismissal – unless, of course, there are other circumstances such as a poor attendance record in the past (see 'Unfair Dismissal', page 435).

The only industries in which the law has laid down the right to minimum holidays, with pay, are those in which Wages Councils have been established (see page 391).

At Work

Giving the employee work to do

Surprisingly there is no general duty on an employer to provide his staff with work. It is sufficient if he pays them. Generally, they cannot complain if they are not given enough to do.

This common-law doctrine has come under increasing attack in recent years, but it is still the law, although there would seem to be three exceptions to it:

1. *Actors, writers.* Some people work not just for the money but for the chance and opportunity of becoming better known. Writers, singers, actors, photographers, and other artists can thus demand the right to work or compensation for not receiving it.
2. *Skilled workers.* An employee who has a skill can demand work so that he will not lose his skill. But the limits of this category are difficult to lay down. It clearly covers such people as airline pilots and surgeons, but it is open to question whether it covers skilled industrial workers. In *Langston* (1974) a car welder was suspended on full pay for two years. Lord Denning said he had the right to work because 'in these days an employer, when employing a skilled man, is bound to provide him with work. By which I mean that the man should be given the opportunity of doing his work when it is available and he is ready and willing to do it.' But Lord Denning was in the minority in that case, so his opinion – whilst of great influence – is not the law.
3. *Piece-rate and bonus workers.* An employee can claim work when his wages are linked to the amount of work he does. But it seems likely that the employee could not complain if his employer simply paid him a reasonable sum instead to cover his lost commission. So, to that extent, it may well be that he does not have a right to actual work. The law is unclear.

If an employee is entitled to insist on work and he is not given it, he can regard himself as having been dismissed. He can thus leave and then claim unfair dismissal; but even this will not guarantee him the right to work. An employer cannot be forced to reinstate an employee and if he defies an industrial tribunal's order to reinstate the worker, the employer can only be forced to pay money compensation.

Inventions at work

The Patents Act 1977 sets out complicated rules as to whether an employee can own a patent over something he invented at work. Generally, the answer will be 'no', because the Act says he cannot claim it as his own if:

• he invented it in the course of his normal duties; so if a research chemist creates a new medical compound for his pharmaceutical employers, the employer can claim the patent rights, *or*

• he is 'in a position of special responsibility'. Just what this means is not entirely clear but it is probably intended to cover senior management staff who instigate research projects.

If the invention belongs to the employer, then the employee can apply for cash compensation if the employer has derived 'outstanding benefit' from the patent, 'having regard among other things to the size and nature of the employer's undertaking'. This is an area for specialist advice, but note that many employees are covered by collective agreements which give more generous terms – so employee inventors should always consider whether they should be in an appropriate union.

A good starting-point for anyone who wants to find out more about patents is to get the free booklet *Introducing Patents – A Guide for Inventors* (from the Department of Trade and Industry).

23 Maternity

A pregnant employee can have time off work for antenatal care; in addition she can claim maternity pay from her employer and she can also claim her job back after the birth of her child.

Further, she can claim unfair dismissal if she is sacked because she is pregnant (see page 442).

Time off for antenatal care

The Employment Act 1980 allows all pregnant women to take time off work, with pay, in order to receive antenatal care. However, after the first appointment the employer can demand a medical certificate confirming that the woman is pregnant, together with an appointment card (or other document confirming the appointment for which she wants time off).

If the employer unreasonably refuses paid leave to the woman, she can complain to an industrial tribunal. Note that this right to take time off is not limited to occasions when the woman has complications – it covers any appointment made on the advice of a doctor, midwife, or health visitor. Also, this is one of the few rights that is available to virtually all employees – even if they are only part-timers, and even if they have only recently started work with that employer.

The employee was allowed time off to go to antenatal and relaxation classes, but the employers refused to pay her during the time off. She complained to an industrial tribunal. Held: By allowing her to take time off, the employers had conceded that it was reasonable for her to have the time off. Under the Act, she must be paid if it is reasonable for her to have the time off – thus, the employers had to pay her. Gregory (1982)

Maternity pay

Most women workers can claim maternity pay – whether or not they intend to return to work after the birth. Maternity pay is 90 per cent of the employee's normal wages for six weeks. It is paid to her by the employer, who is then reimbursed by the state (s. 34, Employment Protection (Consolidation) Act 1978).

But the woman is not automatically eligible for maternity pay. She must follow complicated rules:

Employment: At Work

1. Continue in employment until at least the eleventh week prior to the expected date of birth. If she leaves her job before then she will lose her right to maternity pay. Note that she need not be 'working' at the eleventh week – all that is required is that she should still be employed. So if she is off work sick she will still be employed, and will be eligible even though she is not working. If her employer dismisses her because she is pregnant, and she will thus not be employed on the eleventh week, she should claim unfair dismissal (and also sex discrimination).

   She can, of course, work on after the eleventh week if she wishes; her employer cannot force her to leave before she wants to.

2. She must have been employed by her employer for at least two years (by the beginning of the eleventh week before the baby is due).

3. *She must tell her employer that she intends to stop work because of her pregnancy.* This must be done at least three weeks before she is due to leave. If she does not give this notice, she will lose her right to maternity pay. In exceptional cases, the three-week period can be waived if she gave notice as soon 'as was reasonably practicable' – for example, if she did not know she was pregnant until a few days before she left. Similarly, the three-week period may be waived if the woman did not know she had to give notice to the employer; however, such claims are treated with great scepticism. The notice to the employer need not be in writing, but it is always advisable to give written notice so that there can be no dispute about whether she did give proper notice. (See draft letter on page 408.) If she does not give written notice, the employer can insist on being given written notice. He can also demand to see a medical certificate confirming the expected date of confinement. (This date is important, because it is from this date that the eleven-week period is usually calculated.)

The amount of maternity pay

Maternity pay is six weeks' wages at 90 per cent of the woman's normal weekly wage, minus the DHSS maternity allowance. If the woman's earnings vary from week to week, or include an element of overtime, there are special rules for calculating her 'normal' weekly wage (see page 390).

To calculate the amount due, the employer should:

1. Work out the employee's normal weekly pay.
2. Calculate 90 per cent of that figure.
3. From that figure, deduct the flat-rate maternity allowance (paid by the DHSS) – whether or not the woman is receiving maternity allowance (for instance, she may not have paid enough NI stamps). The employer only pays 90 per cent of wages, less maternity allowance.
4. Multiply that net weekly figure by 6.
5. If the woman is still employed at the time she is paid the maternity pay, the employer should also deduct income tax and national insurance. If she is no longer employed he need not deduct tax. The woman should include the

maternity pay in her income tax return as untaxed income, and the revenue will then ask her to pay any tax direct to them. In short, it is taxable income.

6. The employer should pay the maternity pay in a lump sum as soon as the woman leaves, or on a weekly or monthly basis. Although it would not be unlawful to pay it as a lump sum at the end of the six-week period, this would clearly be contrary to the intention of the Act.

7. The employer can then claim a full refund from the Maternity Pay Fund. The claim is made through the Department of Employment.

8. If the employer does not pay the woman, she should complain to an industrial tribunal within three months. If the employer cannot pay her because he has gone bust, then the government fund will pay her (see page 421).

Ineligible employees. Not all women can claim maternity pay. In particular, part-timers, and those who have not been employed for two years (at the time of the eleventh week before the child is due) cannot claim. For a full list see the chart on pages 376–7.

Other maternity money. The pregnant employee should not forget to claim maternity allowance (a weekly benefit) and maternity grant (a lump-sum benefit) from her local DHSS office (see page 746).

Maternity leave: returning to work

An employee who has left to give birth can claim her job back after the birth (s. 45, Employment Protection (Consolidation) Act 1978), but as with the right to maternity pay, there are complicated requirements to be met. She must:

1. Continue in employment until at least the eleventh week before expected date of birth (as with maternity pay).

2. She must then have been employed for at least two years (as with maternity pay).

3. *She must write to her employer that she intends to stop work because of her pregnancy and that she will want to return to work after the birth.* As with the maternity pay, this notice must be given at least three weeks before she leaves. The notice must be in writing and it must state the expected date of birth (see draft letter below). If he wishes, the employer can insist the woman provides a medical certificate stating the expected date of birth.

4. *The employer can insist that she confirms her intention of returning to work.* The rule is that once seven weeks have elapsed after the expected date of birth the employer can ask her to give written confirmation of her intention to return to work. If she does not give the written confirmation within two weeks of it being requested, she will lose her right to return to work (assuming that the employer warned her that failure to reply within two weeks would result in her losing the right to return). Note that the seven-week period runs from the expected date of birth, as originally notified to the employer, and not the actual date of birth. At this stage she does not have to give a date for her return to work – she simply has to confirm that she still intends to return.

5. *She must return to work within twenty-nine weeks of the birth.* This twenty-nine-week period is strictly enforced and the woman can only extend it if she can produce a medical certificate confirming that she is not well enough to return to work. But a sick note can only extend the period by four weeks so, whatever happens, the woman will lose the right to return unless she does so within thirty-three weeks of the actual date of birth.
6. *She must give her employer at least three weeks' written warning before she does return to work.* She must give a specific date – at least twenty-one days in advance. In practice, therefore, the latest deadline for giving this notice is twenty-six weeks after the start of the week in which the child was born.
7. If she works for a small firm, she may not be able to insist on having her job back. If there were fewer than six employees (including her) in the firm at the time when she left, then the employer need not take her back if it is not 'reasonably practicable' to give her the old job (or another 'suitable' job). It will be for the employer to convince the industrial tribunal of this.

When the woman returns to work

On her return, the employee can claim the same rate of pay and the same terms of employment as if she had not stopped work. Thus she will obtain the benefit of any pay increases that have been made since she left. Normally, her contractual pension and seniority rights will carry on as from the date she left (unless her contract says otherwise), so that the period of absence cannot be counted when later calculating length of service for pension entitlement. Redundancy pay and other statutory benefits, however, will continue to accrue during the period of absence.

But only rarely will the woman be able to insist that she returns to the actual job she was doing prior to her leaving. The law says that she must be employed on the same 'terms and conditions' as previously – in other words, her contract of employment must not be changed. But usually the employment contract only defines an employee's job in wide terms. So unless her contract is very specific in defining her job, she will have to accept another similar job, as long as the pay, hours, holidays and other terms are the same. Thus, in practice, the woman will often find that her new job is not the same as her old job.

In addition, the employer can offer the woman an alternative job if it is 'not reasonably practicable' for her to return to her old job. This is intended to cover the situation in which the employer has had to take on permanent staff to cover for the woman while she was off work or where circumstances have made her old job unavailable. However, the employee must be offered a suitable alternative job instead, and if she is not offered a job, or if she is offered an unsuitable job, she can claim unfair dismissal or redundancy. The only exception is in firms employing fewer than six people: in these small firms if it is not reasonably practicable for the woman to return to her old job, and if she cannot be offered a suitable alternative job, then she need not be re-employed and she will not be able to claim unfair dismissal or redundancy. (See 7 above.)

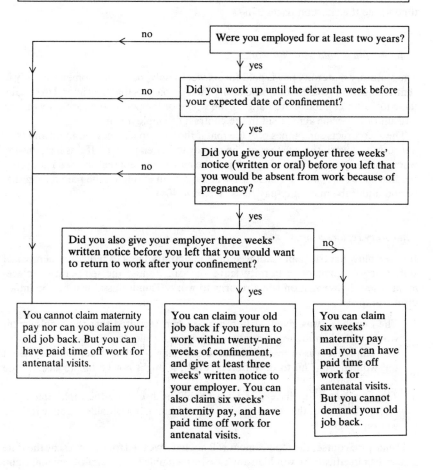

Pregnant?
How to check whether you can claim maternity pay and have your old job back

Were you employed for at least two years?

no

yes

Did you work up until the eleventh week before your expected date of confinement?

no

yes

Did you give your employer three weeks' notice (written or oral) before you left that you would be absent from work because of pregnancy?

no

yes

Did you also give your employer three weeks' written notice before you left that you would want to return to work after your confinement?

no

yes

You cannot claim maternity pay nor can you claim your old job back. But you can have paid time off work for antenatal visits.

You can claim your old job back if you return to work within twenty-nine weeks of confinement, and give at least three weeks' written notice to your employer. You can also claim six weeks' maternity pay, and have paid time off work for antenatal visits.

You can claim six weeks' maternity pay and you can have paid time off work for antenatal visits. But you cannot demand your old job back.

Similarly, if the employer simply refuses to re-employ the woman, the employee can claim unfair dismissal or redundancy.

Ineligible employees. Not all employees can claim maternity leave (e.g. part-timers) see the chart on pages 376–7.

If the woman is paid while off work

The statutory maternity pay is paid for six weeks only, but some women (notably in central and local government) who notify their employers that they intend to reclaim their job after childbirth are paid for the whole of the period they are off work, as a result of a specific agreement in the contract of employment.

These contracts sometimes provide that if the woman changes her mind and does not return to work she must repay the money to her employers. If this happens the woman is almost certainly liable to repay the money (except that she need not repay the first six weeks' wages – since she will have been entitled to be paid during that period under the maternity-pay rules: see page 404).

Temporary replacements

If an employer recruits an employee on a temporary basis to replace a member of staff who is absent on maternity leave, he can dismiss the temporary replacement when the woman on leave returns to work. The dismissal will not be unfair dismissal if:

1. The employee was given written notice when recruited that the employment would end when the woman returned from maternity leave.
2. The employee was dismissed so that the woman could have her job back. So if the woman went on to do different work, it might not be fair to dismiss the replacement.
3. The employer must have acted reasonably in dismissing the replacement. In effect, this means that he must have offered him/her a suitable vacancy if there was one available.

Usually, of course, the replacement will not have worked for two years by the time s/he is dismissed, so s/he would in any case be ineligible for an unfair-dismissal claim (see page 426).

Maternity rights: draft letter to an employer

The legal rules on claiming maternity pay, and on claiming the right to return to work, are very complicated. It is easy to make a mistake – which is why the timetable should be followed very carefully, and why it is best to put everything in writing. For instance:

Dear Sir/Madam,

I wish to inform you that I am pregnant, and that the expected date of my confinement is the week beginning (*date*).

Would you therefore kindly take this letter as notice under the Employment Protection (Consolidation) Act 1978 that:

(a) I wish to claim maternity pay, *and*

(b) I wish to return to work after the birth of my baby.

In addition, I may need to take paid time off work for antenatal visits. I shall, of course give you notice of the appointments as soon as I am able.

I should be grateful if you would acknowledge receipt of this letter.

Yours ...

Note 1. This letter must arrive at least three weeks before you plan to leave work.

Note 2. Even if you have previously told your employer that you will not be claiming maternity pay and/or maternity leave, it seems that you can change your mind – assuming, of course, that you comply with the rules and give the employer proper notice. Obviously, it is better to avoid any dispute by not agreeing to forgo any of these rights in the first place.

Note 3. If you notify your employer that you intend to return, but subsequently change your mind, your employer cannot sue you for compensation. It is, therefore, always advisable to state that you intend to return if there is any possibility that you may wish to do so. Remember that there is always the slight possibility of a miscarriage.

24 Accidents at Work

Every employer has a duty to take reasonable care for the safety of his staff; if he does not, he can be sued for negligence by an injured employee.

But it is for the employee to show that the employer was negligent, for if negligence cannot be shown the employer will not be liable. In addition, if the court finds that the employee himself was partly to blame for the accident, it will reduce his damages by a corresponding amount. For instance, if an employer was negligent, but the employee was one third to blame for the accident, the courts would only award him two thirds of the normal damages.

The employer's duty to take reasonable care of his staff has three elements:
- to provide competent work-mates, *and*
- to provide safe equipment and plant, *and*
- to provide a safe system of working.

Competent work-mates

It is the employer's duty to employ safe and responsible staff. If one employee is negligent and so injures another employee, the injured employee can sue his employer for his work-mate's negligence. The employer is therefore personally liable for the negligence of his staff, although he may – in theory, if not in practice – be able to sue the negligent employee to recover any damages paid to the injured employee (see page 371).

For instance:

Mr Cripps was an electrician. His employers sent him, with an apprentice, to install electric lights in a barn. In the barn were some calves, so Mr Cripps told the apprentice to stand at the foot of the ladder and keep the calves away. A calf bumped into the apprentice, who fell against the ladder knocking it over. Mr Cripps injured his wrist. He sued his employers. Held: The employers were liable because the apprentice had been negligent. They were responsible for his negligence. Cripps (1974)

If an employer knows that a member of his staff is a danger to his work-mates then the employer should remove him from a task where he is likely to injure someone, or even, after warnings, dismiss him. For instance, if the employer knows that someone plays practical jokes, the employer will be liable if an accident occurs:

Mr Hudson was injured when a practical joke went wrong. The person who played the joke on him had been employed for some four years, and over that time he had often tripped people up and engaged in horseplay, despite having been told not to by the employer. Mr Hudson sued the employer, arguing that the employer had failed to provide a safe and competent work-mate. Held: The employer was liable. Hudson (1957)

Many claims arise out of motor accidents, when the injured employee is a passenger in a vehicle driven by a work-mate. In such a case the employer is responsible for the negligent driving of his employee.

If the employer can show that the negligent employee was not acting 'in the course of his employment' at the time of the accident, then he will not be liable. For instance, if the employees without permission leave the work site to drive to the pub and on the way back one of the employees is injured by the other's negligent driving, the employer will not be to blame. He is only liable for the negligence of his staff when the staff are acting in the course of their employment. The same applies if it is a non-employee who is injured:

A bus conductor got into a quarrel with a passenger. The bus conductor assaulted the passenger, injuring him. The passenger then sued the bus company, arguing that it was responsible for the acts of its employees. Held: No. The bus conductor had not been acting in the course of his employment by striking the passenger and so the company was not liable. Keppel Bus Co. (1974)

Similarly, if the negligent person is not an employee but an independent contractor, the employer will not be liable. In some cases, the employer will not be liable if the independent contractor is injured, since there will be no employer/employee relationship between them:

Jones was on the lorry on a building site. When a cement mixer broke down, he was told to use another one which was unsafe. Jones was injured. Held: Jones was not an employee and so the normal duty of care did not apply; he could not recover damages. Jones (1973)

See page 379 for how to decide whether or not a person is an employee.

Safe equipment and plant

The employer is liable if an employee is injured because of faulty equipment, plant, or premises, if the employer was negligent. For instance, if the floor is slippery or uneven, the employer is liable if he knew of the defect or should have known of it.

Similarly, if the employee is injured by defective equipment, he can sue the negligent employer. For instance, if a hammer fractures and a flying piece injures the employee, the employer will be liable if he was negligent; in effect, he will be liable unless he can show that he had inspected the hammer and had no reason to suspect that it was faulty. If the hammer was made in a negligent manner by the manufacturer (e.g. faulty casting, poor-quality metal) then by the Employer's Liability (Defective Equipment) Act 1969, the employer will be liable to the employee for the negligence of the manufacturer. This allows the employee to sue the employer, rather than the manufacturer, who might since have gone out of business or might be based abroad. The employer may, however, be able to make a claim against the manufacturer.

This common-law duty to provide safe working conditions is often backed up by detailed statutory requirements as to the design, layout, and provision of working equipment and facilities. Numerous regulations have been made covering various industries (e.g. under the Offices, Shops and Railway Premises Act 1963; the Mines and Quarries Act 1954; the Agriculture (Poisonous Substances) Act 1952; Mineral Workings (Offshore Installations) Act 1971; Nuclear Installations Acts 1965 and 1969; and so on). Of particular importance is the Factories Act, which covers more than just factories – construction sites, shipyards, docks and warehouses using mechanical power, brickworks, potteries, cement works, paper-making and printing firms, laundries and dry cleaners, garages, power stations, gasworks, slaughter-houses, and railway workshops are all included in the definition of a factory. Amongst the detailed requirements of the Factories Act are the rules that:

• work places shall be properly ventilated and lit
• sufficient washing and toilet facilities must be provided
• moving machinery must be fenced
• fences must be properly maintained
• hoists, lifts, and ropes must be properly constructed and maintained
• floors, passages, and stairs must be kept unobstructed and free of slippery surfaces.
For instance:

> *Mrs Woodward had a lift to work from a colleague. They parked in the factory car park, close to the footpath leading to the factory entrance. She slipped on ice and injured her back. She claimed damages from her employers, arguing that there was a breach of the Factories Act. Held: Yes, the employers should have gritted the footpath and, since they had not, they were liable to Mrs Woodward.* Woodward (1980)

For details of the Factories Act requirements, contact the local health and safety inspector (phone number in the telephone directory). An important point to note about many of the statutory requirements is that the employer is liable even if he was not negligent; for instance, if an employee is injured by an unfenced machine, the employer is liable whether or not he was negligent; he would also be liable if, for example, the fencing was wrongly removed by another employee.

A safe system of work

It is for the employer to supervise how his staff carry out their jobs, and to ensure that they do so in a safe manner. If he negligently fails to ensure that a safe system is in use, then he will be liable in damages to any employee who is injured.

> *Mr Upson was lifting a metal plate with four work-mates. One of the others let go, and as a result the plate slipped and crushed Mr Upson's fingers. He sued his employers, arguing that the system of work was unsafe. Held: The employers were liable. They should have arranged (through their foreman) for someone to act as a coordinator for the lifting operation.* Upson (1975)

Mr Litherland worked for a furniture manufacturer, where he used a glue which was often a cause of dermatitis. The employers did not warn him of this risk, nor did they provide him with gloves or cream to reduce his chances of catching dermatitis. Mr Litherland contracted dermatitis and sued his employers. Held: They had negligently failed to provide a safe system of work and so they were liable. Litherland (1974)

Mr Payne was a labourer in a quarry. One day he was asked to help out by doing the more skilled job of repairing a chain with a steel hammer. He was not supplied with, or told to wear, goggles, nor was he told that if he struck the link-pin, as opposed to the link, it might shatter. Mr Payne hit the link-pin and lost an eye when it shattered. Held: His employers had not provided a safe system of work and so they were liable in damages. A safe system of work requires that untrained workers be told how to look after themselves. Payne (1973)

Mr Charlton was sent by his employers to collect the firm's weekly wages, some £1,500. He was attacked by robbers and injured. He sued his employers, arguing that they had failed to provide a safe system of work. Held: The employers were liable. They should not have sent Mr Charlton alone to collect the wages; they should have made some other arrangement, such as employing a security firm. Charlton (1978)

In many cases the amount of damages the employer has to pay will be reduced because the employee was himself partly to blame. When this happens, the employee forfeits part of his damages for this 'contributory negligence'.

Mr McGuiness was an eighteen-year-old butcher. He was using a new meat cutter when his hand slipped and he lost the tops of two fingers. He had in the past been told to use a pusher to hold the meat but he had not bothered to do so since the manager never used it. He sued his employers. Held: The employers were liable for not providing a safe system of work. But McGuiness himself had been negligent. He was one third to blame and so he only recovered two thirds of the full damages he would otherwise have been awarded. McGuiness (1973)

Suing an employer

An employee who has been injured in an accident at work should always take legal advice as to whether he has the basis of a claim against his employer. It should be borne in mind that the law will often make the employer liable in circumstances in which a layman might not think that he was to blame. Accordingly, it is important always to take legal advice. A trade-union member will usually be able to ask his union to take advice from the union's solicitors, who are likely to have considerable experience of such claims. A non-union member should consult a solicitor privately.

Many employees are very reluctant to sue their employers; they feel that it could cost them their jobs. However, it should be remembered that the employer will be insured against such a claim (the law requires him to be insured) and so the claim will really be against the insurance company: it will be against the employer in name alone. The employee need not fear that the employer will have to pay the damages out of his own pocket.

The injured employee should also claim any welfare benefits that might apply (e.g. injury benefit, disablement benefit). See page 734.

If you are injured at work

1. Note down names of all witnesses. Later obtain written statements from each of them. Try to arrange for photographs to be taken of the scene.
2. Report the accident to the employer. Ensure correct details are entered in the firm's accident book.
3. If the accident involved defective equipment (e.g. broken rope) keep it, or make sure it is not thrown away or repaired until your lawyers have agreed. Take photographs of it.
4. Try to find out whether there have been any similar accidents, and whether anyone has ever complained about the hazard that led to your accident. Obtain a written statement from anyone who complained or who had a similar accident.
5. Contact your trade-union representative and take legal advice.
6. Claim any welfare benefits for which you are eligible.
7. Keep a note of all your losses and expenses (and those of your family) arising out of the accident. These will form part of your claim.
8. See your doctor if the injury is other than trivial.
9. Do not accept any offer of compensation until you have taken full legal and medical advice.

Reporting an accident

An employer must notify the local health and safety executive officer if there is:

• an accident which *causes major injury or death* to anyone (whether he is an employee or not). A 'major injury' means a fracture of the skull, spine or pelvis; a fracture of any bone (except in wrist, hand, ankle, or foot); an injury necessitating the amputation of hand or foot; loss of sight of an eye; or any injury resulting in hospitalization for more than twenty-four hours (unless for observation only). In short, any serious injury must be reported.

• a *major incident* which endangered anyone working there, *even if no one was injured*. (This covers serious incidents such as explosions, collapse of cranes and scaffolding, etc.)

The notification must be made by the quickest possible means, usually the telephone. It must also be reported in writing within seven days (using form F 2508) and an entry should be made in the firm's accident book.

25 Ending the Employment

Neither the employer nor the employee can end the employment contract unless he gives the other proper notice. In other words, the employer cannot sack the employee and the employee cannot resign unless proper notice is given. The amount of notice to be given will be as set out in the contract of employment, provided this is not less than the minimum period required by the law.

Notice by the employer

An employer who wants to dismiss a member of his staff must give proper notice. Unless the employment contract says otherwise, the length of notice will vary with the length of the employee's employment.

Statutory minimum length of notice required

Length of employment	Length of notice by employer
Under one month	Nil
One month to two years	One week
Two years to twelve years	One week for each full year of employment
Over twelve years	Twelve weeks

(s. 49(i), Employment Protection (Consolidation) Act 1978.)

Often there is no written contract of employment and there are no written particulars. In this case the statutory minimum will apply, unless the employee can show it was an 'implied' term of the employment contract that he should receive longer notice. Often an employee who is paid monthly will be able to argue that he should receive at least a month's notice even if the statutory minimum gives him less than a month. It all depends upon what is regarded as 'reasonable' notice in the trade or profession. Generally, the more highly paid and the more senior the position, then the longer the notice to be given to the employee. For instance, three months has been held to be reasonable for a specialist oil salesman, six months for a photographic journalist, and twelve months for a ship's officer.

When an employee is given notice he should ask the employer to give written reason for the dismissal (see page 418). The employer's answers may enable the

415

employee to decide whether he should bring an unfair-dismissal or redundancy claim.

Ineligible employees. The notice provisions do not apply to all staff (e.g. part-timers – for a full list, see the chart on pages 376–7).

Giving wages in lieu of notice

Normally, an employer need not provide his staff with work – he just has to pay them (see page 401). It follows that an employer who wishes to dismiss an employee need not let the employee carry on working during the notice period. The only legal obligation on the employer is to pay him his normal wages during that time. This is called 'giving wages in lieu of notice'.

In practice, the employee need not work out his notice if he does not want to. He can leave (for example, to start a new job) and not lose his right to bring an unfair-dismissal claim (although there are special provisions about redundancy). If he does leave, he will of course lose the right to wages in lieu of notice (see page 419).

When the employer need not give any notice

There are two sets of circumstances in which the employer need not give the employee any notice:

• when the employee's 'gross misconduct' justifies 'summary dismissal';
• when the employment cannot continue – for example if the employee has been sent to prison or is suffering from a major illness.

1. 'Gross misconduct' and 'summary dismissal'

On-the-spot sacking is allowed – without notice – when the employee is guilty of such gross misconduct that it goes 'to the root of the employment contract'. But the employee must have behaved extremely badly for summary dismissal to be justified. Theft at work, assaults on management, or gross breaches of discipline might justify summary dismissal.

Generally, the industrial tribunals regard summary dismissal as being only rarely justified. Even if it is justified, the employer should follow the normal disciplinary procedures – such as allowing the employee to give his side of the story. (See page 395 for the rules on disciplinary procedures.) On the other hand, if the conduct was very bad and a proper disciplinary inquiry would not have made any difference to the outcome, then the employee would still not win an unfair-dismissal claim (see page 447).

If the summary dismissal is unjustified there are two different claims the employee can bring against his employer:

• a *wrongful-dismissal* claim for the wages due to him for the period of notice he should have been given (see page 417);
• an *unfair-dismissal* claim for the employer's having sacked him unreasonably.

2. When the employment cannot continue

Some outside event might occur which is so serious that it automatically brings the employment to an end. The contract becomes impossible to perform, and so lawyers say it has become 'frustrated'. For instance, the employee may receive a long prison sentence, he might become incurably ill, or he might lose a particular skill – an opera singer who loses his voice is an example.

But if it is decided that the contract has been 'frustrated' then it will mean that it has simply come to an end – and so the employer cannot be said to have dismissed or sacked the employee. Thus, no unfair-dismissal claim can be brought by the employee. This is why it is serious for an employee if it is suggested that the employment contract has become frustrated – he runs the risk of not being able to bring an unfair-dismissal claim. Because of the serious effects of holding that employment has been frustrated, the courts have become increasingly reluctant to uphold frustration claims by employers: the courts seem to feel that it is fairer for everyone if the ending of the employment is treated as a dismissal, so the employee can at least argue his case before an industrial tribunal.

In practical terms, therefore, frustration claims are rare – and it is even rarer for them to succeed. It is probably in cases of lengthy absence through ill-health that frustration is most often argued. Each case has to be decided on its own facts and the decision reached in one case is not likely to be of much help in another case (e.g. in one case an absence of eighteen months was held not to be frustration; in another case, an absence of four months did amount to frustration!).

Anyone who is unlucky enough to be involved in an argument as to whether an employment contract has been frustrated should seek expert legal advice.

When proper notice is not given

If an employer does not give proper notice to an employee, he can be sued for breach of contract. He has broken the employment contract and so he must pay damages to the employee. The amount of damages will be the employee's losses arising from the breach of contract – the wages he should have been paid for the proper period of notice or for the remainder of his fixed-period contract.

The employee's claim is called a *wrongful-dismissal* claim. It is brought in a civil court (county court, unless the wages claimed exceed £5,000, in which case it is brought in the High Court, Queen's Bench Division). This is the only employment law claim that is not brought in an industrial tribunal. If he brings a wrongful-dismissal claim, he does not lose his right to bring an unfair-dismissal, or redundancy, claim as well.

The damages claimed by the employee will normally be the wages due for the period of notice. Only exceptionally will they be more. There is one case in the law reports in which the employee in a wrongful-dismissal claim was given additional damages for the 'mental distress' he suffered because of his employer's behaviour:

In July 1963, after seventeen years' service, Mr Cox was promoted and his salary increased by £70 p.a. He was led to believe that he would receive a further substantial increase, and was

417

dismayed when he was only awarded a further £30 p.a. He protested, and the firm retaliated by, in effect, demoting him, although he continued to receive his previous salary. He became depressed and frustrated. In 1975 the firm persuaded him to resign. In effect he had been forced out of his job and so he sued for wrongful dismissal. He was awarded £500 for the depression, frustration, and distress caused by the employer's breach of the employment contract. Cox (1976)

But this case should be treated with caution. Most lawyers feel that it was wrongly decided and, even if it was, it must be borne in mind that the employer's conduct was spread out over a period of ten years. So it is probably of very limited application. However, an employee bringing a wrongful-dismissal claim is probably best advised to claim damages for 'mental distress' in order to inflate his claim, so that he can then negotiate a good compromise settlement.

More often than not, the damages in a wrongful-dismissal claim will be less than the wages due to the employee. This is because the damages are only supposed to compensate the employee for his 'loss'. If he found another job immediately – at a similar or higher salary – he has not suffered any loss, so he will not be able to claim any damages.

Usually, the ex-employers will argue that the employee could have found another job and that any losses are his own fault. If they can prove this, then the employee's claim will be worthless. Often the employee with a wrongful-dismissal claim will have to be prepared to compromise his claim unless he can show that he couldn't be expected to get a job at a similar salary during the period of notice.

Finally, the damages will be reduced by any unemployment benefit received during the notice period, and by the amount of tax and national insurance that would have been deducted from his wages. The justification for reducing the damages in this way is that the damages are only intended to compensate him for his losses; if these items were not deducted he might (theoretically) recover more in damages than he would have in wages.

Wrongful dismissal and unfair dismissal. The two are distinct claims and must not be confused. Wrongful dismissal is for a specific amount of wages owed, whereas unfair dismissal is a claim for general compensation to cover the dismissal. Other differences are that wrongful-dismissal claims are brought in the civil courts, have a six-year time limit, are within the legal-aid system, and normally make the loser liable to pay the winner's legal costs. None of these apply to unfair-dismissal claims.

Giving reasons for a dismissal

An employer must provide written reasons for dismissing an employee – but only if the employee asks him (s. 58, Employment Protection (Consolidation) Act 1978). The employee's request need not be in writing, although it is advisable for a written request to be made so that there is a record. The employer has fourteen days in which to provide written reasons.

The employer's reply must be in sufficient detail. Whilst the reasons need not be exhaustive they must be sufficiently comprehensive to be self-explanatory. The

Employment Appeal Tribunal has said, 'The document must be of such a kind that the employee, or anyone to whom he may wish to show it, can know from reading the document itself why the employee has been dismissed.' In practice, it is sufficient to refer back to the letter of dismissal if that was sufficiently detailed.

If the employer does not provide the written reasons within fourteen days, the employee can then apply to an industrial tribunal. If the tribunal decides that the employer acted 'unreasonably' in not providing the reasons, it will order him to pay the employee two weeks' wages. It may also draw unfavourable conclusions which might damage the employer's credibility if he is trying to show that he acted fairly.

If the employer does provide the written reasons, but they are inadequate or untrue, the employee can complain to the tribunal. The tribunal will decide the issue, and if the complaint is upheld the employee will receive two weeks' wages.

Ineligible employees. Not all employees can insist on being given written reasons for dismissal (e.g. part-timers). For full details, see the chart on pages 376–7.

Notice by the employee

An employee who wants to leave his job must give at least one week's notice if he has been employed for four weeks or more (s. 49(i), Employment Protection (Consolidation) Act 1978). This is unless his employment contract requires him to give longer notice. The *written particulars* of the contract, sent to the employee by the employer (see page 374), should state how much notice he must give, and often this will be more than the statutory minimum.

If there is no written provision as to notice, the law may decide that a senior member of staff should give more than one week's notice during his first two years with a firm.

If the employee resigns without giving proper notice

If an employee does not give notice of his resignation, then he is in breach of contract and can be sued by the employer. The position is similar to a wrongful-dismissal claim brought by an employee who has been sacked without proper notice (see page 417).

The employer can sue the employee for damages. But his provable 'losses' are unlikely to be large. The employee will usually be able to show that the employer could have cut his losses by recruiting a replacement. Even if the employer can show a direct loss (e.g. no replacement was available; a major order was lost; he incurred advertising and job-agency costs) he is unlikely to sue. Firstly, suing the ex-employee might worsen labour relations in the firm. Secondly, the courts tend to be unsympathetic to such claims and usually find a way of ensuring that the employee is not penalized for resigning his job.

In practice, all the employer can easily do is to refuse to provide the employee with a reference and, perhaps, to refuse to pay any wages or holiday pay due to him. In theory the employee could sue for the wages owed, but the employer could then counterclaim for damages in respect of the employee's unannounced resignation. So, unless the wage arrears are substantial, the employee will probably decide it is not worth suing.

Ending a fixed-term contract

A fixed-term contract is for a definite duration. There is no need for either employer or employee to give notice when the fixed term expires since they both know when it is due to end. The only way the contract can be ended before the due date is if the employee is guilty of gross misbehaviour or if 'frustration' – such as serious illness – occurs (see page 417).

Note that an employee with a fixed-term contract may be able to claim unfair dismissal if his contract is not renewed when it runs out (see page 433).

Death of the employer or employee

If either employer or employee dies, the employment contract automatically comes to an end. Note that if an employee is employed by a company, the fact that his own boss dies will not mean that his employer has died. The company is separate from its directors and managers, and cannot die other than by going into liquidation.

If the employer dies

The employee can make a redundancy claim against the employer's estate, unless he decides to carry on working for the business if the estate carries on running it. The employee can carry on with an unfair-dismissal claim made before the employer died, or if he had been given notice of dismissal before the employer's death.

All debts due from the employer (such as wage arrears) can be claimed from the employer's estate.

If the employee dies

The employee's personal representative can carry on with any unfair-dismissal or redundancy claim which the employee had made or could have made.

The insolvent employer

If an employer goes bust, the contracts of employment of the staff automatically come to an end. But special protection is given to employees to ensure that money owed to them by the employer, and any redundancy pay they could claim, is paid. This is done by:

• allowing most claims to be paid by the Department of Employment;
• making some of the claims priority debts.

These various rights can only benefit an employee whose employer becomes insolvent. They do not protect the employee whose employer simply disappears (as sometimes happens in the building trade), unless someone is prepared to start bankruptcy proceedings against the absent employer.

1. Claiming from the Department of Employment

The employee can claim (under s. 122, Employment Protection (Consolidation) Act 1978):

(a) *Wage arrears* for up to eight weeks, at a maximum rate of £152 per week. This includes wages owed in respect of medical suspension payments, guarantee payments for lay-off, pay due for time off to union officials and to redundant staff looking for new jobs

(b) *Notice*: wages due for the period of notice which the employee should have been given (up to £152 per week). But the employee can only claim in respect of the statutory period of notice, not for any longer period allowed under his employment contract.

(c) *Holiday pay* for up to six weeks (up to £152 per week).

(d) *Unfair dismissal* (basic award only) and redundancy payment.

The employee should first ask the liquidator or receiver for the amount due. The liquidator or receiver will calculate the amount due, and if the employee agrees the figures, the Secretary of State sends the money direct to the employee. If the employer does not have a receiver or liquidator, the employee should apply direct to the Secretary of State, via his local Department of Employment office. If payment is still refused, complain to an industrial tribunal.

Ineligible employees. See the chart on pages 376–7.

2. Claiming priority debts from the employer's receiver or liquidator

When a firm goes bust, there is an order of priority amongst the various creditors. Only when the *preferential* creditors have been paid in full can the other creditors claim a share of the remaining assets. Certain debts to employees are preferential debts, but the maximum amount that can be treated as a priority debt is £800. These debts include:

- *wage arrears* for up to four months
- *holiday pay*
- *pension contributions* for up to four months.

Any excess will be an ordinary debt.

Claiming from a liquidator or receiver can take a long time. Also there may be other preferential debts (such as tax owed to the Inland Revenue and claims by other members of staff) so that there may not be sufficient assets to pay all the preferred creditors. When this happens, they all get a percentage of the amount due to them.

References and testimonials

There is no legal obligation on an employer to provide his staff with references or testimonials when they leave his employ.

This can cause hardship. In one case, a man had worked for ten years as a security guard. His immediate superior was replaced by a different person with whom he had a row. So the employee fixed up another job and left. Unfortunately the new job fell through and so he had to look for employment with other security firms. But all the firms he approached contacted his previous employers for a reference, and the supervisor with whom he had argued would reply that 'Mr X worked with us for ten years and left of his own accord'. Whilst this was true, it was a damning reference; by making no mention of his honesty, reliability, and integrity, it by implication cast doubts on his suitability. As a result, he was unable to obtain a job as a security guard despite his excellent record. He was, in effect, unemployable as a security guard because he could not insist on a proper testimonial, and yet he had no legal redress.

If an employer does provide a reference he should tell the truth. But an honest, discreet employer need have no fears as to his legal liability for giving a reference. In theory, the employee could sue him for defamation if the references contained an unprovable allegation. However, references are covered by 'qualified privilege', which means the employer would only be liable if he acted 'maliciously' (i.e. without believing that what he was saying was true; see page 713). The employee's difficulty in proving 'malice' and the absence of legal aid for defamation cases make the chances of his suing the employer very remote. The practical way for employers to avoid even this slight risk is to give the reference verbally on the phone, for the employee will then find it extremely difficult to prove what was said about him.

The employer might also have a legal liability to the person to whom he gives the reference. If he tells the new employer that the employee was 'trustworthy and honest' when in fact he was sacked for stealing at work, he may be liable in negligence. Although in legal theory he would be liable, it seems unlikely that the courts would hold him responsible. Certainly, there is no record of a case in the law reports in which the ex-employer was held liable to the new employer. The ex-employer can avoid any liability by writing 'without responsibility' across the top of the reference. This will make it clear that the new employer relies on the reference at his own risk.

If the employer deliberately provides a false testimonial he can be prosecuted in the magistrates' court under the Servants' Character Act 1792. So also can an employee who forges or alters his employer's reference (maximum penalty for both offences is £50 fine).

Restricting the employee's future work

Sometimes an employer will try to restrict the type of work that his staff can do when they leave his employment. The employer might insert a clause into the contract of employment that an ex-employee is not to work within a stated distance of the employer's office, that he won't set up his own competing business within a stated period, and that he won't approach his ex-employer's customers for business once he has left the firm. Restrictions of this sort are called 'covenants in restraint of trade'. The courts frown on any action that has the effect of limiting a man's freedom of work – to do the work he wants to do, for whomsoever he chooses. This was the principle behind the decision in the Kerry Packer 'cricket circus' case:

Kerry Packer recruited top star cricketers to play for his commercial cricket teams. The Test and County Cricket Board retaliated by altering its rules so that any cricketer who played for Packer would no longer be able to play first-class cricket in the UK. Packer, and several of his recruits, challenged the validity of the action. Held: The bans were in restraint of trade. They prevented the cricketers from seeking employment elsewhere and they were not in the interests of the cricketers or the public. Thus the clauses were invalid and could not be enforced. Greig (1977)

If an employer inserts a restraint-of-trade clause in the employee's contract of employment, the courts will examine it critically. Only if the employer can show that it is reasonable and necessary for the protection of his trade interests will it be upheld – but only if it is not against the public interest. The courts' dislike of these clauses was forcibly expressed by Lord Denning in a 1956 case: 'During the last forty years the courts have shown a reluctance to enforce covenants of this sort . . . if these covenants were given full force they would tend to reduce the employee's freedom to seek better conditions, even by asking for a rise in wages; because if he is not allowed to get work elsewhere, he is very much at the mercy of his employer.'

The more widely drafted the restriction, the more likely it is that the courts will decide that it is unenforceable. In short, the less ambitious the covenant, the more likely it is to succeed. Most clauses fail because:

- they are not *solely* designed to protect trade secrets;
- they last for an unreasonably long time;
- they cover an unreasonably wide geographical area.

The seniority of the employee will often be an important factor in assessing the reasonableness of the clause:

Mr Greer joined a dry-cleaning business in 1924. In 1974 he was offered the chance of becoming a director, which he accepted. His contract of employment as a director contained the following clause: 'In view of the access to trade secrets and secret processes which the employee may have during the course of his employment . . . he shall not within a period of twelve months from the termination thereof either directly or indirectly, neither alone nor in association with any other person, firm or company engage in any part of the United Kingdom in any business which is similar to any business involving such trade secrets and/or secret processes carried on by the company.' Shortly afterwards, Mr Greer left and joined another dry-cleaning firm. Was the clause valid? Held: No, the clause was too wide. Greer (1979)

In this case the main defect was the clause saying that it applied 'in any part of the United Kingdom'. The company could, however, have protected its position by restricting the clause to the local area in which Mr Greer had worked. They had not done so, and so the clause was not binding on him.

By way of contrast is the following case, in which the restriction clause was upheld by the court:

Employment: At Work

Mr Harris was in charge of preparing Littlewoods' mail-order catalogue. It was a senior post, giving him a directorship and a salary of £18,000 p.a. He was approached by Littlewoods' big mail-order rivals, who offered him more money and a company car. He accepted. Littlewoods then sought an injunction to stop him working for the competitors, on the basis that he had signed a restraint-of-trade clause which prevented him joining any rival firm for twelve months. Held: The twelve months' restriction was reasonable for a man of his seniority. The covenant was valid and so he could not join the rival firm. Littlewoods (1977)

Estate agents often seem to have arguments about these restrictions:

Mr Luck was employed by Mr Davenport-Smith in his estate agent's business. Mr Luck left the firm and set up in competition. Mr Davenport-Smith claimed damages on the grounds that Mr Luck was in breach of a covenant that he would not work as an estate agent for three years within one mile of each of Davenport-Smith's offices in Saltdean, Peacehaven, and Patcham. Held: The three-year restriction was unreasonable and so the clause was void. Luck (1977)

A less-ambitious clause would have worked. For instance:

An ex-employee of a firm of estate agents set up in business 150 yards away. He had signed an agreement not to set up in competition within a one-mile radius. His former employers applied for an injunction against him. Held: An injunction would be granted. The one-mile radius was reasonable. Anscombe & Ringland (1984)

The net effect is that most restraint-of-trade clauses are unenforceable. Even clauses drafted by skilled lawyers are often held to be invalid. In practice, these clauses are used more to discourage the employees, rather than to restrain them legally.

26 Unfair Dismissal

The first unfair-dismissal legislation was introduced in 1971. Until then, an employer had been free to dismiss his staff subject only to their being given notice and any redundancy payment that might be due to them. But that was the full extent of the employer's obligations. The fact that he was behaving unreasonably or immorally was irrelevant in the eyes of the law. The Industrial Relations Act 1971 altered this position. The present law on unfair dismissal is contained in the Employment Protection (Consolidation) Act 1978, although that Act has since been altered slightly. But the basic principles of unfair-dismissal compensation remain as they were in 1971.

The employer must be able to justify the dismissal to a public body, the industrial tribunal. If the tribunal finds that the dismissal was unfair, he can be ordered to pay cash compensation to the employee, or even to re-employ him. The unfair-dismissal legislation has thus transformed the law on dismissals. In the early 1970s, the industrial tribunals acquired a reputation of being pro-employee and anti-employer. In recent years, there has been a subtle but marked change in the attitude of the tribunals, and many would now argue that the tribunals have reversed their bias. Be that as it may, there can be little doubt that it is now significantly more difficult to win an unfair-dismissal claim than it was in the 1970s.

Summary: The basic principles of the unfair-dismissal rules are straightforward. An employee who is sacked after two years' service has three months in which to complain to an industrial tribunal. If he can show the tribunal that he has been 'dismissed', the employer will then have to justify the dismissal. To do this, the employer must show that he had a 'fair' reason for sacking the employee (for instance, because the employee was incompetent or dishonest). Then the tribunal will consider whether the employer acted reasonably in deciding to sack the employee; generally, this means checking that a fair procedure was followed. If the tribunal decides that the dismissal was unfair then it can order the employer to give the employee his job back or to give him another job. Usually, though, the employee receives cash compensation. The amount paid to him will reflect the fact that he has now lost his job and will also compensate him for his losses, although the compensation will often be reduced if the employee's own conduct contributed to his dismissal.

The requirements of a successful unfair-dismissal claim

There are four hurdles to be overcome by an employee who brings an unfair-dismissal claim:

Employment: Unfair Dismissal and Redundancy

Hurdle No. 1 Is s/he within the unfair-dismissal legislation? (See page 426.)
Hurdle No. 2 Has s/he been 'dismissed' by the employer? (See page 427.)
Hurdle No. 3 Was there a 'fair' reason for the dismissal (i.e. misconduct, disobeying orders, non-cooperation, poor timekeeping, drunkenness, violence, swearing, dishonesty, incapability, incompetence, lack of qualifications, ill health, industrial action, or some other substantial reason)? (See page 433)
Hurdle No. 4 Did the employer behave 'reasonably'? (See page 446.)

Hurdle No. 1. Is the employee within the unfair-dismissal legislation?

Not all employees can claim for unfair dismissal.

The main requirement is that the employee must have been employed for at least two years, otherwise s/he cannot claim unfair dismissal, however unreasonably his/her employer behaved. Because of this two-year qualifying period many employers review the position of new staff shortly before the two-year period expires.

In deciding whether the employee has worked for two years, the tribunal will add the period of his/her statutory notice on to the time when s/he was dismissed. So, if s/he is dismissed without notice after 103 weeks, then the one week's notice to which s/he is entitled by statute (see page 415) will be added to his/her 103 weeks' service, and s/he will be held to have been employed for two years.

Small firms. The different qualifying period for people working in small firms was abolished on 1 June 1985. But people employed in firms of over twenty people before that date still have a one-year qualifying period.

Part-time workers. Part-timers are defined as those employees who do not work more than sixteen hours a week. If an employee works sixteen hours or more then s/he is a full-timer and thus able to claim unfair dismissal. If s/he works between eight and sixteen hours a week (on average) then he (or more probably, she) can claim unfair dismissal – but only if s/he has worked for the employer for at least five years. So, in such cases, the normal one-year (or two-year) qualification period is extended to five years. If the part-timer works fewer than eight hours a week then s/he cannot claim unfair dismissal – however long s/he has worked for the employer.

Retirement age. If an employee is sacked after s/he has reached the 'normal retirement age' for that category of employee, then s/he is not eligible to claim unfair dismissal. The (rather harsh) rule is that it is the retirement age for similar employees that matters – not the retirement age for that particular employee. So in one case a woman aged sixty-one could not claim unfair dismissal even though her employment contract envisaged her working until age sixty-five, because the 'normal' retirement age was stated to be sixty.

When there is no qualifying period. If the employee claims s/he has been sacked because of his/her trade-union activities, or because of race, sex, or marriage discrimination, then there is no qualifying period (i.e. there is no need to have worked for one, or two, years).

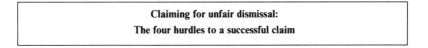

Claiming for unfair dismissal:
The four hurdles to a successful claim

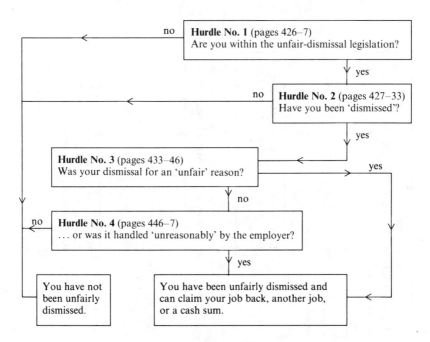

no — **Hurdle No. 1** (pages 426–7)
Are you within the unfair-dismissal legislation?

↓ yes

no — **Hurdle No. 2** (pages 427–33)
Have you been 'dismissed'?

↓ yes

Hurdle No. 3 (pages 433–46)
Was your dismissal for an 'unfair' reason? — yes

↓ no

no — **Hurdle No. 4** (pages 446–7)
... or was it handled 'unreasonably' by the employer?

↓ yes

You have not been unfairly dismissed.

You have been unfairly dismissed and can claim your job back, another job, or a cash sum.

Illegal contracts. If the contract of employment is illegal then no claim for unfair dismissal can be made. This is primarily aimed at tax fiddlers. For instance:

> *An employee brought an unfair-dismissal claim. At the industrial tribunal hearing the employers showed that the employee, as well as being paid her normal wage, had received an extra £5 cash per week gross. No tax or NI deductions were made from that extra £5. Held: There was an agreement to defraud the Inland Revenue and thus, as a matter of public policy, the whole contract of employment was illegal. No unfair-dismissal claim could be brought. Corby (1980)*

Ineligible employees. Not all employees can claim for unfair dismissal. Apart from those who have not worked for long enough, part-timers are the main group that cannot claim. See page 376–7 for a full list.

Hurdle No. 2. Has the employee been 'dismissed' by the employer?

Usually it is obvious whether or not an employee has been dismissed. Normally he is sacked, given proper notice, and handed his P45 tax form.

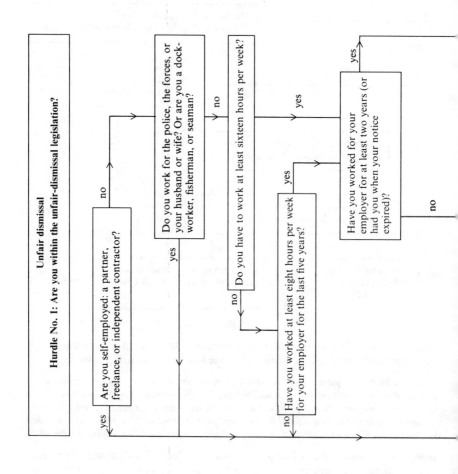

Unfair dismissal

Hurdle No. 1: Are you within the unfair-dismissal legislation?

Are you self-employed: a partner, freelance, or independent contractor?

Do you work for the police, the forces, or your husband or wife? Or are you a dock-worker, fisherman, or seaman?

Do you have to work at least sixteen hours per week?

Have you worked at least eight hours per week for your employer for the last five years?

Have you worked for your employer for at least two years (or had you when your notice expired)?

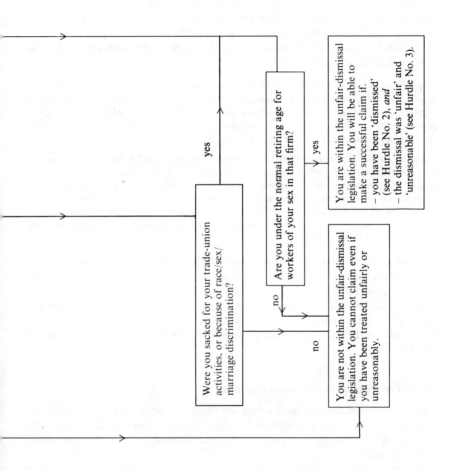

yes

Were you sacked for your trade-union activities, or because of race/sex/marriage discrimination?

no

Are you under the normal retiring age for workers of your sex in that firm?

no

yes

You are not within the unfair-dismissal legislation. You cannot claim even if you have been treated unfairly or unreasonably.

You are within the unfair-dismissal legislation. You will be able to make a successful claim if:
– you have been 'dismissed' (see Hurdle No. 2), *and*
– the dismissal was 'unfair' and 'unreasonable' (see Hurdle No. 3).

429

It is not always so straightforward. If the employer did not specifically tell the employee that he was sacked, the tribunal will have to decide whether or not the employer did mean to sack him. For instance, if the employer tells the employee to 'get out of my factory' it will probably be a dismissal. On the other hand, if the employee is told to 'join a f— union and get some overalls on' the position will be less clear cut; it will depend on the surrounding circumstances (e.g. if the words were said to a manager it would probably be taken as a dismissal, but not if said to a labourer on a building site where such words might be taken as part of everyday vocabulary). So it is not the words alone that matter – you must also look at the surrounding circumstances.

Mrs Simpson had been unwell and she was recovering from a major illness. She overheard an argument between an employee and her son, so she rushed into the room and shouted at the employee 'Go! Get out! Get out!' He left, and claimed unfair dismissal. Held: He had not been dismissed. Mrs Simpson's words had to be looked at in the overall context – she was unwell and they were spoken in the heat of the moment. J & J Stern (1983)

Mr Martin had a heated row with a director of the company; it ended with the director sacking him. Five minutes later – when he had calmed down – the director realized he had not acted properly and so he saw Martin and told him he was suspended for two days, but not sacked. Martin would not accept this, and claimed unfair dismissal. Held: There had not been a dismissal. The surrounding circumstances showed that it would be wrong to treat this as a dismissal – words spoken in the heat of the moment can be withdrawn if a mistake has been made (provided this is done quickly). Martin (1983)

'Dismissal' is not confined to the cases in which the employer sacks the employee. An employee can still regard himself as having been dismissed (and so be eligible for unfair dismissal) if:

• he is entitled to resign because his employer has broken the contract of employment. This is called constructive dismissal, *or*

• the employer fails to renew the employee's fixed-term contract when it expires (but see page 433).

Justified resignation – constructive dismissal

Sometimes the employer does not sack the employee but, instead, behaves in such a way that the employee is justified in leaving. Despite the fact that the employee has not been sacked, it will count as a 'dismissal' and so he will be able to bring an unfair-dismissal claim.

To amount to constructive dismissal, the employer's conduct must be a serious breach of the employment contract (e.g. if the employee is demoted, or has his wages cut). When this happens, the employee can regard himself as having been constructively dismissed by his employer and so he can resign and then claim unfair dismissal.

The employer's conduct must be a breach of the employment contract. The mere fact that the employer is behaving 'unreasonably' will not make it constructive dismissal unless the employer is also breaking the employment contract, or unless the

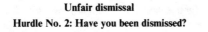

Unfair dismissal
Hurdle No. 2: Have you been dismissed?

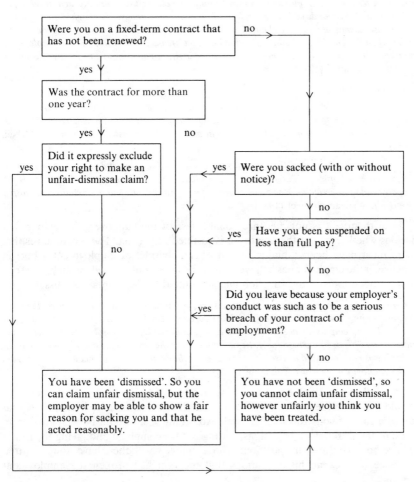

unreasonable behaviour is so grave as to amount to a breach of the contract.

A shop assistant was refused leave to take a day or half-day off work to supervise her son's insulin injection on the day he came out of hospital. She resigned and claimed constructive dismissal. Held: No. However unreasonably the employers might have behaved, the firm was only small and so it could not therefore be an implied term of her contract that she be allowed time off in an emergency. Since there had been no breach of the employment contract, there was no constructive dismissal. Warner (1978)

Sharp was suspended for five days as a disciplinary measure. He did not dispute the suspension, but because the suspension left him short of money he asked for some of his accrued holiday pay to be paid to him in advance. Although this was a reasonable enough request, it was not a term of his employment contract that he be allowed to claim accrued holiday pay before he took his holiday. The firm refused to pay him the money. He resigned saying it was constructive dismissal, and then claimed unfair dismissal. Held: No. Constructive dismissal only arises when the employer is guilty of behaviour that breaks the very basis of the employment contract. Mere unreasonable behaviour would, of itself, not amount to constructive dismissal. Western Excavating (1978)

On the other hand:

A foreman was told to work under the supervision of an ordinary electrician, as a 'temporary' arrangement. He refused, and claimed he had been constructively dismissed. Held: This was a major breach of the contract of employment and so it was constructive dismissal. McNeil (1984)

Mr Jones was a fleet sales director, but he was subjected to gradual demotion, being moved to more cramped offices with fewer and fewer facilities. In the end he was unable to do his job properly and so he resigned. Held: This was constructive dismissal (and so he could claim unfair dismissal). Wadham Stringer (1983)

In legal theory, it is not the unreasonableness of the employer's behaviour that decides whether or not the employee is justified in leaving. The law requires that there must have been a major breach of the contract of employment – but, in practice, if the employer has behaved badly then the employee will probably be seen to have been forced out of his job and so entitled to claim unfair dismissal.

Cedron was a night-club worker. He was insulted by the manager, who used foul and abusive language to him, and said that if he didn't like it he could leave. Cedron left, and claimed unfair dismissal. The employers argued that it was not constructive dismissal because even if the manager had behaved unreasonably, he had not broken the terms of the employment contract. Held: It was constructive dismissal. The manager's behaviour was so bad that it went to the root of the employment contract. Palmanor (1978)

If an employee is thinking of resigning because of his employer's behaviour, he should keep a full record of what has occurred, as it will be up to him to show that it was a case of constructive dismissal. Accordingly, he would be well advised to write to the firm before he resigns, setting out his complaint and giving the firm a chance to reconsider its position. The employee will then have some written evidence to back up his allegations that the firm had broken the employment contract.

'Resign or be sacked.' An employer will often make it clear to an employee that he is to be sacked, but the employer will then suggest that the employee resigns so as to avoid the embarrassment and stigma of having been dismissed. Can the employee claim unfair dismissal – or can the employer argue that the employee left of his own free will, and was not dismissed? The answer is that the tribunal will look at all the circumstances, and if it decides that the employee was pressurized into resigning (i.e. 'resign or be sacked') then it will be treated as a dismissal, and so the employee

can claim unfair dismissal. In practice, though, the employee would be better advised to wait until he is sacked rather than offer his resignation – that way he avoids having to prove that he was, in fact, sacked and that he did not voluntarily resign.

When a fixed-term contract ends

An employee with a fixed-term contract may be able to claim unfair dismissal if the contract is not renewed when it expires. The only exception is when the contract is for a year or more, and when it specifically states that its non-renewal will not give rise to an unfair-dismissal claim. In effect, employees with a contract for more than one year can sign away their unfair-dismissal rights, and if the contract is not renewed when it expires they will not be able to claim unfair dismissal. But, even in this case, if the employee is sacked before the fixed term has expired (e.g. because the employer has less work for him to do), the employee will be able to claim unfair dismissal – provided he will then have worked for two years (the minimum period for being able to bring an unfair-dismissal claim).

If the fixed-term contract is for less than a year then the employee cannot sign away his rights – and so he will be able to claim unfair dismissal if the contract is ended early or if it is not renewed when it runs out.

Hurdle No. 3. Was there a 'fair' reason for the employee's dismissal?

Once the employee has surmounted Hurdle No. 1 (is he within the unfair-dismissal legislation?), and Hurdle No. 2 (has he been 'dismissed' by the employer?), it is for the employer to show that there was a fair reason for his dismissal: this is Hurdle No. 3.

So, once Hurdle No. 2 has been passed, the burden of proof passes on to the employer. It is up to him to show a 'fair' reason for the dismissal.

The usual 'fair' reasons for a dismissal are:
* misconduct by the employee:
  - disobeying orders – *see page 433*
  - non-cooperation – *see page 434*
  - poor timekeeping – *see page 435*
  - drunkenness – *see page 436*
  - violence and swearing – *see page 436*
  - dishonesty – *see page 437*
* the employee is incapable or incompetent, or lacks qualifications – *see page 439*
* other 'capability' problems, such as ill health – *see page 440*
* industrial action, such as striking – *see page 444*
* it would be illegal for the employee to continue working – *see page 444*
* there is 'some other substantial reason' justifying dismissal – *see page 445*

Misconduct by the employee: disobeying the employer's orders

It is an implied term of every employee's contract of employment that he will obey his employer's orders – assuming that the orders are both lawful and reasonable (see page 370). In addition, though, the order must be one that is authorized by the contract of employment. For instance, if a man's employment contract states that his job is to operate a lathe, it will not be an authorized order if he is told to clean the lavatories instead. If the employer insists that the employee obey this unauthorized order, the employee can resign. He can then regard himself as having been constructively dismissed (see page 430) and can claim unfair dismissal.

If the employment contract (and in practice that usually means the *written particulars* sent to the employee) does not define the job, then the employee may well be obliged to obey the employer's instructions. If he refuses to do so, the employer will then have a 'fair' reason for dismissing him. So it can be very important from the employee's point of view that his job be fully described in the *written particulars* (see page 374).

Similarly, if the employee breaks the rules of conduct or disciplinary rules laid down by the employer, his dismissal may not be unfair. Obviously, each case must be decided on its own facts and the tribunal will consider the 'reasonableness' of the decision to sack. For instance:

> *Ladbroke's disciplinary rules forbade the staff from placing their own bets. In the course of an abortive investigation into allegations of fraud it was learnt that several employees had placed bets in breach of the disciplinary rules. They were dismissed, that being the penalty laid down in the disciplinary rules. They claimed unfair dismissal. Held: Their dismissal was unfair. It was not sufficient that the disciplinary rules authorized dismissal for the dismissal to be fair.* Ladbroke Racing (1979)

If an employer is complaining about a particular matter of conduct, it must be related to the employee's job. For instance, in one case a petrol-pump attendant was learning to drive and she drove off from work in the family car – but collided with the petrol pumps, causing damage worth £6,000. It was held that her dismissal was unfair – her bad driving was not relevant to her job.

Misconduct by the employee: non-cooperation

Non-cooperation can take various forms. The mere fact that an employee does not work cheerfully or with good grace does not amount to non-cooperation; an employee is legally obliged to do his work, but he need not do it with a smile on his face.

Whether an employee is not cooperating will depend upon the terms of his employment contract. For instance, if he refuses to cooperate by doing occasional overtime, the position will depend upon whether his contract obliges him to do overtime when required. If overtime is voluntary, then his non-cooperation will not make his dismissal 'fair'.

> *Mr Martin's written terms of employment stated that 'you will be expected to work such overtime as is necessary to ensure continuity of service'. Throughout his employment with the firm, Mr Martin was reluctant to work overtime, but did so on some occasions after persuasion. He was eventually sacked after refusing to work on one Friday or Saturday evening. He claimed*

unfair dismissal. Held: The dismissal was fair because Martin had not complied with what was a term of his employment contract. This was so even though the firm had not sought to force him to work overtime before and had in fact condoned previous refusals. No warning was necessary. Solus (1979)

The tribunal will have little sympathy with an employee who rigidly stands on his contractual rights when it is clear that he is acting unreasonably by not cooperating in a change of contractual arrangements. For instance:

The RAC emergency service was inundated with work. The RAC decided to reorganize the service and reached an agreement with the staff association which was acceptable to the majority of staff. However, it involved staff in working extra hours; three employees refused to agree to the changes, because their thirty-one-and-a-half-hour week was increased to a forty-two-hour week. After being sacked, the three men claimed unfair dismissal. The Employment Appeals Tribunal ruled that it did not necessarily follow that they were entitled to win their claims because their contracts of employment had been altered. As long as the RAC demonstrated to the employees with patience and understanding that the reorganization was sensible and in the interest of employees generally, and had listened to and weighed up their views, then the dismissal would be fair. Martin (1979)

Most cases of non-cooperation take the form of niggling, petty incidents; in short, bloody-mindedness. Only if the conduct continues over a long period of time will it be regarded as a 'fair' reason for dismissal. Even then the tribunal will look closely at the reasonableness of the employer's conduct (Hurdle No. 4, page 446). They will ask why the employee has been behaving in that way. Has the employer been authoritarian, inconsiderate, or rude? Has the employer tried to discuss the problem with the employee? Has the employee been given a chance to explain why he is discontented? Most important of all, has he been given a clear 'this can't go on' warning? In short, what would the reasonable employer have done?

Misconduct by the employee: poor timekeeping

As with bloody-mindedness, poor timekeeping will not be a serious disciplinary matter unless it continues for a long time. Dismissal for lateness will almost certainly be unfair if the employee was not given an express warning and told that he would be dismissed unless his timekeeping improved. Also, the tribunal will want to know why the employee has been arriving late – for instance, is it a temporary problem caused by domestic upheavals?

The nature of the employee's job will also be relevant. It will be a more serious matter if he is a senior employee or in a position of responsibility. An extreme example:

Two maintenance fitters were both long-serving employees with excellent records. But one afternoon they both went absent for two and a half hours without permission and were summarily dismissed. They claimed unfair dismissal. Held: No. They held important positions of responsibility, and as such, were paid to be on call at any time. An absence of two and a half hours could not be excused – especially since there were clearly displayed notices warning staff that they would be instantly dismissed if they went absent without permission. Morrison (1973)

If the tribunal decides that the lateness or absenteeism did not justify dismissal, then the employee will win his unfair-dismissal claim. However, if the employee was persistently late, the tribunal might well find that his own conduct contributed to the dismissal and so reduce the compensation paid to him (see page 460). As always, the tribunal will consider the case by reference to what the 'reasonable' employer would have done. (See Hurdle No. 4, page 446.)

Clocking-in offences are regarded in a different light; they are always serious offences and often justify summary dismissal (because of the 'dishonesty' involved). For instance:

Mr Stewart was a bus driver. Although his shift was due to end at 9.45 p.m. an inspector could not find him at 7 p.m. On the following night he was watched by two inspectors, who saw him hand in his cash and time cards much earlier than he should have done. The same thing happened a few days later. He was reported to the district traffic superintendent and, following a meeting, he was sacked. He claimed unfair dismissal. Held: It was not unfair dismissal. False clocking in and false claims about hours worked are always serious offences of dishonesty, which can often justify instant dismissal. This was so, even though the company had not followed its own disciplinary procedure – in that it should normally have challenged Mr Stewart and asked him for an explanation after he was first seen by the two inspectors. Stewart (1978)

Misconduct by the employee: drunkenness

Drunkenness does not normally, of itself, justify dismissal. But persistent drunkenness will. A lot will depend upon the nature of the employee's job; an airline pilot who is found drunk would be liable to summary dismissal, whereas a packer in a factory should probably only be given a reprimand for a first offence.

The tribunal will want to know whether it was a one-off offence. Has the employee been given a warning in the past and specifically been told that further drunkenness would lead to dismissal? Has the management turned a blind eye to drinking in the past? Did the employer give the employee a chance to sober up and give an explanation before sacking him (perhaps drugs prescribed by a doctor caused 'drunken' behaviour, for example)?

Misconduct by the employee: violence and swearing

These are similar to drunkenness. How serious was the offence? Certainly, bad language of itself must be particularly serious to justify dismissal. Who was the person attacked or insulted? The more senior his status, the more seriously should the offence be regarded. Has such conduct been condoned in the past? Has the employee been given a chance to explain his conduct and to apologize? Was he given a formal warning that repetition would lead to dismissal?

This is the sort of question that the tribunal will want to have answered. The members of the tribunal will be realistic and be aware that some swearing (and even horse-play) is accepted in industry. They will want to be sure that the alleged bad language is not being used as a mere excuse for getting rid of the employee.

Serious fighting at work might be sufficiently grave to justify dismissal for a first offence, although the tribunal might want to check that the employee realized fighting would lead to dismissal. Mere arguing will rarely justify dismissal:

Two employees started arguing. A heated row developed but there was no violence. Both were dismissed. Was it unfair dismissal? Held: Yes. The misconduct was not sufficiently grave to make the dismissal fair. The chairman of the tribunal said, 'Here we have found that there was not a fight, merely a tussle.' Till and Walters (1978)

Misconduct by the employee: dishonesty and other offences

Theft is always a serious matter. Usually a theft at work will justify summary dismissal, but the employer must still act 'reasonably' and handle the incident in the proper way (see Hurdle No. 4, page 446). The amount involved is usually not the important point: it is the principle of dishonesty that matters. Thus, in one case, a dismissal for a fiddled travel-expenses claim of £1·48 was held to be fair.

If an employer suspects an employee of theft, he should not act as an instant prosecutor, judge, and jury. The employee should be given full details of the allegations, all witnesses should be interviewed, and the employee should be given a chance to explain his conduct. If the employer does not follow the proper procedures, he may well lose the unfair-dismissal claim, although it is likely that the tribunal will reduce the employee's compensation because his own conduct contributed to his dismissal (see page 460).

A supermarket cashier failed to ring up eighteen items on a customer's bill. The area controller asked her to explain herself and she said she had been unwell. The police were called and later that day she was sacked. But the police eventually decided not to prosecute. Was it unfair dismissal? Held: Yes. She should have been given a proper chance to explain, since she had 'not been herself' when interviewed by the area controller. The firm should have waited a few days before asking her to explain. Since the proper disciplinary procedures had not been followed, the dismissal was unfair. Obviously, if she had been caught red-handed the position would have been different and she could have been dismissed without an investigation and without being given a chance to explain herself. Tesco (1977)

The employer does not have to wait for the employee to be found guilty in a criminal court before he dismisses the employee. It will be 'fair' for the employer to dismiss the employee if he has 'reasonable grounds' for believing the employee is guilty. He need not have evidence that would convince a jury; all he needs is to have 'reasonable grounds' to believe that the employee is guilty. As Lord Denning has put it, 'If a man is dismissed for stealing, as long as the employer honestly believes it on reasonable grounds, that is enough to justify dismissal. It is not necessary for the employer to prove that he was in fact stealing.'

The rules on how to deal with suspected dishonesty by an employee were laid down in a 1980 case called *Burchell* v. *BHS*. The dismissal will not be unfair if (1) the employer reasonably believed that the employee was guilty, and if (2) he carried out 'as much investigation as was reasonable in the circumstances'. So the important point is not whether the employee was actually guilty or not – it is whether the employer was reasonably entitled to think that he was guilty.

Even if the employee is subsequently acquitted by a court, the dismissal will be 'fair' if the employer can show that he had reasonable grounds, at the time of the dismissal, for thinking the employee was guilty. The Employment Appeals Tribunal has justified this seemingly harsh line:

> At first sight those not familiar with the problem say that it is wrong to dismiss the employee until the guilt has been established. Further experience shows that this is impracticable. In the first place, quite apart from guilt, involvement in the alleged criminal offence often involves a serious breach of duty or discipline. The cashier charged with a till offence, guilty or not, is often undoubtedly in breach of company rules in the way in which the till is being operated. The employee who removes goods from the premises, guilty or not, is often in breach of the company rules in taking his employer's goods from the premises without express permission; and it is irrelevant to the matter that a jury may be in doubt whether he intended to steal the stock.

The same criteria apply to employees who are suspected of vandalism:

> *An employee was suspected of committing acts of vandalism at his work place. He was sacked. Subsequently he was acquitted of the criminal charge brought against him. He claimed unfair dismissal. Held: No. The employer was not required to prove that the employee was the vandal – all that the employer had to do was show that he had reasonable grounds for believing the employee to be guilty.* Ferodo (1976)

Normally, an employer should investigate the alleged offence. He is expected to investigate the most obvious and likely explanations of what happened and should do so with an open mind. He should not set out to prove that the employee was guilty, but simply try to gather evidence from the more obvious sources. At the end of the day the industrial tribunal will ask 'Was there anything more a reasonable employer would have done?' A mere suspicion of dishonesty will not justify a sacking. For instance:

> *An anonymous tip-off led to a spot check being carried out on a till-girl who had worked for the firm for many years. There was a £22 shortfall and the girl offered no explanation. So, she was sacked. Held: It was unfair dismissal. There were no reasonable grounds for suspecting her of dishonesty in view of her previous good work-record, and, most important, there had not been a proper investigation.* Peebles (1984)

Criminal convictions for offences outside the employment can sometimes justify dismissal. But the tribunal will want to be sure that the conviction is relevant to the employment. For instance, does it affect the employer's reputation? (As in the case of a shopfitter who was convicted of stealing from one of his employer's customers: it was held that the dismissal was fair.) If the employee is in a position of trust or responsibility then his dismissal is more likely to be fair, but if the offence does not affect the employer's trust in him, it will probably be unfair to dismiss him.

Sexual offences are regarded in a particularly serious light:

> *A bus conductor was sacked following his conviction for gross indecency in an out-of-work incident. His dismissal was held to be fair. The chairman of the tribunal said that the conductor*

'came into close contact with the public and there would be occasions when the bus would be at lonely spots, and it would be understandable if members of the public should be apprehensive of entering buses where he was a bus conductor'. Potts (1978)

The employee is incapable, incompetent, or unqualified

Even if an employee is clearly incompetent, it is important that the employer acts reasonably (see Hurdle No. 4, page 446).

The most difficult cases are those involving employees who are doing their 'incompetent best'. If the employee is not up to the job, then much will depend upon the wording of his employment contract. If he is employed, for instance, to operate a particular machine and is incapable of doing so, then his dismissal is likely to be 'fair'. On the other hand, if his duties are described in a vague, general way, the employer will probably be unable to dismiss him for not being able to operate one type of machine when he can operate other machines that come within his job description.

The employer will generally be expected to do all he can to help the employee. He should be given a chance to improve his performance, and receive encouragement and training from management. He should also be sent a clear warning letter, making it clear that he will be dismissed if his performance does not improve.

But how long a period should the incompetent employee be given in which to 'pull up his socks'? There is no hard-and-fast rule; much will depend upon the seniority of the job, how long the employee has been doing it, and the other surrounding circumstances. In one case, a three-month period was held to be appropriate for a sales director who had been employed for two years; in another case, six months was appropriate for a works director employed for six years. Conversely, in another case involving a works director of six years' standing, a five-week period between warning and dismissal was not enough and so he won his unfair-dismissal claim.

In fact, there is a further problem for employees in this position. If they are not given enough warning (i.e. sufficient time in which to improve performance), then they may well win an unfair-dismissal claim. But, if the tribunal decides that a longer period of warning would have made no difference – because the employee wouldn't have improved his performance sufficiently – then only limited compensation will be awarded. See page 458 for how compensation is assessed (e.g. if he should have received six months' warning but was only given two months', then the compensatory part of the award will only be four months).

If an employee is promoted, he should be given a fair chance to adjust to his new responsibilities. If he cannot cope then he should be offered his old job back, if at all possible. But if all else fails, the employer will be entitled to dismiss him and the dismissal will be fair. It should be emphasized that this is despite the employee not having done anything 'wrong' or otherwise being at fault; that is not how the unfair-dismissal laws work. For instance:

Mr Cook was manager of a non-food depot. After eight years he was promoted to be manager of a food depot despite his having no experience of managing food depots. He could not cope with the new job and so the firm offered him another job as a non-food depot manager, but at the higher

439

food-depot manager rate of pay. He refused on the grounds that it would involve him in inconvenient travel. He claimed unfair dismissal. Held: No. The employers had acted reasonably.
Cook (1977)

What mattered in this case was that the employer had lost confidence in the employee. The Employment Appeals Tribunal commented, 'It is important that the operation of the unfair-dismissal legislation should not impede employers unreasonably in the efficient management of their business.'

If an employee is dismissed for lack of qualifications, the tribunal will want to know when it was decided that he must have the qualifications. If it was decided after he started the job, then the dismissal is likely to be unfair. On the other hand, if he was told before he started work that he would have to obtain certain qualifications, it will probably be fair to dismiss him if he fails to qualify. But, as always, the employer must act 'reasonably' (see Hurdle No. 4, page 446). In short, what would the reasonable employer have done in these circumstances?

Other capability problems, including temperament and ill health

An employee can be efficient and hard-working, and yet have the wrong personality for the job. If so, it may be 'fair' for the employer to dismiss him.

Industrial tribunals approach such cases with great reserve. The tribunal will want to be sure that it is not the employer who is being unreasonable or 'difficult'. Has the employee been asked to mend his ways? Has the problem been explained to him? Is it possible to transfer him to another job? Has he received a formal, written warning? How long has his personality been tolerated without complaint? But there comes a time when the employer can say 'enough is enough'.

Often the dismissal can be justified on the basis of 'some other substantial reason' (see page 445).

Ill health is another area of difficulty. Employers are expected to provide reasonable job security for sick members of staff. Before sacking a sick employee the employer should:

1. Fully investigate the nature of the sickness and how long it is likely to last. The employee should be consulted and given a chance to give his views as to the prospects for recovery.

> *An employee started work as a cold-metal handler in October 1974. In January 1975 he slipped a disc and went off sick. In March 1976 he told his employer that he was expecting to be operated on soon, and that he would then be able to return to light work. On 28 June 1976 he was given his notice, expiring on 11 July 1976. He claimed unfair dismissal. Held: Yes. There was no reason why the firm should not have consulted with him before deciding to sack him. They had not done so, and so it was unfair dismissal.-*
> Williamson (1977)

Only when consultation would be completely pointless – such as when the employee is seriously ill – can the employer dispense with it. For instance:

Mr McInally was a barman at a camp for North Sea oil workers in Shetland. During the six months prior to his dismissal, he suffered from asthenia, which, in the opinion of both the company doctor and his own doctor, made him unfit to carry out his job. Subsequently, he was dismissed without any further consultation by his employers. He claimed unfair dismissal. Held: Further consultation was unnecessary. Since it had been overwhelmingly established that Mr McInally was medically unsuited to the job, consultation was not needed. The purpose of consultation is to establish the facts of the case, and 'if it is clear that the purpose cannot be achieved, the need for a consultation diminishes or disappears'. Taylorplan Catering (1980)

2. Give the employee written notice that the illness, or repeated absence from work, may lead to his dismissal. But, once again, this might not be necessary if the illness is particularly serious.
3. Obtain full information, usually from proper medical reports.
4. Every effort should be made to find alternative work for the sick employee. For instance, if an employee is no longer able to do heavy work the employer should try to find light work for him, if such work is available. But the employer cannot be expected to create a new job for the employee.

An electricity board inspector had worked for the board for thirty-eight years when he was dismissed. He had been absent for all but two weeks during the last year of employment, because of a heart condition. He claimed unfair dismissal, arguing that his employers should have found him suitable alternative work, especially in view of his long service. The judge who heard the appeal said 'no'. 'It cannot be right that . . . an employer can be called upon by the law to create a special job for an employee, however long serving he may have been. On the other hand, each case must depend on its own facts. The circumstances may well be such that the employer may have available light work of the kind which is within the capacity of the employee to do, and the circumstances may make it fair to at least encourage him or to at least offer him the chance of doing that work.' However, on the facts of this case, the employee was not unfairly dismissed. Mryside & N. Wales E.B. (1975)

5. It is not so important to follow these procedures if the employee is often absent owing to unconnected minor ailments, rather than one major illness. This is so even if the unconnected absences are all covered by medical certificates. In such a case, there comes a time when the employer is entitled to say 'enough is enough' and, assuming warnings have been given, he can fairly dismiss the employee.

Mrs Thompson was absent from work for about 25 per cent of her working time. Throughout this period she had numerous minor illnesses. She was given a number of warnings about her attendance record; eventually she was sacked for failing to improve her attendance. She had been given a final warning. She claimed unfair dismissal. Held: No, it was not an unfair dismissal. In cases of this sort, with intermittent illnesses, 'firstly, there should be a fair review by the employers of the attendance record and the reasons for it, and, secondly, appropriate warnings, after the employee has been given an opportunity to make representations. If there is no adequate improvement in the attendance record, it is likely that in most cases the employer will be justified in treating the persistent absences as a sufficient reason for dismissing the employee.' Int. Sports Co. (1980)

The net effect of these rules is that if the employer follows the proper procedure he can fairly dismiss a sick employee unless there is alternative work that could have been offered to the employee. So the sick employee has relatively little job security. To protect himself as much as he can, the sick employee should ensure that he keeps his employer fully informed of the medical position. He should send in sick notes regularly. He should make it clear that he intends to return to work, and that he does not regard the employment as coming to an end. He should also keep in touch with his work-mates so that he can find out if there is any suitable alternative work available in the firm that he could do.

For rules as to sick pay, see page 386; for SSP, see page 387.

Pregnancy

Normally it will not be fair to dismiss a woman because she is pregnant. So the sacked employee will win her unfair-dismissal claim (provided she has worked for two years).

In fact, relatively few employees are dismissed solely because they are pregnant. It is usually a consequence of the pregnancy that causes the employer to sack the woman. For instance, the pregnancy may affect the woman's concentration, it may increase her absenteeism, or it may make it difficult for her to work without frequent rests. Usually, however, the sacked woman can successfully claim unfair dismissal:

An employee who was pregnant was absent from work for a month, because of hypertension brought on by the pregnancy. Held: She had been dismissed for a reason connected with her pregnancy and so the dismissal was unfair. Elegbede (1977)

And this will be so even if the pregnancy is the 'last straw' for the employer:

An employee had a bad absenteeism record. She had been given a verbal warning and also a final written warning that any further absences would lead to her dismissal. She then became pregnant and went into hospital as a result of a miscarriage. Because of this absence from work, she was dismissed. She claimed unfair dismissal. Held: Yes. She had been sacked as a result of the miscarriage, which was a reason connected with her pregnancy. Accordingly, it was unfair. George (1977)

Compare:

An employee was frequently absent owing to ill health and this caused substantial disruption at her work place. She received several warnings from the employer. In April 1979 she was off sick again, and produced a medical certificate in support. On 10 April her supervisor recommended that she be dismissed. On 11 April she phoned to say she was pregnant. On 17 April she sacked. She claimed unfair dismissal on the basis that the principal reason for her dismissal was her pregnancy. Held: No. The employers only learnt of her pregnancy after it had been decided to sack her. Her pregnancy was not the principal reason for her dismissal. Del Monte Foods (1980)

So, generally, a dismissal for a reason connected with a pregnancy will be unfair. However, there are two exceptions to this, when it will be fair for the employer to dismiss the pregnant woman. But even in these cases, the employer must offer the woman another suitable job, if there is one available:

1. If the woman cannot carry on doing her job without breaking the law, it will not

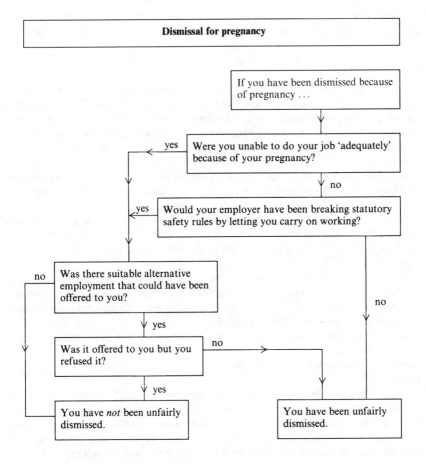

Dismissal for pregnancy

If you have been dismissed because of pregnancy . . .

yes — Were you unable to do your job 'adequately' because of your pregnancy?

no

yes — Would your employer have been breaking statutory safety rules by letting you carry on working?

no — Was there suitable alternative employment that could have been offered to you?

no

yes

Was it offered to you but you refused it? — no

no

yes

You have *not* been unfairly dismissed.

You have been unfairly dismissed.

be unfair to dismiss her. For instance, if her job involves working with radiation levels that could be dangerous to the unborn child.

2. If the woman is incapable of doing her job, or of doing it adequately, the dismissal will not be unfair. In practice, this is the provision that employers use to justify dismissing pregnant women. But it should be noted that the law only requires that the woman be able to do her job 'adequately', which is clearly a lower standard than might otherwise be expected. So, if the woman can show that she is doing a reasonable amount of work, her dismissal would probably be unfair. Also, the 'adequacy' is judged at the time of the dismissal. If the employer rushes in and anticipates that she will become inadequate, it will be unfair dismissal.

Even if the employer can justify the dismissal on one of the above grounds, he still has two more hurdles to cross before he can be sure that the dismissal is fair. Firstly,

443

he must offer the woman a suitable vacancy if one exists in the firm. Secondly, the tribunal will consider whether he acted 'reasonably' (i.e. Hurdle No. 4, page 446).

Industrial action

An employee can be fairly sacked for striking or taking other industrial action while the industrial action is taking place. But he must not be victimized. This means that *all* those striking at the time of the sacking must also be sacked, for otherwise those who are sacked can claim to have been victimized and so unfairly dismissed. Similarly, if all are sacked but some are later given their jobs back, then that too will be victimization, and so the employee(s) not re-employed can bring an unfair-dismissal claim. (But there is a three-month time limit for this rule – so if the employer re-employs some of the strikers, but more than three months after their sacking, then the others will not be able to claim unfair dismissal.)

These victimization rules do not apply only to strikes. They apply to any employees dismissed for industrial action, whether it be a go-slow, a ban on new machinery, or whatever. Unless all the staff involved in the industrial action are dismissed, dismissals may be unfair.

Different rules apply to dismissals that take place after the dispute has been resolved. If an employer sacks a striker after his return to work then the dismissal will have to be justified as being fair. But it may be fair to make former strikers redundant before making 'loyal' employees redundant.

Sometimes an employer will argue that a striking employee has dismissed himself by going on strike, since the strike is in breach of his contract of employment. This argument is totally false – the striking employee is not assumed to have dismissed himself.

Finally, it should be noted that these victimization rules all deal with dismissal (i.e. sacking) – they do not cover less drastic sanctions imposed by an employer. So, docking a day's pay may, for instance, be allowable – since it will not legally count as victimization. In practical terms, therefore, the safeguards that are designed to stop the victimization of those involved in industrial action are of limited effect.

It would be illegal for the employee to do his job

The obvious example of this is the lorry driver who is disqualified from driving. He is thus unable to do his job without breaking the law. His dismissal will therefore probably be fair.

Even so, the tribunal will want to be sure that the decision to sack was a reasonable one (i.e. Hurdle No. 4, page 446). How long would the ban last? Could a temporary replacement be employed? Is there another job that could be given to the employee?

The Hearing Aid Council Act 1968 forbids hearing-aid dispensers from employing unqualified dispensers. An employee who had been a trainee dispenser was sacked after he failed to qualify. He claimed unfair dismissal but the employers argued that the dismissal was fair because it would have been illegal for them to employ him as a dispenser. Held: The employers had not acted reasonably. They could have applied for the employee's training period to be extended and, besides, it was unlikely that they would have been prosecuted. So it was unfair dismissal. Sutcliffe (1977)

There is 'some other substantial reason' justifying the dismissal

This is a catch-all provision. It allows an employer to dismiss an employee when the complaint against him does not fit into any of the normal 'fair' reasons justifying a dismissal.

The courts have not defined what 'some other substantial reason' means. It has deliberately been left vague so that it can continue to be used as a long stop for the unusual cases. It can sometimes be used to justify seemingly hard decisions – as in the case of the fireman who was sacked for refusing to agree to work longer hours under a collective agreement negotiated between his union and his employers. It was held that this was 'some other substantial reason' justifying the dismissal, even though it was accepted that the union could not negotiate as his agent and so bind him to accept the change in his employment contract.

'Some other substantial reason' is often used to justify dismissal when there is an incompatibility between staff. So in one case it made the dismissal of a female employee 'fair' when she had upset her male colleagues by frequently boasting of her sexual exploits with a younger man. In another case it was used to justify the dismissal of an employee in an old people's home whose behaviour upset the aged residents. Another example:

Mr Saunders was a handyman at a children's camp. He was sacked when it was discovered he was a practising homosexual. Mr Saunders argued that he was not interested in young people and was able to keep his private life separate from his work. He claimed unfair dismissal. Held: The dismissal was fair. The tribunal was entitled to find that many employers would feel that the employment of homosexuals should be restricted, especially when they had to work closely with children. Saunders (1981)

In reaching that decision, the Employment Appeals Tribunal made it clear that, in borderline cases, if the employer approaches the matter fairly and properly he cannot be faulted for doing what he considered to be just and proper. Potentially, 'some other substantial reason' can be used to justify a wide range of dismissal. For instance, in one case an employee had been given a wage rise above government guidelines and the firm being threatened with withdrawal of government subsidies. The firm therefore reduced his wages and he resigned. It was held that it was not unfair dismissal.

Occasionally, the tribunals have allowed 'economic necessity' of a firm faced with a crisis to be treated as 'some other substantial reason' justifying dismissal. Staff who have refused to vary their employment contracts to allow more efficient work practices to be introduced have been held to have been fairly dismissed. For instance, see the case of Mr Martin on page 435. Similarly, dismissal may be justified where employers need to reorganize their businesses and an employee refuses to cooperate:

Employment: Unfair Dismissal and Redundancy

Mr Hollister was a local secretary of the farmers' union in Cornwall. His main source of income was commissions from an insurance company. Other local secretaries in Cornwall complained that local secretaries in other parts of the country were able to earn more because they had different insurance commission arrangements. Accordingly, the Cornwall branch agreed to alter the secretaries' contracts of employment so that a new commission scheme could be introduced. Hollister refused to accept the change and was sacked. He claimed unfair dismissal. Held: The dismissal was fair. The reorganization of the business justified the decision to sack him. Hollister (1979)

This was an important decision by the Court of Appeal. The dismissal was held to be fair despite the fact that Mr Hollister was having the terms of his contract of employment changed against his will, and despite the fact that the employers did not carry out the full consultation envisaged by the Code of Practice. The tribunals have made it clear that an employer who has to reorganize his business has little to fear from the unfair-dismissal laws. Thus in one case an employee was sacked for refusing to do voluntary (i.e. not compulsory) overtime and it was held that this was not an unfair dismissal – the needs of the business required that the overtime be worked. Similarly, if the employer comes under pressure from his main customer, then the dismissal will probably be fair – however unfair it may be on the employee. So, in one case a firm of North Sea oil contractors sacked a worker because BP (their main client) wanted the man to be sacked; this was held not to be an unfair dismissal since it had been a 'fair' decision for the employer to make in the light of his business requirements (i.e. the mere fact that it was unfair on the employee did not make it an unfair dismissal).

Hurdle No. 4. Did the employer behave 'reasonably'?

The last hurdle in an unfair-dismissal claim is the 'reasonableness' of the employer's behaviour. Even if the employer has surmounted Hurdle No. 3, and shown that he had a 'fair' reason for the dismissal, he cannot be sure that the dismissal was fair. The industrial tribunal will ask itself whether he acted 'reasonably'.

Of course, if the employer failed to surmount Hurdle No. 3 and was unable to show a 'fair' reason he will have lost the case. There will then be no need to go on and consider whether he acted 'reasonably'.

General guidelines on what is the 'reasonable' behaviour expected of an employer are set out in the various codes of practice published by the Advisory, Conciliation and Arbitration Service. The most important of these codes is the one dealing with disciplinary rules and disciplinary procedures; extracts from it are set out on page 395.

It is important to remember that:

• the decision whether the employer acted reasonably is taken from the employer's point of view. The test is 'What would a reasonable employer have done in these circumstances?' The decision to sack does not have to be fair from the employee's point of view.

• the 'reasonableness' of the decision to sack will occasionally involve a consideration of whether sacking was too severe a penalty. But usually the tribunal will be more concerned to see that the proper procedures are followed.

• the employee must be warned about his conduct in all but the most exceptional cases (e.g. guilty of gross misconduct) or where a warning would have been irrelevant because of the employee's 'irredeemable incapacity'.

• in other cases, consultation may be necessary; for instance, with an employee suffering from long-term sickness. This is also the case when the employer wants to reorganize the business and requires the staff to change the terms of their employment contracts. But in the final analysis, tribunals will not allow the unfair-dismissal legislation to prevent the proper and reasonable reorganization of a business (for instance, see the case of Mr Hollister, page 446).

• generally, the employee must be given a chance to put his side of the story before any decision is made to sack him. But even this may not be necessary if it is obvious that the decision to sack him would have been the same even if he had been allowed to argue his case.

When a proper inquiry would not have made any difference. The Code of Practice sets out the standard of practice and 'reasonableness' expected of employers. When it was first introduced, the code was regarded as the standard expected of all employers, regardless of their circumstances. However, since then, the tribunals have adopted a less rigorous standard. For instance, it is now not unusual for a dismissal to be fair, despite the fact that the proper procedures (e.g. consultation, investigation) were not followed, if the tribunal is satisfied that following the procedures would have made no difference to the eventual decision to sack. In short, if the tribunal feels that dismissal would have resulted even if the employer had followed a proper disciplinary procedure, then the procedural irregularity will probably be ignored. If the procedural shortcomings would have made no difference, then they will probably not make a 'fair' dismissal into an unfair dismissal.

One result of this much-criticized rule has been that the status of the Code of Practice has been undermined. Accordingly, the initial hope that the code would encourage employers to implement a thorough procedure in each and every disciplinary case has not been fulfilled.

Similarly, tribunals are now more ready to take the size and resources of the employing firm into account when deciding whether a dismissal was 'reasonable'. Thus, the code would seem to be no longer the standard required of small firms, but rather an ideal which it is hoped they will eventually attain.

27 Industrial Tribunals: Bringing an Unfair-Dismissal Claim

Industrial tribunals hear virtually all employment law disputes. Most of their work consists of hearing unfair-dismissal and redundancy-payment claims.

The tribunals are designed to be relatively informal and to hear employer/employee disputes with the minimum of cost, delay, and legal formality. To achieve these aims, the tribunals have several important rules:

1. Non-lawyers can represent the parties. So an employer or employee who does not want to act for himself need not instruct a solicitor. Instead he can ask a trade-union official, friend, or other person to act as his advocate.
2. Everybody pays their own legal costs. In other courts, the winner of a case usually has his costs and expenses paid by the loser. But industrial tribunals only award costs in exceptional circumstances. The idea of the no-costs rule is to discourage the use of professional lawyers. In practice, though, employers usually do instruct lawyers, whilst employees often go unrepresented, unless their union provides representation.
3. An unfair-dismissal claim must be made within three months and a redundancy claim must be made within six months.
4. Once the employee has shown that he was 'dismissed' by the employer, it is for the employer to show that the employee is not entitled to an unfair-dismissal or redundancy award. In other words, the burden of proof is, in practice if not in theory, on the employer.
5. The hearing of cases is relatively informal when compared to the procedure in a normal court. Whilst the hearing is not a round-the-table discussion, it will avoid the formalities of a court. In particular, the rules of evidence are less strict and so hearsay and written evidence will usually be allowed.
6. Legal aid is not available. So however poor the employee may be, he cannot get legal aid to finance his claim. However, advice and assistance in filling in the forms and in preparing the case might be available under the green-form scheme (see page 864).

Applying to an industrial tribunal

To claim unfair dismissal, the employee must make his claim within three months of his dismissal. The claim is made by sending in an application form to an industrial tribunal – not to the employer.

The three-month period for claims

The application form must arrive within three months of the dismissal. The tribunal can extend the three-month period, but only when it was 'not reasonably practicable' for the employee to apply in time. The tribunals apply the rules strictly and only allow late claims in exceptional circumstances. The sort of excuse that is likely to be accepted is if the employee has had a serious illness, or if the employer told him to delay starting the industrial-tribunal proceedings because 'we might be able to work something out'. On the other hand, the mere fact that negotiations were taking place, or the fact that the employee had thought he would easily find another job, will not be a reason for extending the time limit – and nor will the employee's ignorance of there being a time limit.

Sometimes the employee does not apply in time because he took advice and was not told that there was a time limit. When this happens, the tribunal will consider the status and qualifications of the person who gave the advice. If it was a 'skilled' adviser (such as a lawyer, trade-union official, or Citizens' Advice Bureau worker) then the late claim may be turned down. The employee will not be able to claim unfair dismissal but he will probably be able to sue the skilled adviser for negligence in giving him bad advice. If the advice came from an 'unskilled' source (such as a work colleague) then a late claim may be allowed.

Before making the claim

To win his claim, the employee will have to show that he was employed for at least two years and also that he was dismissed. It is therefore advisable for him to:

1. Collect together the relevant papers. These will usually include: his letter of appointment, the written particulars of his employment contract, copies of the firm's disciplinary rules and procedures, works rules, and pension booklet; his last wages slip, his P45 form and any letter of dismissal that was sent to him. If necessary he should ask the employer for copies.
2. Ask the employer to provide written reasons for the dismissal. The employer must provide this information (see page 418). The answers will let the employee know how the employer intends to defend the claim. The answers should be checked with any letter of dismissal for any inconsistency.

Filling in the application form

The application form is called an IT 1. Its full title is 'Originating Application to an Industrial Tribunal'. Copies can be obtained, free, from any Job Centre, employment office, or unemployment office.

The IT 1 form is largely self-explanatory. There are only three questions that are worthy of mention:

Employment: Unfair Dismissal and Redundancy

IT 1 question no. 1:
'I hereby apply for a decision of a tribunal on the following question'

Usually the answer will simply be 'whether I was unfairly dismissed and/or I am entitled to a redundancy payment and if so how much'.

IT 1 question no. 12: 'The grounds for the application'

The employee should set out a brief summary of the case. There is no need for him to reveal all the details of his case, but it should provide the employer with enough information to enable him to defend the claim properly.

The employee should remember that the tribunal will look at the IT 1 when it hears his case. They will be looking to see whether he has been consistent in the grounds for his claim, and has not changed his story since filling in the form.

IT 1 question no. 13: '(If dismissed.) If you wish to state what in your opinion was the reason for your dismissal do so here'

Once again the employee should outline the basis of his claim. But he need not reveal all his evidence.

The application form should be sent to the Secretary to the Tribunals, Central Office of the Industrial Tribunals (England and Wales), 93 Ebury Bridge Road, London SW1. For Scotland the address is St Andrew House, 141 West Nile Street, Glasgow. The application will be registered and sent to the employee's local tribunal, who will acknowledge receipt of his IT 1. It is vital that the form arrives within the three-month period.

The employer's response

A copy of the IT 1 is sent to the employer. He then has fourteen days in which to reply to the claim. Usually, this is done by filling in form IT 3 (sent to the employer with the IT 1).

The employer must first decide whether he intends to argue that there was no dismissal – perhaps because the employee resigned. But often the employer will admit that there was a dismissal, going on to argue that it was a 'fair' dismissal.

The employer will need to take great care in stating the reason for the dismissal. The reason given on the IT 3 should be the same as the reason originally given to the worker when he was dismissed or when he was supplied with written reasons for the dismissal. For instance, suppose the original reason was bad timekeeping, but the employer now gives the reason as insubordination. If this happens the tribunal will be suspicious of the employer's consistency and, in addition, it may well decide that the employer never gave the employee a chance to answer the insubordination charge. If that were so, the employer would not have acted 'reasonably' and so the dismissal would be unfair.

Industrial Tribunals: Bringing an Unfair Dismissal Claim

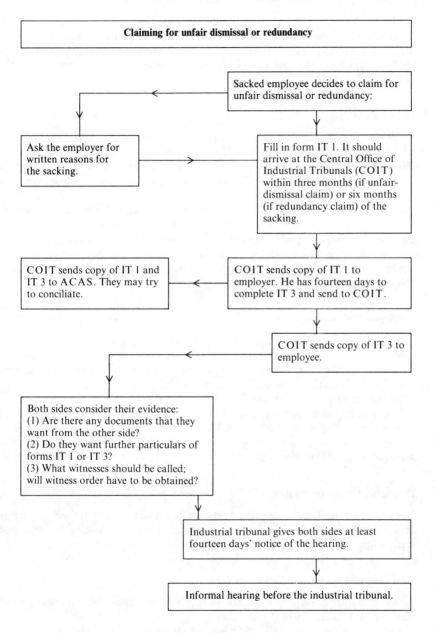

Claiming for unfair dismissal or redundancy

Sacked employee decides to claim for unfair dismissal or redundancy:

Ask the employer for written reasons for the sacking.

Fill in form IT 1. It should arrive at the Central Office of Industrial Tribunals (COIT) within three months (if unfair-dismissal claim) or six months (if redundancy claim) of the sacking.

COIT sends copy of IT 1 and IT 3 to ACAS. They may try to conciliate.

COIT sends copy of IT 1 to employer. He has fourteen days to complete IT 3 and send to COIT.

COIT sends copy of IT 3 to employee.

Both sides consider their evidence:
(1) Are there any documents that they want from the other side?
(2) Do they want further particulars of forms IT 1 or IT 3?
(3) What witnesses should be called; will witness order have to be obtained?

Industrial tribunal gives both sides at least fourteen days' notice of the hearing.

Informal hearing before the industrial tribunal.

The employer should also check whether he gave the employee a reference. If so, he should make sure that the reference is not inconsistent with what is said to be the reason for the dismissal. For instance, if the reference describes the employee as 'reliable and hard-working' the employer can hardly give 'incompetence' as the reason for his dismissal.

Conciliation

A copy of the IT 1 is also sent to a conciliation officer of the Advisory, Conciliation and Arbitration Service. He will try to negotiate a settlement if asked to by either employer or employee, or if he himself 'considers that he could act with a reasonable prospect of success'. He will ask both employer and employee whether he can help by conciliating. There is no obligation on either to discuss the case with the conciliation officer or to cooperate with him in any way. The tribunal will not be told of a refusal to cooperate. Any information given to the conciliation officer is confidential, so there is no danger of it being revealed to the tribunal.

Generally, it is sensible to use the conciliation officer's service. He can provide objective advice (but he will not say if an offer is high enough!) and can have a calming influence on injured feelings.

Settling out of court

Many claims are settled without the case being heard by a tribunal. However, a settlement will not be binding on the employee unless it is approved beforehand by a conciliation officer. This is so even if the employee signs a receipt that he accepts the offer 'in full and final settlement' of his claim.

So any settlement – whether or not it is negotiated through the conciliation officer – should be approved by a conciliation officer. This is so even if the claim is settled before the employee has sent off his IT 1. If the employee should renege on an unapproved settlement and then go on to win his claim, the tribunal will deduct the settlement figure from his compensation.

Preparing for the hearing

Both employer and employee should prepare their cases well in advance. To do this they will want to find out as much as they can about each other's evidence and arguments.

Obtaining all the relevant documents

Either employer or employee can ask for copies of the other's relevant documents. This is called 'discovery of documents'.

For instance, an employee could ask for his personnel file, copies of internal memos, time and motion studies, time sheets, disciplinary records, disciplinary letters sent to him, and the employer's note of what happened at any disciplinary meeting or appeal. He could also ask for a copy of the written particulars of his employment contract (or the employment contract itself, if it was in writing) should he have mislaid his own copy.

An employer might ask to be given copies of sick notes, medical reports, and details of the employee's efforts to find a new job.

In short, any document that is relevant can be asked for. To obtain discovery of documents the employer or employee should first write to the other, setting out the documents required. If the letter is ignored, or the request is refused, the next step is to write to the secretary to the tribunal enclosing a copy of the previous letter and asking that an order be made. Normally, the order will be made without the need for a hearing.

Obtaining further particulars

Either employer or employee can ask for more detail of the other's case. This is done by asking for 'further and better particulars' of the answers given on forms I T 1 and I T 3.

For instance, suppose an employer's I T 3 states that the employee was unable to cope satisfactorily with his duties and that his attitude to the job was wrong. In such a case, the employee can ask for more information – 'In what way is it alleged that I could not cope with my duties'? and 'In what way is it alleged that my attitude to the job was wrong'? The employer will then have to reply with specific instances.

It is often advisable for an employee to ask for further and better particulars to show whether the employer followed the proper disciplinary procedures. If he did not, he may not have acted 'reasonably' and so he may lose the case.

It will therefore often be useful for an employee to ask 'State the date and nature of any warnings that were given to me, by whom they were made, and in whose presence. State when the decision to dismiss me was taken and by whom. State when I was advised that I could appeal against the decision, and by whom.' Questions of this sort can tie the employer down and cause him considerable difficulties.

Applying for 'further and better particulars' is done in the same way as applying for discovery of documents.

Witnesses

It is helpful to go through a witness's evidence with him before the hearing. But a witness cannot be made to cooperate. Although he can be forced to attend the tribunal hearing, he is under no obligation to speak to either employer or employee before the hearing.

The witnesses should be asked to attend voluntarily, without a *witness order* being made. But sometimes it will help the witness if he is ordered to attend. For instance, a shop steward will be reluctant to attend to give evidence for the employer since it may put him in an embarrassing position with his members. By obtaining a witness order, the employer allows the shop steward to say that he had no choice but to attend.

To obtain a witness order the employer or employee should write to the industrial tribunal stating that the witness is unwilling to attend without an order, and also explaining why his evidence is required. The tribunal will normally make the witness order and it will then be for the employer or employee to serve it on the witness. If there is any doubt about the witness being willing to attend, the order should be handed to him in person (not posted). He should also be offered *conduct money* – enough money to cover his travel to and from the hearing.

Working out how much the case is worth

Both sides should decide how much the claim is worth. Many claims are settled at the last minute, often a few minutes before the hearing is due to start. So both employer and employee should know the figure (if any) at which they would be prepared to settle.

In many claims the real issues in dispute will be

* did the employee contribute to his own dismissal?
* has the employee done all he can to reduce his losses?

The employee should therefore go prepared to fight both these suggestions. In particular, he should have written evidence of his efforts to find a new job and the number of interviews he has attended, as well as receipts for all his expenses.

The pre-hearing assessment

Sometimes there will be a preliminary hearing before the case is properly heard. This is an informal hearing designed to weed out the hopeless cases.

A preliminary hearing is not held in every case. It can be held either at the request of one of the parties (usually the employer) or if the tribunal thinks such a hearing would be useful. No evidence is heard and the tribunal members consider the merits of the case on the basis of the originating application (IT 1) and notice of appearance (IT 3). They cannot prevent the applicant from continuing with his claim, nor can he give judgement. However, they can advise either party as to the weakness of a case and remind them that costs can be awarded at the tribunal hearing if the claim (or defence) is 'without merit'.

Indirectly, therefore, hopeless claims are warned off.

The hearing of the claim

Both employer and employee will be given at least fourteen days' notice of the hearing. Both should ensure that their witnesses can attend on that date; if they can't, then the hearing should be postponed.

Who speaks first?

The hearing usually begins with the tribunal chairman making a short introductory speech and then asking both sides to make an 'opening statement'. The idea is that the tribunal, and the other side, should have an idea of what each party will say and the evidence that will be produced. The case then begins in earnest.

Who speaks first will depend upon whether 'dismissal' is at issue. If the employer denies that the employee was 'dismissed' (for instance, it could be argued that he resigned) then the employee presents his case first and calls his witnesses. But if the employer admits that the employee was 'dismissed' then the issue to be decided is whether the dismissal was 'unfair'. So, in that case, the employer presents his case first and calls his witnesses.

When a witness has given his evidence he can be cross-examined by the other side, as in any court case. But the normal rules of evidence are relaxed in tribunal hearings. Thus *hearsay* evidence is allowed (e.g. 'John told me he had seen Brian hit the foreman' will be allowed, although it would still be better to call John to describe what he saw).

Written evidence is also acceptable. But the tribunal will prefer the evidence of a witness in person to that of a written statement, since there can be no cross-examination of what is said in a written document.

The employee should be sure to take all relevant documents to the hearing, such as:

- contract of employment
- pay details (e.g. wage slips, P 60)
- details of fringe benefits (e.g. luncheon vouchers, use of car, travelling expenses)
- pension and superannuation documents
- details of income tax refunds received
- particulars of unemployment benefit received
- receipts and documents connected with expenses in looking for a new job (e.g. travel expenses, household removal expenses).

The decision

When both sides have presented their evidence they will be allowed to make concluding statements. Then the members of the tribunal will retire and probably announce their decision a few minutes later. In complicated cases the tribunal may *reserve* its decision, which means that the parties will be sent a written decision at a later date.

Costs

Each party will normally have to pay his own legal costs (if any) whether he wins or loses. Only when a party has acted *frivolously, vexatiously,* or *unreasonably* will costs be awarded against him. For instance, an employee who presses on with a claim despite being warned at a pre-hearing assessment that the case is hopeless, might well have to pay some of the employer's legal costs.

In addition, costs and expenses can be awarded when a postponement was asked for without good reason. For instance, if the employer turns up at the hearing and then decides that he wants to be legally represented, the tribunal might agree to a postponement but order him to pay the employee's wasted costs. But even these orders are rare.

Limited expenses, however, are often ordered for the parties and their witnesses. The expenses of representatives are only allowed if the representative was not a lawyer or a full-time trade-union or employers' association official.

Anyone thinking of bringing an unfair-dismissal claim should read *Industrial Tribunals Procedure* (free from the Department of Employment or COIT). Another useful book is *Industrial Tribunals: Preparing and Presenting Your Case*, by J. Angel (Tolley, 1984; £14.95).

28 Winning an Unfair-Dismissal Claim

If an employee wins his unfair-dismissal claim, the industrial tribunal can make one of three orders:

1. That he be re-employed by the employer and given his old job back (reinstatement).
2. That he be re-employed by the employer, but given a different job (re-engagement).
3. That he be paid a cash sum.

The decision on which order to make will depend on the wishes of the employee and the circumstances of the case. The tribunal will explain the differences between the three remedies and ask the employee which one he would prefer.

1. Reinstatement in his old job

If the employee asks for his old job back, the tribunal will consider whether it would be practicable and also whether the justice of the situation would make it fair on the employer. For instance, if the employee's own behaviour contributed to his dismissal, the tribunal might well decide it would be unfair on the employer to insist on reinstatement.

The 'practicability' of reinstatement can include such matters as harmony in the work place and the feelings of the other staff. The fact that the employer has taken on a replacement for the dismissed employee can also be relevant, but usually the employer will have to show that he did not realize the employee would ask for the job back. This is why it is advisable for an employee to ask for reinstatement when he fills in the unfair-dismissal application form.

However, in practice, reinstatement is virtually never ordered.

2. Re-employment, but in a different job

This can be ordered by the tribunal at the request of the employee, but only if the job is suitable and the terms and conditions are comparable to those of the employee's old job.

Similar considerations arise as with an order for reinstatement. In practice, it is virtually never ordered.

3. Cash compensation

A cash award is made in over 99 per cent of successful claims.
The total cash sum will be made up of two separate amounts:
- the *basic* award   (up to £4,560).
- the *compensatory* award   (up to £8,000).

In practice, few awards reach these maximum figures; £500 or so is a typical award. The award will be tax-free.

Calculating the basic award

The basic award gives the employee the amount of redundancy payment he would have received if he had been made redundant instead. The size of the redundancy payment (and thus the basic award) will depend upon the age of the employee, the length of his service, and the amount of his weekly net wage. He will receive a certain number of weeks' wages depending on his age and length of service. The table on page 459 sets out how the award is calculated.

The maximum award is thirty weeks' wages. However, an additional restriction is imposed because the maximum net wage allowed is £152 p.w. (1985/86).

Illustration. *Mr Jones earns £65 p.w. net. He is aged twenty-four and has worked with the firm for two years. His basic award is thus two weeks' wages (see table), i.e. 2×65=£130.*

Illustration. *Mr Smith earns £180 p.w. net. He is now aged fifty-five and has been with his employers for seventeen years. His basic award is thus twenty-four weeks' wages (see table), but up to a maximum of £152 p.w., i.e. 24×152=£3,648.*

However, the tribunal can reduce the basic award if it is felt that the employee's own conduct contributed to his dismissal. For instance, if the employer had a fair reason for dismissing him, but failed to follow the proper procedures, the employee might win the case, but forfeit some (or all) of his compensation because of his behaviour. Similarly, the award can be reduced if he unreasonably refuses an offer of his job back. See 'When the Employee's Behaviour Reduces the Compensation', page 460.

Employees near retirement age. An employee who is within one year of state retirement age will lose one twelfth of his/her compensation for each whole month after his/her birthday. (e.g. a woman aged fifty-nine years and three months will lose a quarter of her award).

The basic award will also be reduced by any amount that the employee has received as a redundancy payment. So an employee who is unfairly selected for redundancy would normally receive no basic award.

Calculating the compensatory award

This is intended to cover the employee's losses resulting from his dismissal. The maximum award is £8,000.

Compensation for unfair dismissal: how many weeks' wages?

Age (years)	Service (years) 2	3	4	5	6	7	8	9	10	11	12	13	14	15	16	17	18	19	20
20	1	1	1	1															
21	1	1½	1½	1½	1½														
22	1	1½	2	2	2	2													
23	1½	2	2½	3	3	3	3												
24	2	2½	3	3½	4	4	4	4											
25	2	3	3½	4	4½	5	5	5	5										
26	2	3	4	4½	5	5½	6	6	6	6									
27	2	3	4	5	5½	6	6½	7	7	7	7								
28	2	3	4	5	6	6½	7	7½	8	8	8	8							
29	2	3	4	5	6	7	7½	8	8½	9	9	9	9						
30	2	3	4	5	6	7	8	8½	9	9½	10	10	10	10					
31	2	3	4	5	6	7	8	9	9½	10	10½	11	11	11	11				
32	2	3	4	5	6	7	8	9	10	10½	11	11½	12	12	12	12			
33	2	3	4	5	6	7	8	9	10	11	11½	12	12½	13	13	13	13		
34	2	3	4	5	6	7	8	9	10	11	12	12½	13	13½	14	14	14	14	
35	2	3	4	5	6	7	8	9	10	11	12	13	13½	14	14½	15	15	15	15
36	2	3	4	5	6	7	8	9	10	11	12	13	14	14½	15	15½	16	16	16
37	2	3	4	5	6	7	8	9	10	11	12	13	14	15	15½	16	16½	17	17
38	2	3	4	5	6	7	8	9	10	11	12	13	14	15	16	16½	17	17½	18
39	2	3	4	5	6	7	8	9	10	11	12	13	14	15	16	17	17½	18	18½
40	2	3	4	5	6	7	8	9	10	11	12	13	14	15	16	17	18	18½	19
41	2	3	4	5	6	7	8	9	10	11	12	13	14	15	16	17	18	19	19½
42	2½	3½	4½	5½	6½	7½	8½	9½	10½	11½	12½	13½	14½	15½	16½	17½	18½	19½	20½
43	3	4	5	6	7	8	9	10	11	12	13	14	15	16	17	18	19	20	21
44	3	4½	5½	6½	7½	8½	9½	10½	11½	12½	13½	14½	15½	16½	17½	18½	19½	20½	21½
45	3	4½	6	7	8	9	10	11	12	13	14	15	16	17	18	19	20	21	22
46	3	4½	6	7½	8½	9½	10½	11½	12½	13½	14½	15½	16½	17½	18½	19½	20½	21½	22½
47	3	4½	6	7½	9	10	11	12	13	14	15	16	17	18	19	20	21	22	23
48	3	4½	6	7½	9	10½	11½	12½	13½	14½	15½	16½	17½	18½	19½	20½	21½	22½	23½
49	3	4½	6	7½	9	10½	12	13	14	15	16	17	18	19	20	21	22	23	24
50	3	4½	6	7½	9	10½	12	13½	14½	15½	16½	17½	18½	19½	20½	21½	22½	23½	24½
51	3	4½	6	7½	9	10½	12	13½	15	16	17	18	19	20	21	22	23	24	25
52	3	4½	6	7½	9	10½	12	13½	15	16½	17½	18½	19½	20½	21½	22½	23½	24½	25½
53	3	4½	6	7½	9	10½	12	13½	15	16½	18	19	20	21	22	23	24	25	26
54	3	4½	6	7½	9	10½	12	13½	15	16½	18	19½	20½	21½	22½	23½	24½	25½	26½
55	3	4½	6	7½	9	10½	12	13½	15	16½	18	19½	21	22	23	24	25	26	27
56	3	4½	6	7½	9	10½	12	13½	15	16½	18	19½	21	22½	23½	24½	25½	26½	27½
57	3	4½	6	7½	9	10½	12	13½	15	16½	18	19½	21	22½	24	25	26	27	28
58	3	4½	6	7½	9	10½	12	13½	15	16½	18	19½	21	22½	24	25½	26½	27½	28½
59	3	4½	6	7½	9	10½	12	13½	15	16½	18	19½	21	22½	24	25½	27	28	29
60	3	4½	6	7½	9	10½	12	13½	15	16½	18	19½	21	22½	24	25½	27	28½	29½
61	3	4½	6	7½	9	10½	12	13½	15	16½	18	19½	21	22½	24	25½	27	28½	30
62	3	4½	6	7½	9	10½	12	13½	15	16½	18	19½	21	22½	24	25½	27	28½	30
63	3	4½	6	7½	9	10½	12	13½	15	16½	18	19½	21	22½	24	25½	27	28½	30
64	3	4½	6	7½	9	10½	12	13½	15	16½	18	19½	21	22½	24	25½	27	28½	30

Men only { 60, 61, 62, 63, 64 }

The compensatory award will usually be made up of:

(a) *Lost earnings to the date of the hearing.* This is the net wage loss. It is the amount that the employee would have received had he carried on working, after allowing for tax, national insurance, other deductions, and also any earnings from his new job (if any). If the employee was not paid during the period of notice (see page 415), then he should receive full compensation for those lost wages – even if he found another job and so did not suffer any actual loss during the notice period. But once the notice period ends, other earnings are taken into account. *For example:* An employee should have been given four weeks' notice, but is sacked on the spot. His wages were £100 p.w. but he gets another job paying £70 p.w. for a period of seven weeks, after which he gets another job paying £100 p.w. His lost earnings will be £490 (i.e. 4 × £100, plus 3 × £30).

(b) *Future loss of earnings.* If the employee is still out of work, or if he has taken on a new job at a lower wage, he will have a continuing wage loss. Tribunals are generally reluctant to apply strict mathematical calculations when working out the loss, and will only rarely allow more than five years' loss. In practice, tribunals tend to round down rather than round up, and so employees receive less compensation than a strictly mathematical calculation would entitle them to.

If the tribunal feels that the employee has not done all he could to 'mitigate his loss' (i.e. keep his losses to a minimum) it will usually reduce the award. Thus a tribunal will often decide that an employee should have made greater efforts to find another job or that he should have accepted a lower rate of pay (as in a wrongful-dismissal claim, see page 417).

(c) *Loss of his employment protection rights.* The employee will have lost the right to notice built up by the length of his service. He will also have lost the other employment protection rights which are only given to staff who have worked for qualifying periods (see the table on pages 376–7). For instance, the employee will have no entitlement to redundancy payments in his new job until he has worked there for two years. The standard way of calculating this is to award half the value of the minimum statutory notice period that the employee has accrued. *For example:* An employee has worked for eight years and now earns £140 p.w. He is entitled to eight weeks' notice – see page 415 – and so the likely compensation is £560 (i.e. 4 × £140).

(d) *Expenses in looking for work.* Looking for a new job can be expensive. Travel, phone calls, advertisements, and subscriptions to trade journals can all be expenses arising from the dismissal. Sometimes the cost of moving home to take up a new job will be recoverable in part (£500 is not an uncommon award).

When the employee's behaviour reduces the compensation

The industrial tribunal can reduce the basic award and the compensation if it is felt that the employee's behaviour contributed to his dismissal. The courts have not laid down any guidelines as to what is conduct justifying a reduction in the amount of the award. In practice, the tribunal has a considerable discretion and the 'contributory fault' rule will often be used to reduce an employee's compensation to what the tribunal members regard as being reasonable. This is all part of the rough-and-ready approach that tribunals take when calculating compensation.

The contributory fault need not amount to a deliberate act by the employee, although he must have been blameworthy or culpable. But he can be found to have contributed to his dismissal even when he did not mean to exacerbate the situation.

An employee won his unfair-dismissal claim but had his compensation reduced by 40 per cent because his character and personality had contributed to his dismissal. He appealed, saying that his character and personality were beyond his control and so shouldn't be taken into account. Held: The tribunal acted correctly in reducing the award by 40 per cent. Moncur (1978)

Only exceptionally will contributory fault exceed 80 per cent. But it can be as much as 100 per cent.

The employee was dismissed unfairly. Shortly after his dismissal the employers discovered that he had been taking secret commissions from the customers. He won his unfair-dismissal claim but he received nothing because the contributory fault was assessed at 100 per cent. W. Devis & Sons (1977)

Similarly, if the employer offers to give the employee his job back, but the employee unreasonably refuses to accept, the compensation can be reduced by whatever percentage the tribunal thinks fair. But in this instance, it is only the basic award that can be reduced; the compensatory award cannot be reduced.

Because of the contributory-fault rule, an employee bringing an unfair-dismissal claim should be ready to rebut all allegations that his employers may make against him. The problem is that if the employer makes enough allegations against him, the tribunal may eventually believe some of them, and so reduce his award.

Extra cash in exceptional cases

Occasionally, the employer will have to make an additional cash payment to the employee. This happens when a tribunal has ordered the employer to re-engage or reinstate the employee, but the employer has not done so. The employer can be ordered to pay extra compensation of between thirteen and twenty-six weeks' wages. If the refusal to re-employ is because of sexual or racial discrimination, the extra compensation is between twenty-six and fifty-two weeks' wages. (As usual, there is a maximum rate of £152 p.w.) Exceptionally, the employee may be entitled to even more compensation – if it is a trade-union-related case (i.e. because he was – or was not – a member of a union; or, because of union activities). Special rules apply but the minimum award is £2,100 plus compensation of up to £12,560 (or, exceptionally, 104 weeks' wages, up to a maximum of £33,560 if greater).

Enforcing the cash award

Both employer and employee have six weeks in which to appeal against the tribunal's decision. Once that period has expired, and if no appeal has been made, the employee can sue the employer for the cash owed. If the employer does not pay up, the employee should sue in the civil courts in the usual way for any debt. The claim will be brought in the county court, unless it exceeds £5,000, when it will be in the High Court.

Criticisms of the unfair-dismissal legislation

The major weakness of the legislation is its technicality, which makes it difficult for both employer and employee to know just what the law is. As the president of the Employment Appeals Tribunal has said: 'Unfair dismissal is in no sense a common-sense expression capable of being understood by the man in the street . . . In fact, it is narrowly, and to some extent, arbitrarily, defined.' But it is difficult to see how this complexity can be avoided. The alternative is to scrap the detailed rules and give the tribunals a greater discretion, but at the price of even greater uncertainty as to the law.

Many people argue that the cash awards made by tribunals are too low. Although in theory the awards can run into thousands of pounds, typical awards are well below £1,000. Certainly there are arguments for increasing the amount of the basic award.

Some of the rules as to who is excluded from the legislation are rather arbitrary (see pages 376–7). The exclusion of part-time workers effectively ensures that many women workers have no unfair-dismissal rights. The exclusion of those past retirement age, whilst perfectly logical, often causes a sense of grievance.

Is it fair that employees should have to be employed for two years before they come within the legislation? Why have any qualifying period? The present two-year rule encourages employers to sack staff after one hundred and three weeks and replace them with other temporary staff. This is especially true in the hotel and catering trades.

Even if an employee is within the legislation, will he bother to use it to enforce his rights? There are two disincentives:

1. There is no legal aid for industrial tribunal cases. If he does not have a trade union that will act for him, he will have to act for himself or pay a solicitor to represent him. Many employees are reluctant to act for themselves, and since the sacked employee may well have financial problems, and be living on state benefits, he will be in no position to instruct a solicitor, so incurring legal costs.
2. If he is legally represented, and wins the case, he will not have his legal costs paid by his employer. They will have to come out of his compensation.

Employers also have their criticisms of the legislation. Many argue that it is too easy for an employee to bring an unfair-dismissal claim. They suggest there should be a small registration fee to deter the cranks and those with hopeless cases. Some would like to see the losing employee paying part of the employer's legal costs.

The cost to an employer of defending a claim can be considerable. Apart from the expense of legal fees, the employer may have senior staff and personnel wasting time at the hearing of the case as they wait to give evidence.

Sometimes an employer will decide it is cheaper to 'buy off' the claim, rather than go to the expense and inconvenience of defending it. In short, they argue that they are being blackmailed into settling hopeless cases for their 'nuisance value'. Against this it can fairly be said that many employers incur lawyers' fees unnecessarily, when they could easily defend the case themselves or through a member of staff.

29 Redundancy Payments

The redundancy-payments scheme was introduced in 1965, to compensate redundant workers for the loss of their jobs. This simple aim was initially frustrated by a series of court decisions that applied a narrow, restrictive interpretation to the key sections of the legislation. However, in recent years, most of these difficulties have been overcome, although the redundancy-payments scheme remains a highly technical and complex form of compensation. The modern law is set out in the Employment Protection (Consolidation) Act 1978.

Apart from giving the employee some 'property' rights in his job, the redundancy-payments scheme was also designed to increase job mobility by cushioning the financial effects of redundancy. However, it seems unlikely that the scheme has encouraged mobility of labour, because the mere fact that an employer might have to make a redundancy payment is likely to encourage him to retain his staff rather than to make them redundant.

What is needed for a successful claim?

There are three hurdles that need to be met by an employee who wants to claim a redundancy payment:

Hurdle No. 1. Is he within the redundancy-payments legislation, or is he ineligible?
Hurdle No. 2. Has he been 'dismissed' by his employer?
Hurdle No. 3. Was he dismissed because he was 'redundant'?

Once the employee has cleared the first two hurdles, it is for the employer to show that the employee was *not* dismissed because of redundancy. The burden of proof is on the employer; if he cannot show that it was not a redundancy situation, then he will lose the claim.

If the employee's claim is successful, he is entitled to a cash sum, the amount of which varies with his age and the length of his service with the employer. It is irrelevant that he may have obtained another job, even if it is better paid. He is being compensated for the loss of his job – not for a period of unemployment.

Hurdle No.1. Is the employee within the redundancy-payments scheme?

Not all employees are eligible. Part-timers and those near retirement age are

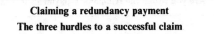

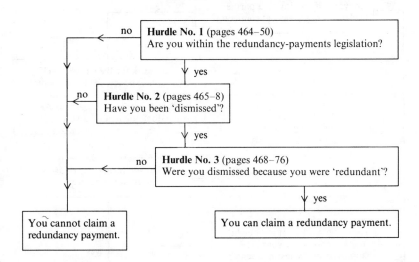

Claiming a redundancy payment
The three hurdles to a successful claim

no → **Hurdle No. 1** (pages 464–50)
Are you within the redundancy-payments legislation?

↓ yes

no → **Hurdle No. 2** (pages 465–8)
Have you been 'dismissed'?

↓ yes

no → **Hurdle No. 3** (pages 468–76)
Were you dismissed because you were 'redundant'?

↓ yes

You cannot claim a redundancy payment.

You can claim a redundancy payment.

amongst those specifically excluded. For full details of ineligible employees see the table on pages 376–7 and the chart on page 466.

In practice, the most important restraint on eligibility is the two-year qualifying period. An employee can only claim a payment if he has been continuously employed, by the employer, for at least two years (note: it is the same period as for an unfair-dismissal claim – see page 426).

The two-year qualification period is therefore the same as with an unfair-dismissal claim – two years.

Hurdle No. 2. Has the employee been 'dismissed' by the employer?

A redundancy payment can only be claimed if the employee has been 'dismissed'. In law, 'dismissal' is not restricted to sackings, but also covers the situation where an employee has been forced to resign because of the conduct of his employer ('constructive dismissal', see page 430). Generally, for the legal meaning of 'dismissal', see 'Unfair Dismissal' (page 427), where similar principles apply. Do not forget that a person with a fixed-term contract will count as having been 'dismissed' if he is not offered a new contract:

> *Mr Lee was taken on as a temporary lecturer in a teacher-training college for one year. At the end of that year he was offered another one year's employment, although he realized that the declining number of students would mean that his services would not be needed in the future. At*

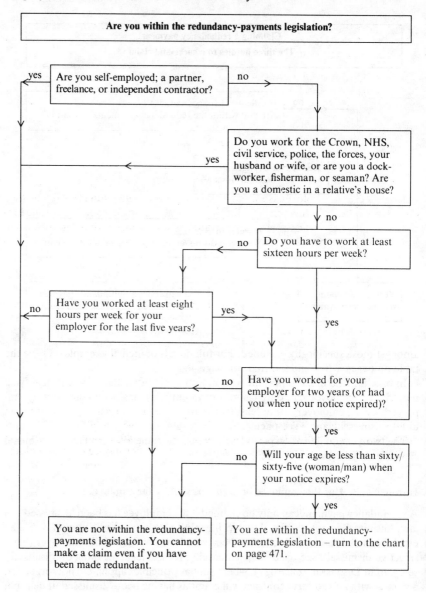

Are you within the redundancy-payments legislation?

yes — Are you self-employed; a partner, freelance, or independent contractor?   no

Do you work for the Crown, NHS, civil service, police, the forces, your husband or wife, or are you a dock-worker, fisherman, or seaman? Are you a domestic in a relative's house?   yes

no — Do you have to work at least sixteen hours per week?   no

Have you worked at least eight hours per week for your employer for the last five years?   yes

no

Have you worked for your employer for two years (or had you when your notice expired)?   no

yes

Will your age be less than sixty/sixty-five (woman/man) when your notice expires?   no

yes

You are not within the redundancy-payments legislation. You cannot make a claim even if you have been made redundant.

You are within the redundancy-payments legislation – turn to the chart on page 471.

the end of the second year he was not offered a new contract. He claimed redundancy payment. Held: The failure to offer him a new contract amounted to a 'dismissal' and so he could claim a redundancy payment. Notts CC (1980)

If the employee is not dismissed he will not be able to claim a redundancy payment. So it is important that an employee does not anticipate his dismissal by resigning before he is dismissed. If he does he will be unable to claim a payment:

The employee was told by his employers that the department in which he worked would be closed down some time in the future. The employee therefore began to look for other work, and when he had arranged another job he left, and claimed a redundancy payment. Held: No. He had not been dismissed by his employers and so he could not claim a redundancy payment, since they had not told him exactly when his department would be closed down. Morton Sundour Fabrics (1967)

However, if an employee is told that there is a redundancy situation and he then agrees to be made redundant, this will not prevent him from claiming redundancy pay. The mere fact that he agrees to the redundancy does not stop it being a dismissal. This also applies to 'volunteers' for redundancy as long as the employer then dismisses them. But:

Liverpool University wrote to its staff saying that cut-backs had to be made and that 300 posts would have to be lost within the next few years. Staff were also reminded that there was an early-retirement compensation scheme, which gave generous benefits if the job was ended by mutual consent of both employer and employee. Some of the staff decided to opt for early retirement under this scheme and they then claimed normal redundancy payments as well. Held: No, they were not entitled to redundancy payments – since they had not been 'dismissed'. The jobs had been ended by mutual agreement, not by dismissal. Liverpool Univ. (1984)

Leaving during the notice period

If an employee has been given notice, and so been dismissed, he need not always work out the period of notice. Provided he gives the employer notice, he can leave early. However, the employer can, in turn, serve a counter-notice on the employee demanding that the employee work out his period of notice or otherwise risk jeopardizing his redundancy claim. If the employee ignores that counter-notice, he can still claim a redundancy payment, but an industrial tribunal might reduce the amount of the payment if it is decided that he acted 'unreasonably'.

The employee must comply with two requirements if his notice is to be valid. Both rules are illustrated by this case:

An employee was given four and a half weeks' notice, although under the statutory rules as to notice (see page 415) he was only entitled to two weeks. The employee found another job and gave his employers oral notice a week after they had given him notice of his dismissal. Held: He was ineligible for redundancy because:

● *the notice to his employers should have been in writing, not oral; and*

● *the notice to his employers had to be served during the statutory period of notice (i.e. the last two weeks). He had served the notice before the statutory period had started and so the notice was invalid.* Lobb (1966)

Employment: Unfair Dismissal and Redundancy

Clearly these rules as to the employee's notice are unnecessarily complicated and are a pitfall for the unwary. Full details are in section 85 of the 1978 Act.

The effect of misconduct and industrial action

An employee may jeopardize his redundancy rights if he is in breach of his employment contract by misbehaving at work or by taking part in industrial action.

The effect of his breach of contract will depend upon whether it takes place before he is dismissed:

• *misconduct and/or strikes before the redundancy is announced* will cause the employee to forfeit his right to a redundancy payment;

• *misconduct and/or strikes after the redundancy is announced* will not necessarily cause the employee to forfeit his redundancy payment. However, an industrial tribunal will only award him what it regards as a 'just and equitable' amount, so the gravity of his breach of contract – and the circumstances in which it occurred – will determine the amount he receives.

The rules on striking against redundancy are complicated and they are a pitfall for the unwary. Workers should take expert advice – but bear in mind that dismissal of all the strikers will not be unfair dismissal (see page 444), so they clearly run the risk of forfeiting both redundancy and unfair-dismissal entitlements.

Hurdle No. 3. Has the dismissed employee been made redundant?

In a redundancy claim, an industrial tribunal will assume that the employee was 'redundant' unless the employer can show otherwise.

Usually it is easy to decide whether an employee has been made redundant. The simple test that will normally answer the question is to ask 'Has the dismissed employee been replaced by another employee?' If he has, it will not be redundancy. If he has not, then it will probably be redundancy.

But this test will not cover every situation. It is possible for an employee not to be replaced and yet not be redundant:

Mr Hindle was a craftsman with a lifetime's experience of boat building. But his employers decided that he was 'too good and too slow' for their requirements. So he was dismissed. No replacement was taken on, but the remaining employees worked overtime to make up for the loss of his services. Held: This was not redundancy. The employer had shown that redundancy was not the reason for the dismissal and that was sufficient to defeat Mr Hindle's claim. The Court of Appeal said, 'All an employer must do is to prove that redundancy was not the main cause and he does this by proving that the requirements of the business for workers of the relevant kind had not diminished. It is not the policy of this Act to reward long service and good conduct, as such, but only to compensate an employee who is dismissed for redundancy.' Hindle (1969)

Note that this decision was reached in 1969, some two years before the unfair-dismissal legislation was introduced. There can be little doubt that if Mr Hindle was dismissed in the same way today, he would be able to claim unfair dismissal and so recover compensation from his employers. This is a point that should always be borne in mind; if an employee is not 'redundant' he may be able to claim unfair dismissal. He will be better off for doing so since unfair-dismissal compensation usually exceeds redundancy compensation.

Unfair dismissal and redundancy

It will be remembered that to defend an unfair-dismissal claim, an employer must show that:

• he had a fair reason for dismissing the employee, *and*
• he behaved reasonably.

'Redundancy' is a 'fair' reason for dismissing an employee. So usually a redundant employee cannot claim unfair dismissal. However, he will be able to do so if the employer did not behave 'reasonably' (if, for instance, the employee was unfairly selected for redundancy). In such a case the employee can claim a redundancy payment and also unfair dismissal, although the amount of his unfair-dismissal compensation will be reduced by the amount of his redundancy payment (see page 458).

So whilst most redundant employees cannot claim unfair dismissal, in the exceptional case the employee who has not been treated 'reasonably' can claim both redundancy and unfair dismissal.

Selection criteria. If the employee is unfairly selected for redundancy then an unfair-dismissal claim may be brought. This will involve looking at the reasonableness of the criteria used by the employer for deciding who should be selected. 'Last in, first out' used to be the usual criterion and tribunals will normally accept this as a fair method of selection. Recently, more discretionary criteria have become widespread (e.g. 'capability, qualification, and performance' of relevant staff) in which case there is much more scope for the employee to argue that the criteria are unfair. For instance, an employee who is generally uncooperative and unhelpful could not be properly selected on the basis of 'performance' since those personal characteristics will not normally be relevant to how he (or she) performs the job.

As a generalization, the tribunals will expect an employer to follow these five principles of good industrial-relations practice:

1. Give as much warning as possible of the possibility of redundancies,
2. Consult with the union as to what should be the selection criteria,
3. Use objective criteria for selection (e.g. attendance record, length of service), not personal opinions.
4. Follow these criteria closely when deciding who is to be made redundant,
5. Check that there are no other alternative jobs available.

One point to note is that a 'part-timers first' rule will almost certainly run into difficulties – not from the redundancy-payments laws, but from the sex-discrimination laws. Nationally, over 80 per cent of part-timers are women, and a 1982 case held that it would therefore be 'grossly discriminatory' to have a 'part-timers first' rule when deciding which staff were to be made redundant (see page 692).

Employment: Unfair Dismissal and Redundancy

When does 'redundancy' exist?

'Redundancy' is defined in section 81 of the Employment Protection (Consolidation) Act 1978. The effect of the section is that redundancy exists when:
- the firm closes
- the business is taken over
- the firm moves
- the employee's work is reduced
- the employee is laid off or put on short time.

The firm closes

There is usually no problem in recognizing a redundancy when the firm closes down. However, complications arise if the firm is taken over.

The business is taken over

If the business is taken over, then, although the employee is dismissed by his old employer, he may not be entitled to a redundancy payment. If the new employer offers him his old job or if he offers him 'suitable alternative' work, then the employee may well be unable to claim a redundancy payment. Instead his service with the old employer will count as service with the new employer, and if he should later be made redundant, he will be able to claim a payment based on the combined total of his years of service.

This is clearly reasonable enough. If the firm is completely taken over, then it would be inappropriate for the employee to be able to claim a redundancy payment just because the name on the factory gate has changed. However, difficulties arise in deciding what is, and what is not, a change in the ownership of the business. If the business is not taken over *as a going concern*, then the change-of-ownership rules will not apply. Accordingly, the employee should claim a redundancy payment from his old employer even if he works at his old job for the new employer.

Mr Passmore was employed in maintaining a steel plant. Every year the contract for the maintenance of the steel plant would be put out, and the incoming contractor would always take on the outgoing contractor's staff – including Mr Passmore. Eventually the steel works were closed down and Mr Passmore claimed a redundancy payment based on his entire period at the plant. Held: No. Despite the fact that he had done the same job, in the same place, under the same conditions, and for the same pay, he could not claim that there had been a change in the ownership of the business each year. The incoming contractors had not taken over a going concern and so Mr Passmore's employment with the previous contractors could not be taken into account. Port Talbot Eng. Co. (1975)

This can put the employee in a difficult position. As Lord Denning has said, 'If the new owner takes over the business as a going concern – so that the business remains the same business but in different hands – and the employee keeps the same job with the new owner, then he is not entitled to a redundancy payment' (1969)

470

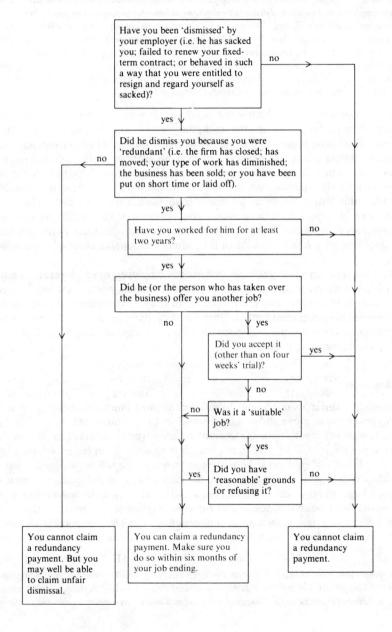

Working out whether you are eligible for a redundancy payment

Have you been 'dismissed' by your employer (i.e. he has sacked you; failed to renew your fixed-term contract; or behaved in such a way that you were entitled to resign and regard yourself as sacked)? → no

↓ yes

Did he dismiss you because you were 'redundant' (i.e. the firm has closed; has moved; your type of work has diminished; the business has been sold; or you have been put on short time or laid off). ← no

↓ yes

Have you worked for him for at least two years? → no

↓ yes

Did he (or the person who has taken over the business) offer you another job?

no ↓   ↓ yes

Did you accept it (other than on four weeks' trial)? → yes

↓ no

Was it a 'suitable' job? ← no

↓ yes

Did you have 'reasonable' grounds for refusing it? → no

yes ←

You cannot claim a redundancy payment. But you may well be able to claim unfair dismissal.

You can claim a redundancy payment. Make sure you do so within six months of your job ending.

You cannot claim a redundancy payment.

Employment: Unfair Dismissal and Redundancy

A mere sale of the physical assets of the business will not be a sale of the business:

A children's clothing firm closed one of its factories. A machinist in the factory was kept on by the new employer and he worked at the same machine as before, but now he was producing men's trousers, not children's clothes. The employee claimed a redundancy payment from the old employers. The industrial tribunal refused his claim, saying that there had been a full transfer of ownership of the business. On appeal, this was overruled. The old employers had just sold the physical assets (i.e. the factory and the machines), not the business, including goodwill and orders. Accordingly, there had not been a transfer of the ownership of the business and so the employee could claim a redundancy payment. Crompton (1975)

So it is important to see whether the purchaser is acquiring more than just the physical assets. Is he also buying the stock, the goodwill, the existing contracts, and customer lists? If he is not, then it will not be a true transfer of ownership, and the employee should claim redundancy – even if his working environment remains unchanged and he is doing the same job as before. His service with the new employer will be completely separate from the service with the old employer, so if he should be made redundant in the future he cannot claim the benefit of his past service.

On the other hand, if the new employer is buying the goodwill, etc., then there will be a transfer of ownership. The employee cannot claim a redundancy payment if the new employer gives him his old job or if he offers him suitable alternative employment.

These laws are ridiculously complicated and few employers or employees have any idea of how they are supposed to work. To make matters worse, new regulations were introduced in 1981 (called the Transfer of Undertakings Regulations) which have clouded the issues even further. Unfortunately, this area of redundancy law has now become so complicated that specialist advice is always needed. So seek expert help in a situation such as this.

The firm moves

A firm may transfer its operations to a different plant in another place. Can the employees refuse to move and declare themselves to be redundant?

The answer will depend upon the terms of the employee's contract of employment. If it contains a job-mobility clause, requiring him to move when requested, then he will be in breach of contract if he refuses to move. So he will be unable to claim redundancy. On the other hand, if it does not contain a job-mobility clause then his employers cannot insist that he move, and he can claim redundancy unless the move is so trivial as to make it unreasonable for him to refuse (e.g. a move to the next street). Relatively few employment contracts have specific job-mobility clauses. Generally, an employer will try to *imply* a job-mobility clause into the contract, but a lot will depend on what is the practice in the particular industry.

Two employees worked in a firm's north-western area office, which covered an area from mid-Wales to Cumberland. The office was in Liverpool, and their work allowed them to return home every day. However, work in the Liverpool area declined and so the employers decided to move the office to Barrow-in-Furness, 120 miles away. The two employees claimed a redundancy payment. The employers argued that it was an implied term of the employment contracts that the men would be prepared to work well away from home. Held: No. The only clause that could be implied was that the men would work within daily travelling distance of their homes. So while the employers could move the office from Liverpool, they could not move it so far away. So the redundancy claims succeeded. O'Brien (1968)

When there is a job-mobility clause, then the employee who refuses to move will have no right to a redundancy payment. So an engineer moved from RAF Marham to RAF Kinloss and an atomic-energy worker transferred from Orfordness to Aldermaston were both unable to claim redundancy.

The employee's work is reduced

Reorganizations, productivity agreements, and new working methods can all lead to a reduction in the number of staff needed, or to a reduction in the need for the particular kind of work done by an employee.

When this happens there will almost certainly be redundancy. But a mere reorganization will not be redundancy unless the amount of work to be done is reduced. Altering the hours of work cannot of itself be redundancy – although if the imposition of a new working schedule is not authorized by the employment contract, the employee may be able to claim unfair dismissal.

An employee worked a five-day week from 9.30 a.m. to 5.30 p.m. Her employers changed her to a six-day week, from 8 a.m. to 3 p.m. and noon to 8 p.m. alternate weeks. She refused to accept the change and was dismissed. She claimed she had been made redundant. Held: No. The employers needed just as many employees as previously, it was just that they were needed at different hours. So this was not redundancy. Johnson (1974)

Even if the reorganization leads to a shorter working week, it will not be redundancy unless the length of the week is reduced below that promised by the employment contract.

The makers of Matchbox Toys reorganized their production system because of a decline in sales. The effect of the changes was to alter the hours of work and, more important, to reduce the overtime that the men worked. Six men refused to accept the changes and claimed redundancy, saying that the decline in overtime resulted from the fall in sales. Held: This was not redundancy because the employers were under no obligation to provide overtime work. Lesney Products (1977)

Difficulties can arise when the employer still needs employees to do a particular type of work, but decides that the employee is no longer suitable for that type of work. An example is Mr Hindle who was 'too good and too slow' and yet his dismissal was not due to redundancy (see page 468). Other examples include:

A barmaid was sacked after eighteen years' service. The management wanted to change the image of the pub and so decided 'young blondes and bunny girls' should serve behind the bar. The sacked barmaid claimed redundancy. Held: No. The employers still needed barmaids so it could not be a case of redundancy. Vaux Breweries (1968)

473

The workshop manager of a garage was dismissed when new owners took over the garage business, despite his having worked there for thirty years. He was unable to do crash-repair estimates, which his previous boss had done, and so his new employers found him to be unsuitable. He claimed redundancy. Held: No. The work of the repair shop had not diminished and so it could not be a redundancy situation. North Riding Garages (1967)

Note that some of these cases were heard before the unfair-dismissal laws were introduced. So, today, those employees would be able to claim unfair dismissal as an alternative to claiming redundancy. Often such a claim will succeed, on the basis that it was unfair to reorganize the working arrangements. But not always: if the bulk of the rest of the staff accept the changes then the tribunal will probably decide that it is not unfair dismissal. For instance, in a 1984 case, a shift supervisor refused to change from night shifts to day shifts because of her family commitments. It was held that this was not redundancy but nor was it unfair dismissal (since the reorganization had been agreed with the unions and supported by 80 per cent of the staff in a ballot).

Generally, if the dismissed employee is replaced by another employee, then that will be clear evidence that the amount of work has not diminished, and so it cannot be a case of redundancy. However, this only applies if the dismissed employee is replaced by another *employee* – not if he is replaced by a self-employed contractor, or lump labour.

Two painters and decorators were sacked by their employer. He replaced them with lump labour (i.e. self-employed contractors), and argued that it could not be redundancy since there had been no decline in the amount of work – as was evidenced by his having replaced the two men. Held: This was redundancy. The two men had not been replaced by employees, so there was a decline in the amount of work available for employees. Bromby (1971)

The employee is laid off or put on short time

Occasionally an employee who has been laid off or put on short-time working can claim a redundancy payment. This is so even if his employment contract allows his employer to lay him off or put him on short time (see page 389). The law is set out in section 88 of the 1978 Act. The section is complicated and an employee who is thinking of making a redundancy claim under it should take advice from a solicitor or trade-union official.

Basically, section 88 allows the employee to declare himself redundant if he has been laid off (i.e. has received no pay) or put on short-time working (i.e. has received half a week's pay or less) for:

• four consecutive weeks, *or*
• six of the last thirteen weeks.

The employee has four weeks in which to serve a notice on his employer. The notice must be in writing and state that he intends to claim a redundancy payment; in addition he must give in his notice of resignation. The employer then has seven days in which to serve a written counter-notice saying that he will dispute the claim and that, within the next four weeks, full-time working will resume and will continue for at least thirteen weeks without lay-off or short time.

If the employer does not serve a counter-notice then the employee is entitled to his redundancy payment. However, if a counter-notice is served the industrial tribunal will consider the matter and the employee may well lose his payment if work was in fact available as promised by the employer.

The offer of another job

An employee may lose his redundancy payment if he turns down the offer of another job from his employer.

If the new job is *identical* to his old job and he refuses it, he will definitely forfeit his redundancy payment.

If the new job is in any way *different* from his old job, then he can try it out for a 'trial period' of up to four weeks. If he decides to reject the job, he will lose his redundancy payment if the job was 'suitable' for him and if he acted 'unreasonably' in refusing it.

The offer must be made by the employer or by the person taking over the firm. The employer cannot try to evade his liability to pay redundancy money by finding a job for the employee with a different firm.

In addition, it will only be a valid offer if:

- it is made before (and not after) the old job ends;
- the new job will start no later than four weeks after the end of the old job;
- the offer describes the new job in sufficient detail. It must be more than a vague offer of employment.

If the employer does not fulfil these conditions then the 'alternative job' rules will not apply. So even if the employer is certain that the employee will reject the new job, he must go through the formalities of offering it to the employee.

Refusing the offer

If the new job is identical to the old job, the employee will lose his redundancy payment if he refuses to take the new job.

The complications arise when the new job differs from the old job. Then the employee can try it out for up to four weeks. If at the end of that four weeks he decides to reject the new job, he can apply for his redundancy payment. He is not obliged to try out the new job on a trial period – he can simply refuse it as soon as it is offered to him. However, if he does this, it is more likely that the tribunal will decide that he acted 'unreasonably' in rejecting the job.

If the employee rejects the new job, he will only forfeit his redundancy payment if:

- the new job was '*suitable*', *and*
- he was '*unreasonable*' in refusing it.

Whether a job is 'suitable' will depend upon its terms and conditions; such matters as pay, fringe benefits, the job description, and the place of work will all be relevant. The question of whether it was 'reasonable' for the employee to reject the job will depend more on the employee's personal circumstances; the travel involved in the new job, its effect on his home life, and any loss of status will all be relevant.

In practice, industrial tribunals treat 'suitability' and 'reasonableness' in similar ways. Rather than consider them as two separate criteria they tend to be amalgamated into a general test of whether the employee should have accepted the new job.

Claiming a redundancy payment

An employee must claim his redundancy payment within six months of the end of his old job. If he does not, he may well forfeit his right to a payment.

The claim can be made either to the employer or to an industrial tribunal. Either way the claim should be in writing and should be made within the six-month period. If the claim is made to the employer and the employer does not make the payment, the employee can then apply to an industrial tribunal even if the six-month period has expired by then.

The time for claiming. The general rule is that redundancy claims must be made within six months of dismissal (unlike unfair-dismissal claims, in which there is only a three-month time period). This six-month period can be extended, but the sensible advice is to avoid any difficulties by making a claim to the industrial tribunal within the six-month period.

The amount of the redundancy payment

The amount of the payment is worked out by allowing the employee a fixed number of weeks' wages for the number of years he has worked for the employer:
- each year worked between the ages of eighteen and twenty-one gives the employee half a week's pay;
- each year worked between the ages of twenty-two and forty gives the employee one week's pay;
- each year worked between the ages of forty-one and sixty-five (sixty for women) gives the employee one and a half weeks' pay.

Service below the age of eighteen does not count, and the maximum number of years of service that can be taken into account is twenty. The table on page 459 sets out how these rules work. When assessing the amount of the payment, any weekly wage in excess of £152 is ignored.

Illustration. An employee joined a firm at the age of fifteen. At the age of thirty-five he is made redundant. At the time of his dismissal he earns £180 p.w. He has twenty years' service but service under the age of eighteen is ignored, so he only has seventeen years' allowable service. Referring to the table, it will be seen that an employee of thirty-five with seventeen years' service is entitled to a payment of fifteen weeks' wages. However, the maximum weekly wage allowed is £152, so his redundancy payment will be 15×152=£2,280.

The redundancy payment will usually be tax-free.

Employees near retirement age

An employee who is near retirement age will lose part of his redundancy payment. A woman aged fifty-nine and a man aged sixty-four will lose one twelfth of the payment for every additional month of their age. Thus, a man aged sixty-four years and nine months will lose three quarters of his redundancy payment, and a woman aged fifty-nine years and two months will lose one sixth of her payment.

If the employer is insolvent, the employee can still claim his redundancy payment. If necessary, the Department of Employment will make the payment to the employee and then try to recover the money from the employer.

The employer's rebate

An employer can reclaim 35 per cent of a redundancy payment from the Redundancy Fund. This is a fund financed by part of the national insurance contributions made by employers. To claim the rebate he sends off form RP 2 within six months of making the payment, together with the employee's receipt (on form RP 3).

Redundancy: the employer's duty to consult

Every employer who is planning to introduce redundancies has a general duty to 'give as much warning as possible to the employees concerned'. This is recommended by a code of practice and if an employer ignores the code he may be found to have behaved 'unreasonably' and so lose an unfair-dismissal claim (see page 469).

In addition, there is a more specific duty to consult with the trade unions, but only if the unions are recognized by the employer. If the employer has recognized union(s) then if he is planning:
- to make a hundred or more employees redundant within a period of ninety days,

or
- to make ten or more employees redundant within a period of thirty days,

then he must notify the union(s) (and the Department of Employment) at least ninety days and thirty days (respectively) beforehand.

Section 99 of the 1978 Act requires the employer to provide the union with details of:
- the reasons for the redundancies;
- the number of employees to be made redundant and the type of work they do;
- the total number of staff doing that type of work;
- how it is proposed to decide who should be selected for redundancy (e.g. 'last in, first out');
- how the dismissals are to be carried out and over how long a period.

Sanctions

If an employer does not comply with these consultation provisions, the union (but not the individual employees) can complain to an industrial tribunal. The employer will lose the case unless he can show that there were 'special circumstances' why he couldn't comply with section 99 (perhaps because of a sudden bankruptcy) and that he took all 'reasonably practicable' steps.

In addition, the tribunal can order the employer to pay compensation to the individual employees. This is called a *protective award* and can be the employees' wages for the length of notice that should have been given (i.e. up to ninety days' pay if ninety days' notice is appropriate; up to thirty days' pay for thirty days' notice; up to twenty-eight days' pay in any other case).

In practice the consultation provisions are largely ignored and most employers simply close down without notice, but pay their staff the compensation which would be required if a protective award were made. Thus the consultation rules are generally a financial rather than a procedural obstacle to declaring redundancies.

Golden handshakes

Redundancy payments are always tax-free. In addition, an employee may receive a termination payment from his employers when made redundant or sacked; generally, this is called a 'golden handshake'. Often the employee will pay little or no tax on this sum because

• the first £25,000 (1985) received is tax-free
• further sums can be free of tax if there is foreign service, 'top-slicing' relief, or superannuation relief. Specialist advice should be sought in these cases.

Note that money in lieu of wages will generally be regarded as a golden handshake and not normal taxable earnings, even though strictly speaking it is taxable. Accrued holiday pay will be taxed.

Time off to look for a job

If an employee with two years' service has been given notice of redundancy, he is entitled to take paid time off work to look for a new job.

The employer must allow time off for the employee to:

• look for new employment, *or*
• make arrangements for job training (note: he is only allowed time off to *arrange* the training – he cannot demand time off for the actual training).

The employer must pay the employee during the time off.

The difficulty arises in deciding what is a 'reasonable' amount of time for the employee to be allowed off. Whilst this will depend on the facts of the individual case, it seems that a total of two days will often be the maximum.

If the employer refuses to allow the employee to take time off, the employee has three months in which to complain to an industrial tribunal. The tribunal will only penalize the employer if it was 'unreasonable' of him to refuse the time off, so if there was a staff shortage or other crisis the employer might be able to refuse time off.

If the employer is found to have been 'unreasonable' he can be 'fined' by being ordered to pay the employee up to two days' wages. Because this is the maximum penalty, the clear implication is that more than two days' leave will be an unreasonable amount of time off.

30 Trade Unionism and the Law

The right to be a trade unionist

Every employee has a legal right to join an independent trade union. An employer who interferes with this right can be ordered to pay compensation to the employee (s. 23, Employment Protection (Consolidation) Act 1978).

It is not only straightforward sacking for trade-union activities that is prohibited. Less draconian measures which amount to victimization of the unionist, such as unfair disciplinary measures, excessive zeal by a supervisor, and unjustified refusal of promotion, are also unlawful.

But the law only protects the employee if the trade-union activities are taking place outside working hours or, if in working hours, the employer had previously given his consent to such activities taking place. So normally the trade-union member who carries out his union activities during working hours will not be protected.

A new employee in a bus firm joined the TGWU and actively tried to recruit new members amongst his work-mates. The firm did not recognize the union and to thwart the employee's efforts he was transferred to another job which isolated him from the other staff. He claimed that the firm had victimized him because of his trade-union activities. Held: Yes. He had been victimized, but he could not receive any redress from the law. His union activities had taken place during working hours and accordingly it was not unlawful for the employers to victimize him. Robb (1977)

Occasionally tribunals have held that management have implicitly given their consent to union activities during working hours, but such cases are rare and the activist would be unwise to rely on such an implied permission.

'Working hours' is confined to the hours when the employee works; it does not include his meal, rest, and tea breaks. So he can complain if he is dismissed or victimized for trade-union activities carried out during off-work periods, even if these activities took place on the employer's premises (e.g. meeting in the canteen during the dinner break).

Unfortunately the Employment Protection (Consolidation) Act does not define what 'trade-union activities' are permitted. It would seem that the usual union organizational work of collecting subscriptions and distributing union literature is protected. But beyond that, the law is unclear; the test laid down in some cases has been that permitted union activities must not cause 'substantial inconvenience' to the firm – hardly a clear guideline to those involved. In practice, the tribunals tend to

479

apply a narrow and restrictive meaning to the phrase so that unofficial action over a pay claim would probably not be a permitted activity.

However, concern over health and safety matters will probably count as trade-union activities.

Mr Drew was a parks gardener. During his three months' employment he frequently made complaints over health and safety matters. He was eventually sacked when he refused to clear snow during an official go-slow. He claimed unfair dismissal, arguing that he had really been sacked because of his health and safety complaints, and that these were trade-union activities. Held: It was not unfair dismissal. While health and safety matters were 'trade union activities', only trade-union officials and safety representatives could bring them forward. Individual union members, such as Mr Drew, could only pursue such matters outside working hours. The 1978 Act protected unionists only if their trade-union activities took place either

- *outside working hours, or*
- *within working hours with the employer's consent.* Drew (1980)

If Mr Drew had been acting in an official trade-union capacity he would, of course, have been protected.

The right to take part in union activities only applies to members of *independent* unions. These are unions that have been certified by the government's certification officer as being independent of employers and employers' organizations. The union need not be recognized for its members to be protected. However, if the union is recognized then additional rights accrue; members can take part in certain activities during working hours and officials can take paid leave to deal with their union duties (see page 485).

When an activist is dismissed or victimized he should complain to an industrial tribunal within three months.

If he has been *dismissed* there is a special procedure available which is designed to reinstate him in his job until the proper, lengthy hearing of his claim. This is called an application for 'interim relief' and it must be made within seven days of the dismissal. At the full hearing of the unfair-dismissal claim it is for the employee to show that the employer dismissed him for trade-union reasons (i.e. union membership or activities). In practice it can be extremely difficult to do this and few employees succeed in doing so. It is usually fairly easy for the employer to argue that there was some other reason for the dismissal, such as misconduct or poor timekeeping.

Do not forget that if the activist is on strike, or taking part in industrial action, it will not be unfair dismissal if *all* those still out on strike are sacked. Mass dismissals are permitted; victimization is not (see page 444).

If the employee has not been dismissed, but has been *victimized*, he has three months in which to apply to the industrial tribunal. It will be for the employer to prove to the tribunal that the action taken against the employee was not motivated by anti-union intentions. If he cannot do so, the employee will win the case (cf. dismissal, above, where it is the employee who must prove his case). But the tribunal will want to be sure that the employer *intended* to victimize the employee; so even though the effect of his actions was to victimize unionists, he will not be liable if he can show that this was not his intention. If the employee's complaint is upheld, the employer can be ordered to pay him compensation (there is no maximum limit).

Ineligible employees. Not all employees are protected against victimization and dismissal for union activities. In particular, part-timers are excluded. For full details see the table on pages 376–7. The protection is also not available to prospective employees.

A well-known trade-union activist used a false name when applying for a job. He did this because he knew that he would not get the job if the employers knew his true identity. But soon the employers found out who he was and told him he could not have the job. He claimed he had been dismissed for his trade-union activities. Held: No. The law only protected staff from dismissal and victimization *resulting from trade-union activities, not against* being refused employment *on those grounds.* City of Birmingham (1977)

Time off work for union duties and activities

If an employer recognizes a trade union, he must be prepared to allow members and officials of the union to take time off work for their duties and activities.

Union officials

Union officials, as opposed to mere members, can take 'a reasonable' amount of *paid* time off work for:

• industrial relations duties between employer and employees (e.g. collective bargaining, talking to members about negotiations, appearing before tribunals, lecturing new employees), *and*

• industrial relations training on a course approved by his union or the TUC.

The description 'union official' is not restricted to paid officials of the union. It covers any lay union official who has been constitutionally appointed or elected. So it includes shop stewards and staff representatives but probably not branch secretaries.

ACAS have published a Code of Practice which gives guidance on how the rules are to be applied. However, the code does not define what is a 'reasonable' amount of time – that will depend on such factors as the size of the firm, the employee's position, the pressure on the firm, etc.

Union members

Union members can take a 'reasonable' amount of *unpaid* time off work to carry out their trade-union activities. The ACAS Code of Practice does not define 'union activities' but the term usually covers attendance at policy-making meetings of the union, representing the union on committees, voting in union elections, and sometimes attendance at union meetings. (For further information, see the ACAS

481

Code of Practice, obtainable from HMSO.) If the employee is not allowed to take time off he can complain to an industrial tribunal within three months. The tribunal can order the employer to award him cash compensation.

Ineligible employees. These time-off provisions only apply if the employer has recognized the union. In addition, certain employees (such as part-timers) are excluded. See the table on pages 376–7.

The closed shop

For decades the closed shop was an integral part of the industrial-relations scene. In the 1960s it was estimated that two fifths of all employees worked in closed shops.

These days the advantages of a closed shop to both unions and management are generally recognized. Accordingly, the law now gives special status to closed-shop agreements (properly called 'union-membership agreements'). An employer can insist that individual employees join a particular union if there is a closed shop in practice – but only if the closed shop has been voted for by the staff in a secret ballot (and approved by a large majority).

An employee who refuses to join the union concerned can be sacked, as can an employee who is expelled from the union. His employer will not be liable to him for unfair dismissal since dismissal for refusing to join a union covered by a union-membership agreement is a 'fair' dismissal, however unreasonably the employer acted.

There are only four exceptions to this, when the employee can refuse to join the closed shop and claim unfair dismissal if he is sacked (or victimized – e.g. paid lower wages) as a result:

• *personal objections*: the Employment Act 1980 allows an employee to refuse to join the union if he 'genuinely objects on grounds of conscience or other deeply held personal conviction to being a member of any trade union whatsoever, or of a particular trade union'. The effect of this is that union membership need not be obligatory if the employee has a genuine and sincere objection to joining. Further, the objection need not be to trade unionism in general, but can be limited to a particular union. So, the employee can say, 'I don't mind joining a union, but I won't join yours.' He can also refuse to join if it would break a professional code.

• *existing employees*: existing employees who are not union members need not join when a union-membership agreement comes into effect. Only new employees, or existing employees transferred into that category of staff, need join.

• *balloting on new UMAs*: any new union-membership agreement must be approved by at least 80 per cent of the work-force in a secret ballot. If it is not, then any employee who is sacked for refusing to join the union can claim unfair dismissal – even if he does not have a personal objection to joining a trade union. If 80 per cent support is obtained, the sacking will only be unfair if the employee could show a personal objection, or if he was already an employee at the time the UMA was introduced.

● *Five-yearly ballots.* Every union-membership agreement must be approved by secret ballot at least once every five years. If it is not, then it will not be a legal closed shop and it will be unfair dismissal to victimize or sack an employee who refuses to join the union. The ballot must result in a vote in favour of 80 per cent of those eligible to vote (or 85 per cent of those actually voting, if there is a small turnout).

If the employee comes within one of these four exceptions, he need not join the union. If he is sacked for his refusal to join, he will be able to obtain unfair-dismissal compensation. Similarly, he can complain to an industrial tribunal if the employer does not sack him but takes other action against him (for instance, demoting him, or denying him overtime). If the employer is forced into sacking the employee, or discriminating against him, by threats or pressure from someone else, the employer can join that person in the unfair-dismissal claim. Thus a union, shop steward, unofficial strike leader, or contractor could be made to pay some or all of the unfair-dismissal compensation awarded to the employee.

Even if an employee is compelled to join a specified union there is nothing to prevent him taking part in the activities of another, different, union.

'Trade union only' contracts. The rules on the closed shop were tightened up even further by the Employment Act 1982. This prevents a businessman from requiring that his contractors operate a closed shop, or that they recognize and consult with a trade union. In short, commercial contracts cannot contain clauses laying down rules as to whether employees are to be (or are not to be) in a union, or which require the firm to deal with a union. If a contract contains such a clause, then it will be invalid. Similarly, it will be illegal for anyone to take industrial action to try to get such a clause put in a contract.

Prior to 1982 it was common in the engineering, printing, and construction industries for potential suppliers to be limited to those who operated closed shops. Also, local-authority contracts often contained clauses requiring a contractor to operate a closed shop (and to require that a sub-contractor also ran a closed shop). Both those practices are now unlawful – as would be a strike designed to force the adoption of such arrangements.

Expulsion or exclusion from the union

If there is a closed shop a union member who is expelled from the union can complain to an industrial tribunal. The same applies to someone whose application for membership is rejected by the union. The complaint must be made within six months, and the tribunal will then consider whether the union acted reasonably and honestly. If the complaint is upheld, the tribunal can order the union to accept the applicant as a member; if this order is not complied with in the next four weeks, the applicant can go back to the tribunal and claim compensation. Even if the order is complied with, the applicant can claim compensation for his losses arising from the original expulsion or exclusion from membership. Specially generous compensation provisions apply in such cases.

Finally, there are two other remedies that might be used:
- the courts may be willing to declare a member's expulsion from a trade union to be invalid. However, the refusal to grant membership cannot be challenged in the courts.
- the Independent Review Committee of the TUC will hear complaints, if the applicant has exhausted the union's complaints procedure. The committee can recommend that the individual be admitted to the union, but the union is not legally obliged to admit him. However, the TUC say that there is a 'clear responsibility' on unions to accept the committee's recommendations.

The right not to join a union

An employee cannot be forced to join a union – unless an approved closed-shop agreement (i.e. balloted and approved by a large majority of the work-force) is in force. See above.

Legal protection for unions and strikers

During the nineteenth century it was virtually impossible for trade unions to take effective industrial action and yet be acting within the law. As soon as they found a means of bringing pressure to bear on employers, the judges would decide that this new activity infringed an old common-law rule. Accordingly, the police could bring prosecutions and the employers could sue the unions and their members, and also obtain injunctions preventing the action from taking place. Such obscure civil laws as conspiracy, procuring breach of contract, intimidation, and unlawful interference with trade were all used to make trade-union activities unlawful.

In the end Parliament had to step in to protect the unions from these common-law offences – and indeed from the ingenuity of the judiciary who kept finding ways of curbing union activities. The first major piece of legislation to protect the unions was the Trade Union Act 1871, which led to the Trades Disputes Act 1906, and the protection given by that Act has survived as the basis of the modern law on trade-union immunity, until rewritten by the 1982 Employment Act.

The 1982 Act gives trade unions immunity from being sued for nearly all the old common-law offences, but only if they are pursuing legitimate trade-union objectives. In the words of the Act, they must be acting 'in contemplation or furtherance of a trade dispute'.

Over the years there have been numerous decisions as to what is, or is not, a 'trade dispute'. Obviously, a trade dispute exists when there is an argument as to the terms of work, allocation of work, sackings, discipline at work, or the provision of union facilities. The 1982 Employment Act gave the phrase 'trade dispute' a narrower meaning than had previously been the case. So an inter-union dispute (i.e. one not involving an employer) is not a trade dispute, and nor is a dispute involving an employer who does not have any staff involved in the dispute (e.g. if he is a supplier of another employer whose staff are on strike). Similarly, if the motives behind the union's actions are political or personal, then it will not be a trade dispute.

The union representing B B C engineers intended to ask its members not to transmit the Cup Final unless the B B C agreed that the programme should not be relayed to South Africa. The B B C sought an injunction preventing the ban. The union argued that there was a trade dispute and so the court could not grant the injunction. Held: There was no trade dispute. The action was due to political motivations and an injunction would be granted. B B C (1977)

Similarly, a one-day protest strike against the Industrial Relations Act was held not to be a trade dispute. In another case, a union strike pressurized an employer into sacking an employee but this was held not to be a trade dispute because the union's action was motivated by the individual officer's personal grudge against the employee concerned.

The important point to grasp is that if it is a 'trade dispute' then the union will be protected from some of the old common-law claims for damages that could otherwise be brought against it – provided there was a strike ballot beforehand (see page 486). But, even then, if it acts unlawfully (e.g. by taking secondary action – such as blacking a firm that supplies the firm whose employees are on strike), then it can be liable in damages. If the union authorizes or endorses such unlawful action then it can be sued. Obviously arguments can then arise over whether the union did approve of the unlawful action, but the Employment Act 1982 tackles this by making it liable for the actions of its 'responsible' officers (e.g. the N E C, general secretary, regional and district secretaries, etc.) unless the union quickly dissociates itself from their actions and repudiates the unlawful acts.

To summarize, one can say that unions now have only limited protection from being sued. If they ballot and they are involved in a genuine trade dispute (i.e. action taken for industrial reasons by staff against their employer) then the union will be exempt from being sued (e.g. for any lost profits caused to the company by the strike). But if the action becomes unlawful, then the union can be sued – for instance, for those lost profits. And even then, the union might be liable if it did not hold a secret ballot before the industrial action took place (see page 486).

One thing that will be obvious to any reader is that the whole area of trade unions and the law has become absurdly complicated – largely because successive governments have altered the law to favour their own views. Specialist advice is needed to anyone who is thinking of entering this legal minefield.

Union recognition

It is to a union's advantage to be recognized by an employer. It then has certain rights that are denied to a union that is not recognized:

1. It can demand to have certain bargaining information disclosed to it.
2. It must be consulted over proposed redundancies (see page 477).
3. Its members and officials can take time off work to carry out their union duties and activities (see page 481).
4. It must be consulted over the provision of occupational pension schemes.
5. The employer must, on request, allow his premises to be used for secret ballots

held by the union (if in connection with strikes, industrial action, union and staff representative elections, or the rules of the union).

6. The union has the right to appoint safety representatives, under the Health and Safety at Work Act.

But an employer cannot be made to recognize a union, even if the majority of his employees are union members. Recognition of a union can only be a voluntary act by the employer.

The legal effects of going on strike

Suing

An employee who goes on strike, or takes other industrial action, is likely to be in breach of his contract of employment. Theoretically then, his employers could bring a civil action against him and sue for breach of contract. However, it is over twenty years since such a claim was brought in the courts and, in practice, the striking worker need have no fear of being sued for breach of contract. If he were sued, the damages payable would be the cost to the employer of hiring substitute labour, but the court might well express its disapproval of the employer's claim by refusing to give him his costs.

Apart from the breach-of-contract claim, the striker (and his supporters) could be sued for various torts – such as inducing breach of contract, interference with trade, and conspiracy. Many of these torts were 'invented' by the judges in the nineteenth century when trying to extend the liability of strikers and unions. However, the Trade Disputes Act 1906 gave a defence to such tort claims if the defendant was acting 'in contemplation or furtherance of a trade dispute'. As we have seen above, the definition of what is a 'trade dispute' has been narrowed in recent years and so too has the extent to which unions (and their officials) are protected from being sued (e.g. by an employer who has lost sales because of a strike). A union will only be safe from being sued if: (1) there is a genuine trade dispute; and (2) a secret ballot was held no more than four weeks beforehand.

The need for a strike ballot. The Trade Union Act 1984 requires there to be a ballot before any strike or industrial action (i.e. anything that breaks the contract of employment) takes place. The ballot must be secret; it must be no more than four weeks before the action is taken; only those likely to take part in the action can vote; postal votes must be accepted. In short, there are detailed rules as to how the ballots are to be held and if these rules are not followed then the union will lose its immunity from being sued (e.g. by an employer who has lost profits because of a strike). So whereas prior to 1984 a union was immune from being sued if the strike was a genuine 'trade dispute', now there is a second hurdle to be overcome – was there a secret ballot?

If there isn't a genuine trade dispute, or if there was not a secret ballot, then the union can be sued for damages.

Secondary disputes. The press often talk about 'secondary action'. This is when union action is taken against an employer who is not a direct party to the dispute (i.e. he does not employ the striking staff, but he might for instance supply their employing firm with materials). The law says that if the employees of A take action against B, this secondary action will only be immune from the civil law if:

- the principal aim of the action is to put pressure on A, not on B, *and*
- it 'is likely to achieve that purpose', *and*
- there is a direct commercial contract between A and B. For instance, it is lawful for the employees of a component firm to strike in support of a strike by workers at a car firm, but it would not be lawful for employees of the component firm's suppliers to strike.

Otherwise, secondary action will be unlawful – and the union can be sued for it. Note in particular that it will never be justifiable legally to use secondary action to force an employer to impose a closed shop.

Wages

The striker loses the right to be paid while he is on strike. Whether or not he will be able to demand strike pay from his union will depend upon whether the union has made the strike 'official' and, if so, whether the union has exercised its discretion to award strike pay.

Dismissal

The employer can dismiss a striker, and if he does so while the employee is still on strike, the dismissal cannot be held unfair, unless the employer did not dismiss *all* the striking employees. (i.e. everyone who is still out on strike). If all the strikers were dismissed they will lose their unfair-dismissal claims (see page 444).

Social-security benefits

Unemployment benefit. People laid off because of a strike cannot claim unemployment benefit if they are either participating in the strike (e.g. on strike, refusing to cross a picket line), or if they are directly interested in the outcome (e.g. if they will receive higher wages themselves through a knock-on effect).

Statutory sick pay. A person receiving SSP when the strike starts will continue to be entitled to it. But a striker who falls ill after the strike has begun cannot then claim SSP unless he can show that he is neither participating in the strike nor directly interested in it (see above). He will still not be eligible for SSP when the strike ends – instead he will be entitled to sickness benefit from the DHSS.

Family-income supplement. A striker receiving FIS when the strike begins continues to be entitled to it until it next has to be renewed (it normally runs in a fifty-two-week period of entitlement). No new FIS claim can be made by a person on strike, but the partner or spouse may be able to claim it.

Education and health benefits. Entitlement to help with fares, free school meals, prescriptions, etc. is unaffected by a strike – and indeed many strikers will immediately become eligible for these benefits.

Housing benefit. Entitlement should not be affected by there being a strike (except that housing-benefit supplement may be lost). Many strikers will find it advisable to claim housing benefit.

Tax rebates. PAYE refunds are no longer made at the start of a strike.

Supplementary benefit. There are severe restrictions on the claiming of SB by strikers and their families. The basic rule is that there is no entitlement to benefit if there is a trade dispute – assuming that the person is participating in the dispute, or is directly involved in it (i.e. as with unemployment benefit – above). As far as single strikers are concerned (i.e. no family), there will be no entitlement to benefit except that in a few urgent cases payments may be available (although housing benefit should be paid in full). For strikers with families, there are complicated rules but the basic effect is that SB is available for the family but not for the striker. Normally, the family will get SB, but without the amount that would usually be included for the striker (generally, of course, the man) and in addition there will be a further deduction of £15 (1985).

Working out entitlement to social-security benefits is always extremely difficult, because the system is so complicated. When strikers are involved the position is even worse and it therefore follows that strikers and their families should always seek expert help on their benefit entitlements (rather than rely on what the DHSS says). Unions, CABs, law centres, and the Child Poverty Action Group are obvious starting-points when looking for this specialist help.

On the picket line

It is on the picket line that trade unionists are most likely to fall foul of the law.

Picketing, of course, can mean different things to different people. The word originates from a military term used to describe guards who man an outpost so as to give advance warning of an attack. Today, simple picketing involves a few strikers standing at the work gates to remind their fellow workers that there is a strike in progress and perhaps to persuade them to support the pickets by not working. 'Mass picketing' is simple picketing but with numerous pickets taking part and so physically blocking the work entrance. In addition, there are 'flying pickets' and 'ghost pickets', each of which has different characteristics.

There are two ways in which pickets can become involved with the law:

- if the picketing is unlawful, the employer can use the *civil* law to obtain an injunction ordering the picketing to stop;
- if the pickets break the *criminal* law, the pickets can be prosecuted.

Picketing and the civil law

The basic rule is that there is no legal right to picket. Thus, the civil courts will grant an injunction ordering the pickets to stop. The only exception is when the picketing comes within section 15 of the Trade Union and Labour Relations Act 1974, which makes it lawful for 'a person in contemplation or furtherance of a trade dispute' to attend at or near his own work-place 'for the purpose only of peacefully obtaining or communicating information or peacefully persuading any person to work or abstain from working'.

In short, a worker can picket his own work-place, but not someone else's work-place. Secondary picketing (i.e. when employees of A picket work-place B) is therefore illegal and the employer can obtain an injunction to stop the picketing.

For the picketing to comply with section 15, it must come within each of the three following categories. If it does not, an injunction can be obtained:

The only people who can picket are:
- employees
- full-time union officers and national officers of the union, who can join their members on the picket line
- ex-employees sacked during the dispute (unless they have since found other jobs).

The only places that can be picketed are:
- the work-place, that is, the entrances to the premises but not inside the premises, since that would be trespass
- if there is more than one place of work (for example, if the pickets are van drivers, building workers) or if it is impractical to picket the work-place (for instance, if the pickets are miners or seamen) then they can picket other premises. The Code of Practice suggests they picket 'those offices of their employer from which they receive their instructions or pay packet, or depot or garage from which their vehicle operates'.

The only picketing that is lawful is:
- for the purpose *only* of peacefully obtaining or communicating information or peacefully persuading any person to work or abstain from working. For instance, if the picket goes beyond peaceful persuasion it will be unlawful. In this respect, the recommendations of the code are of great importance. 'The main cause of violence and disorder on the picket line is excessive numbers . . . This is particularly so whenever people seek by sheer weight of numbers to stop others going into work or delivering or collecting goods. In such cases, what is intended is not peaceful persuasion, but obstruction, if not intimidation . . . Accordingly, pickets and their organizers should ensure that in general the number of pickets does not exceed six

at any entrance to a work-place; frequently a smaller number will be appropriate.' Whilst the code is not legally binding, a court will give great weight to it when deciding whether to grant an injunction to stop the picketing.

• if it is 'in contemplation or furtherance of a trade dispute' (see page 484). Thus political and consumer pickets are unlawful and can be stopped by an injunction.

Section 15 of the 1974 Act does not allow pickets to stop vehicles so that they can then communicate with, or persuade, the drivers of the vehicles not to enter the employer's premises. In theory this seriously limits the protection given by section 15 since the stopping of supplies in lorries is usually a main objective of a picket line. In practice, however, the police use their discretion to allow the stopping of vehicles as long as it is done in an orderly manner.

Broome was picketing a building site. He tried to persuade a lorry driver not to enter but the driver refused. Broome then stood in front of the lorry, still arguing with the driver. He was arrested and charged with obstructing the highway. He was found guilty, for although he was trying to 'peacefully persuade' the lorry driver not to cross the picket line, he was also trying to stop the driver and detain him against his will. It was said that the section 'does not confer any right on any picket to stop anyone or to stop any vehicle in order to try to persuade persons not to work'. Hunt (1974)

Picketing and the criminal law

Completely separate from the civil law (above) is the criminal law. If a picket commits a criminal offence the police can prosecute him irrespective of whether he is protected by section 15 of the 1974 Act from civil action. Thus, a picket can be protected by section 15 and yet act illegally. As the Code of Practice says, 'If a picket commits a criminal offence he is just as liable to prosecution as any other member of the public who breaks the law. The immunity provided by the civil law does not protect him in any way.'

In practice, it is the risk of prosecution for obstruction of the highway and/or breach of the peace that is the real threat to industrial picketing. Generally, the right to picket depends upon the discretion and tolerance of the policemen present. The crucial element is the decision of the police on whether or not to allow the pickets to remain, or to prosecute, although usually the police are prepared to turn a blind eye to what are technical infringements of the law. However, the picket cannot be sure that his picketing will not lead to a criminal charge, however peacefully he may carry out his picketing. The two criminal charges that are most likely to be brought against a picket are obstruction of the highway and/or breach of the peace.

1. Obstructing the highway

It is an offence wilfully to obstruct the highway (s. 137 of the Highways Act 1980 – maximum penalty £400 fine, see page 343). The offence does not apply to *every* obstruction of the highway but only to an *unreasonable* obstruction of the highway.

Lord Parker has said: 'It depends on the circumstances, including the length of time the obstruction continues, the place where it occurs, the purpose for which it is done and, of course, whether it does in fact cause an actual, as opposed to a potential, obstruction.' So it is a question of fact.

But the courts are usually willing to accept the evidence of the police as to whether there was an obstruction of the highway.

Some forty pickets were circling the outside of a factory. A police officer considered that they were obstructing the highway and asked them to stop, saying he would only allow two or three people to picket. The leader of the pickets, Mr Tynan, refused to obey this instruction and was arrested for obstructing the highway. He was found guilty. It was held that section 15 did not protect Tynan because the pickets were there not merely for the purposes allowed by the section, but also in order to block off part of the highway. Tynan (1967)

In that case the pickets were moving; they were circling the factory. They did this because they thought it would reduce their chances of being accused of obstructing the highway. They argued that since they were on the move they were using the highway for a legitimate purpose and so could not be guilty of obstruction. The decision in the case shows that their supposition was wrong.

Mass pickets are usually unlawful because the numbers involved are an indication that there is an intention to block the highway. In practice, though, mass pickets, while often illegal, are usually effective, because mass arrests are rarely carried out for fear of inflaming the situation. However, if picketing takes place on private land (e.g. on a private entrance-way to factory gates) then there can be no obstruction charge (since it is not the public highway that is being obstructed).

2. Conduct likely to cause a breach of the peace

It is the duty of the police to prevent a breach of the peace. 'Breach of the peace' is a very wide term and it allows police to order someone to stop doing something that is itself perfectly legal, if they think that it is likely to lead to a breach of the peace, i.e. it is likely to lead to the commission of any offence (see page 686). So, if an offence is likely to result, the picket can be told to stop. If he refuses he may be charged with conduct likely to lead to a breach of the peace or with obstructing a police officer in the execution of his duty.

The organizers of a picket had agreed with the police that the number of pickets should be limited to two at each of the two entrances to the factory. Bates wanted to join the two pickets at one of the entrances and refused to accept the limitation on numbers imposed by the police. He was not obstructing the highway, nor was he acting violently or threatening violence. He was arrested for obstructing a police officer in the execution of his duty. Held: He was guilty. It was sufficient that the constable could reasonably anticipate a real possibility of a breach of the peace. Piddington (1961)

Even if a picket is able to avoid falling foul of the two offences detailed above, there are other charges that can be used against him – for instance, if there is any violence a charge of unlawful assembly can be brought; if abusive language is used

491

it can be threatening behaviour (see page 688). Similarly intimidation, possession of an offensive weapon (e.g. banner), criminal damage, and obstructing the police, can often be brought into play.

Extracts from the Code of Practice on Picketing

B. Picketing and the civil law

6 S. 15 of the Trade Union and Labour Relations Act 1974 (as amended by the Employment Act 1980) provides the basic rules for lawful industrial picketing:
  (i)   it may only be undertaken in contemplation or furtherance of a trade dispute;
  (ii) it may only be carried out by a person *attending at or near his own place of work*; a trade union official in addition to attending at or near his own place of work may also attend at or near the place of work of a member of his trade union whom he is accompanying on the picket line and whom he represents;
  (iii) its only purpose must be peacefully obtaining or communicating information or peacefully persuading a person to work or not to work.

7 Picketing commonly involves persuading employees to break their contracts of employment by not going into work and, by disrupting the business of the employer who is being picketed, interfering with his commercial contracts with other employers. If pickets follow the rules outlined in paragraph 6 they are protected by section 13 of the Trade Union and Labour Relations Act 1974 (as amended) from being sued in the civil courts for these civil wrongs.

8 These rules apply in the normal cases where employees picket at their own place of work in support of a dispute with their own employer. Cases may arise, however, where employees picket at their own place of work in support of a dispute between another employer and his employees, for example, where employees at one place are involved in a strike in support of a dispute elsewhere and have mounted a picket line at their own place of work in the course of that strike.

9 In such cases the picketing, in order to be protected, must further satisfy the requirements of lawful secondary action contained in section 17 of the Employment Act 1980. In practice this means that these pickets will have to target their picketing precisely on the supply of goods or services between their employer and the employer in dispute. If they impose or threaten an indiscriminate blockade on their employer's premises, they will be liable to be sued in the civil courts . . .

Lawful purposes of picketing

18 The only purposes of picketing declared lawful by section 15 are:
  • peacefully obtaining and communicating information; and
  • peacefully persuading a person to work or not to work.
  Pickets may, therefore, seek to explain their case to those entering or leaving the picketed premises and to ask them not to enter or leave the premises where the dispute is taking place. This may be done verbally or it may involve the distribution of leaflets or the carrying of banners or placards putting the pickets' case. Pickets have, however, no powers to require other people to stop or to compel them to listen or to do what they have asked them to do. A person who decides to cross a picket line must be allowed to do so. . .

C. Picketing and the criminal law

22 If a picket commits a criminal offence he is just as liable to be prosecuted as any other member of the public who breaks the law. The immunity provided under the civil law does not protect him in any way.

23 The criminal law protects the right of every person to go about his lawful daily business free from interference by others. No one is under any obligation to stop when a picket asks him to do so or, if he does stop, to comply with the picket's request, for example, not to go into work. Everyone has the right, if he wishes to do so, to cross a picket line in order to go into his place of work or to deliver or collect goods. A picket may exercise peaceful persuasion, but if he goes beyond that and tries by means other than peaceful persuasion to deter another person from exercising those rights he may commit a criminal offence. . .

25 A picket has no right under the law to require a vehicle to stop or to be stopped. The law allows him only to ask a driver to stop by words or signals. A picket may not physically obstruct a vehicle if the driver decides to drive on or, indeed, in any other circumstances. A driver must – as on all other occasions – exercise due care and attention when approaching or driving past a picket line, and may not drive in such a manner as to give rise to a reasonably foreseeable risk of injury.

D. Role of the police

26 It is not the function of the police to take a view of the merits of a particular trade dispute. They have a general duty to uphold the law and keep the peace, whether on the picket line or elsewhere. The law gives the police discretion to take whatever measures may reasonably be considered necessary to ensure that picketing remains peaceful and orderly.

27 The police have *no* responsibility for enforcing the *civil* law. An employer cannot require the police to help in identifying the pickets against whom he wishes to seek an order from the civil court. Nor is it the job of the police to enforce the terms of an order. Enforcement of an order on the application of a plaintiff is a matter for the court and its officers. The police may, however, decide to assist the officers of the court if they think there may be a breach of the peace.

28 As regards the *criminal* law the police have considerable discretionary powers to limit the number of pickets at any one place where they have reasonable cause to fear disorder. The law does not impose a specific limit on the number of people who may picket at any one place; nor does this Code affect in any way the discretion of the police to limit the number of people on a particular picket line. It is for the police to decide, taking into account all the circumstances, whether the number of pickets at any particular place is likely to lead to a breach of the peace. If a picket does not leave the picket line when asked to do so by the police, he is liable to be arrested for obstruction either of the highway or of a police officer in the execution of his duty if the obstruction is such as to cause, or be likely to cause, a breach of the peace.

E. Limiting numbers of pickets

31 Large numbers on a picket line are also likely to give rise to fear and resentment amongst those seeking to cross that picket line even where no criminal offence is committed. They exacerbate disputes and sour relations not only between management and employees but between the pickets and their fellow employees. Accordingly pickets and their organizers should ensure that in general the number of pickets does not exceed six at any entrance to a work-place; frequently a smaller number will be appropriate.

F. Organization of picketing

Functions of the picket organizer

32 An experienced person, preferably a trade-union official who represents those picketing, should always be in charge of the picket line. He should have a letter of authority from his union which he can show to police officers or to people who want to cross the picket line. Even when he is not on the picket line himself he should be available to give the pickets advice if a problem arises.

33 An organizer of pickets should maintain close contact with the police. Advance consultation with the police is always in the best interests of all concerned. In particular the organizer and the pickets should seek directions from the police on the number of people who should be present on the picket line at any one time and on where they should stand in order to avoid obstructing the highway.

34 The other main functions of the picket organizer should be:

- to ensure that pickets understand the law and the provisions of this code and that the picketing is conducted peacefully and lawfully;
- to be responsible for distributing badges or armbands, which authorized pickets should wear so that they are clearly identified;
- to ensure that employees from other places of work do not join the picket line and that any offers of support on the picket line from outsiders are refused;
- to remain in close contact with his own union office, and with the offices of other unions if they are involved in the picketing;
- to ensure that such special arrangements as may be necessary for essential supplies or maintenance are understood and observed by the pickets. . .

Non-industrial pickets

If the picket is not connected with a 'trade dispute' then the civil immunities conferred by the 1974 Act do not apply. This means that, in addition to the criminal liabilities set out above, the pickets can have civil proceedings taken against them, i.e. they can be sued for damages and an injunction can be obtained ordering them to stop picketing. This also applies to industrial pickets who take action that is not in contemplation or furtherance of a trade dispute.

So political pickets (such as a picket outside an embassy) or a consumer picket (such as a picket outside a shop that charges excessive prices or discriminates against non-whites) are usually unlawful. The leading case involved an Islington firm of estate agents:

Pickets were outside the office of a firm of estate agents which was alleged to be associated with property speculators who winkled out tenants (i.e. bought them out for cash inducements). The picket was peaceful and orderly. The police did not intervene so the firm started civil proceedings. They claimed that the picketing was a 'legal nuisance' (see page 347) and asked for an injunction ordering the picketing to stop. The Court of Appeal granted the injunction, partly because the

pickets would not have had sufficient money to pay any damages awarded to the estate agents.
Hubbard (1975)

Sit-ins and occupations

Until 1977 it was not a criminal offence for a worker (or student) to stage a sit-in or occupation – assuming, of course, that there was no violence and that the premises were not broken into. The only sanction that could be used against them was a civil one; the owners could seek an injunction (and damages) ordering the occupiers to leave or use reasonable force to eject them as trespassers.

The Criminal Law Act 1977 introduced criminal sanctions for sit-ins and occupations in certain circumstances. Section 6 of the Act creates the offence of 'using or threatening violence to secure an entry' (maximum penalty six months' prison and a fine of £2,000). The section has been criticized because it covers the mere threatening of violence when there is someone on the premises – even if the people staging the occupation do not know he is there. For instance, suppose a security guard sees a group of people approaching the premises equipped with what could be taken as offensive weapons, such as spanners; in such a case, the offence has been committed. Mere weight of numbers could also be taken as a threat of violence. So people entering premises should make it obvious that they are not threatening any violence. They should not carry anything that could be mistaken for an offensive weapon and they should enter in small groups.

If, however, workers refuse to leave a factory at the end of their shift they cannot be prosecuted under the 1977 Act, since their entry was not unlawful.

The trade unionist and his union

Disciplinary proceedings against members

When a person joins a trade union he agrees to be bound by its rules, as set out in the rule book. The rule book forms a contract between the member and the union. The rules will usually allow the union to discipline the member for misconduct, failure to pay subscriptions, or 'conduct detrimental to the union'. The ultimate disciplinary sanction is expulsion from the union.

The courts have been very critical of trade-union disciplinary procedures and have always insisted that the strict wording of the rule book be followed. In addition, the courts have repeatedly stated that the rules must comply with the requirements of 'natural justice' – basically that the accused member be given a fair hearing and an opportunity to answer the charges against him.

Thus, in one case, expulsions were set aside because the members had not received advance notification of the charges and because there was no proper hearing. In another case the expulsion was overruled because the general secretary acted as both prosecutor and judge, by presenting the case against the member and then sitting as chairman of the meeting. Another expulsion was invalid because the member had not had a proper opportunity of refuting the allegations. In short, the courts will bend over backwards to ensure that the member is treated fairly by the union. The judicial justification for this was summed up by Lord Denning in a 1952 case: 'A man's right to work is just as important to him as, if not more important than, his rights of property. These courts intervene every day to protect rights of property. They must also intervene to protect the right to work.'

However, some commentators have suggested that the courts have shown themselves to be over-zealous when protecting individual union members by applying the rules of natural justice. They note that the courts seem less concerned in applying the rules of natural justice in other cases, for instance, to immigrants refused entry and to students facing expulsion from college.

When there is a closed shop

When there is a union-membership agreement (i.e. a closed shop) there are special rules governing the expulsion of union members, and the refusal to allow membership of the union (see page 483).

The 'political fund' – 'contracting out'

The Trade Union Act 1913 allows unions to set up separate political funds if a majority of their members approve of such a step. However, not every union member may want part of his subscription to be allocated towards a political party that he opposes. Accordingly, any member can demand to be allowed to contract out of the political fund. He cannot be victimized, punished, or expelled for doing so.

The Trade Union Act 1984 has made it mandatory for unions to hold regular ballots on whether the political levy should continue. There must be a ballot at least every ten years; the first ballot must have been held by 31 March 1986 (unless a ballot was held in the ten years prior to that date).

Trade-union elections

The 1984 Trade Union Act introduced rules requiring that certain trade-union elections be by secret ballot. Note that the rules only apply to the election of voting members of the union's 'principal executive committee' (i.e. usually the NEC) and they must have been elected by secret ballot within the last five years. Similarly, office holders on the committee (typically a president, or general secretary) must have been elected by secret ballot to that office within the last five years.

PART FOUR

CONSUMER AND BUSINESS

31 The Consumer and the Law

Consumers are protected by a variety of laws. The most important of these are:
- *the law of contract* affects the quality of the goods sold or the service provided. Generally, the shopkeeper who sells defective or unsuitable goods is in breach of contract and must compensate his customer (see page 509).
- *the law of negligence* makes sellers and manufacturers of goods liable for defects that ought to have been avoided. So someone injured by a negligently made product can sue the maker, and perhaps the seller (see page 503).
- *the criminal law* lays down minimum standards of quality, hygiene, design, and construction for many products. In addition, it is a crime for the shopkeeper to have false or misleading price and display labels, etc. (see page 576).
- *credit-control laws* impose strict rules as to when and how hire purchase or credit may be offered (see page 564).

Overseeing all these consumer-protection laws is the Office of Fair Trading (OFT) monitoring consumer complaints and seeing how the laws are working. The OFT can also propose new laws to deal with unfair trading practices, although it prefers to persuade trade organizations to introduce voluntary codes of practice for dealing with consumer complaints and so avoid the need for legislation.

These different forms of consumer protection are largely unrelated and frequently they overlap. Unfortunately, consumer law has developed piecemeal over the years; it is not a neatly thought-out structure with a particular remedy for a particular complaint. So the dissatisfied customer will often have several possible remedies to pursue against the trader.

The difference between 'civil' and 'criminal' remedies

Remember that there is a fundamental difference between 'civil' and 'criminal' cases (see page 757). With civil cases it is for the consumer himself to take the trader to court; he cannot expect the police or any other state official to sue for him. On the other hand, with criminal cases it is generally the police (or another state department such as the Trading Standards Department of the local authority) who take action and prosecute.

Often, of course, the two overlap. For instance, if a publican gives short measure to his customer not only is he in breach of contract to the customer (a civil claim) but he is also in breach of the weights and measures laws (a criminal offence).

499

The legal background to consumer protection

The contract between the customer and the trader

Any purchase or sale involves making a *contract*. Contracts do not have to be lengthy, verbose documents drawn up by solicitors, and they generally need not be in writing. Only contracts for the sale of land, HP agreements, and some insurance agreements need be in writing.

So the shopper who buys potatoes from the grocer, meat from the butcher, sweets from a confectioner, papers from the newsagent, and so on, is making a contract with all those retailers. Similarly if he buys cigarettes from a machine, he is making a contract with the machine owner, and if he buys goods through the post he is making a contract with the mail-order firm. In each contract he is contracting to pay the purchase price, whilst they are contracting to supply the goods. Retailers and consumers are repeatedly entering into contracts and if either side breaks the contract, the other can sue for 'breach of contract'.

When is the contract made?

A typical consumer contract will be made informally:
Customer: 'A pound of apples, please.'
Shopkeeper: 'That will be twenty-five pence, please.'
(Customer hands over twenty-five pence and shopkeeper hands over the apples.) In the eyes of the law, the customer and shopkeeper have made a contract: the customer *offered* to buy the apples; the shopkeeper *accepted* the offer; the apples were then exchanged for money. The requirements of a binding contract were present: an offer and an acceptance, together with value given and received by both sides.

Similarly, suppose that a shop has a washing machine marked at £225. If the customer goes into the shop and tells the shop assistant that he will buy the machine, that constitutes his *offer*, the first stage in the making of a contract. But there is *no* contract until that offer has been accepted, so the customer has until then to change his mind and back out of the deal. But when the shop assistant accepts his order there has been an *acceptance* of the offer, and so the contract is made. The customer cannot now change his mind and demand his money back (unless, of course, he takes the machine home and finds it is defective – see page 518). Similarly, the shopkeeper cannot now back out of the contract. If the machine should have been priced at £325 and the £225 was an error, he cannot demand an extra £100 from the customer; it is too late, for a binding contract has been made.

Can the customer change his mind?

It follows from this that the customer cannot call off the deal once his offer has been accepted by the shopkeeper. But if the customer tells the shopkeeper that he has changed his mind before the shopkeeper has accepted the offer, then the customer is free to back out, without cost or obligation.

In practice, therefore, it is important to know when the offer is accepted. Usually this is obvious; it will be when the shopkeeper accepts the money from the customer, for instance, at the check-out till in the supermarket. But it is not always so straightforward.

Mail order. If goods are ordered through the post, the contract is made (i.e. the customer's offer to buy is accepted by the firm) when the firm *posts* an acceptance letter, confirmation, receipt, or goods to the customer, not when the firm's letter is received by the customer. So goods ordered by post can be cancelled without obligation only if the customer notifies the company (by phone or letter) before they post the goods or a letter of acceptance.

Auction. The customer's bid is the offer for the goods. The bid is accepted when the auctioneer knocks down the goods to the bidder, usually by tapping a hammer on the auction desk. So a bid can be withdrawn any time before the hammer comes down.

Buying goods on credit. Special rules apply to goods bought on credit at home (i.e. not in a shop). Although the contract is made when the seller agrees to sell the goods, the customer usually has five days in which he can change his mind and back out of the contract (see page 568).

A customer who tries to back out of a contract after it has been made will be liable to pay compensation, in the form of damages, to the shopkeeper. The amount of the damages will depend on the seller's loss (see page 521).

Can the shopkeeper change his mind?

Similar rules apply to the shopkeeper. Once he accepts the customer's offer, he cannot change his mind. If he does try to back out of the contract, he will be liable in damages.

Note that the shopkeeper is only obliged to sell the product once he accepts the customer's offer. But he is under no obligation to accept the offer. The practical importance of this is that a shopkeeper is not obliged to sell items just because he has them on display. Thus, in the example of the washing machine earlier, if the shopkeeper had realized that the price was incorrectly marked before he accepted the customer's offer, he could have refused to sell it for £225. The mere fact that he has 'For Sale £225' on a sign attached to the machine does not make him legally liable to sell it at that price. His 'For Sale' sign is no more than an 'invitation to treat': an invitation to the customer to make him an offer. In effect, the shopkeeper is saying 'if you make me an offer of £225 I may well accept it, but I need not do so.' The only occasions when a shopkeeper would be in trouble for not selling goods at the marked price would be:

- if his refusal to accept the offer was because of the customer's race or sex (see Chapter 47, page 695).
- if it could be shown that he had never intended to sell the goods at that price: he would then be committing a criminal offence under the Trade Descriptions Act. It is illegal to mislead customers as to the price they can expect to pay, so if the

shopkeeper displayed an item at a cheap price as a 'come-on' to entice customers into his shop, he would be committing an offence (see page 581). Displaying false price labels is a criminal offence.

What are the terms of the contract?

When the consumer bought the washing machine, he did not discuss the terms of the contract with the shop assistant; it was left unsaid that the machine should wash clothes properly and that it should be safe to use. But although these terms were not specifically agreed upon, the law implied them into the contract. These *implied contractual terms* form the basis of the consumer's protection against faulty goods (see page 509).

As long as there is sufficient certainty as to the basics of the transaction, then the law will imply the other terms. But if there is not sufficient certainty, there will not be a contract. For instance, suppose a customer goes into a shop and asks how much shelf units are and then asks whether the shopkeeper could supply them if necessary. In such a case there is insufficient certainty; they have not agreed which shelf units, how many, or at what price. However, if it was only the price that had not been agreed, there might be sufficient certainty for there to be a contract; the law would simply make it an implied term that the customer would pay a 'reasonable' price, bearing in mind what other shops charge for those units. So price need not be agreed in advance – the housewife who orders a pound of carrots without agreeing the price is impliedly agreeing to pay a reasonable price for those carrots – in other words, the 'going rate' for them.

Sometimes the terms of the contract will be expressly agreed between the retailer and his customer. For instance, a hire shop is likely to have a standard order form setting out its conditions of hire. Or a bus company may have a notice on its tickets, reading 'for conditions see over' and then on the reverse side the traveller is told that he travels 'in accordance with the current Conditions of Business laid down by the Company, a copy of which can be inspected at the Company's offices'. These then are express terms. But these express conditions will not necessarily be binding on the customer:

1. The conditions must have been brought to his attention *before* the contract was made. If the customer only learnt of the conditions after the contract had been made, then obviously they cannot form part of the contract. For instance, if a hotel has a notice stating that 'all valuables are left in rooms at owner's risk' then that sign should be displayed in the booking office, not the bedrooms, for the contract has been made by the time the customer enters his room. Similarly, if a dry-cleaner's has a sign limiting its responsibility for damage to clothes, that sign should not be pinned to the back of the entrance door, for then the customer only sees it when he leaves the shop after making the contract.

2. The conditions must be fair. They must not take away his statutory rights – for instance, that goods are of proper quality or that work done will be to a proper

standard. A clause that attempts to do this will be ineffective, and in addition the shopkeeper will be committing a criminal offence (see page 507). Moreover, *any* condition which limits the retailer's liability to his customers is put to a 'fairness' test – if it is 'unfair' then it is ineffective (see page 515).

There are clear advantages in having express terms in a consumer contract. It avoids doubt as to what has been agreed and it reduces the scope for misunderstandings. In large or unusual transactions it is sensible to have comprehensive express terms, rather than have to rely on implied terms. For instance, when arranging for building work to be carried out, it is always advisable to set out the terms in writing before any work is done.

Suing for breach of contract

If either customer or retailer breaks the contract, the other can sue him for breach of contract. For instance, if the washing machine is faulty, the customer can sue the shopkeeper. If the customer's cheque bounces, then the shopkeeper can sue the customer.

But only the parties to the contract can sue for breach of contract. For instance, if the washing machine had faulty wiring and electrocuted the customer when he used it, he could sue the shopkeeper for breach of contract – namely for breach of the implied promises that the machine was reasonably fit for the purpose intended (see page 509) and also that it was of merchantable quality (see page 511). Even if the wiring defect was the fault of the manufacturer, the shopkeeper would be liable. He could not tell the customer to sue the manufacturer. Instead the customer can sue the shopkeeper, and the shopkeeper can then, in turn, sue the manufacturer.

But suppose the machine was bought by a husband and it was his wife who was electrocuted when using it. The wife would not have been a party to the contract made with the shopkeeper and so she could not sue him for breach of contract. Her only remedy would be to sue the manufacturer (and perhaps the shopkeeper) for negligence in marketing an unsafe machine. However, to win a negligence claim she would have to prove that the manufacturer (or the shopkeeper) had not taken sufficient care – something that it is not always easy to show. So, whereas her husband would have a straightforward contract claim to which there could be no real defence, she would have a complicated negligence claim that might be difficult to win.

Negligence claims: the manufacturer's liability for defective products

If a manufacturer produces faulty goods he can be sued by anyone who suffers injury or loss because of those faults – assuming of course that it can be proved to a court that the manufacturer fell below the standard of care expected of a reasonable manufacturer.

In practice, there is a high standard of care expected from manufacturers. But it can be difficult for a plaintiff to prove that the manufacturers were negligent. A

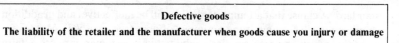

Defective goods
The liability of the retailer and the manufacturer when goods cause you injury or damage

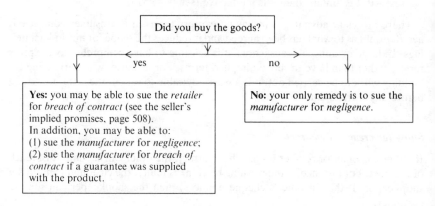

Did you buy the goods?

yes · no

Yes: you may be able to sue the *retailer* for *breach of contract* (see the seller's implied promises, page 508).
In addition, you may be able to:
(1) sue the *manufacturer* for *negligence*;
(2) sue the *manufacturer* for *breach of contract* if a guarantee was supplied with the product.

No: your only remedy is to sue the *manufacturer* for *negligence*.

classic illustration of this was the thalidomide claims; the deformed children would only have been able to win their claims in court if they could show that Distillers had been negligent. Because of their inability to prove negligence the claims dragged on for years as the children's lawyers tried to negotiate a compromise settlement. However, if the mothers who purchased the drug had been injured by it and they – rather than their children – had been suing, it might have been a different matter. The mothers, as customers, might have been able to sue the chemists who supplied the drugs for breach of contract in selling goods that were not of merchantable quality; there would then have been no need to prove negligence.

The negligence laws are aimed at providing compensation for loss, injury, and damage caused by unsafe goods. They are not designed to provide compensation for goods that are shoddy or poor value, unless of course the defects cause loss, injury, or damage. So if a man buys a present for his wife and the present turns out to be shoddily made, the only remedy is for the husband to sue the shopkeeper for breach of contract. The wife cannot sue the shopkeeper since she did not have a contract with him, nor can she sue the manufacturer for negligence, since she has not suffered any loss, damage, or injury.

Reforming the negligence laws

In practice, the negligence laws are applied fairly strictly and the manufacturer of defective goods will probably be able to avoid liability only if he can show that the defect was not his fault or that the plaintiff did not take sufficient care (e.g. did not inspect the goods before using them).

The Council of Europe has proposed that manufacturers should be made strictly liable if they produce defective products. There would, therefore, be no need to show negligence. Thus, the wife electrocuted by the washing machine bought by her husband would not have to prove negligence. All she would have to do would be to show that there was a defect and that it had caused her damage (e.g. injury, time off work, damage to her other property – such as clothes ruined in the washing machine).

This extension of liability is called 'product liability'. It already exists in many American states and if introduced here it would revolutionize legal liability. For instance, in one American case the manufacturers of a 'blow-out-proof' tyre were liable without the plaintiff having to show how or why the tyre burst, as he would have had to do under our laws. In another American case, a car suddenly veered off the road and was so badly damaged that it was impossible to discover what had gone wrong. The court decided that 'something must have been wrong' and that this must, therefore, have been the manufacturer's fault. Such a decision would have been impossible under our negligence laws, for the plaintiff here would have had to prove how the accident happened and why it was the manufacturer's fault.

If (or more probably when) the EEC's draft directive becomes part of our law, it will transform the liability of manufacturers. In effect, they will owe the same duty to the general public as shopkeepers owe to their customers under the law of contract.

The difference between goods and services

Before looking in detail at the legal protection given to consumers, there is a basic point to be considered: different laws apply when buying *goods* from when paying for *services and repairs*. Generally, the customer has more protection if he is buying goods than if he is paying for services or repairs. There is no logical reason why the laws should be different – it is just a by-product of the chaotic way in which our consumer protection laws have evolved over the years.

Is one paying for goods or for services/repairs?

Usually it is obvious whether the contract is for *goods* or for *services/repairs*. For instance:

Buying goods	Paying for services or repairs
Food	Dry-cleaning
Drink	Suit alterations
Paint	Cobbling
Car	Car servicing
Consumer durables	Hiring tools, equipment, etc.
A completed house	Solicitor's fees
Book	Estate agent's fees
Washing machine	Theatre and cinema seats
Piano	Builder's fees

Buying goods	*Paying for services or repairs*
Clothes	Holidays
Light bulbs	Insurance
Electrical goods	Electrical repairs
Spares for a car	Hotel bills
DIY materials	Taxi fare
A painting	Bank services
Off-the-peg suit	A commissioned painting

Sometimes it is often difficult to decide whether one is buying goods or paying for services. For example, when an artist paints a portrait he is supplying services, not goods, because one is paying for his skill and labour in painting the picture, not for the oil paint and canvas that make up the finished item. On the other hand, the tailor who supplies a suit is providing goods, not services, since the customer is really paying for the suit, not his skill. Similarly, if the wing of a car is damaged, the motorist will take it to a garage for repair; the garage will provide a new wing and trim (i.e. goods), and also fit the wing in position and respray it (i.e. service and repair). In this situation the law asks 'What is the customer really paying for – the skill and labour involved or the goods supplied?' Clearly, in that case the motorist is paying for the skill and labour in repairing the car, rather than for the cost of the replacement wing, and so he is paying for services/repairs, not goods.

The important point is that different rules apply: when buying goods the law is as set out on pages 507–29; **when paying for services or repairs** the law is as set out on pages 530–49.

32 Buying Goods

Until recently, shopkeepers could avoid being liable for the quality and fitness of the goods they were selling. Traditionally, the law said that the seller sold the goods, and the buyer bought them, on the terms agreed in their contract. And, although the courts might imply a term that the goods were of proper quality or fit for use, it was possible for these implied terms to be specifically excluded from the contract. So it became common – especially in the motor trade – for receipts and order forms to contain *exemption clauses* which specifically said that there were to be no implied terms as to the quality of the goods. Usually the exemption clause would be in small print and worded in verbose legal jargon that made its effect incomprehensible to all except trained lawyers. All too often the customer did not realize that the exemption clause was taking away his legal rights, but even if he did there was little he could do about it; most retailers sold goods subject to exemption clauses and so the consumer had no choice but to accept the position.

The law's justification for this unfair system was to argue that the customer and shopkeeper had freely entered into a contract with one another and, as adults, they should be bound by the terms of that contract. As Sir George Jessel, a nineteenth-century judge well known for his *laissez-faire* views, put it: 'Contracts when entered into freely and voluntarily shall be held sacred.'

Today we recognize that freedom of contract only exists when there is equality of bargaining power; it is nonsense to suggest that the individual consumer can bargain and negotiate with large retail concerns. But it was not until 1973 that Parliament finally stepped in to safeguard the consumer, and the modern law is set out in the Sale of Goods Act 1979. The consumer is no longer bound by clauses that exempt the shopkeeper from liability for faulty and defective goods. So if a consumer buys shoddy goods the shopkeeper is liable to him, whether or not the shopkeeper knew of the fault, and whether or not he was to blame in any way. Signs and notices saying, for instance, 'all conditions and warranties are hereby excluded' or 'we will not in any case be liable to pay compensation for any loss or damage whatsoever sustained by the purchaser' or 'no money can be refunded' are ineffective; the retailer is still liable for breach of contract if the goods are faulty.

Not only will such a sign be ineffective, but the shopkeepers who display it will be committing a criminal offence. By the Consumer Transactions (Restriction on Statements) Order 1976, it is illegal for a supplier of goods to try to take away a customer's rights under the Sale of Goods Act (see page 509 for details), whether he does

---

Buying Faulty Goods: Is the Shopkeeper Liable?

To find out whether the shopkeeper is liable, ask yourself 'What is the basis of my complaint?'

• 'The goods don't work properly.' The shopkeeper is liable because he has broken Promise No. 1 (see page 509).

• 'Although the goods work properly for their normal use, they are no good for the use I bought them for, which I told the shopkeeper about.' The shopkeeper is liable because he has broken Promise No. 1 (see page 509).

• 'The goods work properly, but they are of poor quality.' The shopkeeper is liable because he has broken Promise No. 2 (see page 511).

• 'There is nothing wrong with the goods, in that they work properly and are of good quality. However, they are not what I asked for.' The shopkeeper is liable because he has broken Promise No. 3 (see page 512).

• 'I was given false information about the goods before I bought them, and this influenced my decision to buy them.' The shopkeeper is liable because he has broken Promise No. 4 (see page 513).

• 'There is nothing wrong with the goods, but I've changed my mind and I no longer want them.' The shopkeeper is not liable (see page 500).

---

so by notice, advertisement, or statement. It is also illegal for him to make statements about the consumer's rights against him over the quality, fitness, and description of the goods unless, at the same time, he tells the customer that his Sale of Goods Act rights are unaffected. A consumer who thinks that a trader has broken the terms of the 1976 Order should contact the local trading standards officer.

The 1976 Order covers any notice that misleads customers as to their Sale of Goods Act rights. For instance, 'no refunds', 'no complaints considered once you have left the shop', 'any complaint must be made within seven days of purchase' are all illegal. For example, in 1978, Abbey Fashions in Leeds had a sign reading 'We willingly exchange goods but regret that money cannot be refunded'. The proprietor was fined £5 and ordered to pay £15 costs since the sign implied that purchasers of defective goods could not claim their money back, which of course they can. Similarly, a Shrewsbury umbrella-maker was found guilty after displaying a sign which read 'All umbrellas must be checked before leaving till. No returns can be accepted after use.'

The 1979 Act and the 1976 Order do not apply to trade purchases – in other words when the goods are bought in the course of business and not as a consumer purchase (see page 515 for how to decide if it is business or not). With a business purchase a trader can insert an exclusion clause, although even then the clause will be subject to a 'fairness' test, and if it is unfair on the buyer it will be ineffective (see page 516).

The Sale of Goods Act

Certain terms as to the quality and fitness of the goods are implied into the contract made between the shopkeeper and his customer. The Sale of Goods Act 1979 implies three terms, which are in effect promises made to the customer by the shopkeeper:

1. The goods are fit for their usual use;
2. The goods are of proper quality;
3. The goods are as described.

In addition to these three promises, the shopkeeper is bound by the Misrepresentation Act 1967 not to misdescribe the goods when he sells them. So there is an additional promise by the shopkeeper:

4. His sales talk is true.

The shopkeeper's promises

Promise No. 1: The goods are fit for their usual use

The customer can assume that a shopkeeper has selected his stock with skill and care, so that the items he sells will be fit for their normal use. For instance, a person who buys a bun from a food shop can assume it is fit to eat. Likewise, a raincoat must at least be showerproof; children's toys must be safe for children to play with; books must be legible; chairs must be safe and comfortable to sit on.

If the item is not fit for its usual purpose then the shopkeeper is in breach of contract. This is the effect of section 14 (3) of the Sale of Goods Act 1979:

> Where the seller sells goods in the course of a business, and the buyer, expressly or by implication, makes known to the seller any particular purpose for which the goods are being bought, there is an implied condition that the goods . . . are reasonably fit for that purpose, whether or not that is a purpose for which such goods are commonly supplied, except where the circumstances show that the buyer does not rely, or that it is unreasonable for him to rely, on the seller's skill or judgement.

For instance:

> *The Frost family bought some milk, but it was contaminated with typhoid germs. Mrs Frost died. Held: Breach of contract since the milk was not fit for the purpose for which it was bought.* Frost (1905)

> *A six-year-old boy bought a 6d. catapult from his local newsagents. The catapult came from Hong Kong and was made of poor-quality plastic. When the boy was using it, it broke in two, and part of the catapult and a stone went in his face, causing the loss of an eye. Held: He could sue the newsagent for breach of contract under s. 14 (3) – the catapult was not fit for its purpose.* Godley (1960)

The shopkeeper is only liable if the goods are not fit for the use for which they were supplied. For instance, if a chair collapses when it is sat on, there is a clear breach of the shopkeeper's promise. But if the chair collapses when it is being stood on by

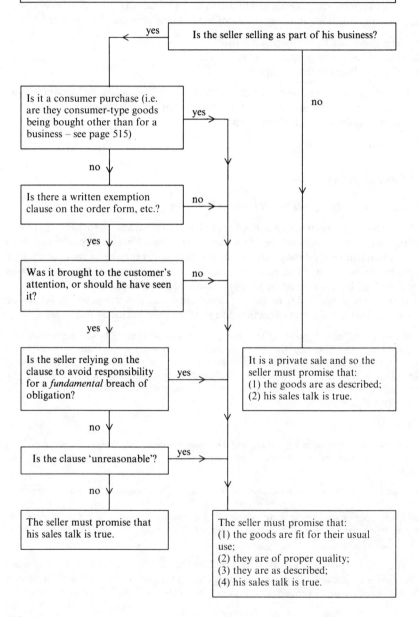

**Buying goods
The seller's promises to the customer**

Is the seller selling as part of his business?

yes

no

Is it a consumer purchase (i.e. are they consumer-type goods being bought other than for a business – see page 515)

yes

no

Is there a written exemption clause on the order form, etc.?

no

yes

Was it brought to the customer's attention, or should he have seen it?

no

yes

Is the seller relying on the clause to avoid responsibility for a *fundamental* breach of obligation?

yes

It is a private sale and so the seller must promise that:
(1) the goods are as described;
(2) his sales talk is true.

no

Is the clause 'unreasonable'?

yes

no

The seller must promise that his sales talk is true.

The seller must promise that:
(1) the goods are fit for their usual use;
(2) they are of proper quality;
(3) they are as described;
(4) his sales talk is true.

510

a painter then the shopkeeper may not be liable, since that is not the usual use to which a chair is put.

However, if the customer makes it clear that he wants the item for an unusual purpose, then the shopkeeper will be liable if he says it will be suitable for that purpose. For instance, suppose the customer wants to stick two pieces of plastic together but the shopkeeper only has wood glue; if the customer asks the shopkeeper if the wood glue will work on plastic, then the shopkeeper will be in breach of contract if he says it will work and it does not.

If the shopkeeper's promise is broken, the customer may be able to reject the goods, although more often he will probably have to accept damages (see page 518).

If the item is bought privately. If the goods are bought from a private individual, as opposed to a trader (for instance, if bought from a private advertiser in the local paper), then Promise No.1 will not apply (see page 515).

Promise No. 2: The goods are of proper quality

The shopkeeper must ensure that the goods he sells are of proper, merchantable quality. 'Where the seller sells goods in the course of a business there is an implied condition that the goods supplied under the contract are of merchantable quality' (s. 14(2), Sale of Goods Act 1979).

It is not always easy to decide if goods are of proper quality, although usually the test is to ask 'Should they have been sold in that condition?' If not, then they are not of merchantable quality. The price of the goods and the way in which they were described will usually be the key factors – basically, the shopkeeper must sell goods that are of a proper standard, bearing in mind their price and description. So one can expect a lower standard from goods bought in a sale and from second-hand goods.

A clock that keeps poor time, a new car that is scratched, shoes that are scuffed, clothes that are torn or stained, china that is chipped, a shirt with a button missing: these will all be goods that are not of merchantable quality.

Often the 'merchantable quality' promise will overlap with Promise No. 1, that the goods are fit for their usual purpose. For instance, if a new car will not start, it is not fit for its purpose nor is it of merchantable quality. Yet an item can be fit for its purpose and not of merchantable quality. For example, if a new car is scratched, that scratch will not affect its performance and so it will be fit for the purpose, yet it will not be of merchantable quality – obviously, a new car should not be scratched.

One difficult question is 'How long can one expect an article to last before faults develop in it?' This will depend upon the facts of the individual case but, as always, the price and description of the item will be crucial. Obviously, a £100 watch should last several years without developing a fault, whereas a £5 watch may only be expected to last six months or so. On the other hand, if the £5 watch was described as 'will last for ever', it might be reasonable to expect it to last a few years. The general test is 'What can you reasonably expect of such an item?' If in doubt, the customer should take it back and complain.

But the merchantable-quality rule does not apply 'as regards defects specifically drawn to the buyer's attention before the contract is made' (s. 14(2)(a)). So if the customer asks for a pair of plimsolls but is told 'We only have one pair in your size, but they have a black mark on them', he cannot later bring them back on the basis of the black mark, because he was specifically told about the defect. However, if he finds some other defect, such as an extra mark that he was not warned about, he could then take them back to the shop.

Similarly, the merchantable-quality rule does not apply 'if the buyer examines the goods before the contract is made, as regards defects which that examination ought to reveal' (s. 14(2)(b)). So if the buyer of the plimsolls had looked at them before buying them he could not bring them back because of an additional mark if he should have seen the mark when he examined them. It is obviously a matter of reasonableness; if the mark was obvious then he cannot complain, but if the mark could not be seen because it was covered by the price-tag, he could complain. The moral of this is: the customer should either not examine goods or, if he does examine them, examine them properly. If he only examines them half-heartedly, he cannot complain about defects that would have been revealed in a more thorough examination.

If the shopkeeper's promise is broken, the customer may be able to reject the goods, although more often he will probably have to accept damages (see page 518).

If the item is bought privately. If the goods are bought from a private individual, as opposed to a trader (for instance, if bought from a private advertiser in the local paper), then the promise will not apply (see page 515).

If it is not a consumer purchase. If the customer buys the goods as a trade purchase, rather than as a consumer purchase, the promise may not apply (see page 515).

Promise No. 3: The goods are as described

Goods must be what they say they are. They must be as described by the shop assistant or by a label or sign. 'Where there is a contract for the sale of goods by description there is an implied condition that the goods shall correspond with the description' (s. 13, Sale of Goods Act 1979).

This is so even when the customer selects the goods himself, for example, off the shelves of a supermarket. Thus, a 'cod steak' must be made of cod, not haddock; a 100 per cent wool pullover must not contain any fibre other than wool; cotton sheets must not contain any nylon; a tin of spaghetti hoops must not contain spaghetti numbers; a 1985 car must not be late 1984; size 7 shoes must not be size 6; and so on. This is so even if there is nothing wrong with the goods. For instance, the customer who orders a pale blue raincoat can refuse to accept a dark blue raincoat, even if the dark blue raincoat is otherwise free of faults.

If the item is bought privately. Unlike Promises 1 and 2, this promise does apply to private sales (i.e. when the goods are bought from a private individual as opposed to a trader). For instance:

Mr Taylor advertised his car as 'Herald convertible, white, 1961, twin carbs.'. Mr Beale bought the car but later discovered that it was an amalgam of two different cars; the rear was from a 1961 Herald 1200 and this was welded to the front end of an earlier Herald 948. Mr Beale sued for breach of contract, saying the car was not 'as described'. Held: Mr Taylor was liable. The car was not as described. Beale (1967)

If the promise is broken, the customer may be able to reject the goods, although more often he will probably have to accept damages (see page 518).

If it is not a consumer purchase. If the customer buys the goods as a trade purchase, rather than as a consumer purchase, the promise may not apply (see page 515).

Promise No. 4: His sales talk is true

Following on from the accuracy of the description of goods is the requirement that any sales talk must be truthful. The customer can sue the seller if false statements are made about the goods.

But not all sales talk is actionable. The law accepts that salesmen often use exaggerated language and meaningless hyperbole – that is all part of the language of the market place. The customer is expected to take phrases like 'she's a beauty'; 'the best around'; 'fantastic value'; 'one of our most popular models', and so on, with a pinch of salt. The law will dismiss that sort of sales talk as mere 'puff', and the customer cannot bring the goods back just because they are not 'the best around'.

But the law will intervene if the salesman makes statements of fact about the goods which induce the customer to buy them. So if the salesman says 'You will get thirty-eight miles to the gallon from this model' or 'The element only needs to be replaced once a year', then the customer can complain if these statements turn out to be untrue. The law calls these 'misrepresentations', and if they induced the customer to buy the goods, then the shopkeeper is liable even if he (or his salesman) did honestly believe that the car would do 38 m.p.g. or that the heating elements would last at least a year. Even if the seller is acting innocently, and to the best of his knowledge, he is responsible should his representation be untrue (Misrepresentation Act 1967). But statements of opinion cannot be representations; for instance, if the salesman says 'This jacket looks better on you' or 'I think the sound quality of this radio is better', the customer cannot complain if he later decides that he does not agree with the salesman's opinion.

If a customer has been given false sales talk, then in addition to a breach of the Misrepresentation Act, there will often have been a breach of Promise No. 1 (the goods are fit for their purpose), and Promise No. 3 (the goods are as described). However, Promise No. 1 does not apply to a purchase from a private individual, as opposed to a purchase from a trader. So if the goods were sold privately, the buyer would have to rely on the Misrepresentation Act (Promise No. 4) and so show that the misrepresentation induced him to buy the item, or rely on there having been a false description of the goods (Promise No. 3).

In practice, the difficulty about bringing consumer claims based on misleading sales talk is that you have to prove that the salesman said what he did. This is why it is usually advisable for the customer to have a friend with him when making major purchases, so that the friend can be a witness as to what was said and promised by the salesman.

If the shopkeeper's promise is broken the customer may be able to reject the goods, although more often he will probably have to accept damages (see page 518). The shopkeeper, apart from being liable to his customer, may well have committed a criminal offence under the Trade Descriptions Acts (see page 577).

Buying goods on credit

The customer does not lose any of his legal rights if he buys goods on credit (e.g. HP, credit sale, or a credit card such as Barclaycard or Access – but not an overdraft or bank loan).

In fact he will usually be better off than if he had paid in cash. This is because the Consumer Credit Act 1974 makes the credit supplier (usually a bank or finance company) equally liable with the shopkeeper for the quality of the goods bought. In other words, the shopkeeper's four promises apply to the credit supplier as well and he can be sued if, for instance, the goods are not fit for their usual purpose. If the shopkeeper is liable for breaking one of the shopkeeper's promises, then so is the credit supplier. The customer can sue either the shopkeeper or the credit supplier.

The legal basis of this liability depends on the type of credit:

• *if the goods are bought on* HP, then the customer's contract will be directly with the finance company (see page 566 for how HP works). Thus, the finance company is, in effect, the seller of the goods and is liable for the shopkeeper's promises. But this only applies if the credit provided was for not more than £15,000.

• *if the goods are bought on another form of credit* (e.g. Access), then the Consumer Credit Act 1974, section 75, makes the credit supplier liable, but only if the cash price of the goods was between £100 and £30,000.

Illustration. *Fred buys a car for £5,000, a suit for £150, and a radio for £45. All three items are defective. The car was brought through a bank loan he had arranged; the suit was bought on Access, and the radio on Barclaycard. He can obviously sue the three retailers, but can he also sue his bank, Access, and Barclaycard? The answer is that he cannot sue his bank since that was a personal loan arranged by himself. Nor can he sue Barclaycard, since the price of the radio was under £100 and thus excluded from the liability rules. But, he can go against Access in respect of the suit, even though Access were in no way to blame for the suit being faulty. He has the same rights against Access as he does against the shopkeeper.*

The moral is clear – always try to pay by credit card, not cheque. This is especially so when buying a second-hand car, or paying for car repairs – those are the sort of transactions in which problems can arise. If there are problems, then you will have a claim against the bank, and not against a dodgy trader. Bear in mind that the bank will not be automatically liable; it will only be liable if the trader is liable (e.g. because the car is not of merchantable quality, the sales talk was not true, etc.). But if the trader is liable, then the bank will be liable as well – and they are more likely to have the money to make it worth suing them!

In practice, few cases are brought against credit suppliers. Few customers seem to realize that credit suppliers are liable for the goods bought with their credit, and those who do generally prefer to pursue their complaint against the shopkeeper who actually sold the item. But the potential right to claim from the credit supplier can be very useful, especially when the shopkeeper is not worth suing, perhaps because he has since gone bankrupt.

If the customer does claim from the credit supplier, the credit supplier can, in turn, sue the shopkeeper for any damages or compensation paid to the customer.

Buying from a private individual

The customer has more rights when buying from a dealer, shopkeeper, or trader than from a private individual. When goods are bought from a trader, all four of the shopkeeper's promises apply; when buying from a private individual the only promises that apply are:

No. 3. The goods are as described (s. 13, Sale of Goods Act 1979) – page 512.
No. 4. The sales talk is true (Misrepresentation Act 1967) – page 513.

The seller will be a dealer or trader even if he only operates a part-time business. For instance, the person who buys cars and does them up at the weekends to sell them will be a dealer and so all four promises will apply. This will be so even if he advertises the cars for sale as though he were a private individual. In addition, he will be committing a criminal offence. Under the Business Advertisements (Disclosure) Order 1977 it is an offence for a person selling goods in the course of a business to publish an advertisement which does not make it reasonably clear that the goods are sold in the course of a business. So, the part-time car dealer should put 'Trade' in his advertisements. In practice, of course, the 1977 Order is largely ignored and many traders still sell their goods through classified advertisements without disclosing that they are traders. The real value of the 1977 Order is that it gives a powerful bargaining counter to the dissatisfied customer, who can demand satisfaction or threaten to report the trader to the trading standards officer for prosecution.

A person can be selling in the course of business even if he is selling an item in which he does not trade. For instance, if a solicitor buys a new desk and decides to sell his old desk, the sale of his old desk will be a trade sale since it is sold by the solicitor as part of his business activities. So, all four of the shopkeeper's promises would apply.

Buying as a consumer, not a trader: exclusion clauses

The customer usually has more legal protection if he buys an item as a 'consumer' than when he buys as a trader or for a business. This is because the seller can insert an exclusion clause excluding Promises 1, 2, and 3 (i.e. all the Sale of Goods Act implied terms) if the buyer is not a 'consumer'. Since such exclusion clauses are commonly found in trade receipts and order forms, it is important to decide whether a customer is a 'consumer' or not.

Consumer and Business: The Consumer and the Law

The Unfair Contract Terms Act 1977, section 12, says a person will be a consumer if the goods are of a type ordinarily bought by private individuals and the seller is in business but the buyer is not (or does not pretend to be).

Illustration. Luigi owns a restaurant. He buys potatoes from his local greengrocer. If the potatoes are for use in his restaurant, it will not be a consumer purchase. If the potatoes are not for use in the restaurant but for Luigi's own home use, it probably will be a consumer purchase. However, if the potatoes are for his home use, but Luigi implies that they are for use in the restaurant (e.g. by receiving a trade discount or by including them in a large order for the restaurant), then Luigi will not be dealing as a consumer.

Illustration. John Evans is going away on holiday, so he decides to buy a camera. If he buys the camera from a discount store it will be a consumer purchase, unless the store is for 'trade only'. If he buys a second-hand camera from a friend who is replacing his camera, it will not be a consumer purchase since the friend is not in the camera business.

If goods are bought at auction, it is automatically assumed that it is not a consumer purchase, even if the purchase is made by a private individual who is not a trade buyer (see page 527).

If the customer is buying as a consumer then the shopkeeper cannot insert an exclusion clause which excludes the shopkeeper's Promises 1, 2, and 3. In fact, it will be a criminal offence if he tries to do so (see page 508). However, if the buyer is not dealing as a consumer, then the seller can exclude those three shopkeeper's promises, although he can never exclude Promise No. 4 (i.e. that his sales talk is true).

Sothebys agreed to sell a diamond; it had a reserve price of £9,000, although it had been valued at £22,500. Unfortunately, it was stolen from Sotheby's offices and so they were sued. They relied on an exclusion clause in the conditions of sale which said that they were not liable for any loss or damage – whether or not it was caused by their negligence. Held: The exclusion clause meant that Sothebys were not liable (so make sure that you insure anything before putting it in auction). Spriggs (1984)

But if an exemption clause does purport to exclude the three promises, it may not necessarily be effective. Firstly, the exclusion clause will be invalid if it was not brought to the customer's attention before he made the purchase (see page 502). Secondly, the court will strike out the clause if its effect is so fundamental that it allows the seller to avoid liability for a basic breach of the contract. The court will ask itself 'What was the presumed intention of the buyer and seller; can they really have both intended that the seller should not be liable for this defect?' So if the breach of contract is absolutely fundamental then the exclusion clause may not work (e.g. if the auctioneer loses the diamond because he leaves it on a bus).

A third way of attacking an exclusion clause in a non-consumer transaction is to argue that it is 'unreasonable'. By section 11 of the Unfair Contract Terms Act 1977 the exclusion clause could be struck out if it was unreasonable. Whether it was unreasonable would be decided in the light of all the circumstances of the case, but the sort of factors that the court would consider include:

• the relative bargaining strength of the buyer and seller; could the buyer have gone elsewhere, or did he have little choice but to accept the seller's terms?

- did the buyer have the choice of paying more in return for having the exclusion clause removed? For instance, could he have gone to the retail counter rather than the trade counter?
- was the customer aware of the exclusion clause? Was it brought to his attention? Did he understand what it meant, or was it in incomprehensible legal jargon? Was it tucked away in the small print?
- has the customer previously bought goods from the seller on similar terms?
- were the goods made, adapted, or designed to the customer's special order?

It is for the seller to show that his exclusion clause is reasonable, not for the customer to show it is unreasonable. For instance:

British Rail were to deliver a suitcase from Stockport to Haverfordwest. Their price was £6·03 and the standard BR conditions exempted BR from any liability unless the customer could show that BR's wilful misconduct had caused the loss – and, in any event, the compensation to be paid was to be by reference to the weight of the goods, not their value. Unfortunately, the suitcase was lost and the customer sued. BR said that the exemption clause prevented them from being liable since the customer could not show that they had been guilty of 'wilful misconduct'. Held: The exemption clause was invalid as it was 'unreasonable'. Thus, BR were liable for £320 damages – which was the value of the suitcase plus its contents. However, the judge refused to give additional compensation to cover the customer's 'distress and inconvenience'. Waldron-Kelly (1981)

Mr Woodman took photos of his friend's wedding, intending to give the photos to the friend as a wedding present. The film was taken to a chemist's shop which acted as collecting agent for a national firm of film processors. On the side of the envelope into which the film was put was an exclusion clause stating that the company was only liable for the value of the film. When the films were returned it was obvious that many of the photos had been lost. Mr Woodman sued but the company merely offered him the value of the ruined film. Held: The exemption clause was 'unreasonable' and so it was invalid. Mr Woodman was awarded £75 damages for the distress and loss of enjoyment arising from the loss of the wedding photos. Incidentally, the judge did go on to say that the exclusion clause would have been reasonable if there had been a two-tier pricing system (i.e. a lower price in which it is made clear that the processing firm is not liable, plus the option of paying more for a service in which the company is liable). Since then some processors have introduced such a system – but many have not, and those that have not are probably operating with exclusion clauses that are invalid. Woodman (1981)

A farmer bought 30 lb of cabbage seeds. But the seeds were useless – they were not cabbage seeds at all! So the farmer sued for his lost profit on the cabbage crop (£61,000). But the seed-suppliers said they were not liable for this amount because an exclusion clause limited their liability to the £130 cost of the seed. Held: The exclusion clause was 'unreasonable' (under the Unfair Contract Terms Act) and so the farmer was entitled to the full amount of his lost profits. George Mitchell (1983)

The rules on exclusion clauses are summarized in the chart on page 510. One point to note is that a trader does not suffer any criminal penalty for 'trying on' an ineffective exclusion clause. All that happens is that it does not work. But why shouldn't it be a criminal offence to try deliberately to mislead the customer as to his rights? In practice, it is all too common to find exclusion clauses on display when the traders must know that they are no more than a con-trick, e.g. wildlife parks which try to disclaim all responsibility for negligence if visitors are injured; ferry companies which say they are not liable if an accident is caused through negligence of the crew or unseaworthiness of the boat; home-improvements firms which say they will only accept responsibility for defects if the customer points them out within seven days of the work being done; car-hire firms which say they will not accept any liability for loss, etc. due to faults in the cars supplied. Why shouldn't these deceitful traders be guilty of a criminal offence?

Taking action over faulty goods

If the goods are faulty, the shopkeeper will probably be in breach of contract for breaking one of the four shopkeeper's promises.

The first thing to be done is to complain. Many shopkeepers will not argue if a reasoned complaint is made to them, but it is always important that the complaint be made without delay. If the shopkeeper refuses to accept responsibility, do not give up. Send him a letter, putting the complaint in writing. Find out whether he is in a trade association; if so, take the complaint up with the association. If the goods were bought on credit, consider claiming from the credit supplier (see page 514).

If all else fails, the customer will have to take the matter to court. For claims involving no more than £5,000, the action is brought in the county court. In addition, if the claim involves no more than £500, there are two rules of court that make it relatively easy for the consumer to sue:

• each side will have to pay its own legal costs. So even if the case is lost, the customer need not fear that he will be landed with paying the shopkeeper's legal costs;

• the case will normally be heard as an arbitration hearing. This is a relatively informal hearing, unlike a more formal court hearing in front of a judge. If the claim exceeds £500, the case can still go to arbitration, but only if the shopkeeper agrees.

For full details of these rules see pages 843 and 872.

The steps to be taken in a DIY county court case are set out on page 872.

Generally, of course, it is not necessary to go to court; the shopkeeper and his customer can usually negotiate a satisfactory compromise. But, when negotiating, it is important that they both know what the law entitles them to.

Damages or your money back?

If the goods are faulty, the customer will often have to accept damages – cash compensation (e.g. the cost of repair) – rather than be able to ask for his money back.

However, the customer may not want damages, he may prefer to have his money back and to take his custom elsewhere. For instance, if he has just spent £500 on a colour TV, but it blows its tube a few weeks later, he might well prefer to buy a different type of set from a different shop, rather than have that TV repaired. Unfortunately, the law is not clear on this point and it is not certain whether the customer is entitled to return the item and have his money back.

The Sale of Goods Act says that a customer loses his right to reject the goods once he has 'accepted' them. Acceptance does not mean a physical acceptance of the goods, such as their being handed over to the customer by the shop assistant. Instead, it means a legal acceptance – when the customer has made it clear that he accepts the goods as satisfactory, or after he has kept them for a reasonable time without rejecting them as unsatisfactory. The difficulty, of course, is in deciding how long is a 'reasonable time'. After how long does the customer lose the right to reject the goods? The answer is that no one knows! Leading lawyers are divided on the question and the only thing that is certain is that the law needs clarifying.

A Daimler was delivered in October. Over the next six months there were several faults, mainly involving oil leaks and brake-judder. In June, the buyer offered to return the car and he stopped paying the HP instalments. Had he left it too late to return the car and have his money back? Held: No. He had acted promptly enough and so he had all his money back. The car was not of merchantable quality. Laurelgates (1983)

Similarly, if the customer has treated the goods as his own (e.g. he has had them repaired, or altered, *before* he complains) then it will be too late to reject the goods. He will have to accept damages – in practice, the cost of repair. Often, though, many shops are prepared to give cash refunds even when the customer has legally 'accepted' the goods; they feel that for reasons of customer goodwill it is better to treat their customers fairly rather than rely on the strict letter of the law. So it is always worth asking for your money back.

How much damages?

If goods are faulty and it is too late to cancel the purchase, the customer can claim damages for all losses naturally and directly flowing, in the ordinary course of events, from the breach.

Illustration. Mrs Jones buys a washing machine. Three months later it overheats, ruining the clothes inside it. Clearly the shop is liable since the machine is not of merchantable quality (see page 511). It is too late for her to get her money back, but she can claim:

- *the cost of the engineer's visits in inspecting the machine and repairing it;*
- *the value of the clothes that have been ruined;*
- *the additional cost of taking her clothes to a launderette while her machine is out of order;*
- *the postage and phone bills involved;*
- *her lost wages while off work (e.g. to let the engineer in).*

If she did not lose time off work she could claim a nominal sum for the inconvenience involved, say £5 per half day. All of these would be losses naturally flowing from the shop's breach of contract. Mrs Jones would, of course, be under a duty to keep her losses to a minimum, so she would be expected to do all she could to keep the damages to a minimum (e.g. postpone doing her washing for a day, rather than incur extra launderette bills).

A garage sold a 1979 car as having been registered in October 1978. Held: The buyer was entitled to damages. These were based on the difference in price between a 1978 and 1979 car in Glass's trade guide. South London Tyre (1984)

In practice few consumers claim for inconvenience. In law, however, there is no reason why they should not:

> *Mr Gascoigne bought a second-hand car for his wife to use, but it gave nothing but trouble. The garage was liable. Mrs Gascoigne had been inconvenienced by the breakdowns – when pregnant she had to use other transport on her hospital visits, and bus and taxi fares had been incurred. Could the Gascoignes claim damages for the inconvenience and frustration, apart from the cost of repairs? Held: Yes. They were awarded £75 for inconvenience and frustration.* Gascoigne (1978)

Damages and cancellation are the only two remedies recognized by the law. In practice, though, it is unlikely that either of these remedies will be offered by the shopkeeper or, indeed, insisted upon by the customer. The shopkeeper will often offer to repair the fault, to replace the item, or to give a credit note. Whilst these may be satisfactory remedies it should be remembered that a court would never make such an order; it would either order damages or money back.

Exchanging goods

It follows that the customer is not obliged to accept a replacement item from the shopkeeper. In law, he is entitled to either damages or money back; he need not accept an exchange. Usually, of course, the customer will be prepared to do so, but if for some reason he does not want to – perhaps because he wishes to take his custom elsewhere – he need not.

A free repair

The same applies if the shopkeeper offers to repair the defect. If the customer has not accepted the goods he can demand his money back. If he has accepted them, he can insist on damages. The damages will usually be the cost of repair, plus any incidental expenses. He need not have the repair carried out by the shopkeeper – he can, if he wishes, have the repair done elsewhere and send the bill to the shopkeeper. If he does this, he must, of course, ensure that the repair work is done at a reasonable price, so he should obtain estimates from several sources.

In practice, of course, there is unlikely to be any reason why the customer will not agree to the shopkeeper doing the repair.

Credit notes

Since a credit note is not one of the two remedies recognized by the law, it will be either less, or more, than the customer is entitled to. If the customer has not accepted the goods he can demand all his money back, in cash. So he need not accept a credit note if he would rather have cash. However, if the customer has accepted the goods, then he will only be entitled to damages. So if the shopkeeper offers him a credit note for the full value of the goods, then this will probably be worth more than the damages he could otherwise demand. Once the customer has accepted a credit note he cannot demand that it be exchanged for cash. He has agreed to accept goods to the value of the credit note and he cannot later change his mind.

Other points to watch

Cancelling an order: the customer's liability

A customer is free to cancel his order before the order has been accepted by the retailer, for until the acceptance there is no binding contract (see page 500). But once the contract has been made, the customer will be in breach of contract if he tries to back out of the purchase. The seller would then be able to sue him for damages – in other words, his losses arising as a direct and natural result, in the ordinary course of events, from the customer's change of mind.

Suppose the customer ordered a new car but changed his mind and cancelled the order after the garage had accepted his order. The amount of compensation he would have to pay the garage would depend upon how easily the garage could find another buyer for the car. So if demand for those cars exceeded the supply, the garage would be able to re-sell immediately without loss; accordingly, no damages would be payable. However, if the supply of those cars exceeded the demand for them, the garage would be unable to sell the car; even if they did sell it, they could argue that they would have been able to supply another car to the new customer if the original customer had not cancelled his order. Thus, they could demand their lost profit.

So, in practice, when a customer cancels his order there can be considerable argument as to the amount due.

Lazenby Garages bought a second-hand BMW for £1,325 on 14 February. Five days later, Mr Wright agreed to buy it for £1,670, to take delivery two weeks later. But on 20 February, he changed his mind and told Lazenby's that he would not accept delivery of the BMW. Six weeks later, Lazenby's sold the car for £1,770 – £100 more than the price agreed with Mr Wright. Lazenby's sued Mr Wright for their 'lost profit' on his contract, some £345. His defence was that Lazenby's had not suffered any loss by his breach of contract. Held: A second-hand car was an individual item, for which there was no available market. But the garage could only recover its true loss, and since it had ended up making a profit, Mr Wright need not pay them any damages. Lazenby Garages Ltd (1976)

If the item involved is a mass-produced consumer item – such as a washing machine – then clearly there can be no argument as to the shopkeeper's loss; it is his lost profit. The shopkeeper can easily obtain washing machines to sell to his other customers, so if a sale is lost, the shopkeeper will have lost his profit. The mere fact that another customer buys that particular machine will not alter the position, since the shopkeeper could have obtained another machine to meet that customer's order. So the shopkeeper is entitled to his lost profit. In practice, he will simply sue the customer for the full price (i.e. the amount the customer agreed to pay); the customer will then have to pay for it, take delivery, and sell it as second-hand.

Buying second-hand goods

The seller of goods makes the same four promises to the buyer whether the goods are new or second-hand (see page 509). All that is different is the standard of quality, durability, and fitness that can be expected from second-hand goods. This will largely depend upon the price paid and the description of the goods. A cardigan bought for 10p in a jumble sale cannot be expected to last as long as a cardigan bought in a 'nearly new' shop for £5. In turn, the nearly new cardigan cannot be expected to be as good as a new £7 cardigan, but the buyer would expect the £5 cardigan to be reasonably sound, bearing in mind that the saving is only £2.

But a more important consequence of buying second-hand is that, more often than not, the seller will be a private individual – for instance, selling through a classified advertisement. If the seller is a private individual (as opposed to a trader), the shopkeeper's Promises No. 1, 'the goods are fit for their usual use', and No. 2, 'the goods are of proper quality', will not apply. So the buyer will have less protection as to the quality and suitability of the goods when buying privately than when buying from a trader (see page 515).

Part-time or full-time traders who advertise as though they were private individuals are committing a criminal offence (see page 515).

Sale goods and seconds

The position is the same as with second-hand goods bought from a trader, namely that all four shopkeeper's promises are valid, but there is a lower standard applied, depending upon the price and description of the goods. See also 'Labels That are Controlled' (page 582).

Paying a deposit

A deposit is usually more than a mere sign of good intentions; it will probably be a commitment to go ahead with the purchase. If a deposit is paid by the customer and accepted by the retailer, there will be a binding contract and neither side can back out, unless the contrary was agreed. For instance, the parties can withdraw without obligation if a deposit for a house is said to be 'subject to contract' or if a deposit note says 'refundable in full if claimed within two weeks hereof'.

If the deposit is a binding commitment to go ahead with the contract, the customer will be liable in damages if he backs out (see page 500). The amount of damages to be paid will depend upon the seller's loss, and this may be more, or less, than the deposit. If it is less, the balance of the deposit must be refunded; if it is more, the customer is liable for the excess. Many traders mistakenly believe they can always claim all of a defaulting customer's deposit. That is not so, but any doubt can be avoided by the customer referring to the money paid as a 'part-payment' and not as a deposit. This will be conclusive proof that the sum paid cannot be automatically forfeited.

Goods on approval

If goods are bought on approval, the customer will usually have to return them to the shop by a certain date if he wants his money back. If this is so, he must ensure that the goods are returned in time; if he is late, he cannot insist on his money back, even if the goods are still in perfect condition. The customer must take proper care of goods on approval, and he will be responsible if they are damaged through his lack of care. The same will apply to goods on 'sale or return'.

Late delivery of ordered goods

Sometimes the customer will order an item and then be told that it is out of stock and cannot be supplied for some time. Can he back out of the transaction and take his custom to another shop that can offer immediate delivery?

Generally, the answer will be 'no', for there is already a binding contract with the shopkeeper and the customer cannot back out – unless, of course, it was specifically agreed that the goods should be ready by a particular date.

If there is no specific agreement, the Sale of Goods Act 1979 just requires that the goods be delivered within a 'reasonable time', which, in practice, is a rather vague and unhelpful phrase. However, if the customer has already waited what he regards as being a reasonable time, his best course of action is to make it clear that he is not prepared to wait much longer. He should notify the shopkeeper that 'time is now of the essence' – in other words, late delivery of the goods cannot be tolerated any longer, and if they are not delivered in time, the customer will regard the contract as having been broken and will withdraw from it. It is best to put the notice in writing – for instance, 'unless the goods are delivered within fourteen days, I shall regard the contract as at an end, since time is now of the essence'. If the goods are not ready at the end of that time, the shopkeeper should be notified that the contract has come to an end. Any deposit should, of course, be returned to the customer. In theory, the customer could sue for breach of contract, but such an action would be unusual. Most customers simply take their custom elsewhere and resign themselves to further delay.

Guarantees

Often a product will come with a guarantee from the manufacturer. The guarantee is not a legal contract: strictly speaking, the manufacturer is not bound by it. But in practice, of course, a guarantee is well worth having. The customer will still have his contract with the shopkeeper and the guarantee may give him an extra claim against the manufacturer. By signing a guarantee, the customer does not forfeit any of his other legal rights. In fact, it is a criminal offence for the guarantee to suggest that it takes away any of the customer's legal rights, which is why most guarantees now have a phrase stating 'This guarantee is in addition to your statutory rights' (see page 507).

Sometimes a guarantee will go further than the statutory rights. For instance, suppose a watch breaks down after four years. It might be that under the shop keeper's Promise No. 2 – 'goods are of proper quality' – three years is a reasonable time for such a watch to last. But if the manufacturer has given a five-year guarantee there will be no need to argue with the shopkeeper about whether the goods are of proper quality – the customer can simply send the watch back to the manufacturer.

These rules as to guarantees only apply to 'consumer' transactions. If the customer is not dealing as a consumer (see page 515) then exclusion clauses which take away the statutory rights may be valid. So when making a trade purchase the customer should always read the small print of the guarantee very carefully, strike out any exclusion clauses, and tell the shopkeeper what he has done. He will then not have accepted the clause and it will not be binding on him.

Stolen goods

It is a basic rule of law that a person can only sell what belongs to him. If the goods do not belong to the seller, then the buyer does not acquire ownership of them – however innocently he may have acted. For instance, if my watch is stolen and then sold to various innocent purchasers, the watch will still belong to me. If I find out where the watch is, I can claim it back. The person who had innocently bought the watch would have to go back to the person who sold it to him and claim his money back (i.e. damages). The seller would have no defence to the claim, for the Sale of Goods Act 1979 makes it an 'implied term on the part of the seller that . . . he has a right to sell the goods'. The seller could, in turn, claim from the person who sold the watch to him, and so on, down the line of innocent buyers and sellers.

In practice, of course, the chain would soon be broken, for one of the buyers would be unable to trace the person who sold it to him. He would therefore go uncompensated.

This rule can cause hardship to innocent purchasers, and there is an arguable case for changing the law so that an innocent purchaser will acquire title to stolen goods. The loss would then fall on the original owner.

There are, however, two anomalous exceptions to the general rule, by which an innocent purchaser can acquire title to a stolen item (and so refuse to return it to the original owner):

1. *An article bought in an ancient market.* Purchases in *market overt* are protected – but it must have been bought in an old-established market, on market day. The market must have been established by Act of Parliament or Royal Charter. For historical reasons, all sales at all times within the City of London are treated as sales in *market overt* (this is a crazy old law that should be abolished).

2. *A vehicle bought on hire purchase.* When an item is on HP or a conditional sale agreement, it belongs to the finance company, not the buyer. Only when all the instalments have been paid off will it become the buyer's property (see page 566). If the item is sold before the HP is paid off, the buyer will not acquire ownership. But exception is made for cars, motor-bikes, and other motor vehicles (by Part III of the Hire Purchase Act 1964). A private purchaser who

buys a car from a hirer (i.e. *not* from a crook) without knowing of the HP agreement (or that it has not been paid off) acquires ownership of the car, and so it cannot be repossessed by the finance company. If the car is bought by a trade purchaser, the trade purchaser will not be protected, but if he then sells it on to an innocent private purchaser, that private purchaser will acquire ownership. The risk of buying a motor vehicle that is on HP can be easily avoided. Hire Purchase Information plc has a full record of all such finance agreements, but its records are not open to the public. However, Citizens' Advice Bureaux and the motoring organizations can make searches for their clients and members, so anyone contemplating buying a second-hand car should ask that a search be made.

Handling stolen goods

A person who buys stolen goods is not committing an offence unless he knows or believes them to be stolen. The circumstances in which he bought them will of course be relevant; if he bought them very cheaply from a stranger he would probably be taken to have believed them to be stolen. Handling charges are tried in the crown court (up to fourteen years' imprisonment and unlimited fine), or if both magistrates and accused agree, in the magistrates' court (maximum penalty six months' prison and £2,000 fine).

Selling techniques

Inertia selling: unsolicited goods

One pressure-selling technique of the 1960s was to send people (especially firms) goods they had not ordered and then to invoice them for the goods. Surprisingly, the goods would often be paid for. To curb this practice, the Unsolicited Goods and Services Act 1971 allows the person to whom the goods are sent to claim them as his own. The recipient has two options. Either:

• he can do nothing; if the goods are not collected within six months they will become his property, *or*

• he can write to the sender; if he informs the sender that the goods are unsolicited, and that they should be collected, then if they are not collected within thirty days they become his property.

The sender of the goods may also be committing a criminal offence. Firstly, any invoice, etc., accompanying the goods must state in bold red letters 'This is not a demand for payment; there is no obligation to pay' and 'This is not a bill'. Secondly, it is an offence to threaten legal proceedings for the amount owed or to start any other collection procedures. Both these offences arise under the Unsolicited Goods and Services (Invoices etc.) Regulations 1975. A third possible offence might be unlawful harassment of the recipient (see page 882).

Pyramid selling

Another dubious sales technique of the late 1960s was direct selling through a pyramid of distributors. Each distributor would sell to other distributors beneath him, so that those at the bottom of the pyramid would be buying unwanted goods at such a high price that they could not hope to re-sell them.

To curb the practice, regulations have been made under the Fair Trading Act which, if observed, would abolish the worst aspects of pyramid selling. Amongst the requirements are:

• a new recruit can withdraw from the pyramid scheme within seven days of joining it;
• it must not be claimed that a particular income can be earned by joining the pyramid scheme;
• there are controls on how much new recruits can pay for goods;
• the promoter must buy back a participant's purchases at 90 per cent of the price paid if the participant wants to leave the pyramid.

Buying from doorstep salesmen

The consumer has the same legal rights when buying from a doorstep salesman as when buying from a shop. The difficulty is that, whereas the shop will still be there if the goods develop a fault, the doorstep salesman will probably have moved on elsewhere. So it is important that the consumer only deals with doorstep salesmen who are known to be reputable and honest.

If the purchase is made on credit (e.g. HP) the customer has the additional advantage of being able to back out of the deal within the next five days. This five-day cooling-off period does not apply to credit purchases made in shops (see page 568).

Buying through the post: mail order

As with doorstep salesmen, so with mail-order firms – most are honest, but some are not. It is important to deal only with reputable firms such as those that state 'money back if not satisfied', or 'goods are sent to you on fourteen days' approval'.

When ordering goods by post it is advisable to keep the catalogue or advert that describes the goods. If the goods should turn out to be defective, the catalogue and advertisement would be useful evidence of what was promised. The mail-order firm must, of course, comply with all the usual shopkeeper's promises, including the promises that 'the goods are as described' and the 'sales talk is true' (see pages 512 and 513).

Mail-order advertisers must make it clear in their advertisements that they are in business (see page 515). In addition, the advertisements and catalogues must contain the firm's name and address.

See also 'Late Delivery of Ordered Goods' and 'Goods on Approval' (page 523).

Buying at auction

An auctioneer need not accept bids. If he does accept a bid, the contract is not made until the hammer drops. Once that happens, neither the auctioneer nor the bidder can back out of the transaction.

Generally, the seller of a lot cannot himself bid for it in an effort to bid up the price. However, this will be legal if the right for the seller to bid is specifically reserved in the auctioneer's conditions of sale.

The disadvantage of buying in auction is that the buyer will usually have to accept the goods even if they are faulty. This is because an auction purchase can never be a 'consumer' purchase (see page 515) and so the auctioneer can rely on exclusion clauses which take away the shopkeeper's Promises Nos. 1, 'the goods are fit for their usual use', 2, 'the goods are of proper quality', and 3, 'the goods are as described' (see page 509).

Mock auctions

A mock auction is an auction at which it is pretended that goods are being sold at very low prices. For example, items worth £5 are sold for £1, and so the public believes that all the other items on offer are being sold cheaply. In fact, the organizers make their money by asking excessive prices for the other items, which the unknowing customers think they are buying at bargain prices. Organizers of mock auctions can be fined up to £2,000.

Shop hours and Sunday trading

Shop hours

The Shops Act 1950 sets out the law on closing hours and early-closing days. However, the Act allows local authorities to grant exemptions from the general rules, so what follows may be subject to local variations.

Every shop must be closed by 8 p.m., except on one late night per week (Saturday unless the local authority fixes another day) when shops must be closed by 9 p.m. However, some items are exempt from this rule, including refreshments, canteens, medical supplies, and car accessories for immediate use.

In holiday resorts, the local authority can alter the closing hours for up to four months of the year. In addition, on special occasions (such as Christmas), any local authority can suspend the normal rules as to late-night closing. The hours for tobacconists and confectioners can also be extended by order of the local authority (generally, to 9.30 p.m., and 10 p.m. on the late day).

Early closing

The general rule is that every shop must be closed by 1 p.m. on one weekday each week. However, Schedule I of the 1950 Act lists various types of shops that are exempted, including the sale of refreshments, car accessories, medicines, newspapers and periodicals, and meat, fish, bread, milk, cream, fruit, vegetables, and other perishables.

The local authority can also exempt other types of shops from the early-closing rules if a majority of those shop-owners agree. In holiday resorts, the early-closing rules can be suspended for up to four months in every year.

Sunday trading

Every shop must be closed all day Sunday. However, various items are exempt, including the sale of liquor, flowers, tobaccos, papers, and magazines. In addition, the local authority can allow opening up until 10 a.m. on a Sunday for specified transactions, such as the sale of bread and groceries. In holiday resorts the rules can be suspended for up to eighteen weeks each year.

Market stalls can count as shops and so be subject to the Sunday trading restrictions. If a Sunday market is held, both the stall-holders and the organizers can be liable.

A company organized Sunday markets where goods were sold in breach of the Shops Act. Both the organizers and a stall-holder were prosecuted in the magistrates' court and fined. In addition, the local authority brought a civil claim against the organizers and obtained an injunction forbidding them from holding any more illegal fairs. Newark D.C. (1979)

In practice, obtaining an injunction is a much more effective remedy than prosecuting in the magistrates' court. An injunction prevents future trading on Sundays and if it is broken the trader will be in contempt of court – and this could lead to imprisonment for persistent breaches. By comparison, prosecution in the magistrates' court is relatively ineffective – the penalty is a fine of up to £1,000.

Jewish shopkeepers can register with the local authority, and so be permitted to open until 2 p.m. on Sundays. However, they must then close all day Saturday. An application for registration must be supported by a sworn statement that the shopkeeper has not worked on the Jewish sabbath in the past.

In practice, of course, the provisions of the Shops Act are often ignored and many shops in the large towns have opening hours that are in clear breach of the rules. It is the duty of the local authorities to enforce the Act but many authorities turn a blind eye to these breaches, believing that the shops provide a useful service to the community. A further complication is that some traders get around the rules by merely taking names from interested customers on a Sunday, and then formalizing the sale on a different day.

As it stands, the law on Sunday trading is chaotic. The list of exempt items that can be sold on a Sunday is full of anomalies. For instance, milk and cream can be sold but not tinned or dried milk or cream (although clotted cream can be sold in tins or otherwise). Chinese and Indian take-away-food shops are allowed, but fish-and-chip shops are not. A chemist's shop can sell medicine, medical and surgical appliances, but not films – although films can be sold by a zoo! There can be little doubt that the law needs overhauling. At the moment much depends upon the attitude of the individual local authority. The effects of this are most noticeable in London where some boroughs enforce the law strictly and prevent Sunday trading, whereas neighbouring boroughs turn a blind eye to infringements by traders.

33 Paying for Repairs and Services

Different rules apply when paying for repairs and services than when buying goods. See page 505 for the difference between 'goods' and 'repairs/services'.

The servicer's/repairer's/contractor's promises are:

1. He will carry out the work to a reasonable standard.
2. Any materials used will be of good quality and reasonably fit for use.
3. He will take reasonable care of the goods while they are in his possession.
4. The work done will be as was agreed.

Paying for Poor Service: Is the Contractor Liable?

To find out whether the servicer/repairer/contractor is liable, ask yourself 'What is the basis of my complaint?'

- 'The work has not been done to a proper standard.' The contractor is liable because he has broken Promise No. 1 (see page 530).

- 'Although he has done the work properly, he used unsuitable or poor-quality materials.' He is liable because he has broken Promise No. 2 (see page 532).

- 'My goods were lost/damaged/stolen while in his care.' He is liable because he has broken Promise No. 3 (see page 533).

- 'There is nothing wrong with his work, but it is not what I asked for.' He is liable because he has broken Promise No. 4 (see page 534).

The contractor's promises

Promise No. 1: The work will be done to a reasonable standard

A person who follows a trade or profession must exercise the skill of a reasonably competent member of that trade or profession. The law says that there is 'an implied term that the supplier will carry out the service with reasonable care and skill' (s. 13, Supply of Goods and Services Act 1982). For instance, a person who employs a carpenter to build cupboards can expect them to be built to the standard normally

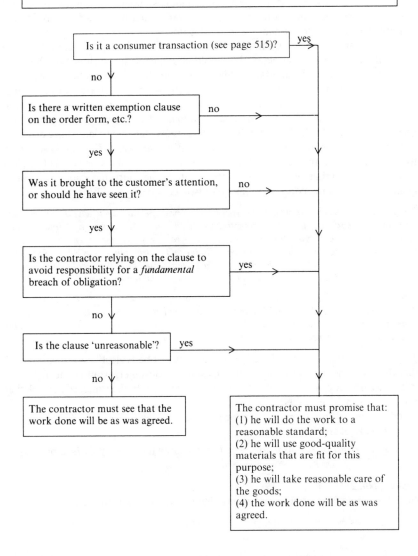

**Repairs and services
The contractor's promises to the customer**

Is it a consumer transaction (see page 515)? — yes →

no ↓

Is there a written exemption clause on the order form, etc.? — no →

yes ↓

Was it brought to the customer's attention, or should he have seen it? — no →

yes ↓

Is the contractor relying on the clause to avoid responsibility for a *fundamental* breach of obligation? — yes →

no ↓

Is the clause 'unreasonable'? — yes →

no ↓

The contractor must see that the work done will be as was agreed.

The contractor must promise that:
(1) he will do the work to a reasonable standard;
(2) he will use good-quality materials that are fit for this purpose;
(3) he will take reasonable care of the goods;
(4) the work done will be as was agreed.

provided by skilled carpenters. However, if the job was given to an odd-job man, the customer would have to apply a lower standard.

Although the customer can expect a 'reasonable standard' of workmanship, this is a notoriously difficult test to apply. It is so vague that it allows for considerable dispute as to what is 'reasonable' and what is not.

If the customer does not think that the work done is of the proper quality, and the firm will not accept his complaint, he should obtain evidence to show that the work was not of a reasonable standard. This is best done by asking another firm, in the same line of business, to inspect the work and say what, in their opinion, is wrong. If they also give a quote for remedying the faults, that will be a good starting-point for deciding how much damages are due. Bear in mind that cases involving claims for no more than £500 (which will be the case with most consumer claims) are not tried in a court but are referred to an informal arbitration (see page 872). This is generally to the customer's advantage since arbitrators tend to take a less legalistic (and less 'fussy') approach than most judges. Unfortunately, the courts have not always been willing to support the consumer – as these two 1983 decisions illustrate:

> One case involved an argument over carpet-laying. The carpet was said to have the pile running the wrong way and the pattern was off-centre. The court took a strict approach. A small amount of compensation was awarded for the pile running the wrong way, but no compensation was given for the pattern being off-centre, even though the judge said 'it strikes the eye as being a little odd'. It was held that there was no implied term that the pattern would be in the middle. The customer should have specifically made it clear that this was an essential requirement.

> A central-heating system was modified, but at the end of the work it was not satisfactory. Could the customer say that the central-heating contractor had broken the implied promise to use 'reasonable care and skill'? Held: No. There was no implied obligation to provide a reasonably satisfactory, well-balanced, and properly regulated system!

These were particularly harsh decisions and may not be typical – but they do show that the law is not always as sympathetic as many consumers would expect.

Trade associations may be able to provide evidence as to the standard of work that can reasonably be expected.

If the servicer's/repairer's/contractor's promise is broken, see page 535, 'When the Promise is Broken'.

If it is not a consumer transaction. The promise may then not apply (see page 515).

Promise No. 2:
He will use suitable materials and ensure that they are of proper quality

The materials used in any repairing or servicing contract must be reasonably fit for their purpose.

> Mr Stewart took his 1929 Bentley in for a service. The garage fitted new brake linings, but unknown to the garage the linings used were not suitable. Next day the brakes failed and the car overturned at 60 m.p.h. Mr Stewart sued. Held: The garage was liable because the materials used were not fit for their purpose. Stewart (1952)

This is very similar to the shopkeeper's Promise No. 1 that 'goods are fit for their usual use', implied by section 14(3) of the Sale of Goods Act 1979 (see page 509). That Act only applies to the purchase of 'goods', not services, but the judges have made it clear that the common law implies a similar duty on the suppliers of services. For instance, in one case, a patient complained about the fit of a set of false teeth and sued the dentist, alleging a breach of section 14(3) of the Sale of Goods Act. The dentist argued that section 14(3) did not apply, since he had been providing services, not goods. The judges held that whilst this was true, there was still an implied term in a contract of service that the teeth would be reasonably fit for their purpose (Samuels, 1943).

Similarly, the judges have also said that any materials used in a service or repair must be of proper quality. This is very similar to the shopkeeper's Promise No. 2: that 'the goods are of proper quality', implied by section 14(2) of the Sale of Goods Act (see page 511).

If the servicer's/repairer's/contractor's promise is broken, see page 535, 'When the Promise is Broken'.

If it is not a consumer transaction. The promise may then not apply (see page 515).

Promise No. 3: He will take care of any goods left in his possession

Suppose a motorist leaves his car in a garage for repairs, but when he returns is told, 'Sorry, we had a fire last night and your car was burnt out.' Is the garage responsible or must the motorist claim on his insurance policy and so lose his no-claims bonus?

The answer will depend upon whether the garage took 'reasonable care' of the car. In effect, this means that they must have taken reasonable steps to stop a fire starting and also to put out the fire once it had started. If they were not negligent, then they will not be liable.

However, it will be for the garage to prove that it was not negligent – negligence is presumed unless the garage can show otherwise. In practice, it is often very difficult to prove a negative, and so, in all probability, the garage will be liable. They could only avoid liability if they could show that they had eliminated all fire hazards and installed a proper water-sprinkling system. This usually means that they must show how the fire started, that it was not their fault, and how their fire-protection systems, whilst being adequate for most purposes, could not cope with such an outbreak of fire.

Similar rules apply when goods are stolen. If a watch is left with a jeweller for repair and then stolen, the jeweller will have to compensate the customer unless he can show that he was not negligent. This means that he must show that he took all reasonable steps to prevent thefts, i.e. installation of proper locks and burglar alarms.

Often, though, goods just 'disappear' from the repairer's premises – it is assumed that they have been stolen, but no one really knows. In these circumstances it is almost impossible for the repairer to show that neither he, nor his staff, were not negligent and so the customer is entitled to compensation.

Some repairers, contractors, and servicers use exclusion clauses in their order forms in an attempt to exclude their liability for lost or damaged goods (e.g. 'Customers' goods and valuables are left at their own risk'). Under the Unfair Contract Terms Act these exemption clauses must pass a 'reasonableness' test; if the clause is unreasonable it will be struck out and so be totally ineffective. For the rules to be applied see page 516.

If the servicer's/repairer's/contractor's promise is broken, see page 535, 'When the Promise is Broken'.

If it is not a consumer transaction. The promise may then not apply (see page 515).

Promise No. 4: The work done will be as was agreed

It may be that there is nothing wrong with the quality of the work done, or the service provided, but it was not what was asked for. For instance, a customer may only have asked for a coat to be dry-cleaned and yet be asked to pay extra because it has been retextured as well.

When this happens, the customer is not responsible for the extra work and need not pay for it. However, this assumes that he can prove what was said when the original order was made. In practice, it may be difficult for the customer to show that he did not ask for the coat to be retextured unless there was a friend or witness who heard him ask for it to be dry-cleaned.

Similar rules apply when a garage carries out expensive work to a car without prior authorization. If the customer takes his car into the garage for them to investigate a particular noise, the garage cannot go ahead and remedy the defect without his authority. He has only asked that the noise be investigated, not that the work be done. Likewise, if the customer asks the garage to contact him if the cost is likely to exceed £25, then the garage must do so. If the garage does work worth £50, then the customer need only pay the first £25 of their bill – he need not even pay them a 'reasonable amount' for the extra work.

This is the legal theory. In practice, of course, things are not as straightforward. Firstly, the garage is likely to deny that a £25 limit was agreed. This is why it is important to put such terms in writing, or to ensure that someone heard the garage being told of the £25 limit. Secondly, the garage is unlikely to allow the customer to collect the car until the full bill has been paid. This can put the customer in some difficulty, but if he is convinced that he is in the right he should write to the garage setting out his position (i.e. he will not pay for the unauthorized work) and specifically state that:

1. He gives them a stated time in which to accept his offer of payment for the authorized work.
2. If he is not allowed to collect the car, he will hire a replacement. The hire fees will form part of his claim against the garage.
3. He will then sue in the county court for damages (i.e. inconvenience and hire charges). Suing in the county court is usually straightforward (see page 872).

If the garage still refuses to be reasonable the customer will have to sue. But first it might be worth checking whether the garage belongs to a trade association and, if so, to complain to the association.

Finally, work done must correspond with the promise made by the contractor – in other words his sales talk must be true. The position is the same as when buying goods (see page 513).

If the servicer's/repairer's/contractor's promise is broken, see below, 'When the Promise is Broken'.

If it is not a consumer transaction. The promise may then not apply (see page 515).

When the promise is broken

If the contractor breaks one of his promises to the customer, he will be in breach of contract. The customer can either reject the finished article, or accept it and claim damages.

The position is the same as when buying goods and the shopkeeper breaks one of his promises (see page 518).

Disputing the bill

Often there is no pre-arranged agreement about the price to be paid for the work done. Either the price is not mentioned, or the contractor says he cannot give a price until he has started work and seen what is involved in the job. The problems arise when the customer thinks the bill is too high.

In the absence of a specific agreement as to the price, the customer must pay a 'reasonable amount' – in other words, the amount that a similar firm would charge for the work done. The law says that when a price is not agreed in advance, then 'there is an implied term that the (customer) will pay a reasonable charge' (s. 15, Supply of Goods and Services Act 1982). So if the customer thinks the bill is too high he should ask other local tradesmen what they would have charged, and then offer the contractor what seems to be the average price.

Obviously, it is important to compare like with like. For instance, a person who employs a twenty-four-hour plumbing service to repair a leaking tap must expect to pay more than if he had employed a local, day-time, plumber. What is a reasonable price for the work done will depend on all the circumstances of the case.

If the parties agreed beforehand on a specific price, the 'reasonable amount' rule does not apply. Both sides are bound by the agreed price. If the price is excessive for the work done then the customer has no legal redress (assuming, of course, that the work is to a standard that one would expect for that price) and, conversely, if the agreed price is very cheap for the work done, the customer cannot be made to pay any more.

If the bill is high because the contractor has done work that he was not asked to do, then the customer need not pay for the extra work (see page 534).

When the problem is not solved

Sometimes a repairer will fail to solve the problem. For instance, the garage cannot trace the source of that squeak! When this happens, the customer cannot refuse to pay for the work and time spent. He must pay a 'reasonable amount' even though the problem has not been solved. The only exception would be if the problem was not solved because of the incompetence of the repairer – but this usually can only be shown by getting another repairer to solve the problem, and for him to state that the fault should have been cured by a reasonably competent member of that trade. In such a case, the customer could obviously refuse to pay for the earlier, abortive, work.

Estimates and quotes

When major work is to be carried out, or if the work is of a technical nature, it is usual for the customer to obtain an estimate or quote from the contractor.

A quote is binding on the parties, even if the job should turn out to involve considerably more, or less, work than was originally envisaged. Few people realize this, and it is not uncommon to find quotes and estimates regarded as being mere guides as to the eventual price. A quote is a fixed price, unless it specifically says that the quotation 'is not a fixed price', or that the quote can be 'increased to reflect increased cost of materials'.

With estimates, the position is less clear-cut. In legal theory, an estimate is similar to a quote in that it is a pre-arranged, fixed price. However, in practice, an estimate is regarded as no more than a 'statement of intent' as to what the price will be and it seems unlikely that a customer could treat an estimate in the same way as a quote. If the eventual bill is higher than the original estimate, then the customer will have to pay the increased amount, assuming, of course, that it is a 'reasonable price' for the work done (see above). If the price greatly exceeds the estimate, it will be for the contractor to justify the increase.

When a customer agrees an estimate it is advisable for him to write 'extra work shall only be carried out on my written instructions'. This will reduce the scope for argument if the contractor should later charge for work that he was not asked to do.

Late completion of work

The general rule is that work must be completed within a 'reasonable time', and if a customer wants time 'to be of the essence', he should make this clear to the contractor. For instance, if a motorist wants the garage to service his car by the Friday evening when he is due to go away on holiday, he should make this clear to the garage. If the car is not ready in time he would be entitled to deduct his damages (e.g. cost of hiring another car) from the bill. If nothing was said to the garage, the customer could not complain if it was not ready in time.

The law says 'there is an implied term that the supplier will carry out the service within a reasonable time' (s. 14, Supply of Goods and Services Act 1982). The position is therefore the same as when goods are delivered late (see page 523). Late delivery can, sometimes, be a criminal offence. For instance, a dry-cleaner who advertises four-hour services can be prosecuted under the Trade Descriptions Acts if cleaning takes longer than four hours (see page 580).

Broken appointments

It is particularly annoying to wait at home for a service engineer or other contractor to call, only to find that he does not turn up at the agreed time. If the contractor had agreed to turn up at that time then he would be in breach of contract. Accordingly, he will be liable to the consumer for the damages flowing in the ordinary course of events from the missed appointment.

For instance, if the customer had taken time off work to keep the appointment, the lost wages could be claimed. Often, though, the customer's financial loss will be minimal: the price of a few phone calls inquiring why the engineer had not turned up. But even in these cases, where the customer has not suffered a wage loss, he has been inconvenienced by having to stay in and being unable to leave the house. Accordingly, he is entitled to damages for general inconvenience, perhaps £5 for a morning or afternoon.

If the customer is planning to take time off work to keep an appointment with a repairer, he should make this clear to the repairer. He will then have no difficulty in justifying a claim for lost wages as damages should the repairer not keep the appointment. It is not always easy to recover damages for a broken appointment, since few contractors are willing to admit legal liability for the inconvenience. In practice, the customer's best remedy is to deduct the damages from the bill, once the work has been done.

Receipts

A customer cannot normally insist on a receipt. He is only legally entitled to a receipt if he needs it to show the VAT paid. Equally, the shopkeeper or contractor cannot insist on the customer producing a receipt before he will entertain a complaint. ('We can't do anything without a receipt' is nonsense!)

Hiring goods

The customer hires the goods on the terms laid down in the hire agreement. Usually these are drafted in favour of the hire shop, so it is advisable for the customer to read them through and strike out any that seem unreasonable. If there is no hire agreement, then the law will make the customer liable for taking reasonable care of the goods, although he will not be responsible for fair wear and tear.

Many hiring agreements contain exclusion clauses limiting the hire firm's liability. These exclusion clauses will be ineffective in so far as they try to take away the Sale of Goods Act promises made to the customer (see page 509). In addition, if a clause tries to limit the hire firm's liability in negligence should the item injure or kill the hirer (or anyone else), that clause will be invalid.

When the customer forgets to collect his property

Sometimes people leave goods in a shop to be repaired or serviced, but do not bother to collect them. Shoe-repairers, in particular, complain about this. When this happens, the shopkeeper can sell the goods, deduct the amount he is owed, and then pay any balance to the customer.

The Torts (Interference with Goods) Act 1977 sets out the rules. If he can, the shopkeeper must give recorded delivery or registered letter notice to the customer that the goods will be sold if he does not collect them within a reasonable time. Usually, though, the shopkeeper does not know how to contact the customer, in which case he should make a reasonable effort to track him down. Only then can he sell the goods. If the goods are of a high value, or if the shopkeeper fears that there may be some difficulty (for instance, do the goods really belong to the customer?) he can ask the court to approve the sale. His legal costs can, of course, be deducted from the proceeds of sale.

The 1977 Act only applies if no other agreement was made between shopkeeper and customer. For instance, if the customer agreed that the shopkeeper could sell the goods and keep any profit if they were not collected, then that agreement would override the less generous provisions of the 1977 Act. Accordingly, the prudent shopkeeper will make it a term of his contract with the customer that he can dispose of uncollected goods within a relatively short time and keep any profit. This is best done by inserting a suitably worded clause into the order form signed by the customer and, perhaps, also displaying an explanatory notice in a place where it can be clearly seen by customers.

Public utilities

Electricity

The owner or occupier of property within fifty yards of an electricity main can demand to be connected to the mains supply. A lawful occupier of the property (such as a tenant) can also demand that the property be connected to the mains, but a squatter cannot. The Electricity Board can charge for installing lines on private land and for the cost of any lines more than sixty feet from the mains.

The board has an obligation to supply electricity, but the supply can be irregular or fluctuating. For instance:

A farmer wanted to breed factory chickens. Infra-red lamps were needed to keep the temperature at the correct level. The Electricity Board's engineer said the supply would be sufficient to run the lamps. The lamps were bought from the board and installed by them. Subsequently, the voltage failed on several occasions, and many chicks died. Held: The Electricity Board were not in breach of their statutory duty to supply electricity. Willmore (1957)

The Electricity Board can usually run electricity lines across private land without the consent of the landowner. If the landowner will not agree, the board must obtain the approval of the Secretary of State and the local authority. The landowner can be paid compensation (usually only a few hundred pounds) for the inconvenience and loss of amenity.

The illegal abstraction of electricity (e.g. by-passing the meter or plugging into someone else's supply) is an offence. The maximum penalty is five years' imprisonment if tried in the crown court, six months' and a £2,000 fine if tried in the magistrates' court (but both the magistrates and the accused must agree if it is to be tried in the magistrates' court).

Gas

The British Gas Corporation has a duty to supply all reasonable demands for gas, so far as it is economical to do so.

The owner, or legal occupier, of premises can demand to be connected to the mains supply if the premises are within twenty-five yards of a main. The customer has to pay the cost of installing the supply over his land, and over thirty feet from the main.

Gas pipes cannot be laid on private land without the consent of the landowner, although the corporation's engineers can enter private land to repair or renew existing pipes.

If gas escapes, the corporation can be liable for negligence or nuisance if damage is caused. The corporation is criminally liable if it fails to stop a gas leak within twenty-four hours of being notified of it, unless it did all that was 'reasonably practicable'.

The Gas Safety Regulations 1972 set out detailed rules as to the use of gas. Customers who break the regulations can be fined up to £1,000. In particular:
- it is illegal to use a gas appliance knowing or suspecting that:
  - there is inadequate ventilation
  - gas is escaping
  - the appliance has a dangerous fault;
- if a gas leak is suspected, the gas supply must be turned off; the gas supply must then not be used until the leak has been fixed; if gas continues to escape, the area board must be notified;
- do-it-yourself installations and repairs are banned; only competent engineers can work on gas supplies and gas appliances.

Illegal abstraction of gas will usually lead to a theft prosecution (up to ten years' prison in the crown court; six months' and £2,000 fine in the magistrates' court).

Cutting off the gas and electricity

Gas and electricity boards can only cut off a supply if the bills for supply are not paid. They cannot cut off a customer who owes them money for some other reason. For instance, if a customer buys a gas cooker from the Gas Board, on credit, the board cannot cut off the gas supply if the customer falls into arrears with payments on the cooker. The board can only cut him off for non-payment of gas-supply bills.

The customer must be given proper notice before the supply is cut off. With *gas*, the customer must be given at least seven days' notice (written), and the bill must be twenty-eight days overdue for payment. With *electricity* the customer must be given at least twenty-one days' notice and then an additional written notice at least seven days' before the cutting off. The notice must specifically state that if the bill is not paid, the supply will be cut off.

The next step will be for a Gas or Electricity Board official to call. He will ask for permission to enter the premises, but the customer can legally refuse him entry (unless he already has an entry warrant – see below). Often the officials use deception to get into the house – for instance, the gas man might say 'I've come to read the meter' and then be let in by the customer who discovers a few minutes later that the gas supply has been disconnected. Accordingly, the customer is always well advised to refuse entry to any official of the Gas or Electricity Board if a notice of intention to disconnect has been given. It is important to stress that the customer is under no legal obligation to allow the official to enter.

If the official is refused access, he will go away and apply to the magistrates for an entry warrant. The Rights of Entry (Gas and Electricity Boards) Act 1954 sets out the rules. The entry warrant will be granted if it can be shown that the customer had been given at least twenty-four hours' notice of the intention to disconnect and that he refused entry to the official.

When the official returns with his warrant, the customer should allow him to enter and cut off the supply. The official need not give the customer any notice before he calls. If the customer obstructs the official, he can be fined up to £400. A similar penalty applies when the householder refuses to let an official in when there is an emergency and, in such a case, there is no need for the official to have a warrant.

A customer who is facing disconnection should contact the local CAB to see whether they can persuade the board to postpone disconnection. Often they can negotiate an agreement for the customer to pay off the arrears by instalments.

Because of complaints about the arbitrary cutting off of supplies, the Gas and Electricity Boards have a joint Code of Practice setting out their guidelines. This states:

Your supply will not be cut off if you agree to make regular payments for your electricity or gas and to pay off the debt by instalments in a reasonable period. This would have regard to what you tell us about your circumstances and income. You must keep your side of the agreement.

Your supply will not be cut off if there is real hardship and it is safe and practical to install a slot meter. This would be set to collect the debt in a reasonable period. We would have regard to what you tell us about your circumstances and income.

Your supply will not be cut off between 1 October and 31 March if all the people living in the house who have an income are old-age pensioners. But this will not apply if it is clear that they can pay but haven't, and in these cases the supply may not be reconnected for the following winter.

Your supply will not be cut off if the debt is in the name of a past customer. But you must have made proper arrangements to take over the supply.

Your supply will not be cut off if there is no adult at home at the time unless we have got an entry warrant.

If we do have to come to cut your supply off we may find that your circumstances have changed. We may leave your supply on and look at your case again.

Your supply will be cut off if you do not pay your bill or keep to an agreed arrangement with us to pay it, and if Social Security or Social Services cannot help you.

Before reconnecting a disconnected supply, the Gas or Electricity Board can ask for a deposit; there is no control on the size of the deposit. However, if the customer offers to pay by slot meter, rather than by quarterly bill, this may persuade the board to reduce the amount of the deposit. The Electricity Board cannot charge for reconnecting the supply unless the supply was previously cut off for non-payment of bills, or if the premises are more than fifty yards from the mains. A squatter cannot legally demand a supply to the house he is squatting in although, in practice, many boards will agree to connection if a suitable deposit is given. On the subject of deposits, the Code of Practice says:

Usually we only ask for deposits from short-stay customers or from customers who have been bad payers in the past. We will not ask for a deposit if a customer:

(a) keeps to an agreed arrangement to pay an amount each week or month, *or*
(b) has a slot meter put in, *or*
(c) gives an acceptable credit reference or guarantor.

Arrangements must be made to pay off any arrears.

If we have asked you for a deposit and you disagree with the amount you can, if you wish, have the amount decided by arbitration. We will tell you about this and the possible alternative arrangements if we ask for a deposit.

Tenants

The law on charging tenants for gas and electricity is set out on page 283.

Water

Each of the nine regional water authorities has a statutory duty to supply 'wholesome' water. If the water is not wholesome, the authority can be sued, as in a 1938 case when a girl contracted typhoid from contaminated tap-water (*Read*, 1938).

The authority must supply water to houses in its area if this can be done at 'reasonable cost'. Otherwise it is for the landowner to provide his own supply of wholesome domestic water (i.e. water for drinking, washing, cooking, and sanitation). If the house does not have a proper water supply it is quite likely that the local authority will declare it unfit for human habitation (see page 315) and make a demolition or closing order.

Water rates are not payable on premises that are not connected to the mains. When supply can be laid on at reasonable cost, the owner (or legal occupier) of a property can demand to be connected. The cost of laying on the pipes is paid by the customer.

The authority can lay mains (but not service pipes) on private land without the consent of the landowner, since although the authority needs the landowner's consent, the Secretary of State can overrule an unreasonable withholding of consent. The landowner will be entitled to compensation, although this will usually be a nominal amount unless real loss is caused.

Refuse collection and litter

Under the Control of Pollution Act 1974, a local authority has a duty to collect household waste free of charge. The only time when the authority need not collect the waste is when the place is so isolated or inaccessible that the cost of collection would be unreasonably high and adequate arrangements could be made by the resident.

The free collection service only applies to household waste. It does not apply to office or industrial waste, even if it is a house that is being used as an office or industrial base. 'Waste' includes all normal household items and any scrap item which needs to be disposed of since it is 'worn out, contaminated, or otherwise spoiled'. Rubble from home building improvements is not household waste.

Local authorities also have a duty to collect non-household waste, but they can charge for this service.

Various statutes control the dumping of litter. The basic offence is contained in the Litter Act 1983, which makes it illegal to discard litter (maximum penalty £400 fine). In practice, this piece of legislation is virtually useless as a sanction against litter-louts. Not only must the litter be discarded in a public place which is in the open air (cf. a shop), but it must be shown that not only was the litter dropped but that it was intended to leave it there and not pick it up again – something that it is usually difficult to prove. In addition, it is not an arrestable offence (see page 778) and the offender need not give his name and address when challenged. Not surprisingly, successful prosecutions are rare.

The Refuse Disposal (Amenity) Act 1978 makes it illegal to dump abandoned cars (or parts of cars) in the open air, whether on public or private land. It is also an offence deliberately to abandon any other item in the open air. The maximum penalty on a conviction is a £100 fine and three months' prison. In addition, the defendant can be ordered to pay the local authority's costs for removing the dumped materials and disposing of them elsewhere. If it is a car that is abandoned, the owner may still be obliged to have insurance and road tax for it, unless it is in such a state that it could not be got going (see pages 609).

Railways

In the eyes of the law, a passenger travels on the railways in accordance with the contract made between himself and the British Railways Board. In other words, the passenger travels on the conditions laid down in the BRB regulations.

By buying a ticket, the passenger does not become entitled to insist that the trains run on time or even that he has a seat on the train. A person with a second-class ticket cannot sit in an empty first-class seat, just because all the second-class seats are occupied. If he does he can be asked to pay the excess fare (or all the first-class fare if he has a second-class season ticket), although BRB does have a discretion to waive the excess if all the second-class seats are full. In these circumstances, the passenger should give his name and address to the ticket inspector and say that he will be asking BRB to exercise its discretion and not charge him.

A passenger who travels without a ticket commits an offence if he does not *intend* to pay the fare. Similarly, it is an offence, for example, to use a £1 ticket on a £1.50 journey if there is no intention to pay the extra 50p. The prosecution must show that the passenger did not intend to pay the fare, so a genuinely forgetful passenger will have a defence to the charge. In practice, it can be difficult to raise this defence successfully; nearly all fare-dodgers use it, and the courts treat it with great scepticism. The maximum penalty for fare-dodging is a £400 fine, or three months' imprisonment.

If luggage is lost or damaged through the railway's negligence the passenger can claim damages for his loss. If the luggage was in the guard's van, the onus is on the railway to show that the loss or damage was not its fault; if it was in a passenger compartment, the onus is on the passenger. Generally, the railway's liability is limited to a relatively small amount, unless it can be shown that such an exclusion of risk is unreasonable. (But BR now has a more generous Voluntary Code of Practice.)

Other services

Taxis

Taxis are licensed by local authorities and their activities are controlled by statutes and by local by-laws. The taxi licence number must be displayed, both on the rear of the taxi and in the passenger compartment.

A taxi need not stop to pick up a customer even if it has its 'For Hire' sign on. The only exceptions are when the taxi is at a cab rank, parked and awaiting passengers, or is stationary (but a taxi which is 'stationary' at traffic lights or when dropping passengers need not accept a fare).

Taxi fares are controlled and the taxi driver commits an offence if he charges more than the displayed price on the meter. If the journey is outside the range of the meter, the taxi driver can negotiate a fare with the customer. However, this must be done in advance.

In London special rules apply. Once a taxi has stopped to pick up a fare, the driver must accept that fare, assuming that:
• the destination is within the Metropolitan Police district, *and*

- the destination is less than twenty miles away, or will take less than an hour to reach, *and*
- it is not a multiple fare involving any detours.

A customer who wishes to complain about a London taxi driver should complain within seven days to the Public Carriage Office, Penton Street, London N1, preferably quoting the number of the taxi, the taxi licence, and the driver's badge number. The taxi driver can be fined up to £400 for refusing to accept the passenger, and up to £400 for overcharging.

Hotels, etc.

The law distinguishes between 'hotels' and other places of accommodation. 'Hotels' (which, in law, are referred to as 'inns') are places that offer food and liquor and, if requested, sleeping accommodation to any traveller. So an establishment that does not have a liquor licence, or which does not accept guests except by prior arrangement or booking, will not be a hotel. Thus, a pub, a lodging house, a bed-and-breakfast establishment, or a private hotel are not 'hotels', and so different legal rules apply.

When service is refused

If the establishment is a hotel, it must be prepared to provide reasonable accommodation for the traveller. The only exceptions are when the hotel has no room for him or he is in an unfit state (e.g. drunk or disreputable-looking). In addition, the hotelier can refuse accommodation if he has reasonable grounds for thinking that the guest will be unable to pay the bill.

However, if it is not a hotel, the owner need not offer accommodation to anyone. He is in the same position as a shopkeeper – he can choose whom he sells his goods or services to (see page 501) subject, of course, to the race and sex discrimination laws (see Chapter 46, page 690).

Similar rules apply to the provision of food and meals. A hotelier must provide food, at any reasonable time, for any of his guests, assuming that he has food in the building. If the establishment is not a hotel, the owner need not serve food or drink on demand. Thus, a publican can refuse to serve a customer unless the pub is a hotel, or unless his refusal of service is based on sexual or racial discrimination.

Display of charges

Any hotel or establishment that is in the business of providing sleeping accommodation has to display its prices (either in reception, or in the entrance) – provided it has at least four bedrooms or eight beds. The notice must give details of prices for single and double accommodation, including service charge, and VAT must be included (or marked separately). This law therefore covers many small establishments, such as bed-and-breakfasts. In practice, the rules, which are enforced by local trading-standards officers, are not widely known (they are in the Tourism (Sleeping Accommodation Price Display) Order 1977!).

Overbooking

If a person books accommodation in any establishment – whether it be a hotel, guest house, bed and breakfast, etc. – and turns up only to find that no room has been reserved for him, he can claim damages for breach of contract.

But this only applies if his booking has been *accepted* by the proprietor. There would be no contract if the guest had simply written to the proprietor telling him of his imminent arrival, unless the hotelier had notified his acceptance of the booking.

Any damages will be the loss incurred by the guest (e.g. cost of driving to another hotel and of phoning them; the extra cost of staying at a similar establishment whose prices are higher). But the guest must act reasonably, and not stay in a superior hotel unless it is the only one available.

Similar rules apply if the guest arrives at the establishment only to find that the accommodation is inferior to that booked.

When the standard of accommodation is poor

The proprietor is providing a service, and if the accommodation is not of a sufficient standard he will be in breach of contract. As a supplier of services he makes the four contractor's promises set out on page 530.

Cancelling the booking

Once the intending guest's booking has been accepted by the proprietor, there is a binding contract. So if the guest cancels he will be in breach of contract and will have to pay damages to the proprietor.

The amount of the damages will be the proprietor's loss naturally following from the cancellation. If the room is immediately re-let, the loss will be minimal, and the damages should be just a nominal sum to cover the inconvenience caused. If the room is not re-let, the hotelier is entitled to his lost profit and often this will be approximately assessed at the amount of the guest's deposit.

Compensation for ruined holidays

If a holiday does not live up to its promise (i.e. the description in the brochure) then the customer can sue for breach of contract: the tour operator is providing a service and his failure to honour the contract makes him liable (see pages 530–35 for the law on 'services'). But the disappointed holiday-maker will probably want more than a refund of the cost of his holiday. He will probably feel that a holiday has a special value to it – after all, it is not as if he can just go out and buy another one, as he could with a car or other faulty consumer item. In short, he will probably want compensation for the disappointment and distress caused by the ruined holiday – and the court will probably give it to him. The principle that a ruined holiday is worth more than a refund of its price was established in 1973 by a Mr Jarvis, who sued Swans Tours over a disappointing holiday in a European winter ski-resort, and in 1974 by a Mr Jackson, who sued Horizon Holidays:

> *Mr Jarvis booked a four-week holiday in Ceylon, which was described as being 'of the highest standard'. The brochure described the hotel as having a mini-golf course, an excellent restaurant, a swimming pool, and beauty and hairdressing salons. None of these existed. The travel firm was guilty of breach of contract, but argued that the damages should be minimal and for Mr Jarvis only. Held: No. Mr Jarvis was awarded £1,100 damages for the inconvenience and disappointment suffered by himself and his family.* Jarvis (1975)

Most ruined holidays are not as badly ruined as this holiday was. Thus, the level of compensation is unlikely to be as high. The amount that should be accepted will all depend upon the facts (i.e. just how bad was the inconvenience? Was there any way that the tour operator could have avoided it?). In typical cases, one might be thinking in terms of some £300 compensation – but obviously this is no more than a very rough guide and it does assume that there was some substantial disruption and inconvenience caused.

ABTA, the Association of British Travel Agents, run an arbitration scheme for customers who think they are entitled to compensation. It obviously only applies when the tour operator is a member of ABTA. The customer has to put down a deposit and the dispute then goes to an arbitrator who decides the case by looking at the documents only (i.e. there is no hearing). It should be remembered that this ABTA scheme is optional – the customer need not use it and he may well be happier to go for arbitration in the county court (i.e. the small-claims procedure) which provides a fairly cheap and easy service – and has the added advantage of there being a hearing in front of the arbitrator (see page 872 for details and procedure). One point worth noting is that the deposits for the ABTA scheme (if the claim is over £1,000) are more than the fee needed to sue under the small-claims scheme – and for many people that alone will be sufficient to put them off the ABTA scheme.

Lost property

There are different rules for 'hotels' and for other establishments such as lodging houses and pubs.

The Hotel Proprietors Act 1956 makes a hotelier liable for the first £50 loss on any one item, up to a total of £100. This is so even if the item was not stolen, lost, mislaid, or damaged through his negligence. But if the guest wishes to recover more than £50 for an item (or £100 altogether), he must show that the loss, damage, etc., was caused by the negligence or fault of the hotel or its staff. If so, the hotelier is liable for the full loss.

However, the hotelier can still limit his liability to £50 (and £100) by exhibiting a notice at the entrance or reception desk stating that all valuables must be deposited with the proprietor for safe-keeping. So hoteliers are usually not liable for items stolen from hotel bedrooms, because they nearly always display a properly worded sign. Of course, if the goods were left with the proprietor for safe-keeping and then stolen, the hotelier would be liable for the *whole* of the loss.

With establishments that are not hotels the rules are different. A guest must take care of his own property. Only if the proprietor or his staff were negligent can they be liable. Generally, though, it is difficult to recover compensation in these circumstances.

The £50 (and £100) limits are of course very much out of date and need to be increased to take account of inflation.

Pubs

The Licensing Act 1964 sets out the general rule on pub hours:

	London	*Outside London*
Monday to Saturday	11 a.m. to 3 p.m. 5.30 p.m. to 11 p.m.	11 a.m. to 3 p.m. 5.30 p.m. to 10.30 p.m.
Sunday	Noon to 2 p.m. 7 p.m. to 11 p.m.	10 a.m. to 2 p.m. 7 p.m. to 10.30 p.m.

In areas outside London, the licensing magistrates can extend the evening hours to 11 p.m.

Further, the licensing magistrate can vary these hours so long as the total opening hours do not exceed nine hours per day (or nine and a half hours if the evening hours have been extended to 11 p.m.). The Sunday hours cannot be modified, except for extending the evening hours to 11 p.m.

A publican is not obliged to be open during these hours. However, if he is regularly closed during licensed hours he might find that the licensing magistrates will refuse to renew his annual licence, on the ground that he is failing to provide a reasonable service to the public.

The opening hours are extended by ten minutes to allow for the drinking-up of liquor bought during licensed hours. The drink must be finished within the ten-minute period – if the customer continues drinking outside that time, he commits an offence (fine of up to £400). If the customer has not finished his drink he must leave it in the pub – he cannot take it with him. The drinking-up time is extended to thirty minutes if the the drink was supplied to go with a meal being eaten on the premises.

If intoxicating liquor is drunk outside the permitted hours, both the customer and the publican can be fined up to £400.

Consumer and Business: The Consumer and the Law

Refusing service

Every publican has the right to refuse to serve any customer if he so wishes. The only exception to this is if the refusal is based upon racial or sexual discrimination (see page 690). In addition to his common-law right to refuse service, any publican can refuse to admit, and may throw out, anyone who is 'drunken, violent, quarrelsome or disorderly' (Licensing Act 1964).

Previous offenders can also be banned from certain pubs. When sentencing for an offence that occurred on licensed premises, the magistrates can ban the defendant from specified pubs for a period of between three months and two years. If the ban is broken, there is a maximum penalty of £400 fine or one month in prison.

Children in pubs

Children under fourteen cannot go into a bar during opening hours (up to £50 fine for publican; no offence is committed by the child). A 'bar' is a part of the licensed premises that is mainly used for the sale or drinking of intoxicating liquor, so whilst it may be legal for the child to stand in the hallway of a pub, it may well be technically illegal for him to be in a beer-garden.

Surprisingly, children over five can have alcoholic drinks in licensed premises as long as they do not buy the drinks and the drinks are drunk other than in the bar – for instance, in an attached restaurant.

Young people aged fourteen and over can go into a bar. When under sixteen, they can only buy soft drinks. Once sixteen, a young person can buy beer, cider, perry, or porter if it is to be drunk with a meal eaten on the premises; he cannot buy wine to drink with the meal. Otherwise, a person under eighteen cannot buy alcoholic drinks in a pub (maximum fine £400) nor can he drink them if they are bought for him by an adult (maximum fine £400 each for the child and the adult). Once the age of eighteen is reached, there are no restrictions.

Pawnbrokers

The Consumer Credit Act 1974 has repealed the Pawnbrokers Acts of 1872 and 1960. Pawnbrokers are regarded as another part of the credit industry, and as such are subject to strict controls when the amount lent does not exceed £15,000.

The customer must always be given a 'pawn receipt' for his goods. The pawnbroker commits an offence (maximum fine of £200) if no receipt is supplied.

The pawn must be redeemable for at least six months from the date it was taken, which means that the pawnbroker cannot sell it within that period. At the end of that period:
● *if the loan was for up to £25*, the item pledged becomes the pawnbroker's property;
● *if the loan was for more than £25*, the pawnbroker can sell the item, although he must first notify the customer of his intention to sell. The pawnbroker can deduct the amount he is owed from the sale proceeds, and any excess must be paid to the

customer. The customer must also be given a statement of account showing the sale price, the expenses of sale, and the net amount left. If the customer thinks that the item has been undersold by the pawnbroker it is for the pawnbroker to justify his price by showing he took 'reasonable care' over the sale. Similarly, it is for the pawnbroker to justify any expenses incurred in the sale (e.g. transportation, auction fees). If the sale realizes less than the amount of the debt, the customer still owes the balance to the pawnbroker.

If the pawnbroker refuses to allow the customer to redeem the pawn within the six months' period (or before the item is sold) he can be fined up to £200. He may also be guilty of theft.

Pawnbrokers are not allowed to take pawns from people under eighteen years old (maximum penalty £1,000 fine in a magistrates' court; one year's prison and unlimited fine if tried in the crown court).

Lost tickets

The customer does not lose his right to redeem the pawn if he loses his pawn ticket. The customer completes a form if the loan was for no more than £25, and swears a statutory declaration if it was for more than £25. The pawnbroker must then allow him to redeem the pawn.

TV licences

Every household using a TV should have a TV licence. The licence attaches to the household not to the individual TV set. So if the TV is lent to a friend, the friend cannot rely on the owner's TV licence. One licence covers all the sets in that household: you do not need one licence for each set.

Students in a hall of residence who have sets in their own rooms will all require their own licences. They are not covered by the college's licence or their parents' licences.

In rented premises, it is for the tenant to obtain a licence, whether or not the set was supplied by the landlord. Each flat or bed-sit should have its own licence, but flat-sharers will need one licence between them since together they comprise only one household.

A licence is not needed in a holiday let. The tenant is assumed to be covered by his own licence, at home.

Hotel guests do not need separate licences for their sets, unless they reside permanently in the hotel. But the hotel may well need extra licences. It will need one licence for the first fifteen sets; and a further licence for each additional five sets.

Finally, note that the detector-van does not have to find you actually watching an unlicensed TV for you to be guilty of an offence. It is enough if the set is ready for use.

34 Using a Bank

The bank and its customer

When a customer opens a bank account he is entering into a contract with the bank. Two of the terms of this contract are:

● *the bank will honour the customer's instructions* by meeting his cheques when there is money in the account, and also by only paying money out of the account on his instructions.

● *the bank will act confidentially* by not revealing the customer's financial affairs to anyone without his prior permission.

Cheques

Stopping a cheque

A bank must obey its customer's instructions. So if a customer writes a cheque but later decides to stop it, he can order the bank not to honour it. If his instructions reach the bank before the cheque is met, the bank must not pay out on it. This does not apply to cheques supported by a cheque card. They cannot be stopped.

The bank will usually want written instructions from the customer. However, if the order to stop it is phoned through, the bank will normally act immediately and postpone payment until written instructions are received.

If the bank receives the customer's instructions to stop the cheque, but for some reason allows the cheque to be met, then the bank must bear the loss. The bank will have acted against the customer's instructions and so he cannot be liable for the sum paid out. It is the bank's loss – whether the mistake was intentional or not.

The same applies if the bank pays out by mistake:

> *Husband and wife opened a joint account and told the bank that all cheques must be signed by both of them. The bank mistakenly paid out on cheques signed by the husband alone and so the wife sued the bank. Held: The bank was liable. The bank had not followed the customer's instructions.* Catlin (1983)

If a customer does stop a cheque, it does not absolve him from liability for paying the money to the payee (i.e. the person who was supposed to receive payment). If the cheque was part of a contract to pay the money, then by stopping the cheque the customer has acted in breach of contract. He will thus be liable in damages and must pay the sum due to the payee (e.g. if a person pays a deposit for a new car by cheque, he cannot back out of the transaction by simply stopping his cheque – he will still owe the money due under the cheque and he will still be committed to buying the car). In addition, if he had no intention of meeting the cheque when he wrote it out, he may also be liable for the criminal offence of fraud.

When the customer dies

The bank will stop all a customer's cheques when notified of his death (unless it is a joint account). Similarly, all cheques will be stopped if the bank learns that he is an undischarged bankrupt, or that he has committed an act of bankruptcy.

Post-dated cheques

A post-dated cheque is a cheque that is not to be met by the bank until a future date. That is the customer's instructions and, if the bank acts otherwise, it does so at its own risk.

Thus, if a cheque is written on 1 January, but dated 30 January, it should not be paid until then. But suppose the customer instructs the bank to stop the cheque before the 30 January only to find that the bank has mistakenly paid out the money already. The question then arises of who bears the loss. The answer is simple: the bank has failed to obey the instructions of its customer and so it bears the loss. The bank must credit the customer's account with any money wrongly paid out.

When a cheque 'bounces'

A bank must honour its customer's cheques but only if there are sufficient funds in his account. So if a customer has £399 in his account and writes out a cheque for £400, the bank can refuse to meet the cheque; it does not have to pay £399, and just leave the £1 unpaid. The unpaid cheque will be sent to the payee with a note stating 'R/D' – refer to drawer. Similarly:

> *The National Westminster did not pay a customer's mortgage standing order, because she had insufficient money in her account. Later (after the building society had repossessed her house) she sued the bank, arguing that they should have paid the standing orders as soon as sufficient money had been paid into the account. Held: No. A bank need not continuously monitor a customer's account. If there are not sufficient funds on the date the standing order arises then the bank need not pay.* Whitehead (1982)

Obviously if the customer has negotiated an overdraft with his bank, this rule will not apply until the customer comes to the limit of his overdraft. The bank cannot refuse to meet a cheque because it will put the customer's account into the red if a sufficient overdraft has already been negotiated.

Occasionally, a bank will refer a cheque back to the drawer by mistake, when there are sufficient funds in the account to meet it. This may cause acute embarrassment to the customer, especially if the bouncing cheque is for only a small amount. The extent of his legal redress against the bank will depend upon whether it was drawn on a private or business account. If it was a business cheque then a court may well award him several hundred pounds damages, for it will be accepted that a business man's financial standing can be seriously damaged by a bounced cheque. But if it was a private cheque, the customer will usually receive no more than nominal damages of a pound or two, unless real loss can be proved. The private customer is expected to dismiss the incident as a mere annoyance.

Mrs Gibbons paid her rent by cheque. But her cheque bounced because the bank had mistakenly credited a payment in the wrong account. As a result Mrs Gibbons's landlord insisted that in future she pay her rent in cash. Mrs Gibbons sued the bank for damages. Held: The bank was liable, but Mrs Gibbons was only awarded £2 damages. Gibbons (1939)

Exceptionally, a bank can be liable for defamation if it wrongly refuses to pay out on a cheque:

Mr Davidson was in business as a bookmaker. He stopped payment of a cheque by writing to the bank, but the bank mistakenly paid out on the cheque. As a result, when his next cheque was presented there was not enough money to meet it and, as it was returned to the payee with 'not sufficient' written on it, Mr Davidson sued for libel. Held: Yes, this was libel. Damages of £250 were awarded. As a result of this case, banks now write 'refer to drawer', rather than 'not sufficient', on unmet cheques in the hope that it will not be defamatory. Davidson (1940)

When the customer's signature is forged

When the customer opens his account he supplies specimen signatures to the bank. The law takes this as meaning that the bank should therefore know the signature of each of its customers, even if the signatures have changed in style since the specimen signatures were supplied! Clearly, this piece of legal logic is in reality a nonsense, but it is the law and, from the customer's point of view, it is a good law.

So if someone finds or steals the customer's cheque book, and draws a cheque in his own favour by forging the customer's signature, the bank bears the loss if it pays out on the cheque. Even if the forgery is a masterpiece and cannot be distinguished from the proper signature, it is the bank's loss and not the customer's. The only exception to this would be when the customer was aware that someone was forging his signature on cheques. Clearly, it is only reasonable to expect the customer to notify the bank if that is so. If he does not, then any future losses will be borne by him.

If a cheque book is lost, the customer should tell the bank immediately; he will not, of course, be liable for the forged cheques used (cf. lost credit cards, see page 565).

If the signature is forged then the bank need not pay out on the cheque – even if it was backed up by a cheque card. This is because the signature on the cheque is not that of the customer and so the cheque card does not guarantee the cheque. A cheque card only guarantees a cheque that is properly signed.

When the amount to be paid is altered

What if the amount to be paid is falsely increased, and the bank pays out that larger sum? Generally, it will be the bank's loss. If it pays out the larger amount it will not have done so on the instructions of its customer, and so he cannot be liable. So if the customer writes a cheque for 'Seven pounds', but someone alters it to 'Seventeen pounds', the bank can only debit the account £7 and they, not the customer, lose the £10. However, this rule is subject to the customer having taken reasonable care not to facilitate fraud. If he had left a large space between the word 'Seven' and the word 'Pounds', then clearly he would be inviting fraud. Similarly, if he wrote the amount as £ 7— rather than £7—, he would not be taking sufficient care, and would have to bear the loss.

The care expected of the customer is a matter of degree to be decided on the facts of each case. For instance:

A clerk at the firm of MacMillan & Arthur was responsible for writing out the firm's cheques, which were then signed by one of the partners in the firm. One day the clerk carefully prepared a cheque so that it read £2.0.0., but he did not insert the amount in words. The cheque was for cash. The cheque was signed by the partner. The clerk then went away, altered the figures to read £120.0.0. and inserted 'one hundred and twenty pounds' in words. The clerk cashed the cheque for £120. MacMillan & Arthur sued the bank saying that the bank should only have debited their account by £2, not £120. Held: Customers should draw cheques so that they cannot be altered if they fall into dishonest hands. The bank was allowed to deduct the full £120. London Joint Stock Bank (1918)

When a cheque, already written out, is stolen or lost

Suppose someone is given a cheque, but before paying it into his bank account it is stolen or he loses it. Normally he could go to the person who gave him the cheque (i.e. the drawer), tell him to stop that cheque, and ask for a replacement. But suppose that someone else pays the cheque into an account before the lost or mislaid cheque is missed. He will do this either by opening a false account in the person's name, or by signing that name on the back of the cheque and so endorsing it to himself for payment into his own account. The drawer will have paid out the money from his account, but the original payee will have received nothing. What is the position?

Usually the original payee will bear the loss. The drawer of the cheque has discharged his liability to him and he cannot now ask for a replacement cheque. Nor can he go to his bank and complain that they wrongly paid out on the cheque (unless he could show that they had not acted in good faith or in accordance with normal practice). Thus, the loss would fall on the original payee who lost the cheque or had it stolen from him. (But see also 'Not Negotiable', page 556.)

Lost traveller's cheques. Different rules apply to lost traveller's cheques, and the small print on the order form will set out who is to bear any loss. Usually, the cheques will be replaced if the loss was reported to the police, and if they had not been countersigned in advance – unless the customer was 'excessively careless' (in one case it was held that a customer had not been excessively careless when he lost traveller's cheques which fell from his pocket when he took his coat off on a hot afternoon).

Lost electronic cash-cards. Many banks issue cards that enable customers to withdraw cash from electronic terminals. If one of these cards is stolen, there will normally be no maximum limit to the customer's liability – if the thief uses it to take a large amount of money from the account, then it is the customer who will bear the loss, not the bank. However, if the customer's account is programmed to allow withdrawals into overdraft by use of the card, then the card would be treated as a credit card – in which case, the normal £50 maximum limit of liability would apply. But, if the card does not permit an overdraft, it cannot be treated as a credit card – and then there will be no maximum liability. This seems to be a flaw in banking legislation.

Secrecy and confidentiality

The customer's financial affairs are private and are not to be disclosed without his prior consent – for instance, if he gives the bank as a reference. Despite this it seems that banks frequently give confidential information about their customer's creditworthiness to other banks. This practice is probably unlawful and could give rise to a damages claim.

> *Mr Tournier's account was in the red. His bank manager allowed him to pay it off by instalments. But Tournier fell into arrears with the instalments. So the bank manager phoned Tournier's employers to discover his latest address. In passing, the manager mentioned that Tournier's cheques showed he had been gambling heavily. His employer then refused to renew Tournier's employment contract. He sued the bank, arguing that there was an implied contract that they would not disclose his affairs. Held: Yes, unless there was an implied consent to the disclosure, the bank would be liable.* Tournier (1924)

Exceptionally the courts will say that a bank does have implied consent to reveal information. For instance:

> *Mrs Sutherland's cheque bounced because she was overdrawn. The bank manager did not give her an overdraft because he knew that she gambled. Mrs Sutherland complained to her husband, who phoned the manager. The manager then told Mr Sutherland of his wife's gambling. Mrs Sutherland sued the bank. Held: There was an implied authority for the bank to disclose her affairs. Since Mr Sutherland had phoned, the bank manager was justified in assuming that Mrs Sutherland did not mind his referring to her gambling. The bank was not liable. The judge said that even if the bank had been liable, the damages would have been a nominal £2.* Sutherland (1938)

There are a few exceptions to the secrecy rule. For example, the Inland Revenue can obtain a court order to inspect a bank account. In addition, a bank is obliged to notify the Revenue of some interest payments received by its customers.

Taking the bank manager's advice

If a customer asks his bank manager for expert financial advice, or employs him to handle his financial affairs for him, the bank may be liable for negligent advice.

Obviously, the bank is not liable just because the advice it gave, say as to good investments, turns out to be wrong. But if the advice should never have been given in the first place (e.g. because a particular company was known to be in financial difficulties) then the bank may be liable for negligent advice.

An advertising agency placed adverts for a client. To ensure that the advertising fees would be met, the agency asked the client's bankers for a reference. The bank replied that the firm was respectable and considered good, although the reference was said to be made 'without responsibility'. The agency then placed newspaper and TV advertisements for which they were personally liable to pay. The client's firm went bust and the agency lost £17,000. It became clear that the bank's reference had been wrong. The agency sued the bank. Held: A bank could be liable to an outsider for negligent advice, and they would have been liable in this case had it not been for the 'without responsibility' disclaimer. Hedley Byrne (1963)

A glossary of banking terms

A/C payee. 'Account payee' written on a cheque means that the cheque can only be paid into the payee's (i.e. the person to whom the cheque is made out) bank account. It cannot be endorsed to someone else, nor can it be exchanged for cash.

& co. These words are often written on a crossed cheque. They have no legal significance and are of no effect. Contrary to popular belief, the words do not have the effect of making the cheque not negotiable.

balance. If there is a debit balance the account is overdrawn; if there is a credit balance it is not.

banker's card. Usually called a cheque card; see below.

banker's draft. A cheque drawn by the bank on its own (not a customer's) funds. In effect, it is as good as cash since there is no risk of it bouncing. Used when completing major purchases (e.g. buying a house) when the seller wants a cheque that is as good as cash, but which does not have the disadvantages of cash.

banker's order. Usually called a 'standing order'; see below.

cheque card. This gives a guarantee that any cheque supported by a cheque card will be met by the bank, even if the cheque-card holder does not have sufficient money in his account. The card is valid for individual cheques up to £50. It also allows the holder to draw up to £50 in cash from any branch of any bank in the UK.

credit entry. A payment into an account (cf. 'debit entry').

crossed cheque. A cheque is crossed when it has two parallel lines drawn across it. A crossed cheque cannot be cashed; it must be paid into a bank account. These days most cheques are crossed cheques.

debit entry. A payment out of an account (cf. 'credit entry').

direct debit. Similar to a standing order, except that the debit is made on the initiative of the payee and not automatically.

drawer. The person on whose account the cheque is drawn (i.e. payable).

endorsing. A cheque is endorsed by the payee signing it on the back. This allows it to be paid into someone else's account. But this will not be so if the cheque is marked 'A/C payee'.

not negotiable. If a cheque marked 'not negotiable' is stolen, then the drawer is not legally liable if it is paid into a thief's account or the account of someone to whom the thief has endorsed the cheque. So the drawer can recover any money mistakenly paid out by the bank.

open cheque. The opposite of a crossed cheque, in that it is exchangeable for cash at the drawer's bank and need not be paid into an account.

'or order'. Most cheques have the words 'Pay . . . or order'. This allows the payee to endorse the cheque to someone else.

payee. The person who receives the money.

refer to drawer (R/D). Marked on a cheque that has bounced.

specially presented cheques. Specially presenting short-cuts the normal clearing operation. The cheque goes direct to the drawer's branch and so there is a quick decision as to whether or not it will be met.

standing order. An instruction to the bank for them to pay a fixed sum, at regular intervals, to a named payee.

35 Insurance

Few commentators would deny that insurance law is weighted in favour of the insurance companies and against the interests of the customer.

In most consumer transactions, the law is prepared to modify the contract made between the customer and the seller in order to protect the customer. Minimum standards of work, quality, fitness, and description are implied into the contract, and the consumer thus has legal safeguards against the seller avoiding liability. But, in insurance, the position is different. The insurance contract is construed strictly as a legal document, and the usual result is that it is construed against the consumer. In fact, the law takes this further by deliberately tipping the scales of justice in favour of the insurer, by over-emphasizing the duty of the customer to disclose everything to the insurer.

How the law is weighted in favour of insurance companies

1. Disclosing all 'material' facts

The contract made between the insurer and the customer differs from a normal contract in that it is a contract of 'the utmost good faith' (in Latin, a contract *uberrimae fidei*). This means that the customer must act with the 'utmost good faith' towards the insurance company. In particular, he must tell the insurers of *all* material facts relevant to his application for insurance. It is up to him to tell the insurers of *anything* that would influence a 'prudent insurer' in deciding whether to take on the risk or, alternatively,·in deciding the amount of the premium. In effect, then, the criterion used for deciding whether a fact is 'material' is the normal practice of insurers, which ensures that the rule is applied very strictly. Any material fact must be disclosed. If it is not disclosed the customer will be uninsured.

To make matters worse, it makes no difference that the customer is unaware of the significance of a particular fact. Even if he does not realize it is 'material' he must tell the insurers of it. This is so even if he is not asked about it. In short, he must volunteer all relevant information.

Illustration. *Harry Evans smokes ten cigarettes a day. He decides to take out life insurance but he is not asked any questions about his smoking habits and so the matter is never raised. Subsequently, he is killed in a motor accident. The insurers then discover that Harry used to smoke. Since this was something that would have affected the decision whether to insure him (or the price for doing so), the insurers can repudiate the policy. The policy is invalid, and the insurance company need pay nothing to Harry's widow, except a refund of his premiums. The fact that his smoking was irrelevant to how he died makes no difference.*

Following a theft, diamond merchants claimed on their insurance policy. The insurers repudiated liability because the firm's sales manager had been convicted of smuggling diamonds in the USA some eight years previously. They argued that this was a material fact that should have been disclosed to them even though there was no suggestion that the sales manager was involved in the theft. The diamond merchants said they had thought that their employee's conviction was irrelevant. Held: No, it was a material fact. The insurers did not have to pay up. Roselodge (1966)

Arterial Caravans' premises were burnt down. The insurers then discovered that there had been a serious fire five years earlier in other premises owned by the firm's proprietor. The insurance company refused to pay out, saying that this was a material fact that they should have been told about. Held: Yes, the previous fire was material and so it should have been disclosed even though no one had asked about it. Arterial Caravans were uninsured. Arterial Caravans (1973)

The customer's duty of good faith continues after he has filled in the application form, up until the time the insurance company agrees to insure him. For instance:

Mr Looker applied for life insurance. The company agreed to accept him, and issued a receipt in the standard form stating that it was a condition that he remained in good health until the first premium was paid. Mr Looker then became ill, but he did not notify the company and he sent off his cheque for the first premium. Three days later he died. Held: He was not insured – he should have told the company of his illness. Looker (1928)

2. The proposal form

Insurance companies give themselves additional protection by the way in which they word their proposal forms. The final sentence of the form will often read 'the insured's answers form a part of the insurance policy'. The effect of this innocent-looking phrase is to make the proposal form part of the policy itself. So if any of the answers are incorrect the insurance company can declare the policy to be null and void, and so refuse to pay out on it. The catch is that the rule applies even when the customer does not realize that his answer is incorrect, so although he may have acted with the 'utmost good faith' he can still be uninsured.

Illustration. *Peter Brown takes out life insurance. The proposal form has a question 'Are you in good health?' Mr Brown, believing himself to be in good health, answers 'yes'. A year later he is killed in an accident at work. A post-mortem discloses that he had a malignant brain tumour which was obviously getting worse and which existed at the time he took out the insurance. The insurance company could then argue that his statement that he was in good health was wrong and declare the policy to be null and void.*

This is, of course, a scandalous situation. In practice most disputes over the proposal form arise because the customer was careless when filling it in. However, if he puts down a slightly inaccurate answer it may invalidate his insurance, even if it is irrelevant to his claim.

Dawsons took out motor insurance for a lorry. However, the address at which the lorry was garaged was incorrectly entered, by mistake, in the proposal form. Later the lorry was destroyed by fire and so Dawsons claimed on the policy. Held: The wrong address was not a material fact so the insurers could not repudiate for failure to disclose a material fact. However, the proposal form contained a provision that 'the proposal shall be the basis of the contract and shall be held as incorporated therein'. This allowed the insurers to repudiate. So Dawsons were uninsured, despite the mistake having been unintentional and despite it not having been 'material'. Dawsons (1922)

So it is important to be careful when filling in a proposal form.

When there is a claim on an insurance policy, the company will usually ask the customer to fill in a lengthy form, which largely repeats the questions asked in the proposal form. The insurers will then be able to compare the two sets of answers to see whether the proposal form contained any inaccuracies. For this reason it is wise to keep a copy of any proposal form.

3. Renewing the policy

If the insurance policy is renewed each year (as with a car or house-contents policy), then each renewal is a new contract. Thus, the customer's duty to act with the 'utmost good faith' and to disclose all 'material' facts applies anew. Accordingly, the customer must tell the insurers of anything that has happened within the last year that is a 'material' fact. Usually, of course, the insured is not asked directly whether any new facts have arisen. More often than not, he simply sends off his renewal cheque and assumes that his insurance is validly renewed. However, if he forgets to tell the insurers of any material fact, he will be uninsured.

Mrs Lambert took out insurance to cover her own and her husband's jewellery. The proposal form did not ask whether Mr and Mrs Lambert had ever been convicted for an offence of dishonesty. The policy was renewed year after year, until nine years later when Mrs Lambert claimed £311 for stolen jewellery. The insurers then discovered that Mr Lambert had been convicted for a dishonesty offence before the insurance was taken out, and also for an offence during the period of cover. Held: The insurers could repudiate on two grounds. Firstly, Mrs Lambert should have mentioned her husband's earlier conviction on the proposal form; since she had not, the policy was void. Secondly, Mrs Lambert should have told the insurers of his second conviction when renewing the policy. It was a material fact and so it should have been mentioned on renewal – even though the insurance company had never mentioned that the Lamberts should tell them of any criminal conviction. Lambert (1975)

4. Narrowly interpreting the cover given

Generally, insurance policies are construed very narrowly: the customer does not get the benefit of any doubt.

Mr Young took out a householder's insurance policy to cover himself against risks to his house. Amongst other things, the policy covered him against loss from 'storm tempest or flood'. Subsequently, Mr Young claimed on the policy because the floor of a downstairs lavatory had three inches of water in it. This was due to the gradual seepage caused by the blocking of an underground water supply. The insurers said this was not a 'flood'. Held: They were correct. This was not a 'flood', since a flood meant a large movement of water, and did not cover seepage. So although the floor was under water, Mr Young could not claim. Young (1976)

Problems of construction and interpretation often arise under motor policies. For instance, what is 'social and domestic use' of the car?

Mr Binions was a carpet layer. One day he was working on a job with an employee of his, and Mr Binions's father had also called in to help out. The employee had a bad toothache so it was agreed that Mr Binions senior would drive the employee home in his son's car. On the way to lunch, the car crashed. Mr Binions senior's policy only covered 'social and domestic use'. Held: His policy did not cover him, since he was using the car for two purposes. Firstly, the social use of going to lunch and, secondly, the non-social use of taking the employee home. The material character of the journey was to take the employee home and so his insurance did not cover the accident. Seddon (1977)

Another case illustrated how the wording of a policy can be of crucial importance. The owner of a Rolls-Royce was tricked into parting with it by a con-man, in return for a forged bank draft. He then claimed on his insurance policy with the Commercial Union, only to be told that the policy covered 'theft', but his car had not been stolen – it had been obtained by fraud, and, in addition, he had parted with it voluntarily!

Sometimes the insurance company can declare the policy void on the grounds of 'public policy' – i.e. that it would be wrong for the customer to be allowed to claim.

Mr Geismar took out insurance for some valuable items. When they were stolen, he claimed on the policy. The insurance company discovered that he had imported them into the UK without having paid customs duty on them. So they refused to pay up, arguing that it would be wrong to compensate him for the loss of 'illegal' items. Held: They need not pay him! Geismar (1977)

5. Insurance brokers and the insurance company

Most insurance is effected through insurance brokers. Not unnaturally, most people regard their broker as a representative of the insurance company and accordingly they follow his advice and trust his judgement. For instance, if the customer mentions some fact but is told 'Oh, they won't want to know about that', or if the broker puts down his answers incorrectly, he regards the agent as being someone in authority – someone who can take decisions on behalf of the insurance company. But this is not so; the insurance broker is not an agent of the insurance company and he cannot speak on the company's behalf. This is so even if the insurance agent is employed by the insurance company.

Mr O'Connor went to an insurance broker to take out insurance on his car. The brokers filled in the proposal form incorrectly, saying the car was garaged whereas it was parked on the road at night. Subsequently, Mr O'Connor's car was damaged, but the insurers refused to meet the claim, because of the incorrect answer on the proposal form. Mr O'Connor argued that the insurance brokers were the agents of the insurers and so the insurance company was bound. Held: No, the insurance broker was not the company's agent. Mr O'Connor was uninsured. O'Connor (1971)

So if the broker fills in the proposal forms incorrectly, the customer will be uninsured. His only remedy will be to sue the broker for negligence – assuming that he can prove that it was the broker's error, not his own, and that the broker has enough money to be worth suing.

Mr McNealy was an insurance broker. A client, who was a part-time musician, asked for motor insurance. The client disclosed his full-time job but was not asked about, nor did he mention, his part-time job as a musician. Mr McNealy arranged insurance on a policy that did not apply to certain occupations, including part-time musicians. When there was an accident, the insurance company refused to pay up. Mr McNealy was sued by his client for negligence. Held: He was liable. He knew of the terms of the policy and should have checked that his client did not come within one of the excluded categories. McNealy (1978)

Often, of course, insurance is arranged by part-time brokers who are not reputable firms and so, when a mistake is made, the customer has no one to sue. He is left uninsured and without compensation.

Reform

Clearly the law is weighted in favour of insurance companies and against the consumer. There is no reason why the law should not be brought up to date. Why not simply say that the insurance company can only repudiate liability if the customer was guilty of fraud?

Until the law is reformed, all the customer can do is to take great care when filling in the proposal and claim forms. In addition, it is advisable to deal only with the large, reputable firms which will often honour policies even when their lawyers have advised them that they can technically repudiate liability.

(For more insurance 'horror' stories, see the section on car insurance, page 610).

Claiming on an insurance policy

The idea of insurance is to put the customer in the same position as he would have been before the accident or loss occurred. This means that the customer cannot be better off as a result of claiming on the policy. So he will not receive the replacement cost of, for instance, a stolen TV, but only its second-hand value. If he was paid the replacement value (i.e. the cost of buying a new TV) he would end up better off than before the theft and that is not the purpose of insurance. This is the 'principle of indemnity'.

These days 'replacement policies' are becoming more popular and may become normal for house contents insurance. This is obviously more sensible, but the drawback is the ever-increasing premium.

Many people are confused as to the difference between a house contents policy and a house buildings policy. The basic distinction is simple: a house contents policy covers the personal possessions of the householder and his family against damage and theft (but theft will not be covered if the house is sublet or lent unless there was a forcible entry); a buildings policy covers damage to the buildings and its fittings (decorations, ceilings, fixtures and fittings, paths, fences, garages, etc.).

Betterment

If the customer does end up in a better position than before the claim was made, he may be liable to pay 'betterment' to the insurance company unless he has a replacement policy. Thus, a motorist who has an old car may have the front wing replaced by the insurers after an accident. Clearly, he is better off than he was before the accident, since he now has a new wing rather than an old one. So he must pay for the difference in value between the two – even if he did not want the new wing. He cannot argue that there was nothing wrong with the old wing before the accident, and so he did not need a new wing. In terms of common sense that is clearly correct, but in terms of insurance law and the principle of indemnity, it is wrong. The law prevails and so he must pay for the betterment.

Average clause

If a customer has £10,000 worth of property, but he insures it for £5,000, what happens if £5,000 worth is stolen? The answer is that he receives £2,500. This is because his insurance policy will almost certainly contain an 'average clause', which allows the insurance company to pay a proportion of the value of the stolen goods in relation to the proportion by which he was under-insured.

Delay

Insurance companies are notoriously slow at replying to letters and in paying out money. Their policy seems to be one of delay, delay, delay, when it comes to dealing with any matter that might involve them in paying out money. Any solicitor with experience of insurance claims knows that it is often necessary to commence legal proceedings in order to put pressure on insurance companies to pay out, even in cases when they are clearly liable.

If a local office is being very slow in processing the claim, it is often advisable to send a letter of complaint to the head office. If the claim is sound, the customer may like to threaten legal proceedings and remind the insurance company that they may well have to pay the resulting legal fees. The British Insurance Association can also help if an insurance company is ignoring letters.

When an insurance company goes 'bust'

The collapse of such companies as Fire, Auto & Marine and the Vehicle & General Insurance Co. led to considerable public outcry as to the plight of those customers who were left uninsured. As a result, the Policyholders Protection Act 1975 was passed, to give some protection to the customers of insurance companies that 'fail' or get into serious financial difficulties.

Generally, if the company goes into liquidation, the policyholder will be paid 90 per cent of any sums due to him or, in the case of life assurance, 90 per cent of the value of the policy, if alternative insurance cannot be arranged. Exceptionally, if the insurance was compulsory by a statute (for instance, employers have to insure against liability to pay damages to injured employees) then the policyholder receives 100 per cent, not 90 per cent, of his entitlement.

Any inquiries concerning the scheme should be addressed to the Policyholders Protection Board, at Aldermary House, Queen Street, London EC4 (01-248 4477). Note that corporate policyholders are excluded from the scheme, so a company will not be protected if its insurers go out of business. Similarly, if the whole insurance scheme was illegal (e.g. the company was not a registered insurance company) then the board will not help.

The Insurance Ombudsman

If you are involved in a dispute with an insurance company, you might be able to refer the dispute to the Insurance Ombudsman. He is an arbitrator, whose salary is paid by the insurance industry. Most insurance companies subscribe to the scheme.

Disputes can be referred to the Ombudsman within six months of the final decision of the insurance companies (e.g. the letter saying that they will not pay you any more money). The Ombudsman will consider the papers you have sent him, and ask the company for its side of the argument. Generally, there will be no hearing or meeting, and the Ombudsman will simply consider the papers before him. He will then come to a decision. If he finds in your favour, he can order the company to pay you a reasonable sum in settlement (up to £10,000). The important point to note is that the Ombudsman's arbitration will be binding on the company – but it need not be binding on you. You, as the customer, can simply reject his findings if you do not like them. On the other hand, if you want to accept what he says, then the insurance company have no choice – it must pay out the amount ordered by the Ombudsman. If you do not wish to follow the Ombudsman's decision, you can simply proceed with a court claim against the insurance company, in the usual way. It therefore follows that you have nothing to lose by going to the Insurance Ombudsman – and in practice he can provide a simple, free remedy. The Insurance Ombudsman can be contacted at 31 Southampton Row, London WC1B 5HJ (01-242 8613).

36 Consumer Credit and Hire Purchase

Our credit laws are still undergoing a radical overhaul as a result of the recommendations of the 1971 Crowther Committee. The committee's recommendations were largely enacted in the Consumer Credit Act 1974, but only parts of that Act have been brought into operation, and it will be several years before all the provisions of the 1974 Act are in force. Accordingly, the law is still in a state of flux, but only those sections of the 1974 Act that have been brought into operation are referred to here.

The obvious advantage of credit, to the consumer, is that it allows him to 'buy now and pay later', which in a time of inflation can be a great benefit. On the other hand, the disadvantages can be obvious; one judge is reported as having neatly summarized them thus: being persuaded by a man you don't know, to sign an agreement you don't read, to buy furniture you don't need, with money you haven't got.

The most common types of credit for personal borrowing

Overdraft

This allows the customer of a bank to overdraw his current account up to an agreed level. The customer need not use the full credit facility and he will be charged interest on the amount of credit he actually uses. The rate of interest is usually variable, often being 2 per cent above the bank's current base rate. The money can usually be spent on anything the customer chooses. Overdrafts are described as 'running-account' credit in the Consumer Credit Act. One disadvantage is that the customer will probably have to pay bank charges, as well as interest charges, when he might otherwise have avoided them.

Bank loan

This is usually a loan of a stated amount for a particular purpose, for instance, to buy a car; such loans are referred to as 'restricted-use' credit agreements in the 1974 Act. The loan is a separate account with the bank and the customer is required to pay it off in regular instalments over an agreed period, usually of no more than three years. The rate of interest is usually fixed.

Personal loan

This is similar to a bank loan, and in fact personal loans are often made by banks.

Insurance policy loan

This is a loan given on the security of the cash-in value of an endowment or whole-life policy, and is lent by the insurance company.

Credit cards

Access and Barclaycard are the best-known credit cards. The customer pays the trader by producing his card, and the trader then invoices the credit-card company, paying a small percentage to the company as commission. If the customer settles his monthly account with the credit-card company by the correct date, he will pay no interest. He will thus have had interest-free credit for several weeks. If he does not settle his account, he will be charged interest on the amount due, at a rate of interest varying with the banks' base rate, but probably between 22 and 25 per cent per annum.

The card-holder's liability

Until he signs the card, the card-holder is not responsible for it. So if it is lost before he signs it and an unauthorized person uses it to buy goods, the card-holder is not liable, and the loss falls on the credit-card company. Thus, the instructions to a new card-holder always say 'sign the card immediately'.

Once the card-holder signs the card, he becomes bound by the conditions set out in the 'Conditions of Use' sent to him with his card. By section 85 of the 1974 Act, the card-holder must be sent a fresh copy of the conditions every time his card is renewed; if he is not, the card company cannot enforce the agreement against him.

If the card is mislaid after it has been signed, the card-holder will only be liable for the first £50 of losses if it is misused (ss. 83 and 84, 1974 Act). This is even if the card-holder does not notify the card company that he has lost the card. The only exception is when the card is misused by someone who acquired it with the card-holder's consent. (For instance, if the card is lent to a friend, who then misuses it, the card-holder is liable for all the purchases made.)

As a matter of practice, the credit-card companies generally limit the card-holder's liability to the first £50 of loans if the card-holder promptly notifies them of the loss of the card. For instance:

If the Access card is lost or stolen the card-holder will notify the bank's Access department immediately. If such notification is given orally it shall be treated as not taking effect if not confirmed in writing to the bank's Access department within seven days thereafter. Subject to such notification, the maximum liability of the card-holder shall be £50 for loans to the bank arising from use of the Access card by any other person . . .

565

This condition is, however, subject to sections 83 and 84 of the Consumer Credit Act, and the customer's maximum liability will never exceed £50, unless he gave the card to the person who misused it.

Under the Conditions of Use, the card-holder is not responsible for any losses once he has notified the card company of the card's disappearance. It can therefore be important to prove exactly when the card company was notified. For instance, if the card is stolen at 10 a.m. and the card was misused by the thief at 12 o'clock, it is important to know whether the customer phoned the card company before 12 o'clock. The problem is, of course, that purchases are not usually timed to the minute. However, section 171 (4) of the Consumer Credit Act says that it is for the card company to prove that the purchase was made before the card-holder notified the company of the card's loss. So, in practice, if the loss is reported to the company on the same day as the card is used, the company will probably find it difficult to make the card-holder responsible.

If the goods are defective

If the goods bought with the card are faulty or defective in any way, then the card-holder has equal rights against the card company and against the shopkeeper. By section 75 of the 1974 Act, the card company is jointly liable with the shopkeeper for the shopkeeper's breach of contract if it was a consumer purchase and the cash price of the goods was between £100 and £30,000 (see page 514).

It is now illegal for a credit-card company to send a credit card to someone who has not asked for it (s. 51, 1974 Act). This provision was the direct result of the outcry when Access was introduced and cards were sent to many people who had not asked for them.

Hire purchase and credit sale

What is a hire-purchase agreement?

When a consumer signs a hire-purchase agreement he does not become the owner of the goods he is buying. What happens is that the shopkeeper sells the goods to the finance company, not the customer. The finance company then hires out the goods to the customer in return for the HP instalments. Only when the customer has paid off all the instalments does he become the owner of the goods. Until then, they belong to the finance company, and since they are not the customer's he cannot sell them.

It is easy to tell whether a credit agreement is an HP agreement. If it is, it will contain this warning, printed in a red box:

> This is a Hire Purchase Agreement regulated by the Consumer Credit Act 1974. Sign it only if you want to be legally bound by its terms.
>
> Signature of debtor
>
> Date of signature
>
> The goods will not become your property until you have made   payments. You must not sell them before then.

Also, if it is an HP agreement, the finance company will be referred to as 'the owner', whereas the customer will be called 'the hirer'.

The laws set out in this chapter only apply to HP agreements in which the amount of credit does not exceed £15,000. It is the amount of credit, not the price of the goods, that decides the £15,000 limit. For instance, an £18,000 car bought on £14,000 worth of HP will come within the rules.

What is a credit-sale agreement?

With credit sale, the customer becomes the owner of the goods as soon as he buys them. What happens is that the shopkeeper sells the goods to the finance company, which then sells them to the customer. The customer, in return, undertakes to pay back the finance company in five or more instalments.

Since the customer acquires immediate ownership of the goods, he can sell them before he has paid off all the loan – unlike goods bought on HP – although he will of course be liable to pay off the outstanding instalments. However, it will probably be a term of the credit-sale agreement that he pays off all the remaining instalments as soon as he sells the goods.

It is easy to tell whether a credit agreement is a credit-sale agreement. If it is, it will contain this warning, printed in a red box:

This is a Credit Sale Agreement regulated by the Consumer Credit Act 1974. Sign it only if you want to be legally bound by its terms.
Signature of buyer   Date of signature

In a credit-sale agreement, the finance company is usually referred to as 'the seller', whilst the customer is called 'the buyer'.

The laws set out in this chapter only apply to credit-sale agreements in which the amount of credit is not less than £50 and not more than £15,000.

As with HP, the laws on credit sale are now contained in the Consumer Credit Act 1974. However, since the customer is the immediate owner of goods bought on credit sale, the provisions as to ending the credit agreement and repossession by the finance company (see below) which apply to HP do not apply to credit sale. However, the other Consumer Credit Act provisions do apply.

Entering into the credit agreement

Before the customer signs the HP or credit-sale agreement, he must be notified of the cash price of the goods and also the rate of interest and the total credit price, for instance by means of a label. This information must also be set out in the credit agreement, although it may well be buried in a maze of legalistic jargon.

If, by some mischance, the information was not set out in the agreement, the finance company would be unable to enforce the agreement against the customer or make him pay the instalments.

Trying to back out of the credit agreement

Normally, once the credit agreement has been made, it is too late for the customer to change his mind and cancel the agreement. He will have made a binding agreement with the finance company and will be in breach of contract if he defaults. However, despite this, there are two occasions when the customer can back out.

1. Backing out before the company agrees to provide credit. The credit agreement is only finalized when the customer's proposal form, in which he asks for credit, is approved and accepted by the company or other credit supplier. Often, there will be a delay of several days while the company checks the customer's creditworthiness and processes his application for credit. Only when the company approves the application is a legally binding agreement made. It follows that the customer can back out at any time before the credit supplier approves his application for credit.

2. Backing out when the customer signed the agreement 'off trade premises'. Special protection is given to customers who sign a credit agreement 'off trade premises' (i.e. anywhere other than in a shop, showroom, or finance company office). For instance, the exception will apply if the agreement is signed at home with a doorstep salesman. If the agreement was signed off trade premises, then:

• a copy of the agreement must be left with the customer when the sale is made, *and*

• another copy of the signed agreement must be posted to him within seven days, *and*

• the customer has five days in which to back out. The five-day 'cooling-off period' runs from the date when he receives the second copy of the agreement (i.e. the one that had to be posted to him). He can cancel the agreement by posting a letter of cancellation within five days of his receiving the copy agreement sent to him by the finance company. This will usually only be received by him several days after he signed the agreement, so he may well end up with considerably more than five days in which to cancel. The five-day period is enforced strictly; for instance, if the copy agreement is received on Monday morning, the letter of cancellation must be *posted* by Saturday evening. It is advisable for the customer to send the letter of cancellation by recorded delivery, or to obtain a certificate of posting from the post office. This will avoid argument as to whether the letter was posted in time.

The letter of cancellation need not be in any particular form, although it is obviously desirable to give the reference number of the agreement and for the customer to make it quite clear that he is cancelling the agreement.

It is important to note that the cooling-off period only applies to agreements signed *'off* trade premises'. If the agreement is signed on trade premises, the customer cannot cancel. Some less reputable traders try to avoid the provisions of the Act by advising the customer 'to come down to the shop to sign the agreement'. The customer should, of course, refuse to do so.

The customer's right to cancel must be mentioned in the credit agreement. Regulations have laid down the detailed wording that must be used, and the notice must be printed in a red box on the agreement. To ensure that the regulations are complied with, most finance companies have pre-printed forms of agreement containing the red box. However, if the form is mistakenly used for an 'on trade premises' agreement (i.e. no right of cancellation) and the red box is not crossed out, then the customer will acquire the right to cancel in the cooling-off period.

The effect of cancellation

If the agreement is cancelled, the position is as though it had never existed. So all money must be refunded, except for a £3 fee. Any guarantor or surety is released from his obligations. If there is a linked transaction, then they are both cancelled. (For instance, if the customer bought a TV he might have taken out a maintenance contract at the same time; by cancelling the purchase of the TV he also cancels the maintenance agreement.)

If the credit purchase involved a trader in a part exchange, those goods must be returned to the customer. If they are not returned within ten days in the same condition, the customer can claim the agreed cash trade-in value from the dealer.

Illustration. Jane Jones buys a new fridge from a door-to-door salesman and she signs the credit agreement at home. He allows her a credit of £25 on her old fridge. However, she cancels the agreement within the cooling-off period. Two weeks later, the salesman returns her old fridge to her, but Jane no longer wants it. She can claim £25 cash instead since the fridge was not returned within the ten-day period.

When a credit agreement is cancelled, the customer must take reasonable care of the goods bought. However, it is not for the customer to return them; the seller must collect them. The customer is only required to allow the seller to collect them, having given written notice, at the seller's expense. Generally, the customer's duty to take reasonable care of the goods only lasts for twenty-one days after the cancellation, unless he failed to allow the goods to be collected during that time, when requested.

Lost agreements

The customer can always obtain a copy of the credit agreement (for instance, if he mislays his original copy). If he writes to the owner or seller of the goods, a copy must be supplied, although a fee of up to 50p can be charged. The customer cannot ask for another copy within the next month.

Statement of payments

The customer can always ask for an up-to-date statement of his account. For a fee of up to 50p, the company must tell him:
- the amount he has paid so far;
- the amount he should have paid so far and when instalments that are unpaid become due;
- the total amount to be paid under the credit agreement, including the various amounts, and when they are due.

Trying to reduce the rate of interest

The rate of interest can be reduced, by the courts, if it is 'extortionate'. This means that it has to be more than merely a high rate of interest, but such that the rates are 'grossly exorbitant' or rates that grossly contravene ordinary principles of fair dealing. Accordingly, this provision only applies in exceptional circumstances.

The Consumer Credit Act does not define what is an 'extortionate' rate of interest, but it does set out some guidelines for deciding whether an agreement is extortionate. The court will look at:

- *the borrower*: his age, experience, business capacity, and health; also the degree of financial pressure on him when he made the agreement, together with the nature of that pressure;
- *the lender*: the risk he accepted (bearing in mind any security taken); his relationship to the borrower; whether or not the cash price of the goods was inflated to make the credit price seem reasonable;
- *the rates of interest current* when the agreement was made.

If a customer thinks the agreement is extortionate, he can apply to the county court. The judge will not confine himself to the rate of interest when he looks at the agreement – he will look at all the terms. In particular, he will look at the total charge for the credit, including any price paid for compulsory insurance and for a compulsory maintenance contract. It is the agreement as a whole that is looked at, not just the rate of interest. Generally it is for the finance company to show that the agreement is not extortionate.

There is no going rate as to what is extortionate. This is because the circumstances of every loan vary and all the factors have to be taken into account. For instance:

Mr and Mrs Scott were sitting tenants. Their landlord offered them the chance to buy the flat for £22,500, which was £1,500 below the market price. The Scotts signed a purchase contract without having arranged finance in advance. They failed to complete the purchase on time and were at risk of losing their £2,500 deposit. Mr Scott was then introduced to a finance firm which obtained a loan of £20,500 to help the Scotts. The firm had no time to make proper inquiries about the Scotts' finances, make an inspection of the property or carry out the usual conveyancing searches. The loan was for three months at 12 per cent (an annual rate of 48 per cent). Subsequently, the Scotts argued that the rate of interest was extortionate. Held: No, taking all the circumstances into account, the rate was not extortionate. Mr Scott was an educated man, he knew what he was doing; the risk to the lenders was considerable in this case – they were putting up over 80 per cent of the value of the property and they were not being given sufficient time in which to carry out the usual conveyancing procedures. In the circumstances, 48 per cent p.a. was not extortionate. A. Ketley Limited (1980)

A loan of £400 was made, repayable by twelve monthly instalments of £66·66 – a true annual interest rate of 184 per cent, and an APR of 320 per cent. Held: This was an extortionate rate, and the court reduced the rate to 40 per cent. It was also suggested that a true annual rate of 100 per cent would generally be regarded as extortionate. Note that this loan offer had been advertised in the national press – so, presumably, many other people were needlessly paying an extortionate rate of interest (and perhaps still are!). Barcabe (1982)

Working out the true rate of interest

Anyone buying on credit should distinguish between the annual or monthly rate of interest (the flat rate) and the true rate of interest. They are not the same. The difference arises because the customer is paying off the debt in instalments over the period, and not just in one lump sum at the end of the period. As a rough guide, the true rate of interest is approximately 1·8 times the flat rate of interest.

Illustration. *A householder borrows £2,000 from his bank to pay for a new extension to his home. The loan is to be repaid over one year, by monthly payments of £200. Thus, at the end of the year he will have paid £2,400, making a flat rate of interest of 20 per cent. But the true rate of interest is 20 × 1·8, some 36 per cent.*

Sending the goods back and cancelling the agreement

What happens when the agreement has been in force for some time, but the customer wants to cancel it? The position depends on whether a credit-sale agreement or a hire-purchase agreement is involved (see page 566–7 for the difference).

Under a *credit-sale agreement* the goods are already the customer's property, so clearly he cannot return them to the finance company and cancel the deal – unless of course, the goods are faulty (see page 514). With *hire purchase*, however, the goods are not the customer's property until all the instalments have been paid. The Consumer Credit Act allows the customer to end the H P agreement and return the goods to the finance company, but only if:

• he has paid all instalments due up to the time he cancels, *and*
• he has paid at least half the credit price of the goods. If he has not paid half the price, then he must pay the extra amount needed to bring his payments up to that level, unless the company's loss will be covered by the amount he has already paid, in which case he need not pay any more.

The finance company can then sell the returned goods and that will be the end of the customer's obligations unless he did not take reasonable care of the goods while he had them, in which case he will be liable for the decrease in their value.

The customer will often, therefore, have paid more than half the price of the goods and now be left with nothing to show for his payments. But that is the price he must pay for being allowed to cancel the H P agreement. If the finance company's loss on the cancelled transaction is more than covered by the customer's payments, he can apply to the court and ask that the excess be refunded.

Illustration. *Brian buys a second-hand car on H P for £2,000. He has paid instalments of £600, and has arrears of £150. Because of his financial difficulties, he returns the car and cancels the H P agreement. The car is subsequently sold for £1,200. What is his liability?*

By applying the 'half credit price' rule, he owes the finance company a total of £400 (i.e. arrears of £150, plus extra instalments of £250 needed to bring the instalments up to half the credit price). But what is the finance company's loss? They have received £600 from Brian and £1,200 from the sale of the car. They have lost only £200 of their £2,000, and so the court would probably order that Brian need only pay his £150 arrears, plus another £50.

Illustration. *Mike buys a motor-bike on* HP *for £1,000. He crashes the bike and cancels the* HP *agreement. He pays half the price (£500) to the finance company and says that is the limit of his liability. The finance company sell the wrecked bike for £50 – had it been in good condition it would have been worth £400. Mike is liable for half the payments and, in addition, the loss arising from his not having taken reasonable care of the bike: £350.*

Paying off the debt

The customer can pay off the amount owed at any time, whether it be an HP or credit-sale agreement. He will be entitled to a rebate for early settlement.

Falling into arrears with payments

If the customer gets into arrears, the legal position will depend upon whether the agreement is for credit sale or HP (see page 566–7 for the difference).

Under a *credit-sale agreement*, the goods already belong to the customer and so the finance company cannot reclaim them or sue for their return. All the company can do is to start court proceedings for the amount still due.

With a *hire-purchase agreement*, the position is different. The goods will not be the customer's property until all the instalments have been paid. Accordingly, the goods still belong to the finance company and they can be repossessed, or reclaimed, if the customer falls into arrears.

However, to protect the customer, when goods are on HP:

• if an instalment is overdue, the finance company must give the customer seven days' notice before it takes any steps against him;

• if the customer has paid one third (or more) of the credit price, the finance company must obtain a court order before it repossesses the goods. If less than one third has been paid, the company need not apply for a court order, although its representatives are not allowed to enter the customer's home (or other premises) to seize the goods, unless the customer agrees.

If the finance company applies to the county court for a repossession order, the judge will not necessarily make the order. He will listen to the customer's explanation and, if there is any reasonable prospect of the money being paid off, he will probably make a 'time order'. This is an order for the debt to be paid in instalments.

If the case does go to court, the customer will probably have to pay the company's legal costs. However, if the customer previously makes a written offer of smaller instalments over a longer period, and that offer is similar to the order eventually made by the judge, it is unlikely that he will be ordered to pay the legal costs. It is, of course, illegal for a finance company to harass a customer who is in arrears (see page 882).

Standing surety for someone else's credit agreement

Often a finance company will only provide credit if the customer can persuade a friend or relative to be a 'surety' for him. This is usually done by the surety being a 'guarantor' – he agrees to pay if the customer defaults on the credit agreement (e.g. is in arrears with the instalments). Alternatively, the surety may be asked to give an 'indemnity', in which case he agrees that the finance company can approach him direct for payment, without involving the customer. Another possibility is that he is asked to deposit money to cover the customer's possible default.

A person who acts as a surety must be given a copy of the customer's credit agreement, which is the source of his own liability. In addition, the finance company must provide him with two copies of the surety agreement, one signed by the company and the other by himself. If these copy documents are not provided, the surety cannot be sued for the customer's debts.

The surety (or guarantor) is liable for the customer's default, and to this extent he stands in the shoes of the customer. He cannot be made to pay more than the customer would have had to pay. For instance, if the customer legally cancels the agreement because it was signed 'off trade premises' (see page 568) then the surety cannot be sued to meet the company's loan. The surety is no more liable than the customer.

However, being a surety can often be very risky. It is unwise to stand surety unless one is sure that the customer – even if he is a friend – can, and will, pay the instalments. If he does not, and the surety has to cover the finance company's losses, the surety can sue the customer for the amount paid out. Often, of course, this right to sue is valueless since it is usually the customer's lack of money that led him to default in the first place.

Finance companies do not hesitate to enforce agreements against sureties. Once the surety has agreed to stand surety, he cannot later change his mind and demand to be released from his obligation. So, beware of being a surety!

If the goods are faulty or unsatisfactory

When a customer buys goods, the shopkeeper makes several promises as to their quality, fitness, and description. If the goods are faulty or unsatisfactory, the customer can either claim compensation or demand his money back (see page 518).

The position is no different when goods are bought on credit; the shopkeeper is liable. However, the credit customer gets additional protection because the finance company is also liable, along with the shopkeeper, for the quality, fitness, and description of the goods. So the customer can sue the shopkeeper or the finance company, whichever he prefers. This joint liability is not restricted to goods bought on HP or credit sale. It applies to all credit purchases, including goods bought with a credit card, and even goods bought with a bank loan given to enable that purchase to be made. It does not, however, apply to goods bought on a normal overdraft, since although bought on credit, the credit was not specifically supplied to finance that particular purchase (see page 514).

Licensing of lenders

The Consumer Credit Act 1974 has introduced an extensive system of licences for all people and firms who provide credit, hireage services, credit brokerage, debt-counselling and debt-collecting services. In effect *anyone* who provides credit, or lends money (e.g. under an HP agreement), must have a licence from the Office of Fair Trading. If there is no licence, then any credit agreement will be *unenforceable*, and so the customer can simply refuse to pay the instalments due. Then the lender can only enforce the agreement if the Director-General of Fair Trading says so. In addition, the lender commits a criminal offence.

Whilst all the reputable credit firms do have licences, some of the 'fringe operators' have not obtained licences, either because they do not realize that they need them or because their unsatisfactory credentials would bar them from obtaining a licence. A customer who is in dispute with such a firm might find it worthwhile checking whether they do have a consumer credit licence.

Certain agreements are valid even if there is no licence. For instance, building societies do not need a licence. Nor is a licence needed if the rate of interest was relatively low. In addition, the Consumer Credit Act only applies when credit of up to £15,000 is involved. So if more than £15,000 is lent (for instance, on a second mortgage) no licence is needed.

Credit brokers and mortgage brokers

Anyone who finds credit facilities for someone else is a 'credit broker'. For instance, a mortgage broker who arranges mortgages and an electrical dealer who arranges HP finance for his customers are credit brokers.

The Consumer Credit Act imposes restrictions on the charges that can be made by credit brokers. But these restrictions only apply if the credit involved does not exceed £15,000. If it does, then there are no restrictions on fees. However, a major exception to this is for mortgages; mortgage brokers' fees are controlled whatever the size of the mortgage.

If the credit broker fails within six months to obtain credit for the customer, his fee cannot exceed £3. The same applies if the broker raises credit for the customer, but the customer then decides not to enter into the agreement. For instance, if a mortgage broker finds a mortgage for his client, but the client then decides not to take up the mortgage, the most the broker can charge him is £3. However, if the credit broker finds credit for the customer, and the customer takes it up within six months, the credit broker can charge a fee, and then there is no restriction on the fee that can be charged – however high it may be.

Being refused credit

Before selling goods on credit, many firms check the customer's creditworthiness with a credit reference agency. The agency will tell the retailer whether the customer has ever defaulted on a credit payment or been taken to court for debt. Occasionally mistakes can be made and the credit reference agency has false information on its files. For example, it may confuse the customer with someone else of a similar name who has a poor credit history. To minimize the likelihood of consumers being denied credit because of incorrect credit records, the Consumer Credit Act allows a consumer to demand to see his credit file at any time.

But usually it will be when a shop has denied him credit that the customer will wonder whether there is a file on him. If the credit application was for not more than £15,000, the customer can ask the shopkeeper whether he approached a credit reference agency for information. If the request is made within twenty-eight days of their last having had dealings, the shopkeeper has seven days in which to supply the name and address of any agency he consulted. If he does not provide the information, he is committing a criminal offence (maximum penalty £1,000 fine).

The customer can then, at any time, write to the agency requesting a copy of the file on him – enclosing a fee of £1. The agency must send the file (or a letter stating there is no file) to the customer within seven working days.

The customer can then tell the agency if he thinks any of the information is incorrect. The agency then has twenty-eight days in which to notify the customer of its decision. If he is not satisfied with the steps taken, the customer then has twenty-eight days in which to send a notice of correction to the agency for placing on his file. This notice cannot be more than 200 words long and gives the customer a chance to have his views placed on record.

If the agency is not prepared to put the notice of correction on file, it can refer the matter to the Director-General of Fair Trading for a decision – as can the customer. If the credit reference agency fails to comply with any of these requests, it can be fined up to £1,000 for each offence.

37 Crimes against Consumers

The criminal law also intervenes to regulate the way that traders conduct their business. Usually, though, these laws can only be enforced by state officials, not by private individuals. A lot therefore depends upon the willingness of the local officials to prosecute for infringements.

Generally, there is no way that the individual consumer can force them to prosecute, although there is an important exception to this rule with trade-description offences. In those cases, the local authorities are under a legal duty to enforce the legislation and can themselves be taken to court if they do not prosecute when there are reasonable prospects of securing a conviction.

Weights and measures offences

The Weights and Measures Act 1963 and numerous detailed regulations set out specific rules to be observed by retailers. Full details can be obtained from local Weights and Measures Departments, but these are the sort of topics covered:
* regulations on pre-packed foods;
* strict rules as to the giving of short weights and short measures – making it a crime even if it happens accidentally;
* the requirement that certain foods should be sold by weight, not by volume (e.g. tea, cheese, meat);
* the testing and inspection of weighing and measuring equipment by local-authority inspectors.

One point to note is that there is no duty on manufacturers to put 'sell-by' dates on their foods. As regards labels, there are all sorts of complicated rules (e.g. yogurt can only be called 'strawberry-flavoured' if its flavour comes mainly from real strawberries; otherwise it must be called 'strawberry flavour').

Food and Drug Act offences

The Food Act 1984 and numerous detailed regulations set out rules relating to the purity and quality of food and drugs and the hygiene standards to be observed. For example, it is illegal to:
* treat food so that it is harmful to health;
* sell food that is unfit for human consumption.

All food for human consumption must be of the 'nature, quality, and substance' demanded. This is a very wide-ranging provision, covering such things as watered-down milk, meat that is off, and beer that is flat. A customer who buys poor-quality food or who is concerned at the hygiene levels in a particular shop should complain. The environmental health officer will inspect the premises and can force the shop to improve the standards.

In addition, if a customer buys food that is bad, the shop should refund his money. Buying food that has gone off is just the same as buying any faulty goods, and the customer has the same legal redress against the shopkeeper (see page 518) under civil law; the environmental health officer will be enforcing a remedy under criminal law.

Safety regulations

The Consumer Safety Act 1978 allows the Secretary of State for Prices and Consumer Protection to make any regulations he 'considers appropriate for the purpose of securing that goods are safe, or that appropriate information is provided and inappropriate information is not provided'. This allows him to lay down standards for the production, inspection, and marketing of whole classes of goods. If he considers that goods are 'not safe' he can ban their sale. He can also make a manufacturer publish a public warning that particular goods are not safe.

Also, regulations made under the earlier Consumer Protection Acts lay down detailed safety rules for the manufacture and sale of certain items, including carry-cots, nightdresses, electric blankets, oil heaters, and babies' dummies.

Fireworks. For safety reasons, no fireworks can be sold to children under age sixteen (maximum fine of £400; Explosives (Age of Purchase) Act 1976). There are similar penalties for anyone – of whatever age – who sets off a firework in the street.

Trade descriptions

The Trade Descriptions Acts of 1968 and 1972 make it illegal for traders to:
- describe *goods* falsely;
- describe *services* falsely;
- display misleadingly low *prices*.

What was designed as clear, straightforward legislation has become a complicated and specialized area of law. This is mainly because large retail concerns have paid for top lawyers to fight cases for them, and to persuade the courts that the defences allowed should be construed liberally in favour of their clients. As a result it can often be exceedingly difficult to secure a conviction.

The legislation is enforced by the Trading Standards Department. Private prosecutions are allowed, but these are rare. Most consumers complain to the trading standards officer and leave it to him to decide whether there should be a prosecution. Generally, the maximum penalty on conviction in the magistrates' court is £2,000 fine, but if tried in the crown court it is two years' prison and an unlimited fine.

There are different rules for 'goods' and for 'services'. See page 505 for the distinction between the two.

Falsely describing 'goods'

The 1968 Act lists the various characteristics of goods that must be accurately described:

- the size, quantity, or gauge of goods (e.g. 'enough for two square yards' on a can of paint; 'half a pint' on a bottle of beer; 'two dozen sheets' on a writing pad);
- the method of manufacture, production, or of reconditioning (e.g. 'hand-made'; 'cut-glass'; 're-textured'; 'heat-sealed');
- composition of the goods (e.g. 'all wool'; '100 per cent beef'; '5 per cent proof'; 'four-star' petrol);
- misleading pictures on wrappers and packets;
- how well the goods will do their job (e.g. 'kills all germs'; 'will clean your oven in fifteen minutes');
- the strength, accuracy, or behaviour of the item (e.g. 'machine-washable'; 'waterproof'; 'unbreakable');
- testing or appraisal by an organization, or a claim that it is of an approved type (e.g. 'conforms to British Standard'; '*Which?* Best Buy');
- the previous history of the goods (e.g. 'army surplus'; 'unused'; 'one lady owner'; '2,000 miles only');
- the manufacturer, and the date and place of manufacture (e.g. 'over a hundred years old'; 'made in England'; '1984 car').

In short, virtually any false description of his goods made by a trader can be a criminal offence.

Reported cases include:

An electric bulb was described as 'special long-life bulb with a maximum guarantee of 2,500 hours'. When tested, the average deficiency was 24 per cent. Guilty. Fined £50.

1 cwt bag of coal was 71 lb underweight. Guilty. Fined £7.

An engaged couple decided to buy an antique engagement ring since it would appreciate in value. They went to an antique shop and chose a 'Victorian' ring for £40, which was described on the receipt as 'circa 1830'. In fact, it was a 1961 reproduction. The dealer, a specialist in antique jewellery, pleaded guilty. Fined £75.

A customer was visited by a salesman and he signed a contract for 'full central heating' without reading it. When the system was fitted the customer discovered that all he had was four electric convector heaters – not even one in each room. Guilty. Fined £200.

A door-to-door salesman sold sponges claiming that they were being sold to benefit disabled children. The managing director of the firm responsible was found guilty and fined £100.

A kettle manufacturer had printed 'slightly imperfect' on a kettle's ticket. The seller put his price label on top of the 'slightly imperfect' sign. Guilty of falsely implying that the kettle was in perfect condition. Fined £100.

A bulldog was advertised as having 'no vices', yet it habitually bit people who tried to stroke it. Guilty. Fined £25.

Cars are a particularly common source of complaint. Many convictions have been recorded, and the consumer who buys a faulty car from a motor trader can often use the Trade Descriptions Acts to advantage. For instance:

A car was advertised as being in 'immaculate condition'; the log book showed it had had nine owners and been written off. Guilty. Fined £40.

A car bought from a leasing company was sold as having 'one previous owner'. Held: This was a false description.

A car was sold as being 'a real beauty', and 'it's in real good condition'. In fact, the seller had bought it knowing it needed a lot of repairs. It was unsound and had numerous defects. Guilty. Suspended prison sentence of six months.

A second-hand car was sold as having a new crankshaft, pistons, and rings. In fact it had the original pistons and rings and the crankshaft had probably done 15,000 miles. Guilty. Fined £100.

A second-hand car was described as 'mechanically perfect'. It had twenty-four faults including oil leaks, weak suspension, broken springs, and battery faults. Guilty. Fined £35.

With milometer readings the car trader must take positive steps to negate the effect the milometer readings might have on purchasers. A casual remark during the sales talk and a clause in small print on the receipt would not be sufficient. More important, nor would a small sticker which is stuck over the milometer – the courts have held that stickers disclaiming responsibility are no defence to a trade descriptions prosecution, unless it is made absolutely clear that the milometer cannot be relied upon (i.e. the sticker must be bigger and make more of an impression on the customer than the milometer).

Remember that these trade descriptions laws only apply to sales by dealers and traders. If a private individual sells something, he is not bound by the trade descriptions laws. For instance, in one case a courier sold his car on the basis that it had done 18,000 miles – in fact it had done 118,000 miles. It was held he could not be guilty of an offence under the Trade Descriptions Act because he was not in business selling cars. On the other hand, of course, the person who bought the car would have had a claim (for compensation) if the courier had wrongly said that the car had only done 18,000 miles (see page 515 for the promises made by someone who sells items privately).

Defences to prosecutions

There are two different defences to a prosecution. Firstly, that the offence was someone else's fault, and, secondly, that it was not realized that the description was false.

To argue that the offence was someone else's fault, the defendant must show two things: firstly, he must show that the offence was due to either:

- a mistake, *or*
- his relying on information given to him, *or*
- the default of some other person – which could be his employee.

Secondly, he must go on to prove that he took all reasonable precautions to avoid the offence.

The scope of the defence was considerably widened by a 1971 case.

Tesco had set up a careful and elaborate system of supervising its employees to check that no Trade Descriptions Acts offences were committed. However, a store manager failed to check the work of his staff (as he was supposed to) and a 'special offer' poster was displayed on a range of goods when there were none available at the special price. When prosecuted, Tesco argued that the offence was due 'to the default of another person' (their manager), and that they had done all they could to prevent offences being committed. The House of Lords held this was a valid defence. Not guilty. Tesco (1971)

So a large organization can avoid liability if it can show that its staff had clear instructions about labelling goods, and this is a major inroad into the scope of the legislation; previously, it had been held that firms were responsible for the mistakes of their staff. However, if a firm wishes to raise this defence it must identify the employee concerned. It is not sufficient to say it was one of several employees.

The only other defence to a prosecution is for the trader to show that he did not know, and could not with reasonable diligence have found out, that his description was false. But this can be difficult to prove.

Mr Mahoney was a motor dealer. While he was on holiday a friend bought a three-year-old car for him but did not tell Mahoney that the milometer reading was false. Mahoney drove the car, inspected it, and satisfied himself that the reading was true. He then sold the car. Subsequently, it was discovered that the car had done considerably more than the recorded 26,000 miles. When prosecuted, Mahoney argued that he did not know of the false reading and, furthermore, that there was no way that he could, with 'reasonable diligence', have found out that it was wrong. Held: He was guilty. He should not have assumed that a three-year-old car would only have done 26,000 miles and, since he had not made any inquiries or issued a disclaimer, he was guilty. Lewis (1977)

Falsely describing 'services'

The laws on falsely describing services are not as strict as the laws on falsely describing goods. This is because the trader will only be guilty if:
- *either* he knew the description was false
- *or* he made the statement 'recklessly' (e.g. he didn't bother to check the truth, but shut his eyes to the possibility of it being untrue).

Accordingly, convictions are more difficult to obtain than with goods.

Reported cases of false descriptions of services include:

Thomson Holidays described the Hotel Golden Coast in Greece as having a private swimming pool, a children's paddling pool, and a night club on the beach. The swimming pool was not private and there was no night club or paddling pool. Guilty. Fined £450 and £1,000.

A firm of dry-cleaners advertised a 'two-hour service'. Three items took 3 hours 30 minutes, 2 hours 30 minutes and 2 hours 17 minutes. Guilty on all three counts.

When selling a washing machine, a shop assistant said there was a 'same-day or next-day service' for repairs. In fact, this was not true; asked if it was possible, the shop manager agreed it was unusual and unlikely. Guilty. Fined £10.

A garage agreed to rebore and overhaul a car engine, and the work was paid for in advance. Six months later the work had still not been done. Guilty. Fined £10.

A holiday brochure described a villa as being a 'stone's throw from one of the beaches of St Jean'. The beach was one mile away. Guilty.

A travel brochure falsely claimed that a hotel in Spain had a swimming pool, that there was English food with special meals for children, and that push chairs could be hired. Guilty. Fined £5,000.

One problem is that the courts take a very strict line when deciding what amounts to a 'service' – the point being that if something is neither a 'good' nor a 'service' then it is not caught by the trade description laws. For instance, in one case Dixons were prosecuted because a 'never knowingly undersold' type of offer (i.e. refund the difference if bought cheaper elsewhere) was said to apply to a range of goods that, in fact, were not covered by it. The court held that a 'service' means (at least in the eyes of the law) doing something for somebody and a mere offer to refund money could not amount to doing something for someone! Thus, the offer was not a 'service' and so the trade descriptions prosecution failed. Many non-lawyers would probably dismiss the decision (and the law) as a nonsense.

Misleading price and sale labels

The Trade Descriptions Acts also control the use of misleading price and sale labels. This is because shoppers often regard the price of an item as a guide to its quality. For instance, a radio marked '£50, reduced to £25' may seem more attractive than a similar radio marked '£25'.

It is an offence for a shopkeeper to indicate falsely that goods were sold at a higher price – so, for instance, the shopkeeper would be committing an offence unless the radio had previously been on offer at £50. However, the position is made more complicated because the Acts require the prosecution to prove that it was not offered for £50 for a continuous period of twenty-eight days during the last six months. Thus, it is not for the shopkeeper to prove that he had it on sale at £50 for twenty-eight days during the last six months, but for the prosecution to show he did not. This is usually very difficult to prove.

It is also illegal for a shop to mislead a customer as to the price he is likely to have to pay. For instance, if an item is marked at £2.50 in the window, but at £2.60 in the shop, that will be an offence. Similarly, price displays which are misleading will be illegal; for instance, if the price only applies when more than one item is bought or if it is paid for with cash. Unless the 'catch' is clearly displayed, the trader will be committing an offence.

Labels that are controlled	
Reduced: £12	Illegal: the old price or the amount of the reduction must be stated (1979 Bargain Offers Order).
~~£25~~ £12	The items must have been on sale at £25 in that shop (or in a shop in the chain of shops) for a twenty-eight day period during the last six months. But it is for the prosecution to prove that they were not (Trade Descriptions Act).
Last Week's Price £25 now £12	As above, except that the shop need only have sold the item for £25 on one day of the previous week. Once again, it is for the prosecution to prove that this is not so (Trade Descriptions Act).
Sale Special Purchase £12	This label must be used when goods are specifically bought for a sale. Otherwise, customers may be misled into thinking that the item is normally sold in that shop, but at a higher price (Trade Descriptions Act).
Recommended Price £25 Our Price £12	A 'recommended price' is the price set by the manufacturers. The statement on the card must be true. (But often manufacturers inflate their recommended prices so that reductions look better value.) Illegal if the item is a bed, consumer electrical item, carpet, furniture, domestic electrical appliance, or similar appliance run on another fuel, e.g. gas cooker (1979 Bargain Offers Order).
Seconds/ Sub-standard £12	The label need not give the price of the 'perfect' goods.
~~Perfect £25~~ Imperfect £12	The item, in perfect condition, must have been sold at £25 in that shop (1979 Bargain Offers Order). The item, in perfect condition, must have been for sale in that shop (or another in the group) for at least twenty-eight days during the last six months (Trade Descriptions Acts).

All the following signs are illegal (1979 Bargain Offers Order).

Worth £30 Only £20	Comparative Price £30 Sale Price £20	Normally £30 elsewhere Only £20 here

At least £30 elsewhere Only £20 here	Up to £10 off	Up to 33% off usual price

Another problem area is 'worth or value' claims where traders indicate that their goods are a bargain by reference to some vague comparison, for instance: 'worth £40, only £25'; 'comparative price £19.75 – sale price only £13.50'; 'normally £5 elsewhere, only £2.50 here'; 'up to 33 per cent off the usual price'; 'up to £4 off'; 'save up to £5'.

The details are set out in the Price Marking (Bargain Offers) Order 1979. This is a ridiculously complex order, but its overall effect is to make it illegal to claim – or even imply – that:

● prices are lower than for similar goods (or services) elsewhere, *or*
● the goods (or services) offer better value than elsewhere,

unless the claim is justified.

The order covers all price and value claims, whether made in advertisements, on price labels, or orally by the shopkeeper.

The 1979 Order has acquired the reputation of being one of the most confusing laws in existence. In theory, the test is whether a reasonable shopper would find the label misleading, but the wording of the Order (coupled with some extraordinary decisions by the judges) has made a nonsense of the intention behind the regulations. Thus, 'end of range clearing price', 'special clearance offer', 'special clearance price' were all held to be illegal, whereas 'bargain price', and 'Britain's lowest price' were not.

In fact, the 1979 Order has been so criticized that it is likely that it will soon be replaced – probably with regulations that do not impose such stringent requirements on shopkeepers.

No-refund notices. These are illegal (see page 508).

Compensation for the customer

If a trader is convicted under the Trade Descriptions Acts, the magistrates can make a 'compensation order' against him. This is an award of compensation to the

583

customer who suffered loss through the false trade description. However, the magistrates are not compelled to make a compensation order – they have a discretion in deciding whether to do so (see page 714).

If they do not make a compensation order (or if they do not make a large enough order), the customer will have to sue the trader for breach of contract. He will claim damages for his losses and the inconvenience suffered (see page 519). The fact that the trader was convicted by the magistrates will make it virtually impossible for him to successfully defend the customer's civil claim for damages.

The rules of legal tender in England and Wales

Notes

Only Bank of England notes are legal tender. Accordingly, Scottish and Irish notes can be refused.

Coins

There are maximum numbers of coins that can be offered as payment:
- 20p and 50p pieces are legal tender up to £10;
- 10p and 5p pieces (separate or mixed) are legal tender up to £5;
- 2p and 1p pieces (separate or mixed) are legal tender up to 20p.

However, this does not mean that (for example) a bus conductor need accept a £5 note for a 5p bus fare. He can refuse to accept the passenger's offer, in which case no contract is made (see page 500) and the passenger must leave the bus.

Consumers' rights: who's who in the Town Hall

Environmental health officers

Environmental health officers used to be called public health inspectors. The change of name was introduced to reflect the wide-ranging scope of their duties, which are not confined to traditional public health matters. Included in their workload is the enforcement of the Food Act and the hygiene of shop premises. They can be contacted at the offices of the local district council (or London borough council) in the Environmental Health Department, or, sometimes, in the Housing Department or Trading Standards Department.

Trading standards officers

These officers enforce the Trade Descriptions Acts and the consumer safety legislation. Sometimes they are called consumer protection officers. In some areas they have a wider brief and perform some environmental health duties, such as the enforcement of hygiene standards in shops. They can be contacted in the

Trading Standards Department of the district council (or London borough council).

Weights and measures inspectors

The weights and measures legislation is enforced by these officers. Often one officer will be both the trading standards officer and the weights and measures inspector. They can be contacted in the Trading Standards Department.

38 Bankruptcy

To be unable to pay a debt is no longer a crime, and generally it cannot lead to the debtor being sent to prison (but see page 66). However, it can result in a court declaring the debtor to be bankrupt, which will result in the loss of his property and assets, as well as considerable embarrassment, distress, and inconvenience.

Bankruptcy should not be confused with 'liquidation'. Liquidation occurs when a receiver is sent into a company to wind it up, but it is not necessary for the company to be in financial difficulties for it to be wound up. For instance, it may have been formed in connection with a specific project that has now come to an end and so the company is to be wound up.

When can bankruptcy arise?

A person who cannot pay his debts is *insolvent*; he will not be *bankrupt* until the court makes an adjudication order against him (see Step 11, page 592). But the process leading to the adjudication order can begin as soon as the debtor commits an *act of bankruptcy*. This allows a creditor to present a bankruptcy petition to the court, which will then make a receiving order, and finally an adjudication order. But unless there is an act of bankruptcy, the process cannot be started; so the mere fact that a creditor is owed money will not, of itself, enable him to start bankruptcy proceedings. Moreover, even if there is an act of bankruptcy, a creditor cannot petition for bankruptcy unless he is owed at least £750. If he is not owed that much, he will have to use another remedy to recover his money (see page 882).

Summarized, the basic position is that you cannot petition for someone's bankruptcy unless he has a creditor owed at least £200, and unless the bankruptcy proceedings are started within three months of an 'act of bankruptcy'.

There are nine *acts of bankruptcy* that allow a bankruptcy petition to be presented:

1. If a creditor has obtained a court judgement for a debt of £750 or more which remains unpaid. See page 876 for how to obtain judgement over a debt. Petitioning for bankruptcy is only one of several alternatives available to the creditor (see page 882), and he may well decide to use one of the other, less drastic, remedies first.

   This is the most common way of starting bankruptcy proceedings. The creditor serves a formal notice on the debtor ordering him to pay the judgement debt and telling him that if he does not pay he will be committing an act of bankruptcy. If the debtor does not pay up within ten days, the creditor can present a bankruptcy petition to the court.

2. If the debtor fraudulently disposes of his property, so as to delay or defeat his creditors. Any creditor can then present a bankruptcy petition.

3. If the debtor leaves the country to avoid his debts. Any creditor can then present a bankruptcy petition.

4. If the debtor fraudulently gives preference to one debtor over his other debtors. Any debtor can then present a bankruptcy petition.

5. If the debtor announces that he will not be paying any of his debts. Any debtor can then present a bankruptcy petition.

6. If the debtor conveys all (or substantially all) of his property to trustees to hold for his creditors. Any debtor who did not agree to this arrangement could then present a bankruptcy petition.

7. If the debtor's goods are seized by the sheriff to pay a judgement debt, and they are then sold by the sheriff, or held by him for more than twenty-one days. Any creditor can then present a bankruptcy petition.

8. If the debtor is convicted of a criminal offence and the criminal court makes a criminal bankruptcy order against him.

9. If the debtor himself presents a bankruptcy petition to the court. He may do this to relieve himself of the pressure of being insolvent, so that matters can be properly sorted out (e.g. if he has multiple debts; has no prospects of being able to work out an agreement with his creditors; and has debts of over £5,000 – if the debts are less, then an administration order might be a better step; see page 886). If it is the debtor who presents the bankruptcy petition, the court will immediately make a receiving order against him.

It is not cheap to petition for bankruptcy. Apart from paying court fees (£25), the petitioner must leave a deposit with the court (£200 if a creditor; £100 if the debtor). Many people who are owed money naïvely think that they can use bankruptcy to force the debtor to pay off the debt. Often, however, this is a forlorn hope, for the courts do not encourage bankruptcy. The deposit (which should eventually be returned) is, in effect, an interest-free loan to the court of £200. Only fairly large debts (i.e. at least £750) count for starting the bankruptcy. In addition, the creditor's solicitors will almost certainly charge him much more than the amount of the legal costs (if any) than he can ever hope to recover from the debtor – the debtor will have to pay legal costs as set out in a scale laid down in 1952 (!), whereas the creditor's solicitor is obviously not going to be content with a 1952 scale of pay, and the extra amount will have to be paid by the creditor himself.

The position of the bankrupt

The mere presenting of a bankruptcy petition does not, of itself, affect the legal status of the debtor. But he will eventually lose his property:

- when a *receiving order* is made all his property and assets will pass into the possession and control of the official receiver. For the time being, though, the debtor will remain the legal owner of the goods. As soon as the receiving order is made the electricity, gas, and water companies will be told. They will read the meters and probably refuse further supplies until a slot-meter is installed, or unless someone else will guarantee the bills.
- when an *adjudication order* is made the ownership of all his property and assets, as well as the possession and control of them, will pass to his trustee in bankruptcy. From now on, he will be a bankrupt, and until the adjudication order is discharged by the court he will be an undischarged bankrupt.

The undischarged bankrupt

An undischarged bankrupt
- cannot be a company director;
- cannot manage a company, directly or indirectly;
- cannot be an M P, a J P, or a local councillor;
- cannot carry on a trade or business unless he uses the same name as that in which he was declared bankrupt (or if he uses a different name, he must tell all customers his correct name);
- cannot obtain credit for £50 or more (e.g. overdraft) without revealing that he is an undischarged bankrupt (oddly, this does not apply to H P agreements);
- can open a bank account but the bank must inform the trustee, who will usually order the account to be closed and any money in it to be handed over;
- if he receives or earns any money it will be the property of the trustee. It must pass to the trustee. The trustee will only allow the bankrupt to keep as much of his earnings, profits, pension, etc., as are reasonably necessary to support himself and his family. In practice, this is a small amount, and allows the bankrupt no luxuries.

The bankrupt's wife

In law, the bankrupt and his/her spouse are two different people. Many bankrupts try to use this rule to their advantage by putting property in the name of the spouse and then arguing that it cannot be seized on bankruptcy. But this is not always a successful ruse. The trustee can take back anything that was given to the spouse by the bankrupt within two years of the bankruptcy. In addition any gift made by the bankrupt to his spouse within the ten years prior to the bankruptcy can be taken back by the trustee unless the bankrupt was solvent at the time of the gift.

But, otherwise, the bankrupt's husband or wife is treated as a separate person and so his or her assets cannot be taken to pay the debts. If the family home is in their joint names then the spouse will normally have a 50 per cent share and this will be paid to him or her if the house is sold (although the court might decide to refuse a sale of the home if it would cause exceptional hardship to the innocent spouse). If the property is not in their joint names, the other spouse (usually the wife) will

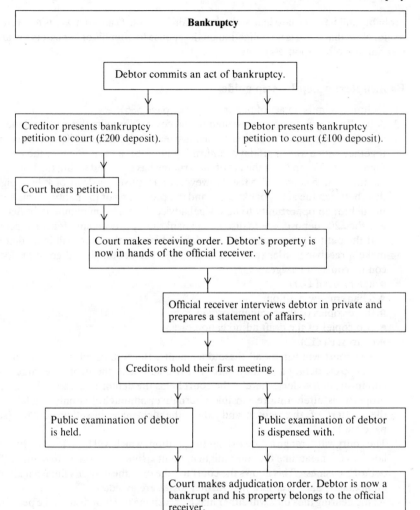

Bankruptcy

Debtor commits an act of bankruptcy.

Creditor presents bankruptcy petition to court (£200 deposit).

Debtor presents bankruptcy petition to court (£100 deposit).

Court hears petition.

Court makes receiving order. Debtor's property is now in hands of the official receiver.

Official receiver interviews debtor in private and prepares a statement of affairs.

Creditors hold their first meeting.

Public examination of debtor is held.

Public examination of debtor is dispensed with.

Court makes adjudication order. Debtor is now a bankrupt and his property belongs to the official receiver.

probably still have a share in it and, once again, the court can – if it wants to – refuse a sale. Note that there is no obligation on the spouse to offer his or her assets towards clearing the other spouse's debts.

Bankruptcy: a step-by-step guide

1. Debtor commits an act of bankruptcy (see page 586).
2. A bankruptcy petition is presented to the court. Normally this will be done by a creditor (a 'creditor's petition') who must leave a deposit of £200 with the court, together with a sworn affidavit confirming his debt, and stating that the debt is for at least £750 and that the act of bankruptcy has occurred within the last three months. There is also a £25 fee. However, there must be a delay of at least eight days between the act of bankruptcy and the presenting of the petition; this gives the debtor an opportunity to take legal advice. The £750 minimum debt figure, and the £200 deposit, are to discourage bankruptcy proceedings for small debts.

   If the petition is presented by the debtor himself, the court will immediately make a receiving order (proceed to Step 4). The debtor should go to his local county court and lodge:
   - a deposit of £100
   - a bankruptcy petition
   - three copies of the receiving order
   - two copies of the draft adjudication order
   - court fee (£12).

   The court will supply all these documents. Because of the large amount of the deposit, debtor's petitions are inadvisable unless the debts are large. An administration order, whereby the court helps the debtor to organize his affairs properly, is often a more sensible alternative, although it is only available at the request of the debtor and when the debts are less than £5,000 (see page 886).
3. The court will arrange a date to hear the petition, which will be at least eight days later. In the meantime the court might appoint an interim receiver to manage the debtor's business. This allows the court to take over the debtor's financial affairs immediately and so ensure that further losses are avoided.
4. At the hearing the court will either make a receiving order or dismiss the petition. A receiving order gives the official receiver possession and control of the debtor's goods and property, so that they are protected from dealings by the debtor and the creditors. Other creditors are thus unable to take action against the debtor (except that secured debtors can realize their security, e.g. a mortgage on a house) and must simply notify the official receiver of their claim; this is done by giving him written notice and is called proving the debt.

   Instead of making a receiving order, the court might dismiss the petition. It might do this, for instance, if the debtor had no assets and no prospects of having any, for then making him bankrupt would be a pointless exercise. Similarly, if it was felt that the creditor was presenting the petition for an ulterior motive (e.g. to extract other money from the debtor improperly or to injure his commercial reputation unfairly), the petition might be dismissed.

5. The receiving order is advertised in the *London Gazette* and in a local paper.
6. The debtor will be interviewed, in private, so that a 'statement of affairs' can be drawn up. This will list all his assets, liabilities, and debts, as well as the names, addresses, and occupations of the creditors (and any securities held by them). In addition, it will often give a brief summary of the events leading up to the act of bankruptcy and perhaps offer reasons why the debtor has become insolvent.

    The official receiver will usually employ an accountant to interview the debtor and, indeed, his wife or anyone else who may have relevant information or papers. If the debtor does not cooperate, he can be declared bankrupt immediately. Amongst other things, the official receiver will want to check that the debtor does not have money or assets salted away, or 'warehoused', with friends and relatives. He will also be considering whether there was any fraud.

    The official receiver will aim to draw up the statement of affairs within seven days of the receiving order being made (three days if it was the debtor who presented the petition).
7. The official receiver will then write to every creditor notifying him of the time of the first creditors' meeting, and giving a summary of the statement of affairs, plus his comments. If the debtor has suggested a 'scheme of arrangement' to pay the creditors, the creditor will then be given a voting slip so he can approve, or disapprove, of the scheme.

    The first meeting of the creditors will be advertised in the *London Gazette* and in a local paper.
8. The first meeting of the creditors will be held within fourteen days of the receiving order having been made.

    The official receiver will be chairman of the meeting, which will give the creditors an opportunity of collectively discussing what ought to be done. The debtor need not attend. The meeting will generally:
    - go through the statement of affairs in some detail, to verify it and see what can be done about the position;
    - decide whether the debtor should be declared bankrupt. Sometimes it will be better if he is allowed to carry on in business;
    - perhaps consider any composition or scheme put forward by the debtor (this should not be confused with a Deed of Arrangement). But the scheme must give all creditors at least 25p in the £, and be approved by at least 50 per cent of creditors, and 75 per cent in value.
9. Next, a date will be fixed for the public examination of the debtor. This will generally take place as soon as is practicable after the creditors' meeting. Once the date for the public examination has been fixed, the official receiver will notify the debtor and the creditors, and advertise it in the *London Gazette* and a local paper.
10. The public examination of the debtor will take place in open court. It will be an exhaustive examination of his conduct and also an inquiry into his financial

affairs. The debtor will be on oath and he will be required to sign a written transcript of his evidence. It will only end when the court is satisfied that his affairs have been sufficiently investigated.

The public examination can be a distressing and emotional experience for the debtor. Until the Insolvency Act 1976 was passed it was mandatory that there should be a public examination, but now the court can order that it need not be held. Generally, this will happen if the debtor has been blameless or the debts are very small. An examination will always be ordered in cases of fraud or recklessness. The court will also be influenced by whether the debtor has cooperated in disclosing his affairs, and whether he has been declared bankrupt before.

11. At the end of the public examination, the court will decide whether to make an adjudication order. It is the adjudication order that turns the debtor into a bankrupt, and which makes the trustee in bankruptcy the owner of all the bankrupt's possessions. He will remain an undischarged bankrupt until the court agrees to discharge the adjudication order – see 'Getting Discharged' below.

12. The trustee will begin administering the bankrupt's estate by realizing the assets and selling them off. The trustee need not take over all the bankrupt's assets; he can disclaim 'onerous' assets (e.g. if the item is subject to a mortgage, if it cannot be sold easily, if it would be more trouble than it is worth), and also renounce unprofitable contracts.

Then he will distribute the estate. The debtor will only be allowed to keep necessary bedding and clothing for himself and his family, plus the tools of his trade, up to a total value of £250. The rest of his assets will go to the creditors once the legal and accountancy fees have been paid. There is an order of priority between the creditors:

(a) First, the *secured creditors* are paid (i.e. those who lent on the security of a particular asset, for instance, a mortgage on a house).

(b) Next, the *preferential creditors* are paid off. This covers:

- rates
- tax
- arrears of pay due to an employee, up to £800 (see page 421 for details)
- NI contributions due on employees' wages.

(c) Then the *ordinary creditors* are paid. Often, of course, there is no money left to pay these or, if there is, it is not enough, and so the creditors will each receive *x* pence in the £ (a 'dividend'). Generally, the amount of the first dividend will be announced within four months of the first meeting of the creditors (Step 8 above).

(d) Finally, if there is any money left, the *deferred creditors* are paid. These will include the bankrupt's spouse if claiming the return of a loan made to help the bankrupt's business; anyone who lent money to the business in return for a share of the profits; claims by creditors for interest.

Getting discharged

The bankrupt will want to be discharged so that he is no longer subject to the restraints suffered by an undischarged bankrupt (see page 588). Discharge will wipe the slate clean and mean that all his debts are discharged (except for certain tax arrears and liability to make affiliation payments, etc.).

The bankrupt can apply to the court to be discharged at any time after the end of the public examination. To apply to the court, he submits a form (obtainable from the court), together with a certificate from the official receiver listing the names and addresses of all known creditors. The court then fixes a date for the hearing, and gives the official receiver twenty-eight days' notice and the creditors fourteen days' notice. The hearing is also advertised in the *London Gazette*. At least a week before the hearing, the official receiver sends a report on the bankrupt to the court, and a copy is also sent to the bankrupt.

The opinion of the official receiver as to whether a discharge should be granted will be of great importance. If the report does not approve of a discharge, the court is very unlikely to make an order of discharge. Thus, there is little point in the debtor applying for discharge unless the official receiver will support him. In practice, it is usually better not to apply for discharge – see below, for the reasons why.

The court can refuse the application, or grant:
- an unconditional discharge;
- a conditional discharge (i.e. the bankrupt has to comply with conditions; for instance, that he pays off certain debts by instalments from future earnings);
- a suspended discharge (i.e. the discharge will not come into effect until a certain date or until a certain dividend has been paid to creditors).

The court cannot grant an unconditional discharge if:
- less than 50p in the £ dividend has been paid (unless he was not to blame for this);
- he did not keep proper books for the three years prior to his bankruptcy;
- he continued trading after he knew he was insolvent;
- he incurred debts without any reasonable expectation of being able to pay them;
- he has failed to account for missing money;
- gambling, extravagance, or culpable neglect caused the bankruptcy;
- he put creditors to needless expense by pointlessly defending actions brought against him;
- within the three months before the receiving order he gave unfair preference to a particular creditor, or he incurred unreasonable expense by suing in a hopeless claim, or he borrowed to bring his dividend up to 50p in the £;
- he has previously been bankrupt (or entered into an arrangement with creditors);
- he has been guilty of fraud, or destroying papers, etc.

Automatic discharge

Many bankrupts never apply for discharge and so the Insolvency Act 1976 introduced provisions that enable certain undischarged bankrupts to be automatically discharged. The rule now is that a bankrupt will be automatically discharged five years after the date of the adjudication order, unless any of the above circumstances apply. Whether or not the automatic discharge provisions are to apply will be announced by the court at the end of the public examination (or when ordering that there need not be a public examination).

Even if the automatic discharge rule does not apply, the bankrupt may still be discharged without his or her having to apply to the court. Within twelve months of the fifth anniversary the official receiver will go to the court, bring it up to date on the position, and ask whether the bankrupt should be discharged. The court can then decide whether to grant a discharge and, if so, whether it should be unconditional, conditional, or suspended.

Because most bankrupts are automatically discharged, there is usually little point in applying for discharge (above). A disadvantage of applying for discharge is that if it is refused then the automatic discharge provisions do not apply – so the bankrupt will then have to make repeated applications for discharge (and, also, conditions might be imposed, whereas no conditions would be imposed on an automatic discharge).

39 Deciding Whether to Form a Company

Anyone who sets up in business will want to know whether he should form a company or remain as a sole trader (or a partner if his business is shared with someone else). The answer will depend largely upon such factors as the size of the business, the risks of the business, and tax advantages.

The main differences between companies and sole traders or partnerships

The risk of bankruptcy

In a limited company, the shareholders' and directors' personal liability is limited to their shares. The sole trader, or partner, risks bankruptcy if his business fails, and the effects of bankruptcy will not be confined to the loss of his own money and property; it will have other disadvantages such as making him ineligible to be a company director and unable to obtain credit of more than £50 without disclosing that he is a bankrupt. He will find it difficult to borrow money in the future – for a house mortgage, for example.

The equivalent of bankruptcy for a company is insolvency. Generally, the director or shareholder of an insolvent company will not face any personal stigma as a result of the company's failure – apart, of course, from the loss of his share capital. However, in practice, the small businessman who forms a company will often find that he has to guarantee personally any loans made to the company, so if the company becomes insolvent he will be liable to pay the debts. If he cannot do so he will be declared bankrupt, and so he will have been no better off than if he had not formed a company.

Death and retirement

A company is a legal entity in its own right. As such it can never die, for it can only come to an end when it is wound up. The company is therefore unaffected by the death or retirement of directors or shareholders; the company continues with new directors and new shareholders.

If a sole trader or partner dies, the firm will also die. The remaining partners will have to reconstitute the partnership and there may be difficulties in the valuation and transfer of assets such as buildings, plant, and bank accounts.

Raising money

Because the sole trader, or partner, is personally liable for his business's debts one would have thought that he would find it easier to borrow money than would a company. Surprisingly, this is not so. This is because of a device known as a *floating charge* which provides an effective security for a loan, but which can only be created by a company. A floating charge gives the lender a continuing security against all the assets of the company, including, for example, stock in trade. The company can deal with its assets in the usual way by buying and selling its assets as it chooses even though there is a floating charge on them. This would not be possible with a normal mortgage of property, for the lender's consent would be needed to the sale of each item – something that would clearly be impracticable with the changing stock in trade of a business.

A floating charge is therefore a very effective, but flexible, form of security. It allows the company to trade in the normal way without having to obtain consents from the lender, and conversely, it provides the lender with a security tied to all the assets of the firm.

In legal theory, both sole traders and partnerships could create floating charges, but detailed provisions in the Bankruptcy Act make it uncertain whether the lender would have a complete safeguard for his security. The practical effect of this is that floating charges are not available to sole traders or partners, and are confined to companies.

Remember that if a small company borrows money, the directors will probably be asked to provide personal guarantees and thus their personal fortunes will be at risk if the company fails.

Publicity of accounts

All limited companies must file audited accounts with Companies House each year (unlimited companies need not). These accounts are open to public inspection. Conversely, the sole trader or partner can keep his accounts confidential and need not disclose them to anyone.

In practice, this is not an important point. Most accounts at Companies House are a year or two out of date, for most companies fail to file their accounts on time. Thus, the information on file is likely to be of limited value. The sole trader or partner may well find, in practice, that he has to disclose his accounts to lenders and they are probably the main category of people who are likely to want to refer to a company's accounts anyway. In addition, the activities of credit-rating agencies and credit reference agencies are such that it is usually possible to find out the financial standing of a person or firm, even if he is a sole trader or partner. In some ways, it could be argued that it is better to have the accounts on public view, and so reduce the risk of unjustified assumptions as to financial standing being made on the basis of gossip, rumour, and false deduction.

For the small businessman, the expense of having his accounts audited each year, together with the fee for filing the accounts, may be a consideration when deciding whether it is worth forming a company.

The size of the firm

There is no restriction on the size of any firm in terms of number of employees, value of assets held, etc. But there is a restriction on the numbers who can be partners in a partnership (the maximum is twenty), and the number of people who can be directors in a private company (the maximum is fifty).

In practice, these restrictions are of little importance. Most companies have less than twenty shareholders and so the firm could be a partnership if that were thought to be preferable.

The expenses of formation

It is easy for a sole trader to start business, and the same applies to a partnership. The position is much more complicated for a company: there are sizeable fees to be paid (see below), documents to be drawn up, and procedures to be followed. There is no doubt that it is more expensive and inconvenient to form a company.

The extra formalities of forming a company make it more expensive than setting up as a sole trader or in partnership. The formation of a company requires the preparation of two documents, the Memorandum and the Articles, plus a registration fee (currently £50). Off-the-shelf companies can be bought for some £100 or so. There is also the additional expense of having the accounts audited each year, which is not necessary for a sole trader or partner. The audited accounts have to be filed with the Register of Companies (annual fee currently £20).

Against these expenses of forming a company, a sole trader need not incur any expenses (except perhaps a solicitor's or accountant's fee for drafting a partnership agreement).

Taxing the firm's profits

The sole trader, or partner, pays tax on all his profits, even if the profits are not taken out of the business. The rate of tax can be as much as 60 per cent. In a company, the directors pay tax on their earnings in the same way as any other employee but the excess profits can be kept in the company, where they will be subject to corporation tax (currently 30 per cent unless annual profits exceed £100,000 – 1985 figures).

The net effect of these tax rules is that if the firm's profits are such that the sole trader or partners are in the higher tax bands, they would be well advised to convert the business into a company.

There are three tax advantages that the sole trader or partner has over a company:
- the sole trader, or partner, will pay less in national insurance contributions as a self-employed person than the combined contributions of the company and himself if he were a director employed by the company;
- the sole trader, or partner, pays his tax on a preceding-year basis; this means that he pays last year's tax this year (if incomes are growing this gives a useful cash-flow advantage); the employee of a company pays his tax as he earns it under the PAYE system;

- it is easier for the sole trader or partner to claim that his wife works in the business and so justify employing her to use up her married woman's earned-income allowance (see below);
- a sole trader or partner can offset his losses in one business against the profits in another; this cannot be done with a company;
- the sole trader or partner can generally claim more expenses and fringe benefits than if he were a company director.

Using the firm's money

A sole trader can draw money and capital out of his business as and when he wishes; so, too, can a partner, if the other partners do not object. The director or shareholder in a company is in a less flexible position; there are rules in the Companies Act which forbid loans to directors and a reduction in the capital of the company. If shares are sold to raise the money, there might be a liability to capital gains tax and corporation tax.

Value added tax

Any business which has an annual turnover of £19,500 or more is liable to pay VAT. This is so whether the business is run by a sole trader, partnership, or company. However, when a person operates several different businesses, he may find that each has a turnover below the VAT limit, but that their combined turnover is over the VAT limit. It is therefore advantageous for him to be able to separate the different businesses so that they are not treated as one single business. Although this can be done by a sole trader or partnership, if different companies are formed there can be no argument that they are trading separately.

Employed or self-employed?

A sole trader, or a partner, will be self-employed; a company director will normally be employed. See the table on page 379 for the main differences between the two. Note in particular:
- the combined national insurance contributions of an employer and an employee are more than those of a self-employed person;
- a self-employed person is not eligible for as many welfare benefits as an employed person – in particular, unemployment benefit and sickness benefit are denied to the self-employed;
- pension arrangements for an employed director can be more generous than those for a self-employed person; pension planning is a highly specialized topic and expert advice is needed when considering which company gives better pension prospects;
- a director, as an employee, can receive a golden-handshake of up to £25,000, tax free, on retirement; there is no such golden-handshake provision for the sole trader or partner, who would have to pay income tax on the amount received.

Bringing a husband or wife into the business

Many married men have wives who are not earning because they are bringing up the children. The wife is therefore unable to use the married woman's earned-income allowance (£2,205 in 1985). However, if the husband is self-employed (as a sole trader or partner) he can bring his wife into the business and pay her for all the work she does as a self-employed assistant. Usually, he will pay her just enough to use up the married woman's allowance. In fact he may pay her slightly less, so she is under the limit for liability to pay national insurance contributions (see page 729). Generally, the Inland Revenue accept this as a legitimate ploy, although obviously the wife should do some work for her money.

A company director, as an employed person, cannot do this unless the company employs his wife, but then there would be an immediate liability to pay national insurance contributions.

If a spouse can put a considerable amount of time into the business, the best arrangement is for her to be in partnership with her husband, if her husband would otherwise be in a high tax bracket. Half his earnings can then go to his wife and the two of them can elect for separate taxation ('wife's earnings election', see page 52), thus reducing their total tax bill.

Forming a co-op

A cooperative is an enterprise which is controlled by all its members. Co-ops are primarily of two kinds – workers' co-ops (in which all the staff own a stake in the business), and consumer co-ops (such as housing co-ops in which the members jointly purchase, develop, and manage a pool of properties). A legal structure is usually necessary and there are two main alternatives:
- registration as a Friendly Society (under the Industrial and Provident Societies Acts). Most co-ops which adopt this form of structure will use model rules prepared by the Industrial Common Ownership Movement (ICOM).
- registration as a company limited by guarantee. This is the same as an ordinary company except that no shares are issued. All members guarantee a nominal sum (usually £1) towards the company's debts and that is the extent of their personal liability.

Both these legal structures ensure that there is a written framework for running the co-op and both offer the advantages of limited liability to the participants. In practical terms there is virtually nothing to choose between the two methods – although it is cheaper to form a company limited by guarantee and accordingly that method is now becoming more popular. (£100 would probably cover the formation costs.)

Finding out about a business

It is not always easy to find out who owns a business – even though this may be vital information for a supplier or customer. In most cases it is possible to check the position by simply looking at the firm's notepaper – if the name ends in 'Ltd' or 'plc' then it is probably a company (although this is not a foolproof check since some businesses wrongly claim to be companies when they are not). The next step is to check with the records at Companies House. Postal and phone searches are no longer possible so it is necessary either to go to the Registry (in London or Cardiff – see page 893) or to check if the main local library has an index of all registered companies.

In theory, all limited companies should put their registered number (where registered) plus their registered office address on notepaper, invoices, etc., although not all do so. There is no need for director's names to be included. Similar rules apply to businesses that are not companies (e.g. a one-man business, a partnership) which do not operate under the name of the owner; such firms must have the owner's name and address displayed on invoices, letters, etc. and at the place of business. In theory, therefore, it should be possible easily to find out who owns a business – but in practice it is not. This is because the sort of businesses that are disreputable (and which are therefore likely to be sued or to have complaints made against them) are just the sort of firms that will not bother to display the owner's name and address. In such cases it can be extremely difficult to find out exactly who runs the business, even though the trader is probably committing a criminal offence by failing to provide his name. In fact, a person who felt strongly about it could bring a private prosecution against the suspected owner for his failure to display the name (such a private prosecution would be for breach of section 29 of the Companies Act 1981; see page 779 for how to bring a private prosecution). In practice, a private prosecution would probably be a waste of time. It is better to complain to the trading-standards officer, and hope that he prosecutes.

40 Renting Business Premises

The Rent Acts only apply to residential lettings. The law on business lettings is set out in the Landlord and Tenant Act 1954. It applies to all commercial lettings, whether the premises be an office, factory, studio, shop, warehouse, or whatever. If the premises are used partly for residential purposes and partly for business purposes, the tenant will not be able to claim Rent Act protection (see page 237), but he will be able to claim business-tenancy protection unless his lease specifically prohibits the premises being used for business purposes. In that case he will not have protection under either Act (unless the landlord has implicitly acquiesced in the business use) and so he will have to leave when his lease expires, or when his periodic tenancy (e.g. weekly, monthly, etc.) is brought to an end by a notice to quit.

For the Rent Acts see Chapter 16; for the meaning of a 'fixed-term tenancy' and a 'periodic tenancy', see page 236.

Anyone taking on a business lease should take legal advice from a solicitor; business leases are complicated and many landlords impose extremely harsh terms on their tenants. In practice, most business tenants are fully liable to maintain and repair their premises (as though they owned them), and it is usual to have a rent review after, say, five years. The solicitor will be able to advise as to whether the repairing obligations, the rent-review provisions, and the other terms of the lease (e.g. any restrictions as to the type of business that can be carried on) are acceptable.

When the Landlord and Tenant Act applies

The 1954 Act applies to all business lettings with two exceptions:
- if the tenant is given a fixed-term tenancy of up to six months, the Act will not apply. Thus he will have no security of tenure. The landlord can only use this way of evading the Act twice: once the tenant has been in occupation for more than twelve months, he acquires full rights under the Act.
- if the tenant is given a fixed-term tenancy and the court has agreed that the 1954 Act should not apply. Both landlord and tenant must together apply to the court, before the tenancy begins, for formal confirmation that the tenant will not have the right to stay on at the end of the lease. In practice, the courts usually rubber-stamp these agreements and the whole procedure need only take a month or so. But note that this procedure only applies to a fixed-term letting (e.g. a lease for a year) – it

cannot be used for a periodic letting (e.g. a weekly, or quarterly, letting that could be ended on a week's or quarter's notice).

How the 1954 Act works

The business tenant's main concern will usually be that he cannot be evicted at the end of his lease or by service of a notice to quit. The tenant is likely to have built up a clientele and goodwill at the premises and therefore he will probably want to be able to stay in occupation. The 1954 Act usually gives him this security.

If the tenant has a fixed-term tenancy, it will carry on when the term expires. The landlord can only end an expired fixed-term tenancy, or a periodic tenancy, by serving a special notice on the tenant and then applying to the court.

The procedure is:

1. The landlord must serve a statutory notice to quit (in a prescribed style and format) on the tenant. This must state a date when the tenancy is to end, and this date must be between six and twelve months ahead. The notice must also state whether the landlord would oppose an application by the tenant to the court for a new tenancy and, if so, on what grounds.
2. Within two months of receiving the notice, the tenant must give a written counter-notice stating whether or not he will give up possession. The time limit is applied strictly – if the tenant does not serve his notice in time, then he loses the right to claim a new tenancy (it is a mistake that is often made).
3. Unless the tenant comes to a satisfactory agreement with the landlord, the tenant must, within two to four months of receiving the notice, start county-court proceedings for a new tenancy. Once again, the tenant must make sure he does not miss the time limits – if he does, he will lose the right to demand a new lease.
4. The court will grant the tenant a new tenancy unless the landlord can show that one of the following grounds for possession exists:
   - failure to repair and maintain, as required;
   - persistent delay in paying rent;
   - other substantial breaches of the tenancy;
   - suitable alternative premises can be provided;
   - the tenant is a subtenant of part only of the premises and the landlord needs possession so he can sell the whole premises;*
   - the landlord wants to demolish or reconstruct the premises and he needs access to do so;*
   - the landlord wants the premises for his own business or residential use (unless he purchased his interest as landlord from the previous landlord within the last five years).*

   *Note. In these cases the landlord must compensate the tenant for evicting him. The compensation will depend upon how long the tenant has been in business in the premises: *less than fourteen years:* compensation is usually two and a quarter times the rateable value of the premises; *fourteen years or more:* compensation is usually four and a half times the rateable value.

5. If the court grants a new tenancy, it will fix the terms of the tenancy. These need not necessarily be the same as those of the old tenancy, although the court will 'have regard' to them, as well as to 'all relevant circumstances'. The new tenancy will start three months after the court hearing, and in the meantime the old tenancy will continue (except that the court may order a new rent level to apply in the interim). The new rent will be an open market rent (i.e. what the premises would be let for, disregarding the fact that the tenant has been in occupation and that he has built up goodwill; improvements carried out by the tenant are also ignored).

If the court refuses to grant a new tenancy, the tenant will have up to twenty weeks in which to leave. If he does not leave by then, the landlord can apply for him to be evicted.

All the time limits given above are applied strictly. For instance, a tenant who does not apply to the court within two to four months of receiving the landlord's notice will forfeit the right to apply to the court for a new tenancy.

If the tenant's original tenancy was for a fixed term of over one year, or if he has continued from year to year, he can himself initiate the procedure under the 1954 Act; he need not wait until the landlord serves a notice on him (i.e. Step 1 above). Instead, the tenant can serve a notice on the landlord (the notice must be in a special prescribed form) asking for a new tenancy; the landlord then has two months in which to serve a counter-notice stating whether he opposes the application and, if so, why. The procedure then continues in the usual way (i.e. Steps 3, 4, and 5 then follow).

If, for some reason, the tenant does not want his tenancy to continue he should give his landlord at least three months' notice before the date it is due to expire. If he waits until after that time, he must give at least three months' notice, expiring on a quarter day.

The above is just a summary of the provisions of the 1954 Act. It is a complex piece of legislation: there are time periods to be observed and special forms to be used. Accordingly, it is important to obtain legal advice when dealing with any business-tenancy matter.

Assigning a lease

It is not uncommon for a businessman to sell off his business together with his tenancy. Usually, he will have to obtain his landlord's consent to the assignment, but the standard arrangement is that the landlord should not be able to 'unreasonably withhold' his consent (see page 276). The assignee (the purchaser) will usually have to provide the landlord with three or four business references to prove his suitability as a tenant. The landlord will then sign a formal licence which authorizes the assignment (his solicitor's fees will probably have to be paid by the existing tenant). Only then can the existing tenant sign a deed assigning the tenancy to the purchaser.

The parties will have to pay their own solicitor's fees unless there is an agreement

Consumer and Business: Business

in writing to the contrary (Costs of Leases Act 1958). It is not uncommon for the seller to insist that the purchaser pays the seller's and the landlord's legal fees. When this happens, the purchaser should insist that a maximum figure be agreed in advance, for otherwise he runs the risk of being overcharged by the solicitors; if he is overcharged he will not have the usual remedies against the seller's and landlord's solicitors that he would have against his own solicitor (see page 835).

Legal fees when buying a lease

Generally, a solicitor will work out his fees in the same way as he would for the purchase of a residential property. (See page 222 for how these fees are calculated.) The charge is likely to be on the basis of the time spent, plus 25–35 per cent for typing etc., plus ½ per cent of the purchase price, plus 1 per cent of half the annual rent multiplied by the length of the lease, up to a maximum of twenty years. For instance, on the purchase of a shop lease for twenty-one years for £20,000 with the rent at £5,000 p.a., the work involved being nine hours at an hourly charge of £30, the fee might be:

9 × £30	£270
plus 30 per cent	81
plus ½ per cent of £20,000	100
plus 1 per cent of £2,500 × 20 years (= £50,000)	500
	£951 (excl. VAT and disbursements)

In fact, many solicitors would charge less than this; by shopping around it should be possible to get a cheaper price (probably more like £400–£500 not including VAT). As always, it is best to obtain a firm estimate from the solicitor before instructing him.

If the client thinks the fee is too high, he can ask the solicitor to obtain a remuneration certificate from the Law Society (see page 836).

PART FIVE

MOTORING

41 Putting the Car on the Road

The driving licence

Anyone over the age of seventeen can apply for a driving licence unless suffering from disease, epilepsy, mental illness, or bad eyesight (i.e. unable to read a number-plate at twenty-five yards in daylight while wearing glasses).

A learner only receives a provisional licence (valid until age seventy), but is required to display L-plates and be accompanied by a driver in possession of a full licence (who must be registered with the Department of Transport if he is a professional driving instructor). On passing the driving test, the motorist is entitled to a full driving licence, and this will not need renewal until s/he reaches his/her seventieth birthday. After seventy, it can be renewed every three years, but the applicant must disclose any disabilities and may be required to submit to a medical examination and agree to his/her doctor's medical records being examined.

A licence must be signed as soon as it is received by the licence-holder. If the licence-holder changes his address (or name) he must return the licence and supply the new particulars. The penalties for driving-licence offences are set out in the penalty chart (page 637 below; in particular, see pages 638 and 643).

Producing a driver's licence

A policeman can demand to see a motorist's driving licence if:
- the motorist has been *driving* on the road (or supervising a learner who was driving), *or*
- the policeman reasonably believes that either:
  – the motorist was the driver of a motor vehicle when an *accident* occurred because of its presence on the road, *or*
  – the motorist had committed a *motoring offence*.

The main point to note is that anyone driving a car can be asked to produce his or her licence, however unreasonably the policeman may be acting. When asked to produce his licence the motorist can either produce it there and then, or he can select a police station where he will take it within the next five days. However, he cannot send the licence to that police station; he must take it in person.

Road fund licence

Road tax must be paid for any vehicle kept, parked, or used on the road – and this includes an 'old banger' that needs mechanical attention before it will go. The only occasions when a licence is not needed are when the motorist is driving to and from a pre-arranged MoT test, or when the car is being used during the fourteen days' grace allowed after expiry of the last licence; note that the period of grace only applies if a new licence was applied for before the old one expired – not if the application is made in the fourteen days following expiry of the licence. During the fourteen-day period the old licence should be displayed on the windscreen; it is not enough to display a 'licence applied for' sign.

Application for a new licence can be made by post, or in person at a post office; documents required are the vehicle registration document, insurance certificate, MoT certificate (if applicable), the completed form and requisite fee, and the old licence (if applying at a post office). Failure to tax a car, and failure to display the tax disc, are separate offences – see the penalty chart on page 646.

If a tax disc is lost, a replacement can be obtained by completing form V 20. If a licence is surrendered before its expiry date, a refund can be obtained for complete calendar months by completing form V 14.

MoT certificate

A current MoT certificate is needed for any vehicle that has been registered for three or more years. Note that the requirement arises as from the vehicle's third anniversary – it is not sufficient to wait until the next Road Fund licence application after that date. Similarly, cars imported from abroad need an MoT certificate as soon as they are three years old; the three years does not run from the date of importation.

The test covers steering, brakes, tyres, lights, seat belts, exhaust, flashers, washers, wipers, warning lights, body and suspension. It is not a certificate of road-worthiness, and the possession of a current MoT certificate will not be a defence in a prosecution for having an unroadworthy vehicle.

A policeman can ask a motorist to produce the MoT certificate on the same occasions as when he can ask to see a driving licence (see page 607). Penalties for MoT offences are set out in the penalty chart, on page 646.

Registration document

This is often called the log-book. It shows who is the registered keeper of that vehicle but it does not show who is the owner. Although a registration document should always be handed over when a car is sold, it is not proof that the seller owns the car. When a car is sold the DVLC must be told immediately – by both the seller (who fills in the tear-off part of the log-book), and the buyer. The buyer cannot simply wait until he next needs to tax the car.

The number of former owners of a vehicle is noted on the log-book but their names and addresses are not stated (except for the last owner). The registered keeper can obtain these details, free of charge, by writing to the DVLC.

Lost registration documents can be replaced by applying on form V 62. Penalties for registration-document offences are set out in the penalty chart (page 646).

Insurance

The law tries to ensure that anyone who suffers injury through a motorist's negligent driving should recover damages. Since most people would be unable to meet an award of damages made against them for serious personal injury, Parliament has insisted that all motorists insure against that possible liability. This is all that the law requires – it does not require any more than insurance against injury to other people (including passengers), and so the motorist need not be insured for damage to other people's property and possessions – although in practice most policies do cover damage to property and possessions.

Prosecutions for failure to insure

Using a vehicle without insurance

Whilst this offence clearly covers the person who drives a car without insurance, it goes further and includes a person who has a car which is capable of being used.

A car was left jacked up on the road, without it being covered by a valid certificate of insurance. The defendant argued that he could not be guilty of 'using' the car since it could not be driven. Held: He was guilty. The car could be moved and so insurance was needed and he was guilty of 'using' it without insurance. Elliott (1959)

On the other hand, if a car is completely immobile, and cannot be driven or moved, then the owner cannot be said to be using it.

The compulsory-insurance laws are applied strictly. Even if a motorist believes he is insured but in fact is uninsured, he will still be committing an offence even if he made an honest and genuine mistake. For instance, if Smith borrows a car from Jones after being told by Jones that the insurance covers Smith, then both will be guilty of breaking the compulsory-insurance laws.

Failure to have insurance is a serious offence, and will nearly always lead to penalty points (between 4 and 8), and sometimes disqualification (see the penalty chart on page 639). However, there is a special defence for employees who innocently drive their employer's vehicles without insurance. For this defence to succeed, the employee must satisfy the court that it was 'probably true' (*not* the stiffer test of 'beyond reasonable doubt') that:

- the vehicle did not belong to him, and he had not hired or borrowed it, *and*
- he was using the vehicle in the course of his employment (see page 411 for what this means), *and*
- he did not know, and had no reason to believe, that he was not insured.

Motoring

Causing or permitting a vehicle to be used without insurance

This is aimed at the person who lends out his car without checking that the driver is insured. If the owner tells the driver that he cannot use the car until he obtains insurance, then the owner will not be liable.

The obligation to insure (and indeed to have a driving licence and MoT certificate) only applies to a vehicle that is on a 'road', as opposed to private land. In 1968 a classic borderline case arose when a lorry was half on private land and half on a road at the time of an accident; it was held that the lorry was on the road and so insurance, tax, and MoT certificate were all needed.

How the motorist's insurance can be invalid

The law on motor insurance is no different from that on other types of insurance. Chapter 35 sets out the position. The basic rule is that the insured person must act in the utmost good faith and so tell his insurers of anything that could be relevant to their insuring him. Thus he must tell them of all accidents and convictions even if he is not asked about them, and the information he gives to the insurers (for instance, as to where the car is to be garaged) must be 100 per cent correct. Otherwise his insurance will be invalid. Thus, the insurance company may not have to pay out if sued, or if they do pay out then the unfortunate motorist may have to reimburse the insurers. However, if the insurance policy is invalidated in this way it is most unlikely that the motorist will face a criminal prosecution for not being insured. The police will take the view that he was insured until the time when the insurance company repudiated liability or cancelled the policy. Therefore, whilst the insurance policy may be invalid as regards a civil claim for damages, it will be valid against a criminal prosecution for being uninsured.

The law reports contain many cases of motorists who thought they were insured but whose insurers were entitled to repudiate liability. Generally, this was because they had fallen foul of one of the following insurance rules:
• the duty to disclose everything (even when you are not asked about it, see page 557). For instance:

The motorist failed to disclose that a previous proposal for a different type of policy had been turned down. Locker (1936)

The insured did not mention that her husband would be driving the car and that he had a bad accident record. Dunn (1933)

The bookmaker described himself as a dealer, since he knew that the company would not insure him as a bookmaker. Holmes (1949)

• false statements (even when you don't know they are false, see page 558). For instance:

The insured completed the proposal form and in reply to 'Has anyone who to your knowledge will drive the car been convicted of driving offences?', he put 'no'. However, unknown to him, his son, who would drive the car, did have several motoring convictions. Held: The answer was

610

wrong and so the insurers could cancel the policy and repudiate liability. M.&M. Insurance (1941)

A motorist who knowingly makes a false statement to obtain insurance commits an offence.

● breaking one of the conditions of the policy. Motor policies always contain small print imposing various conditions on the motorist. The motorist will often be unaware of these conditions and so may not realize that he is invalidating his insurance. For instance:

– the use to which the vehicle is put. If the policy is limited to 'social, domestic and pleasure' purposes, it will not cover a business trip.

> *Mrs Levinger's motor policy was limited to use on 'the business of the insured'. Mrs Levinger then turned her business into a company, so legally it was no longer her business. Held: The insurers could repudiate liability since the car was no longer being used on 'the business of the insured'.* Levinger (1936)

– that the vehicle be kept in roadworthy condition. Many policies require that the car be kept 'in a proper state of repair', and that it is not used 'in an unsafe condition'.

> *A car was carrying several extra passengers so that it was overloaded and this affected the steering. It was involved in an accident. The insurers then claimed that the insured had been in breach of the roadworthiness condition in his policy. Held: Yes. He was uninsured.* Clarke (1964)

In one case, the front brakes of a coach became worn because the owners failed to carry out normal maintenance; the insurers were able to avoid liability when the defective brakes caused an accident. Even worse, it seems that the insurers can escape liability even if the defect was not the owner's fault because no amount of maintenance would have prevented the defect (e.g. if lights fail). This is, of course, a ridiculous situation.

Also, the defect need not even cause the accident or be responsible for the claim being made. For instance, if a car with faulty lights is stolen, the insurers can repudiate liability – even though the failure to maintain was unconnected with the theft! In short, the law is unfairly biased in favour of the insurance companies.

The companies argue that they rarely enforce their policies in such a strict way; their Code of Practice says that in the absence of fraud, deception, or negligence they will not unreasonably repudiate liability to indemnify a policy-holder where the circumstances of the loss are unconnected with the breach.

But why should motorists have to rely on the good practice of insurers? Why not alter the law and remove the privileged legal position of insurers?

– time limits for claiming. Most policies require the insured to notify the company of an accident or claim within seven or fourteen days. This provision can be applied strictly:

> *Mr Brooke went to see the branch manager of his insurers to make a claim. He told the manager about the claim and the manager gave him a claim form to complete. He went away, filled in the form and returned it, but by then the time limit had expired. Held: The insurers could repudiate liability.* Brooke (1946)

Motoring

The duty to report any accident to the insurance company applies even when the motorist does not want to claim under the policy: for instance, if he has a comprehensive policy but decides to claim from the other motorist involved, or when the motorist decides to pay the other motorist's damage himself rather than lose his no-claims bonus. In such a case the motorist might write to his insurers: 'I am reporting this accident to you as required by the terms of my policy; however, please note that I am not making a claim under the policy and I should therefore be grateful for your confirmation that my no-claims bonus will not be affected by my reporting this accident to you.'

For how to make a claim after an accident, and the apportionment of blame for accidents, see Chapter 43, page 650.

The effect of motor insurance being invalidated

If a motorist's insurance policy is invalid for some reason, then he will be committing a criminal offence if he uses the car after the insurance company has cancelled the policy or repudiated liability. But until that time he will not be criminally liable. But what about the injury or damage he causes – can the insurance company avoid paying compensation to the innocent parties? The answer is partly yes and partly no:

• as regards claims for personal injury, the insurance company must pay any damages awarded against the uninsured motorist. So the innocent person who is injured can be sure that he will receive compensation from the insurance company. However, the insurance company can – in turn – sue the uninsured motorist in an attempt to get him to reimburse them (in practice, of course, he probably won't have enough money to make it worth suing him).

• if the claim is not for personal injury, but is for damage to property or possessions, the insurance company need not pay any damages awarded against the motorist. The innocent person will therefore only receive compensation if the motorist has sufficient assets to pay the damages.

Illustration. *Mr Brown had his car insured for 'social, domestic and pleasure use'. One day he delivered a package for his employer in the car, but had an accident on the way. The accident was his fault. His insurers repudiated liability because the car was not being used for social, domestic, or pleasure purposes. In the accident Mr Brown drove into a car driven by Mr Smith, who claimed damages for:*
(1) pain and suffering caused by a broken leg;
(2) lost wages for the time he was off work;
(3) the cost of a suit ruined in the accident;
(4) the value of his written-off car.
Items (1) and (2) will have to be paid by the insurance company, although they can claim reimbursement from Mr Brown. Items (3) and (4) will have to be paid by Mr Brown. If Mr Brown does not have sufficient money to pay (3) and (4), Mr Smith will go uncompensated unless he himself had a comprehensive insurance policy that he could claim on. This would, of course, probably involve him in paying an excess (see below) and also in the loss of his no-claims bonus.

Uninsured motorists. If Mr Brown had never taken out the insurance policy then

Mr Smith would obviously have been unable to claim any of his damages from the insurance company. However, he would not have gone uncompensated. He could claim from the Motor Insurers Bureau (MIB) which exists to compensate the victims of uninsured and untraced motorists. The MIB would meet Mr Smith's claim for damages under items (1) and (2), although it would of course be able to claim reimbursement from Mr Brown assuming he had sufficient assets.

'No claims' and 'excesses'

Most motor policies offer a 'no-claims' discount, whereby the premium is reduced according to the number of preceding years in which no claim was made. Typical reductions are:

1 year – 30 per cent reduction
2 years – 40 per cent reduction
3 years – 50 per cent reduction
4 years – 60 per cent reduction.

The important point to note is that the no-claims bonus, or a proportion of it, is lost as soon as a claim is made. It is wrong to suppose that the bonus is only lost if the accident was not the insured's fault; it is a no-claims bonus, not a no-fault bonus. However, many insurance policies now provide that only a part of the no-claims bonus is lost in the event of a claim. A further deterrent to small claims is the 'excess'. This usually requires the policy-holder to pay the first £25 or £50 of any claim.

A complication can arise, however, because of 'knock-for-knock agreements'. These are agreements between insurance companies, whereby they agree to meet claims made by their own insured motorists even when, legally speaking, the accident was the fault of a motorist insured by another insurance company. In effect, each company pays out on its own claims and so all the companies avoid the expense and inconvenience of claiming from one another. So a motorist may have his claim paid by his own insurers even though it is the other negligent motorist's insurers who should really be paying him. He will, of course, lose his no-claims bonus and his excess since a claim has been made on his policy. However, if he can convince his insurers that he was in no way to blame for the accident the insurers will agree to reinstate his no-claims bonus, but in practice he can only do this by recovering his own excess from the other motorist (or the insurers). Thus, the innocent motorist may have to sue for the few pounds of his excess if he is to preserve his no-claims bonus.

Car sharing

It used to be unlawful for a motorist to share the cost of travel with his passengers. Since 1978, non-profit car-sharing has been allowed if:
- no more than eight people travel in the vehicle;
- charges are agreed before the journey starts. There must be no profit, but the driver can charge for more than just the petrol; for instance, he can recover a contribution towards servicing, insurance, and road tax proportionate to the use of

the car. But the owner must incur these expenses – he cannot charge his passengers for costs that he does not incur (e.g. if his employer provides him with free petrol) since he would then be making a profit.

The driver's insurance will not be invalidated by car-sharing if it meets the above requirements.

Advertising for car-sharers is allowed, provided the advertisements do not amount to plying for hire, like a taxi.

Vehicle maintenance

The duty to have a safe and roadworthy vehicle is not limited to the time of the annual MoT test. The Motor Vehicle (Construction and Use) Regulations set out – in some 146 provisions and 11 schedules – the legal standards required at all times from any car on the road. Many of these detailed regulations will be met by the vehicle manufacturer and are unlikely to concern the motorist (e.g. the requirement that flashing winkers have between 60 and 120 flashes per minute). However, the Regulations insist that these requirements are met at all times and both the owner and the driver of the vehicle can be prosecuted for any breach.

The Construction and Use Regulations cover virtually all aspects of vehicle design, safety, and maintenance; the provisions on horns, brakes, overloading, lights, steering, tyres, mirrors, and noise are of particular importance. Most of the offences do not carry penalty points (or endorsement), although the rules on dangerous loads, brakes, steering, and tyres are exceptions to this. Only in a very few cases (involving trade vehicles) can penalty points be imposed. For penalties, see page 645.

A motorist can be convicted of using a vehicle in breach of the Construction and Use Regulations even when he did not know of the vehicle's fault. This is because they are *absolute offences* – either the offence was committed or it was not, for there can be no half-way house. The charge is one of 'being in breach of the Regulations', not 'knowingly being in breach of the Regulations'. For instance, headlights must be in perfect working order during the day, and not just at night; a motorist driving in the daytime may not know if his headlight bulb has broken since he last used the lights, but he will still be guilty of an offence. However, in such a case, the court will usually find the motorist guilty, but give him an absolute discharge (see page 805).

If the charge is one of 'permitting or causing' the vehicle to be used in breach of the Regulations, then the defendant must be shown to have 'known' of the fault. Whereas 'using' the vehicle is an absolute offence, 'causing or permitting' its use is not.

Spot checks

Breaches of the Construction and Use Regulations usually come to light when the police inspect a vehicle after an accident or during a spot check. A uniformed policeman can, *at any time*, stop a vehicle and ask to check its brakes, steering, silencer, tyres, exhaust, lights, and reflectors. However, the driver can say that it would be inconvenient to have an immediate inspection and can insist that it be arranged at any convenient time in the next thirty days, unless the policeman feels that the vehicle should be checked immediately either because it has been in an accident or because it seems to have a serious defect. If so, the inspection cannot be postponed.

Brakes. The handbrake and the brakes on the four wheels must be effective and capable of stopping the car in a reasonable distance. As a guide, the Highway Code gives the shortest stopping distance of a typical car with good brakes, including thinking time, as 75 ft at 30 m.p.h., 175 ft at 50 m.p.h., 315 ft at 70 m.p.h.

Horn. All private motor vehicles must have a horn. Bells, two-tone horns, and sirens are not allowed. There are restrictions on sounding horns at night and sounding them unnecessarily (see page 351).

Lights. Both lights and reflectors must be kept clean and in full working order, even in daytime. It is illegal to have a red light at the front of a car or a white light at the rear (except when reversing). It is also illegal to have rear fog lights that are wired to the brake lights. Lighting-up time is the period between half an hour after sunset and half an hour before sunrise. Dipped or full headlights are compulsory at night outside built-up areas (i.e. when the street-lights are more than 200 yards apart), and in all areas if there is poor visibility, such as fog or heavy rain.

When parked at night, a car must have sidelights on unless it is on a road with a 30 m.p.h. speed limit, in the light of a street lamp, and not on a main bus route. It must also be parked at least fifteen yards from any junction and be facing the correct direction.

Mirrors. All vehicles must have a rear-view mirror, but only goods vehicles and large passenger vehicles need wing mirrors.

Number-plates. These must have the vehicle's number in regulation approved size and style of lettering. An offence is committed if the vehicle is driven with number-plates that are so dirty as to be unreadable.

Silencer. An effective silencer is compulsory.

Speedometer. A speedometer must be fitted to all post-1937 vehicles, except motor-cycles of less than 100 cc. The speedometer must be accurate to within 10 per cent at speeds over 10 m.p.h.

Windscreen wipers. Wipers are compulsory unless the driver can see clearly over or through the windscreen without them. Windscreen washers are also compulsory.

Seat belts. The fitting of seat belts in new cars has been compulsory for many years (generally, since 1964). But it is only since 1983 that the wearing of seat belts in the front of a car has been compulsory. There are only a few exceptions – when reversing; delivery roundsmen; taxi-drivers; police and other emergency services; if a medical exemption certificate can be produced. In practice, few people are entitled to medical certificates, since most GPS apply the rules strictly. If a person does have a certificate then it must be shown to a policeman on request (or produced at a police station within five days).

Children under twelve months are not allowed to travel in a front seat (even if securely held by an adult). Children aged between one and thirteen (inclusive) are allowed in front seats, but must be strapped in – as of course must any adult. If a child is not strapped in then the driver can be prosecuted.

Penalties for seat-belt offences are set out in the penalty chart, page 643.

The motorist as consumer

A car is a consumer item and thus its purchase and sale is subject to the consumer laws set out in Chapter 32. One point to watch particularly carefully is that many second-hand cars are bought and sold from private individuals, not from motor-traders. That being so, the purchaser will not have the benefit of the Sale of Goods Act protection which would apply to a purchase from a trader (see 'Buying from a Private Individual', page 515; 'Buying Second-hand Goods', page 522).

If repair work is carried out by a member of the Motor Agents' Association (MAA) or of the Society of Motor Manufacturers and Traders (SMMT), there may be an additional remedy. These bodies have produced a Code of Practice which, among other provisions, sets out minimum standards expected of their members. If a customer feels that a member has broken the code he can apply for arbitration. Even if the garage is not a member of one of these organizations, the code can be relevant because it shows the standards expected of a 'reasonable' garage and this can be extremely useful to the consumer who is suing in the county court.

Major recommendations in the code

Repairs and servicing (excluding work carried out under a manufacturer's warranty)

Dealers must bear in mind that when supplying parts or accessories in connection with repairs or servicing work for consumers, they have a similar responsibility to that which exists under a contract for the sale of goods to ensure that the goods are of merchantable quality and fit for the purpose for which they are required and that work is performed in a proper and workman-like manner.

Manufacturers accept a responsibility for ensuring the reasonable availability of spare parts to the distribution chain.

Dealers will provide at least an estimate of the cost of labour and materials for all major repairs and manufacturers' recommended servicing. A firm quotation should be offered wherever possible. It must be made clear to the customer whether an estimate or quotation is being made and whether it is inclusive of VAT and where applicable the rate at which this is chargeable. Quotations should always be in writing identifying the dealer. If requested, estimates will be in writing. It should be remembered that an estimate is a considered approximation of the likely cost involved whereas a quotation constitutes a firm price for which the work will be done. If a charge is to be made for the estimate or quotation this must be made known to the customer before his instructions are accepted. Any dismantling costs which are necessary to arrive at such estimates or quotations should be notified to the customer in advance on the clear understanding whether or not dismantling costs are to be charged on an estimate or quotation which is refused. If, during the progress of any work, it appears that the estimate will be exceeded by a significant amount, then the customer should be notified and asked for permission to continue with the work.

Parts replaced during service or repair will be made available for return to the customer until the customer has taken delivery of the car unless a warranty claim is involved or unless the parts have to be submitted to the supplier because replacement parts are being supplied on an exchange basis. Dealers should notify customers in advance of work being done what their arrangements are in regard to retention and disposal of parts replaced.

Invoices should be clearly written or typed and give full details of the work carried out and materials used. The amount and rate of VAT should be clearly indicated. Dates and recorded mileages should always be noted where applicable.

Dealers should exercise adequate care in protecting customers' property while it is in their custody, and must not seek by disclaimers to avoid their legal liability for damage or loss. Dealers should carry adequate insurance to cover their legal liability and should strongly advise customers to remove any items of value not related to the car.

Repairs must be guaranteed against failure due to workmanship for a specific mileage or time period which should be stated on the invoice. Dealers are advised to ensure that they are adequately insured against consequential loss claims arising from any such failure.

A dealer's rules as to the method of payment he will require on completion of the work should always be notified to the customer before the work is accepted.

When it is necessary to subcontract work, the dealer will agree to be responsible for the quality of the subcontractors' work. Any estimate given to the customer must include the subcontracted work and in the event of any increase in charge for the work, the principles in para 5.4* must apply.

Handling complaints

Manufacturers and dealers must ensure as appropriate that effective and immediate action is taken with a view to achieving a just settlement of a complaint. To this end there will be, from the point of view of the customer, an easily identifiable and accessible arrangement for the reception and handling of complaints. In addition, manufacturers must give every assistance to their dealers in handling complaints under warranty, or those in which the manufacturer is otherwise involved.

When complaints are raised through a third party (e.g. the Automobile Association, the Royal Automobile Club, a trading standards officer or a Citizens' Advice Bureau), willing guidance must be given to that body and every attempt should be made to re-establish direct communication with the complaining customer and to reach a satisfactory settlement with him.

In the event that a complaint is not resolved manufacturers and dealers must make it clear to a customer that he has a right to refer the complaint to the appropriate trade association.

Where conciliation has failed to resolve a dispute the SMMT, the MAA and the SMTA have agreed to cooperate in the operation of low-cost arbitration arrangements which will be organised by the Chartered Institute of Arbitrators.

Customers must always be advised that they have the option of taking a claim to the courts. The award of the arbitrator is enforceable in law on all parties.

*Not printed here.

Motoring

Arbitration

1   A customer who has a complaint about the quality of the goods or service to his motorcar should in the first place and at the earliest opportunity refer it to the dealer concerned.

2   The complaint, preferably in writing, should be addressed to a senior executive, a director, a partner or the proprietor. Some dealers will have an executive specially appointed to deal with complaints.

3   If the complaint relates to warranty on a new car and the dealer is unable to resolve the matter, the customer should take his complaint direct to the manufacturer concerned.

4   If attempts to reach a satisfactory solution fail, the customer has a right to refer his complaint to one of the trade associations which subscribe to the Code of Practice for the motor industry, if the dealer concerned is a member of that association. Any such complaint must be in writing.

5   All complaints referred to the appropriate trade association (SMMT, MAA or SMTA) within a reasonable time of the cause for complaint arising will be considered.

6   If the trade association fails to resolve the complaint, its members will agree to go to arbitration except in those cases where the trade association is of the opinion that it would be unreasonable for the member to be required to do so.

7   The award of the arbitrator is enforceable in the courts by any party.

42 Prosecutions for Motoring Offences

In the eyes of the law, motoring offences are no different from other offences; if the defendant is guilty then he is a criminal. Society, of course, generally takes a more lenient view and regards motoring offences as being different from other criminal offences, presumably on the basis of 'there, but for the grace of God, go I'. This ambivalent attitude to motoring offences is reflected in the fact that Parliament has had to create a special offence of 'causing death by reckless driving' because of the refusal of juries to convict motorists for manslaughter, even when there is clear evidence of gross negligence.

However, there is one legal difference between many motoring offences and most other offences, in that motoring offences are generally not concerned with the intention or knowledge of the accused. Whereas most crimes involve, firstly, an illegal act and, secondly, an intention to commit the illegal act, most motoring offences need only the illegal act and not the intention to commit it. For instance, the motorist who drives at 40 m.p.h. in a 30 m.p.h. zone cannot expect to be acquitted because he did not know there was a 30 m.p.h. limit, or because his speedometer was working incorrectly (in itself an offence under the Construction and Use Regulations). The court would only be concerned to know: (1) was there a 30 m.p.h. limit in force and (2) was the accused exceeding 30 m.p.h. – if so, then a conviction must result, although obviously the circumstances of the offence would be relevant when deciding on a suitable penalty.

Similarly, take the example of the motorist who does not know that his insurers have 'gone bust', and that he is therefore driving without insurance. He may be morally blameless but in the law's eyes he will be guilty of driving without insurance and a conviction must result. His excuses will only be relevant after conviction, when the court is considering what penalty to impose.

However, this is not an absolute rule, for there are some motoring offences that require a guilty knowledge or intent on the part of the accused before he can be convicted. But such offences (e.g. reckless driving, 'causing or permitting' charges) are the exception rather than the rule, whereas in non-motoring offences the reverse applies.

Whilst in legal theory all motoring convictions are criminal convictions, a distinction is in fact made between the various categories of motoring offences, and this distinction is reflected in the way in which they are recorded:
- convictions usually regarded as 'criminal' are recorded at the Criminal Record Office at Scotland Yard and at the regional police headquarters around the country.

Motoring

Thus, offences such as causing death by reckless driving, and taking a vehicle without consent, would be recorded in the national criminal records.
● convictions resulting in an endorsement or in disqualification are recorded on the DLVC computer at Swansea. Every driver has a driver number, and the police can apply for a computer print-out of his driving record.
● minor offences are not recorded in a central register.

When proceedings are begun

Because motoring offences are, in the eyes of the law, similar to other criminal offences, proceedings are begun in the same way (see page 777 for ways in which criminal proceedings can be commenced). However, since most motoring offences carry relatively small penalties, they are usually begun by a summons. Only in the more serious cases (such as reckless driving or breathalyser offences) is the motorist likely to be arrested and taken to the police station.

When served with a summons there are two preliminary points that the motorist should consider before he decides whether to plead guilty or not guilty.

1. What exactly is the charge against him?

The charge will often be set out in legalistic language, so the motorist should read it carefully and, if necessary, seek legal advice. Often it will be important to check whether he is being prosecuted for 'using' the car, 'driving' the car, 'being in charge' of the car (e.g. when it is parked), or 'permitting' its use (e.g. when he allows an employee to use it). It is worth checking that the correct wording is used for the facts of the particular case.

2. Should the police have notified him of likely prosecution?

With certain offences, the motorist must be warned that he might be prosecuted so that he can take steps to contact witnesses and collect evidence before too much time elapses. The warning can either be a verbal warning from the policeman at the time of the offence (typically: 'the facts will be reported with a view to consideration of the question of proceedings being taken against you') or a written notice of intended prosecution (or even a summons), served within fourteen days of the offence. The notice is usually sent by recorded-delivery post and will simply state that the police intend to prosecute. But just because a notice of intended prosecution is served, it does not necessarily mean that the police will prosecute, for the service of the notice simply allows the police to keep their options open while they decide whether or not to prosecute.

A warning of possible prosecution is only needed for:
● reckless, careless, or inconsiderate driving;
● failure to comply with a traffic sign;

- failure to comply with the directions of a policeman regulating traffic;
- parking in a dangerous position;
- speeding offences.

However, no notice is needed if an accident occurred at the time of the offence. So if, for instance, a motorist is involved in a collision, however slight, he need not be warned that he might be prosecuted for careless driving. However, if he had not hit the other vehicle and there had been no accident, then he would have to be warned.

In practice it is difficult for a motorist to have a summons dismissed because no notice of intended prosecution was given. It is for him to show that the notice was not delivered and if the police can show that the notice was sent by recorded delivery to his address, the court will usually assume that it was served properly.

Should the motorist defend the charge?

Once the motorist has checked these technicalities, he will have to decide whether to defend the charge and whether to instruct a solicitor. In all but the most obvious cases it is advisable to take legal advice, either from a solicitor, a Citizens' Advice Bureau, or from the AA or RAC (if he is a member). If the prosecution follows a serious accident, the motorist's insurance company may be prepared to instruct a solicitor to represent him, since their liability to pay damages could be affected by the outcome of the criminal prosecution.

Points to be borne in mind at this stage

- is it worth incurring legal fees to defend the charge? In a magistrates' court prosecution the motorist will only rarely recover all his legal costs if he is acquitted (see page 845). Also, legal aid will only be available for the more serious motoring offences.
- what is the maximum possible penalty, and also what is the likely penalty? Refer to the penalty chart on pages 637–46.
- does he have any previous motoring convictions that will affect the penalty? In particular, does he have penalty points that could lead to disqualification under the 'totting-up' rules (see page 626).
- if the offence is very trivial, is it worth incurring the inconvenience of defending it? For instance, with a parking summons it might be cheaper and more convenient to plead guilty rather than go to the inconvenience of attending court to defend the charge.
- does he have a defence to the charge? There is no point in pleading not guilty when there is no hope of acquittal. Indeed, such a course of action usually rebounds; the court may feel its time has been wasted and so impose a stiffer penalty, as well as ordering the defendant to pay the costs of the prosecution (which he would probably have avoided had he pleaded guilty). This is especially true of breathalyser prosecutions, where many defendants plead not guilty when they clearly are guilty.

- if the motorist is going to plead guilty, can he do so by post? It is possible to plead guilty by post to most motoring offences, but it is important that the defendant writes to the court in good time and that he encloses his driving licence. See page 790 for the procedure. Remember that it is not possible to plead 'not guilty' by post. A 'not guilty' plea means an attendance at court by the defendant.

Penalties

The penalty chart on pages 637–46 sets out typical penalties for first-time offenders. But it does not set out the possible maximum penalties – which may well be much greater. This is because the vast majority of motorists are not fined the maximum amount (for instance, some obstruction charges can carry a maximum penalty of up to £2,000 but, in practice, typical penalties are in the £10–£25 bracket). So, maximum penalties are usually misleading.

Bear in mind that the typical penalties set out in the penalty chart are no more than very rough guidelines. Different courts take different attitudes to the same case – it is not uncommon for a solicitor to have two clients with seemingly identical cases, and find that one client, in one court, gets a sentence twice that of the other client who had the good fortune to appear in a different court. In any event, the penalty imposed will depend on the facts of the incident, the court's impression of the accused, any previous convictions, and also that particular court's view of the seriousness of the offence in question. It is, therefore, impossible to set out a list of normal penalties, but the penalty chart does set out 'typical penalties' as a rough-and-ready guide, although the limitations of these figures should always be borne in mind.

Apart from fine or imprisonment, endorsement and disqualification are usually the major penalties that can be imposed on motoring offenders.

Endorsement

An endorsement can be imposed for most motoring offences, the major exceptions being for parking, obstruction, no road-fund licence, no MoT certificate, no lights, and most construction and use offences.

Otherwise an endorsement will be ordered unless the court decides that there are *special reasons* (see page 625) for not endorsing. The endorsement is entered on the motorist's driving licence and also on police records, although the motorist can apply for it to be removed from the licence after four years (eleven years if endorsement was for a drink-driving offence).

What is an endorsement? An endorsement means that the conviction is 'endorsed' (i.e. written) on the motorist's driving licence. As such, an endorsement is not – by itself – much of a penalty. There was a time when endorsement could lead to disqualification (i.e. loss of driving licence). Under the old rules, a motorist who had three endorsements in a three-year period would automatically lose his licence, and so motorists used to do all they could to avoid having their licences endorsed. But the law was changed in 1982 and now it is the number of penalty points that decides whether a motorist should be disqualified – not the number of endorsements. If an endorsement is imposed, then the motorist will nearly always get some penalty points. So, the motorist will want to do all he can to avoid getting an endorsement.

How can an endorsement be avoided? The court nearly always has power to endorse if it wants to, but on many other occasions it has very little discretion to refuse to endorse. In the penalty chart on pages 637–46 there is a column headed 'Compulsory Endorsement?' and this shows the offences for which the court has to endorse. However, even in those cases, the court can refuse to endorse if it is convinced that there are 'special reasons' surrounding the way in which the offence was committed. So, if the motorist can convince the court that there were special reasons, then the court will not endorse his licence, and – probably more important – the court cannot then impose any penalty points. In practice, very few motorists are able legitimately to argue that there were special reasons – see below (page 625) for the rules on special reasons.

Penalty points

Before 1982, the rule used to be that a motorist would lose his licence if he had three endorsements in three years; now it is if he has 12 penalty points in three years.

It is not every motoring conviction that leads to penalty points being imposed. Only the more serious offences carry points. To see whether a particular offence carries points, refer to the penalty chart on pages 637–46. If the offence is listed as having a compulsory endorsement, then points will normally have to be imposed.

Most offences carry a fixed number of penalty points (e.g. dangerous parking carries 3 points). But a few offences – in practice, probably the most important offences – carry a range of penalty points and the court has a discretion as to the number of points to impose. The offences are:

careless driving	2–5 points
failing to stop after an accident	5–9
failing to report an accident	4–9
driving while uninsured	4–8

In these cases, the court has a discretion. It will obviously take into account the circumstances of the case, the seriousness of any damage caused, and the previous driving record of the motorist. So if a motorist is being prosecuted for one of these offences he would be unwise to plead guilty by post, in case the court imposes maximum penalty points. He should appear in court to explain the mitigating circumstances and why a lower number of points should be imposed.

Convictions for more than one offence. Often a motorist will face more than one charge as a result of one incident. The question then arises of how many points should be imposed. The answer is that he will only get the points for the most serious offence – he will not also get points for the other offences.

623

Penalty points	
Any offence involving automatic disqualification (see page 627)	4
Reckless driving	10
Careless or inconsiderate driving	2–5
Being in charge when unfit through drink	10
Being in charge with alcohol above prescribed limit	10
Failure to supply specimen for breath test	4
Failure to supply specimen for analysis	10
Illegally carrying passenger on motor cycle	1
Failure to comply with traffic directions	3
Leaving vehicle in dangerous position	3
Failure to stop after accident	5–9
Failure to give particulars or report accident	4–9
Contravention of Construction and Use Regulations	3
Driving without a licence	2
Failure to comply with conditions of licence	2
Driving with uncorrected defective eyesight	2
Refusal to submit to eyesight test	2
Driving when disqualified as under age	2
Driving when disqualified by court order	6
Using/causing/permitting use of uninsured motor vehicle	4–8
Contravention of motorway traffic regulations	3
Contravention of pedestrian-crossing regulations	3
Failure to obey school-crossing patrol sign	3
Contravention of street playground order	2
Exceeding speed limit	3
Taking a conveyance without consent	8
Going equipped for stealing with reference to theft or taking of motor vehicle	8
Stealing or attempting to steal motor vehicle	8
Each endorsement under old totting-up rules	3

Illustration. *A motorist is stopped on the motorway for speeding. When the police examine his car they discover that his brake lights are not working. He is subsequently convicted of speeding (which carries 3 points), and for a breach of the Construction and Use Regulations (which also carries 3 points). In fact, he will only receive 3 points – he will not have 6 points.*

Illustration. *A motorist is involved in a serious accident and subsequently prosecuted for reckless driving (which carries 10 points), and for speeding (3 points). He will receive 10 points (i.e. not 13 points).*

This rule only applies if the offences are 'committed on the same occasion'. For instance, suppose a motorist drives from Bristol to London, and is seen driving carelessly in Bath, and speeding near Heathrow. The offences were not committed on the same occasion and so he will incur points (between 2 and 5) for the careless driving, and 3 points for the speeding. On the other hand, if the two offences had happened at more or less the same time then it would count as only one conviction for points purposes. The difficulty, of course, lies in deciding when offences are 'committed on the same occasion' and when they are different occasions. When there is a dispute on this point, the court has to decide the issue.

Can points be avoided? If the offence carries penalty points then the court must normally impose those points – it cannot decide that the offence was not serious enough to merit points. Refer to the penalty chart on pages 637–46 to see which offences carry penalty points. But points can only be imposed if the motorist's licence is also endorsed. So if the motorist can persuade the court not to endorse his licence then he will also avoid incurring points. However, an endorsement can only be avoided if the motorist can persuade the court that there were 'special reasons' in his particular case. This is not as easy as it may seem because it is not the hardship to the individual motorist that matters (e.g. it may threaten his job), but the circumstances of the offence.

Special reasons

The fundamental rule on special reasons is that the circumstances *must be connected with the offence, and not with the offender*. The reason must be special to the offence – not the offender. Thus, the mere fact that the offender will lose his job if his licence is endorsed cannot be a special reason, as it is a circumstance that relates to the offender, not the offence. On the other hand, the fact that the offence was committed after the motorist had drunk laced drinks could be a special reason, since it relates to the circumstances of the offence, and not the offender's own personal circumstances.

Many motorists convince themselves that there are special reasons why they should not have an endorsement, but only occasionally will they be correct. The best way to illustrate how strictly the rules on special reasons are applied is to consider **examples of what have been held *not* to be special reasons:** the fact that:

- he has been driving for many years without complaint or accident;
- he is a professional driver and will otherwise lose his job;
- he is disabled and relies on his car for transport, or he is disabled and only drove the car at the time of the offence because there was no public transport available;
- he will suffer financial hardship, or it will cause serious hardship to the defendant's family;
- he is a doctor and endorsement resulting in disqualification would cause medical services in his area to deteriorate;
- he is a soldier serving in Northern Ireland and must be able to drive on duty;
- domestic circumstances (such as a baby-sitter waiting at home) forced him to drive the car at the time of the offence;
- endorsement would result in disqualification and that would be too severe a penalty;
- any accident that occurred was not his fault;
- the offence occurred late at night when there were few people about.

Special reasons are not just important when an endorsement is being considered. In the more serious motoring offences for which disqualification is mandatory (for instance drunken driving, see page 633) the motorist can argue that there are special reasons why he should not be disqualified. Once again, the principle to be applied is that the special reason must be relevant to the offence, not to the offender. See page 635 for more examples of special reasons.

Twelve points equals disqualification

The basic rule is that a motorist who acquires 12 penalty points in a three-year period will lose his licence for at least six months. This is what is sometimes called 'totting-up'. In fact, it is an oversimplification to say that 12 points in three years equals six months' disqualification. In many cases it will, but often the rules are complicated to apply.

The three-year period. In most cases, it is simply a matter of seeing whether the motorist has had points within the last three years. But special provisions have had to be built into the rules so as to prevent cunning lawyers from trying to get an advantage by postponing their clients' court appearances (and so dragging out the three-year period). However, the basic rule is that offences committed within three years of the date of the latest offence – not the date when it comes to court – are taken into account. (In fact, the rules can be difficult to apply, so anyone with a borderline case should take legal advice.) Nevertheless, if the motorist has already been disqualified in the last three years, then that disqualification wipes the slate clean as regards points incurred before disqualification. So if a motorist had 10 points one year ago, but was disqualified nine months ago, then only points imposed in the last nine months – since his disqualification – will be counted against him.

The length of disqualification. The normal rule is that 12 points in three years leads to a minimum of six months' disqualification. Note that this is the *minimum* period, although, in practice, it is usually six months (not longer) that is imposed. But, if the motorist has been disqualified before, within the last three years, then the minimum period is longer:

– no disqualification in last three years	*six months minimum*
– one disqualification in last three years	*one year minimum*
– more than one disqualification in last three years	*two years minimum*

A disqualification has two consequences. Firstly, it wipes the slate clean so that past penalty points no longer count. Secondly, it means that if there is another disqualification in the three-year period, then the court must impose a longer disqualification next time.

These minimum periods of disqualification apply in the vast majority of totting-up cases. But, the court does have a discretion, and it is allowed to impose a shorter period (or indeed, not to disqualify at all) if it can be persuaded that there are *mitigating circumstances*. This allows the court to take into account the personal circumstances of the motorist. But it must be emphasized that the court will look for serious and exceptional hardship if that is to be sufficient reason for not disqualifying. It will not be impressed by vague talk of hardship and inconvenience – it will want clear evidence of exceptional hardship.

'Mitigating circumstances' for not disqualifying under the totting-up rules should not be confused with 'special reasons' for not endorsing a licence (see above for 'special reasons'). The important restriction on 'special reasons' is that they must be special to the circumstances of how the offence was committed (e.g. laced drinks) and not to the offender himself (e.g. he is a commercial traveller). With 'mitigating circumstances' for not disqualifying, it is different – the personal circumstances of the motorist are relevant. Thus, every example on page 625 of what was *not* a 'special reason' could be a valid example of a 'mitigating circumstance' for not disqualifying.

Anyone who is facing disqualification under the totting-up rules should consider instructing a solicitor to argue his case, if he thinks he might be able to raise mitigating circumstances as to why he should not be disqualified.

Summary: endorsements, points, and totting-up

The sequence of events is:

1. The motorist is convicted of an endorsable offence (see the penalty chart on pages 637–46 to check whether an offence is endorsable or not).

2. The magistrates will then endorse his licence, unless he can show there are *special reasons* for not doing so (see page 625 for what counts as a special reason).

3. If his licence is endorsed, the magistrates will then impose penalty points. Refer to the penalty chart to see whether an offence does carry points. But, if no endorsement was ordered, then no points can be imposed.

4. If points are imposed, the magistrates will then go on to see whether he should also be disqualified, under the totting-up rules (i.e. 12 points in three years). If so, he will normally be disqualified for at least six months, unless he can show that *mitigating circumstances* apply (see page 626 for what this means).

Automatic disqualification for serious offences

There are two ways in which a motorist can be disqualified from driving. Firstly, he can be disqualified under the totting-up rules, i.e. because he has received 12 penalty points in the last three years (see above). Secondly, he may be disqualified for a single offence, if it is serious enough.

Some offences are so serious that they normally result in automatic disqualification. Drunk driving is the most well-known example. That offence and certain others (e.g. death by reckless driving) carry an automatic twelve months' (minimum) ban. However, even with these serious offences, the court can decide not to ban if there are 'special' reasons relating to the offence (e.g. laced drinks). Refer to page

625 for examples of what can be (and more important, what cannot be) special reasons. There are more examples of special reasons in the section on drunk driving, page 635.

Apart from these serious offences, when disqualification is the norm, the court often has power to ban if it wishes. A glance at the penalty chart (pages 637–46) will show that the court, surprisingly often, has the power to disqualify – if it wants to. In practice, of course, the court will only occasionally disqualify for these offences and much will depend upon the circumstances of the particular case. But there is a growing school of thought that a short period of disqualification can be a far more effective penalty than a fine, and so it is becoming more frequent for courts to impose short disqualifications for these offences. The sort of offences that come within this category are: failing to stop after an accident; driving while disqualified; crossing double white lines; reckless driving; deliberate no-insurance; speeding if more than 30 m.p.h. over the limit; traffic-light offences; and taking a vehicle without consent. In practice, the chances of disqualification vary enormously from court to court, and from offence to offence (e.g. about 1 per cent of traffic-light offenders are disqualified; about 2 per cent of those convicted of careless driving; and about 11 per cent of no-insurance offenders).

The effect of disqualification. If a court disqualifies, then the ban comes into effect immediately – the motorist cannot even drive home from the court-house to garage his car! If he defies the ban, and is caught, there is a fair chance of his going to prison (about a 10 per cent chance, if he is tried in the magistrates' court). Even when the period of disqualification ends, he cannot simply get in his car and start driving again: in any event he will have to get a new licence from the DVLC, at Swansea, and he may even have to take a driving test (if that was ordered by the court).

Removing the disqualification

A motorist who has been disqualified can apply to the court for the ban to be lifted early. The application is made to the court that imposed the ban and it will be for the offender to convince the court that his character and recent conduct justify the return of his licence; the seriousness of the original offence and any pressing reason why he needs his licence back will also be taken into account. The application cannot be made until at least two years have expired:

• *disqualified for under four years:* can apply after two years;
• *disqualified for four to ten years:* can apply when half the period has expired;
• *disqualified for over ten years:* can apply after five years.

When the court hears the application, the procedure is that the police outline the circumstances of the original offence (including any mitigating or aggravating circumstances). They will also say whether the applicant has been in trouble since his disqualification. Next, the applicant will be asked to state the grounds of his application, and why he needs to be able to drive. Usually, this will be because it will increase his chances of getting a job, in which case it is advisable to have strong supporting evidence from a prospective employer. Instead of removing the disqualification the magistrates may decide to simply reduce its length. Alternatively, of course, they may refuse to change the length of the ban (if so, the applicant cannot appeal, but he can apply again in three months' time).

The principal motoring offences

Reckless driving

Section 1 of the Road Traffic Act 1972 creates the offence of causing death by reckless driving, and section 2 covers reckless driving when death does not result.

For a motorist to be guilty of reckless driving, it must be shown that more than mere carelessness or bad driving was involved. The driving must have involved the motorist in knowingly taking an obviously serious risk. One judge has defined it as deliberately doing something knowing that there was a risk of losing control of the vehicle. In effect, the driving must have created an obvious risk – which the motorist did not give any thought to (or if he did realize the risks, then he simply carried on regardless). For instance:

A motor-cyclist sped through Lowestoft at about 75 m.p.h. He was in a 30 m.p.h. speed limit. He hit, and killed, a pedestrian. Held: This was reckless driving. It was such an excessive speed as to amount to a serious and obvious risk. Lawrence (1981)

The sort of situations that lead to a reckless driving charge (as opposed to the less serious charge of careless driving) are: a major accident caused by going through red lights; overtaking on a bend; going the wrong way on a dual carriageway, and so on.

Often the charge is brought with a charge of the lesser offence of 'careless driving' and it is then left to the court to decide whether the driving was so bad as to be reckless.

Reckless driving is an offence that can be tried in either the crown court or the magistrates' court (see page 785). The charge of causing death by reckless driving can only be heard in the crown court. Disqualification will always be considered and often the court will disqualify and order the offender to retake the driving test. A fine will also be imposed, and this is unlikely to be less than £250. If the motorist is not disqualified, then 10 points will normally be imposed. Refer also to the penalty table, page 643.

Careless driving

This offence derives from section 3 of the Road Traffic Act 1972, where it is described as driving 'without due care and attention, or without reasonable consideration for other persons using the road'.

This is a charge that is frequently brought after a minor accident. The test to be applied is: did the motorist exercise the care and attention that a prudent driver would have done? If the answer is 'no', he is guilty. Thus, bad driving can lead to a conviction even if there was no accident. Basically, even the most minor error of judgement will be careless driving, and although not every breach of the Highway Code will be sufficient for a conviction, the offence is one that it is easy to commit, for the 'prudent motorist' is assumed to observe the Highway Code. Many motorists commit the offence every day of the week. It is all a matter of degree. For instance, in the case of the motor-cyclist driving through Lowestoft at 75 m.p.h. (above), that was reckless driving; if he had been doing 40 m.p.h., then that would have been careless driving. Similarly, running into the back of the car in front is careless driving; but driving into the back of it at a high speed, after a dangerous overtaking manoeuvre, would be reckless driving.

Learner drivers doing their incompetent best are subject to the same standards as other drivers (see page 654). So, too, are the drivers of emergency vehicles. A policeman, fireman, or ambulance driver cannot, for instance, jump red lights; he is subject to the same standard of driving care as other road users.

A policeman answered an emergency call on a motorway. He drove along the hard shoulder and collided with a stationary lorry. The policeman was prosecuted for careless driving but argued that he was on an emergency call and so had a defence to the charge. Held: No. The policeman's standard of driving must be the same as that of other road users. There are no special standards for policemen. (Note that with speeding there is an exception, for emergency vehicles can exceed the speed limit if their use would otherwise be 'hindered'.) The policeman was guilty. However, the fact that he was on an emergency would be very relevant in determining what was the proper sentence. Wood (1977)

In practice, careless driving is a difficult charge to defend. Endorsement will be ordered unless there are special reasons. A fine of between £40 and £70 (plus 2–5 points) will usually be imposed (see the penalty chart, page 637).

The allied offence of inconsiderate driving covers the driver who (for example) does not bother to dip his headlights at night or does not slow down to avoid splashing pedestrians.

Speeding

The opinion of two people (whether policemen or not) is enough to secure a conviction. Alternatively, the court will usually accept the evidence of one policeman who followed the accused for three tenths of a mile and was watching a speedometer, or who noted the speed on radar equipment. If the limit was exceeded by only 5 m.p.h., the motorist will usually be let off with a caution.

Since speeding is an absolute offence, it is no defence to argue that the speeding did not cause danger to anyone; if the speeding was dangerous then the more serious charges of careless or reckless driving may also be brought.

In built-up areas, if the street lights are less than 200 yards apart one can be fairly sure that there is a 30 m.p.h. speed limit unless there is a sign to the contrary; if the lights are over 200 yards apart then it will usually be a de-restricted zone.

It is notoriously difficult to defend a speeding charge successfully. Police officers have little difficulty in finding motorists who are speeding and so it is difficult to persuade a court that the policeman is committing perjury and that the offence was not committed. Usually, it is alleged that the motorist was breaking the limit by at least 10 m.p.h. and so it is difficult to argue that there was a mistake, or that the policeman's speedometer was inaccurate. It is particularly difficult to defend the charge if the motorist was caught in a radar trap. Then the only hope is for the motorist to suggest that the police pulled in the wrong car, but few magistrates are impressed by such an argument.

A conviction will result in endorsement, and 3 penalty points, unless special reasons apply; see the penalty chart, page 644.

Taking a motor vehicle without consent

The Theft Act 1968 created a special offence of taking a vehicle without consent. This is because the normal charge of theft can only apply when the offender intended to *'permanently* deprive' the owner of his vehicle. Obviously, the joy-rider has no intention to permanently deprive, and so he cannot be guilty of theft (unless it is theft of the petrol used – but even that would not apply if he replaced the petrol).

The defendant will have a defence if he can show that he believed he had the owner's permission to take the vehicle, or that the owner would have consented had he known the circumstances. The defendant only has to prove one of these points on a 'balance of probabilities' (see page 759) to be acquitted.

If the owner's consent is obtained by trickery then the offender cannot be prosecuted for taking the vehicle, although he can be prosecuted for deception.

Endorsement is always ordered unless there are special reasons, and disqualification is common. Since joy-riders often damage the cars they borrow it is worth remembering that the court can order the offender to pay compensation to the victim. For the penalties, see the penalty chart, on page 646.

Parking

The mere absence of a 'no parking' sign does not mean parking is always permitted. Local by-laws will often lay down the details of parking zones and ignorance of these is no defence.

Similarly, the rules as to parking meters vary from place to place, but generally the motorist cannot feed the meter (i.e. add money for a second time) or move his car directly into a bay in the same group of meters (a different group will be marked by two white lines). When a ticket is written out, the motorist can opt to pay the fixed penalty (usually £10) within twenty-one days, and if he does so there will be no offence and no conviction. However, if he does not pay the fixed penalty and is subsequently fined in the magistrates' court, it will count as a criminal conviction and, theoretically, will need to be reported to his insurers before the policy is renewed. For meter-offence penalties, see the penalty chart, page 642.

If the parked car causes an obstruction the motorist can be prosecuted for the offence of obstructing the highway (see page 343). In practice, though, he is more likely to be charged with a breach of Regulation 114 of the Motor Vehicles (Construction and Use) Regulations 1973. This covers 'causing unnecessary obstruction of a road'. It is for the magistrates to decide whether the car did cause an 'unnecessary obstruction', but it can be applied strictly. For instance, in one case a taxi driver was found guilty when he had waited in the road to turn right, so holding up heavy traffic. In another case, a doctor who was answering an emergency call parked his car so as to cause an obstruction and was found guilty. Likewise, a motorist who boxed in another car by bad parking was convicted of causing an obstruction, and fined.

The offence is not endorsable, and the typical fine is about £20. If the obstruction involved a complete disregard for other people (e.g. blocking a fire-station access) a heavy fine would be imposed. See the penalty chart, page 641.

Failing to stop and give particulars after an accident

A motorist whose vehicle is involved in an accident must stop for long enough to allow the other people concerned to ascertain his name and address. Not only must he stop, but he must exchange particulars with anyone reasonably requesting them. In addition, even if the motorist does stop he may be obliged to report the accident to the police – and if he fails to do so this would be another charge that could be brought against him (see below).

The sensible motorist will, of course, stop after any accident, however small, and exchange particulars with anyone else involved. Legally, though, the obligation to stop and to provide particulars only exists if the accident caused:
• *injury* to anybody or to an animal (which is restricted to horse, cattle, ass, mule, sheep, pig, goat, or dog but not a cat), *or*
• *damage* to any vehicle (except the motorist's own car) or to other property which is attached to the road or adjoining land (e.g. if a wall, fence, tree, building, or street furniture is damaged).

So, to take an extreme example, a motorist who runs over a cat, and then collides with a piece of furniture left on the pavement, damaging both it and his own car, need not stop to provide particulars; nor, indeed, need he report the accident to the police.

If the motorist is obliged to stop he must give his name and address and that of the owner of the vehicle, plus the vehicle number, to anyone who reasonably requires it – in practice, other motorists and those who have suffered injury or damage. He is not required to give particulars of his insurance or to produce his driving licence. In practice, of course, the sensible motorist will do so, if only because by producing his insurance certificate he will usually remove the need for him to report the accident to the police (see below).

Both failure to stop and failure to provide particulars are endorsable offences, and an endorsement (plus 5–9 points) will be imposed unless there are special reasons (see page 625). If the motorist can satisfy the court that he did not realize there had been an accident he must be acquitted, but in practice that is a difficult defence to prove. See the penalty chart, page 637.

Failing to report an accident

An accident must be reported to the police if:

- someone was injured and at the time of the accident the motorist did not produce his insurance certificate to a policeman or someone reasonably entitled to ask for it, e.g. a traffic warden, someone injured, *or*
- he did not give his name and address at the time of the accident to someone reasonably entitled to ask for it.

So if full particulars were exchanged at the time of the accident (including insurance details if someone was injured) the motorist need not report the accident to the police. If there was no one present at the scene of the accident, and so there was nobody to ask for the particulars, the motorist must report it to the police.

If the accident has to be reported, the motorist should do so as soon as possible, and in no circumstances can he wait more than twenty-four hours. The accident must be reported in person – it is not good enough to phone the police station. If the motorist is found guilty of failing to report an accident, his licence will be endorsed (and he will receive 4–9 points) unless he can show special reasons for not endorsing.

Note: for what to do when there is an accident, see page 651.

Drunk driving

Every solicitor has a steady flow of clients who come into his office with a drunk-driving summons, expecting that some sort of defence can be put up to the charge. For the vast majority of these people, the best advice that can be given is to plead guilty and not waste money on legal fees. It may be a difficult fact for the disgruntled motorist to accept, but in the *overwhelming majority of drunk-driving cases there is no defence to the charge.*

In practical terms, once the police can show that the motorist was 'over the limit' then the chances of an acquittal are virtually nil. The only possible defences are based on legal and scientific technicalities – but these only apply in the most exceptional cases.

There are two basic offences: driving with excess alcohol; and being in charge of a car when suffering from excess alcohol. The 'being in charge' offence covers the motorist who is not driving – perhaps because he is so drunk that he is slumped across the steering-wheel.

The offence must have been committed in a public place. So, if the motorist was on private property all the time, no charge could be brought. In practice, of course, this is virtually inconceivable. Note that whether a place counts as 'private' or 'public' does not depend upon whether it is privately owned – if the public have access then it is likely to be a 'public' place (e.g. a pub car park is likely to be a public place during opening hours).

In theory, the police cannot carry out random breath tests. In practice, however, they need have very little justification to carry out a test – all the police need to show is that they had suspicions that the driver had consumed alcohol (note: they needn't have suspected that he was over the limit – it is enough that they suspect he has had some alcohol, and so merely leaving a pub car park may be sufficient grounds for suspicion). Alternatively, they can always carry out a test if there has been an accident or if the motorist has committed a moving-traffic offence (e.g. one wheel crossing over a white line). It can be seen that these powers are extensive, and whilst the police cannot simply set up random breath tests as and where they wish, they do – in practical terms – have more than sufficient powers to stop drunk drivers. The net effect is that it is almost impossible for a motorist to raise a legal defence based on the argument that the breath test was not legally justified.

Under the old breathalyser laws there were various technical defences that were successfully put up to breathalyser charges. However, the law was changed in 1983, with the result that it is now much more difficult to find a loophole. The net effect is that the drunk driver will almost certainly be convicted. For instance, there used to be a dodge known as the 'hip-flask defence', under which the motorist would have a quick drink between being stopped by the police and before having the breath test. Under the new law, the chances of that defence working have been drastically reduced since the motorist must now *prove* that he would otherwise have been under the limit – and in practical terms that is often very difficult to prove. Similarly, under the old law there were complicated procedural steps that the police had to take, and a minute breaking of those rules would make the breath test invalid; under the new rules, minor procedural mistakes are ignored.

The level of alcohol. There are various ways of measuring the alcohol level, but they are all equivalent. The motorist will be guilty if he has more than 80 milligrams of alcohol in 100 millilitres of blood; 107 milligrams of alcohol in 107 millilitres of urine; or 35 micrograms of alcohol in 100 millilitres of breath. In practice, it is the last of these three levels that is applied, usually via use of the Intoximeter machine. To avoid the risk of mistakes, the police do not prosecute if the breath reading is less than 40 micrograms (even though the legal requirement is only 35 micrograms). In practice, therefore, there is little chance of a motorist being wrongly convicted.

The penalty. A motorist convicted of driving with excess alcohol faces a maximum penalty of up to six months in prison, a fine of £2,000, and disqualification for at least one year. The penalties for being in charge of a vehicle (i.e. not driving) are less. Note that there is a separate offence to cover the motorist who refuses to provide a breath specimen – he is still likely to be disqualified. In practice, these maximum penalties are rarely imposed. But disqualification is nearly always ordered – and it will be for at least twelve months (three years if the second disqualification in a ten-year period). Refer to the penalty chart on page 638 for typical sentences for first-time offenders.

The crucial question for the motorist is not likely to be 'Will I be found guilty?' (because, in practice, he will almost certainly be found guilty), but 'Will I be disqualified?' Once again, the answer is that it is extremely likely that he will be disqualified. However, there are occasions when the court can agree that it would be wrong to disqualify, in which case there is no need to disqualify. This is when the court decides that there were *special reasons* surrounding the commission of the offence.

But the special-reasons argument can only be raised in a few cases. This is because the 'special reasons' must apply to the way in which the offence was committed – and not to the effect that disqualification will have on the motorist. (Refer back to page 625 where there is a section on what can be a special reason for not having an endorsement, since identical principles apply when arguing that there are special reasons for not disqualifying for drunk driving.) The essential point to grasp is that the special reasons must, in some way, explain how the offence was committed – they are not to be confused with the special circumstances of the individual motorist that would make disqualification particularly inconvenient for him.

In practice, few motorists are able to argue 'special reasons'. For instance, these are all examples of cases in which motorists were not able to show special reasons (and so they lost their licences):

- the defendant is a careful person who would not have driven had he realized that he had drunk too much;
- he is a diabetic;
- although he failed the breathalyser tests, his driving ability was unimpaired;
- the excess alcohol level in the defendant's blood or urine was very small;
- drinking on an empty stomach caused the drinks to have an unusually powerful effect.

However, a sudden emergency can amount to a special reason. But it is for the defendant to prove that he would not otherwise have driven, and that he was forced to do so by a sudden medical emergency. A mere errand of mercy, or other non-medical emergency, will not be a special reason. For instance:

A motorist had been drinking. He heard that his business partner was stranded with his aged and ailing mother in a remote part of the country, having run out of petrol. He went to fetch them but was breathalysed en route. Held: This was not an emergency, since a garage, the AA, the RAC, or the police could have assisted. Bains (1970)

The court considers the acuteness of the emergency, whether there was an alternative means of transport or help, and the standard of the defendant's driving.

Laced drinks can also be a special reason. But it is for the defendant to prove that his excess alcohol level is due to drinks that were put into his glass unknown to him. So in one case when a defendant thought he was drinking lager and lime, whereas in fact the drink contained vodka, he was able to claim a special reason and persuade the court not to disqualify him. The following was a borderline case:

Mr Krebs was given a Harp lager by a friend. His glass was refilled four times and Mr Krebs thought the refills were also Harp. In fact they were Löwenbrau, a stronger lager. When breathalysed, his reading was 92. Expert evidence was given that if the drinks had been Harp, as Krebs believed, the reading would have been only 20. Held: Mr Krebs had shown a 'special reason' and so he was not disqualified. Krebs (1977)

Motoring

Since drunk driving is an absolute offence, it makes no difference whether the prescribed limit is exceeded by a large or small amount; in either case the accused is guilty and the court will only consider the amount of the excess when deciding on the length of disqualification and the amount of the fine. Similarly, it is irrelevant that the drink consumed did not affect the driving of the accused. Disqualification is automatic on conviction (see penalty chart on page 638) for at least twelve months, unless the conviction is the motorist's second drunk-driving conviction in the last ten years, in which case the disqualification will be for at least three years.

Prison for drunk drivers. Occasionally, the courts have a blitz on drunk drivers. This will usually be in the run-up to Christmas, and the courts will get publicity by sending some first-time offenders to prison. The power to do this is based upon a 1980 Act which allows courts to impose up to four days' detention in police cells (i.e. not in prison). So a short sharp shock can be imposed.

Penalties for motoring offences: how to use the penalty chart

The penalty chart on the next few pages sets out the main motoring offences and gives rough guidelines for sentences on first offenders. It cannot be emphasized too strongly that these are no more than very approximate guidelines, and under no circumstances should they be seen as definite recommendations. Some courts are stricter, others softer. Each case depends upon its own facts – and upon the characters involved in it. The aim of the penalty chart is simply to give an approximate indication of the author's guess of 'going rates' in 1985.

Penalty Chart: Motoring Offences

Offence	Typical penalty for first offender	Penalty points	Compulsory endorsement?	Disqualification?
Accidents				
Failing to stop after accident	£125 fine, endorsement, and penalty points (or perhaps disqualification)	5–9	yes	at the court's discretion
Failing to report accident within twenty-four hours	£100 fine, endorsement, and penalty points	4–9	yes	at the court's discretion
Failing to produce certificate of insurance after accident	£15 fine	0	yes	at the court's discretion
Failing to give name and address after accident	£25 fine	0	yes	at the court's discretion
Careless driving				
Driving without due care and attention (careless driving)	£60 fine, endorsement, and penalty points	2–5	yes	at the court's discretion
Inconsiderate driving	£60 fine, endorsement, and penalty points	2–5	yes	at the court's discretion
Leaving vehicle without stopping engine or setting hand brake	£10 fine	0	no	no
Driver not in control of the vehicle	£10 fine	0	no	no
Reversing vehicle for an unreasonable distance	£10 fine	0	no	no

(Continued)

Offence	Typical penalty for first offender	Penalty points	Compulsory endorsement?	Disqualification?
Opening vehicle door causing injury or danger	£25 fine	0	no	no
Driving on footway	£10 fine	0	no	no
Driving in street designated as a play street	£10 fine	0	yes	at the court's discretion
Drink and drugs				
Driving with alcohol in the blood above the prescribed limit – 80 mg of alcohol in 100 ml of blood or 107 mg of alcohol in 100 ml of urine	£200 fine, endorsement, and one to three years' disqualification, depending on the excess amount of alcohol (e.g. eighteen months over 150 mg; two years over 200 mg; three years over 300 mg)	0 (usually)	yes	yes minimum twelve months
Failing to provide specimen of blood or urine for laboratory test	£120 fine, endorsement, and eighteen months' disqualification	0 (usually)	yes	yes, minimum twelve months
In charge of vehicle while unfit through drink or drugs	£75 fine, endorsement, and six months' disqualification	10	yes	at the court's discretion
Driving licence				
Driving while disqualified	£120 fine, but probably detention-centre or prison sentence instead	6	yes	at the court's discretion
Driving without a licence when no licence could have been granted	£20 fine and endorsement	2	yes	at the court's discretion

Causing or permitting a person to drive without a licence	£20 fine and endorsement	0	yes	at the court's discretion
Driving with uncorrected eyesight	£20 fine and endorsement	0	yes	at the court's discretion
Refusing to submit to an eyesight test	£20 fine and endorsement	0	yes	at the court's discretion
Failing to produce licence to police	£5 fine per document	0	no	no
Obtaining licence while disqualified	£50 fine	0	no	no
Failing to produce licence to court for endorsement	£20 fine	0	no	no
Forging licence	£50 fine	0	no	no
Making false statement to obtain licence	£50 fine	0	no	no
Failure to sign licence	£5 fine	0	no	no
Failure to state date of birth or sex when required	£10 fine	0	no	no
Insurance				
Using vehicle uninsured against third-party risks	£100 fine and endorsement (but if deliberate, then also disqualification, or 7–8 points)	4–8	yes	at the court's discretion
Forging insurance document	£100 fine	0	no	no

(Continued)

Offence	Typical penalty for first offender	Penalty points	Compulsory endorsement?	Disqualification?
Lighting				
When parked	£15 fine (£8 if lit road)	0	no	no
When moving	£50 fine (£25 if lit road)	0	no	no
Loads				
Causing danger by carrying too many passengers	£40 fine	3	yes	at the court's discretion
Causing danger by having an insecure load	£30 fine (higher if goods vehicle)	3	yes	at the court's discretion
Long and projecting loads	£75 fine	0	no	no
Exceeding the maximum gross weight or axle weight	£200 fine	0	no	no
Motorways				
Excluded traffic using a motorway	£40 fine, endorsement, and points	3	yes	at the court's discretion
Parking on hard shoulder	£20 fine (perhaps £15 on slip road)	0	no	no
Reversing vehicle, making U-turns, or driving in the wrong direction on main motorway	£150 fine, endorsement, plus points (might be disqualified for three months)	3	yes	at the court's discretion

Reversing vehicle, making U-turns, or driving in the wrong direction on slip roads	£50 fine and endorsement	0	yes	at the court's discretion
Vehicles over three tons using third lane	£60 fine and endorsement	3	yes	at the court's discretion
Walking on motorway or slip-road	£25 fine	0	no	no
Walking on hard shoulder or verge	£20 fine	0	no	no
Noises				
Sounding horn in a built-up area between 11.30 p.m. and 7 a.m.	£10 fine	0	no	no
Sounding horn when stationary	£10 fine	0	no	no
Noise caused by faulty silencer	£10 fine	0	no	no
Use of vehicle or trailer which causes excessive noise	£10 fine	0	no	no
Parking				
Leaving vehicle in a dangerous position	£25 fine, endorsement, and points	3	yes	at the court's discretion
Wilful or unnecessary obstruction	£15 fine	0	no	no
Failing to park on the nearside after dark	£15 fine	0	no	no

(Continued)

Offence	Typical penalty for first offender	Penalty points	Compulsory endorsement?	Disqualification?
Stopping on a clearway	£25 fine	0	no	no
Offences against waiting restrictions	£15 fine	0	no	no
Failure, without reasonable excuse, to make a statutory statement of ownership	£20 fine	0	no	no
Making a false statement of ownership	£50 fine	0	no	no
Failure to pay initial parking-meter charge	£15 fine	0	no	no
Exceeding excess period	£10 fine	0	no	no
Returning to a parking-meter bay within one hour	£10 fine	0	no	no
Parking on a suspended meter	£15 fine	0	no	no
Improperly parked	£10 fine	0	no	no
'Feeding' parking meter by putting in more coins	£20 fine	0	no	no
Failure to pay excess charge	£15 fine	0	no	no
Tampering with a meter	£25 fine	0	no	no

Pedestrian-crossings

Offence	Penalty	Points		
Breach of zebra regulations by a stationary vehicle	£25 fine, endorsement, and points	3	yes	at the court's discretion
Breach of zebra regulations by a moving vehicle	£30 fine, endorsement, and points	3	yes	at the court's discretion

Provisional licences

Provisional licence holder not accompanied by a qualified driver	£50 fine, endorsement, and points (and possible disqualification from driving)	2	yes	at the court's discretion
Provisional motor-cycle licence holder carrying a passenger who is not qualified	£25 fine, endorsement, and points (and possible disqualification from driving)	2	yes	at the court's discretion
Driving without L plates	£15 fine, endorsement, and points	2	yes	at the court's discretion

Reckless driving

Reckless driving	£300 fine, endorsement and six months' disqualification (or points)	10	yes	yes
Causing death by reckless driving	Penalty (will be severe) depends on circumstances	0 (usually)	yes	yes

Seat belts

Not wearing belt in front of car	£10 fine	0	no	no

(Continued)

Offence	Typical penalty for first offender	Penalty points	Compulsory endorsement?	Disqualification?
Child not wearing in front of car (driver liable)	£10 fine	0	no	no
Speeding				
Exceeding speed limit on a motorway	£2 fine for every mile per hour above speed limit (and possible disqualification if over 100 m.p.h.)	3	yes	at the court's discretion
Exceeding speed limit on other roads	£2 fine for every mile per hour above the speed limit, plus endorsement and points	3	yes	at the court's discretion
Exceeding goods-vehicle speed limit	£2 fine for every mile per hour above speed limit, plus endorsement and points	3	yes	at the court's discretion
Passenger-carrying vehicles limited to 50 m.p.h.	£2 fine for every mile per hour above speed limit, plus endorsement and points	3	yes	at the court's discretion
Traffic directions				
Disobeying a constable directing traffic	£25 fine, endorsement, and points	3	yes	at the court's discretion
Disregarding a school-crossing-patrol sign	£25 fine, endorsement, and points	3	yes	at the court's discretion
Disregarding traffic-light signals	£25 fine, endorsement, and points	3	yes	at the court's discretion

Disregarding a stop sign	£25 fine, endorsement, and points	3	yes	at the court's discretion
Disregarding double white lines	£25 fine, endorsement, and points	3	yes	at the court's discretion
Disregarding other road signs – for example, 'Give Way' and 'No Entry'	£20 fine	0	no	no
Vehicle condition				
Defective brakes	£50 fine, endorsement, and points	3	yes	at the court's discretion
Defective steering	£25 fine, endorsement, and points	3	yes	at the court's discretion
Defective tyres	£25 fine, endorsement, and points	3	yes	at the court's discretion
Tyres of different types fitted to the same axle	£25 fine, endorsement, and points	3	yes	at the court's discretion
Other vehicle parts in dangerous condition	£25 fine, endorsement, and points	3	yes	at the court's discretion
Windscreen not maintained so that driver's vision is obscured	£25 fine	0	no	no
No seat-belts or anchorage points	£25	0	no	no
Unladen weight not marked on goods vehicle	£25 fine	0	no	no

(Continued)

Offence	Typical penalty for first offender	Penalty points	Compulsory endorsement?	Disqualification?
Vehicle registration				
Failure to pay duty on motor-vehicle licence (i.e. no road tax)	fine of twice the unpaid duty (plus the unpaid duty)	0	no	no
Registration mark obscured or missing	£10 fine	0	no	no
Failure to register change of ownership	£50 fine	0	no	no
Fraudulent use of licence	£50 fine	0	no	no
No MoT certificate	£10 fine – more if over three months overdue	0	no	no
Vehicle theft				
Taking a vehicle	£100 fine, endorsement, and points (perhaps twelve months' disqualification). But if a passenger, then £75 (perhaps six months' disqualification)	8	yes	at the court's discretion

Motor cyclists

Typical penalties for the principal motor-bike offences are set out below. Note, in particular, that crash helmets are compulsory for both riders and passengers.

Motor-cycling offences

	Offence	Typical penalty for a first offender
Brakes	Riding or permitting use with defective brakes	£25 and endorsement
Helmet	Riding with no helmet – even as a pillion passenger	£25
Lights	Riding or permitting use with defective lights	£15 parked £20 moving
Mirror	Riding or permitting use of cycle first used after 1 October 1978 without rear-view mirror	£15
Noise	Adapting silencer to increase noise level	£20
Passenger	Carrying a pillion passenger without footrests	£15
	Carrying an unqualified pillion passenger when only a provisional-licence holder	£10 plus endorsement and 1 point
Speedometer	Riding or permitting use of motor cycle with no, or defective, speedometer	£10
Trailer	Towing a trailer by solo motor cycle	£20
Tyres	Riding or permitting use with defective tyre	£25 and endorsement for each tyre

Motoring

Cycling offences

	Offence	*Maximum fine*
Brakes	Riding or permitting use with defective brakes	£400
	Selling or offering for sale bicycle with defective brakes	£400
Lights	Riding or permitting use of bicycle with defective lights at night	£1,000
	Riding or permitting use of bicycle with defective lights in poor visibility	£1,000
Parking	Leaving bicycle in a dangerous position	£400
	Leaving bicycle on footpath	£400
	Leaving bicycle on clearway	£400
Riding	On footpath	£400
	Careless or inconsiderate riding	£50
	Reckless riding	£400
	Riding while unfit	£400
	Taking hold of another vehicle	£50
	Carrying a passenger	£50
	Unauthorized racing	£50
Signs and signals	Disobeying signal given by police constable or traffic warden	£400
	Disobeying traffic signs, traffic lights, or white lines	£400
	Failing to accord precedence to pedestrian, or overtaking on approach to crossing	£400

Cyclists

Cyclists are subject to the same laws as other road users and, although they cannot be imprisoned or disqualified, they can be fined. For instance, a cyclist who disobeys a policeman's signal is subject to the same maximum fine, £400, as a car driver.

There are, of course, various provisions that apply only to cyclists. Points worth noting include:

- a dismounted cyclist who is pushing his bike is legally a 'rider', not a 'pedestrian'. Thus, he commits an offence if he wheels his bike past red traffic lights. However, there is an exception for cyclists who wheel their bikes over pedestrian crossings; for those purposes they are not cycling.
- cycles are subject to special parking controls. It is illegal to leave a bike in a dangerous position, on a footpath, or on a traffic clearway. But cyclists need not obey painted yellow lines; thus a cyclist can leave his bike on the kerb beside a double yellow line unless it is a dangerous position or a clearway.
- a cyclist can be convicted of being drunk in charge of a bike. But the normal breathalyser laws do not apply, and of course there can be no disqualification (merely a fine of up to £400).

43 Road Accidents

Most drivers like to think that accidents happen to other people and not to them. This is, of course, nonsense. Even the most careful motorist can be involved in an accident and it is only sensible to know what to do when an accident occurs.

See page 651 for what to do and what not to do when an accident happens.

The lawyer's basic advice is 'say nothing – write down everything'. Remember that responsibility for the accident (and for the resulting losses, expenses, and injuries) will depend upon who was to blame. What the motorist says in the heat of the moment can be distorted and used against him in a court months or even years later. For instance, most people's natural inclination when speaking to a person injured by a collision with their car is to say 'I'm sorry', but this can easily be misconstrued as meaning 'I am sorry I caused the accident', rather than 'I am sorry you have been injured'.

The motorist should take a note of the names and addresses of the other parties. Vehicle registration numbers and insurance details should also be recorded, if possible. The names and addresses of witnesses should also be obtained or, failing that, a note should be made of their car numbers so they can be traced through the Vehicle Records Office (see page 892). All the details of the accident should be recorded. There should be a sketch plan showing the positions of all vehicles, road signs, road widths, obstructions to vision, position of witnesses, the location of any wreckage or debris, and so on. It is also useful to make a note of the road and weather conditions, the damage to other vehicles, and the apparent extent of anybody's injuries.

The cars should not be moved until their positions have been recorded on a plan or marked on the road surface; evidence as to the point of impact is often crucial in working out how an accident occurred and whose fault it was.

Unless the accident is trivial, it is advisable to call the police, although they are not obliged to attend and may refuse to do so if there are no injuries and if the damage is small. If the police do attend, it is advisable to make a note of the officers' numbers. The police will probably ask those involved to make short statements, but the motorist should remember that what he says will be written down and a copy will eventually be supplied to the other motorist's insurers and lawyers. That being so, it is best to say nothing at this stage, beyond politely explaining to the policeman that one would rather not make a statement for the moment. However, the policeman can demand to be told the motorist's name and address (and that of the owner, if different), plus the vehicle, insurance and MoT particulars; this information should obviously be provided if requested.

If you are involved in a road accident

Don't

- assault or abuse the other driver;
- apologize, offer excuses, or say anything that could later be used to suggest that you admitted responsibility for causing the accident – unless, of course, you clearly were to blame;
- move the vehicles until their positions have been recorded;
- make a statement to the police at this stage; wait until you have calmed down. However, you are obliged to give your name, address, and vehicle registration number, and to produce your driving licence, MoT certificate and (if anyone has been injured) your insurance certificate (see page 632).

Do

- stop;
- call the police and note number of policeman attending;
- note names and addresses of everyone involved: the other drivers must give you their names, addresses, and vehicle registration numbers, and (if anyone has been injured) produce insurance certificates; similarly, you must provide them with this information on request;
- ask witnesses for their names and addresses; if these are not available note their vehicle registration numbers if they are in cars, so that they can be traced at a later date;
- write down any comments or explanations made by any party to the accident or by a witness;
- note the apparent damage to any vehicles and the apparent extent of injuries suffered.

Afterwards

- while the facts are still fresh in your mind, make a full description of exactly what happened; note time, road conditions, road layout, signposts, damage to vehicles, any vision obstructions, other traffic, road markings, point of impact, etc.; if you have a camera, take photos;
- report the accident to your insurance company;
- write to the motorist who is to blame, claiming damages for any loss, expenses, and injury suffered.

Reporting the accident

To whom should the accident be reported? If the police attend then there will be no need to notify them, but if they did not attend and particulars were not given to the other people involved, then the accident will have to be reported as soon as possible. See page 632 for the duty to stop after an accident, to provide particulars to other people, and to report the accident to the police.

It will also be necessary for the motorist to report the accident to his insurers. Most policies require that the accident be reported within seven days or else the insurance will not cover that accident or future accidents. Further, if the policy is renewed with no mention of the accident having been made to the insurers, then the motorist will not have acted in 'perfectly good faith' and so the insurers will be able to declare that the policy is invalid (see page 559). 'Reporting' an accident to insurers is, of course, different from 'claiming' under the policy and will not, itself, affect the motorist's no-claims bonus. For a specimen letter to the insurance company, see page 612.

When filling in the insurer's accident report form, the motorist should be perfectly honest and provide them with all the information that supports his version of how the accident happened. If the accident was not his fault then he should say so clearly and unambiguously. The accident report form will contain questions similar to those asked when the proposal form was completed on the insurance being taken out. The insurers may well compare the two sets of answers to check that the motorist has not been in breach of the policy in any way (e.g. by using the car for unauthorized business travel) and that full and truthful answers were given when the insurance was first taken out. Any discrepancies may allow the insurers to 'repudiate liability' under the policy and so refuse to meet any claims (see page 610).

Apportioning the blame

A motorist who has been involved in a road accident will only recover compensation for his injuries, losses, and other damage if he has a comprehensive policy or if he can show that someone else was to blame for the accident.

If he has a comprehensive policy. Generally if he claims on the policy he will lose part of his no-claims bonus and he will have to pay the excess – the first few pounds of the claim. If the motorist has a third-party policy it will only indemnify him for damages due to other people as a result of his own negligent driving; it will not compensate him for his own losses, however caused.

If he can show that someone else was to blame for the accident. If so, he will be able to claim from that person's insurers.

So unless a motorist has a comprehensive policy he will have no automatic right to compensation. Generally, therefore, the right to compensation will be dependent upon showing that someone else was to blame for the accident; if that can be proved, then that person (and his insurers) will have to pay compensation.

Before dealing with the mechanics of making a claim against another motorist, one must first understand how the law apportions and fixes 'blame' for motoring accidents.

'Negligence'

The law says that every motorist has a duty to take reasonable care to avoid injury, loss, and damage to other road users; if he does not, he must compensate those other road users for the injury, loss, and damage incurred. In short, he must pay them damages for his negligence.

The problems arise when one tries to apply that seemingly simple idea to practical events, for it is always a question of deciding whether or not the duty to take care has been broken. Clearly, if the 'reasonable' man would not have acted as the motorist did, then there will have been a breach of the duty of care, and thus negligence – but the concept of the (mythical) 'reasonable' man is not as simple as it sounds. As a starting-point, ask yourself 'Who was to blame, bearing in mind that the "reasonable" motorist never disobeys the Highway Code and is always alert to the possibility of other motorists being less careful than they should be?' Usually, common sense will supply the answer. Frequently, an accident will not be due to the 'negligence' of just one motorist; the other motorist(s) may have contributed to the accident by being less careful than they should have been, and so they are – to a degree – to blame themselves. In such cases, the law apportions the blame between the motorists and each will lose a corresponding proportion of his damages for this 'contributory negligence'.

Illustration. *A Ford pulls up and a Vauxhall runs into the back of it. Every motorist has a 'duty of care' to drive in such a way that he can pull up in an emergency without hitting the car in front. The Vauxhall's driver is in breach of this duty and thus negligent, and so liable to pay damages to the Ford's owner.*

But suppose the accident occurred on the motorway and that the Ford stopped in the carriageway without giving any signal. Then the Ford's driver would have been in breach of his duty, firstly, not to stop on the motorway and, secondly, to signal his intentions, whilst the Vauxhall would have been in breach of his duty to keep a lookout for obstructions on the road and to take avoiding action. Thus, a court might find both sides equally to blame and give them both only 50 per cent of their full damages.

However, suppose that the Ford had pulled up at a pedestrian crossing, and that the Vauxhall's driver had seen this and tried to brake but hit the Ford because of a brake failure. If the Vauxhall owner had no way of knowing that the brakes were faulty, and had his car serviced regularly, he could not be said to be to blame. He had taken 'reasonable care to avoid injury, loss, and damage to other road users' and this accident arose through an entirely unforeseeable failure of his brakes. Thus, the Vauxhall would not be negligent and the Ford could not recover damages from him. The only way the Ford would be able to recover any compensation is if he could:

(a) *claim under his own comprehensive policy (but this would cost him his excess and no-claims bonus), or*

(b) *show that someone else, other than the Vauxhall, was negligent and that this negligence caused what was a reasonably foreseeable accident. For example, if the Vauxhall was new then the Ford might have a claim against the Vauxhall manufacturers because they were in breach of their duty to the general public to fit sound brakes to new cars. Alternatively, if the Vauxhall was not new, a garage that had recently serviced its brakes might owe a duty to the Ford's driver (as a road user) to ensure that the Vauxhall brakes were working correctly.*

Motoring

All road users, whether motorists or pedestrians, have a duty to take care. For instance, if a careless pedestrian is injured by a careless driver, then the pedestrian will forfeit some, if not all, of his damages.

Mrs Clifford stepped on to a pedestrian crossing when Mr Drymond's car was some 25–30 yards away, and travelling at 26–30 m.p.h. She was hit by the car when she was on the crossing. Held: Mr Drymond was negligent because the reasonable motorist keeps a proper lookout for pedestrians when approaching a pedestrian crossing. But Mrs Clifford was also negligent because the reasonable pedestrian does not step on to a crossing without first checking that oncoming cars can stop in time. Liability was apportioned with Mr Drymond being 80 per cent to blame and Mrs Clifford 20 per cent to blame. So Mrs Clifford only recovered 80 per cent of the normal damages. Clifford (1976)

What about learners?

The duty of care owed by a learner driver is the same as that owed by any other 'reasonable' motorist. The learner cannot escape liability by arguing that he was doing his incompetent best.

Mr Nettleship agreed to give Miss Weston driving lessons. She was a careful learner but on the third lesson she failed to straighten out after turning left; the car hit a lamp standard and Mr Nettleship's kneecap was broken. He sued Miss Weston for damages but she argued that she was not in breach of her duty to take care – she had taken all the care that she, as a learner, could take. Held: No. She was liable. As a motorist, she was required to drive to the standard of the 'reasonable' motorist, not the 'reasonable learner motorist'. Nettleship (1971)

Breaking the Highway Code

Generally, the fact that a motorist did not obey the Highway Code will be a good starting-point for fixing blame. But it does not always follow that the 'reasonable road user' would have observed the Highway Code and so negligence may not attach. For instance:

Miss Powell was struck by a car while walking along the left-hand side of the road at night. She had not been walking on the pavement because it was covered by snow, and she was not wearing light-coloured clothes. The car had been travelling quickly and without proper lights. The motorist argued that she was 25 per cent to blame for not observing the Highway Code. Held: No. Whilst she was in breach of the Highway Code she had not been negligent, and so she recovered 100 per cent damages from the negligent motorist. Powell (1972)

Mechanical defects

The essence of attaching blame is that the defendant failed to take proper care. Generally, therefore, if an accident happens because of a latent mechanical defect that he could not have known of, he cannot be liable in negligence. However, it will be for the defendant to show that he took all necessary steps to stop the danger arising, for otherwise he will be liable.

A five-year-old lorry suffered a brake failure and killed George Henderson. His widow sued the owners of the lorry for negligence. They argued that they were not to blame since the accident had been caused by a latent defect in the brakes. They had visually inspected the brakes every week, but the failure occurred in a hidden pipe that could not be seen. Held: They were liable, since they had not conclusively shown that they had taken all steps to avoid the risk of brake failure. Henderson (1969)

On the other hand:

Mr Saville bought a seven-year-old car (which had done about 75,000 miles) for £650. It went well enough; there were no odd noises, and it had eight months' MoT left. Three weeks later he lost control of the steering and crashed into a parked car. Examination then showed that the steering arm had collapsed. Was he liable (in practice, of course, was his insurance company liable) in damages to the owner of the parked car? Held: No. In the circumstances, he had acted reasonably since he had no reason to think there was any problem with the car. It was unreasonable to expect anyone who bought a car with a recent MoT to have it examined by an expert engineer. So, he was not to blame – and the innocent motorist went uncompensated. Rees (1983)

When both motorists could have been to blame

Often there is no clear proof of who was to blame, perhaps because there were no witnesses and the drivers cannot clearly recall what happened. When this happens, liability is often divided fifty-fifty between them and they both recover half their normal damages from each other. This is often applied when two vehicles meet head-on in a narrow country road or collide at cross-roads of equal status.

Two cars collided head-on at night; there were no witnesses and one driver was killed and the other was so seriously injured that he had no recollection of what happened. There was no evidence of what happened apart from marks on one side of the road. Held: it was no more probable that the accident had occurred on one side of the road than in the middle of the road, and accordingly both drivers were equally to blame. Both had to pay 50 per cent damages. Howard (1973)

Flashing headlights

It is common for motorists to flash their headlights as a 'come on' sign; what happens if a driver obeys the signal only to find that it is not safe to do so and collides with another motorist? The answer is that the mere flashing of lights does not absolve that motorist from his normal duty of care to other road users. In fact the motorist who is hit by the car will usually be able to sue the motorist who acted on the flashing lights, and occasionally even the motorist who negligently flashed his lights when it was not safe. However, this presupposes (as always) that they were negligent, but exceptionally this will not be so:

A car was in a side street, waiting to cross a congested main road. A bus driver in the main road stopped and flashed his headlights at the car to indicate that he would let him cross. The car pulled out very slowly but collided with a motor-cyclist that was overtaking the stationary bus. Could the motor-cyclist sue the car driver and/or the bus driver? Held: No. On the particular facts of the case neither driver had been negligent. The car driver had come out with very great care and so did nothing wrong. The bus driver was also not negligent because the court held that the flashing of lights did not mean 'it is safe for you to cross', but merely 'come on as far as I am concerned'. The motor-cyclist did not receive any compensation. Clarke (1969)

Not wearing seat-belts

Whilst every road user has a duty to take care not to harm other people, he also has a duty to look after himself. An obvious way of reducing the severity of injuries received in a car accident is to wear a seat-belt; a person who does not do so will probably be held not to have taken sufficient care to look after himself. Thus, he too will have been negligent and so any damages he receives will be reduced proportionately to allow for his own negligence.

This assumes, of course, that there were seat-belts fitted to the car, and also that wearing the seat-belt would have minimized the injuries. If it can be shown that the seat-belt would not have prevented injury, then the negligence in not wearing it will be ignored as being irrelevant. But such cases are rare and the general rule is that failure to wear a seat-belt will result in a 25 per cent reduction in damages.

Mr Froom was injured in a car crash but he was not wearing the seat-belt fitted to his car. He suffered head and chest injuries and also a broken finger. The medical evidence was that, apart from the broken finger, the injuries would probably have been prevented if he had been wearing the seat-belt. In reply, Mr Froom argued that he did not like wearing a belt for fear of being trapped in the vehicle after a crash and, besides, he did not drive at more than normal speed. Held: The reasonable motorist guards against the possibility of negligence by other road users by wearing a seat-belt, since statistics show that the chance of injury increases fourfold when a seat-belt is not worn. Where injuries would have been totally prevented by wearing a seat-belt, the damages should be reduced by 25 per cent. When the injuries would have been 'a good deal less severe', the damages should be reduced by 15 per cent. In Mr Froom's case a reduction of 20 per cent should be made. Froom (1975)

For the criminal penalties on not wearing seat-belt, see page 615.

When the negligent motorist cannot be traced

The victim of a hit-and-run accident may have no one to sue, since the negligent motorist will have disappeared. Similarly, if the motorist stopped but gave false particulars, the victim will be unable to sue him.

When this happens the Motor Insurers' Bureau (MIB) will compensate him. The MIB is funded by the insurance industry and it will nominate an insurance company to deal with the claim as though the untraced motorist was insured with them. However, as with claims against uninsured motorists, the claim must be restricted to compensation for personal injury and consequential loss, rather than direct financial loss (e.g. the value of a car written off in the accident). See page 612.

Changing the 'negligence' basis of compensation

Under our legal system the victim of a road accident has no automatic right to compensation. Unless he can show that someone else was to blame for the accident his only source of financial help is likely to be DHSS benefits such as sickness benefit, and perhaps some compensation from his insurance company if he was a motorist with a comprehensive insurance policy. If no one else can be blamed for the accident, then the law will not entitle him to receive compensation.

A five-year-old boy ran out into the road from behind a parked car; he was running to an ice-cream van on the other side of the road. He was seriously injured by a passing car – even though the car was only travelling at 15 m.p.h. He sued (through his parents), arguing that the motorist had been negligent. Held: The motorist had not been negligent and so the little boy was not entitled to any compensation. The only way the motorist could have avoided hitting the boy would have been if he had been driving at 5 m.p.h. It was not reasonable to expect that, and so he was not liable. The five-year-old went without compensation. Kite (1983)

Even if the injured person can show that someone else was to blame he may be held to have been negligent himself and so forfeit some of his damages. For instance, the motorist who does not wear his seat-belt is likely to lose between 15 and 25 per cent of his damages (see page 656).

The present system of compensation based on blame and negligence denies compensation to thousands of people every year. There are some 400,000 road-accident injuries every year, including 7,600 fatal accidents. Of these, only about one quarter of the victims obtain compensation. The others either are unable to show that anyone else was negligent or do not bother to sue – presumably because of the costs and delay involved.

The remedy would seem to be to abolish the present system of compensation based on negligence. This has been done in New Zealand. The Pearson Commission investigated the possibility of abolishing our negligence system in 1978, but it came out with a compromise solution – introduce a far more generous welfare benefit for all road-accident victims, but retain the negligence principle. Many commentators felt that this compromise was not what was needed and that instead an injury board should be created to compensate the victims of all accidents in the same way that the Criminal Injuries Compensation Board compensates victims of violent crime (see page 717). At present, there are no plans to implement the Pearson proposals.

Claiming compensation

If you intend to make a claim against another road user, then:

1. Drive or tow the car home or to a garage and keep any towage receipt.
2. Report the accident to your own insurers. If you have a comprehensive policy, notify them that no claim is being made against them (see letter on page 612).
3. If the claim is substantial or involves anything other than very minor personal injury, consult a solicitor. If the claim is successful, and it is for more than £500, the other side will have to pay most of your legal costs (see page 843).

4. Ask the garage for a written estimate of the cost of repairs. If the vehicle is a write-off ask for their written confirmation that it is 'beyond economical repair', and their estimate of its pre-accident value.
5. Write to the other motorist claiming damages. A typical letter might read:

I refer to the accident on — at — involving motor car no.— This accident was caused by your negligent driving of a motor vehicle and accordingly damages are claimed for the personal injury, losses, expenses, and inconvenience arising therefrom.

The wreckage is at present with Messrs — at — and can be inspected by you or your insurers on an appointment being made with Mr —. Please ensure that an inspection is made within the next fourteen days, failing which the necessary repairs will be put in hand (or the wreckage will be disposed of).

Yours faithfully

6. Keep a full note of all losses and expenses arising out of the accident.
7. Do not have the repairs carried out until you are fairly sure that the insurers will meet the cost or that your claim will be successful, for the garage bill will be your responsibility.

The insurers will be evasive and slow correspondents; but do not let them slow down the handling of the claim – if necessary, you should pester them with letters. If the repairs will involve replacing worn parts with new parts, the insurers will expect you to pay 'betterment' (i.e. a contribution to the cost) since the car will now be in a better condition than it was before the accident. They are entitled to insist on such a contribution (see page 562) but always check that they are not charging too much.

8. Alternatively, if the vehicle is a write-off, try to agree a figure for its pre-accident value. Use local-newspaper advertisements and garage estimates to support your valuation. Also check your insurance proposal form to see what valuation you placed on the car then. Do not be unrealistic about the valuation; insurance engineers can accurately assess the pre-accident condition of a vehicle from the wreckage and will detect untrue statements about the car's recorded mileage, interior condition, etc. Once the insurers agree that the vehicle is 'beyond economical repair' then take steps to dispose of the wreckage, for the insurers will not be liable for storage charges as from that date.

It may be that you cannot afford to buy a replacement vehicle until the insurance moneys are received. But you probably cannot recover extra compensation for the increased period of inconvenience when you are without a car, nor for the cost of interest on money borrowed to buy the replacement car. As far as the law is concerned, your financial status (or lack of it) is irrelevant and the defendant should not have to pay higher damages just because you are hard up.

9. If the car has been repaired, you will generally be expected to pay the garage and to recover the amount afterwards from the insurers. Losses and expenses incurred in collecting the car will form part of the claim.
10. Formulate the amount of the claim. Include all losses and expenses reasonably incurred as a result of the accident, unless they are too unlikely. Items that can be legitimately claimed include the cost of travel home after the accident, travel

to pick up the car, wages lost, stamps, telephone calls, private medical fees, prescriptions, new clothing to replace clothing damaged in the accident (but allow something for the fact that the damaged clothing was not new), cost of hiring a replacement vehicle (it must be of a suitable type, i.e. a Mini owner shouldn't hire a Rover), and also losses and expenses incurred by members of your family, although strictly speaking, they should be separate claims. If a vehicle isn't hired while the damaged car is being repaired, then claim the cost of bus, rail, and taxi fares incurred, plus a small amount for inconvenience. However, allowance must be made for the money saved on not having to buy petrol, oil, etc. A figure of £20 p.w. for inconvenience and compensation for loss of use of the car is generally reasonable.

If possible, all these items of expense should be proved by receipts. Wage losses can be proved by a letter from the employer setting out the net (i.e. after-tax) loss. If any DHSS benefits were received (such as sickness benefit, invalidity benefit) as a result of the accident, then one half of their total should be deducted from the wage loss; unemployment and supplementary benefits are deducted in full when working out the wage loss.

Set out all these financial losses (called 'special damage' by lawyers) in list form and send them to the insurers. If there was any injury sustained in the accident, try to negotiate a suitable figure for that as well, but it is important to remember that all but the most trivial personal-injury claims should be handled by a solicitor. As a layman you may, unwittingly, settle your case for less than it is worth or you may not appreciate that what seems to be a trivial injury could have serious long-term consequences.

11. The insurers will probably handle the claim very slowly. If you have a claim that is sound on liability (i.e. the other motorist was definitely to blame) you may well find it best to commence county-court proceedings against the other motorist. This will almost certainly cause the insurance company to deal with the claim without any further delay. The steps to be taken to sue in the county court are set out on page 872. The specimen pleadings on pages 911–12 are from a claim arising out of a minor road accident.

Insurance brokers

Sometimes a motorist's insurance broker will offer to negotiate the claim with the insurance company for him. The motorist should check, in advance, what the broker's fee will be.

These brokers do not have to belong to a professional body and accordingly the motorist should try to ensure that his broker is competent and honest, for otherwise he may find that his claim has been under-settled. If the accident involved any personal injury it is advisable to use a solicitor rather than a broker.

If the broker cannot negotiate a proper settlement and the next step is to start court proceedings, he will no longer be able to act; only a solicitor can sue on behalf of someone else. There is thus a temptation for brokers to under-settle claims and so recover commission when a solicitor might have commenced proceedings and ended up with a larger amount of compensation for his client.

On-the-spot settlements

When the accident happens the negligent motorist may offer the innocent motorist an immediate cash settlement on a 'let's not bother with the police' basis. If a motorist is offered such a settlement he should reject it. Firstly, it may be an offence not to report the accident to the police (see page 633), and secondly, the claim may be worth much more than he is being offered; only when a mechanic has inspected the car and a doctor checked any injuries should such a settlement be contemplated. Whether or not the offer is accepted, the accident will still need to be reported to the motorist's own insurers (see page 612).

The negligent motorist who offers an on-the-spot settlement may do so because he wants to retain his no-claims bonus. If so, he should settle the claim by writing to the other motorist as follows:

I refer to the motor accident at — on —. As agreed, although I am not admitting any liability, I am prepared to pay you £— in full and final settlement of all your claims arising from that accident, and accordingly I enclose a cheque for that amount. Please acknowledge safe receipt by signing the attached copy of this letter and returning it to me.

This ensures that the other motorist cannot come back and claim more money at a future date.

PART SIX

CIVIL LIBERTIES AND THE WELFARE STATE

44 Police Powers and Individual Liberty

Here we are concerned with the law's futile attempt to reconcile two contradictory aims – firstly, the need to catch criminals and, secondly, the desire to allow citizens to go about their business without interference by the police.

The law has never satisfactorily come to terms with the problem. The law is often very confused and obscure on some of these 'civil liberty' issues but, frequently, it seems that the courts are prepared to ignore what few rights the individual has if it will help the police to catch wrongdoers. So the citizen who proclaims 'I know my rights' is probably unaware of just how limited those rights are.

Helping the police

The general rule is that no one is obliged to help the police with their inquiries. It may be one's social or even moral duty to do so but there is no law which says that one must; all the law requires is that one should not give false information to the police or waste police time (anyone who does is liable to a fine of up to £200 and up to six months' imprisonment).

But of course most people do help the police; if everyone stood on their constitutional rights and refused to cooperate, the task of the police would become impossible.

When the police stop someone in the street and ask him to 'come down to the station and help us with our inquiries', that request can be refused. The only way the police can make someone accompany them to the police station is to *arrest* him, and that can only be done in certain circumstances (see page 777). As Lord Devlin has put it: 'You may sometimes read in novels and detective stories . . . that persons are sometimes taken into custody for questioning. There is no such power in this country. A man cannot be detained unless he is arrested.' But few people know that this is the law and of course the police do not tell suspects of their right to refuse to go to 'the station'.

The Police and Criminal Evidence Act 1984 tidied up the rules on the treatment of people who are 'helping the police with their inquiries'. But it still preserves the right of the suspect to refuse to help the police with their inquiries – and to leave the police station. The Home Office Code (issued under that Act) says:

Any person attending a police station voluntarily for the purpose of assisting with an investigation may leave at will unless placed under arrest. If it is decided that he should not be allowed to do so then he must be informed at once that he is not under arrest. ... If he is not placed under arrest but is cautioned ... the officer who gives the caution must immediately inform him that he is not under arrest and is free to leave if he wishes and remind him that he may obtain legal advice if he wishes.

So the basic rule is that the police can only keep someone in the police station if they arrest him or if he voluntarily agrees to being held by them. (But see 'Searching Someone', page 670.)

A suspect's rights

Police questioning

If a person agrees to help the police (or if he is arrested), there are rules of conduct governing the manner in which he is to be questioned. The Police and Criminal Evidence Act 1984 sets out basic guidelines that have to be followed, and these are backed up by a detailed Home Office Code on the Detention, Treatment and Questioning of Detainees (generally called The Detention Code). The code sets out the rules that the police should follow, but these rules are not totally binding on the police. So if a policeman conducts an interview that does not follow the rules, it does not necessarily follow that the evidence obtained will be inadmissible – that is for the trial judge to decide. The judge will probably only rule it out if it would be oppressive or unfair to include it.

Rights on detention

As soon as a suspect is detained, he must be told why – and also that he has:
- the right to see a solicitor (see page 668);
- the right to have someone told of his detention (see page 669);
- the right to look at the Code of Practice that the police should follow (in particular, to read the detailed Detention Code – see above).

In addition, the custody officer (i.e. the policeman responsible for all detained suspects – a different policeman from the one dealing with the suspect's case) must give him a written note of these three legal rights. That written note will also give him the usual caution (i.e. 'You do not have to say anything unless you wish to do so, but what you say may be given in evidence.')

Police questioning

A suspect cannot be made to help the police: if he simply refuses to answer the police questions then there is nothing (in theory, anyway) that the police can do about it. Firstly, there is a fundamental legal principle which says that a suspect's silence is not to be held against him – in other words, the mere fact that he did not answer questions is not to be used as an argument that he must have something to hide! Secondly, the police should not use force or pressure to get answers to their questions. For instance, the code says: 'No police officer may try to obtain answers to questions . . . by the use of oppression, or shall indicate, except in answer to a direct question, what action will be taken if . . . the person makes a statement or refuses. . . .'

There are other rules that the police have to observe, many of which are aimed at ensuring that unfair pressure is not put on suspects. For instance, cells must be clean. There should be two light meals, and one main meal, each day. The suspect must be allowed at least eight hours' rest each day; interview rooms must be properly heated; suspects are not to be made to stand; there must be a break from interviewing at normal meal times and – as a general rule – there should be short refreshment breaks every two hours. The code sets out extremely detailed guidelines that should be followed. Another safeguard for the accused is that the police must give him a verbal 'caution'. The caution reminds the suspect of his fundamental legal right to not answer the police question – 'you do not have to say anything unless you wish to do so, but what you say may be given in evidence.' If the suspect has not been arrested, but is merely 'helping the police with their inquiries' (i.e. voluntarily agreeing to be questioned – see above), then the caution must also remind him of his other fundamental legal right: the right to leave the police station if he wishes (and also to take legal advice).

To summarize: The caution always tells the suspect that he does not have to answer questions. But if the suspect has not been arrested, then he must also be told that he is free to leave if he wishes. The caution has to be repeated at various stages of the police investigation. In particular, it has to be given (and repeated):

● when a suspect is arrested;

● when a suspect is about to be interviewed; *and*

● if there is a short break in the interview then he must be reminded he is still under caution when the interview restarts. If the break is of more than an hour, then the whole caution must be repeated.

Many lawyers with large criminal practices say that the police often ignore these rules. Certainly, there is some evidence that the rules are not always followed. If the police should conduct their questioning in an improper manner, it is usually almost impossible for the suspect to prove afterwards that the rules were broken. And, of course, even if he can prove that the rules were not followed, the judge who hears his case may still allow the evidence against him to be heard.

Statements

A suspect need not give a statement to the police and, unless there is a straight-forward explanation, he is usually best advised to 'say nothing'. There are several reasons for this:

● he will probably be upset and shaken at having been held in a police station and questioned. It would be unwise to make a statement in this disturbed condition – much better to wait until he has received legal advice and had a day or two in which to recover his composure.

● the statement will probably reveal how he intends to defend himself should the case go to court. Since the whole procedure at a criminal trial is based on the adversarial principle of 'your side' against 'their side', it is obviously bad tactics to reveal one's case this early in the proceedings.

• if the suspect does make a statement he should check it is accurate, or write it out himself (and so avoid arguments about its accuracy).

Obviously, the police will urge the suspect to make a statement, but he should not be afraid to insist on his legal right to remain silent – even if it means that he remains in custody for a longer period. For instance, the police may refuse to grant him 'police bail', which may mean that he has to stay in custody overnight (see page 781).

Finally, a suspect should not be tempted to 'make a deal' with the police whereby he makes a statement admitting guilt, in return for the police not bringing a more serious charge, unless he has taken legal advice – as is his right.

Verbals

Following on from the problem of statements to the police is the vexed question of *verbals*. This is the word used to describe admissions, or incriminating statements, that the police falsely allege to have been made by the accused.

When the police question, arrest, or charge a person, they keep a written record of the events and conversations. For example, the notebook might read, 'When charged, the accused said, "Fair enough, I did it",' but the accused may later deny ever having said those words. Either he is lying, or he has been verballed by the police.

The end result has been that many criminal trials have revolved around whether the accused did make an admission – or whether he was 'verballed' by the police. In effect, there have been mini-trials within the main trials, with police officers being accused of giving false evidence. The Police and Criminal Evidence Act 1984 has set about introducing changes that will remove this problem, by tape-recording police interviews with suspects. At the moment this is only being done on a trial basis in a few parts of the country, but within a relatively short time it should be the norm for all police interviews to be tape-recorded. The hope is that this will reduce the verbal-ling problem, although the likelihood is that tape-recording will simply create new problems of its own (through e.g. the mischievous suspect who shouts out 'stop hitting me'; the fear that defendants will try to use the recording to show a threatening tone in the police officer's voice – as evidence of coercion and oppression; and the doubt about whether defence lawyers be paid for the extra time spent in going through transcripts of the recordings).

Being held by the police

We have already seen that there are two fundamental rights given to all suspects:

• you cannot be detained and held by the police unless you have been arrested (unless, of course, you are prepared to help voluntarily by answering questions),

• you need not answer any police questions.

In fact, there is another basic right given to people held in detention against their will (i.e. arrested). This is the right not to be held for an unreasonably long time before being charged in writing for a specific offence. In general, a suspect cannot be held for more than twenty-four hours between being taken to the police station after his arrest and his being charged with a specific offence. At the end of that twenty-four-hour period the police should either charge him or release him – unless he is being held for a 'serious' offence (see below), in which case they may be able to hold him for longer. In these 'serious' cases, a senior police officer can authorize detention for up to thirty-six (not twenty-four) hours, and at the end of that time the police can ask a magistrates' court to agree to further detention without charging (up to thirty-six hours, per application) up to a maximum time of ninety-six hours – i.e. four days of detention and questioning without being charged. This court hearing is in private (i.e. relatives and friends cannot attend) but the suspect's lawyer can appear and argue why the detention should not be extended any further.

What happens if the police hold someone for longer than they should (e.g. for more than twenty-four hours)? The answer lies with the ancient remedy of *habeas corpus*. This is a written application to the High Court which complains that the detained person is being held against his will and without lawful authority. If the judge thinks that the application is well founded, he will order the police to appear and to justify the detention, for otherwise the suspect must be released.

But, as with so many of the citizen's rights vis-à-vis the police, this is often an illusory right. First, habeas corpus applications are rare and time-consuming. It may therefore be difficult to find a solicitor able and willing to take the case on and to act quickly – assuming, of course, that the suspect can get word to him from the police station. Secondly, the police may well charge him so as to give themselves 'lawful authority' for holding him. Often a holding charge of this sort will be made purely as a device to allow the suspect to be held in custody; more often than not, the holding charge will later be dropped. Nowadays it seems that the courts are not sympathetic to habeas corpus applications. In the last twenty years, whilst the number of applications has doubled, the success rate has fallen from 22 per cent to 8 per cent. It is common for a solicitor to present the court with an affidavit in which he sets out the circumstances which make it clear that his client is being held illegally, and yet the usual practice is for the court to adjourn the hearing for twenty-four hours so that the police can appear before the court to put their side of the case. Thus, illegal detention continues for another day at least, which gives the police extra time in which to extract a confession.

Suing for wrongful arrest. If a person is wrongly arrested and detained by the police then he may be able to sue for damages. However, he will only be able to do this if the police acted unreasonably – in other words, if they did not have reasonable grounds for the arrest. Just because a person is detained, and subsequently released, it does not follow that he is entitled to compensation from the police. In practice, it is only in the most exceptional case that a person is entitled to sue for wrongful arrest.

Civil Liberties and the Welfare State

A respectable antique dealer was carrying a suitcase in Portobello Road. The police stopped him, and the end result was that he was taken to the police station and held for five hours. The police had made a mistake and there had been no grounds for holding him. He sued and was awarded £1,750 compensation (i.e. £350 per hour!). Hayward (1984)

Suspect's rights

Apart from the right to refuse to answer questions (see above), all detainees are entitled to:
- see a solicitor;
- have someone told about the arrest;
- be released if not charged within twenty-four hours (see above).

'Serious' offences: when the suspect has fewer rights. For serious offences, these rights are not taken away – but they are reduced, largely because the police can postpone them. For instance, the police can delay the suspect's right to see a solicitor, or to have someone told of his detention. But this only happens if he is suspected of a 'serious arrestable offence'. Unfortunately, the law does not set out a neat, clear-cut, definition of what is a 'serious' offence (i.e. a 'serious arrestable offence'). Obviously, some particularly grave crimes are specifically mentioned (e.g. murder, rape, incest, death by dangerous driving), but generally each individual crime has to be looked at on its own merits to see whether it is 'serious'. The Police and Criminal Evidence Act 1984 gives only vague guidance – for instance, has the offence caused serious harm or financial loss to anyone? If so, then it will be a 'serious' offence, and so the police will be able to postpone some of the detainee's legal rights. However, pause for a moment and consider what amounts to a serious financial loss: to a millionaire the loss of £50 is not serious, but to his hard-up au pair it might be a disaster! So, are we to say that the theft from the millionaire is not 'serious', but the theft from the au pair is? – for, if so, the thief who stole from the millionaire has more legal rights than his companion who stole from the au pair! Nonsense it may be, but it seems to be the law.

The right to see a solicitor

The Detention Code (made under the 1984 Act – see page 664) is quite clear about the right to see a solicitor. 'Any person at a police station may consult and communicate privately, whether in person, in writing or on the telephone, with a solicitor of his own choice.' In fact, when the suspect arrives at the police station, the custody officer must give him a written notice setting out his legal rights (including the right to see a solicitor): see page 664. The suspect must be asked whether he wants to see a solicitor; if he says no, then he should sign so there is a written record of this. If he refuses to sign then the police must assume that he does want to see a solicitor and they must make the necessary arrangements. In short, the general rule is that the suspect must specifically sign away his right to see a solicitor.

668

However, as is usually the case, there are major exceptions to this basic rule. If it is a 'serious' offence then a police officer can give authority for the suspect to be denied access to a solicitor (see above for what is a 'serious' offence). The senior officer can do this if he thinks that allowing access to a solicitor would:
– interfere with the evidence, *or*
– alert other (unarrested) suspects, *or*
– hinder the recovery of stolen property.

Perhaps more important, in any case (i.e. whether or not it is 'serious') a senior officer can decide that the interviewing of the suspect can go ahead – even though the solicitor has not yet arrived – if he thinks 'there is a risk of harm to persons or serious loss of or damage to property, or that *awaiting the arrival of a solicitor would cause unreasonable delay to the processes of investigation*'. So, the theory is that the suspect is entitled to legal advice, but the police can simply press on with the interview before the solicitor arrives – provided they feel that these vague criteria (e.g. 'unreasonable delay') apply. In practice, the net effect is that access to a solicitor can often be indirectly thwarted.

If the suspect wants to see a solicitor (assuming that the police are not going to use one of these exceptions to delay access to a solicitor) then he can choose any solicitor he likes (assuming he can persuade the solicitor to come down to the police station!). To simplify matters, the Police and Criminal Evidence Act 1984 envisages a nation-wide network of duty solicitors who will be on call in the major police stations, and able to help suspects. These would be private solicitors (i.e. not connected with the police), from local firms, who would take it in turns to go on the duty-solicitor rota. A suspect would not be forced to use the duty solicitor, and could opt to use another solicitor – although the police might then suggest that this would cause 'unreasonable delay' (see above)!

The right to have someone told of his detention

The code explains that the suspect has 'the right not to be held incommunicado'. It goes on to say, 'a detained person may on request have one person known to him or who is likely to take an interest in his welfare informed at public expense as soon as practicable of his whereabouts. If that person cannot be contacted the detained person may choose up to two alternatives.' But, as expected, there is an important exception. If it is a 'serious' offence that is being investigated (see above for what this means), then a senior police officer can decide that the right is not to apply – on the same basis as he can deny access to a solicitor (i.e. in order not to interfere with evidence; alert suspects; hinder recovery of property – see above). However, the senior officer cannot do this simply because he thinks it would cause 'unreasonable delay' – although he can use this ground to deny access to a solicitor (see above).

The code also says that the suspect should be given writing materials to write letters or messages, if he asks for them; those letters are then to be sent (at the suspect's expense) as soon as is practicable, although the police can read them. Likewise, the code says that a suspect can speak on the phone to one person, although the police can listen in to the conversation. Once again, if it is a 'serious' offence, a senior officer can take away these rights (i.e. on the grounds given above). Similar rules apply when relatives or friends of a detainee inquire of the police if they are holding him; the basic rule is that they must be told (assuming the detainee agrees), but this need not happen if it is a 'serious' offence.

Bail

For the rules on granting bail, see page 781.

Taking fingerprints and photos

Prior to 1985, the police had very limited fingerprinting rights. However, the law now gives a wide right to take fingerprints. A senior police officer can authorize the taking of a suspect's fingerprints if he thinks the person has been involved in an offence, provided the taking of the fingerprints may tend to prove (or disprove) that guilt. Once a suspect has been charged, in writing, with a specific offence, the police have even greater powers – if the offence is of the sort that is recorded in police records (most non-trivial offences) then they can take fingerprints.

If a suspect is subsequently acquitted of the charge against him, then the fingerprints must be destroyed. The suspect can insist on witnessing the destruction.

Roughly similar rules apply to the taking of photos. If it is a recordable offence that he has been charged with, then the police can take photos; once again, the photos must be destroyed if he is subsequently acquitted of the charge. In addition, there is a general right for the police to photograph groups of people when arresting several people at a time (i.e. they can photograph each person at the time of arrest, so there is a record of who was arrested, where, and by whom). Although the police can use force to take a suspect's fingerprints there seems to be no legal right for them to use force to take a photograph. So, if a suspect refuses to cooperate (e.g. puts his hands in front of his face) then – in theory – there is nothing the police can do, and if they use force the suspect would be able to sue for damages.

Searching someone

The police do not have a general power to search members of the public. However, the Police and Criminal Evidence Act 1984 does give them fairly extensive powers to stop and search suspected individuals. Detailed guidelines are set out in a Code on Stop and Search, but the basic effect is that a policeman can search someone if the policeman has reasonable grounds for thinking the person is carrying certain ('prohibited' is the word the Act uses) items. This covers offensive weapons (e.g. knife, razor, sharpened comb, etc.), or any item that could be used to commit an offence involving dishonesty – such as theft, stealing a car, burglary, etc. It follows that this could cover a screwdriver (i.e. which could be used to force a window), or a bundle of car keys. In practice, it is a vague criterion, and it gives the police a wide discretion in deciding whether to search.

The code says that the citizen must be told why he is being searched and why the constable is entitled to carry out the search; the constable must also identify himself. The search can extend to the suspect's car; in public, the search is limited to removal of outer coat, jacket and gloves. But a more detailed search – as far as a complete strip search – can be carried out, in which case it must be by a police officer of the same sex and out of public view (e.g. in a police van or at the police station).

The code lays down detailed guidelines for the police to follow (but remember that the courts can still allow evidence to be given even though it was obtained by breaking one of the codes – see page 664). In particular, it says that the powers of stop and search should be used 'responsibly and sparingly. Over-use of the powers is as likely to be harmful to police effort in the long-term as misuse. It is also particularly important to ensure that any person searched must be treated courteously and considerately if police action is not to be resented.'

These words are obviously aimed at the over-use of police powers against young blacks. In this connection it is necessary to remember that a policeman can only stop and search if he has 'reasonable grounds for suspicion': if he does not have those grounds then the search will be unlawful. What the code says is that

reasonable suspicion cannot be supported on the basis simply of a higher-than-average chance that the person has committed or is committing an offence, for example, because he belongs to a group within which offenders of a certain kind are relatively common, or because of a combination of factors such as these. For example, a person's colour of itself can never be a reasonable ground for suspicion, and young blacks should not be stopped and searched on the basis that statistics show that they have a higher-than-average chance of being involved in arrests for certain types of offence. The mere fact that a person is carrying a particular kind of property or is dressed in a certain way or has a certain hairstyle is likewise not of itself sufficient. Nor is the fact that a person is known to have a previous conviction for possession of an unlawful article.

The vital point is in deciding what are 'reasonable grounds' for suspicion, for the mere fact that the policeman does not find what he is looking for will not, of itself, mean that he did not have reasonable grounds for carrying out the search. But how is the citizen to know whether the policeman has 'reasonable grounds'? For example, the police may have just received a report that someone looking like the citizen recently committed a theft in that vicinity; in those circumstances they might well be acting reasonably in searching him, but it puts the individual citizen in an impossible position.

Apart from this general power of stopping and searching, the police have additional powers that come into effect as soon as someone is arrested. The policeman can carry out a search straight away – for evidence, or for weapons, etc. Once at the police station, the police have further rights to search – and the custody officer can authorize a strip search, as well as a search of intimate parts of the body.

Entering and searching property

The same basic rule applies as with the searching of a person, namely that the police have no general right of search. If they carry out an unauthorized search they will be trespassers, and so can be physically ejected and sued for damages (see page 339).

But, as always, there are exceptions. The best-known exception is when the police obtain a search warrant. For a search warrant to be granted the policeman will have to show that a 'serious' offence has been committed (see page 668 for what this means), and that there is likely to be relevant evidence obtained by a search. He will also have to explain why a warrant is necessary (e.g. the owner of the house cannot be contacted; the owner should not be given any advance warning, etc.). Unless the policeman can satisfy the court on all these points, then no search warrant should be granted. One point to note is that there must have been a 'serious' offence – so the police cannot get a search warrant for a trivial offence.

In addition, there are certain occasions when the police can carry out a search without a court search warrant. For instance: to catch an escaped prisoner; to save life or prevent injury; to prevent serious property damage; to arrest a trespasser who has an offensive weapon; to prevent a breach of the peace (see page 686); to arrest someone for an 'arrestable' offence (see page 778 for what this means – basically, it is an offence that could lead to more than five years in prison).

Finally, the police also have a right to search the home (or other premises) of anyone who has committed an arrestable offence, to look for evidence.

Whenever the police carry out a search they should comply with the Home Office Search Code. For instance, this says

premises may be searched only to the extent necessary to achieve the object of the search. . . . Searches must be conducted with due consideration for the property and privacy of the occupier . . . and with no more disturbance than necessary. . . . If the occupier wishes to ask a friend, neighbour or other person to witness the search then he must not be discouraged or prevented from doing so, unless the officer in charge has reasonable grounds to believe that this would seriously hinder the search. A search need not be delayed for this purpose.

Bear in mind, however, that this code (as with all codes) is not totally binding on the police; if they break the code they cannot necessarily be sued, and – more important – the chances are that any evidence improperly obtained will still be usable against the suspect (see page 664).

Police seizure of property

Generally, if the police carry out a lawful search (i.e. a search authorized by search warrant, written authority, etc.) then they can take anything they find which is material evidence or the fruit of a crime. This can be evidence of any crime – not just the crime for which the person has been arrested, or for which a search warrant was granted. The property can be kept for as long as is necessary for the police to complete their investigations. In practice, it seems that the police sometimes seize goods when they have no clear authority for doing so. When this happens the owner of the property should apply to the magistrates' court for an order that the police return his property to him (see page 716).

Identification evidence

A suspect cannot be made to take part in an identification parade. However, if he refuses the police may well arrange for him to be seen amongst a group of other people by the witness, in which case the witness may well identify him. So it is generally advisable for a suspect to agree to an ID parade rather than allow an informal identification to take place. A suspect should always take legal advice before agreeing to take part in an ID parade.

A suspect can insist upon there being an ID parade in any case, unless it would be 'impracticable'. Basically, this means that if identification may be an issue at the trial, the defendant can insist on an ID parade.

There is a Home Office Identification Code, which sets out the detailed rules on how an ID parade should be conducted. Perhaps its most important statement is that 'a suspect must be given a reasonable opportunity to have a solicitor or friend present': the fundamental piece of advice for anyone asked to take part in an ID parade is to consult a solicitor as to whether he should agree, and also to arrange for the solicitor to be present.

The code also says that:
- the suspect should be given a leaflet setting out his rights;
- the witness should not be allowed a chance of seeing the suspect before the parade takes place;
- 'the suspect should be placed among persons (at least eight or, if practicable, more) who are as far as possible of the same age, height, general appearance – including standard of dress and grooming – and position in life as the suspect. Members of a homogeneous group such as the police or the army should not usually be used as participants in an identification parade unless the suspect is a policeman or a soldier. One suspect only should be included in a parade unless there are two suspects of roughly similar appearance in which case they may be treated together with at least twelve other persons';
- 'the suspect should be allowed to select his own position in the line and should be expressly asked if he has any objection to the other participants in the line or the arrangements. Any objections should be recorded and, where practicable, steps should be taken to remove the grounds for objection';
- the line should be visited by only one witness at a time; the witness should be told that the suspect may, or may not, be in the line;
- if the witness asks to see members of the line moving, or to hear them talking, he should first be asked whether he can identify the suspect by appearance only; the witness should then be told that the members of the line were selected for their physical appearance only – not their similar voices;
- once the witness has left, the suspect should be told that he can change his position in the line before the next witness inspects the line;

- at the end of the ID parade, the suspect can have his comments on the parade noted by the officer in charge.

If the guidelines are not followed, the trial judge may decide that the identification evidence obtained should be ignored. In effect, therefore, the position is the same as with a breach of any other Home Office code.

In practice, it can often be difficult for a suspect to refuse to take part in an ID parade. The police will say that if he refuses then they will confront the witness with him and ask the witness whether he is the correct person – which can be extremely risky from the suspect's point of view! Another practical problem can arise when (e.g.) a young black is held as a suspect, because the police might have great trouble in finding enough black youngsters to make up an ID parade. When this happens, the suspect is often offered a 'group identification', as an alternative to an ID parade. For instance, if someone claims to have been mugged by a black youth on a tube train, the police might offer a group identification to the suspect – the witness will wait beside the ticket barrier and the suspect will walk out of the station, mingling with the other passengers. The Home Office Identification Code sets out guidelines on how such group identifications are to be conducted, and any suspect who is offered one should seek the help of a solicitor who can give practical help (e.g. he will make sure the identification takes place at a time of the day when the tube station is likely to be busy!).

The Home Office code also lays down guidelines for when a witness is shown a selection of photographs:

- photo-identification should not be allowed if an ID parade can be arranged;
- the witness should be shown not less than twelve photos at a time; 'the photographs used should as far as possible all be of a similar type', for instance, a snapshot should not be included in a bundle of 'mug-style' criminal photographs; when shown a photo of a suspect, the other photos should 'have as close resemblance to the suspect as possible';
- the witness should be told that the suspect's photo may or may not be included in the bundle;
- once a witness makes a firm identification by photo, he should then be asked to attend an ID parade.

Identification evidence in criminal trials

Identification evidence is notoriously unreliable. It has been shown on many occasions that people who positively identify a suspect are wrong because the suspect could not have been present at the time of the original sighting.

In the mid-seventies, following several wrong convictions based on identification evidence, Lord Devlin was asked to review the law on the subject. His report, published in 1976, led to several changes to ensure that identification evidence is thoroughly tested before a suspect is convicted on the basis of it. To this end, the following safeguards were introduced. Firstly, if identification evidence is being given, the accused can insist on a full old-style committal before the magistrate commits him for trial in the crown court; a simplified committal must not be used (see page 796). Secondly, 'dock identifications' are banned (except on 'old style' committals – see page 796 for what this means). This means that the witness cannot be asked if he can see in court the person he saw, unless he has previously picked out the suspect in an ID parade. Thirdly, judges must remind jurors of the weaknesses and dangers of identification evidence. The judge should go through the identification evidence during his summing up, reminding the jury of any weaknesses in it.

Prisoners

Generally, prisoners do not have rights, they just have privileges, as set out in the 1964 Prison Rules. Until a case in 1978 the courts had always held that the rules had no legal force and so a prisoner could not take the prison authorities to court if they failed to comply with the rules. However, it now seems that the courts will enforce the rules, but only in exceptional circumstances, such as when the prisoner is being disciplined by the board of governors. But, otherwise, the rules are no more than recommendations from the Home Office to the prison authorities. In addition, to make the prisoner's legal position even more difficult, the rules are interpreted and construed by reference to internal Home Office circulars, many of which are confidential; neither the prisoner nor his legal adviser can demand to see them.

What follows is not so much an account of 'prisoner's rights' as a description of the normal administrative procedures applicable to prisoners.

Unconvicted prisoners

Many prisoners have not been convicted of an offence; they are held in custody while awaiting trial. They have special privileges not given to ordinary, convicted prisoners.

In particular, remand prisoners can wear their own clothes, have clothing sent in to them, refuse to work, and may send and receive as many letters as they like – although their letters are liable to be censored by the prison authorities. They are usually allowed a visit each day, and can have any writing or reading material they wish, unless it is considered 'objectionable'. They are allowed to retain a watch, battery shaver, battery radio, calendar, and also photographs. They are usually allowed to have tobacco and cigarettes and meals sent in to them. They can also be treated, at their own expense, by outside doctors.

Convicted prisoners

Visiting

Generally, they are allowed one visit every four weeks, although some prisons have now increased this to one visit every two weeks. Young people are always allowed a visit every two weeks, and all prisoners may be granted extra visits at the discretion of the authorities.

The Home Office can restrict access to prisoners as it thinks fit. Thus, governors usually refuse visits to prisoners who have been disciplined (see page 677) until the disciplinary period has been served.

To visit a prisoner it is first necessary to write to the governor for a visiting order, which gives authority for up to three visits. The visit will be within the sight and hearing of a prison officer, and will normally be at least thirty minutes long. Visitors can only give cigarettes to prisoners, and they are not allowed to take notes of their conversations. Personal contact (e.g. hugging, kissing) is only allowed at the beginning and end of a visit. It is often possible for relatives or friends of a prisoner to get help with the cost of prison visits (i.e. travel, etc.). A wife (or other close relative) who is on supplementary benefit should automatically be entitled to help. For those not on SB, the position is more complicated. However, the Home Office can pay for visits; for details, contact the local probation office, although it should be remembered that help is only available to those on very small incomes.

Correspondence

A convict can send one letter per week, and also receive one letter per week, although extra letters may be allowed to enable him to keep in touch with his family. All letters to and from prisoners must be read and examined by a member of the prison staff, and can be censored if necessary; in practice, prisoners are given an opportunity of re-writing censored letters. A letter should not describe prison conditions and should not be longer than the equivalent of four sides of 7 × 5 in. paper. Generally, permission is needed to write to anyone other than the prisoner's spouse, girl-friend, close family, friends known to him at the time he entered prison, and his MP.

Property

Convicts can only have those reading and writing materials that the prison authorities are prepared to make available to them. They are usually allowed to bring some books, a watch, and a calendar into the prison with them.

When the prisoner is received at the prison, he will be searched and all his property removed from him. The property will be returned on his release. If he is sent money or gifts during his sentence, these will normally be kept for him until his release. Gifts sent to the prisoner will be examined and only handed to him if he is entitled or privileged to receive such items. Money is usually returned, or kept in the prison bank account.

Other privileges

Governors can grant other privileges, such as possession of a typewriter or attendance at lectures and evening classes in the prison. Prisoners who are not in local prisons who have served three years or more are often allowed to have items such as flowers, bedspreads, and mats in their cells.

Discipline

This is imposed by the governor and the Board of Visitors; the board is usually composed of magistrates. Prison rule 47 sets out over twenty offences against prison discipline, ranging from swearing, lack of respect, and other minor offences, through to mutiny.

When a charge is made against a prisoner he is entitled to be present at the hearing. Often the prisoner will be able to insist upon having a lawyer or friend represent him at the hearing. However, there is no hard-and-fast rule about this; it depends upon the seriousness of the charge, the complexity of the case, etc. In a straightforward and simple case, no representation will be necessary – but in a complicated or serious case, it should be allowed. The press and the public are excluded from any disciplinary hearing.

Most disciplinary offences are tried before the governor, who can impose a maximum penalty of twenty-eight days' loss of remission. The more serious offences go to the Board of Visitors, who can impose up to 180 days' loss of remission. Rule 49(2) states that 'at any inquiry into a charge against a prisoner he shall be given a full opportunity of hearing what is alleged against him and of presenting his own case'. However, until 1978 the courts refused to enforce this rule and governors and Boards of Visitors were left to run their disciplinary hearings as they thought fit; the rules of natural justice and of normal court procedures need not apply. However, one case changed that, and now disciplinary hearings of the Board of Visitors must be conducted in a proper judicial manner.

Following a riot at Hull prison, numerous prisoners were disciplined by the Board of Visitors. Seven prisoners complained to the High Court that the disciplinary hearings had been in breach of rule 49(2) and also failed to follow basic rules of justice. In particular, they complained that they had not been allowed to cross-examine witnesses, or to call witnesses to prove their evidence. The High Court threw out the prisoners' application, saying that the Board of Visitors were immune from control by the courts. The prisoners appealed to the Court of Appeal. Held: The Board of Visitors had acted wrongly and they would be ordered to re-try the cases. The Board of Visitors had to act judicially and the courts could control its activities – 'the rights of a citizen, however circumscribed by a penal sentence or otherwise, must always be the concern of the courts'. Hull Prison (1978)

Work

A prisoner must work if required. If he has no outdoor work and he is not in an open prison, he should be allowed one hour of exercise each day.

Hair

A man's hair or beard can be cut against his wishes, but a woman's hair can never be cut without her consent.

Civil Liberties and the Welfare State

Voting

Convicts cannot vote. Unconvicted (remand) prisoners can use a postal vote.

Release from prison

Apart from release at the end of his term, there are four ways in which the prisoner can be released from prison (excluding escape).

Remission of sentence. Up to one third of a fixed-term sentence can be remitted for 'industry and good conduct'. Time spent in custody counts for remission. The sentence cannot be reduced to less than five days.

Parole. After serving at least one third of the sentence, the prisoner can be released, subject to keeping in touch with the Probation and After Care Service until such time as he would have been eligible for remission. The sentence served cannot be reduced to less than one year. The decision whether to grant parole is at the discretion of the Parole Board; there is no appeal from a refusal of parole. 'Lifers' do not get parole but may go out on licence.

Licence. This is release subject to compulsory supervision and care. In particular, it applies to lifers and offenders under twenty-one when they were sentenced.

Home leave. This is temporary release for employment or training to 'assist in the transition from prison life to freedom'. Several prisons allow inmates who are nearing the end of their terms to go out in the day and work at normal jobs, and also to go home at the weekend.

Our system of criminal law takes great pride in the many protections and rights that are given to accused people prior to their trial and conviction: see 'The Law's "Fair Deal" for Criminals', on page 776. However, it seems that as soon as the accused is found guilty and put in prison, the legal system loses interest in him; prisoners have few rights that are legally enforceable, and they are treated as second-class citizens. It is difficult to see why the imposition of a custodial sentence should not only deprive a man of his liberty, but also take away some of his basic legal rights, such as the automatic right to legal advice when being disciplined.

The ex-offender

Once an offender has served his sentence, whether it be a term in prison, probation, or even a fine, it would be reasonable to allow him to put the conviction behind him and live in peace. Unfortunately, the law gives him only limited protection from having his criminal past revealed against his wishes.

Rehabilitation of offenders

The aim of the 1974 Rehabilitation of Offenders Act is that ex-criminals should be able to 'wipe the slate clean' and be allowed to forget their past convictions. Thus the offender would be able to fill in an insurance form, a mortgage application, apply for a job, and so on, without having to reveal his criminal past. In practice, though, the Act is subject to major exceptions that limit its effectiveness:

- anything more serious than a two-and-a-half-year prison sentence cannot be wiped out;
- if the press reveal an old, spent conviction, the offender can sue for defamation but he will only win if he can show that the paper acted 'maliciously'; this is usually very difficult to prove. (See page 712.)

How a sentence becomes spent

The Act lays down a table of rehabilitation periods for different types of sentence. Once the rehabilitation period has expired, the offence becomes 'spent' and so need not be revealed in the future. Shorter rehabilitation periods apply if the offender was a juvenile (under seventeen) when he was sentenced.

What matters is the length of the sentence, not the time served in prison. For instance, a person sentenced to three years will normally be released after two years for good conduct; however, his sentence will count as a three-year sentence, and since that exceeds the two-and-a-half-year maximum, it can never become spent. If an offender is sentenced for several offences at one time, the position will depend upon whether the sentences are concurrent (i.e. they run together) or consecutive (i.e. one runs after the other has finished).

Illustration. *Mr Jones receives three months for theft, nine months for assault and two years for robbery, to run concurrently. The sentence is therefore for two years and a ten-year rehabilitation period applies. If the sentences were to run consecutively, there would be a total sentence of three years and so the offence could never become spent.*

Difficulties can arise with suspended sentences and the position here seems unduly hard. An example will show how it works:

Illustration. *Mr Brown is sentenced to nine months' prison suspended for two years. He commits another offence and so the original sentence comes into effect, but the court reduces it from nine months to six months. For rehabilitation purposes it still counts as a nine-month sentence and so the rehabilitation period is ten years, not seven years as would be the case if it was treated as a six-month sentence.*

Complicated rules also apply when the offender is convicted for another offence before the previous offence has become spent. The position then depends upon whether or not the subsequent offence is summary (i.e. can only be tried in the magistrates' court, see page 785). If the offence is summary then it will not affect the rehabilitation period for the previous offence. If the offence is not summary, then the previous offence will only become spent when the subsequent offence becomes spent.

Illustration. *Mr Smith is sentenced to one year; thus there is a rehabilitation period of ten years. Eight years later he is convicted of theft (not a summary offence) and sentenced to another one-*

year term (another ten-year rehabilitation period). The first conviction will only become spent when the second one does – that is ten years after the second conviction, which is eighteen years after the first conviction.

If the second conviction had been for a summary offence, it would not have affected the first conviction, which would thus have become spent in the normal way, ten years after conviction.

When a sentence becomes spent

Sentence	Rehabilitation period	
	for person over 17	*for person under 17*
Prison: over 2½ years	never	never
Prison: over 6 months but no more than 2 years	10 years	5 years
Prison: not over 6 months	7 years	3½ years
Fine	5 years	2½ years
Borstal	7 years	7 years
Detention: over 6 months, but no more than 2½ years	5 years	5 years
Detention (or Detention Centre Order): not over 6 months	3 years	3 years
Absolute discharge	6 months	6 months
Conditional discharge; binding over; probation order; care order; supervision order	1 year after date of conviction/order or after the date when it ends – whichever is later	1 year
Disqualification	the length of the disqualification	the length of the disqualification

Exceptions, when convictions can be revealed

Apart from its obvious complexity, the Act contains major exceptions which severely restrict its effectiveness as an instrument of rehabilitation:
1. Sentences of more than two and a half years cannot be rehabilitated.
2. When applying for certain jobs, the Act does not apply. Thus, the prospective employee must reveal his spent convictions, although only if asked to do so. The

main categories are: doctors, dentists, dental auxiliaries; barristers; solicitors; vets; nurses; midwives; opticians; chemists; the police and armed forces; staff in a prison, remand centre or detention centre; traffic wardens; probation officers; teachers; lecturers and youth workers who come into contact with people under eighteen; social workers who might deal with people who are under eighteen, over sixty-five, or are handicapped, seriously ill, or addicts.

3. Spent convictions can be revealed in the course of a criminal trial. However, the Lord Chief Justice has ordered that: 'Both court and counsel should give effect to the general intention of Parliament by never referring to a spent conviction when such reference can be reasonably avoided. If unnecessary references to spent convictions are eliminated much will have been achieved. No one should refer in open court to a spent conviction without the authority of the judge, which authority should not be given unless the interests of justice so require. When passing sentence the judge should make no reference to a spent conviction unless it is necessary to do so for the purpose of explaining the sentence passed.'

Spent convictions cannot normally be revealed in civil cases, but this does not apply if the court is hearing an application for custody, adoption, wardship, or guardianship.

When a spent conviction is improperly revealed

The Act does not provide a very satisfactory remedy to the ex-offender whose spent conviction has been wrongly revealed. Generally, all he can do is to sue for defamation and, of course, the defendant will not be able to plead that what he said was true; for the purposes of the defamation case the spent conviction never occurred. However, the ex-offender will only win if he can show that the defendant acted 'maliciously' – basically if he can show that it was done deliberately to injure his reputation. In practice, this is usually difficult to prove. (See page 712.)

The only real sanctions provided by the Act apply to officials who wrongly disclose spent convictions (maximum penalty £1,000 fine) and those who dishonestly try to obtain such information (maximum penalty £2,000 fine and six months' prison). This is aimed at curbing the activities of over-zealous private investigators and, even, reporters.

Reporting convictions to employers

A convicted person has no redress if someone tells his employer of the conviction. The law does not recognize such a 'right to privacy'. However, if the employer dismisses the employee because of the conviction, the employee should consider bringing an unfair-dismissal claim. The prospects of success will depend upon the nature of the job and the offence (see Chapter 26).

A Home Office circular asks the police to report convictions of people in specific jobs if the offence:

1. *Is punishable by a month (or more) imprisonment without the option of a fine.* Jobs

covered are: a doctor or medical practitioner, a dentist, certified midwife, state registered nurse, state enrolled nurse, student nurse, or a special assistant nurse.

2. *Is such that it is believed to render a person unsuitable to teach or care for children* (in particular, sexual offences or indecency against, cruelty to, or neglect of, children). Jobs covered: teacher; those employed in the care of children in a residential school, remand home, approved school, probation school, or home; the resident proprietor of a private school; a youth leader; a clergyman.

3. *Involves fraud, dishonesty, or moral turpitude.* Jobs covered: barrister.

4. *Involves money or property.* Jobs covered: solicitor or solicitor's clerk.

5. *For any offence.* Jobs covered: a magistrate.

6. *Is relevant to fitness to drive, or to sexual or indecency offences.* Jobs covered: a driver or conductor of a public-service vehicle.

7. *Any offence other than a minor traffic offence* (i.e. if there has been no imprisonment or disqualification). Jobs covered: all civil servants – that is, any person in government service, except the armed forces, temporary employees, and those in nationalized industries or the NHS.

If the police leak information about a conviction to the employer of a person who does not come within the above categories, a complaint should be made against the police.

45 Political Demonstration and Protest

The public right to meet and demonstrate

Strictly speaking, it is incorrect to talk of 'the public right to meet and demonstrate', for there is no such right. In fact, we are only permitted to do what is not expressly prohibited by the law, so that meetings and demonstrations are only legal if they do not involve a breach of the law, however trivial that breach may be – for instance, obstructing the highway.

But although we have no inviolable right to hold political rallies or to demonstrate in the streets, we are – in practice – usually allowed to do so. This is because the police generally use their discretion wisely and do not prosecute for every act that is technically an offence. If they did choose to apply the law rigorously it would probably be impossible to hold demonstrations and rallies as we know them; one can say that our cherished 'right' of protest is held at the discretion of the police, to be taken away if they so choose.

Therefore this chapter is concerned not so much with the right to organize and demonstrate as with the offences that demonstrators might commit. The hope is that awareness of the possible charges will enable them to minimize their chances of acting illegally. The main offences are:

- committing a breach of the peace (page 686)
- obstructing the highway (page 687)
- obstructing/assaulting a P C (page 687)
- insulting words and/or behaviour (page 688)
- unlawful assembly (page 688)
- affray (page 689)
- riot (page 689)
- picketing offences (page 490).

Meetings and processions

No meeting can be held without permission or prior notice.

If the meeting is to be on private property, the permission of the owner of the land must be obtained first, for otherwise the people at the meeting will be trespassers (see page 339); they can be thrown off the land and sued in the civil courts for any loss occurring. Usually, though, they will not have committed a criminal offence (but see page 280).

683

If the meeting is to be on public land there may be a local by-law or a local Act that requires the organizers to give the local authority and the police thirty-six hours' notice; failure to do so will be a criminal offence (usual maximum penalty £50 fine).

The same is true of processions. But with processions there is a greater risk of a prosecution for obstructing the highway; see page 687 for how easily the offence can be committed.

In addition, the police have various powers under the Public Order Act 1936, which was rushed through Parliament in the wake of the battle of Cable Street:

• a chief officer can impose conditions on the organization and route of a procession if he has grounds for suspecting that it may cause 'serious public disorder'; *and*

• if that power is not enough, the chief officer can apply to the local authority for an order banning all or some processions for up to three months and he can impose conditions on the slogans or banners used. The Secretary of State's consent is needed before the ban can come into effect.

In London, further restrictions apply, mainly derived from nineteenth-century Acts:

• when Parliament is sitting, no open-air meeting of a 'political nature', with more than fifty participants, can be held north of the Thames within one mile of the Houses of Parliament.

• any open-air meeting or procession that obstructs the free passage of MPs to the House, or which causes disorder or annoyance in the neighbourhood, is illegal.

• special Department of the Environment permits are required for meetings, etc., in Hyde Park and Trafalgar Square.

Cooperating with the police

In the face of these extensive police powers, it is clearly wise for organizers to cooperate with the police and do more than merely notify them of the intention to hold a public meeting or procession. For, however well-intentioned the organizers may be, they cannot foresee how their supporters (and, indeed, their opponents) will behave. So it is only common sense to liaise with the police before the event. 'The right of public meeting then is dependent almost entirely on the police exercising their discretion in a reasonable manner. The promoter should cooperate with the police in the expectation that they will treat him fairly; if he proceeds in defiance of their wishes, conviction is likely' (Harry Street, *Freedom, the Individual and the Law*).

Private meetings

If the meeting is on private premises, anyone present can be told to leave; if he refuses, the organizers can eject him as a trespasser. Note that if he has paid to enter the meeting he might have a contractual right to stay; to avoid this, the organizers would be well advised to display a notice at the entrance reserving their right to refund money and to ask people to leave.

One would have thought that the owner of private property could also exclude the police and that they would be trespassers if they entered without his permission. But the law is not clear on this point and the police will generally argue that they can enter any private meeting if they apprehend that any offence is likely to be committed (for instance, if they think there will be a breach of the peace – see page 686 for how a small disturbance can be a breach of the peace). Whilst there is no clear legal authority to support this view, the organizer would be rash to exclude them – for if they are entitled to enter he would, at the least, be prosecuted for obstructing the police in the execution of their duty.

A Home Office circular in 1909 expressed what is still the police point of view, namely a 'preference for the policy of non-interference in ordinary political meetings, although on exceptional occasions it may become necessary to station police inside a meeting for the purpose of maintaining order'. Whether that is police practice, as opposed to police policy, is open to doubt.

Organization

Stewards

Stewards can be appointed at both public and private meetings. In practice, stewards are a very important means of controlling a crowd. The organizers should liaise with the police as to the number and organization of the stewards. Obviously, the stewards have the same status as other private individuals and are not accorded any special legal powers; thus, they cannot use force to ensure compliance with their wishes.

Fly-posting

Sticking posters in public places is illegal under the Town and Country Planning Acts (i.e. because they are treated as adverts – and planning permission is needed for any advertising hoarding), and often under local by-laws as well. Exceptions are advertisements for non-commercial events, including political, educational, social, and religious meetings, if the prior consent of the owner of the hoarding, window, etc., is obtained. There are usually other detailed requirements, the most important of which is that the poster should be no more than six square feet in size. The local authority will provide further details. Posting an advertisement on someone else's property (e.g. window, lamp-post) without permission is punishable – under the planning-permission laws – by a fine of up to £400 in the magistrates' court.

Spray painting

Painting slogans is likely to be illegal under local by-laws. In addition, it is likely to be criminal damage. The cost of repairing the damage can be high; water-based paint soaks into brickwork.

Collecting signatures

A person organizing a petition should take care not to obstruct the highway (see below).

Selling pamphlets, etc.

This does not require a street-trading licence, but there is always the risk of obstructing the highway. In the Metropolitan Police area, a licence is needed for charitable (or other benevolent) collections – but not for selling political papers, etc.

Picketing

Whilst there is no specific right to demonstrate, protest, hold rallies, etc., it would seem, at first sight, that there is a right to picket. But the right to picket is restricted to industrial disputes involving those doing the picketing, and in particular does not cover non-industrial pickets (e.g. consumer picket; political picket). In any event, even authorized pickets can fall foul of several criminal offences. See page 490 for details of the law on picketing.

Offences arising from meetings, demonstrations, etc.

Committing a breach of the peace

Anything that disturbs the 'Queen's peace' is an offence. Since the 'Queen's peace' has been defined as 'the preservation of law and order', it can be appreciated that many seemingly trivial disturbances are thus offences.

Generally, though, there must have been some physical force used or at least some behaviour that would lead one to expect a disturbance involving force – but even with that qualification it is still a widely drawn offence. The offence ranges from minor assaults, threats, or obstructions through to more serious offences such as riot and affray (see page 689); in practice, of course, a person committing a more serious offence would be prosecuted for that offence rather than face the more minor charge of breaking the peace. Whilst every crime is technically a breach of the peace, it is when no crime has been committed that the charge is often used. The test is: 'Was there conduct amounting to, or likely to cause, an outbreak of violence?' If so, there has been a breach of the peace (e.g. when two opposing groups of demonstrators are shouting slogans at each other – no specific offence is committed, but if the tension is raised there could be a breach of the peace).

A person who is guilty of a breach of the peace will be bound over to keep the peace or to be of good behaviour. If he refuses to be bound over he can be sent to prison (see page 807).

Obstructing the highway

In the eyes of the law, the highway (including the pavement) is to be used for 'passing and re-passing' – a quaint phrase which means that it is only to be used for travelling from one place to another. Thus, it is not to be used for parking one's car, holding a meeting, talking to a neighbour, or selling newspapers from a stand, since all of these activities do not involve the use of the highway for 'passing and re-passing'. All are thus obstructions of the highway.

To make the offence even wider, the courts have held that it is not even necessary for anyone to have actually been obstructed by the unauthorized act.

It is thus an offence that is easily committed. In practice, though, the court will consider whether the defendant was using the highway 'reasonably', and this will mean taking into account the amount of traffic present, the time of day, and the size of the road; thus a person washing his car in a suburban road on a Sunday morning may be technically obstructing the highway, but will generally be held to have been using the highway 'reasonably', and so he would not be prosecuted by the police. But for demonstrators who may be peacefully taking part in a demonstration or lobby the law is usually less understanding. The very vagueness of the charge makes it difficult to defend, and if a policeman tells the court that he thought the demonstrator was causing an obstruction, it will be extremely difficult for the demonstrator to avoid conviction. For this reason, an 'obstruction of the highway' charge is probably the most frequently used charge against demonstrators. Also, it has the added advantage from the police point of view that the offender can be arrested on the spot, without the need for a warrant.

A procession which keeps moving is less likely to be an obstruction of the highway, for the participants can then argue that they were indeed using the highway for 'passing and re-passing'. For this reason, a procession or march is usually a legally safer form of protest than a rally or a lobby. The maximum penalty for obstructing the highway is a fine of £400. (See also page 490.)

Obstructing/assaulting a police officer in the execution of his duty

The important words here are 'in the execution of his duty'. If the policeman was not acting in accordance with his legal powers and duties, then the charge must fail. For example, the person who refuses to allow a PC to search his bags will not be obstructing the policeman in the execution of his duty, unless the PC has legal authority to search the bags.

Policemen saw two teenagers going from house to house, so one of the policemen challenged the boys and asked them what they were doing. The boys ran off thinking that the policemen were thugs. The policemen gave chase and caught the boys, who then hit them. When prosecuted for assaulting an officer in the course of his duty, the boys argued that the policemen were not acting in the course of their duty, since the police can only use force to arrest someone, not to detain him for questioning. Held: This was correct, and the boys were acquitted. Kenlin (1967)

A youngster was shouting and swearing on a bus. A plain-clothes policeman told him to get off. He began to do so, but then the policeman tried to detain him; the youth hit the policeman. Was he guilty of assaulting a policeman in the execution of his duty? Held: No. The policeman had not arrested the youth and had no legal right to detain him. The policeman was therefore acting illegally in trying to detain the youth – and so was not 'acting in the execution of his duty'. Ludlow (1983)

Note that the accused need not know that the PC was, in fact, a policeman for an offence to be committed. So if I hit someone who turns out to be a plain-clothes policeman on duty, I can be prosecuted for the offence; but if he is not on duty, I will only face prosecution for simple assault. Both offences can only be tried in the magistrates' court. It has often been suggested that the offences should be triable in the crown court, before a jury, since they are both of a serious nature. The maximum penalty for assaulting a police officer is six months' prison and £2,000 fine; the maximum for obstructing a police officer is one month's prison and £400 fine.

Insulting words and/or behaviour

Section 5 of the Public Order Act 1936 creates an extremely wide offence. The section is rather a mouthful, but it bears careful reading:

it is an offence for any person in any public place, or at any public meeting, to use threatening, abusive, or insulting words or behaviour, or to distribute or display any writing, sign, or visible representation which is threatening, abusive, or insulting with intent to provoke a breach of the peace, or whereby a breach of the peace is likely to be occasioned.

Thus, it is an offence to say anything insulting in public if it is likely to cause someone else to break the peace. This is a very widely drawn offence (maximum penalty six months' prison and £2,000 fine).

Worse still, a 1963 case decided that the offence can be committed if the words used are likely to cause hooligans in the audience to commit a breach of the peace, even if they have come to the meeting intent on preventing the speaker from making himself heard! So the speaker at a meeting may have the most peaceful intentions and yet be guilty of an offence just because part of the audience is disruptive.

Fortunately, the police do not use the section as ruthlessly as they could if they so wished. It places speakers at meetings in an almost impossible position, and this brings us back to the common thread running through all our so-called civil liberties – namely, that these 'liberties' are generally enjoyed by us at the whim and discretion of the police. If the police did enforce all these laws, all the time, nearly all demonstrations and protests would be illegal.

Unlawful assembly

An offence is committed if three or more people meet to do an unlawful act, or a lawful act by unlawful means, causing reasonable people to fear a breach of the peace.

The common purpose that the people meet for must be such that it is likely to involve a breach of the peace – in other words, it could lead to violence. Thus this charge can be brought against people at counter-demonstrations and rallies at which trouble is expected. But if the demonstrators behave peacefully and do nothing to make the meeting unlawful, they will not commit the offence. For instance:

In the 1880s marches by the Salvation Army had frequently run into violent opposition from the 'Skeleton Army'. To avoid further trouble the police asked the Salvation Army to call off a march, but they insisted on it going ahead. After the march the leaders were charged with unlawful assembly. Held: Since they had assembled for a lawful purpose, and with no intention of carrying it out unlawfully, they could not be guilty of unlawful assembly – even though a breach of the peace was likely to result from their actions. Beatty (1882)

Riot

A riot is an unlawful assembly that becomes violent. It is an old offence and one that had fallen into disuse until the Cambridge Garden House trial of 1970 (arising out of a student protest). Lord Justice Sachs distinguished unlawful assembly and riot as follows:

The moment people in a crowd, however peaceful their original intentions, come together to act for some common purpose in such a way as to make reasonable citizens fear a breach of the peace, then the assembly becomes unlawful. It becomes riotous when alarming force or violence is used, and anyone who actively encourages such an assembly by words, signs, or actions, or by participating in it, is guilty.

Fortunately, riot prosecutions are few and far between although the offence has recently been reactivated, and prosecutions were brought (unsuccessfully) against miners involved in the mass pickets of 1984.

Affray

An affray is a fight that might intimidate onlookers. 'If two lads indulge in a fight with fists, no one would dignify that as an affray, whereas if they used broken bottles or knuckle-dusters, and drew blood, a jury might well find it was, as a passer-by might be upset and frightened by such conduct' (Lord Goddard).

Affray is often the half-way house between unlawful assembly and riot.

Picketing offences

See page 490.

46 Discrimination and the Law

Libbaty's a kind o'thing
Thet don't agree with niggers.
(James Lowell, 1819–91)

The law is prepared to intervene to remedy three types of discrimination: namely, discrimination based on a person's race, sex, or marital status. But the law never makes it a criminal offence to discriminate. If the discrimination is unlawful, the person discriminated against may be able to bring a civil claim for damages but no criminal prosecution can be brought (although, exceptionally, there might be a prosecution for inciting racial hatred).

The anti-discrimination laws are set out in the Race Relations Act 1976 and the Sex Discrimination Act 1975. Both Acts adopt a similar approach, and so the same basic principles apply in all discrimination cases. The Acts tackle discrimination at two levels; firstly, they allow an individual to take legal action against someone who has discriminated against him/her and, secondly, each creates an overall watch-dog body to monitor and advise on the general problems of discrimination. For racial discrimination, the national body is the Commission for Racial Equality, whilst its equivalent for sex and marital discrimination is the Equal Opportunities Commission.

But the primary responsibility for enforcing the legislation rests with the individual, and this is probably the major weakness of the laws, for many people will simply not bother to take action against a discriminator. To win the case, the complainant must not only show that s/he has been discriminated against, but that the act of discrimination was unlawful and not exempted from either of the two Acts.

What is 'discrimination'?

Unlawful discrimination occurs when a person is treated *less favourably* than s/he would otherwise be, simply because of his/her:
- *race* (i.e. because of colour, race, nationality, or citizenship, or ethnic or national origin);
- *sex* (i.e. because s/he is a man or a woman);
- *married status* (i.e. because s/he is married and not single).

Discrimination can be *direct* or *indirect*. Direct discrimination is straightforward intentional discrimination (e.g. advertising a flat with a 'no blacks need apply' sign). Indirect discrimination is more subtle, and may even be unintentional: a person may appear to treat people equally but, in fact, be indirectly discriminating because s/he imposes an unjustifiable condition that effectively limits the opportunities of a particular sex, racial group, or of married people. For instance, if eligibility for membership of a club is dependent upon a certain number of years' residence in the UK, that condition may well be indirect racial discrimination. Likewise, it would be indirect sex discrimination if an employer unreasonably insisted that all his staff be at least six feet tall.

The headmaster of a private school would not allow a Sikh boy to attend unless he removed his turban and cut his hair, since turbans and long hair were against the school's rules. Held: These rules amounted to indirect discrimination against Sikhs. In addition, the House of Lords held that Sikhs did make up an 'ethnic' group – the Act did not just protect those of a particular race, but extended to groups with a definite cultural tradition, such as the Sikhs. Thus, the school rules had to be changed. Mandla (1983)

When deciding whether there is indirect discrimination, the court will want to know whether 'in practice' it is harder for the discriminated-against group to comply with the conditions than other people. For instance:

The Civil Service laid down an upper age limit of twenty-eight for entry into the service as an executive officer. Ms Price was thirty-five and she complained that this was indirect sex discrimination since many women gave up work to look after their children during their twenties. Held: It was clear that 'in practice' it was harder for women to comply with the age limitation than it was for men. Thus, it was indirect sex discrimination and the Civil Service was asked to review its policy on age restrictions. Price (1977)

When it is not unlawful to discriminate

The Race Relations Act and the Sex Discrimination Act do not ban *all* racial, sex, and marital discrimination. There are exceptions when discrimination is allowed.

Sport. Sporting teams can be selected on the basis of nationality, birthplace, and residence, but not colour; competitive events can be limited to one sex if physical stamina or physique is important (so single-sex tennis is allowed, but single-sex snooker is not).

Insurance. Sex and marital discrimination is allowed if justifiable on statistical grounds (e.g. women live longer than men, so they can be charged less for life insurance).

When required by an Act of Parliament. Discrimination is not unlawful if it is authorized by a statute. For instance, women are not allowed to work in underground mines.

Marital discrimination. The laws on marital discrimination only apply in the employment field. So discrimination on marital grounds in non-employment matters is allowed when racial and sex discrimination would be unlawful.

Communal accommodation. Residential accommodation is exempted from the sex and marital discrimination laws if it is communal, and if, for reasons of privacy and decency, it should be used by one sex only. But racial discrimination on this ground is not allowed.

Positive discrimination. Training boards, employers, and trade unions can take limited action to encourage the training of groups that have been under-represented

691

in certain fields. But this provision is of limited effect and does not permit reverse discrimination (e.g. employer recruiting staff so as to achieve a balance between the sexes).

Charitable bequests and foundations. Generally charities can discriminate in handing out benefits, unless they impose a colour bar.

Employment. Additional exceptions apply in the employment field (see below).

Discrimination in the employment field

The racial/sex/marital discrimination laws apply throughout the employment field. They cover all steps from the recruitment of staff (e.g. notifying only boys' schools of vacancies might be discrimination against girls), the advertising of vacancies (e.g. wording of the advertisement; instructions to an employment agency), the selection of applicants for interviews and the actual hiring to treatment of employed workers, including selection for training, transfers, and promotion, as well as selection for lay-off, redundancy, short-time working, etc. For instance:

Workers had to be laid off. Instead of a 'first in, last out' rule, the firm decided to make part-timers redundant before full-time staff. Held: This was sex discrimination. In practice, it is women who are part-timers (nationally, 80 per cent are female) and so this was indirect discrimination against the women members of staff. Clarke (1983)

Following theft by a black employee, BL planned to increase security by requiring all its black workers to be searched on leaving work. Held: This would be racial discrimination, since white workers were not being treated in the same way. BL Cars (1983)

A new head was to be appointed to a school. Four men and one woman were interviewed; the woman was asked about her relationship with her husband, whether she was Miss or Mrs, was she legally separated from her husband, and did she intend to have a family in the future. The men were not asked questions of this sort. Held: The questions were discriminatory and should not have been asked. Gates (1983)

But there are *exceptions* when the discrimination will not be unlawful. These are in addition to the general exceptions listed above.

Private households. Jobs in private houses (e.g. cook) are outside the legislation.

Small firms. If there are no more than five staff, the firm is exempt from the sex and marital laws, but not from the racial laws.

Certain jobs. Some jobs are partially excluded from the sex and marital discrimination laws, but not from the racial laws. For instance, the police force and prison service can lay down height requirements; whilst both men and women can be midwives, sex and marital discrimination is permitted when recruiting staff. Employees of religious bodies are outside the sex discrimination laws if their employment would conflict with their religious doctrine or offend a significant number of the religion's followers. In addition, the forces are excluded from the sex and marital discrimination laws.

Pregnancy, childbirth, death, retirement. Employers can give special treatment to women in connection with pregnancy and childbirth. Discrimination between the sexes is allowed by employers in deciding their entitlement to death or retirement benefits (e.g. age of retirement) but both men and women must have equal access to a firm's pension schemes. In practice, disputes over pension arrangements often arise when people are being laid off – if so, it is really a redundancy problem and discrimination laws may not apply (so the 'pensions' exception will not be relevant).

Genuine occupational qualifications

It may be that being of a particular racial group or sex is a necessary qualification for the job – but marital status can never be a genuine qualification (e.g. 'single men only' is unlawful) unless it is a married couple that is to be employed (e.g. 'married couple required' is lawful).

Racial group. This can be a qualification when selecting actors for a play or choosing a model, when authenticity requires someone from that racial group. Similarly, bars and restaurants can select a person from a particular racial group (e.g. a Chinese waiter in a Chinese restaurant).

Sex. Sex can be a genuine occupational qualification when selecting actors and models. Also, if a job involves physical contact with the opposite sex (e.g. frisking staff for security checks) or if the work is such that members of the opposite sex might object to a person of that sex (e.g. woman attendant in a male lavatory), then the discrimination will not be unlawful. In addition, there are detailed exceptions for single-sex establishments, such as hospitals.

These anti-discrimination laws do not apply to employees only; they also cover the self-employed, including contract workers and partners. Trade unions, employers' organizations, and professional bodies are also forbidden to discriminate in, for example, the terms of membership, benefits for members, expulsion, and so on. One point to note is that physical strength and stamina can never be a 'genuine occupational qualification' – so a woman cannot be turned down for a labourer's job merely because she is a woman (but she can be turned down if she isn't strong enough).

Pay

Sex discrimination in the employment field is also governed by the Equal Pay Act 1970. This was passed before the Sex Discrimination Act and it bans sexual discrimination in respect of pay rates and other terms of a contract of employment (see page 391). If the jobs are similar, or of equal value, then a man and woman of similar status (e.g. qualifications, length of service) must work on equal terms unless there is a 'material difference' in what they do. The Sex Discrimination Act did not repeal the Equal Pay Act, and so both Acts work side by side. However, it would have been much simpler if Parliament had tidied up the legislation so that there was only the one Act covering sex discrimination in employment. Under the present law,

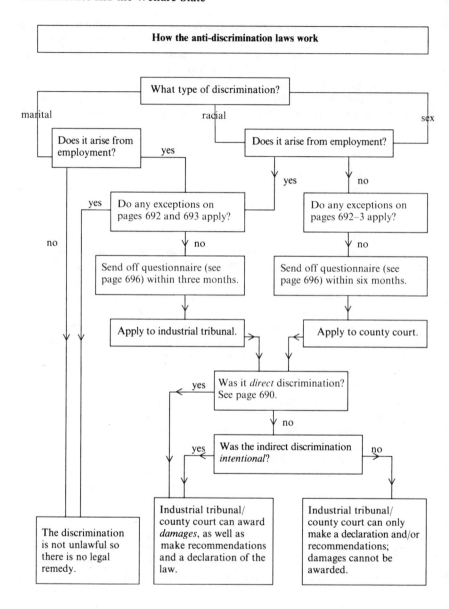

How the anti-discrimination laws work

What type of discrimination?

marital   racial   sex

Does it arise from employment?   yes

Does it arise from employment?

yes   no

yes   Do any exceptions on pages 692 and 693 apply?

Do any exceptions on pages 692–3 apply?

no   no   no

Send off questionnaire (see page 696) within three months.

Send off questionnaire (see page 696) within six months.

Apply to industrial tribunal.

Apply to county court.

yes   Was it *direct* discrimination? See page 690.

no

yes   Was the indirect discrimination *intentional*?   no

The discrimination is not unlawful so there is no legal remedy.

Industrial tribunal/ county court can award *damages*, as well as make recommendations and a declaration of the law.

Industrial tribunal/ county court can only make a declaration and/or recommendations; damages cannot be awarded.

if the discrimination arises before a job is given (e.g. a woman is refused an interview) that is under the Sex Discrimination Act; but if it arises during the employment (e.g. a woman not given a pay rise) then it comes within the Equal Pay Act!

Discrimination in providing goods, facilities, services, and premises

The sex and race discrimination laws – but not the marital discrimination laws – apply in all these fields, subject to the general exceptions listed above.

Goods, facilities, and services

This covers an enormously wide field, such as access to and use of hotels, restaurants, boarding houses, shops, public buildings, schools, night classes, cinemas, pubs, theatres, and banking services, as well as credit, finance, grants, mortgages, and insurance.

El Vino's wine bar refused to serve women at the bar; they had to sit down at tables. Held: This was less favourable treatment of women, and so it was sex discrimination. Gill (1983)

Mrs Quinn bought a suite of furniture in a department store. She asked to pay by HP. The store agreed – provided her husband would guarantee the loan, even though Mrs Quinn had a steady job. The store admitted it would not have asked for a woman to guarantee a husband's HP agreement. Held: This was sex discrimination. Quinn (1981)

Clubs

If a club is genuinely private, and not public, it is not unlawful to discriminate on the grounds of sex in the selection of members and the provision of facilities, including drinks. So a men's bar will probably be legal in a private golf club, but unlawful in a pub.

Special rules apply to racial discrimination in clubs; the basic rule is that racial discrimination laws apply unless *all* the following are met:
- the club is not an organization of workers, employers or a trade body, *and*
- it is not open to the public or a section of the public, because it has a constitution limiting admission to members, and 'membership' is defined so that 'members' do not constitute a section of the public, *and*
- it has fewer than twenty-five members.

Otherwise, racial discrimination in a club is unlawful. It is worth noting that the Race Relations Act contains detailed provisions to ensure that membership rules cannot be abused so as to avoid the legislation. However, special rules apply to clubs for people of a particular group (e.g. a club for Welsh people), but not if it is a colour bar.

Selling, letting and managing property

An owner-occupier may be able to discriminate when selling or letting his property, but only in certain well-defined cases. If the property is residential accommodation in a small dwelling, the person disposing of it can discriminate if s/he (or a near relative) will be living on the premises, and be sharing accommodation (other than means of access) with people who are not members of his or her household.

If a property is being sold, the anti-discrimination laws are only excluded if the seller does not employ an estate agent and does not advertise the property as being for sale.

These property provisions only apply to sex and race discrimination, and not to marital discrimination. It is therefore lawful to advertise a flat with a 'no married couples' sign.

Enforcing the anti-discrimination laws

It is up to the individual who has been discriminated against to take action. He brings a *civil* complaint, not a criminal charge, and so the police will not be interested in his case. Discrimination can never be a criminal offence (unless it goes so far that it is inciting racial hatred). However, he may be able to obtain assistance from the Equal Opportunities Commission or the Commission for Racial Equality if his case is particularly complex, or raises important issues.

If the complainant is a member of a trade union, they may provide legal assistance. Legal aid (see Chapter 57) will only be available in non-employment cases.

Both the Race Relations Act and the Sex Discrimination Act encourage the use of a standard-form questionnaire to be sent by the complainant to the discriminator. Copies can be obtained from the commission and from most Citizens' Advice Bureaux. The form sets out the details of the discriminatory act and the discriminator is asked to agree or deny the facts. He is then told why the facts amount to discrimination, and asked to comment. The answers given can be used as evidence when presenting the case; if the answers are evasive or abusive, this might be held against the discriminator.

Use of the questionnaires usually clarifies the issues, and can help the complainant to decide whether it is worth taking the case any further. But the questions must be served, and so the complaint started, within a short period of the act of discrimination. In an employment case there is a three-month time limit, whereas in other cases the period is six months.

Discrimination claims are normally brought in the county court (see page 759). But all employment cases (e.g. equal pay, race or sex discrimination) are heard before industrial tribunals (see page 391).

The hearing

Whether the case is heard in an industrial tribunal or a county court, the complainant will have to prove his/her case 'on a balance of probabilities' (see page 759).

If the tribunal or court decides that there has been discrimination, it will have to decide what to do about it. It may simply make a declaration setting out the rights of the parties in the hope that the parties will, in the future, behave themselves, and it may also recommend that the discriminator takes certain action (e.g. that the discriminating employer recruits the complainant by a certain date).

Damages can often be awarded to a complainant. In cases of *direct* discrimination damages can always be awarded; but in cases of *indirect* discrimination damages can only be awarded if the discriminator acted 'intentionally' – i.e. he knew he was discriminating (see page 690 above for the distinction between direct and indirect discrimination). The damages can cover loss of earnings, expenses incurred, etc. and also a sum for injured feelings. Generally, the amount awarded for injured feelings is not large, but in one recent sex discrimination case it was valued at £200.

Bringing a discrimination claim . . . a word of warning

The anti-discrimination legislation is very modern in concept. In fact, to lawyers of the old school, it is almost revolutionary, for it interferes with the freedom of the individual to decide who he wants to employ, sell his goods to, have in his restaurant, and so on. It is thus a complete departure from the sort of *laissez-faire* legislation that was so prominent in the nineteenth century and the early part of this century.

Perhaps this is why the judges have still not come to terms with it. In practice, it is notoriously difficult to win a discrimination case, and the judges seem only too anxious to give a narrow, restrictive interpretation to both the Race Relations Act and the Sex Discrimination Act. Generally, race discrimination cases are harder to win than sex discrimination cases.

47 The Mentally Ill

The law on mental health is set out in the Mental Health Act 1983. This brought up to date the changes that had been made by the Mental Health Act 1959, which had been a pioneering Act, for it attempted to shift the care of the mentally ill out of special institutions and into the community, through the services of social workers. Also, as much treatment as possible was to be on a voluntary basis, with compulsory hospitalization being used only when essential. In the words of the 1957 Percy Report which led to the 1959 Act, 'compulsory powers should be used in future only when they are positively necessary to override the patient's own unwillingness or the unwillingness of his relatives, for the patient's own welfare or for the protection of others'.

The 1983 Act deals with 'mental disorders' (defined as 'mental illness, arrested or incomplete development of the mind'). In fact, the Act deals with four different subcategories of mental disorder, but the important point to realize is that only people who are *abnormally aggressive or seriously irresponsible* can be detained against their will for long periods of time. It therefore follows that many people who are mentally ill – but harmlessly so (e.g. schizophrenic, depressed, senile) – cannot be compulsorily detained. Note also that someone is not to be treated as having a mental disorder merely because of their sexual behaviour, or because of a dependency on alcohol or drugs.

These definitions of 'mental disorder' are narrower than the definitions that were in the 1959 Act. This was partly because the 1983 Act was intended to curb the extent to which mentally ill (but not dangerous) people could be compulsorily put away. It was felt by many people that the 1959 Act powers were being misused and that compulsory admittance was often being used for reasons of mere administrative convenience; thus, the 1983 Act tightened up the definitions to restrict the powers to detain patients compulsorily.

Admission to a mental hospital

Admission can be voluntary (informal) or compulsory (formal). About 90 per cent of admissions are voluntary and, in these cases, the patients are free to discharge themselves at any time – even against medical advice (but see page 699).

Although most admissions are voluntary, it has been suggested that some social workers do not bother to persuade patients to agree to admission, but simply use the

698

compulsory procedures to save themselves work. The 1983 Act did try to reduce the dangers of this happening but there can be little doubt that it still occurs.

There are several ways in which compulsory admission can be authorized; each method is derived from a particular section of the 1983 Act, and so compulsorily admitted patients are frequently referred to as 'section patients'. The question of which section was used to authorize the admission becomes important when considering whether the decision to detain the patient can be reviewed and how he may be discharged.

The types of compulsory admission

Admission for assessment (s. 2). Application is made by the *nearest relative* or an approved social worker, supported by a recommendation of two doctors that voluntary admission is not appropriate. A patient admitted for *assessment* cannot be held for more than twenty-eight days without his case being reviewed. This is the most frequently used ground for compulsory admission. The patient's 'nearest relative' will be, in this order, his: spouse, child, parent, brother or sister, grandparent, grandchild, uncle, or aunt. The criterion for admission is that the patient *ought* to be detained either in the interests of his own health and safety or for the protection of other people. The patient can challenge the detention by applying to a Mental Health Review Tribunal within the first fourteen days. In addition, the *nearest relative* has the right to discharge the patient.

Admission for treatment (s. 3). Application is made by the *nearest relative* or an approved social worker, plus the evidence of two doctors. The section is used for the more serious cases of mental disorder – about 3 per cent of all compulsory admissions. Here the criterion for admission is that detention is *necessary* either in the interests of his own health and safety or for the protection of other people. Thus, the doctors' certificates must specifically state why treatment in hospital is necessary and why no other action will suffice. The initial admission can be for up to six months; that can be renewed for a further six months, and then extended for a year at a time. The patient can apply for his detention to be reviewed once during each of these periods.

Emergency admission (s. 4). Application is made by the *nearest relative* or an approved social worker, and one doctor (who must have seen the patient within the last twenty-four hours). A patient admitted in an emergency can only be detained for seventy-two hours, unless a second doctor gives his recommendation; if he does, the patient can then be held for up to twenty-eight days (i.e. under s. 2, admission for assessment, above). The procedure is designed to deal with emergency cases in which the normal procedures for admission for assessment would involve undue delay.

Compulsory detention of voluntary patients (s. 5). A patient who was voluntarily admitted can usually discharge himself at any time. However, if the staff think he should be compulsorily detained, they can detain him for up to three days while they apply for a compulsory admission order. A doctor's certificate will be needed; if there will be delay in fetching a doctor, then a senior nurse is authorized to detain the patient for up to six hours. People who are thinking of going voluntarily into a hospital should bear in mind that they may not be free to leave as and when they wish. Often a patient who intends to leave will be told that unless he agrees to remain in the hospital as a voluntary patient, he will be 'sectioned' (i.e. a compulsory order will be made), and the threat of this will induce many people to agree to stay in. Obviously, if the patient feels that there are no medical reasons justifying a formal (compulsory) admission then he should apply to the Mental Health Review Tribunal.

Detention by police or social worker. An approved social worker can apply to a JP for the police to be allowed to enter premises and take someone to a 'place of safety' (i.e. hospital, police station, residential home). This is done when the patient has been ill-treated, neglected, or is living alone and unable to care for himself (s. 135). But, more important, a policeman can detain any person found in a public place whom he reasonably believes to be mentally disordered, and put him in a 'place of safety' (e.g. a cell) for up to seventy-two hours (s. 136). This is potentially a very wide power for it allows the police virtually to arrest and imprison someone who has not committed an offence. Note that it is entirely a lay decision by the policeman; no proper medical evidence is needed to justify his decision. This is an unnecessarily wide power. Apparently, it is used most in the Greater London area.

Criminal court admissions. Any criminal court can make a *hospital order*, which is a compulsory admission order on a defendant. In addition, a crown court can add *restrictions;* there are also provisions allowing unconvicted defendants to be remanded in hospital, and for existing prisoners to be transferred to hospitals.

Detention in the hospital

The compulsorily admitted patient cannot choose which hospital to go to. Once in the hospital, the patient must be told – as soon as is practicable – which section of the 1983 Act is being used to justify the detention. Written information must also be given about discharge, appeals, legal aid, etc.

It will be seen from the summaries above that there are different periods for the detention of different categories of patients (e.g. seventy-two hours for emergencies; twenty-eight days for assessment; six months for treatment). But, once the patient is in hospital, the hospital can extend the period of detention, so these are in no way maximum periods. If a patient wrongly discharges himself, then he can be brought back by the police, an approved social worker, or a member of the hospital staff. However, there is a twenty-eight-day time limit for doing this; after that time, a fresh compulsory-detention order has to be made.

The patient's *nearest relative* (see page 699 for who this is) can sometimes discharge the patient. This applies to patients who are in for assessment or treatment, but it does not apply to an emergency admission. The nearest relative has to give at least seventy-two hours' advance notice of the intention to discharge the patient, so that the doctor can have sufficient time to decide whether to block the discharge (by issuing a 'barring certificate'). This prevents the relative discharging the patient, and all the relative can do is to appeal to the Mental Health Review Tribunal (unless the patient is in for assessment, in which case the relative cannot appeal).

Treatment in hospital

In a general hospital a patient can refuse treatment. If the staff ignore his wishes and carry out the treatment, they can be sued for assault if it can be shown that the staff 'touched' the patient without his informed consent. If the patient is unable to give his consent, for instance if he is unconscious, the doctor can proceed without consent if treatment is urgently necessary. But it will then be for the doctor to defend his actions; he will have to show that the urgency of the need for treatment and the impracticability of obtaining consent left him with no choice but to carry out the treatment. This is usually best done by showing that if he had not carried out the treatment he would have been guilty of professional negligence.

Usually, of course, consent will be given by the patient. But such consent must be real: the doctor must explain, in broad terms, what he intends to do, and what are the implications of those actions – in effect, the patient must be told of the risks involved. If the patient is not given this information then he cannot be said to have consented to the operation, and so an action will lie. Thus, a proforma signed by the patient consenting to the operation 'the effect and nature of which has been explained to me' will not deprive the patient of his/her right to sue if, in fact, no explanation was given.

In a mental hospital the position is different.

Patients with mental disorders can be treated against their will for those disorders – but they cannot normally be treated for unrelated complaints. For instance, if a mental patient needs a leg operation (i.e. unconnected with the mental disorder), then the hospital cannot force the operation on to him, unless the patient is not 'competent' to make a decision, and, in addition, the illness threatens his life.

In addition, there are restrictions on forcing certain types of treatment for the mental disorder on to the patient:
- brain surgery, and the implanting of hormones to reduce the male sex drive, can only be done with consent, doctor's approval, and the approval of two independent qualified persons;
- ECT, and drug treatment, is also controlled. Either consent is needed, or a doctor must certify that the patient is incapable of consenting and will otherwise deteriorate. However, even the above treatments can be forced on to the patient if it is a matter of life and death.

The patient's civil rights

There are various restrictions on the civil liberties of in-patients in mental hospitals. Generally, these restrictions apply whether the patient is formal or informal.

The right to visits. The patient has no legal right to visits, except to give him assistance where the decision to discharge him is involved, or when he makes a complaint.

Correspondence. Letters addressed to any patient can be withheld if a medical officer thinks it 'would be calculated to interfere with the treatment of the patient or cause him unnecessary distress'. Letters sent by any patient can be withheld if the medical officer thinks it would be 'unreasonably offensive to the addressee, or is defamatory of other persons . . . or would be likely to prejudice the interests of the patient', unless the letter is addressed to an MP, the Mental Health Review Tribunal, or certain other official bodies.

Voting. Compulsorily detained patients cannot have their names on the electoral roll and so cannot vote. Voluntary patients can register on the electoral roll, and can have postal votes.

Jury service. Mentally disordered people who are resident in a psychiatric hospital, or who regularly receive mental treatment from their GPs, cannot serve on a jury.

Driving licences. An applicant for a driving licence (or a person applying to renew a licence) must declare whether s/he is receiving in-patient treatment for a mental disorder, or is suffering from a mental disorder that could lead to his/her being detained. In such a case the Secretary of State for the Environment will usually refuse to grant a licence.

Clothes. Both compulsory and voluntary patients have the right to wear their own clothes, and cannot be forced to wear bedclothes (or hospital-provided clothes) all the time.

The Mental Health Review Tribunal

Mental Health Review Tribunals (MHRTs) are independent bodies, and they are there to safeguard the proper use of the extensive powers given by the Mental Health Act. Each MHRT has a legal member, a medical member, and a lay member, and it will review decisions on detaining patients. The 1983 Act sets out the occasions when the patient and/or the patient's nearest relative can apply to the MHRT. The main occasions are:

Type of case	Who can apply to MHRT?
Assessment (s. 2)	Patient can apply in first fourteen days. Nearest relative cannot apply.
Treatment (s. 3)	Patient can apply once in first six months, once in next six months, and once a year thereafter. Nearest relative cannot apply.
Emergency (s. 4)	Patient cannot apply. Nearest relative cannot apply.

Barring of relative's discharge	Patient cannot apply (except in first fourteen days of assessment). Nearest relative can apply within twenty-eight days (unless patient is being assessed).
Reclassification of type of mental disorder	Patient can apply within twenty-eight days. Nearest relative can apply within twenty-eight days.

The hearing. The patient can be represented by anyone (whether lawyer, friend, or whoever). Legal aid is available for MHRT hearings (see page 865); it is important to find a solicitor who takes on these sorts of cases (the local library or CAB will probably have a list of solicitors who are competent to handle such a case). The legal aid can cover the cost of obtaining an independent medical report. When the application is made the MHRT will send a copy to the hospital and ask for a medical report together with a statement of reasons why the patient should not be discharged. The hospital must provide the report within three weeks, but it can ask that certain parts of it are not shown to the patient. The MHRT can override the hospital's objections, but one advantage of the patient having his own solicitor is that the solicitor will usually be able to obtain a complete copy of the report, in return for promising not to show it to the patient. The solicitor will then be able to make sure that any independent evidence to be put forward on the patient's behalf does adequately answer the points made in the hospital's report.

The tribunal hearing will probably be very informal. At the end of the hearing the tribunal will decide whether the continued detention of the patient is justified in accordance with the terms of the Mental Health Act. If it is not, then the hospital will be ordered to release the patient. Note that, in general, the tribunal must discharge a patient if it is satisfied that he is no longer mentally disordered, or – and this is important – if it is not necessary in the interests of the patient's health or safety, or for the protection of other people, that he should be detained. So if a person has a perfectly harmless belief (e.g. 'I am Napoleon') then there will be no justification for compulsorily detaining him in hospital.

The Court of Protection

If a person is certified by his doctor as being incapable of administering his property and affairs because of mental disorder, the Court of Protection can take control of them for him. Anyone can apply to the court for appointment as 'receiver' of the property, although the court prefers applications to be made by close relatives of the patient. Being a receiver is similar to being a 'trustee' (see page 158) and the patient loses virtually all control over his property and affairs.

48 Immigration

Immigration law is incredibly complicated. It is an area in which specialist advice is needed, and no one should think that a layman can work out nationality, citizenship, and immigration status in any but the most straightforward cases. A CAB will generally be able to give advice on immigration matters, or at least be able to refer one on to a specialist adviser. Thus what follows is merely a summary of answers to some of the most commonly asked questions – it is not a comprehensive guide. In addition, throughout this chapter we have assumed that the necessary passports are available; if (as often happens), they are not, then it is more essential than ever to take specialist advice.

The fundamental point to realize is that a person can have a British passport and yet not be a British citizen. There are five different types of British *nationality*, but only one of these (called British *citizenship*) gives complete freedom to enter and leave Britain at will. So, whilst a British *national* will have a British *passport*, s/he is not necessarily a British *citizen*.

Who is a British citizen?

The easiest way of working out whether someone is a British citizen is to look at their passport. But, remember, the mere fact that someone has a British passport does not mean that they are a British citizen. Basically, the person will be a British citizen if the British passport says:
- 'British citizen' at the foot of page 1, *or*
- 'Citizen of the UK and Colonies' at the foot of page 1, and if there is also a 'certificate of patriality' or a 'certificate of entitlement' stuck to one of the other pages, *or*
- 'Citizen of the UK and Colonies' at the foot of page 1, plus 'holder has right of abode in UK' on page 5, *or*
- 'Citizen of the UK and Colonies' at the foot of page 1, and it is clear from the stamps in the passport that at least five continuous years were spent in this country before 1 January 1983 (and there must have been no limit attached to those periods here). When the passport expires, the new passport will confirm that the holder is a British citizen, since it will then state 'British citizen' at the foot of page 1 (as above).

These then are the basic rules (although there are complicated exceptions for people like Falkland Islanders, and for people from former UK colonies). The important point is that only a person in one of the above categories is likely to be a British citizen – and it is only a British citizen who has full rights to live, work, and move freely in and out of the UK. Thus, only British citizens are exempt from immigration controls.

There are four other categories of people who might have British passports, but who will not be British citizens. Those categories are:

• *British Dependent Territories Citizen.* The person will be a national of this country, but will be subject to immigration control. If the person is settled here, with no restrictions on working, then he may be able to apply for British citizenship.

• *British Overseas Citizen.* The person will be a national of this country, but will be subject to immigration control. If the person is settled here, with no restrictions on working, then he may be able to apply for British citizenship. Vouchers may be available for a limited number of such people to settle here.

• *British Subject.* This is similar to the two above categories, in that a person settled here may be able to apply for British citizenship.

• *British Protected Person.* Such a person has very few rights and cannot apply to become a British citizen.

Commonwealth citizens

Commonwealth citizens may have British passports but that does not mean that they will be British citizens – and it is only a British citizen who is exempt from immigration control (see above). A person is treated as a Commonwealth citizen if s/he has either:

• a British passport (provided it does not say 'British Protected Person' on page 1), *or*

• a passport from a Commonwealth country.

If a person is a Commonwealth citizen, then their immigration rights will depend upon whether they have a 'right of abode' in the UK. This can usually be checked by looking in the passport – if there is a 'certificate of entitlement' or a 'certificate of patriality' stuck to one of the inside pages then there will be a right of abode.

If a Commonwealth citizen has a right of abode, then he or she is free from immigration controls – and can leave and re-enter the UK at will, and also be free to work here. The only restrictions that might affect a 'Commonwealth citizen with a right of abode' are those on bringing dependants into the UK, and on bringing in a non-British spouse (i.e. it must be proved that there will be sufficient accommodation and money for them – so they will not be claiming welfare benefits). Fiancés (male and female) are only admitted for a genuine marriage – temporary admission will only become permanent if they marry and are continuing to live together one year later.

Who has a right of abode? Usually there will be a certificate of patriality or a certificate of entitlement pasted on one of the inside pages of the British passport, and this will prove that the person has a right of abode. If there is no certificate, then the person will have to show that either:

(1) he or she was born before 1 January 1983 and has a parent who was born in the UK, *or*

(2) she (note, women only – not men) married, before 1 January 1983, a man who qualified under (1) above, or who was then a 'citizen of the UK and Colonies with the right of abode'.

Proof of this will enable the person to obtain a certificate of entitlement from the Home Office, which will then be stuck into the passport.

EEC nationals

It will usually be obvious whether a person is an EEC national – a glance at the passport or national identity card should confirm the position.

EEC nationals are not totally free from immigration controls. The basic rule is that an EEC national who is a worker (or self-employed) can move freely from one EEC country to another. Normally, leave to enter the UK will be given for six months, and this will extend to immediate members of the family – even if they are not EEC nationals. During this six-month period there will be no restriction on working. In practice, the six months will be extended without difficulty, whether or not the person has a job; only if the person has 'recourse to public funds' is an extension likely to be refused. The only two grounds for deporting an EEC national are the 'recourse to public funds' argument, or if it is not in the 'public interest' for the person to stay here.

If a person is a dependant of an EEC national already in the UK, then permission to enter should be obtained. This will normally be no more than a formality and a 'letter of consent' should be granted without difficulty. Alternatively, the dependant can enter the UK as a visitor and then ask to be able to stay on as a dependant.

Irish citizens

Here we are dealing with people from Eire (i.e. Southern Ireland). People from the North are normally British citizens and thus have free rights of entry and work. However, the Prevention of Terrorism Act provisions could enable a British citizen to be deported.

British subjects and Irish citizens travelling from Eire are theoretically subject to immigration controls – but, in practice, these are of limited effect. They can live and work in the UK without restriction, and can generally bring in dependants. They may also be able to apply for British citizenship after five years of being settled in the UK, and in any event all people from Eire have full voting rights in the UK (and can serve on a jury, stand for local or parliamentary elections, and join the forces). They are fully entitled to welfare benefits (including use of the NHS), and educational facilities and grants.

British passports

There are several types of British passport:

- the standard passport lasts ten years, and is 30 pages long (although 94-page passports can be obtained). Anyone who is within one of the five categories of British national (i.e. a British citizen, or one of the four categories listed on page 705) can apply. But only a British citizen will have free and unhindered rights to enter and leave the UK at will (see above). Thus, a person who is subject to immigration control – and therefore not able to enter and leave at will – may be able to obtain a British passport.
- the family passport covers both husband and wife. The first-named on the passport is its holder, and so the other spouse cannot travel abroad unless accompanied by that spouse.
- a British Visitor's passport is a simple fold-out card, and it is valid as a passport for one year. It can only be used in certain countries where visas and entry permits are not needed. The applicant must be at least eight years old, and a British citizen, a British Dependent Territories Citizen, or a British Overseas Citizen (see page 705 for what these phrases mean).
- a collective passport can be issued for an approved school party (or guides, scouts, etc.). It can cover from five to fifty children, all of whom must be under eighteen. Children (i.e. under sixteen) can be put on a standard passport for no extra fee (unless application is made after the standard passport has already been issued, in which case a fee is payable). Alternatively, a passport can be applied for in the child's own name; this will initially be for five years, but will be extended for a further five years (free of charge) even if the child is then over sixteen.

Illegal immigrants

An illegal immigrant is liable to be deported. There is no right to remain after a certain number of years of illegal immigration – the illegal immigrant can never legitimize his position by 'getting away with it' for a long period of time. Sometimes a person will be let into this country by mistake – is that person then an illegal immigrant? If he acted in good faith then he is likely to be allowed to remain here since he will not have been an illegal immigrant. On the other hand, if he lied to the immigration officer, or forged a document, then he will be an illegal immigrant.

Difficulties have arisen when the immigrant has not told the immigration officer of relevant facts – not because of any fraud or deception, but simply because he was not asked the right questions. Thus, in one case a man who had been given an entry certificate as a single man did not mention to the immigration officer that he had since married. It was held by the House of Lords that he should have volunteered this information, and so he was liable to be deported as an illegal immigrant. But this decision was much criticized and it does not follow that the incoming immigrant has to volunteer all relevant information to the immigration officer – it is a matter of degree as to what he should disclose.

Appeals against deportation orders can normally be made to an Immigration Appeals Tribunal.

People who help illegal immigrants to enter the UK can be prosecuted (maximum penalty in magistrates' court is six months' prison and £2,000 fine; in the crown court it is seven years' prison and unlimited fine). 'Harbouring' (i.e. giving shelter) to an illegal immigrant is a separate offence (maximum penalty £2,000 and/ or six months).

Help on immigration problems: UKIAS and JCWI

UKIAS and JCWI may be able to help with immigration problems, although both are extremely over-worked and operating on limited resources (the initials stand for United Kingdom Immigration Advisory Service, and the Joint Council for the Welfare of Immigrants). Also, a local CAB may be able to give advice and/or refer to a local specialist agency.

49 Defamation

Defamation is the collective word for libel and slander. It is the medium through which the defamation is made that determines whether it is libel or slander.

Traditionally, the law distinguished between the spoken word (slander), and the written word (libel), with libel being regarded as the more serious because of the permanence of the written word, as opposed to the transience of the spoken word. However, that classification broke down with the introduction of new forms of communication in the twentieth century. As for films, it was decided in a 1934 case that defamation in a film was libel, even though it was based on the spoken word. Similarly, it has been decided (this time by Act) that defamation on the TV is libel, and not slander. Defamation in cable, video, and satellite transmissions are best seen as being libel, not slander. Despite these complications, the basic distinction remains between spoken and written defamation (including TV, films, etc.); spoken is slander, written is libel.

With libel, the plaintiff (i.e. the person suing) need not show that the defamation caused him loss or damage; it is enough for him to show that the words were defamatory. But with slander the position is different; the plaintiff can only sue if the spoken defamation caused him loss or damage (e.g. it led to the loss of a contract). Mere injured feelings, embarrassment, or hurt pride are not sufficient to justify a slander action. Slander, by its nature, is spoken and thus is only temporary, and so the plaintiff is encouraged to forget the incident rather than litigate.

However, if he can show loss or damage then he can sue, and, in addition, certain types of slander are assumed to cause damage and so he can sue even if he cannot prove direct loss or damage:
- an allegation that he has committed an imprisonable offence (e.g. 'you are a thief');
- an allegation that the plaintiff has VD;
- disparaging comments about the plaintiff's office, profession, trade, or business;
- that an unmarried woman is not a virgin; that a married woman has committed adultery; or that a woman is a lesbian. Verbal allegations of male homosexuality are not actionable unless loss or damage can be proved – but a written allegation would be actionable as libel.

Otherwise, the same laws apply to slander as to libel. In practice, though, it is libel that is the more important of the two; few people litigate over verbal insults and so slander actions are rare.

Suing for defamation

Defamation cases are relatively few. There are two reasons for this:

1. Legal aid is not available for defamation actions. However bad the libel or the slander, the plaintiff cannot get legal aid to help him sue. Thus he will usually have to finance the case himself. This effectively dissuades most private people (apart from the rich) from suing for defamation.
2. A defamation action is a civil case (see page 757). But it can only be brought in the more senior (and more expensive) of the civil courts, namely the High Court. The plaintiff cannot sue in the cheaper county court, however small his claim for damages.

Anyone who thinks he has been defamed should bear these two points in mind. This is why few allegations of defamation get past the stage of the solicitor's letter.

What is a defamatory statement?

There is no simple nutshell test for deciding whether a statement (whether written or spoken) is defamatory, but a good general rule is to ask: 'Is it a false statement that discredits the plaintiff?' If so, it will almost certainly be defamation.

When a defamation case is tried, the judge sits with a jury – one of the rare occasions when a civil case has a jury. The judge decides whether the statement is capable of being defamatory, but it is the jury that then decides whether it was actually defamatory – and if so, how much damages the plaintiff should receive.

Bringing a defamation action

The plaintiff has to prove two things: firstly, that the statement had a defamatory meaning and, secondly, that it referred to him.

The statement is defamatory

Usually, showing that the statement had a defamatory meaning is not sufficient. More often than not, the defendant agrees that the words might be defamatory but he argues that he has a defence to the action because the statement was justified (e.g. the plaintiff *is* a drunkard). See below for defences.

Sometimes the meaning is less clear-cut, and the plaintiff argues that by implication the words are defamatory. In effect, it is the innuendo that causes the defamation:

In the 1920s Tolley was a famous amateur golfer. Fry's, the chocolate makers, produced an advertisement which showed Tolley playing golf, with a bar of Fry's chocolate sticking out of his pocket. A limerick on the advertisement suggested that the chocolate was as good as Tolley's drive. Tolley sued for defamation because the advertisement had been prepared without his knowledge or consent. Fry's argued that the advertisement was not defamatory. Held: The advert was defamatory. The implication behind the advert was that Tolley had been paid to consent to its publication, and so he had prostituted his reputation as an amateur golfer. Tolley (1931)

A racetrack photographer took a photo of a couple. The man said his name was Corrigan and that he was engaged to the lady. Subsequently, the photo appeared in the Daily Mirror *under the caption 'Mr Corrigan and Miss X, whose engagement has been announced'.*

In fact, Corrigan's real name was Cassidy and he was separated from his wife. Mrs Cassidy sued the Daily Mirror *for libel, arguing that the implication behind the photograph was that she was not married to her husband, but was merely his mistress. Held: The photograph and caption were defamatory. Mrs Cassidy was awarded £500 damages.* Cassidy (1929)

The Daily Mail *published an article in which it was alleged that Michael Foot, MP, had received private treatment in an NHS hospital. Held: This was defamatory. The implication was that Mr Foot was hypocritical and insincere in his advocacy of equality.* Foot (1978)

The plaintiff is the subject of the statement

Apart from showing that the statement is defamatory, the plaintiff must also show that he was identified as the subject of it. Often this will be obvious, as when the plaintiff is referred to by name. But if his identity is ascertainable then that will be sufficient. This is so even if the defamation was unintentional. For instance:

The Sunday Chronicle *published an account of a Dieppe motor-racing event. In describing the crowd, the correspondent wrote, 'There is Artemus Jones with a woman who is not his wife . . . Who would believe, by his goings-on, that he was a churchwarden at Peckham? . . . Here, in the atmosphere of Dieppe, he is the life and soul of a gay little band that haunts the casino and turns night into day, besides betraying a most unholy delight in the society of female butterflies.'*

In fact, the correspondent made all this up; it was a figment of his imagination. But there was in North Wales a barrister called Artemus Jones who used to write for the Sunday Chronicle. *He sued for libel saying that although he was not a churchwarden and not resident in Peckham, people would take the article as referring to him. Held: It was defamatory. He was awarded £1,750 damages. (Note: today, the paper could have avoided paying damages by printing an apology; see below.)* Jones (1909)

The Observer *had an article with the headline 'Corruption: three MPs escape prosecution – exclusive', and in the article was a large photograph of Reginald Maudling, MP. Although the article made it clear that he was not one of the MPs referred to, Maudling sued for libel. Held: The* Observer *was liable. The position of the photo was such that readers could have inferred that Mr Maudling was one of the corrupt politicians.* Maudling (1978)

Defences to a defamation claim

Anyone who is threatened with proceedings for defamation or libel should take legal advice. If the complaint is justified and the statement was defamatory, the best course of action is to write a letter of apology immediately.

If the action is to be defended, there are five main defences that can be raised: justification, fair comment, absolute privilege, qualified privilege, and, finally, that the defamation was unintentional.

Justification

This means that the statements are true. For instance:

> A newspaper article stated that Mr Loughans, who had a criminal record, had committed a murder. In fact, Loughans had been acquitted on that murder charge in 1944. He sued for libel. The paper pleaded justification as a defence. It was pointed out that in a criminal case (which the murder trial had been) a very high standard of proof was needed to secure a conviction – the jury had to be convinced 'beyond reasonable doubt' that he was guilty. But in a civil case (such as the defamation trial) a lower standard applies; the jury simply had to be satisfied on 'a balance of probabilities' that Loughans had committed the murder. This the jury did by upholding the plea of justification and so defeating the claim for defamation. Loughans (1963)

The Rehabilitation of Offenders Act 1974 has complicated the defence of justification. The Act provides that a criminal can sue for defamation if a 'spent' conviction is revealed and if he sues the defendant cannot plead justification (i.e. that the allegation is true). However, the plaintiff can only win his defamation case if he can show that the defendant acted maliciously in publicizing the conviction (see 'Rehabilitation of Offenders', page 678). In practice, the courts are reluctant to find that a newspaper was acting maliciously and so it is very difficult for the ex-offender to obtain an injunction to stop a paper publishing details of his previous convictions – especially when there is some 'public interest' justification.

Fair comment

It is a complete defence to a defamation claim if the statement was made on a matter of public interest, in good faith, and without malice. The logic behind this defence is that a man is entitled to his own opinions and he is free to tell people of them if, but only if, they are on a matter of public concern. For instance:

> A newspaper wrote, 'Sugar for Silkin. From these humble Tories I turn to a lordly Socialist. Forward the first Baron Silkin. Observe the return to Britain of the Heinkels. Not in the skies but on the rolling roads. These economical little runabouts are selling briskly in the petrol famine. They are seen everywhere – even in New Palace Yard, Westminster, where MPs park their cars. What has this to do with Lord Silkin? Why, he is Chairman of Noble Motors, who market the Heinkels in Britain. And his son, former socialist candidate Mr John Silkin, is a director. Oh, the eloquence that solemn portly Lord Silkin has churned out in the House of Lords against arming the Germans. He has said that part of his case is "emotional". "I feel it is wrong that so soon after the events of the war, we should join hands with them today for the purposes of combining our forces." Of course, when Lord Silkin joins hands with the Germans now, he represses his emotion. It is just good solid business. From which, no doubt, he makes a fine profit.'
>
> Lord Silkin sued. Held: The defence of fair comment applied. What mattered was not whether the jury agreed with the opinion expressed, but whether the writer had honestly held that opinion. The claim failed. Silkin (1958)

Absolute privilege

A defamation claim cannot be brought against statements made:

- in the House of Commons or the House of Lords;
- in connection with judicial proceedings (e.g. by a witness in a court case);
- in newspaper, radio, and TV reports of judicial proceedings.

All such statements and reports have absolute privilege. Their originators cannot be sued, even if the statements are totally untrue and are said out of spite or malice.

Qualified privilege

This protects statements made in circumstances that demand they be privileged. For instance, reports of parliamentary proceedings, reports of meetings of public concern (e.g. a TUC conference), or of official bodies; also the reference given by an ex-employer to another employer. Similarly, statements genuinely made on matters of public concern can be privileged, e.g. an allegation of misconduct by a public officer or statements given to the police to help them catch criminals.

The general principle is that society recognizes that there must be occasions when the public interest demands that honest beliefs (even if mistaken) should be reported. Only when the plaintiff can show that the defendant acted out of malice can he succeed in a defamation claim if qualified privilege exists. For instance, if your employer wrongly described you as a 'bad timekeeper' in a reference, you could not sue for defamation unless you could prove that he had said this maliciously – i.e. in order deliberately to hurt you, rather than through an innocent mistake.

Unintentional defamation

The fact that the defamation was not intentional is no defence to a defamation claim. For instances of this, see *Cassidy* and *Jones* above. But since the Defamation Act 1952, the defendant has been able to make amends and so avoid having to pay heavy damages to the plaintiff.

If the defamation arose innocently, the publisher of a libel can immediately make a suitable 'offer of amends', such as an offer to publish a suitable correction and apology. If this is done, the plaintiff will not be entitled to damages.

50 Victims of Crime

Compensating the criminal's victim

The criminal law is concerned with bringing offenders to justice and ensuring that they do not go unpunished. The criminal law is therefore dealing with the *offender* rather than with the victim.

But what of the victim? He will want compensation if he has been injured or if his property has been stolen or damaged. There are three ways in which he can go about obtaining compensation:

1. He can ask the criminal court to order the criminal to pay him compensation – a criminal compensation order.
2. He can sue the criminal for damages in the civil courts. Exceptionally, he might even be able to sue the police for not taking steps to prevent the offence.
3. He can claim from the state-financed Criminal Injuries Compensation Board if he suffered personal injury.

1. Obtaining a criminal compensation order

The criminal court that convicts the offender can order him to pay compensation of up to £2,000 to the victim (Powers of Criminal Courts Act 1973, section 35). In principle, this sounds an excellent scheme, and indeed Lord Scarman has described section 35 as 'a convenient and rapid means of avoiding the expense of resorting to civil litigation when the criminal has the means which enable the compensation to be paid'. Actually, the section is not as useful as it would appear, partly because few offenders have 'the means which enable the compensation to be paid' and partly because the criminal courts have been reluctant to use their powers to the full. In practice, orders are made mainly in cases of criminal damage, fraud, burglary, theft, and robbery. In fact, about 70 per cent of magistrates' court convictions for criminal damage lead to compensation orders being made, although the vast majority are for less than £50. The power to order compensation is surprisingly wide. For instance, in one case a man had wandered into a garden and thrown a stone through a window; the terrified (but uninjured) householder was awarded £25 for the terror he had suffered.

Whether or not to order compensation is entirely at the discretion of the court. But it cannot give compensation after a road accident, and it will not do so if:

● there is some doubt as to the defendant's responsibility for the damage or loss (for instance, if he denies that he stole some of the items), *or*

● it seems unlikely that the defendant will be able to pay the compensation. An order will not be made if it would have to be paid by instalments over a long period of time, or if its effect on the accused would be so serious that it might encourage him to commit further crime to pay off the compensation order.

The full rules were set out in a 1976 case:

Mr Miller was an account supervisor. He had been convicted of two offences of theft (with fifteen others taken into consideration) involving £6,100. He was sentenced to fifteen months in prison, and a compensation order for £6,100 was made against him. He appealed. The Court of Appeal quashed the compensation order. The court pointed out that when defendants come up for sentence, they are normally anxious to persuade the court that they are willing to make restitution as soon as possible. Courts had to be careful and bear in mind that:

● *a compensation order is not an alternative to a sentence*

● *it should take into account the defendant's finances*

● *the amount of compensation must not be oppressive; the court should bear in mind that discharged prisoners are often short of money and if ordered to pay compensation they might be encouraged to commit further offences*

● *the amount of the order must be realistic; an order for payment by instalments over a long period should be avoided*

● *a compensation order should only be made when it is clear that the defendant is under a legal liability to compensate.*　　　　　　　　　　　　　　　　　　　　　　　　Miller (1976)

The main points to note are that the court must be clearly satisfied that the accused is liable for the damage – and it must be quite clear how much the damage is worth. The court cannot make an 'informed guess' as to the right level of compensation. For example, in one case the owner of a car valued it at £3,000, but the defendant had sold it, in bits, for £600. The JP decided it was worth £1,000, without having heard any further evidence – the court of appeal overturned that compensation order since an order should only have been made if the value was clear.

Often the court will have to choose between imposing a fine and making a compensation order, since it will feel that the defendant is too poor to be able to afford both. When this happens the court should opt for the compensation order (although, in practice, it has to be said that most courts are reluctant to order compensation).

Compensation in the magistrates' court: guidelines suggested by the Magistrates Association

Type of injury	Assumption as to pain	Suggested sum
Graze	Considerable pain for a few days; a little after a week.	£35
Bruise	More variable. Generally speaking, the closer to a bone the more painful. Likely to be painful for a couple of weeks.	£50
Cut	Depends on size and whether stitched. Pain likely to have gone in two weeks.	£50–£150

Type of injury	Assumption as to pain	Suggested sum
Sprain	Likely to be painful for three or more weeks.	£75–£150
Fracture	Arms around four weeks. Legs or ribs around six weeks.	£150–£400
Head injury	Headaches unpredictable, average of a month. More serious if knocked out.	£100–£400
Scarring	Important to consider position and likelihood of permanency, especially on face and if young.	£200–£500
Loss of tooth	Depends on position and age of victim.	£60–£150

Note

1. More compensation is likely if the victim is elderly or infirm, or if the injury is in a particularly sensitive area of the body.
2. Less compensation is likely if there was provocation by the victim or if the injury was less serious than might normally be expected.

Restitution orders

A restitution order is an order that stolen property be restored to its owner. As with compensation orders, the criminal courts seem very reluctant to use these powers and the result is that a restitution order will only be made in the plainest of cases, when there can be absolutely no doubt as to where the property is and to whom it belongs.

A restitution order can also be made when the property has come into the hands of the police (Police Property Act 1897). In this case there is no need for the property to have been stolen; it might, for example, be an item that was taken by the police to use as evidence. So the order can be made in favour of the accused, as well as the victim or a witness.

2. Suing for damages

A crime of violence will give the victim a civil claim for assault, and a crime involving theft of property or damage to property will usually give the victim a civil claim for trespass. The victim of crime will thus always have a civil remedy which he can pursue in the civil courts where he will, of course, ask for damages against the offender.

In practice, civil claims by victims are rare, presumably because few victims realize they can sue the offender and also because few offenders are worth suing. There is little point in suing an offender who does not have the resources to pay the damages (and any legal costs incurred).

If the offender is insured then it would, of course, be a different matter, for his insurers will usually have to meet any judgement obtained against him. The usual instance of this is in motoring cases; the offender will have committed a criminal offence by his reckless driving and the victim can bring a claim for negligence. The damages will probably be paid by the offender's insurers.

Suing the police

One other civil remedy that may be open to the victim is to sue the police. An obscure piece of nineteenth-century law (The Riot (Damages) Act 1886) allows the owner of property damaged in a riot to obtain compensation from the police (in effect, from the local ratepayers). But, for the claim to succeed, it must be shown that:

1. There was a 'riot' – in other words, there were at least three people who acted together and used force or violence that alarmed at least one reasonable bystander (see page 689). Football hooligans could come within this category.
2. The rioters behaved 'tumultuously'. This means that the number of people, or the way in which they were behaving, should have put the police on their guard and so they should have taken steps to stop the damage occurring.

There is no need for the rioters to have been prosecuted for riot. For instance, if a gang of hooligans are only prosecuted for criminal damage, or even if they escape detection, the police can still be liable if there was legally a 'riot' and it was 'tumultuous'.

Claims should normally be made within fourteen days.

3. Applying to the Criminal Injuries Compensation Board

The Criminal Injuries Compensation Board (CICB) is a state-run body that pays compensation to people injured as a result of crime.

The crime must be a 'crime of violence', but the courts have interpreted this phrase widely, so that a non-violent crime which leads to injury can come within the scheme.

The occupant of a house committed suicide by breaking a gas pipe. Subsequently, the police were called to the house and PC Clowes went inside. There was a gas explosion and he was injured. He claimed from the CICB but it was argued that his injury did not result from a crime of violence but merely from an act of criminal damage. Held: The CICB should pay him. The person who had killed himself had been reckless as to whether the escaping gas would injure someone else and so it amounted to a 'crime of violence'. Clowes (1977)

The fact that no one was prosecuted or convicted for the offence does not affect the CICB's obligation to compensate the victim. Indeed, the CICB are obliged to pay out even when the injury arose out of a 'suspected crime'. So compensation can be paid even when it turns out that no crime was actually committed:

PC Ince was driving a Panda car in central London when he received a call that people were breaking into a Territorial Army depot. PC Ince rushed towards the scene, but was killed in a collision when he jumped a red traffic light. In fact, the alarm call was a false one – there was no break-in. His widow claimed compensation from the CICB, but the CICB argued that the death did not result from an offence or an attempted offence. Mrs Ince appealed. Held: The CICB should compensate her. It was sufficient that PC Ince had honestly believed that an offence was taking place and had taken action to prevent it. Although his negligent driving had been the direct cause of his death, the suspected break-in had been an indirect cause and so his death was within the CICB scheme. Ince (1973)

Thus the CICB often pay out in cases that do not – at first sight – seem to involve crimes. It should also be remembered that many trivial actions are in fact crimes and so give rise to a CICB claim. For instance:

Tony Killingbach was playing soccer for his office team. During the game, which was a hard one, Killingbach was deliberately kicked in the course of a high tackle when he was off the ball. Killingbach fell and broke his arm. After the game, Killingbach's team mates reported the incident to the police but Killingbach decided not to press charges. Subsequently, he claimed from the CICB. Held: He had been injured as a result of a crime of violence (the high tackle was legally an assault) and so he was entitled to compensation from the CICB. Killingbach (1978)

On the other hand:

A train driver suffered shock and depression after seeing the headless body of a suicide beside the railway track. Could he bring a CICB claim? Held: No. Although the suicide victim had broken the law and committed a criminal offence, the driver's illness was not directly attributable to that crime and so no CICB claim could be brought. Webb (1985)

A final example involved a claimant who was awarded over £7,000 compensation after having had a lump of mud thrown at his back by a work-mate (because, of course, that amounted to an assault – a crime of violence!). So any injury that results from unlawful force can lead to a CICB claim.

Cases that are excluded from the CICB scheme

Cases worth less than £400. In order to cut down administrative work and expense, these small-value claims are excluded. For instance, a grazed ankle, a black eye or a minor cut is unlikely to reach the £400 (1984) limit unless there was also a substantial wage loss involved.

Claims for damages to property or for loss of property. The CICB scheme is primarily designed to compensate for bodily injury and losses resulting from those injuries (e.g. loss of earnings while off work; cleaning bloodstained clothes). It does not cover loss or damage to valuables. So if someone is mugged, they cannot claim compensation for their lost wallet and money, but they can claim compensation for any injury suffered.

Offences not reported to the police. The CICB will not pay compensation unless the crime was reported to the police 'without delay'. Any delay in reporting the offence can result in failure of the CICB claim. This rule is applied very strictly and the offence must be reported even when the victim knows that the police will not be able to help – for instance, if the attacker was not seen by the victim and he has since disappeared. In practice, it is vitally important that the victim reports the incident without delay.

Claims not made within three years. A claim must be made to the CICB within three years. This rule is similar to the three-year limitation period that applies to the bringing of court proceedings in injury cases (see page 773).

Traffic offences. Generally, traffic offences are excluded because the victim will usually be able to claim from the offender's insurance company or, if he is uninsured, from the Motor Insurers' Bureau (see page 612).

Provocation and misconduct by the victim. If the victim provoked the violent crime, he cannot expect CICB compensation. Similarly, if he was misbehaving himself he will not come within the scheme; for instance, a participant in a gang fight cannot expect compensation if he is injured in the course of the fight. However, it is not clear to what extent 'contributory negligence' (see page 653) by the victim will apply. It might be thought that the victim would lose some of his compensation if he himself was negligent, as, for instance, in the case of PC Ince who was killed as a result of his negligent driving when rushing to the scene of a crime (above). But this is not so. In Ince's case, Lord Denning specifically said that the CICB 'should not be influenced by concepts of contributory negligence unless the conduct of the applicant involves something reprehensible or provocative'. So it seems that only 'reprehensible' negligence should be taken into account. In practice, one feels that the CICB do take into account contributory negligence even when it is not 'reprehensible' and award lower sums to such applicants.

Dubious characters. Finally, the CICB has a wide discretion to refuse compensation (or to reduce the amount awarded) because of the 'conduct of the applicant before, during or after the events giving rise to the claim, or to his character and way of life'. What this means is that the CICB has an extremely wide discretion to penalize claims by 'doubtful characters' – generally, people with criminal records, those who associate with criminals, or who lead a debauched life. For instance, one man was refused compensation for a broken leg caused through an assault by his drinking companion – he had convictions for dishonesty both before and after the incident, and even though those convictions were irrelevant to his claim, he was refused compensation. Not surprisingly, many commentators feel that this is too wide a discretion and that it is open to abuse.

Violence in the family

Until 1979, the victim could not make a CICB claim if s/he was living with the assailant as part of the same family. Battered wives and children were thus excluded. This was obviously unfair and the position now is that a victim can make a claim even if living with the offender as 'members of the same family'. But to guard against fraud (i.e. mum falsely saying she has been assaulted by dad) the CICB will only pay out if:

- the offender was prosecuted (but he need not have been convicted), *and*
- the injuries justify compensation of at least £500, *and*
- the offender will not benefit from the award, *and*

- when the victim is a child, the CICB will want to be sure that it is in the child's best interests that an award is made.

How much compensation?

In theory, the CICB aims to pay the victim a sum roughly equal to the damages which he would be awarded if he sued the offender in the civil courts. In practice, the CICB is much less generous than the courts. The CICB award will cover:
- compensation for the pain and suffering caused by the injury, *plus*
- lost earnings resulting from the injury (net wage loss, minus all social security and NI benefits received by the victim), *plus*
- a sum to cover his loss of earnings in the future and perhaps an additional sum to reflect the difficulty he will have in obtaining a job in the future.

The difficulty usually arises in assessing the compensation for the pain and suffering. Each case has to be judged on its merits and the CICB try to ensure that their awards reflect the amounts being awarded by the courts in civil claims. Some guidance as to amounts paid was given by the CICB in 1984:

Undisplaced nasal fracture	£450
Displaced nasal fracture	£700
Wired jaw	£1,250
Rape (no physical injuries and psychological consequences no more serious than usual)	£2,750
Loss of two front upper teeth:	
No bridge inserted	£1,200
Bridge inserted	£1,000
Loss of sight in one eye	£12,000
Total loss of hearing (twelve-year-old girl)	£32,000
Exploratory operation (no other injury)	£2,500
Scar across face, from ear to mouth:	
Young man	£4,500
Young woman	£7,000

But these figures are only a guide. Each injury has to be assessed individually – for instance, stab wounds can vary enormously in severity. Also, awards increase with inflation each year. See also suggested levels of compensation for magistrates on page 715.

Making the claim

An application form should be obtained from the CICB at 10–12 Russell Square, London wc1 (01-636 2812 or 01-636 4201). This should be completed and returned as soon as possible; there is no fee. The board staff are helpful and will deal with any questions.

A member of the board's staff will investigate the application and collect together all the relevant papers (e.g. proof of loss of earnings from employers, record of the offence being reported to the police, medical reports). In serious cases it is often worth the applicant obtaining his own medical report from a consultant to ensure that the medical evidence before the board is complete.

The papers then go before a member of the board, who makes an award, generally without having seen the applicant. The applicant is then told how much he is being offered. If he is dissatisfied with the amount he can ask a three-member hearing of the board to review the award. This is, in effect, an appeal and both the board and the applicant can supply further information (such as additional medical reports) for the hearing. The applicant can attend the hearing and he can bring a lawyer or friend if he wishes. The decision of the board is final and cannot be appealed to the courts unless there is a dispute over the application of the scheme, not just the amount awarded.

In most serious cases it is advisable to have the help of a solicitor. He has experience in presenting claims and collecting evidence, and his knowledge of levels of damage may well be invaluable.

Unfortunately, legal aid is not available for CICB claims. However, the green-form scheme, which generally allows up to £50 worth of legal advice, can be used. In practice, the solicitor may well be able to have the £50 extended to £125 or more, but if compensation is awarded the money will have to be used to repay the cost of the free legal advice to the Law Society (see page 869).

Overall, the CICB scheme is a good starting-point for compensating victims of crime. However, it could be considerably improved – and it could be made the basis of a more generalized compensation scheme. For instance, why not allow legal aid to be granted for CICB applications? Why not allow CICB cover to be extended to cover all claims in which insurance does not apply (e.g. if an employer does not insure against accident claims by his staff? Why not allow the compensation to be paid in instalments, rather than simply by lump sum? Why not allow the damages to be awarded on exactly the same basis as a court would (e.g. allow compensation for bereavement on death; no upper maximum on loss-of-earnings figures)? Many of these may seem detailed points, but, in practice, they do seriously limit the effectiveness of the CICB scheme. Many commentators feel that if these changes could be introduced, we would have the basis of a system that could replace the present antiquated procedures for suing for personal injury in ordinary accident claims.

51 Homelessness

Prior to 1977 the legal responsibility of local authorities to house the homeless was muddled and confused. There was never more than an obligation to provide temporary accommodation (e.g. in a hostel, bed and breakfast) and the council's duties were divided between the Housing Department and the Social Services Department, which led to endless wrangling over which department was responsible for a particular homeless family.

The Housing (Homeless Persons) Act 1977 imposes a legal obligation on local-authority Housing Departments to rehouse certain homeless people. These are people who have a priority need, and they must be rehoused by the council. The Act is backed up by a Department of Environment Code of Guidance, which does not have the force of law but is extremely influential. It sets out what should happen in practice.

The 1977 Act is not a straightforward piece of legislation. How it applies to a particular situation can only be worked out by following the correct step-by-step procedure, which is summarized in the chart on pages 724–5. Key concepts that must be grasped are:

1. Who is covered by the *obligation to rehouse*?
2. Who has a *priority need*? A person who is not a priority need cannot claim even temporary accommodation.
3. What is *'intentional' homelessness*? This will disqualify the applicant from permanent accommodation and entitle him to temporary accommodation only.
4. Does he have a *'local connection'* with another area? If so, he need only be given temporary accommodation while the other authority arranges permanent accommodation.

1. Who needs to be rehoused?

A person is homeless when he has no accommodation that is sufficient for himself, plus those of his family who live with him, plus any other person who normally lives with him. Generally, therefore, mistresses and common-law wives are included as part of the family unit. Families must not be split; as the code says:

The practice of splitting families is not acceptable, even for short periods. The social cost, personal hardship, and long-term damage to children, as well as the expense involved in

722

receiving children into care, rules this out as an acceptable course, other than in the exceptional case where professional social-work advice is that there are compelling reasons, apart from homelessness, for separating a child from his family.

2. Who has a priority need?

Unless there is a priority need the council need not provide accommodation. The authority's legal responsibility is then limited to providing advice to the applicant (e.g. addresses of lodgings or hostels, an appointment with a housing-aid centre).

A person has a priority need if:

- s/he has dependent children, under sixteen (nineteen if at school or training), *or*
- s/he (or one of his/her family, etc.) is vulnerable because of old age, disability, etc., *or*
- she (or one of the family, etc.) is pregnant, *or*
- s/he became homeless because of an emergency such as flood, fire, or other disaster.

The important point to note is that single people – especially single men – are not likely to qualify as having a priority need (unless 'vulnerable' through old age, illness etc.). Thus, single men can rarely expect to be rehoused, and single women can only expect to qualify if they have children or are at risk – it is specifically provided that a battered woman without children can be regarded as 'vulnerable' if she would face violence if she returned home.

If an applicant is homeless but is not a priority, then all the council has to do is to give general advice and assistance about finding accommodation – in practice, this means handing out a printed list of local housing associations and accommodation agencies!

3. What is intentional homelessness?

Intentional homelessness deprives the applicant of the right to permanent accommodation. Even if he has a priority need, all he can demand is temporary accommodation for long enough to give him a reasonable chance of finding his own accommodation, usually for a month or six weeks.

A person who sells his house or who is evicted from rented accommodation because of persistent rent arrears may be treated as intentionally homeless. But if the rent arrears were the result of genuine financial difficulties, that should not be seen as intentional. The authority ought to look at the reasonableness and genuineness of the applicant's behaviour. For instance, if he gave up a tenancy because of continuing harassment, that should not be seen as intentional homelessness. But tenants should be careful not to give up their rented accommodation too easily – if they do, the council will say they are intentionally homeless and thus not entitled to be rehoused.

Other examples of intentional homelessness include the family who were evicted because of persistent misbehaviour by their children; the family who gave up their home to move abroad and who then changed their minds and came back to live in

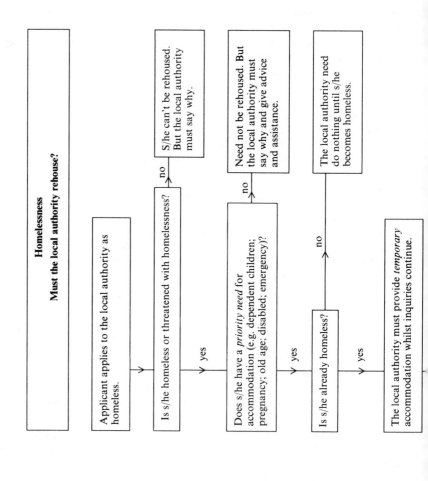

Homelessness

Must the local authority rehouse?

Applicant applies to the local authority as homeless.

Is s/he homeless or threatened with homelessness?

— no → S/he can't be rehoused. But the local authority must say why.

— yes →

Does s/he have a *priority need* for accommodation (e.g. dependent children; pregnancy; old age; disabled; emergency)?

— no → Need not be rehoused. But the local authority must say why and give advice and assistance.

— yes →

Is s/he already homeless?

— no → The local authority need do nothing until s/he becomes homeless.

— yes →

The local authority must provide *temporary* accommodation whilst inquiries continue.

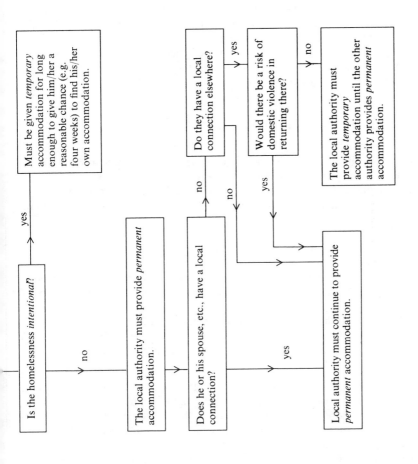

Is the homelessness *intentional*?

yes → Must be given *temporary* accommodation for long enough to give him/her a reasonable chance (e.g. four weeks) to find his/her own accommodation.

no → The local authority must provide *permanent* accommodation.

Does he or his spouse, etc., have a local connection?

no → **Do they have a local connection elsewhere?**

no → Local authority must continue to provide *permanent* accommodation.

yes → Local authority must continue to provide *permanent* accommodation.

Do they have a local connection elsewhere?

yes → **Would there be a risk of domestic violence in returning there?**

no → The local authority must provide *temporary* accommodation until the other authority provides *permanent* accommodation.

yes → Local authority must continue to provide *permanent* accommodation.

the UK; the family who swapped their accommodation for a caravan in the country and who then found that conditions in the caravan were too hard for them to endure.

If a tenant faces eviction proceedings and it is clear that the court will make an eviction order (e.g. because there is a resident landlord), the tenant need not wait until the order is made before leaving. He should not be counted as intentionally homeless because he has given up possession in such circumstances. However, some councils adopt a harsh approach to the Act and the tenant should check the position with the council before giving up the tenancy.

There is little doubt that many councils apply the 'intentionally homeless' provisions very strictly in an attempt to avoid the obligation to house. In case of doubt, specialist legal advice should be sought.

4. Does he have a local connection elsewhere?

If the applicant does not have a local connection (and none of his family, etc. has) but he (or one of his family, etc.) has a local connection elsewhere, it will be for the other authority to provide permanent accommodation. The only exception to this is when the applicant (or one of his family, etc.) would run the risk of domestic violence by returning to that area; this provision is obviously designed to protect battered wives.

A local connection exists if a person:

● was normally resident there in the past, *or*
● he has a job there, *or*
● he has family associations there or some other special connection with the area.

If an authority thinks the applicant has local connections with another authority it will notify that other authority, but in the meantime it must provide temporary accommodation. If the other authority accepts its responsibility then that authority will have to provide permanent accommodation. If the other authority disputes the local connection, the Department of the Environment will arbitrate and decide which authority is responsible.

Summary. Many people naïvely think that their local council has an obligation to rehouse them if ever they become homeless. It can be seen from the above that this is not so – only those with a priority need (i.e. the old, the infirm, and those with children) have to be rehoused, and even they will not have to be rehoused if they are intentionally homeless (for instance, if they were evicted from their last home because of rent arrears). The 1977 Act is a complicated piece of law and specialist legal advice is needed by anyone who has the misfortune to become involved with it.

A final point to note is that the Act does not lay down the standard of accommodation that has to be provided. Accordingly, many councils have been able to get away with putting homeless families in bed-and-breakfast, or other 'temporary' accommodation. Although such accommodation may be totally unsuitable, it is all that is needed for the council to be complying with its legal duties. Also, homeless families are not entitled to jump to the top of the housing waiting list – the Act merely says that the council has to give the homeless 'reasonable preference' when allocating housing, but this phrase is so vague as to be virtually meaningless.

52 Social-Security Benefits

'Social security' is the general phrase used to describe cash benefits. The Department of Health and Social Security (DHSS) is responsible for the administration of all the social security schemes. There are two main categories of social-security benefits: means-tested and non-means-tested benefits.

Means-tested benefits

Supplementary benefit (see page 744) and family income supplement (see page 742) are the principal means-tested benefits. Both aim to help the poor.

Non-means-tested benefits

The other benefits are designed to deal with particular events and situations, such as widowhood, unemployment, retirement, sickness, or the birth of a child. The criterion for determining eligibility is not poverty but whether the particular situation has arisen. Most of these benefits are at least partly financed by the National Insurance Fund, which receives a substantial proportion of its income from the national insurance contributions paid by employers, employees, and the self-employed. Accordingly, eligibility for some of these non-means-tested benefits is conditional on the applicant having paid sufficient national insurance (NI) contributions.

Benefits that are dependent on sufficient NI contributions having been paid

Child's special allowance, page 737
Death grant, page 738
Invalidity benefit, page 741
Maternity allowance, page 747
Retirement pension, page 748

Sickness benefit, page 741
Unemployment benefit, page 750
Widow's allowance, page 753
Widowed mother's allowance, page 753
Widow's pension, page 754

Benefits that do not depend on the amount of NI contributions paid

Attendance allowance, page 738
Child benefit, page 735
Disablement benefit, page 734

Guardian's Allowance, page 736
Housing benefit, page 743
Industrial death benefit, page 735

728

Invalid care allowance, page 739   One-parent benefit, page 736
Maternity grant, page 746   Severe disablement allowance, page 742
Mobility allowance, page 739

Other benefits

There are, of course, other benefits available, such as redundancy payments (see page 464), and criminal injuries compensation (page 717), but traditionally these are not included in the term 'social-security benefits'.

The four categories of national insurance contributions

It can be seen from the list above that many benefits are paid only if the applicant has paid sufficient NI contributions. Most people pay contributions (or have them credited to their record) from the time they leave school until the time they retire. However, before 1978 women who stayed at home to bring up children did not have contributions credited to them while they were not in paid employment. There are four categories of contributions.

Class 1 contributions: employees and office-holders

By the Social Security Act 1975, Class 1 contributions have to be paid by 'a person who is gainfully employed . . . either under a contract of service or in an office . . . with emoluments chargeable to income tax under Schedule E'. The two essential requirements are, therefore, that he is 'gainfully employed' (in other words, he receives some remuneration, however small), and that he has a 'contract of service' or that he holds an office (in other words, he is an employee, not a self-employed person – see page 379).

The amount of the contribution is earnings related, being a percentage of gross income between the current lower and upper earnings level. The employee's contribution is deducted at source by the employer, who pays over the employee's contribution when he pays his own share of the Class 1 contribution. The total NI contribution is paid by the employer to the Inspector of Taxes, along with the usual PAYE tax payments.

If the employee's earnings are below a certain level, called the lower earnings limit (£1,846 in 1985) then he pays no Class 1 contribution. If he earns more than that, he will pay a contribution – on a sliding scale of between 5 and 9 per cent – on his gross earnings, up to the upper earnings limit (£13,780 in 1985, at 9 per cent). The employer also pays a contribution – initially on a sliding scale at the lower earnings limit, which then increases up to a maximum of 10·45 per cent (1985). Unlike the employee, the employer pays the contribution on all a higher-paid employee's earnings; his contribution does not stop at the upper earnings limit.

A Class 1 contributor is eligible for all those benefits listed above which are dependent on sufficient NI contributions having been paid. But if the employee earns less than the current lower earnings limit, and so need not pay Class 1 contributions, he cannot claim any of those benefits. However, if he wishes he can pay voluntary Class 3 contributions, which will safeguard his entitlement to retirement pension, widow's benefit, death grant, and child's special allowance.

Class 2 contributions: the self-employed

Under the 1975 Act Class 2 contributions have to be paid by 'a person who is gainfully employed . . . otherwise than in employed earner's employment (whether or not he is also employed in such employment)', in other words, the self-employed. The contribution is paid at a flat rate, and is paid by direct debit through a bank or by sticking stamps on a NI contribution card.

Those with small earnings (less than £1,925 for the 1985/86 tax year) can apply for exemption and so not have to pay Class 2 contributions (full details in DHSS leaflet NI 27A). Those with larger earnings have to pay additional, Class 4, contributions (see below).

A Class 2 contributor is eligible for all those benefits listed above which are dependent on sufficient NI contributions having been paid, *except* unemployment benefit.

Class 3 contributions: voluntary contributions

If a person's contribution record is patchy, he can pay Class 3 contributions and so fill in gaps in the contribution record. Of the benefits that are dependent on sufficient NI contributions having been paid, Class 3 contributions can only give entitlement to child's special allowance, death grant, and retirement and widow's benefits.

Class 4 contributions: the self-employed with higher earnings

A self-employed person paying Class 2 contributions will also have to pay Class 4 contributions if his profits exceed a certain level. The amount to be paid is a fixed percentage of profits between a lower and upper limit (in the 1985/86 tax year, 6·3 per cent of earnings between £4,150 and £13,780).

Further information on national insurance contributions

A person can be liable to pay more than one class of NI contribution. For instance, an employed person (liable to pay Class 1) may also have a part-time business, in which case he will have to pay Class 2 on his self-employed earnings, unless the small-earnings exemption applies. He could also be liable to pay Class 4 contributions if his self-employed earnings were sufficiently high.

A person who does not pay his contributions can be prosecuted in the magistrates' court; generally the maximum penalty is £50 and an order that the arrears of contributions be paid off. Re-using NI stamps or fraudulently trying to reduce liability to pay contributions is punishable with up to three months' prison and a fine of £400.

Women and NI contributions

Prior to the introduction of the 1975 legislation, women were often entitled to lower rates of benefit than men. The position has now been changed so that insured men and women generally receive the same benefits. However, until May 1977 married women could opt for a reduced range of benefits and a reduced liability to make NI contributions. If the option has been exercised the woman loses the right to claim invalidity benefit, maternity allowance, sickness benefit, unemployment benefit, and retirement pension (unless she can qualify by virtue of her husband's NI contributions).

If a woman did not opt for reduced liability by 11 May 1977, she will now have to pay the full NI contributions – assuming of course that she is earning, either as an employed person (Class 1) or a self-employed person (Class 2 and Class 4). It is too late for her to opt out now.

If she did opt out she can change her mind and opt back in. This will happen automatically if she divorces or if she has been neither employed nor self-employed for two or more consecutive tax years. She will then be liable to pay full contributions (assuming she is employed or self-employed) but in return she will be eligible for more benefits.

As can be seen, the position is absurdly complicated.

The married woman's entitlement to the various NI benefits

Invalidity benefit Maternity allowance Sickness benefit Unemployment benefit	She will not be eligible for these benefits if she has opted out.
Death grant Retirement pension	As above, except that she might be eligible by virtue of her husband's contributions even if she has opted out.
Child's special allowance Widow's benefits	Eligibility is based on her late husband's contribution record, so opting out does not affect eligibility.
Attendance allowance Child benefit Family income supplement Guardian's allowance Industrial injury benefits Invalid care allowance Maternity grant Mobility allowance One-parent benefit Severe disablement allowance Supplementary benefit	Eligibility is determined by a means test or by a specific situation having arisen. There is no need for NI contributions to have been paid, so a woman is eligible whether or not she has opted out.

Divorced women

When a working woman divorces she will have to change from paying a married woman's stamp to a full-rate contribution. Otherwise, she may lose entitlement to benefits (in particular, maternity allowance, unemployment benefit, and additional retirement pension).

A divorced woman may find that she is eligible for some benefits that she was not eligible for when married (in particular, child's special allowance, one-parent benefit, invalid care allowance, and severe disablement allowance). In any event, a divorced woman under the age of sixty can still rely on her ex-husband's contributions when calculating eligibility for the basic retirement pension, death grant, and some other benefits.

As always, the rules are extremely complicated. DHSS leaflet NI95 gives full details of the rules for divorced women.

Contribution conditions for NI benefits

There are some ten welfare benefits that become due only when sufficient NI contributions have been paid (see list above, page 728). Generally, there are two contribution requirements to be satisfied:
- a minimum amount must have been paid in *any* one previous tax year, *and*
- a minimum amount must have been paid or credited in the *relevant tax year*.

The minimum amounts to be paid are expressed in terms of the 'earnings factor'. This is simply the earnings on which contributions were calculated in the year in question. So if someone at the lower earnings level – the minimum wage at which contributions become payable – needs an earnings factor of at least fifty times the lower earnings limit, then he will have had to have worked and contributed (or had contributions credited) for at least fifty weeks in that year. But since contributions are usually a percentage of earnings, a person who earned twice as much per week would satisfy the earnings factor after only twenty-five weeks' work.

Another phrase that needs explanation is the 'relevant contribution year'. This will be the year in which sufficient contributions must have been paid. The general rule is that the 'relevant contribution year' is the last completed tax year (April–April) before the beginning of the year (January–December) in which the claim is being made. This is best explained by a table:

Date of claim	The relevant tax year for working out whether sufficient NI contributions have been paid or credited
January 1984 to December 1984	April 1982 to April 1983
January 1985 to December 1985	April 1983 to April 1984
January 1986 to December 1986	April 1984 to April 1985

The effect of this can be that eligibility is decided on the basis of contributions paid 1¾ to 2¾ years ago! So someone who has not contributed for some two years may be eligible, whereas a person who has been working for some two years but who was previously not contributing may be unable to claim the various benefits.

Going into hospital

Some benefits can be reduced or withdrawn if the claimant goes into hospital.

Supplementary benefit	reduced immediately
Unemployment benefit	usually stopped (as unavailable for work)
Attendance allowance Constant attendance allowance Invalid care allowance	withdrawn after four weeks
Invalidity benefit Industrial death benefit Non-contributory retirement pension Retirement pension Severe disablement allowance Sickness benefit Unemployability supplement Widow's benefits	reduced after eight weeks

The following benefits are usually unaffected by hospitalization: child benefit, FIS, maternity allowance, maternity grant, guardian's allowance, disablement benefit, mobility allowance.

Further information. Ask for DHSS leaflet NI 9.

Taxation of benefits

As the years go by, more and more welfare benefits are becoming taxable (i.e. the benefits count towards total taxable income in that tax year). The following are taxable: industrial death benefit (if paid as a pension); invalid care allowance; invalidity allowance when paid with retirement pension; job-release allowance; old person's and/or retirement pensions; SSP; supplementary benefit if paid to a striker or to the unemployed; unemployment benefit; widowed mother's allowance; widow's allowance; widow's pension.

Finding out about welfare benefits

The details of the various benefits are summarized in this chapter. More detailed information can be obtained from the excellent DHSS leaflets which can be obtained free of charge from any DHSS office or by post from DHSS (Leaflets), PO Box 21, Stanmore, Middlesex HA7 1AY. Local offices of the DHSS are listed in the phone book. It will generally be necessary to phone or call in to find out which local office covers a particular area. Claims for benefits should be made to that local office, except that unemployment-benefit claims are made to the Department of Employment.

A guide to the principal social-security benefits

Remember that social-security rules and regulations are constantly being changed. It is always essential to check the up-to-date position. A CAB should be able to provide detailed information on the latest changes, and it should also be able to advise on general problems (e.g. lost giros, failure by DHSS to answer queries etc.).

Accidents at work

Disablement benefit

This is payable to employees injured at work (or who contract a prescribed industrial disease), and the amount paid varies with the level of disablement.

Eligibility conditions. Only employees are eligible; there is no need for NI contributions to have been paid. The main requirement is that the disablement arises from an accident at work (or from a listed disease – such as dermatitis). To be eligible, the employee must be suffering a continuing disability ninety days later (i.e. from the date of the accident or beginning of the industrial disease), although there are special rules for industrial deafness. If there is disability beyond the ninety-day period, the employee is not eligible for disablement benefit.

The extent of the disablement is assessed by reference to a scale of injuries. For instance, loss of sight (for work purposes), deafness, or loss of both hands is rated 100 per cent disablement. Loss of an eye is 40 per cent; loss of a thumb 30 per cent; loss of all toes of one foot is 20 per cent; loss of an index finger 14 per cent. If a particular injury (such as backache) is not in the table, it is rated on an equivalent basis.

The effect of the disablement on that particular employee is not relevant. For instance, the loss of a little finger is worth 7 per cent whether the injured employee be a concert pianist whose career is ruined by the injury, or a clerk whose career is unaffected by the loss of the finger. Both would receive the same award.

If the disablement is assessed at less than 20 per cent, the disablement benefit will normally be paid in the form of one lump sum. If the disablement is 20 per cent or more, the benefit will be paid as a weekly pension.

Additions to the disablement benefit. Additional benefits can be paid to supplement the disablement benefit:

• *special hardship allowance*: paid when the injury or disease prevents the employee from returning to his job, and he cannot do work of a similar standard. Details in DHSS leaflet NI 6.

• *constant attendance allowance*: if the employee is receiving 100 per cent disablement benefit, then an additional sum is payable if he needs constant care and attention. Details in DHSS leaflet NI 6. In exceptionally severe cases, where the need for attendance is likely to be permanent, the constant attendance allowance may be supplemented by the *exceptionally severe disablement allowance*, which allows a larger amount to be paid. Details in DHSS leaflet NI 6.

• *hospital treatment allowance*: when the employee is in hospital receiving treatment for his injury or disease, he can be paid an additional allowance which raises the amount of his disablement benefit to the 100 per cent rate. Details in DHSS leaflet NI 6.

• *unemployability supplement*: paid when the injury or disease makes the employee permanently unfit for work. Details in DHSS leaflet NI 6.

Claiming. To claim disablement benefit obtain an application form from any DHSS office. Send the completed form to the local DHSS office.

Further information. Ask for DHSS leaflet NI 6.

Industrial death benefit

A weekly benefit paid to the widow (or dependants) of an employee who died as a result of an accident at work or an industrial disease. The higher rate of benefit for a widow is paid during the first twenty-six weeks.

Eligibility conditions. The requirements are similar to those for disablement benefit (see above), namely that the deceased must have been an employee who died as a result of an industrial accident or disease, arising out of and in the course of his employment.

Claiming. When the death is registered, the free certificate of death should be sent (with the form on the back completed) to the local DHSS office. The office will send form BW 1 for the widow to complete and return, together with the marriage certificate and a full death certificate. If the person claiming the benefit is not the widow, she should obtain claim form B I 200 from the local DHSS office.

Consider also claiming damages from the employer if the accident was caused by the negligence of the employer or a fellow-worker (see page 410).

Further information. Ask for DHSS leaflet NI 10.

Injury benefit. This used to be paid to employees injured in industrial accidents. It was abolished in 1983 when Statutory Sick Pay (SSP) was introduced. Now, most employees receive SSP for eight weeks and then transfer to sickness benefit. In 1986, the rules will be changed, so that SSP is paid by the employer for twenty-eight weeks. At the end of that time, most employees will transfer to invalidity benefit. See page 387 for SSP, page 741 for sickness benefit.

Children

Child benefit

A flat-rate benefit paid to the person bringing up the child. There is a fixed amount per child. It is not means-tested; it is payable whatever the level of the adult's income.

Eligibility conditions. The benefit is paid to the person bringing up a child under sixteen (or under nineteen if still at school full-time). Usually, the benefit is paid to the mother, but it can be paid to any person who lives with the child or who contributes substantially towards its support (such as a grandparent). There is no means test for eligibility, nor is there any need for national insurance contributions to have been paid.

Single parents (i.e. those who are single, widowed, permanently separated, or divorced) are entitled to an extra weekly payment called the *one-parent benefit*, which used to be known as *child-benefit increase*. This is an additional amount that is paid irrespective of the number of children in the family. It can also be claimed by other single people bringing up a child (e.g. single grandparent or friend of the family who is bringing up the child). Note that the one-parent benefit cannot be claimed by a married couple or by a parent who is living with someone as husband or wife. Neither is it payable to a parent who is receiving an increase for a child with certain specified benefits (e.g. widowed mother's allowance). Where a lone parent is receiving a benefit such as sickness, unemployment, invalidity benefit, or maternity allowance, then the one-parent benefit will be reduced by the amount of the other benefit(s).

Claiming. Obtain claim form CH 2 from your local DHSS office together with slip CH 3. If possible, the child's birth certificate should be enclosed with the application. When claiming for subsequent children refer to the notes in the existing child-benefit order book.

Further information. Ask for DHSS leaflets CH 1 (child benefit) and CH 11 (one-parent benefit).

Guardian's allowance

A flat-rate benefit, paid weekly, to adults who look after an orphan.

Eligibility conditions. The benefit is only payable if both parents are dead, or if one parent has died and the other parent cannot be traced or is serving a long prison sentence. If the parents are divorced, then the benefit can be paid on the death of one parent if the other parent was not awarded custody and is not paying any maintenance towards the child's upkeep. Thus, a step-parent will often be able to claim the guardian's allowance when his/her spouse (the child's parent) dies, even if s/he is not the legal guardian of the child. There are two other requirements:

• at least one of the parents must have been born in the UK, or have lived here for fifty-two weeks in any two-year period (since reaching age sixteen); *and*
• they must be eligible for child benefit (see page 735) for that child.

There is no means test for eligibility, and there is no need for any national insurance contributions to have been paid.

Claiming. Obtain form BG 1 from any DHSS office and send to the local DHSS office.

Further information. Ask for DHSS leaflet NI 14.

Child's special allowance

A flat-rate benefit, payable weekly, to a divorced woman with a child and whose ex-husband has died.

Eligibility conditions. The divorced woman's child must have been receiving at least 25p a week in maintenance payments from the ex-husband who has now died. The woman must not have remarried, although it will not matter if the husband re-married before he died. The benefit is only payable if sufficient national insurance contributions were paid by the husband – it cannot be earned on the basis of the woman's own contributions. He must have paid at least fifty contributions (of any class) at any time before April 1975, or have an earnings factor of at least fifty times the lower earnings limit in any one tax year before he died (see page 732).

Claiming. Obtain form CS 1 from any DHSS office and return it to the local DHSS office. Preferably, the marriage certificate, proof of divorce or annulment, and evidence of the husband's maintenance obligations should be enclosed with the form. However, if these papers are not available, the application form should be sent in without them.

Once the benefit is granted it will be paid until the child is sixteen (or nineteen if still at school) or until the woman remarries, ceases to be eligible for child benefit, or cohabits with a man as his wife.

Further information. Ask for DHSS leaflet NI 93.

School and college benefits

Free school meals. For families on supplementary benefit, or FIS, or (in some areas) who have a low income. Eligibility is subject to a means test, but is automatic for those on supplementary benefit or family income supplement.

School fares. Normally free transport is provided for children aged between five and sixteen who live more than three miles (two miles if under eight) from their nearest school. Some local authorities help with the cost of fares even when these conditions are not satisfied.

Educational maintenance allowance. Low-income parents who keep a child at school beyond the age of sixteen may qualify for help. Any allowance is at the discretion of the local authority and is means tested.

School uniform and clothing grants. Low-income parents may qualify for help. Any allowance is at the discretion of the local authority and is means tested. Families on supplementary benefit may be able to obtain payments from the DHSS for clothing, but not normally for school uniform, nor if clothes are worn out or outgrown.

For further information on these educational benefits, contact the local authority's Education Department (or DHSS for supplementary benefit).

Death

Death grant

This is a lump sum paid to help with funeral expenses.

Eligibility conditions. The grant is only payable if sufficient national insurance contributions have been paid. There must have been at least twenty-five contributions (of any class) paid at any time before April 1975, or contributions on twenty-five times the lower earnings limit in any one tax year since then (see page 732 for what this means). The contributions can have been paid either by the deceased or by the surviving husband or wife. If the deceased was handicapped and unable to work, contributions of a close relative can be used. Special rules apply when children die. The amount of the grant is small; because of this it is possible that death grant will be abolished and replaced with a more generous – but means-tested – grant.

Claiming. The grant is paid to the deceased's executors or administrators. If there are no executors or administrators it is paid to the next of kin or other person who accepts responsibility for paying the funeral expenses.

The claim should be made within six months of death. A claim form can be obtained from the local DHSS office. In addition, the applicant will usually have to produce the death certificate, any marriage certificate (if the applicant is the spouse), an undertaker's bill or estimate, and any DHSS order books in the name of the deceased.

Further information. Ask for DHSS leaflet NI 49. See also 'Widowhood', page 753.

Other benefits. A death in the family may lead to eligibility for many other benefits (in particular, see: 'Widowhood', page 753; 'Industrial Death Benefit', page 735; 'One-Parent Benefit', page 736).

Handicapped or disabled people

Attendance allowance

A weekly benefit payable to the severely handicapped.

Eligibility conditions. Payable to people (including children over the age of two) who are severely disabled (mentally or physically), and who have needed a lot of day-time and/or night-time care for the last six months. Kidney patients who dialyse at home may qualify. A higher rate of benefit is paid if attendance is needed both day and night. There is no means test, nor is there any need for national insurance contributions to have been paid.

Claiming. Fill in form DS 2, which is attached to DHSS leaflet NI 205.

Further information. Ask for DHSS leaflet NI 205.

Invalid care allowance

A weekly benefit payable to someone who is looking after a severely disabled person. *Eligibility conditions*. The carer must be aged between sixteen and sixty (sixty-five if a man) and not be employed or in full-time education. The carer must be providing substantial care to the invalid for at least thirty-five hours per week. The invalid must be receiving attendance allowance or constant attendance allowance. There is no means test, nor is there any need for national insurance contributions to have been paid. It is not payable if the carer is receiving another benefit, such as unemployment, sickness or widow's benefit, or goes into hospital. A woman cannot receive the benefit if she lives with her husband (or her common-law husband) or if she receives maintenance equal to the amount of the benefit.

Claiming. Fill in form D S 700, which is attached to D H S S leaflet N I 212.

Further information. Ask for D H S S leaflet N I 212.

Mobility allowance

A weekly benefit paid to those, aged five to sixty-five, virtually unable to walk.

Eligibility conditions. The applicant must be under sixty-six and the inability to walk must be likely to persist for at least twelve months. However, the applicant must not be so severely incapacitated that s/he would be unable to use the allowance to help get about. There is no means test, nor is there any need for national insurance contributions to have been paid.

Claiming. Fill in form M Y 1, which is attached to D H S S leaflet N I 211.

Further information. Ask for D H S S leaflet N I 211.

Other benefits

1. Handicapped children who do not go to school can receive free milk.
2. Registered disabled workers can get help with the cost of travel to work if public transport is not available. This is a Department of Employment, not a local authority, benefit and is payable even if the disabled person is receiving the mobility allowance.
3. Social services departments have numerous benefits for the disabled, such as meals on wheels, home helps, laundry service, and help with the cost of installing a telephone.
4. Assistance through 'Motability' with buying or leasing a car.
5. There are various other benefits that may be available (e.g. vaccine-damage payments; tax reliefs; rate concessions). It is best to contact a specialist group for advice.

Health and sickness

See also 'Handicapped or Disabled People', above.

Free dental treatment

Eligibility conditions. Families receiving supplementary benefit or FIS or free milk or prescriptions because of low income are automatically entitled to free NHS dental treatment. Other low-income families may be eligible – there is a sliding scale of benefits, dependent on the family's income. Women who were pregnant at the start of a course of treatment, or who have had a baby in the last year, and children under sixteen are also entitled to free dental treatment. Those aged sixteen to eighteen (nineteen if in full-time education) get free treatment but, if they have left school, may have to pay for dentures.

Claiming. Those on supplementary benefit or FIS and those entitled for reasons other than low income should tell their dentists. Others should ask the dentist for application form FI D.

Further information. Ask for DHSS leaflet D 11.

Free glasses

Eligibility conditions. Children under sixteen (under nineteen if in full-time education) and families receiving supplementary pension or allowance (including housing-benefit supplement), FIS, or free milk or prescriptions because of a low income, are entitled to free NHS glasses. Other low-income families may be eligible for help with all or part of the cost; there is a means test similar to that for free dental treatment.

Claiming. Those automatically entitled to free glasses should tell their optician. Others should ask the optician for form F 1.

Further information. Ask for DHSS leaflet G 11.

Free prescriptions

Eligibility conditions. Families receiving supplementary benefit (including housing-benefit supplement) or FIS are automatically entitled to free prescriptions, as are pregnant women, mothers with a child under one, children under sixteen, pensioners, and those with certain medical conditions (see DHSS leaflet P11 for details). Other low-income families may be eligible for free prescriptions on a means test.

Claiming. Fill in the details requested on the back of the prescription form. Expectant mothers should first obtain form FW 8 from a doctor or health visitor and send it to the Family Practitioner Committee, and mothers with children under one should fill in Form A in leaflet P 11 unless they already have an exemption certificate. Those on a low income, and subject to the means test, should use Form B in leaflet P 11.

Further information. Ask for DHSS leaflet P 11.

Hospital patient's travelling expenses

Eligibility conditions. Those receiving supplementary benefit (including housing-benefit supplement) or FIS can claim a full refund of their public transport fares to hospital, and, if necessary, those of an escort, whether they are an in-patient or out-patient. Other low-income families may be eligible for help with fares on a means test.

Claiming. Those on supplementary benefit or FIS should take their order book to the hospital to claim. Others on a low income should claim on the form attached to DHSS leaflet H 11.

Further information. Ask for DHSS leaflet H 11.

Sickness benefit

A weekly benefit paid to those who are unable to work because of illness. In practice, most employees will receive statutory sick pay (SSP) for the first eight weeks of their sickness and only then transfer to sickness benefit. In 1986 the rules will be changed, so employees will get SSP from the employer for twenty-eight weeks; after that, they will transfer to invalidity benefit, or perhaps supplementary benefit (but not to sickness benefit).

Eligibility conditions. The claimant must either (1) have been injured through an accident at work or contracted a prescribed industrial disease (when he was an employee – not self-employed), or (2) have paid sufficient NI contributions.

Class 1 and Class 2 NI stamps count towards eligibility – so a self-employed person can claim sickness benefit if he has paid sufficient NI contributions. If he has not then he may be eligible for some other benefit (e.g. supplementary benefit).

Sickness benefit cannot be paid for more than twenty-eight weeks; the claimant may then be able to claim invalidity benefit (see below). From 1986, most employees will receive SSP (for the first twenty-eight weeks) rather than sickness benefit. In effect, the only people who will then get sickness benefit will be the self-employed (who obviously do not get SSP), and those few employed people who are ineligible for SSP. As a result, the importance of sickness benefit will be vastly reduced – and it may well be that sickness benefit will eventually be phased out.

Claiming. If you are working for an employer you will probably get SSP (see above). If not, ask your employer for Form SSP 1(E) (or Form SSP 1(T)) if your period on SSP is running out. If you are self-employed, then complete Form SC 1 (Rev.), obtainable from doctors' surgeries, hospitals, or social-security offices. You will not need a doctor's certificate for the first week's absence.

Further information. Ask for DHSS leaflet NI 16.

Invalidity benefit

Invalidity benefit is made up of:
- *invalidity pension*: a flat-rate, weekly benefit paid to the ill when sickness benefit

runs out, plus an earnings-related additional pension (based on Class 1 contributions paid since April 1978), *and*

• *invalidity allowance*: an additional flat-rate, weekly benefit, paid to those who were more than five years away from retirement age when the invalidity began. The younger the claimant, the larger the allowance (the allowance may be reduced if the pension exceeds certain levels).

Eligibility conditions. The requirements are the same as for sickness benefit. When sickness benefit runs out after twenty-eight weeks of illness, invalidity benefit commences automatically.

Claiming. Continue sending in doctor's statements, as for sickness benefit.

Further information. Ask for DHSS leaflet NI 16A.

Severe disablement allowance

A weekly, flat-rate benefit paid to people who are too ill to work, but who are ineligible for sickness benefit or invalidity benefit. However, the benefit is not paid for the first twenty-eight weeks of incapacity for work, so it often becomes payable when a person receiving sickness benefit would have started receiving invalidity benefit.

Eligibility conditions. The main requirement is twenty-eight weeks' continuous incapacity for work. Generally, there is a requirement that the claimant be 80 per cent disabled – a doctor should be able to give advice on this point.

Claiming. Fill in form SDA 1 attached to leaflet NI 252.

Further information. Ask for DHSS leaflet NI 252.

Poverty

Family income supplement (FIS)

A weekly benefit paid to low-income families in which the man or woman is working.

Eligibility conditions. Since supplementary benefit is not available to people who are in full-time work, there is a separate benefit available for those who are in full-time work but who are still poor. Family income supplement (FIS) is payable when the claimant

• has at least one dependent child, *and*

• works at least thirty hours per week, whether he or she be employed or self-employed. If the claimant is a single parent the weekly hours figure is only twenty-four.

Claims can be made by single parents, married couples, and unmarried couples. The amount of FIS to be paid will be half the difference between the family's gross income (not counting child benefit) and the amount fixed by Parliament as the income appropriate to a family of that size. In 1986 that was £86 per week, plus £11.50

for each child under eleven (£12.50 if aged eleven to fifteen; £13.50 if aged sixteen or more). For instance, a family with two children under eleven and earnings of £95 would receive (1986) £7 per week (i.e. £109 less £95, divided by 2). There is a maximum amount that can be paid (e.g. in 1986 a family with one child under eleven could not receive more than £25).

The family's income is worked out on a gross (i.e. before-tax) basis. Maintenance payments and most welfare benefits are taken into account (except that child benefit and housing benefit are ignored).

In addition to receiving the cash from FIS, a person on FIS is automatically entitled to free:

- NHS prescriptions, glasses, and dental treatment
- milk and vitamins for expectant mothers and children under school age
- school meals
- fares to and from hospital
- legal advice and, in most cases, legal aid (unless too much capital).

Because of these additional benefits it is often worth claiming FIS even when the amount of FIS payable is very small.

Claiming. Complete the application form attached to DHSS leaflet FIS 1. The form, signed (where applicable) by both the man and the woman, should be sent to the FIS Freepost address at Blackpool. Evidence of income should be sent with the form (pay-slips for the last five weeks for those paid weekly; two months for those paid monthly; the last profit and loss account for the self-employed). The claim should always be made at once, even if evidence has to be sent on later. This is because no arrears are paid if a claim is delayed. With seasonal workers, earnings are usually averaged out over a six-month period.

The claim is dealt with by post and there is usually no need for the claimant to be interviewed.

The claimant will be sent an order book of weekly allowances. The benefit is usually payable for fifty-two weeks, and continues to be payable even if the claimant's income increases or decreases during that period.

Further information. Ask for DHSS leaflet FIS 1.

Housing benefit

Housing benefit can help with the cost of both rent and rates. The details of how the complicated rules work will depend upon whether the claimant is receiving SB (i.e. supplementary benefit).

SB claimants. The local authority (note – not the DHSS, who administer SB) will allow a 100 per cent rate rebate so that no rates will have to be paid. Similarly, a 100 per cent rebate will be made for rent (whether it is paid to the council or to a private landlord). This is called certificated housing benefit (because the DHSS gives the local authority a certificate confirming that SB is being claimed). In addition, there is the unlikely possibility that the claimant may receive an extra payment called housing-benefit supplement instead of normal supplementary benefit (which is paid to people who were worse off as a result of housing benefit being introduced as a replacement for the old rent and rates rebates).

People who are not claiming SB. Eligibility will depend upon a very complex means test (the rules are applied differently by different local authorities). This is called standard housing benefit.

Claiming. Apply to the local authority (or DHSS if on SB). As always, it is often best to ask a CAB for advice on eligibility and on how the local council administers the scheme.

Supplementary benefit

A weekly benefit paid to people over sixteen who are not in full-time work. These are the rates from November 1984; they are increased each November.

	Ordinary rate	*Long-term rate*
Husband and wife	£45.55	£57.10
Single householder	£28.05	£35.70
Any other person aged		
18 or over	£22.45	£28.55
16–17	£17.30	£21.90
11–15	£14.35	
0–10	£9.60	

Eligibility conditions. Eligibility is assessed by working out the claimant's *resources* and comparing them with his *requirements*. The shortfall will normally be the amount of supplementary benefit to be paid.

A claimant's resources will be based on his:
1. *Income*, plus that of his spouse (or cohabitee) if they are living together; all income is counted including cash benefits, except that the following are disregarded:
   - the first few pounds of a claimant's earnings (£4, in 1985)
   - educational grants, maternity grant, death grant, attendance and mobility allowances
   - small gifts from friends or relatives (unless they are given to pay for an item covered by supplementary benefit, e.g. rent)
   - the first few pounds of any other income.
2. *Capital*: the capital value of an owner-occupied house is ignored; all other capital is taken into account; anyone with more than £3,000 capital (1985) cannot claim supplementary benefit.

A claimant's requirements will be based on the amount that Parliament has accepted that he and his family need to be able to live on. The figures (1985) are set out above.

744

Apart from the 'ordinary rate' there is a higher 'long-term rate', which is paid if:
- the claimant (or partner) is aged sixty or over;
- both claimant and partner are under sixty and have been receiving SB or invalidity benefit (or certain other invalidity payments) for a year without having to sign on for work;
- both claimant and partner are under sixty and have been signing on quarterly for at least a year and have now been told they need no longer sign on at all.

Note that the figures above do not include anything for housing costs (i.e. rent or mortgage, plus rates). These will usually be paid as part of housing benefit (see page 743) – unless the claimant is paying a mortgage, in which case the interest payments will normally be paid by the DHSS, together with a nominal sum to cover insurance and maintenance costs.

So the amount of benefit will be the 'requirements' (i.e. the figures set out above), less the 'resources'. For instance:

Wife lives with two children aged twelve and nine. Husband pays maintenance of £15 p.w. to wife, and £5 p.w. for each child

	'Requirements'	*'Resources'*
Wife	£28·05	£15·00
Twelve-year-old	14·35	5·00
Nine-year-old	9·60	5·00
Heating allowance	5·20	
Child benefit		13·70
One-parent benefit		4·25
	57·20	42·95

Wife can therefore claim SB of £14·25. (Note: 1985 figures.)

Being available for work. The general rule is that SB cannot be claimed by anyone who is in full-time work (i.e. working thirty hours per week). Part-timers working fewer than thirty hours can claim SB but their earnings will be deducted from the benefit (save for a small allowance). Unemployed claimants must be available for work, and if offered a suitable job will be expected to take it. Single parents, pregnant women, and the elderly do not have to be available to work.

Part-time earnings. The basic rule is that if a claimant earns money then her benefit will be reduced accordingly. But the first few pounds of the earnings will be ignored. The first £4 (1985 figure) will always be ignored and if the claimant is a single parent then up to £12 can be ignored (strictly speaking, the single parent can exclude £4, plus half the amount between £4 and £20; all figures are for 1985). A child's earnings are always ignored (e.g. if a child earns £5 from a paper round, there is no danger of the family's SB being reduced).

Extra Payments from the DHSS

The normal requirements (i.e. the figures set out above) will often be insufficient to meet the day-to-day living expenses of particular claimants. For instance, an individual may have greater heating requirements than average and so the nominal sum allowed for heating in the normal requirements may have to be increased (e.g. if the household includes a person under five, or over sixty-five; or if the house is hard to heat). These additional requirements are calculated by referring to a fixed scale of additional amounts that can be allowed. Thus, in this example, the claimant might be able to claim an additional requirements payment, either towards the extra heating costs of the young/old person or because of illness – but s/he can only claim one additional heating allowance, so s/he cannot claim both extra sums (thus s/he will simply receive whichever is the higher amount allowed).

Additional requirements payments can also be made for items such as special diets, laundry, a private home help, blindness, baths, special wear and tear on clothes, hire-purchase instalments, furniture storage, and fares to visit someone in hospital. A CAB will be able to give details of eligibility and the amounts payable.

In addition, 'single payments' may be made to cover one-off items of expenditure (e.g. cooker, heater, maternity costs, bedding, essential redecoration, clothing and footwear, funeral expenses). Once again, a CAB can give detailed advice as to eligibility for these single payments, and an indication of the amount that might be allowed. Note that a claimant with capital over £500 may be expected to use the excess over £500 towards paying for these items.

Claiming. Complete the form attached to DHSS leaflet SB 1, and take or send this to the local DHSS office. Personal claims are dealt with more quickly. Claimants who are out of work should complete form BI (obtainable from the unemployment-benefit office) and take or send it to the local DHSS office.

The claimant may be visited at home by a DHSS officer or asked to call at the office. A provisional payment may be sent by post soon after the application is received and the balance due will be adjusted when full supporting evidence for the claim has been supplied.

*Further information.*The regulations governing payment of supplementary benefit are extremely complicated. For guidance, refer to the *National Welfare Benefits Handbook*, published by the Child Poverty Action Group (1 Macklin Street, London wc2) or, for more detail, *The Penguin Guide to Supplementary Benefits*, by Tony Lynes.

Pregnancy

Maternity grant

A lump-sum grant of £25 to help with the costs of having a baby.

Eligibility conditions. Paid to anyone having a child in Great Britain. Two or more grants can be claimed if the mother has twins, triplets, etc.

Claiming. Apply in the period of fourteen weeks before the baby is due, and three months after the birth. Fill in form BM 4 (from the DHSS or maternity clinic) and send it to the local DHSS office.

Further information. Ask for DHSS leaflet FB 8 or NI 17A.

Maternity allowance

A weekly benefit paid for eighteen weeks (and more, if the birth is later than expected).

Eligibility conditions. The benefit is only payable if sufficient national insurance contributions have been paid and if the woman has given up work. Contributions on twenty-five times the lower earnings limit (see page 732) must have been paid in any previous tax year, and in addition, contributions on fifty times the lower earnings limit must have been paid or credited in the 'relevant tax year'.

Date on which baby is born or is due	The relevant tax year for working out whether sufficient contributions have been paid or credited
24 March 1985 to 22 March 1986	6 April 1983 to 5 April 1984
23 March 1986 to 21 March 1987	6 April 1984 to 5 April 1985

The contributions must have been Class 1 (employed) or Class 2 (self-employed) and eligibility is on the basis of the mother's contribution record. She cannot claim on her husband's contributions.

Claiming. Apply in the three-week period between fourteen and eleven weeks before the baby is due. A late claim may be accepted but benefit will probably not be paid for the missed weeks unless there is a good reason for the delay. Fill in form BM 4 (as for the maternity grant).

Further information. Ask for DHSS leaflet FB 8 or NI 17A.

In addition

1. Women at work may be entitled to maternity pay from their employers (see page 404).
2. Expectant mothers receiving supplementary benefit or FIS, or who have a low income, can obtain free milk and vitamins. Ask for DHSS leaflet MV 11 at any post office.
3. See also, 'Children', page 735.

Retirement

A weekly benefit is paid to women of sixty or more and men of sixty-five or more. As well as the basic pension, the pensioner can be paid:

additional pension	dependent on earnings and NI contributions since April 1978
guaranteed minimum pension	this is paid instead of all or part of the 'additional pension' and arises under a contracted-out occupational pension scheme;
graduated pension	dependent on NI contributions paid between 1961 and 1975;
invalidity addition	paid if the pensioner was entitled to invalidity allowance (page 741) before he retired.

Basic pension

Eligibility conditions. Apart from the age requirements, the pensioner must also have:
1. *Retired or reached the age of sixty-five for a woman or seventy for a man*: it is not necessary to have completely stopped work to be 'retired'. A working pensioner can be treated as having retired if:
   - his earnings do not exceed the earnings rule (see below) or only occasionally do so, *or*
   - he generally does not work more than twelve hours or so per week
   - she is widowed when over sixty, in which case she can carry on working and claim a pension on the basis of her late husband's NI contributions.
2. *Paid sufficient NI contributions*: the two NI contribution conditions for the basic pension are:
   - at least fifty contributions must have been paid at any time before 6 April 1975, or contributions on fifty times the lower earnings limit (fifty-two times since 1978) must have been paid in any one tax year since then, *and*
   - the same level of contributions must have been paid or credited for

Length of working life	Number of years' contributions that must have been paid
Up to 10 years	working life minus 1
10–20 years	working life minus 2
20–30 years	working life minus 3
30–40 years	working life minus 4
41 or more years	working life minus 5

approximately 90 per cent of the pensioner's working life. (Since 1977, women who pay the full NI contributions – see page 731 – before they leave paid employment to have a family can have contributions credited to them until their youngest child reaches sixteen, for a maximum period of twenty years.)

The working life theoretically starts at sixteen, but since the national insurance scheme was only introduced in 1948, the date will be whichever is the later of:

• the date when s/he started pension insurance, *or*

• July 1948.

If the pensioner cannot satisfy the second NI contribution requirement, he may still be entitled to a basic pension but at a reduced rate. The amount of the pension is reduced in proportion to the number of his qualifying years, down to a minimum 25 per cent level, below which no pension is paid.

Illustration. Arthur Jones was born in 1920. He started work in 1937, but he had no pension insurance. He was sixty-five in 1985. How is his pension entitlement calculated? His 'working life' will have started in 1948 when the national insurance scheme was first introduced. This gives him a 'working life' of thirty-seven years, which in turn means that he needs the necessary level of contributions for thirty-three (thirty-seven less four) years. If he only had fourteen years prior to 1975 during which fifty-two contributions were paid, he would receive only 43 per cent of the basic pension.

The earnings rule. The basic pension, any invalidity addition, and any increment for deferring retirement (but not other pension payments) are reduced if the pensioner earns more than a certain amount per week (£75 in 1985/6). But this only applies to women between sixty and sixty-five, and to men between sixty-five and seventy. The deduction is 50 per cent of the first £4 over the limit and thereafter 100 per cent of any excess. Earnings are determined on the basis of the gross figure subject to the deduction of:

• reasonable expenses connected with the job (e.g. union subscriptions, fares, overalls, clothes)

• up to 15p per meal eaten during working hours (unless luncheon vouchers are provided)

• reasonable costs of paying for someone to look after other members of the family because the pensioner is out at work.

Claiming. The DHSS usually contact the pensioner some four months before his/ her sixty-fifth/sixtieth birthday. If the pensioner has not received a letter three months before that birthday, s/he should contact the local DHSS office. The pension is claimed by completing and returning the claim form sent to the pensioner by the DHSS.

Further information. The DHSS publish several free leaflets on pensions. Unfortunately, this is a complex topic and the pamphlets must be studied carefully. The main leaflets are:

NP 32, *Your Retirement Pension*
NP 32A, *Your Retirement Pension if You are Widowed or Divorced*

NP 32B, *Retirement Benefits for Married Women*
NI 92, *Earning Extra Pension by Cancelling Your Retirement*
NI 184, *Retirement Pensions for People over Eighty.*
All are obtainable from any DHSS local office.

Other benefits

Pensioners whose income is below the supplementary-benefit levels. This is determined by their *resources* and *requirements* (see page 744). Pensioners can have the shortfall met by claiming supplementary benefit, which when paid to a pensioner is called *supplementary pension.*

Pensioners over eighty who are not receiving the basic pension. They can apply for the *over-eighties' pension.*

Divorcees and widows. Women who are divorced (but not remarried) and widows can claim a basic pension on the basis of their husband's NI contribution record.

Extra pension for deferring retirement. Pensioners who do not retire and so claim their pensions get an increased pension when they do retire. Their basic pension is then increased by about 7½ per cent for each year that the pension was deferred. However, deferment cannot continue after age seventy (sixty-five for women) so the maximum increment for deferring retirement is about 37½ per cent.

Free prescriptions. Anyone over pensionable age is entitled to free prescriptions (see page 740) and reduced fares on public transport. Pensioners are also entitled to free (or cheap) dental treatment.

Unemployment

Unemployment benefit

Usually paid fortnightly in arrears, to employees who are now out of work. Payable for up to fifty-two weeks (excluding the first three days of unemployment).

Eligibility conditions. Unemployment benefit is only payable if sufficient national insurance contributions have been paid. There are two requirements:
• *either* twenty-six Class 1 contributions must have been paid at any time before April 1975, *or* in any one tax year since that date the claimant must have had an earnings factor of twenty-five times the lower earnings limit (see page 732 for what this means); *and*
• the earnings factor during the 'relevant tax year' (see page 732) must be at least fifty times the lower earnings limit (or twenty-five times for a reduced rate of benefit). The relevant tax year will be the tax year ending in the year before the claim is made.

Date of claim	*The relevant tax year for working out whether sufficient national insurance contributions have been paid or credited*
January 1984 to January 1985	April 1982 to April 1983
January 1985 to January 1986	April 1983 to April 1984
January 1986 to January 1987	April 1984 to April 1985

Only Class 1 contributions count, so only employees can claim unemployment benefit – the self-employed are not eligible. The contribution rules are relaxed for those people who have not been able to pay contributions for a sufficiently long period, namely the young, people arriving from abroad, widows, and divorced women. People over retirement age who have not claimed their pension are not subject to the normal contribution conditions for unemployment benefit.

Disqualifications. The claimant can be refused benefit if he places 'unreasonable restrictions' on the sort of work, pay and conditions which he is prepared to accept if offered a job. However, the claimant can insist that his physical condition be taken into account when considering his refusal to accept jobs, and also he can demand that regard be had to the nature of his usual occupation and the time which has elapsed since he became unemployed.

Up to six weeks' benefit can be withheld if the claimant left his last job because:

1. He was sacked for 'misconduct'. 'Misconduct' does not necessarily mean that moral blame can be attached to the employee. The behaviour must be such that it made him unfit to hold the job, and it will usually take the form of 'industrial shortcomings, disobedience, faulty workmanship, idleness, unauthorized absence, some types of carelessness, and conduct . . . adversely affecting the proper discharge of his duties' (R (U) 2/77). If the employee has won an unfair-dismissal claim against his sacking, it is most unlikely (but not impossible) that his unemployment benefit could be withheld because of misconduct.

2. He left the job voluntarily and without a good reason. Once it becomes clear that the claimant left the job voluntarily (i.e. was not dismissed) it is for him to show that he had 'just cause' for leaving. For instance, a reduction in wages, constructive dismissal (see page 430), inability to do the job, difficulty with travelling to work, reluctance to join a trade union, and general grievances about the job would all be sufficient justification for leaving the job. But even if the claimant can show that he had a good reason for resigning, he may still be denied his first six weeks' benefit if he failed to look for another job *before* leaving. It has been held that the claimant need not have actually fixed up a new job, but he should have good prospects of finding one. However, this condition is not always enforced and the claimant who had a good reason for leaving his last job, but no prospects of finding another job, will not always forfeit his first six weeks' unemployment benefit.

In addition, up to six weeks' benefit can be forfeited if the claimant:

- Unjustifiably refuses a suitable job or offer of training, *or*
- Does not attend an interview arranged for him, or attends the interview but does not try to get the job. In addition, benefit can be forfeited if the claimant does not carry out job-seeking steps recommended by the Job Centre, although this only happens rarely.

Strikers are not usually eligible for unemployment benefit (see page 487).

Working while unemployed. A claimant will normally lose one sixth of his weekly unemployment benefit for every day he works.

Pensions. Claimants aged sixty or more who are receiving an occupational pension forfeit their unemployment benefit to the extent that their pension exceeds £35 per week.

Claiming. The claimant should go, in person, to his local Unemployment Benefit Office on the first day of his unemployment. If possible, he should take his P 45 or national insurance number with him. However, he should not delay claiming benefit if he does not have the P 45 or national insurance number, since unemployment benefit cannot be backdated and so he would lose benefit for every day of delay.

TOPS training allowances

A weekly benefit paid to those on a Training Opportunities Scheme (TOPS) course to learn a new skill.

Eligibility conditions. The applicant must be unemployed and have been out of full-time education for at least three years.

Claiming. Ask for an appointment with the TOPS officer at a Job Centre or employment office.

Further information. Ask for free leaflets TSA L 79 and L 91 from a Job Centre or employment office.

Job search and employment transfer benefits

A grant to help the unemployed (or redundant) with the expense of finding a new job and moving to a different part of the country.

Eligibility conditions. The claimant must be unemployed or facing redundancy.

Claiming. The claimant should tell the Job Centre or employment office as soon as he decides to look for a job in another area.

Further information. Ask for free leaflets EPL 65, EPL 66, and EPL 67 from a Job Centre or employment office.

Employment rehabilitation allowance

A weekly benefit paid during rehabilitation courses to encourage a return to work.

Eligibility conditions. The applicant must be on a rehabilitation course for people who have been sick, disabled, or unemployed.

Claiming. Inquire at the Job Centre or employment office.

Further information. Ask for free leaflets EPL 30 and EPL 57 from a Job Centre or employment office.

Note

Consider also redundancy payments (page 464) and an unfair-dismissal claim (page 425).

Widowhood

There are three widow's benefits.

Widow's allowance

This is a flat-rate benefit paid for the first twenty-six weeks after the husband died. However, it is not paid if the husband was a retirement pensioner or if the widow was over sixty at the time of her husband's death. Benefit will be lost if the widow remarries or starts to live with another man.

Eligibility conditions. The benefit is only payable if sufficient national insurance contributions were paid by the husband (not by the widow). However, the qualifying conditions are not onerous and are usually satisfied. The husband must have paid either at least twenty-five contributions (of any class) at any time before April 1975 or contributions on twenty-five times the lower earnings limit (see page 732 for what this means) in any one tax year since then.

Claiming. When the death is registered, the registrar provides a free certificate. On the back of the certificate is a form which should be completed and sent to the local DHSS office. The DHSS office will then send the widow a claim form (BW 1) which she should complete and return as soon as possible. Benefit may be lost if the claim form is submitted more than three months after the death.

Further information. Ask for DHSS leaflet NP 35.

Widowed mother's allowance

This is a flat-rate benefit paid weekly to a widow who has one or more children under nineteen. The benefit becomes payable when the widow's allowance runs out – twenty-six weeks after the death. As with widow's allowance, benefit will be lost if the widow remarries or lives with another man. If the widow is over forty when the widowed mother's allowance runs out, i.e. when all the children have reached nineteen, she may be entitled to widow's pension (see below).

Eligibility conditions. The benefit is only payable if sufficient national insurance contributions were paid by the husband (not by the widow). The rules are stricter than those for widow's allowance. There are two conditions to be met:

1. He must have paid fifty contributions (of any class) at any time before April 1975, or contributions on fifty times the lower earnings limit (fifty-two times from 1978 on) in any one tax year since then.
2. He must have paid at least fifty contributions a year for most of his working life. The working life of a person usually begins at age sixteen, but since the national insurance scheme was only introduced in 1948 the 'working life' may well date from the time when the husband first had to join the scheme. The rules are similar to those for retirement pensions – see page 748.

If the husband did not pay contributions for a sufficient number of years, his wife will only receive a proportion of the usual flat-rate benefit, assuming he satisfies condition 1 above.

Claiming. Same as widow's allowance (above). No claim is needed if widow's allowance is being paid.

Further information. Ask for DHSS leaflet NP 36.

Widow's pension

This is a benefit paid weekly, but the widow must have been aged forty or more when her husband died (or her widowed mother's allowance, if she received it, ran out). A widow then aged fifty or more receives the full-rate widow's pension. Widows under fifty lose 7 per cent for each year under fifty (for instance, a widow of forty-three loses 49 per cent and so receives 51 per cent of the full pension).

Eligibility conditions. The rules are the same as for widowed mother's allowance (above).

Claiming. Same as for claiming widow's allowance and widowed mother's allowance (above). No claim is needed if widow's allowance is being paid.

Further information. Ask for DHSS leaflet NP 36.

Further information

Even this brief introduction to the social-security system will have made it obvious that it has developed on an *ad hoc* basis over the years – so it is now an absurdly complicated and confusing mass of rules and regulations. Claimants must not think that they can guide themselves through this maze; expert help is needed, and for most people the local CAB will be the first place in which to seek help. For those who want to read more, there are the relevant government pamphlets, which are often useful and which are free. For specialist help refer to the excellent *Disability Rights Handbook* (which covers virtually all benefits except retirement pensions) or the CPAG *National Welfare Benefits Handbook* and *Rights Guide to Non-Means Tested Social Security Benefits*.

PART SEVEN

THE LEGAL SYSTEM

53 The Courts

There are different courts for different types of cases. Basically, there is a hierarchy of courts, with the senior courts hearing the more important cases and, also, appeals from the lower courts. However, the position is made more complicated because some courts hear only civil cases, others hear only criminal cases, whilst some hear both civil and criminal cases.

The hierarchy in **civil** cases is:

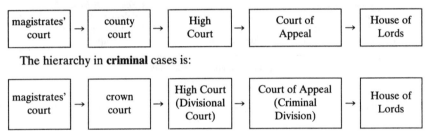

The hierarchy in **criminal** cases is:

Civil or criminal?

The starting-point in any case is to decide whether it is civil or criminal. Really, it is a distinction between criminal and non-criminal, since civil cases are all those cases that are not criminal.

Usually, the distinction will be obvious; it is the difference between being *prosecuted* (for a criminal offence) and *sued* (for a civil wrong – also called a tort). If the aim of the person bringing the case is to punish the defendant then it will probably be a criminal case. However, if his aim is to obtain compensation, or some other benefit for himself, it will generally be a civil case.

One incident can lead to both civil and criminal proceedings. For instance, suppose a pedestrian is injured by the negligent driving of a drunken motorist. The police will prosecute the motorist for drunken driving, and that will be a criminal case. The injured pedestrian will sue the motorist for damages to compensate him for his injury and lost wages, and that will be a civil case. The two cases will be heard in different courts: they cannot be heard in one combined trial – although, one might ask, why not?

To underline the difference between civil and criminal cases, it is possible for there

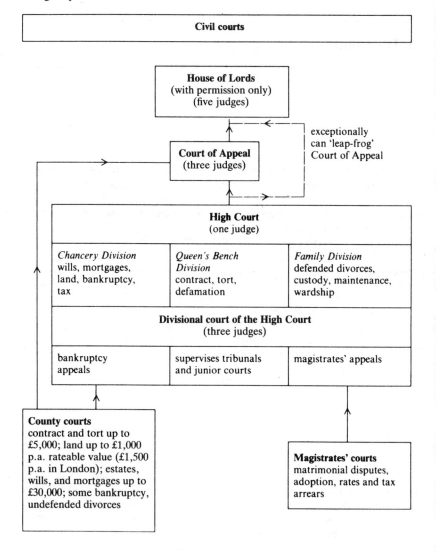

Civil courts

House of Lords
(with permission only)
(five judges)

Court of Appeal
(three judges)

exceptionally
can 'leap-frog'
Court of Appeal

High Court
(one judge)

Chancery Division wills, mortgages, land, bankruptcy, tax	*Queen's Bench Division* contract, tort, defamation	*Family Division* defended divorces, custody, maintenance, wardship

Divisional court of the High Court
(three judges)

bankruptcy appeals	supervises tribunals and junior courts	magistrates' appeals

County courts
contract and tort up to
£5,000; land up to £1,000
p.a. rateable value (£1,500
p.a. in London); estates,
wills, and mortgages up to
£30,000; some bankruptcy,
undefended divorces

Magistrates' courts
matrimonial disputes,
adoption, rates and tax
arrears

to be different verdicts in the two cases. For instance, the motorist might be convicted of drunken driving in the criminal case, and yet be held not liable in the civil case (e.g. if the accident was the pedestrian's own fault). The case of the alleged murderer, Mr Loughans, quoted on page 712, is another example. Quite simply, the courts are concerned with different questions in the different cases. In addition, the courts will apply a different standard of proof in the two cases. In the criminal case, the defendant will only be found guilty if it is shown *beyond all reasonable doubt* that he committed the offence. However, in the civil court he will be held liable if it is shown *on a balance of probabilities* that he was to blame. So the courts use different criteria in judging the two types of cases.

'Beyond all reasonable doubt' is a stiffer test than 'on a balance of probabilities'. Not surprisingly, lawyers have frequently argued over the exact semantic difference between the two, and it is fair to say that no one has ever arrived at a satisfactory brief explanation. However, for most purposes it is the difference between 'definitely' and 'probably' – or, perhaps, the difference between '90 per cent sure' and '60 per cent sure'.

The courts: an A–Z guide

County courts

Most civil cases are heard in the county court. It is the junior of the two principal civil courts: the county court and the High Court. It hears everything from landlord-and-tenant disputes, hire-purchase repossessions, undefended divorces, debt claims, and personal injury claims through to bankruptcy and income-tax arrears. The following types of cases are heard in the county courts.

1. *Claims for up to £5,000 damages.* Any money claim for a civil wrong (i.e. breach of contract or tort) where no more than £5,000 is claimed. This covers a whole host of claims, such as consumer complaints, accident and injury claims, debt cases, negligence, and nuisance. The only real exception is defamation claims which must be brought in the High Court, even when less than £5,000 damages is claimed.

    If the claim is worth more than £5,000 the plaintiff must sue in the High Court, unless he is prepared to abandon the excess over £5,000. To encourage the use of the county court, there are costs penalties for those who sue in the High Court when they should have sued in the county court (see page 843).

2. *Landlord and tenant disputes,* and any other actions involving houses and buildings. However, the net annual rateable value of the land in question must not exceed £1,000 (£1,500 in Greater London); if it does, the case must be heard in the High Court. Most of these cases are actions by landlords to recover possession of premises after serving a notice to quit – generally called 'possession actions'. All cases involving the Rent Acts (private residential lettings) and the business tenancies legislation must be heard in the county court.

The Legal System

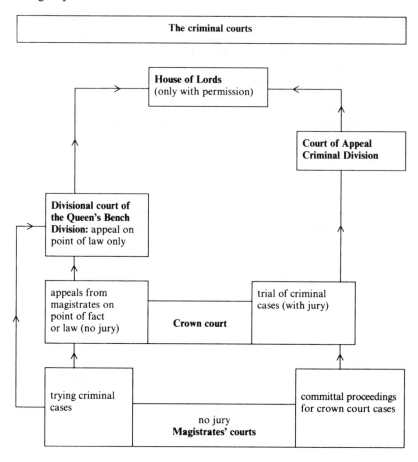

The criminal courts

House of Lords
(only with permission)

Court of Appeal
Criminal Division

Divisional court of
the Queen's Bench
Division: appeal on
point of law only

appeals from
magistrates on
point of fact
or law (no jury)

Crown court

trial of criminal
cases (with jury)

trying criminal
cases

no jury
Magistrates' courts

committal proceedings
for crown court cases

3. *Mortgage claims.* But only if the amount left to be paid off does not exceed £30,000. If more than £30,000 is involved, the case must go to the High Court. Most of these cases involve building society repossessions after the borrower has failed to pay the mortgage instalments (see page 199).

4. *Equity trusts and probate.* But only if the amount in dispute does not exceed £30,000 (if it does, the case is tried in the High Court). This covers disputes over the terms of a will, the distribution of an estate, and the management of property held in trust for someone else.

5. *Bankruptcies and winding up.* Some county courts deal with bankruptcies, although bankruptcies in the London area are dealt with by a branch of the High Court. County courts can also deal with the winding up of companies that have a paid-up capital of no more than £10,000.

6. *Undefended divorces.* If a divorce is undefended it is heard in the county court; if defended, it is tried in the High Court. When granting the divorce, the county court can decide questions over the family assets and property, maintenance, and also custody of the children.

   Adoption applications can be heard in the county court, although they can also be made in the magistrates' court and the High Court.

7. *Domestic violence.* County courts can grant injunctions against wife-batterers and violent boy-friends (see page 83).

Procedure in the county courts

County-court cases are heard either by a judge or by a registrar. The registrar is a junior judge, hearing the less important cases, such as those in which the defendant admits liability. He will often fix maintenance payments and attachment of earnings payments, and hear trials involving no more than £500.

There are some 340 county courts in England and Wales. For how to bring a simple county-court claim, see page 872.

Most appeals from county-court decisions are heard by the Court of Appeal.

Crown courts

The crown courts hear the more serious criminal cases. They are of relatively recent origin, having been introduced by the Courts Act 1971, which abolished the old quarter sessions and assizes, and introduced a more rational and flexible structure.

The crown courts hear all criminal cases that are not tried in the magistrates' courts. Some offences can be tried only in the crown court, others can be tried only in the magistrates' courts, whilst some can be tried in either court (see page 785). In addition, the crown courts hear appeals from convictions by magistrates' courts. Only the defendant can appeal, and the appeal involves a rehearing of the evidence, usually before a judge and two JPs, but not a jury.

Crown courts are located throughout the country. There are three grades of crown court, the grading depending upon the seniority of the judge staffing the courts, and this in turn decides the seriousness of the offence tried at a particular court. For instance, particularly serious crimes are tried at the Old Bailey, the best-known of the crown courts.

Appeals from crown-court convictions (and sentences) are heard by the Court of Appeal, Criminal Division.

Court of Appeal

The Court of Appeal is made up of two distinct courts, one for civil appeals and the other for criminal appeals.

Court of Appeal

The civil-appeals court is known simply as the Court of Appeal. It can hear appeals from county-court decisions and civil decisions of the High Court. The appeal is technically a 'rehearing' of the case but this is a misnomer, for the court does not hear the witnesses again. The court mainly listens to legal argument from counsel and any dispute as to the evidence is decided by reference to the notes or transcript taken at the previous trial. Most appeals relate to points of law, but some appeals are based on the argument that the judge drew the wrong inference from the facts or that the 'learned judge misdirected himself'.

The jurisdiction is based on hearing appeals from:
● the county court, on all matters except bankruptcy;
● the High Court, on all civil matters;
● various tribunals, in particular the Employment Appeals Tribunal, the Lands Tribunal, and the Restrictive Practices Court.

Most appeals are heard by three judges, although some (e.g. appeals from county-court decisions) can be heard by only two judges. Decisions need not be unanimous. The head of the court is the Master of the Rolls – arguably the most influential appointment in our legal system.

Court of Appeal, Criminal Division

It was not until 1907 that there was an appeal system for the more serious criminal cases. The Court of Criminal Appeal was then established, but it was abolished in 1966 when the Court of Appeal took on a dual role of hearing both civil and criminal cases, and was split into two divisions to hear the different cases. Accordingly, criminal appeals now go to the Court of Appeal, Criminal Division.

This court hears appeals from crown court decisions. Only a convicted defendant can appeal – the prosecutor cannot appeal if the accused is acquitted. The court can dismiss the appeal, quash the conviction, or vary the sentence, and even substitute a conviction for another offence (e.g. quash a conviction for burglary but find the defendant guilty of theft instead). In addition, the court need not allow the appeal just because the defendant is technically not guilty. Even if the defendant succeeds, the court can dismiss his appeal if 'no miscarriage of justice has actually occurred'. This process is often used so that the court need not release a defendant because of a minor irregularity in the hearing of his trial.

Although the prosecution cannot appeal against the accused's acquittal, there is a procedure that allows a point of law raised in the crown court hearing to be referred to the Court of Appeal, Criminal Division. If the Attorney-General feels the point is of sufficient importance, he can refer the matter to the court, which will then consider it. The position of the acquitted defendant is not affected by this – he remains 'not guilty' even if the Court of Appeal's decision makes it clear that his acquittal was a wrong decision.

Most appeals are heard by two judges; if they cannot agree there will be a re-hearing in front of three judges. The head of the court is the Lord Chief Justice.

Appeals from decisions of the Court of Appeal (on both civil and criminal matters) are made to the House of Lords, although leave must first be obtained.

European courts

European Court of Human Rights

The European Convention for the Protection of Human Rights and Fundamental Freedoms requires the UK government to comply with the standards set out in the convention.

Individual citizens can complain to the European Commission on Human Rights, in Strasbourg, and the complaint can then proceed to either the Court of Human Rights or the Committee of Ministers at the Council of Europe.

The application will be considered initially by the commission. The application will only be considered if the applicant has used all the legal remedies available to him in the UK; in effect, this means he must have appealed his case through the hierarchy of courts, although he need not have exhausted all non-legal remedies (e.g. complaint to MPs or the Ombudsman). In addition, the application must be made within six months of the final appeal decision that is now being appealed against. If the application meets these requirements, the commission's staff investigate it. Both the applicant and the UK government submit written arguments and there will usually be a hearing in Strasbourg. The commission then announces a provisional opinion, which is not published, and tries to negotiate a settlement between the parties.

If no settlement can be negotiated, the commission draws up a formal report, stating whether there has been a breach of the convention. This report is published. The case can then be referred to the Court of Human Rights, but only by the commission or the UK government (or another government involved in the case). The individual who made the application cannot take the case to the court. In practice, very few cases reach the court. Usually governments abide by reports of the commission for fear of adverse publicity.

The Convention on Human Rights cannot be enforced through our own domestic courts – it can only be enforced by the European Court. For instance:

An antique dealer was charged with handling stolen property, but was subsequently acquitted. However, it became clear that the police had been tapping his phone and so he claimed damages for this from the police. He relied, in part, on the European convention which allows everyone 'the right to respect for his private and family life, his home, and his correspondence'. Held: The European Convention on Human Rights was not recognized by our courts and so it could not make the phone-tapping illegal. The convention could only be enforced by going to the European Court. The English courts therefore did not recognize the European convention – in fact, the antique dealer did take his case to the European Court (and won!). Metropolitan Police (1979).

The European Court of Human Rights has no connection with the EEC, or its own court, the European Court of Justice.

European Court of Justice

This is the Common Market's court of law. It can decide disputes over the interpretation and application of any of the EEC's regulations or institutions. Member states and affected individuals can bring cases before the court.

In practice, the main users of the court are companies affected by the commercial provisions of the Treaty of Rome and the EEC's regulations. Since the Treaty of Rome has little to say about human rights and the administration of justice, the court is rarely used by individual citizens.

The High Court

The High Court hears all the more important civil cases, and it also has a small criminal-appeals jurisdiction.

The work of the High Court is split between its three divisions. Before 1972 the High Court was in four divisions whose different workloads were largely derived from historical distinctions that were no longer of importance. The allocation of work has now been reorganized on a more rational basis between three divisions.

Queen's Bench Division

This division (known as the QBD) is the busiest. It hears all contract cases, tort claims (such as claims for negligence or nuisance), and claims for the recovery of land, such as the eviction of squatters. However, it only hears the cases that are not brought in the county court, for the county court can hear claims for up to £5,000. Whilst claims for £5,000 or less can be brought in the High Court they are discouraged, for the High Court litigant with a small-value claim will usually forfeit all, or part, of his legal costs (see page 843).

There are also two specialist courts within the QBD. The Commercial Court hears major commercial disputes, usually in private, with the judge hearing the case in the more informal role of an arbitrator. The Admiralty Court hears maritime disputes.

Chancery Division

This specializes in 'equity' matters such as:
- contracts for the sale and purchase of land (but not eviction cases)
- mortgage repossessions
- disputes over wills and the administration of estates
- trust fund disputes
- bankruptcy and winding up of companies
- Inland Revenue disputes
- administering the affairs and property of the mentally disordered. When doing this, the court is called the Court of Protection.

Family Division

This court hears all family disputes. The bulk of these are defended divorces. In addition, it deals with separation, custody of children, maintenance, adoption, and applications for wardship. It also decides arguments over the division of the family assets and property when the marriage breaks down.

The Divisional Courts

Each of the three divisions of the High Court has what is called a Divisional Court attached to it. In practice, the same judges will sit in these Divisional Courts, and the only difference will be that the court has a different name – such as the Divisional Court of the Queen's Bench Division. However, whereas High Court cases are usually tried by only one judge, when the court sits as a Divisional Court, there must be three judges.

The Divisional Courts are the appellate part of the High Court.

QBD. Hears appeals on points of law from criminal decisions of magistrates' courts. In addition it has an important function as overseer of the junior courts and tribunals. If someone wishes to complain about what a court or tribunal has done (or not done) he can make an application for judicial review to the QBD.

Chancery Division. Deals with appeals from county courts on bankruptcy matters.

Family Division. Hears appeals from magistrates' courts in domestic and matrimonial cases.

The House of Lords

This is the final appeal body for both civil and criminal cases. A case can only be 'taken to the Lords' if permission has been given, either by the Court of Appeal or by the Appeals Committee of the House of Lords. Permission is only given if the appeal is of general legal importance.

The normal rule is that a case can only go to the Lords after it has been heard by the Court of Appeal, so the case progresses slowly up the judicial hierarchy. Occasionally, this delay causes problems and so a special procedure was introduced in 1969 to allow an appeal direct from the High Court to the House of Lords, so 'leap-frogging' the Court of Appeal. However, this is only allowed in exceptional circumstances, and both the High Court judge and the Lords must certify that there is a legal point of general public importance involved, which indicates that previous judicial decisions need to be reconsidered. In practice, the leap-frogging procedure is rarely used.

The judges in the House of Lords are called Lords of Appeal in Ordinary, although they are more popularly called the Law Lords. They are paid professional judges who are given life peerages. In addition, the Lord Chancellor and peers who have held high judicial office (such as ex-Lord Chancellors) are qualified to sit as judges. In legal theory, any ordinary member of the House of Lords (a lay lord) could take part in the hearings but there is a strictly applied convention that, in practice, excludes them – when one lay lord did express an opinion he was completely ignored.

The court used to sit in the chamber of the House of Lords but since 1948 it has usually sat as an Appellate Committee in a committee room in the Palace of Westminster and only occasionally sits in the chamber (for instance, during the summer recess). There must be at least three judges for a committee to be quorate, although, in practice, appeals are heard by five judges. The judgements of the individual judges are described as 'speeches', but this is no more than a remnant of the days when the court was the Lords and sat in its chamber. Nowadays the judgements are not even read out, but copies are distributed.

In practice, the high cost of taking a case to the Lords leads to its case-load having a high proportion of tax, commercial, and property disputes. Very few criminal cases reach the Lords.

Do we need a Court of Appeal and a House of Lords?

We have two major appellate bodies: the Court of Appeal and, for a few cases, the House of Lords. Is there any justification for retaining the House of Lords? Why not abolish its judicial functions and retain the Law Lords as members of the Court of Appeal, whose experience and intellect can be called upon as necessary?

The present system causes delay and it can drastically increase legal costs. It can also lead to a sense of unfairness, when a person wins the hearings in all the lower courts only to lose in the Lords; he then has to pay the costs of all the earlier hearings, even though he won them.

More important, many lawyers would say that the House of Lords is out of touch with the practical realities of everyday law. In recent years there have been several House of Lords' decisions that have thrown accepted legal practices and procedures into chaos and which have shown that the Lords give little thought to the practical consequences of their decisions. Far from clarifying the law (which one would have thought to be a major objective of the supreme court in the land) the House of Lords has tended to confuse and further obscure it.

The Judicial Committee of the Privy Council

The Judicial Committee does not fit neatly into any part of the courts structure. It is an anachronism, and yet it can wield enormous influence and in many ways it is the ultimate judicial body.

Since 1833, the Judicial Committee has been the final appellate court for cases heard in the dominions and colonies. During the second half of the nineteenth century its importance increased, as the Empire developed and expanded. Generally, British-dominated countries would adopt our legal system (or have it imposed on them) and so the legal principles raised, for instance, in an Indian case might be of great importance to legal thought in this country and also in the other parts of the Empire. So the Judicial Committee became the appellate body for the Empire.

In practice, its judges are the same judges that sit in the House of Lords; since 1962 some Commonwealth judges have been able to sit as judges, although few have done so.

As the Empire split up, so many of the newly independent countries decided that it would be wrong to retain the Judicial Committee as their final appeal court. So the number of countries that send cases to the Judicial Committee has declined. The Committee is now the ultimate appellate Court for the Channel Islands, Isle of Man, the Colonies, the Protectorates, the Australian States, New Zealand, Jamaica, Trinidad, Tobago, Mauritius, Malaysia, Singapore, Gambia, Barbados, Fiji, and Granada. Appeals can only be made with leave from the Crown.

Decisions of the Judicial Committee are accorded great respect by all countries whose legal systems are based on our own. Thus, English, Indian, Pakistani, and even Canadian lawyers will treat the committee's decisions as being of great persuasive authority. In effect, the Judicial Committee is the same as the House of Lords (but with their lordships wearing different legal hats!).

The magistrates' courts

These are the most junior courts and yet they are the most important. There are over 650 magistrates' courts throughout the land and it is in these courts that the vast majority of court cases are heard.

Most magistrates are amateurs. They act as unpaid judges, receiving only their travelling expenses and a subsistence allowance. Only in the big cities are there a few professional, full-time magistrates, known as 'stipendiaries'.

Magistrates' courts can hear both civil and criminal cases. About 98 per cent of all criminal cases are heard in the magistrates' courts, and every criminal prosecution must be commenced there, even if the case is eventually tried in the crown court. See Chapter 54 for how criminal proceedings are begun and for how committal proceedings take place.

On the civil side, magistrates' courts have an extensive matrimonial and family jurisdiction. They can make maintenance and affiliation orders and adoption orders, and can also make orders restricting a violent husband's access. In addition, they have jurisdiction to hear other miscellaneous civil matters, such as rates arrears, and recovery of unpaid income tax and national insurance contributions. Sitting as a juvenile court, the magistrates can order that a child be put into care.

Committees of local magistrates also deal with such things as liquor and betting-licence applications.

Although there are now training courses and instruction books for magistrates, most JPs have little knowledge of the law, other than what they have picked up over the years as they hear cases. For legal advice they go to the clerk who sits in every magistrates' court and who is there to advise and assist the magistrates. Generally, the clerk will be a solicitor or barrister of at least five years' experience.

The justices' clerk is in a position of some power, for he may easily influence the magistrates in their decision, although, of course, he should not do so. In theory, the clerk's role is limited to advising the magistrates as to questions of law, practice, and procedure, and at the same time to giving general advice as to sentencing practices. The clerk should not be involved in the magistrates' decision as to guilt or innocence, or as to the sentence to be imposed. In practice, however, the justice's clerk is in an extremely influential position and many observers feel that they often play a more active role in the decision-making process than is theoretically permitted. Certainly, it takes a strong-minded JP to stand up to an experienced clerk!

Tribunals

Tribunals are unlike the other courts since they are, strictly speaking, not courts at all. They are specially constituted bodies for deciding disputes in a particular area of the law. For instance, industrial tribunals settle employment disputes; rent tribunals fix fair rents. All tribunals have a specialized jurisdiction.

Although there were some tribunals in the nineteenth century, they are largely a twentieth-century phenomenon. In particular, the post-war period has seen a substantial increase in the numbers of tribunals and in the types of work they do. The expense, inaccessibility, and formality of the conventional courts has led to the introduction of more and more tribunals, aimed at providing a cheap and informal means of resolving disputes. This, indeed, is the justification for not allowing legal aid for tribunal cases; the argument is that an extension of legal aid would result in the tribunals becoming over-lawyered, and that, in time, the tribunals would acquire the less desirable features of ordinary courts. The counter-argument is, of course, that it is absurd to allow legal aid for a trivial magistrates' court or county-court case, and yet deny it for a tribunal case which might be of great significance (for instance, industrial tribunals can award thousands of pounds compensation – much more than the £5,000 limit in the county court).

Although the tribunals are outside the conventional courts system, they are subject to control by the courts. Some tribunal decisions can be appealed direct to the courts, but usually a question of law (not fact) must be involved.

In addition, the Divisional Court of the Queen's Bench Division exercises a general supervisory role over all tribunals and will quash the decision of a tribunal that exceeds its powers, acts improperly, or refuses to hear a claim.

The press, the public, and the 'open court' principle

It is a fundamental principle that justice should not only be done, but should be seen to be done. Thus, trials and court hearings are usually conducted in open court so that the press and the public can attend.

Over the years it has become necessary to restrict this open-court policy in order to protect people from unfair publicity. The result is that there are now various types of cases from which the press or the public are excluded, or in which reporting restrictions apply.

Juvenile cases

There are restrictions placed on who is eligible to attend a juvenile-court hearing (see page 147, for those who can attend). In addition, the press cannot report the name, address, or school of the accused child, nor publish a photograph or any particulars which could identify anyone under seventeen, whether the accused or a witness (the age limit is eighteen if the child is in care). The maximum penalty for breaking these reporting restrictions is a £2,000 fine.

The juvenile court has a discretion to allow these reporting restrictions to be lifted. But this should only be done in the exceptional case. For instance, it might be used to allow the press to publicize the acquittal of an accused child where he comes from a small community in which everyone knows he is on trial. However, the reporting restrictions cannot be lifted to help a child who is not the accused. For instance, if it is thought in the community that a particular boy is being prosecuted, whereas in fact it is a different boy, the court cannot allow the name of the boy to be published in order to protect the other boy.

Obviously, the juvenile court must not use the lifting of reporting restrictions as an indirect way of punishing the juvenile offender. These restrictions also apply in the crown court if the case is on appeal from a juvenile-court decision.

In addition to these restrictions on juvenile-court cases, there are other restrictions that apply in any court; for instance, if a juvenile is tried in the crown court, or if he sues in the High Court or county court. It is an offence to 'reveal the name, address or school, or otherwise give information which might identify any child or young person' involved in *any* court case, but this only applies if the court specifically directs that reporting restrictions shall apply. (Maximum penalty for breach is a £2,000 fine.) This is called a 'section 39 order' since it derives from section 39 of the Children and Young Persons Act 1933.

Domestic proceedings in the magistrates' court

Magistrates' courts can hear various 'domestic' cases: for instance, maintenance, custody, affiliation, guardianship, and consent-to-marry applications.

All these matters are heard in private; the public is not admitted, although the press is. Exceptionally, even the press can be excluded if the evidence is 'indecent' and the interests of justice or public decency dictate that the press should not hear the indecent evidence. In guardianship applications and in applications by young people for consent to marry (see page 18) the magistrates can exclude the press if the court feels it is in the interests of the minor for the case to be heard in private.

Generally, therefore, the normal rule is for the public to be excluded but for the press (as the representatives of the public) to be allowed to stay. However, the press can only publish:

- the names, addresses and occupations of the parties and witnesses;
- the grounds of the application, and a concise statement of the charges and counter-charges (but only if the various charges are backed up by evidence – so unsubstantiated charges cannot be reported; the actual evidence supporting the charges cannot be reported);
- submissions made on points of law and the court's decision on them;
- the court's decision and any observations made by the magistrates when giving their decision. So if the magistrates describe the wife as 'an immoral hussy' the press can report it.

A journalist who breaks these restrictions can be fined up to £1,000. The Attorney-General's consent must be obtained for a prosecution.

In practice, papers very rarely publish any details of domestic cases.

Divorce and matrimonial cases

In the same way that domestic proceedings in magistrates' courts are subject to reporting restrictions, so are divorce petitions and other matrimonial cases in the various other courts. This includes defended and undefended divorce petitions, maintenance, custody, legitimacy, and also applications for the family assets and property to be divided between the spouses. The reporting restrictions are identical to those in magistrates' courts' domestic proceedings (see above).

Divorce, judicial separation, and nullity orders are made in open court, but the written evidence in support will usually have been gone through in private. Matters relating to children and finances are always heard separately, usually in chambers (i.e. a private room) so that neither the public nor the press can be admitted.

Committal proceedings

The more serious criminal cases are tried in the crown court. But before the case can go to the crown court it must first be vetted by the magistrates who can check that there is the basis of a case against the accused. If so, it will be 'committed' to the crown court for trial (see page 795).

The public can attend committal proceedings but there are restrictions on what the press can report. The purpose of the restrictions is to avoid adverse publicity for the defendant prior to the crown-court trial. However, these reporting restrictions can be lifted if the accused wishes; for instance, he might hope that publicity given to the committal proceedings will lead to witnesses coming forward to prove that he was not present at the scene of the crime.

The reporting restrictions are set out in section 3 of the Criminal Justice Act 1967. They restrict press reports of the committal to:
- the name of the court, and of the justices;
- the names, ages, addresses, and occupations of the parties and the witnesses, and their lawyers;
- the decision of the court;
- whether bail or legal aid was granted;
- if the accused is committed, the charges against him.

(Maximum penalty for breach is a £2,000 fine. Prosecutions can only be brought with the consent of the Attorney-General.)

Note that these restrictions only apply to committal proceedings; they do not apply to the actual trial of a criminal case, whether it be in the magistrates' court or the crown court. Nor do they apply if the magistrates find that there is no case to answer, and so do not commit the accused to the crown court; when this happens the press can report the full facts of the case. The logic behind this is that the reporting restrictions are designed to prevent adverse pre-trial publicity – not to protect acquitted defendants from publicity. However, this can often be very hard on the acquitted defendant.

Rape cases

The public are always admitted to rape cases unless the evidence is 'indecent' (see below). However, special restrictions apply to the press reporting of rape (and attempted rape) cases:

Identifying the accused man
- the accused man cannot be identified in the press once he has been arrested, or if a warrant has been issued for his arrest;
- he cannot be identified at the committal proceedings unless he asks to be;
- at the trial (in the crown court) he can only be identified if he so requests, unless the judge decides that identification is in the public interest;
- if acquitted, he cannot be identified;
- if convicted, he can be identified.

Identifying the woman
- the woman cannot be identified at any stage of the proceedings unless the crown-court judge directs otherwise; he will only do this if identification is in the public interest;
- if the accused is convicted and appeals, the Court of Appeal can allow the woman to be identified if this may produce evidence needed for the man's appeal.

These restrictions are set out in the Sexual Offences (Amendment) Act 1976. The Act also introduced restrictions on cross-examination of rape victims as to their previous sexual experiences. The judge should only allow this if it would be unfair to the defendant not to allow such questions. Many people suspect that the discretion is exercised too often because, in practice, most judges tend to think there is a link between sexual experience and the likelihood of the woman having consented to the rape she is now complaining about. Incidentally, the police are also supposed not to ask about irrelevant sexual history when investigating a rape allegation (according to a Home Office circular) but, once again, one doubts whether that applies in practice.

Official secrets

Normally the public and press can attend an official-secrets trial, and the press can report the proceedings in the normal way. However, the court can exclude both the public and the press, on application by the prosecution, if satisfied that national safety would otherwise be prejudiced. Sentencing must always take place in public.

Indecent evidence

The press are prohibited from reporting 'any indecent matter or indecent medical, surgical, or physiological details being matters or details the publication of which would be calculated to injure public morals' (Judicial Proceedings (Regulation of Reports) Act 1926). Maximum penalty on conviction is a £2,000 fine; prosecutions can only be brought with the consent of the Attorney-General.

This restriction applies in all court cases, civil or criminal, and whatever the subject matter of the dispute, be it a defamation action, a nullity claim, or whatever. Thus, indecent language and four-letter words can be used in the courtroom, but it may be an offence for the press to publish that evidence.

Sub judice: when publication is contempt of court

A newspaper may also be restricted in what it can report by the contempt laws. This will generally cover reporting which prejudices the fair trial of a case, for instance by interviews with the witnesses, analysis of the evidence, or ignoring a direction by the judge.

> *Distillers were being sued for negligence as a result of the thalidomide tragedy, but the proceedings had been in progress for a long time. The* Sunday Times *wanted to publish an article which attempted to show that Distillers had not taken sufficient care to check the safety of the drug before marketing it. Distillers sought an injunction preventing the publication of the article on the ground that it would be a contempt of court. The House of Lords held: The article would be in contempt and so should not be published. It would be contempt to publish an article expressing an opinion when this could give rise to a 'real risk' that the fair trial of the case would be prejudiced. It was also contempt to use improper pressure to induce a party to settle on terms that he did not want.*
> Times Newspapers (1973)

Although this decision was criticized later by the European Court of Human Rights, the principles laid down by the House of Lords still apply.

Another example involved a blackmail case:

In the course of a well-publicized blackmail trial, evidence was given by several well-known people as to how they had been blackmailed over their sexual activities. The witnesses were allowed to give evidence without their names being mentioned in court. The judge asked the press not to report the names of the witnesses if the press found out their identity. The judge did not order that the names should not be published and the Socialist Worker *ignored the request and disclosed the true identity of a 'Mr Y'. Held: This was contempt.* Socialist Worker (1975)

Because of cases such as this, the *sub judice* rule was altered by the Contempt of Court Act 1981. This makes it contempt of court to publish anything which 'creates a substantial risk' that the court proceedings will be prejudiced. But if the editor does not know that there are relevant court proceedings under way, or if he merely publishes a fair and accurate report of the case, then he cannot be in contempt. For instance, a paper that published details of someone's previous convictions will only be in contempt if it knows that he is currently being prosecuted for another offence – since the publication of his 'form' would obviously prejudice him at his trial. On the other hand, if the paper did not know of the court case then it would not be in contempt (although it might fall foul of the rules on Rehabilitation of Offenders – see page 678).

The 1981 Act also allows the court (i.e. the judge or magistrates) to order that the press should not publish a witness's name (or should not publish certain parts of the evidence). This provision was a direct result of the *Socialist Worker* case (above) and it has been severely criticized. It is said to be too far-reaching, in that it allows courts to gag the press when there is no real justification for doing so.

Time limits on suing and prosecuting

There are different time limits for different types of legal claims. A person who has a claim should ensure that he commences proceedings within the appropriate 'limitation period' – if he waits until the limitation period has expired, he is unlikely to be able to sue:

contract claims (e.g. debt)	six years
tort claims (e.g. nuisance, negligence, defamation)	six years
squatters	twelve years
unpaid rent	six years
personal-injury claims (i.e. accidents)	three years (but see below)
criminal prosecutions	six months for summary offences; no time limit for other offences.

Note that the limitation period only lays down the time within which the claim must be started. For instance, a consumer who sues a shopkeeper for breach of contract over a faulty appliance has six years in which to sue. As long as he starts suing within that time, it does not matter that the trial of the case takes place more than six years after the date of purchase.

In practice, the courts disapprove of 'stale' claims, even when brought within the limitation period. Clearly, the consumer who sues over a faulty appliance should bring the claim as soon as possible, for the longer the delay, the less favourably will the case be received.

Minors. People under eighteen cannot sue in the courts. They have to sue via an adult (see page 124). Because of this, the limitation periods are extended for minors – the period only starts when the child reaches its eighteenth birthday. So a child of fifteen who wants to sue over a contract matter can, in theory, claim a limitation period of nine, not six, years (see page 125).

Similar rules apply to the mentally ill.

Suing for personal injury. The time limit for bringing a personal-injury claim (i.e. claiming damages for injury suffered in an accident) was traditionally three years from the date of the accident. However, this simple rule led to hardship in two types of cases:

1. When the injured person did not know he could sue. Often, an injured worker would not realize that he could sue his employer if he was injured at work by a careless fellow-worker or if the equipment was defective. By the time the injured person discovered his right to sue, it was often too late.
2. When the injured person did not realize he was injured or ill. A person might be exposed to a health hazard, such as radiation, coal dust, or asbestos dust, and not become ill until more than three years later. It would then be too late to sue.

These problems were only partly dealt with by the existing law, and to remedy the position the law was changed. The Limitation Act 1980 allows a personal-injury claim to be made within three years of:

● the date of the accident, *or*

● the date when the injured person first realized that he was ill or injured and that, in addition, he might be able to sue.

The Act also gives the courts a general power to waive the three-year rule in exceptional cases. In deciding whether to waive the three-year period the court considers the reasons for the delay, the conduct of the defendant, the seriousness of the injury, whether the evidence is still available, and the steps taken by the plaintiff to obtain advice.

Mr Buck first contracted pneumoconiosis in 1959. By 1963 he had realized that he could sue, but he did not bother, mainly because the disease caused him little discomfort at that time. However, the disease became worse and by 1970 he was very ill, and he finally had to give up work in 1973. He was then advised to sue his employers and in 1975 he started proceedings. His employers said that he was too late. Held: The general rule was that he should have sued within three years of discovering he had a claim (i.e. 1963). So normally the limitation period would have expired in 1966. However, the court exercised its discretion and allowed him to sue even though the three-year period had expired nine years previously. He was seriously ill and, more important, the employer would not be put at a disadvantage by the lateness of the claim; all the relevant information was available. Buck (1977)

So a person with a personal-injury claim should take legal advice about suing, even if the accident happened more than three years ago. Note that there is a special scheme which allows accident claimants to obtain a free initial interview from a solicitor. See page 871.

54 The Criminal Law

Everyone knows what a 'crime' is; in the words of the *Oxford English Dictionary*, it is an 'act punishable by the law'. But people usually associate the word 'crime' with the more sensational or serious offences, such as murder, manslaughter, and arson, and forget that such petty offences as careless driving, parking violations, and leaving litter are also crimes – the only difference being in the severity of the punishment meted out to the offender.

The same principles of criminal justice apply to mass-murderers as to shoplifters and others accused of comparatively trivial crimes. In the eyes of the law, a crime is a crime – however grave or trivial the offence may be.

The law's 'fair deal' for criminals

- the accused is presumed innocent until proved guilty;
- to prove his guilt, the prosecution must show *beyond reasonable doubt* that he committed the offence. This means that if there is a reasonable doubt as to his guilt, then he must be acquitted (cf. the lighter burden of proof in civil cases, page 759);
- he need not help the police with their inquiries, or make a statement to them; further, this lack of cooperation cannot be held against him at the trial;
- he can remain silent and it will not be held against him;
- he is tried on the facts of the case, not on the evidence of his previous convictions; the court will not be told of his 'record' since that might create a prejudice against him. Only if he is found guilty will his 'form' be relevant, when it may influence the court's sentence; but the accused will forfeit the benefit of this rule if he falsely tells the court he is of good character, or if he attacks the character of the prosecution witnesses;
- he is tried on the oral evidence of witnesses; generally, written evidence is not allowed since there is no opportunity for its maker to be cross-examined; also, the evidence of a witness must be of what he himself saw or heard and not *hearsay* (i.e. second-hand evidence). For instance, A cannot say that B told him that the accused had admitted committing the crime: only B, or the accused, can give that evidence;
- he is protected from trial by newspaper; the *sub judice* rules prevent the papers from reporting anything other than the evidence given in the case; speculation by the press is prohibited (see page 769 for the restrictions on press reporting);
- he has various 'civil liberties' that regulate the manner in which the police can question him (see Chapter 44).

These safeguards are given to all people, whether they be mass-murderers or litter-bugs. The underlying principle is that it is better for several guilty people to go free rather than take the risk of one innocent person being wrongly convicted.

Criminal proceedings

There are two ways of bringing the suspect before the court: either by a *summons* or, alternatively, by *arresting* and then *charging* him (see the chart on page 780).

Issuing a summons

Firstly, there is the *summons* to appear in court at a certain date and time. To obtain a summons, the police go before a magistrate and state where and when the accused committed the offence; this is called laying an *information*, and must be done within six months of the offence. If the magistrate thinks there is a prima facie case (which he nearly always does) he will sign and issue the summons, commanding the accused to appear in court, usually at least one week later. The police then serve the summons on the accused, usually by post.

Obviously, this procedure is only used in the less serious cases where there is no risk of the offender absconding as soon as he receives the summons. The accused person must attend the court on the dates given in the summons; if he does not, a warrant can be issued for his arrest. The only exception to the rule is when the summons states that he can plead guilty by post, in which case he need not attend court in person (see page 790).

Arresting and charging

The second way of starting criminal proceedings is to *arrest* the suspect and then *charge* him. This is normally done in more serious cases, when a summons would be inappropriate. However, there are some occasions when an offence is not serious, but when a summons would not be suitable (e.g. the suspect's name and address may be false – in which case the police will want to be able to hold him while they check the details). But, except in those few cases, the general rule remains that a summons is used for the less serious cases, whereas arrest and charging is used for the serious cases. Arresting and charging are two different steps in the prosecution process. The suspect is arrested when a policeman takes him into custody – in other words, by making it clear that the suspect has to accompany him to the police station. The charging occurs when he is in the police station and the custody officer reads out the formal description of the offence, hands him a copy of the charge, and gives him a notice setting out his legal rights. It is thus a two-stage process – arresting, followed by charging at the police station.

But a policeman cannot arrest anyone unless he has lawful authority to do so, for otherwise he runs the risk of being sued for damages in respect of false imprisonment. With the more serious offences (generally those for which the maximum sentence could be five years or more in prison), a policeman automatically has power to arrest a suspect; see the list below. However, if the offence does not automatically entitle the policeman to arrest the suspect, then he must first obtain the consent of a magistrate. This is done by the magistrate issuing an arrest warrant. The procedure is basically the same as when laying an information for the issue of a summons, although this time the policeman will hand in a written statement and give his evidence on oath. If the magistrate decides that there is a prima facie case against the accused, he will issue the warrant. The police can then serve the warrant on the accused and arrest him.

Once the police have arrested the suspect, they should charge him as soon as is reasonably possible.

At this stage, the accused can:

- demand to phone a solicitor (see page 668);
- refuse to answer any questions (see page 664);
- ask that a friend or relative be told of his arrest (see page 669).

Arrest without a warrant

A policeman can arrest someone without the need for a warrant if the person is:

1. *Seen* committing any of these offences: obstructing the highway; being drunk and incapable; refusing to take (or failing to take) a breath test; committing any indictable offence (see page 785) at night; soliciting; refusing to give his name and address when legally obliged to (for instance, a motorist involved in an accident); committing certain immigration offences; assault.
2. *Suspected* of committing either of these offences: loitering with intent to commit an arrestable offence (i.e. an offence for which you could get more than five years in prison); driving while disqualified.
3. *Seen committing, or reasonably suspected* to be committing, a breach of the peace or any offence that could lead to five years', or more, imprisonment. These offences are called 'arrestable offences'. Included are: armed assault; arson; actual bodily harm; burglary; death by reckless driving; demanding money with menaces; dishonest handling; drug offences; grievous bodily harm; living off immoral earnings; manslaughter; murder; some firearm offences; rape, indecent assault, and other serious sex offences; taking a motor vehicle without authority; theft; wounding. (Note: this is not a complete list of all arrestable offences.)

A private individual can arrest someone without the need for a warrant (a 'citizen's arrest') if the offence comes within paragraph 3 above.

Time limits on criminal prosecutions

There are different rules for magistrates' court cases and for other cases.

Offences that must be tried in the magistrates' court

These must generally be prosecuted within six months of the offence being committed. This means that the prosecutor must lay information before the magistrates and ask that a summons be issued within six months of the offence. However, there is no need for the summons to be served on the accused within the six-month period, let alone for him to be tried within that period. But, if the information is not laid within the six months, the offender cannot be prosecuted for the offence.

However, with certain motoring offences the prosecution must be careful to give the accused notice of intended prosecution. This must be in the form of an oral warning at the time of the offence or a written warning (or summons) served within fourteen days of the offence being committed (see page 620).

The six-month rule in the magistrates' court is subject to a few minor exceptions, when statutes lay down longer periods. For instance, offences under the Obscene Publications Act can be prosecuted up to twelve months after commission; and summary offences under the Companies Acts have a time limit of three years.

Offences that need not be tried in the magistrates' court

These are not, generally, subject to any time limit. Thus, a person can be charged with a serious offence that he committed many years ago, although often it is decided not to prosecute if the time-lag is substantial.

However, there are a few offences that are subject to specific time periods. For instance, Trade Descriptions Act offences can only be prosecuted within three years of their commission or within one year of the discovery of the offence, whichever is later. But such a time limit is very unusual.

Bringing a private prosecution

The vast majority of criminal prosecutions are brought by the police – in fact, about 99 per cent of the total. But the law allows private individuals to prosecute for most offences, for it has long been a principle of our laws that all citizens should have access to the criminal courts.

Most private prosecutions are started by the issuing of a summons in the magistrates' court. (See page 886 for the procedure to be followed.) Once a summons has been issued, the case will proceed in the normal manner for any magistrates' court case. The only difference would be that the private individual would be prosecuting instead of a policeman or prosecuting solicitor.

Mischievous private prosecutions can be stopped in an indirect way. The Director of Public Prosecutions has the power to take over the conduct of any criminal prosecution if he so chooses. Thus, if a private prosecution was thought to be against the public interest the DPP might take over the case, but then not present any prosecution evidence when it came to trial. The accused person would, of course, have to be acquitted.

The Legal System

How criminals are taken to court

Criminal proceedings are started in one of three ways

Magistrates issue a summons.	Police arrest suspect without a warrant (page 777)	Magistrate issues warrant for arrest of suspect.

Warrant is served and accused is arrested.

Suspect is charged at the police station.

Is the offence summary (magistrates' court only), indictable (crown court only), or triable either way (magistrates' court or crown court)?

summary   triable either way   indictable

Accused attends magistrates' court. Charge put to him. Prosecutor and defendant say which court they would prefer. Magistrates decide. But if they order magistrates' court trial, the defendant can override this and insist on crown court trial.

Magistrates examine the evidence against the defendant. If there is a prima facie case, he is committed for trial in the crown court. If not, he is acquitted.

Accused is tried before the magistrates.

Accused is tried in crown court before judge and jury.

Accused is found guilty and sentenced, or he is acquitted.

No one should embark on a private prosecution lightly. It is always preferable to get the police to prosecute. The private prosecutor should bear in mind that:

- if he loses the case he may have to pay the accused's legal costs;
- if he loses, he may be sued for damages if it can be shown that he acted 'maliciously' in bringing the prosecution. In addition, if a citizen's arrest was made, a damages claim for false imprisonment could follow;
- even if he wins, the prosecutor is unlikely to recover all his legal costs and expenses;
- often the accused will make counter-allegations against the prosecutor (e.g. in the typical dispute between two neighbours who are both making accusations against each other). When this happens, the magistrates frequently find it impossible to sort out who is in the right and who is in the wrong; in these circumstances, it is common for the magistrates to bind over (see page 807) both the prosecutor and the accused;
- if the accused is able to opt for a crown-court trial (see page 786) and does so, the private prosecutor will have to instruct a solicitor and barrister to act for him in the crown court. This could be very expensive.

Shoplifting. Nearly all shoplifting charges are brought by the individual shop-owner (i.e. as a private prosecution) rather than by the police. So the normal rules about private prosecutions will generally apply. If the prosecution fails (i.e. the accused person is acquitted by the court), then the shop could well face a damages claim, for malicious prosecution, and false imprisonment (see above). In practice, of course, most people would rather simply forget about the whole affair, rather than start fresh court proceedings!

Bail

Once the accused has been arrested and charged, the question arises of whether he is to be released or held in custody. In legal terminology: he is either *remanded on bail* or *remanded in custody*. If the prosecution was started by summons the problem will not arise for he will not have been taken into custody; instead, he will simply have been told when he is to appear in court.

If the arrest was by warrant, the magistrate who issued it may have written on the back that the accused should have bail; if the warrant is 'backed for bail' in this way, the police have no choice but to release the accused after charging him. If it is not backed for bail then the police cannot release the accused on bail.

Otherwise it is for the police to take the initial decision whether to remand the accused in custody. Bail is granted entirely at their discretion and it is then called *police bail*. But if police bail is refused, the prisoner must be brought before a magistrate within twenty-four hours (forty-eight hours at weekends and public holidays) and given a chance of asking the magistrate for bail. So when an accused person is arrested and charged, the power to hold him in custody is initially with the police.

Special rules apply to children and young people:
- children under fourteen must be granted police bail unless charged with murder or manslaughter;
- a young person between fourteen and seventeen must be granted police bail unless a senior police officer believes
    - that the young person should be detained in his or her own interest, *or*
    - the young person would not turn up in court if released, *or*
    - it would defeat the ends of justice to grant bail, *or*
    - the young person has committed murder, manslaughter, or some other 'serious offence'.

Being detained in custody. There are detailed rules on how long a suspect can be held in custody. See page 666.

Asking the magistrate for bail

To refuse a man bail is to keep him in custody for an offence that he may not have committed. Apart from the social stigma of being kept in custody, the accused may well suffer through losing his job, in which case his family may be forced to live on supplementary benefit.

Accordingly, the basic principle is that no one should be refused bail unnecessarily. Apart from the libertarian reasons for this, there are also practical (and financial) reasons for not putting remand prisoners into the already overcrowded prisons. The aim is that 'the number of persons remanded in custody should be kept to the minimum compatible with the interests of justice'. The Bail Act 1976 sets out the rules.

When deciding whether to grant bail, the magistrate will first look at the offence with which the accused is charged:

1. *If the offence does not carry a possible prison sentence*, bail should only be refused if the accused has previously been given bail and failed to turn up in court when required *and* the court now believes that he will do so again.
2. *If the offence could carry a prison sentence* the magistrate need not grant bail if:
   - there are *substantial grounds* (i.e. more than mere suspicion) for believing he would abscond, commit an offence, or obstruct the course of justice (e.g. 'get at' witnesses), *or*
   - there has been insufficient time since charging for the police to have collected information about his suitability for bail, *or*
   - he has previously jumped bail, *or*
   - if the case has been adjourned for a report to be prepared (such as a social-welfare, medical, or probation report) then bail can be refused if it would be impracticable to make the inquiries or the report without his being in custody.

In all other cases, the accused must be granted bail.

If bail is refused

The court must give its reasons for refusing bail, and a written note of these must be given to the defendant. The defendant will then go to prison, but as a remand prisoner he will have special privileges not enjoyed by convicted prisoners (see page 675). The time spent as a remand prisoner will count as time served if he should subsequently be convicted and sent to prison for the offence.

The remand in custody is normally for eight days at a time, and the prisoner will then come back before the magistrates (whereupon he will normally be remanded for a further eight days, and so on, until his case is ready for trial). However, the accused can opt to avoid these eight-day remands, by agreeing to the remand being for a longer time: this will save him the inconvenience of trips from prison to the court, and should not delay the trial of his case in any way.

A prisoner cannot make repeated applications for bail – unless he has new grounds. If there is a change of circumstances (e.g. he now has someone who will stand surety; he has fixed up a job) then he can make a fresh application for bail – but not otherwise. In practice, therefore, most prisoners see little point in insisting that they be re-remanded every eight days, and so they will often agree to being remanded for a longer time.

Appealing. If the magistrates refuse bail, then their decision can be appealed to the crown court. The legal aid will normally cover the legal costs.

A prisoner's friends and relatives will often urge his solicitor to appeal straight away, but this is not always wise. If the crown-court judge should uphold the magistrate's decision, it is unlikely that the magistrate will be persuaded to change his mind at a later date. So it might be much better to collect evidence that answers the magistrate's reasons for refusing bail and present this at the next hearing, rather than rush off and appeal to the crown court.

If bail is granted

The defendant will be given a written note of the court's decision and told when he should next appear in court. If he does not turn up on that day but absconds, he will be guilty of an offence (maximum penalty three months' prison and £2,000 fine in a magistrates' court, twelve months' prison and an unlimited fine in a crown court). In addition, he is unlikely to be granted bail again.

Often the bail will be granted subject to conditions. For instance, the defendant may have to surrender his passport, report to the police station once a day, agree to live in a certain place, agree not to go near a particular place, or deposit cash or valuables as security. The Bail Act states that 'no condition should be imposed unless it is necessary', but it seems clear that many magistrates impose conditions when they are not strictly necessary. When this happens, the accused should tell the magistrate that he regards the conditions as being unnecessary. He can refuse to accept the conditions and if remanded in custody, can apply to the crown-court judge for bail to be granted free of conditions. Not surprisingly, few defendants are prepared to do this, and most simply accept the magistrate's conditions, however unreasonable they may be.

Usually bail will only be granted if the defendant can find one or more sureties. A surety is a person who agrees to forfeit a fixed sum should the accused not answer his bail. He does not have to deposit any money with the police while the accused is on bail, for it is only if the accused fails to answer bail and the magistrates decide to enforce the surety's bond that he has to produce the money. The amount at risk is called the 'recognizance'.

The surety will have to go to the court, as the magistrate will want to check that he is a suitable surety. The Bail Act says that a surety's suitability will be based primarily on:

● his financial resources (does he have the money to pay the recognizance if it should be enforced against him?);

● his character and any criminal record;

● his proximity (whether in terms of kinship, place of residence, or otherwise) to the person for whom he is to be surety.

The correct procedure is for the court to decide on the amount of the recognizance required, bearing in mind the nature of the offence, the defendant's record, and so on. The court should then consider the suitability of the sureties. The court should not decide that a large recognizance is needed simply because a particular surety is well off.

If the accused absconds and does not answer the bail, the surety may forfeit the sum due; he is said to have his 'recognizance estreated'. He will have to appear before the magistrates and argue why he should not forfeit the recognizance. Forfeiture is not automatic, for the court will want to know the extent to which the surety was to blame for the defendant absconding.

Mrs Green stood surety for her husband who was accused of importing cannabis. She told the court that her share of the family home was worth £3,000 and so she was accepted as surety for a recognizance of £3,000. Her husband later absconded. The magistrates ordered Mrs Green to forfeit the full £3,000, and she appealed against that decision. Held: The magistrates' decision would be overturned. They should have considered the extent to which Mrs Green was to blame for her husband defaulting. Moreover, magistrates should not accept a wife as a surety on the basis of matrimonial property. Since Mrs Green had done all she could to secure her husband's attendance, Lord Denning ordered that the recognizance should not be estreated. Green (1975)

However, that decision was very much a borderline case and subsequent decisions have made it clear that the 'blameworthiness' of the surety is not the only factor to be considered. Strictly speaking, if the surety has any doubts as to whether the accused will answer bail, he should take the accused to the police station and ask to be released from his surety. The police will then, of course, take the accused into custody until a suitable replacement surety can be found. In practice, magistrates are reluctant to allow sureties to be let off if the defendant absconds. Clearly, therefore, no one should stand surety unless he is sure that the accused will not abscond.

If the magistrates do insist that bail will only be granted subject to a surety, the defendant must be told why this is so, and then be given a written note of the reasons.

Legal aid

The vast majority of people who are prosecuted for the more serious criminal offences get legal aid. See page 862 for the procedure. But legal aid is not available for all criminal charges. Many magistrates take a fairly tough line and refuse to grant legal aid unless the charge is particularly serious. What one can say is that anyone who is tried in the crown court can expect to receive legal aid (assuming he passes the means test), and he can also expect to receive legal aid if he is up on a serious charge in the magistrates'. If there is an element of dishonesty involved in the offence (e.g. theft, fraud, taking a car, etc.) then legal aid will probably be granted. But someone charged with (e.g.) drunk driving would not normally get legal aid.

The trial of the case

Where will the case be tried?

What happens next will depend upon the type of offence, for this will determine whether the case is tried before the magistrates in a magistrates' court or before a judge and jury in the crown court. Basically, the magistrates hear the less serious cases – some 96 per cent of all criminal cases.

The offence will be:
- triable in the magistrates' court only (a *summary* offence); *or*
- triable in the crown court only (an *indictable* offence); *or*
- triable in the crown court or the magistrates' court (an offence *triable either way*).

All criminal cases start in the magistrates' court. If the offence is *summary*, then the trial will also take place in the magistrates' court. If it is *indictable*, the trial will usually take place in the crown court, but only after the magistrates have confirmed that there is the basis of a case against the accused and committed him for trial in the crown court.

With offences *triable either way*, the position is more complicated. First, the charge is put to the accused in the magistrates' court. Second, both the accused and the prosecutor can say which court they think should hear the case. Third, the magistrates then say where they think the case should be tried. If that is in the magistrates' court, the fourth step is for the accused to be given the chance of overriding the magistrates' decision and insisting on his right to a jury trial in the crown court. Note that if he insists on a crown-court trial against the wishes of the magistrates, he might be penalized by the crown court should he subsequently be found guilty. With juveniles (i.e. under seventeen) different problems arise: see page 146 for juvenile-court cases.

Opting for magistrates' court or crown-court trial

If the defence is *triable either way* the defendant has to weigh up the pros and cons of trial in the magistrates' court and in the crown court.

Advantages of trial in the magistrates' court

• *speed:* if the plea is guilty. If the plea is not guilty, it can take just as long (or even longer) to get the case heard by magistrates as in the crown court.

• *costs:* it is cheaper to run a case in the magistrates' court. Many defendants obtain legal aid and then cost is not a major factor, although if found guilty they are likely to pay a significantly larger contribution towards legal aid costs in the crown court than in the magistrates' court.

• *penalty:* generally, lighter penalties are imposed in the magistrates' court. But sometimes the magistrates commit the defendant to the crown court for sentencing, in which case that advantage is lost.

Advantages of trial in the crown court

• *acquittal:* the chances of being found not guilty are considerably higher in the crown court. Thus if the defendant is a professional person or person with a lot to lose if convicted, he should always opt for crown-court trial if it is available.

• *evidence:* the defence will see the prosecution's case in advance because all the evidence will have been supplied when the case is committed from the magistrates' court (see page 795). In a magistrates' court trial the defendant does not always see the prosecution evidence in advance, which can be a serious disadvantage. But this is changing – some of the evidence can now be disclosed if the offence is 'triable either way' (see page 785).

• *legal aid:* there is much more chance of getting legal aid if the case is to be tried in the crown court.

Trial in the magistrates' court

Whether the accused is being prosecuted by way of summons, or by arrest and charge, the day will come when the case is listed for hearing in the court's daily case list – the list of cases to be tried on that day.

Generally, the defendant must attend court on the date fixed for trial. The only exceptions are where he intends to plead *guilty* and:

• he has been offered the choice to plead guilty by post and he has done so (see page 790), *or*

• he sends a solicitor or barrister to represent him in court, assuming he wishes to plead guilty.

Otherwise the court will usually issue a warrant for his arrest should he not appear, although sometimes the case will simply be heard in his absence and he will be found guilty. However, this will normally only be done for a petty offence and when it is clear that the summons was properly served on him.

It may be that either the prosecution or the defence is not ready to proceed with the trial, perhaps because witnesses are not available or because the lawyers have not had sufficient time in which to investigate the case. If so, they may be able to persuade the magistrates to grant an adjournment and fix a new date for the trial.

The prosecution case will usually be presented by the police officer who arrested, or summonsed, the defendant. However, if the case is at all serious, then a solicitor from the national prosecution service will probably prosecute.

The officer in charge of the case will have obtained full statements from all the witnesses. He will also have prepared a brief summary of the facts, setting out the main circumstances of the crime. This will have been served on the accused, usually with the summons, but he may not have been given a copy of the witness statements. Thus, he may not know the evidence against him until it is revealed in the course of the trial as the prosecution witnesses give their evidence. This makes it extremely difficult for the defence to prepare its case in advance (cf. the position in the crown court, where the defence always receives the prosecution statements before the trial begins). But this is changing and defendants facing more serious charges are often given copies of the statements (see page 786).

If the offence is at all serious, the accused will probably have taken legal advice, although he need not be represented by a lawyer and can act for himself if he so wishes.

He may be tempted to plead 'guilty' just to 'get it all over and done with', but he should avoid this temptation unless he really is guilty. Conversely, he may have a hopeless case but decide to plead 'not guilty' on the basis that he has nothing to lose; this is wrong, for he does have something to lose. On conviction, the magistrates are unlikely to be sympathetic to a defendant who has wasted their time and that of the police and witnesses. In addition, he may well be ordered to contribute to prosecution and witness costs – something that would probably have been avoided if he had pleaded guilty.

The procedure in the magistrates' court is fairly informal. In fact, the *OED* definition of 'summary' is a fair description of magistrates' court summary trials – 'brief, dispensing with needless details and formalities: done with dispatch'. Lawyers have long argued about the quality of trials in the magistrates' courts, with many practitioners arguing that the magistrates are too willing to accept police evidence, and that they are too overworked to be able to give each case the care and attention it deserves. Whether these criticisms are well founded it is impossible to say, for no scientific research has been done on the point. However, it is probably true to say that there are very few lawyers who would happily accept a magistrates' court trial in preference to a jury trial in the crown court!

The case begins with the prosecution giving a brief explanation of the case to the magistrates. Prosecution witnesses are then called to give evidence, with the defence being able to cross-examine each of them. After all the prosecution witnesses have given their evidence, the defence can call its witnesses. They, in turn, can be cross-examined by the prosecution. At the completion of their evidence, the prosecution and the defence both make short speeches summarizing the reasons why the magistrates should return a verdict of guilty or not guilty.

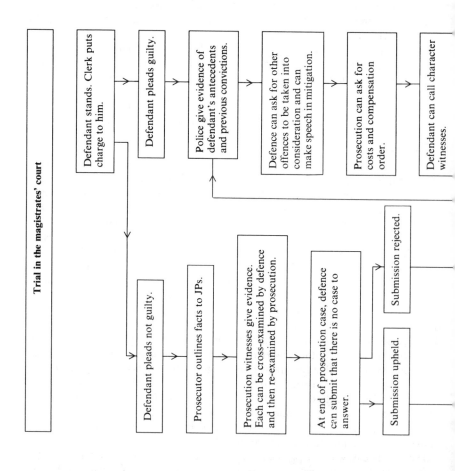

Trial in the magistrates' court

Defendant stands. Clerk puts charge to him.

Defendant pleads guilty.

Police give evidence of defendant's antecedents and previous convictions.

Defence can ask for other offences to be taken into consideration and can make speech in mitigation.

Prosecution can ask for costs and compensation order.

Defendant can call character witnesses.

Defendant pleads not guilty.

Prosecutor outlines facts to JPs.

Prosecution witnesses give evidence. Each can be cross-examined by defence and then re-examined by prosecution.

At end of prosecution case, defence can submit that there is no case to answer.

Submission rejected.

Submission upheld.

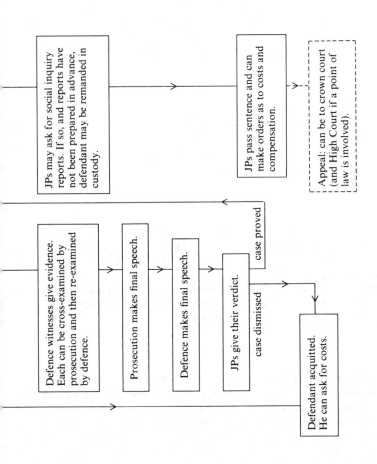

JPs may ask for social inquiry reports. If so, and reports have not been prepared in advance, defendant may be remanded in custody.

JPs pass sentence and can make orders as to costs and compensation.

Appeal: can be to crown court (and High Court if a point of law is involved).

Defence witnesses give evidence. Each can be cross-examined by prosecution and then re-examined by defence.

Prosecution makes final speech.

Defence makes final speech.

JPs give their verdict.

case proved

case dismissed

Defendant acquitted. He can ask for costs.

The magistrates then give their verdict. If they find the accused guilty, the police officer in charge of the case will read out any previous convictions recorded against him. The defence can then make a speech in mitigation, arguing for a light sentence. (See 'Sentencing Offenders', page 802.) It will probably be useful to produce evidence of the accused's employment prospects, his earnings, and family commitments; character witnesses can also be called.

Before passing sentence, the magistrate may want a medical or social inquiry report prepared. If so, the case will have to be adjourned for a week or so if the report was not prepared in advance. Sentence will then be passed (see pages 802–9). See the chart on pages 788–9 for full details of the procedure.

Acquittal

If the verdict is not guilty, the defendant should ask that his legal costs be paid for him. Unfortunately, this is rarely ordered unless the magistrates feel that the case against the defendant was so weak that he should never have been prosecuted (see 'Legal Costs', page 845). In no circumstances is the acquitted defendant entitled to any compensation for the strain of being wrongly accused of a criminal offence.

Appeals

The prosecution cannot appeal if the accused is acquitted, except on a point of law. If he is found guilty, the accused can only appeal against the conviction if he pleaded 'not guilty' to the charge. But the severity of the sentence can always be appealed, whether he pleaded guilty or not guilty. The appeal is to the crown court, and must be made within twenty-one days of the magistrates' decision. Special points of law may be appealed direct to the Divisional Court of the High Court (Queen's Bench Division) by either the prosecutor or the defendant.

Pleading guilty by post

The defendant may be given the opportunity to plead guilty by post if the charge against him is for a summary offence that does not carry a maximum penalty of more than three months' imprisonment. Generally, the option of pleading guilty by post is only offered in the less serious motoring offences (e.g. careless driving). It is never possible to plead *not guilty* by post: to plead not guilty, you should appear in court in person. Also, it is not every defendant who can opt to plead guilty by post; it is for the prosecutor (usually the policeman involved) to decide whether to allow the defendant the choice to plead guilty by post. If he decides to, the sequence of events is:

1. The prosecutor serves on the accused:
    • a statement of facts, being a short summary of the facts of the case. This will form the basis of the evidence against the accused should he agree to plead guilty by post, *and* *(Continued on page 794)*

Criminal Penalties

Maximum penalties for criminal offences tried in the magistrates' courts

---

Abusive words or behaviour: £2,000 and 6 months
Actual bodily harm: £2,000 and 6 months
Air guns: £400, forfeiture
Ammunition: £2,000 and 6 months, forfeiture
Animals (cruelty to): £1,000 and 3 months
Animals straying on highway: £400
Assault on police constable or person assisting police constable: £2,000 and 6 months

Bankrupt (undischarged, obtaining credit): £2,000 or 6 months
Begging: £1 or 14 days before one magistrate; £400 or 1 month if before two or more magistrates
Brothel: £200 and 3 months; £1,000 and 6 months
Builder's skip:
depositing on highway: £400
not complying with a condition: £400
unlit on highway: £400
Burglary: £2,000 and 6 months

Children (cruelty to): £2,000 and 6 months
Common assault: £400 or 2 months. Indictable common assault, £2,000 and 6 months;
    aggravated assault, £1,000 or 6 months
Cruelty to animals: £1,000 and 3 months
Cruelty to children: £2,000 and 6 months
Customs duty (avoiding): three times value of goods or £2,000 and 6 months

Dangerous machinery: £2,000
Deception (obtaining by): £2,000 and 6 months
Dishonestly handling: £2,000 and 6 months
Dogs:
dangerous, no penalty only an order
dog licence £50
dog worrying livestock £400
Drunk: £50
Drunk and disorderly: £400

Earnings of prostitution (living on): £2,000 and 6 months
Enclosed premises (found on): £400 or 3 months
Evasion of liability, obtaining by deception: £2,000 and 6 months
Exposure (indecent): £400 or 3 months

False alarm of fire: £1,000 and 3 months
False statement to obtain social security: £2,000 and 3 months
False weighing or measuring equipment: £2,000 (and six months if deliberate
    fraud)

Maximum penalties for criminal offences tried in the magistrates' courts – contd

---

Firearm: Forfeiture for each of the following:
in public place: £2,000 and 6 months
purchasing, possessing, etc., without certificate: £2,000 and 6 months
trespassing in a building: £2,000 and 6 months
trespassing on land: £1,000 and 3 months
Food (selling food not of quality demanded): £2,000
Forgery: £2,000 and 6 months
Found on enclosed premises: £400 or 3 months

Game (trespassing on land in daytime in search of game): £50; £400 if five or more trespassers
Going equipped to steal: £2,000 and 6 months
Grievous bodily harm: £2,000 and 6 months

Handling stolen goods: £2,000 and 6 months
Harassing residential occupier: £2,000 and 6 months
Highway:
builder's skip (depositing or leaving unlit): £400
straying animals on: £400
wilful obstruction: £400

Indecency (gross between males): £2,000 and 6 months
Indecency with child: £2,000 and 6 months
Indecent assault: £2,000 and 6 months
Indecent exposure: £400 or 3 months
Insulting words or behaviour: £2,000 and 6 months
Intoxicating liquor:
selling outside permitted hours: £400
selling to persons under 18: £400 (and forfeiture of licence on second conviction)
selling without a licence: £1,000 and 6 months. Forfeiture of liquor and containers

Jay-walking: £400

Landlord and tenant: Unlawful eviction or harassment: £2,000 and 6 months
Liability, obtaining evasion of by deception: £2,000 and 6 months
Litter (including car dumping):
(1) Litter Act 1983: £400
(2) Refuse Disposal (Amenity) Act 1978: £1,000 and 3 months
Living on earnings of prostitution: £2,000 or 6 months

Making off without payment: £2,000 and 6 months
Measuring equipment (false or unjust): £2,000 (plus 6 months if fraud) and forfeiture

National Insurance:
(1) Failing to pay contributions: £400 plus two years' arrears
(2) Failing to return card: £50
Noise: £2,000

Obscenely exposing person: £400 or 3 months
Obstructing a constable (or a person assisting a constable): £400 and one month
Obstructing highway: £400
Obtaining evasion of liability by deception: £2,000 and 6 months
Obtaining pecuniary advantage: £2,000 and 6 months
Obtaining property by deception: £2,000 and 6 months
Obtaining services by deception: £2,000 and 6 months
Offensive weapon: £2,000 and 3 months, forfeiture

Payment, making off without: £2,000 and 6 months
Pecuniary advantage (obtaining by): £2,000 and 6 months
Pedlar (trading without licence): £1 or 14 days before one magistrate; £400 or one
    month before two or more magistrates
Poaching: £50, £400 if five or more trespassers
Possessing anything to damage or destroy property: £2,000 and 6 months
Prostitutes:
living on earnings of: £2,000 and 6 months
soliciting by prostitutes: £100/£400

Railway offences:
avoiding fare: £400 or 3 months
giving false name or address: £400 or 3 months
Resisting a constable or a person assisting a constable: £400 and one month

Shotgun:
purchasing or possessing, etc., without licence: £2,000 and 6 months, forfeiture
loaded shotgun in a public place: £2,000 and 6 months, forfeiture
Skip:
depositing on highway: £400
not complying with condition: £400
unlit: £400
Smuggling: three times value of goods or £2,000 and 6 months
Social security:
false statement to obtain: £2,000 and 3 months
persistently refusing or neglecting to maintain oneself or a dependant: £1,000 and 3 months
Statutory nuisance (noise): £2,000
Stealing: £2,000 and 6 months
Straying animals on highway: £400

Taking motor vehicle or conveyance: £2,000 and 6 months, plus endorsement and 8 penalty
points
Tattooing a minor: £400
Telephone:
fraudulent use of public telephone: £2,000 and 3 months
indecent or false calls: £400
Television licence: £400

(Contd)

Maximum penalties for criminal offences tried in the magistrates' courts – contd

---

Theft: £2,000 and 6 months
Threatening to damage or destroy property: £2,000 and 6 months
Threatening words or behaviour: £2,000 and 6 months
Trade description:
applying false trade description: £2,000
supplying goods with false description: £2,000
Trespassing on land during daytime in search of game, etc.: £50, £400 if five or more trespassers

Undischarged bankrupt obtaining credit: £2,000 and 6 months

Wilful obstruction of highway: £400
Wilful obstruction of police constable (or person assisting police constable): £400 and one month
Wounding: £2,000 and 6 months

NOTES
Bear in mind that:
– These are the maximum penalties that can be imposed by magistrates. Most offenders will get a sentence that is way below the maximum figure. However, some charges can also be heard in the crown court, in which case higher maximum penalties can apply.
– The figures for maximum penalties are revised periodically. To check the current figures, refer to a book such as Anthony & Berryman's *Magistrates Court Guide* (published annually by Butterworths).
– Many offences have penalties that are set by reference to scales of fines. Those scales are (maximum fines):

Level	1	2	3	4	5
Fine	£50	£100	£400	£1,000	£2,000

(Continued from page 790)

    • a notice explaining that he can plead guilty by post if he wants to, but that he is not obliged to do so.
2. The defendant then decides whether he wishes to plead guilty by post. If so, he writes to the clerk of the court telling him of his decision and completing the form attached to the notice of prosecution, which allows him to set out any mitigating circumstances. In motoring cases, the driving licence will usually have to be sent. It is advisable for the defendant to reply well before the date fixed for the hearing, for otherwise he may have to pay the costs and expenses of witnesses who attend court unnecessarily. The defendant can withdraw his postal plea at any time before the trial of the case.
    The defendant need not agree to plead guilty by post. He can, if he prefers, attend in person to plead either guilty or not guilty. However, he cannot plead not guilty by post.

3. If a postal plea is received, the court notifies the prosecutor.
4. When the case is tried, the clerk of the court will read to the magistrates the statement of facts and the defendant's plea in mitigation.
5. The magistrates then find the defendant guilty and consider the appropriate sentence. Usually the magistrates will pass sentence straight away, but sometimes they will adjourn the hearing so that the defendant can be present when he is sentenced. This will often be done if the magistrates feel they need more information, but it must be done if a severe sentence is to be imposed. The accused must be present in court if he is to be sentenced to:

• prison, detention centre, or a suspended prison sentence, *or*
• disqualification. This is usually a disqualification from driving, but it also includes disqualification from owning an animal.

For instance, if the defendant pleads guilty by post to a charge of speeding, but he already has 10 penalty points, the magistrates would then adjourn the hearing for up to four weeks so that a new date could be fixed when the defendant could attend court and argue why he should not lose his licence. If the accused does not appear at the new hearing date, or send a solicitor to represent him, a warrant may be issued for his arrest. More usually, though, the court will then simply pass sentence in the absence of the defendant, which it can do if he was properly notified of the later hearing.

Trial in the crown court

Every case that is tried in the crown court must first pass through the magistrates' court. The magistrates will check that there is sufficient evidence against the accused to justify his being tried for the offence; if there is, they will commit him for trial in a crown court, but if there is not they will release him.

The committal proceedings

The committal proceedings are not a trial of the case by the magistrates. The magistrates' function is to see whether there is a prima facie case against the accused – in other words, to weed out the prosecutions that have no real chance of success. Thus, the purpose of the committal is to test the strength of the prosecution evidence and so, indirectly, to give the defendant a warning of the evidence that the prosecution will bring against him in the crown-court trial. The defence is thus given a preliminary view of the prosecution evidence and an opportunity to prepare its defence. This, of course, cannot be done in a magistrates' court trial since then the accused is only given limited advance notification of the evidence against him.

In the old days, committals were always lengthy and time-consuming. The prosecution had to call its witnesses to give oral evidence to the magistrates and the evidence would be written down. This was so even when the defence agreed that there was a case to answer and had no objection to the case being committed to the crown court. To remedy this situation, the Criminal Justice Act 1967 introduced an alternative procedure. The position now largely depends upon whether the defendant agrees that there is a prima facie case justifying committal – as usually he does.

When the defence agrees to the committal

The 1967 Act introduced a short form of committal for such cases. This allows the magistrates to commit the accused without their having to consider the strength of the evidence against him. Thus, the defendant voluntarily forgoes the examination of the evidence by the magistrates, but the court will only let him do this if he (and all his co-defendants) are legally represented at the committal hearing.

For the short form of committal to be available the prosecution must have previously served the defence with copies of all the statements made by relevant prosecution witnesses. The defence can then consider the strength of the prosecution evidence beforehand and so be able to decide whether there is the basis of a case against the accused. If there is, then they will almost certainly agree to a short-form committal. These days this is the usual form of committal, and it is called a 'section 6(2)' since it derives from this section of the Magistrates' Courts Act 1980.

When the defence oppose the committal

If the defence does not believe that there is a prima facie case, a full committal can be held. This can take two forms:
- all the prosecution witnesses attend the magistrates' court. They give their evidence and are cross-examined by the defence, with all their evidence being written down and then read over to them. This was the standard form of committal prior to 1967. Accordingly, it is still referred to as an 'old-style committal', *or*
- the prosecution evidence is in writing, being copies of statements previously taken from witnesses; these will also have been served on the defence. This allows the magistrates to examine the prosecution evidence without the need for the witnesses to attend court. This is called 'committal on the documents'.

Whichever method of committal is chosen, the defence can submit that there is no case to answer. This is, of course, the sole issue before the magistrates; they are not considering whether he is guilty or not, and if they commit him for trial it will in no way be taken as an indication of guilt. Generally, it is for the defendant to decide on the type of committal since the prosecution will only rarely demand a full, old-style committal.

Note also that to protect the defendant from adverse publicity which might affect the crown-court trial, there are restrictions on what the press can report if the case is committed by the magistrates. See page 770.

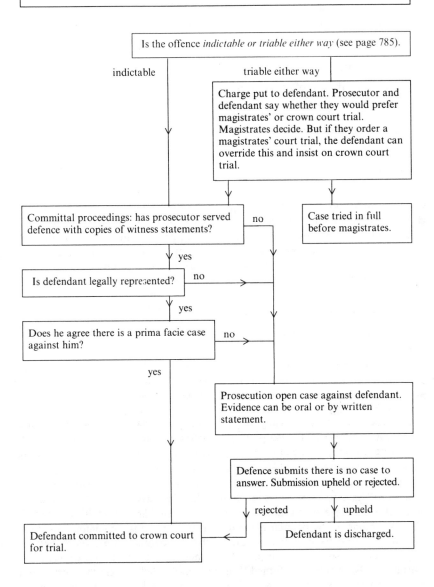

Committal proceedings

Is the offence *indictable or triable either way* (see page 785).

indictable | triable either way

Charge put to defendant. Prosecutor and defendant say whether they would prefer magistrates' or crown court trial. Magistrates decide. But if they order a magistrates' court trial, the defendant can override this and insist on crown court trial.

Committal proceedings: has prosecutor served defence with copies of witness statements?

no

Case tried in full before magistrates.

yes

Is defendant legally represented?　no

yes

Does he agree there is a prima facie case against him?　no

yes

Prosecution open case against defendant. Evidence can be oral or by written statement.

Defence submits there is no case to answer. Submission upheld or rejected.

rejected | upheld

Defendant committed to crown court for trial.

Defendant is discharged.

Bail after committal

If the magistrates refuse to grant the accused bail, he can appeal to the crown court (see page 783). Legal aid is available for this appeal.

Delays in coming to trial

Unfortunately, there is often a considerable time-lag between the magistrates' court committal and the trial in the crown court. During this time the memories of the witnesses will start to fade, and the defendant will have the worry of the case hanging over him, whether or not he is held in custody.

Preparing for trial

After his committal from the magistrates' court the accused will probably be granted legal aid (only about 2 per cent of applications are turned down), which will cover the greater part – if not all – of his legal costs (see 'Legal Aid', page 862). His solicitor will go through the prosecution statements and prepare the defence accordingly. Note that the defence does not have to disclose any of its evidence to the prosecution unless there is an alibi defence, in which case the prosecution must be given advance warning. This is to stop the defendant concocting a false alibi and then springing it on the prosecution during the crown-court trial, when it would be too late for the police to obtain evidence to refute it. Accordingly, if the defendant intends to rely on an alibi he must give details of it to the prosecution within seven days of his committal by the magistrates.

The accused's solicitor will instruct counsel (i.e. a barrister) to appear at the crown-court hearing since the solicitor is not allowed to do the court work himself. If the case raises any difficult points the solicitor may well have a conference (i.e. a meeting) with counsel, probably with the accused also present.

There will normally be little warning before the case comes up for hearing; cases come on in turn and not by pre-arranged appointments. Thus, the defendant and his lawyers may only be told of the trial a few days before it is due to start, and so have to arrange for all their witnesses to come to court at short notice. Frequently, the barrister instructed by the solicitor will be engaged in another case and so be unable to represent the accused at the trial; if so, the brief (i.e. the barrister's bundle of papers) will have to be passed on to another barrister who will have no knowledge of the case and have only a short time in which to familiarize himself with the facts. 'Brief swapping' is the popular name for this practice. It is a common sight in any court to see barristers quickly reading through the papers in a case in which they have only just been instructed. That barristers generally only meet their clients on the morning of the trial was confirmed by a study in Sheffield; in crown-court cases in which the accused was planning to plead not guilty, 79 per cent met their barrister for the first time on the morning of the trial; in 'guilty' cases, the figure was 96 per cent.

The trial

When the day for the trial arrives the accused will be brought before the judge and the charge will be read out in the form of an indictment; it is possible that this will contain additional charges that have been added since the committal. If so, the accused can apply for an adjournment so as to prepare a proper defence, but usually his lawyers advise him to accept the position, and so the trial proceeds.

The accused then pleads to the charge – either guilty or not guilty. If the plea is 'not guilty' a jury will be sworn in with twelve members. The prosecution barrister begins the case by outlining the facts of the crime to the jury. He then calls his witnesses, who are cross-examined by the defence barrister. Once all the prosecution evidence has been heard, the defence counsel presents his witnesses who are, in turn, cross-examined by the prosecution barrister. The two barristers then make closing speeches to the jury urging them to acquit/convict the defendant. It then remains for the judge to *sum up* the case to the jury, by reviewing the evidence and advising the jury on the law.

The jury's verdict

After the judge has finished his summing-up, the jury retire to consider their verdict, preferably a unanimous one. But if they have not all agreed on a verdict within two hours, the judge may – if he so wishes – call them into court and tell them that he will accept a majority decision of ten of the jury. The jury then retire again to see if they can now reach a verdict. But if they still cannot reach a verdict, they will have to sit on until the judge agrees that no decision can be reached; when that happens the hung-jury is discharged and a new trial is ordered.

The verdict

If the defendant is acquitted, he will be freed and that will be the end of the case; the prosecution cannot appeal. Surprisingly, though, the accused will not receive any compensation for the worry, strain, inconvenience, and loss he has suffered, even if he has been kept in prison for several months. Only if he can show that the police acted 'maliciously' in prosecuting him could he sue them for damages – and usually the chances of proving 'malice' are extremely remote, even when it undoubtedly exists. However he will probably be awarded his costs (i.e. his legal expenses). See page 845.

If the defendant is convicted (i.e. found guilty), the judge will ask the police what is known about the prisoner. This is a request for details of the prisoner's criminal record. The prisoner's barrister will then make a speech in mitigation asking for a lenient sentence. At this stage, the judge may well adjourn the case so that a medical or social inquiry report can be prepared on the prisoner. Often this will have been prepared in advance, but if not, the hearing will be adjourned, probably for a week or two. The defendant may be released on bail during this time but it is more usual for him to be remanded in custody since it will be administratively more convenient to prepare the report if he is in prison.

The report will be of vital importance. The judge will pay great attention to it when deciding on his sentence. It is therefore surprising that a copy of the report is usually not given to the defence before the trial even when it is known that the accused intends to plead guilty. Moreover, it is usually the case that the social worker who wrote the report is not in court to be cross-examined on his conclusions, prior to sentencing.

Appealing

The defendant can appeal to the Court of Appeal, Criminal Division, against the severity of the sentence, the decision of the jury, or on a point of law.

The jury

> Now, jurymen hear my advice –
> All kinds of vulgar prejudice
> I pray you set aside:
> With stern judicial frame of mind,
> From bias free of every kind
> This trial must be tried!
>
> (*Trial by Jury*, Gilbert and Sullivan)

Eligibility to serve

Anyone between the ages of eighteen and sixty-five and who is on the electoral register is liable to jury service. In addition, the person must have lived in the UK for a continuous period of five years since the age of thirteen; this condition is aimed at weeding out those people who do not have a proper understanding of the English language.

But certain groups of people may be excused from serving, or may be unable to serve:

Ineligible people. Judges, JPs, solicitors, barristers, policemen, the clergy, legal executives, prison officers, prison governors, probation officers and members of boards of prison visitors are amongst those whose jobs make them ineligible for jury service. The person remains ineligible for ten years after leaving the job, except for ex-judges and JPs, who remain ineligible for life.

Disqualified people. Anyone who has been sentenced to prison (or detention centre, youth custody, community service, or a suspended sentence) within the last ten years is disqualified from jury service. So too is anyone put on probation within the last five years. Also, a person sentenced to more than five years in prison is disqualified for life.

Excused people. Peers, MPs, members of the forces, doctors, dentists, nurses, midwives, chemists, and vets can apply to be excused from jury service if they wish. So also can a person who has sat on a jury (excluding a coroner's jury) within the last two years.

Being called for service

Usually about six weeks' notice is given. A person who is ineligible or disqualified should notify the court office. He must do this, for if he sits on the jury he will be committing an offence (maximum fine of £100 if an ineligible person; £400 if a disqualified person). The summoning officer can excuse a person from jury service if there is 'good reason' for doing so. However, mere inconvenience will not be sufficient and the officer will want to be satisfied that severe inconvenience or great hardship would be caused. Good reasons would generally include holiday arrangements, exams, an illness in the family, pregnancy, or a one-man business that would otherwise have to close down. If the officer refuses to excuse the juror, application can be made to the High Court for the jury summons to be set aside. If the juror is excused service, it is likely to be only a temporary reprieve.

A person who fails to comply with a jury summons can be fined up to £100. The mere fact that his employer will not release him from work is not a defence; however, the employer might well be punished for contempt of court.

On the date stated in the jury summons, the juror should attend court. He will form part of the jury panel – namely all the prospective jurors. The jury for a case is selected by ballot, and once the twelve jurors needed for a jury have been selected they take the juror's oath, in turn. Once the oath has been taken, the juror cannot be challenged but at any time before then either the defence or the prosecution can challenge the juror. The defence can challenge up to three jurors without giving any reason; thereafter any challenges must be justified to the judge. The prosecution can also challenge jurors by asking them to 'stand by for the Crown' which means that the juror goes back to the jury panel and will only have to serve if there are insufficient people in the panel to make up a jury. Like the defence, the prosecution is also able to challenge 'for cause'.

Although a jury is normally composed of twelve jurors, it can be made up of fewer. At the start of the case there must be twelve jurors, but the trial can continue as long as there are nine jurors. So up to three jurors can fall ill or be released.

The judge has power to release a juror during the course of a trial if it would not interfere with the administration of justice to do so. This favour is only exercised occasionally; for instance, if a juror faces a domestic crisis or if he falls ill. However, it can also be exercised to allow a juror to go on holiday:

A juror was called for jury service on 16 July and was told that she would probably not be needed after 30 July. Her first case, on the 16 July, was a theft offence, and the trial was only expected to last three or four days. But it had still not finished on 30 July. The juror told the judge that she had arranged to go on a camping holiday in Somerset with her family on the next day. She asked to be discharged and the judge agreed. The trial continued with eleven jurors. The defendant was convicted and appealed to the Court of Appeal, arguing that there had been an irregularity in the trial, namely the releasing of the juror. Held: No. 'Those summonsed to serve as jurors are entitled to such consideration as it is within the power of the courts to give them. If the administration of justice can be carried on without inconveniencing jurors unduly it should be. Discharging a juror whose holiday arrangements would be interfered with by having to stay on the jury after being sworn no longer hinders the administration of justice: trials can go on as long as there are nine jurors. Anyway an aggrieved and inconvenienced juror is not likely to be a good one.' Hambery (1977)

The finances of jury service

Compensation is fairly limited. It is made up of three different elements:
- *daily travelling allowance*: second-class rail or bus fare or, for car users, a specified rate per mile (but parking fees may not be recoverable); *plus*

- *subsistence allowance*

  If absent from home:

for up to five hours	£1.15
five to ten hours	£2.25
over ten hours	£4.70
overnight (inner London)	£40.75
overnight (elsewhere)	£34.15

- *loss of earnings:* the actual net loss (i.e. after tax, etc.) but up to a maximum of £21 per day (or £10.50 if absent four hours or less). (1985 figures).

The importance of jury service

Each jury is a little Parliament. The jury sense is the parliamentary sense. I cannot see one dying and the other surviving. The first object of any tyrant in Whitehall would be to make Parliament utterly subservient to his will; and the next to overthrow or diminish trial by jury, for no tyrant could afford to leave a subject's freedom in the hands of his countrymen. So that trial by jury is more than one wheel of the constitution; it is the lamp that shows that freedom lives. (Lord Devlin)

Sentencing offenders

The punishment of offenders has four main aims: to deter the offender and others from committing crimes; to prevent him from committing further crimes (for instance, by taking away his driving licence); to exact retribution for society; to reform the offender via rehabilitation and training.

Prison

Most offences have a fixed maximum prison sentence, but usually the offender will receive less than that maximum period. It is possible for an offender to be released after as little as one third of his sentence has been served, since he can have up to one third taken off for parole and one third for remission (see page 678). Generally, a magistrates' court cannot impose a sentence of more than six months per offence, although the magistrates can sometimes get around this by committing the prisoner to the crown court for sentence in the hope that the judge will pass a longer sentence. If the accused is being sentenced for several offences, the maximum magistrates' court prison term is a total of twelve months.

If a prisoner is sentenced to prison for several offences at the same trial, the judge will say whether the sentences are to run *concurrently* or *consecutively*. This is best explained by an example: if a prisoner receives two sentences of one year each, he will only serve one year if the sentences run concurrently, but he will serve two years if the sentences are to be consecutive. Most prison sentences are concurrent.

Prison is seen as the last resort when sentencing an offender these days. This is partly because prison is not generally regarded as a reforming influence and, perhaps more important in practice, partly because of the high cost of keeping someone in our crowded prisons. Accordingly, there are three rules that limit the powers of the courts to send offenders to prison:

1. *First-time offenders* must normally have a prison sentence suspended (see below).
2. *First-time imprisonment* cannot be imposed unless the accused is legally represented (unless he did not bother to apply for legal aid or he was rejected on financial grounds) and, in addition, the court feels that no other sentence would be appropriate. If the court feels that only prison would be appropriate, it must say why. Usually it will be because of the gravity of the offence or because of the defendant's previous record. Normally, first-time prison cannot be imposed unless a social-welfare report has been prepared.
3. *An offender under twenty-one* is sentenced to youth custody, not prison (youth custody was introduced in 1982, as a replacement for prison and for borstal). But the minimum sentence for boys is four months (twenty-one days for girls); so a boy under twenty-one will only go into youth custody if the offence was so serious that it justified a four-month-plus sentence. The effect, of course, is that most young people convicted of less serious offences do not lose their liberty.

An alternative to sending someone to prison is for the magistrates to have him held in the police cells (i.e. not in prison) for up to four days. It amounts to a short sharp shock, and some magistrates have started to use this tactic as a weapon against drunk drivers who, apart from losing their licences, are given four days in the police cells.

Suspended sentence

Rather than send the offender to prison, the judge may sentence him to prison but say that the sentence will not come into effect if he behaves himself for a fixed period of between one and two years. This option of suspending the prison sentence is only available if the sentence is for no more than two years. If the offender commits another imprisonable offence during the fixed period, the court may bring the suspended sentence into effect and send him to prison.

If the prison sentence is for six months or less (as any magistrates' court prison sentence must be), the judge *must* suspend the sentence unless one of several exceptions applies. The most important exceptions cover crimes of violence and criminals who have previously received prison or borstal sentences; the net effect is that most first-time offenders in the magistrates' court do not go to prison. Another possibility is for part only of the prison sentence to be suspended: in other words, the defendant goes to prison for part only of the term, and will not serve the rest of the term if he behaves himself. This is called a partially suspended sentence. It is particularly suitable for a first offender whose offence is so serious that he must go to prison, but when the court feels that he will probably behave in the future. If a partially suspended sentence is imposed, then the court will say how long the offender is to spend initially in prison: it must be at least twenty-eight days, but it cannot be more than three quarters of the total sentence.

The basic rule with any suspended sentence is that if the offender commits another imprisonable offence within the one-to-two-year period, he will go to prison for the original offence. However this will not always be so, for the court:

• *cannot activate* the suspended sentence if he receives an absolute discharge, conditional discharge, or probation for the subsequent offence;

• *need not activate* the suspended sentence if it would be 'unjust' to do so. Thus, the court has a wide discretion, and often this will be exercised in the offender's favour if the subsequent offence is of a different type and nature from the first offence, or if the court does not feel that the subsequent offence by itself justifies a term in prison.

Probation

Probation can be for up to three years. But if the offender is over seventeen years old, he cannot be put on probation unless he agrees. Sometimes conditions are imposed, such as residence in a probation home, or that he will keep in touch with the probation officer as required by the officer, or that he attend a day centre.

If the offender commits further offences while on probation, the court can impose a fresh punishment for the original offence. Similarly, if the offender does not comply with the terms of the probation order (for instance if he does not attend appointments with the probation officer) he can be re-sentenced for the offence. Alternatively, the court might leave the probation order in force and fine him (up to £400).

Conditional discharge

If probation would be inappropriate, the offender may receive a conditional discharge instead. The conviction will stand but he will be released without punishment for a period of up to three years. If, during that time, he commits any other offence then he may be brought back and given a sentence for the original offence; this may or may not be prison.

Absolute discharge

Although the offender has been convicted of the crime, the court may feel that it would be wrong to punish him; if so, he may receive an absolute discharge.

For example, the driver of a fire-engine might pass through red traffic lights on the way to an emergency call; technically, he is guilty of an offence, for the law does not allow drivers of emergency vehicles to drive with any less care than ordinary road users (see page 630). But the court may feel that the police should have turned a 'blind eye' to the offence, or perhaps merely cautioned the driver, rather than prosecuted him. If so, the court might give the driver an absolute discharge.

Fine

In practice, this is by far the most important form of sentence, since 80 per cent of magistrates' court sentences are fines. The means of an offender may affect the amount of a fine, but it should not influence the basic decision of whether or not to fine him.

Magistrates cannot impose fines of more than £2,000. It is usual for the court to allow the fine to be paid off by weekly instalments; an offender who wants 'time to pay' should produce evidence of his weekly income (after tax), his weekly expenditure, and his family commitments. Generally, the court must give the offender time in which to pay the fine. However, the court is not always obliged to do so and can order an immediate prison sentence if the fine is not paid there and then, but only if:
● the offence is punishable with imprisonment and the offender appears to have sufficient means to pay immediately, *or*
● he is unlikely to remain in the UK, *or*
● he is serving (or about to serve) a prison or detention sentence.

However, if the offender does not pay the fine by the date laid down, or if he does not keep up with the instalments due, the court is likely to allow him further time in which to pay or to reduce the size of the instalments. Sometimes a fines supervision order will be made, which requires the offender to be placed under the care of a probation officer, who can encourage him to sort out his financial affairs so that he can then pay off the instalments.

But, if all else fails, the offender who does not pay his fine can be sent to prison. The Magistrates' Court Act 1980 lays down the maximum sentence:

Amount due in £s	Prison sentence up to
0–50	7 days
50–100	14 days
100–400	30 days
400–1,000	60 days
1,000–2,000	90 days
2,000–5,000	6 months
5,000–10,000	9 months
over 10,000	12 months

Generally, these periods of imprisonment only apply to unpaid fines, costs, compensations, and legal-aid contributions. However, they are also used when sentencing those in default with rates arrears and, more important, with maintenance arrears; in such cases the maximum sentence is six weeks.

In addition, magistrates' courts have various other powers against fine-defaulters. In particular, they can order the offender to be searched while in court, and any money on him can be used to pay the fine. Also, the offender can be put in the cells for the rest of the day (but not beyond 8 p.m.) and this then wipes out the arrears.

Scales of fines. Different offences have different maximum-fine levels. Generally, these maximum amounts are fixed by reference to one of five scales of fines (e.g. assault carries up to three months' prison or a fine up to the maximum on scale 3). Those scale figures are changed periodically, to allow for inflation. The current (1985) figures are set out on page 794.

Community service order

For *imprisonable* offences the defendant can do 'hours instead of time'. If he is willing, he can be required to perform unpaid work for a stated number of hours (between 40 and 240 hours) within the next twelve months. However, the offender cannot insist on being able to do community service. It is only available when offered by the court, and this will only be done when a social inquiry report has recommended him for it.

If the offender does not carry out the terms of the community service order, the court can impose a fresh sentence for the offence. Alternatively, they can order him to persevere with the community service order and, in addition, he can be fined up to £400.

Deferred sentence

The court may decide to postpone sentencing for up to six months. But this can only be done so that the court can take into account:
• his conduct after conviction (for instance, making reparation for the offence), *or*
• any change in his circumstances (e.g. he may have a more settled home life or a new job).

806

A sentence can only be deferred once – it cannot be deferred for successive periods of up to six months.

Binding over

Strictly speaking, an order that a person be 'bound over to keep the peace' is not really a sentence at all. It is more in the way of preventive justice, for it allows the magistrates to warn citizens as to their future good conduct. If the person fails to keep the peace or to be of good behaviour during a stated period (up to twelve months) he may forfeit a sum of money. This sum is called a recognizance. Thus, a typical order would be to be 'bound over for nine months in the sum of £25'.

Before the binding-over order is made, the court must allow the person a chance of arguing against it. If the person does not agree to being bound over, he can be sent to prison for up to six months.

The important point to note is that one does not have to commit a criminal offence to be eligible for binding over. The court has wide powers to bind over, given by two different Acts:

- the Justices of the Peace Act 1361 allows an order to be made whenever the magistrates think there is likely to be a further breach of the peace;
- the Magistrates' Courts Act 1980 allows an order to be made if the magistrates hear evidence that satisfies them that the original complaint against the person was justified.

These are, then, extensive powers. They are often used in inter-neighbour disputes. The typical course of events is that Mr A issues a summons for assault against Mr B; but Mr B then replies with a summons for assault against Mr A. Both cases are heard together and the magistrate is faced with two families arguing out their private feud in the courtroom. He finds it impossible to decide who is in the wrong, and so he orders both Mr A and Mr B to be bound over. Naturally, both Mr A and Mr B are furious with the outcome, since they interpret the binding-over order as a finding of guilt.

In addition, binding-over orders are often used against peeping toms, poison-pen writers, and rejected suitors who will not take 'no' for an answer. About eight thousand orders a year are made under the 1361 Act.

Clearly, there is a danger that magistrates might misuse their wide powers. Civil-liberties groups have often complained that demonstrators and protestors have been bound over for no good reason and that, in effect, the powers have been used to take away the right of free speech and protest (e.g. it was frequently used against Greenham Common women during the peace demonstrations in 1984).

Young offenders. There are various rules about the sentences that can be imposed on people aged under twenty-one. See page 148.

Making a speech in mitigation

Before a convicted person is sentenced he (or his lawyer) can make a speech in mitigation to the court. The purpose of mitigation is to persuade the court to impose a lighter sentence than it might otherwise have done. It is not an occasion for the defendant to repeat 'I didn't do it'; it is too late to argue about guilt, for the only matter to be decided is the sentence.

There are two elementary rules of mitigation:

1. Do not say too much – as Wilfred Fordham QC has put it, 'pleas in mitigation do not get any better the longer they go on'.
2. Do not call too many character witnesses. Usually one will suffice. But make sure that the character witness is unrelated; for instance, the mother of the accused is hardly likely to be viewed by the court as an impartial observer.

Sentencing offenders: the sentence that can be imposed

	Age of the offender						
	under 10	10–13	14	15	16	17–21	over 21
Absolute discharge (no punishment imposed)		•	•	•	•	•	•
Attendance centre order (attendance for several hours per week in leisure time)		•	•	•	•	•	
Binding over (offender or sureties forfeit money if he misbehaves)		•	•	•	•	•	•
Care order (child goes into care of local authority)	•	•	•	•	•		
Community service order (unpaid community work)					•	•	•
Compensation order (compensation to the victim)	•	•	•	•	•	•	•
Conditional discharge (no punishment if offender behaves himself)		•	•	•	•	•	•
Criminal bankruptcy (denying the offender the proceeds of his life of crime)						•	•
Deprivation of property (offender loses property used when committing the crime)		•	•	•	•	•	•

Sentencing offenders: the sentence that can be imposed – contd

	Age of the offender						
	under 10	10–13	14	15	16	17–21	over 21
Detention centre (males only; full-time detention: aim is short, sharp lesson)			●	●	●	●	
Fine (financial penalty)		●	●	●	●	●	●
Guardianship order (commits the accused as a mental patient)					●	●	●
Prison (full-time detention)							●
Probation (supervision by a social worker)						●	●
Restitution order (restores stolen property to its owner)	●	●	●	●	●	●	●
Supervision order (a junior form of probation)		●	●	●	●		
Suspended prison sentence (threat of prison if offender commits further offence)						●	●
Youth custody (detention for young people)				●	●	●	

55 The Lawyers

It is no coincidence that 'the law' is an anagram of 'wealth'.

Solicitors

There are nearly sixty thousand solicitors in England and Wales. They are the lawyers that the public most frequently meets and, as such, are the GPs of the legal profession.

The work that solicitors do

A solicitor's work falls into two categories:

1. *Court work.* A solicitor can appear as an advocate only in the magistrates' court, the county court, and, exceptionally, in the crown court. Solicitors cannot appear in the more senior courts. In practice the vast majority of court cases are heard in the magistrates' court and the county court, so solicitors are able to appear in most court cases.
2. *Non-court work.* This is all the other legal work, such as conveyancing, probate and wills, business advice, and also, of course, preparing for court cases.

Unlike the barrister, a solicitor is in many ways like a businessman, with an office to run, clients to see, and correspondence to be answered. There is no such thing as a typical firm of solicitors, for the categories of legal work undertaken by different firms vary enormously. A few solicitors operate as one-man businesses, where one solicitor, with a typist, comprises the whole firm. At the other end of the scale are the large city firms with twenty or so partners, which only act for commercial clients. In between are the medium-size practices with perhaps five partners, willing to take on all types of legal work, from conveyancing to legal-aid criminal cases.

Traditionally, property (conveyancing and probate) has been the main fee-earner for solicitors. A Prices and Incomes Board survey in 1968 showed that 71 per cent of solicitors' fees came from this source and it seems that the proportion has changed little since then. A Law Society survey in 1976, found that the typical solicitors' firm derived its income from:

Conveyancing	52%	Matrimonial	7%
Other non-court work	24%	Criminal	5%
Total non-court work	76%	Personal injury	4%
		Other court work	8%
		Total court work	24%

Obviously no one solicitor can be sufficiently knowledgeable to be able to give proper advice on every field of law; with the complexity of modern law, specialization is inevitable. Thus, the different partners within a firm tend to have their own speciality, but if no one in the firm is sufficiently knowledgeable to give advice, the papers can always be sent to a barrister for him to advise. Sometimes, of course, the solicitor will simply tell the client that he does not take that type of work and refer the client to a firm that does.

Solicitors' monopolies and restrictive practices

The Solicitors Act 1974 gives solicitors three monopolies, namely over
- conveyancing
- probate
- suing and starting court proceedings.

The conveyancing monopoly

This was always the most well known – and most criticized – of the professional monopolies. Under the Solicitors Act (s. 22) it was illegal for a non-solicitor to draw up the transfer or conveyance on the sale of land, or to lodge a document at the Land Registry, if he did so 'in the expectation of any fee, gain or reward' (maximum penalty for breach, £50). But that monopoly was significantly eroded by the Administration of Justice Act 1985. This allowed 'licensed conveyancers' to do this work, and so the present position is that either a solicitor or a licensed conveyancer may draw up the transfer or conveyance, or lodge the document at the Land Registry. But if anyone else does it (e.g. an unlicensed conveyancer) then that person will be committing an offence under the Solicitors Act.

At the moment, only one step in the conveyancing process is subject to the solicitors/licensed conveyancers' monopoly (i.e. step number 14 in the conveyancing table on page 216). An unqualified person can take all the other steps in the conveyancing process apart from drawing up the transfer. However, since no conveyance can proceed without the transfer or conveyance being prepared there is, in effect, a ban on conveyancing by unqualified people. Thus, whilst the solicitors' monopoly over conveyancing is being abolished, it is only being partially abolished – so as to allow licensed conveyancers to do the work as well. It is not a free-for-all – unlicensed people still cannot do conveyancing.

It is too soon to say whether allowing licensed conveyancers to do conveyancing work will bring down the cost of conveyancing. In fact, the main changes have been made by allowing solicitors to advertise – the result has been increased price-competitiveness among solicitors, with a general lowering of fees. It looks as though the introduction of licensed conveyancers will not have any further impact on the level of fees. See page 222 for conveyancing fees in general.

The probate monopoly

Only a solicitor can take instructions for taking out a Grant of Probate or letters of administration, and only a solicitor can draw up the necessary papers. An offence is committed under section 23 of the Solicitors Act 1974 if a non-lawyer does this work for 'fee, gain or reward' (maximum penalty for breach is £50 fine). It is not illegal for a non-lawyer to do the other work involved in administering an estate, or for a non-lawyer to take all the steps if he does not charge for doing so.

In fact many solicitors delegate the preparation of these documents to law agents – unqualified firms that attend the Probate Registry regularly and specialize in this sort of work. The law agent acts on the instructions of the solicitor and does the work in his name and so, technically, there is no breach of the Solicitors Act. But in practice, the law agent does virtually all the work on his own initiative and the solicitor leaves it to him to decide what has to be done. This practice makes the probate monopoly hard to justify. Many banks and other trust corporations act as executors for people who appoint the bank or corporation by will. When this happens, the bank or corporation can take all steps except the preparation of the executors' affidavit which is the document that must be sworn before a Grant of Probate can be issued. To overcome this restriction, the bank or corporation has to appoint a solicitor to do this stage of the work for them and the solicitor's fees are charged to the estate. This restrictive practice was recommended for abolition by the 1979 Royal Commission on Legal Services.

Note that there is no restriction on non-solicitors charging for drawing up wills. This is why banks have executor and trustee departments that are able to draw up wills for customers. A point to watch out for is that the bank will then usually name itself as an executor of the will – and its charges on administering the estate (i.e. sorting it out after the death) are likely to be much higher than those of a solicitor (see page 174).

The monopoly over court work

The Solicitors Act 1974 contains two provisions designed to stop non-lawyers from being involved in legal proceedings:

1. It is an offence for anyone other than a solicitor or barrister to prepare 'any instrument relating to any legal proceeding', if he does so for 'fee, gain, or reward' (maximum penalty for breach is a £400 fine).

   Mr Powell ran a non-profit-making organization called 'Assistance in Divorce'. For a flat fee of £25 he helped people obtain undefended divorces from the courts. Mr Powell hoped that his organization would act in such a way that the divorcing couple would remain friends after the divorce, something that frequently does not happen if solicitors act. After some 750 court cases he was prosecuted by the Law Society. Held: He was guilty and was fined £20. But as the chairman of the magistrates told him: 'We have a certain amount of sympathy for the work you have been doing.' Powell (1978)

If no fee is charged then no offence is committed. Thus, Citizens' Advice Bureaux and other free advice agencies that fill in court forms (such as divorce forms) for people do not commit an offence.

2. It is an offence for a non-lawyer to act as a solicitor in any civil or criminal matter (maximum penalty, two years' imprisonment), for instance by pretending to be a solicitor. Apart from a solicitor or barrister, the only people who can appear in court are a litigant in person or his friend (but the friend cannot address the court; see page 875).

Few people criticize the monopoly on court work. It is generally accepted that it is desirable to have professionals conducting court cases; they weed out the hopeless cases and ensure that cases are conducted efficiently and fairly. The counter-argument is that many court cases (especially in the magistrates' court) do not require specialist advocates and that lay advisers, trade-union representatives, and social workers would be capable of making speeches in mitigation and of defending in the more straightforward cases. They might also encourage demystification of the legal process and reduce the amount of legalese used in the courts. The 1979 Royal Commission came out against altering the present monopoly rules.

Restrictive practices

The Law Society lays down several rules on professional practice which restrict free competition between solicitors. These are set out in the Solicitors Practice Rules. The most important of these is Rule 1, which prohibits touting for business or unfair attraction of business. Thus, price-cutting and sharing offices with non-lawyers are banned as being 'unprofessional'. Some advertising is allowed. Solicitors can advertise in the press and on the radio, but they must be careful what they say about themselves. They cannot claim to specialize in certain types of work, and nor can they claim to be better than other solicitors (although, in practice, if a solicitor advertises that he takes particular types of cases then most members of the public will take this as implying that he specializes, and that he thinks he is better than many other firms of solicitors!).

Whether one approves of these restrictions depends upon whether one sees competition as being a good or bad thing for professional standards.

Solicitors' fees

See 'Legal Costs', pages 832–45.

Complaints against solicitors

The Law Society is the solicitors' professional body. As such it has two roles: firstly, to act as the representative body of solicitors, and, secondly, to ensure that proper professional standards are maintained and that defaulting solicitors are disciplined.

In the public mind these two roles can sometimes conflict, and the person who makes a complaint may feel that the Law Society is protecting the solicitor. The basic problem is that the Law Society has to wear two different hats. On the one hand it is a virtual trade union or pressure group for solicitors; on the other hand, it has to discipline solicitors who break the rules and who step out of line. Not surprisingly, many non-lawyers feel that these two jobs are contradictory.

The vital point is that – at the moment – the Law Society can only investigate professional misbehaviour – it cannot investigate professional negligence. So if the complaint is, in essence, that the solicitor has bungled the case or given bad advice, the Law Society will not help. Instead, the Law Society will simply advise the complainant to see another solicitor who can then advise whether the original solicitor should be sued for negligence. But, this is likely to change soon. The Administration of Justice Act 1985 may allow the Law Society to hear complaints about bad work. As yet, the details have not been worked out – but the changes should be in force shortly.

The Law Society can (for instance) investigate complaints that a solicitor has:
- persistently delayed in replying to letters;
- not accounted to a client for money held for the client;
- failed to keep the client's business confidential and secret;
- acted for both sides to a dispute when there was a conflict of interest;
- taken advantage of a client's age or inexperience;
- overcharged (but first the client should have asked for a remuneration certificate, or had the costs taxed; see 'Legal Costs', page 835);
- behaved dishonestly.

The Law Society cannot (for instance):
- investigate allegations of incompetence or negligence by the solicitor (but, this may soon change – see above);
- order the solicitor to pay compensation to his client; only a court can do that (but, this may soon change – see above);
- tell a solicitor he must act for a particular client;
- force the solicitor to return a client's papers to the client unless the client has already paid the solicitor's bill;
- tell the solicitor how to do his job (unless he is behaving unprofessionally – see above);
- investigate an allegation of overcharging until all of the remedies available to the client have been exhausted (see 'Legal Costs', page 833).

If the complaint is one that can be heard by the Law Society, the client should write to The Secretary, Professional Purposes, The Law Society, 113 Chancery Lane, London W C 2, setting out the complaint and authorizing the Law Society to send a copy of the letter to the solicitor. The staff of the Law Society will then send a copy of the letter to the solicitor and correspond with both solicitor and client. The solicitor may be asked to give his version. If the Law Society staff feel that the

The Lawyers

complaint is not well founded, they will usually send a copy of the solicitor's letter to the client and state that they regard the explanation as satisfactory. However, if the client is still not satisfied, or if the Law Society staff are not satisfied with the solicitor's explanation, the papers will go to the Professional Purposes Committee of the Law Society. This committee is made up of solicitors and it will examine the papers in the case; it will not interview the solicitor or the client.

If the committee rejects the complaint, the client is told that he can appeal to the Lay Observer. This is a layman appointed by the Lord Chancellor, and he can give the Law Society his comments on a complaint. The Lay Observer very rarely finds the Law Society was wrong to reject a complaint.

If the Professional Purposes Committee upholds the complaint it can discipline the solicitor, but it cannot order that compensation be paid by the solicitor to the client. The main punishments that the committee can impose are:
• a reprimand;
• setting conditions on the granting of the solicitor's annual practising certificate (e.g. that he acts only as an employee, not a partner);
• investigation of the solicitor's accounts with a view to checking whether he has broken the accounting rules.

In addition, the committee can order that formal disciplinary proceedings be begun before the solicitors' disciplinary tribunal. The tribunal sits as a court and both the Law Society and the solicitor will usually retain counsel to present their arguments. If the complaint is proved beyond reasonable doubt (see page 759), the tribunal can:
• impose a reprimand;
• fine the solicitor up to £750 (the money goes to the Crown);
• suspend the solicitor from practice for up to five years;
• order the solicitor to pay the costs of the tribunal hearing;
• strike the solicitor off the Roll. This is the ultimate sanction and the solicitor will remain struck off until such time (if ever) that he can persuade the tribunal to restore his name to the Solicitors' Roll. In the meantime he cannot practise as a solicitor, although he can work as a non-solicitor in a solicitor's office if he first obtains the Law Society's consent.

The solicitor can appeal the decision to the Divisional Court of the Queen's Bench Division.

The punishments imposed by the disciplinary tribunal are published in the *Law Society's Gazette*, and this publicity will, in itself, often be a considerable punishment for a solicitor.

Most complaints that are upheld relate to delay by the solicitor and other acts of professional misconduct. It is breaches of the accounting rules that are regarded as most serious, and a solicitor who (for instance) invests clients' money for his own benefit can expect to be struck off by the disciplinary tribunal.

In theory, these controls over solicitors sound admirable. In practice, of course, adverse publicity has led to the general public having little confidence in the Law Society's ability (or willingness) to investigate complaints against solicitors. These problems may have been exaggerated but it is clear that changes will have to be made. Certainly, the Law Society itself has belatedly woken up to these problems and seems to be trying to improve its internal procedures. One constructive suggestion made by the Law Society has been that it should be able to order solicitors to make good their errors, and to refund their fees, when work has been done badly since, surprisingly, the Law Society is presently unable to do this. Perhaps a more sensible and far-reaching reform would be to take the job of handling complaints against solicitors away from the Law Society and hand it to an independent body of non-lawyers. As with the tricky problem of complaints against the police, that is the only real way to ensure that justice is actually seen to be done.

Changes. The Administration of Justice Act 1985 will change the rules on complaints against solicitors. In particular, it will be possible to complain about the bad work done by a solicitor. At the present time, you can only complain if the solicitor has been guilty of professional misconduct – not just because he has done a bad job. When the 1985 Act is fully in force, you may be able to complain if the solicitor has not done the job to a proper standard. In addition, there may soon be an Arbitration Scheme (as an alternative to court proceedings) for claims against negligent solicitors. This, it is hoped, will provide a quicker, more informal remedy.

Suing a negligent solicitor

The Law Society may uphold a complaint but it will not compensate the client. The client's remedy, if he has suffered loss, is to sue the solicitor in the courts, either for breach of contract or for negligence.

Every solicitor must have insurance to meet claims made by clients. Thus, the client is unlikely to go without compensation if he can show negligence or breach of contract. In addition, of course, the solicitor (and the solicitor's partners) will be personally liable to pay the damages. If both the insurance and the personal liability of the firm are insufficient to compensate the client, he may be able to obtain money from the compensation fund. This is a Law Society fund to which all practising solicitors contribute and it pays compensation to clients who have lost money because of fraud by their solicitors (e.g. if the solicitor has run off with the client's money or gambled it away). So there can be no danger of a solicitor going 'bust' and the public losing out.

If a solicitor is disciplined by the Law Society it is likely that he will be liable for professional negligence to his client. But the solicitor need not have been disciplined by the Law Society for the client to be able to sue him. If the solicitor has fallen below the standard of competence and expertise expected of a typical solicitor, then he is liable to his client. The client will therefore be able to sue for his losses, although he will have to show that the solicitor's negligence did cause him a loss.

Illustration. *Mark Evans's car is damaged in a road accident in 1979. He instructs a firm of solicitors to obtain compensation for him. Unfortunately, the solicitors do very little until 1983 by which time it is too late to sue the other motorist (see page 773). Clearly the solicitors have been negligent and they are liable to Mr Evans for his losses – the amount he would have recovered from the other motorist had he sued.* But if the solicitors can show that the other motorist would probably not have been to blame (and so not liable to pay Mr Evans any damages) then they themselves will not have to pay him damages, except for his inconvenience and the mental distress.

Solicitors messed up a wife's claim against her husband on divorce. They failed to ask for a large enough share of the family business, accepting only £12,000. It later became clear that it was worth more. She sued for negligence and the judge held that £24,000 would have been a reasonable figure, but £20,000 would certainly have been realizable. So he awarded her £8,000 damages from her solicitors. McNamara (1983)

The courts accept that the negligence of a solicitor can cause the client considerable upset and mental distress and he should be compensated for this.

Miss Heywood was being pestered by a former boy-friend. She went to local solicitors and asked them how the boy-friend could be prevented from pestering her. She was seen by an unqualified clerk, who bungled the case; he spent eleven months trying to obtain an injunction in the High Court, whereas an efficient solicitor would have successfully obtained an injunction from the county court in two or three weeks. She sued the solicitors for professional negligence. Held: The solicitors were liable. She was awarded £125 damages for the distress and upset caused to her. Heywood (1976)

Mr and Mrs Buckley were selling their house and buying another. They told their solicitor not to exchange contracts for one without simultaneously exchanging contracts on the other. Negligently, the solicitor exchanged on their sale but not on their purchase, which subsequently fell through. The Buckleys were eventually forced to buy a completely unsuitable property because nothing else was available. They sued the solicitor for negligence. Held: The solicitor was liable. The judge awarded them £355 for out-of-pocket expenses such as removal fees, petrol, and phone calls, and £1,000 for the loss of money on their new house. In addition, he awarded them £750 each for the distress, anguish, and inconvenience: they had been living in an unsuitable house for two years, Mrs Buckley had suffered from anxiety, and Mr Buckley had been forced to store his business tools (he worked at home) fifty yards away. Buckley (1977)

The real difficulty may be in finding another solicitor who one can be sure will not be reluctant to sue the negligent solicitor. Often this is not as difficult as it sounds. Firstly, the Law Society has a Negligence Panel of solicitors who are experienced in this sort of work and who have made it clear that they will not shrink from suing other solicitors. Secondly, a local CAB may well know of a sympathetic solicitor who can be trusted to take on the case. One point to bear in mind is that solicitors in small towns tend to know each other and it is generally better to go to a solicitor in a different town – and specifically ask whether he does know the negligent solicitor; if he does, then it is probably in everyone's interests that he is not asked to handle the negligence claim.

Changing solicitors

A person who is not happy with the advice and service being provided by a solicitor should think about changing to a different solicitor. But changing solicitors is not something that should be done without good reason. A useful first step is to go to the CAB and discuss the position with them; they may have more experience and be able to provide a yardstick against which the solicitor's competence can be measured (e.g. they may know how long similar cases take to get to court). Also, they may be able to help by making contact with the solicitor to see whether the difficulty can be sorted out – all too often, the problem boils down to a failure by the solicitor to communicate with the client (e.g. failing to tell the client what is happening, or why things are taking so long).

Bear in mind that there is no point in changing solicitors just because one does not like the advice given. Some people become annoyed when their solicitor gives them unwelcome advice (e.g. you will lose the case). In short, there is no point in shooting the piano player when you don't like the tune!

The solicitor's lien. A solicitor can hold on to a client's file of papers until his bill is paid. In practice, this can make it difficult to change solicitors – the sacked solicitor may take his revenge by refusing to release the papers until his fees are paid. If the fees are correct (see page 835 for how to query solicitor's charges) then the solicitor is entitled to hang on to the papers – he is said to have a lien over them. But, once the bill is paid, then the solicitor must release them. Note also, that in a legal-aid case the lien should not be a problem; the client should ask the legal-aid authorities to change the legal-aid certificate, and once that is done the first solicitor must send the papers to the new solicitor. He cannot hold on to them.

Becoming a solicitor

These days, most intending solicitors have law degrees. The law graduate then takes a thirty-six-week Law Society approved course at which the academic knowledge he acquired during his degree course is supplemented by practical teaching. This is called the 'vocational course'. Having passed the exam at the end of this course, the trainee can start his articles of clerkship. After two years of articles, he will be a qualified solicitor.

The 'articles' stage is the period of training on the job. Ideally, the academic emphasis of the degree course and the practical emphasis of the vocational course will be supplemented by the real-life experience of working in a solicitor's office. The trainee solicitor will sit in with his employer, see how the office is run, and gradually build up an expertise and clientele of his own. Unfortunately, it is rarely like that. The quality of the articled clerk's training varies enormously, and it is often a matter of luck, depending upon the particular solicitor to whom the trainee is articled. Often the articled clerk is given the menial tasks that none of the qualified solicitors want to do, and there is no Law Society supervision of the quality of the training given. (For example, is the clerk given his own cases? Is he allowed an opportunity to ask his employer for advice and guidance? Is he given a wide variety of work or is his training specialized in a particular branch of the law?)

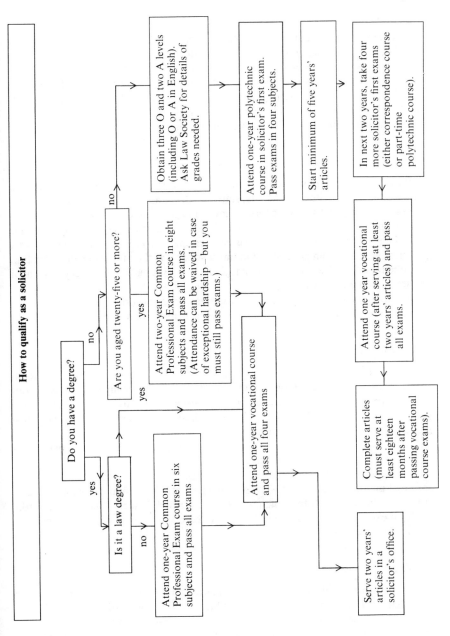

How to qualify as a solicitor

Do you have a degree?

— no → Are you aged twenty-five or more?

— no → Obtain three O and two A levels (including O or A in English). Ask Law Society for details of grades needed.

→ Attend one-year polytechnic course in solicitor's first exam. Pass exams in four subjects.

→ Start minimum of five years' articles.

→ In next two years, take four more solicitor's first exams (either correspondence course or part-time polytechnic course).

→ Attend one year vocational course (after serving at least two years' articles) and pass all exams.

→ Complete articles (must serve at least eighteen months after passing vocational course exams).

Are you aged twenty-five or more? — yes → Attend two-year Common Professional Exam course in eight subjects and pass all exams. (Attendance can be waived in case of exceptional hardship – but you must still pass exams.)

Do you have a degree? — yes → Is it a law degree?

Is it a law degree? — yes → Attend one-year vocational course and pass all four exams

Is it a law degree? — no → Attend one-year Common Professional Exam course in six subjects and pass all exams

→ Attend one-year vocational course and pass all four exams

→ Serve two years' articles in a solicitor's office.

Traditionally, articled clerks are poorly paid. Many solicitors would justify the low wages by pointing out that an articled clerk is unproductive for a considerable portion of the period of articles and thus the firm cannot afford to pay more. No doubt there are occasions when that is so, but it is clear that many articled clerks are exploited as a cheap form of legal labour. The desperate shortage of vacancies for articled clerks encourages this underpayment, and it is likely to continue until such time as the Law Society lays down a binding minimum rate of pay.

See the chart on page 819 for how to qualify as a solicitor.

Commissioners for oaths

Until 1975, only commissioners for oaths (solicitors specially appointed by the Lord Chancellor) could witness affidavits, statutory declarations, and other official documents. Now all practising solicitors are given the power of a commissioner for oaths and so they too can witness affidavits and other documents. The only restriction is that the solicitor cannot witness documents prepared by his firm; thus a client of a solicitor who needs an affidavit sworn must swear it in the offices of a different firm of solicitors. The fee for swearing an affidavit is £3 (plus 75p for every document attached to the affidavit).

A notary public is a lawyer who witnesses deeds and other documents for use abroad; most notaries are solicitors, but few solicitors are notaries.

Legal executives

Most solicitors' offices employ unqualified legal staff. In theory, they are there to do the routine, run-of-the-mill legal work but it is clear that many of them carry out responsible and complex tasks. The typical job-recruiting advertisement for a legal executive will state that he 'must be able to work without supervision', and many such executives do the job of a qualified solicitor.

The most fitting analogy of the relationship between a legal executive and a solicitor is that of a junior executive and a managing director.

The Institute of Legal Executives was formed in 1963 to be the representative body of these unqualified legal staff. The institute has set up an examinations structure so that the competence of their members can be verified. It seems likely that the role of legal executive will increase in the future, especially now that many can become licensed conveyancers.

Finding a solicitor

Different firms of solicitors do different types of work: for instance, the solicitor who handled a friend's conveyance may be of little help in a domestic-violence dispute. It is therefore essential to find a solicitor with the right sort of experience. Sometimes friends and acquaintances can recommend a solicitor; but if not, the best source of advice is likely to be the local Citizens' Advice Bureau (CAB). The CAB is likely to have considerable experience of the type of work handled by local lawyers and they will probably have had a fair amount of feedback as to the quality of service provided by particular solicitors. Some CABs are reluctant to recommend specific firms of solicitors, in case other firms accuse them of favouritism; nevertheless, in practice, the CAB staff are usually able to give inquirers a fair idea of which are the most suitable firms.

Similarly, specialist advice agencies (e.g. a housing-aid centre) will usually be able to recommend a lawyer who is experienced in that particular type of work.

Before making an appointment with a solicitor it is sensible to phone and check that the firm handles work of that sort. Unfortunately many people are reluctant to ask solicitors whether they do a particular type of work and how much they charge.

Finally, do not forget that solicitors are not the only source of legal advice.

CABs. Many CABs have professional staff who can provide a skilled, free service.

Law Centres. These are usually in inner-city areas. They tend to specialize in the type of work found in such areas which is not adequately serviced by solicitors (e.g. tenants' cases, welfare-benefit claims, consumer complaints). They are staffed by qualified lawyers, and if they take the case they will provide a service similar to that of a private solicitor – except that it may be free!

Advice Centres. These are usually only open part-time, in the evenings for instance. Typically, local solicitors will provide free legal advice, but the solicitors cannot start court proceedings for the inquirer; if court work is needed, the client will have to see the solicitor privately in his office as a normal fee-paying client (unless legal aid is available).

Trade unions. Many trade unions provide legal advice on employment-related matters (e.g. accidents at work, unfair-dismissal claims). The advice is usually free to union members.

Specialist advice centres. There are numerous advice centres giving specialist advice in particular areas of the law, especially in the housing and consumer fields.

Barristers

There are some four thousand barristers in England and Wales. They are the specialist advocates and specialist advisers of the legal profession.

The work that barristers do

A barrister's work falls into two main categories:

1. *Court work*: barristers can appear as advocates in any court in the land and they have a monopoly over appearing in the higher courts.

2. *Non-court work*: not all barristers spend their working day in court. Barristers are asked by solicitors to advise on difficult points of law or on how a particular case should be conducted. In addition, barristers prepare formal pleadings, the documents submitted in the more important court cases.

Barristers cannot form partnerships with other barristers. Several barristers will, however, share a set of rooms, known as 'chambers', and employ clerical staff and a clerk between them. But they will not share their earnings in the way that partners in a firm of solicitors would.

The clerk is the barrister's managing agent. He deals directly with solicitors and negotiates the barrister's fees, for it is not etiquette for a barrister to discuss his fee with a solicitor. The clerk will take a commission (often 10 per cent) from the fee.

Since barristers can only be instructed by solicitors, a barrister is largely dependent upon his connections with solicitors until he has made a name for himself. This makes the first few years of practice difficult.

Queen's Counsel

About 10 per cent of the Bar is made up of Queen's Counsel (QCs). QCs are known as 'leaders' because until 1977 a QC could only appear in court if a junior barrister (i.e. a barrister who is not a QC) also appeared with him. These days a QC can appear without a junior, but it is not encouraged. In any event, the QC can refuse to appear by himself if he would otherwise be unable to:
- 'conduct the case, or *other cases*', or
- 'fulfil his professional or semi-professional commitments'.

In short, the QC must insist that he has a junior if he is already overworked! In practice, therefore, one finds it rare for a QC to appear in court without a junior.

Becoming a QC usually results in an increase in the barrister's income, because he can charge higher fees and, by delegating to a junior, he can spend less time on research and preparation. However, there is a risk that his clients will go elsewhere rather than pay his increased fees plus those of a junior, in which case the QC may find that he has priced himself out of the market.

The earnings of barristers vary enormously. It is a profession of extremes. A 1981 survey showed the top QCs earning over £150,000 p.a., although the average was around £46,000. The average barrister earned £17,700, but this figure conceals wide fluctuations.

Barristers' monopolies and restrictive practices

The main monopoly enjoyed by barristers is their monopoly over rights of audience in the higher courts. Barristers can appear in all the courts, whereas solicitors can only appear in the magistrates' courts, county courts, and, exceptionally, crown courts (if the hearing involves an appeal or committal for sentence from a magistrates' court case at which the solicitor appeared as advocate). Thus, barristers have a monopoly over appearing in the higher courts.

The arguments in favour of the Bar's monopoly are that:
- it is in the public interest that the more important cases should be handled by independent experts; it ensures a more efficient hearing of the case and a weeding out of the hopeless cases;
- it is in the client's interest that his case should be handled by a barrister; apart from being a specialist in advocacy, the barrister can look at the case objectively and give sensible advice; a solicitor cannot do this because he has handled the case from the beginning and he is often emotionally involved in it.

The arguments against the monopoly would seem to be more convincing:
- many solicitors are as competent advocates as are most barristers;
- many clients would prefer to be represented by the solicitor they know, rather than a barrister they do not know;
- it is wasteful in that two lawyers have to be retained to do the work that one lawyer could do. Since over 40 per cent of barristers' fees come from legal-aid work, financed by the state, this represents a substantial waste of public money.
- most solicitors are experienced enough to know when a case is so difficult that a specialist advocate is needed; the solicitor could then advise his client that a barrister should be retained.

The 1979 Royal Commission on Legal Services, however, recommended that the monopoly should remain.

Of the allegations of restrictive practices raised against the Bar, the main ones are:
- the informal rule that a QC will not normally appear without a junior; thus, a client who wants to instruct a senior barrister will often have to instruct (and pay for) two barristers (see page 823);
- the complex rules on qualifying as a barrister place unfair obstacles in the way of those without private financial backing (see page 825).

Complaints against barristers

These are heard by the Professional Conduct Committee of the Senate (the Senate is a body comprising representatives of the four Inns of Court and of the Bar Council). Its members come from the Bar Council, and all are practising barristers.

When a complaint is made, a member of the committee examines it and reports to the committee, which then decides what to do. The committee can ask the barrister for his comments and it can ask for information from the client, the solicitor in the case, and anyone else concerned; this information is supplied to the barrister as a matter of course, but the complainant does not normally see it. The committee does not hear witnesses, the complainant, or the barrister. If the complaint is upheld, the committee can:
- admonish the barrister;
- report the matter to the barrister's Inn;
- present a charge before the Disciplinary Committee if the complaint seems to justify suspension or disbarment.

The Disciplinary Committee is made up of members of the Senate. The hearing is like a court hearing and the barrister will usually be legally represented. The committee can, if it upholds the complaint:

- suspend the barrister (i.e. a temporary sanction)
- disbar him (i.e. a permanent sanction)
- reprimand him
- order him to forgo his fee.

In a typical year there are only about 100 complaints against barristers, so it is difficult to come to firm conclusions as to the main cause of complaints. However, evidence from the Bar Council shows that about 66 per cent of complaints relate to the quality of work done (e.g. bad advice, acting without instruction, acting contrary to instruction, lack of courtesy, inadequate representation, undue influence, poor conduct of the proceedings, late return of briefs, delay, absence); 15 per cent relate to professional etiquette (e.g. advertising, touting, abuse of qualifications, refusing to act); and only 1 per cent relate to fees. Generally, the complaints system is designed to deal with unprofessional behaviour rather than negligence and a poor standard of work. As the Secretary of the Senate has said, 'a barrister's success or failure may well govern whether or not he gets work, but as a general rule it cannot be a matter for disciplinary action', and he added that it 'would almost certainly be inappropriate' to take disciplinary action over 'inefficiency, delay, undue cost, etc.'

Suing a negligent barrister

Until recently it was thought that a barrister could not be sued for professional negligence. The leading case was a House of Lords decision of 1967:

> *Rondel was facing criminal charges and he selected a barrister, Michael Worsley, to represent him. Following his conviction, he blamed Worsley, and argued that Worsley had failed to present his case properly. Rondel sued Worsley for professional negligence. Although it was clear that Worsley had not been negligent, the case went to the House of Lords to decide whether a barrister could be sued for professional negligence. Held: No, as a matter of public policy, he was immune from being sued for his alleged incompetence in court.* Rondel (1967)

However, a 1978 case makes it clear that this immunity only covers advocacy, and not the pre-trial work done by a barrister:

> *Saif Ali was injured in a car accident. He instructed a firm of solicitors to represent him and they, in turn, asked a barrister to advise. The barrister failed to suggest that certain steps be taken and Saif Ali subsequently found that it was too late for him to sue the other motorist. Instead, he sued his solicitors for professional negligence; they, in turn, sued the barrister. The question put to the House of Lords was whether the barrister could be sued over the non-advocacy side of his work. Held: No advocate could be sued for professional negligence (whether he be a barrister or a solicitor) for his performance as an advocate. But he could be sued for other negligent work. The immunity from being sued only covered court work and work intimately connected with the conduct of the case in court. Thus, the barrister could be sued by the solicitors for his bad advice.* Saif Ali (1978)

The Lawyers

Becoming a barrister

As with the solicitors' branch of the legal profession, most intending barristers are law graduates. The law graduate has to join one of the Inns of Court and then attend a course for the Part II and Practical Exercises exam, which is similar to the vocational course for solicitors. After passing this exam, he serves as 'pupil' to a qualified barrister for twelve months, although he can take cases of his own (if he is sent any) after six months. During his pupillage he is not paid and so he must be able to maintain himself for at least six months, although in practice it is more likely to be two years or so before he has sufficient brief fees to maintain himself.

This training system is full of anachronisms that have no place in the 1980s. In particular, to qualify he has to:
- eat at least twenty-four 'dinners' (a meal at his Inn of Court); he can eat three per legal term (there are four terms to the year). Apart from being a waste of the student's time, the eating of these dinners can impose a financial burden on those who have to travel up to London from the provinces.
- pay two fees:
  – an £85 fee on admission to the Inn;
  – a £75 fee when he qualifies and is called to the Bar.
- buy a wig and gown (approximately £150 if new).

By comparison, the only fees paid by a prospective solicitor are £40 enrolment fee and £15 admission fee.

Judges

All professional judges are recruited from the legal profession. The only non-lawyers with a judicial role in our legal system are lay magistrates (see page 767).

Appointment

The general rule is that judges are appointed from the ranks of barristers of at least ten years' standing. However, either a solicitor or a barrister can be appointed a recorder (a part-time judge, hearing mainly crown-court cases) and after five years as a recorder, he can be promoted to circuit judge. Thus solicitors can, exceptionally, join the ranks of the junior judges. In practice, most judges have been in practice at the Bar for over twenty years before they are appointed.

The appointment of judges is in the hands of politicians, not of other judges (e.g. when Sir John Donaldson was suggested as Master of the Rolls, the Lord Chancellor told Mrs Thatcher that the judiciary thought he was the wrong man; the reply was said to have been, 'Fortunately, Lord Chancellor, your judges do not appoint the Master of the Rolls. I do.') Appointment to the Court of Appeal, to the House of Lords, or as Lord Chief Justice or President of the Family Division, is made by the Prime Minister after consultation with the Lord Chancellor, who is alone responsible for all other judicial appointments. The Lord Chancellor is, of course, a political appointee, with a seat in the Cabinet, who will previously have been in practice as a barrister.

In practice, the Lord Chancellor has only a limited number of names to choose from when he is selecting a High Court judge. He will be looking for an able barrister (almost certainly a QC) aged at least forty-five, who is prepared to take on the job; the salaries of judges are not high when compared with the earnings of many QCs. However, the attraction of a knighthood (for senior judges) and a state pension is usually sufficient to ensure that few QCs turn down a judicial appointment. But the Lord Chancellor will probably have fewer than a dozen or so suitable contenders from whom to choose.

Social background

Many commentators have pointed out that the judges tend to come from the upper echelons of society. There can be little argument about this. In 1969 Henry Cecil carried out a random survey of thirty-six judges in the High Court and Court of Appeal: 86 per cent had been to public school, and 92 per cent were Oxbridge graduates. In a random survey of county-court judges, the figures were 75 per cent from public school, and 81 per cent from Oxbridge.

It is unlikely that these percentage figures will change before the end of the century. In practice, only barristers can become senior judges and the financial restrictions on entry to the Bar (see page 825) ensure that the Bar remains, overall, an upper-middle-class profession, whereas solicitors are more middle-middle class. Only recently has the extension of higher education, the introduction of more scholarships for young barristers, and the growth of legal aid to provide income for the junior Bar meant that those without private incomes have been able to contemplate becoming barristers. Until those barristers reach middle age in the next decade, the social composition of the judiciary cannot change. And who is to say that those barristers will not be upper middle class after twenty years or so at the Bar?

This assumes, of course, that the criteria for selecting judges remain unchanged. An obvious reform would be to make experienced solicitors and academics eligible for senior judicial posts. More radically, consideration could be given to appointing laymen as judges, or even to holding elections for judicial office – as happens in the USA. Consideration might also be given to recruiting younger people as judges; at the moment, the average age on appointment is fifty-three. Not surprisingly, the judges at the top of the judicial hierarchy are the oldest: the average age of Court of Appeal judges is sixty-five, and that of Law Lords sixty-eight.

Retirement

Magistrates must retire at seventy; circuit judges at seventy-two (exceptionally this can be extended to seventy-five); and the senior judges must retire at seventy-five.

It is difficult to sack a judge once he has been appointed. Circuit judges and recorders can be removed by the Lord Chancellor for incapacity or misbehaviour, but other senior judges hold office 'during good behaviour' and can only be removed by the sovereign following a vote by both Houses of Parliament – something that has not happened in modern times.

Suing a judge

A judge cannot be sued for his bad decisions or for the mistakes he makes in court. This has long been a principle of our law:

> *William Penn, the Quaker leader, was on trial. The judge ordered the jury to find Penn guilty but they refused, and acquitted him. The judge showed his displeasure by fining, and subsequently imprisoning, the jurors. One of the jurors sued the judge for false imprisonment. Held: His claim must fail since judges of the senior courts could not be sued for acts done while acting judicially.* Bushall (1671)

Since then the principle has been refined somewhat, but the basic rule remains the same; a judge has immunity from liability, if the acts complained of were done by him in his capacity as a judge, in good faith, albeit mistakenly.

> *A judge was hearing an appeal against deportation. The appellant was on bail but the judge ordered him to be kept in custody although the judge had no power to do so. The judge was subsequently sued for false imprisonment. Held: Although the judge had clearly acted wrongly, he could not be sued because he had been acting in a judicial capacity. Lord Denning said: 'Every judge of the courts of the land – from the highest to the lowest – should be protected to the same degree. If the reason underlying this immunity is to ensure "that they may be free in thought and independent in judgement", it applies to every judge, whatever his rank. Each should be protected from liability to damages when he is acting judicially . . . So long as he does his work in the honest belief that it is within his jurisdiction, then he is not liable to an action. He may be mistaken in fact. He may be ignorant in law. What he does may be outside his jurisdiction – in fact or in law – but so long as he honestly believes it to be within his jurisdiction, he should not be liable.'* Sirros (1974)

How judges make law

Judges are able to use their position to make new law, but they do so in a roundabout way – by the manner in which they interpret the two principal sources of our law:
- the common law, *and*
- statutes.

The common law

The origins of our common law can be traced back to the Norman era. Prior to the arrival of the Normans, there was little contact between the various villages and towns scattered throughout the country; each shire and each hundred had its own local court, dispensing its own justice in accordance with local custom and the wishes of the local barons.

The Normans set about imposing a national system of law instead of the local variations. By the Assize of Clarendon (1166) and the Assize of Northampton (1176) the basis was laid of a system whereby judges of the realm went on regular journeys throughout the country, to bring the king's justice to every citizen. The aim was that there should be a common system of law throughout the land, and so the common law began. These developments took place at a time when there were few statutes or other forms of written law and so a body of principles and maxims (clichés, some would say) evolved which provided an answer to most legal problems. In time, the decisions of the judges were written down and their decisions would subsequently be used by other judges as evidence of what the law was. Thus, as the common law evolved, the decisions of one generation of judges would be followed by later generations.

But obviously the law could not remain static; there had to be some flexibility to meet the needs of changing times. Thus the judges would still follow earlier decisions but they would distil a general principle from the decision which would then be adapted to meet the new circumstances. Thus the common law is never static; it changes from day to day as it evolves in the courts.

As a hierarchy of courts developed it was natural that the decisions of the senior courts should be regarded as binding on the junior courts. Thus, the doctrine of *precedent* was created, whereby the decisions of the House of Lords are binding on all the other courts trying similar cases; if there is no relevant House of Lords decision on record, then it is the decision of the Court of Appeal that is binding, and so on, down through the hierarchy of courts.

The advantage of such a system is that there is a unanimity of approach by the courts, and a consistency in the way the courts apply the law. The disadvantage is that it can lead to inflexibility, if a junior court is bound by an old House of Lords decision that has not been reviewed by the Lords for a long time. Unfortunately, this is what tended to happen and, to make matters worse, the doctrine of precedent was extended by the notion that the House of Lords and the Court of Appeal were bound by their own previous decisions. Thus, change became impossible unless the judges could use some semantic device to justify not following the old decision. It was not until 1966 that the House of Lords finally decided that it was not bound by its old decisions and that it could reinterpret the law if it wished. The Court of Appeal has never formally announced that it no longer regards its old decisions as binding but it is now generally accepted that it can revise its previous decisions if it wishes.

The common law allows considerable scope for judicial law-making. By its very nature, the common law is constantly evolving and changing; it can only change through the decisions of the judges, and so they directly alter the law of the land.

The classic illustration of how the judges have made law is the history of the 'negligence' claim. Basically, the law of negligence allows a victim to sue someone who has taken less care than he should have done (see page 653). But this is a relatively recent concept. Until the nineteenth century there was no such action; there was merely a variety of situations in which negligence might give rise to liability. But the nineteenth century saw a drawing together of these various actions under the overall category of the negligence claim, and slowly standardized tests for determining liability were worked out. It was not until 1932 that the House of Lords finally laid down a system of principles for the negligence claim that was the real starting-point of the law of negligence as we know it today. The House of Lords decision in *Donoghue* v. *Stevenson* (1932) created the modern law of negligence. But as the years have gone by *Donoghue* v. *Stevenson* has been amended; for instance, in 1932 the negligence action did not apply to negligent statements as opposed to negligent acts, but in 1964 the judges of the House of Lords held that it did cover negligent statements. Thus the common law constantly changes, and it is the judges that change it.

Statutes

A statute is an Act of Parliament. An Act is the law; the judges must follow the law as stated in an Act of Parliament. Thus, if the common law says one thing and an Act says something else, the judges must follow the Act.

The judges are bound by the Acts passed by Parliament. But who is to decide what these Acts *mean*? The answer, of course, is that it is for the judges to decide, and so the judges are left with considerable scope for judicial law-making. For instance:

• the judges have consistently refused to apply the Sex Discrimination Act as it was intended by Parliament; Lord Denning, in particular, consistently defied the clear wording of that Act.

• the history of legal protection for trade unions is one of constant conflict between the unions and the judges. When Parliament has passed laws to protect the unions, the judges have interpreted the Acts so as to minimize (if not emasculate) the intention of Parliament.

It is, however, inevitable that judges should be able to mould the law by the way they interpret statutes. Words are necessarily an imperfect vehicle for setting out the law; it is a difficult task for the drafters of a statute to prepare an Act that covers all possible circumstances. It is inevitable that there will be some ambiguities and some unforeseen situations and then one has to rely upon an arbitrator, the judge, to decide what the law should be. The skill and foresight of the parliamentary draftsman is therefore of considerable importance. Standards vary. Sometimes the wording is appalling:

> The following provisions of this Act shall extend only to shops that is to say those provisions of section six and section eight which relate to the approval by occupiers of shops of orders made under these sections the provisions of paragraph (c) of subsection 1 of section seven and the provisions of paragraph (a) of section 12.

Small wonder that with passages like that to interpret, the judges are left by Parliament to make the law. As Lord Justice Mackinnon said of another Act, the Trade Marks Act 1938, 'In the course of three days' hearing of this case, I have, I suppose, heard section 4 read, or have read it for myself, dozens if not hundreds of times. Despite this iteration, I must confess that, reading it through once again, I have very little notion of what the section is intended to convey and particularly the sentence of 253 words, as I make them, which constitute subsection 1.'

Fortunately, some of our present parliamentary draftsmen are trying to improve the standard of legislative drafting. Mr Francis Bennion, in particular, has produced the Consumer Credit Act 1974 which is little short of a masterpiece; despite having to deal with topics of great complexity, he has produced an Act that is clear, logical, and seemingly free of ambiguities. However, it should not be forgotten that it was Mr Bennion who drafted the Sex Discrimination Act 1976, and it seemed that it too was a model of legislative clarity. Indeed it was, but that did not prevent the Court of Appeal (under Lord Denning) from defying the clear wording of the Act and giving decisions that made nonsense of Parliament's intention. So, in the final analysis, however well drafted the Act may be, the judges can interpret it as they will and then it is up to Parliament to pass another Act which closes the loophole opened by the judges.

The greatest exponent of judicial freedom in interpreting statutes (and indeed the law in general) was Lord Denning. Throughout his long career as a judge he was always innovative and controversial. Never afraid to speak his mind, he has changed the law on numerous occasions by simply reinterpreting old court decisions or by a piece of semantic cunning. What is more, he did not deny that, as a judge, he made the law. Once, he remarked that some lawyers believe

we should go by the literal words of a statute and simply follow what they call the 'formal' view. I may be in a minority. I take a different view. I think the primary object of the law is to do justice. Therefore, we ought to mould it, as far as we can, and develop it so as to do justice not only in the particular case, but in succeeding cases too. I would rather mould the law. Others would keep it static. [Justice and law] should be almost the same, but it was William Temple, when Archbishop, who went to the lawyers and said: 'I can't say I know much about the law, having been far more interested in justice' . . .

Law is a rigid thing. Justice is a flexible thing: doing what is just in a particular case.

I would say: 'Let's do what's just in this case and let other cases follow.' For instance, a very important case we had a few years ago was when a house was built on what had been a rubbish heap – apparently quite satisfactorily but, after a few years, the foundations gave way and it collapsed. The householder brought a claim against the local authority whose inspector had passed the bad foundations. Were the local authority liable for the negligence of their inspector? All the previous cases would have said no. But we held that the local authority were liable if they passed foundations which were bad. That case, I'm glad to say, was affirmed by the House of Lords. That was certainly an innovation.

Again, when the borstal boys got out of Portland, got into Poole Harbour and wrecked one of the yachts, the owner of the yacht sued the Home Office for the negligence of the staff who'd failed to supervise the borstal boys properly. It had never been done before. Were the Home Office liable to the owner of the yacht whose boat was damaged? We held they were. You see: that is how it happens. The law of negligence has gradually been expanded by the decisions of the courts.

In short, Lord Denning preferred flexibility (with which he implicitly equated 'justice') to certainty (with which he implicitly equated 'injustice').

The counter-arguments against Lord Denning's flexible approach have been well summarized by Lord Hailsham, who wrote:

Lord Denning's strength lies in his rugged independence and his unwillingness to tolerate injustice or pettifogging technicality in any form. His weakness lies largely in an inability to appreciate the need for certainty and coherence in any complicated body of jurisprudence which is going to serve the needs of a community requiring to stand on solid ground . . . Public policy is indeed an unruly horse for judges to ride and sometimes best left to committees or commissions set up by the legislature to look all round a jurisprudential question before hitting on a solution. It has always seemed to me that Lord Denning has more than once shown himself slow to appreciate the inherent limitations of the judicial process as a source of new law. To begin with, judicial legislation is always retrospective legislation, and the objections to retrospective legislation are often as serious when the victims are parties to litigation (for which they have usually paid) as when they are other members of the public acting on the innocent assumption that if what they are doing is legal at the time they do it, it will not turn out to be illegal about two years later when it comes into court. Secondly, I think he does not fully appreciate that, as a general rule, law-making is essentially a function which cannot be accomplished properly when apart from a panel of three judges the only parties to the process are the advocates representing two or three out of a great number of potentially interested parties and arguing particular points relating to an individual dispute . . . It is also to be remembered that there is an irreducible residuum of subjectivity inherent in all creative genius. We recognize it in politicians like Winston Churchill or Lloyd George, but we are apt to overlook it when we become judges . . . But I was aware also of a certain subjectivity in his value judgements which . . . made me sympathize, at least to a small extent, with his less inventive and more orthodoxly conservative colleagues whom he castigates as 'timorous souls'.

The difference between these two views is a fundamental one: should the judiciary play an active or passive role?

56 Legal Costs

What are 'costs'?

To a solicitor, his 'costs' are the total amount he will charge his client. The word 'costs' is, therefore, a confusing term for it is not limited to court fees and other out-of-pocket expenses; it describes all the solicitor's fees, including, of course, his own fee for doing the work. The final bill – the solicitor's costs – will be made up of disbursements, profit costs, and VAT:

Disbursements. These are the solicitor's out-of-pocket expenses. They are sums spent by the solicitor on the client's behalf. For instance, in a house purchase the solicitor might pay search fees to the local authority, the Land Charges Registry; and the Land Registry; he will also pay stamp duty and a Land Registry fee for registering the buyer as the owner; in addition, there will be miscellaneous expenses, such as travel costs, phone calls, and stamps. In a High Court case, the disbursements might include court fees, barrister's fees, expert witnesses' fees, expenses incurred by other witnesses, and so on.

Profit cost. This is the term used to describe the solicitor's professional charge for doing the work. It is his fee, excluding his out-of-pocket expenses (i.e. disbursements). However, the phrase 'profit cost' is unnecessarily complicated and, in addition, it is misleading. It is wrong to describe it as a 'cost' since it has not cost the solicitor anything (except his time), and it is wrong to describe it as a 'profit'. It is the solicitor's gross profit; but from it he will pay his rent, rates, office machinery expenses, insurance, staff salaries, and so on. Only then will his net profit emerge.

VAT. Finally, the client will have to pay VAT on the whole of the solicitor's profit cost, and on those of the disbursements which are 'VATable' (for instance, a barrister's fee).

Argument over the bill

Any argument over the amount of a solicitor's bill will usually be based on his profit cost figure, since both the disbursements and VAT are generally not disputed. Machinery exists to control the amount of the profit cost, there being three different ways in which this is done. Usually, only one of these procedures will be available in a particular case.

Fixed fees. For some legal work (in particular, undefended divorces and debt-collection cases) there are fixed fees setting out the amount a solicitor can charge. Generally, though, these fixed fees only apply when the costs are paid by someone other than the solicitor's own client; for instance, when the loser of a case is told to pay the winner's legal costs. If the solicitor's costs exceed the fixed fee he can usually charge the excess to his client.

Scale fees. For some legal work there are scale fees, under which the fee increases with the value of the item involved. For instance, there is an unofficial scale governing solicitors' costs in work done for a client's building society when a property is being bought (see page 224).

Control by the Law Society and the courts. In court cases (properly called 'contentious cases') the court can check a solicitor's bill. This is called 'taxing costs'. In non-court work (properly called 'non-contentious cases') the bill can be referred to the Law Society, who will decide whether it is fair and reasonable, and issue a remuneration certificate setting out a proper fee. If necessary, the Law Society decision can be reviewed by asking the court to 'tax' the costs.

Contentious and non-contentious costs

All work done by a solicitor can be described as either 'contentious' or 'non-contentious'. 'Contentious' means that court proceedings have been begun and accordingly 'non-contentious' means that court proceedings were not commenced. So the distinction is really between court work and non-court work. However, the solicitor's fee for such work is described as contentious or non-contentious costs. Examples of the different categories of legal work include:

Contentious	*Non-contentious*
Defended divorce	Conveyancing
Undefended divorce	Drawing up a will
Applying for maintenance	Probate and administering an estate
Suing over a debt	Advising on letting property
Suing for breach of contract	Legal advice on anything, even if it
Suing for negligence	might have led to court proceedings
Suing for accident compensation	Compulsory purchase
Defamation cases	Tax advice
Any court case	Taking a case to a tribunal (e.g. an
An arbitration hearing	unfair-dismissal or redundancy claim)

The importance of the contentious/non-contentious distinction is that they involve different methods of working out legal costs. A solicitor's bill in a contentious case will be totally different from his bill in a non-contentious case. The way in which it is calculated will be different, and so also will be the way in which the solicitor's client can complain about it.

Solicitors' costs: how much?

It is impossible to give guidance as to the likely charge for different types of work. Most solicitors charge largely on the basis of the time spent on that particular task, and hourly rates vary between £20 and £50 in most firms. Rough guidance can be obtained from the amounts that solicitors are paid for work done under the green-form scheme (see page 864) and in the magistrates' court. Legal-aid pay rates are:
- travelling and waiting time, £17 per hour
- preparation and green-form work, £27 per hour
- time in court, £33 per hour
- letters and phone calls, £2.15 each

However, most solicitors' firms regard these rates as uneconomic and the private client will generally have to pay more.

Legal costs: (1) Non-contentious (non-court) legal work

The solicitor's bill

The first stage is for the solicitor to send a bill to the client. A written bill must always be made out, and it must show disbursements, profit costs, and VAT separately. It (or the covering letter) must be signed by a partner in the firm. The bill must be fairly detailed but it need not itemize everything. In a 1955 case, Lord Denning said a non-contentious bill:

> must contain a summarized statement of the work done, sufficient to tell the client what it is for which he is being asked to pay. A bare account 'for professional services' between certain dates, or for 'work done in connection with your matrimonial affairs' would not do. The nature of the work must be stated, such as, advising on such and such a matter, instructing counsel to do so and so, drafting such and such a document, and so forth.

A person who is unhappy with his solicitor's bill should first check the bill itself. Does it set out what the solicitor did for his money? If not, the client should ask for more detail.

The bill need not set out how the solicitor has calculated his profit cost figure. It only needs to describe the work – not how it is charged. For instance, the solicitor is not required to say how much time he spent on the case or what he charges per hour.

What is a 'fair and reasonable' fee?

A solicitor should only charge his client a 'fair and reasonable' fee, taking into account all the circumstances.

The Solicitors Remuneration Order 1972 sets out eight criteria which are to be taken into account when deciding what is a 'fair and reasonable' fee:

(i) the complexity of the matter or the difficulty or novelty of the question raised;

(ii) the skill, labour, specialized knowledge and responsibility involved on the part of the solicitor;

(iii) the number and importance of the documents prepared or perused, without regard to length;

(iv) the place where and circumstances in which the business or any part thereof is transacted;

(v) the time expended by the solicitor;

(vi) where money or property is involved, its amount or value;

(vii) whether any land involved is registered land;

(viii) the importance of the matter to the client.

These factors, and any other relevant considerations, decide what is a 'fair and reasonable' charge.

In practice, of course, this is a hopelessly vague test and of little assistance to the client who thinks he has been overcharged. In reality, all he can do is ask 'What is the going rate for work of this sort?' If he inquires of other solicitors and their estimates are considerably less than his bill, he might well conclude that his solicitor's bill is not 'fair and reasonable'.

Time costing

It is becoming increasingly common for solicitors to keep time records of how long they spend on each individual case. If records have been kept the solicitor can use the hourly rate as the basis for his charge. In such a case, the Law Society will generally uphold a solicitor's bill charged on a time basis, plus a 25–35 per cent sum to cover typing and overheads, plus an additional sum to reflect the value of the work done (e.g. ½ per cent in conveyancing matters). For instance, on this basis if the sale of a £50,000 house involved seven hours' work, at £25 per hour, the bill could be:

7 × £25	£175.00
plus 30 per cent	52.50
plus ½ per cent of £50,000	250.00

£477.50 not including VAT and disbursements

The amount of the hourly rate is the debatable factor; £15 might be appropriate for an articled clerk and £40 for a senior solicitor in London. Generally, £30 per hour can be regarded as a fair average.

Querying the solicitor's bill

A client who thinks his bill is unreasonable should raise the matter with the solicitor. If necessary, he should ask the solicitor for more information about the work done.

If the solicitor is not prepared to reduce his charge, then the client can either:

• accept defeat, and pay the full bill, *or*

• not pay, and ask the solicitor to submit the bill to the Law Society for them to check what is a 'fair and reasonable' charge. This is called 'obtaining a remuneration certificate'. But there is a time limit so the client should make sure that he does not wait too long (see below), *or*

• do nothing and not pay the bill. The solicitor cannot sue for the money owed without giving the client formal notice of his right to apply for a remuneration certificate from the Law Society and to have the bill taxed by the court. If the solicitor does give this notice to the client, the client should act quickly.

Remuneration certificates

In any non-contentious case, a client can ask his solicitor to obtain a remuneration certificate from the Law Society. This is a certificate stating what, in the Law Society's opinion, is a 'fair and reasonable' charge for the work done. From the client's point of view this is an excellent remedy, since:

• the Law Society cannot increase his bill; the Law Society can only reduce the bill or uphold it at its present level, so the client cannot lose.

• there is no fee payable. Nor can the solicitor charge him for the extra cost and inconvenience of obtaining a remuneration certificate, even if the Law Society upholds the solicitor's bill.

But he must request this within twenty-eight days of the solicitor giving formal notice to the client of his right to apply for a remuneration certificate and have his costs taxed (see page 838). If the client delays beyond this twenty-eight-day period he loses the right to ask for a remuneration certificate, although he can still ask for the costs to be taxed.

All the client need do is to ask the solicitor to obtain a remuneration certificate from the Law Society. The solicitor will then fill in a form and send it to the Law Society. The Law Society will ask the client for his comments and then ask the solicitor to forward his file for inspection. The file may be examined by members of the Council of the Law Society, but more usually it goes before a member of a special committee of the Law Society formed for this purpose. The committee members are all practising solicitors. The Law Society will then issue a remuneration certificate stating what is a 'fair and reasonable' charge, although this cannot be more than the amount originally asked for in the bill, so the client cannot lose. One problem is delay – it usually takes a few months for the file to be gone through (but, presumably, the client will not mind the delay since it postpones the time when he has to pay!).

Generally, both the solicitor and the client will accept the remuneration certificate as conclusive. However, either can take the matter further by commencing High Court proceedings and asking for the bill to be taxed – i.e. vetted – by a court official. The court can reduce or approve (but not increase) the amount of the bill, and can order that the costs involved in the application be paid by one of the parties. Generally, if the original bill is reduced by more than a fifth, the solicitor pays all the costs, but if it is reduced by less than a fifth, the client pays. With large bills the costs can include a sizeable court fee – 5 per cent of the bill. In practice, few clients (or solicitors) apply to the High Court for taxation. There are usually only some 150 such applications each year.

The remuneration-certificate procedure is potentially an excellent safeguard against overcharging in non-contentious work. However, one has the impression that relatively few members of the public know of it and that the legal profession does little to advertise it. The small number of remuneration certificates is not proof that all the other solicitors' bills are regarded as 'fair and reasonable' by clients. There are no figures on how many solicitors' bills are reduced without a remuneration certificate being obtained. However, it is probably a sizeable number, if only because most solicitors would rather reduce their bill than go through the inconvenience, delay, and expense of applying for a remuneration certificate. To this extent the system is unfair on the solicitors and it might be fairer if the procedure was taken over by some independent body (i.e. including non-solicitors) who could then increase the bill if it thought a larger fee was 'fair and reasonable'. In return, one might then require solicitors to tell their clients of the remuneration-certificate procedure – something that they do not have to do at the moment, unless suing for the unpaid costs.

Another criticism of the remuneration-certificate system is that it only applies to unpaid bills. If a client has paid the bill (even if he pays it under protest) he loses the right to insist on a remuneration certificate. Unfortunately, it is not uncommon for the client to pay the bill and only later to find out that he could have asked for a remuneration-certificate. So if a client is unhappy with his solicitor's bill, he should not pay it.

Sometimes the client will 'pay' the bill unknowingly. For instance, if the solicitor receives money for the client (say on the sale of a house) he may well send his bill to the client and, at the same time, deduct his costs from the client's money. The client will then be sent a cheque for the net amount – the sale proceeds minus the solicitor's costs. When this happens, the deduction of the costs by the solicitor is not regarded as a payment of the bill by the client, and so the client does not lose his right to call for a remuneration certificate. However, the client should act quickly and call for a remuneration certificate without delay, for otherwise his silence will be taken to be tacit acceptance of the solicitor's bill.

The big problem with the remuneration-certificate scheme is the twenty-eight-day period – if the client does not ask for the certificate within that time, it will then be too late.

Paying someone else's costs

A more fundamental criticism of the remuneration-certificate system is that it is not available to someone who has agreed to pay another person's legal costs. A remuneration certificate can only be called for by a 'client' of the solicitor, and in this case the person who has agreed to pay the costs will not be the 'client' and so cannot demand a remuneration certificate. All he can do is call for a High Court taxation – a much more expensive and hazardous procedure.

It may seem strange for someone to agree to pay another person's legal costs, but it does happen, especially when commercial premises are let and the tenant agrees to pay the landlord's costs, or when a leaseholder buys out his landlord's freehold. Exploitation and overcharging is all too easy in these circumstances. The only way the problem can be solved is by trying to· get the solicitor to give a firm quote in advance, or by trying to limit one's liability to an agreed maximum amount.

Being sued for an unpaid bill

If a solicitor's client refuses to pay his bill for non-contentious work the solicitor may eventually decide to sue for his fee. However, the client is given some protection against this happening without his knowledge, for the solicitor must first give the client written notice of his right to apply for a remuneration certificate and to have the bill taxed. The solicitor cannot sue for the unpaid costs until at least one month after the notice is given to the client. This gives the client a breathing space in which he can decide what to do. If he decides to ask for a remuneration certificate he should do so quickly, for once the month expires he will lose the right to demand a remuneration certificate. He may, however, still be able to apply for a High Court taxation, but in practice he is unlikely to want to do that. So it is important that the client decide what he wants to do when he receives the solicitor's notice. (For what a remuneration certificate is, see page 836).

The notice given by the solicitor need not state that the solicitor intends to sue, nor need it describe the remuneration-certificate and taxation provisions in detail. Often, the notice will be printed on the reverse side of the bill, in which case the twenty-eight-day period for applying for a remuneration certificate starts running straight away. Frequently the notice will be in a form that is virtually unintelligible to the client. More often than not he will simply be told, 'You have the right under para (i) of article 3 of the Solicitors Remuneration Order 1972 to require us to obtain a certificate from the Law Society and there are provisions in the Solicitors Act 1957 relating to the taxation of costs.' The solicitor need not tell the client what the remuneration-certificate provisions are, that he should apply within the next month, or what the taxation provisions are, as long as he refers to the Solicitors Remuneration Order and the Solicitors Act, as above.

A firm of solicitors were considering suing a client for an unpaid bill. They wrote to the client: 'We are now considering the institution of proceedings against you for the recovery of these costs. We accordingly draw your attention to your rights to require us to obtain a certificate from the Law Society, certifying that the sum charged in our bill is fair and reasonable and your right to apply to the court that our bill of costs be taxed by a taxing officer of the Supreme Court if you wish.' The solicitors sued, but the client said this was not a proper notice. Held: It was not a proper notice. A notice would only be valid if it either (1) specifically told the client of his remuneration-certificate and taxation rights (as was done here) and also told the client of the one-month rule (which was not done here), or (2) specifically referred to the Solicitors Remuneration Order and the Solicitors Act. The notice in this case did neither; and so it was invalid and accordingly the solicitors could not sue for their costs. Clement-Davis (1979)

So, the rules are complicated – and anyone being sued for unpaid legal costs should check that the solicitors did follow the rules. If they didn't, then the proper notice must be given and fresh court proceedings will have to be started (and, of course, the client can apply for a remuneration certificate).

Agreeing a fee in advance

A solicitor and his client can agree on a fixed fee rather than a fee on the usual 'fair and reasonable' basis. The agreement can be made before the work is done or while it is being done. However, to be enforceable it must be set out in writing and signed by both solicitor and client.

Generally, such an agreement will be binding on both solicitor and client, although the court can overrule it if the solicitor obtained the client's agreement unfairly, or if the terms are not 'reasonable'.

In practice such agreements are rare. Few solicitors will act for a fixed fee because they have no way of knowing, in advance, how much work a client's problem will involve.

Interest on unpaid costs

A solicitor cannot automatically charge his clients interest on their unpaid bills. Interest only becomes payable one month after the solicitor has served a proper notice on the client (as above). The rate of interest will be at the High Court's 'judgement debt' rate – 15 per cent (1985).

Money on deposit: when a solicitor should pay interest

What happens when a solicitor holds money for a client; does he have to give the client the interest that could have been earned by putting the money on deposit?

There is no simple answer to this question. It all depends on what is reasonable. Thus, if a substantial sum was left with the solicitor, or even if a relatively small amount was left for a long time, then the solicitor should put the money on deposit and account to the client for the interest. This would be so even if the solicitor omitted to put the money on deposit; in those circumstances, he would have to pay the interest out of his own pocket.

The difficulty lies in deciding when 'in fairness' the client ought to be entitled to the interest. The Law Society Rules suggest that if £500 or more is to be held for two months or more, then the client should be entitled to the interest; presumably, the same would apply if £1,000 was held for one month, etc. However, these suggested figures are merely guidelines and, in practice, the Law Society regards them as being out of date (because of inflation, one can probably double them).

If a client thinks he is entitled to interest from his solicitor, he can demand that the solicitor apply to the Law Society for a Certificate of Interest. The Law Society will then decide whether the money should have been put on deposit and, if so, whether 'in fairness' the client should be paid interest, and if so how much.

Bearing in mind the administrative inconvenience and expense of banking money, keeping accounts, and writing letters, it is probably unreasonable to expect a solicitor to account for interest when money is held for no more than a few days – unless, of course, the sums involved are very large.

Many people think that solicitors do too well out of pocketing the interest they receive on clients' money. The National Consumer Council has suggested that the existing rules should be changed, so that solicitors would have to hand over any interest of £10 or more, provided the money on deposit was £500 or more. Incidentally, on the most conservative estimates, solicitors receive over £40 million a year from moneys they hold on deposit!

Legal costs: (2) Contentious (court) legal work

In court cases, the general rule is that the loser pays the winner's legal costs. This is called the 'indemnity principle', for the loser indemnifies the winner for his legal fees. The loser, therefore, ends up paying two sets of legal costs: those of his own lawyers and those of the winner's lawyers.

This seemingly simple rule is complicated by the fact that there are several different ways of assessing the legal costs, and the amount to be paid will depend largely upon the basis used.

The three main ways of assessing costs

The party-and-party basis

If the judge orders the loser to pay the winner's costs, he will probably direct that they be paid on the 'party-and-party basis'. This allows the winner to claim all his legal costs which were 'necessarily or properly incurred for the attainment of justice'. In short, the work must have been 'necessary'. Work that was not strictly 'necessary' will not be allowed and so cannot be included in the party-and-party costs to be paid by the loser. For instance, suppose the winner had instructed a QC for what was not a difficult case; it might well be decided that the QC was not 'necessary' and so his fee would not be allowed on party-and-party costs. Instead, the winner would be allowed the fee that a suitably competent junior barrister would have charged. Suppose, also, that the winner insisted on seeing his solicitor unnecessarily often; these extra, unnecessary, visits could not be charged up to the loser as party-and-party costs.

The loser's costs liability is therefore likely to be restricted to the 'necessary' costs of the winner.

The solicitor-and-client basis

A client is liable to pay all his own solicitor's legal fees and these will be assessed on the 'solicitor-and-client basis'. This makes the client liable for all the solicitor's fees in conducting the case in the way that the client expressly or impliedly authorized. Generally, then, the client must pay all his own solicitor's costs unless the costs were 'unreasonably incurred'.

The important point here is that solicitor-and-client costs (all costs except those 'unreasonably' incurred) will usually be more than party-and-party costs (all costs that were 'necessary'). For instance, if the winner briefed a Q C and that fee was disallowed as being 'unnecessary' for party-and-party costs, it would probably be allowed as solicitor-and-client costs, since the solicitor would have incurred it reasonably on the client's express (or more usually implied) authority.

So the winner would not recover the full amount of the Q C's fee from the loser, and yet he would have to pay the full fee to his solicitor. The result is that a person can win his case, have his party-and-party costs paid by the loser, and yet still have to pay some legal costs to his own solicitor. Solicitor-and-client costs usually exceed party-and-party costs. So the 'indemnity principle', whereby the winner's costs are paid by the loser, is not a complete indemnity. The winner is only indemnified for his 'necessary' legal costs.

The common-fund basis

A third way of assessing costs is the common-fund basis. This will usually allow all costs 'reasonably' incurred and so it is similar to solicitor-and-client costs. In practice, the common-fund basis produces a figure that is more than a party-and-party amount, but less than the amount that would be allowed on a solicitor-and-client basis.

A solicitor who acts in a legal-aid case will be paid on the common-fund basis and so will have to forgo the extra amount that he might have received from a private client, when his costs would have been worked out on the solicitor-and-client basis. This is the main use of the common-fund basis. It is also used when an infant's claim for damages is settled; the loser will usually pay common-fund costs (not party-and-party costs) and the infant's solicitor will accept the common-fund costs and forgo the extra solicitor-and-client costs from his infant client. The result is that the infant does not lose any of its damages in legal costs.

How the winner can end up out of pocket

Because there are three different ways of calculating legal costs, the winner can still have to pay some costs.

If the loser was not ordered to pay the winner's legal costs

Usually, the loser is ordered to pay the winner's costs, but not always. For instance, the winner may have had an unmeritorious claim, or the claim may have been so small that the winner loses his right to costs. (See page 842 for 'When the Loser Need not Pay the Winner's Costs'.)

When this happens, winner and loser will usually have to pay their own legal costs.

If the loser is ordered to pay the winner's costs on the party-and-party basis

This is the usual order. However, the winner will be liable to pay his solicitor on the more generous solicitor-and-client basis, unless he is on legal aid, in which case his solicitor will be paid on the common-fund basis. Any shortfall between the two figures will have to be paid by the winner himself.

If the loser does not pay the costs

The loser may be ordered to pay the winner's costs (either on the party-and-party basis or the common-fund basis) and yet not do so. For instance, he may have gone bankrupt or simply disappeared. However, this will not affect the winner's liability to pay his own solicitor's costs. So the winner will have to pay his own legal costs out of his own pocket. The solicitor can use any damages recovered by the winner towards paying his own fees.

In legal-aid cases, the shortfall in costs is met by the client forfeiting his 'contribution', and also his damages – the statutory charge. See page 857 for details.

When the loser need not pay the winner's costs

The normal principle is to apply the indemnity rule and order the loser to pay the winner's costs. But there are some occasions when the court will not do this:
- when the winner did not deserve to win;
- when the loser had previously offered a fair settlement of the claim;
- when the claim is for a small amount.

When the winner did not deserve to win

If the court is not impressed with the merits of the winner's claim, it can indirectly show its disapproval by refusing him his costs:

> Exodus *was a novel about the Second World War. In it, the author, Leon Uris, said that a Dr Dering had taken part in 17,000 experimental operations at Auschwitz. Dr Dering sued for libel and was able to show that although he had performed many experimental operations at Auschwitz, the figure was not 17,000. Accordingly, he won the case, but the court showed its disapproval by only awarding him ½d. in damages. More important, he was ordered to pay all the legal costs.* Dering (1964)

When the loser previously offered a fair settlement

The loser will not have to pay the winner's costs if he previously paid the court a larger amount than the winner eventually received in damages.

Illustration. *Peter Jones was injured in a car accident and he sued the negligent driver. Peter's solicitors valued his claim at about £5,000 but the driver's solicitors thought he would only receive £4,000 damages. So they paid £4,000 into court. Peter then had a choice. He could accept the £4,000 and the driver would have to pay all Peter's legal costs to date. Alternatively, he could reject the £4,000. If he rejected the £4,000, the case would go to trial but the judge would not be told how much had been paid into court. If he awarded Peter £4,000 or less then Peter would receive the lesser figure, and more important, would have to pay all the legal costs (not just his own, but those of the driver as well) as from the day the money was paid into court. Peter decided to reject the £4,000. The trial judge awarded him £3,900 damages. Peter received £3,900 but only recovered his legal costs up to the date of the payment into court. He had to pay all the legal costs arising since the payment in, and since that included the trial (always the most expensive part of a case) it was a sizeable sum. So, although he won the case, he had little to show for it.*

By making a payment in at an early stage of the case, a defendant can put the plaintiff in considerable difficulty. If the amount paid into court is slightly less than the claim is worth, the plaintiff will probably accept it. He will probably decide that he dare not risk taking the case to court and, by coming before a mean judge, or as a result of his witnesses not giving evidence well, recover less than the payment in. If that happens, he may lose a sizeable part of his damages in legal costs.

Small-value claims

In cases worth no more than £500, the winner will not normally be awarded his legal costs. The justification for this rule is that the costs awarded would be an unduly large amount in relation to the value of the claim. So the litigant in a claim for £500 or less must either act for himself or be reconciled to paying his lawyer's fees himself.

In any case involving £500 or less:
• the case will be heard informally by an arbitrator. It will not be tried in open court by a judge in a formal trial.
• no legal costs will be allowed other than the court fees (e.g. fee on issuing the claim, see page 879).

However there will always be a few exceptional cases in which it would be wrong to expect the parties not to use lawyers. In these cases either the plaintiff or the defendant can ask the court to rule that the case be heard in open court (not as an arbitration) and that legal costs be allowed (no small-claims rule). Thus the rule is that cases involving £500 or less are subject to the small-claims rule unless either party can persuade the court otherwise.

A variation on the small-claims rule is the provision which penalizes litigants who bring small-value claims in the higher courts. In particular, if a litigant could have sued in the county court, but instead sued in the more senior (and more expensive) High Court, he may forfeit all, or part, of his right to costs, depending upon the amount of damages he is awarded.

The county court can hear claims for up to £5,000, but if the litigant sues in the High Court when he could have sued in the county court:

- if he recovers less than £600 he will not recover any costs at all;
- if he recovers between £600 and £3,000 he will usually have his costs paid by the loser, but only up to the amount that would have been payable had he sued in the county court.

How the court vets legal costs

When the loser of a case is ordered to pay the winner's legal costs, the loser's solicitor will try to negotiate an acceptable figure with the winner's solicitor. If they cannot reach agreement, the winner's solicitor will have to 'tax' his costs.

Taxation of costs is the legal term for describing the checking and assessing of costs by the court. It has nothing to do with the Inland Revenue!

The winner's solicitor will draw up a detailed bill setting out how his costs are made up. Usually his bill will be divided into sections covering his fees for preparing paperwork and documents, attending barrister's chambers and court, preparing for the trial, and a sum covering general care and attention. The bill is lodged with the court and will be vetted by a court official, who can disallow certain parts of the bill, for instance, if the work was not 'necessary'.

Thus, the level of costs is ultimately in the hands of the courts, although the courts have to follow scales and maxima laid down for them.

In addition, fixed party-and-party costs are laid down for some common types of claim. For instance, the maximum a solicitor is allowed for an undefended divorce is usually £47 if counsel is briefed, or £55 if the solicitor takes the case himself. This is all that the loser can be charged in a party-and-party taxation, and since the solicitor's fee will usually exceed that, the client will have to pay the shortfall himself. Similarly, there are fixed party-and-party costs laid down for most debt cases; generally, the fixed fee is so low that the creditor is almost certain to have to pay additional solicitor-and-client costs to his solicitor.

In the same way that the loser can have the winner's costs taxed, so can any client – whether he wins or loses – have his own solicitor's costs taxed. This taxation will, of course, be on the solicitor-and-client basis. In practice, this happens very rarely, for it is more usual for the solicitor to agree his fee with the client. In addition, of course, few clients know that they can have their solicitor's bill taxed, for the solicitor need not tell the client of the procedure unless the solicitor is planning to sue the client for the unpaid costs (see page 838).

In non-contentious matters, a client can avoid the expense and risks of having his solicitor's costs taxed by applying to the Law Society for a remuneration certificate (see page 836). This procedure is not available in a contentious case.

Costs in criminal cases

In civil cases the general rule is that the loser pays the winner's costs. In criminal cases, this rule cannot be applied as rigidly, because often the convicted defendant will have no money or he will be going to prison and so be unable to pay any costs.

On the other hand, the mere fact that a defendant has been acquitted does not mean that the prosecutor was wrong in bringing the prosecution, so it might be unfair to order the prosecution to pay all the legal costs.

Criminal cases: the costs of the acquitted defendant

If the accused is acquitted the court can either:
- award him no costs, so he pays his own costs, *or*
- order the prosecutor to pay his costs – in effect this means they are paid by the police, out of the local rates, if the prosecution is brought by the police, *or*
- order that they be paid from central funds. This means they are paid by central government. However, this option is not available if the defendant has been tried in the magistrates' court for a summary offence (i.e. an offence that is not capable of being tried in the crown court), although this will change soon.

The court has a considerable discretion in deciding which order to make. Generally, magistrates' courts are more reluctant to award costs than are the crown courts. In fact, in many magistrates' courts it is relatively rare for an acquitted defendant to be awarded his costs. As another general rule, one can say that an order for costs to be paid by the prosecution, rather than out of central funds, is an indication of the court's disapproval of the prosecution, often showing that the case should never have been brought.

In the crown court, the basic rule is that an acquitted defendant should receive his costs and these should be paid from central funds. But the court always has a discretion in deciding what order to make as to costs. For instance, the court might make a different order if:
- the prosecution acted spitefully or brought the prosecution without reasonable cause. In such a case the defendant's costs would normally be paid by the prosecutor and not out of central funds;
- the defendant brought suspicion on himself by his own conduct, and so misled the prosecution into thinking that it had a stronger case against him than it really did. In such a case, it would be normal for the defendant to have to pay his own costs
- there was ample evidence to convict the defendant, but he was acquitted on a technicality, without merit. In such a case the defendant will have to pay his own costs.

Criminal cases: the costs of the successful prosecutor

If the defendant is convicted, then, as regards the prosecution's costs, the court can order either
- that no order is made; the prosecution costs are borne by the local police, in effect the ratepayers, *or*
- that they are paid by the defendant; in practice, this will usually mean that the defendant is ordered to contribute a specified amount towards the costs, *or*
- that they are paid out of central funds, i.e. by the government. This order can also be made if the defendant is acquitted.

57 Legal Aid

There are four different schemes which offer subsidized legal aid and advice. The schemes are mutually exclusive, so the person who wants to use the services of a solicitor must decide which is the most appropriate scheme for him.

If court proceedings have begun

Civil legal aid. This is generally called 'legal aid' and is available for those involved in civil (i.e. non-criminal) cases. The applicant can apply for legal aid whether he is suing or being sued. Eligibility will depend upon the merits of the case and a means test (see page 850). If the case is to be in the magistrates' court (e.g. paternity suits, some maintenance applications), different rules apply; then legal aid is available under the simpler *green-form scheme* (see below).

Criminal legal aid. This is for people involved in criminal proceedings. However, only a defendant can apply, so legal aid cannot cover the costs of a private prosecution. Eligibility will depend upon the requirements of 'justice' and a means test. In practice, it is virtually always granted for crown-court cases, but the position in magistrates' court cases is less certain (see page 862).

If court proceedings have not begun

If the applicant merely wants legal advice and perhaps help, there are two alternatives.

The green-form scheme. This provides legal advice and assistance for those of limited means. There is a strict means test and a sliding-scale of contributions, depending upon the applicant's income. This is the main form of legal advice for people who are not involved in a court case but who need general legal help, as in writing letters (see page 864).

£5 for half an hour scheme. This allows the applicant to see a solicitor at the cheap rate of £5 for the first half an hour. Thereafter he has to pay the normal going rate. In practice this scheme is little used, and is second best to the green-form scheme (see page 870).

Finally, there are various voluntary and charitable bodies and organizations which can offer free legal advice.

Legal aid, advice, and assistance

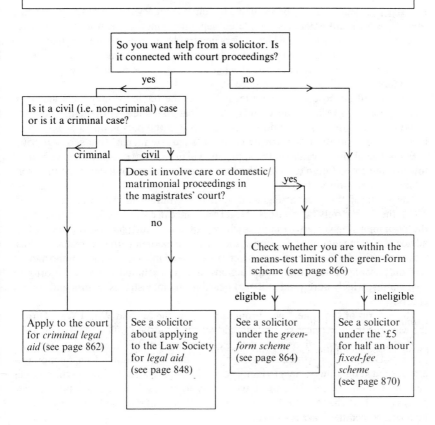

So you want help from a solicitor. Is it connected with court proceedings?

yes / no

Is it a civil (i.e. non-criminal) case or is it a criminal case?

criminal / civil

Does it involve care or domestic/matrimonial proceedings in the magistrates' court?

yes

no

Check whether you are within the means-test limits of the green-form scheme (see page 866)

eligible / ineligible

Apply to the court for *criminal legal aid* (see page 862)

See a solicitor about applying to the Law Society for *legal aid* (see page 848)

See a solicitor under the *green-form scheme* (see page 864)

See a solicitor under the '£5 for half an hour' *fixed-fee scheme* (see page 870)

Legal aid in civil cases

In civil cases, legal aid may be available to help pay the legal costs of suing, or being sued. This legal-aid scheme is completely separate from the green-form scheme for legal advice and assistance, which covers general legal costs before it is decided to start court proceedings (see page 864). The civil legal-aid scheme is also completely separate from the criminal legal-aid scheme, which helps meet the legal costs of defendants in criminal cases (see page 862).

The overall purpose of the civil legal-aid scheme (called simply legal aid) is to enable people to sue in the courts and to defend claims made against them, when they could not otherwise afford to do so. The aim is that the person on legal aid should be in the same position as a private client of 'adequate means' (but see page 856).

Even if legal aid is available, the applicant will usually have to pay a 'contribution' towards the costs. Often this contribution is so substantial that it deters people from taking up their offers of legal aid.

The roots of the present legal-aid system are buried in the inter-war period. Then, there were only two sources of legal assistance in civil cases. Firstly, there were the 'poor man's lawyer' advice centres where solicitors would voluntarily dispense free advice at evening meetings. Secondly, there was the 'poor person's procedure', which was a primitive form of legal aid, subject to a stringent means test. More important, it was only available for High Court actions, and so excluded the vast majority of civil claims, which were (and still are) heard in the magistrates' courts and county courts.

The reform of the system was brought about by the Second World War. During the war, the three services set up legal-aid schemes for their officers and men. Most of the cases involved divorce, and to ease the burden, the Law Society set up a Services Divorce Department which took over this work. Soon a Civil Section was established at the Law Society to handle cases for people who were not in the services and, by the end of the war, the Law Society found itself with a substantial legal practice. It had changed from being the solicitors' professional body into a state-financed body of practising solicitors.

Clearly, changes were needed and the Rushcliffe Committee was appointed to review the position. It reported in 1945, and set out recommendations which became the basis of the Legal Aid and Advice Act 1949. Rushcliffe proposed:

(a) Legal aid should be available in all courts and in such a manner as will enable persons in need to have access to the professional help they require;

(b) This provision should not be limited to those who are normally classed as poor, but should include a wider income group;

(c) Those who cannot afford to pay anything for legal aid should receive this free of cost. There should be a scale of contributions for those who can pay something towards costs;

(d) The cost of the scheme should be borne by the state, but the scheme should not be administered either as a department of state, or by local authorities.

These are the fundamental principles of the present-day legal-aid scheme.

Applying for legal aid

A person who wants to apply for civil legal aid fills in a blue form, known as Legal Aid Form No.1 (see illustration on page 908). Copies of this form can be obtained from most Citizens' Advice Bureaux, and from solicitors' offices.

There is nothing to prevent the applicant from filling in the form himself, without his having taken legal advice. However, it is advisable to see a solicitor first and arrange for him to fill in the form. He will know the best way to complete the form, the way the questions should be answered, and the sort of information that should be attached in support of the application. The form should set out the basis of the claim and unless all the relevant facts are marshalled in support, the application might be rejected because the case looks weaker than it is. For instance, in an accident case, the applicant may not have obtained a statement from a witness who will confirm that the accident was not his fault. By going to a solicitor, the applicant reduces the chances of his not presenting his case in the best light, and so he increases his prospects of being granted legal aid. For how to find a solicitor, see page 820.

The cost of employing a solicitor to help complete the form will not be covered by legal aid. A legal-aid certificate does not cover legal work done prior to the date it was issued. So the solicitor's fee cannot be paid for by the legal-aid certificate. Instead, the applicant will either have to:

• pay the solicitor himself, at the normal rate charged by the solicitor; however, he may be able to find a solicitor who operates the '£5 for half an hour' scheme (see page 870);

• or apply for legal advice and assistance under the green-form scheme. This will cover some, or all, of the solicitor's fee, but only if the applicant comes within the strict financial limits of the green-form scheme (see page 866).

Often though, a solicitor will not charge for helping to complete a legal-aid application form. Many solicitors will do the work free, knowing that if legal aid is granted they will act for the client and so perhaps earn other fees, which will be paid for.

The completed application form is sent to the Law Society's Legal Aid Office (address in the telephone directory). There is no fee to be paid. They send the (separate) form which sets out details of the applicant's finances to the Department of Health and Social Security (DHSS). The DHSS will then check whether the applicant is financially eligible for legal aid and, if so, whether he ought to pay a contribution towards the expected legal costs. The remainder of the application form goes before a Certifying Committee of the Legal Aid Committee. The Certifying Committee is made up of local barristers and solicitors who look at the merits of the application to see whether the case is worthy of legal aid – is there a strong enough case?

The applicant therefore has to surmount two hurdles before he can be granted legal aid. He must show that his case merits legal aid and also that he is financially eligible.

Hurdle No.1: the merits of his case

Does the applicant deserve legal aid? By section 7(5), Legal Aid Act 1974, 'a person shall not be given legal aid in connection with any proceedings unless he shows that he has reasonable grounds for taking, defending, or being a party thereto, and may also be refused legal aid if it appears unreasonable that he should receive it in the particular circumstances of the case'. In short, does he have reasonable prospects of success and is it reasonable to pursue it?

The 1982 Act does not lay down any criteria or guidelines for deciding these questions. It is entirely within the discretion of the Certifying Committee. But, over the years, since these principles were first introduced in 1949, the lawyers on the committees have decided the issue by asking themselves: 'What advice would I give to the applicant if he were a private client possessed of sufficient means to pay his costs?' If a private client would be advised to press on with the claim, then legal aid should be granted. If he would be advised to take no further steps, then legal aid should not be granted.

The size of the potential benefit from winning the case can be relevant; one of the criteria in section 7(5) is that it should not be 'unreasonable' to pursue the claim. So if the potential benefit is small, the legal-aid application can be rejected. For instance, it would not be worth suing over a debt of £10. Nor would it be worth suing if the defendant was known to be bankrupt and there was no hope of his ever being able to pay any damages; nor if the case involved a small amount, but raised complicated legal issues which would have to be resolved by the senior courts. In short, a cost/benefit test is applied.

Limited certificates. If the committee has doubts as to the merits of a case, they may grant a 'limited certificate'. This is a grant of legal aid which runs out once a certain stage of the case has been reached. The applicant then has to go back to the committee and ask them to extend the certificate so he can press on with the case. This gives the committee a chance of reviewing the case at a later date. For instance, if a case does not look very strong the committee may issue a certificate limited 'to investigating the case and obtaining counsel's opinion'. This would allow the solicitor to investigate the evidence and interview witnesses. The papers would then go to a barrister, who would give a written opinion on the prospects of success. Once that was done the papers would go back to the committee and they would decide – largely on the basis of the barrister's opinion – whether the legal-aid certificate should be extended to cover the commencement of court proceedings.

Hurdle No.2: financial eligibility

Even if the applicant merits legal aid, he will still have to show that he comes within the current means-test limits.

The last page of the legal-aid application form sets out the applicant's finances and those of his/her spouse. This information is sent by the Legal Aid Office to the DHSS, which checks the applicant's financial eligibility (usually this is done by asking for a form to be completed, and letters being sent to employers, etc.).

Financial eligibility will be worked out by calculating the applicant's 'disposable income' and 'disposable capital'.

'Disposable income' is worked out on the basis of the applicant's likely income during the next twelve months. From his gross income are deducted tax, national insurance contributions, work expenses (usually fares), rent or mortgage payments. Also, an allowance is made for each dependant. The final, net, figure is called the 'disposable income'. See page 855 for a specimen calculation showing how these rules work. Eligibility will depend upon the amount of the disposable income. If it is (1985 figures) more than £5,155 then the applicant is not eligible for legal aid. If it is less than £2,145 then the applicant receives free legal aid. Between those two figures, the applicant will be offered legal aid but will be expected to make a contribution towards the costs (one quarter of the amount over £2,000 – see page 852).

'Disposable capital' is the value of all the applicant's possessions (e.g. cash, bank accounts, national savings, shares; value of antiques, boats, caravan, etc.; amount that could be borrowed on security of existing life policy), minus certain specified items. In particular, he can disregard the value of his house, household furniture, personal clothes, car, tools and trade equipment, and a specified amount for each dependant. The net figure is called the 'disposable capital'. For a specimen calculation, see page 855.

Eligibility will also depend upon the amount of the disposable capital (1985 figures). If it is over £4,500 the applicant is unlikely to be eligible for legal aid, although there is a discretion. If it is less than £3,000 he will be eligible for free legal aid (provided he does not have too much disposable income – see above). If the disposable capital is between these two figures then he will be offered legal aid but will be expected to make a contribution towards the costs (this will be the amount over £3,000 – see page 853). Once again, this is provided that he does not have too great a disposable income (see above).

The husband's or wife's income and capital

If an applicant is married, the income and capital of his (or her) spouse will be taken into account, unless the couple have separated and are living apart. So a housewife who does not work will have her financial eligibility assessed on the basis of her husband's income and their joint capital. The only time when the financial resources are not aggregated is when the husband and wife have 'a contrary interest' – i.e. they themselves are in dispute. So if a wife wants legal aid to divorce her husband, her financial eligibility will be based solely on her own income and capital. Her husband's finances will be ignored, since the couple are in dispute. The effect of this is that most housewives involved in a matrimonial dispute get free legal aid without having to pay any contribution.

The income or capital of a cohabitee is never taken into account.

Similar rules apply when a child applies for legal aid. For instance, suppose a child is injured in a car accident and wishes to sue the negligent driver. The legal-aid application form will be submitted by his parents on his behalf and the parents' income will have to be taken into account when deciding whether the child is eligible. However, if the negligent driver was the child's own father and legal aid was needed to sue the father (and, indirectly, to recover the money from the father's insurance company), then the father's income would not be taken into account. Since the child has a 'contrary interest' to his father, the father's income is ignored.

When the case involves property or money

When calculating disposable income and disposable capital, the DHSS disregard the value of anything that is 'the subject-matter of the proceedings'. For instance, if the applicant wants legal aid to sue a marina over a defective boat which he bought from them, then the value of the boat will not be taken into account when working out his disposable capital.

It is not always easy to decide whether something is the subject matter of the proceedings. The test for deciding is to ask the question: 'Is it in jeopardy as a result of the case?' If it is, then it should be ignored when assessing financial eligibility. Maintenance paid to a spouse under a court order is, however, taken into account even when the legal-aid application relates to fresh maintenance proceedings.

Illustration. *Mrs Jones receives £30 p.w. maintenance from her ex-husband. However, Mr Jones is not as well off as he was and so he applies for the maintenance order to be varied (i.e. he wants the weekly payment reduced). Mrs Jones applies for legal aid to defend the case. When working out her disposable income, the £30 p.w. maintenance will be taken into account, even though the maintenance payment is put in jeopardy by the court proceedings.*

Illustration. *A husband and wife both agree to a divorce. Since it is an undefended divorce, legal aid will not be available (page 41). However, they cannot agree on how to divide up the family property – including the properties they own, their savings in the building society, and cash in the bank. Accordingly, the wife applies for legal aid so that she can ask the court to make a property order dividing the family assets between the two of them. When working out the wife's financial eligibility, the DHSS assessment officer will:*
- *ignore the husband's income since 'they have a contrary interest', and*
- *ignore the value of all the family property (e.g. houses, savings, cash, furniture) which is 'the subject matter of the dispute'.*
So unless the wife has income or capital of her own she will almost certainly be eligible for free legal aid.

Contributions

If the applicant is financially eligible, he will have to pay a 'contribution' if his disposable income exceeds £2,145 and/or if his disposable capital exceeds £3,000 (1985 figures).

The size of the contribution will depend upon the amount by which these figures are exceeded. Usually, the contribution is:

- *disposable income* will be a quarter of the excess over £2,145;
- *disposable capital* will be all the excess over £3,000 (although the DHSS do have a discretion to ask for less).

The illustration on page 855 shows how the contribution is worked out in a typical case.

If legal aid is granted, the applicant will be sent an offer of legal aid, setting out the amount of his contribution, if any. It will also state how the contribution is to be paid. Generally, contributions based on disposable capital must be paid in a lump sum straight away, but contributions from income are normally paid in twelve monthly instalments.

There is no right of appeal against the amount of the contribution, but the committee will usually check their figures if asked.

The amount of the contribution will not necessarily be the maximum amount that the applicant will have to pay in legal costs, although often it will be. If he loses the case he is likely to have to pay something towards the winner's legal costs. If he wins the case he will usually receive his contribution back, unless the loser does not pay all the legal costs. For instance, suppose the contribution is £50 and the costs £100, but the loser only pays £80 towards the cost; the applicant will have £30 of his contribution returned to him. If the loser paid nothing towards the cost, the applicant would lose his £50 contribution and also £50 of his damages (see page 857 below).

Sometimes the contribution will exceed the estimated costs of the case. For instance, the contribution may be £1,000, and yet the committee estimates that the legal costs will not be more than £750. At first glance, there might seem no point in the applicant's accepting the offer of legal aid. But there is. If the case is appealed to the higher courts, and even to the House of Lords, his maximum contribution will still only be £1,000. By accepting legal aid – even with a large contribution – he has some safeguard against escalating legal costs. Moreover, by being on legal aid his liability to pay his opponent's costs should he lose is, in practice, drastically reduced.

Emergency applications

Normally, it takes two months or so for a legal-aid application to be processed. But not all legal claims can wait that long. For instance, if a tenant is illegally evicted by his landlord he needs an injunction immediately, to order the landlord to allow him back into his home. For cases of this sort, legal aid can be granted without delay, and usually within the space of a few hours.

When there is an emergency the applicant should first find a solicitor who is prepared to act for him and to apply for an injunction as soon as legal aid is granted. Once the solicitor has taken a note of the facts of the case, and checked the client's financial eligibility, he will phone the Law Society Office and ask for legal aid. Often the office will insist that the applicant delivers a completed legal-aid application form, whereupon they will consider it immediately. However, if the solicitor can

	Income from all sources (including child benefit) before deduction of income tax, national insurance contributions, and rent	
	Maximum gross income permitting free legal aid	Minimum gross income which makes applicant ineligible for legal aid
Type of applicant		
1. Single person	£4,235 (£81 p.w.)	£9,171 (£176 p.w.)
2. Married couple	£6,419 (£123 p.w.)	£11,355 (£218 p.w.)
3. Married couple 1 child aged 6	£7,419 (£143 p.w.)	£12,355 (£238 p.w.)
4. Married couple 2 children aged 4 and 8	£8,420 (£162 p.w.)	£13,355 (£257 p.w.)
5. Married couple 3 children aged 4, 8 and 13	£10,026 (£193 p.w.)	£14,847 (£285 p.w.)
6. Married couple 4 children aged 4, 8, 13 and 15	£11,634 (£224 p.w.)	£16,293 (£313 p.w.)
7. Married man apart from wife, paying court order of £1,200 per annum	£5,612 (£108 p.w.)	£10,548 (£203 p.w.)
8. Single parent with 2 children aged 4 and 8	£5,529 (£106 p.w.)	£10,465 (£201 p.w.)
9. Single parent with 3 children aged 4, 8 and 13	£7,135 (£137 p.w.)	£12,071 (£232 p.w.)

Note. These figures are for rough guidance only. They assume that rent or mortgage payments are about £20 per week. If they were more, then the figures would have to be increased (the gross earnings figures would go up by approximately £145 for each extra £100 of housing costs). The figures are for 1985.

convince the office that the case is a real emergency and that legal aid would definitely be granted, they will grant legal aid at once. (Financial eligibility will be checked on the phone, with contributions being paid in the usual way.) The solicitor can then begin to act for the client and take the steps necessary to obtain an injunction immediately.

This emergency procedure is mainly used on behalf of illegally evicted tenants and women who have been beaten up by their husbands or lovers.

Illustration. *Mark Evans is married, with a boy of six and a girl of twelve. He also supports his mother-in-law. He pays mortgage repayments of £40 p.w., rates of £15 p.w., and he has work expenses of £10 p.w. His gross weekly wage is £250. He pays tax and NI of £40 p.w. He has £1,300 in a building society and his wife has shares worth £1,800.*

Disposable income	£	£
gross wage	250	
child benefit	£13.70	
		263.70
Deduct		
tax and NI	40.00	
mortgage	40.00	
rates	15.00	
work expenses	10.00	
allowance for wife	32.25	
allowance for six-year-old	14.40	
allowance for twelve-year-old	25.95	
allowance for mother-in-law	33.67	
		211.27
weekly disposable income		52.43
multiply by 52		× 52
annual disposable income		£ 2,726.36

Contribution from income will be a quarter of the excess over £2,145 (i.e. a quarter of £581)=£145. This will be payable by twelve monthly instalments of £12.10.

Disposable capital: total disposable capital is £3,100. Contribution from capital will be excess over £3,000=£100. This will be payable in one lump sum. Mark Evans's total contribution to his legal-aid costs will therefore be £245 payable by a lump sum of £100 and twelve monthly instalments of £12.10. These figures are, of course, the maximum sums he can be asked to pay. If the costs of the case are likely to be less, then he will only be asked for the lesser amount. (Even so, it may still be to his advantage to accept an offer of legal aid, see page 853.) These are 1985 figures.

When legal aid is granted

If legal aid is granted, the applicant will be sent a formal offer setting out the amount of the contribution he must make. If he accepts, the legal-aid certificate will be issued and sent to his solicitor.

Any contributions are paid to the Accounts Office at the Law Society's Legal Aid Office. The client does not pay any money to the solicitor, for the solicitor will apply to the office for his fees at the end of the case.

The legally aided client can expect much the same service from the solicitor as if he was a private client, paying for the case himself. However, there is one complication, because apart from having a duty to help his client, the solicitor will also have a duty to avoid wasting the public money in the Legal Aid Fund. Occasionally, the solicitor's two duties clash and he will then have to put his duty to the Legal Aid Fund above his duty to the client. For instance, suppose the client is suing his employer over an accident that occurred at work. Legal aid is granted, but the solicitor then interviews the witnesses and discovers that the accident was the client's own fault and clearly the employer is not to blame; the case is hopeless. He must then tell the Legal Aid Committee what the witnesses say, although the probable result will be that his client's legal-aid certificate will be withdrawn, so as to avoid wasting any more money on the case.

The same applies if the client refuses to accept a reasonable offer in settlement. The extra cost of taking the case to trial might not justify refusing the offer and the solicitor must put his duty to the Legal Aid Fund above his duty to the client.

So it is not correct to say that the legally aided client is in the same position as the private, paying client. With a private client, money is no object – assuming he can afford it.

When the case is over: the total cost of being on legal aid

Not until the end of the case does the legally aided litigant know exactly how much he will have to pay. He will probably have already paid a 'contribution', but whether he has to pay any more will depend upon whether he wins or loses the case and on the amount of costs paid by his opponent.

Winning a case on legal aid

The general rule is that the winner's legal costs are paid by the loser. If the legally aided client wins his case he will probably find that the judge orders the other party (the loser) to pay all his costs.

Any damages awarded will go to the solicitor and not the client. The solicitor will then pass the money on to the Legal Aid Office and it will not be paid out to the client until all the legal fees have been paid.

The solicitor will work out his costs on what is called the common-fund basis (see page 841). This is the amount that he will receive from the Legal Aid Fund for acting on behalf of the client. The loser will have to pay the solicitor's costs, but not on such a generous basis as the common-fund basis. Instead, the loser need only pay the costs on what is called the party-and-party basis (see page 840). Basically, the party-and-party costs will be slightly less than the common-fund costs. The loser will pay the party-and-party costs to the solicitor who will then pass them on to the Legal Aid Office. The office will then pay the solicitor his common-fund costs. The money to pay the solicitor will come from:

1. The party-and-party costs paid by the loser. But usually there will be a small shortfall, and the balance will be taken from:
2. The client's contribution. So if the contribution was £100 and the shortfall was £30, the client would receive a refund of £70 from his contribution. But if the client did not pay a contribution, or if the contribution is not enough to pay the shortfall, the balance will be taken from:
3. The damages. The damages and other proceeds of the case will have been paid by the solicitor to the Legal Aid Office. The office can take any shortfall on costs from this money. The office is said to have a *statutory charge* over the proceeds, and it can use this statutory charge to claim a share of the proceeds to pay any unpaid costs.

Illustration. *Suppose the shortfall between the costs due to the solicitor and the costs paid by the loser is £50. The client had paid a £30 contribution, and won £1,000 damages. The shortfall of £50 is met firstly, by using the £30 contribution and, secondly, by using the damages. So the client loses his contribution and receives only £980 damages.*

Complications arise when the loser does not pay the party-and-party costs. This can be either because:

• he is ordered to pay the costs but doesn't (e.g. he has not got the money to do so, or he goes bankrupt, or he disappears) *or*

• he is not ordered to pay the costs. Although the loser is usually ordered to pay the costs, there are occasions when he is not (see page 842).

When this happens, the shortfall between what the Legal Aid Office receives and the amount they pay the solicitor for his common-fund costs can be considerable. As always, the shortfall will be met, firstly, from the client's contribution and, secondly, from the damages and proceeds of the case. The end result can be that the winner loses all his damages.

Illustration. *Mr Evans was granted legal aid to sue Second-Hand Carsales Ltd over a defective car which he bought from them. His contribution was £75. Mr Evans wins the case, is awarded £600 damages and Second-Hand Carsales Ltd are ordered to pay Mr Evans's costs. Mr Evans's solicitor's costs are £400. Second-Hand Carsales Ltd pay £350 of the damages but then go bankrupt. The Legal Aid Office will pay the solicitors their £400, and recover that money from the contribution (£75) and the damages (£350). Mr Evans is then left with £25 (i.e. £50 less than if he hadn't bothered).*

It is because the damages might have to go towards the legal costs that they are paid by the solicitor to the Legal Aid Office, and not to his client. The solicitor has no choice; he must pay the money to the Legal Aid Office. The Legal Aid Office will only release the money to the client when it is clear that there will not be a shortfall. This will usually be some time after the hearing. So the client may well feel aggrieved that, having won his case, he has to wait several months before his damages are paid to him.

The statutory charge – the right to take the legal costs out of the damages – can cause great hardship, as well as great bitterness. To a limited extent the hardship is mitigated since some damages and awards (such as maintenance payments) are exempt (see below). However, the Legal Aid Office has no power to waive the statutory charge, however much hardship it causes. All it can do is to agree to postpone the statutory charge.

Illustration. Mr and Mrs Brown have divorced. The court has ordered that the family house should be sold so that Mrs Brown can use her share of the proceeds to buy a flat in which to live with the children. No order for costs was made, so the proceeds of sale are liable to be used to pay Mrs Brown's solicitor's costs, although the first £2,500 of the marital settlement is exempt (see below). However, to do this would defeat the purpose of the court order. So the Legal Aid Office agrees that Mrs Brown can buy a flat, and the Law Society will then have a charge on the flat. If the flat is sold, the debt must be paid off. In effect, Mrs Brown is able to postpone paying the legal costs.

The statutory charge in matrimonial cases. It is in matrimonial cases (i.e. when husband and wife go to court to sort out who has what) that the statutory charge causes the greatest problems. The first difficulty is that the wife will normally have been awarded free legal aid (i.e. legal aid without having to make any contribution towards the costs). This is because the husband's income is ignored, and because the value of the family assets is also ignored (see page 851). The wife may therefore be misled into thinking that she will never have to pay anything towards the legal costs (after all she has free legal aid!), and her solicitor may well forget to tell her that this is not necessarily so.

In matrimonial cases the court often decides that each side (i.e. husband and wife) should pay their own legal costs – rather than order that one spouse pays all the costs. So if a wife (or husband) is legally aided, then the proceeds of the case (i.e. the share in the family home, any lump-sum settlement etc.) will be subject to the statutory charge – and be liable to be used towards paying the legal-aid costs. Thus, the legal aid will not be free – it might have been free initially, but the wife (or husband) will have to pay for that legal aid if s/he receives any of the family assets as a result of the court case. For instance:

In 1972 Mrs Hanlon started divorce proceedings. The case was not finished until 1977 by which time it had been to the Court of Appeal. Mrs Hanlon was on legal aid but so was her husband and thus he was not ordered to pay her costs – amounting to some £8,000. In the course of the divorce hearing, the court had ordered that the matrimonial home (worth some £10,000) be transferred to Mrs Hanlon. The Law Society claimed that the £8,000 costs should be paid by Mrs Hanlon from the proceeds of the litigation. Accordingly, a charge was registered against the house. Mrs Hanlon contested the Law Society's right to do this. Held: The statutory charge applied. Only the first £2,500 was exempt (see below) and the balance could be used to meet the legal fees. Thus, after five years' litigation, Mrs Hanlon had virtually nothing to show for it. Hanlon (1980)

If the house is to be sold straight away then the Law Society will demand immediate repayment of the legal costs. But if the house is not to be sold (usually because it is to be transferred into the sole name of the wife) then the Law Society will not insist that the house is sold. Instead, it will register a mortgage against the house and wait until it is eventually sold. Further, it may even agree to wait an even longer time and allow its mortgage to be put on the replacement home instead. But, it will only agree to this if:

• the new home will have sufficient equity (i.e. value, after repaying mortgages) to cover the amount of the statutory charge, *and*

• the new home is to be occupied as the sole residence of the applicant, together with at least one unmarried child who is under eighteen (or in full-time education if over eighteen), or if it is necessary for the applicants or their dependants to move for reasons of health, disability, or employment, *and*

• it will be just and reasonable to agree to postponing the charge again and it would cause 'hardship' to the applicant if that were not done.

Only in the most exceptional circumstances will further postponements be granted (i.e. on a sale of the substituted property).

So a wife (or husband) will be much better off if she receives the house in the matrimonial proceedings rather than a mere share in the house. For instance, if she has the whole house put into her name then the Law Society will normally agree to postpone the repayment of the legal-aid costs until it is sold (or even later – see above). On the other hand, if the outcome is that she has a percentage of the value of the house, and it is to be sold and the proceeds split, then the Law Society will demand immediate repayment of the legal-aid costs – it will not accept a mortgage on her own house (i.e. bought with the proceeds of the old house) instead. The moral is that it will often be better for a wife to take the whole of the house (and so avoid it being sold), and 'buy out' her husband's share by agreeing to go without maintenance.

The fundamental point to grasp is that legal aid is not necessarily free – the proceeds of the case will be subject to the statutory charge, and so be used to pay the legal-aid costs. The answer is to keep the legal costs to a minimum – it is crazy for husbands and wives to litigate over the family assets, since they are merely increasing the legal costs and reducing the amount that will be left to be divided between themselves.

Exemptions from the statutory charge

The proceeds of the case are exempt from being used to pay the legal costs in a few instances. The main exemptions are:

• maintenance payments to a wife or child;

• the first £2,500 of a matrimonial settlement, i.e. when the family property is divided up and some of it is transferred to the wife (or husband). Only the excess over £2,500 can be used to pay outstanding legal costs;

• various social-security benefits (e.g. disablement benefit, industrial death benefit).

Illustration. *Mr and Mrs Jones both agree to a divorce based on two years' separation. However, they cannot agree over the family property and so Mrs Jones is granted legal aid to cover the costs of applying to the court for a property order. The judge awards her maintenance of £1,000 p.a. plus £5,000 cash, but does not make any order as to costs. Her solicitor's costs are £500. The*

The Legal System

Legal Aid Office can apply the statutory charge but the maintenance is exempt and so is the first £2,500 of her cash. However, the balance of the cash is sufficient to pay the £500, and so she only receives £4,500 cash. If the judge had ordered that she receive £2,000 p.a. maintenance and no cash lump sum, she would not have had to pay anything towards the costs since all the maintenance would be exempt.

Losing a case on legal aid

Normally, the loser of a case is ordered to pay the winner's costs. But when the loser is on legal aid the rules have to be altered.

The judge will only order the legally aided loser to pay 'a reasonable amount' towards the winner's costs. In deciding what is a reasonable amount, the judge will consider the financial resources of the winner and the loser, and also their conduct in the case. More often than not, the judge will decide that a reasonable amount for the loser to pay would be an amount equal to the contribution he made when granted legal aid. The loser's total expenditure on legal costs will then be twice his contribution (i.e. his original contribution to the Legal Aid fund towards his own costs and the contribution ordered by the court towards his opponent's costs). That will be the limit of the legally aided loser's liability. His own solicitor's costs will be paid by the Legal Aid Fund and he will not have to make another contribution to cover those costs.

Legal aid costs: a summary

Winner	Loser	By whom winner's costs paid
Assisted	Assisted	By the loser, on the party-and-party basis, up to an amount considered reasonable by the court given his means. The balance, on the common-fund basis, is found by the winner out of his contribution and the statutory charge.
Assisted	Unassisted	By the loser, on the party-and-party basis, to the limit of his means. The balance, on the common-fund basis, is paid by the winner out of his contribution and the statutory charge.
Unassisted plaintiff	Assisted defendant	By the loser, on the party-and-party basis, up to an amount considered reasonable by the court given his means. The balance of the costs incurred are paid by the winner out of his own resources or damages recovered.
Unassisted defendant	Assisted plaintiff	By the loser, on the party-and-party basis, up to an amount considered reasonable by the court given his means. The balance of the costs incurred are paid by the winner out of his own resources unless the court makes an order against the Legal Aid Fund on the ground of hardship.

What of the winner? If the loser is only ordered to pay a reasonable amount of the winner's costs (usually equal to the contribution) who pays the balance of the winner's legal costs? The answer is that, usually, the winner will have to pay them himself, so even though he has won the case he incurs legal costs. The only exception is that if he was the defendant in the case, he can recover his costs from the Legal Aid Fund if he would otherwise suffer 'severe financial hardship'. Generally, this means that the winner will have to pay his own costs if he is wealthy or if a company. If the winner is a private individual of limited means he can expect to recover his costs from the Legal Aid Fund.

The opponent of a legally aided litigant is therefore at a disadvantage. Even if he wins the case he is likely to have to pay some legal costs. In short he cannot win! If the opponent is also on legal aid, then the winner will probably have to pay his costs out of his damages.

Civil legal aid: what needs to be done

The principles behind the legal-aid system, as set out in the Rushcliffe Committee's Report (page 848), are a sound foundation for the present scheme. The weakness lies in the means test.

The financial eligibility limits have not kept pace with inflation. The result is that only the poor can be sure of qualifying, leaving the vast bulk of the population ineligible. For most people, the practical consequence of being outside the legal-aid limits is that they cannot take a case to court if that should be necessary. The rights given to citizens are of limited value if they cannot be enforced in the courts. The solution must be to increase the legal-aid limits and to peg them to the national average wage level. Need contributions be as high as they are? To expect applicants to contribute a quarter of their excess income and all their excess capital is unduly harsh. Research shows that there is an alarming drop-out rate for those who are offered legal aid with a contribution. Many applicants decide that they cannot afford the contribution and so they abandon their cases, despite the fact that their cases must have had reasonable prospects of success; this is a strong argument for abolishing contributions.

The legal-reform group, Justice, have proposed that a new form of legal aid be introduced, which could run alongside the existing system. This would allow solicitors to take cases on a 'payment-by-results' basis. If the case is lost, the solicitor recovers nothing; if the case is won, the solicitor takes a percentage of the damages. The suggestion is that the system would be administered by the Law Society, who would ensure that professional standards were maintained and also assess the solicitor's percentage. At the moment, a solicitor cannot act on a payment-by-results basis. Indeed until 1967 he could have been prosecuted for 'champerty' if he had done so. Whilst it is no longer a crime, such an arrangement is 'professional misconduct' by a solicitor, and would lead to disciplinary action being taken by the Law Society.

A payment-by-results system (called a contingency-fee arrangement) operates in the USA. Whilst it seems to work in the USA, many commentators feel that it is an immoral and dangerous principle. They argue that it can put the solicitor in a position where his own interests are in conflict with those of his client. For instance, if a client has a claim worth £5,000 and he is offered £4,000 at an early stage in the case, the solicitor might be tempted to advise the client to accept. From the solicitor's point of view he will get the bulk of his fee if the case is settled for £4,000, whereas if it goes to trial he will have to do a lot more work for little extra money. Consequently, the solicitor might be tempted to under-settle his client's case.

On the other hand, one would have thought it possible to introduce a contingency-fee system that, properly policed by the Law Society, could overcome these risks. Certainly, if the legal-aid financial limits are to remain as low as they are, then contingency fees must surely merit careful consideration. If such a system would enable people to litigate when they could not otherwise afford to, then it must be beneficial.

The only real solution, of course, is to raise the legal-aid eligibility limits.

Legal aid in criminal cases

An accused person can apply for legal aid to pay all, or part, of his legal costs. The decision whether to grant legal aid is taken by the courts themselves.

Legal aid has been available in criminal cases since 1903, when the Poor Prisoners Defence Act provided a limited legal-aid scheme for those accused of serious crimes. Prior to that date, the only form of criminal legal aid was the 'dock brief' (see page 916). In 1930 criminal legal aid was extended to the magistrates' court and the test for eligibility was whether it was 'desirable in the interests of justice'. This remains the overall test for eligibility under the present legal-aid provisions, which are set out in Part II of the Legal Aid Act 1974.

In addition to this statutory criterion, the courts generally follow principles laid down by the Widgery Committee of 1966, which carried out a review of the criminal legal-aid system. Widgery recommended that criminal legal aid should be granted – subject to a means test – in cases:

(a) where the charge is a grave one in the sense that the accused is in real jeopardy of losing his liberty or livelihood or suffering serious damage to his reputation; *or*
(b) where the charges raise a substantial question of law; *or*
(c) where the accused is unable to follow the proceedings and state his own case because of his inadequate knowledge of English, mental illness, or other mental or physical disability; *or*
(d) where the nature of the defence involves the tracing and interviewing of witnesses or expert cross-examination of a witness for the prosecution; *or*
(e) where legal representation is desirable in the interests of someone other than the accused as, for example, in the case of sexual offences against young children where it is undesirable that the accused should cross-examine the witness in person.

What this means in practice is that legal aid is granted by magistrates for the more serious cases – or to someone who faces a serious penalty if convicted (i.e. because of previous convictions). But, those charged with relatively minor offences will not get legal aid. This is especially true with motoring prosecutions – very few accused motorists can get legal aid (even if they qualify financially).

A further complication is that different courts take different attitudes to the granting of legal aid. Some are more generous – others are less generous. A local solicitor should be able to advise on the prospects of getting legal aid for a particular offence. Virtually any case that goes to the crown court is likely to be serious – and have possibly serious results for the defendant. So legal aid is nearly always granted (over 97 per cent of crown-court defendants receive legal aid).

Legal aid in magistrates' court cases can be granted either by the magistrates or by their clerk. Only the magistrates – not their clerk – can refuse legal aid.

Legal aid in crown court cases can be granted either by the magistrates, when they commit the defendant for trial to the crown court, or by the crown court.

The means test in criminal legal aid

Criminal legal aid is only granted to defendants who meet the means test. The rules on financial eligibility are similar to those for civil legal aid – see page 850.

Anyone on SB or FIS will automatically receive free legal aid. Otherwise, a means test is applied – the figures are roughly the same as those in civil legal-aid cases (see page 854). If it is a juvenile who is applying, then the parents' finances will be taken into account (unless the juvenile is aged sixteen or more, in which case the parents' finances may not apply).

A defendant can be ordered to make a contribution to his legal-aid costs, either when he is granted legal aid or when the case is finished – even if he is acquitted. If a contribution is asked for, when legal aid is granted, the defendant will normally be able to pay it in instalments over twenty-six weeks. In addition, after the case has been heard, he may then be asked to pay additional costs. The sentence imposed on a guilty defendant will have to be taken into account when deciding whether to order a contribution to the legal-aid costs. Clearly, if he is sentenced to prison, and he has no savings, there will be no point in ordering him to make a contribution.

There is no appeal against a contribution order. This can cause hardship and it seems an unfair rule. For instance, a defendant might be prosecuted and, because of the nature of the case, his trial could last several weeks. He may be found guilty and given a relatively minor punishment (such as a fine or conditional discharge); nevertheless the judge can punish him indirectly by imposing a high costs contribution. The defendant cannot appeal against that contribution order, even though it may amount to a much more serious penalty than the sentence imposed on him by the court – against which, of course, he could appeal.

An example of criminal legal aid

Mr Jones is arrested and taken to the police station. Mrs Jones arranges for a solicitor to visit the police station to advise Mr Jones while he is being questioned. The solicitor's fee can be paid under the green-form scheme (page 864). Eventually, Mr Jones is charged and next day he appears before the magistrates. They refuse him bail and order that he be kept in custody.

Mr Jones's solicitor applies to the magistrates (or their clerk) for legal aid. This is granted in principle and the magistrates order him to make a contribution. If he had been on supplementary benefit he would not have had to pay a contribution; however, in Mr Jones's case, he is earning, and is expected to pay a contribution. This is paid in instalments over twenty-six weeks.

If Mr Jones had not found a solicitor who was willing to come down to the police station, then he might well have used the duty solicitor at the magistrates' court. Duty solicitors are available in most magistrates' courts, to help defendants who do not yet have a solicitor. The duty solicitor would have seen Mr Jones under the green-form scheme. Probably, that solicitor would have taken the case on, and acted for Mr Jones in subsequent magistrates' court and crown-court hearings. However, Mr Jones would have been able to insist upon a different solicitor – if he did not want to use the duty solicitor.

His solicitor decides to appeal against the refusal of bail. The appeal is to a judge in the crown court. The costs of this are covered by the legal aid granted by the magistrates.

Eventually the date for the committal hearing is arranged. At this hearing the magistrates will decide whether Mr Jones should be committed to the crown court for trial. His solicitor represents him, his fees being paid by the legal-aid order. When the magistrates commit Mr Jones, his legal aid is extended to cover the costs of the crown-court case.

If Mr Jones is acquitted *at the crown-court hearing he may still have to make a contribution to the costs of his defence. However, if the case is such that the court feels the defence's costs should be paid from central funds (see page 845) he will not be ordered to make a contribution and any money he has paid will be returned to him.*

If Mr Jones is convicted *he will probably have to make a contribution to his legal costs, unless he is sent to prison. Should Mr Jones decide to appeal to the Court of Appeal, his existing legal aid order will cover advice from his lawyers as to the prospects of his appeal. But it will not cover the costs of the appeal. He would have to make a separate application and this would only rarely be successful.*

Advice and assistance under the green-form scheme

The green-form scheme was designed as a simple way of giving legal aid to people who were not involved in court proceedings, but who needed general legal advice and assistance. Thus, it is mainly for non-court work, and if a court case is involved then it will normally be necessary to apply for civil legal aid (page 848) or criminal legal aid (page 862). The general rule is that the green-form scheme will cover the first £50 of the solicitor's fees (but this figure can be increased – see below).

The green-form scheme can be used to pay all, or part of, a solicitor's fees for a whole host of different legal problems. For instance, the green-form scheme can cover the solicitor's fees in:

- writing letters;
- negotiating;
- preparing and drafting documents, including a will, and even a conveyance;
- helping complete a legal-aid application form;
- helping a do-it-yourself litigant who wants advice on how to fill in court forms and how to present his case;
- going to a police station to advise a suspect who is 'helping the police with their inquiries', but who has not been charged.

● some court work – but not much is covered. Although the green-form scheme was originally designed to exclude anything that involved court work, it has been altered over the years and can now cover the cost of legal representation for:
  - parents when the local authority wants to take their child into care. The child will have its own solicitor and will be eligible for civil legal aid (see page 141) but the parents will be able to use the green-form scheme to cover their legal costs.
  - a husband or wife (usually a wife) who wants to bring domestic proceedings in the magistrates' court (e.g. applying for maintenance, or for a protection order).
  - a person facing a criminal charge in the magistrates' court, when the court asks a solicitor who is at the court to represent him. In practice, this covers the costs of representation by a duty solicitor (i.e. a solicitor who attends court specific- ally to help people who are not already represented by a solicitor – see page 864.
  - prisoners who are facing disciplinary charges before a prison board of visitors (see page 677), and mental patients who are applying to the Mental Health Review Tribunal (see page 703).

The green-form scheme is a relatively recent innovation. When civil legal aid was introduced in 1949 it had been planned to introduce a type of green-form scheme then; the proposal was that salaried solicitors would have offices at the Legal Aid Area Committee office, and dispense general legal advice for 2s.6d. a session. But economy cuts prevented that scheme from being introduced, and although a sub- sidized legal-advice scheme was introduced by the Law Society in 1958, it was not a satisfactory answer to the problem. So in 1968 the Law Society proposed a new scheme, which would apply a simple means test and which would involve low admin- istration costs. The proposal was accepted, and the Legal Advice and Assistance Act 1972 launched what was formally known as the Legal Advice and Assistance Scheme. In practice, it became known as the green-form scheme, after the colour of the application form.

How the green-form scheme works

Anyone who wants legal advice can go into a solicitor's office and ask for advice under the green-form scheme. Most solicitors' offices operate the green-form scheme (look for the Legal Aid logo).

When the applicant is interviewed by the solicitor, the first thing the solicitor will do is to start filling in a green form. After writing down the applicant's name and address, he will take details of his (or her) finances to see whether the applicant is financially eligible. He will also check that the applicant's problem is within the scope of the green-form scheme.

Hurdle No. 1: financial eligibility

The applicant must pass the means test. Eligibility will be determined on the basis of the applicant's weekly 'disposable income' and 'disposable capital'.

Disposable income is the applicant's income from all sources, minus tax, national insurance contributions, and a specified allowance for each dependant, such as wife and children. If the applicant is on supplementary benefit or FIS, his disposable income is taken to be nil, and so he is automatically eligible for free advice unless he has too much capital. Otherwise a sliding scale applies and the applicant will have to make a contribution towards the legal costs (see table below).

Disposable capital is the value of the applicant's possessions, excluding his furniture, clothes, tools of his trade, and his house. If the applicant has more than the prescribed amount of disposable capital, then he will not be eligible under the green-form scheme. For a person with no dependants, the maximum amount (1985) is £765; if one dependant, £965; two dependants, £1,085; three dependants, £1,145 (plus £60 for each extra dependant). If the applicant has disposable capital under these amounts, he will be eligible (provided he does not have too much income – see above) and will not have to use any of the capital towards paying for the legal costs.

Once weekly disposable income and disposable capital have been assessed, the solicitor can work out whether his client is eligible under the green-form scheme and, if so, whether the advice will be free, or subject to the client paying a contribution.

The figures for financial eligibility vary from year to year. The amount of the contribution is worked out on a sliding scale, increasing with the amount of the disposable income:

Weekly disposable income	Maximum contribution
under £51	nil (i.e. free)
£51–£59	£5
£59–£63	£11
£63–£67	£15
£67–£71	£20
£71–£75	£24
£75–£79	£28
£79–£83	£33
£83–£87	£37
£87–£91	£41
£91–£95	£46
£95–£99	£50
£99–£104	£55
£104–£108	£60
over £109	not eligible

A typical green form is illustrated on pages 909–10 and it shows how the means test is applied.

As with an application for civil legal aid, the finances of a spouse are usually taken into account, unless the couple are in dispute (see page 851).

Once the solicitor has worked out his client's financial eligibility, he will probably ask for any contribution there and then. The amount of the contribution will be the total cost to his client of the legal advice, unless the solicitor manages to recover money or property for him, in which case that may have to be put towards the solicitor's fees (see below).

Hurdle No. 2: is the problem covered by the green-form scheme?

The two basic requirements are, firstly, that the problem must involve a question of English law and, secondly, that it must not involve the solicitor in commencing court proceedings (unless one of the above exceptions applies, in which case the green-form scheme can cover the cost of legal representation).

The first requirement is unlikely to cause difficulties. Occasionally, though, it does. For instance, if a woman asks for advice on how to divorce her husband in Eire, she cannot be eligible under the green-form scheme.

The second requirement is less clear-cut. The green-form scheme was not designed to cover a solicitor's fees in starting court proceedings or in running a court case. However, the regulations do not prevent a solicitor from using the scheme to advise a client how he himself can start court proceedings or how he should run his own court case. So it is acceptable for a solicitor to tell his client how to start a court case and how to conduct the case, but if the solicitor himself starts the case or conducts it, the green-form scheme cannot apply.

Illustration. Mr Jones has been sacked and he wants to claim unfair dismissal. He goes to a solicitor for advice. If the solicitor fills in the unfair-dismissal application form and signs it on Mr Jones's behalf, then his fee cannot be covered by the green-form scheme. However, if the solicitor discusses the claim with Mr Jones, and tells him how best to fill in the application form, and it is Mr Jones who signs the form, then the solicitor's fee will be covered by the green-form scheme – providing Mr Jones is financially eligible. This is because the solicitor has merely given advice – he has not started legal proceedings for his client.

Another example of when a solicitor uses the green-form scheme to help his client start proceedings is with undefended divorces. Civil legal aid is not available for undefended divorces and so the only way a person involved in an undefended divorce can get free (or partly free) legal advice is to use the green-form scheme. However, since the green-form scheme does not allow the solicitor to start divorce proceedings, he cannot use the green-form scheme to cover his fees in handling the divorce for his client. All he can do is to tell the client how to do his (or her) own divorce. In effect, it is the solicitor who fills in the divorce forms, but it is the client, not the solicitor, who signs the forms. When another step has to be taken the client sees the solicitor again, and is told what to do next. But throughout the proceedings the client is technically handling the case him/herself.

The Legal System

How much legal advice can be obtained under the green-form scheme?

The green-form scheme covers the first £50 of the solicitor's fees (i.e. the first £50 plus VAT). Once the solicitor's fees reach £50 he must tell the client that the green-form scheme no longer applies and that any extra legal advice will have to be paid for by the client, in full.

In practice, however, the £50 limit is of little effect. Firstly, the solicitor can often arrange for the £50 limit to be raised. Secondly, the £50 limit becomes £90 in undefended divorces. Thirdly, there is no maximum limit if the green-form scheme is being used to pay for court work.

Increasing the £50 limit

As soon as the solicitor realizes that his fees will be more than £50, he will contact the Law Society's Legal Aid Office. He will explain the position and suggest an increased maximum figure. If the Area Office agree that the advice is necessary, and the solicitor's estimate of the fees seems reasonable, it will agree to increase the limit and 'grant an extension' to a specified amount. The client will not have to pay an increased contribution even if the £50 limit is increased by a substantial amount.

Illustration. A woman goes to a solicitor and explains that her husband has been taken away by the police and is being held by them. The solicitor calculates that the woman is eligible under the green-form scheme with a contribution of £5. He phones the police station and it becomes clear that he ought to go to the police station to advise the man as to his rights. It seems likely that the police interviews will take several hours. Clearly, the solicitor's fee in going to the police station and remaining there for some hours will exceed £50. So he phones the Legal Aid Office, explains the position, and asks for an 'extension to £75'. This is granted. His fee will be paid by the office, and the client's contribution will remain at £5.

£90 in undefended divorces

For straightforward, undefended divorces, legal aid is not available. To compensate for this, the £50 limit under the green-form scheme has been raised to £90 for advice in connection with an undefended divorce. However, the solicitor cannot issue the divorce petition for his client; that must be done by the client personally (see above).

No limit in court cases

Although the general rule is that the green-form scheme does not cover court work, there are exceptions (see page 865). In those cases, the legal fees can be covered by the green-form scheme, although technically it is referred to as 'assistance by way of representation'. The rules on financial eligibility are identical to those under the normal green-form scheme. The one important difference is that there is no £50 ceiling on the amount of legal fees provided by the scheme. There is no maximum level and so the eligible client can get legal representation costing well over £50.

When the case is over: the total cost of the advice

When the case is over, and the solicitor has finished his work, he will calculate his fees. If the fee is less than the amount of the contribution paid by the client, the solicitor will refund the balance of the contribution to the client. Accordingly, the client will have paid the full cost of the legal advice himself. For instance, if the contribution is £40, and the solicitor's fee £30, the solicitor will refund £10.

Usually, though, the contribution will be less than the solicitor's bill. The solicitor can take the shortfall from any money or property which he has recovered for the client or which he has successfully defended for the client. The solicitor is said to have a *statutory charge* over the money and property, in the same way that the Legal Aid Fund has a statutory charge over property recovered in a civil legal-aid case (page 857).

Illustration. *Mrs Smith consulted a solicitor over the cost of repairs to a coat which was damaged by dry-cleaners. Her contribution under the green-form scheme was nil since she was on supplementary benefit. The solicitor wrote to the dry-cleaners and persuaded them to settle Mrs Smith's claim for £22. The solicitor's fee is £15. He can deduct the £15 from the £22 and so Mrs Smith only receives £7.*

The effect of the statutory charge is that it is rarely worth using the green-form scheme for small-value claims. If the claim is successful, the legal fees are likely to swallow up any money received.

Note that when the statutory charge applies, the client does not receive free (or even partly free) legal advice. If necessary, all the settlement money is used to pay the legal fees.

If no money or property is recovered then there can be no statutory charge. There is no money or property for the solicitor to take his fees from, and so the shortfall is paid to him by the Legal Aid Office. The client need not pay any more than the amount of the original contribution.

Illustration. *Mr Evans was sacked by his employers and went to see a solicitor about claiming unfair dismissal. The solicitor saw him under the green-form scheme and collected Mr Evans's contribution of £8. It became clear that the advice would exceed the £50 limit so the solicitor arranged for the limit to be extended to £75. Mr Evans claimed unfair dismissal and followed the advice and instructions of the solicitor, but it soon became clear that Mr Evans had a hopeless case because of his previous misconduct at work. However, the solicitor persuaded the employers to pay Mr Evans £50. The solicitor's bill was £70. The solicitor's fee was paid, firstly with the £8 contribution, secondly by using the £50 compensation, and thirdly by claiming the remaining £12 from the Legal Aid Fund. Mr Evans was left with nothing.*

The right of the solicitor to claim his costs out of the settlement moneys can cause his client great bitterness and a feeling of 'having been done'. To ease the hardship it can cause, some moneys are exempt from the statutory charge. If the solicitor recovers any of the following items for his client, he cannot take his fee out of the money:

– maintenance payments,
– the first £2,500 in any family proceedings (e.g. if husband agrees to give a lump sum to wife to cover her share of the family home; see page 859),
– the first half of a redundancy payment,
– household goods and furniture, or tools of the applicant's trade.
– most welfare benefits.

Illustration. A wife and her two children have been abandoned by her husband. Her solicitor advises her under the green-form scheme and as a result she successfully claims supplementary benefit; she also goes to the magistrates' court and obtains a maintenance order against her husband. Altogether these give her an income of £45 p.w. The solicitor's fee is £35. The fee will not come out of her supplementary benefit or her maintenance. Both are exempt from the statutory charge and so the solicitor's fees are paid in full by the Legal Aid Office.

In addition, the statutory charge can be waived in any case if it 'would cause grave hardship or distress to the client to enforce' it, or if it could only be enforced with 'unreasonable difficulty because of the nature of the property' (e.g. as in the case of a valuable pet dog that was recovered for a client – the Law Society agreed it would be unreasonable to expect the dog to be sold to pay for the legal costs!). So a person who receives advice under the green-form scheme, and who thinks he comes within these exceptions should ask the solicitor not to apply the statutory charge. The solicitor will then apply to the Legal Aid Office for permission to waive the statutory charge.

Half an hour's advice for £5

Most solicitors are prepared to give preliminary advice under the '£5 for half an hour's advice' scheme. This is a fixed-fee arrangement whereby the solicitor will give legal advice and not charge his client more than £5 for the first half hour. There is no means test, so the fixed-fee offer is available to both rich and poor. However, if the client is hard up, he (or she) may be eligible under the green-form scheme (see page 864). If so, the maximum charge for the half hour's advice will be £5 or the green-form contribution, whichever is the lesser.

Once the first half hour has been used, the client will have to pay the solicitor on a normal commercial basis, which will usually be much more than £5 per half hour. A person who wishes to use the £5-for-half-an-hour scheme should make it clear to the solicitor that he is seeing him under the scheme. Otherwise the solicitor will assume that the client is a private client, prepared to pay the going commercial rate.

A client cannot insist that a solicitor allows him an interview under this fixed-fee scheme. The Law Society has told solicitors that 'in appropriate circumstances the solicitor may decline'.

Despite its limitations the £5 scheme is of considerable value. It allows a person who is of limited means, but outside the green-form eligibility limits, to take legal advice at a 'bargain' price. Half an hour will usually be sufficient time for the solicitor to give basic advice to his client and advise him whether he has a claim worth pursuing and, if so, whether he should apply for legal aid. Unfortunately, the scheme has received little publicity and so few people know of it.

Free help with accident claims

In some parts of the country it is possible for an accident victim to have a free initial interview with a local solicitor. This will enable the solicitor to advise as to whether there is a basis of a claim. Leaflets describing the scheme are distributed in hospitals, doctors' surgeries, and CABs. If it is available locally, a form has to be sent to the local law society who will then allocate the client to a local solicitor. But there is no guarantee that the solicitor will be experienced in personal-injury cases, although in practice most are.

58 DIY: Legal Action without a Lawyer

There is no rule of law which says that a litigant must employ a solicitor or barrister to act for him, although in practice most people do. The litigant can act for himself if he wishes, whether the case be in the magistrates' court, the county court, or even the senior courts.

Cases where litigants are encouraged to act for themselves

Industrial tribunals. These hear, amongst other things, unfair dismissal, redundancy, and allegations of sex discrimination in employment. Legal aid is not available (although it may be possible to get an extension under the green-form scheme – see page 868). Alternatively, a trade union may help a member. If he wins the claim, he will have to pay his own legal costs, for the normal rule that the 'loser pays the winner's costs' does not apply in the industrial tribunals (see page 455). By this means the use of lawyers is discouraged.

Undefended divorce. These cases are heard in the county court. Legal aid is not available to help with the legal costs (see page 41), but the court procedures have been simplified so as to encourage people to do their own divorces (see page 44). However, if children are involved or if large sums of money are in dispute, legal advice should always be obtained. If there is an argument over the children or money legal aid will usually be available.

Claims for no more than £500. These claims are also heard in the county court, by an arbitrator. Whenever the amount claimed is no more than £500, each side will have to pay its own legal costs, so the normal rule that the 'loser pays the winner's costs' will not apply. This is called the small-claims rule (see page 843). It is designed to discourage the use of lawyers in claims that involve relatively small amounts, when the legal costs could exceed the amount in dispute. The small-claims rule applies to all actions in which the plaintiff (the person suing) claims damages only, whether the damages are for breach of contract, negligence, trespass, or whatever. However, the rule does not apply to:
- *complex cases:* in difficult and unusual cases either party can ask the court to order that legal costs be awarded, even if no more than £500 is involved.
- *claims for an order other than damages*: the small-claims rule is restricted to damages-only claims. For example, it would not apply to cases in which a battered wife obtained an injunction against her husband or a landlord obtained a possession

872

order against his tenant, for those claims would be for something other than money damages.

DIY litigation: the arguments for and against

The main reason for acting for oneself is to save money; most solicitors charge between £25 and £45 per hour. In addition, of course, much of the work involved in preparing a case for trial is routine – writing to witnesses, preparing copies of relevant papers, etc. – and can be done as well by a layman as by a lawyer. A solicitor is likely to charge £150–£200 for handling an undefended divorce and a similar amount for a consumer claim worth several hundred pounds. His fee for a morning in the magistrates' court might well be £60. So the savings that can be made by DIY litigation are worth while.

Many people have little choice but to act for themselves. If they cannot obtain legal aid or legal assistance from a trade union, they have no real choice. No one should be frightened of acting for themselves; any reasonably intelligent person can be a DIY litigant and present the case in a satisfactory way. The main piece of advice is to 'know your limitations', and so prepare the case properly; try to discuss it with a lawyer; be prepared to put in a lot of work; do not try to be Perry Mason in the courtroom; present the case in a logical and coherent way; and ask the judge if in any doubt as to what to do next in court.

The disadvantages

Competence. The layman cannot expect to know the law and the court procedure as well as a lawyer. Whilst he can read law books and rehearse his presentation of the case, he can never be sure that he has not – through ignorance – overlooked a basic flaw in his case. Similarly, when he gets to court, the layman is bound to be nervous and apprehensive. He is unlikely to be able to present his case and his evidence to the judge as expertly as would a lawyer. He will not know how to cross-examine witnesses, how to address the judge, or how best to present his case. However enthusiastic he may be, as an inexperienced amateur he cannot expect to perform as well as a professional, and the danger is that he will lose the case when a lawyer might have won it.

Against this, though, it must be said that it is easy to exaggerate the difficulties facing the DIY litigant; these days judges are sympathetic to laymen who handle their own cases and will often go out of their way to help DIY litigants. Also, the layman will have one advantage over a lawyer; he will know the facts of the case intimately, whereas the lawyer is likely to have only a cursory knowledge of them.

Detachment. One of the reasons for employing a solicitor is to be given objective advice: a detached, realistic opinion of the prospects of success. The DIY litigant will be very closely involved in his own case and he will find it difficult to stand back and look at his claim in an objective way – and it is only by doing so that the weaknesses of a claim can be seen.

Of course, one way for the layman to overcome this problem is to discuss the case with a lawyer. Rather than asking the lawyer to handle the claim, he simply asks him to advise on the weaknesses of the claim, how those weaknesses can be strengthened (e.g. what new evidence should he try to obtain?), and the tactics he should adopt (e.g. should he be prepared to negotiate or should he put on a show of toughness by pressing on with the proceedings?). By taking legal advice in this way the layman can go some way to overcoming the disadvantages that he faces.

Time. The layman will take considerably more time to prepare his case than would a lawyer. The layman will have to start from the beginning: first, finding out the law; secondly, applying it to the case; and thirdly, collecting the relevant evidence. The lawyer will be able to do the first and second steps in a very short time; he is likely to have the general legal knowledge and experience to enable him to assess the prospects of success in a few minutes. The layman, of course, does not have this advantage.

He must be prepared to spend time researching the law, finding out about court procedure, and, probably, in rehearsing the presentation of his case. In addition, there will be the worry and strain of the case; many people become very anxious about their claims.

The DIY litigant must accept that he will have to spend a considerable amount of time on his case. In fact, if he puts a money value on his leisure time he might find it cheaper to employ a solicitor. However, the DIY litigant may be able to obtain some compensation for his lost time if he wins the case (see page 875).

When not to act for yourself

Part of 'knowing your limitations' is to accept that there are some cases that should only be handled by lawyers unless there is absolutely no alternative.

It is not advisable for the layman to act for himself when there are important matters at stake or when the case involves complicated legal issues. On this basis, DIY litigation is not for:

Defended divorces. These are heard in the High Court. The procedure is more complicated than in the county court.

Children and property disputes. Even in undefended divorces there can be disputes over custody of the children and division of the family assets. These are important matters, best left to a professional lawyer. Legal aid may be available.

Injunctions. Injunctions are for emergencies only, such as to stop an illegal eviction or to prevent further wife-battering. The procedure to be followed is fairly complicated, even in the county court, so it is advisable to retain a lawyer.

Rent Act cases. The Rent Acts are notoriously complicated. Whilst it is possible for a landlord to act for himself in possession proceedings if the tenant is not disputing the claim, he would be best advised to retain a solicitor if the tenant does defend the case. A tenant should always take legal advice if possession proceedings are begun; he may well have a legal defence under the Rent Acts that he, as a layman, does not know of.

Finally, it is obviously pointless to act for oneself if free legal aid is available. The DIY litigant should check that he, or she, is not eligible for legal aid (see page 846).

How a friend can assist in court

Most DIY litigants are nervous when they first go into the courtroom. It is difficult to take a note of what the witnesses say, to decide what questions to ask in cross-examination, and to follow the arguments of the other side. Yet all of these things have to be done.

It is advisable for the DIY litigant to take a friend or helper into court who can sit beside him, taking notes of evidence, making suggestions, and quietly prompting if mistakes are made. Few DIY litigants take a friend into court, but it is a sensible step. Because so few people do it, some courts might challenge the litigant's right to have a helper. It is true that the court has a discretion to regulate its affairs – but it must act 'reasonably'. So if the court seems reluctant, ask them why it would be unreasonable to have a friend in court, and refer to the case of *McKenzie* (1970). This was a Court of Appeal decision which confirmed the right of a layman to have a helper in court, who can take notes, quietly make suggestions, and give advice. However, the friend cannot address the court or examine the witnesses.

Mr McKenzie was petitioning for divorce, but he was not on legal aid. The facts were complicated and his wife defended the divorce proceedings. Mr McKenzie decided to act for himself, despite the fact that the case would be complicated; in fact it lasted ten days. At the start of the case Mr McKenzie went into the court with a clerk who worked for Mr McKenzie's ex-solicitors. The clerk came as a friend – the solicitors were not acting for Mr McKenzie – and he intended to advise Mr McKenzie on how to present the case. The trial judge ordered the clerk to leave, saying that Mr McKenzie must either act for himself or use a lawyer; he could not have help from another layman. Mr McKenzie lost the case and appealed, saying that he should have been allowed the assistance of the clerk. Held: Yes. Every litigant can have a friend beside him. This was a right that had existed for years although it was rarely used. What had been said in an 1831 case was correct: 'Any person, whether he be a professional man or not, may attend as a friend of either party, may take notes, may quietly make suggestions, and give advice; but no one can demand to take part in the proceedings as an advocate.' McKenzie (1970)

Since this case, such lay advisers are generally called 'McKenzie men'. Every DIY litigant should take advantage of this decision and ask the court to let him (or her) have a McKenzie man.

Being paid for the work involved

The usual rule in civil cases is that the loser pays the winner's legal costs (see page 840). But what happens if the winner has no legal costs because he acted for himself? Until 1975 the answer was that the loser did not have to pay any costs to the winner, even if the winner had devoted hours of his spare time to preparing the case. Partially to remedy this unfair situation, the Litigants in Person (Costs and Expenses) Act 1975 was passed to allow the DIY litigant to claim reasonable compensation for the work put in to the case.

To ensure that the loser is no worse off paying costs to a DIY litigant than he would have been to a legally represented opponent, the Act restricts the costs that are payable. Firstly, the DIY litigant can only claim costs when he could have claimed costs if legally represented; in particular, this means that the small-claims rule applies and so the DIY litigant cannot recover costs in claims of £500 or less (see page 872). Secondly, the DIY litigant's costs cannot exceed those of a solicitor; the loser is not to be made to pay extra because the DIY litigant put a disproportionately high number of hours' work into the case. Also, whilst he can claim up to £6 per hour for the time reasonably spent on the case, he cannot claim more than two thirds of the amount a solicitor could charge for handling the case.

In short, therefore, the litigant's bill can be cut down because he is claiming for too many hours' work, and/or his hourly wage loss exceeds two thirds of the amount a solicitor would have charged. His disbursements (see page 832) will normally be allowed in full if they would have been reasonably incurred by a lawyer. However, if he spends money unnecessarily (for instance, on expert's reports) the expense will not be allowed. Nor will he be able to recover the cost of law books bought for the case.

If the claim is worth no more than £1,000 the DIY litigant's costs will be assessed by the judge at the end of the case, so he should have a log of the time he has spent working on the claim. If the claim exceeds £1,000, the costs will normally be 'taxed' at a later date by a court official (see page 844), although the litigant can avoid the inconvenience of this by asking the trial judge to assess them at the end of the case. Generally, assessed costs are lower than taxed costs.

DIY in the county court

The county courts hear nearly all civil cases involving £5,000 or less (see page 759). Accordingly, this is the court that the DIY litigant with a civil claim is likely to sue in. In addition, county courts hear undefended divorce petitions (see page 44 for the steps to be taken in an undefended divorce).

The DIY litigant will usually want to sue for damages. Typical DIY claims are for:

- non-payment of a debt, e.g. for money lent and not repaid; for payment of a bill delivered for work done or for goods supplied;
- faulty goods, e.g. defective electrical items or poor-quality consumer goods;
- poor service, e.g. failure to repair a car or radio properly; failure to do the job to a proper standard;
- negligence, e.g. a motorist's car is damaged by the negligent driving of another motorist; whilst he may be insured, he might decide to sue the negligent motorist and so avoid claiming on his policy, which might lose him his no-claims bonus;

• wages owed; an employee may be sacked without proper notice, in which case he can claim the wages due; this is a 'wrongful-dismissal' claim – not to be confused with an 'unfair-dismissal' claim which is brought in an industrial tribunal.

Who to sue

The person sued is called the defendant. It is important that he is named properly in the court papers and that the address is correct. A private individual's name and address can often be checked from the telephone directory or the electoral register kept at the town hall.

Businesses

With businesses it is important to sue the correct person(s) or firm.

Partnerships. All the partners in a firm are responsible for each other's business debts and liabilities incurred on the firm's behalf. However, the claim must be against the firm name or against all the named partners, for otherwise the other partners will not be liable. For instance, if Brown, Smith, and Jones carry on business as 'BSJ Builders', the action should be against 'BSJ Builders' (a firm) or against 'Brown, Smith, and Jones'. If it was against 'Brown and Smith', Jones would not be liable.

Companies. A company can only be sued if its registered office is stated. This can be found out by writing to the Registrar of Companies. A company can usually be identified by the fact that it has 'plc', 'Ltd' or 'Limited' in its name. Many firms use 'and Co.' in their names, but this does not necessarily mean that they are companies (see page 600).

Firms. If a business is not a company it will be a one-man business or a partnership. If the name of the firm does not consist of the full names of all the partners, or of the sole trader, the firm should be sued in its business name. See page 599 for the problems that can arise when trying to trace the owner of a business.

Which court to sue in?

There are county courts throughout the country. However, you cannot bring your claim in whichever court is the most convenient for you. You are limited to suing in either the court for the area where the defendant lives (or carries on business) or the court for the area where the cause of action arose.

Illustration. *John Jones lives in Newcastle. He is driving through Gloucester when his car is hit by a lorry driven by a Mr Smith of Brighton. John Jones cannot sue in Newcastle County Court, but he can sue in Brighton County Court (where the defendant carries on business) or in Gloucester County Court (where the cause of action arose – i.e. where the accident happened).*

Illustration. *Jane Jones buys a TV set in an electrical shop in Bristol, although she lives in Bath. The shop is a company whose registered office is in London. Jane can sue in either Bristol or London.*

The Legal System

An action begun in the court for the area where the defendant lives or works is called an *in district* claim; if begun in the court where the cause of action arose it is an *out of district* claim.

Setting out the claim in writing

As the plaintiff, you must set out your claim in writing. This document is called the 'Particulars of Claim'.

The document should set out neatly and concisely the basis of the claim. It should state what is claimed and why the defendant is liable, but it need not give the evidence in support of your claim.

It is a good idea to set out the Particulars of Claim in numbered paragraphs. This is how lawyers do it – and it has the advantage of making the document more easy to understand. In addition, lawyers usually set out the claim in the third person (e.g. 'on the 3rd of May 1986 the plaintiff purchased . . .'). However, this is no more than a legal convention – if you prefer, you can set it out in the first person (e.g. 'on the 3rd of May 1986 I purchased . . .'). Look at the Specimen Particulars of Claim on page 911 to see how the document should be set out. You will also find a selection of useful precedent Particulars of Claim in the free booklet *Small Claims in the County Court* (from your local county court).

Your claim will be for damages – in other words, money compensation. To pursue this, you must bring a 'default' action.

Bringing a default action in the county court

1. Write to the defendant setting out details of the claim and asking whether he admits liability.
2. If the letter is ignored or if the correspondence does not look like leading to a settlement, write to the defendant giving him fourteen days' notice of your intention to commence county-court proceedings. It is a good idea to send the letter recorded delivery and to keep a copy.
3. Prepare the Particulars of Claim. Ensure that it is neatly typed. See page 911 for a typical Particulars of Claim. Put the name of the court in the top left, and then put the names of the parties in the centre – as in the specimen. Write 'Case No. . . .' in the top right corner; the court will insert the reference number of the case. You will need at least three copies: one for you, one for the defendant, and one for the court. Consider whether you should abandon any part of the claim that exceeds £500 (see page 872).

   To help DIY litigants, many county courts have standard Particulars of Claim forms which cover the usual DIY claims. Ask for copies of these standard forms and, if suitable, use them.
4. You can now start the court proceedings. Decide which court you are going to sue in (see page 877). The address of the court will be in the phone directory under 'courts'. Take, or send, to the court:

(a) *Request Form* (obtainable from the court) – this is your request that proceedings be commenced. The court will supply the correct form (there are different forms for in-district and out-of-district claims).

(b) *Two copies of the Particulars of Claim.*

(c) *Court fee*, paid in cash or postal order (not by cheque). The fee is not small. In 1985, the fee in claims of up to £300 was 10 per cent of the amount claimed. Between £300 and £500, the fee was £35; over £500, the fee was £40.

5. The court official will then prepare a Plaint Note and a summons. The Plaint Note will be sent to you, to confirm that proceedings have been begun and that the summons has been sent to the defendant. The summons is sent to the defendant, together with a copy of the particulars of claim.

6. What happens next will depend upon what the defendant decides to do.

If the defendant does nothing. If the defendant does not answer the claim within fourteen days of the service of the summons, you can enter judgement in default. You can do this by sending a form to the court (form N30, obtainable free from the court) together with the Plaint Note. You can ask that the defendant pay the amount owed immediately, or in instalments at a frequency you suggest. The court will then make this its order and tell the defendant. Experience shows that it is often unwise to ask for the whole sum to be paid immediately – if you have any doubts as to the defendant's ability to pay, it is better to accept realistic instalments.

If the defendant admits the claim. One of the forms sent to the defendant is an Admission Form. The defendant can admit the claim and, if he wishes, ask for time to pay. He sets out his income and financial liabilities on the form, and can make an offer in payment – for example, £5 per month. The defendant returns the form to the court, which then sends a copy to you.

As the plaintiff, you then have to decide whether to accept the defendant's proposal. If 'yes', write to the court (quoting the plaint number) saying you accept the offer; this should be done within eight days of your receiving the copy admission. If you do not want to accept the defendant's proposals, write to the court saying so (once again, quote the plaint number). The court will then fix a 'disposal date'. This is the date for an informal hearing when the registrar can decide how the defendant should pay off the debt. You can question the defendant as to his finances, but, in general, it is better to accept an offer of realistic instalments rather than obtain an order for instalments that the defendant cannot meet. You need not attend the 'disposal' but if not, it is essential that you write to the court asking that the registrar deal with the case in your absence, otherwise he may dismiss your case.

If the defendant denies the claim. The defendant may deny liability. Often, he will simply fill in the form that was sent to him by the court. On the other hand, he might instruct solicitors – in which case, they will probably prepare a formal typewritten defence (a specimen is shown on page 912). If he does put in a defence, then the court will fix a date for a preliminary hearing – a pre-trial review.

7. The date fixed by the court for the preliminary hearing – properly called the pretrial review – arrives. If the plaintiff has not heard from the defendant he should attend court with any paperwork needed to prove his claim (e.g. receipts, bills) and ask for judgement in default of defence.

The pre-trial review is not a formal court hearing. It is an informal meeting between the parties and a registrar of the court. The aim is not to determine liability or who is in the right. The pre-trial review is an opportunity to make the necessary preparations and orders for the full hearing of the case. For instance, either party could ask the registrar to order:

• more detail of the opponent's case. This is done by asking for 'Further and Better Particulars' of the defence or particulars of claim (e.g. if you say the defendant's negligent driving was in breach of the Highway Code, the defendant might write asking which paragraphs of the Highway Code you are referring to);

• supplying copies of relevant documents (e.g. copy letters from employers, showing wage loss; or copy receipt for work carried out).

If the claim is for no more than £500, the court will normally refer the case to arbitration, although either plaintiff or defendant can object and ask for it to be tried by the court in the usual way. It will be for him to show that the case is not suitable for hearing by an arbitrator (for example, because it is particularly complicated or involves difficult questions of law). If the claim is for more than £500, then arbitration will not be ordered unless either plaintiff or defendant makes an application to the court asking for arbitration.

Arbitration is a much more informal county-court hearing than the normal trial of a case. Rather than being a formal trial with all the rules of evidence (e.g. no hearsay evidence) arbitration is more relaxed and provides a less legalistic hearing. This is usually less intimidating to the DIY litigant. It will normally be advisable for the DIY litigator to have his case heard by an arbitrator, rather than by a county-court registrar or judge as a trial. The two important points about arbitration are:

• only rarely can an arbitrator's decision be appealed

• solicitors' costs will not normally be allowed if the claim is for not more than £500.

8. Both you and the defendant should prepare for the trial (or the arbitration hearing). All evidence should be collected together in readiness. Witnesses should be warned of the date of the trial – the parties will be notified of the date shortly after the pre-trial review.

As a DIY litigant you might find it useful to sit in on another county-court trial to see how the case is presented and how the court procedure works.

9. Next there is the trial. You can take a friend along to advise and assist (see page 875). You and your witnesses give evidence first. The defendant can cross-examine the witnesses. Then the defendant and his witnesses give evidence and

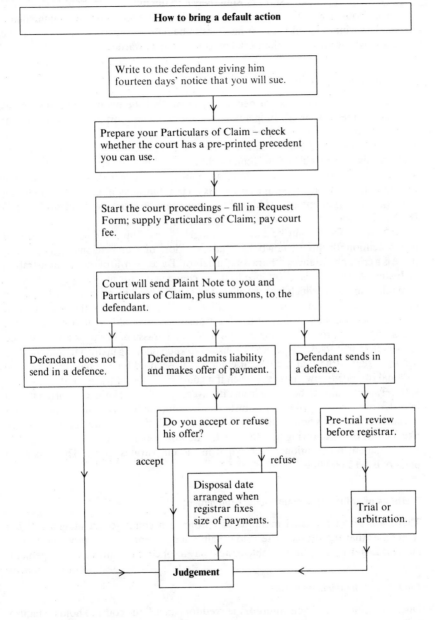

How to bring a default action

Write to the defendant giving him fourteen days' notice that you will sue.

Prepare your Particulars of Claim – check whether the court has a pre-printed precedent you can use.

Start the court proceedings – fill in Request Form; supply Particulars of Claim; pay court fee.

Court will send Plaint Note to you and Particulars of Claim, plus summons, to the defendant.

Defendant does not send in a defence.

Defendant admits liability and makes offer of payment.

Defendant sends in a defence.

Do you accept or refuse his offer?

Pre-trial review before registrar.

accept   refuse

Disposal date arranged when registrar fixes size of payments.

Trial or arbitration.

Judgement

they can be cross-examined by you. At the end of the evidence, both you and the defendant can make a short closing speech to the judge, who should be referred to as 'Your Honour'. The judge will probably deliver his judgement immediately. The winner should ask for his costs to be paid by the loser. However, if the claim was for no more than £500 no costs will be awarded.

Enforcing a money judgement

Obtaining judgement does not necessarily mean that the plaintiff will recover his damages or the debt owed. Judgement is no more than a court pronouncement that the money is owed. If the defendant does not pay the amount due, the plaintiff will have to go back to the court and ask that the judgement be enforced. There are various ways of enforcing a judgement but it should not be forgotten that they are all useless if the debtor does not have any money or assets with which to meet the judgement. If a debtor is penniless there is no point in suing him, let alone in trying to enforce a judgement against him: the money spent on court fees (and any lawyer's fees) will be wasted.

Judgements should only be enforced by legal means. Threats of violence may lead to prosecution for threatening behaviour, extortion, or even blackmail. In addition, there is a criminal offence of 'harassing' a debtor. By section 40 of the Administration of Justice Act 1970 it is an offence to try to coerce a debtor into paying up by:
● making demands which 'are calculated to subject him, or members of his family or household to alarm, distress, or humiliation'. The frequency of the demands and the way they are made will be crucial. For instance, it would be harassment to call late at night with rough-looking men; it might be harassment to park a van marked 'debt collector' outside the debtor's house or to keep phoning up throughout the day.
● falsely suggesting that the debtor could be prosecuted for not paying. It is not a criminal offence to owe money – even if a court has entered judgement.
● falsely pretending to be acting in an official capacity or to have an official document in order to enforce payment. For instance, it would be harassment for the creditor to call at the debtor's home claiming to be a court bailiff, and producing what looked like a court order allowing him to seize the debtor's possessions.

Harassment prosecutions are brought in the magistrates' court. The maximum penalty is a £2,000 fine.

Methods of enforcing a county-court judgement

There are seven principal methods of enforcing a county-court judgement; but remember that the prerequisite is to obtain a judgement (see the procedural steps above). Legal aid may be available to help pay a solicitor to enforce the judgement.

Finding out the debtor's means

Once judgement has been entered, the creditor can ask the court to hold an inquiry as to the debtor's means. The debtor can be ordered to produce his books and papers. He can be asked relevant questions if 'fairly pertinent and properly asked'. The hearing is intended to be a searching cross-examination as to the debtor's property and means. In an extreme case, refusal to answer a proper question could result in the debtor being sent to prison by a judge.

The hearing is in chambers in front of a court officer. The debtor's answers are written down and then read over to him. He will be asked to sign the transcript.

To apply for an oral examination the creditor applies to the county court covering the area where the debtor lives or carries on business. The application is made on form N316 (obtainable from the court) and a fee of £12 is payable. The creditor will then have to attend court to ask that an appointment be made. Usually the court will serve the attendance order and the expenses on the debtor. The debtor and creditor then attend the oral examination at the time stated on the order. At the examination the creditor should ask for an order that the debtor pays his legal costs.

Often the debtor will fail to attend the examination. When this happens, the court will adjourn to a new date and give notice to the debtor that he may be committed to prison if he does not attend. This court notice must be served personally on the debtor, at least five days before the new hearing date. In practice, this firm warning is usually enough to persuade the debtor to attend the new hearing. The debtor is then taken before the judge and suitably admonished and immediately ordered to attend before the registrar or higher executive officer straight away, so that the oral examination can take place without delay.

Putting a charge on the debtor's home

If the debtor owns a house or flat, the creditor can apply to the court for an order charging, i.e. mortgaging, the property with the judgement debt. If the judgement debt remains unpaid, the ultimate sanction is for the creditor to apply to the court for the debtor's property to be sold to pay the debt. This is so even if the debtor owns the property with someone else (e.g. if jointly owned with his/her spouse).

If the debtor does own property, this can be an effective sanction; the possibility that he might lose his home will often ensure that the debtor does all he can to pay off the debt. However, in practice the court will very rarely order the property to be sold.

To apply for a charging order, the creditor must swear an affidavit. The county court staff can advise on the correct wording. Form N393 is also needed; court fee is £12.

Sending in the bailiff

The creditor can ask the court to send the bailiff in, to seize the debtor's goods, and then auction them off to meet the judgement. This is called *levying execution*, or if the judgement is for arrears of rent, *distress against goods*. The creditor fills in form N323 (obtainable from the court), produces the Plaint Note to the court staff, and

The Legal System

pays a fee (15 per cent, up to a maximum fee of £30). There is no court hearing. The court will then 'issue execution' which authorizes the bailiff to enter the debtor's premises, which he will usually do two or three weeks later.

The bailiff can enter the premises either by day or by night, but not on a Sunday. He cannot break into the premises, although he can climb through an unlocked window. Once inside the building he can break down internal doors, if necessary. He can seize any goods or possessions belonging to the debtor, except essential clothes and tools and implements of trade up to the value of £250. However, he cannot seize goods belonging to someone else, so if the debtor's wife says they belong to her, the bailiff will probably not risk taking them. Similarly, hire-purchase items (which legally belong to the finance company, see page 566) cannot be seized.

It is usually advisable to have an oral examination of the debtor before sending in the bailiff (see above). Then if, for instance, the debtor claims his car is on hire purchase the creditor can demand to see the HP agreement. Note that HP is not the same as credit sale (see page 567) and goods being bought on credit can be seized. In recent years HP has declined in popularity (although many people who buy goods by instalments mistakenly think they are on HP whereas they are often being bought on credit sale).

When sending in the bailiff give him as much information as possible (e.g. colour, make, registration number of the debtor's car).

The bailiff impounds the goods, and if the debt is not paid off within five days, they can be sold off by auction. In practice, the goods are usually left on the debtor's premises rather than being carried away, and he will then have five days before the goods are taken from him.

Attachment of earnings

The court can make an order that regular deductions be made from the debtor's pay-packet by his employer, and that the debt be paid off in this way. In effect, it is Pay As You Earn via the courts.

However, an attachment of earnings order is only of use if the debtor has a steady job. If he is out of work, or if he changes jobs frequently, an order will be of no effect.

The creditor applies for an order by sending two copies of form N337 (obtainable from any county court) to the county court where the debtor resides (this may not be the same court, in which case ask that the proceedings be transferred to that court), together with the Plaint Note and court fee (usually 10 per cent of the amount due, up to a maximum of £30). A copy of the form is sent to the debtor, together with a reply form. The reply form requires the debtor to set out details of his employment, his income, and his financial commitments. The debtor is also asked how much he would be prepared to have deducted from his wages, on a regular basis.

If the court feels that more information is needed, it can ask the debtor, his employer, and other people, to provide information.

A hearing date is fixed, when the registrar will decide how much the debtor can afford to pay. This will be done by, first, calculating the 'protected earnings' figure – the amount below which the debtor's income should not fall. Often this will be equal to the supplementary-benefit rates for the debtor and his family. Then, the registrar will fix the 'normal deduction rate', which will be the amount usually deducted from the debtor's wages.

The debtor can never be left with less than his protected earnings figure. For instance, suppose the debtor earns £40 p.w. on average, and the registrar fixes a protected earnings figure of £30 p.w. and a normal deduction rate of £10. If in a particular week the debtor only earns £35, the deduction will be £5. If, next week, he earns £45, the deduction will still be £10 – not £15.

Once the registrar makes an order, a copy is sent to the debtor's employer. The employer then has seven days in which to start making the deductions. The money is sent direct to the court, which then forwards it to the creditor. The employer must tell the debtor of the deductions, and he can charge the debtor 50p for the administrative work of each deduction.

If the employee leaves his job, the employer has ten days in which to notify the court; failure to do so is an offence carrying a fine of up to £100. The debtor can also be fined up to £100 (and sometimes even sent to prison) if he does not tell the court when finishing and starting jobs.

In practice, attachment-of-earnings orders are usually of limited value. The sort of people who tend to get into debt rarely have steady jobs. Those that do often change jobs and simply disappear.

Maintenance arrears can be enforced by a magistrates' court attachment-of-earnings order (see page 66).

Intercepting money owed to the debtor

A creditor can apply to the court for an order that debts owed to the debtor be paid direct to the creditor, and that money in a bank account be paid out to him. This is called a garnishee order.

Generally, garnishee orders are little used. In fact, they can be very useful against a debtor who has the money to pay, or who is so hopelessly in debt that he does not bother to collect the few debts that are owed to him. Garnishee orders are usually used against firms and companies.

In practice, of course, the difficulty for the creditor is to find out who does owe money to the debtor or whether he has a bank account which is in credit.

The creditor applies for a garnishee order by swearing an affidavit on form N349 (obtainable from any county court), and delivering this to the court, with the Plaint Note, and fee of £12. If the proceedings are in a different court, he should ask the original court for a certificate of judgement and produce this when applying for the garnishee order. This is then served on the person who owes the debtor the money or the bank holding his money. If this person – called the garnishee – does not pay up, the case proceeds to a full trial, when the judge decides whether the garnishee should pay the money to the creditor.

Bankruptcy

This is a drastic step, and it will rarely be worth making the debtor bankrupt unless the sums involved are large. A bankruptcy petition is best handled by a solicitor. Note that a creditor can only petition for bankruptcy if he is owed £750 or more, unless he is petitioning with other creditors and between them the debts are £750 or more. The court fees are substantial when compared with the fees for other methods of enforcing a judgement. Accordingly, bankruptcy is rarely a realistic way of enforcing a judgement. However, merely taking the first step (i.e. serving a formal bankruptcy notice on the debtor – see page 590) can sometimes bring a result, assuming of course that the debtor has the money. This first stage costs little and may be a worthwhile ploy, but it is usually not worth going further and actually commencing bankruptcy proceedings. Generally, see page 586.

Making an administration order

A debtor can ask the court to help him organize his liabilities. The debtor tells the court of all his liabilities and the court then stays all other proceedings against him. Arrangements are then made for the debtor to pay off the debts in instalments often by an attachment-of-earnings order. So, the debtor can get his creditors 'off his back' by telling the court of his financial problems – and the court will then fix a realistic timetable for repayment of the debts by instalments.

The application for an administration order can only be made by the debtor himself. However, it might be worth while a creditor suggesting to the debtor that an administration order might give him a breathing space and a chance to put his affairs in order – which would be to the benefit of both debtor and creditor.

Starting proceedings in the magistrates' court

The DIY litigant will find that the procedure for commencing proceedings in the magistrates' court is straightforward. Typical DIY cases include:
- wife's application for maintenance
- affiliation application by mother of illegitimate child
- private prosecutions (see page 779)
- complaints about noise
- footpath and highway obstructions.
The procedure in all cases is basically the same.

1. Telephone the local magistrates' court and ask at what time of the day the court hears applications for summonses. This varies from court to court, but usually it is either 10 or 10.30 a.m., although some courts hear them at 2 p.m., the start of the afternoon session.
2. At the court, ask for the warrant officer's office. Tell him you want a summons issued and ask which court to go to.

3. Go to that court. There will probably be a policeman at the door of the court. Tell him you want to issue a summons. He will want to know your name, address, and the nature of your application. It is helpful if you can give the statutory authority for your application, but this is not essential (e.g. if you were a tenant applying for a statutory nuisance order against your landlord, you would say you wanted to issue a summons under section 99, Public Health Act 1936).

4. Wait inside the court. Eventually, your turn will come and your name will be called out by a police officer. You should then go to the front of the court and explain to the magistrate (or his clerk, if the magistrate is not sitting) why you want a summons issued. By telling the magistrate about the case you are said to be 'laying information' in a criminal case (i.e. a private prosecution), or 'making a complaint' in any other case. The magistrate will want to be sure that you have the basis of a case, although he will not expect you to prove your case at this stage. It might be useful to show him any documentary evidence in support of your application, and offer to call witnesses to support you.

   The magistrate should be referred to as 'Your Worship', unless s/he is a stipendiary (professional magistrate) in which case use 'Sir' or 'Madam'.

   If the magistrate decides that you have an arguable case, he will agree that a summons should be issued. If he turns down your application you will have to obtain more detailed and convincing evidence, and then apply again.

5. The police officer in the court will have written down details of the magistrate's order. He will give you his note. Take it to the general office of the court and tell the clerk that you have been granted a summons. Discuss the wording of the summons with them and ask them to issue the summons against the defendant.

6. The clerk (or sometimes the warrant officer) will fix a date for the hearing of the case. He will then issue the summons and serve it on the defendant for you.

7. Attend court on the date of the hearing with your witnesses. Don't forget that you can take a friend or helper into court with you (see page 875). The trial will be as in a criminal prosecution (see page 786).

More serious crimes

Private prosecutions can also be brought for cases that are tried in the crown court, but once the magistrates have committed the case to the crown court for trial (see page 795), the Crown will take over the prosecution and the private prosecutor will play no further part, unless, of course, he is called as a witness by the prosecution. If the Crown does not approve of the prosecution it can simply offer no evidence when the case comes before the crown-court judge; the prosecution will then be dismissed.

APPENDICES

Appendix 1
Useful Sources of Information

There are numerous records and registers that are open to public inspection. What follows is an A–Z summary of the more useful of these sources of information.

Unless otherwise stated, a fee is usually payable but details of fees and charges are not given here because they change so frequently. It is advisable to phone before making a search, to ascertain the amount of the fee.

Highly recommended is the *Directory of Registers and Records*, by Trevor Aldridge (Oyez Longman, 1984; £6.95), which contains full details of virtually all the numerous types of records that can be made available.

Addresses

The DHSS has an address for nearly every person over the age of fifteen. However, this address will normally only be revealed if it is needed for court proceedings (such as maintenance, affiliation, divorce cases).

The DHSS will sometimes forward letters to the recorded address if a sufficiently good reason is provided. The letter to be forwarded should be in a sealed envelope, and it should be sent with a covering letter to the DHSS, Special Section A, Records Branch, Newcastle-upon-Tyne. There is no fee.

Other possible sources of a person's address are the NHS records and the military sources. However, an address will normally only be revealed for the purpose of court proceedings.

See also 'Electoral Register'.

Adoption

There are two registers. The Registrar-General has kept the Adopted Children Register since January 1927 and a copy certificate (showing date and court of adoption, child's adopted name, names and addresses of adopting parents) can be supplied to any applicant. The second register cross-references the entry in the Adopted Children Register to the Births Register and enables the child's parent(s) to be identified. The cross-reference register is not open to the public although the adopted person may be able to make a search in it (see page 109).

Certificates from the Adopted Children Register can be obtained either in person (from the Registrar-General's office – see address in 'Births, Marriages and Deaths') or by post from the General Register Office, Registration Division, Titchfield, Fareham, Hants.

Bankruptcy

The presentation of bankruptcy petitions and the making of receiving orders are recorded in

Appendix 1

a central registry. Anyone can make a postal search of the alphabetical index by writing to the Superintendent, Land Charges Dept, Burrington Way, Plymouth.

Receiving orders are recorded in a register at Thomas Moore Building, Law Courts, Strand, London WC2, which is open to personal inspection by anyone.

Births, marriages, deaths

Copy certificates are available from the Registrar-General, General Register Office, St Catherine's House, 10 Kingsway, London WC2 (01-242 0262). Personal searches can be made on weekdays between 8.30 a.m. and 4.30 p.m. Search can also be made by post, either using the free application form or by sending a letter stating (at least) the date and place of the event and the full names.

Generally, the registers only date back to 1 July 1837; where the event occurred abroad, registers were only kept from July 1849. A separate register of still-births was started on 1 July 1927, but this register is not open to inspection unless the Registrar-General's permission is obtained.

See also 'Adoption'; 'Divorce'; 'Inquests and Post-Mortems'; 'Parish Records'; 'Probate and Letters of Administration'; 'Wills'.

Business names

Partnerships and sole traders used to have to register their business names (unless the business was in their proper names). The register was abolished in 1982, but records for 1972–82 were transferred to Business Registry Searches of Greyhound Chambers, Chepstow, Gwent (02912 70138). Post, phone, or telex searches can be made.

Cars

The name and address of the registered owner of a car can be obtained from the Drivers and Vehicle Licensing Centre, Swansea (0792 782576). The names and addresses of previous owners can also be supplied. Application can only be made by someone with reasonable cause for needing the information.

See also 'Hire Purchase'.

Change of name

There is no comprehensive register of changes of name. If the change of name was by deed poll it may have been enrolled with the Supreme Court, but this is not compulsory. Personal search can be made at Room 81, Royal Courts of Justice, Strand, London WC2 or if the deed poll was enrolled more than three years ago, at the Public Record Office, Chancery Lane, London WC2.

Other sources of information are:
● *An Index to Change of Name 1760–1901* (W. P. W. Phillimore and E. A. Fry, 1905) lists changes recorded in private Acts of Parliament, publications, etc., but is not completely comprehensive;
● Private Acts of Parliament;
● Register of Change of Name by Royal Licence kept by the College of Arms, Queen Victoria Street, London EC4.

Charities

Many charities are registered with the Charity Commissioners. Anyone can apply for the name of the charity, its constitution, objects, approximate annual income and the name and address of the person to whom any correspondence should be addressed.

A personal search should be made at the Charity Commission (Registration Division), St Alban's House, 57–60 Haymarket, London SW1 (01-214 8773).

Common land

County councils keep records of all common land and village greens, showing the land affected and the rights claimed, and giving details of anyone claiming to be the owner of the land.

Anyone can search in the register. Apply by post on form CR1 to the county council (they will supply the form).

Companies

Every company has a file with the Registrar of Companies. This gives detailed information as to its constitution, capital structure, shareholders, directors, secretary, registered office, accounts, auditor's reports, director's reports, mortgages and debentures, and associated companies.

A personal or postal search can be made with the Companies Registration Office, Cardiff (0222 388588). Copies of some of the documents on file are also available for inspection in Companies House, 55–71 City Road, London EC1 (01-253 9393).

In addition, every company has to keep a register of charges, register of members, register of directors and secretaries. These registers can be inspected by anyone, even if not a shareholder. Often these records are more up to date than those on the files of the Registrar of Companies.

Divorce

Anyone can apply for a copy of a decree nisi or decree absolute. The decree will show the name of the parties to whom the decree was granted, the grounds, and the date.

Personal application is made to the Principal Registry, Family Division, Room A44, Somerset House, Strand, London WC2 (01-405 7641). Once the applicant has found the entry in the index he can ask for a copy.

Doctors

The General Medical Council keeps a register of all medical practitioners, showing their names, address, qualifications, and date of first registration. Apply to General Medical Council, 44 Hallam Street, London W1 (01-580 7642).

Electoral Register

Anyone can inspect the Electoral Register, compiled by the appropriate local authorities. Copies are usually available for inspection in main post offices, public libraries, and the town hall. The register shows the names of every person living at a particular address who is eligible to vote.

893

Appendix 1

Highways and rights of way

Every district council and London borough council keeps a list of the highways in that area that are maintainable at public expense. Inquiry can be by post or in person; there is no fee. Rights of way are shown on the 1:50,000 Ordnance Survey maps, and on the statutory maps kept by the local authority under the National Parks and Access to the Countryside Act 1949 (see page 341).

Hire purchase

There is no general index of items that are currently on HP. However, there is a register of cars that are on HP (see page 525).

Housing associations

Housing associations are required to register with the Housing Corporation. This register can be inspected by anyone. It shows the association's registered office, its address for correspondence, the type of dwellings provided, its constitution, and accounts for the last three years.

Application is made to the Housing Corporation, Registration and Supervision Division, 149 Tottenham Court Road, London W1 (01-387 9406). More limited information is available from the regional offices of the Housing Corporation.

Inquests and post-mortems

A coroner is obliged to keep all documents concerning an inquest, including any post-mortem report. These will include the coroner's own notes of the evidence given by witnesses at the inquest.

The documents can be inspected free of charge by a person with a legitimate interest, but not by any person who is merely curious. Copies can usually be supplied on payment of a fee. The documents are kept for fifteen years and then may be destroyed.

Legal stationery

Legal forms and books on law can be obtained from any Oyez shop (head office: Oyez House, 237 Long Lane, London SE1 (01-407 8055).

Naturalization

When a person is naturalized, details of his or her full name, address, country of origin, and date of naturalization are published.

Prior to 1961 annual lists were published by HMSO, but since then monthly lists have been published in the *London Gazette*. Inquiries to Home Office, Lunar House, Wellesley Road, Croydon (01-681 3421).

Parish records

Records of burials, marriages, and baptisms are kept in many parish churches, but the extent and completeness of the records varies considerably.

Anyone can apply to inspect the records. Application is made to the incumbent, but if he does not have the records, or does not know where they are, application is made to the Diocesan Record Office or the County Record Office.

Many nonconformist registers are now in the Public Record Office.

Planning applications

Local planning authorities keep registers of all applications for planning permission, and records of whether they were granted. Anyone can inspect the register and obtain copies for a fee.

Probate and letters of administration

Records are kept of every grant, including the name and address of the deceased and the personal representatives, and the value of the estate. Postal or personal application should be made to the Principal Registry, Family Division, Somerset House, Strand, London W C2 (01-405 7641).

Registered land

Anyone can inquire whether a particular piece of land has a registered title. Apply in writing to the appropriate Land Registry (see page 201). The register itself, showing who is the owner of the land and any mortgages or charges affecting it, is not open to public inspection. Only the proprietor (i.e. the owner), or someone applying with his written consent, can obtain a copy.

Registered rents

The rent tribunal fixes rents for tenants with resident landlords; the rent officer fixes rents for other tenants. (See Chapter 16). The rent officer keeps records of all rents he has fixed, including a brief description of the premises, the rent payable (and whether it includes rates), any part of the rent which is for services provided by the landlord, the names and addresses of the tenant and the landlord, and particulars of any furniture and services provided by the landlord.

In the same way, the rent tribunal keeps a register of the rents they have fixed. The rent tribunal's register will also specify which parts of the property are occupied by the tenant alone and which parts are occupied jointly with the landlord.

The registers can be searched by anyone on personal application.

Road accidents

If the police took details of an accident a copy of the policeman's notes and any witness statements can be obtained. The notes will usually show the names and addresses of those involved and any witnesses, the time, place, and date of the accident, any injury or damage caused, and the insurance particulars of the driver. The report will generally not be provided until any criminal prosecution arising from the accident has been completed.

Apply by letter to the chief constable of the district, specifying the date, time, and location.

Appendix 1

Service records

Army. Full service records of non-officers who were discharged before 1900 are kept in the Public Record Office, Chancery Lane, London WC2 (01-405 0741). These records are open to anyone.

Post-1900 records and the records of officers are only available to the soldier, someone applying with his consent, or to his next-of-kin. The inquiry should be addressed to the record office of the regiment or corps concerned unless it relates to an officer, in which case application is made to the Army Records Centre, Hayes, Middlesex.

Navy. Similar restrictions apply as with the army, above.

Air force. Records can only be inspected by the serviceman or someone applying with his written consent. For officers, application is made to PM(AR)1b(R.A.F.), R.A.F. Barnwood, Eastern Avenue, Gloucester. For airmen, apply to P(Man)3e(2)a, R.A.F. Personnel Management Centre, R.A.F. Innsworth, Glos.

Sewers and pipelines

Local authorities keep maps showing the routes of sewers and pipelines. Anyone can inspect these maps free of charge.

Solicitors

The Law Society keeps a computerized roll of the names of all solicitors. Anyone can search the roll, free of charge, at the Law Society, 113 Chancery Lane, London WC2 (01-242 1222).

Tree-preservation orders

If a local authority has made a tree-preservation order, anyone can inspect the order at the council's office and pay for a copy. The order will identify the tree concerned.

Wards of court

A Ward Book is kept of all infants who have been made wards of court. Application for information can only be made by a person with a legitimate interest.

Apply in person to Room 169, Royal Courts of Justice, Strand, London WC2. There is no fee.

Wills

Copies of wills lodged when probate or letters of administration were taken out can be obtained by any applicant.

A personal search is first made at the Principal Family Registry, Family Division, Strand, London WC2 (01-405 7641), for the reference number of the will. A copy can then be inspected. Application can also be made by post.

Wills and Their Whereabouts, by B.G. Bourne, revised by Anthony J. Camp (3rd edn, Phillimore, 1965), has details of the location of wills of people who died before 1858.

The Principal Probate Registry operates a scheme that allows people to deposit their will with the registry so that there is no danger of its being lost on their death (see page 161). The index of people who have deposited a will is open to inspection by anyone (apply in person to Room 28, Somerset House, or by post to the Record Keeper, the Principal Probate Registry) but the will cannot be inspected.

Appendix 2
Specimen Legal Forms

Acknowledgements

The forms on pages 899–901, 903 and 907 are Crown copyright and are reproduced with the permission of the Controller of Her Majesty's Stationery Office; the forms on pages 904–6 are reproduced with the permission of HM Land Registry, whose help in preparing the forms is gratefully acknowledged; the legal-aid forms, pages 908–10, are reproduced with the permission of the Law Society; the form of Contract of Sale by reference to the National Conditions of Sale, pages 210–11, and the actual conditions themselves, are the copyright of the Solicitors' Law Stationery Society plc, and may not be reproduced without permission.

Divorce Petition — Matrimonial Causes Rules

(1) Delete as appropriate.

IN THE .... COUNTY COURT[1]

No. 89D0703

IN THE DIVORCE REGISTRY[1]

(1) On the 16th day of March 19?, the petitioner PETER MORRIS was lawfully married to MICHAEL MORRIS (hereinafter called the respondent) at the Register Office in the District of Paddington in the City of Westminster

(2) The petitioner and the respondent last lived together at 4 Abingdon Cottages, London NE1.

(3) The petitioner is domiciled in England and Wales, and is by occupation a Kitchen assistant and resides at 4 Abingdon Cottages, London NE1 and the respondent is by occupation a Mechanic and resides at 93 Clifton Road, London NE5

(4) There are no children of the family now living (except) Michael Joseph Morris, born 12th February 1969

(5) No other child now living has been born to the (petitioner)* (respondent)† (so far as is known to the petitioner)† during the marriage (except—

(6) There are or have been no other proceedings in any court in England and Wales or elsewhere with reference to the marriage (or to any child of the family) or between the petitioner and the respondent with reference to any property of either or both of them (except)

(7) There are no proceedings continuing in any country outside England and Wales which are in respect of the marriage or are capable of affecting its validity or subsistence (except)

(8) No agreement or arrangement has been made or is proposed to be made between the parties for the support of the (respondent)† (petitioner)* (and the said children) (except)

(9) The said marriage has broken down irretrievably.

(10) The respondent has committed adultery with a woman unknown (hereinafter called the co-respondent) and the petitioner finds it intolerable to live with the respondent.

SPECIMEN

SPECIMEN

Statement of arrangements for children (see p.46)

Statement as to Arrangements for Children—Matrimonial Causes Rules—Form 4

*) Delete as appropriate.

IN THE   **COUNTY COURT**[1]

No. 8400708

~~IN THE DIVORCE REGISTRY~~[1]

Between   PETER MORRIS   Petitioner

and   MICHAEL MORRIS   Respondent

and   WORRA VARAKORN)   Co-Respondent

State in respect of each child.

The proposed arrangements for the children of the family under 16 and those over 16 but under 18 who are receiving instruction at an educational establishment or under-going training for a trade, profession or vocation are as follows:—

(i) residence : The child, Michael Joseph Morris, aged 11, resides in a house at 4 Abingdon Cottages, London NE1 which is council accommodation. It is intended that he will continue to reside there. The premises comprise two bedrooms, a kitchen, living room, bathroom and toilet.

(ii) education etc. The said Michael Joseph Morris attends St George's School, Cambridge Road, London NE1

Divorce petition (continued)

The petitioner therefore prays:

(1) That the said marriage may be dissolved.

(2) That the petitioner may be granted the custody of Michael Joseph Morris

(3) That the   may be ordered to pay the costs of this suit.

(4) That the petitioner may be granted the following ancillary relief:

(a) an order for maintenance pending suit
     a periodical payments order
     a secured provision order
     a lump sum order

(b) a periodical payments order
     a secured provision order   } for the children of the family
     a lump sum order

(c) a property adjustment order

signed   Peter Morris

The names and addresses of the persons to be served with this petition are:—

Respondent: Michael Morris, 93 Clifton Road, London NE5

Co-respondent:

The petitioner's address for service is   4 Abingdon Cottages London NE1

Dated this 4th day of November 1985

Address all communications for the court to: The Registrar, County Court,

The court office at

is open from 10 a.m. to 4 p.m. (4.30 p.m. at the Divorce Registry) on Mondays to Fridays.

Statement of arrangements for children (continued)

(iii) financial position

The petitioner supports the said child on supplementary benefit, and it is intended to make a claim for financial relief.

(iv) access

At present the respondent enjoys reasonable access and the petitioner has no objection to reasonable access continuing.

SPECIMEN

Statement of arrangements for children (continued)

State whether or not the said child(ren) are suffering from serious disabilities or chronic illness or from the effects of such illness.

The said child is not so suffering or so affected by illness.

State whether or not the said child(ren) are under the care or supervision of a welfare officer or officer appointed by a local authority or other person or organisation.

The said child is not under care or supervision as so stated.

Dated this *4th* day of *November* 19 *86*

Signed *Petra Morris*

petitioner

Address all communications for the court to: The Registrar, County Court

The court

office at

is open from 10 a.m. to 4 p.m. (4.30 p.m. in the Divorce Registry) on Mondays to Fridays.

SPECIMEN

Appendix 2

Affidavit (see page 88)

In the matter of the Domestic Violence and Matrimonial Proceedings Act 1976

B E T W E₋,E N :

PETRA MORRIS   Applicant

- and -

MICHAEL MORRIS   Respondent

A F F I D A V I T

I, PETRA MORRIS unemployed of 4 Abingdon Cottages, London NE1 the above-named Applicant, herein MAKE OATH and SAY as follows:

1.   On the 16th March, 1968 I married Michael Morris, the above-named Respondent. There is one child of the marriage, Michael Joseph Morris born on the 12th February, 1969.

2.   For a very long period of time I have been subjected to violent assaults and abuse by the Respondent. On the 19th December, 1983 I petitioned in the Willesden County Court for divorce on the grounds that my marriage had irretrievably broken down by virtue of the Respondent's behaviour towards me. A copy of that Petition is now produced and shown to me marked 'PM1' the contents of which are true and to which I crave leave to refer...

4.   In the course of the divorce proceedings before the Willesden County Court I agreed to attempt a reconciliation with the Respondent and the said Petition was dismissed by consent before the Learned Registrar on the 5th September, 1984.

5.   The reconciliation never really worked and the Respondent continued his drunken violent behaviour towards me. The Respondent has received I estimate between £17,000 to £18,000 at the end of 1984 for agreed damages for injuries sustained in an accident and he is in the process of drinking his way through that money. I estimate he has about £4,000 remaining. He has continued to get drunk almost every day and every night and the beatings have hardly stopped...

11.   I have myself been drinking heavily recently because I am so shattered by the Respondent's behaviour. My General Practitioner has now prescribed tablets to prevent me drinking so heavily which have been successful. I remain terrified of the Respondent and dread him coming home...

13.   The Respondent is not working at all. He is just drunk the whole time and frequently collapses unconscious in the matrimonial home, defecating and vomiting over his clothes and the furniture. I understand that the Respondent draws Supplementary Benefit in respect of me and the child.

14.   I have attempted on several occasions now to reconcile with the Respondent. I now believe that my marriage to him is completely at an end and I shall instruct my Solicitor shortly to prepare a Petition for divorce. I also believe that unless restrained by order of this Honourable Court the Respondent will continue to assault and injure on every occasion that the opportunity to do so arises. I accordingly pray for an order in the terms of my application.

SWORN at   100 Hill Street, London NE 1
this 23rd day of October 1986

Before me J Jones, SOLICITOR

Petra Morris

Injunction (see pages 85, 88)

BEFORE <u>HIS HONOUR JUDGE TAYLOR</u> SITTING IN CHAMBERS

County Court

No. of Matter: 89356247

Power of arrest attached to injunction under Section 2 of
Domestic Violence and Matrimonial Proceedings Act 1976.

Applicant: PETRA MORRIS

SEAL.

Respondent: MICHAEL MORRIS

[here set out the injunction]

UPON HEARING Counsel for the Applicant and the Respondent in person and on the
Respondent undertaking for a period of six months from today.

1)   Not to assault or molest the Applicant PETRA MORRIS.

2)   To vacate the premises situate at 4 ABINGDON COTTAGES, LONDON NE1 by not
later than 2.00 p.m. on the 14th September 1986.

3)   Not to enter or attempt to enter the said premises after he has vacated
them as aforesaid except for the purpose of access to <u>MICHAEL JOSEPH MORRIS</u>
in accordance with arrangements agreed to in writing by the Applicant and/or
her Solicitors or a Court Order.

AND IT IS FURTHER ORDERED

that there be no order as to costs (save that the costs of the Applicant be
taxed on a Common Fund Basis in accordance with the provisions of the 2nd
Schedule to the Legal Aid Act 1974)

AND LET THE RESPONDENT <u>MICHAEL MORRIS</u> TAKE NOTICE THAT UNLESS HE OBEYS THE
DIRECTIONS CONTAINED IN THIS ORDER HE WILL BE GUILTY OF CONTEMPT OF COURT AND
WILL BE LIABLE TO BE COMMITTED TO PRISON.

DATED THIS 12th DAY OF SEPTEMBER 1986

~~POWER OF ARREST~~

~~AND the Judge being satisfied that the Respondent has caused actual bodily harm to the Applicant [or the child concerned]
and being of opinion that he is likely to do so again, a power of arrest is attached to this injunction whereby any constable
may arrest without warrant a person whom he has reasonable cause for suspecting of being in breach of the injunction as
mentioned in Section 2(3) of the Domestic Violence and Matrimonial Proceedings Act 1976.~~

Address all communications to the Chief Clerk, County Court,
quoting the number of the matter mentioned above.
The Court Office is open from 10 am - 4 pm, Monday to Friday.

Form 411: Order 46, Rule 28(3): Power of Arrest attached to Injunction, DV&MP Act 1976.

MCR 25703/1/8093730 650 2/80 TL

SPECIMEN

Draft transfer for registered land (see page 216)

Draft transfer for registered land (continued)

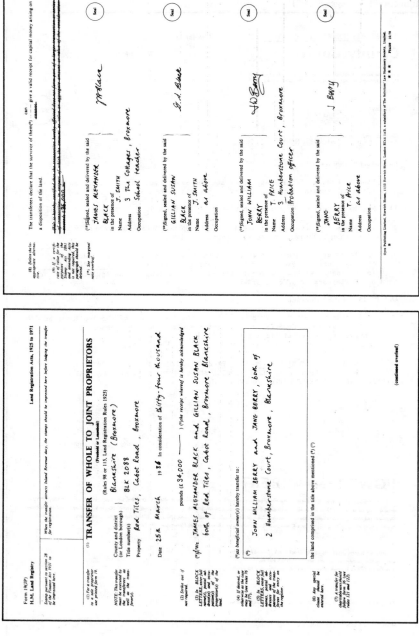

SPECIMEN

Land Registry certificate (see page 209)   Land Registry certificate (continued)

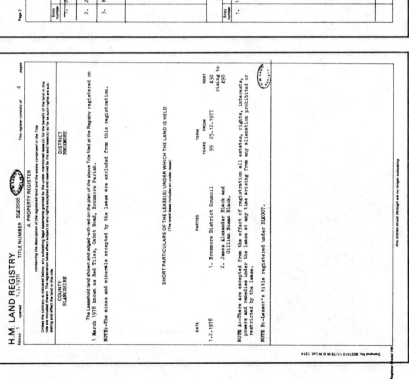

H.M. LAND REGISTRY
Edition 1 opened 1.3.1978 TITLE NUMBER BLK2088 This register consists of 4 pages

A. PROPERTY REGISTER
containing the description of the registered land and the estate comprised in the Title

Unless the contrary is indicated below, any subsisting legal easements granted by the under-mentioned lease(s) for the benefit of the land in this title are included therein. The registration takes effect subject to any rights excepted and reserved by the said lease(s) so far as such rights are subsisting and affect the land in this title.

COUNTY BLANKSHIRE

DISTRICT BROXMORE

The Leasehold land shown and edged with red on the plan of the above Title filed at the Registry registered on 1 March 1978 known as Red Tiles, Cabot Road, Broxmore Parish.

NOTE—The mines and minerals excepted by the lease are excluded from this registration.

SHORT PARTICULARS OF THE LEASE(S) UNDER WHICH THE LAND IS HELD
(The word lease includes an under-lease)

DATE	PARTIES	TERM		RENT
		YEARS	FROM	
1.2.1978	1. Broxmore District Council	99	25.12.1977	£30 rising to £90
	2. James Alexander Black and Gillian Susan Black.			

NOTE A:—There are excepted from the effect of registration all estates, rights, interests, powers and remedies under the lease at any time arising from any alienation prohibited or restricted by the lease.

NOTE B:—Lessor's title registered under BLK007.

Any entries struck through are no longer subsisting

SPECIMEN

Demand No 8037410117/79 W B W Ltd 1314

Page 2   TITLE NUMBER BLK2088

B. PROPRIETORSHIP REGISTER
stating nature of the Title, name, address and description of the proprietor of the land and any entries affecting the right of disposing thereof

TITLE ABSOLUTE

Entry number	Proprietor, etc.
1.	~~JAMES ALEXANDER BLACK and GILLIAN SUSAN BLACK, his wife, both of Red Tiles, Cabot Road, Broxmore, Blankshire. SUBJECT TO ... as on 1 March 1978~~
2.	JOHN WILLIAM BERRY and JANE BERRY, his wife, both of Red Tiles, Cabot Road, Broxmore, Blankshire, 2BR 9LA, registered on 1 May 1986
3.	RESTRICTION registered on 1 May 1980:—No disposition by one proprietor of the land (being the survivor of joint proprietors and not being a trust corporation) under which capital money arises is to be registered except under an order of the registrar or of the Court.

C. CHARGES REGISTER
containing charges (and registered dealings therewith), private easements, restrictive covenants, under-leases and other incumbrances

Entry number	The date at the beginning of each entry is the date on which the entry was made on the edition of the register	Remarks
1.	March 1978:—A Conveyance of the land in this title dated 27 April 1918 and made between (1) James Brown (Vendor) and (2) John Daniel Smith (Purchaser) contains the following covenants:—	

"And the Purchaser for himself his heirs and assigns hereby covenants with the Vendor and his assigns at all times hereafter to observe and perform all and every of the stipulations and conditions contained in the Schedule hereto.

THE SCHEDULE above referred to

1. No building to be erected on the land shall be used other than as a private dwellinghouse.

2. No building to be erected as aforesaid shall be converted into or used as a boarding house.

3. The front garden of the premises shall at all times be kept in neat and proper order and condition.

4. No aerial posts or wires erected upon or over the premises shall be of an unsightly appearance or be otherwise calculated to cause any annoyance or damage to the owners or occupiers of any adjoining property."

Any entries struck through are no longer subsisting

SPECIMEN

Land Registry certificate (continued)

Land Registry certificate (continued)

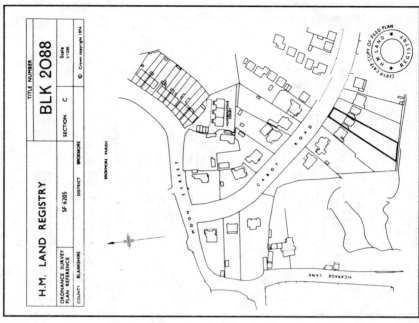

H.M. LAND REGISTRY

	TITLE NUMBER
	BLK 2088

ORDNANCE SURVEY PLAN REFERENCE	SF 6205	SECTION C	Scale 1/1250
COUNTY BLANKSHIRE	DISTRICT BROXMORE		© Crown copyright 1974

CERTIFIED COPY OF FILED PLAN
H M LAND REGISTRY

BROXMORE PARISH

LEWES MOON STREET

CABOT ROAD

VICARAGE LANE

SPECIMEN

TITLE NUMBER BLK2088

Page 3

C. CHARGES REGISTER

containing charges, incumbrances etc. adversely affecting the land and registered dealings therewith

Entry number	The date at the beginning of each entry is the date on which the entry was made on this edition of the register	Remarks
2.	~~March 1986—Charge dated 30 December 1985 registered on 1 March 1986~~ to secure the moneys including the further advances therein mentioned.	
3.	PROPRIETOR—THE NATIONAL BUILDING SOCIETY of Society House, The Avenue, ~~Weyford~~ Blankshire, 1WY 2AB, registered on 1 March 1974.	
4.	1 May 1986—CHARGE dated 25 March 1986 registered on 1 May 1986 to secure the monies therein mentioned.	
5.	PROPRIETOR—REPUTABLE BUILDING SOCIETY (Account No.12670) of Plumb Lane, High Street, Weyford, Blankshire, 1WY6DB registered on 1 May 1986.	
6.	1 December 1986—CHARGE dated 30 November 1986 registered on 1 December 1986 to secure the moneys including the further advances therein mentioned.	
7.	PROPRIETOR—SAFEWAY BANK LIMITED (Co.Regn. No.4761) of 17 Church Street, Weyford, Blankshire, 1WY 5AB, registered on 1 December 1986.	

Any entries struck through are no longer subsisting

Demand No 8706652 8/80 W B W Ltd 1314

IR 25

SPECIMEN

Rent registration certificate (see pages 254–5)

Rent Act 1977	**⌐RENT REGISTER**

Registration Area: Registration No:

PREMISES

Address
and
description:

Clifton Road, Hill Park, London NE5. Non self-contained 2nd
floor flat over shop comprising 1 room, kitchen, separate w.c.
and shared bathroom/w.c.

TENANCY

Tenant's name
(and address if different from above):

Landlord's name and address: Landlord's agent's name and address:

		Commenced on:	Term:
~~Contractual~~	*Statutory	——	——
Rental Period:	General Rate borne by: † Landlord	Other rates borne by: † Landlord	Present Rateable Value:

Allocation of liability for repairs:

In accordance with agreement between A——— Esq. and B——— Esq. for one year
from 21.6.83. Copy in possession of the Rent Officer. Section 32 & 33 of the
Housing Act 1961 apply to the tenancy.

Services provided by landlord:

Constant hot water in shared bathroom/w.c.
Lighting and furnishing of common parts.

Furniture provided by landlord:

In accordance with inventory in possession of the Rent Officer.

Other terms of tenancy taken into consideration in determining fair rent:

None

REGISTRATION	Application made by:	Application received on: 15.12.85	Supported by Certificate of Fair Rent No: ——
Certificate of Fair Rent issued on:	Last Registration dated:	Effective from:	Registration No:

Rent Register Sheet	(a) RENT determined by RENT OFFICER (EXCLUSIVE of rates †): £65 per calendar month	(d) Amount due to furniture and/or services not counting for rent allowance purposes: £20
		(e) Noted Amount attributable to services: £5 per month

(b) Registered on: 9.6.86	(c) Effective from: 15.12.85	(f) Service Element: Nil

(g) REMARKS: Rates are payable from the landlord and are recoverable from the tenant.	If this case has been referred to a RENT ASSESSMENT COMMITTEE or there has been an application for CANCELLATION insert a cross in the box below. Details of RAC decision or CANCELLATION are specified overleaf.

* *Delete as appropriate*
† Where a tenant pays rent inclusive of rates the landlord is entitled to collect the rates in addition to the rent and may increase the rent
to cover increases in rates.
Particulars of INITIAL REPAIRS (where a statutory tenancy has arisen by virtue of Part I, Landlord and Tenant Act 1954) are
DETAILED OVERLEAF where appropriate.

Appendix 2

Legal Aid Form No. 1 (see page 849)

Form A1
GENERAL

THE LAW SOCIETY
LEGAL AID ACT 1974

 LEGAL AID
ENGLAND and WALES

APPLICATION FOR
LEGAL AID CERTIFICATE

OFFICIAL
USE
ONLY

Surname (Block Letters)   ~~Mr.~~ Mrs. ~~Miss.~~
MORRIS

Forenames
PETRA

Permanent Address
4 Abingdon Cottages,
London NE1

Address for correspondence if different from Permanent Address

Occupation **Unemployed**

Date of Birth **27 June 1949**

(side text, rotated): If you have difficulty in completing this form you may be eligible for advice and assistance from a solicitor under Section 1 of the Legal Aid Act 1974 (known as the "Green Form" Scheme).

The proceedings for which I apply for legal aid are:—

To apply for an injunction and other relief under the Domestic Violence and Matrimonial Proceedings Act 1976

Have the proceedings already begun? **YES** | NO

Are you covered by insurance wholly or in part in respect of the claim? **YES** | NO

My opponent(s) is (are):—

Name
Michael Morris

Address
4 Abingdon Cottages, London NE1

The solicitor I wish to act for me is
John White   Has he agreed to act for you? YES | NO

Firm's name and address
Smith and Jones,
12 Park Road, London NE1

List of papers which accompany this Application Form:—

Affidavit of applicant

Any correspondence relating to an attempt to settle the claim **must** be forwarded.

Have you previously applied for a legal aid certificate in this or any other matter? **YES** | NO

If you have
—please give the reference number(s):

or please give as many particulars as you can, including the approximate date on which the application was made, your surname (if it was different from your present surname) and address at the time.

Have you received advice and assistance from a solicitor under the "Green Form" Scheme in respect of the matter for which you now apply for legal aid? YES | **NO**

October 1977

SPECIMEN

908

LA/Rep/6A
GREEN FORM

THE LAW SOCIETY

LEGAL AID
ENGLAND and WALES

Key Card

SOLICITOR'S REPORT ON LEGAL ADVICE AND ASSISTANCE GIVEN UNDER
THE LEGAL AID ACT 1974

PLEASE USE BLOCK CAPITALS

Surname	BROWN	Forenames	Male/Female	AREA REF No.
		Jane Mary		
Address	3 Clifton Avenue, London W9		

CAPITAL		CLIENT	£ 50	Ⓐ
TOTAL SAVINGS and OTHER CAPITAL		SPOUSE	£ 100	
		TOTAL	£150	

INCOME
State whether in receipt of Supplementary Benefit or Family Income Supplement.
YES/NO   If the answer is YES ignore the rest of this Section.   Ⓑ

Total weekly Gross Income

Client	£ nil
Spouse	£ 100
TOTAL	£ 100

Allowances and Deductions from Income

Income tax	£ 14	Ⓒ
National Health Contributions, etc.	£ 2·50	Ⓓ
Spouse	£ 32·25	Ⓔ

Dependent children and/or other dependants	Number		
Under 5		£	
5 but under 11	2	£ 28·80	
11 „ „ 13		£	Ⓕ
13 „ „ 16		£	
16 „ „ 18		£	
18 and over		£	

LESS TOTAL DEDUCTIONS	➡	£77·55
TOTAL WEEKLY DISPOSABLE INCOME		£ 22·45

TO BE COMPLETED AND SIGNED BY CLIENT

I am over the compulsory school-leaving age.

I have/have not previously received help from a solicitor about this matter under the Legal Aid and Advice Schemes.

I am liable to pay a contribution not exceeding .. .. £ nil   Ⓖ

I understand that any money or property which is recovered or preserved for me may be subject to a deduction if my contribution (if any) is less than my Solicitor's charges.

The information on this page is to the best of my knowledge correct and complete. I understand that dishonesty in providing such information may lead to a prosecution.

Date 18/4/86   Signature J. M. Brown

NOTE TO SOLICITORS
With effect from 1st April 1977

Where advice and assistance are being given in respect of divorce or judicial separation proceedings and the work to be carried out includes the preparation of a petition, the solicitor will be entitled to ask for his claim for Costs and Disbursements to be assessed up to an amount referred to in a general authority given by the Area Committee to exceed the prescribed basic sum in such cases.

Appendix 2

LEGAL AID
ENGLAND and WALES

THE LAW SOCIETY

Please see over for
explanatory notes.

Green Form

GREEN FORM KEY CARD
(No. 15)
Effective from 26th November 1984

CAPITAL means the amount or value of every resource of a capital nature
In computing Disposable Capital disregard
(i) the value of the main or only dwelling house in which the client resides, and
(ii) the value of household furniture and effects, articles of personal clothing and tools or implements of the client's trade, and
(iii) the subject matter of the advice and assistance.

Maximum Disposable Capital for Financial Eligibility
£765 client with no dependants.
£965 „ „ 1 dependant (whether spouse, child or other relative)
£1085 „ „ 2 such dependants
£1145 „ „ 3 such dependants
(Add £60 for each additional dependant.)

The capital and weekly income of both husband and wife must be taken into account, unless:
(a) they have a contrary interest;
(b) they live apart; or
(c) it is inequitable or impracticable to aggregate their means.
If a housewife living with her husband is seeking advice in connection with a matter in which he has a contrary interest, the money which she receives from him for normal household expenses should not be included as part of her own separate income.

INCOME means the total income from all sources which the client received or became entitled to during or in respect of the seven days up to and including the date of this application.

Note – a client in receipt of supplementary benefit or family income supplement is entitled to advice and assistance without contribution provided that his disposable capital is within the limits set out in **A** above.

In computing Disposable Income deduct:-
(i) Income Tax
(ii) Payments under the Social Security Acts 1975-80

These deductions also apply to the spouse's income if there is aggregation.

(iii) £32.25 in respect of either husband or wife (if living together) whether or not their means are aggregated. Where they are separated or divorced, the allowance will be the actual maintenance paid by the client in respect of the previous 7 days.

(iv) £14.40 for each dependant child or dependant relative of the household under 11 years of age
£21.52 for each dependant child or dependant relative of the household of 11 but under 16 years of age
£25.95 for each dependant child or dependant relative of the household of 16 and 17 years of age
£33.67 for each dependant child or dependant relative of the household of 18 years of age or over

There is no deduction in relation to a foster child.

Client's Contributions

Disposable Income	Maximum Contribution	Disposable Income	Maximum Contribution
Not exceeding £51 a week	nil	Not exceeding £79 a week	£28
„ £59 „	£5	„ £83 „	£33
„ £63 „	£11	„ £87 „	£37
„ £67 „	£15	„ £91 „	£41
„ £71 „	£20	„ £95 „	£46
„ £75 „	£24	„ £99 „	£50
		„ £104 „	£55
		„ £108 „	£60

Where the initial green form limit is £50 client's contribution in excess of this amount can only be called for if a financial extension has been obtained from the general committee.

Note

The green form must be signed by the client at the initial interview as soon as his eligibility has been determined except in the case of an authorised postal application.

SPECIMEN

IN THE SHOREDITCH COUNTY COURT   Plaint No. 891234567

B E T W E E N

                    MICHAEL MORRIS   (Plaintiff)
                          and
                    BRIAN EVANS   (Defendant)

                    PARTICULARS OF CLAIM

1. The Plaintiff is and was the owner of a Cortina motor vehicle registration number ABC 123

2. On or about the 7th April 1985 the Plaintiff was driving his motor vehicle on a road known as Ritson Road, London W8. As he was making a right turn into Stannard Road, W8 a Mini motor vehicle, registration number XYZ 789 driven by the Defendant reversed and collided with the Plaintiff's motor vehicle.

3. The collision was caused by the negligence of the Defendant.

                    PARTICULARS

The Defendant was negligent in that he:

(a) Failed to keep any or any proper lookout.

(b) Failed to take any or any adequate precautions to ascertain whether the road behind was clear before reversing his vehicle.

(c) Reversed and continuing to reverse the vehicle without first ascertaining or ensuring that it was safe to do so.

(d) Failed to give any or any adequate warning of his intention to reverse.

(e) Collided with the Plaintiff while reversing the vehicle.

(f) Failed to heed the presence of the Plaintiff.

(g) Drove too fast in the circumstances.

(h) Failed to stop, to slow down or in any other way so to manage or control the vehicle or to avoid the collision.

4. As a result the Plaintiff has suffered loss and damage.

                    PARTICULARS

Cost of repair to Plaintiff's motor vehicle   £161.65

Bus fares of a friend of the Plaintiff who lent his
car to him while it was being repaired   £ 12.00

Loss of use of the vehicle   £

AND THE PLAINTIFF CLAIMS:

1. Damages not exceeding £400

2. Costs.

30th November 1985
                                          Michael Morris
                                          93 Clifton Road
To the Registrar of the Court   London NE1
and to the Defendant

SPECIMEN

Appendix 2
Defence (see pages 878–82)

IN THE SHOREDITCH COUNTY COURT   Plaint No 891234567

BETWEEN

MICHAEL MORRIS   Plaintiff

and

BRIAN EVANS   Defendant

D E F E N C E

---

1. The Defendant admits that on 7th April 1985 a collision occurred between the Plaintiff at the junction of Ritson Road and Stannard Road, London W8 between the Plaintiff's Cortina and the Defendant's Mini car.

2. The Defendant denies that this collision was caused by his negligence as alleged in paragraph 3 of the Particulars of Claim. The Defendant denies that he was guilty of any negligence.

3. The collision was solely caused, or alternatively contributed to, the negligence of the Plaintiff.

PARTICULARS OF NEGLIGENCE

The Plaintiff was negligent in that he:

(a) Drove too fast.

(b) Failed to keep a proper lookout.

(c) Drove on the wrong side of the road.

(d) Drove on to and across the white line on the road.

(e) Ran in to the front of the Defendant's Mini car.

(f) Failed to slow down, stop, swerve, or take such other action as was necessary to avoid the collision.

4. The Defendant does not admit that the Plaintiff suffered loss and damage alleged in paragraph 4 of the Particulars of Claim.

BRIAN EVANS of
104 Coventry Grove,
LONDON E10

DATED 12th day of November 1985

TO the Registrar of the Court and to
the Plaintiff

SPECIMEN

912

Appendix 3
Legal Jargon: An A–Z Guide

abate. To reduce or make less (e.g. general *legacies* are abated – reduced proportionately – when the deceased's estate is insufficient to pay all the general legacies in full; a nuisance is abated when it is reduced).

abstract of title. A summary of the legal title to *unregistered land*. The abstract shows the history and validity of the title; cf. an epitome of title, which lists all the documents going back to the *root of title*.

accord and satisfaction. When a creditor accepts an agreement suggested by the debtor, which satisfies the debt and so prevents the creditor from suing the debtor.

acknowledgement of service. When the defendant is served with a *writ* he should enter a written acknowledgement of service with the court. If he does not do so within fourteen days, the plaintiff may be able to obtain *judgement in default* against him.

action. Civil proceedings in a court of law.

act of God. 'An extraordinary circumstance which could not be foreseen, and which could not be guarded against' (Pandorf (1886)). Insurance policies do not usually cover acts of God.

actus reus. The guilty act; cf. *mens rea.*

administrator, administratrix. The personal representative appointed by the court to administer the estate of someone who has died intestate (i.e. without a will) or who left a will which did not appoint executors.

ad valorem. According to the value; e.g. stamp duty on sale of land is charged according to the price paid.

affidavit. A written statement to be used as evidence in court proceedings. The deponent swears (or affirms) as to its truth before a commissioner of oaths, a solicitor, or a court official, who then witnesses the deponent's signature.

amicus curiae. A friend of the court. A barrister appointed in certain cases to assist the court who can bring matters that have been overlooked to the court's attention.

ancient lights. Windows which have had an uninterrupted access of light for at least twenty years. Buildings cannot be erected which interfere with this right of light.

annul. When court proceedings, or their outcome, are declared no longer to have effect.

antenuptial. Before marriage.

Anton Piller order. A search warrant allowing the papers of a defendant in a civil (*not* criminal) case to be seized and his premises searched. Usually applies when the court thinks the defendant might destroy incriminating evidence.

913

arraign. To bring an accused person to the bar of the court so that the indictment can be read to him.

arrestable offence. A criminal offence carrying a maximum penalty of five years' or more imprisonment. All arrestable offences allow the offender to be arrested without a warrant. See page 778.

assault. Strictly speaking, merely attempting to strike another person is an assault. If touching takes place, then it is *battery*. In practice, the word assault is always taken to include the battery.

attestation. The signature of a witness to the signing of a document by another person.

attorney. Since the Judicature Act 1875, attorneys have been officially called solicitors.

Attorney-General. The chief law officer of the Crown and head of the barristers' profession.

automatism. An involuntary act done by a person who is not aware of what he is doing or who is unable to control his muscles.

autrefois. A person cannot be tried for the same offence twice.

bailiff. A person employed by the sheriff to serve and enforce court documents and processes.

bailment. When goods are left by one person (the 'bailor') with another (the 'bailee') to hold in accordance with instructions; e.g. leaving luggage at railway luggage offices.

bank holidays. In England and Wales, these are laid down in the Banking and Financial Dealings Act 1971 as Easter Monday, the last Monday in August, 26 December and, if either 25 or 26 December is a Sunday, then also 27 December.

bankruptcy. When a court takes over a debtor's assets on behalf of his creditors. See page 586.

battery. Using force on another person, whether or not harm results.

bench. The term used to describe the magistrates and judges in a court.

beneficiary. A person who is entitled to property which is held for him by trustees. Also, someone who receives a gift under a will.

bequeath. To leave *personal* (cf. *real*) *property* under a will. The gift is called a *legacy*.

bona vacantia. Goods that do not have an owner. Generally, they go to the finder except in cases of shipwreck and treasure trove, when they go to the Crown.

brewster sessions. Annual meeting of licensing justices to consider applications (and renewals) for licences to sell alcoholic liquor.

bridle way. A public right of way to pass on horseback.

burden of proof. The obligation of proving the case.

by-law. Rules laid down by a local authority or other body in accordance with powers given to them by an Act of Parliament. These local rules have the full force of law.

capital punishment. Death by hanging is now restricted to high treason and piracy with violence.

case stated. When a case is submitted by a court to a higher court for its opinion, the lower court will summarize the facts of the case and the relevant points of law. Most commonly arises when a magistrates' court decision is appealed to the Divisional Court of the Queen's Bench Division.

caveat emptor. Let the buyer beware.

certiorari. An order of the High Court to review and quash the decision of the lower court which was based on an irregular procedure.

champerty. Financing another's legal action in return for a share of the profits. Such a contract is unenforceable, but is not a criminal offence.

charge on land. A *mortgage*.

charity. A body that has legally charitable objectives. Only bodies which are for the relief of poverty, the advancement of education, the advancement of religion, or for other purposes beneficial to the community, can qualify as charities.

chattels. All property other than *freehold* real estate. Chattels can be 'chattels real' (leaseholds) or 'chattels personal' (all other property – also called pure personalty).

c.i.f. Cost, insurance, freight. The cost of the goods includes these items.

civil law. The law administered by the civil courts (i.e. non-criminal law).

Class F. A spouse whose name is not on the title deeds of the matrimonial home can register a Class F charge which warns all purchasers that she claims the right to live in the home, even if it is sold by the other spouse. See page 78.

codification. The bringing together into one Act of Parliament of all the law on one topic without altering the law.

commorientes. When people die together at the same time, their deaths are presumed to have occurred in order of seniority by age.

complaint. The initial step in beginning civil proceedings in the magistrates' court.

condonation. When one spouse forgives the other's matrimonial misconduct. It is no longer a bar to divorce, but see Chapter 2.

consideration. If a person promises to do something for another (e.g. pay money) that promise can only be enforced if the other person gave, or promised, something of value in return; that is said to be the consideration for the promise. Thus, every contract requires consideration. The only exception is when the promise is in a *deed*.

conversion. A tort which arises when someone's title to his chattels is denied or if a bailee negligently allows his bailor's goods to be damaged.

conveyance. A written document transferring ownership of *land* from one person to another.

corporeal hereditaments. Visible, tangible property (e.g. house, car, books).

costs. The expenses relating to legal services. See Chapter 56.

counterclaim. When a defendant is sued he can include in his defence any claim that he may have against the plaintiff, even if it arises from a different matter.

coverture. Legal status of a married woman.

crime. Defined in Halsbury's *Law of England* as an unlawful act or default which is an offence against the public and which renders the person guilty of the act liable to legal punishment.

curtesy. An ancient right whereby a widower had a life estate in the land of his late wife. Very rare nowadays.

curtilage. The garden, field, yard, etc., surrounding a house and which belongs to the house.

custom. An unwritten law dating back to time immemorial.

damage feasant. Damage by animals of A on the land of B. If B seizes the animals (distress damage feasant) he cannot sue for damages.

Appendix 3

declaratory judgement. When the court makes a declaration as to the law, or rights between parties, without making an order to enforce those rights.

deed. A written document that has been signed, sealed, and delivered by its maker. The signature is witnessed. These days, the maker only signs for there is rarely any need for him formally to *seal* or deliver the deed.

defendant. A person who is sued or prosecuted, or who has any court proceedings brought against him.

demise. The grant of a lease in land.

deposition. A statement made on oath by a witness.

detinue. An action formerly brought to recover chattels wrongly detained, but abolished by the Torts (Interference with Goods) Act 1977.

devise. A gift of *land* in a will (if not land, it is a bequest).

Director of Public Prosecutions. The DPP is a solicitor or barrister of at least ten years' standing who works under the Lord Chancellor. Only he can prosecute for certain serious crimes.

discovery of documents. In many civil actions the parties disclose all their relevant documents to each other, even if the disclosed documents injure their case.

distrain. To levy *distress*.

distress. Seizing a personal chattel from a debtor or wrongdoer in satisfaction of the debt, etc.

dock brief. A prisoner being tried on indictment (i.e. in the crown court) can request any robed barrister in court to represent him for a nominal fee. The practice has become rare since the introduction of legal aid.

domicile. Where a person has his permanent home. See page 21.

dominant tenement. Land which has the benefit of rights over another piece of land; e.g. if plot A has a right of light over plot B, plot A is the dominant tenement and plot B is the *servient tenement*.

duty solicitor. Many magistrates' courts have rotas of solicitors who attend the court and give advice and help to unrepresented defendants.

easement. The right which an owner of land (called the *dominant tenement*) has over the land of another person, called the *servient tenement* (e.g. right of way, light, support).

enactment. An Act of Parliament, or part of an Act.

encumbrance. A liability affecting property (e.g. a lease, *mortgage, restrictive covenant*).

engross. When a draft document has been approved by everyone concerned, it is then re-typed in its final form. That is the engrossment.

equity. Body of doctrines and maxims which developed alongside the common law, and which aimed to mould the rigid and inflexible common-law principles into a more just and equitable legal system.

equity of redemption. The right of a mortgagor (i.e. borrower) to redeem his *mortgage* after the date stated in his mortgage deed.

estate. An interest in *land* (e.g. a lease).

estoppel. A rule which prevents a person denying the truth of a statement or the existence of facts which he has led another to believe; e.g. if X spends money on Y's property because Y says he will give it to X, then Y may not be able to change his mind and refuse to give the property to X.

execution. Enforcing a court's judgement by compelling the defendant to comply with it; e.g. a bailiff who seizes goods by *distress* is executing the judgement.

executor (executrix). A personal representative appointed by will.

ex parte. An application to the court by one party to the proceedings, without the other party being present. See page 87.

expert witness. An expert witness can give his opinion on a subject. This is an exception to the general rule that witnesses must not tell the court their opinions; e.g. a witness cannot say 'I thought he was driving dangerously.'

extinguishment. When a right or obligation ends; e.g. a debt is repaid and so the right to sue for recovery of the debt is extinguished.

fatal accident. When a person is killed by the negligence of another, his dependants can sue for their financial loss arising from his death. Only the spouse, parent, grandparent, child, grandchild, nephew, niece, or cousin can sue: a common-law spouse cannot sue (Fatal Accidents Act 1976).

fee simple. The absolute ownership of land. Basically the same as a freehold.

fee tail. An interest in land which descends to the direct issue (i.e. children) of the owner, and which he cannot give to anyone else.

feme covert. A married woman.

feme sole. An unmarried woman (i.e. spinster, widow, divorced woman).

fieri facias. A court order to the sheriff requiring him to seize a debtor's goods to pay off a creditor's judgement.

foreclosure. When a mortgagee (e.g. a building society) forecloses on a *mortgage*, the mortgagor (the borrower) forfeits his *equity of redemption*. The court therefore allows the mortgagee to take possession of the property, sell it, and deduct the amount it is owed from the proceeds of sale. Any balance goes to the mortgagor.

freehold. cf. *leasehold*, under which property is held for a specified period of time.

frustration. A contract is frustrated if it becomes impossible to perform because of a reason that is beyond the control of the parties (e.g. war). The contract is cancelled.

garnishee order. When a creditor commences proceedings against someone who owes his debtor money, so as to intercept the repayment before it reaches the debtor; e.g. A is owed money by B, but B is owed money by C; A can obtain a garnishee order against C. See page 885.

good faith. Honestly.

goodwill. 'The whole advantage, wherever it may be, of the reputation and connection of the firm' (Trego (1896)).

ground rent. The rent paid by a person with a long lease (commonly ninety-nine years) to the freeholder.

guarantor. A person who guarantees another's debts; also called a *surety*. See page 572.

Appendix 3

habeas corpus. (Latin for 'that you have the body'.) A court order which requires that a named individual be produced before the court; applied for when a person is illegally detained (see page 667).

half-blood. The relationship between people who have one common ancestor; e.g. between A and B who have the same father, but different mothers.

heirloom. 'Any piece of household stuff which, by custom of some countries, having belonged to a house for certain descents, goes with the house after the death of the owner, unto the heir and not to the executors.'

high seas. The seas more than five kilometres from the coast.

holding charge. A minor charge used as a device for holding a suspect while a more serious offence is investigated.

holograph. A document written in the maker's own handwriting; e.g. a holograph will.

hostile witness. A court can declare a witness to be hostile if it believes that he is hostile to the party calling him and that he is unwilling to tell the truth. This then allows the witness to be cross-examined by the party who called him. (Parties cannot usually cross-examine their own witnesses.)

ignorance of the law is no excuse. 'Every man must be taken to be cognizant of the law, otherwise there is no knowing of the extent to which the excuse of ignorance might be carried. It would be urged in almost every case' (Bailey (1800)).

illegal. An act is illegal when it involves breaking the criminal law; cf. an *unlawful* act.

immovables. *Land* and the property attached to it.

in camera. When evidence is not heard in open court (see page 772), for instance because it relates to a person's sexual capacity or to official secrets.

indictable offence. An offence which could be tried on indictment in the crown court.

indictment. The written accusation, prepared by the Crown, charging a crown-court defendant. It is read out at the beginning of the trial.

infant. A person under eighteen. Also called a minor.

information. Strictly speaking, an information is any proceeding brought by the Crown other than by *indictment*. In practice, the word is now mainly used to describe a statement placed before a magistrate which informs him of the commission of an offence for which a summons or warrant must be issued by the magistrate. This is called 'laying an information'. See page 777.

injunction. A court order requiring someone to do, or to refrain from doing, something. See page 85.

interim. In the meantime. An 'interim order' in an action is made prior to the full hearing of the case, when a 'final order' will be made. The hearing of the application for an interim order will be an *interlocutory* proceeding.

interlocutory. An interim stage in the course of the action (e.g. interlocutory injunction). 'Interlocutory proceedings' usually describe the events in a civil case between its commencement (by issuing a *writ* or summons) and its ending (by judgement being given).

interpleader summons. When a person holds property to which he has no claim, but two or more people claim it from him, he can issue an interpleader summons asking the court to decide who has the best claim to the property.

interrogatories. In the course of a civil action a party can ask the court for leave to put written questions to the other party. Their purpose is to narrow down the differences between the parties by asking the other party to make admissions.

intervener. A person who intervenes in an action to which he is not a party. Generally applies to a woman accused of adultery in another's divorce and who wishes to intervene to deny that allegation.

inter vivos. Made between people who are alive (e.g. a gift inter vivo); cf. a testamentary gift.

intestate. Dying without leaving a will. See page 180.

invitation to treat. An offer to receive an offer; e.g. a shopkeeper's display of goods in a window is an invitation to treat – he is offering the customer an opportunity to offer to buy those goods, whereupon he might accept that offer. See page 500.

issue. Offspring (i.e. children, grandchildren, etc.).

jactitation of marriage. If A wrongly claims to be married to B, then B can ask the court to confirm that they are not married.

jointly and severally. If A and B are jointly and severally liable to C, then C has three possible courses of action: he can sue A, or B, or A and B.

joint tenancy. When two or more people hold property as joint tenants, they own it between them, and if one dies the other(s) take his share; e.g. A, B, and C own a house; if C dies his share passes to A and B who now have half each, instead of one third each. The alternative to having a joint tenancy is to have a *tenancy in common*.

joint tortfeasors. Two or more people who are responsible for a tort. For example, A negligently drives his car into B. But A was acting in the course of employment for C, his employer, who therefore has a *vicarious liability* for A's negligence. Thus, as far as B is concerned, A and C are joint tortfeasors. They are *jointly and severally* liable.

judgement debtor. A debtor who has had a court judgement for the debt made against him, but who has not yet paid off the debt.

judgement in default. A plaintiff can enter judgement in default against a defendant who fails to carry out a procedural step in time; e.g. fails to file a defence to the claim.

judicial review. Application for judicial review is made to the Divisional Court when a lower court or tribunal has behaved incorrectly. The court can make an order of *certiorari*, *mandamus*, or *prohibition*.

judicial separation. Similar to divorce in that it makes both husband and wife single persons again for all legal purposes. However, unlike a divorce, it does not allow either party to remarry.

jurat. The sentence at the end of an affidavit or statutory declaration which shows when, where, and before whom it was made.

jurisdiction. Our courts have jurisdiction over England, Wales, Berwick on Tweed, territorial waters, and English boats on the *high seas*.

kin. Blood relatives.

knock for knock. Agreement between insurance companies to pay claims made by their own insured and so avoid the expense of claiming from each other. See page 613.

laches. Unreasonable delay in pursuing a legal right. See *limitation*.

land. 'Land in the legal signification comprehendeth any ground, soil or earth whatsoever, as meadows, pastures, woods, moors, waters, marshes, furzes and heath . . . It legally includeth also all castles, houses and other buildings' (Coke).

Land Charges Register. A register of all adverse rights and interests affecting *unregistered land* (e.g. *mortgages, restrictive covenants, easements, Class F*, etc.). Unless the right or interest is registered it will not bind an innocent purchaser of the property.

laying an information. Starting magistrates' court criminal proceedings. See *information*.

leading question. One which suggests the answer or which only allows a 'yes' or 'no' answer; e.g. 'Were you scared?' Only allowed in cross-examination.

leasehold. An estate in land that is less than a *freehold*. Generally used to describe an interest for a fixed term (e.g. for ninety-nine years).

legacy. A gift of *personal property* by will (cf. *devise*).

legal separation. The same as *judicial separation*. See page 48.

legitimation. Legitimization of a bastard by the subsequent marriage of the parents. See page 100.

lessee. Person who takes a lease (i.e. the tenant).

lessor. Person who grants a lease (i.e. the landlord).

lien. A creditor has a lien over property of the debtor until the debt is paid off; e.g. if a solicitor holds title deeds to a house for a client who has not paid the solicitor's bill; the solicitor need not release the title deeds until the bill has been paid.

limitation. Court proceedings must be begun within the limitation period. There are different periods for different types of claims. See page 773.

liquidated sum. A specific sum, or a sum that can be worked out as a matter of arithmetic; cf. *unliquidated damages* when the amount is not easily ascertainable.

liquidator. Person who winds up a company.

London Gazette. Government journal for publication of official notices (e.g. proclamations; winding up; receivership orders).

long vacation. Generally, the whole of August. The Supreme Court only transacts urgent business during this time.

McNaghten Rules. Three rules for use when deciding whether an accused person can plead insanity as a defence.

maintenance pending suit. In divorce, nullity, or separation proceedings the court can order maintenance to be paid before the full hearing of the petition. See page 67.

mandamus. A command from the Divisional Court of the High Court that a lower court does something; e.g. hears a claim which it denied having jurisdiction to hear.

Mareva injunction. A court order freezing assets so they cannot be taken out of the country (if the court thinks the defendant might try to thwart a claim by moving all his money abroad).

master. A practice master deals with routine *interlocutory* proceedings in a High Court action.

mens rea. The 'criminal intention' to commit a crime. The mens rea and the *actus reus* together make the crime.

mesne profits. Damages payable by a trespasser who has stayed in possession after his right to occupy the land has ended; e.g. a tenant who stays on after the end of his tenancy. Generally, the mesne profits will equal the rent for the premises.

messuage. A dwelling-house with its *curtilage*.

minor interest. An interest in *registered land* (e.g. *mortgage*) which only binds purchasers if it is registered on the title register.

misdemeanour. Criminal offences used to be either misdemeanours or (more serious) felonies. The classification was abolished in 1967.

misfeasance. The improper or negligent carrying out of a legal act (e.g. a company director who misapplies the company's money).

moiety. One half.

mortgage. A loan of money on the security of a property. The lender is the mortgagee and the borrower is the mortgagor.

naturalization. Whereby an alien becomes a citizen and subject of his adopted country.

negotiable instrument. A transferable security (e.g. cheque, promissory note, bill of exchange).

nemo dat quod non habet. No one can give what does not belong to him. So a thief cannot pass ownership of property to a person who buys it from him: it still belongs to the person from whom it was stolen. See page 524.

next friend. Person through whom either an *infant* or a mental health patient acts in a legal action. See page 124.

nolle prosequi. The plaintiff discontinues his action. More usually in a criminal case when the *Attorney-General* stays a prosecution; he has power to do this in any indictable prosecution.

non-cohabitation order. Magistrates' court order releasing a spouse from the obligation to live with the other spouse.

non-contentious business. Non-court legal work (e.g. conveyancing, probate). See page 833.

nuncupative will. An oral will. Only valid if made while on active service.

obiter dictum. A statement of opinion by a judge which is not relevant to the case being tried. It is not of such authority as if it had been relevant to the case being tried. (See *ratio decidendi*.)

official referee. Layman appointed by the High Court to try complex matters in which he is a specialist (e.g. accountancy disputes).

official solicitor. Acts in High Court cases as a *next friend* for those who have no one to assist them.

Old Bailey. The Central Criminal Court, one of the crown courts.

option. A right to buy something.

originating summons. Similar to a *writ* in that it commences proceedings in the High Court. For instance, when an *infant* is injured and his *next friend* wants the court to approve a settlement.

parol. An informally made contract. Previously used to describe any contract not under *seal* but now generally taken to mean an oral contract.

passing off. A tort whereby A passes off his goods or business as being that of B (e.g. by using a similar name or label). B can apply for an *injunction* and damages.

peppercorn rent. A nominal rent which it is not intended that the landlord will collect (e.g. a red rose on Midsummer Day). But it preserves the landlord's legal title.

per incuriam. A mistaken decision by a court; other courts need not follow it.

periodic tenancy. A tenancy which is not for a fixed term. The tenant pays rent periodically (e.g. weekly, monthly) and the tenancy continues until notice is given by either party. See page 236.

personal property. All property except *land*. Also called personalty.

plaintiff. Person who sues (i.e. brings a civil action).

plc. A public limited company. Most used to have 'Ltd' after their names, but changed this to plc when UK company law was brought into line with EEC law in 1981.

pleadings. Formal written documents in a civil action. The plaintiff submits a statement of claim, the defendant a defence.

polygamy. Legally having more than one spouse.

portion. Parental gift to establish a child in life.

possessory title. Title acquired by a squatter through adverse possession. See page 340.

pre-emption. A right of first refusal if a property is sold.

premium. In a tenancy, the premium is the price paid other than in rent; e.g. a flat is sold on a ninety-nine-year lease at an annual rent of £50, for £15,000 – the £15,000 is the premium.

prescription. Method of acquiring rights over another's land by usage over a period of time. See page 195.

presumption of death. 'If a person has not been heard of for seven years, there is a presumption of law that he is dead' (Lal Chand (1925)).

pre-trial review. Preliminary meeting of parties in county-court action to consider administrative matters and what agreement can be reached prior to the trial. See page 880.

privacy. There is no *tort* of interfering with another's privacy, although the European Convention on Human Rights states that 'everyone has the right to respect for his private and family life, his home and his correspondence'.

profit a prendre. The right to take something off someone else's *land* (e.g. collect firewood).

prohibition. An order of a Divisional Court of the High Court preventing an inferior court from doing something (e.g. hearing a case that is outside its jurisdiction).

public policy. Acts which are against public policy are illegal (e.g. gambling debts cannot be sued for; nor can a prostitute sue for her payment).

purchaser. Generally taken to mean one who buys property, but, strictly speaking, it covers any person who acquires the *fee simple* in *land* other than by descent (for instance, a person who receives the land as an *inter vivos* gift).

putative father. The man who is alleged to be the father of an illegitimate child.

quantum meruit. As much as he has earned.

Queen's Proctor. A solicitor representing the Crown who can intervene in divorce cases (for instance, if the divorce was obtained on the basis of false evidence) before the decree is made absolute.

rack rent. 'A rent that represents the full annual value of the holding' (Newman (1975)).

ratio decidendi. The reason for a judicial decision. A statement of legal principle in a ratio decidendi is more authoritative than if in an *obiter dictum*.

real property. Freehold estates in *land*; it is often used to describe any interest in land.

recognizance. Sum of money that will be forfeited by an accused person who fails to answer to his bail. See page 784.

re-examination. Examination of a witness by the party calling him, after his cross-examination by the other party.

registered land. Land that is registered under the Land Registration Act 1925. See page 201.

relator. A private individual on whose suggestion the *Attorney-General* brings an action for the public good – a relator action.

remainder. When a person has an interest in land that will come into his possession when someone else's interest ends, he has an interest in remainder; e.g. A gives land to B for life, the remainder to C. (See *reversion*.)

rentcharge. A rental payment on freehold land. Largely abolished in 1977 except when used to enforce covenants between freeholders.

replevin. Recovering goods seized by the sheriff or bailiff, after paying off the *judgement debt*.

requisition. An inquiry by a purchaser of *land* concerning the vendor's title to that land. See page 216.

res ipsa loquitur. The matter speaks for itself. Normally a plaintiff must prove his case, but in accident claims in which the circumstances raise a prima facie indication of negligence, the defendant has to prove he was not negligent. The circumstances indicate negligence – it speaks for itself.

restitutio in integrum. Restoring the status quo.

restrictive covenant. A covenant that allows one landowner to control the use of another's land. See page 335.

retrospective legislation. An Act that applies to a period before the Act was passed.

reversion. If an owner of land disposes of it for a period, after which it will revert back to him, he is said to hold the reversion; e.g. a landlord grants a lease for twenty years; he will acquire the freehold in twenty years' time. See also *remainder*.

right of re-entry. Right of landlord to take possession if tenant breaks the terms of the tenancy.

riparian. Connected with the bank of a river or stream.

root of title. Title deed which forms the basis of the vendor's title to the *land*. Must be at least fifteen years old. See page 201.

salvage. The right of a person who saves a ship or its cargo from shipwreck to receive compensation. Usually assessed by the court.

seal. Used to be the impression of a piece of wax on to a document. Now a small red sticky label is used instead, although the absence of the seal will not invalidate the document, since 'to constitute a sealing neither wax nor wafer nor a piece of paper, not even an impression is necessary' (Sandilands (1871)).

section 6(2) committal. Short form of committal by magistrates. See page 796.

servient tenement. See *dominant tenement*.

settlement. Tying *land* up for the future by leaving it to trustees to hold for successive limited owners.

sine die. Indefinitely.

small claim. Colloquial phrase generally referring to consumer claims for no more than £500 in the county court. (Above that figure, the loser usually has to pay the winner's legal costs; see page 872.)

solus agreement. When a retailer agrees to buy all his goods from one supplier. Common in the petrol-supply business.

special damage. Financial loss that can be proved (e.g. wage loss).

specialty contract. A contract under seal.

specific performance. When a party to a contract is ordered to carry out his part of the bargain (e.g. to sell a house). Only ordered if damages (money) would be an inadequate remedy.

stakeholder. One who holds money as an impartial observer. He will only part with it if both parties agree or if ordered by the court.

stare decisis. To stand by decided matters. Alternative name for the doctrine of precedent. See page 828.

statute. An Act of Parliament.

statute-barred. When there has been so much delay before commencing proceedings that the *limitation* period has expired.

statutory instrument. Subordinate legislation made by the Queen in Council or a minister, in exercise of a power granted by *statute*.

stay of proceedings. When a court action is stopped by the court.

subpoena. A court order that a person attends court, either to give evidence (subpoena ad testificandum) or to produce documents (subpoena duces tecum).

substituted service. When a document cannot be served on the defendant or his solicitor, the court may allow substituted service by, for example, its being sent to his last known address, or advertised in newspapers.

summary judgement. If the defendant does not show an arguable defence to the claim, the plaintiff can apply for summary judgement. Also known as 'Order 14' (after the Rule of the Supreme Court that lays down the procedure).

surety. A *guarantor*.

taxation of costs. Examination and approval by the court of legal fees. See page 836.

tenancy in common. When two or more people hold land as tenants in common, they each have equal shares in it. If one dies his share does not pass to the other (cf. *joint tenancy*). For example, A, B and C own a house. If C dies, his share will pass under his will to his family, etc. A and B will still own one third each of the house; the other third will be owned by the person who inherited C's share. Joint owners are presumed to be joint tenants, not tenants in common.

term of years. A lease for a fixed period of duration.

testate. Dying having left a will.

testator. The person who makes a will.

third-party proceedings. When a party to an action sues someone else. For example, A sues B for damages after B drove his car into A. But B's negligent driving was partly caused by C, a pedestrian, who was jay-walking. B starts third-party proceedings against C, and if the court orders B to pay damages to A, it can also order C to pay damages to B.

tort. A civil wrong (other than breach of contract) giving rise to the right to bring an action in the civil courts (e.g. nuisance, negligence, trespass, defamation).

Treasury counsel. Barristers who receive briefs from the *Director of Public Prosecutions* for *Old Bailey* prosecutions. They are nominated by the Lord Chancellor.

uberrimae fidei. Of the utmost good faith. See page 557.

ultra vires. Outside the powers (e.g. of a company).

unenforceable. A contract or other right that cannot be enforced because of a technical defect (e.g. *statute-barred*).

unlawful. An act is unlawful when it involves a breach of the law and so allows civil proceedings to be brought. It does not involve a breach of the criminal law (cf. *illegal*).

unliquidated damages. Damages which cannot be arithmetically calculated in advance and are dependent upon the opinion (and generosity) of the court (e.g. for the loss of a limb). (See *liquidated sum*.)

unregistered land. *Land* that is not *registered land*. See page 201.

unsound mind. As defined in the Mental Health Act 1983. See page 698.

vendor and purchaser summons. Procedure whereby parties to a contract for the sale of *land*, who are in dispute, can apply relatively speedily to a judge in chambers for a decision.

vexatious litigant. A person who cannot bring any action without the permission of the court, because he has previously brought vexatious or frivolous proceedings.

vicarious liability. When one person is responsible for the actions of another because of their relationship; e.g. an employer is liable for the actions of his employee – see page 370. The plaintiff can sue either, or both, of them.

void. Of no legal effect. If a marriage is void it is as though it had never taken place (cf. *voidable*).

voidable. Capable of being set aside. A voidable marriage will end when it is annulled (i.e. avoided) but it will be recognized as having existed until that time (cf. *void*).

volenti non fit injuria. A person cannot sue over an injury to which he has consented. 'Knowledge of the risk of injury is not enough. Nor is a willingness to take the risk of injury. Nothing will suffice short of an agreement to waive any claim for negligence' (Nettleship (1971)).

volunteer. A person who is given, or who inherits, property without giving any *consideration*.

wager. A bet. A betting or gambling debt is *unenforceable* as being contrary to *public policy*.

waste. Causing lasting damage to land (e.g. by a tenant).

with costs. If judgement is entered 'with costs', it means that the winner's *costs* will be paid by the loser. See Chapter 56.

writ. Document for commencing many High Court actions. It commands the defendant to file an *acknowledgement of service*.

Index of Cases

927

Index of Cases

Index of Cases

Index of Cases

General Index

Abandoned cars, 542
Abatement notice, 310
Abortion, 104–5; advice to under-sixteens, 120
Absolute discharge, 148, 805, 808
Absolute privilege, *see* Defamation
Abstract of Title, 913
ACAS (Advisory, Conciliation, and Arbitration Service): conciliation by, 452; picketing (Code of Practice), 492–4; and time off work, 481; *see also* Discipline at work
Access, 126
Accidents: to burglars and squatters, 362; in the home, 362–4; insurance against, 364; landlord's responsibility, 363; to trespassing children, 363; uninsured motorists, 612–13; *see also* Accidents at work; Negligence; Road accidents
Accidents at work, 410–14; defective equipment, 411–12; liability of employee to employer, 370; negligent work-mate, 410; reporting, 414; safe system of work, 370, 412; suing after, 413; welfare benefits, 734–5; what to do after, 414
Accommodation agencies, 282–3
Acknowledgement of service, 913
Addresses, tracing, 891
Administration order, 886
Administrator, 913; *see also* Executors
Adoption, 142, 143; and birth certificate, 109; as legitimation, 101; registers, 891; by step-parent, 107
Adultery, 30–32; co-respondent, 31; effect on maintenance, 60; six-month rule, 31
Adverse possession, *see* Squatters
Advertisements, planning permission for, 330

Affidavit, 913; specimen, 902
Affiliation, *see* Illegitimacy
Affray, 689
Aircraft, and airspace, 344–5
Airspace, trespass into, 344
Alibi, 798
Animals, 358–62; dangerous animals, 359; dangerous wild animals, 360; guard dogs, 360; when harmless animal is dangerous, 359; licences 360; negligent owner, 358–9; quarantine, 360–61
Anton Piller order, 913
Arbitration, 880
Arrest, 777–8; arrestable offence, 778, 914; citizen's arrest, 778
Arrestable offence, *see* Arrest
Assault, 914
Assigning a tenancy, *see* Council tenants; Rent Acts
Assured tenancy, 236
Attachment of earnings, 66, 884–5; protected earnings, 884
Attendance allowance, 738
Attendance centre, 149, 808
Attestation clause, *see* Wills
Auction, 501, 527
Automatism, 914

Bail, 781–5; appeals, 783; children and, 782; conditions of, 783; entitlement to, 782; police bail, 781; refusal of, 783; sureties, 784
Bailiff, 883; eviction by, 260; obstruction of by squatter, 281; powers of, 884
Bank holidays, 914
Banker's draft, 555

937

General Index

care, 403; time off for jury service, 801;
time off for trade-union officers, 481; time
off to look for new job, 478; unpaid time
off for union members, 481; women, 398;
in written particulars (employee's), 378;
young people, 398; see also Holidays
House of Lords, 765–6
Housing Action Areas: grants in, 323, 325;
landlord's notice to quit, 261
Housing associations, 296–9; charities, 299;
eviction, 298; grounds for evicting, 298;
Housing Corporation, 296–7; as new
landlord, 297; passing on rate increases,
298; protection of mistresses, 298;
redevelopment by, 298; register, 894;
rent levels, 297–8; right to buy, 299;
shared ownership, 299; succession, 298;
swapping homes, 299; if the tenant dies,
298; see also Repair of rented
property
Housing benefit, 743–4
Human habitation, fitness for, 315, 316; see
also Repair of rented property

Identification: evidence of in trials, 674–5;
group identification, 674; parades, 673–4;
photos, 674
Illegitimacy, 99–101; access by father, 128;
affiliation and maintenance, 101–4;
affiliation agreement, 101; birth
certificate, 108; blood tests, 99; bringing
affiliation proceedings, 101–2; illegitimate
child, 99; inheritance, 104; legitimation,
100–101; mother's sole responsibility,
106; nationality, 120
Immigration, 95, 704–8; British citizen, 704;
Commonwealth citizens, 705; E E C
(European Economic Community), 706;
fiancés, 705; illegal immigrants, 707;
Irish, 706; passports, 707
Improvement grants, 324–6; see also Grants
Indecency, penalties for, 792
Indecent evidence, 772
Indictable offence, 785
Industrial action: no victimization, 444;
redundancy and, 468; secondary action,
487; sit-ins, 495; strike ballots, 486; suing,
486; trade dispute, 489; unfair dismissal

and, 444; welfare benefits, 487–8; see also
Picketing
Industrial death benefit, 735
Industrial disputes (trade dispute), 484–5
Industrial tribunals: chart of procedure, 451;
conciliation, 452; discovery, 452; Form
IT1, 449–50, 453, 454; Form IT3, 450,
453, 454; the hearing, 454–6; legal advice,
448; no costs, 448, 455; pre-hearing
assessment, 454; settlement, 452;
witnesses, 453
Infant, 156; see also Children
Information, 918
Injunction, 85–9; harassment of tenant,
272–3; landlord's failure to repair, 307;
noise, 350; on notice or ex parte, 87;
persistent trespassing, 339–340; power of
arrest, 86, 88–9; procedure, 88–9;
specimen documents, 902–3
Inns, see Hotels
Insolvency, 586; acts of, 586–7
Insulting behaviour, 688
Insurance, 557–63; accident, 364; average
clause, 562; 'betterment', 562; brokers,
560; claiming, 561–2; construction, 560;
disclosure, duty of, 557–8; failed
companies, 562–3; when house-buying,
215; Insurance Ombudsman, 563;
material facts, 557; no insurance
(motorists), 609; proposal form, 558–9;
public policy, 560; reform, 561; renewal,
559; theft cover, 560; see also Car
insurance
Insurance brokers, see Insurance
Interlocutory stage, 918
Intermediate grants, see Grants
Interpretation, 829–30
Intervener, 919
Intestacy, 151–2, 180–82; children and
grandchildren, 181; mistresses, common-
law spouses, 182; other relatives, 181;
partial intestacy, 182; surviving spouse,
181; see also Death; Executors; Family
provision; Wills
Invalid care allowance, 739
Invalidity benefit, 741
Inventions, 401–2
Invitation to treat, 919

Solicitors, 810–21; advertising, 813; changing, 817; complaints, 813–16; conveyancing monopoly, 811; criminal-duty solicitors, 669; detainee's right to see, 668; discipline, 815; finding a, 820–21; interest on deposit money, 839–40; Law Society role, 813–14; Lay Observer, 815; legally aided clients, 856; Practice Rules, 813; probate monopoly, 812; qualification chart, 819; qualifying, 818–20; records, 896; solicitors' lien, 818; suing negligent, 816–17; types of work, 810; *see also* Solicitors' fees

Solicitors' fees: the bill, 834; for business leases, 604; contentious or non-contentious? 833; costs, 832; for divorce, 40–41; fixed-price agreements, 839; hourly charges, 834; interest on, 839; legal aid, 856; paying someone else's bill, 837; for probate work, 174; suing for unpaid fees, 838; taxing costs, 836; time costing, 835; 'fair and reasonable' criteria, 834–5; *see also* Costs

Special grants, 326

Speeding, 630–31; penalties for, 644

Spot checks on vehicles, 614

Squatters, 280–82; adverse possession, 340; criminal offences, 280; eviction, 281–2; residential occupier, 280–81; sit-ins, 495; as trespasser, 280; *see also* Prescription

Stakeholder, 924

Stamp duty, 225

Standard amenities, 312–13, 322

Statutory charge, 75; *see also* Legal advice; Legal aid

Statutory nuisance, 310

Statutory sick pay, 387–8; qualifying days, 387; self-employed, 382; strikers, 487; table of eligibility, 388

Statutory tenancy, 250–51

Step-parents, 106–7

Stolen goods, 524–5; handling, 525; HP vehicles, 524; markets, 524; penalties, 791

Straying livestock, 359–60

Strict liability, 357

Strikes, *see* Industrial action

Sub judice, 772–3

Subletting, *see* Council tenants; Rent Acts

Subsidence, 353; *see also* Trees

Succession to a tenancy, 265, 269–70, 292–3, 295

Suing for assault, 716

Summary offence, 785

Sunday trading, *see* Shops

Supervision order, 149, 809

Supplementary benefit: additional requirements, 746; availability for work, 745; earnings, 745; effect of care order, 138; long-term rate, 745; mortgage interest, 200; rates, 744; requirements, 744; resources, 744; single payments, 746; strikers, 488; *see also* Liable-relative proceedings

Support, right of, 353–4

Sureties, 784

Surveys, 204–5; costs, 205; limitations of, 205; mortgage surveys (limited scope), 207

Suspended sentence, 803, 809; rehabilitation of, 679

System-built properties, 327

Taking motor vehicle, 631; penalties, 793; penalty for first offender, 646

Tax: businesses, 597–8; CGT and owner-occupiers, 197–8; effect of separation or divorce, 74; employed and self-employed, 382; free of tax, 156; golden handshakes, 478; marriage, 52–3; mortgage payments, 196–7; personal allowances, 52, 94; redundancy, 478; separate assessment, 52; separate taxation, 52; strikers, 488; tax fiddlers, 427; tax-relief for owner-occupiers, 196–8; welfare benefits, 733; *see also* Stamp duty

Taxis, 543–4

Telephones, penalties for offences, 793

Temporary employees, 408

Tenancy in common, 924

Tenant's exchange scheme, 299

Theft, penalties for, 794

Third-party proceedings, 925

Threatening behaviour, penalties for, 794

Time limits for suing, 773–5

Time-sharing, 190